FAMILIES OF ANCIENT NEW HAVEN

Compiled by
DONALD LINES JACOBUS

With Cross-Index
by Helen Love Scranton

Nine Volumes in Three

Volumes IV-VI

GENEALOGICAL PUBLISHING Co., Inc

Originally published as
New Haven Genealogical Magazine, Volumes I-VIII
Rome, NY and New Haven, CT, 1922-1932
Cross-Index, New Haven, CT, 1939

Reprinted nine volumes in three by
Genealogical Publishing Co., Inc.
Baltimore, 1974, 1981, 1997
Library of Congress Catalogue Card Number 73-22149
International Standard Book Number 0-8063-0607-6
Set Number: 0-8063-0953-9
Made in the United States of America

The publisher gratefully acknowledges the loan
of the original volumes from the New Haven Colony
Historical Society, New Haven, Connecticut

FAMILIES
of Ancient
NEW HAVEN

Volume IV

COMPILED BY
DONALD LINES JACOBUS

PRINTER
CLARENCE D. SMITH
ROME, NEW YORK
1927

Contents

Families of Ancient New Haven

COMPILED BY DONALD LINES JACOBUS

ABBREVIATIONS

b.	born	Lieut.	Lieutenant
Bapt.	Baptist	m.	married
bp.	baptized	Maj.	Major
bu.	buried	Meth.	Methodist
c.	"circa"-about	nat.	"natural"-illegitimate
Capt.	Captain	N. S.	New Style
Col.	Colonel	O. S.	Old Style
Cpl.	Corporal	Rev.	Reverend (clergyman)
d.	died	R. W.	Revolutionary War
da.	daughter of	rem.	removed
Dea.	Deacon	res.	resided, residence
div.	divorced	s.	son of
Dr.	Doctor (physician)	s. p.	"sine prole"-without issue
Ens.	Ensign		
F. & I. W.	French & Indian Wars	Sgt.	Sergeant
Gen.	General	w.	wife of
hr.	hour	wid.	widow of
k.	killed	wk.	week

ABBREVIATIONS FOR SOURCES OF INFORMATION

These abbreviations are made up of two parts, the first signifying the town, the second, the kind of record. Thus, in *NHV*, *NH* means New Haven and *V* the vital statistics of that town. In *WdT1*, the *Wd* means Woodbridge and *T* a gravestone inscription, the figure following the *T* designating a particular graveyard. In *HC2*, the *H* stands for Hamden and *C* for a Congregational church there, the figure following the *C* specifying the particular church. *NoHx* means the Episcopal church of North Haven, *x* always standing for an Episcopal church and *NoH* for North Haven. A list of general symbols for towns and kinds of record are given below, followed by a list (arranged alphabetically by symbols) of the specific record sources.

SYMBOLS FOR TOWNS

B	Bethany	Mid	Middletown	S	Southington
Bd	Branford	My	Middlebury	St	Stratford
C	Cheshire	NH	New Haven	Sy	Southbury
D	Derby	NM	New Milford	W	Wallingford
EH	East Haven	NoB	North Branford	Wat	Waterbury
Farm	Farmington	NoH	North Haven	Wd	Woodbridge
G	Guilford	O	Orange	WH	West Haven
H	Hamden	Oxf	Oxford	Wol	Wolcott
L	Litchfield	P	Plymouth	Wtn	Watertown
M	Milford	Ppt	Prospect	Wy	Woodbury

SYMBOLS FOR KIND OF RECORD

C	Congregational Church record
CCt	County Court record
F	Family, private or Bible record (this symbol always stands alone)
SupCt	Superior Court record
T	Gravestone record
V	Vital (town) record
x	Episcopal Church record

SPECIFIC SOURCES

BAlm	Beckwith's Almanac
BD	Mortality List of Bethany, 1788–1793
BT1	"Cemetery in the Hollow", Bethany
BT2	Episcopal graveyard, Bethany
BT3	"Sperry Cemetery", Bethany
BT4	"Carrington Cemetery", Bethany
BT5	Methodist graveyard
BV	Vital statistics, Bethany
Bx	Christ Church (Prot. Ep.), Bethany
BdV	Vital statistics, Branford
CC	Congregational Society, Cheshire
CT1	Old graveyard, Cheshire
CT2	Episcopal graveyard, Cheshire
CV	Vital statistics, Branford
Cx	St. Peter's Church (Prot. Ep.), Cheshire
ColR	"Columbian Register", contemporary newspaper
ConnH	"Conn. Herald", contemporary newspaper
DC	Congregatiohal Society, Derby
DT1	Old graveyard, Derby
DT2	Episcopal graveyard, Derby
DT3	"Great Hill Cemetery", Seymour
DT4	Graveyard, Beacon Falls
DT5	Cemetery in North Derby on the Housatonic
DV	Vital statistics, Derby
Dx	St. James' Church (Prot. Ep.), Derby
EHC	Congregational Society, East Haven
EHR	"East Haven Register", by Rev. Stephen Dodd
EHT	Old graveyard, East Haven
EHV	Vital statistics, East Haven
F	Family, Bible or private records
F&IWRolls	Muster Rolls of Conn. Troops, French and Indian Wars
FarmV	Vital statistics, Farmington
HC1	Congregational Society, Mount Carmel (in Hamden)
HC2	Congregational Society, "East Plain" or Whitneyville (in Hamden)
HT1	"Centerville Cemetery", Hamden
HT2	"Hamden Plains Cemetery", Highwood (in Hamden)

HT3	Old graveyard, Mount Carmel (in Hamden)
HT4	"State Street Cemetery", Hamden
HT5	"Whitneyville Cemetery", Hamden
HT6	"West Woods Cemetery", Hamden
HV	Vital statistics, Hamden
LT	"Litchfield and Morris Inscriptions", by Charles Thomas Payne
LV	Vital statistics, Litchfield
MC1	First Congregational Society, Milford
MC2	Second Congregational Society, Milford
MT	Old graveyard, Milford
MV	Vital statistics, Milford (including mortality lists)
MidV	Vital statistics, Middletown
MyT	Graveyard, Middlebury
NHC1	First Congregational Society, New Haven
NHC2	Second Congregational Society, New Haven
NHT1	City Burial Ground ("Grove Street Cemetery"), New Haven, including stones in Center Church crypt and those removed from the Green
NHT2	"Westville Cemetery", New Haven
NHT3	"Union Cemetery", Fair Haven (in New Haven)
NHT4	"Evergreen Cemetery", New Haven
NHV	Vital statistics, New Haven
NHx	Trinity Church (Prot. Ep.), New Haven
NMV	Vital statistics, New Milford
NoBC1	Congregational Society (1725), North Branford
NoBC2	Congregational Society (1745), Northford (in North Branford)
NoBT1	Graveyard, Northford
NoHC	Congregational Society, North Haven
NoHD	Mortality list of North Haven
NoHT1	Old graveyard, North Haven
NoHT2	Old graveyard, Montowese (in North Haven)
NoHT3	Modern graveyard, North Haven
NoHV	Vital statistics, North Haven
NoHx	St. John's Church (Prot. Ep.), North Haven
OC	Congregational Society, Orange
OT	Graveyard, Orange
OxfC	Congregational Society, Oxford
OxfT1	Two graveyards (close together), Quaker Farms (in Oxford)
OxfT2	"Zoar Bridge Cemetery", Oxford (now removed)
OxfV	Vital statistics, Oxford
PC	Congregational Society, Plymouth (formerly Northbury)
PT	Graveyard, Plymouth
PptT	Graveyard, Prospect
SC	Congregational Society, Southington
SalemC	Congregational Society, Naugatuck
Salem x	St. Michael's Church, (Prot. Ep.), Naugatuck
StC	First Congregational Society, Stratford

StV	Vital statistics, Stratford
Stx	Christ Church, (Prot. Ep.), Stratford
SyV	Vital statistics, Southbury
WC1	First Congregational Society, Wallingford [records not includ ed]
WC2	First Congregational Society, Meriden
WT1	"Center Street Cemetery", Wallingford
WT2	Old Graveyard, Meriden
WV	Vital statistics, Wallingford
Wx	St. Paul's Church (Prot. Ep.), Wallingford [records not included]
WatT1	City Cemetery (now destroyed), Waterbury
WatT2	"East Farms Cemetery" Waterbury
WatT3	Old Graveyard and Hillside Cemetery, Naugatuck
WatV	Vital statistics, Waterbury
Wat x	St. John's Church, (Prot. Ep.), Waterbury
WdC	Congregational Society, Woodbridge
WdD	Mortality List, Woodbridge
WdT1	"Middle Cemetery", Woodbridge
WdT2	Graveyard, "Milford side", Woodbridge
WdT3	Graveyard (near Seymour), Woodbridge
WdV	Vital statistics, Woodbridge
WHD	Mortality lists of Philemon Smith and "Aunt Lucena" Smith, West Haven
WHT1	Congregational graveyard, West Haven
WHT2	Episcopal graveyard, West Haven
WHT3	"Oak Grove Cemetery", West Haven
WolT	Graveyard, Wolcott
WtnD	Mortality lists (Judd and Skilton), Watertown
WtnT	Graveyard, Watertown
WyC	First Congregational Society, Woodbury
WyV	Vital statistics, Woodbury

ADDITIONAL ACKNOWLEDGMENT

Mr. Newton J. Peck, of Woodbridge, Conn., has kindly permitted the use of private mortality lists in his possession which cover a period when deaths were seldom entered in the public town records.

***HITCHCOCK.** (CONTINUED FROM PAGE 762.)

FAM. 10. BENJAMIN & ELIZABETH (IVES) HITCHCOCK:

1 BELA, b 27 Oct 1719 *WV*, d 13 Oct 1796 *CC*, æ. 77 *CT1;* Census (C) 2-0-3; m (1) 25 Dec 1744 *WV*—Sarah da. John & Elizabeth (Mix) Atwater, b c. 1724, d 23 Oct 1746 *WV;* m (2) 24 Nov 1747 *WV*—Hannah da. John & Elizabeth (Mix) Atwater, b 28 Dec 1722 *WV*, d 28 June 1805 æ. 83 *CT1.*

(By 1): *i* Isaac, b 11 Jan 1745/6 *WV*, bp Mar 1746 *CC*, d 23 June 1746 *WV*, "child" d 1746 *CC.*

(By 2): *ii* Isaac, b 26 Oct 1748 *WV*, *CT1*, bp 18 Dec 1748 *CC*, d 27 May 1749 *WV*, æ. 0-7-1 *CT1.*

iii Bela, b 21 Sep 1750 *WV*, bp Aug (?) 1750 *CC;* m 2 June 1779 *CC*—Comfort da. Ebenezer & Jane (Andrews) Atwater, b 16 Mar 1757 *WV.*

iv Hannah, b 31 Dec 1752 *WV;* m 17 Sep 1783 *CC*—Joseph Atwater.

v Asa, b 11 Feb 1755 *WV;* Census (C) 1-1-1; m 3 Dec 1789 *CC*—Asenath da. Eli & Ruth (Hill) Doolittle, b 13 Apr 1766 *WV.*

vi Sarah, b 1 Aug 1757 *WV;* [m 30 Jan 1799 *CV*—Phinehas Ives].

vii Aaron, b 6 Dec 1759 *WV*, d 9 Jan 1835 æ. 75 *CT1;* m 13 Jan 1785 *CC*—Ruth da. Ephraim & Thankful (Preston) Tuttle, b 3 Jan 1763 *WV*, d 13 May 1831 æ. 68 *CT1.*

viii Joseph, b 26 Sep 1761 *WV*, d 23 Oct 1839 æ. 78 *CT1;* m (1) 14 Sep 1795 *CC*—Rachel Johnson da. Charles Chauncey & Lydia (Holt) Hall, b 4 July 1764 *WV*, d 17 Dec 1809 æ. 45 *CT1;* m (2) 10 Jan 1811 *CC*—Charlotte da. Chauncey & Lydia (Holt) Hall, b 20 Jan 1769 *WV*, d 5 Jan 1846 æ. 77 *CT1.*

ix Eunice, b 16 Sep 176[4] *WV*, d 15 Sep 1826 æ. 62 *CT1;* m 12 Mar 1797 *CV*—Titus Atwater.

2 HANNAH, b 12 Sep 1721 *WV*, "da." bp 21 Mar 1726 *CC*, d 28 Apr 1809 æ. 87 *CT2;* m 26 May 1740 *WV*—Elnathan Andrews.

3 BENJAMIN, b 23 Feb 1724 *WV*, d 1792; m 27 Feb 1744/5 *WV*—Rhoda da. Samuel & Hannah (Lewis) Cook, b 22 Oct 1724 *WV.*

i Thaddeus, b 13 Dec 1745 *WV*, bp Dec 1745 *CC*, d 8 Aug 1752 *CC.*

ii Hannah, b 9 Mar 1747/8 *WV.*

iii Samuel, b [24 Jan 1751], d 2 Feb 1751 æ. 1 wk. 3 days *CT1.*

iv Benjamin, b 24 Nov 1752 *WV*, d 1809; m 21 Apr 1774 *CC*—Eunice da. Daniel & Eunice (Doolittle) Hotchkiss, b 8 Jan 1755 *WV.*

v Rhoda, b 24 Nov 1752 *WV;* m 20 Apr 1774 *CC*, 15 Apr *WV*—Obed Doolittle.

vi Lucy ("Lue"), b 24 Mar 1755 *WV*, d 1819; m 13 Feb

1775 *CC*—Joel Merriman.

vii Damaris, b 5 Dec 1756 *WV;* m 6 Feb 1778 *CC*—Reuben Thorpe of S.

viii Thaddeus, b 10 Dec 1760 *WV*, d 11 Dec 1809; m Abigail Arnold.

4 ELIZABETH, b 23 Feb 1726 *WV*, "da." bp 21 Mar 1726 *CC*, d s. p.

5 ABIGAIL, b 10 May 1728 *WV*, bp June 1728 *CC*, d 5 Nov 1782 æ. 55 *HT3;* m 9 Dec 1747 *NHV*—Daniel Bradley.

6 SAMUEL, b 1 Apr 1730 *WV*, bp Apr 1730 *CC*, d 8 May 1798 æ. 68 *SC;* m Tamar da. Caleb & Tamar (Thompson) Doolittle, b 12 Aug 1736 *WV*, d 7 Dec 1816 æ. 80 *SC*.

7 NATHANIEL, b 30 June 1732 *WV*, bp July 1732 *CC*, d 12 Mar 1734 *WV*.

8 DAMARIS, bp July 1785 *CC*, "child" bu. 19 July 1737 *CC*.

9 JOSEPH, b 12 or 13 July 1737 *WV*, bp July 1737 *CC*, d 1 July 1760.

10 NATHANIEL, b 2 or 12 Sep 1739 *WV*, bp 2 Sep 1739 *CC*, d s. p. 30 Mar 1770 *WV*, æ. 32 *CT1;* m 4 May 1763 *WV*—Lydia da. David & Lydia (Cook) Dutton, b 27 Apr 1738 *WV*, d 29 Oct 1774 *CC;* she m (2) 30 Jan 1772 *CC*—Enos Tyler.

11 DAVID, b 29 June 1742 *WV*, bp July 1742 *CC*, d 27 July 1814 æ. 72 *SC;* m Hannah da. Caleb & Tamar (Thompson) Doolittle, b 8 Apr 1746 *WV*, d 21 Dec 1815 æ. 70 *SC*.

12 DAMARIS, b 23 Sep 1744 *WV*, bp Sep 1745 *CC*, d 25 Nov 1756 *WV*, 20 Nov æ. 12 *CT1*.

FAM. 11. JAMES & PHEBE (LEEK) HITCHCOCK:

1 MARY, b c. 1754, d 5 Sep 1837 æ. 83 *NHV;* m 15 July 1780 *NHC2*—Eldad Mix.

2 PHEBE; m 7 Mar 1779 *NHC1*—Henry Brown.

3 JAMES. [James Hitchcock, said to be a native of NH, impressed on board a British ship of war *ConnJournal*, 4 Feb 1802].

4 ELIZABETH.

FAM. 12. JACOB & PHEBE (IVES) HITCHCOCK:

1 ABIGAIL, b 8 Nov 1761 *NHV*, bp 16 June 1765 *NoHC*.

2 JACOB, b c. 1763, bp 16 June 1765 *NaHC*, d 4 Mar 1769 *NoHC*.

3 ENOCH, bp 26 July 1765 *NoHC*, d 26 July 1765 *NoHC*.

4 PHEBE, bp 16 Nov 1766 *NoHC*.

5 ABIGAIL, b c. 1768, d 5 Mar 1769 *NoHC*.

6 ABIGAIL, bp 18 Feb 1770 *NoHC*.

7 JACOB, bp 19 Jan 1775 *NoHC*.

8 CALEB, bp 3 May 1778 *NoHC*.

9 JOHN, bp 18 Mar 1781 *NoHC*.

FAM. 13. STEPHEN & SARAH (BROCKETT) HITCHCOCK:

1 STEPHEN; m Damaris da. David & Damaris (Sanford) Sanford, b [June 1773], d 21 Sep 1854 æ. 81-3 *HV*.

i Eliza; m Peter Joice.

ii Emeline, b [Jan 1809], d 22 Nov 1895 æ. 86-10 *HV;* m (1)

Gilbert Root of D; m (2) 15 Aug 1847 *HV*—Henry Peck.
iii Orrin, b [June 1812], d 16 Aug 1883 æ. 71-2 *HV;* m.
iv George; m & had 5 children.

2 JOHN, d s. p.

3 EUNICE; m Seymour Sanford; res. Wd. 1806, H 1812, rem. to Dryden, N. Y.

4 SARAH; res. H 1812.

FAM. 14. ISAAC & HANNAH [STILES] HITCHCOCK:

1 PETER.

2 ISAAC, b c. 1775, d 25 June 1863 æ. 88 *BT2;* m Mary da. Abraham & Rebecca (Johnson) Carrington, b c. 1778, d 22 Nov 1855 æ. 78 *BT2*.

3 LYDIA, b 21 Aug 1776 *NHV*.

4 ICHABOD, b 8 May 1777 *HV*, d 9 Sep 1824 *HV;* m (1) 13 Mar 1800 *HV*—Roxana Thompson, b c. 1781, d 26 July 1816 *HV*, æ. 33 *HT3;* m (2) 19 June 1817 *HV*—Fanny Brockett.

(By 1): *i* Lewis, b 6 Aug 1801 *HV*, bp 5 Sep 1802 *HC1*.
ii Leverett, b 12 Apr 1803 *HV*, bp 29 Oct 1803 *HC1*, d 7 June 1881 æ. 78 *HT1;* m 7 Sep 1828 *HV*—Emily Chapman, who d 3 Aug 1872 æ. 60 *HT1*.
iii Hannah, b 28 Apr 1805 *HV*, bp 18 Aug 1804 *HC1*, d 27 Sep 1824 *HV*.
iv Stiles, b 9 Feb 1807 *HV*, bp 26 Apr 1807 *HC1*, d 30 Aug 1824 *HV*.
v Henry, b 5 Mar 1809 *HV*, bp 7 May 1809 *HC1*.
vi Merrit, b 31 Oct 1811 *HV*, bp 26 Jan 1812 *HC1*.
vii Albert, b 26 Dec 1814 *HV*, d 16 May 1893 æ. 76 *HV;* m Pamelia da. Leverett & Pamelia (Hotchkiss) Dickerman, who d 1 Nov 1893 æ. 78 *HV*.

(By 2): *viii* Horace, b 12 May 1818 *HV*.
ix William, b 9 Mar 1820 *HV*.
x Roxana, b 24 Dec 1821 *HV*.
xi Harriet, b 6 Mar 1824 *HV*.

FAM. 15. SAMUEL & HANNAH (BASSETT) HITCHCOCK:

1 SARAH, b 3 Jan 1771 *NHV*, bp 15 Mar 1772 *HC1*, d 25 Jan 1852 æ. 81 *HT1;* m 9 May 1790 *HV*—Elam Ives.

2 MARY, b 9 Aug 1772 *NHV*, bp 27 Sep 1772 *HC1*, d 1814; m Eli Goodyear.

3 SAMUEL, b [Nov 1775], bp 14 Jan 1776 *HC1*, "son" d 26 Jan 1777 æ. 1-2 *NoHC*.

4 SAMUEL, b c. 1777; m Mabel [?perhaps da. Hezekiah & Sarah (Ives) Bassett].
i Nancy. bp 10 Nov 1799 *HC1*.
ii Polly Maria, bp 18 May 1800 *HC1*.
iii Linda, bp 11 Dec 1803 *HC1*.
iv Nancy, bp 22 Dec 1804 *HC1*.
v Samuel Bassett, bp 1808 *HC1*, d s. p. 9 Oct 1881 æ. 73 *NHV*.

vi Chester, bp 13 May 1810 *HC1*.

5 Hannah, b c. 1778, d 26 Dec 1806 æ. 29 *HT3*.

6 Amasa, b c. 1780, d s. p. 24 Aug 1846 æ. 66 *HT3;* m (1) Phebe ——, who d 19 Mar 1833 æ. 64 *HT3;* m (2) 26 May 1833 *HV*—Phebe da. Timothy & Elizabeth (Alling) Leek.

FAM. 16. David & Lydia (——) Hitchcock:

1 Rhoda, b 12 Sep 1772 *NHV*, bp 18 June 1777 *HC1;* m Phinehas Beach of W.

2 David, b 17 Nov 1773 *NHV*, bp 18 June 1777 *HC1;* res. H 1797.

3 Lydia, bp 18 June 1777 *HC1;* res. Unadilla, N. Y., 1799.

FAM. 17. Amos & Sarah (Sperry) Hitchcock:

1 Sarah Minerva, d s. p.

2 Hannah, b c. 1795, d s. p. 7 Aug 1842 æ. 47 *BT1*.

3 Lewis.

4 Ransom; m 30 Oct 1828 Nancy Perry.

5 Amos, b c. 1804, d 27 Apr 1878 æ. 74 *BT1;* m 30 Aug 1830 Louisa N. Judson.

6 Lucien.

FAM. 18, Elihu & Hannah (Hotchkiss) Hitchcock:

1 Levi; rem. to N. Y. City.

2 Eliab, d s. p.; perhaps the "youngest child" of Elihu who d 2 May 1813 *ColR*.

FAM. 19. Eli & Abigail (Sperry) Hitchcock:

1 Elihu.

2 Grant; m 22 Mar 1823 *HV*—Anna da. Jesse Doolittle.

3 Miles, b c. 1802, d s. p. 9 June 1880 æ. 78; m Ursula ——, who d 21 Apr 1867 æ. 63½.

4 Zada; 17 Sep 1820 *WdV*—Ira Smith of Ppt.

FAM. 20. William & Phebe (Hotchkiss) Hitchcock:

1 Nancy, b 4 May 1788 *F*, d 27 Dec 1863 æ. 76 *NHT1;* m Joel Osborn.

2 Betsey, b 28 June 1790 *F*, d 2 Aug 1862; m William Hargill.

3 William, b 7 Mar 1793 *F*.

4 John, b 3 Mar 1796 *F*, d 24 Jan 1829 æ. 33 *NHT1*, 26 Jan æ. 34 (*NHC2*) *NHV;* m Harriet Louisa da. Joab & Elizabeth (Sperry) Way, b 21 Nov 1794 *F*, d 14 Nov 1867 æ. 33 (i. e. 73) *NHT1*.

i Edward DeForest, b 12 Aug 1815 *F*, d 17 Nov 1816 *F*.

ii Edward DeForest, b 21 Feb 1817 *F*, d 4 May 1884 æ. 67 *NHT1;* m (1) 21 Oct 1840 *NHV*—Lydia A. Fuller, who d 20 Oct 1842 æ. 23 *NHT1;* m (2) Carolyn Amelia da. Eleazer & Fanny (Osborn) Hotchkiss, b 8 Feb 1824 *F*, d 29 July 1859 *F* (Norfolk, Va.); m (3) Phebe A. Everitt.

iii Rebecca Fayette, b 13 Aug 1818 *F*, d 1 Sep 1822 *F*, "child" æ. 4 (*NHC2*) *NHV*.

iv Lewis Merritt, b 13 July 1820 *F*, d 1 June 1834 *F*, æ. 14 *NHV*.

v Albert F., b 2 May 1822 *F*, d 15 Aug 1854 (at Utica, N. Y.) *F*.

5 LUTHER, b 30 Sep 1799 *F*, d 21 Apr 1826 æ. 26 *NHV*.

FAM. 21. TIMOTHY & ABIGAIL (CLARK) HITCHCOCK:

1 ABIGAIL, b 15 Nov 1773 *F*, d 20 Aug 1864 æ. 91 *Bx*.

2 ANNA, b 7 Oct 1775 *F*, d 23 May 1831 æ. 56; m John Delavan Wooster.

3 LYDIA, b 1 July 1779 *F*.

4 TIMOTHY, b 5 Aug 1781 *F*, d 5 Dec 1878 æ. 97-4 *NHV*, *SeymourT;* m (1) 6 Jan 1803 Urania Twitchell, who d 4 Jan 1843; m (2) 2 Aug 1843 Miranda, wid. Bassett, who d 21 Jan 1867.

5 BETHIA, b 19 June 1784 *F*, d 21 June 1841; m Aaron King of Tallmadge, Ohio.

6 DENZEL, b 7 Dec 1786 *F*, d 24 Jan 1850 æ. 63 (Seymour); insane; m Betsey [da. David & & Thankful (Tolles)] Carrington, b [18 Aug 1789 *F*].

7 CLARK, b 8 Mar 1789 *F;* rem. to Norfolk, Va.; m (1) Abigail da. Peter & Asenah (Beecher) Perkins, b c. 1792, d 23 Nov 1827 æ. 35 (at Norfolk, Va.) *BT2;* m (2) ——— .

8 ELIZABETH, b 3 July 1794 *F*, d 19 May 1861 æ. 66 *Bx;* m Darius Driver.

FAM. 22. JOSEPH & CATHERINE (SMITH) HITCHCOCK:

1 LETTY; m David Rockwell.

2 CATHERINE; m Benjamin Coats.

3 EUNICE, b c. 1788, d 13 Mar 1832 æ. 44 *BT2;* m Eli Terrill.

FAM. 22. JOSEPH & MABEL (HOTCHKISS) HITCHCOCK:

4 URSULA; m Jesse Gregory.

5 MABEL; m Edmund Hagen.

6 MERRIT, b 26 Sep 1793 *F*, d 26 Sep 1842 *F;* m (1) Polly Taylor, b 1 July 1794, d 11 May 1818; m (2) Mahala Sessions, b 20 Feb 1797, d 26 June 1869.

7 MARY, b c. 1801, d 6 Oct 1854 æ. 53; m Nathaniel Platt.

8 MARSHALL, b 29 Mar 1804 *F*, d 7 Apr 1854 (at Herrick, Pa.); m 10 Dec 1825 (Pike, Pa.)—Julia Ann Taylor.

9 JONATHAN, d s. p.

10 BETSEY, b c. 1812, d 1 May 1879 æ. 66; m Lynder Fletcher.

11 JOSEPH, b 26 Feb 1814 *F*, d 5 Mar 1867 (at Le Raysville, Pa.); m 4 Sep 1836 Alvira Lines.

FAM. 23. AMASA & SARAH (BRADLEY) HITCHCOCK:

1 LURA, b 22 June 1766 *WV*, bp 14 Mar 1773 *CC*, d 15 July 1829 æ. 63 *CT1;* m 11 Mar 1792 *CC*—Reuben Preston.

2 AMASA, b 17 Feb 1768 *WV*, bp 14 Mar 1773 *CC*, d 30 Apr 1835 æ. 67 *CT1;* Census (C) 1-0-1; m (1) 10 June 1790 *CV*—Anna da. Moses & Hannah (Dunbar) Blakeslee, b 9 Aug 1768 *WV*, d 6 Oct 1795 æ. 27 *CT1;* m (2) 6 Dec 1796 *CV*, 4 Dec *CC*—Abigail Mary Ann da. Rev. John & Abigail (Hall) Foote, bp 22 Sep 1776 *CC*, d 9 Aug 1798 æ. 22 *CT1;* m (3) 13 Jan 1800 *CV*—Elizabeth Austin, who d 29 June 1854 æ. 85 *CT1*.

3 HANNAH, b 25 Dec 1769 *WV*, bp 14 Mar 1773 *CC*, d 2 Oct 1825 æ. 56 *CT1;* m 23 Dec 1789 *CC*—Elias Gaylord.

4 SARAH, b 29 Dec 1771 *WV*, bp 14 Mar 1773 *CC*, d 10 Aug 1844

æ. 74 *CTI*; m 5 Dec 1792 *CC*—Joseph Ives.

5 ABIGAIL, b 4 Dec 1773 *WV*, bp 19 Dec 1773 *CC*; m 7 Apr 1799 *CC*—Benjamin Lewis.

6 MARY, b 13 Nov 1775 *WV*, bp 19 Nov 1775 *CC*; m 16 July 1797 *CC*—Amasa Doolittle.

7 RUTH, b 1 Feb 1779, bp 21 May 1779 *CC*, d c. 1871; m 16 Jan 1800 *CC*—Joseph Moss.

8 SILAS, b 9 June 1781, bp 22 July 1781 *CC*, d 18 July 1784 æ. 3 *CTI*.

9 JAIRUS, b 28 Mar 1783, bp 29 Mar 1783 *CC*, d 31 Mar 1783 æ. 0–0–2 *CTI*.

10 SILAS, b 1 June 1784, bp 1 Aug 1784 *CC*, d 26 Sep 1849 æ. 65 *CTI*; m 22 Oct 1806 *CV*—Polly da. Aaron & Patience (Todd) Bradley, bp 2 July 1786 *HCI*, d 13 Dec 1860 æ. 74 *CTI*.

11 JAIRUS, b 13 Aug 1786, bp 8 Oct 1786 *CC*, d 15 Feb 1853 æ. 67 *CTI*; m 8 Mar 1815 *CV*—Amelia da. Amos & Abigail (Bristol) Andrews, b 17 Jan 1787 *CV*, d 29 Dec 1853 æ. 67 *CTI*.

12 LOUISA, b 16 Sep 1789, bp 19 Sep 1789 *CC*, d 20 Sep 1789 æ. 0–0–4 *CTI*.

FAM. 24. VALENTINE & SARAH (HOTCHKISS) HITCHCOCK:

1 REUBEN, b 4 Jan 1764 *WV*, d s. p. 3 July 1794 æ. 30 *CTI*; Rev.; res. Sunbury, Ga., & Ppt.

2 ROGER, b 8 July 1766 *WV*, d 30 Jan 1823 æ. 57 *CTI*; Rev.; m 11 Feb 1808 *CV*—Sophia Hickox, who d 15 June 1850 *CTI*.

3 CYNTHIA, b 11 July 1769 *WV*, bp 20 Aug 1769 *CC*, d 29 May 1800 æ. 30 *CTI*.

4 SARAH, b 30 Mar 1773 *WV*, bp 4 Apr 1773 *CC*, d 15 Mar 1817 æ. 44 *CTI*; m 8 Nov 1795 *CV*—Jared Moss.

5 PATIENCE BENHAM, b 1 Oct 1775 *WV*, bp 26 Nov 1775 *CC*, d 29 Nov 1820; m 2 Feb 1794 *CC*—Jared Moss of Augusta, N. Y., & Sandusky, O.

6 HENRY LAWRENCE, b 17 Nov 1778 *WV*, bp 17 Jan 1779 *CC*, d s. p. 30 Apr 1812 æ. 34 *CTI*; Dr.; res. Wat; m 23 Nov 1809 *CC*—Abigail da. Asahel & Abigail (Law) Hitchcock, bp 1 Feb 1784 *CC*, d 31 Mar 1855 æ. 71 *CTI*.

7 PETER, b 19 Oct 1781, bp 28 Oct 1781 *CC*, d 4 Mar 1854; (Yale 1801); res. Burton, Ohio; Chief Justice, Sup. Ct., Ohio; m 12 Dec 1805 *CC*—Nabby da. Elam & Abigail (Hall) Cook, b 10 July 1784, d 26 July 1867.

8 MELISSA, b c. 1786, d 5 Aug 1794 æ. 8 *CTI*.

FAM. 25. DAVID & LOIS (COOK) HITCHCOCK:

1 DAVID, b 18 Dec 1771 *WV*, bp 6 Dec 1772 *CC*, d 1 Sep 1803 æ. 32 *CTI*, 31 Aug *CC*; m 9 Oct 1793 *CC*—Hannah da. Nathan & Phebe (Thompson) Andrews, b 12 Sep 1773 *WV*; she m (2) 19 Apr 1804 *CC*—Roswell Smith.

2 URANIA, b 4 Jan 1774 *WV*, bp 9 Jan 1774 *CC*, d 8 June 1843; m 12 Jan 1795 *CC*—Joseph Hall Cook.

3 ABNER, b 4 Sep 1777 *CV*, *WV*, bp 7 Sep 1777 *CC*, d 31 Aug 1810;

m Mary Warner.

4 LOIS, b 2 Sep 1781 *CV* [?1779], bp 30 Apr 1780 *CC;* m 15 June 1806 *CV*—Ephraim Tuttle.

5 MARCUS, b 4 Mar 1783 *CV*, bp 27 Apr 1783 *CC*, d 21 May 1852 (at Burton, Ohio); m 31 Mar 1808 *CV*—Marena da. Nathan & Ann (Atwater) Gaylord, b 16 July 1786 *CV*.

6 LEE, b 9 Apr 1788 *F*, "child" d 28 June 1788 *CC*.

7 GAIUS, b 15 Feb 1791 *F*, bp 1 May 1791 *CC*, d 27 May 1862 æ. 71 *CTI;* m 14 Oct 1814 *CV*—Lavinia Tuttle, who d 11 Oct 1878 æ. 87 *CTI*.

(The Hitchcock Genealogy adds a da. Lucy Ann who d young. A Marcus bp 20 May 1781 *CC* was perhaps a child of David. A "child" d 9 Nov 1781 *CC*).

FAM. 26. ASAHEL & ABIGAIL (LAW) HITCHCOCK:

1 MILES, b 5 Oct 1762, d 14 May 1767 æ. 5 *CTI*.

2 CHARLOTTE, b 23 Apr 1765, d 21 June 1765 æ. 0-2 *CTI*.

3 MILES, b 4 Feb 1767 *WV*, bp 14 June 1767 *CC*, d 9 Dec 1843; m (1) ——— ; m (2) 25 Oct 1825 Caroline Aertse.

4 MARY ANN, b 19 Nov 1769 *WV*, bp 4 Mar 1770 *CC*, d 12 Jan 1848 æ. 77 *CTI;* m Wm. Carrington.

5 NABBY, b 7 Feb 1773 *WV*, bp 21 Feb 1773 *CC*, d 16 Sep 1775 æ. 2-6 *CTI*.

6 ANDREW LAW, b 23 May 1779 *WV*, bp 30 May 1779 *CC*, d 22 Dec 1804 æ. 25 *CTI;* m Katharine ———, who d Dec 1807 æ. 27 *CTI*.

7 ABIGAIL, bp 1 Feb 1784 *CC*, d 31 Mar 1855 æ. 71 *CTI;* m 23 Nov 1809 *CC*—Henry Lawrence Hitchcock.

FAM. 27. ELIAKIM & LOWLY (HULL) HITCHCOCK (incomplete):

1 DAUGHTER, d 6 Apr 1774 *NHCI*.

2 LOWLY, bp 26 May 1776 *NHCI;* m 5 Feb 1804 *CC*—Moses Bunnell.

3 CHILD, d 5 Sep 1779 *NHCI*.

4 NANCY, b 27 Oct 1784 *F* [1783], bp 9 Nov 1783 *NHCI*, d 1864; m Cyrus Baldwin of Wtn.

5 SARAH, bp 30 Apr 1786 *NHCI*.

6 ALFRED, bp 31 May 1789 *NHCI*.

7 BETSEY, bp 29 July 1792 *NHCI*.

FAM. 28. DAN & ANNA (PERKINS) HITCHCOCK:

1 REBECCA, b 4 May 1775 *WV;* m ——— Perkins.

2 SAMUEL, b 22 June 1776 *WV;* res. Ppt; m 7 May 1809 *CC*—Sybil da. Josiah & Hannah (Blakeslee) Talmadge, b 9 May 1788 *CV*.

3 BETSEY, b 16 May 1779 *WV*, d 10 Dec 1826 æ. 46 *CTI;* m Amos Bristol.

4 CHAUNCEY, b 17 July 1781 *WV*, d 1852 (Fabius, N. Y.); m Jan 1802 *CC*—Sarah da. Augustus & Sarah (Preston) Bristol, b 27 Aug 1786 *CV*, d Apr 1868 (at Bristol) *F*.

i Rebecca, b 6 Aug 1802 (at C) *F*, d 7 Oct 1864 (Ithaca, N.

Y.) *F;* m 5 Oct 1819 (at B) *ColR*—George W. Wilmot.

ii Mary Ann; m Jacob Curtis; res. Carbon Cliff, Ill.

iii George; m Nancy A. Hart of Bristol.

iv Matilda, b 13 Oct 1810 (Butternuts, N. Y.); m (1) Lyman Litchfield; m (2) 7 Oct 1868 Alfred Cooper of Forestville.

v Sarah M., b 14 Dec 1816; m 28 May 1843 Robert Ezra Sloper.

vi Benajah, b 24 Dec 1824 (at C), d 22 Oct 1903 æ. 78–10–28 *BristolV;* m 4 Sep 1849 Nancy A. da. Asahel & Anna (Judd) Mix, b 1 July 1831, d 30 Nov 1906 æ. 75–4–28 (Montgomery, Mass.) *BristolV.*

5 LYMAN, b 2 Jan 1784 *WV*, d 21 Oct 1862; m 1 Jan 1809 *CC*—Amy da. Ebenezer & Patience Hull, b c. 1791, d 22 Nov 1827 *CT2.*

6 ANNA, b 19 Oct 1785 *WV;* m John Reed of Mansfield, Eng.

7 DAN, b 23 Jan 1788 *WV;* rem. to Baltimore, Md.

8 ESTHER, b 12 May 1790 *WV;* m Amasa Perklns.

9 MATILDA, b 5 May 1793 *WV.*

10 CLARISSA, b 3 June 1795 *WV*, d 22 Jan 1876 æ. 80–5–19 *HV;* m (1) Levi Perkins; m (2) Sylvester Sherman.

FAM. 29. MATTHIAS & MARY (THOMPSON) HITCHCOCK:

1 CLARISSA, bp 15 Aug 1803 *NHx.*

2 HARRIET, b c. 1790, bp 15 Aug 1803 *NHx*, d 24 June 1870 æ. 80 *NHV;* m 12 July 1821 *NHV*—Benjamin Bradley.

3 ABIGAIL, b 15 Jan 1795 *F*, bp 15 Aug 1803 *NHx*, d 20 Aug 1876; m 2 Apr 1833 Lyman Brockett.

4 LUTHER, b c. 1798, bp 15 Aug 1803 *NHx*, d 28 June 1826 æ. 28 *NHT2.*

5 FANNY, b c. 1800, bp 15 Aug 1803 *NHx;* m 27 Aug 1821 *NHV*—William Thomas.

6 WILLIAM, b [Jan 1803], bp 15 Aug 1803 *NHx*, d 31 Aug 1803 æ. 0–7 *NHx.*

7 EMILY, b c. 1807, d 5 Oct 1840 æ. 33 *NHT2.*

FAM. 30. ELIADA & ESTHER (WARNER) HITCHCOCK:

1 COMFORT, b 24 July 1786 *F*, d 30 Apr 1849; m Lyman Munson.

2 ESTHER, b c. 1788, d 22 Mar 1874 æ. 86 *HT2, HV;* m Asa Alling.

3 HANNAH, b c. 1798, d 14 Oct 1821 æ. 23 *HT2.*

4 SARAH, b c. 1802, d 14 Oct 1835 æ. 33 *HT2.*

HITCHESON. ——— m Agnes ———, who d before 1685 (at NH); she m (2) ——— Sutton.

1 SARAH; m Thomas Leek.

2 THOMAS, d s. p. before 1685 (at NH).

HITFIELD. MATTHIAS m 25 Aug 1664 *NHV*—Maria da. Cornelius & Jannekin Melyn, wid. ——— Pardice.

***HODGE.** FAM. 1. THOMAS, s. of John & Susanna (Denslow), b 13 Feb 1668/9 *Windsor*, d 2 May 1712 æ. 43 *WHT1;* m Judith da. Benjamin & Rebecca (Mallory) Bunnell, b 13 Apr 1672 *NHV*, d 21 July 1746 æ. 4 *h HT1;* she m (2) Daniel Bristol.

1 DANIEL, b 28 Jan 1693/4 *NHV*, bp 27 Oct 1734 *Stx*, d 10 June 1777 *WHD;* m Eleanor da. Ebenezer & Eleanor (Lane) Brown, b 1 Mar 1698/9 *NHV*.

i Sarah, b 19 May 1726 *NHV*, bp 27 Oct 1734 *Stx*, d 20 Mar 1802 æ. 76 *WHD;* m Jonathan Brown.

ii Jesse, b 11 Mar 1727/8 *NHV*, bp 27 Oct 1734 *Stx*.

iii Daniel, b 12 Dec 1729 *NHV*, bp 27 Oct 1734 *Stx*, d 29 Aug 1787 æ. 58 *WHD;* m Sarah da. Josiah & Mary (Arnold) Platt, b 17 Feb 1741/2 *NHV* [O. S.], 28 Feb 1742 *OC* [N. S.], d 7 Apr 1825 æ. 83 *OC*. **FAM. 2.**

iv Benjamin, b 22 Feb 1731/2 *NHV*, bp 27 Oct 1734 *Stx*, d 20 Sep 1776 *WHD*.

v Eleanor, b 25 May 1734 *NHV*, bp 27 Oct 1734 *Stx*, d 20 Sep 1745 æ. 11 *WHT1*.

vi Mary, b 24 July 1736 *NHV*, d 8 Oct 1805 æ. 70 *WHD;* m Nathaniel Downs.

vii Martha, b 24 Apr 1740 *NHV*.

viii Rebecca, b 26 May 1743 *NHV*.

2 JESSE, b 17 Nov 1695 *NHV*, d s. p. before 1725.

3 JUDITH, b 8 Oct 1697 *NHV;* m 29 June 1720 *NHV*—Samuel Hale.

4 THOMAS, b 28 Mar 1701 *NHV*, d c. 1736; m Ann da. Daniel & Esther (Sperry) Bristol, b 12 Feb 1701 *NHV;* she m (2) 8 Nov 1737 *NHV*—George Clinton.

i Esther, bp 11 Sep 1729 *Stx*, d 27 Feb 1802 æ. 73 *WHT1;* m 14 Feb 1751 *NHV*—Isaac Beecher.

ii Thomas, bp 16 Apr 1731 *Stx;* said to have left s. David.

iii William, bp 27 Oct 1734 *Stx*, d c. 1779 in (RW); m 12 June 1755 *NHC2*—Lucy da. Nathan & Rachel (Painter) Smith, b 16 Nov 1737 *NHV;* she m (2) 4 Aug 1783 *Wat V*—Johnson Anderson. **FAM. 3.**

iv Mary, b 24 July 1736 *NHV*.

5 MIRIAM, b 18 Aug 1703 *NHV*, d soon.

6 SUSANNA, b 7 Sep 1705 *NHV;* m William Beardslee of Stratfield.

7 MARY, b 5 Nov 1707 *NHV;* m 15 Oct 1724 *NHV*—Samuel Seward of L. I.

8 MARTHA, b 18 Feb 1709/10 *NHV;* m 19 Jan 1726/7 *NHV*—Benjamin Jones.

9 MIRIAM, b 2 Mar 1712 *NHV;* m 22 Dec 1731 *NHV*—Daniel Blakeslee.

FAM. 2. DANIEL & SARAH (PLATT) HODGE:

1 DANIEL, b [8 Jan 1765], d 18 Jan 1832 æ. 68 *WHT2*, 20 Jan *WHD;* m May 1796 Betsey da. Chauncey & Dorcas [Stevens] Smith, b c. 1774, d 28 Oct 1843 æ. 69 *WHT2*.

i Mehitabel; m Hershel Stevens of WH.

ii Laura; m Seymour Brockett of NH.

iii Elias; res. Bridgeport 1848.
iv James, b c. 1808, d July 1327 æ. 19 (at sea) *WHT2*
v Martha; res. NH 1848.
vi David; res. Augusta, Ga., 1853.
vii William, b c. 1817, d 29 Dec 1833 æ. 17 (at sea) *WHT1*.

2 SARAH, b 8 Jan 1765 *OC;* m Amos Mallory; rem. to P.

3 BENJAMIN, b c. 1768,; res. D; m Eliphal Mallory; she m (2) —— Eels of Macon, Ga. Family incomplete.

PAGE 946

i Benjamin, b c. 1792, d 26 July 1868 æ. 76 *DT2;* m Ann da. Jerrod & Mary (Wooster) Barthelme, b 24 July 1795 *F*, d 2 Jan 1856 æ. 60 *DT2*.

4 REBECCA.

5 MARTHA, b 19 Oct 1771 *OC*, d 9 Mar 1813 *OC*.

6 JESSE, "child" bu. 26 Sep 1776 *NHx*.

7 ELEANOR, bp 1 Sep 1776 (sponsor, Sarah Brown) *NHx*, d 20 July 1792 æ. 16 *WHD*.

8 MEHITABEL, d 23 Sep 1787 *WHD*.

9 JESSE, b 29 Apr 1780 *OC*, "son" bp 4 June 1780 *NHx;* rem. to M 1813; m (1) Nancy Hooker, who 6 July 1807 æ. 23 *OC;* m (2) Lucy da. David & Lucy (Catlin) Trowbridge, wid. Zaccheus Candee, b c. 1783.

(By 1): *i* Nancy Selina, b 10 Apr 1806 *OC*.

10 SON, bp 28 Sep 1783 *NHx*.

FAM. 3. WILLIAM & LUCY (SMITH) HODGE:

1 (probably) PHILO, b 9 Jan 1756 *F*, d 30 Jan 1842 (Roxbury); Census (Wy) 2-1-4; m (1) 12 Sep 1778 Keturah Armstrong; m (2) 1 Jan 1788 Lucy Newton.

2 EUNICE, b 9 Sep 1758 *F*, d 10 Aug 1843; m 30 Dec 1778 *WatV*—Joel Terrill.

3 CHESTER SMITH.

4 MABEL; m (1) 14 May 1783 *NHSupCt*—Nathaniel Tyler; he div. her 1799; m (2) Jan 1797 (Durham, N. Y.) *F*—Jeremiah Hotchkiss.

5 STATIRA; m —— Gunn.

6 DAUGHTER; m —— Smith.

7 JEREMIAH, bp 11 Feb 1776 *NHx*.

8 BELINDA, b c. 1779, d 3 Mar 1865; m David Beebe of Lorain Co., Ohio.

HODGE. MISCELLANEOUS. ANN, b c. 1750, had a nat. child b 1767 *NHC Ct;* she m 9 Feb 1775 *NHC2*—Joseph Thomas....... JOHN BELDEN, m 14 Sep 1806 *OC*—Violet Northrop of Wd.

HODGES. CHARLES m 1 July 1686 *LymeV*—Ann ——. Another Ann (sister of Charles?) m 28 Feb 1710/1 *NHV*, 1 Mar 1711 *EHV*—William Luddington. Charles rem. to EH & in 1719 with w. Ann conveyed property bounded by land of "brother Luddintons."

1 ABIGAIL; m 29 July 1713 *NHV*—Henry Nails.

2 THOMAS, b 12 July 1692 (at Lyme) *NHV;* m Jane da. Matthew & Mary (Brockett) Moulthrop, b 13 Dec 1694 *NHV*.

i Lydia, b 12 Aug 1718 *EHV.*

ii Jane, b 17 Apr 1720 *EHV.*

iii Hannah, b 21 Sep 1722 *EHV.*

iv Job, b 24 Apr 1726 *EHV;* rem. to New Fairfield. A Job appears, Census (Norwalk & Stamford) 1-2-2.

v Kezia, b 12 Aug 1729 *EHV.*

vi Abel, b 8 Mar 1730/1 *EHV,* d 25 Apr 1802 æ. 72; Census (New Fairfield) 1-1-2; m Rebecca da. Caleb & Jemima (Keeler) Trowbridge. [Census, Thaddeus (New Fairfield) 1-1-1; Census, Thomas (New Fairfield 1-3-2; perhaps sons of Abel].

3 ABRAHAM; rem. to Phillips Precinct, N. Y.; m Abigail da. John & Hannah (Moulthrop) Russell, b 19 May 1701 *NHV.*

i Abraham, b 23 June 1726 *NHV;* Census, (Cambridge, N. Y.) 2-0-2.

ii Isaac, b 7/13 June 1729 *NHV.*

iii Abigail, b 13 Apr 1732 *NHV,* 1731 *WatV.*

iv David, b 7 Feb 1733/4 *NHV.*

v Samuel, b Aug 1736 *NHV;* Census (Cambridge, N. Y.) 1-0-4.

4 JOHN, d 1735; m ——— .

i Mary, d 29 Mar 1784 *HCl;* m 4 May 1735 *NHV*—Caleb Andrews.

5 RICHARD; m Mary da. Nathaniel & Elizabath How.

HODSHON. Variants, HODSON, HUDSON. JOHN, b c. 1616, d Oct 1690 *NHV,* 14 Oct æ. 74 *NHTl;* m 2 Sep 1651 *NHV*—Abigail da. Nathaniel Turner, who d 1693.

1 ABIGAIL, b 25 Mar 1654 *NHV,* bp 8 Feb 1656 *NHCl;* m 8 Dec 1680 *StV*—Richard Blackleach of St.

2 SARAH, b 5 Apr 1657 *NHV,* bp 12 Apr 1657 *NHCl;* m 11 Nov 1684 *NHV*—Rev. Israel Chauncey.

3 MARY, bp 8 July 1660 *NHCl,* d soon.

4 JOHN, b [1663] *NHV,* d 4 Nov 1663 *NHV.*

5 SAMUEL, b Sep [1664] *NHV,* bp 12 Nov 1664 *NHCl,* d 26 Aug 1673 æ. 9 *NHTl.*

6 JOHN, b 7 Apr 1667 *NHV,* d 2 Nov 1711 *NHV,* æ. 44 *NHTl;* m 5 Apr 1691 *NHV*—Elizabeth da. Thomas & Sarah (Rutherford) Trowbridge, b 30 June 1676 *NHV,* bp 30 Apr 1687 *NHCl,* d 1 Dec 1711 *NHV,* æ. 35 *NHTl.*

i John, b 5 Feb 1693 *NHV,* 6 Feb *NHTl,* d 1693 *NHV,* 18 Dec 1693 æ. 1 *NHTl.*

ii John, b c. 1694, d 15 Feb 1720/1 *NHV,* 14 Feb æ. 27 *NHTl.*

7 MARY, b 17 Apr 1670 *NHV,* d Mar 1670/1 *NHV.*

8 ANNA, b Feb 1671 *NHV* [1671/2], d 20 Feb 1672 *NHV.*

9 NATHANIEL, d s. p. c. 1701; Dr.; res. St; m Abigail da. Rev. Nathaniel & Abigail (Strong) Chauncey, b 14 Oct 1677; she m (2) 12 Jan 1703/4 *StV*—Samuel Gaskell; she m (3) 20 Apr

1710 *StV*—Edward Burroughs.

HODSHON. Elizabeth m 30 Mar 1681 *NHV*—John Watson.

HOLABIRD. HANNAH m 15 Oct 1750 *NHV*—Gershom Brown.

HOLBROOK PAGE 1244

HOLCOLM. JOEL m 20 Nov 1745 *WV*—Sarah Bull.

1 SARAH, b 3 Mar 1746/7 *WV*, d 26 July 1751 *WV*.

2 SARAH, b 25 Feb 1754 *WV*.

3 LUCY, b 5 Mar 1761 *WV*.

HOLLINGWORTH. ABIGAIL of M m 21 May 1741 *NHV*—Samuel Munson

HOLMES. JEHIEL m Martha ——, who bp 24 Nov 1776 *NHC2*.

1 LUCY, bp 24 Nov 1776 *NHC2*.

2 JOHN LEE, bp 24 Nov 1776 *NHC2*.

3 SIMEON, b c. 1778, bp Nov 1789 (æ. 11) *NHx*.

4 BENJAMIN, b c. 1780, bp Nov 1789 (æ. 9) *NHx*.

5 ELIZABETH, b c. 1789, bp Nov 1789 (æ. 6) *NHx*.

6 JEHIEL, b c. 1786, bp Nov 1789 (æ. 3) *NHx*.

HOLMES. MISCELLANEOUS. JUDAH, admitted inhabitant of NH, perhaps father of JANE, who m 26 June 1695 *NHV*—William Wooding. Prior to marriage, Jane had a nat. child by John Alling, viz.: Mary, b 26 Aug 1693 *NHV* [p. 18].......COL. JAMES d 8 July 1824 æ. 87 *NHT1*; his w. Tamar d 11 Oct 1778 æ. 30 (at Montreal) *NHT1*.

***HOLT.** FAM. 1. WILLIAM, b c. 1610, d 1683 æ. 73 *WT1*, 1 Sep *WV*; m Sarah ——, who d 1717; she m (2) William Peck.

1 JOHN, b c. 1645, d [16] June 1733 æ. [—] *EHT*; m Jan 1673 *NHV*—Elizabeth da. John & Tabitha Thomas, b 15 May 1648 *NHV*.

i Elizabeth, b 28 Sep 1674 *NHV*, d 19 Dec 1751 æ. 78 *EHV*; m 23 Feb 1691/2 *NHV*—John Potter.

ii John, b 23 Mar 1678/9 *NHV*, d s. p.

iii Joseph, b 22 Jan 1680 *NHV* [1680/1], bp (Aged) 18 Apr 1756 *EHC*, d 25 May 1770 *NorfolkC*; m (1) 28 Feb 1705/6 *NHV*—Abigail da. Samuel & Sarah (Cooper) Hemingway, bp 8 July 1688 *NHC1*, d 1736 *EHV*, 10 Feb æ. 49 *EHT*; m (2) Mary ——, who d 10 June 1743 *EHV*, æ. 44 *EHR*; m (3) 19 Dec 1745 *WC2*—Joanna da. Joseph & Sarah (Stanley) Gaylord, wid. Robert Royce & John Johnson. **FAM. 2.**

iv Daniel, b 30 Mar 1689 *NHV*.

2 NATHANIEL, b c. 1647, d 28 May 1723 æ. 77 (at Newport, R. I.) Sgt.; rem. to New London; m (1) 5 Apr 1680 (at New London)—Rebecca da. Thomas & Millicent (Ash) Beebe, who d 1689; m (2) —— ; had issue.

3 MERCY, b c. 1649, d c. 1688; m 9 Nov 1680 *WV*—Abraham Doolittle.

4 ELEAZER, b 5 Apr 1651 *NHV*, bp July 1656 *NHC1*, d 24 June 1736 æ. 86 *NHT1*; Ens.; m (1) 5 Nov 1674 *NHV*—Tabitha da. John & Tabitha Thomas, b 18 Dec 1653 *NHV*, d 18 Aug 1725 æ. 71 *NHT1*; m (2) Mary da. Ephraim & Mary (Powell) San-

PAGE 946

ford, wid. Joseph Ashburn & Joshua Hotchkiss, b Oct 1670 *NHV*, d 1750.

(By 1): *i* William, b 25 Sep 1675 *NHV*, d 28 Nov 1675 *NHV*.

ii Thomas, b 4 Nov 1676 *NHV*, bp 29 July 1688 *NHCl*, d s. p. 13 Mar 1758 æ. 82 *NHTl*; m 9 May 1722 *NHV*—Abigail da. John & Abigail (Sherman) Johnson, b 28 Sep 1695 *NHV*, d 5 Mar 1778 æ. 83 *NHTl*.

iii Sarah, b 2 Apr 1679 *NHV*, bp 29 July 1688 *NHCl*, d 29 Mar 1743 *NHV*; m 22 Sep 1698 *NHV*—John Bradley.

iv Susanna, b 21 Oct 1681 *NHV*, bp 29 July 1688 *NHCl*, d 4 June 1712 *NHV*, 7 June *NHTl*; m 5 Feb 1707/8 *NHV*—Roger Alling.

v Tabitha, b 30 Jan 1683 *NHV*, bp 29 July 1688 *NHCl*, d 4 Oct 1743 æ. 60 *NHTl*; m (1) 30 June 1709 *NHV*—Samuel Whitehead; m (2) 2 Dec 1718 *NHV*—David Atwater.

vi Abigail, b 17 Nov 1686 *NHV*, bp 29 July 1688 *NHCl*, d 1760; m Enos Pardee.

vii Elizabeth, bp 12 Jan 1690 *NHCl*, d 21 Apr 1718 *NHV*.

viii Lydia, bp 5 Nov 1693 *NHCl*, d 31 Aug 1776 æ. 83 *NHTl*; m (1) 4 Feb 1724/5 *NHV*—John Bassett; m (2) Stephen Sperry.

5 THOMAS, b 31 July 1653 *NHV*, bp July 1656 *NHCl*, d 3 June 1676 *NHV*.

6 JOSEPH, b 2 Apr 1655 *NHV*, bp July 1656 *NHCl*, d 19 Dec 1697 æ. 41 *WV*; m 20 Nov 1684 *WV*—Elizabeth da. Francis & Lydia (Bunnell) French, b 20 June 1664 *DV*, d 18 Nov 1739 *WV*, æ. 76 *WTl*.

i Joseph, b 10 June 1685 *WV*, d 2 June 1767 æ. 82 *WV*; m (1) 8 June 1709 *WV*—Abigail da. Thomas & Mary (Merriman) Curtis, b Nov 1689 *WV*, d 12 Jan 1730 *WV*; m (2) 13 July 1730 *WV*—Mary Benedict, wid. Isaac Royce, who d 10 Feb 1748/9 *WV*; m (3) 25 July 1749 *WV*—Mary Roberts, who d 10 Sep 1761 *WV*; m (4) 9 Feb 1762 *WCl*—Elizabeth ——, wid. Barnabas Lewis & Daniel Merwin, b c. 1703, d 26 July 1766 æ. 63 *WV*. **FAM. 3.**

ii Daniel, b 6 Oct 1687 *WV*, d 1749; m 2 Mar 1716 *WV*—Rebecca da. Thomas & Grace (Watson) Hall, b 6 Jan 1691 *WV* [1691/2], d 30 Mar 1760 *WV*. **FAM. 4.**

iii Benjamin, b 3 Sep 1690 *WV*, d 28 Oct 1742 *WV*, æ. 53 *WTl*; Capt.; m 14 Dec 1726 *WV*—Abigail da. Jacob & Abigail (Hitchcock) Johnson, b 1699 *WV*, d 4 Nov 1742 *WV*, æ. [—] *WTl*. **FAM. 5.**

iv Mary, b 29 Jan 1693/4 *WV*, d c. 1729; m 23 Dec 1714 *WV*—Thomas Royce.

v Elizabeth, b 23 Mar 1696 *WV*, d 3 June 1768 æ. 73 *WV*, *WTl*; m 5 Oct 1720 *WV*—Joseph Doolittle.

7 BENJAMIN, b 6 Mar 1656/7 *NHV*, bp July 1656 *NHCl*, d s. p. 2 Aug 1690 æ. 32 *WV*.

FAM. 2. JOSEPH & ABIGAIL (HEMINGWAY) HOLT:

1 JOHN, b 26 Aug 1706 *NHV*.

2 JOSEPH, b 30 Oct 1708 *EHV*, d s. p.

3 DANIEL, b 6 Sep 1711 *EHV*, d 11 June 1756 æ. 45 *EHT;* Ens.; m 12 Feb 1735/6 *NHV*—Anna da Samuel & Anna (Morris) Smith, b 17 May 1719 *NHV*, d 7 Dec 1798 æ. 80 *EHC;* she m (2) 25 Jan 1758 *EHC*—Timothy Andrews.

i Abigail, b 22 Nov 1736 *NHV*, d 3 Oct 1828 æ. 91-5 *EHC;* m (1) John Moulthrop; m (2) 17 Nov 1785 *EHC*—Samuel Shepard.

ii Anna, b 27 Mar 1741 *NHV*, d 22 Sep 1751 *NHV*.

iii Dan, b 18 Oct 1744 *NHV*, d 31 Jan 1829 æ. 84 *EHT*, *EHC;* Census (EH) 2-2-6; m 5 Dec 1765 *EHC*—Anna da Daniel & Abigail (Chidsey) Hitchcock, b 24 Sep 1746 *EHV*, d 3 Mar 1818 æ. 71 *EHT*, *EHC*. **FAM. 6.**

iv David, b 24 Oct 1751 *NHV*, d 31 Oct 1751 *NHV*.

v Anna, b 14 Mar 1752 *NHV* [1752/3]; m 2 Jan 1772 *EHC*—Timothy Dawson.

4 SAMUEL, b 30 July 1713 *EHV*, d 1753; m 13 Oct 1737 *NHV*—Mercy da. David & Abigail (Peck) Austin, b c. 1710.

i Joseph, b 8 Aug 1738 *NHV*, d 10 July 1826 æ. 88 *WatV;* Census (EH) 2-0-2; m 1759 Hannah da. Isaac & Mary (Frost) Blakeslee, b 29 Aug 1741 *NHV*, d 25 Aug 1794 æ. 53 *EHT*, æ. 50 *EHC*. **FAM. 7.**

ii Samuel, b 24 Mar 1740/1 *NHV*, d 29 Sep 1742 *EHV*, *NHV*.

iii Samuel, b 10 Dec 1743 *NHV*, d 10 Feb 1831 æ. 87 *EHT*, *EHC;* Census (EH) 2-1-2; m (1) 10 Oct 1765 *EHC*—Mary da. John & Hannah (Smith) Rowe, b 22 Mar 1744 *NHV*, d 16 Nov 1778 æ. [—] *EHT*, 17 Nov æ. 37 *EHC;* m (2) Lydia da. Deodate & Lydia (Woodward) Davenport, b c. 1746, d 17 Apr 1801 æ. 55 *EHT;* m (3) 3 May 1802 *EHC*—Ann da. Oliver & Lois Atwood, wid. Simeon Martin of Bethlehem, b 3 June 1747 *WyV*, d 29 Oct 1826 æ. 80 *EHC*, 1827 *EHT*. **FAM. 8.**

iv Thomas, b 12 Mar 1747/8 *NHV*, d 22 Sep 1751 æ. [—] *EHT*.

5 ABIGAIL, b 4 Aug 1716 *EHV*, d 27 Oct 1782 æ. 63 *EHC;* m (1) 1 June 1732 *NHV*—John Howell; m (2) Nathaniel Barnes.

6 ELIZABETH, b 21 Apr 1718 *EHR*.

7 ISAAC, b c. 1721, d Nov 1806 æ. 86 *NorfolkC;* Capt.; Census (L) 4-0-3; m Mercy da. Eleazer & Mercy (Ball) Morris, b c. 1725, d Oct 1801 æ. 77 *NorfolkC*.

i Isaac, b 1 Jan 1743 *EHV*, d s. p. 1 Oct 1797 æ. 55 (Norfolk); Census (L) 5-1-3; m 8 May 1764 *NorfolkC*—Mabel Doud.

ii Desire, b 10 Dec 1744 *EHV;* m 18 Nov 1767 *NorfolkC*—John Phelps, Jr.

iii Mercy, b 24 July 1747 *EHV;* m 1 Apr 1768 *NorfolkC*—Samuel Knapp.

iv Jacob, b 13 Jan 1750 *EHV*, d c. 1775; m Lucy ——— ; she m (2) 13 Aug 1778 *NorfolkC*—Gideon Lawrence. Children, bp *NorfolkC:* 1 Abigail & Ammi 26 Feb 1775; Jacob Selah 15 May 1775.

v Eleazer, b 1 Aug 1752 *EHV*, d 1835; Census (L) 1-1-2; m 16 Feb 1775 *NorfolkC*—Elizabeth Stone. Children recorded *NorfolkC:* 1 Eleazer, bp 20 June 1784, d Feb 1786. 2 Allen Stone, bp 20 June 1784; m Feb 1801 Elizabeth Butler. 3 Samuel, bp 11 June 1785, d June 1785. 4 Cynthia, bp 19 Feb 1789.

vi Nicholas, b 4 Oct 1755 *EHV*, bp 6 Oct 1756 *EHC*, d 16 Apr 1832; Census (L) 1-3-4; m (1) 22 June 1778 Keturah Pratt, b 15 Mar 1757, d 27 Feb 1798; m (2) Feb 1799 Sarah da. John Phelps, wid. ——— Phelps, who d 11 May 1821; m (3) June 1824 Lydia da. Reuben Gaylord, wid Jedediah Phelps, who d 27 Feb 1828; had 10 children.

vii Lois, b 14 Jan 1758 *EHV*, bp 29 Jan 1758 *EHC*, d Sep 1777 *NorfolkC*.

viii Stephen, b 16 Sep 1760 *F*, bp 26 Apr 1761 *NorfolkC*, d 12 June 1855; m Elizabeth Bunce, b 26 Mar 1760, d 31 Oct 1848; had 8 children.

ix Morris, bp 26 June 1763 *NorfolkC*, d 19 Mar 1815 æ. 56 *NorfolkC;* m Sarah Kingsbury, b 1 Dec 1770, d 9 Apr 1835 (at Austerlitz, N. Y.); had 7 children.

x Ammi Robbins, bp 30 Aug 1767 *NorfolkC*, d 3 Sep 1770 *NorfolkC*.

FAM. 3. JOSEPH & ABIGAIL (CURTIS) HOLT:

1 SYBIL, b 16 Mar 1710 *WV*, d 5 Aug 1738 *WV;* m 5 Aug 1730 *WV*—Josiah Mix.

2 TAMAR, b 31 Oct 1711 *WV;* m William Johnson of Durham.

3 MARY, b 9 Feb 1714 *WV;* m 17 June 1735 *NHV*—Abel Matthews.

4 SUSANNA, b 12 Feb 1716 *WV*, d 24 Sep 1742 *WV;* m 15 Oct 1739 *WV*—William Beach.

5 SAMUEL, b 14 May 1718 *WV*, d c. 1775; m 6 Nov 1740 *WV*—Abigail da. James & Sarah (Mitchell) Hough.

i Moses, b 11 Feb 1741/2 *WV;* m 15 May 1760 *WV*—Desire da. Caleb & Esther (Humphreville) Hall, b 20 June 1740 *WV*. Child: Bede, b 28 Oct 1762 *WV*.

ii Tamar, b 14 Aug 1744 *WV*.

iii Benjamin, b 9 Mar 1747 *WV;* m 2 May 1770 *WV*, *DurhamC*—Ann Merwin.

iv John, b 2 Dec 1749 *WV*.

v Abigail, b 30 Sep 1752 *WV*, or 11 Oct *WV*.

vi Eunice, b 15 May 1755 *WV*, bp 22 June 1755 *NoBC2*.

vii Rhoda, b 11 Feb 1758 *WV*.

viii Samuei, b 23 Feb 1761 *WV;* [?m 27 May 1779 *WV*—Jerusha Griswold].

ix Aaron, b 6 July 1768 *WV*,

6 JUSTUS, b 19 Oct 1720 *WV*, d c. 1790; res. 1786 Adams, Mass.; m 26 Apr 1749 *WV*—Thankful da. Samuel & Elizabeth (Doolittle) Blakeslee, b 26 Nov 1729 *WV*, d 1788.

i Stephen, b 9 Apr 1750 *WV;* res. Whitestown, N. Y.; had 4 children.

ii Joseph, b 14 Aug 1755 *WV*.

iii Susanna, b 22 Nov 175[7] *WV*.

iv Phebe, b 16 Jan 17[60] *WV*.

v Titus, b 9 Apr 17[62] *WV*.

vi Esther, b 9 Mar 17[64] *WV*, d Feb 1841; m 1788 Philo White.

vii Mary, b 8 June 17[66] *WV*, d 1823; m Nathan Smith.

viii Amos; res. Farmington, Ontario Co., N. Y.; had 7 children.

ix Isaac, b 7 Feb 1772 *WV*, d Sep 1826 (at New Hartford, N. Y.); m 1793 Elizabeth Sayles; she m (2) Henry Wilbur; had 5 children.

7 LUCY, b 12 Dec 1722 *WV;* m 13 Mar 1748/9 *WV*—Caleb Lewis.

8 LYDIA, b 24 Apr 1725 *WV;* m 16 Dec 1747 *WV*—Ephraim Beach.

9 ABIGAIL, b 20 July 1727 *WV*, d c. 1808; m (1) 24 Apr 1746 *WV*—Amos Johnson; m (2) Jonah Todd.

10 MEHITABEL, b 26 Dec 1729 *WV*, d 28 Dec 1729 *WV*.

FAM. 4. DANIEL & REBECCA (HALL) HOLT:

1 PHEBE, b 24 Dec 1716 *WV*, d 23 Mar 1744 *WV*.

2 MARAH, b 21 May 1718 *WV*, d 21 May 1718 *WV*.

3 HANNAH, b 28 Apr 1719 *WV;* m James Corbet.

4 (?ZURIEL), b 22 Jan 1721 *WV*, Thomas d 27 Feb 1745/6 (at Cape Breton) *WV*.

5 SARAH, b 23 Nov 1722 *WV*.

6 EUNICE, b 26 Nov 1725 *WV;* m (1) David Way; m (2) 26 Dec 1766 *WV*—Philip Shea.

7 LOIS, b 30 Oct 1726 *WV;* m 3 Sep 1747 *WV*—Samuel Dunbar.

8 DANIEL, b 27 May 1729 *WV*, d 20 Dec 1806 æ. 78 *WT1*, æ. c. 80 *WC2;* Census (W) 1-1-2; m 6 June 1753 *WV*—Mary da. Nathaniel & Mary (Russell) Barnes.

i Abigail, b 6 Mar 1754 *WV*.

ii Daniel, b 20 Mar 1756 *WV*, d 15 July 1802 æ. 48 *WT2;* Census (W) 1-0-1; m 17 July 1777 *WV*—Sarah da. Samuel & Susanna (Beadles) Johnson.

iii Benjamin, b 27 June 1759 *WV;* Census (W) 1-0-1; m 2 Dec 1784 *WV*, *CC*—Abiah da. Charles Chauncey & Lydia (Holt) Hall, b 20 Nov 1759 *WV*, d 31 Oct 1793 æ. 32 *WT2*.

iv Thomas, b 9 Nov 1762 *WV*, d 1836 (at Hartwick, Mass.); B. A. (Yale 1784), M. A. (1793); Rev.; m May 1796 (at Sutton, Mass.)—Sarah da. Rev. Ebenezer Chaplin, who d 4 July 1854 æ. 84-2 (at Hartwick). Child: Sarah Chaplin, b c. 1798, d 13 July 1848.

v Nathaniel, b 17 Oct 1765 *WV*, d 5 Feb 1770 *WV*.

vi Nathaniel, b 29 Jan 1771 *WV*.

9 JOSEPH, b 25 Feb 1733 *WV*, d s. p. 1754.

10 REBECCA, b 11 May 1738 *WV;* m 6 Sep 1768 *WV*—Thomas Bunn.

11 ABIGAIL, b 11 May 1738 *WV*, d 3 June 1738 *WV*.

FAM. 5. BENJAMIN & ABIGAIL (JOHNSON) HOLT:

1 PATIENCE, b 29 Dec 1727 *WV*, "Prudence" d 23 May 1737 *WV*.

2 ELIZABETH, b 25 Dec 1729 *WV*, d 17 Sep 1742 *WV*, æ. [—] *WT 1*.

3 LYDIA, b 15 Aug 1732 *WV*, d 31 Jan 1808 æ. 75 *CT1;* m 5 Dec 1751 *WV*—Charles Chauncey Hall.

4 BENJAMIN, b 14 June 1734 *WV*, d 2 May 1735 *WV*.

5 BENJAMIN, b 22 Aug 1737 *WV*, d 6 Aug 1742 *WV*.

6 PRUDENCE, b 30 May 1740 *WV*, d 30 Nov 1807 æ. 67 *WT1;* m 28 Nov 1759 *WV*—Caleb Hall.

FAM. 6. DAN & ANNA (HITCHCOCK) HOLT:

1 DANIEL, b 5 July 1767 *EHV*, bp 19 Sep 1773 *EHC;* m 10 Jan 1789 *EHC*—Hannah da. Joseph & Hannah (Blakeslee) Holt, b 17 Aug 1767 *EHV*.

2 SARAH, b 25 Nov 1769 *EHV*, bp 19 Sep 1773 *EHC;* m 20 Apr 1786 *EHC*—Samuel Thompson.

3 LYDIA, b 25 Aug 1770 *EHV*, bp 19 Sep 1773 *EHC;* m 4 May 1788 *EHC*—Jesse Bradley.

4 HEMINGWAY, b 26 Feb 1772 *EHV*, bp 19 Sep 1773 *EHC*, d 7 Oct 1810 (at sea) *EHC;* m 2 Dec 1795 *EHC*—Lorinda da. Jared & Sarah (Smith) Bradley, b 9 Oct 1772 *F*, d 5 Aug 1864; had 7 children.

5 ANN, b 18 May 1773 *EHV*, bp 19 Sep 1773 *EHC*, d 26 July 1795 æ. 22 *EHT*, æ. 29 *EHC;* m 16 Dec 1793 *EHC*—John Forbes.

6 PHILEMON, b 21 July 1775 *EHV*, *EHT*, bp 10 Sep 1775 *EHC*, d 12 Dec 1864 *EHT;* m 8 Apr 1802 *EHV*, *EHC*—Desire da. Benjamin & Lydia (Gates) Smith, b c. 1781, d 17 June 1866 æ. 84 *EHT*.

i Dan, b 1 Feb 1803 *EHV*.

ii Benjamin S., b 8 Mar 1805 *EHV*.

iii Charlotte E., b 6 Mar 1809 *EHV*.

iv Lydia G., b 2 Nov 1812 *EHV*.

v Henrietta D., b 16 Aug 1817 *EHV*.

vi Anna C., b 2 July 1820 *EHV*.

vii Sally A., b 2 July 1820 *EHV*.

viii Philemon, b 13 Nov 1822 *EHV*.

7 AMY, b 26 Feb 1778 *EHV*, bp Apr 1778 *EHC;* m John Forbes.

8 LOIS, b 19 Feb 1780 *EHV;* m 21 June 1801 *EHC*—Horatio G. Street.

9 BETSEY, b 2 Oct 1781 *EHV*, bp 10 Feb 1782 *EHC*, d 8 Mar 1866; m 23 [Jan] 1800 *EHC*, 26 Jan *EHV*—Samuel Chidsey.

10 Jared, b 3 Feb 1783 *EHV*, bp 8 [——] 1783 *EHC*, "son" d Oct 1804 æ. 21 *EHC*.

11 Abi, bp 16 [Mar] 1788 *EHC;* m 1806 *EHC*—Jared Goodsell.

12 Abigail, bp 1 Mar 1789 (12th child) *EHC*.

FAM. 7. Joseph & Hannah (Blakeslee) Holt:

1 Mercy, b 6 Jan 1760 *EHV*, bp 12 June 1774 *EHC*, d 12 Sep 1819 æ. 60 *WatT2;* m 2 Jan 1783 *EHV, EHC*—Hezekiah Todd.

2 Ebenezer, b 6 June 1761 *EHV*, bp 12 June 1774 *EHC*, d 21 Oct 1835 æ. 74 (Harwinton); m (1) Olive da. Joseph & Olive (Luddington) Grannis, b c. 1763, d 17 Sep 1804 æ. 41 *WatT2;* m (2) Mary Wilcox, who d 11 Feb 1816 æ. 51 (Harwinton); m (3) Ruth H. Adsell, who d 2 Nov 1858 æ. 77 (Harwinton).

(By 1): *i* Philemon, b Oct 1781 *WatV;* m 17 Aug 1806 *WatV*—Abby da. Ambrose & Beulah (Blakeslee) Barnes, b 15 Feb 1780 *WatV;* had 7 children.

ii Abigail, b c. 1783, d 27 Sep 1853 æ. 70 *CTI;* m Joseph Beecher.

iii Joseph, b 1788 *F*, d 1823; m 29 Jan 1809 Lydia Todd, b 7 Dec 1789, d 1860.

iv Child, d Aug 1792 *EHC*.

v Elizabeth, b 4 Dec 1792 *F;* m Jonas Smith.

(By 2): *vi* Henry (adopted), b Dec 1809 *F*.

(By 3): *vii* Olive M., b 25 Jan 1821 *F;* m 28 May 1846 Jacob W. Hemingway.

3 Hannah, b 17 Aug 1767 *EHV*, bp 12 June 1774 *EHC;* m 10 Jan 1789 *EHC*—Daniel Holt.

4 Joseph, b 5 June 1773 *EHV*, bp 12 June 1774 *EHC*, d 19 Mar 1845 æ. 70 *NHT3;* m 20 Mar 1797 *EHC*—Amy da. Edward & Lydia (Luddington) Goodsell, b 7 Feb 1776 *EHV*, d 11 Nov 1843 æ. 65 *NHT3*.

i Laban, b c. 1797, d 17 Oct 1850 æ. 53 *NHT3;* m 25 May 1823 *NHV*—Sylvia da. Russell & Mary (Bradley) Grannis, b c. 1802.

ii Lucretia; m Edward Blakeslee.

iii Nancy.

iv Edward, b c. 1807, d 11 Mar 1899 æ. 92 *NHT3;* m Mehitabel Clark, who d 29 Nov 1900 æ. 81 *NHT3*.

PAGE 946

v Mary.

FAM. 8. Samuel & Mary (Rowe) Holt:

1 Samuel, b c. 1770, bp 30 Aug 1773 *EHC*, d 23 June 1803 æ. 33 *E HT, EHC;* m 12 May 1796 *EHC*—Abigail da. Josiah & Comfort (Hitchcock) Bradley, b 22 Oct 1776 *EHV*, d 24 Sep 1834 æ. 58 *EHT;* she m (2) 10 Feb 1806 *EHC*—John Hemingway.

i Alfred, b 16 Jan 1797 *EHV*, bp 4 Sep 1800 *EHC*, d 8 Nov 1827.

ii Jeremiah, b Dec 1798 *EHV*, bp 4 Sep 1800 *EHC*, d 4 Feb 1850.

iii Mary Rowe, bp 31 Oct 1802 *EHC*.

2 ELIZABETH, b [Sep 1773], "child" d 25 Feb 1774 æ. 0-5 *EHC.*
3 MARY, bp 21 Dec 1777 *EHC;* m Joseph Bishop.

HOOD. RICHARD; Census (NH) 3-0-3; m Aug 1760 *NHC1*—Sarah da. Josiah & Elizabeth (Miles) Thompson, b c. 1735, bp 21 Oct 1788 *NHx*, bu. July 1805 æ. 70 *NHx.* The 7 children were bp (adults) with the mother.

1 RICHARD, b 22 Jan 1761 *NHV*, d c. 1793; m 12 Feb 1791 *NHx*—Abigail da. Joshua & Martha (Minor) Ray, b 20 July 1763 *NHV*, d 15 June 1796 *F;* she m (2) 24 Jan 1795 *NHx*—Ezra Lines.
i Esther, b [c. 1 Jan 1791], bp 12 Feb 1791 (æ 6 wks.) *NHx.*
ii Richardson, b [1 Sep 1793], bp 8 Sep 1793 (æ. 7 or 8 days) *NHx*, d 26 Nov 1793 (æ. 11 wks.) *NHx.*

2 SAMUEL, b c. 1763; Census (NH) 1-1-2; m 17 Mar 1784 *NHC2*—Sarah da. Eleazer & Elizabeth (Cook) Brown, b 13 Nov 1760 *NHV*, d 24 Feb 1839 æ 78 *NHT1*, *NHV.*
i Sarah, b c. 1784, bp 21 Oct 1788 *NHx*, d 5 Jan 1833 æ. 49 *NHT1*, 6 Jan (*NHx*) *NHV;* m 15 May 1805 *NHx*—James Gorham.
ii John, b c. 1786, bp 21 Oct 1788 *NHx*, d 31 Oct 1862 æ. 76 *NHT1*, *NHV;* Capt.; m 10 May 1809 *NHx*—Delia S. Brown.
iii Abigail, b [Dec 1788], bp 6 May 1789 *NHx*, bu. 10 May 1789 æ. 0-5 *NHx.*

3 MARY, b c. 1765; m Solomon Davis.

4 WILLIAM, b 16 Apr 1776 *NHT1* [error for 1767], d 26 Dec 1842 æ. 76 *NHT1;* Census (NH) 1-0-1; m 31 July 1790 *NHC1*—Elizabeth da. Timothy & Susan [Gordon] Bonticou, b 20 Sep 1770 *NHT1*, d 11 Apr 1837 æ. 67 *NHT1.* Family incomplete.
i Susan Maria, bp 27 Jan 1793 *NHx*, d 5 July 1873 æ. 81 *NHV.*
ii Roswell, b c. 1806, d 7 Jan 1875 æ. 69 *NHT1;* m Abby M. Beach, who d 25 Nov 1852 æ. 36 *NHT1.*

5 ELIZABETH, b c. 1769.

6 EASTON, b c. 1771, d 5 Nov 1828 æ. 57 (*NHx*) *NHV;* m Henrietta ——, probably the Harriet who d 11 Dec 1842 æ. 67 *NHV.* Family incomplete.
i George A., b c. 1804 (at EH), d 13 Dec 1881 æ. 76 *NHV.*

7 SARAH, b c. 1779, d July 1805 æ. 26 *NHx.*

HOOD. MISCELLANEOUS. BENJAMIN, b c. 1789, d 30 Sep 1871 æ. 82 (of Sumter, S. C.) *BAlm;* m 9 Aug 1827 *NHV*—Susanna Bonticou......ELIZABETH, b c. 1789, d 28 Feb 1852 æ. 63 *NHT1;* m Zaccheus Naples......NANCY, b 1796, d 17 Apr 1884 æ. 87 *NHT1*, æ. 88 *NHV;* m Marcus Merriman. The above 3 were probably gr.children of Richard (FAM. 1).

HOOKE. REV. WILLIAM had children recorded *NHC1*: 1 Elizabeth 14 Dec 1645; 2 Mary 5 Sep 1647.

HOOKER. MISCELLANEOUS. MARY da. Samuel & Mary (Willet), b 3 July 1673, d 1 Nov 1740 æ. 68 *NHT1;* m 26 July 1698 *NHV*—James Pierpont....

ESTHER of Farm m Oct 1728 *NHV*—Isaac Stiles.

HOPKINS. MISCELLANEOUS. SAMUEL of NH, returned to Eng.; m 5 Dec 1667 *NHV*—Hannah da. Nathaniel Turner. Children recorded *NHV:* 1 Wait Samuel 30 Aug 1668; Hannah 2 May 1670......MOLLY bp 2 June 1786 *NHx* (with her sister Bridget Fanning, both adults).

HORTON. FAM. 1. JEREMIAH, of Springfield, Mass., d 1682; m 5 May 1664 *NHV*—Mary da. William & Anna (Tapp) Gibbard.

1 JEREMY, b 1665; m Mary Terry.

2 SAMUEL, b 1667; res. NH; m Sarah da. William & Sarah (Hall) Johnson, b 6 Nov 1676 *NHV*.

i John, b 27 Nov 1700 *NHV*, d 4 Feb 1787 *SalemC;* m (1) 18 Aug 1726 *NHV*—Obedience da. Thomas & Elizabeth (Farnes) Sperry, b 23 Jan 1700 *NHV*, d 14 May 1767 æ. 68 *WdT1;* m (2) 1770 Susanna (probably wid. —— Morehouse of Danbury). **FAM. 2.**

ii Mary, b 24 Feb 1703 *NHV;* m Nov 1728 *NHV*—Noah Wolcott.

iii Sarah, b 17 May 1712 *NHV*, d soon.

iv Abigail, b 4 July 1714 *NHV*.

v Samuel, b 21 Aug 1716 *NHV*, bp 1716 *NHC1*, d 1800; Census (NH) 2-0-2; rem. to Wol; m (1) Sarah da. Abraham & Elizabeth (Glover) Dickerman, b 22 Dec 1716 *NHV*, d c. 1759; m (2) 7 Aug 1760 *NHC2*—Susanna Cooper, wid. Stephen Howell, b c. 1714, d 2 Sep 1771 æ. 57 *NHC1;* apparently divorced; m (3) 9 Oct 1765 *NoHC*—Elizabeth da. James & Elizabeth (Clinton) Bishop, b c. 1746. **FAM. 3.**

vi Sarah, b 4 Apr 1718 *NHV*, bp Apr 1718 *NHC1*.

3 THOMAS, b 1668; m (1) Sarah Warner; m (2) Mercy, wid. Kilburn.

4 TIMOTHY, b 1670, d 1740.

5 JOHN, b 1672, d 1689.

6 MARY, b 1674.

7 BENJAMIN, b 1682; m Mary Glover.

FAM. 2. JOHN & OBEDIENCE (SPERRY) HORTON:

1 PATIENCE, b 9 May 1728 *NHV*, bp 2 Jan 1736/7 *NHC1*, d 24 Dec 1769 æ. 41 *WdT2;* m Stephen Hine.

2 RACHEL, b 1 Mar 1730/1 *NHV*, bp 2 Jan 1736/7 *NHC1*, d 1787; she had a nat. child:

i Timothy Gibbud, bp 28 Mar 1762 *WdC*, d 26 Nov 1825 æ. 64 *WatT3;* m Rejoice Terrill.

3 JOHN, b 28 Sep 1735/6 *NHV*, bp 2 Jan 1736/7 *NHC1*, d 14 May 1799 *SalemC*, æ. 64 *WatT3;* Census (Wat) 3-0-3; m 1 Dec 1762 *WdC*—Mary da. Joseph & Elizabeth (Alling) Beecher, b 20 Dec 1740 *NHV*, d 20 Dec 1804 æ. 64 *WatT3*.

i Calvin; Census (Wat) 1-3-1.

ii Elizabeth; m 25 Oct 1786 *SalemC*—Ezekiel Porter.

iii John, b c. 1769, d 19 Sep 1837 æ. 68 *WatT3;* m Sarah J.

da. Amos & Sarah (Hopkins) Culver, b c. 1775, d 10 Apr 1867 æ. 92 *WatT3*. **FAM. 4.**

iv Benjamin.

v Polly; m Stiles Hotchkiss.

4 Obedience, bp 6 July 1740 *NHC1*, d s. p 1 Oct 1826 æ. 87 *WatT3;* m ——— Smith.

5 Eunice, bp 14 Nov 1742 *WdC*, d soon.

6 Eunice, bp 1 Apr 1748 *WdC;* m 13 Mar 1774 *WdV*—Joseph Merwin.

FAM. 3. Samuel & Sarah (Dickerman) Horton:

1 Naomi, b 23 Sep 1738 *NHV*, bp 5 Nov 1738 *NHC1*, d 4 Aug 1751 æ. 13 *NHT1*.

2 Elisha, bp 11 May 1740 *NHC1*, d 12 Aug 1744 æ. 4 *NHT1*.

3 Samuel, b 26 July 1743 *NHV*, d 6 Aug 1751 æ. 8 *NHT1*.

4 Elisha, b 2 Dec 1745 *NHV*, bp 11 June 1749 *NHC2*, d 1826; Census (S) 1-2-4; res. Wol; m 24 June 1772 *NoHC*—Ruth da. Joy & Miriam (Perkins) Bishop, b 1 June 1752 *NHV*. Family incomplete.

i Samuel, b 4 Dec 1773 *NHV*, d 1834; m Hannah ——— .

ii (probably) Alfred, b [3 Sep 1773?], d 26 Apr 1858 æ. 84-7-23 (b at Wol) *NHT1;* m.

iii Elisha.

5 Sarah, b 3 Nov 1747 *NHV*, bp 11 June 1749 *NHC2*, d 25 July 1751 æ. 4 *NHT1*.

6 Timothy, b 26 Dec 1749 *NHV*, d 7 Aug 1751 æ. 2 *NHT1*.

7 Sarah, b 13 Sep 1751 *NHV*, d 15 Feb 1832 æ. 80 *NHT1*, 17 Feb (*NHC2*) *NHV;* m Martin Parrot.

8 Naomi, b 14 Nov 1753 *NHV*, d young.

9 Mary, b 22 Aug 1755 *NHV*, bp 21 Sep 1755 *NHC2*, d 23 Nov 1825 æ. 70 *NHT1*, 25 Nov (*NHC2*) *NHV*.

10 Mehitabel, b 2 Apr 1757 *NHV*, bp 19 June 1757 *NHC2*, d 11 Jan 1826 æ. 69 *RoxburyC;* m 22 Apr 1795 *NHC1*—David Bots-ford.

11 Abigail, b 2 Feb 1759 *NHV*, bp 30 Sep 1759 *NHC2*, d 4 Dec 1829 æ. 70 *NHT1;* m Joseph Hotchkin.

FAM. 3. Samuel & Elizabeth (Bishop) Horton:

12 Elizabeth, b 22 Mar 1769 *NHV*, bp 3 Sep 1769 *NHC1*, d 1805; she had a nat. child:

i Almira Pond, b c. 1800, d 29 May 1891 æ. 91 *NHV*, *NHT1*.

FAM. 4. John & Sarah J. (Culver) Horton:

1 Miles, b c. 1794, d 28 Oct 1867 æ. 73 *WatT3;* m Polly ———, who d 16 Apr 1883 æ. 88 *WatT3*.

2 Mary; m 6 Nov 1823 *WatV*—Samuel A. Bunnell.

3 Emily; m 5 Dec 1821 *WatV*—Lewis M. Hoadley.

4 Lucius B.

5 Laura A.

HORTON. FAM. 5. Ebenezer, d 14 Feb 1773 *WV;* m (1) 28 Oct 1766 *W*

V—Abigail [da. Samuel & Mary (Bassett)] Alling; m (2) Phebe da. Samuel & Mary (Bassett) Alling; she m (2) 19 Dec 1773 *WV*—Abel Alling. Perhaps Hannah who m 3 Feb 1768 *WV*—Archibald Clark was sister of Ebenezer.

(By 1): 1 Mary, b 21 Apr 1767 *WV*, d 21 Apr 1767 *WV*.

2 Luman, b 12 May 1768 *WV*.

PAGE 1789 (By 2): 3 Christopher, b 30 Dec 1769 *WV*; m 8 Aug 1792 *NoHV*—Esther da. Joseph & Martha (Hart) Curtis, "wife" d [June] 1826 *WV*.

i Ruth, b 25 Sep 1793 *NoHV*.

4 Christian, b 29 June 1771 *WV*.

5 Ebenezer, b 5 Apr 1773 *W*, d 10 Apr 1773 *WV*.

HOSFORD. Gideon, s. of Benjamin & Experience (Smith), b (at L); Census (Woodstock, N. Y.) 2-1-2; m 23 Feb 1757 *WV*—Jerusha da. Isaac & Jerusha (Sexton) Cook, b 19 Nov 1736 *WV*.

1 Reuben, b 6 Sep 1760 *WV*; m 1 Mar 1779 *WV*—Olive da. Laban & Prudence (Stanley) Andrews, b 2 May 1761 *WV*.

2 Sirajah, b 16 Dec 1762 *WV*; m 1 Oct 1786 *WV*—Jane Wilson of Georgetown, S. C.

3 Joel, b 9 Feb 1769 *WV*.

4 Lucy, b 5 Jan 1771 *WV*, d 13 Mar 1774 *WV*, æ. 4 *WTI*.

5 Lucy, b 1 Feb 1774 *WV*.

6 George, b 6 Feb 1779 *WV*.

HOSMER. Aged Wid. d 23 Feb 1787 æ. 84 *NHCI*.

HOSSINGTON. John; m Mary ——— ; they rem. before 1777 from W to Woodstock, N. Y. [Mary, perhaps sister of John m (1) 18 Oct 1769 *WV*—Francis Hendrick; m (2) 8 Oct 1772 *WV*—Edward Cleaveland].

1 Mary, b 26 Apr 1758 *WV*.

2 Ann, b 26 Apr 1758 *WV*.

3 Ellethine, b 24 Jan 1760 *WV*.

4 John Smith, b 8 Aug 1761 *WV*.

5 Vespasian, b 8 June 1763 *WV*.

6 Diana, b 28 June 1765 *WV*.

7 Salmon, b 29 Apr 176[7] *WV*.

†HOTCHKIN. Variant, Hodgkin. fam. 1. Oliver, s. of Abraham Jr. of G, b 16 Oct 1774 *GV*, d 2 Jan 1861 æ. 87 *NHTI*; m Cynthia ———, who d 2 Feb 1849 æ. 68 *NHTI*.

1 Harmon J., b c. 1799, d 25 Feb 1833 æ. 34 *NHTI*.

2 Jaherzy S., b c. 1803, d 18 Oct 1822 æ. 19 *NHTI*.

3 Daughter, b c. 1806, d 8 Nov 1822 æ. 16 *NHV*.

HOTCHKIN. fam. 2. Joseph, s. of Abraham Jr. of G, b 17 Nov 1758 *GV*, d 29 Apr 1827 æ. 68 *NHV*, 28 Apr æ. 67 *NHTI*; m Abigail da. Samuel & Sarah (Dickerman) Horton, b 2 Feb 1759 *NHV*, d 5 Dec 1829 æ. 70 *NHTI*.

1 Elias, b c. 1783, d 14 Aug 1824 æ. 39 *NHTI*; m Clarinda ———, who d 23 Jan 1819 æ. 33 *NHTI*.

i Charles, b c. 1810.

ii Mary Ann, b c. 1812.

iii Amanda Charlotte.

2 TABITHA; m ——— Gaston.

3 LOVINA; m Adonijah Kingsley.

4 ABIGAIL; m ——— Dudley. PAGE 2046

†**HOTCHKISS.** Considerable material on this family was kindly furnished by Mr. O. E. Hotchkiss of Oakland, Calif., & Mr. Clarence D. Smith of Rome, N. Y.

FAM. 1. **SAMUEL, d 28 Dec 1663 *NHV;* m Sep 1642 Elizabeth Cleverly, who d 1681 *F*.**

1 JOHN, d 1689; m 4 Dec 1672 *NHV*—Elizabeth da. Henry & Joan Peck, b 16 Mar 1649 *NHV*, bp 24 Mar 1650 *NHCl*, d 1730 *F*.

i John, b 11 Oct 1673 *NHV*, d 17 Apr 1732 æ. 59 *CTl;* Capt. & J. P.; m Mary da. William & Mary (Clark) Chatterton, b 29 Nov 1673 *NHV*, d 26 July 1741 æ. 68 *CTl*. **FAM. 2.**

ii Joshua, b c. 1675, d 14 Aug 1741 æ. 66 *NHTl;* m Susanna da. William & Mary (Clark) Chatterton, b 17 Sep 1678 *NHV*, d Sep 1766 æ. 88 *NHCl;* she m (2) Abraham Dickerman. **FAM. 3.**

iii Joseph, b 8 June 1678 *NHV*, d 31 July 1740 *G;* m Apr 1699 *G*—Hannah da. Isaac Cruttenden, b 27 Mar 1678, d 28 Mar 1756. **FAM. 4.**

iv Josiah, b 24 Jan 1680 *NHV* [1680/1], d 13 July 1732 *CC;* m 8 Dec 1715 *WV*—Abigail da. John & Hannah (Bassett) Parker, who d c. May 1732 *WV*. **FAM. 5.**

v Caleb, b 18 Oct 1684 *NHV*, d 4 Apr 1763 æ. 79 *NHCl;* m (1) 14 Feb 1705/6 *NHV*—Mehitabel Cruttenden, b 11 Apr 1682, d 30 Nov 1750 æ. 69 *NHTl;* m (2) ———, who d 23 Aug 1759 *NHCl*. **FAM. 6.**

vi Elizabeth, b 18 Jan 1686 *NHV*, d 13 Sep 1723 *NHV*.

vii Ruth, b c. 1688, d 24 Mar 1773 æ. 85 *NHCl;* m (1) 12 Mar 1717/8 *NHV*—Jonathan Sackett; m (2) 11 Dec 1728 *NHV*—Benjamin Dorman.

viii Child, probably da., living 1723.

2 SAMUEL, b c. 1645, d 29 Dec 1705 *EHR;* Lieut.; m (1) 18 Mar 1678/9 *NHV*—Sarah da. Robert & Sarah (Nash) Talmadge, b 19 Sep 1652 *NHV;* m (2) Hannah da. John & Dorothy Thompson, wid. Matthew Moulthrop, who d 19 Jan 1712/3 *EHV*.

(By 1): *i* Mary, b 1 Jan 1679 *NHV* [1679/80], bp 9 May 1686 *NHCl*, d 12 Nov 1723 *NHV;* m 1 Mar 1699 *NHV*—Caleb Tuttle.

ii Sarah, b 7 Apr 1681 *NHV*, bp 9 May 1686 *NHCl;* m ——.

iii Samuel, b 6 Mar 1682/3 *NHV*, bp 9 May 1686 *NHCl*, d 22 Dec 1740 *EHV*, æ. 57 *EHT;* m Mary ———; she m (2) 26 Oct 1745 *NHV*—Henry Tolles. **FAM. 7.**

iv James, b 8 Dec 1684 *NHV*, bp 9 May 1686 *NHCl*, d soon.

v Abigail, b 12 Feb 1686 *NHV* [1686/7], bp 12 Feb 1686/7 *NHCl*.

vi Ebenezer, bp 16 Dec 1688 *NHCl*; res. NM; m ——— .
FAM. 8.

vii Robert, bp 8 Sep 1690 *NHCl*, probably d young.

viii James, bp 8 Sep 1690 *NHCl*, probably d young.

ix Enos, bp 8 Sep 1690 *NHCl*, probably d young.

3 SARAH; m Jeremiah Johnson of D.

4 JOSHUA, b 16 Sep 1651 *NHV*, bp (adult) 18 Feb 1693/4 *NHCl*, d between 7 Apr & 1 Oct 1722; Sheriff; m (1) 29 Nov 1677 *NHV*—Mary da. George & Martha (Miles) Pardee, b 18 Apr 1658 *NHV*, d c. 1684; m (2) c. 1685 Hannah da. Thomas & Hannah (Powell) Tuttle, b 24 Feb 1661 *NHV* [1661/2], bp (adult) 24 Mar 1693 *NHCl*, d 17 Feb 1718/9 *NHV*; m (3) [c. 1719], *NHV*—Mary da. Ephraim & Mary (Powell) Sanford, wid. Joseph Ashburn of M, b Oct 1670 *NHV*, d 1750; she m (3) Eleazer Holt.

(By 1): *i* Mary, b 30 Apr 1679 *NHV*, d young.

ii Stephen, b 25 Aug 1681 *NHV*, bp 18 Feb 1693/4 *NHCl*, d 5 Mar 1755 *WV*, 1755/6 *CC*, 1755 æ. 74 *CTl*; Dea.; m 12 Dec 1704 *NHV*—Elizabeth da. John & Elizabeth (Post) Sperry, b 17 Jan 1683 *NHV*, d 17 May 1760 *WV*, æ. 77 *CTl*. **FAM. 9.**

iii Martha, b 14 Dec 1683 *NHV*, bp 18 Feb 1693/4 *NHCl*, d c. 1755; m 25 Mar 1702 *NHV*—Thomas Brooks.

(By 2): *iv* Hannah, b c. 1686, bp 24 Mar 1693 *NHCl*, d 3 Aug 1723 *NHV*; m 10 May 1709 *NHV*—Ebenezer Peck.

v Priscilla, b 30 Dec 1688 *NHV*, bp 24 Mar 1693 *NHCl*; m John Sperry.

vi Abraham, bp Mar 1694 *NHCl*, d 1725; m Deborah da. Joseph & Abigail (Preston) Thomas, bp 27 May 1694 *NHCl*, d 5 Jan 1790 æ. 96-6-[28] *BD*; she m (2) John Carrington. **FAM. 10.**

vii Abigail, b 12 Oct 1695 *NHV*, bp 19 May (?) 1695 *NHCl*, d 30 Aug 1735 *WV*; m 2 Jan 1721/2 *NHV*, 7 Jan 1722 *WV*—Daniel Winston.

viii Mary, bp 11 July 1697 *NHCl*, d 12 July 1763 *WV*; m 22 Apr 1734 *WV*—Moses Atwater.

ix Desire, bp 1 Jan 1698/9 *NHCl*, d Oct 1702 *NHV*.

x Isaac, b June 1701 *NHV*, d c. Sep 1750; Sgt.; res. B; m 22 Apr 1725 *NHV*—Rachel da. Thomas & Anna Carnes. **FAM. 11.**

xi Jacob, b Feb 1704 *NHV*; res. B; m 30 Apr 1729 *NHV*—Elizabeth da. Abraham & Elizabeth (Glover) Dickerman, b 12 June 1706 *NHV*. **FAM. 12.**

5 THOMAS, b 31 Aug 1654 *NHV*, d 27 Dec 1711 *NHV*, æ. 58 *NHTl*; m 27 Nov 1677 *NHV*—Sarah da. William & Sarah (Thomas) Wilmot, b 8 Mar 1662/3 *NHV*, bp (adult) 23 June 1695 *NHCl*, d 1731; she m (2) c. 1713 Daniel Sperry.

i Samuel, b 7 Sep 1680 *NHV*, d 1730; m 10 Jan 1705 *NHV*—Sarah da. Benjamin & Elizabeth (Thompson) Bradley, b 7 June 1680 *NHV*, d before 1730. **FAM. 13.**

ii Sarah, b 18 Feb 1682/3 *NHV*, bp 23 June 1695 *NHCl*; m 3 Feb 1708/9 *NHV*—Joseph Turner.

iii Anna, b 12 Dec 1684 *NHV*, bp 23 June 1695 *NHCl*; m 13 Dec 1705 *NHCCt*—Samuel Johnson.

iv William, bp 7 Oct 1695 *NHCl*, d s. p. 1731.

v Abraham, bp 7 Oct 1695 *NHCl*; m Elizabeth da. William & Sarah (Hall) Johnson, b 10 May 1685 *NHV*. **FAM. 14.**

vi Dorcas, bp 7 Oct 1695 *NHCl*, d 17 Mar 1744 (Southold, L. I.); m John Youngs.

vii Lydia, bp 23 June 1695 *NHCl*, d 15 Jan 17[60?] *WV*; m (1) Ebenezer Johnson; m (2) 15 Sep 1736 *WV*—Nathaniel Hall.

6 Daniel, b 8 June 1657 *NHV*, d 10 Mar 1712 *NHV*; m 21 June 1683 *NHV*—Esther da. Richard & Dennis Sperry, b Sep 1654 *NHV*.

i Elizabeth, b 30 Aug 1684 *NHV*, bp 12 Aug 1688 *NHCl*, d 11 Jan 1736 æ. 62 (?) *CTl*; m 13 Jan 1702 *NHV*—Caleb Matthews.

ii Daniel, b Aug 1687 *NHV*, bp 12 Aug 1688 *NHCl*, d 1733; m 5 Feb 1711/2 *NHCCt*—Susanna da. Benjamin & Elizabeth (Thompson) Bradley, b 10 July 1684 *NHV*, d 25 July 1751 æ. 67 *NHTl*; she m (2) John Blakeslee. **FAM. 15.**

iii Obadiah, b 20 Mar 1690 *NHCl*, bp 1690 *NHCl*; m Jan 1716 *WV*—Eunice da. Benjamin & Mary (Hitchcock) Beach, b 3 Aug 1698 *WV*. Child: 1 Lois, b 11 Jan 1717 *WV*; m 20 July 1735 *WV*—Abner Matthews.

iv Esther, b 25 Nov 1693 *NHV*, bp 26 Nov 1693 *NHCl*.

v (perhaps) Rebecca, bp 7 June 1696 *NHCl*, d soon.

vi Rebecca, b 14 Feb 1697 *NHV* [1697/8], bp Feb 1697/8 *NHCl*, d 23 Feb 1762 *WV*, 25 Jan æ. 65 *CTl*; m (1) 15 Nov 1720 *WV*—Thomas Ives; m (2) 1 Dec 1748 *WV*—Edward Parker.

vii Jemima, b 26 Nov 1702 *NHV*, d 28 Jan 1779 *CC*; m 11 Apr 1727 *WV*—Jonathan Andrews.

FAM. 2. John & Mary (Chatterton) Hotchkiss:

1 John, b 27 June 1694 *NHV*, bp (adult) May 1726 *CC*, d 3 Feb 1777 *CC*; Capt.; m 10 Mar 1719 *WV*—Miriam da. Richard & Sarah (Clark) Wood, b 10 Dec 1700 *WV*, d 10 Jan 1765 æ. 65 *WV*, *CTl*.

i Jason, b 12 May 1719 *WV*, bp May 1726 *CC*, d 19 May 1776 *CC*, *WV*; m (1) 27 Dec 1744 *WV*—Abigail da. Moses & Sarah (Merriman) Atwater, b 13 Sep 1725 *WV*, d 23 Feb 1773 *WV*, *CC*; m (2) 17 Feb 1774 *WV*—Thankful da. Samuel & Ruth (Peck) Sedgwick, wid. Jehiel Preston & Ephraim Tuttle, b 21 Apr 1721 *HartfordV*, d 5 Oct

1806 æ. 85 *CT1;* she m (4) 4 June 1778 *CC*—John Hall. **FAM. 16.**

ii Sarah, b 13 July 1721 *WV*, bp May 1726 *CC*, d 7 Aug 1784 æ. 64 *HV;* m (1) 14 June 1738 *WV*—Augustus Bristol; m (2) Cornelius Brooks.

iii Dorothy, b 28 Dec 1723 *WV*, bp May 1726 *CC*, d c. 1751; m 27 Dec 1742 *WV*—Samuel Benham.

iv Hannah, b 3 July 1726 *WV*, bp 10 Aug 1726 *CC*, d 13 Mar 1798 æ. 72 *SC;* m 28 Feb 1744/5 *WV*—Joseph Bunnell.

v Miriam, b 10 Sep 1728 *WV*, bp Sep 1728 *CC;* m 16 June 1747 *WV*—Gideon Curtis.

vi Naomi, b 23 Feb 1731 *WV*, bp 28 Feb 1730/1 *CC*, d 1796 æ. 70 *BristolC;* m 6 Nov 1749 *WV*—Samuel Adams.

vii Lydia, b 19 Feb 1733 *WV*, bp Feb 1732/3 *CC*, d 27 Aug 1798 æ. 66 *BristolT;* m (1) Thomas Hart; m (2) Sep 1777 Ladwick Hotchkiss.

viii John, b 16 Sep 1735 *WV*, bp 21 Sep 1735 *CC*, d 27 June 1800 æ. 65 *CT2;* Census (C) 4-1-3; m 14 Feb 1756 *WV*—Phebe Gillam. **FAM. 17.**

ix Elijah, b 6 Mar 1738 *WV*, bp 29 Jan 1737/8 *CC*, d 11 June 1797 *CC;* Census (C) 1-0-0; m 8 June 1758 *WV*—Elizabeth da. Benjamin & Elizabeth (Curtis) Kellogg, b 21 May 1738 *WV*. **FAM. 18.**

x Mary, b 1 Dec 1740 *WV*, bp 30 Nov (?) 1740 *CC*, d 3 May 1798 *CC*, æ. 59 *CT1;* m 12 May 1757 *WV*—Thomas Brooks.

xi Child, d 1747 *CC*.

2 Lydia, b 31 Aug 1697 *NHV*, d 9 Nov 1737 *CC*, æ. 41 *CT1;* m 12 Sep 1716 *NHV*—Stephen Clark.

3 Mary, b 1 Apr 1701 *NHV*, d 13 Nov 1787 *CC*, æ. 88 *CT1;* m 2 Feb 1732 *WV*—Joshua Hotchkiss.

4 Amos, b 27 June 1704 *NHV*, d 17 Jan 1773 *CC;* Capt.; m (1) 25 Feb 1731 *WV*—Elizabeth da. Caleb & Elizabeth (Hotchkiss) Matthews, b 6 Oct 1705 *NHV*, d 17 Sep 1731 æ. 26 *CT1;* m (2) Obedience da. Samuel & Martha (Farnes) Munson, b 13 Oct 1702 *WV*.

(By 1): *i* Amos, bp Sep 1730 [1731?] *CC*, d soon.

(By 2): *ii* Elizabeth, bp 23 Dec 1733 *CC;* m (1) 6 May 1752 *WV*—Jonathan Bristol; m (2) 1 Mar 1769 *WV*—Abner Blakeslee.

iii Robert, bp June 1736 *CC*, d Apr 1750 *CC*.

iv Amos, b 27 Mar 1738 *WV*, bp 26 (?) Mar 1738 *CC*, d 24 July 1784 *CC;* m 6 Apr 1758 *WV*—Elizabeth da. Nathaniel & Elizabeth (Hitchcock) Beadles, wid. Ichabod Merriam, b 12 Dec 1731 *WV*. **FAM. 19.**

v Obedience, b 7 Jan 1740 *WV*, bp Jan 1739/40 *CC*, d 1806; m 23 Feb 1769 *WV*—Abner Austin. She had a nat.

child: 1 Roswell, b 4 July 1765 *WV*.

vi Lois, b 2 July 1743 *WV*, bp July 1743 *CC*, d 14 Dec 1773 *CC*, 16 Dec *WV;* m 14 Nov 1765 *WV*—William Jones. She had a nat. child: 1 Tryal Hitchcock, b July 1759 *WV*, who in turn had a nat. child, Lois, b 27 Sep 1774 *WV*. Tryal m 24 Dec 1778 *WV*—Samuel Anthony.

vii Marlow, b 20 June 1745 *WV*, bp June 1745 *CC*, d 9 Nov 1808 *CC;* m (1) 13 Nov 1764 *WV*—Titus Lines; m (2) 12 Oct 1775 *CC*—James Jones.

5 **James**, b 24 Nov 1706 *WV*, d 6 Mar 1781 *CC;* m 23 July 1728 *WV*—Tamar da. Samuel & Martha (Farnes) Munson, b 5 Dec 1707 *WV*, d 2 Oct 1788 *CC*.

i James, b 16/17 Feb 1729 *WV*, bp Oct 1731 *CC*.

ii Benjamin, b 3 Mar 1730 *WV*, bp Oct 1731 *CC*, d c. 1803; Census (C) 1-1-1; m 12 Dec 1751 *WV*—Martha da. Thomas & Desire (Bristol) Brooks; she res. Whitehall, N. Y., 1803. **FAM. 20.**

iii Asa, b 24 Nov 1731 *WV*, bp Nov 1731 *CC*, d 1 July 1763 *WV;* m 2 May 1752 *WV*—Mary da. Giles & Abigail (Curtis) Andrews, b c. 1737, d 20 Nov 1806 æ. 79 *PptT;* she m (2) 26 Jan 1775 *CC*—Enos Tyler. **FAM. 21.**

PAGE 946

iv Robert, b 17 June [?Jan] 1733 *WV*, bp Jan 1732/33 *CC;* there was a Robert, Census (Southold, L. I.) 2-0-3.

v Eunice, b 28 Mar 1734 *WV*, bp 30 Mar 1733/4 *CC*, d 16 Jan 1737 *WV*, "child" d 5 Jan 1736/7 *CC*.

vi Tamar, b 24 Apr 1736 *WV*.

vii Eunice, bp 29 Jan 1737/8 *CC*, d 19 Sep 1801 æ. 65 *CTI;* m 15 Feb 1758 *WV*—Andrew Durand.

viii Waitstill, bp Oct 1740 *CC;* Census (C) 3-1-2; m 23 Feb 1764 *WV*—Eunice da. Moses & Mary (Rowe) Bradley, b 12 Dec 1743 *WV*. **FAM. 22.**

ix Reuben, b 5 Feb 1742 *WV* [1742/3], bp Feb 1742/3 *CC*.

x Lydia, b 21 Aug 1745 *WV*, bp Sep 1745 *CC*, d 7 Feb 1833 æ. 89 *PptT;* m 7 Oct 1774 *WdC*—Hezekiah Beecher.

xi Lois; m 1 Jan 1770 *WV*, 3 Jan *CC*—John Ives.

6 **Robert**, b 12 May 1709 *WV*, d Apr 1732 *WV*, 23 Apr æ. 23 *CTI*.

7 **Miriam**, b 20 Feb 1712 *WV;* m 4 June 1730 *WV*—Abel Sperry.

8 **Henry**, b 1 Apr 1715 *WV*, d 9 June 1799 *CC*, æ. 84 *CTI;* Capt.; Census (C) 1-0-2; m (1) 23 Nov 1736 *WV*—Sarah da. Nathan & Sarah (Beecher) Benham, b c. 1712, d 13 Nov 1751 æ. [5]0 (?) *CTI;* m (2) Lydia da. Joseph & Susanna Morgan, wid. Isaac Ives, b c. 1719, d 8 May 1793 *CC*, 7 Mar (?) æ. 74 *CTI*.

(By 1): *i* Henry, b 2 Sep 1737 *WV*, bp Sep 1737 *CC*, d 10 Mar 1821 (at Paris, N. Y.); Census (C) 1-1-2; m 4 Jan 1759 *WV*—Esther da. Joseph & Esther (Ives) Smith, b 8 Dec 1737 *WV*. **FAM. 23.**

ii Joseph, b 18 Dec 1738 *WV*, d 28 Mar 1783 (k. by a cart) *CC;* m (1) 4 Mar 1761 *WV*—Mary da. Miles & Mary

(Tuttle) Hull, b 15 July 1740 *WV*, d 14 Feb 1776 *WV;* m (2) 1 Jan 1778 *CC*—Ruth Hill, wid. Eli Doolittle, who d 19 May 1807 *CC*. **FAM. 24.**

iii Jonah, b 26 Jan 1741 *WV*, bp Jan 1740/1 *CC*, d 26 July 1741 *WV*.

iv Sarah, b 5 Feb 1742/3 *WV*, bp Feb 1742/3 *CC*, d 21 Sep 1802 æ. 59 *CT1;* m 9 Dec 1762 *WV*—Valentine Hitchcock.

v Jonah, b 28 Oct 1745 *WV*, bp Nov 1744 (?) *CC*, d 19 Sep 1812 *CC*, æ. 68 *CT1;* Census (C) 2-3-2; m 14 Aug 1764 *WV*—Eunice da. Nathan & Rachel (Tuttle) Tyler, b c. 1743, d 12 Feb 1835 æ. 93 *CT1*. **FAM. 25.**

vi Mary, b 1 Feb 1746/7 *WV*, bp Feb 1745/6 (?) *CC*, "child" d 1747 *CC*.

9 Benjamin, b 10 May 1718 *WV*, d Aug 1718 *WV*.

FAM. 3. Joshua & Susanna (Chatterton) Hotchkiss:

1 Thankful, b 15 June 1701 *NHV*, d 1757; m (1) 10 June 1725 *NHV*—James Gilbert; m (2) 30 Dec 1731 *NHV*—Caleb Bradley.

2 Caleb, b 27 July 1703 *NHV*, d 27 Oct 1785 æ. 83 *NHT1;* m 19 Dec 1728 *NHV*—Ruth da. John & Sarah (Cooper) Munson, b 30 Jan 1707/8 *NHV*, d 21 May 1785 æ. 81 *NHT1*, 23 Apr æ. 77 *NHC1*.

i Hezekiah, b 27 Sep 1729 *NHV*, bp 5 Oct 1729 *NHC1*, d 8 May 1761 (at N. Y.) *NHT1;* m (1) 12 Dec 1751 *NHV*—Sarah da. Abraham & Sarah (Wilmot) Bradley, b 12 Mar 1728/9 *NHV*, d 3 Sep 1753 *NHV*, æ. 24 *NHT1;* m (2) 19 June 1754 *NHV*, *NHC2*—Mary da. John & Desire (Cooper) Wooding, b 20 Nov 1731 *NHV;* she m (2) Enos Johnson. **FAM. 26.**

ii John, b 12 Nov 1731 *NHV*, bp 14 Nov 1731 *NHC1*, d July 1779 æ. 47 *NHT1;* m 28 Aug 1755 *NHV*—Susanna da. Timothy & Jane (Harris) Jones, b 10 Aug 1732 *NHV*, d 6 May 1813 æ. 81 *NHT1;* Census, Susanna, (NH) 0-0-3. **FAM. 27.**

PAGE 946

iii Sarah, b 12 Nov 1731 *NHV*, bp 14 Nov 1731 *NHC1*.

iv Joshua, b 12 Feb 1733/4 *NHV*, bp 16 Feb 1733/4 *NHC1*, d 3 June 1795 æ. 62 *NHT1;* Rev. soldier, at West Point 1781, by family record; Census (NH) 2-0-1; m Mary da. Thomas & Mary (Miles) Punderson, b 28 Jan 1737/8 *NHV*, d 1 Mar 1821 æ. 84 *NHT1*, æ. 83 (*NHC2*) *NHV*. **FAM. 28.**

v Susanna, b 12 Feb 1733/4 *NHV*, bp 16 Feb 1733/4 *NHC1;* m 17 July 1754 *NHC2*—Ezra Dodge.

vi Lemuel, b 10 Aug 1737 *NHV*, bp 12 Sep 1737 *NHC1*, d 6 Jan 1820 æ. 82 *NHV;* Census (NH) 3-1-4; m (1) 2 Jan 1757 *NHV*—Mary [da. Peter & Mary] Mallory, who d 19 Apr 1762 *NHV;* m (2) 6 Mar 1765 *NHV*—Parthena da. Joseph & Hannah (Patterson) Murray, bp 16 June

1741 *NMC*. **FAM. 29.**

vii Ruth, b 3 June 1740 *NHV*, bp 13 July 1740 *NHC1*, d 1835; m 15 Nov 1763 *NHC2*—Ichabod Page.

viii Caleb, b 7 Sep 1742 *NHV*, bp 10 Oct 1742 *NHC1*; d before 1781; an old family record says k. 5 July 1779 æ. 37 & was army Dr. under Gen. Spencer in R. I. 1776–1778; is there confusion with Caleb (FAM. 6, 3) ?; m 31 Mar 1778 *F*—Rosetta Owen, wid. Elisha Phelps; she m (3) ——— Guernsey. Child: 1 Lorinda; m ——— Fabridge.

PAGE 1245

ix Esther, b 5 Aug 1745 *NHV*, d 6 Oct 1831 æ. 86 *LT*; m Philemon Murray.

3 JOSHUA, b 22 Dec 1707 *NHV*; res. Washington 1785; m 18 Dec 1732 *NHV*—Obedience da. Samuel & Elizabeth (Smith) Cooper, b 25 July 1712 *NHV*, d 14 Dec 1771 æ. 59 *NHC1*.

i Hannah, b 14 Jan 1733/4 *NHV*, bp 10 Mar 1733/4 *NHC1*.

ii Charles, b 8 July 1736 *NHV*, bp 11 July 1736 *NHC1*; Census (Hebron, N. Y.) 3-2-2; m 11 Feb 1762 *NHC1*—Elizabeth da. John & Sarah (Potter) Harris. **FAM. 30.**

iii Timothy, b 16 Mar 1742 *NHV*, bp 21 Mar 1741/2 *NHC1*, d s. p. 1776.

iv Eunice, b 11 July 1745 *NHV*, bp 14 July 1745 *NHC1*, d 29 Mar 1824 æ. 79 *Washington*; m 5 Aug 1762 *NHC1*—John Davies of L, who d 20 Apr 1799 æ. 63 *Washington*.

v Lois, b 16 Aug 1749 *NHV*, bp 20 Aug 1749 *NHC1*; m 29 Dec 1772 *NHC1*—Aaron Smith of New Fairfield.

4 RUTH, b 16 Mar 1712 *NHV*, d 30 Mar 1773 æ. 62 *NHC1*; m Thomas Gilbert.

FAM. 4. JOSEPH & HANNAH (CRUTTENDEN) HOTCHKISS:

1 JOSEPH, b 3 Sep 1700 *GV*, d 5 Sep 1740; m Thankful Stone, b 5 Dec 1711, d 14 Sep 1751.

i Ezekiel, b 14 Mar 1726 *GV*, d 5 July 1779 (k. by British at NH); m 25 Jan 1749/50 *NHV*—Hannah da. Nathan & Hannah (Todd) Alling, b 4 Oct 1727 *NHV*; Census, Hannah (NH) 1-0-2. **FAM. 31.**

ii Daniel, b 2 July 1728 *GV*, d 13 Sep 1807 *CC*, æ. 81 *CT1*; Census (C) 2-1-2; m Eunice da. Moses & Lydia (Richason) Doolittle, b 27 Oct 1733 *WV*, d 5 July 1811 æ. 77 *CT1*. **FAM. 32.**

iii Rachel, b 18 Mar 1730 *GV*, d 15 Aug 1802; m 1 Dec 1748 Miles Hotchkiss.

iv John, b c. 1732, d 30 Oct 1799; m 20 Apr 1756 Obedience da. Joseph & Hannah (Hotchkiss) Stone, b 12 Dec 1731, d 28 May 1797.

v Mary, b c. 1734, d 18 Mar 1743.

vi Thankful, b 22 Oct 1736 *F*, m 3 Sep 1755 Elihu Stone of L.

vii Joseph, b 22 Oct 1736 *GV*; res. C & Harpersfield, N. Y.;

m 30 July 1761 *WV*—Hannah da. Moses & Mary (Hotchkiss) Atwater, b 1 May 1739 *WV*, d 28 Aug 1825 *F*. **FAM. 33.**

viii Amos, b 2 Jan 1739 *GV;* rem. to Vt.; m (1) 12 Mar 1760 Desire da. Janna & Desire (Cornwell) Dowd, b 1736, d 1 Feb 1797 *F;* m (2) Hannah ——, who d 25 Aug 1805 *F*.

ix Ebenezer, b 5 Jan 1741 *GV*, d 23 Nov 1760 *GV*.

2 Isaac, b 25 Dec 1702 *GV*, d 17 Sep 1752; m 8 July 1724 Elizabeth Avered.

i Isaac, b 1 July 1725 *GV*, d 26 Oct 1755 *GV*.

ii Miles, b 11 Feb 1728 *GV*, d s. p. 13 May 1810; m 1 Dec 1748 Rachel da. Joseph & Thankful (Stone) Hotchkiss, b 18 Mar 1730 *GV*, d 15 Aug 1802.

iii Elizabeth, b 7 Oct 1731 *GV*, d 29 Mar 1818; m 16 May 1750 Elon Lee of Meriden.

iv Lucy, b 1 Dec 1736 *GV;* m —— Norton of Winchester.

3 Wait, b 18 Jan 1704 *GV*, d 30 July 1778 æ. 74 *Wol;* m 2 Nov 1731 *GV*—Sarah Bishop, who d 24 Apr 1761 *G;* [perhaps m (2) Abigail Dudley, wid. Daniel Bishop, who d 1787 at Bethlehem].

i Wait, b 18 Nov 1733 *GV*, d 15 Oct 1799 æ. 66 *WolT;* Census (Wat) 2-3-2; m (1) 16 Oct 1759 *GV*—Lydia da. Thomas & Lydia (Lyman) Webster, b 4 Feb 1730 (at Hebron), d 26 Apr 1776 *WatV;* m (2) 10 Oct 1776 *WatV* —Deborah da. John & Deborah (Blakeslee) Alcott, wid. Isaac Twitchell, b c. 1742, d 18 June 1831 æ. 89 *WolT*. **FAM. 34**

ii Lois, b 5 Oct 1735 *GV*, d 9 Mar 1818; m 11 Dec 1760 Phinehas Johnson.

iii Sarah, b 5 June 1738 *GV*, d 5 Feb 1746 *GV*.

iv Selah, b 24 Dec 1742 *GV;* m Rebecca ——.

4 Hannah, b 13 Sep 1707 *GV*, d 20 July 1793; m 7 Jan 1730 Joseph Stone.

5 Deborah, b 18 Jan 1710 *GV*, d s. p.

6 Miles, b 28 July 1712 *GV*, d s. p.

7 Mark, b 1 July 1714 *GV*, d 19 Nov 1775; m (1) 25 Dec 1739 Margaret Crawford, who d 7 Jan 1750; m (2) 8 Jan 1751 Miriam da. Joseph & Lois (Pond) Lee, who d 31 Mar 1788.

(By 1): *i* Deborah, b 23 Feb 1741; m —— Sanford of NM.

ii Mary, b 13 Oct 1746, d young.

(By 2): *iii* Timothy, b 11 Jan 1752, d in R. W.

iv Eunice, b c. 1754, d 27 Feb 1827; m 23 May 1770 William Lee.

v Isaac, b 7 Oct 1756, d 28 Aug 1835; m 5 Jan 1783 Ann da. Nathaniel & Anna (Talman) Spinning, who d 17 Aug 1844.

vi Ira, b 10 May 1758, d 1826; res. Bd; m (1) between 1775

& 1779 Mary Rose; m (2) 30 Mar 1782 *BdV*—Abigail Frisbie, who d 18 Feb 1836. Child: 1 Lancelot, b 19 Oct 1783 *BdV*.

vii Eber, b 26 May 1762, d 2 Sep 1832; m (1) Leah Page, who d 11 Sep 1794; m (2) Sarah Whiting, b 14 July 1758, d 29 Jan 1830.

FAM. 5. JOSIAH & ABIGAIL (PARKER) HOTCHKISS:

1 JOSIAH, b 13 Oct 1716 *WV*, d 29 Dec 1716 *WV*.

2 ELIZABETH, b 25 Jan 1718 *WV*, bp 8 Jan 1726/7 *CC*; m 3 July 1734 *FarmV*—Abram Hills.

3 JOSIAH, b 3 Apr 1720 *WV*, bp 8 Jan 1726/7 *CC*, d 17 Aug 1796 *CC*; Census (C) 1-0-1; m 8 Dec 1741 *WV*—Abigail Bartholomew, b 23 Jan 1724/5 *BdV*.

i Josiah, b 26 Dec 1742 *WV*, bp Sep 1745 *CC*, d 1812; Census (C) 4-0-4; m Sarah da. Elisha & Eunice (Perkins) Perkins, b 28 Aug 1741 *Hadley, Mass., V*. **FAM. 35.**

ii Benoni, b 4 Aug 1752 *WV*, bp 11 July (?) 1752 *CC*, d 27 Feb 1835 æ. 82 *CTI*; Census (C) 1-1-4; m (1) 5 Sep 1771 *KensingtonC*—Hannah Norton, b 1748, d 16 May 1788 *F*; m (2) Lucy ——, b 1764, d 23 Nov 1821 *F*. **FAM. 36.**

4 LADWICK, b 13 Jan 1723 *WV*, bp 8 Jan 1726/7 *CC*, d 7 Mar 1803 æ. 81 *New Durham, N. Y.*; Capt.; Census (Farm) 1-0-1; res. New Britain; m (1) 22 Dec 1743 *FarmV*—Molly da. Nathaniel & Margaret (Holcolm) North, b 18 Mar 1716/7, d 21 Feb 1775; m (2) 9 Aug 1775 Mercy, wid. Moses Hills, who d 7 1777 æ. 49 *F*; m (3) Sep 1777 Lydia da. John & Miriam (Wood) Hotchkiss, wid. Thomas Hart, b 19 Feb 1733 *WV*, d 27 Aug 1798 æ. 66 *BristolT*.

(By 1): *i* Lemuel, b 8 Nov 1744 *FarmV*, d 18 Feb 1802 æ. 58 *New Durham, N. Y.*; Census (Berlin) 3-2-6; m 26 Mar 1764 Penelope da. Joseph & Anna (Booth) Mather, b 27 May 174[-]. **FAM. 37.**

ii Mary, b 21 July 1747 *FarmV*; m 17 Dee 1769 John Stedman.

iii Ladwick, b 25 May 1752 *FarmV*, d 1 Dec 1823; Census (Berlin) 1-3-4; m 17 May 1773 Martha da. Stephen & Catherine Lee, who d 20 Feb 1813. **FAM. 38.**

iv Josiah, b 7 Nov 1757 *FarmV*, d 14 Apr 1832; Census (Farm) 2-1-3; m (1) 22 Feb 1781 Mary da. John Root; m (2) Esther (——) Carrington. (Had Jeremiah, b 1787, d 1834, & others.)

5 LENT, b 2 June 1726 *WV*, bp 8 Jan 1726/7 *CC*, d 8 Apr 1760 *WV*, 7 Apr 1759 æ. 34 *CTI*; m 20 Dec 1750 *WV*—Abigail Chauncey; she m (2) Isaac Tyler.

i Ruth, b 29 Oct 1751 *WV*; m 20 Dec 1775 *CC*—William Perkins.

ii Abigail, b 2 Sep 1753 *WV*.

iii Lent, b 2 Sep 1753 *WV*, d 2 Dec 1805 æ. 5 *NHT1;* Census (NH) 2-0-3; m 21 Sep 1788 *NHC1*—Sarah da. Stephen & Abigail (Atwater) Ball, b 19 Oct 1765 *NHV*, d 29 May 1803 æ. 37 *NHT1*, æ. 38 *NHC1*. **FAM. 39.**

iv Martha, b 2 Aug 1757 *WV*, d 31 May 1821 æ. 65 *WatT1;* m 15 June 1775 *WatV*—Simeon Nichols.

6 TRIAL, b 20 Mar 1728 *WV*, bp 21 Mar 1728/8 *CC*, "child" d 1732 *WV*.

FAM. 6. CALEB & MEHITABEL (CRUTTENDEN) HOTCHKISS:

1 MEHITABEL b 20 Nov 1706 *NHV*, d 2 Nov 1725 æ. 18 *NHT1*.

2 RACHEL, b 26 Oct 1709 *NHV*, d 6 May 1774 *MV;* m (1) Ebenezer Wolcott; m (2) 28 Oct 1731 *NHV*—Thomas Humphreville; m (3) 7 Nov 1745 *NHV*—Samuel Pardee.

3 CALEB, b 6 June 1712 *NHV*, d 5 July 1779 æ. 68 *NHT1*, æ. 67 (k. by enemy) *NHC1;* m 6 Jan 1736/7 *NHV*—Phebe da. Jonathan & Abigail (Bradley) Atwater, b 9 Oct 1714 *NHV*, d 19 Feb 1795 æ. 81 *NHT1*, *NHC1*.

i Stephen, b 4 Feb 1737/8 *NHV*, bp 5 Feb 1737/8 *NHC1*, d 19 Dec 1800 æ. 63 *NHT1;* Capt.; Census (NH) 3-3-3; m (1) 9 Dec 1767 *NHV*, 10 Dec *NHC1*—Abigail da. William & Abigail (Hitchcock) Scott, b c. 1747, d 4 May 1789 *NHC1*, æ. 42 *NHT1;* m (2) 15 Nov 1789 *NHC1*—Elizabeth da. Jeremiah & Elizabeth (Sperry) Osborn, wid. James Miles, b 29 Apr 1750 *NHV*, d 14 Feb 1820; she m (3) Thomas Rogers of NoB. **FAM. 40.**

ii Phebe, b 12 Oct 1739 *NHV*, bp 13 Oct 1739 *NHC1*, d young.

iii Mehitabel, b 20 Mar 1741/2 *NHV*, d 18 Mar 1804 æ. 62 *DT1;* m 11 Nov 1761 *DV*, *NHC1*—Elijah Hotchkiss.

iv Jonah, b 12 June 1745 *NHV*, bp 16 June 1745 *NHC1*, d 15 Nov 1811 æ. 66 *NHT1;* m 18 Mar 1772 *NHC1*—Elizabeth da. David & Elizabeth (Bassett) Atwater, b 30 Jan 1747/8 *NHV*, d 16 Apr 1827 æ. 79 *NHT1*, 17 Apr (*NHC1*) *NHV*. **FAM. 41.**

v Amos, b 22 May 1750 *NHV*, bp 27 May 1750 *NHC1*, d 17 Nov 1797 æ. 48 *NHC1;* Census (NH) 1-1-1; m 12 Sep 1773 *NHC1*—Rebecca da. David & Elizabeth (Gorham) Gilbert, b 29 May 1754 *NHV*, she m (2) Bishop Dodd. Child: 1 Henry, bp 30 July 1780 *NHC2*.

vi Asa, bp 3 June 1755 *NHC1*, d 2 Sep 1800 æ. 45 *NHC1*.

4 ELIPHALET, b 28 June 1714 *NHV*, d 31 Mar 1726 æ. 11 *NHT1*.

5 JOEL, b 18 Mar 1716/7 *NHV*, bp 1717 *NHC1*, d 1777; m (1) 5 Nov 1741 *NHV*—Mary da. Daniel & Mary (Bassett) Sherman, b 19 Mar 1718/9 *NHV;* m (2) Sarah ——— .

(By 1): *i* Elihu, b 16 Aug 1742 *NHV*, bp 10 Oct 1742 *NHC1*, d 12 May 1835 æ. 93 *LT;* Census (L) 2-1-5; m 1769 Lydia da. Eliakim & Lydia (Moulthrop) Robinson, b 13 Apr 1743, d 2 June 1836 æ. 93 *LT*. **FAM. 42.**

ii Joel, b 9 Nov 1745 *NHV*, bp 29 Dec 1745 *WdC*, d 13 Feb 1819 æ. 73 *BTI*; Census (Wd) 1-2-6; m Martha da. Timothy & Lydia (Lines) Peck, b c. 1748, d 13 Nov 1831 *BTI*. **FAM. 43.**

iii Mary, b 25 Jan 1747/8 *NHV*, bp 20 Mar 1748 *WdC*, d 31 Dec 1834 æ. 87 *CTI*; m 1 July 1773 *NHV*—Stephen Ives.

iv Eliphalet, b 14 Apr 1750 *NHV*, bp 20 May 1750 *WdC*, d 29 Mar 1835 *F*; Census (L) 1-3-1; m 1772 Esther da. Daniel & Esther (Baldwin) Beecher, bp 26 Aug 1752 *WdC*, d 21 May 1833 *F*. **FAM. 44.**

v Elias, b 18 Mar 1752 *NHV*, bp 3 May 1752 *WdC*, d 18 Feb 1821 *F*; Census (Wd) 1-2-1; m 19 Jan 1780 *F*—Eunice da. Jonathan & Miriam (Canfield) Atwater, b 24 Aug 1753, d 18 Aug 1838 æ. 85 *NHTI*. **FAM. 45.**

vi Rachel, b 21 Feb 1754 *NHV*, d 19 Nov 1828 æ. 75 *NHTI*; m Medad Osborn.

vii Eldad, b 21 Apr 1756 *NHV*, d 5 Sep 1832 æ. 76 *PptT*; Census (Wat) 1-1-2; m Abigail da. Jonathan & Miriam (Canfield) Atwater, who d 2 Jan 1826 æ. 67 *PptT*. **FAM 46.**

viii Medad, b 21 Apr 1758 *NHV*, d soon.

ix Medad, b 7 Oct 1760 *NHV*, d 1828 *F*; m 7 Feb 1787 *WatV*—Rebecca da. Isaac & Temperance (Goodspeed) Spencer, b 18 Sep 1759 *F*. An infant s. d 13 Feb 1788 æ. 0-0-1 *BD*.

x Mehitabel, b 14 July 1764 *NHV*, d Nov 1827 æ. 65 *BTI*; m 25 Sep 1793 *NHCI*—Stephen Hawley.

6 Nehemiah, b 20 Apr 1719 *NHV*, bp 3 May 1719 *NHCI*, d 21 Oct 1768 æ. 50 *NHCI*; m 8 Nov 1739 *NHV*—Mary da. Arthur & Elizabeth (Stevens) Rexford, b c. 1720, bp (adult) 26 Oct 1760 *NHCI*, d 2 Aug 1770 æ. 50 *NHCI*.

i Naomi, b 15 Mar 1740/1 *NHV*, bp 26 Oct 1760 *NHCI*, d 23 Jan 1774 æ. 33 *NHTI*; m 13 Dec 1764 *NHCI*—James Bradley.

ii Nehemiah, b 11 Jan 1744/5 *NHV*, bp 26 Oct 1760 *NHCI*, d 30 Mar 1798 *NHx*, æ. 56 *ConnJournal*; Census (NH) 1-3-4; m (1) 25 Jan 1768 *NHCI*—Rebecca da. Jeremiah & Elizabeth Osborn, bp 14 Aug 1743 *NHCI*, d 3 Dec 1781 æ. 38 *NHCI*; m (2) 3 Nov 1784 *NHCI*—Hannah Johnson; m (3) Mary ——— . **FAM. 47.**

iii Mary, b 2 Jan 1746/7 *NHV*, bp 26 Oct 1760 *NHCI*, d 17 Feb 1826 æ. 79 *NHTI*; m 17 Mar 1768 *NHCI*—Enoch Moulthrop.

iv Arthur, d June 1760 *NHCI*.

v Amy, b c. 1753, bp 26 Oct 1760 *NHCI*, d 24 Aug 1825 æ. 71 *NHTI*, 26 Aug æ. 72 (*NHCI*) *NHV*; m John Bradley.

vi Martha, bp 16 Nov 1760 *NHCI*; m 7 Sep 1783 *WyV*—Jonathan Sperry.

FAM. 7. SAMUEL & MARY (———) HOTCHKISS:

1 JAMES, b 11 Feb 1709 *EHV*, d 19 Feb 1709 *EHV*.

2 JAMES, b 17 Mar 1711 *EHV*, d 10 May 1711 *EHV*.

3 SARAH, b 20 May 1712 *EHV*, d 17 Sep 1773; m (1) Thomas Shepard; m (2) 26 May 1757 *EHC*—Caleb Hitchcock.

4 SAMUEL, b 5 June 1715 *EHV*, d 31 Aug 1774 æ. 59 *NoBC2;* m 16 July 1744 *EHV*—Mary da. Samuel & Mary (Frisbie) Goodsell, b 17 Dec 1719 *EHV*.

i Mary, b c. 1745, bp 19 Apr 1752 *NoBC2*, d 17 June 1779 æ. 34 *NoBC2*.

ii Samuel, b c. 1747, d 22 Aug 1751 æ. 5 *NoBC2*.

iii Sarah, b c. 1749, d 29 Aug 1751 æ. 3 *NoBC2*.

iv Sarah, bp 19 Apr 1752 *NoBC2*.

v Samuel, bp 19 May 1754 *NoBC2*, d 13 Nov 1803 æ. 53 (?) *NoBC2*.

vi Ebenezer, bp 17 Sep 1758 *NoBC2*, d 7 Oct 1774 æ. 16 *No BC2*.

vii Hannah, bp 1 Nov 1761 *NoBC2*, d 13 July 1788 æ. 27 *NoB T1;* m 28 Sep 1786 *NoBC2*—Jacob Bunnell.

5 MARY, b 5 Mar 1718 *EHV*, d c. 1745; m Samuel Goodsell.

6 ABIGAIL, b 27 Feb 1721/2 *EHV*, d 3 Sep 1743 *EHV;* m Nathaniel Barnes.

7 JOSEPH, b 15 Feb 1724/5 *EHV*, d 27 Apr 1776 æ. c. 50 *EHC;* m Esther da. Samuel & Mary (Hemingway) Russell, b c. 1729, d 14 Sep 1788 æ. 59 *EHC*.

i Abigail, b 6 May 1748 *EHV*, d 16 Nov 1816 æ. 69 *WolT;* m (1) 1 May 1769 *EHC*—Benjamin Bishop; m (2) 24 Oct 1782 *EHC*—Eliphalet Pardee.

ii Mary, b 24 June 1750 *EHR*, d 30 Mar 1826 æ. 76 *WolT;* m (1) 21 Nov 1770 *EHC*—Elihu Moulthrop; m (2) 24 Nov 1784 Charles Upson of Wol.

iii Isaac, b 10 Dec 1773 *EHV*, d [1 Oct] 1784 æ. 30 *EHC;* m 4 Dec 1775 *EHC*—Lydia da. Ezra & Sarah (Chidsey) Fields, b c. 1757, d 24 May 1812 æ. 55 *EHC;* she m (2) 4 Feb 1790 *EHC*—Chandler Pardee. **FAM. 48.**

iv Joseph, b 31 July 1756 *EHR*, bp 8 Aug 1756 *EHC*, d 2 May 1825 æ. 68 *EHC*, 1 May æ. 69 *EHT;* m 27 Jan 1780 *EHC*—Temperance da. Timothy & Anna (Smith) Andrews, b [28 Nov 1760], d 7 Jan 1846 æ. 85-0-38 *EHC*. **FAM. 49.**

v Esther, b 13 Apr 1759 *EHR*, bp 20 May 1759 *EHC*, d 1 Oct 1825 æ. 66 *EHC*, *NHT3;* m 29 [Oct] 1778 *EHC*—John Rowe.

vi Samuel, b 26 Aug 1763 *EHR*, bp 16 Oct 1763 *EHC*.

vii Heman, b 1 July 1765 *NHT3*, [bp 10 June 1770 (at EH) *NoBC2*?], d 20 Feb 1836 *NHT3*, æ. 70 *EHC;* m 28 July 1793 *EHC*—Elizabeth da. Ezra & Huldah (Chidsey) Rowe, b 11 July 1774 *EHV*, 12 July *NHT3*, d 5 Dec

1851 *NHT3*. **FAM. 50.**

viii Asaph, b 7 Oct 1767 *EHR*, bp 17 Jan 1768 *EHC*, d 20 Oct 1813 æ. 46 *WolT;* m 15 May 1788 *EHC*—Hannah da. Edward & Mary (Pardee) Russell, b c. 1767, d 16 Aug 1830 æ. 63 *WolT*.

ix Gideon, b 25 Dec 1769 *EHR*, bp 7 Jan 1770 *EHC*, d 30 Oct 1788 æ. 19 *EHC*.

8 JAMES, b 13 Jan 1727/8 *EHV;* rem. to Norfolk; Census (Benson, Vt.) 3-1-3; m Dorothy da. Aaron & Sarah Aspinwall, b 10 Nov 1733 *WV*.

i (probably) Samuel, b c. 1753, d Jan 1799 *NorfolkC;* Census (L) 1-3-3; m Elizabeth ——— .

ii (probably) Josiah, b c. 1755; m Asenath ——— .

iii Levi, b c. 1757, bp 2 Oct 1763 *NorfolkC*.

iv Mary, b c. 1760, bp 2 Oct 1763 *NorfolkC*.

v Sarah, bp 2 Oct 1763 *NorfolkC*.

vi Rebecca, bp 6 May 1764 *NorfolkC*.

vii David, bp 29 June 1766 *NorfolkC;* Census (Benson, Vt.) 1-1-2.

viii Asenath, bp 30 Oct 1768 *NorfolkC*.

ix Cyrus, bp 29 July 1770 *NorfolkC*.

x James, bp 16 Aug 1772 *NorfolkC;* rem. to Georgia, Vt.; m Alice Storey.

xi Phebe, bp 19 June 1774 *NorfolkC*.

xii Ira, bp 14 June 1778 *NorfokC*.

xiii Charlotte, bp 16 Apr 1780 *NorfolkC*.

9 ENOS, b 13 May 1731 *EHV;* res. Norfolk & EH; m 5 Feb 1756 *EHC*—Elizabeth da. John & Sarah (Russell) Shepard, b 20 July 1734 *EHV*.

i Elihu, b 25 Jan 1757 *EHV*, bp 2 Oct 1763 *NorfolkC;* Census (Halifax, Vt.) 2-1-2; rem. to Brattleboro, Vt.

ii Elizabeth, bp 2 Oct 1763 *NorfolkC;* m Jonathan Finch.

iii Child, d 17 Jan 1763 *NorfolkC*.

iv Ruth, bp 2 Oct 1763 *NorfolkC;* m ——— Warner.

v John, bp 17 June 1764 *NorfolkC*, d s. p.

vi Stephen, b 30 Oct 1772 (?at Bennington, Vt.) *F*, bp 9 Oct 1772 *EHC*, d 11 Nov 1851 (at Mexico, N. Y.) *F;* m 1800 Sally Lamb.

vii Hannah, bp 14 Aug 1774 *EHC*.

viii Samuel, b 25 Apr 1778.

FAM. 8. EBENEZER & ——— (———) HOTCHKISS (family incomplete):

1 EBENEZER; Dea.; Census (NM) 1-1-2; m 10 Jan 1741/2 *NMV*—Hannah Terrill, who d 29 Dec 1782 *NMV*.

i Solomon, b 18 Sep 1742 *NMV*, bp 24 Oct 1742 *NMC;* Census (NM) 1-1-2.

ii Asahel, b 16 Aug 1744 *NMV*.

iii Hannah, b 9 Apr 1746 *NMV*.

FAM. 9. STEPHEN & ELIZABETH (SPERRY) HOTCHKISS:

1 JOSHUA, b 26 Aug 1705 *NHV*, d 29 Dec 1788 *CC*, æ. 84 *CT1*; m 2 Feb 1732 *WV*—Mary da. John & Mary (Chatterton) Hotchkiss, b 1 Apr 1701 *NHV*, d 13 Nov 1787 *CC*, æ. 88 *CT1*.

i John, b 27 Feb 1733 *WV*, bp Mar 1732/3 *CC*, d 9 Nov 1794 *CC*; Census (C) 2-0-4; m (1) 25 Oct 1756 *WV*—Abigail da. Ebenezer & Hannah (Smith) Smith, b 31 Aug 1725 *NHV*, d 19 Apr 1760 æ. 35 *CT1*; m (2) 26 Jan 1761 *WV*—Sarah Gillam. **FAM. 51.**

ii Elizabeth, b 30 Mar 1735 *WV*, bp Mar 1735 *CC*; m (1) 23 Nov 1752 *WV*—Ebenezer Benham; m (2) 25 Mar 1758 *WatV*—Amos Osborn.

iii Mary, b 11 Aug 1737 *WV*, bp 12 Aug 1737 *CC*, d 19 June 1738 *WV*.

iv Mary, b 5 June 1739 *WV*, bp 3 June 1739 *CC*; m 10 Jan 1760 *WV*—Willam Wheeler.

2 MARY, b 1 Jan 1707/8 *NHV*, d 15 Aug 1764 æ. 57 *CT1*; m (1) 27 Feb 1735 *WV*—Abraham Barnes; m (2) 30 May 1745 *WV*—Joseph Ives.

3 HANNAH, b 10 Jan 1710 *WV*, d Mar 1717 *WV*.

4 ESTHER, b 18 Feb 1712 *WV*, d 22 July 1732 *CC*; m 16 June 1731 *WV*—Ephraim Tuttle.

5 ELIZABETH, b 25 Aug 1714 *WV*, d 13 Apr 1732 æ. 18 *CT1*.

6 GIDEON, b 5 Dec 1716 *WV*, d 3 Sep 1807 æ. 91 *PptT*; Dea.; Capt.; Census (Wat) 4-0-2; m (1) 18 June 1737 *WatV*—Anna da. John & Huldah (Earl) Brockett, b 2 Feb 1716 *WV*, d 1 Aug 1762 æ. 47 *PptT*; m (2) 22 Feb 1763 *WatV*—Mabel da. Isaac Stiles, who d 15 Oct 1824 æ. 95 *PptT*.

(By 1): *i* Jesse, b 9 Oct 1738 *WatV*, bp 5 Nov 1738 *CC*, d 29 Sep 1776 (in Army) *WatV*; m 2 Oct 1759 *WatV*—Charity da. Peter Mallory, [possibly the "Widow" who d 27 Dec 1826 æ. 89 *SalemC*]. **FAM. 52.**

ii David, b 5 Apr 1740 *WatV*, bp 11 May 1740 *CC*, d 8 May 1826 *Windsor, N. Y, T*; Dea.; rem. 1788 to Onondagua, now Windsor, N. Y.; m (1) 21 Nov 1763 *WatV*—Abigail da. Alexander & Sarah (Ballard) Douglas of Lynn, Mass., who d 5 Apr 1775 æ. 36 *WatT3*; m (2) 5 July 1775 *WatV*—Penina da. Timothy & Lydia (Lines) Peck, wid. Charles Todd, b c. 1740, d 11 May 1817 æ. 77 *Windsor, N. Y., T*; m (3) Jane Campbell, wid. ——— Dyer. **FAM. 53.**

iii Abraham, b 3 May 1742 *WatV*, d 3 May 1742 *WatV*.

iv Abraham, b 25 Mar 1743 *WatV*, d 29 Oct 1806 *WatV*, 29 Oct 1807 æ. 64 *PptT*; Census (Wat) 3-2-3; m 28 Dec 1767 *WatV*—Hannah da. John & Alice (Clark) Weed, b 18 Nov 1744 *WatV*, d 26 Dec 1824 æ. 80 *PptT*. **FAM 54.**

v Gideon, b 31 Dec 1744 *WatV*, d 6 Jan 1819; res. Wtn; m Mary Scott.

vi Huldah, b 27 June 1747 *WatV*, d 28 Mar 1774 *WatV*; m.

8 Apr 1773 *WatV*—Joseph Payne.

vii Anna, b 22 Oct 1749 *WatV*, d 17 Feb 1835 æ. 87 *WatT3;* m 16 Mar 1775 *WatV*—Reuben Williams.

viii Amos, b 24 Nov 1751 *WatV*, d 13 May 1820 æ. 70 *PptT;* Census (Wat) 2-2-3; m 24 Dec 1772 *WatV*—Abigail da. Gershom & Mary (Fenton) Scott, b c. 1752, d 8 Apr 1844 æ. 92 *PptT*. **FAM. 55.**

ix Submit, b 2 June 1753 *WatV*, d 10 Dec 1844 æ. 91-6 *PptT;* m 15 June 1775 David Payne.

x Titus, b 26 June 1755 *WatV*, d 29 Jan 1835 *F;* Census (Wtn) 1-1-3; m Rachel Guernsey.

xi Eben, b 13 Dec 1757 *WatV*, d 26 July 1853 æ. 95 *PptT;* Census (Wat) 1-1-2; m (1) 15 Feb 1781 *WatV*—Mary da. Gideon Sanford, who d 18 Jan 1835 æ. 73 *PptT;* m (2) Ruth ——, who d 6 Mar 1842 æ. 76 *PptT*. **FAM. 56.**

xii Child, stillborn 27 July 1762 *WatV*.

(By 2): *xiii* Mabel, b 23 May 1764 *WatV*, d c. 1799; m 15 Sep 1785 *WatV*—Chauncey Judd.

xiv Phebe, b 29 Aug 1765 *WatV;* m Reuben Williams.

xv Hannah, b 14 Oct 1766 *WatV*, d 26 Nov 1766 *WatV*.

xvi Stiles, b 30 Jan 1768 *WatV;* rem. to Greene, N. Y.; m Polly da. John & Mary (Beecher) Horton.

xvii Olive, b 21 Nov 1769 *WatV;* m William Jones.

xviii Millicent, b 6 May 1771 *WatV*, d 9 Oct 1849 æ. 79 *PptT;* m David Sanford.

xix Amzi, b 3 July 1774 *F;* rem. to Meriden.

7 STEPHEN, b 1 Dec 1718 *WV*, d 16 May 1807 æ. 89 *Burlington;* Census (Bristol) 1-0-1; m (1) 31 Dec 1742 *WV*—Thankful da. Samuel & Elizabeth Cook, b 14 Nov 1718 *WV*, d 14 Sep 1760 *WV*, æ. 42 *CTI;* m (2) 2 Mar 1762 *WV*—Ann da. Evan & Rachel (Parker) Royce, wid. Daniel Johnson, b 23 June 1727 *WV;* m (3) 13 Sep 1782 (?)—Thankful da. John & Mary (Gaylord) Hickox, wid. Benjamin Brooks, b 30 Mar 1722 *WV*, d 18 Aug 1812 æ. 89 *Morris, N. Y., T.* Family perhaps incomplete.

(By 1): *i* Esther, b 23 Oct 1742 *WV*, bp Oct 1742 *CC*, d 15 Oct 1749 *WV*, æ. 7 *CTI*.

ii Thankful, b 14 Mar 1744/5 *WV*, bp Mar 1744/5 *CC*, d 20 Sep 1776 *WV;* m (1) 5 May 1767 *WV*—Titus Preston; m (2) 21 Mar 1771 *WV*—Stephen Cook.

iii Susanna, b 3 Aug 1747 *WV*, bp Aug 1747 *CC*, d 15 Oct 1749 *WV*, æ. 3 *CTI*.

PAGE 946 *iv* Esther, b 9 June 1750 *WV*, bp June 1750 *CC;* [m Abner Johnson].

v Susanna, b 20 July 1752 *WV*, bp July 1752 *CC*.

vi Stephen, b 15 July 1754 *WV*.

vii Samuel, b 22 Oct 1755 *WV*, d 1843; Census (Bristol) 1-3-4; m Rachel Upson, who d 1833 æ. 79 *BristolC*.

viii (perhaps) Jeremiah, b 30 Apr 1759 (at C)*F.* d 14 Mar 1842; m (1) ——— ; m (2) Jan 1797 (Durham, N. Y.)—Mabel da. William & Lucy (Smith) Hodge, div. w. Nathaniel Tyler. Children by 1st w.: Ransom, Willis, Harriet, Jeremiah.

8 Silas, b 20 Nov 1719 *WV,* d 9 Jan 1783 æ. 64 *WatTI;* m (1) 12 May 1748 *WatV*—Lois da. Thomas & Hannah (Upson) Richards, wid. Benjamin Bronson, b 1 Nov 1719 *WatV,* d 7 Feb 1766 æ. 47 *WatTI;* m (2) Abigail ———, who d 31 Aug 1794 *WatV.* She was perhaps Abigail Humiston, wid. Stephen Alcott, Thomas Vergison & David Barnes, b 3 Dec 1715 *NH V.*

(By 1): *i* Chloe, b 19 Jan 1748/9 *WatV.*

ii Hester, b 2 Jan 1750/1 *WatV,* d 23 Feb 1787 æ. 37 *WatTI;* m 21 Nov 1774 *WatV*—Joseph Payne.

iii Stephen, b 24 Aug 1753 *WatV,* d 9 Sep 1826 æ. 73 *WatTI;* Census (Wat) 1-1-5; m 31 Dec 1778 *WatV*—Tamar da. Nathaniel & Phebe (Bronson) Richardson, b 13 Sep 1758 *WatV,* d 29 Mar 1853 æ. 94½ *WatTI.* FAM 57.

iv Truman, b 18 June 1760 *WatV,* d 30 May 1833 æ. 73 *Wat TI;* Census (Wtn) 1-0-3; m Ruth ———, who d 24 Nov 1838 æ. 75 *WatTI.*

v Lois, b 21 Mar 1763 *WatV,* d 23 Aug 1763 *WatV.*

9 Hannah, b 23 Feb 23 1722 *WV,* d 9 Oct 1779 æ. 58 *CTI;* m 23 Feb 1743/4 *WV*—Stephen Atwater.

10 Abraham, bp 28 Dec 1724 *CC,* d young.

11 Bathsheba, b 1 Sep 1726 *WV,* bp Sep 1726 *CC,* d 8 Aug 1813 æ. 87 *SyT;* m Ralph Lines.

12 Benjamin, b 1 Feb 1728 *WV,* bp Feb 1727/8 *CC,* d 13 Apr 1815 æ. 88 *WatV;* Census (C) 1-0-1; m 16 Apr 1751 *WV*—Elizabeth da. Abiel & Hephzibah (Prindle) Roberts, b 15 Nov 1727 *W V.* Family perhaps incomplete.

Abraham Barnes, b 21 Jan 1752 *WV,* bp Dec 1721 (?) *CC,* d 3 Feb 1752 *WV.*

ii Elizabeth, b 15 Feb 1753 *WV;* m 19 Mar 1781 *CC*—Zenas Andrews.

iii Hannah, b 14 June 1755 *WV.*

13 Noah, b 24 Mar 1730 *WV,* bp 1 (?) Mar 1729/30 *CC,* d s. p. 13 Jan 1760 *WV,* æ. 30 *CTI.*

FAM. 10. Abraham & Deborah (Thomas) Hotchkiss:

1 Mabel, b c. 1719, bp 29 Mar 1730 *NHCI,* d 19 Feb 1798 æ. 80 *B TI;* m 6 Apr 1738 *NHV*—Isaac Beecher.

2 Hannah, b c. 1721, bp 29 Mar 1730 *NHCI,* d before 1748; m 1 Sep 1743 *WdC*—James Sherman.

3 Deborah, b c. 1723, bp 29 Mar 1730 *NHCI;* m 29 Mar 1743 *NH V*—John Lines.

4 Dorcas, b c. 1725, bp 29 Mar 1730 *NHCI,* d 1790.

FAM. 11. Isaac & Rachel (Carnes) Hotchkiss:

1 Abraham, b c. 1727, bp 31 Aug 1735 *NHCI,* d young.

2 ISAAC, b c. 1729, bp 31 Aug 1735 *NHC1*, d 1777; m Anna da. Daniel & Zerviah (Canfield) Terrill.

i Lorania, bp 30 Aug 1752 *WdC;* m 14 May 1777 *WatV*—Amos Osborn.

ii Abraham, b c. 1754, d 24 Nov 1802 æ. 48 *WatT3;* Census (Wd) 1-4-2; m Rosetta da. Ezra & Ruth (Sperry) Sperry, b c. 1758, d 9 Sep 1841 æ. 83 *WatT3.* **FAM. 58.**

iii Peter.

iv Isaac, b c. 1758, d 11 May 1828 æ. 70 *WdT3;* Census (Wd) 1-2-3; m Elizabeth da. Hezekiah & Mary (Peck) Clark, b 9 May 1762 *F*, d 6 Jan 1859 æ. 97 *WdT3.* **FAM. 59.**

v [Anna].

vi [Susanna].

vii [Rachel].

viii Ichabod.

3 MARTHA, b c. 1731, bp 31 Aug 1735 *NHC1;* m 26 Oct 1749 *WdC*—Josiah Lounsbury.

4 RACHEL, b c. 1734, bp 31 Aug 1735 *NHC1*, d 17 Jan 1767 *SalisburyV;* m 19 Feb 1754 *SalisburyV*—Moses Reed.

5 JACOB, b c. 1736, bp 23 May 1736 *NHC1*, d 26 June 1825 æ. 89 *BT1;* Census (Wd) 2-1-4; m 25 Jan 1763 *WdC*—Mary da. Thomas & Rachel (Peck) Perkins, b 20 Aug 1744 *NHV.*

i Mary; m —— Thomas.

ii Huldah; m —— Hull.

iii Zedekiah; m Anna da. Timothy & Ann (Russell) Brown, b c. 1770, d 30 Mar 1842 æ. 72 *BT2.*

iv Rhoda; m —— Warner.

v Zaccheus, b c. 1774, d 18 Feb 1856 æ. 82 (at B); m Martha da. David & Mabel (Beecher) Thomas. Children: 1 Wales; res. WH. 2 Guy, d s. p. 3 Spencer, b c. 1804, d 7 Nov 1856 *F;* m Rhoda da. Zedekiah & Anna (Brown) Hotchkiss, who d 5 Mar 1856 *F.*

vi Lucy; m —— Warner.

vii Hannah; m —— Thomas.

6 JOSEPH, bp 11 June 1738 *NHC1;* m 10 June 1760 *GlastonburyC*—Elizabeth Brooks. Family incomplete.

i Lois, b 6 June 1761 *MV.*

7 LORANA, bp 4 Oct 1741 *NHC1.*

8 ABIGAIL, bp 11 Mar 1744 *WdC*, d soon.

9 ABIGAIL, bp Apr 1746 *CC.*

10 REUBEN, bp May 1749 *CC.*

11 LOIS, bp May 1749 *CC.*

FAM. 12. JACOB & ELIZABETH (DICKERMAN) HOTCHKISS:

1 JABEZ, b 4 Aug 1729 *NHV*, bp May 1735 *CC*, d 10 July 1816 æ. 87 *WolT;* Cpl.; Census (Wd) 1-0-2; m Lydia da. Stephen & Lydia (Holt) Sperry, b c. 1735, d 4 Sep 1817 æ. 82 *WolT.*

i Stephen, b 31 Oct 1761 *F*, d 4 Nov 1847 æ. 87 *BT2;* Census (Wd) 1-0-1; m Hannah da. Timothy & Ann (Russell) Brown, b c. 1767, d 26 Feb 1847 æ. 80 *BT2*. **FAM. 60.**

ii Mary, b 3 June 1762 *F* [1763?].

iii Timothy, b 22 Jan 1766 *F*, d 14 June 1843 æ. 77 *WolT;* m Lucy ———, who d 23 Aug 1837 æ. 67 *WolT*.

iv Lydia, b 1 Apr 1768 *F*.

v Eleazer, b 4 June 1770 *F*.

vi Lydia, b 7 June 1774 *F*.

2 TIMOTHY, b 11 Apr 1731 *NHV;* m 4 Mar 1762 *WV*—Lucy Andrews, who d 27 Apr 1772 *WV*, *CC*.

i Samuel, b 14 Dec 1762 *WV*, bp 23 Aug 1767 *CC*.

ii Ambrose, b 14 Jan 1765 *WV*, bp 23 Aug 1767 *CC*, d 25 Jan 1825 æ. 58 *WT2;* Census (C) 1-0-0; m 25 Dec 1791 *CC*—Lucretia Baldwin, who d 9 Oct [——] æ. 73 *WT2*.

iii Aner, b 24 Dec 1766 *WV*, bp 23 Aug 1767 *CC*.

iv Bryant, b 31 May 1769 *WV*, bp 2 July 1769 *CC*.

v Lucy, b 23 Apr 1772 *WV*, bp 28 Apr 1772 *CC*, d 6 May 1772 *WV*.

3 ELIJAH, b 13 May 1733 *NHV*, bp May 1735 *CC*, d 2 Sep 1806 æ. 72 *DT1;* Census (D) 2-1-6; m 11 Nov 1761 *DV*—Mehitabel da. Caleb & Phebe (Atwater) Hotchkiss, b 20 Mar 1741/2 *NHV*, d 18 Mar 1804 æ. 62 *DT1*.

i Leverett, b 6 Oct 1762 *DV*, bp 10 Oct 1762 *DC*, d 3 Oct 1826 æ. 64 *DT1;* Census (D) 1-1-2; m 14 Aug 1785 *DV*—Sarah da. William & Mary (French) Burritt, b 3 Jan 1763 *DV*, d 8 Jan 1842 æ. 79 *DT1*. **FAM. 61.**

ii Phebe, b 2 Aug 1764 *DV*, bp 5 Aug 1764 *DC*, d 13 Mar 1850 *F;* m 22 Oct 1804 *F*—Reuben Tucker.

iii Elijah, b 16 Nov 1766 *DV*, bp 30 Dec 1766 *DC;* m (1) 19 Apr 1795 *WatV*—Polly da. David Clark, who d 28 Oct 1808 *WatV;* m (2) 7 June 1809 *WatV*—Lucinda da. James & Eunice (Dutton) Warner, b 20 Sep 1765 *WatV*, d 22 Dec 1845 æ. 81 *WatT1*. **FAM. 62.**

iv Elizabeth, b 17 June 1769 *DV*, bp 23 July 1769 *DC*, d 29 Aug 1794 æ. 25 *DT1*.

v Mehitabel, b 22 July 1772 *DV*, bp 23 Aug 1772 *DC*, d 4 Nov 1833 æ. 62 *DT1*.

vi Cyrus, b 16 July 1774 *DV*, bp 24 Aug 1774 *DC*, d 27 Jan 1846 æ. 72 *DT1;* m 29 Jan 1800 *MC2*—Catherine Fowler, who d 24 Feb 1832 æ. 58 *DT1*.

vii Nabby, b 30 Aug 1777 *DV*, bp 5 Oct 1777 *DC*, d 2 Feb 1846 *F;* m 8 May 1796 *F*—Ezra Lewis.

viii Rebecca, b 7 Nov 1779 *DV*, bp Feb 1780 *DC*, d 3 July 1866 *F;* m (1) 20 Feb 1819 *F*—Levi Smith; m (2) 11 May 1851 *F*—Erastus Merrells.

ix Beers, b 5 May 1787 *DV*, d 21 Mar 1835 æ. 48 *DT1*.

4 MARTHA, b 26 June 1735 *NHV*, bp July 1735 *CC;* m 18 Oct 1758 *NHV*—Timothy Leek.

5 ELIZABETH, b 9 Apr 1738 *NHV*, bp 7 May 1738 *CC*.

6 HANNAH, b 18 Apr 1740 *NHV*, [?d 27 Mar 1802 æ. 60 *NoHC*; m Noah Barnes].

7 ABRAHAM, b 9 Feb 1743 *NHV*, bp Mar 1742/3 *CC*, d 8 June 1778 æ. 34 *HT1*; m 7 Feb 1769 *WdC*—Phebe da. Abraham & Elizabeth (Bradley) Augur, b c. 1752, d 29 Mar 1813 æ. 74 *HT1*; Census, Phebe (H) 0-0-2.

i Mary, b 13 Nov 1770 *NHV*, d 28 Sep 1826 æ. 57 *CT2*; m 9 Mar 1809 *CV*—Tillotson Bronson.

ii Elias, b 13 Aug 1772 *NHV*, d 7 July 1830 æ. 56 *HT3*; m (1) Chloe da. Abner & Mary (Tuttle) Todd, bp 8 Oct 1778 *HC1*, d 27 July 1797 æ. 18 *HT3*; m (2) Esther da. James & Lois (Bradley) Dickerman, b c. 1779, d 2 Nov 1826 æ. 47 *HT3*. **FAM. 63.**

iii Huldah, b 22 July 1774 *NHV*, d young.

8 MARY, b 30 Mar 1745 *NHV*, bp May 1745 *CC*.

9 JACOB, b 2 June 1747 *NHV*, bp 21 June 1747 *CC*.

10 ABIGAIL, b 7 May 1750 *NHV*.

FAM. 13. SAMUEL & SARAH (BRADLEY) HOTCHKISS:

1 THOMAS, d 7 Sep 1756 *F&IWRolls*; m 3 Dec 1730 *NHV*—Lydia da. Benjamin & Ruth (Johnson) Dorman, b 2 Aug 1706 *NHV*. Family incomplete.

i Samuel, b 7 July 1732 *NHV*; [perhaps it was he who m Phebe da. Andrew & Jane (Gilbert) Goodyear, b 7 Oct 1737 *NHV*]. **FAM. 64.**

2 DESIRE; m Daniel Rexford.

3 WILLIAM, d s. p. 1745.

4 JOSEPH; res. B; m (1) c. 1737 Lydia da. John & Mary (Ford) Thomas, b 28 Sep 1709 *NHV*, d c. 1738; m (2) 15 Oct 1738 *NHV*—Patience da. Joseph Collins, b 8 Oct 1719 *NHV*, d 8 Jan 1754 *NHV*.

(By 1): *i* Joseph, b 21 May 1739 *NHV*, bp 10 Apr 1748 *WdC*, d 26 Apr 1800 æ. 62 *BT1*; Census (Wd) 3-1-2; m 10 June 1762 *WdC*—Hannah da. Joseph & Dorcas (Richardson) Thomas, b c. 1737, d c. 1821. **FAM. 65.**

ii Samuel, b 19 June 1741 *NHV*, bp 10 Apr 1748 *WdC*, d 1804; Census (Wd) 1-1-2; m 23 Dec 1762 *NHV*, *WdC*—Lydia da. Timothy & Lydia (Lines) Peck, b 13 Mar 1738/9 *NHV*, d c. 1804. **FAM. 66.**

iii Patience, b 22 Apr 1743 *NHV*, bp 10 Apr 1748 *WdC*; m Samuel Hine.

iv William, b 9 Oct 1744 *NHV*, bp 10 Apr 1748 *WdC*, d before 1793; m Eliphal da. George Hine, b 8 Mar 1747 *MV*, bp 6 Feb 1775 *NHx*. **FAM. 67.**

v Jonas, b 20 Aug 1746 *NHV*, bp 10 Apr 1748 *WdC*; Census (Wd) 1-2-4; rem. to Bristol, Ontario Co., N. Y.; m Mabel ——— . **FAM. 68.**

vi Benjamin, b 2 June 1748 *NHV*, bp 7 Aug 1748 *WdC*, d 20 Mar 1809 æ. 62 *BT1*; Census (Wd) 2-1-4; m Sarah da. Samuel & Sarah (Humphreville) Downs, b 29 Nov 1747 *NHV;* she m (2) Ephraim Buckingham.

FAM. 69.

vii Joel, b 19 Mar 1751/2 *NHV*, bp 3 May 1752 *WdC*, d 29 Jan 1816 æ. 64 *LT;* Census (Wd) 1-1-7; m 16 Jan 1777 *WdC*—Abigail da. David & Abigail (Perkins) Sperry, b 16 May 1753 *WdV*, d 15 Aug 1837 æ. 83 *LT;* had issue.

viii Ezekiel, b 5 Jan 1754 *NHV;* Sgt.; Census (Wd) 1-2-2; m Rebecca da. Gershom & Mabel (Dorman) Thomas, b c. 1756, d 20 Nov 1834 æ. 78 *WdD*. **FAM. 70.**

5 Sarah; m 16 Mar 1731/2 *NHV*—Nathaniel Turner.

FAM. 14. Abraham & Elizabeth (Johnson) Hotchkiss:

1 Abigail, b c. 1710, bp (adult) 20 June 1736 *NHC1*, d 1792; m 20 Sep 1737 *NHV*—Ebenezer Munson.

2 Elizabeth, b c. 1721, bp (adult) 13 Dec 1736 *NHC1*, d 17 Feb 1802 æ. 81 *WatT1;* m 8 Feb 1744/5 *WatV*—George Prichard.

3 David, b 19 Aug 1724 *NHV*, bp 13 Dec 1736 *NHC1*, d 24 June 1777 *Wy;* m (1) 10 Nov 1748 *BethlehemC*—Submit Hill, who d Sep 1756 *BethlehemC;* m (2) 21 Sep 1757 *SC*—Lucy Newell.

(By 1): *i* Sybil, b 29 May 1749 *WyV*, bp 23 July 1749 *WyC;* m 7 Oct 1772 *Wy*—Simeon Taylor.

ii David, bp 20 Jan 1751 *WyC*.

iii Huldah, b 16 Apr 1752 *WyV*, bp 31 May 1752 *WyC;* m ——— Yale.

iv Elizabeth, b 11 Feb 1754 *WyV*, bp 17 Feb 1754 *WyC;* m (1) Jesse Munger; m (2) ——— Hine.

v Reuben, b 8 Mar 1756 *WyV*, d 27 June 1834 æ. 78 *Wy;* Census (Wy) 1-3-1; m 1783 Thankful Minor, who d 4 May 1842 æ. 78 *Wy;* for descendants, see Cothren's "Woodbury," I, 579.

FAM. 15. Daniel & Susanna (Bradley) Hotchkiss:

1 (probably) Esther, bp (adult) Mar 1732 *CC*, d Apr 1734 *CC*, m 20 Jan 1733 *WV*—Nathan Andrews.

2 (perhaps) Elizabeth; m 11 Aug 1742 *NHV*—Ebenezer Bishop.

3 Daniel, bp (adult) 31 Jan 1741/2 *CC;* Census (C) 2-0-0; m Mamre da. Ephraim & Lydia (Merriman) Cook, b 21 Dec 1723 *WV*.

i Daniel, b 19 Aug 1744 *WV*, bp Aug 1744 *CC*, d 21 July 1827 æ. 83 (at Wd) *ConnH;* [Census (Wd) 2-3-2]; m 24 Aug 1769 *CC*—Sarah da. Joseph & Esther (Ives) Smith, bp 6 Apr 1746 *CC*, d after 1804.

ii Susanna, b 2 Mar 1745/6 *NHV*, bp 6 Apr 1746 *CC*, d 6 June 1789 *CC;* m 28 Sep 1769 *CC*, 27 Sep *WV*—Ephraim Smith.

iii Ephraim, b 16 Aug 1747 *NHV*, bp Sep 1747 *CC*, d 6 June 1815 æ. 68 *CT2;* Census (C) 1-1-2; m (1) Elizabeth ———, who d 27 Jan 1786 æ. 36 *CT2;* m (2) 10 May 1787 *CC*—Sarah Hopkins, wid. Josiah Talmadge. His adopted da. Molly, b 29 May 1784 *CV*, d 1 Oct 1818 æ.

34 *BT2;* m 16 Mar 1806 *CC*—Archibald Abner Perkins.

iv Lydia, b 9 Mar 1748/9 *NHV*, bp Apr 1749 *CC*, d 11 Feb 1800 *CC;* m 8 Apr 1774 *CC*—William Jones.

v Esther, b 23 Sep 1750 *NHV*, bp Aug (?) 1750 *CC*, d 14 Mar 1838 *New Hartford, Oneida Co., N. Y., T;* m 7 Jan 1773 *CC*, Jan 1773 *WV*—Jotham Gaylord.

vi Mamre, b 15 July 1752 *NHV*, bp July 1752 *CC*, d Sep 1804; m 14 Mar 1776 *WV*, *CC*—Lemuel Hitchcock.

vii Robert, b 4 Apr 1754 *NHV*, d 2 May 1829 æ. 75 *Wells, Vt.;* m (1) Hannah da. John & Phebe (Gillam) Hotchkiss, who d 6 Aug 1786 *CC;* m (2) Lucy da. Gideon & Miriam (Hotchkiss) Curtis, b 29 Mar 1747/8 *WV*, d 1 Mar 1821 æ. 73 *Wells, Vt.;* m (3) Sarah da. Moses & Hannah (Dunbar) Blakeslee, b [1 Apr 1758 *WatV*], d 1834 æ, 76 *Wells, Vt.* **FAM. 71.**

viii Solomon, b 20 June 1756 *NHV*, bu. 20 Apr 1849 æ. 93 *Bx;* Census (Wd) 1-1-2; m.

ix Elizabeth, b 4 Dec 1757 *NHV*, d 29 June 1808 *CC*, æ. 49 *CT1;* m 20 Nov 1775 *CC*—Ezra Bristol.

x Tirzah, b 14 Aug 1759 *NHV*, d 6 Sep 1786 *F;* m Elijah Wooding.

xi Salmon, b 14 Nov 1761 *WV*.

xii Candace, b 14 Apr 1763 *WV;* m 5 May 1783 *NHV*—Enos Tuttle.

xiii Rebecca, b 5 Jan 176[5] *WV;* m [(1) 9 Dec 1781 *Hartford SupCt*—Enos Atwater; he div. her; m (2)] Joel Wilmot.

xiv John Cook, b 8 Sep 1767 *WV*, d Sep 1813; Census (C) 1-1-2; m (1) July 1785 *F*—Mary Crittenden; m (2) Aug 1790 *F*—Abigail Smith da. Johh & Sarah (Gillam) Hotchkiss, b 8 July 1769 *WV*. **FAM. 72.**

4 (probably) SUSANNA, bp (adult) Oct 1741 *CC;* m 25 Dec 1746 *WV*—Joel Parker.

5 SOLOMON, d Apr 1763 *WdT1;* m 16 Dec 1748 *NHV*—Eleanor da. Seth & Elizabeth (Munson) Perkins, b 3 Sep 1726 *NHV*, d 9 May 1816 æ. 90 *WdT1*, æ. 89 *WdC*.

i Elizabeth, b 5 Dec 1749 *NHV;* m 16 Mar 1777 *WdC*—Daniel Johnson.

ii Solomon, b 20 Mar 1752 *NHV*, d 6 Apr 1793 æ. 43 *WdT1;* Census (Wd) 1-2-3; m [Anna da. Oliver & Hannah Pierson, b c. 1756]. **FAM. 73.**

iii David, b 26 Oct 1754 *NHV*, d 5 June 1823 æ. 69 *WdT1;* Dea.; Census (Wd) 1-2-6; m (1) 15 May 1777 *WdC*—Lydia da. Thomas & Elizabeth (Terrill) Beecher, b c. 1756, d 28 June 1785 æ. 29 *WdT1;* m (2) 27 Feb 1788 *CC*—Abigail da. Abraham & Mary (Ball) Atwater, b 26 Oct 1754 *F*, d 17 Oct 1845 æ. 91 *WdT1*. **FAM. 74.**

6 ELIPHALET, b 1 Nov 1727 *DV*, d 5 July 1803; Lieut.; Census (D) 1-0-1; m 26 Dec 1751 *DV*—Comfort da. Jabez & Ann (Gil-

bert) Harger, b 10 Sep 1720 *DV*, d 11 Mar 1802.

i Susanna, b 6 Jan 1753 *DV*, d 19 Jan 1798 æ. 45 *DT1;* m 13 June 1774 *DV*—Dan Tomlinson.

ii Levi, b 2 May 1754 *DV*, d c. 1832; Census (D) 2-2-5; m (1) Phebe da. Jonathan & Abigail (Beecher) Hitchcock, b 11 Dec 1755 *DV*, d 3 Apr 1789; m (2) Betsey ——, who d 8 Apr 1791; m (3) Sarah ——, who d 1 Dec 1801; m (4) Susanna ——, who d 1839. **FAM. 75.**

iii Eliphalet, b 1 Apr 1756 *F*, d 24 Feb 1775 æ. 19 *DV*.

iv Moses, b 28 Dec 1757 *DV*, bp 19 Feb 1758 *DC*, d 9 May 1799 *F;* Census (D) 1-0-2; m 25 Jan 1787 Sarah Bryan of M. A child, Sally M., d 29 Apr 1828 æ. 38 *DT1*.

v David, b 30 Dec 1759 *DV*, bp 17 Feb 1760 *DC*, d 30 Aug 1776 æ. 17 *DV*.

vi Philo, b 26 Nov 1761 *F*, bp Jan 1762 *DC*, d 22 June 1787 *F;* m ——. **FAM. 76.**

7 OBADIAH, b 9 Apr 1731 *NHV*, bp (adult) 12 Apr 1761 *NHC2*, d 23 Mar 1805 æ. 74 *NHT1;* Census (NH) 1-0-1; m 16 Nov 1758 *NHV*—Mercy da. Daniel & Martha (Elcock) Perkins, b 30 Jan 1730 *NHV*, d 14 Feb 1797 æ. 66 *NHT1*.

i Eli, b 18 Sep 1758 *NHV*, bp 12 Apr 1761 *NHC2*, d 13 May 1813 æ. 55 *NHT1;* Census (NH) 2-0-3; m 24 Feb 1783 *NHC1*—Eunice da. David & Elizabeth (Bassett) Atwater, b 2 June 1762 *NHV*, d 13 Feb 1817 æ. 55 *NHT1*. **FAM. 77.**

ii Lydia, b 26 Jan 1761 *NHV*, bp 12 Apr 1761 *NHC2*, d 2 Mar 1793 æ. 32 *NHT1;* m 26 Sep 1782 *NHC2*—Jared Thompson.

iii Obadiah, b 4 Sep 1762 *NHV*, bp 5 Sep 1762 *NHC2*, d 28 Jan 1832 æ. 69 *NHT1;* Dr.; m 12 Feb 1782 *F*—Hannah da. Nathaniel Sherman Lewis, who d 22 Nov 1831 æ. 74 *NHT1*, 23 Nov(*NHC1*) *NHV*. **FAM. 78.**

iv Silas, b 16 Mar 1765 *NHV*, bp 17 Mar 1765 *NHC2*, d 24 Sep 1776 æ. 11-6 *NHT1*.

v Justus, bp 6 Dec 1772 *NHC2*, d May 1812 *NHC1*, 6 May æ. 39 *NHT1;* m (1) 15 Feb 1794 *NHC1*—Elizabeth da. Jonah & Elizabeth (Atwater) Hotchkiss, b 10 June 1773 *F*, d 15 Apr 1796 æ. 23 *NHT1*, *NHC1;* m (2) 27 Apr 1800 *NHC1*—her sister Susanna Hotchkiss, b 24 June 1775 *F*, d 1 Mar 1825 æ. 50 *NHT1*. **FAM. 79.**

FAM. 16. JASON & ABIGAIL (ATWATER) HOTCHKISS:

1 ABIGAIL, b 12 July 1746 *WV*, bp Apr 1747/8 *CC*, d young.

2 SARAH, b 1 May 1750 *WV*, 2 May *CT1*, bp June 1750 *CC*, d 21 July 1823 æ. 73 *CT1;* m 10 July 1771 *WV*, *CC*—William Law.

3 DAVID, b 28 Mar 1752 *WV*, bp May 1752 *CC;* rem. to Ky.; m 26 Dec 1771 *WV*, *CC*—Abigail da. Ichabod & Elizabeth (Beadles) Merriam; b 27 Nov 1753 *WV*. Child: Miles, b 20 Sep 1772 *WV*, d 2 Sep 1774 *WV*.

4 JONATHAN, b 7 May 1754 *WV;* res. NH 1787; rem. to Me.
5 ABIGAIL, b 19 Sep 1756 *WV;* rem. to Watertown, N. Y.; m 21 Sep 1775 *CC*—Bennett Royce.
6 JASON, b 13 May 1759 *WV*, d 19 Nov 1816 *F;* Census (C) 1-2-2; m Ursula da. Andrew & Lowly (Cook) Hull, b 10 Nov 1760 *WV*, d 8 May 1822 æ. 61 *BristolT.*
7 MERRIMAN, b 28 Apr 1762 *WV*, d 16 June 1812 *CC*, æ. 50 *CT1;* Census (C) 2-2-1: m (1) 30 Dec 1785 *CC*—Esther da. Andrew & Lowly (Cook) Hull, b 24 Oct 1764 *WV*, d 19 Feb 1789 æ. 24 *CT1;* m (2) 17 Nov 1791 *WC2*—Keturah da. John & Lois (Merriam) Hough, b 4 Mar 1773 *WV*, d 2 Mar 1795 *CC;* m (3) 27 Mar 1796 *CC*—Betsey da. Andrew & Eunice (Hotchkiss) Durand, b 26 Feb 1773 *WV*, d 9 Apr 1848 æ. 75 *CT1*.
(By 1): *i* Sherlock, b c. 1786, d 11 Nov 1862 æ. 76 *CT1;* m (1) 21 Jan 1816 *CV*—Betsey Dibble, who d 20 Mar 1821 æ. 25 *CT1;* m (2) 2 Dec 1824 *CV*—Roxanna da. Roswell & Susanna (Matthews) Bradley, b c. 1799, d 5 May 1878 æ. 79 *CT1*.
ii Horace.
(By 2): *iii* Child, d 4 Aug 1794 *CC*.
iv Child, d 5 Aug 1794 *CC*.
(By 3): *v* William, b c. 1797, bp 17 July 1803 *CC*.
vi Esther, b c. 1798, bp 17 July 1803 *CC;* m ——— Plumb.
vii Lambert, b c. 1800, bp 17 July 1803 *CC*, d 31 Sep 1806 æ. 7 *CT1*.
viii Betsey, bp 17 July 1803 *CC;* m Frederick Winchell.
ix [Clarina, bp 4 May 1806 *CC*].
x Merriman Lambert, b 16 Nov 1807 *CT1*, bp 12 Jan 1808 *CC*, d 3 Jan 1887 æ. 79 *CT1;* Dea.; m 25 Jan 1841 *CV*—Eliza J. Benham, b 15 Mar 1811 *CT1*, d 13 Dec 1888 æ. 78 *CT1*.
8 LYDIA, b 22 July 1764 *WV;* m Thomas Humphreville.
9 RUFUS, b 29 Mar 1769 *WV*, bp 2 Apr 1769 *CC;* res. 1798 Hampton, Washington Co., N. Y.; m 27 Dec 1792 *CC*—Lowly da. Ambrose & Martha (Munson) Doolittle,
10 ANNA, b 23 Feb 1773 *WV*, bp 25 Feb 1773 *CC;* rem. to Ohio; m Joseph Hart of NH.

FAM. 17. JOHN & PHEBE (GILLAM) HOTCHKISS:
1 HANNAH, d 6 Aug 1786 *F;* m Robert Hotchkiss.
2 JOHN, b 4 Jan 1758 *WV*, d 30 June 1798 æ. 39 *CT2;* Census (C) 1-1-2; m Lois da. John & Sarah (Johnson) Hopkins, b 13 Nov 1757 *WatV*, d 15 Oct 1805 æ. 48 *CT2*.
i Charles, b 16 Dec 1789 *CV*, name changed to John.
ii Cleora, b 8 Apr 1791 *CV*, d 6 Apr 1808 æ. 17 *WtnT*.
iii Sarah, b 1 Sep 1793 *CV;* m Zina Andrews of Wd.
iv Clarissa, b 28 May 1796 *CV*.
3 REBECCA, b 31 Mar 1760 *WV*, d 3 July 1836 æ. 76-3 *Wells, Vt.;* m 24 Nov 1785 *F*—David Lewis.

4 LUKE, b 9 Apr 176[2] *WV*.
5 AARON, b 20 Apr 1764 *WV*, d s. p.
6 MIRIAM WOOD, b 1 Mar 1767 *WV;* m Caleb Smith of Wells, Vt.
7 CORNELIUS, b 29 Oct 1769 *WV*, d s. p.
8 SOCRATES, b 11 May 1774 *WV*, d 27 Feb 1810 *Wells, Vt.;* Dr.; m (1) 1 Dec 1796 Bethia da. Samuel Lathrop, who d 24 June 1803 æ. 24; m (2) Mary Ann da. Ambrose & Martha (Munson) Doolittle, b 28 Feb 1771.

FAM. 18. ELIJAH & ELIZABETH (KELLOGG) HOTCHKISS:
1 DOROTHY, b 22 May 1759 *WV*, d 7 Aug 1828 æ. 69 *CTI;* m 2 May 1785 *CC*—Lyman Atwater.
2 ADA, bp 16 Apr 1769 *CC;* m Munson Durand.
3 SAMUEL, b 22 May 1763 *WV*, ["Sarah" bp 16 Apr 1769 *CC*]; m 12 Feb 1784 *CC*—Miriam da. Amos & Elizabeth (Beadles) Hotchkiss. b 10 Jan 1764 *WV*.

FAM. 19. AMOS & ELIZABETH (BEADLES) HOTCHKISS:
1 ROBERT, b 11/27 June 1760 *WV;* Census (C) 2-0-2; m 25 Nov 1779 *CC*—Lowly da. Asa & Mary (Andrews) Hotchkiss.
2 SAMUEL SHARP BEADLES, b 24 Mar 1762 *WV*.
3 MIRIAM, b 10 Jan 1764 *WV;* m 12 Feb 1784 *CC*—Samuel Hotchkiss.
4 LOUISA, b 10 Jan 1766 *WV*, d 4 Aug 1832 æ. 67 *CTI;* m 16 June 1784 *CV*—Cornelius Brooks Cook.
5 AMOS, b 13 Apr 1768 *WV*, bp 24 June 1768 *CC*.
6 MARLOW, b 22 Feb 1770 *WV*, bp 15 Apr 1770 *CC*, "child" d 12 Feb 1774 *CC*.
7 GEORGE, b 4 June 1772 *WV*, bp 26 July 1772 *CC*.
8 MARLOW, bp 11 Sep 1774 *CC*.

FAM. 20. BENJAMIN & MARTHA (BROOKS) HOTCHKISS:
1 MARTHA, b 27 Dec 1752 *NHV;* m 16 Nov 1773 *WV*, 17 Nov *CC*—Elisha Jones.
2 SIMEON, b 26 Nov 1754 *NHV;* res. 1840 Whitehall, N. Y.; Census (Bristol) 1-2-2; m Jerusha da. Henry & Mary (Cooper) Brooks, b c. 1754.
3 JERUSHA, b 10 Mar 1756 *NHV;* m 30 Oct 1775 *CC*—Samuel Bassett of M.
4 DESIRE, b 10 June 1758 *NHV;* m 16 Sep 1782 *CC*—Isaac Bassett of M.
5 STATIRA, b 16 Nov 1765 *NHV*, d 11 Aug 1846 (at S. Livonia, N. Y.,) *F;* m Jehiel Bunnell.
6 BENJAMIN, b 17 Dec 1767 *NHV;* Census (C) 1-0-3; res. 1803 Whitehall, N. Y.; m 20 May 1787 *CV*—Lucy da. Samuel & Experience (Tyler) Clark, b 8 May 1767 *WV*. Family incomplete.
i Axcilla, b 17 Nov 1787 *CV*.
ii Patty, b 7 Nov 1789 *CV*.
iii Hiram, b 25 Jan 1791 *CV*.
iv David, b 27 Jan 1794 *CV*.

7 David Brooks, b 7 Aug 1769 *NHV*, probably d s. p.

FAM. 21. Asa & Mary (Andrews) Hotchkiss:

1 Sarah, b 6 Mar 1753 *WV*, d 23 May 1776 *CC;* m 8 Dec 1773 *CC*—Joseph Doolittle.

2 Robert, b 14 June 1755 *WV*, d 6 Jan 1826 æ. 72 next June *PptT;* Census (C) 1-0-4; m Jerusha da. Aaron & Mary (Brooks) Cook, b 17 Sep 1759 *WV*, d 19 May 1824 æ. 65 *PptT.*

3 Giles, d 1798; Census (C) 1-1-3; m Esther ——, who d 1810.

i Esther; [?m Linus Atwater].

ii Polly; [?m Linus Atwater].

iii Sally.

4 Lowly; m 25 Nov 1779 *CC*—Robert Hotchkiss.

5 Jared, b 12 Sep 1761 *WV.*

6 Chloe, b 2 Mar 1763 *WV.*

FAM. 22. Waitstill & Eunice (Bradley) Hotchkiss:

1 Asa, b 23 Nov 1764 *WV*, d s. p.; res. 1807 Cazenovia, N. Y.

2 Eunice, b 25 Mar 1768 *WV;* m 26 Oct 1789 *CC*—Munson Merriam.

3 Waitstill, b 18 May 1771 *WV*, bp 30 June 1771 *CC*, d 17 Apr 1846 (Canaan, Ohio); res. 1807 Cazenovia, N. Y.; m 25 May 1800 *CC*—Phebe Cowell, who d 1835.

4 Lydia, b 30 June 1775 *WV*, bp 6 Aug 1775 *CC*, d 6 May 1827 æ. 52 *CTl;* m 12 Oct 1796 *CV*—Benoni Plumb.

5 Alva, bp 18 Mar 1781 *CC;* res. Cazenovia, N. Y.; m 5 June 1809 Huldah da. Rev. Roswell & Lydia (Dorr) Beckwith, b 14 Nov 1785 (Lyme).

FAM. 23. Henry & Esther (Smith) Hotchkiss:

1 Mary, b 29 Sep 1760 *WV;* m 13 Dec 1781 *WatV*—Samuel Mix.

2 Esther, b 1 Mar 1763 *WV*, d 20 Dec 1778 *WV.*

3 Chauncey, b 10 Feb 1765 *WV*, d 11 May 1853 *Paris, N. Y., T;* Census (C) 1-0-2; m Thankful ——.

4 Lyman, b 20 Feb 1768 *WV*, bp 10 Apr 1768 *CC*, d 1825 *Paris, N. Y., T;* Census (C) 1-0-1; rem. to Paris, N. Y., & "farther West"; m 28 Oct 1790 *CC*—Olive da. Nathaniel & Bethia (Hackley) Brown, b 7 July 1771 *WV.*

5 Amasa, b 26 Nov 1769 *WV*, bp 3 Dec 1769 *CC.*

6 Freeman, bp 17 July 1774 *CC.*

FAM. 24. Joseph & Mary (Hull) Hotchkiss:

1 Zurah, b 15 Dec 1761 *WV*, d 19 Oct 1777 *WV, CC.*

2 Sarah, b 27 Aug 1764 *WV.*

3 Miles, b 27 Dec 1766 *WV*, d 12 Oct 1777 *WV.*

4 Mary, b 12 Mar 1769 *WV*, bp 16 Apr 1769 *CC*, d 4 Dec 1777 *WV.*

5 Chloe, b 30 July 1771 *WV*, bp 15 Sep 1771 *CC*, d 31 Aug 1837 æ. 66 *LT;* m Levi Bristol.

6 Martha, b 1 July 1773 *WV*, bp 11 July 1773 *CC*, d 24 Jan 1805 æ. 31 *LT;* m 21 Nov 1791 *CC*—Levi Bristol.

7 Joseph, b 13 Feb 1776 *WV*, bp 15 Feb 1776 *CC;* res. P; m 10 May 1797 *CC*—Nabby da. Reuben & Eunice (Rowe) Bunnell,

16 Mar 1776 *CV*.

FAM. 25. JONAH & EUNICE (TYLER) HOTCHKISS:

1 AZUBA, b 2 June 1765 *WV*, d 17 Nov 1803 æ. 38 *CTI*; m 30 June 1785 *CC*—Job Sperry.

2 ADONIJAH, b 19 Jan 1767 *WV*; Census (C) 1-0-2; m 28 May 1788 *CV*—Sylvia Seymour.

3 EUNICE, b 21 Oct 1768 *WV*, bp 22 Oct 1768 *CC*, d 17 June 1771 æ. 3 *CTI*, "child" *CC*.

4 JONAH, b 13 Apr 1771 *WV*, bp 25 May 1771 *CC*, d 7 Jan 1850 æ. 79 *CTI*; m 6 Oct 1794 *CV*, *CC*—Chloe da. Reuben & Hannah (Gaylord) Bradley, b 8 Oct 1775 *WV*, d 20 Oct 1862 æ. 87 *CTI*.

5 ABNER, b 30 Apr 1774 *WV*, bp 8 Mar [error for May] 1774 *CC*, d 10 May 1774 æ. 0-0-10 *CTI*, "child" d 10 Mar [error] *CC*.

6 HENRY, b 13 Sep 1775 *WV*, bp 5 Nov 1775 *CC*, d 24 Aug 1794 æ. 19 (at Whitestown, [N. Y.]) *CTI*; Dr.

7 MILES, b 28 Aug 1778 *WV*, bp 1 Nov 1778 *CC*, d 23 Nov 1839 æ. 64 *CTI*; m (1) 4 Dec 1800 *CC*—Polly Ives, b c. 1783, d 22 Nov 1815 æ. 33 *CTI*; m (2) Joanna ——, b c. 1784, d 4 Nov 1830 æ. 46 *CTI*.

8 (probably) ABNER, bp 7 Oct 1781 *CC*, d 20 Nov 1805 æ. 25 *CTI*.

FAM. 26. HEZEKIAH & SARAH (BRADLEY) HOTCHKISS:

1 HEZEKIAH, b 25 Dec 1752 *NHV*, d 1 Apr 1827 æ. 74 *NHTI*; Census (NH) 2-2-5; m 6 May 1781 Grace Wilcox, b c. 1759, d 9 June 1829 æ. 70 *NHTI*, 11 June æ. 71 (*NHCI*) *NHV*.

i Sally, b [31 May 1782], d 9 Sep 1782 æ. 0-3-9 *NHTI*.

ii Sarah, b c. 1783, d Oct 1857 æ. 74 *NHTI*.

iii Grace, b c. 1786, d 16 July 1863 æ. 77 *NHTI*, æ. 76-9 *NHV*.

iv Hezekiah, b c. 1789, d 24 Aug 1819 æ. 30 *NHTI*; m Elizabeth da. Jacob & Esther (Mansfield) Thompson, b c. 1785, d 6 Dec 1834.

v Philemon, b [Mar 1791], d 3 May 1794 æ. 3-2 *NHTI*.

vi Mary, b c. 1793, d 29 Mar 1855 æ. 62 *NHTI*; m Marcus Merriman.

vii Edward, b 1796, d 1855.

viii Child, b [July 1798], d 15 Aug 1798 æ. 4 wks. *NHTI*.

ix Horatio Nelson, b c. 1799, d 14 June 1821 æ. 22 *NHTI*.

x Adeline Lucette, b 1803, d 1878; Charles B. Granniss.

FAM. 26. HEZEKIAH & MARY (WOODING) HOTCHKISS:

2 DANIEL, b 1 Apr 1755 *NHV*, d 19 Nov 1800 *NoHC*: Census (H) 1-2-2; m 20 Aug 1782 *NHC2*—Achsah da. Caleb & Mary (Hodges) Andrews. Family incomplete.

i Child, bp 16 May 1784 *HCI*.

ii Daniel, bp 12 Oct 1788 *HCI*.

iii Augustus, bp 14 June 1795 *HCI*.

3 JARED, b 15 Mar 1757 *NHV*, d 20 Feb 1758 *NHV*.

4 JARED, b 6 Mar 1761 *NHV*.

FAM. 27. JOHN & SUSANNA (JONES) HOTCHKISS:

1 LOUISA, b 3 Mar 1756 *NHV*, bp 7 Aug 1757 *NHC2*, d 17 Mar

1822 æ. 66 *NHT1;* m 12 Jan 1777 *NHV*—Daniel Bishop.

2 **Gabriel**, b 15 Sep 1757 *NHV*, bp 18 Sep 1757 *NHC2*, d 24 Jan 1819 æ 61 (at NH) *ColR;* Census (NH) 1-1-2; m Hilpah Rosetta da. Elisha & Rosetta (Owen) Phelps of Simsbury, b 17 Oct 1763, d 19 Mar 1838; she m (2) B. B. Stanwood.

3 **Susanna Augusta**, b 6 Aug 1759 *NHV*, bp 12 Aug 1759 *NHC2*, d 2 Sep 1759 *NHV*.

4 **Sophia Charlotte**, b 3 Mar 1761 *NHV*, bp 8 Mar 1761 *NHC2*, d 27 July 1845 *F*.

5 **Frederick William**, b 30 Oct 1762 *NHV*, bp 31 Oct 1762 *NHC 2*, d 31 Mar 1844; Rev.; rem. to Saybrook; m 29 Aug 1790 Amelia da. Rev. William & Mary (Blague) Hart, b 27 Jan 1761 *F*, d 8 Aug 1845 *F*.

6 **Susanna Caroline**, bp 15 Apr 1764 *NHC2*, d soon.

7 **Lewis George**, bp 1 Dec 1765 *NHC2*, d young.

8 **George Lewis**, bp 12 Apr 1767 *NHC2;* m 6 Feb 1785 *NoHC*—Eunice Cook of W.

9 **Susanna Jane**, bp 28 May 1769 *NHC2*.

10 **Timothy John**, bp 2 June 1771 *NHC2;* m Esther Judd.

11 **Maria Jane**, bp 13 June 1773 *NHC2;* m 20 Dec 1800 *F*—David Starr.

(3 sons & 3 das. d young *NHT1*).

Fam. 28. Joshua & Mary (Punderson) Hotchkiss:

1 **Silas**, b 10 Aug 1755 *NHT1*, bp 7 May 1758 *NHC2*, d 22 May 1848 æ. 93 *NHT1*, *NHV;* Census (NH) 3-3-2; m 17 Dec 1777 *NHC2*—Esther da. John & Lydia (Ives) Gilbert, b 6 Mar 1756 *NHT1*, *NHV*, d 11 Sep 1841 æ. 86 *NHT1*.

i Elisha, b 11 Oct 1778 *F;* 1st Mayor of Cincinnati, Ohio; m 21 Oct 1804 Phebe Gallup of Hartland, Vt. A s. John G., "formerly of Cincinnati," d 3 Dec 1844 æ. 36 *NHT1*.

ii Lydia, b 30 June 1781 *F*, d 10 Oct 1813 æ. 32 *NHT1;* m 28 Nov 1801 *NHV*—Matthew Read.

iii Silas, b 18 Feb 1785 *F*, d 3 Nov 1809 æ. 24 (at St. Bartholomew) *NHT1;* m 28 May 1809 Clarissa da. Ezra & Nancy (Stevenson) Ford, b c. 1785, d 28 Mar 1868 æ. 82 *NH T1*. Child: 1 Clarissa Elizabeth, b 10 Apr 1810 *F*, d 1889; m 1831 Henry Murray.

iv Marcus, b 15 May 1789 *F*, d 27 Feb 1826 æ. 37 *NHT1;* m 12 Sep 1811 Sally Fenn Miles of M, b 2 Jan 1790 *NHT 1*, d 23 Jan 1869 æ. 79 *NHT1*. Children: 1 James Gilbert, b 20 Jan 1812, d s. p. 7 Apr 1882; twice m. 2 Sarah Fenn, b 21 May 1815, d 3 May 1891; m 19 Jan 1835 John Adams Blake. 3 Elizur Miles, b 14 Mar 1818, d 18 Sep 1894; m 31 May 1843 Antoinette Augusta Dunning.

v Minor, b 3 June 1791 *NHT1*, d 21 Oct 1825 (at Mid) *NHT 1*, 22 Oct æ. 38 (*NHC2*) *NHV;* B. A. (Yale 1813); m Clarissa da. Eli & Eunice (Atwater) Hotchkiss; she m (2)

5 Nov 1826 *NHV*—Reuben Skinner of Granville, N. Y.
vi Esther, b 17 Oct 1795 *F*, d Oct 1878; m Philos Blake.
vii Henrietta Maria, b 15 Feb 1802 *F*, d 31 July 1824 æ. 22 *NHT1*; m 30 Jan 1824 *NHV*—Andrew Benton.

2 ELEAZER, b 4 Sep 1757 *F*, bp 7 May 1758 *NHC2*, d 30 Oct 1822 æ. 65 *NHT1*, æ. 67 (*NHC2*) *NHV*; m Naomi da. Michael & Betty (Potter) Gilbert, b c. 1760, d 28 Mar 1836 æ. 76 *NHT1*.
i Betsey, bp 20 Aug 1780 *NHC2*; m 14 Mar 1804 *NHC1*—Malachi Tyler.
ii Michael Gilbert, bp 12 Oct 1783 *NHC2*, d 9 Dec 1848 æ. 65 *NHT2*; m Asenath ——, who d 20 Dec 1861 æ. 78 *NHT2*.
iii Parmelia, b 19 Apr 1785 *HT3*, d 1 Jan 1866 *HT3*; m 12 Oct 1806 *HV*—Leverett Dickerman.
iv Eleazer, bp 5 Aug 1792 *NHC2*, d 13 Apr 1841 æ. 49 *NHT1*; m Fanny Louisa da. Medad & Rachel (Hotchkiss) Osborn b 20 Aug 1796 *NHT1*, d 20 Oct 1882 *NHT1*, æ. 86-2 *NHV*; she m (2) —— Crandall.
v Sherman, b c. 1796, d 28 Feb 1797 æ. 0-10 *NHT1*.
vi Child, b [5 Dec 1800], d 11 Dec 1800 æ. 0-0-6 *NHT1*.

3 LUCINDA, b 28 Nov 1759 *F*, bp 6 Jan 1760 *NHC2*, d 30 July 1805 æ. 46 *NHT1*; m 19 Apr 1780 *NHC2*—James Thompson.

4 ELIJAH, b 14 Feb 1762 *F*, bp 4 Apr 1762 *NHC2*, d Sep 1849 æ. 87 *NHT2*; Census (NH) 2-1-3; m 3 Mar 1782 *NHC2*—Rebecca da. Jehiel & Rebecca (Sperry) Osborn, b c. 1764, d Dec 1842 æ. 79 *NHT2*.
i Mary; m —— Frisbie.
ii Rebecca; m —— Sperry.
iii Rufus, b c. 1791, d 6 Mar 1863 æ. 72 *NHT2*; m Priscilla Nichols, who d 15 June 1847 æ. 47 *NHT2*.

5 ELISHA, b 14 Feb 1762 *F*, bp 4 Apr 1762 *NHC2*, d 17 Apr 1762 *F*.

6 JOSEPH PUNDERSON, b 21 Apr 1764 *F*, bp 27 May 1764 *NHC2*, d 14 Mar 1838 æ. 74 *NHT1*; Census (NH) 2-0-3; m (1) Rhoda da. John & Hannah (Holbrook) Wooding, b c. 1765, d 1 Feb 1823 æ. 58 *NHT1*; m (2) 11 May 1823 *NHV*—Sarah (——) Tuttle, who d 31 Oct 1841 æ. 65.
(By 1): *i* Clarissa, b 18 Dec 1786 *F*, d 17 Sep 1846; m 10 Jan 1808 Lyman Atwater.
ii Henry, b c. 1791, d 9 Apr 1826 æ. 35 (*NHC2*) *NHV*; m Polly ——.
iii Anna, b 5 Nov 1795 *F*, d 26 Feb 1836 æ. 41 *NHT1*; m 12 Dec 1813 Medad Atwater.
iv Walter P., b c. 1812, d 7 Mar 1833.

7 ELISHA, b 4 Aug 1767 *F*, bp 26 Sep 1767 *NHC2*, d 9 Feb 1775 *F*. [Who then was Elisha, bu. 9 July 1839 æ. 72 *Bx*; Census (NH) 1-0-3?]

8 CALEB, b 30 Jan 1770 *F*, bp 4 Mar 1770 *NHC2*, d 16 Mar 1819 æ. 49 *NHT1*; Census (NH) 1-0-1; m Hannah ——, who d 2

Oct 1809 æ. 39 *NHT1*, bu. 3 Oct *NHx*. Family incomplete.

i John, b c. 1801, d Aug 1803 æ. 2 *NHT1*.

ii Evelina, bp 18 June 1805 *NHx*.

iii Daughter, bp 30 June 1808 *NHx*, d 21 July 1808 *NHx*. (Perhaps Lucinda Thompson Hotchkiss who m 27 June 1810 *NHx*—Ebenezer Harvey Bishop was da. of Caleb).

9 MILES, b 1772 *NHT2*, 26 May 1772 *F*, bp 28 June 1772 *NHC2*, d 1837 *NHT2*, 14 Feb *F;* m 18 Nov 1792 *M*—Aner da. Joseph & Eunice (Burton) Hepburn, b c. 1771, d 12 Mar 1836 æ. 65 *NHT2*.

i Zina, b 7 Sep 1793 *F*, d 10 Jan 1860 æ. 67 *NHT1*, 11 Jan *F;* m July 1815 *ColR*—Permena Bradley, who d 3 Mar 1877 æ. 87 *NHV*. Children: 1 Cornelia, d 31 Aug 1819 æ. 1-8 *NHT1*. 2 Caroline, d 12 May 1821 æ. 1-3 *NHT1*. 3 George Morse, d 31 May 1822 æ. 0-5 *NHT1*. 4 George. 5 Alfred.

ii Sally, b 22 June 1795 *F*, d 17 Oct 1874 æ. 79 *NHT2;* m George Morse.

iii Eunice, b 27 Aug 1798 *F*, d 23 May 1884 æ. 85 *NHT1*, æ. 85-9 *NHV;* m (1) Rukard Burke Mallory; m (2) John B. Lewis.

iv Caroline, b 27 Aug 1802 *F;* m 1 Nov 1820 *NHV*—Clark Smith Dunning.

v Miles, b 31 Dec 1804 *F*, bp 18 June 1805 *NHx*, d 27 May 1848 æ. 43 *NHT3;* m 31 Dec 1826 *ConnH*, 1 Dec *NHV*—Eliza D. Cadwell of E. Hartford, b 18 Sep 1807 *F*, d 31 Mar 1869 æ. 61 *NHT2;* she m (2) ——— Bodge. Children (from Bible record): 1 Edward Oscar, b 27 Nov 1827, d Mar 1889. 2 Louisa Minerva, b 25 Dec 1828. 3 Eliza Amelia, b 22 Mar 1830, d 10 Feb 1832. 4 Mary Augusta, b 21 Sep 1837, d 18 Oct 1914; m Andrew W. Hendryx. 5 Charles Burke, b 17 Jan 1840, d 28 Sep 1846. 6 Elisha Miles, b 28 July 1843, d 17 Jan 1846. 7 John Burton, b 22 Aug 1845. 8 Lenora Adele, b 21 Sep 1848, d 23 Sep 1888; m Lyman Dann White.

vi Cornelia, b 12 Apr 1808 *F*.

vii Alfred Edwin, b 30 Dec [1809] *F*, bp 1 Feb 1810 *NHx*, d 4 Feb 1810 *NHx*.

viii Emma Minerva, bp 19 July 1812 *NHx*, d 23 May 1884 æ. 72 *NHV*.

FAM. 29. LEMUEL & MARY (MALLORY) HOTCHKISS:

1 THADDEUS, b 24 Sep 1757 *NHV*, bp 9 Apr 1758 *NHC2*, d 1787; m.

i Parthena; m 1804 *F*—Truman Sperry of Wd.

ii Thaddeus, b 11 Feb 1783 (at NH) *NHT1*, d 14 May 1850 æ. 67 (at B) *NHT1;* m Harriet [da. Timothy & Abigail] Ball, b 7 Mar 1785 (at B) *NHT1*, d 12 Mar 1870 æ. 85 (at NH) *NHT1*.

2 HEPHZIBAH, b 14 Mar 1760 *NHV*, bp 22 June 1760 *NHC2;* m (1)

1 Jan 1777 *NHC2*—David Moulthrop; m (2) 14 Nov 1780 *NH C2*—Phinehas Andrus.

3 MARY, b 3 Apr 1762 *NHV*, bp 7 Nov 1762 *NHC2*, d 11 Aug 1787 æ. 25-4 *NHT1*; m 26 Oct 1780 David Bunce.

4 AMARYLLIS, b 3 Apr 1762 *NHV*, bp (as "Parmelia") 7 Nov 1762 *NHC2*.

FAM. 29. LEMUEL & PARTHENA (MURRAY) HOTCHKISS:

5 LYMAN, b 9 Jan 1766 *NHV*, bp 31 May 1767 *NHC2*; Census (NH) 1-1-3; m 11 May 1786 *NHC1*—Molly da. Phinehas & Martha (Sherman) Bradley, b 28 Apr 1767 *NHV*, d 18 Nov 1844 æ. 78 *NHT2*.

6 HULDAH; m 4 Apr 1788 *NHC2*—Lewis Hepburn.

7 RUTH.

8 HANNAH, bp 2 Apr 1775 *NHC2*.

9 LEMUEL, b 20 Dec 1779 *F* [1778], bp 21 Mar 1779 *NHC2*, d Oct 1845 (Evansburg, Pa.) *F*; m Oct 1801 *F*—Charlotte da. Lemuel & Eunice (Durand) Bradley, b 14 June 1783 *F*, d 5 Apr 1878 (Warren, Ohio) *F*. Children: Harriet; Mireth; Rice; Charlotte; Francis Durand; Caroline; Jane Parthenia; Eunice Emeline.

FAM. 30. CHARLES & ELIZABETH (HARRIS) HOTCHKISS (fam. incomplete):

1 HARRIS, bp 3 July 1763 *NHC1*; Census (Argyle, N. Y.) 2-1-5; it is said he res. Ft. Edward, N. Y., & Tioga, Pa., m Lucy Carey & had 17 children.

2 ELIZABETH, bp 29 Dec 1765 *NHC1*, d 14 Feb 1766 æ. 0-1 *NHC1*.

3 JEREMIAH, bp 14 June 1767 *NHC1*; Census (Hebron, N. Y.) 1-0-2.

4 ARCHIBALD, bp 12 Nov 1769 *NHC1*, d 9 Oct 1772 æ. 3 *NHC1*.

5 CHRISTOPHER, bp 2 Feb 1772 *NHC1*.

6 ELIZABETH, bp 20 Dec 1774 *NHC1*.

FAM. 31. EZEKIEL & HANNAH (ALLING) HOTCHKISS:

1 ENOS, b 6 June 1751 *NHV*, bp 29 Sep 1751 *NHC1*, d 1792; Census (NH) 1-1-4; m Esther da. Isaac & Sarah (Mix) Bradley, b c. 1753, [d 11 Sep 1841 æ. 86 *NHV*].

i Esther.

ii Sarah.

iii Rebecca, b c. 1785, d 8 July 1847 æ. 62 *NHT1*; m Whiting Ives.

iv Ezekiel, b c. 1785, d 12 June 1849 æ. 64 *NHT1*; m 30 Nov 1809 *NHx*—Sarah Larabee, who d 4 May 1852 æ. 66 *NH T1*. Children: 1 Enos Thompson, b 8 Mar 1811 *NH V*, d 8 Oct 1856 æ. 45 *NHT1*; Capt. 2 Leonard Larabee, b 9 Dec 1812 *NHV*. 3 Richard Bradley, b 10 Sep 1814 *NHV*, d 2 Apr 1840 æ. 26 (at sea) *NHT1*. 4 Mary E., b [Oct 1816], d 15 Apr 1882 æ. 65-6 *NHV*; m 19 Nov 1840 *NHV*—William J. Thompson. 5 George L., b c. 1818, d 17 Sep 1849 æ. 32 *NHT1*. 6 Martha A., b c. 1822, d 16 Nov 1853 æ. 31 *NHT1*; m George Terrell.

2 MARY, b 14 May 1753 *NHV;* m 9 Nov 1774 *NHV*—Israel Bradley.

3 HANNAH, b 9 Jan 1755 *NHV;* m 22 Jan 1778 *NHV*—Glover Ball.

4 RACHEL, b 1 Jan 1757 *NHV*, bp 9 Jan 1757 *NHC1*, d 1831; m James Brannen.

5 RHODA, b 10 Feb 1759 *NHV*, bp 18 Mar 1759 *NHC2*, d 7 Jan 1803 æ. 44 *NHT1;* m (1) Samuel Chatterton; m (2) 20 Oct 1792 *N Hx*—Benjamin Brown.

6 LOIS, b 17 July 1761 *NHV*, bp 6 Sep 1761 *NHC2*, d 26 Nov 1828 æ. 70 (at NH) *ColR;* m Samuel Hibbart.

7 EBER, b 26 Nov 1764 *NHV*, bp 23 Dec 1764 *NHC2*.

8 PHEBE, b 6 Nov 1766 *NHV*, bp 16 Nov 1766 *NHC2*, d 27 June 1825 æ. 59 *BT2;* m William Hitchcock.

9 EZEKIEL, b 6 Nov 1768 *NHV*, bp 15 Jan 1769 *NHC2*, d s. p. after 1779.

FAM. 32. DANIEL & EUNICE (DOOLITTLE) HOTCHKISS:

1 THANKFUL, b 15 Feb 1753 *WV;* m 15 Feb 1776 *CC*—David Webb.

2 EUNICE, b 8 Jan 1755 *WV;* m 21 Apr 1774 *CC*—Benjamin Hitchcock.

3 ISAAC, b 4 Mar 1757 *WV;* m 18 Aug 1784 *WashingtonC*—Olive [?da. John & Sarah (Munger)] Twiss.

4 LUCY, b 7 Mar 1759 *WV;* m 2 May 1785 *CC*—Laban Hall.

5 HANNAH, b 5 June 1761 *WV*.

6 THOMAS, b 25 Nov 1763 *WV*.

7 LYDIA, b 30 Mar 1766 *WV;* m 24 Jan 1791 *CC*—Josiah Remington Graves.

8 DANIEL, bp 10 July 1768 *CC*.

9 MOSES, bp 5 Aug 1770 *CC*, "child" d 5 Aug 1770 *CC*.

10 MOSES, b 23 Aug 1771 *WV*, bp 6 Oct 1771 *CC;* m Elizabeth Clarina Amelia da. Ephraim & Elizabeth (Hull) Cook, b 22 Jan 1773 *WV*.

11 DAMARIS, b 27 Feb 1776 *WV*, bp 28 Apr 1776 *CC*.

FAM. 33. JOSEPH & HANNAH (ATWATER) HOTCHKISS;

1 ROZEL [Roswell], b 24 July 1762 *WV*, d 28 Dec 1845 (Harpersfield, N. Y.); m 16 May 1786 *F*—Margaret Harper, b 8 Jan 1766 *F*, d 22 Jan 1845 *F*.

2 THELUS, b 19 May 1764 *WV;* Census (Wat) 1-0-2; res. 1831 Harpersfield, N. Y.; m Sarah da. Asa & Lois (Warner) Scovill, b 1 Nov 1766 *WatV*. A child, Molly, b 1 Feb 1789 *F;* m 27 Apr 1809 Newton Morris.

3 EBENEZER, b 3 Sep 1766 *WV*, d 16 Jan 1826 *F*.

4 SALINA, b 7 Nov 1768 *WV*, bp 13 Nov 1768 *CC*.

5 HANNAH, b 17 Jan 1771 *WV*, bp 20 Jan 1771 *CC*, d 9 July 1824 *F*.

6 JOSEPH, b 17 Mar 1773 *WV*, bp 21 Mar 1773 *CC*, d 27 Feb 1825 *F*.

7 MARY ATWATER, b 16 July 1775 *F*, d 17 Jan 1778 *F*.

8 MARY ATWATER, b 31 Jan 1778 *F*.

9 SARAH H., b 26 Aug 1781 *F*, d 26 July 1796 *F*.

FAM. 34. WAIT & LYDIA (WEBSTER) HOTCHKISS:

1 JOEL, b c. 1760, d 21 Feb 1798 æ. 38 *WolT;* m 6 Feb 1785 *WatV*—Mary da. Josiah & Sarah (Ives) Rogers, b 24 Oct 1758 *WatV*, d 22 Nov 1836 æ. 78 *WolT;* she m (2) Stephen Carter.

i Asenath, b 23 Mar 1787 *WatV*, d 31 Aug 1810 æ. 24 *WolT;* m Ira Hough.

2 LYDIA, b c. 1762, d 25 July 1838 æ. 76 *WolT;* m David Harrison.

3 SARAH, b 27 Mar 1765 *WatV*, d 7 June 1804 æ. 39 *WolT.*

4 ABNER, b 24 May 1771 *WatV*, d 21 Mar 1846 æ. 75 *WolT;* m 19 Nov 1805 Mary da. Judah & Hannah (Baldwin) Frisbie, who d 3 Feb 1852 æ. 72 *WolT.*

5 LUCY, b 24 May 1771 *F*, d soon.

FAM. 34. WAIT & DEBORAH (ALCOTT) HOTCHKISS:

6 LUTHER, b 19 Dec 1778 *WatV*, d 14 Apr 1863 *F;* Maj.; m 24 Nov 1800 Ann da. Curtis Hall, b 1781, d 3 Mar 1864 *F.*

7 MILES, b 23 July 1783 *WatV.*

8 ISAAC, b 16 Oct 1787 *WatV*, d 31 Aug 1870 æ. 82 *WolT;* m Mary ——, who d 12 Dec 1840 æ. 56 *WolT.*

FAM. 35. JOSIAH & SARAH (PERKINS) HOTCHKISS:

1 ABIGAIL, b 12 Dec 1765 *WV*, d 19 Dec 1847 æ. 82 *CT2;* m 4 Dec 1788 *CC*—Joel Moss.

2 ISRAEL, b 30 May 1767 *WV*, bp 2 Aug 1767 *CC*, d 21 Feb 1840 æ. 73 *CT2;* m 20 Sep 1792 *CV*—Martha da. Nathaniel & Lois (Hull) Royce, b 7 Mar 1765 *WV*, d 15 Mar 1840 æ. 75 *CT2.*

i Nathaniel Royce, b 6 Sep 1793 *CV*, d s. p.; m Mary Elizabeth Douglas.

ii Josiah, b 24 Jan 1795 *CV*, d 30 Aug 1832.

iii Elizur, b 8 Oct 1797 *CV*, d 8 Oct 1834 (Lancaster, S. C.); m Agnes Douglas.

iv Martha Maria, b 26 Jan 1800 *F*, ("Maria" b 26 Jan 1801 *CV*), d 26 Sep 1890 *F;* m 6 Apr 1825 *CV*—Hiram Andrews.

v Israel, b 28 Aug 1802 *F*, d 13 July 1842 *F;* m 3 Sep 1828 *CV*—Elizabeth Beach, who d 2 Oct 1860 æ. 57 *F.*

vi Caroline, b 1 Mar 1804 *F;* m Aaron Brooks.

vii Sybil, b 20 June 1806 *F*, d 7 Mar 1808 *F.*

viii Seth, b 18 Sep 1808 *F*, d 7 Dec 1886 (Fort Mill, S. C.); m (1) Olivia Fleming Davidson; m (2) Rebecca (Blount) Steele.

ix Charles Lester, b 16 Mar 1813 *F;* m Annie MacCroskie.

3 JOSEPHUS, b 2 Aug 1768 *WV*, bp 7 Aug 1768 *CC*, d 28 Mar 1821 æ. 58 *CT1;* m 11 Nov 1790 *CV, CC*—Sarah da. Uri & Lois (Doolittle) Benham, b 11 Oct 1769 *WV.*

i Benoni, b 8 May 1794 *CV;* rem. to Ky.

ii Lois, b 27 Oct 1795 *CV;* m Alfred Blakeslee.

iii Sarah, b 13 Dec 1799 *CV*, d 22 Apr 1867 *F;* m 14 Aug 1822 *F*—Willis Laribee.

iv Delos, b 25 Oct 1802 *CV;* m 13 Sep 1827 *CV*—Philocia Moss.

v Mary, b 6 July 1807 *CV;* m 29 Sep 1828 *CV*—William Hotchkiss.

vi Emma, b 16 Nov 1809 *CV;* m Joseph T. Doolittle.

4 Eunice, b 28 Aug 1770 *WV*, bp 14 (?) Aug 1770 *CC;* m 12 Mar 1792 *CC*—Samuel Clark.

5 Salma, b 17 May 1772 *WV*, bp 26 July 1772 *CC;* m 27 Nov 1794 *CC*—Rebecca [da. Jonathan & Abigail (Hall)] Hall, b 16 Dec 1775 *WV*.

6 Sarah, b 13 Dec 1777 *WV*, bp 8 Mar 1778 *CC;* m —— Merriam.

7 Sybil, bp 16 June 1782 *CC;* m Mark Doolittle.

Fam. 36. Benoni & Hannah (Norton) Hotchkiss:

1 Huldah Ann, b 11 Sep 1772 *WV*, bp 7 (?) Sep 1772 *CC*.

2 (probably) Esther, bp 23 Oct 1774 *CC*.

3 (probably) Susanna, bp 17 Nov 1776 *CC;* m 17 Apr 1800 *CC*—Jason Beach.

4 Isaac Norton, bp 16 May 1779 *CC*.

5 William, bp 14 May 1781 *CC*, d 4 Sep 1785 æ. 5 *CT1*.

6 Albert, bp 14 Dec 1783 *CC*, d 12 Mar 1786 æ. 3 *CT1*.

7 Mary, b 6 Dec 1786 *CV*, bp 4 Feb 1787 *CC*.

Fam. 36. Benoni & Lucy (———) Hotchkiss:

8 Eliza, b c. 1793, d 20 Aug 1795 æ. 2 *CT1*.

9 Albert, b [July 1795], d 15 Sep 1795 æ. 0-2 *CT1*.

10 Frederick, b 12 Aug 1803 *CV*.

Fam. 37. Lemuel & Penelope (Mather) Hotchkiss:

1 Lemuel, b 11 July 1764, d 13 July 1766.

2 Chloe, b 24 Apr 1767; m 18 Jan 1792 Abijah Smith.

3 Lydia, b 15 Mar 1769; m 18 Jan 1791 Harvey Peck.

4 Penelope, b 25 June 1771, d 6 Nov 1830; m Joseph Crane.

5 Lemuel, b 30 Nov 1773; m Abigail Ellis.

6 Joseph, b 28 Oct 1775, d 24 May 1786.

7 Nancy, b 16 Feb 1778, d 16 June 1786.

8 Jason, b 30 Nov 1779, d 1828; m Nancy Parker.

9 Anna, b 22 June 1782.

PAGE 946 10 Henry, b 9 Aug 1785.

11 Nancy, b 18 Feb 1788; m Rev. John B. Whittlesey of York, N. Y.

12 Joseph, b 24 July 1791, d 13 Sep 1794.

Fam. 38. Ladwick & Martha (Lee) Hotchkiss:

1 Ladwick, b 6 Dec 1773; went west.

2 Seth, b 3 June 1775; m Temperance Kelly of Yarmouth, Mass.

3 Orren, b 26 Feb 1778.

4 Jesse, b 4 Dec 1780.

5 Sally, b 26 Aug 1782, d 9 Feb 1857; m 15 Apr 1804 Reuben Gladden.

6 Abi, b 15 Aug 1784, d 21 July 1812; m 1 Dec 1805 Joseph H. Flagg.

7 Levi, b 12 June 1786; m Abigail Jones of Newburyport, Mass.

8 **Alvin**, b 1 May 1788, d 11 Sep 1863; m (1) 31 Jan 1810 Sally Williams, who d 5 Oct 1824; m (2) 24 Aug 1825 Mary P. Roberts, b 18 July 1798 (Deerfield, Mass.), d 21 Sep 1854.

9 **Mabel**, b 11 Dec 1791, d 13 Jan 1859; m June 1813 Ira Bronson.

10 **Daniel**, b 22 Aug 1794, d 1821.

Fam. 39. Lent & Sarah (Ball) Hotchkiss:

1 **Anna**, b 8 Sep 1789 *F*, bp 30 July 1794 *NHC1*, "da." d 30 July 1794 æ. 5 *NHC1*, æ. 4–10 *NHT1*.

2 **Sarah**, b 19 July 1791 *F*, bp 28 Aug 1794 (æ. 1) *NHx*, "da." d 28 May 1794 æ. 4 *NHC1*, 28 Aug 1794 æ. 3–1 *NHT1*.

3 **John Ball**, b 18 June 1793 *F*, bp 3 May 1795 *NHC1*, d 24 Aug 1836 æ. 46 *NHT1*; m Harriet da. Earl & Rhoda (Ford) Stevens, b 12 May 1796 *NHV*, d 5 Nov 1893 æ. 96–5–23 *NHT1*.

i Maria, b 18 Apr 1821 *F;* m 20 Sep 1843 Thomas W. Ensign.

ii John Ball, b 16 Oct 1824 *F;* m 21 Apr 1851 *NHV*—Ellen Jane Thomas.

iii Harriet, b 18 May 1827 *F;* m Howard P. Marsh of New Hartford.

4 **Anna**, b 17 Jan 1796 *F*, bp 13 Mar 1796 *NHC1*, d 5 May 1849 æ. 53 *NHT1*; m Abel Burritt.

5 **Sarah**, b 11 June 1798 *F*, bp 19 Aug 1798 *NHC1*, "da." d 7 June 1803 æ. 5 *NHC1*.

6 **Charles**, b 4 Dec 1800 *F*. bp 8 Feb 1801 *NHC1*, "son" d 5 June 1803 æ. 3 *NHC1*.

7 **Edward**, b 11 Feb 1803 *F*, bp 21 Mar 1803 *NHC1*, d 11 Dec 1803 æ. 0–10.

Fam. 40. Stephen & Abigail (Scott) Hotchkiss:

1 **Lucy**, b 4 Sep 1769 *NHV*, bp 10 Sep 1769 *NHC1*, d 5 Mar 1852 æ. 82 *NHT1*; m 25 Oct 1789 *NHC1*—Abraham Dummer.

2 **William Scott**, b 29 Jan 1772 *NHV*, bp 16 Feb 1772 *NHC1*, d 27 July 1834 æ. 62 *NHT1*; m 12 Dec 1795 *NHC1*—Mary da. Isaac & Elizabeth (Thompson) Thompson, b 8 May 1773 *NHV*, d 29 Oct 1841 æ. 68 *NHT1*.

i Mary, b 26 Oct 1796 *F*, bp 23 Sep 1804 *NHC1*, d 4 June 1866 æ. 70 *NHT1*; m Jotham C. Fenn, who d 8 Nov 1835 æ. 39 (at Antigua, W. I.).

ii William Townsend, b 17 May 1798 *F*, bp 23 Sep 1804 *NHC1*, d 16 Aug 1835 æ. 37 *OxfT1*; m 25 Dec 1823 Jennette A. Tomlinson, who d 13 Apr 1847 æ. 43 *OxfT1*.

iii Thomas T., b c. 1798, d 4 Mar 1865 æ. 67 *NHT1*.

iv Susan, b 31 July 1800 *F*, d 3 Apr 1801 æ. 0–10 *NHT1*, "da." d 6 May æ. 0–9 *NHC1*.

v Susan, b [Mar 1802], d 24 Aug 1803 æ. 0–17 *NHT1*, "son" d 25 Aug æ. 2 *NHC1*.

vi Isaac Thompson, b 9 Feb 1804 *F*, bp 23 Sep 1804 *NHC1*, d 22 Sep 1870 æ. 66 *NHT1*; m 7 Nov 1827 Eliza C. Tomlinson, who d 21 Feb 1881 æ. 75 *NHT1*.

vii Wyllys Henry, b 28 Oct 1805 *F*, d 15 Dec 1805 æ. 0–2 *NH*

T1.
viii Amelia Scott, b 16 Mar 1810 *F*, d 30 May 1853 æ. 43 *NHT1*.
ix Elizabeth, b 14 Sep 1812 *F*, d 27 Jan 1816 *F*.
x James, b 25 May 1814 *F*, d 26 June 1815 æ. 0-13 *NHT1*.
3 PHEBE, b 11 July 1773 *NHV*, bp 8 Aug 1773 *NHC1*, d 21 May 1793 æ. 20 *NHT1*, *NHC1*.
4 BETSEY, bp 4 June 1775 *NHC1*, d 4 Oct 1856 *F*; m Henry Wells.
5 STEPHEN, b 22 Sep 1777 *NHV*, bp 25 Sep 1777 *NHC1*, d 10 Aug 1857 æ. 80 *NHT1*; m 15 Feb 1801 *NHC1*—Mary da. Samuel & Lucy (Phipps) Griswold, bp 8 Sep 1782 *NHC2*, d 15 Apr 1856 æ. 74 *NHT1*. Family incomplete.
i Charles, b c. 1802, d 6 June 1834 æ. 33 *NHT1*.
ii [Stephen, b 6 Feb 1805 *NHT1*, d 17 Apr 1868 *NHT1*; m Anna Maria da. Simeon & Hannah (Beardsley) Goodyear, b 7 Feb 1804 *NHT1*, d 2 Apr 1876 *NHT1*].
iii Frederick, b c. 1807, d 17 May 1831 æ. 24 *NHT1*.
iv Mary G., b c. 1809, d 1 Sep 1829 æ. 21 *NHT1*.
v Harriet, b c. 1811, d 29 May 1815 æ. 5 *NHT1*.
vi Harriet, b c. 1820, d 9 Sep 1880 æ. 61 *NHT1*.
vii Robert, b c. 1825, d 26 Dec 1836 æ. 12 *NHT1*.
6 GEORGE, b 6 Mar 1780 *NHV*, bp 23 Apr 1780 *NHC1*, d 15 Apr 1813 æ. 33 *NHT1*; m 26 Sep 1802 *NHx*—Peggy da. Daniel & Elizabeth Collis, b 20 June 1773 *F*, d 9 June 1839 (at Cincinnati, Ohio) *F*.
i Daniel Collis, b [Dec 1803], bp 4 Mar 1804 (æ. 0-3) *NHx*, d 16 June 1834 *F*; m 19 Sep 1827 *NHV*—Elizabeth da. Russell & Mary (Oakes) Hotchkiss.
ii George Wyllys, b c. 1805, d 17 Nov 1886 æ. 81 *NHT1*; m 11 May 1828 *NHV*—Julia E. da. William & Julia (Pardee) Gilbert, b c. 1805, d 14 Mar 1887 æ. 82 *NHT1*.
iii Henry Scott, bp 27 Sep 1807 *NHx*, d 1 Oct 1825 æ. 18 *NHT1*.
iv Elizabeth Davis, bp 15 Apr 1810 *NHx*; m 26 Mar 1834 *NHV*—William T. Truman of Cincinnati, Ohio.
v William Dummer, b 17 Dec 1811 *F*, bp 16 Apr 1812 *NHx*; res. Binghamton, N. Y.; m 28 Sep 1840 *NHV*—Sarah da. Isaac & Esther (Alling) Gilbert.
7 WYLLYS, b 20 Dec 1782 *NHV*, *NHT1*, bp 26 Jan 1783 *NHC1*, d 9 June 1852 *NHT1*; m Nov 1806 *NHC1*, 12 Nov *F*—Lucretia da. Ezekiel & Mary (Hemingway) Hayes, b 24 Apr 1784, d 12 Apr 1859; had 7 children who d s. p.

FAM. 40. STEPHEN & ELIZABETH (OSBORN) HOTCHKISS:
8 DAUGHTER, d 24 July 1791 æ. 0-0-1 *NHC1*.

FAM. 41. JONAH & ELIZABETH (ATWATER) HOTCHKISS;
1 ELIZABETH, b 10 June 1773 *F*, bp 20 June 1773 *NHC1*, d 15 Apr 1796 æ. 23 *NHT1*, *NHC1*; m 15 Feb 1794 *NHC1*—Justus Hotchkiss.

2 SUSANNA, b 24 June 1775 *F*, bp 2 July 1775 *NHC1*, d 1 Mar 1825 æ. 50 *NHT1*; m 27 Apr 1800 *NHC1*—Justus Hotchkiss.

3 EZRA, b 3 Feb 1778 *F*, bp 8 Feb 1778 *NHC1*, d 11 Feb 1866 æ. 88 *NHT1*; m 24 Sep 1800 *F*—Nancy da. John & Elizabeth (Farrand) Mix, b 14 June 1781 *F*, d 26 Dec 1821 æ. 40 *NHT1*, 28 Dec æ. 44 (*NHC1*) *NHV*; m (2) 30 Oct 1825 *NHV*—Nancy da. Levi & Lydia (Augur) Ives, b [14 Nov 1785], d 19 Apr 1836 æ. 50 *NHT1*; m (3) 15 May 1839 (at N. Y.) *ConnH*—Katharine Farrand, who d 2 Feb 1872 æ. 74 *NHT1*.

(By 1): *i* Daughter, b 20 July 1801 *F*, d soon.

ii Daughter, b 20 July 1801 *F*, d soon.

iii James Edward, b 17 May 1803 *F*, bp 11 Sep 1803 *NHC1*, d 10 July 1835 æ. 32 *NHT1*.

iv Charles Farrand, b 4 Nov 1805 *F*, d 31 Mar 1883 (at Bd); rem. to Rochester, N. Y., & Vineland, N. J.; m 30 Oct 1827 *NHV*—Olivia Eunice Trowbridge, b 31 May 1806.

v Maria, b 1 Mar 1809 *F*, d 21 June 1817 æ. 8 *NHT1*.

vi Daughter, b 11 Sep 1811 *F*, d 24 Sep 1811.

vii Frederick Atwater, b 31 Mar 1813 *F*, d 24 Feb 1842 æ. 29 *NHT1*.

viii Ezra Augustus, b 8 Nov 1816 *NHT1*, d 7 June 1846 æ. 30 *NHT1*.

ix Leonard Stanley, b 19 Nov 1818 *F*, d 8 Nov 1894 *F*; m 27 June 1833 *NHV*—Louisa Hubbard.

4 RUSSELL, b 15 Sep 1781 *NHT1*, bp 21 Oct 1781 *NHC1*, d 1 Jan 1843 *NHT1*; m (1) 27 Apr 1807 *F*—Mary Oaks, b 9 Feb 1786 *NHT1*, d 19 Mar 1834 *NHT1*; m (2) 9 June 1835 *NHV*—Elizabeth Ann da. William Gold & Elizabeth (Douglas) Hubbard, b 29 July 1798 *NHT1*, d 8 July 1881 *NHT1*.

(By 1): *i* Russell, b 6 Nov 1809 *F*, d 11 Jan 1881 *F*; m 25 Dec 1833 *NHV*—Catherine E. Wadsworth, who d 29 Jan 1875.

ii Elizabeth, b 19 Mar 1808 *NHT1*, d 6 June 1834 *NHT1*; m 19 Sep 1827 *NHV*—Daniel Collis Hotchkiss.

iii Mary, b 12 Sep 1811 *NHT1*, d 9 June 1837 *NHT1*; m 23 Dec 1829 *NHV*—David Hoadley, Jr., of N. Y. City.

iv Justus, b 24 Aug 1815 *F*, d 21 Nov 1815 æ. 0-3 *NHT1*.

v Susan, b 2 Oct 1816 *NHT1*, d 4 Nov 1835 *NHT1*.

vi Henry O., b 27 Sep 1818 *NHT1*, d 4 Dec 1883 *NHT1*; m Mary A. Sawyer, b 27 Dec 1822 *NHT1*, d 17 May 1912 *NHT1*.

vii Edward, b 15 Oct 1822 *F*, d 25 Oct 1824 æ. 2 *NHT1*.

viii Edward, b 19 June 1824 *F*; m 21 Dec 1859 *F*—Anna Elizabeth, da. Jacob Campbell.

5 ELIAS, b 27 Aug 1786 *F*, bp 1 Oct 1786 *NHC1*, d 25 Nov 1865 æ. 79 *NHT1*; m (1) Mar 1810 Almira Woodward, b c. 1789, d 3 Jan 1848 æ. 58 *NHV*, *NHT1*; m (2) Julia (———) Belden.

(By 1): *i* Caroline W., b 30 Sep 1811 *F*; m (1) 1 Aug 1838 *NHV*—Gustavus C. Bradley; m (2) ——— True.

ii Thomas Woodward, b 9 Jan 1814 *F*, d 20 July 1815 æ. 0-18 *NHTI*.

iii Frances Elizabeth, b 22 Nov 1816 *F*, d 21 Feb 1876 (at New Orleans, La.) *F;* m 4 July 1841 *F*—Rev. Allen B. Hitchcock.

iv Nancy, b 17 Jan 1819 *F;* m 6 Nov 1838 *NHV*—Henry Wheeler of D.

v Maria Woodward, b 10 Sep 1821 *F*, d 21 June 1849 *F;* m Rodney D. Baldwin.

vi William, b c. 1824, d 17 Apr 1845 æ. 21 (at sea) *NHTI*.

vii Thomas Woodward, b 26 Apr 1826 *F;* m (1) 21 Nov 1847 *WHx*—Emma Burrill, who d 31 Mar 1860 *F;* m (2) Jeannie Jewell.

viii Elias, b 28 Feb 1828 *F;* m (1) 15 Aug 1850 Mary Ann Wooster, who d 6 Apr 1851; m (2) Eunice A. Hubbard, who d 5 July 1858; m (3) Mary Landon Hubbard, wid. ——— Pratt.

ix George William, b 16 Oct 1831 *F;* res. Bay City, Mich.; m 14 Aug 1856 Elizabeth St. John.

x James Frank, b 21 May 1834 *F;* m 12 Feb 1857 *F*—Mary R. Babcock.

FAM. 42. ELIHU & LYDIA (ROBINSON) HOTCHKISS:

1 SALLY, b Nov 1769, d 3 June 1818 æ. 49 *LT;* m Benjamin Webster.

2 ELIHU, b 28 May 1771, d 9 May 1813; m c. 1800 Huldah da. Joel & Martha (Peck) Hotchkiss.

3 LYDIA, b 23 Apr 1775, d 4 June 1860.

4 MARY, b 25 Dec 1776, d 9 Sep 1851.

5 RACHEL, b 28 Feb 1779; m Miles Carrington.

6 LYMAN, b 26 May 1781, d 15 Mar 1861 æ. 80 *LT;* m 13 Nov 1804 Clarissa da. Midian & Annie (Watkins) Griswold, b 22 June 1785, d 7 Mar 1855 æ. 70 *LT*.

7 BETSEY, b 5 Apr 1783; m Appleton Marsh.

FAM. 43. JOEL & MARTHA (PECK) HOTCHKISS:

1 MARY, b c. 1773, d 27 Aug 1848 æ. 75 *LT;* m Wheeler Beecher of P.

2 MARTHA, b 18 Apr 1775 *F*, d 12 Oct 1856 æ. 82 *NHTI*, æ. 81-6 *NHV;* m 26 Jan 1800 John Humphreville.

3 HULDAH, b c. 1776, d 28 Mar 1844; m Elihu Hotchkiss.

4 JOEL, b 28 Apr 1778 *F;* rem. to Mosiertown, Pa.; m Mary da. Isaac & Polly (Tuttle) Sperry, b 27 Sep 1785 *F*.

5 LUTHER, b c. 1780, d 8 Oct 1803 æ. 23 *BTI*.

6 ANNA, b 29 Oct 1783 *F*, d 15 June 1814 æ. 32 *BTI;* m 29 Sep 1803 James Terrill.

7 ABIAH, b c. 1785, d 18 May 1865 æ, 81 *NHTI*, æ. 80-9 *NHV;* m (1) Zina Bradley; m (2) 1820 Benjamin Webster of L.

8 CONTENT, b c. 1787, d 29 Oct 1838 æ. 52 *NHTI*, 30 Oct *NHV*.

9 PENINA, b c. 1789, d 8 Feb 1858 æ. 69 *NHTI;* she had a nat.

child: Jane.

10 MEHITABEL, b c. 1793, d 7 Mar 1858 æ. 65 *NHT1*.

FAM. 44. ELIPHALET & ESTHER (BEECHER) HOTCHKISS:

1 ZINA, b 15 Jan 1773 (at Salem) *F*, d 7 May 1829 *F*; m Miranda Hibbard.

2 WILLIAM, b 14 Sep 1775 (at Salem), d 22 July 1848; res. Clinton, N. Y.; m Jemima Hart.

3 ELIPHALET, b 9 Apr 1778 (at L), d 11 Feb 1842; res. Vernon, N. Y.; m 1803 Mary Youngs.

4 CHAUNCEY, b 17 Sep 1780 (at L), d 15 Oct 1827; m 1819 Sophia Thomas.

5 CLARISSA BEECHER, b 2 Feb 1783 (at L), d 22 Aug 1861; m 24 Mar 1817 Claudius V. Boughton.

6 LEMAN, b 29 June 1785 (at L), d 28 Dec 1826; m (1) 19 June 1809 Theodosia da. Joseph & Merriam (Sedgwick) Gilbert, b 28 Apr 1787, d 4 Apr 1813; m (2) 13 Oct 1813 Chloe Gilbert (sister of Theodosia), b 21 Apr 1796, d 16 May 1859; she m (2) Joel Stearns.

7 CALVIN, b 29 Jan 1790, d 13 June 1791.

8 CALVIN, b 12 Aug 1792, d s. p. 28 June 1866.

FAM. 45. ELIAS & EUNICE (ATWATER) HOTCHKISS:

PAGE 946

1 SEYMOUR, b c. 1781, d 28 Oct 1822 æ. 41 *BT1*; m Eunice da. Hezekiah & Philena (Johnson) Beecher, b 9 July 1786 *F*.

i Ransom, b c. 1803, d 20 Aug 1828 æ. 25 *BT1*.

ii Lauren, b c. 1808, d 26 Oct 1834 æ. 26 *BT1*.

iii Sophronia.

iv Atlanta.

v Maria.

vi Rebecca.

2 SHELDON, b [Apr 1783], d 6 Feb 1852 æ. 68-10 *NHT1*; m (1) Clarissa da. Isaac & Polly (Tuttle) Sperry, b c. 1784, d 7 Mar 1839 æ. 55 *NHT1*, *NHV*; [?m (2) Louisa (Peck) Thomas].

FAM. 46. ELDAD & ABIGAIL (ATWATER) HOTCHKISS (family incomplete):

1 NANCY, b c. 1782, d 14 Nov 1794 æ. 13 *WatT1*.

2 SHERMAN, bp 3 Nov 1799 *WatC*, d 6 Aug 1870 *F*; m 27 Dec 1820 *CC*—Eudocia Brooks, who d 7 June 1872 *F*.

3 ELDAD, bp 3 Apr 1803 *WatC*, d 26 Sep 1835 æ. 33 *PptT*; m 26 Nov 1823 *WatV*—Nancy da. Amos & Hannah (Ives) Atwater. [Nancy Hotchkiss w. Benjamin Doolittle, d 21 Jan 1883 æ. 88 *PptT*].

FAM. 47. NEHEMIAH & REBECCA (OSBORN) HOTCHKISS:

1 KETURAH, b c. 1770, d 30 Oct 1776 æ. 6 *NHC1*.

2 NAOMI; m (1) 14 June 1798 *ConnJournal*—Isaac Johnson; m (2) 1819 John Thomas of B.

3 (perhaps) ARTHUR, b c. 1775; res. Albany, N. Y.

4 NEHEMIAH; res. Laprairie, Lower Canada.

5 KETURAH; m Isaac Smith of Odelltown, Lower Canada.

6 (perhaps) BETSEY; m ——— Russell; res. Albany, N. Y.

FAM. 47. NEHEMIAH & HANNAH (JOHNSON) HOTCHKISS:

7 POLLY, b c. 1787, d 17 Sep 1795 æ. 8 *NHx*.

8 LUCIUS, bp 19 July 1795 *NHx;* res. Northeast, Dutchess Co., N . Y

FAM. 47. NEHEMIAH & MARY (———) HOTCHKISS:

9 MARY, bp 29 Oct 1797 *NHx;* res. Northeast, Dutchess Co., N. Y.

FAM. 48. ISAAC & LYDIA (FIELDS) HOTCHKISS:

1 LYDIA, b 12 Dec 1776 *EHR*, bp 16 [Feb] 1783 *EHC;* m 20 May 1795 *EHC*—Titus Sanford.

2 BETSEY, b 2 May 1779 *EHR*, bp 16 [Feb] 1783 *EHC;* m 19 Jan 1800 *EHC*—Samuel Tuttle.

3 SARAH, b 19 Mar 1781 *EHR*, bp 16 [Feb] 1783 *EHC*, d 15 Dec 1838 æ. 57 *EHC;* m 5 June 1806 *EHC*—Isaac Holt Pardee.

4 LOIS, b 26 Aug 1783 *EHR*.

FAM. 49. JOSEPH & TEMPERANCE (ANDREWS) HOTCHKISS:

1 ANNA, b 22 Sep 1780 *EHR*, bp 3 May 1784 *EHC*, d 4 Dec 1852 æ. 72 *EHT;* m 4 June 1806 *EHC*—Abraham Pardee.

2 LYMAN, b 20 Mar 1784 *EHR*, bp 3 May 1784 *EHC*, d 16 July 1861 æ. 77 *EHT;* m 17 Nov 1806 *NoHC*—Sybil da. Daniel & Eunice (Ives) Bradley, b 7 Nov 1784 *F*, d 21 Nov 1855 æ 71 *EHT*.

i Grace Anne, b 25 Apr 1808, d 4 Apr 1885 æ. 77 *NHV;* m Samuel C. Thompson.

ii Sophronia, b 1 May 1812.

iii Joseph Ives, b 24 Apr 1814; m 24 Oct 1836 Sarah Ann da. Roswell & Polly (Potter) Bradley, b 2 Jan 1811.

iv Lyman, b 24 Apr 1816.

v Samuel Russell, b 2 Aug 1819, d 1 July 1850.

vi Elizabeth Amelia, b 9 Aug 1822, d 15 Apr 1825.

vii Daniel Bradley, b 20 June 1825, d 14 Nov 1825.

viii Elizabeth Amelia, b 28 Oct 1827.

3 ESTHER, b 28 June 1787 *EHR*, d 2 Apr 1869 æ. 82 *NHT1;* m John Smith Bradley.

4 ORILLA, b 14 Apr 1791 *EHR*, bp 17 Apr 1791 *EHC*, d 8 Nov 1838 æ. 47 *EHC;* m 16 Oct 1808 *EHC*—Thomas Barnes.

5 POLLY, b 15 May 1793 *EHR*, bp 23 June 1793 *EHC*, d 9 Nov 1826 æ. 33 *NHT1;* m 29 Jan 1815 Henry Oaks.

6 HULDAH, b 11 Oct 1798 *EHR*, bp 3 Dec 1797 *EHC*.

FAM. 50. HEMAN & ELIZABETH (ROWE) HOTCHKISS:

1 HARRIET.

2 HORACE R., b 15 Apr 1799 *NHT3*, d 21 Apr 1849 æ. 50 *NHT3;* m 22 Feb 1824 *EHV*—Charlotte A. Street, who d 12 Sep 1859 æ. 57 *NHT3*.

3 SAMUEL RUSSELL, b c. 1801, d 30 Oct 1844 æ. 43 *NHT3;* m 13 Nov 1822 *EHV*—Eliza da. John & Mary (Davenport) Woodward, bp 12 July 1801 *EHC*.

FAM. 51. JOHN & ABIGAIL (SMITH) HOTCHKISS:

1 MARY, b 23 June 1758 *WV*, d 7 Nov 1846 (Camden, N. Y.); m Joseph Johnson.

FAM. 51. JOHN & SARAH (GILLAM) HOTCHKISS:

2 SARAH, b 28 Oct 1761 *WV*.

3 NOAH, b 9 Jan 1763 *WV*, d s. p. 25 June 1812 æ. 50 *CT2;* Census (C) 2-0-4; m 17 Apr 1782 *CC*—Abigail da. Matthias & Eunice (Hull) Hitchcock, b 12 Dec 1762 *WV*.

4 JOSHUA GILLAM, b 6 Oct 1764 *WV*, d s. p. 1781.

5 EBENEZER, b 18 Jan 1768 *WV*, bp 27 Mar 1768 *CC;* Census (C) 1-1-1; probably had sons John Gillam & Joshua.

6 ABIGAIL SMITH, b 8 July 1769 *WV*, bp 10 Sep 1769 *CC;* m Aug 1790 *F*—John Cook Hotchkiss.

7 BENJAMIN, b 15 Apr 1771 *WV*, bp 9 June 1771 *CC*.

8 SUSANNA, b 18 July 1773 *WV*, bp 1 Sep 1773 *CC*.

FAM. 52. JESSE & CHARITY (MALLORY) HOTCHKISS:

1 ASAHEL, b 15 Feb 1760 *WatV*, d after 1840 (at Sharon); Census (Wat) 2-2-3; m (1) 22 Mar 1781 *WatV*, *CC*—Sarah da. James & Katharine Williams, b c. 1759, d 28 Mar 1794 æ. 35 *WatT3;* m (2) 7 June 1794 *WatV*, 6 July *CC*—Phebe da. Jehiel & Hannah (Jones) Merriman, b c. 1759, d 13 Sep 1829 æ. 71 *SalemC;* m (3) ——— (———) Cowles; m (4) ——— (———) Wakeman.

(By 1): *i* Sally, b 27 Oct 1781 *WatV*.

ii Curtis, b 4 May 1783 *WatV;* m Eunice ———, who d 22 Nov 1834 æ. 52 *WatT3*, 14 Nov *SalemC*.

iii Dyer, b 24 June 1785 *WatV*, d 15 Nov 1862 æ. 77 *WatT3;* m Orra ———, who d 19 Nov 1872 æ. 89 *WatT3*.

iv Esther, b 21 May 1788 *WatV*.

(By 2): *v* Tempy, b 27 Feb 1797 *WatV;* m ——— Andrews.

vi Asahel Augustus, b 30 June 1799 *WatV*, d 21 Apr 1885 (at Sharon); m 3 Oct 1821 Althea da. Abijah & Anna (Hotchkiss) Guernsey; their sons were noted gun and cannon inventors.

vii Marcus, b 1 Sep 1801 *WatV*.

viii Phebe Maria, b 5 Aug 1805 *WatV*.

2 CHARITY, b 24 Mar 1761 *WatV;* m Riverus Russell of Homer, N. Y.

3 BEULAH, b 13 Mar 1762 *WatV*, d 24 Oct 1776 *WatV*.

4 GABRIEL, b 13 Aug 1763 *WatV*, d 22 Jan 1765 *WatV*.

5 REBECCA, b 7 Jan 1765 *WatV*.

6 TEMPERANCE, b 3 Dec 1767 *WatV*.

7 APALINA, b 3 Jan 1769 *WatV;* res. Windsor, N. Y.; m 1792 Amraphel Hotchkiss.

8 CHLOE, b 5 Jan 1771 *WatV*.

9 ANNA, b 19 May 1772 *WatV*, d 26 Mar 1855 *F;* m 16 Apr 1797 *WtnV*—Abijah Guernsey.

10 HULDAH, b 9 Mar 1774 *WatV*.

11 JESSE, b 3 Aug 1776 *WatV*, d 1833; Dr.

FAM. 53. DAVID & ABIGAIL (DOUGLAS) HOTCHKISS:

1 ASENATH, b 11 July 1764 *WatV;* m 15 Dec 1783 *CC*—Elmore Russell; rem. to Windsor, N. Y.

2 SARAH, b 20 Mar 1766 *WatV;* m Justus Beecher of Homer & Windsor, N. Y.

3 FREDERICK, b 6 Mar 1768 *WatV*, d 25 Mar 1846 *Windsor, N. Y., T;* Census (Wat) 1-0-1; rem. to Windsor, N. Y., after 1826; m (1) 9 Mar 1790 *WatV*—Rhoda da. John & Patience (Frost) Hopkins, b 29 Sep 1767 *WatV*, d 12 Mar 1814 *WatV*, æ. 47 *PptT;* m (2) Tabitha da. Phinehas & Mary (Dickerman) Castle, wid. ——— Barrett, b 19 Mar 1772 *NHV*, d 1850.

(By 1): *i* Marilla, b 11 Mar 1791 *WatV*, d 7 Apr 1873; m 4 Oct 1812 Lebbeus Sanford.

ii Chloe, b 16 Apr 1794 *WatV*, d 22 Apr 1812 *WatV*, æ. 18 *PptT*.

iii Julia, b 7 Feb 1796 *WatV*, d 10 Nov 1883; m Jonah Woodruff of Naugatuck.

iv David Miles, b 27 Nov 1797 *WatV*, *PptT*, d 15 Apr 1878 *PptT;* m (1) 1 Dec 1819 Zerviah da. Martin Stevens, b 9 Dec 1797 *PptT*, d 28 Aug 1849 *PptT;* m (2) 1 May 1850 Hannah da. Joseph Ives & Abigail (Bryan) Doolittle, wid. ——— Bristol, b 25 Dec 1812 *PptT*, d 25 Dec 1893 *PptT*.

v Laura, b 4 Sep 1800 *WatV*, d 14 May 1817 æ. 17 *PptT*.

vi Clarissa, b 6 Jan 1806 *WatV*, d 16 Jan 1873; m 27 Sep 1829 Elisha Hall of Windsor, N. Y.

vii Frederick Hopkins, b 5 Nov 1808, d 1808.

4 LAVINIA, b 9 Jan 1770 *WatV;* m Stephen Williams of C.

5 AMRAPHEL, b 25 June 1772 *WatV;* m 1792 Apalina da. Jesse & Charity (Mallory) Hotchkiss.

i Stiles, b 7 Jan 1793 *F*, d 1869; m 19 Oct 1813 *F*—Lydia Beecher, b 6 Dec 1794 *F*.

ii Frederick, b 1794, d 1865 æ. 71 *Windsor, N. Y., T;* m Jemima da. Abner & Anna (Bacon) Comstock, b c. 1808 *F*.

iii Olive, b 1796; m Jedediah Smith.

iv Gideon, b 23 Aug 1797 *F;* m Ann Everett.

v Harry, b 16 June 1803 *F*, d 13 Sep 1873 *F;* m Amanda Hempstead.

vi Amraphel, b 1809; insane.

vii Jesse, b 1814; res. Cornwall, N. Y.; m Betsey Hempstead.

6 CYRUS, b 15 Apr 1774 *WatV;* m Sally Andrus.

i Carver.

ii Clarissa; m Jeffrey Sage.

iii Giles.

iv Parthenia, b 1806 *F;* m Julius Edwards.

v Sophronia; m ——— Orton of Brooklyn, N. Y.

FAM. 53. DAVID & PENINA (PECK) HOTCHKISS:

7 CHARLES TODD, b 24 June 1776 *WatV;* m Rhoda Barrett.

PAGE 946

i Milo.

ii Luke.

iii Titus.
iv Calvin; rem. to Homer, N. Y.
v Flora.

8 ABIGAIL, b 25 Apr 1778 *WatV;* m William Coburn.

9 GILEAD, b 12 Oct 1780 *WatV*, d 1871; m Sarah Hoadley.
i David, b 29 May 1804, d 14 Oct 1868.
ii Orson, b 3 Oct 1808, d 23 Nov 1810.
iii Wallace, b 14 May 1810, d 26 Dec 1863.
iv Harvey Bishop, b 23 Sep 1820, d 20 Aug 1868.

10 PENINA, b 21 Feb 1783 *WatV*, d 19 Jan 1841 *F;* m 1 June 1803 *F*—Sylvester Hulse of Deposit, N. Y.

FAM. 54. ABRAHAM & HANNAH (WEED) HOTCHKISS:

1 JOHN, b 16 Nov 1768 *WatV;* m 3 May 1790 *WatV*—Susanna da. Daniel Williams.
i Levi, b 18 Jan 1791 *WatV*, d 8 Oct 1859 æ. 69 *PptT*
ii Ransom, b 11 Feb 1793 *WatV*, d 8 Aug 1855 æ. 62 *PptT.*
iii Hannah, b 5 July 1797 *WatV*, d 18 Aug 1821 æ. 24 *PptT.*
iv Fanny, b 29 Nov 1801 *WatV.*
v Bronson, b 25 May 1805 *WatV.*

2 EZRA, b 2 Mar 1772 *WatV*, d 10 Oct 1820 *WatV;* m 31 Oct 1796 *WatV*—Melita da. John Beecher.
i Lois, b 19 Dec 1797 *WatV*, d 5 Aug 1804 *WatV.*
ii Sukey, b 19 Dec 1799 *WatV.*
iii Tempy, b 8 Sep 1803 *WatV.*
iv Ansel, b 20 June 1806 *WatV*, d 8 Dec 1827 æ. 21 *WtnT.*
v Samuel, b 20 Nov 1810 *WatV*, d 21 Dec 1830 æ. 20 *WtnT.*
vi Lois, b 8 Apr 1813 *WatV.*
vii Daughter, b 2 Feb 1816 *WatV*, d 9 Feb 1816 *WatV.*

3 LOIS, b 2 June 1773 *WatV*, d Nov 1842; m 1 June 1795 *WatV*—Joseph Payne.

4 HANNAH, b 5 July 1775 *WatV.*

5 JOEL, b 29 Nov 1781 *WatV;* m 16 June 1803 *WatV*—Esther da. Benjamin & Esther (Barrett) Beecher, b 1 Mar 1783 *CV.*

6 BENJAMIN, b 15 June 1786 *WatV*, d 1 Feb 1842 æ. 56 *PptT;* m 26 July 1807 *WatV*—Hannah da. Benjamin & Esther (Barrett) Beecher, b 1 June 1789 *CV.*

FAM. 55. AMOS & ABIGAIL (SCOTT) HOTCHKISS:

1 WOODWARD, b 19 Oct 1773 *WatV*, d 4 Sep 1861 æ. 88 *PptT;* m 2 Apr 1797 *WatV*—Mary da. Phinehas & Mary (Dickerman) Castle, b 24 Feb 1770 *NHV*, d 22 Jan 1870 æ. 100 *PptT.*
i Castle, b 10 May 1798 *WatV*, rem. to Ohio; m Artemisia Stillman of Burlington.
ii William, b Aug 1800 *WatV*, d 25 Mar 1842 æ. 42 (in Ohio) *PptT;* m Elizabeth Thorndike of Va.
iii Rhoda, b 25 Jan 1803 *WatV;* m F. M. Benham of Ohio.
iv Polly, b 3 July 1805 *WatV;* m Hervey Norton.
v Julius, b 11 July 1810 *WatV;* first Mayor of Wat; m 29 Apr 1832 *WatV*—Melissa Perkins of Oxf.

vi Albert, b 10 Apr 1813 *WatV*, d 22 Jan 1844 æ. 31 *PptT;* m Abbie Benio of Mid.
vii Sarah C., b 8 Sep 1818 *WatV*, d 16 Nov 1848 æ. 30 *PptT.*
2 SABRA, b 19 July 1777 *WatV;* m Stephen Russell.
3 AVERY, b 5 Apr 1779 *WatV;* m Philena Judd.
i Marvin.
ii Abigail.
iii Harris, b [4 May 1808], d 9 Oct 1863 æ. 55-5-5 *PptT;* m (1) 20 Nov 1830 *WatV*—Ann J. Martin; m (2) Harriet ———, who d 27 Nov 1841 æ. 28 *WatT3;* m (3) Lucinda ———, who d 30 May 1849 æ. 28 *PptT.*
iv Lucien.
v Charlotte.
vi Mary.
vii Charles.
viii Jane.
4 MOLLY, b 9 Feb 1783 *WatV;* m Joseph Bronson.
5 OREL, b 11 Apr 1785 *WatV*, d 5 Apr 1789 *WatV.*
6 AMOS HARLOW, b 18 Feb 1788 *WatV;* m (1) Almira Wheeler; m (2) 29 Aug 1837 Sarah M. Scott.
i Orel.
ii Marilla, bp 1812 *PptC;* m 17 Nov 1833 *WatV*—Isaac George Smith.
iii Wheeler.
iv Andin.
v Althea, bp 5 Aug 1821 *PptC;* m 18 Apr 1851 *WatV*—Joseph Beardsley.
vi Sylvia, bp 17 Nov 1822 *PptC.*
vii Almira.
viii Amos Frederick.
ix Olive Maria.
x Burr Mallory.
xi Sabra Jane.
7 ORRIN, b 1 Apr 1792 *WatV*, 16 Apr *WatT3*, d 27 Mar 1846 æ. 54 *WatT3;* m (1) Frances Atwater; m (2) Polly M. Hicock, b 27 June 1794 *WatT3*, d 18 Apr 1852 æ. 58 *WatT3.*
8 ABIGAIL OREL, b 10 Sep 1799 *WatV*, d 1804.

FAM. 56. EBEN & MARY (SANFORD) HOTCHKISS:
1 ANNA, b 23 Dec 1781 *WatV;* m 25 Mar 1806 *WatV*—John Prichard.
2 GIDEON MILLS, b 11 Nov 1784 *WatV*, d 27 Jan 1864 æ. 79 *PptT;* m 30 Nov 1809 *CC*—Arvilla da. Joel & Miriam (Moss) Brooks, b 3 Oct 1788 *CV.*
i Brooks, bc. 1812, d 6 Apr 1874 æ. 62 *PptT;* m Laura L. ———, who d 30 July 1858 æ. 48 *PptT.*
ii Harry.
iii Mary; m George Sloper.

FAM. 57. STEPHEN & TAMAR (RICHARDSON) HOTCHKISS:

1 JOSEPH, b 13 Feb 1781 *WatV*, d 12 Mar 1786 *WatV*, æ. 5 *WatT1*.

2 CLARISSA, b 11 July 1784 *WatV*.

3 ESTHER, b 11 Sep 1787 *WatV*, d 29 Oct 1837 *WatV*; m 16 Feb 1807 *WatV*—Humphrey Nichols.

4 CHLOE, b 18 Feb 1790 *WatV*; m 27 Feb 1813 *WatV*—William Baldwin.

5 LOIS, b 28 Nov 1795 *WatV*.

6 IRENE, b 29 Apr 1798 *WatV*, d 8 Sep 1800 *WatV*, æ. 3 *WatT1*.

7 PHEBE IRENE, b 3 Nov 1800 *WatV*; m (1) 1 Dec 1829 *WatV*—Joseph Edward Chatfield; m (2) 23 May 1838 *WatV*—Humphrey Nichols.

FAM. 58. ABRAHAM & ROSETTA (SPERRY) HOTCHKISS:

1 BELA; m [Rachel ———].

i Thomas.

ii William.

2 IRA, b 4 Mar 1781 *F*, d 26 July 1844 (Sheffield, Mass.); m (1) 24 May 1805 Sally da. David & Ruth (Smith) Prichard, who d 9 Nov 1811 æ. 31 *WatT3*, 6 Nov *SalemC*; m (2) 7 June 1812 Roxana Talmadge, b 4 July 1791 *F*, d 21 June 1844 *F*.

(By 2): *i* Chauncey Holden, b 1 Sep 1813, d Feb 1882; m 1838 Sarah Newton Woodruff.

ii Sophia, b 7 May 1815, d 21 Nov 1841.

iii Jane, b 18 June 1817, d 14 July 1857.

iv Augustine, b 5 Dec 1818, d 22 June 1887; m (1) 6 June 1846 Maria Briggs, b 26 Aug 1824, d 16 Aug 1853; m (2) 22 Apr 1857 Clarinda Maria Catlin, b 17 June 1825.

v Mary, b 24 Aug 1820, d 14 Mar 1843.

vi Martha, b 20 Sep 1822, d 25 Sep 1842.

vii Caroline, b 22 May 1824, d 19 Dec 1849,

viii Emily, b 1829, d 12 Mar 1846.

3 CHAUNCEY, b c. 1785, d 10 Nov 1803 æ. 19 *WatT3*, *SalemC*.

4 MARK; m Polly Hotchkiss.

5 ANN, b 3 Aug 1791 *F*, d 14 Feb 1859 (St. Johnsville, N. Y.); m 4 Jan 1817 Anthony Healy.

6 RACHEL, b c. 1793, d 5 Feb 1845 æ. 51 *WolT*; m after 1840 Gates Upson.

7 CALVIN, b c. 1795, d 26 Aug 1815 æ. 20 *WatT3*.

8 ABRAHAM, b 22 Jan 1798 *WatT3*, d 7 Aug 1857 *WatT3*.

FAM. 59. ISAAC & ELIZABETH (CLARK) HOTCHKISS:

1 PATTY, b 9 May 1781 *F*, d 10 Sep 1865; m 9 Feb 1802 John White.

2 PHILO, b 19 May 1783 *F*, d 16 Jan 1837 æ. 54 *WdT3*; m Elizabeth da. Elijah & Sarah (Beecher) Thomas, b c. 1790, d 13 May 1838 æ. 48 *WdT3*. Philo's estate distributed to Jairus, Aaron, Elizabeth (w. ——— Alling) & Rebecca.

3 ELIZABETH, b 8 Aug 1785 *F*, d 5 Sep 1810 *F*; m Erastus Sperry.

4 ISAAC, b 12 Jan 1788 *F*, d 24 Nov 1879 æ. 89 *PptT*; m (1) 5 Dec

1811 *F*—Rhoda da. Amos & Hannah (Ives) Atwater, b 5 Mar 1791 *F*, d 2 Feb 1851 æ. 60 *PptT;* m (2) Ann ——, who d 8 Nov 1874 æ. 78 *PptT*.

5 FANNY, b 14 Feb 1790 *F*, d 7 Mar 1852 *F*, bu. 9 Mar æ. 58 *Bx;* m Abel Prince.

6 REBECCA, b 2 Jan 1794 *F*, d 28 Sep 1849 *F;* m Hiram Hotchkiss.

7 CLARK, b 25 Mar 1803 *F*, d 3 July 1890 æ. 87 *WdT3;* m 25 Apr 1828 (in B) *F*—Caroline A. da. Chilion Sperry, b 1810, d 30 Dec 1894 *F*.

FAM. 60. STEPHEN & HANNAH (BROWN) HOTCHKISS:

1 HARRIET.

2 HARLEY, b 12 Sep 1791 *F*, d 26 Mar 1860 æ. 70 *BT2;* m Patty H[arriet Collins], who d 27 Mar 1864 æ. 71 *BT2*.

3 REBECCA; m Minott Collins.

4 WEALTHY, d s. p.

5 EBER, b c. 1796, d 26 Nov 1851 æ. 55 *BT2;* m Thirza Driver, who d 20 July 1892 æ. 90 *BT2*.

6 STEPHEN; b c. 1799, d 3 June 1842 æ. 42 *BT2;* m 10 Sep 1837 Abigail da. Avery & Philena (Judd) Hotchkiss of Ppt.

7 HANNAH, b 10 June 1801 *BT2*, d 20 July 1887 *BT2;* m John Russell.

8 JARED, b c. 1803, d 24 Aug 1854 æ. 51 *BT2;* m 13 Sep 1840 Amy French.

9 JESSE, b c. 1806, d 25 Dec 1856 æ. 50 *BT2;* m Caroline Sperry, who d 30 Apr 1852 æ. 34 *BT2*.

10 GEORGE, b c. 1809, d 2 Sep 1878 æ. 69 *BT2;* m 4 Apr 1841 Laura da. Jeremiah & Dorcas (Prince) Sperry, who d 31 Mar 1899 æ. 79 *BT2*.

FAM. 61. LEVERETT & SARAH (BURRITT) HOTCHKISS:

1 WYLLYS, b 25 Apr 1788 *DV*, d 24 Nov 1872 æ. 84-7 *DT1;* m (1) Sarah Horsey, who d 1 July 1866 æ. 85-8 *DT1;* m (2) Hannah Tibbals, who d 2 Dec 1875 æ. 73 *DT1*.

2 MARY, b 1 Feb 1790 *F*, d 21 Oct 1873; m 15 Aug 1814 *F*—Isaac Dickerman.

FAM. 62. ELIJAH & POLLY (CLARK) HOTCHKISS:

1 CLARK BEERS, b 17 Mar 1796 *WatV*, d 1 Feb 1857 *F;* m 4 Dec 1823 *F*—Caroline Bennett.

2 HORACE, b 11 July 1799 *WatV*, d 9 Mar 1879 *F;* m (1) 1 June 1826 Lucy Dutton, b 17 Feb 1801, d 27 Sep 1839; m (2) 6 Sep 1841 Mary B. Squires, b 21 Sep 1806, d 17 Feb 1881.

3 REBECCA, b 18 Mar 1805 *WatV*, d 7 Dec 1873 *WatV;* m 24 Nov 1859 (at Plainfield, N. J.) *WatV*—Charles D. Kingsbury.

FAM. 62. ELIJAH & LUCINDA (WARNER) HOTCHKISS:

4 HENRY, b 12 Mar 1810 *WatV*, d 21 Mar 1810 *WatV*.

FAM.. 63. ELIAS & ESTHER (DICKERMAN) HOTCHKISS:

1 LEVERETT, b 24 Mar 1800 *HV;* m (1) Lydia da. Samuel & Susanna (Humiston) Mix, b 1 Feb 1801 *NoHV*, d 24 May 1833 æ. 32 *NoHT1;* m (2) 10 Nov 1833 Ruth Dickerman da. Jared &

Lucy (Hull) Atwater, b 11 Apr 1812 *F*, d 9 July 1835 *F*.

2 MARY C., b 19 Nov 1801 *HV*, d 14 Apr 1856 æ. 54 *HT3;* m 15 May 1822 *HV*—Jotham Bradley.

3 MABEL, b 19 Nov 1801 *HV*, d 13 July 1884 æ. 82-8 *NHV;* m 1 June 1825 *HV*—Josiah Brinsmade.

4 CHLOE, b 18 Feb 1805 *HV;* m Roswell Jacobs.

5 LAURA, b 12 July 1811 *HV*, d 29 May 1897; m 27 Sep 1829 Edward Dickerman.

FAM. 64. [SAMUEL & PHEBE (GOODYEAR) HOTCHKISS]:

(The above Samuel is not known to have married, but was very likely the deceased husband of the widow Phebe Hotchkiss who appears in the conveyance of Goodyear property in Hamden. They may have been parents of the following, who is otherwise unplaced).

1 SAMUEL, of H, d before 1816 (called Samuel Jr.); m ———

i Mary, d before 1816; m ——— .

ii Samuel.

iii Amasa.

iv Sarah.

FAM. 65. JOSEPH & HANNAH (THOMAS) HOTCHKISS:

1 SILAS, b 1766, d c. 1848; m Susanna Peck.

i Temperance; m William Andrew.

ii Wooster, b c. 1793, d 8 Oct 1849 æ. 56 *NHV;* m (1) Mary Loring Bass, who d 22 Dec 1831 æ. 36 (*NHC1*) *NHV;* m (2) 25 Nov 1832 *NHV*—Jennette Tyler, who d 15 Jan 1847 æ. 45 *NHV;* m (3) 23 Jan 1849 *NHV*—Mary Atwater Bradley.

PAGE 1245 *iii* Hiram, b c. 1795, d 22 Jan 1850; m Rebecca da. Clark & Caroline A. (Sperry) Hotchkiss.

iv Deborah; m 25 July 1820 *WdV*—Solomon Terrill.

v Martha; m Lewis Hine.

2 TEMPERANCE, b c. 1767, d 4 Dec 1843; m Strong Sanford.

3 DAVID ELISHA; m before 1792 Betty Sperry [da. Joseph & Phebe (Sperry) Downs]; perhaps m (2) 5 Oct 1820 *WdV*—Larzaretta Clark.

4 HANNAH, d 3 May 1813 *ColR;* m Elihu Hitchcock.

5 JOSEPH; m Elizabeth da. David & Martha (Downs) Beers.

PAGE 1245 6 LYMAN.

FAM. 66. SAMUEL & LYDIA (PECK) HOTCHKISS:

1 LYDIA, b c. 1765, d 13 July 1815 æ. 50; m John Thomas.

2 MOSES; res. Cortland Co., N. Y.; m Sally ——— .

3 JAMES, d 1813; rem. to Homer, N. Y.; m Lucy da. Timothy & Hannah (Smith) Lounsbury. Probate record gives children: Fanny; Micah; Lucy; Leviah; Lydia; Mary; Eunice.

4 ABNER; res. 1800 Homer, N. Y.; m Bathsheba ——— .

5 AARON, d 1849; res. Cortland Co., N. Y. Probate record gives children: Alfred; Miles; Laura; Harriet; Lola.

6 BILDAD; res. Cortland Co., N. Y.

7 MARY.

PAGE 1245 8 HEPHZIBAH.

9 SAMUEL; res. 1800 Homer, N. Y.; m Sally ——— .

10 ZIBA; res. Cortland Co., N. Y.; m Milla ——— .

FAM. 67. WILLIAM & ELIPHAL (HINE) HOTCHKISS:

1 ELIPHAL; m 3 Apr 1782 *WdC*—Francis Moore.

2 JANE, b c. 1765, d 1849; m David Hine.

3 JOHN; Census (NH) 1-1-1; m 2 May 1785 *WdC*—Huldah Sperry.

i Ira, b c. 1790, bp 15 Sep 1804 (æ. 14) *NHx*.

ii Obedience, b c. 1791, bp 15 Sep 1804 (æ. 13) *NHx*.

iii Sally Almira, bp 15 Sep 1804 *NHx*.

iv John Miles, bp 15 Sep 1804 *NHx*.

4 DAVID, b c. 1769, bp 31 Jan 1775 *NHx*, d 12 Jan 1846 æ. — *DT* (Oak Cliff Cem.); m Mercy da. Hezekiah & Eunice (Johnson) Bradley, b c. 1766, bp 15 Aug 1803 *NHx*, d 30 Jan 1854 æ. 88 *DT*.

i Lucy, b c. 1792, bp 15 Aug 1803 (æ. 11) *NHx;* m Isaac Blake.

ii Lewis, b c. 1797, bp 15 Aug 1803 (æ. 6) *NHx*, d 17 Aug 1803 æ. 6 *NHx*.

iii Hannah, b c. 1799, bp 15 Aug 1803 (æ. 4) *NHx*.

iv Willis, b 29 Mar 1803 *DT*, bp 15 Aug 1803 *NHx*, d 18 Sep 1884 *DT;* m Mary A. Kimberly.

v Lewis, b 14 Oct 1806 *DT*, d 19 Feb 1887 *DT;* m Eliza Hull.

vi Eunice; m 23 Sep 1830 Sheldon Moulthrop.

vii Sarah M., b 17 Feb 1814 *DT*, d 14 Apr 1895 *DT;* m William Baldwin.

5 ANNA, bp 31 Jan 1775 *NHx*, d 1828 æ. 60 *MV;* m 2 Oct 1788 *MC1* Isaac Fenn of M.

6 GEORGE, bp 31 Jan 1775 *NHx*, d 31 Jan 1775 *NHx*.

7 SARAH, bp 31 Jan 1775 *NHx*.

FAM. 68. JONAS & MABEL (———) HOTCHKISS:

1 JONAS, b c. 1783, d 6 Mar 1850 æ. 67 *WdD;* m Sally ——— , who d 6 Dec 1852 æ. 65 *WdD*. Family incomplete.

i Minerva, b c. 1809, d 2 Sep 1824 æ. 15 *WdD*.

ii Maria, b c. 1816, d 10 Dec 1852 æ. 37 *WdD*; m Daniel Lyon.

2 SILAS, d before 1818; m Lydia da. Ebenezer & Susanna (Tuttle) Warner, b 5 May 1773 *NHV*, d 21 Dec 1857 æ. 84-6-16 *HV*, æ. 85 *HT2*.

i Lyman, b [Oct 1798], d 11 Jan 1878 æ. 79-9 *HV;* m (1) Harriet Munson, who d 18 Feb 1833 æ. 23 *HT2;* m (2) Luna ——— , who d 24 July 1850 æ. 48 *HT2;* m (3) 21 Jan 1853 *HV*—Charlotte Williams of Fair Haven.

ii Bede.

iii Lydia, d 26 July 1869; m 16 July 1837 Roswell Humiston.

iv Betsey, b c. 1805, d 3 Mar 1877 æ. 72 *HT2;* m Ira Warner.

v Harriet; m 6 Sep 1829 *NHV*—George Goodsell of Bridgeport.

vi Silas, b 19 July 1812 *BT5*, d 20 Jan 1899 *BT5;* m Elitha da. Jonah & Olive (Sanford) Warner, b c. 1812, d 16 May 1886 æ. 74 *BT5*.

3 Thomas, d 17 Feb 1863 æ. 65 to 70 *WdD*.

4 Nicodemus; m Charlotte Porter.

i Jeremiah.

ii Charles.

iii Porter Allen.

iv Mary.

v Jeannette.

5 Martha; m July 1804 *WdC*—William Eaton Jones.

FAM. 69. Benjamin & Sarah (Downs) Hotchkiss:

1 Amos, b 6 Feb 1777 *NHV;* m Lois da. Joel & Elizabeth (Peck) Todd.

2 Sally, b 16 Aug 1778 *NHV*, d Oct 1817 *SalemC;* m 25 Jan 1797 *SalemC*—Samuel Osborn.

FAM. 70. Ezekiel & Rebecca (Thomas) Hotchkiss:

1 Selden.

2 Mabel, d 1833 (at Pike, Pa.); m Joseph Hitchcock.

3 Silliman, b c. 1785, d 27 Aug 1842 æ. 57 *BT2;* m Jeannette da. Philo & Hannah (Lines) Alling, b c. 1790, d 29 Oct 1842 æ. 53 *BT2*.

4 Miles, b c. 1790, d 19 Oct 1843; res. S; m Harriet Grannis.

5 Hubbard, b c. 1798, d 26 Oct 1849 æ. 52 *WdT1;* m 9 Aug 1820 *WdC*—Hannah da. Philo & Hannah (Lines) Alling, b c. 1799, d 20 Apr 1856 æ. 57 *WdD*. Child: Hannah E., bp 3 Aug 1828 *WdC;* m Wm. A. Warner.

FAM. 71. Robert & Hannah (Hotchkiss) Hotchkiss:

1 Raymond, b c. 1779, d s. p. 8 Feb 1855 (Granville, N. Y.); m (1) 2 Feb 1800 Lovina [or Viana] Goodrich, who d 20 Apr 1804 æ. 23 *Wells, Vt.,T;* m (2) 12 July 1804 Polly Parmalee da. Jason Tyler, who d 1861 æ. 76 (Castleton, Vt.).

2 Malinda, b c. 1781; m 29 Dec 1799 *CC*—Silas Gaylord.

3 Oliver, b c. 1784, res. Burton, Ohio; m 26 Dec 1805 *CC*—Polly [da. Henry & Content (Andrews)] Brooks, b [2 Nov 1787 *CV*].

FAM. 71. Robert & Lucy (Curtis) Hotchkiss:

4 Hannah D., b c. 1790, d 13 July 1842 æ. 52; m Sep 1811 Elijah Park.

FAM. 72. John Cook & Mary (Crittenden) Hotchkiss:

1 Mamre, b 30 May 1786 *F;* m 13 Feb 1806 *F*—John Knapp.

2 Lauren, b 22 Aug 1788 *F;* Rev.; m (1) Lucy Roundy, b Mar 1787 *F*, d June 1851 *F;* m (2) 3 June 1852 *F*—Sally Jewell, wid. Cook Hotchkiss.

FAM. 72. John Cook & Abigail Smith (Hotchkiss) Hotchkiss:

3 Mary.

4 Ephraim.

5 COOK, b 14 Sep 1797 *F*, d 28 Aug 1839 *F;* res. Medina, Mich.; m 19 Dec 1818 *F*—Sally da. Joseph & Mary (Crane) Jewell, b 24 July 1797 *F*, d 19 Dec 1859 *F;* she (2) Rev. Lauren Hotchkiss.
6 NANCY, d soon.
7 NANCY; m (1) Lewis Ingersoll; m (2) Elias Baldwin.
8 SARAH; m 1 May 1828 *F*—John Redfield of Equinunk, Wayne Co., Pa.
9 CYNTHIA.
10 JOHN CRITTENDEN; res. Medina, N. Y., & Medina, Mich.; m 17 Oct 1832 Ann Eliza da. Joel & Nancy (Bailey) Peck, b 3 Mar 1815; she m (2) 8 May 1853 Avery S. Hutchins.

FAM. 73. SOLOMON & [ANNA (PIERSON)] HOTCHKISS:
1 LEVINA, d s. p. 1795.
2 JOHN, b c. 1775, d 22 Feb 1842 æ. 66 (at DeWitt, N. Y.) *WdD;* m 16 Oct 1796 *DV*—Betsey da. Joseph & Rachel (Chatfield) Riggs, b 11 June 1775 *F*, d 1 June 1842 æ. 65 *WdC.*
i Truman, b c. 1797, d 28 May 1842 æ. 45 *WdT1*, 29 May æ. 46 *WdC;* m (1) 3 Apr 1823 Emily da. Luther & Susanna (Sperry) Lines, b c. 1797, d 8 Mar 1841 æ. 44 *WdT1*, 18 Mar *WdC;* m (2) Lydia C. da. Ephraim & Sarah (Beecher) Beecher, b c. 1808, d 5 Nov 1852 æ. 44 *WdD;* she m (2) 19 Apr 1846 *WdC*—Stephen Dickerman.
ii Jennet, b c. 1804, d 27 July 1827 æ. 23 *WdT2.*
iii Eliza Ann, b c. 1807, d 15 Feb 1844 æ. 37 *OT;* m 2 Nov 1826 *OC*—Jesse Seymour Pardee.
3 ANNA; m William Merriam.
4 SOLOMON LUCIUS, d s. p. c. 1803.

FAM. 74. DAVID & LYDIA (BEECHER) HOTCHKISS:
1 LYDIA, b 15 Dec 1777 *F;* m Ira Baldwin.
2 DAVID, b 15 Sep 1779 *F*, d 24 June 1842 æ. 63 *WdT1;* m Huldah da. Alling & Sarah (Collins) Bradley, b c. 1782, d 21 July 1836 æ. 54 *WdT1.*
i Maria, bp Oct 1803 *WdC*, d 17 July 1884 æ. 80-1-16 *HV;* m Lewis Sanford.
ii Cordelia, b c. 1805, d 24 Feb 1877 æ. 72 (at NH) *WdD;* m Stephen Sanford.
iii Sally Caroline, bp 31 Aug 1806 *WdC*, d 28 Mar 1872 æ. 66 *WdD.*
iv Henrietta, bp 26 June 1808 *WdC*, d 3 Jan 1887 *WdD.*
v Henry Lucius, b 10 May 1810 *F*, d 26 May 1861; m Lucy da. David & Sally (Downs) Cowell, b 28 Apr 1815 *F*, d 21 Nov 1896; she m (2) ——— Webster. Children: 1 Child, d 13 Sep 1837 æ. 0-6 *WdD.* 2 Sarah, d 23 Jan 1839 æ. 4 *WdD.* 3 George Henry, b 6 Mar 1840, d 28 June 1904; m Caroline Austin.
3 HARVEY, b 17 Sep 1781 *F*, d 9 Dec 1855 æ. 74-2-22 *BT2;* m 1805 Sarah da. Gideon & Sarah (Russell) Alling, b c. 1786, d 21

Sep 1862 æ. 77 *BT2.*

i Son, b 23 Sep 1806 *BT2,* d 28 Sep 1806 *BT2.*

ii Sheldon Alling, b 22 Apr 1808 *F,* d 23 Apr 1889 *F;* m Eunice Perkins.

iii Eliza Samantha, b 18 Sep 1810 *F,* d 14 Feb 1876 *F,* m Crownage Lounsbury.

iv Solomon, b 18 June 1813 *F,* d 6 June 1886 æ. 72–4 *WdD;* m Charlotte Hemingway, b c. 1821, d 28 May 1893 æ. 72 *WdD.*

v Beecher Delos, b 11 Feb 1815 *F,* d 30 Oct 1866 æ. 53 *BT 2;* m Betsey da. Guy Perkins, b c. 1821, d 1 Oct 1863 æ. 42 *BT2.*

vi Julius Leonard, b 17 June 1817 *F,* d 17 Feb 1879; m Sophronia Maria Hotchkiss.

vii Theodore Nelson, b 20 Dec 1819 *F,* d 27 Feb 1888; m Lucia da. Alvin & Sally (Nettleton) Sperry.

viii Sarah Finette, b 29 Oct 1822 *F,* d 15 Jan 1878; m 5 Mar 1848 DeWitt Clinton Castle of Seymour.

ix Orlando Thomas, b 8 Aug 1825 *F,* d 11 Dec 1828 æ. 3–3 *BT2.*

x Harvey Harpin, b 16 Feb 1828 *F;* res. Ppt; m 15 Feb 1852 Charlotte Eliza da. Justus & Rebecca (Sperry) Alling.

xi Margaret Dianthe, b 16 June 1830 *F,* d 14 Feb 1872; m Matthew Trewhella of C.

4 **Eleanor**, b 23 Mar 1783 *F;* m 1805 Abner Baldwin.

5 **Elizabeth**, b 25 Apr 1785 *F,* bp 8 May 1788 *WdC.*

FAM. 74. DAVID & ABIGAIL (ATWATER) HOTCHKISS:

6 **Mary**, b 19 Feb 1790 *F.*

7 **Martha**, b 12 Jan 1792 *F,* d 9 Apr 1843 æ. 52 *WdD;* m Anson Sperry.

8 **Harriet**, b 29 Mar 1798 *F,* bp 27 May 1798 *WdC;* m 1 May 1816 *WdC*—Garry Johnson.

FAM. 75. LEVI & PHEBE (HITCHCOCK) HOTCHKISS:

1 **Elipha**, bp Feb 1778 *DC,* d 21 Sep 1858 æ. 81 *DT;* m Nancy Folsom, b 10 May 1780, d 15 Nov 1865 æ. 86.

i William; m.

ii Albert, d 1864; m 1825 Sally M. Curtis.

iii Burr, b 6 July 1806 *DT1,* d 30 Dec 1854 *DT1;* m.

iv John, b c. 1808, d 23 Aug 1831 æ. 23 *DT1;* m Clarissa Curtis.

v Mary Ann; m David L. Parmelee.

vi Harriet; m Lucius Alling.

vii Eli; m m Susan Kimberly, b 12 Sep 1814.

viii Phebe, b 1 Mar 1814; m 21 Mar 1834 William M. French.

ix Amelia.

x Jane, b 26 Dec 1820, d 12 Aug 1870; m 12 Feb 1841 Augustus Parker.

xi Harvey, b 1822; m Augusta A. Kimberly, b 8 June 1823.

2 **Lucy**, bp 28 May 1780 *DC.*

3 BETSEY, bp 18 Aug 1782 *DC*, d 21 Aug 1819 æ. 37 *DT1*.
4 PHEBE, b c. 1784, d 19 Aug 1873 æ. 89 *DT*.

FAM. 75. LEVI & —— (——) HOTCHKISS:
5 LEVI; m Grace ——, who d 30 Aug 1863 æ. 72 *DT1*.
6 DAVID.
7 ABIGAIL; m Isaac Thompson.

FAM. 76. PHILO & —— (——) HOTCHKISS:
1 PHILO.
2 NANCY.

FAM. 77. ELI & EUNICE (ATWATER) HOTCHKISS:
1 HARRIET, b 12 Nov 1786 *NHT1*; d 15 Mar 1869 æ. 82 (at Canterbury) *NHT1*; m Justus Harrison.
2 CLARISSA; m (1) Minor Hotchkiss; m (2) Reuben Skinner of N. Y. City.
3 LYDIA, bp 21 Sep 1794 *NHC1*, d 2 Sep 1826 æ. 32 *NHT1*; m James Bradley.
4 ELIZABETH M., b c. 1797, d 30 Aug 1803 æ. 6 *NHT1*.

FAM. 78. OBADIAH & HANNAH (LEWIS) HOTCHKISS:
1 SILAS, b 11 Oct 1784 *F*, d 2 Oct 1795 æ. 11 *NHT1*, *NHx*, 3 Oct æ. 12 *NHC1*,
2 LEWIS, b 25 Dec 1786 *NHT1*, d 14 Oct 1859 *NHT1*; m Hannah da. Joseph & Olive (Clark) Trowbridge, b 24 Mar 1792 *NHT1*, d 24 Aug 1873 *NHT1*.
3 HANNAH FRANCES, b 7 Apr 1796 *F*, d 4 May 1815 æ. 19 *NHT1*.

FAM. 79. JUSTUS & ELIZABETH (HOTCHKISS) HOTCHKISS:
1 SON, stillborn 11 Apr 1796 *NHC1*.

FAM. 79. JUSTUS & SUSANNA (HOTCHKISS) HOTCHKISS:
2 HENRY, b 29 Apr 1801 *F*, bp 8 Nov 1801 *NHC1*, d 15 Dec 1871; m 22 May 1823 *NHV*—Elizabeth Daggett da. Benjamin & Hannah (Blakeslee) Prescott.
3 LUCIUS, b 1 Mar 1803 *F*, bp 22 July 1804 *NHC1*, d 29 Nov 1880 æ. 77-9 *NHV*; m (1) 18 Oct 1827 Maria Melcher Street, who d 3 Sep 1833 æ. 36 *NHV*; m (2) 28 Sep 1834 *NHV*—Catherine Ladd Street.

HOTCHKISS. MISCELLANEOUS. ENOCH of NH m 28 Oct 1783 *WatV*—Lois Wolcott; rem. to Mich. 1819 & d near Pontiac......HENRY of G m 13 Oct 1793 *EHC*—Liza Barnes......RUTH m 26 June 1784 *EHC*—Roger Lord......ROBERT m Clarana Turner of Bristol......ELIPHALET m Hannah da. Eli Smith of Wd, b c. 1775; had Juliana, b 30 July 1799 *CV* & Elizabeth, b 8 Aug 1801 *CV*; rem. to Stamford, N. Y.......LYMAN, b 1764, d 15 May 1830......PHILO, b c. 1778, d 16 July 1858 æ. 80 *BT4*; m Patty da. Abel & Anna (Chatfield) Lines, b c. 1783, d 10 Mar 1864 æ. 81 *BT4*. (Probably, Lewis Hotchkiss, who d 17 Aug 1890 æ. 71 *BT4* was a s. of Philo). Children: 1 Laura, b 21 June 1809 *CV*. 2 Emily, b 23 Jan 1813 *CV*.......MAJOR, b c. 1788, d 29 June 1851 æ. 63 *BT4*; m Ada ——, b c. 1787, d 8 May 1845 æ. 58 *BT4*.

HOUGH. We are indebted to E. C. Hough, Esq., of Washington, D. C., for some of the records included in the following account of the Wallingford branch of the Hough family.

FAM. 1. SAMUEL, s. of William & Sarah (Caulkins), b 9 Mar 1653 (at New London), d 14 Mar 1718 *WV;* m (1) 25 Nov 1679 *Farm*—Susanna da. Simon Wrotham, who d 5 Sep 1684; m (2) 18 Aug 1685 Mary da. James & Ann (Withington) Bate, bp Jan 1654/5 *Haddam.*

(By 1): 1 WILLIAM, b 22 Aug 1680 *Norwich,* d [9 Oct 1765]; Dr.; res. W 1710, Norwich 1732, W 1745, Saybrook 1754; m (1) Mehitabel da. John & Sarah (Jones) Pratt, b 6 Sep 1685 *Saybrook,* d 5 Feb 1726 *WV;* m (2) 14 Dec 1726 *WV*—Elizabeth da. Eleazer & Mary (Bunnell) Peck, wid. Samuel Abernathy, who d 8 June 1740 *WV, WC2.*

(By 1): *i* Mary, b 10 Sep 1710 *WV.*

Samuel, b 5 July 1712 *WV,* d 8 Oct 1713 *WV.*

iii Mehitabel, b 15 Aug 1714 *WV;* m 14 May 1741 *WV*—Ichabod Starke of Lebanon.

iv Deborah, b 17 Dec 1716 *WV;* m 20 June 1737 *WC2*—Nehemiah Pratt of Saybrook.

v Ann, b 28 Dec 1718 *WV;* m 27 Oct 1737 *WV*—Samuel Austin.

vi Abiah, b 15 May 1721 *WV,* d 18 Aug 1797 æ. 77 *WC2;* m 17 Dec 1746 *WC2*—Noah Austin.

vii Temperance, b 25 Feb 1724 *WV,* d 12 Oct 1759 *WV, WC 2;* m 16 Oct 1745 *WV*—Abel Austin.

(By 2): *viii* Samuel, b 28 Dec 1727 *WV,* d 1746 (at Cape Breton).

ix Susanna, b 30 Mar 1730 *WV,* d 30 July 1752 *WC2.*

x William, b c. 1732, d 3 Feb 1816; res. Stafford 1773; m 20 Dec 1752 *WV*—Mary da. Daniel & Martha (Doolittle) Hall, b 17 Sep 1733 *WV,* d c. 1817 (insane). **FAM. 2.**

xi Simon, b 11 Jan 1734 *WV,* d 15 Dec 1819 (Richmond, Mass.); res. Saybrook, rem. to Richmond 1784; m (1) 13 Dec 1759 Lucy Pratt, who d 11 Aug 1761 æ. 28, by whom he had 1 child (d in infancy); m (2) 27 Oct 1763 Hannah ———, who d 17 Jan 1777 æ. 45, by whom he had 5 children; m (3) 20 Apr 1777 Lucy Sherrill, who d 13 Nov 1836 æ. 97-6.

xii Benjamin, bp 16 Oct 1738 *WC2.*

2 SAMUEL, b 15 Feb 1681 *WV* [1682], d 30 Nov 1702.

3 SUSANNA, b 27 Nov 1683 *WV;* m 10 Feb 1707 *Saybrook*—Joseph Andrews of Farm.

(By 2): 4 HANNAH, d s. p.; m John Lathrop.

5 JAMES, b 15 Dec 1688 *WV,* d 20 Oct 1740 *WV;* m (1) Hannah Clark, who d 3/4 Mar 1718 *WV;* m (2) 9 July 1718 *WV*—Sarah da. Michael & Sarah Mitchell; she m (2) 16 Jan 1754 *WC 2*—Matthias Hitchcock.

(By 1): *i* Samuel, b 12 July 1712 *WV,* d 26 Aug 1776 æ. 66 *WT2;* m 7 Nov 1734 *WV*—Mehitabel da. Samuel & Hannah (Benedict) Royce, b 2 Sep 1712 *WV,* d 25 Dec 1774 æ.

62 *WT2*. **FAM. 3**.

ii Phineas, b 11 Apr 1714 *WV*, d 11 Sep 1797 æ. 85 *WT2*, 2 Sep æ. 84 *WC2;* m (1) 5 Jan 1737 *WV*—Hannah da. John & Prudence (Royce) Austin, who d 25 Mar 1778 *WV;* m (2) 22 Oct 1779 *WV*—Sarah, wid. Stanley, "wife of Phinehas" d 24 Aug 1791 æ. 67 *WC2;* m (3) Lydia ——. **FAM. 4.**

iii Joseph, b c. 1716, d 5 Jan 1809 æ. 92 *WV;* Census (W) 1-1-2; m (1) 27 June 1745 *WV*—Katharine da. Theophilus & Sarah (Street) Yale, b 25 May 1720 *WV*, d 5 Oct 1767 æ. 48 *WV;* m (2) 17 Apr 1768 *WV*—Ruth Beardslee, b c. 1730, d 6 Aug 1812 æ. 83 *WV*. **FAM. 5.**

iv Hannah, b c. 1718; m 15 Jan 1736 *WV*—Ephraim Andrews.

(By 2): *v* Ephraim, b 9 Apr 1719 *WV*, d 16 Feb 1781 æ. 62 *WT2;* m (1) 12 Nov 1739 *WV*—Hannah da. Robert & Joanna (Gaylord) Royce, b 1 July 1716 *WV*, d 16 Feb 1777 æ. 61 *WT2;* m (2) 5 June 1777 *EHC*—Lydia da. James & Dorothy (Morris) Denison, wid. Jacob Goodsell; Census, Lydia (W) 0-0-1. **FAM. 6.**

vi Daniel, b 6 Mar 1721 *WV*, d 25 July 1768 *WV*, *WC2*, æ. 49 *WT2;* Ens.; m (1) 20 Jan 1741 *WV*—Mindwell da. Nathaniel & Lydia (Hall) Judd, b 10 Apr 1719 *WV*, d 21 Mar 1741/2 *WV;* m (2) 29 Nov 1743 *WV*—Violet Benton. **FAM. 7.**

vii Abigail; m 6 Nov 1740 *WV*—Samuel Holt.

viii Ebenezer, b 22 Jan 1726 *WV;* Census (C) 2-2-5; m (1) Lydia ——, who d 20 July 1757 *WV*, 21 July æ. 35 *NoBC2;* m (2) 17 Nov 1757 *WV*—Abigail Plumb. **FAM. 8.**

ix David, b 28 Feb 1728 *WV*, d 18 Oct 1729 *WV*.

x Sarah, b 18 Oct 1730 *WV*, d 10 Nov 1741 *WV*.

xi David, b 28 Jan 1733 *WV*, d 27 June 1752 *WC2*, æ. 20 *WV*.

xii James, b 24 Mar 1735 *WV*, d 9 Nov 1754 *WC2*.

xiii Barnabas, b 5 Sep 1737 *WV;* m 29 Jan 1760 *WC2*—Esther Weeks. **FAM. 9.**

xiv Mary, b 25 Nov 1739 *WV*.

FAM. 2. WILLIAM & MARY (HALL) HOUGH:

1 SUSANNA, b 24 May 1755 *WV*, bp 26 Aug 1756 *WC2*, d 24 Nov 1756 *WV*, "child" 25 Nov *WC2*.

2 MARY, b 22 June 1756 *WV*, bp 26 Aug 1756 *WC2;* [m 28 Feb 1776 *WV*—Moses Hall].

3 BENJAMIN, d 1840 (Quebec); m Phebe Crane.

4 ELIZABETH, b 30 July 1762 *WV*.

5 HULDAH, b 28 July 1765 *WV;* m Winslow Heath.

6 WILLIAM, b 24 Apr 1767 *F*, d 29 Aug 1854 (W. Leyden); res. Cambridge, N. Y.; m 18 Aug 1791 Eunice da. John Skiff, b

10 Sep 1772 (Adams, Mass.), d 25 May 1845 (Queensbury, N. Y.)

7 SAMUEL, b 25 Jan 1770*F*, d Nov 1843 (Saybrook); m Phebe Root.

FAM. 3. SAMUEL & MEHITABEL (ROYCE) HOUGH:

1 JOHN, b 20 Sep 1735 *WV*, bp 21 Sep 1735 *WC2*, d 24 Feb 1788 æ. 53 *WT2*, æ. 52 *WC2;* Lieut.; m 10 Jan 1760 *WV*, *WC2*—Lois da. Nathaniel & Elizabeth (Hull) Merriam, b 28 July 1740 *WV.*

i Samuel, b 4 Nov 1760 *WV;* Census (W) 1-0-2; m 19 July 1787 *WC2*—Anna Page.

ii Matthew, b 1 Mar 1763 *WV;* Census (W) 1-2-1; m 15 Nov 1787 *WC2*—Mercy Cowles.

iii Chauncey, b 14 June 1765 *WV.*

iv John, b c. 1767, d 5 Dec 1776 æ. 10 *WT2.*

v Asahel, b 1 Dec 1769 *WV.*

vi Keturah, b 4 Mar 1773 *WV*, d 2 Mar 1795 *CC;* m 17 Nov 1791 *WC2*—Merriman Hotchkiss.

vii Mehitabel, b 9 July 1775 *WV.*

viii Lois.

FAM. 4. PHINEAS & HANNAH (AUSTIN) HOUGH:

1 HANNAH, b 13 Mar 1738 *WV*, bp 19 Mar 1737/8 *WC2;* m (1) 10 Dec 1755 *WV*, *WC2*—James Scofield; m (2) 25 Dec 1777 Moses Hall.

2 LYDIA, b 27 May 1740 *WV*, bp 1 June 1740 *WC2;* m 7 June 1759 *WV*, *WC2*—Ezekiel Royce.

3 JAMES, b 31 July 1743 *WV*, bp 31 July 1743 *WC2*, d 14 Sep 1794 æ. 51 *WT2;* Census (W) 2-4-3; m (1) 15 Dec 1768 *WV*—Lucy da. Theophilus & Hannah (Avery) Hall, b 20 Aug 1741 *WV*, d 5 Oct 1775 *WV*, æ. 34 *WT2;* m (2) 6 Nov 1777 *WV*—Deborah da. Joseph & Deborah (Royce) Merriam, wid. Alling Royce, b 18 Oct 1743 *WV*, d 18 Aug 1780 *WV;* m (3) Martha ——, who d 1811.

(By 1): *i* James Avery, b 21 Mar 1770 *WV*, d 9 May 1827 æ. 57 *WT2;* m 19 Apr 1792 *WC2*—Sarah Todd, who d 21 Nov 1842 æ. 75 *WT2;* she m (2) —— Merriam.

ii Lucy, b 23 Mar 1772 *WV* d 16 Dec 1774 *WV.*

iii Hannah, b 31 Jan 1774 *WV;* m Asahel Royce.

(By 2): *iv* Deborah, b 29 July 1780 *WV;* m 10 Nov 1803 *WC2*—John Way.

(By 3?): *v* Phineas; m 21 Nov 1804 *WC2*—Desire Cook.

vi John.

vii Theophilus.

viii Reuben.

4 PHINEAS, b 16 Sep 1745 *WV*, bp 22 Sep 1745 *WC2*, d 1 Aug 1776 *WV*, æ. 31 (in Army, bu. at N. Y.) *WT2;* m 17 Feb 1768 *WV*—Huldah da. Ebenezer & Abigail (Root) Royce, b 10 May 1749 *WV;* she m (2) 4 Sep 1777 *WV*—John Merriam.

i Oliver, b 1 Mar 1770 *WV;* Census (W) 1-0-0.

ii Levi, b 2 May 1773 *WV;* m 14 Nov 1793 *WC2*—Lucretia Merriam.

iii Huldah, b 16 July 1776 *WV*, d 2 Apr 1777 *WV*.

5 MERCY, b 14 Aug 1747 *WV*, bp 9 (?) Aug 1747 *WC2*, d 6 Feb 1820 æ. 72 *WT2;* m Ensign Hough.

6 RACHEL, b 22 Apr 1750 *WV*, "child" bp 8 (?) Apr 1750 *WC2;* m 2 Nov 1769 *WV*—Joseph Shailer.

7 ANN, b 18 Apr 1752 *WV*, bp 19 Apr 1752 *WC2;* m 28 May 1772 *WV*—Timothy Hall.

FAM. 5. JOSEPH & KATHARINE (YALE) HOUGH;

1 MARY, b 15 July 1746 *WV*, d 29 Nov 1769 *WV*.

2 LOIS, b 24 June 1747 *WV*, d 12 Nov 1748 *WV*.

3 JOSEPH, b 12 Sep 1748 *WV*, d 11 Sep 1811 æ. 63 *WT1;* Census (W) 2-1-5; m 8 Nov 1770 *WV*, 9 Nov *CC*—Elizabeth da. Ebenezer & Jane (Andrews) Atwater, b 13 Apr 1748 *WV*.

i Molly, b 11 Sep 1771 *WV*, d 24 Feb 1839 æ. 67 *WT1;* m Salmon Carter.

ii Chauncey, b 17 Nov 1773 *WV*, d 18 May 1815 æ. 41 *WT1;* m Lura da. James & Mary (Tyler) Hough, b 26 Nov 1775 *WV*.

iii Esther, b 24 Mar 1777 *WV;* m Joel Tyler.

iv Horace.

v Elizabeth; m Dan Andrews.

vi Selina; m ——— Blakeslee of Catskill, N. Y.

4 LENT, b 4 Apr 1750 *WV*, d 8 Oct 1837 æ. 87; Census (W) 1-1-3; m (1) 20 Jan 1774 *WV*—Rebecca da. Jonathan & Hannah (Barnes) Tuttle, b 29 Aug 1755, d 22 Aug 1798 æ. 44 *WT1;* m m (2) 6 Jan 1799 *NoHC*—Mary [da. James & Lydia (Mansfield)] Pierpont, wid. Timothy Andrews, b c. 1757, d 27 June 1832 æ. 75 *WT1*.

(By 1): *i* Lucy, b 27 Nov 1774 *WV*, d 28 July 1802 æ. 28 *WT1;* m Dickerman Hall.

ii Hannah, b 27 Nov 1776 *WV*, d s. p.; m Ira Hall.

iii Serajah, b 26 Mar 1780 *WV*, d 3 Aug 1853; m 18 Feb 1801 Elizabeth Avery, b 27 Sep 1782, d 14 Aug 1870.

(By 2?): *iv* Almeria, b 6 Nov 1797 *F*, bp 29 Dec 1799 *NoHC*.

5 LOIS, b 5 Dec 1752 *WV*, bp 10 Dec 1752 *WC2;* m 27 Oct 1774 *WV*—Andrew Hough.

6 DAVID, b 2 Nov 1754 *WV*.

7 JOEL, b 27 Jan 1757 *WV*, d 9 Sep 1843 æ. 87 *HT3;* m (1) 30 Mar 1780 *WV*—Sarah da. Amos & Sarah (Moss) Royce, b 3 Sep 1754 *WV*, d 20 Sep 1801 æ. 47 *HT3;* m (2) Dec 1801 Thankful da. Amos & Sarah (Moss) Royce, b 19 Oct 1769 *WV*, d 14 Apr 1820 æ. 51 *HT3;* m (3) 20 Dec 1820 Ruth Hart, wid. Asahel Munson, b c. 1770, d 8 Jan 1837 æ. 67 (at H) *NoBT1*.

(By 1): *i* Harvey, b 26 June 1781 *NHV*, d 7 July 1854 (Summer Hill, Cayuga Co., N. Y.); m 27 July 1802 Lucy (Adams) Stoddard, b 23 May 1776, d 17 June 1854.

ii Ira, b 7 Mar 1783 *NHV*, d 13 June 1851 æ. 68 *WolT;* m (1) 15 Nov 1808 Asenath da. Joel & Mary (Rogers) Hotchkiss, b 23 Mar 1787 *WatV*, d 31 Aug 1810 æ. 24 *WolT;* m (2) 1 Jan 1812 Mary da. Isaac & Jane (Berry) Hubbard, b 24 Dec 1785, d 6 Mar 1869 æ. 83 *WolT.*

iii Ezra, b 29 Apr 1784 *HV*, bp 27 June 1784 *HC1*, d 22 Apr 1854 (Summer Hill, N. Y.); m 3 Apr 1806 Sally Honeywell.

iv Joel, b 28 Dec 1785 *HV*, bp 19 Feb 1786 *HC1*, d 28 Jan 1800 æ. 15 *HT3.*

v Julia, b 23 Dec 1787 *HV*, d 1818; m Samuel Atwater.

vi Sally, b 20 Aug 1789 *HV*, bp 25 Oct 1789 *HC1*, d 24 Oct 1829 æ. 40 *HT3.*

vii Joseph, b 21 Feb 1791 *HV*, bp 10 Apr 1791 *HC1;* res. C; m Esther Ulyssa da. Bowers Moss, b 13 Dec 1795, d 11 June 1863.

viii Mary, b 25 Nov 1793 *HV*, bp 26 Jan 1794 *HC1*, d 29 Mar 1851; m Parsons Ives.

ix Amos Rice, b 30 Jan 1797 *HV*, bp 9 Apr 1797 *HC1*, d 13 Dec 1869 æ. 73 *HT3*, æ. 72–10–17 *HV;* m Nancy da. Nehemiah Royce, b 28 Sep 1797, d 11 Sep 1870.

x Joel, b 14 Aug 1801 *HV*, bp 27 Sep 1801 *HC1;* res. N. Y. State; m 31 Dec 1829 (Fabius, N. Y.)—Emily Winegar.

(By 2): *xi* Alma, b 4 Nov 1802 *HV*, d s. p. 14 Dec 1829; m 2 Feb 1824 Chauncey Munson.

xii Sylvester, b 4 Feb 1809 *F*, d 19 Feb 1895; res. Rochester, N. Y.; m 12 Feb 1832 Sally Mitchell, who d 7 Mar 1894.

8 KATHARINE, b 5 May 1759 *WV;* m Edmund Smith.

9 JAMES, b 6 Dec 1761 *WV*, d 3 Dec 1762 *WV*.

10 JAMES, b 1 June 1764 *WV*, d 16 Jan 1826 æ. 62 *WT1;* Census (W) 1-2-3; m Mary da. Divan & Lydia (Yale) Berry, b 1 Apr 1768 *WV*, d 13 Apr 1840 æ. 72 *WT1.*

i Divan B., b c. 1788, d 5 Oct 1795 æ. 7 *WT1.*

ii David, b c. 1791, d 11 Oct 1795 æ. 4 *WT1.*

iii James, b c. 1794, d 11 Oct 1795 æ. 1 *WT1.*

iv Mary, b c. 1797, d 2 May 1881 æ. 83 *WT1.*

v James, b 5 Mar 1799, d 25 Apr 1855; m Mary Tyler da. Nehemiah Rice.

vi Joel, d 30 Sep 1886; m June 1836 Mary da. Silas & Rebecca (Hubbard) Rice, b 9 Mar 1809, d June 1878.

vii Caroline, b [Apr 1802], d 1 July 1803 æ. 0-15 *WT1.*

viii Emeline, b [Apr 1802], d 29 June 1803 æ. 0-14 *WT1.*

ix Isaac, b c. 1804, d 1804 æ. 5 wks.

x Lucy, d s. p.; m Hezekiah Root.

xi Emeline; m Wm. Bunce of Kensington.

11 SARAH, b 26 May 1767 *WV*, d 11 Mar 1832 (Jewett, Greene Co., N. Y.); m 31 Jan 1793 Benajah Royce.

FAM. 6. EPHRAIM & HANNAH (ROYCE) HOUGH:

1 ABIGAIL, b 29 Nov 1740 *WV*, d 10 Aug 1743 *WV*.

2 SARAH, b 16 Jan 1741/2 *WV;* m 24 Mar 1761 *WC2*—John Denison.

3 ABIGAIL, b 21 Feb 1743/4 *WV*, bp 26 Feb 1744 *WC2;* m 19 June 1766 *WV*—John Carter.

4 EPHRAIM, b 6 Jan 1745/6 *WV;* Census (W) 2-3-5; m (1) 3 Oct 1766 *WV*—Eunice da. Andrew & Esther (Royce) Andrews, b 6 Dec 1746 *WV*, d 16 Dec 1774 *WV*, æ. 27 *WT1;* m (2) 24 May 1775 *F*—Sarah da. Samuel & Mary (Alling) Dickerman, wid. Joel Munson, b 29 Dec 1741 *NHV*, d 7 Mar 1784 *WV;* m (3) 19 Jan 1785 *WV*—Lydia da. Samuel & Mary (Leek) Alling.

(By 1): *i* Robert Royce, b 22 July 1767 *WV*.

ii Eliakim, b 27 July 1769 *WV;* m 12 Feb 1795 *CC*—Sarah da. Barnabas & Rachel (Curtis) Lewis, b 15 Sep 1770 *WV*.

iii Sarah, b 27 Oct 1772 *WV*.

iv Eunice, b 5 Dec 1774 *WV*.

(By 2): *v* Ephraim, b 28 Sep 1777 *F*, d 24 Jan 1783 *F*.

vi Isaac, b 17 June 1779 *F*.

vii Levi, b 24 Jan 1783 *F*.

(By 3): *viii* Lydia, b 23 Nov 1785 *WV*.

ix Ephraim, b 9 Oct 1787 *WV*, d 3 Feb 1789 *F*.

x Ephraim, b 27 Oct 1789 *WV*, d 1876; m 16 July 1816 *F*—Jerusha da. Abel & Deborah (Sperry) Sanford. **FAM. 10.**

xi Alling, b 3 Nov 1791 *F*.

xii Phebe, b 6 Mar 1796 *WV*.

xiii James, b 22 July 1798 *WV*.

5 ANDREW, b 27 Dec 1747 *WV*, bp Dec 1747 *CC*, "child" d 10 Sep 1748 *WC2*, d July 1748 *CC*.

6 ANDREW, b 17 Dec 1749 *WV*, bp Feb 1749/50 *CC;* Census (W) 1-1-4; m 27 Oct 1774 *WV*—Lois da. Joseph & Katharine (Yale) Hough, b 5 Dec 1752 *WV*.

i Thankful, b 26 Aug 1775 *WV*.

ii David, b 3 Aug 1777 *WV*.

iii Lois, b 11 May 1781 *WV*, d Summer 1802 *WC2*.

iv Kate, b 21 Aug 1783 *WV*.

v Andrew, b 3 July 1785 *WV*.

vi Amy, b 4 Oct 1788 *WV*.

7 HANNAH, b 17 June 1751 *WV;* m ——— Parker.

8 THANKFUL, b 29 Mar 1753 *WV*, bp 17 June 1753 *WC2*, d 18 Aug 1753 *WV*, *WC2*.

9 AMBROSE, b 2 Sep 1754 *WV*, *WT2*, d 30 June 1825 æ. 70 *WT2;* Dea.; Census (C) 1-1-5; m (1) 14 Mar 1776 *WV*—Eunice da. Samuel & Abigail (Hough) Holt, b 15 May 1755 *WV;* m (2) Abigail da. Andrew & Esther (Morris) Goodyear.

10 LOIS, b 3 June 1756 *WV*, bp 11 July 1756 *WC2*, "child" d 2 Aug

1757 *WC2*.

FAM. 7. DANIEL & VIOLET (BENTON) HOUGH:

1 MINEWELL, b 5 May 1745 *WV*, bp 5 May 1745 *WC2*, d 8 June 1807 æ. 63 *WT2;* m 31 Mar 1763 *WV*—Benjamin Curtis.

2 ENSIGN, b 1 Sep 1746 *WV*, bp 7 Sep 1746 *WC2*, d 3 Dec 1813 æ. 67 *WT2;* Dr.; Census (W) 1-2-4; m (1) 27 Apr 1769 *WV*—Chloe da. Moses & Mary (Clark) Yale, b 20 Nov 1745 *WV*, d 24 June 1771 æ. 26 *WT2;* m (2) Sarah da. Abel & Sarah (Atkins) Yale, b 1 Feb 1744/5 *WV*, d 11 Jan 1775 æ. 31 *WT2;* m (3) Mercy da. Phineas & Hannah (Austin) Hough, b 14 Aug 1747 *WV*, d 6 Feb 1820 æ. 72 *WT2*.

(By 1): *i* "Roscilla", b 15 June 1770 *WV*, Rosetta d 9 Mar 1778 æ. 8 *WT2*.

(By 2): *ii* Ira, b c. 1772, d 27 July 1777 æ. 5 *WT2*.

iii Yale I., b c. 1775, d 23 Apr 1819 æ. 44 *WT2;* m Lucy ———, who d 4 Feb 1807 æ. 28-2 *WT2*.

(By 3); *iv* Chloe, b c. 1777, d 1 Feb 1820 æ. 42 *WT2;* m Samuel Tibbals.

v Sally, b c. 1779, d 11 Aug 1864 æ. 85 *WT2;* m 24 Feb 1795 *NHSupCt*—Abijah Bradley; she div. him 1814.

vi Isaac J., b c. 1781, d 26 Feb 1852 æ. 71 *WT2;* Dr.

vii Rosetta; m Allen A. Cowles.

3 ELIJAH, b 23 Jan 1747/8 *WV*, bp 24 Jan 1748 *WC2;* Lieut.; Census (Southwick, Mass.) 2-4-3; m 27 Apr 1769 *WV*—Mary da. Gideon & Eunice (Tuttle) Ives, b 5 Aug 1746 *WV*. Child: Lemuel, b 23 June 1770 *WV*.

4 THOMAS, b 27 Oct 1750 *WV*, bp 29 Oct 1749 *WC2;* Dea.; Census (Southwick, Mass.) 1-5-3; m 30 Sep 1772 *WV*—Rebecca da. David & Elizabeth (Merriam) Ives, b 7 Mar 1752 *WV*. Children recorded *WV:* Elizabeth 24 Feb 1774, Bezaleel 27 Mar 1776, Horatio 5 Jan 1778.

5 SAMUEL, b 12 Mar 1751 *WV*, bp 17 Mar 1751 *WC2;* Census (W) 1-2-3; m 20 Sep 1776 *WV*—Thankful da. Phineas & Anna Hall, b 27 Jan 17[50] *WV*.

6 EUNICE, b 30 Mar 1753 *WV*, bp 25 Mar 1753 *WC2;* m 22 Dec 1774 *WV*—Giles Griswold.

7 DOLLY, b 30 Jan 1755 *WV*, bp 2 Feb 1755 *WC2;* m 25 Sep 1771 *WV*—David Ives.

8 CALEB, b 13 Feb 1757 *WV*, "child" bp 1757 *WC2;* m 27 Nov 1777 *WV*—Rebecca [da. Benjamin & Susanna (Morgan)] Andrews.

9 LYDIA, b 9 Nov 1759 *WV*, d s. p.; "infant" d 23 Dec 1758 *WC2*.

10 HANNAH, b 4 Feb 1762 *WV*, d s. p.

11 DANIEL, b 2 Nov 1763 *WV*, d 8 Sep 1803 (Charlotte, Vt.); Dr.; Census (Charlotte, Vt.) 2-2-3; m Mary da. ——— & Mary (Yale) Barker, b c. 1765, d 20 Mar 1826 æ. 61 (Delaware, Ohio) *F;* she m (2) c. 1805 Levi Foote.

i Sylvester, b 19 June 1785 (at Meriden) *F*, d 28 Feb 1836

(Delaware, O.); m 1 May 1806 (Charlotte, Vt)—Sarah da. John & Joanna (Taylor) Williams, b 15 Jan 1786 (at L), d 1 Oct 1868 (Delaware, O.).

ii Daniel, d 5 Nov 1849 (Ohio); Dr.; m Sophronia Sheldon.

iii Polly, b c. 1790 (Charlotte, Vt.), d 1 Oct 1803.

iv Sally, b c. 1792 (Charlotte), d 27 Sep 1803.

v Hannah, b c. 1795 (Charlotte), d 9 Jan 1866 æ. 71; m Eleazer Copeland of Delaware Co., O.

FAM. 8. EBENEZER & LYDIA (———) HOUGH:

1 BUEL, b 25 Mar 1748 *WV*, bp 27 Mar 1748 *WC2*, d c. 1835 (Alexandria Bay, N. Y.); Census (Wy) 1-3-5; m 5 Sep 1770 *Roxbury C*—Elizabeth Torrance.

i Lydia.

ii Polly.

iii Betsey.

iv Joel, d 1843; res. Williamstown & Floyd, N. Y.; joined the Mormons 1840; m Sarah Stimson.

v Amos; res. Cold Water, Mich.; m.

vi David, b 9 Apr 1790 (Roxbury) *F*, d 26 Aug 1852 (Williamstown, N. Y.); m 24 Mar 1813 *F*—Sarah Filkins.

vii Asel, b 12 Aug 1792 *F*, d 9 Sep 1874 (Alexandria, N. Y.; m Susanna C. Russell, b 3 Sep 1795, d 3 Feb 1854.

2 LYDIA, b 28 Aug 1749 *WV*, d 19 July 1759 *WV*, 10 July æ. 8 *NoB C2*.

3 EBENEZER, d 1830; m (1) ——— da. Abraham Tyler, "wife" d 17 June 1786 *HCl*; m (2) 13 Nov 1786 *HCl*—Lois da. Jonathan & Amy (Beecher) Alling, wid. Enos Dickerman, b 22 Feb 1747/8 *NHV*, d between 1821 & 1824; m (3) 9 Dec 1824 *CV*—Abi, wid. Pond of P.

(By 1): *i* Lucinda, b c. 1780, d 16 Mar 1858; m Amos Abiathar Harrison of Northford.

ii Polly; m John Sanford of Rupert, Vt.

iii Mary; m Seth Johnson of Bainbridge, N. Y.

iv Harvey; res. S; m 25 Mar 1804 Margaret Curtis.

(By 2): *v* Chloe, bp 25 Nov 1787 *HCl*; m Eli Pond of Burlington.

(Phebe da. Ebenezer d 14 Feb 1821, mentally deranged, drowned herself near Hough's Mill in C *ConnH*).

4 LUCY, b 23 Apr 1756 *WV*, bp 23 May 1756 *NoBC2*; m (1) 3 Aug 1775 *CC*—Silas Bellamy; m (2) c. 1779 Elihu Lawrence.

FAM. 9. BARNABAS & ESTHER (WEEKS) HOUGH:

1 JOTHAM, bp 1 Apr 1761 *WashingtonC*.

2 BRENEN, b 3 Sep 1762 *WyV*, "Brevin" bp 5 Sep 1762 *Washington C*.

3 ASA, b 14 Apr 1764 *WyV*, bp 19 Aug 1764 *RoxburyC*.

4 SARAH, b 20 Nov 1766 *WyV*, bp 25 Jan 1767 *RoxburyC*.

5 SARAH, bp 29 May 1768 *RoxburyC*.

6 HULDAH, bp 1 Apr 1770 *RoxburyC*.

7 PHEBE, bp 5 Apr 1772 *RoxburyC*.

FAM. 10. EPHRAIM & JERUSHA (SANFORD) HOUGH:

1 ALVIRON SANFORD, b 20 May 1817, d 26 Oct 1889; m 25 Apr 1844 Sarah Anderson Burch.

2 OLIVER PERRY, b 3 Aug 1818, d 10 Jan 1859.

3 HARRIET EMILY, b 11 Feb 1820, d 3 Aug 1843.

4 JAMES EDWIN, b 26 Oct 1821.

5 SYLVIA CAROLINE, b 11 Mar 1823, d 9 Sep 1844.

6 SYLVESTER ALLING, b 4 Dec 1824.

7 EMMA SYLVIRA DARNALL, b 1 May 1842.

8 MARY SYLVIRA NICHOLSON, b 26 Aug 1844.

HOW. Variant, HOWE. EDWARD of Lynn, Mass., by w. Elizabeth, had with others, sons JEREMY (FAM. 1) and EPHRAIM (FAM. 2).

FAM. 1. JEREMY, b 1614, d 16 Jan 1690/1 *NHV;* m Elizabeth ——, who d 23 Jan 1695/6 *NHV*.

1 ZACHARIAH, d June 1703 *WV;* m 22 Mar 1666/7 *NHV*—Sarah niece of Matthew Gilbert, who d 2 Feb 1713 *WV*.

i John, b 21 Dec 1667 *NHV*, d 8 Nov 1732 æ. 65 *EHT;* m Hannah da. Samuel & Sarah (Cooper) Hemingway, b 14 Sep 1670 *NHV*, d 1740. **FAM. 3.**

ii Zachariah, b 31 Mar 1670 *NHV*, d 15 May 1712 *WV;* m 17 Dec 1702 *WV*—Elizabeth da. Samuel & Sarah (Cooper) Hemingway, div. w. Nathaniel Finch, b 16 Feb 1672 *NHV;* she m (3) 5 Aug 1718 *WV*—Samuel Brockett. **FAM. 4.**

iii Matthew, b 2 Jan 1672/3 *WV* ("son" b Jan 1672 *NHV*), d 24 Dec 1727 *WV;* m 31 Dec 1717 *WV*—Elizabeth da. John & Elizabeth (Daniel) Winston, b 13 Mar 1682/3 *NHV*. **FAM. 5.**

iv Sarah, b 30 Oct 1675 *WV*, d 4 Jan 1740 *WV;* m 9 July 1702 *WV*—Nathaniel Curtis.

v Mary, b 14 Dec 1677 *WV*, d 4 Oct 1708 æ. 29 *WV*.

vi Samuel, d s. p. 9 Feb 1713 *WV*.

2 NATHANIEL, d 12 Feb 1723 *WV;* m (1) Elizabeth Curtiss, b c. 1644, d 29 Dec 1713 æ. 69 *WV;* m (2) 9 Aug 1714 *WV*—Sarah da. Robert & Sarah (Potter) Foote, wid. Isaac Curtis, b 12 Feb 1661 *NHV* [1661/2].

(By 1): *i* Elizabeth, b 27 July 1666 *NHV;* m 15 Jan 1684 *WV*—John Martin.

ii Son, b 20 Sep 1669 *NHV*.

iii Son, b July 1671 *NHV*.

iv Elijah, b 9 Sep 1673 *WV*, d 1 Mar 1748/9 *WV;* m 28 Jan 1703 *WV*—Mary da. Matthew & Bethia (Ford) Bellamy, b c. 1676. **FAM. 6.**

v Lydia, b 6 Nov 1675 *WV*.

vi Daniel, b 18 Mar 1677/8 *WV*, d 1705; m Margery da. Samuel & Elizabeth (Peck) Andrews, b 15 Jan 1681 *WV*, d 1710. **FAM. 7.**

vii Abigail, b 7 Aug 1680 *WV*, d 26 Mar 1722 *WV;* m 2 Dec

1702 *WV*—Thomas Twiss.

viii Nathaniel, d before 1736; m 15 Oct 1711 *WV*—Mary Gray. **FAM. 8.**

ix Mary; m Richard Hodges of EH.

4 ELIZABETH, bp 30 Mar 1645 *NHCl;* m May 1669 *NHV*—James Redfield.

5 BATHSHUA, b (as "Bethia"?) 15 May 1648 *NHCl*, bp 1648 *NHCl*, d 27 Dec 1729 æ. 83 (at Mid); m 23 Oct 1677 *NHV*—Col. John Dixwell (under his pseudonym of James Davids).

6 JEREMIAH, b 8 July 1650 *NHV*, bp 1650 *NHCl*. d 22 Sep 1740 æ. 90 *WV;* m (1) 29 Oct 1674 *WV*—Elizabeth [da. Paul & Martha Peck of Hartford], who d 4 Oct 1704 *WV;* m (2) 9 Apr 1705 *WV*—Mary da. Peter & Mary [Preston] Mallory, wid. Eli Roberts & Samuel Cook, b 28 Nov 1656 *NHV*, d 17 Sep 1752 æ. 96 *CTl*, 7 Sep *WV*, 8 Aug æ. 97 *CC*.

(By 1): *i* Jeremiah, b 15 Sep 1675 *WV*, d 12 Sep 1749 æ. 75 *WV;* m (1) 17 Dec 1701 *WV*—Elizabeth da. Joshua & Elizabeth (Ford) Culver, b 21 Aug 1678 *NHV*, d 17 June 1703 *WV;* m (2) 20 Apr 1704 *WV*—Judith da. Samuel & Hope (Parker) Cook, b 29 Feb 1679 *WV*, d 20 Mar 1708 *WV;* m (3) 7 July 1708 *WV*—Mary da. Henry & Mary (Hall) Cook, b 15 July 1678 *Salem, Mass.,V*. **FAM. 9.**

ii Bathsheba, b 13 Sep 1677 *WV;* m (1) John Stow of Mid; m (2) Daniel Hubbard of Haddam.

iii Ephraim, b 20 Feb 1681 *WV*, d 22 July 1684 *WV*.

iv Martha, b 2 Aug 1684 *WV*, d s. p.; m Francis Hendrick.

v Mary, b 22 Sep 1687 *WV*, [bp 27 Apr 1690 *NHCl*?]; m 23 Apr 1713 *MidV*—John Allin of Mid.

vi Ebenezer, b 3 Mar 1690 *WV*.

vii Ruth; m 18 Oct 1716 *WV*—Daniel Tuttle.

viii Elizabeth; m Theophilus Doolittle.

7 JOSEPH, b 22 Oct 1653 *NHV*, bp Sep 1653 *NHCl;* d 1703; m Esther da. Elnathan & Hannah (Baldwin) Botsford, b 18 Oct 1668 *MV*, bp 31 Mar 1669/70 *MCl;* she m (2) Thomas Humiston.

8 JOHN, b 26 June 1656 *NHV*, bp June 1656 *NHCl;* m ——— . Either he or his brother Joseph was probably father of:

i John of Durham, d c. 1744; m 3 Apr 1714 *NHV*—Lydia Seward. Children (incomplete): 1 John, b 24 Dec 1714 *NHV*, bp 8 May 1715 *DurhamC*, d c. 1743. 2 Lydia, b 28 Mar 1717 *NHV*, bp 1717 *NHCl*. 3, 4 Bathsheba & Naomi, b 20 Apr 1720 *NHV*, bp Apr 1720 *NHCl*. 5 Ephraim, bp 24 May 1730 *DurhamC*. Bathsheba m 1737 *NHCCt*—Jeremiah Griswold.

9 EBENEZER, b 26 June 1656 *NHV*, bp June 1656 *NHCl*, d s. p.

FAM. 2. EPHRAIM, b 1625, d 8 Sep 1680 *NHV;* m Ann Hough, b 1630 *F*, d 1712.

1 EPHRAIM, b 3 Apr 1653 *NHV*, d s. p.

2 Sarah, b 25 Jan 1654 *NHV*, [1654/5], d Nov 1743; m 10 Aug 1682 *NHV*—Nathaniel Tuttle.
3 Mary, b 17 Jan 1656 *NHV* [1656/7], d s. p.
4 Samuel, b 1 Sep 1658 *NHV*, d s. p.
5 Daniel, b 1 Jan 1663 *NHV*, d s. p. before 1690.
6 Isaac, b 22 Aug 1666 *NHV*, d s. p. before 1690.
7 Abigail, b 23 Apr 1669 *NHV*, d s. p.
8 Esther, b 18 Nov 1671 *NHV;* m 29 Sep 1692 *NHV*—James Trowbridge.
9 Mary, b 8 Dec 1674 *NHV*, d 6 Apr 1761 (at St)*F;* m Daniel Brown.

FAM. 3. John & Hannah (Hemingway) How:
1 Hannah, b 9 Feb 1693 *NHV*, bp 26 Nov 1699 *NHCl;* m Thomas Robinson.
2 Sarah, b 20 Nov 1695 *NHV*, bp 26 Nov 1699 *NHCl*, d s. p.
3 Mary, b 9 Mar 1697/8 *NHV*, bp 26 Nov 1699 *NHCl;* m Stephen Pardee.
4 John. b 13 Sep 1700 *NHV*, d 7 Jan 1767 *WatV*, 8 Jan *PC;* m (1) 1729 *NHCCt*—Abigail da. John & Hannah Sutliff, who d 22 Jan 1749 *WatV;* m (2) 17 July 1754 *WatV*—Hannah da. Edmund & Sarah Scott, wid. Ebenezer Elwell, b June 1700 *Wat V.*

(By 1): *i* Abigail, b 21 Apr 1729 *WV*, d 16 May 1799 æ. 71 *ThomastonT;* m 18 May 1752 *WatV*—David Blakeslee.
ii Samuel, b 24 July 1730 *WV*, d 22 Jan 1804 *PV;* Census (Wtn) 1-0-4; m (1) 16 Apr 1750 *WatV*—Mary da. Gideon Allyn, wid. ——— Coben; [m (2) Amy da. Josiah & Naomi (Luddington) Tuttle, b 5 May 1745 *WatV*]; m (3) 14 Nov 1780 *WatV*—Elizabeth Benedict **FAM. 10.**
iii Sarah, b 1 Mar 1732 *WV;* m (1) 18 May 1752 *WatV*—Cephas Ford; m (2) 19 Feb 1761 *WatV*—Aaron Luddington.
iv Martha, b 15 Feb 1734 *WV*, d 13 Oct 1814 æ. 80 *Thomaston T;* m 8 July 1752 *WatV*—Ebenezer Ford.
v Hannah, b 6 Mar 1736 *WatV;* m 10 Mar 1755 *WatV*—Obadiah Scott.
vi John, b 6 Apr 1738 *WatV*, d 6 Dec 1758 *WatV.*
vii Elizabeth, b 3 Mar 1740 *WatV.*
viii Mary, b 1 May 1742 *WatV;* she had nat. children: 1 Timothy Humiston, b 6 Nov 1761 *WatV.* 2 Mary, b 8 Nov 1767 *WatV.*
ix Lydia, b 10 Apr 1744 *WatV*, d 20 Apr 1796 æ. 52 *ThomastonT.*
x Zaccheus, b 14 Aug 1746 *WatV*, d 17 Dec 1820 æ. 74 *ThomastonT;* Census (Wtn) 2-0-2; m 7 Dec 1772 *EHC, WatV*—Esther da. Samuel & Hannah (Hemingway) Thompson. A child, John, b 8 Nov 1773 *WatV.*
xi Ephraim, bp 6 Nov 1749 (at Wat)*Dx*, d [c. 1749] *WatV,*

5 ELIZABETH, b 19 Dec 1702 *NHV*, d 8 Jan 1767 æ. 65 *EHT*; m (1) Isaac Penfield; m (2) 9 Dec 1762 *EHC*—Caleb Chidsey.

6 ISAAC, b 18 Feb 1706 *EHV*, d 1759; m Thankful Rogers, who d 1761.

i Joseph, d s. p.

ii Thankful, b 28 Dec 1731 *EHV*, d 1736 æ. 5 *EHV*.

iii John, b 22 May 1734 *EHV*, d 18 Apr 1781 æ. c. 45 (k. by enemy) *EHC*.

iv Isaac, d s. p. 1762.

v Andrew, d s. p. 1762.

vi Samuel; res. Bd, & Claverack, N. Y.; perhaps the Samuel, Census (Hudson, N. Y.) 3-2-7; m 11 Jan 1770 *BdV*—Sarah Rose; had s. Samuel b 30 May 1770 *BdV*.

vii Elizabeth.

viii Sarah.

ix Hannah, b c. 1747, d 7 Nov 1775 æ. c. 28 *EHC*.

x Joshua; m 12 Jan 1778 *WethersfieldC*—Phebe Weaver.

xi William, d s. p.

7 ABIGAIL, b 3 June 1709 *EHV*.

8 LYDIA, b 19 Dec 1711 *EHV*, d 12 Feb 1760 æ. 43 (48?) *EHR*.

9 BATHSHEBA, b 25 June 1715 *EHV*, d 1761; she had a nat. child by Benjamin Robinson, b 1739 *NHCCt*.

FAM. 4. ZACHARIAH & ELIZABETH (HEMINGWAY) HOW:

1 THANKFUL, b 25 Sep 1705 *WV*; m John Parmelee of Bd. PAGE 1245

2 ZACHARIAH, b 22 Feb 1708 *WV*, d 29 Sep 1740 *WV*; m 25 Nov 1729 *WV*—Mary da. Ebenezer & Mary (Harrington) Frisbie, bp 6 Oct 1711 *BdC*; she m (2) 6 Oct 1741 *WV*—Caleb Jones.

i Ebenezer, b 2 Nov 1730 *WV*, d 4 Jan 1731 *WV*.

ii Mary, b 16 Nov 1731 *WV*; m 7 May 1753 *WV*—Stephen Royce; rem. to Tinmouth, Vt.

iii Elizabeth, b 7 Feb 1734 *WV*; m Joseph Wilford of Bd.

iv Lucy, b 27 Oct 1736 *WV*; m 31 Aug 1758 *CornwallC*—John Pierce.

v Abigail, b 2 Aug 1738 *WV*; m 31 Aug 1758 *CornwallC*—Thomas Carter; rem. to Tinmouth, Vt.

vi Mercy, b c. 1740; m (1) 31 May 1759 *CornwallC*—William Johnson; m (2) ——— Winegar of Kent.

3 ELIZABETH, b 5 Apr 1711 *WV*, d s. p.; m 21 Dec 1726 *WV*—Moses Hall.

FAM. 5. MATTHEW & ELIZABETH (WINSTON) HOW:

1 ELIZABETH, b 20 Nov 1719 *WV*; m 8 Oct 1741 *WV*—William Davidson.

2 MARY, b 21 Dec 1721 *WV*; m 1 July 1746 *WV*—Peter Roberts.

FAM. 6. ELIJAH & MARY (BELLAMY) HOW (family incomplete?):

1 ANNA, b 18 Oct 1704 *WV*; m 12 Nov 1729 *NHV*—Stephen Perkins.

2 ELIJAH, b 6 May 1706 *WV*, d 10 Nov 1771 *WV*; m 9 Oct 1744 *WV*—Hannah da. Samuel & Hannah (Thompson) Thorpe, b 11

Feb 1722 *WV;* she rem. to New Hartford 1778.

i Esther, b 25 Dec 1747 *WV;* m 10 Aug 1772 *WV*—Tenance Edson.

ii Martha, b 14 May 1749 *WV*.

iii Mary, b 14 May 1749 *WV*.

iv John, b 22 Oct 1750 *WV*.

v Aaron, b 24 May 1752 *WV*.

vi Lydia, b 1 Apr 1754 *WV*, d soon.

vii Lydia, b 14 Nov 1757 *WV*.

viii Elijah.

3 AARON, b 4 July 1715 *WV*, d 18 Dec 1738 *WV*.

4 EUNICE; m 4 Aug 1736 *WV*—Richard Hackley.

FAM. 7. DANIEL & MARGERY (ANDREWS) HOW:

1 ELIZABETH, b 28 Jan 1700 *WV;* m 18 Dec 1718 *StV*—Thomas Gilbert of St.

2 DANIEL, b 5 July 1701 *WV* (name changed from Waitstill), d 22 Apr 1745 *WtnD;* m (1) Sarah ——— ; m (2) 3 July 1734 *WatV* — Ann da. Isaac & Mary (Morgan) Bronson, b 28 Aug 1709 *WatV;* she m (2) Isaac Tuttle.

(By 1): *i* Elnathan, b 23 Nov 1722 *WV*, d s. p. c. 1781; "incapable".

ii Elizabeth; m 6 Nov 1756 *WatV*—Caleb Clark.

(By 2): *iii* Aaron, b 23 July 1735 *WatV*, d 2 Apr 1737 *WatV*.

iv Ann, b 2 Sep 1737 *WatV*.

v Huldah, b 24 Aug 1739 *WatV*.

vi Daniel, b 4 Oct 1741 *WatV;* Census (Wat) 1-0-0; m 23 June 1763 *WatV*—Damaris da. David & Sarah (Abernathy) Dutton. Children: 1 Elizabeth, b 31 May 1765 *WatV*. 2 Aaron, b 12 Feb 1766 *WatV*.

vii Elizabeth, b 16 Oct 1743 *WatV*, d 7 May 1745 *WatV*, *WtnD*.

3 LOIS, b c. 1703, d 30 Aug 1749 *WtnD;* m 19 June 1722 *WV*—Caleb Clark.

4 DELIVERANCE, b c. 1705, d Dec 1749 *WtnD;* m (1) 26 Oct 1721 *WV*—Gershom Beach; m (2) Daniel Andrews.

FAM. 8. NATHANIEL & MARY (GRAY) HOW:

1 ELIZABETH, b 1 July 1712 *WV*, bp 26 July 1730 *CC;* she had a nat. child by Moses Atwater: Mabel, bp Apr 1734 *CC*.

2 NATHANIEL, b 29 Oct 1714 *WV*, d 27 Feb 1745/6 (at Cape Breton) *WV;* m Mary da. Nathaniel & Sarah Sutliff, b 16 July 1708 *DurhamV;* she rem. after Nathaniel's death to Durham.

i Aaron, b 16 Jan 1739 *WV;* res. Durham & Wat; m (2nd m?) 27 May 1773 *WatV*—Martha [Scott, wid. Hezekiah] Rogers. Children: 1 Mary, b 16 Apr 1774 *WatV;* probably the Mary Howe of C who d 1822, "no near relatives in this district;" estate ordered distributed to 4 heirs, one of whom was Sally Howe. 2 Calvin, b 20 Feb 1776 *WatV*. The w. of Calvin d 12 Nov 1805 *CC*.

ii Zechariah, d 28 Sep 1760 *F&IWRolls*.

iii Noah, b 13 Oct 1745 (at W) *DurhamV;* res. Bristol & P; Census (W) 1-1-4; m (1) Lydia ——— ; [probably m (2) Lydia Scott, wid. Ebenezer Way]. Children by 1st w.; 1 Mary, bp 19 Aug 1770 *Bristolx.* 2 Azor, bp 3 May 1772 *Bristolx;* had a nat. child by Sally Conkling ("Samme Howe", b 1 Mar 1795 *CV*). 3 Lydia, b 24 May 1784 (at P) *CV*, d 5 Apr 1847 æ. 64 *CTI;* m 5 Aug 1817 *CV*—Samuel Atwater.

3 **Sarah**, b 2 Jan 1717 *WV*, d soon.

4 **Susanna**, b 16 Mar 1720 *WV*, d 24 Dec 1773 *WV*.

5 **Sarah**, b 28 July 1722 *WV*, d s. p.

6 **Philip**, b 30 July 1726 *WV;* Census (L) 1-3-3; m 7 Sep 1748 *Bd C*—Elizabeth Pierce.

FAM. 9. Jeremiah & Elizabeth (Culver) How:

1 **Joshua**, b 2 Dec 1702 *WV*, d 13 June 1760 *WV;* m 7 July 1730 *WV*—Elizabeth da. Thomas & Sarah (Gaylord) Judd, b 18 Oct 1695 *WatV*, [bu. 8 May 1768 *NorfolkC*].

i Joshua, b 14 Sep 1731 *WV*, d 1800; Census (Wells, Vt.) 2-1-2; m 14 Oct 1756 *WV*—Miriam da. Samuel & Elizabeth (Doolittle) Blakeslee, b 4 Oct 1735 *WV;* she m (2) Matthias Button. **FAM. 11.**

FAM. 9. Jeremiah & Judith (Cook) How:

2 **Jeremiah**, b 17 Feb 1704/5 *WV;* rem. to Goshen; m 11 Mar 1730 *WV*—Elizabeth da. John & Elizabeth (Hickox) Gaylord.

i Judith, b 19 Dec 1730 *WV;* m 8 Aug 1754 *Goshen*—Jonathan Wadhams.

ii John, b 1 Oct 1732 *WV;* Census (L) 2-1-2; m 15 Apr 1766 *Goshen*—Lydia Norton.

iii Jeremiah, b 24 Dec 1734 *WV*, d 25 Jan 1736 *WV*.

iv Jeremiah, b 17 Nov 1736 *WV;* rem. to Canaan; Census (L) 4-1-3; m 6 Aug 1761 *Goshen*—Martha North.

v Elizabeth, b 18 Sep 1738 *WV*, d 1 Nov 1738 *WV*.

vi Benjamin, b 26 Oct 1739 *WV*, d 22 Jan 1740/1 *WV*.

vii Benjamin, b 15 Sep 1741 *WV*, d 18 Jan 1741/2 *WV*.

viii Elizabeth, b 15 Sep 1742 *WV;* m 27 May 1762 *Goshen*—Daniel Norton.

ix Esther, b 5 Mar 1743/4 *WV;* m 26 Nov 1766 *Goshen*—David Merrills.

x Joel, b 17 Mar 1744/5 *WV*, bp 28 Apr 1745 *WC2*, d 28 June 1745 *WV*.

xi Joseph, b 9 Oct 1746 *WV;* Census (L) 2-1-6; m 24 Oct 1768 *Goshen*—Prudence Norton.

xii Ruth, b 4 Oct 1748 *WV;* m 27 Feb 1766 *Goshen*—Royce Orvis.

3 **Judith**, b 22 Oct 1706 *WV;* m (1) 19 Jan 1732 *WV*—Elihu Yale; m (2) 13 Oct 1747 *WC2*—David Dutton.

FAM. 9. Jeremiah & Mary (Cook) How:

4 **Sarah**, b 16 Apr 1709 *WV;* m 30 Jan 1734 *WV*—Joseph Preston.

5 Dinah, b 28 Feb 1716 *WV*.
6 Ichabod, b 11 Sep 1717 *WV*.
7 Bathsheba, b 1 Apr 1720 *WV*.

FAM. 10. Samuel & Mary (Allyn) How:
1 & 2 Twins, d soon after born.
3 Ephraim, b 19 Dec 1750 *WatV;* m 10 Mar 1781 *WtnV*—Abigail Hubbard.
4 Abigail, b 8 Jan 1753 *WatV*.
5 Mary, b 7 Nov 1754 *WatV*.
6 Eunice, b 24 Nov 1756 *WatV*.
7 John, b 22 Oct 1762 *WatV*.
8 Abigail, b 13 Sep 1764 *WatV*.

FAM. 10. Samuel & [Amy (Tuttle)] How (family incomplete):
9 Chloe, b 29 Jan 1779 *PV;* m 2 Apr 1797 *PV*—Jesse Clark.

FAM. 11. Joshua & Miriam (Blakeslee) How:
1 David, b 11 Aug 1757 *WV;* Census (Wells, Vt.) 1-2-6; m Phebe Cole.
2 Elizabeth, b 8 Apr 1759 *WV*, d 15 Apr 1759 *WV*.
3 Asa, b 30 Mar 1760 *WV;* m Eunice Buck.
4 Samuel, b 26 Apr 1762 *WV;* Census (Wells, Vt.) 1-2-1.
5 Elizabeth, b 20 May 176[-] *WV*, d 2 June 176[-] *WV*.
6 Eunice, bp 25 June 1769 *NorfolkC;* m Michael Clemons.
7 Joshua, bp 20 Oct 1771 *NorfolkC*.
8 Ruth, bp 10 July 1774 *NorfolkC;* m Samuel Stevens.
9 Joseph, bp 23 Feb 1777 *NorfolkC;* m Annis Paul.

HOW. miscellaneous. Samuel & Elizabeth Jackson of Sheffield, Mass. conveyed right in estate of father How, dec'd (W. Deeds, 1749). Elizabeth was FAM. 8, 1, unless this was a second marriage of FAM. 1, 6, *viii*.

HOWE. Hezekiah, s. of Sampson & Sarah (Sabin), b 28 Aug 1741 (Mid), d 1775; m Hannah da. Nathan & Hannah (Nichols) Beers, b 19 Nov 1748 *StV*, d 4 July 1796 æ. 48 *NHT1;* she m (2) Elias Stillwell.
1 Hannah, b 22 Feb 1773 *NHT1*, d 16 Jan 1854 æ. 81 *NHT1;* m 29 Aug 1795 *NHx*—Solomon Collis.
2 Sally, b 22 Feb 1773 *NHT1*, d 22 Feb 1826 æ. 53 *NHT1;* m Amos Townsend.
3 Hezekiah, b 24 Mar 1775 *F*, d 26 May 1838 æ. 63 *NHT1;* m 21 Apr 1800 *NHV*—Sally Townsend; left issue.

HOWD. Anthony of Bd, d 1676; m Jan 1672 *NHV*—Elizabeth da. Matthias & Elizabeth Hitchcock, b 4 June 1651 *NHV;* she m (2) 22 Aug 1677 *BdV*—John Nash. Issue, 3 sons.

HOWELL. FAM. 1. Stephen, s. of John & Martha (White), b 10 May 1683 (at Southampton, L. I.), d 23 Nov 1770 æ. 87 *NHT1*, *NHC1;* m (1) 4 Mar 1707/8 *NHV*—Desire da. John & Hannah (Bishop) Morris, b 29 Mar 1687 *NHV;* m (2) 21 Aug 1758 *NHC1*—Elizabeth da. Thomas & Mary (Winston) Trowbridge, wid. Joseph Miles, b 29 Mar 1693 *NHV*, d 23 Jan 1783 æ. almost 90 *NHC1*.

(By 1): 1 John, b 8 May 1709 *NHV*, d 23 June 1744 *NHV*, *EHV;* m 1 June

1732 *NHV*—Abigail da. Joseph & Abigail (Hemingway) Holt, b 4 Aug 1716 *NHV*, d 27 Oct 1782 æ. 63 *EHC;* she m (2) 22 Mar 1744/5 *NHV*—Nathaniel Barnes.

i Timothy, b 24 Oct 1732 *NHV*, *EHV*, d 25 June 1771 æ. 39 *NHC1;* m (1) 7 Aug 1755 *NHV*—Sarah da. James & Hannah (Rowe) Peck, b c. 1732, d 1758 *NHC1;* m (2) 9 Nov 1758 *NHV*—Eunice da. Samuel & Bathsheba (Thomas) Tolles, b c. 1739, d 7 May 1777 *NHC1*, bu. 8 May æ. 38 *NHx*. **FAM. 2.**

ii Joseph, b 7 Nov 1734 *NHV*, *EHV*, d 15 May 1742 *NHV*.

iii Henry, b 10 Apr 1736 *NHV*, 1737 *EHV*.

iv Desire, b 27 July 1738 *NHV*, 1739 *EHV*, d 12 Sep 1742 *NHV*, *EHV* .

v Samuel, b 29 Nov 1741 *NHV*, *EHV;* Capt.; Census (NH) 1-0-3; m (1) 5 Aug 1769 *NHC1*—Sybil Starr of Mid, who d 9 Apr 1779 æ. 35 *NHC1;* m (2) 2 Oct 1783 *NHC1*—Obedience da. Dan & Philena (Killam) Carrington, b 7 Dec 1753 *NHV*, d 1836. **FAM. 3.**

vi Joseph, b 8 Jan 1743/4 *NHV*, *EHV*, d 22 Jan 1810 æ. 66 *NHT1;* Census (NH) 3-2-4; m (1) 22 Apr 1766 *NHC1*—Hannah da. Amos & Dorcas (Foote) Hitchcock, b 31 Dec 1748 *NHV*, bp 26 Apr 1772 *NHC1*, d 19 June 1787 æ. 38 *NHT1*, *NHC1;* m (2) Sarah da. John & Abiah (Macumber) Hall, bp 26 Mar 1758 *NHC1*, d 2 Apr 1821 æ. 62 *NHT1*. **FAM. 4.**

2 Hannah, b 25 May 1711 *NHV;* m (1) 6 Mar 1739/40 *NHV*—Daniel Sherman; m (2) 29 May 1764 *WdC*—William Hine.

3 Desire, b 12 July 1713 *NHV*, d 12 Aug 1713 *NHV*.

4 Stephen, b 3 Sep 1714 *NHV*, d 1757; m 23 Sep 1736 *NHV*—Susanna Cooper of Southampton, L. I., who d 2 Sep 1771 æ. 57 *NHC1;* she m (2) 7 Aug 1760 *NHC2*—Samuel Horton.

i Stephen, b 6 Sep 1737 *NHV*, bp 6 Nov 1737 *NHC1*, d young.

ii Susanna, b 7 Jan 1738/9 *NHV*, bp 7 Jan 1738/9 *NHC1*, d 21 Apr 1803 æ. 64 *NHT1;* m 15 Mar 1761 *NHC1*—Eneas Munson.

iii Nathan, b 1 Jan 1740/1 *NHV*, d 23 Dec 1784 æ. 44 *NHC1;* m (1) 13 Nov 1766 *NHC1*—Susanna da. Benjamin & Abigail (Punderson) Munson, b c. 1745, d 15 Dec 1770 æ. 25; m (2) 14 Jan 1778 *NHC1*—Anna Cook; she m (2) 5 Feb 1786 *NHC1*—Asa Blakeslee. **FAM. 5.**

iv Rebecca, b 27 Mar 1746 *NHV*, bp 30 Mar 1746 *NHC1*, d 17 Dec 1786 æ. 41 *NHC1;* m 11 July 1771 *NHC1*—Paul Noyes.

v Desire, b 7 Feb 1749/50 *NHV*, bp 11 Feb 1749/50 *NHC1*, d 11 Sep 1775 æ. 25 *NHC1*.

5 James, b 1 June 1717 *NHV*, bp 1717 *NHC1*, d young.

6 Thomas, b 30 Apr 1719 *NHV*, bp 3 May 1719 *NHC1*, d 18 May 1797 æ. 78 *NHT1*, æ. 79 *NHC1;* Dea.; Census (NH) 1-0-3; m

(1) 1 Mar 1743/4 *NHV*—Mary da. John & Susanna (Alling) White, b 22 Apr 1720 *NHV*, d 27 Mar 1776 æ. 56 *NHT1*, æ. 55 *NHC1*; m (2) 12 Apr 1779 *NHC1*—Hannah da. Jehiel & Mary (Miles) Thomas, wid. Samuel Tolles, b 2 Apr 1737 *NHV*, d 16 Jan 1812 æ. 75 *NHT1*.

(By 1): *i* Hannah, b 1 Jan 1744/5 *NHV*, bp 6 Jan 1744/5 *NHC1*, d 9 Dec 1827 æ. 83 *NHT1*; m 29 July 1767 *NHV*, *NHC1* —Richard Cutler.

ii John, bp 3 May 1747 *NHC1*, d 22 June 1776 æ. 29 *NHT1*, 23 June *NHC1*.

iii Mary, bp 15 Apr 1750 *NHC1*, d [1750] *NHT1*.

iv Mary, b [July 1752], d 11 July 1752 æ. 1 wk. *NHT1*.

v Timothy, b 29 Aug 1753 *NHV*, bp 2 Dec 1753 *NHC1*, d 24 Sep 1782 æ. 29 *NHT1*, *NHC1*.

vi Thomas, bp 18 July 1756 *NHC1*, d 20 May 1798 æ. 42 *NHT1*, *NHC1*; Census (NH) 2-1-3; m 28 Mar 1776 *NHC1* —Sarah da. Ezekiel & Rebecca (Russell) Hayes, b c. 1758, d 23 Aug 1786 æ. 28 *NHC1*, 22 Aug *NHT1*. **FAM. 6.**

vii Mary, bp 17 Aug 1760 *NHC1*, d 6 May 1798 æ. 38 *NHT1*, æ. 39 *NHC1*.

viii Susanna, bp 20 Nov 1763 *NHC1*, d 26 Aug 1798 *NHT1*, æ. 35 *NHC1*.

7 SAMUEL, b 23 Apr 1721 *NHV*, bp 7 May 1721 *NHC1*, d s. p.

8 DESIRE, b 20 Mar 1722/3 *NHV*, bp 24 Mar 1723 *NHC1*, d 10 Apr 1726 *NHV*.

9 TIMOTHY, b 31 Jan 1725/6 *NHV*, bp 6 Feb 1725/6 *NHC1*, d s. p.

10 SYBIL; m Eleazer Brown.

FAM. 2. TIMOTHY & SARAH (PECK) HOWELL:

1 JAMES, b 1 June 1756 *NHV*, bp 29 Aug 1756 *NHC1*; m 31 Oct 1779 *NHC2*—Rhoda da. Abraham & Elizabeth (Bradley) Augur, b c. 1760, d Dec 1818 æ. 58 *ColR*.

2 ELIHU, b 20 Apr 1758 *NHV*, probably d s. p.

FAM. 2. TIMOTHY & EUNICE (TOLLES) HOWELL:

3 CHAUNCEY, b 9 Oct 1759 *NHV*, bp 23 Oct 1759 *NHC1*; Census (NH) 1-2-1; m.

4 BATHSHEBA, b c. 1761; m 29 Sep 1780 *NHC2*—Benjamin Grannis; div.; she had a child bu. 30 Sep 1792 æ. 0-3 (unbaptized) *NHx*.

5 STEPHEN, bp 13 Mar 1763 *NHC1*, d 23 Aug 1764 æ. 0-17 *NHC1*.

FAM. 3. SAMUEL & SYBIL (STARR) HOWELL:

1 SAMUEL, b c. 1770, d 30 Aug 1771 æ. 2 *NHC1*.

2 SAMUEL, bp 28 Feb 1773 *NHC1*.

3 SYBIL, bp 7 Aug 1774 *NHC1*.

FAM. 3. SAMUEL & OBEDIENCE (CARRINGTON) HOWELL:

4 JULIA, bp 30 May 1784 *NHC1*, d 21 Sep 1865 æ. 81-6 *NHV*; m ——— Armstead.

5 MARIA, bp 9 Jan 1791 *NHC1*.

FAM. 4. JOSEPH & HANNAH (HITCHCOCK) HOWELL:

1 ALMIRA, b c. 1767, bp 26 Apr 1772 *NHC1*; m 16 June 1783 *NHC1* —Samuel Russell Jocelyn.

2 HANNAH, b 26 May 1768 *NHT1*, bp 26 Apr 1772 *NHC1*, d 15 Sep 1848 *NHT1*; m 4 Dec 1790 *NHC1*—Daniel Green.

3 WILLIAM, b 30 Oct 1769 *NHT1*, bp 26 Apr 1772 *NHC1*, d 16 Mar 1813 *NHT1*; m 7 May 1792 *NHC1*—Anna Fairchild, b 3 Dec 1771 *NHT1*, d 29 Mar 1809 *NHT1*.

i Frances, b 29 Mar 1796 *NHT1*, d 27 July 1875 *NHT1*; m William A. Bronson, b 14 June 1796 *NHT1*, d 30 Oct 1870 *NHT1*.

ii Nancy A., b c. 1798, d 5 May 1863 æ. 65 (at Guadalajara, Mexico) *NHT1*; m Daniel Loweree.

iii William, b 22 Feb 1800 *NHT1*, d 1816 (at sea) *NHT1*.

iv Robert E., b 27 July 1802 *NHT1*, d 8 July 1862 *NHT1*.

v Harry G., b 11 Oct 1805 *NHT1*, d 2 July 1817 *NHT1*.

4 TIMOTHY, b [May 1771], d 9 Sep 1771 æ. 0-4 *NHT1*, *NHC1*.

5 TIMOTHY, b 25 Jan 1773 *NHT1*, bp 31 Jan 1773 *NHC1*, d 10 Dec 1839 *NHT1*.

6 JOSEPH, bp 5 Mar 1775 *NHC1*, d 5 Sep 1777 æ. 2-6 *NHT1*, 15 Sep æ. 2 *NHC1*.

7 AMELIA, b 14 Nov 1776 *NHT1*, bp 17 Nov 1776 *NHC1*, d 4 Mar 1827 *NHT1*, "Augusta" d 5 Mar 1827 æ. 51 (*NHx*) *NHV*.

8 ELIZABETH, bp 18 Oct 1778 *NHC1*, d 21 Aug 1779 æ. 0-11 *NHT1*, æ. 1 *NHC1*.

9 JOSEPH, bp 9 Apr 1780 *NHC1*.

10 ELIZABETH, bp 29 Sep 1782 *NHC1*, d 5 Aug [1783] æ. 1 *NHT1*.

11 STATIRA, b 26 Mar 1784 *NHT1*, bp 3 Apr 1784 *NHC1*, d 1 Apr 1847 *NHT1*, 2 Apr æ. 63 *NHV*; m —— Phelps.

FAM. 4. JOSEPH & SARAH (HALL) HOWELL:

12 JOHN, bp 28 Mar 1790 *NHC1*.

13 SARAH, bp 15 May 1791 *NHC1*, d 19 July 1875 æ. 84 *NHT1*.

14 MORRIS, bp 15 Jan 1792 *NHC1*.

15 ELIZABETH, bp 15 Dec 1793 *NHC1*, d July 1870 æ. 76 *NHT1*.

16 NANCY, b [Nov 1794], bp 14 Sep 1795 *NHx*, d 22 Sep 1795 æ. 0-9 or 10 *NHT1*, "child" d 23 Sep æ. 0-11 *NHC1*.

17 GEORGE, bp 24 Apr 1796 *NHC1*.

18 HENRY, bp 2 Sep 1801 *NHC1*, "son" d 4 Sep 1801 æ. 1 *NHC1*.

FAM. 5. NATHAN & SUSANNA (MUNSON) HOWELL:

1 STEPHEN, b c. 1768, bp 3 June 1770 *NHC1*.

2 NATHAN, bp 12 Aug 1770 *NHC1*, d 19 Jan 1811 æ. 41 (at Nassau, New Providence) *NHT1*; m 13 Oct 1792 *NHC1*—Lucinda da. James & Ann (——) Thomas, bp 22 Oct 1775 *NHC1*, d 24 Oct 1850 æ. 75 *NHT1*.

i Leverett, bp 24 Nov 1793 *NHC1*, d 20 May 1821 æ. 28 (*NHC1*) *NHV*.

ii Susanna, b 8 Feb 1795 *NHT1*, bp 12 Apr 1795 *NHC1*, d 6 Apr 1864 *NHT1*; m Elihu Sanford.

iii Wealthy, bp 25 June 1797 *NHC1*.

iv Abraham, bp 1800 *NHC1*, d 12 Apr 1864 æ. 64 *NHV;* m.

v Mehitabel, b [Oct 1802]. d 13 Apr 1892 æ. 89-6; m 25 Nov 1828 *NHV*—Miles Tuttle.

vi Harriet, bp 8 July 1804 *NHC1*, d 16 July 1859 æ. 56 *NHT1*.

vii Mary Ann, d 15 Jan 1808 æ. 5 wks. *NHT1*.

FAM. 6. THOMAS & SARAH (HAYES) HOWELL:

1 THOMAS, b c 1776, bp 26 June 1778 *NHC1*, d s. p. 29 Aug 1844 æ. 69 *NHV*.

2 HARRIET, bp 15 Nov 1778 *NHC1*, d 3 Nov 1786 æ. 8 *NHC1*, æ. 9 *NHT1*.

3 JOHN, bp 30 Mar 1781 *NHC1*, d 5 Apr 1781 æ. 3 wks. *NHC1*.

HOWELL. FAM. 7. NICHOLAS, Census (H) 3-0-3; m Mabel ——, bp (adult) 29 Dec 1776 *NHC2*.

1 NICHOLAS, b c. 1762, bp 18 May 1777 *NHC2*, d 22 Jan 1847 æ. 85 *NHV*.

2 LOIS, bp 18 May 1777 *NHC2;* m 23 Nov 1788 *NHC2*—Samuel Thomas.

3 BENJAMIN, bp 18 May 1777 *NHC2;* m 10 July 1791 *NHC1*—Elizabeth da. John & Anna (Morrison) Wilson, b 15 June 1774 *NHV*.

4 ELIJAH, bp 18 May 1777 *NHC2*.

5 ANN, b c. 1776, bp 18 May 1777 *NHC2*, d 27 Nov 1805 æ. 30 *NHT1;* m 19 Apr 1794 *NHx*—Philemon Peckham.

6 RICHARD, bp 27 Sep 1778 *NHC2*.

7 POLLY, bp 7 July 1785 *NHC2*.

HOY. JOHN; m Eleanor ——, who d 15 Aug 1798 æ. 72 *NHx;* Census, Nelly (NH) 0-0-1.

1 (perhaps) SARAH; m 25 June 1789 *NHx*—Constant Abbott of W.

2 WILLIAM EVANS, bp 9 Apr 1769 (sponsor, Catherine Mills) *NHx;* m Bathsheba ——.

i John, bp 31 Jan 1796 *NHx*.

3 ELIZABETH HOBBS, bp 5 Sep 1773 *NHx*.

4 ELEANORA CLIFFORD, bp 5 Sep 1773 *NHx*.

5 MARY BURTON, bp 10 Dec 1774 *NHx*, bu. 20 Jan 1775 *NHx*.

HUBBARD. FAM. 1. JOHN, s. of John & Mabel (Russell), b 30 Nov 1703 (Jamaica, L. I.), d 30 Oct 1773 æ. 70 *NHC1;* M. A. (Yale 1730); Lt. Col.; Dr.; Rep.; Judge of Probate; m (1) 30 Aug 1724 Elizabeth da. Samuel & Melatiah (Bradford) Stevens, who d 25 Aug 1744 æ. 42 *NHT1;* m (2) 13 Sep 1745 *NHV*—Mary da. Abraham & Elizabeth (Glover) Dickerman, wid. Michael Todd, b 1703 *NHV*, d 2 Nov 1760 *NHV*, æ. 56 *NHT1;* m (3) 10 Nov 1761 *NHV*, *NHC1*—Mary, wid. Stevens, who d 27 Apr 1794 æ. 76 *NHC1;* Census, Mary (NH) 0-0-2.

(By 1): 1 LEVERETT, b 21 July 1725, d 1 Oct 1794 æ. 70 *NHT1*, *NHC1;* B. A. (Yale 1744); Dr.; Col.; Census (NH) 2-1-3; m (1) 22 May 1746 *NHV*—Sarah da. Stephen & Mary (Miles) Whitehead, b 27 Oct 1729 *NHV*, d 5 Dec 1769 æ. 40 *NHC1;* m (2) 13 Feb 1771

NHCl—Hester da. Benjamin & Katharine (Durand) Robinson, b c. 1749, d 19 Oct 1800 *NHCl*, æ. 51 *NHTl*.

(By 1): *i* Stephen Whitehead, b 16 June 1747 *NHV*, bp 21 June 1747 *NHCl*, d s. p. 1 July 1771 æ. 25 *NHTl*, 1 Sep 1771 æ. 24 *NHCl*; B. A. (Yale 1766); m 15 May 1771 *NHV*—Eunice White.

ii Leverett, b 7 Sep 1749 *NHV*, bp 10 Sep 1749 *NHCl*, d 14 Apr 1787 æ. 38 *NHTl*, Apr *NHx*; Capt.; m Juliana ——, b c. 1745, d 28 Sep 1813 æ. 69 *NHTl*; Census, Juliana (NH) 0-1-2. **FAM. 2.**

iii Mary, bp 5 Apr 1752 *NHCl*; m John Lewis; res. 1786 Stepney in Wethersfield.

iv Wyllys, b 25 Feb 1755 *NHV*, bp 2 Mar 1755 *NHCl*, d 29 Mar 1774 æ. [19] *NHTl*, æ. 19 *NHCl*.

v Sarah, b 31 May 1758 *NHV*, bp 4 June 1758 *NHCl*; m 21 Nov 1776 *NHCl*—John Trumbull; res. 1797 Hartford.

vi Bradford, bp 23 Aug 1761 *NHCl*, d 16 June 1825 æ. 64 *NHTl*; Bradford d Oct 1826 æ. 49 (*NHCl*) *NHV*, perhaps in error for death of his widow.

vii Nathaniel, bp 11 Aug 1765 *NHCl*, [d 16 June 1825 æ. 65 (*NHCl*) *NHV*, but this this was the death of his brother Bradford]; Dr.; m 6 Dec 1789 *NHCl*—Phebe da. John & Mabel (Miles) McCleave, b 10 Aug 1767 *NHV*, d after 1830. Children: 1 Jane W., d s. p.; m —— Moore of Salisbury. 2 Alfred Stephen Whitehead, bp 1 June 1794 *NHCl*. 3 John Trumbull, bp 8 Oct 1798 *NHCl*.

(By 2): *viii* Elizabeth, bp 1 Dec 1771 *NHCl*, d 3 Dec 1771 æ. 0—0-5 *NHCl*.

ix Elizabeth, bp 11 Apr 1773 *NHCl*, d 18 Jan 1787 æ. 14 *NHTl*, æ. 13 *NHCl*.

x Juliana, bp 8 Oct 1775 *NHCl*, d 22 Jan 1778 æ. 2 *NHCl*, æ. 2-4 *NHTl*.

xi Juliana, bp 14 Feb 1779 *NHCl*, d 29 Mar 1794 æ. 16 *NHTl*, *NHCl*.

xii Lucretia, bp 12 Aug 1781 *NHCl*; m 29 Aug 1799 *NHCl*—Irah Isham of New London.

xiii Wyllys, bp 28 Mar 1784 *NHCl*; res. 1805 Colchester.

2 JOHN, b 24 Jan 1727/8 *NHV* [1726/7?], bp 29 Jan 1726/7 *NHCl*, d 18 Nov 1786 æ. 60 *WT2*, *WC2*; Rev.; m (1) 25 Jan 1749/50 *NHV*—Rebecca da. Isaac & Mary (Atwater) Dickerman, b 2 July 1726 *NHV*, d 24 Nov 1768 æ. 42 *NHCl*; m (2) 20 Sep 1770 *WV*—Mary Russell, wid. George Frost, who d 2 Mar 1806 æ. 70 *WT2*.

(By 1): *i* John, b 3 Jan 1750/1 *NHV*, d 1837; Gen.; Census (H) 2-4-3; m (1) 4 Apr 1774 *NHCl*—Anna da. David & Elizabeth (Bassett) Atwater, b 3 May 1755 *NHV*, d 2 Feb 1778 æ. 23 *NHTl*, æ. 22 *NHCl*; m (2) 13 May 1780 *NHV*

—Martha da. Phinehas & Martha (Sherman) Bradley, b 26 Oct 1750 *NHV*, d 6 June 1811 æ. 61 *HV;* m (3) 1 Jan 1812 *HV*—Sally, wid. ——— Thompson of L. **FAM. 3.**

ii Isaac, b 23 Nov 1752 *NHV*, bp 7 Jan 1752/3 *NHCl*, d 15 July 1796 æ. 44 *WC2*, 5 July 1806 (*sic*) æ. 44 *WT2;* Dea.; m 5 Dec 1782 *WV*—Jane da. Thomas & Ann (Merriam) Berry. **FAM. 4.**

3 DANIEL, b 24 Dec 1729 *NHV*, bp 28 Dec 1729 *NHCl*, d 28 Aug 1765 æ. 36 *NHCl;* m (1) 13 Sep 1750 *NHV*—Martha da. John & Desire (Cooper) Wooding, b 11 Mar 1729/30 *NHV*, d 17 May 1760 *NHCl*, æ. 30 *NHTl;* m (2) Rachel ———, who d 1773 (at Marblehead, Mass.); she m (2) ——— Proctor.

(By 1): *i* Daniel, b 26 May 1756 *NHV*, bp 5 Oct 1760 *NHCl*, d 8 June 1792 æ. 36 *NHTl*, æ. 37 *NHCl;* Census (NH) 1-2-1; m 26 Nov 1778 *NHC2*—Sarah da. John & Abiah (Hitchcock) Alling, b c. 1752, d 16 June 1794 æ. 42 *NHCl*. **FAM. 5.**

ii, iii, iv Infants, d soon *NHTl*.

4 ELIZABETH, b 3 July 1731 *NHV*, bp 27 June (?) 1731 *NHCl*, d May 1775; m 10 Feb 1757 Rev. Ezra Stiles.

5 WILLIAM, b 20 Mar 1732/3 *NHV*, bp 26 Mar 1733 *NHCl*, d 14 Nov 1736 *NHV*, æ. 4 *NHTl*.

6 WILLIAM ABDIEL, b 15 Dec 1736 *NHV*, bp 19 Dec 1736 *NHCl*, d 25 Apr 1772 æ. 36 *NHTl*, *NHCl;* m 14 Feb 1759 *NHV*—Sarah da. Thomas & Ruth (Hotchkiss) Gilbert, b c. 1732, d 14 Sep 1776 æ. 44 *NHCl*.

i Elijah, b 14 Sep 1761 *NHV* [error for 1759?], bp 10 Feb 1760 *NHCl*, d 1 Sep 1776 æ. 17 *NHTl*, *NHCl*.

ii Rachel Lorana, bp 29 May 1763 *NHCl;* m 30 Jan 1783 *NHCl*—David Atwater.

7 NATHANIEL, bp 12 Nov 1738 *NHCl*.

8 AMELIA, bp 24 Oct 1742 *NHCl;* m 1 Jan 1765 *NHCl*—Hezekiah Silliman.

FAM. 2. LEVERETT & JULIANA (———) HUBBARD:

1 DAUGHTER, d 12 Nov 1771 æ. 1 wk. *NHCl*.

2 JULIANA, bp 16 Aug 1778 *NHCl*.

3 LEVERETT, bp 11 Mar 1781 *NHCl*.

FAM. 3. JOHN & ANNA (ATWATER) HUBBARD:

1 JOHN, b 14 Jan 1778 *NHV*, bp 8 Feb 1778 *NHCl*, d 26 May 1861 *F;* res. O; m 15 Dec 1802 *F*—Sally da. Stephen & Eunice (Bradley) Peck, b 1783.

i Anna, b 24 Aug 1809 *F*, d 7 July 1838 *F;* m Sep 1831 *F*—John W. Merwin.

ii John Peck, b 23 July 1811 *F*, d 4 Sep 1880 *F;* m 9 Apr 1843 *F*—Sarah Anna Clarke.

FAM. 3. JOHN & MARTHA (BRADLEY) HUBBARD:

2 RUSSELL, b 1 Mar 1780 *NHV*, bp 16 Apr 1780 *NHCl*, d 10 Sep

1781 æ. 0-18 *NHC1*, æ. 0-18-9 *NHT1*.

3 ANNA, b 15 June 1782 *NHV*, d 10 Apr 1868 æ. 86 *HT1*; m 5 Jan 1803 *NHC1*—Jesse Cooper.

4 RUSSELL, b 18 Oct 1784 *NHV*, bp 5 Dec 1784 *NHC1*, d 1810 at sea; B. A. (Yale 1806).

5 WILLIAM, b 24 July 1787 *HV*, d 1810 at sea; m Abigail da. Timothy & Elizabeth (Stiles) Heaton, bp 1786 *NoHx*.

i Stiles, b c. 1808, d 9 Nov 1822 æ. 14 *HV*.

ii William, b 1 Nov 1810 *F*; m 11 Oct 1832 *F*—Nancy Conaway.

6 DANA, b 17 Aug 1789 *HV*, bp 11 Oct 1789 *NHC1*, d 16 Sep 1852 (at Wheeling, W. Va.); m 16 Oct 1811 *F*—Asenath da. Roger & Rebecca (Gilbert) Dorman.

i Chester Dorman, b 25 Nov 1814 *HV*, d 23 Aug 1891 (at Wheeling, W. Va.); W. Va. Sen. & U. S. Rep.; m 29 Sep 1842 Sarah Pallister.

ii Henry Baldwin, b 23 Oct 1816 *F*.

iii William Dana, b 11 Sep 1818 *F*, d 12 June 1834 *F*.

iv John Rogers, b 8 Nov 1825 *F*; m 9 Oct 1855 *F*—Lucy Ann Clark.

v Martha Rebecca, b 9 Nov 1829 *F*, d 4 Aug 1832 *F*.

FAM. 4. ISAAC & JANE (BERRY) HUBBARD:

1 REBECCA, b 25 Nov 1783, d Feb 1855; m 18 Mar 1802 Silas Rice.

2 MARY, b 24 Dec 1785, d 6 Mar 1869 æ. 83 *WolT*; m 1 Jan 1812 Ira Hough.

3 THOMAS, b 9 Jan 1788; Col.; m 28 Nov 1810 Lydia da. Timothy & Mary (Pierpont) Andrews, bp 19 July 1789 *NoHC*.

4 ISAAC, b 7 July 1790, d 17 Feb 1812.

5 JOHN, b 21 Apr 1792; m 26 Nov 1816 Eunice Merriman.

6 EZRA STILES, b 13 May 1794, d Aug 1861; m Eliza Church, who d Sep 1867.

7 ELIZABETH, b 20 Sep 1796; m 12 Sep 1816 Ira Merriman.

FAM. 5. DANIEL & SARAH (ALLING) HUBBARD:

1 DANIEL, b c. 1780, bp 28 Nov 1784 *NHC1*; m 1 Mar 1801 *NHC1*—Hannah [da. Stephen & Elizabeth (Phipps)] Brown, [bp 21 Apr 1782 *NHC2*].

2 WILLIS, b c. 1782, bp 28 Nov 1784 *NHC1*, d 16 June 1794 æ. 12 *NHT1*.

HUBBARD. FAM. 6. LEVI, b c. 1735, d 21 Aug 1825 æ. 90 *NHT1*, 22 Aug æ. 80 (*NHx*) *NHV*; res. G & NH; Census (NH) 2-1-2; m Anna da. Hezekiah & Mary (Ruggles) Gold, b 14 May 1740 *StV*, d 13 Feb 1826 æ. 85 *NHT1*, 15 Feb (*NHx*) *NHV*.

1 WILLIAM GOLD, b 16 June 1766 *F*, d 18 Feb 1846 æ. 79 *NHT1*; Census (NH) 1-0-3; m 24 May 1789 *F*—Elizabeth da. Benjamin & Elizabeth (Smith) Douglas, b 18 May 1770 *NHV*, d 3 Sep 1834 æ. 64 *NHT1*.

i Benjamin Douglas, b 1 May 1792 *F*, bp 17 June 1792 *NHx*, d 27 Sep 1811 æ. 19 *NHT1*.

ii Henry William Smith, b 24 June 1794 *F*, bp 27 July 1794 *NHx*, d 9 Nov 1813 æ. 19 *NHTI*.

iii Charlotte, bp 18 Sep 1796 *NHx*, d soon.

iv Caroline, bp 18 Sep 1796 *NHx*, d soon.

v Elizabeth Ann, b 29 July 1798 *NHTI*, d 8 July 1881 *NHTI*, æ. 83 *NHV;* m 9 June 1835 *NHV*—Russell Hotchkiss.

vi Anna Woodworth, b 2 Dec 1806 *F*, d 27 July 1837 *F*, 28 July æ. 32 *NHV*.

2 Nancy, b c. 1769, d 6 Nov 1802 æ. 33 (at Troy) *ConnJournal;* m 8 Mar 1794 *NHx*—John Woodworth.

3 Ruggles.

4 Henry, b c. 1774, d 20 June 1794 æ. 20 *NHTI*, 21 June (at D) *NHx*.

HUBBARD. fam. 7. Bela, b 27 Aug 1739 (at G) *NHTI*, d 6 Dec 1812 *NHTI;* Rev.; Census (NH) 1-4-5; m 15 May 1768 (at Fairfield) *NHx*—Grace Dunbar Hill.

1 John James, b 17 Mar 1769 *NHx*, bp 26 Mar 1769 *NHx*, d 14 June 1823 æ. 54 (at Jamaica) *NHTI*.

2 Nancy, b 12 Nov 1770 *NHx*, bp 25 Nov 1770 *NHx*, d 8 Sep 1796 æ. 25 *NHTI*, æ. 26 *NHx*.

3 Grace, b 17 Apr 1772 *NHx*, bp 19 Apr 1772 *NHx*, d 1772 æ. 0-8 *NHTI*, 14 Dec *NHx*.

4 Bela, b 18 Dec 1773 *NHx*, bp 6 Feb 1774 *NHx*, d 30 Aug 1841 æ. 68 *NHTI*.

5 Grace, b 29 Aug 1775 *NHx*, bp 3 Sep 1775 *NHx*, d 23 July 1777 *NHx*, 1777 æ. 2 *NHTI*.

6 Elizabeth, b 9 Nov 1777 *NHx*, *NHTI*, bp 16 Nov 1777 *NHx*, d 17 Oct 1858 *NHTI;* m 6 June 1801 Timothy Pitkin.

7 Frederick, b 29 Nov 1779 *NHx*, bp 19 Dec 1779 *NHx*, d Jan 1822 æ. 42 (at Jamaica) *NHTI*.

8 Thomas Hill, b 5 Dec 1781 *NHx*, bp 23 Dec 1781 *NHx*.

9 William Henry, b 1 Feb 1786 *NHx*, bp 2 Mar 1786 *NHx*, d 13 May 1792 æ. 6-3-12 *NHx*, æ. 7 *NHTI*.

HUBBARD. miscellaneous. Mary m 26 June 1675 *NHV*—Thomas Barnes......Mary w. William d 17 Mar 1710 *NHV*......Margery m 27 Nov 1700 *NHV*—John Glover [probably Margery da. Richard Hubbell of St, b 1681].

HUBBELL. Nathaniel m 5 Mar 1721/2 *NHV*—Esther Mix.

HUDSON. Lot, d 29 Jan 1771 *WV;* m 19 Nov 17[61] *WV*—Ann da. Jonathan & Elizabeth (Thompson) Prindle, b 30 Dec 1740 *WV;* she m (2) 6 Jan 1783 *CC*—Elihu Atwater.

1 David, b 2 Mar 1763 *WV;* Census (C) 1-1-3; m Mary da. Caleb & Mary (Street) Hull, b 14 Aug 1767 *WV*.

2 Amos, b 29 Dec 1766 *WV;* [m Eliphal Atwater].

3 Eunice, b 13 Sep 1767 *WV;* m John Lee Hitchcock.

4 Ann, b 20 Mar 1769 *WV;* m Abiather Hull.

HUDSON. See Hodson.

HUGGINS. JOHN, b c. 1704, d 16 Sep 1757 *BdV*, æ. 53 *BdT;* m 25 Sep 1729 *BdV*—Sarah da. Nathaniel & Mary (Todd) Heaton, b 14 June 1712 *NHV*, d 27 Sep 1799 æ. 88 *NHV*, æ. 87 *NHT1;* she m (2) 26 Nov 1766 *BdC*—John Blackstone.

1 **JOHN**, b c. 1733, d 21 Apr 1773 æ. 40 *BdT;* m (1) 14 Apr 1756 (at E. Guilford) *BdV*—Esther Hand; m (2) 26 Mar 1783 *BdV*—Sybil Kassam; "Wid. of John" d 22 Jan 1797 æ. 72 *NHC1*. Children recorded *BdV:* 1 John, b 29 Dec 1758. 2 William, b 20 Aug 1765. A John had children John Thason & Mary Esther bp 11 Jan 1795 *NHC1*.

2 **CHARLES**, b c. 1735, d 1 July 1737 æ. 2 *BdT*.

3 **SAMUEL**, b c. 1739, d 27 Oct 1811 æ. 72 *NHT1;* m (1) 3 July 1760 *BdV*—Elizabeth Guy, b c. 1739, d 17 Mar 1773 æ. 34 *NHV*, *NHC1*, *NHT1;* m (2) 23 Mar 1774 *NHV*—Mary Collins, b [20 Dec 1747], d 23 Jan 1775 æ. 27-1-3 *NHV*, 10 Jan *NHC1;* m (3) 11 Apr 1775 *NHV*, *NHC1*—Sarah da. Joseph & Ann (Bishop) Miles, b 22 Nov 1754 *NHV*, d 24 Dec 1831 æ. 76 *NHT1*, 26 Dec (*NHC1*) *NHV*.

(By 1): *i* Rebecca, b 1 Mar 1761 *NHV*.

ii Miliscent, b 24 Sep 1763 *NHV;* m 12 Sep 1786 *NHC1*—David Gilbert.

iii Samuel, b 19 Nov 1765 *NHV*, d 29 Aug 1768 æ. 3 *NHC1*, 28 Aug *NHV*.

iv Heaton, b 14 June 1768 *NHV*, d 6 Oct 1794 *NHV*, æ. 27 *NHC1;* Census (NH) 1-0-1; m Rachel da. Abraham & Amy (Hemingway) Bradley, b c. 1768, d 11 Oct 1794 æ. 28 *NHC1*. Children: 1 James Sidney, b c. 1790, bp 31 Aug 1794 *NHC1*, d 18 Aug 1823 æ. 39 (*NHC1*) *NHV*. 2 William, b c. 1792, bp 14 Aug 1794 *NHC1*, d 24 Sep 1794 æ. 2 *NHC1*.

v Sarah, b 12 Dec 1770 *NHV*, bp 23 Dec 1770 *NHC1*.

vi Samuel, b 8 Mar 1773 *NHV*, *NHT1*, bp 21 Mar 1773 *NHC1*, d 29 Mar 1849 æ. 76 *NHT1;* m Martha D. ———, b (at Mid). A da. Jane, b [17 Feb 1805], d 3 Apr 1880 æ. 75-1-16 *NHV;* m Wm. M. Smith.

(By 2): *vii* Mary, b 12 Dec 1774 *NHV*, bp 12 Mar 1775 *NHC1*, d 22 Feb 1776 æ. 0-14-10 *NHV*, æ. 0-14 *NHC1*.

4 **SARAH**, b 29 Feb 1743/4 *BdV*, d s. p.; m Robert Brown.

5 **EBENEZER**, b 17 Dec 1748 *BdV*, d 15 Oct 1825 æ. 77 *NHT1*, 17 Oct (*NHC2*) *NHV;* Census (NH) 1-4-4; m 29 July 1776 *NHC1*—Mary da. Stephen & Eunice (Tuttle) Dickerman, b 17 Jan 1758 *NHV*, d 11 Nov 1837 æ. 80 *NHT1*.

i Mary, b 9 Feb 1777 *F*, bp 5 Dec 1789 *NHC2*, d 25 Oct 1805 *F*.

ii Esther, b 23 Nov 1778 *NHT1*, bp 5 Dec 1789 *NHC2*, d 23 Feb 1845 æ. 66-3 *NHT1;* m 9 Jan 1803 Timothy Bishop.

iii Ebenezer, b 11 May 1781 *F*, bp 5 Dec 1789 *NHC2*, d 16

Aug 1838 æ. 57 *NHT1;* m Sarah W. Alvord.

iv Nancy, b 14 July 1783 *F,* d 9 Aug 1783 æ. [—] *NHT1.*

v Stephen, b 17 Nov 1785 *F,* bp 5 Dec 1789 *NHC2,* d 25 Nov 1825 æ. 41 *NHT1*, 28 Nov (*NHC2*) *NHV;* m 16 Nov 1807 Elizabeth Beers; she m (2) 16 Dec 1846 Timothy Bishop.

vi Henry, b 9 May 1787 *F,* bp 5 Dec 1789 *NHC2,* d 9 Aug 1867 æ. 80 *NHT1;* m 25 Dec 1809 *NHx*—Sarah Maria da. Frederick & Elizabeth Hunt, b c. 1792, d [28 Nov 1863 æ. 71] *NHT1.*

PAGE 2046

vii Louise Caroline, b 6 July 1798 *NHT1*, d 1 June 1879 (at Princeton, N. J.) *NHT1;* m 6 Aug 1817 Cornelius Tuthill.

6 JAMES, b 19 May 1752 *BdV,* d 26 Aug 1819 (Granby); m (1) 14 Feb 1781 Nancy Smith, b 7 June 1760, d 16 Mar 1792; m (2) 17 Oct 1796 Chloe Pratt, who d 8 Apr 1811. A child, Sarah Heaton, bp 18 Aug 1783 *NHC1*, d 21 Aug 1783 æ. 2 *NHC1.* Children by 1st w. are stated as: Sarah Heaton, Nancy Smith, James. By 2nd w.: William Heaton, Sarah, John Lincoln, Chloe, Mary Olivia.

7 WILLIAM CHARLES, b 27 Nov 1756 *BdV,* d 14 Oct 1757 *BdV,* æ. 0-10-14 *BdT.*

***HUGHES.** FAM. 1. HENRY FREEMAN, b c. 1723, d 13 Oct 1791 æ. c. 68 *EHC,* bu. 14 Oct *NHx;* Census (EH) 1-0-1; m 19 July 1745 *NHV*—Lydia da. Noah & Rachel (Hoadley) Tuttle, b 23 June 1722 *BdV,* d 2 Aug 1794 æ. 73 *EHC.*

1 HENRY, b 7 July 1751 *NHV,* d 31 Oct 1785 (at Russell, Mass.); m 17 June 1772 *F*—Grace da. Daniel & Abigail (Granger) Wheaton, who d c. 1823 (at Camillus, N. Y.).

i Stephen, b 8 Apr 1773 *F,* bp 21 Nov 1775 *NHx,* d 3 Feb 1861 *F;* m (1) 1794 *F*—Prudence Newton; m (2) 16 June 1819 *F*—Nancy Crosby; m (3) Anna Stoddard.

ii Samuel, b 10 Apr 1775 *F,* bp 21 Nov 1775 *NHx,* d 1847 (at Defiance, Ohio); m Betsey Wheaton.

iii Henry, b 10 May 1777 *F,* bp 6 June 1778 *NHx,* d 14 Dec 1848 (at Bellevue, Mich.); m (1) May 1796 Sally Wheaton; m (2) Mar 1822 Hannah (Bowen) Earll.

iv Abigail, b 2 Sep 1779 *F,* d 19 Aug 1861 *F;* m Abner Carpenter.

v Freeman, b 21 Apr 1781 *F,* d 30 Aug 1856 (at Geddes, N. Y.); m (1) 2 Nov 1802 Abigail Wheaton; m (2) 1824 Mary Grinnell.

vi Grace, b 9 Oct 1783 *F,* d s. p. 24 Mar 1800; m Augustus Wheaton.

vii Lucretia, b 25 Apr 1785 *F,* d 10 May 1793 *F.*

2 FREEMAN, b c. 1753, d after 1791; loyalist; rem. to St. Johns, New Brunswick; m 24 Nov 1774 *EHC*—Mary da. Benjamin & Katharine (Durand) Robinson (she is called Richards at

marriage).

i Mary, bp 22 Nov 1778 *EHC.*

ii Hannah, bp 22 Nov 1778 *EHC.*

iii John, bp 22 Nov 1784 *NHx.*

3 John, b 7 Sep 1757 *F*, d 1 June 1846 æ. 89–9 *EHC*, æ. 90 *EHT;* Census (EH) 1-1-5; m (1) 10 [Oct] 1778 *EHC*—Mary da. Russell & Lucy (Luddington) Grannis, b 17 Aug 1757 *F*, d 7 Dec 1804 æ. 47 *EHT*, *EHC;* m (2) 1805 Mabel Baldwin, b c. 1757 (at NoB), d 20 June 1833 æ. 76 *EHT*, 19 June *EHC.*

(By 1): *i* Lydia, b17 Aug 1779 *EHV*, d 9 July 1852 (at N. Y. City); m 12 Aug 1802 Henry Welton.

ii Lois, b 12 Sep 1782 *EHV*, d 25 Sep 1829 æ. 48 *EHC;* m Thomas Landcraft.

iii Russell, b 6 Nov 1784 *EHV*, d 15 June 1832 æ. 48 *EHC;* m Betsey da. Levi & Sarah (Tuttle) Forbes.

iv Huldah, b 25 Feb 1787 *EHV*, d 7 Mar 1841 æ. 53 *EHC;* m Orrin Flagg.

v Polly, b 20 June 1789 *EHV*, d 17 Mar 1812 æ. 22 *EHC.*

vi Henry, b 20 Sep 1791 *F*, "child" d 8 Oct 1795 æ. 4 *EHC.*

vii John, b 14 Jan 1794 *F*, d s. p.; m 3 Dec 1821 *NoHV*, *NoHC*—Zeruiah da. Ezekiel & Eleanor (Walter) Jacobs, b 6 Sep 1792 *F*, d 6 Dec 1866.

viii Abigail Rowe, b 23 Feb 1797 *F*, d s. p. 16 July 1874.

4 Daniel, b 17 June 1759 *F*, d 8 Nov 1842 æ. 83 *EHT*, æ. 83–4 *EHC;* Census (EH) 1-1-2; m (1) Lucy da. Russell & Lucy (Luddington) Grannis, b c. 1760, bp (adult) 27 Aug 1788 *NHx*, bu. 18 June 1791 æ. 31 *NHx*, "wife of John" (*sic*) d 25 June 1791 æ. 30 *EHC;* m (2) 24 Dec 1795 *CC*—Sarah da. Benjamin & Phebe (Moss) Atwater, b 26 Apr 1756 *WV*, d Jan 1817 æ. 60 *EHC;* m (3) 5 Apr 1818 Rachel Shailor, b c. 1773 (at Bristol), d 26 Mar 1844 æ. 71 *EHT*, *EHC.*

(By 1): *i* Sarah, b 13 Oct 1782 *F*, bp 8 Dec 1787 *NHx*, d 12 Apr 1808 æ. 25 *EHC;* m 22 Feb 1807 William Woodward.

ii Roswell, bp 8 Dec 1787 *NHx*, d 1815 (at Georgetown, S. C.); res. D; m 1810 Betsey da. Joshua & Anna (Miles) Sears, b 22 Feb 1788 *NHV*, d 7 Oct 1864 æ. 74 *EHT.*

iii Daniel, b 20 June 1791 *F*, d 26 Nov 1791 æ. 0–6 *EHC.*

(By 2): *iv* Aaron Atwater, b 20 Jan 1797 *EHV*, d 14 July 1833 æ. 36 *EHC;* m Lydia Caroline Tuttle.

5 Abigail, b 2 Oct 1761 *NHV*, d 16 Sep 1813 æ. 52 *NHT3;* m 6 Dec 1781 *EHC*—Stephen Rowe.

HUGHES. fam. 2. Bodwell, res. EH & Ohio; m 15 Apr 1760 *EHC*—Mercy da. Abel & Rebecca (Bartholomew) Collins, b 15 Sep 1737 *EHC.*

1 Rebecca, b c. 1761, bp 19 Oct 1765 *EHC*, d soon.

2 Ann, b c. 1763, bp 10 Nov 1765 *EHC;* m 28 Oct 1784 *EHC*—Samuel Brown of Bd; rem. to Greene Co., N. Y.

3 Collins, bp 10 Nov 1765 *EHC*, d 30 Sep 1818 æ. 53 *EHC;* m 2 Jan 1790 *EHC*—Abigail da. Simeon & Abigail (Denison)

Bradley, b 6 Jan 1762 *EHV*, d 20 Aug 1840 æ. 78-7 *EHC*.
i Huldah, b 18 June 1793 *EHV*, d 7 Apr 1812 æ. 19 *EHC*.
ii Nancy, b 11 May 1796 *EHV;* m 15 Oct 1812 *EHC*—Stephen Thatcher.
iii Collins, b 24 Jan 1798 *EHV*, d 1815 (at sea) *EHC*.
iv Sarah Bradley, b 28 June 1801 *EHV*, "child" d 24 Mar 1805 æ. 4 *EHC*.
v Susan, b 19 July 1804 *EHV;* m 29 Oct 1825 *EHV*—Wickham Mills.
vi John, b 21 July 1806 *F*, "child" d May 1816 æ. 10 *EHC*.
4 REBECCA, bp 1 Nov 1767 *EHC;* m (1) Thomas Howell; m (2) 14 Aug 1794 Josiah Moulton.
5 ISRAEL, bp [1771] *EHC*, drowned.
6 JOSEPH, bp 4 July 1773 *EHC*, d s. p.

HUGHES. FAM. 3. CHRISTOPHER, res. NH, d c. 1785; m Abigail da. Joseph & Elsie (Munson) Miles, b 24 Oct 1741 *NHV*, d 3 May 1787 æ. 46 *NHC 1*.
1 SAMUEL, b 28 Mar 1768 *NHT1*, d 25 Mar 1838 *NHT1*, æ. 73 *NHV;* m 10 Nov 1792 *NHV*, *NHx*—Philomela da. John & Mehitabel (Brooks) Miles, b 2 Mar 1769 *NHV*, *NHT1*, d 14 Oct 1844 *NHT1*, æ. 75 *NHV*.
i Mehitabel, b 30 Sep 1793 *NHV*, d 2 Nov 1815 æ. 22 *NHT1;* m Edwin Potter.
ii John Miles, b 2 Oct 1795 *NHV*, bp 24 Oct 1795 *NHx*, d 21 Oct 1799 *NHV*, *NHT1*.
iii Enos Brooks Miles, b 17 Mar 1797 *NHV*, *NHT1*, bp 11 June 1797 *NHx*, d 7 Oct 1864 *NHT1;* m 27 July 1828 *NHV*—Louisa W. da. Timothy Bishop, b 24 May 1804 *NHT1*, d 6 Oct 1872 *NHT1*.
iv Grace, b 23 Jan 1800 *NHV*.
2 CHRISTOPHER, b c. 1771, bp 29 May 1785 (æ. 13 or 14) *NHx*.
3 ELIZABETH, bp 29 May 1785 *NHx*.
4 ABIGAIL, bp 29 May 1785 *NHx*.

HULBURT. WILLIAM m Mary ——, who d 17 Mar 1710 *NHV*.
1 EBENEZER, b 15 July 1705 *NHV*.
2 ANNA, b 6 Apr 1707 *NHV*.
3 BENJAMIN, b 13 Mar 1710 *NHV*.

HULL. FAM. 1. ANDREW, b c. 1606, d 1640; res NH; m Katharine ——, b c. 1612; she m (2) Richard Beach.
1 HANNAH, bp 4 Oct 1640 *NHC1*.
2 SARAH, bp 4 Oct 1640 *NHC1*.

FAM. 2. RICHARD HULL, brother of Andrew above, d c. 1 Sep 1662 *NHV;* m.
1 MARY, d 26 Feb 1664 *NHV;* m 1 Mar 1653/4 *NHV*—John Jackson.
2 JEREMIAH, d 13 June 1700 *NHV;* m 6 May 1658 (at M) *NHV*—Hannah Baldwin.

i Jeremiah, b 2 June 1663 *NHV*, d s. p.
ii Hannah, b 22 Oct 1664 *NHV;* m Nathaniel Prichard.
iii Mary, b 8 Aug 1666 *NHV*, d 12 Nov 1750 *G;* m 10 Mar 1697 *G*—John Hotchkin.
iv John, b 13 Nov 1668 *NHV*, bp 30 Nov 1746 *NHCl*, d 1755; m 1 Jan 1695 *NHV*—Mercy da. Bartholomew & Mercy (Barnes) Jacobs, b 8 Sep 1674 *NHV*. **FAM. 3.**
v Elizabeth, b 27 Feb 1670 *NHV*, d 16 Mar 1670/1 *NHV*.
vi Joseph, b 11 Aug 1672 *NHV*, d 25 Feb 1745/6 *NHV;* m 12 July 1722 *NHV*—Lydia da. John & Lydia Blakeslee, b 25 Mar 1700 *NHV*, d 16 Jan 1784 æ. 83-10 *NoHC*. **FAM. 4.**
vii Sarah, b 4 Mar 1674/5 *NHV*, bp 8 July 1688 *NHCl;* m Joseph Chidsey.
viii Martha, b 25 Nov 1677 *NHV*, bp 8 July 1688 *NHCl;* d after 1713.

3 JOHN, bp 24 May 1640 *NHCl*, d 6 Dec 1711 *WV*, æ. 80 *WTl;* Dr.; res. St, D & W; m (1) Mary [da. Richard & Katharine Beach, b June 1642 *NHCl*], d between 1685 & 1690; m (2) c. 1690 Tabitha da. Henry & Alice Tomlinson, wid. Edward Wooster, who d 1691; m (3) 21 Sep 1699 *WV*—Rebecca Turner [?perhaps Wid. Towner of Bd]. Other wives have been assigned to Dr. John in published accounts, but no record proof for them has been found.

(By 1): *i* John, b 14 Mar 1661/2 *StV*, d 9 Nov 1714 *DV;* m Mary da. Miles & Sarah (Platt) Merwin, b 23 Jan 1665/6 *MV*, bp 28 Jan 1665/6 *MCl*. **FAM. 5.**
ii Samuel, b 4 Feb 1663 *StV* [1663/4], d s. p.
iii Mary, b 31 Oct 1666 *StV*, d 5 Sep 1696 *DV;* m 23 Dec 1685 *DV*—John Prindle.
iv Joseph, b 16 Feb 1668 *StV* [1668/9], d 5 Oct 1744 æ. 76 *DV*, 15 Oct 1745 æ. 75 *DTl;* Capt.; m (1) 20 Jan 1691 *DV*—Mary da. Caleb & Anna (Ward) Nichols, b c. 1666, d 5 Apr 1733 *DV*, 6 Apr æ. 68 *DTl;* m (2) Nov 17[35] *DV*—Hannah Botsford, wid. John Prindle. **FAM. 6.**
v Benjamin, b 10 Apr 1672 *StV*, d 30 Mar 1741 *WV;* Dr.; m (1) 14 Sep 1693 *WV*—Elizabeth da. Samuel & Elizabeth (Peck) Andrews, b 17 July 1674 *WV*, d 27 Apr 1732 *WV;* m (2) 22 Jan 1733 *WV*—Hannah, wid. Parmalee. **FAM. 7.**
vi Richard, b 16 Oct 1674 *DV*, d s. p.
vii Ebenezer, b 16 Mar 1678/9 *DV*, d 9 Nov 1709; m 7 Mar 1706 *WV*—Lydia da. Daniel & Ruth (Rockwell) Mix, b end of July 1682 *WV*, d 1710. **FAM. 8.**
viii Jeremiah, b 28 Sep 1679 *DV* [?1680], d 11 May 1736 *WV;* Dr.; m 24 Mar 1711 *WV*—Hannah da. Samuel & Hannah (Ives) Cook, b 28 May 1693 *WV*, d 22 Nov 1735 *WV*, æ. 43 *WTl*. **FAM. 9.**

ix Andrew, b 15 July 1685 *DV*, d s. p.

4 **Hannah**, bp 26 Feb 1641 *NHC1;* m 25 Dec 1662 *NHV*—Edmund Dorman.

Fam. 3. John & Mercy (Jacobs) Hull:

1 **Lydia**, b 26 Sep 1696 *NHV*, bp (adult) 25 Nov 1733 *NHC1*, d s. p.

2 **Mary**. b 8 Sep 1698 *NHV;* m Oct 1724 *NHV*—Samuel Sperry.

3 **Hannah**, b 11 Apr 1701 *NHV;* m 4 Nov 1756 *NHV*—Caleb Ball.

4 **John**, b 22 Oct 1703 *NHV*, d 22 Apr 1760 *NHV;* m (1) 14 Mar 1738/9 *NHV*—Jane da. Samuel & Anna (Hotchkiss) Johnson, who d 29 Mar 1751 *NHV;* m (2) Elizabeth ——— .

(By 1): *i* Lois, b 21 Jan 1739/40 *NHV*, d 7 Jan 1833 æ. 94 *OT;* m 29 Dec 1763 *NHC2*—Jonathan Beecher.

ii Isaiah, b 25 Apr 1743 *NHV*, bp 29 May 1743 *WdC*, d s. p 1783.

iii Ezra, b 12 Aug 1747 *NHV*, bp 20 Sep 1747 *WdC*, d 20 July 1818 æ. 69 *WatT1;* Census (Wat) 2-2-4; m 18 July 1771 *WatV*—Annis Johnson, b c. 1752, d 19 May 1820 æ. 68 *WatT1*. **FAM. 10.**

5 **James**, b 27 Nov 1705 *NHV*, d 1782; m (1) 22 Aug 1733 *WatV*—Susanna da. Nathaniel Arnold, bp 23 May 1708 *Hartford*, d 9 Dec 1736 *WatV;* m (2) 8 June 1738 *WatV*—Jane da. John & Mary (Washburn) Johnson.

(By 1): *i* James, b 25 July 1734 *WatV*, d 4 Dec 1736 *WatV*.

6 **Sarah**, b 26 Jan 1707/8 *NHV*, bp (adult) 13 Dec 1736 *NHC1;* m 25 Oct 1752 *NHC2*—Stephen Johnson.

7 **Mercy**, b 17 Feb 1709/10 *NHV*, bp (adult) 13 Dec 1736 *NHC1*, d 13 June 1793 æ. 83 *WtnD;* m 14 Nov 1739 *WatV*—Ebenezer Porter.

8 **Esther**, bp (adult) 7 May 1738 *NHC1*, d after 1782; m ——— Churchill of M.

9 **Ebenezer**, b 18 Oct 1715 *NHV*, bp (adult) 24 July 1737 *NHC1*, d 1783; m 31 Aug 1743 *NHV*—Lydia da. John & Elizabeth (Beecher) Dunbar, b 1 Oct 1714 *NHV*, d 24 Aug 1798 æ. 84 *NHT1*.

i Lydia, b 12 Mar 1743/4 *NHV*, d 1 July 1744 *NHV*.

ii James, b 16 June 1745 *NHV*, bp 16 June 1745 *NHC1;* m 16 Jan 1766 *NHC2*—Mary da. John & Mary (Blakeslee) Ball, b 23 Aug 1745 *NHV*, bp 11 July 1773 *NHC1;* she m (2) Moses Sanford. **FAM. 11.**

iii Joseph, b 8 Aug 1747 *NHV*, bp 13 Sep 1747 *NHC1*, d 5 June 1810 æ. 63 *NHT1;* Census (NH) 2-0-2; m (1) Mar 1773 *NHV*—Abiah da. John & Abiah (Hitchcock) Alling, who d c. 1774; m (2) 14 Dec 1775 *CC*—Damaris da. Andrew & Lowly (Cook) Hull, b 18 Sep 1751 *WV*, d 4 Mar 1829 æ. 78 *NHT1*, 6 Mar æ. 79 (*NHC2*) *NHV*. **FAM. 12.**

iv Lydia, b 6 Apr 1749 *NHV*, bp 28 May 1749 *NHC1*, d 17 June 1841 æ. 93 *NHV;* m John Alling.

v David, b 17 Sep 1751 *NHV*, d 27 May 1815 æ. 66 *NHT1;* Census (NH) 2–4–1; m Hannah da. Thomas & Mary (Miles) Punderson, b 18 Aug 1749 *NHV*, d 10 July 1828 æ. 78 *NHT1*, 12 July 1827 æ. 76 (*NHC2*) *NHV*.

FAM. 13.

vi Samuel, b 9 Feb 1754 *NHV*, bp 7 Apr 1754 *NHC2*, d 29 Sep 1836 æ. 82 *NHT1;* Census (NH) 1–3–2; m Mabel [possibly da. Griffin & Mabel (Thompson) Bradley, bp 13 Aug 1758 *NHC2*], d 28 Aug 1845 æ. 87 *NHT1*.

FAM. 14.

vii Rebecca, b 5 Aug 1756 *NHV*, bp 19 Sep 1756 *NHC2*, d Sep 1802 æ. 46 (at NH) *ConnJournal;* m Bishop Dodd.

FAM. 4. JOSEPH & LYDIA (BLAKESLEE) HULL:

1 JOSEPH, b 2 Feb 1722/3 *NHV*, d Dec 1801 æ. 79 *NorfolkC;* Census (NoH) 1–0–3; m 6 June 1751 *NHV*—Hannah da. Joseph & Sarah (Dorman) Wooding, b c. 1734, d Feb 1806 æ. 70 *NorfolkC*.

i Joseph, b 2 May 1754 *NHV;* Census (NoH) 1–5–3; rem. to Norfolk; m 1 Jan 1777 *NoHC*—Sarah da. John & Sarah (Frost) Pardee, b 31 July 1753 *NHV*. Children (incomplete): David; Hannah: James: Joseph: Wooden: Sally: Joel.

PAGE 2047

ii Hannah, b 17 Oct 1756 *NHV*, d 22 July 1760 *NHV*.

iii Mary, b 13 June 1760 *NHV*, d 6 Oct 1761 æ. 0–16 *NoHC*.

iv Hannah, bp 18 Sep 1763 *NoHC;* m 6 Oct 1783 *NoHC*—
——— Butler of Farm.

v Mary, bp 27 Dec 1767 *NoHC*.

vi Esther, bp 2 Sep 1770 *NoHC;* [?m Joshua Atwater].

2 DANIEL, b 29 Sep 1724 *NHV*, d soon.

3 BENJAMIN, b 7 Aug 1726 *NHV*, d 1782; m Mar 1746 *NHV*—Amy da. Stephen & Rebecca (Bishop) Hill, b 29 May 1726 *NHV*, d 1 Dec 1826 æ. 100-5-25 (at NoH) *ColR;* Census, Amy (NoH) 1–0–3.

i Hannah, b 8 June 1746 *NHV*, d 26 Oct 1746 *NHV*.

ii John, b 17 Oct 1747 *NHV*, d 21 Mar 1823 æ. 75 *NoHT1;* Census (NoH) 2–4–3; m 9 Feb 1769 *NoHC*—Martha da. John & Sarah (Frost) Pardee, b 6 July 1747 *NHV*, d 28 Feb 1815 æ. 68 *NoHT1*. **FAM. 15.**

iii Elijah, b 13 Oct 1750 *NHV*, d s. p. before 1798.

iv Benjamin,, b 22 May 1753 *NHV*, d 1817; Census (NoH) 1–2–2; m Hannah da. Joy & Hannah (Grannis) Humiston, b 11 Dec 1758 *NHV*, bp (adult) 1781 *NoHx*, d Dec 1845 æ. 87 *NoHD*. **FAM. 16.**

v Amy, b 3 Aug 1757 *NHV*, d 14 Dec 1853 æ. 98 *WolT;* m 21 Dec 1791 *NoHV*—Ezra Todd.

vi Rebecca, b 12 May 1761 *NHV;* m ——— Barker.

vii Ruth, b 27 Nov 1763 *NHV*, bp 4 Feb 1764 *NoHC*, d 13 June 1789 æ. 27 *NoHC;* m 12 Feb 1787 *NoHV*—Solomon Sackett.

viii Philip, b c. 1767, d 5 Apr 1847 æ. 80 *NoHD.*

4 Daniel, b 23 May 1728 *NHV;* Census (NoH) 2-0-3; rem. to L; m 28 Dec 1752 *NHV*—Eunice da. Obadiah & Hannah (Frost) Hill, b 28 Mar 1731 *NHV,* "wid." d 4 Mar 1808 æ. 77 *WatV.*

i Lydia, b 15 Nov 1753 *NHV,* bp 14 Feb 1762 *NoHC,* d Mar 1807 æ. 53 *WatV.*

ii Eunice, bp 14 Sep 1761 *NoHC.*

iii Abigail, b 20 Feb 1757 *NHV,* bp 14 Sep 1761 *NoHC,* d 16 Sep 1761 *NoHC.*

iv Abner, b 4 May 1759 *NHV,* bp 14 Feb 1762 *NoHC;* Census (NoH) 1-0-2.

v Phebe, b 3 Dec 1760 *NHV,* bp 14 Feb 1762 *NoHC.*

vi Daniel, bp 16 Jan 1763 *NoHC,* d c. 1846; m 1795 Lucretia Hoffman.

vii Abigail, b 16 Jan 1765 *NHV*

viii Asaph, "son" bp 26 July 1767 *NoHC,* d 1831 æ. 65 (at Wat) *NHTI;* m Lydia da. James & Patience (Todd) Bishop, b 20 Feb 1770 *NHV.* Children: (1) Lucinda, b c. 1798, d 2 Oct 1847 æ. 49 *NHTI.* (2) Sophronia, b 15 Sep 1800 *NHTI,* d 14 May 1884 *NHTI.* (3) Justus Bishop, b c. 1803, d 1 Dec 1820 æ. 17 *NHTI.*

ix Jesse, bp 29 Oct 1769 *NoHC,* d 14 July 1787 æ. 17-10 *NoH C.*

x Daughter, bp Nov 1772 *NoHC,* d 23 Feb 1773 *NoHC.*

5 Abner, b 21 Dec 1730 *NHV,* d 18 Oct 1755 *NHV.*

6 Lydia, b 15 Oct 1734 *NHV,* d 4 Sep 1750 *NHV.*

FAM. 5. John & Mary (Merwin) Hull:

1 Deborah, b 26 Dec 1691 *DV,* d 17 Feb 1772 æ. 81 *DV.*

2 John, b 9 Jan 1693/4 *DV,* d s. p. 25 May 1753 *DV.*

3 Mary, b 16 July 1696 *DV,* d after 1754.

4 Martha, b c. 1698; m Abraham Wooster of Wat.

5 Daniel, b 15 Mar 1699/1700 *DV,* d 1768; m 2 Mar 1733/4 *DV*—Elizabeth da. Jonathan & Sarah (Riggs) Lum, b 15 Mar 1712/3 *DV.*

i Daniel, b 20 Dec [1734] *DV,* d 8 Feb 17[38] *DV.*

ii Lemuel, b 7 Nov 1735 *DV,* bp 18 Jan 1736 *DC,* d 15 Feb 17[38] *DV.*

iii Elijah, b 7 Nov 1738 *DV,* bp 12 Nov 1738 *DC,* d s. p.

iv Elizabeth, b 7 Nov 1738 *DV,* bp 12 Nov 1738 *DC,* d 9 Oct 1822 æ. 88 *OxfV;* m (1) 11 Oct 1764 *DV*—Wooster Twitchell; m (2) 22 Oct 1775 *OxfC*—Ichabod Dean.

v Ebenezer, b 22 Dec 1741 *DV,* d 18 Jan 1764 *DV.*

vi John, b 7 June 1744 *DV.*

vii Jeremy, b 22 Oct 1752 *DV;* loyalist.

6 Priscilla, b 3 June 1702 *DV,* d 23 Sep 1755 *WatV,* 25 Sep æ. 54 *WatTI;* m 26 Sep 1727 *WatV*—Samuel Scott.

7 Miles, b 6 July 1704 *DV,* d 20 Jan 1775 *CC,* 19 Jan *WV;* m 4 Dec 1729 *WV*—Mary da. Timothy & Thankful (Doolittle)

Tuttle, b 3 Oct 1712 *WV*, d 21 Apr 1770 *CC*, *WV*.

i Martha, b 29 Nov 1730 *WV*, bp Jan 1730/1 *CC*, d 14 June 1769 *WatV;* m 14 Aug 1750 *FarmV*—Abial Roberts.

ii Esther, b 15 Sep 1733 *WV*, bp Sep 1733 *CC*, d 21 Nov 1751 *WV;* m 23 Jan 1751 *WV*—Josiah Smith.

iii Elijah, b 10 Nov 1735 *WV*, bp Dec 1735 *CC*, d 19 May 1736 *WV*.

iv Eunice, b 27 Mar 1738 *WV*, "child" bp 7 May 1738 *CC;* m 28 Jan 1762 *WV*—Matthias Hitchcock.

v Mary, b 15 July 1740 *WV*, bp 10 Aug 1740 *CC*, d 14 Feb 1776 *WV*.

vi Miles, b 24 Mar 1742/3 *WV*, bp Mar 1742/3 *CC*, d 26 Jan 1808 *CC;* Capt.; Census (C) 2-0-2; m 4 Dec 1761 *WV*—Eunice da. Ebenezer & Anna (Bates) Hull, b 7 Oct 1736 *WV*. **FAM. 17.**

vii Abigail, b 11 June 1745 *WV*, bp June 1745 *CC;* [m 8 Feb 1764 *WatV*—Joshua Moss].

viii Abijah, b 10 June 1747 *WV*, bp 21 June 1747 *CC;* m 20 Apr 1774 *WV*, *CC*—Rachel da. Samuel & Rachel (Bunnell) Thompson, b 20 Apr 1755 *WV*. **FAM. 18.**

8 ELIJAH, b 25 Mar 1707 *DV*, d 23 July 1709 *DV*.

9 EBENEZER, b 8 July 17[09] *DV*, d 19 Jan 1722/3 (drowned in Naugatuck River) *DV*.

FAM. 6. JOSEPH & MARY (NICHOLS) HULL:

1 SAMUEL, b 15 Nov 1692 *DV*, d 8 Sep 1751 æ. 59 *DT2;* m (1) 15 Jan [1724] *DV*—Anna da. John & Elizabeth (Tomlinson) Riggs, b 10 June 1704 *DV*, d 22 Mar 1730/1 æ. 27 *DT1;* m (2) 25 Sep 1735 *Stx*—Sarah da. Abraham & Hannah (Riggs) Harger, b 4 Aug 1716 *DV;* m (3) Hannah Curtis.

(By 1): *i* Child, b 25 Jan 1725 *DV*, "Ann" d 24 Feb 1737 æ. 17 (?) *DT1*.

ii Hannah, b 11 May 1726 *DV*, d 13 Dec 1737 æ. 12 *DT1*.

iii Eunice, b 19 Nov 1727 *DV*, d 17 Nov 1799 æ. 74 *DT3;* m 18 June 1746 *DV*, *Stx*—John Wooster.

(By 3): *iv* Samuel, b c. 1743, d 23 Oct 1806 *F*, 1806 æ. 63 *DT2;* Census (D) 2-4-5; m Abigail da. Jonathan & Abigail (Beecher) Hitchcock, b 15 July 1751 *DV*, d 20 Mar 1819 æ. 68 *DT2*. **FAM. 19.**

v Abijah, b June 1745 *F*, d 5 Jan 1814 *F;* Census (D) 3-2-6; rem. to Beever, Pa.; m 22 Dec 1773 *F*—Caty Curtis; had issue.

2 JOSEPH, b 28 May 1694 *DV*, d 12 June 1778 æ. 85 *DT1;* Capt.; m Sarah ——— .

i Sarah, b 7 Sep 1726 *DV*, d 7 May 1808 æ. 82 *WatT1;* m 4 Dec 1750 *WatV*—Mark Leavenworth.

ii Joseph, b 17 Feb 1727/8 *DV*, d 24 Sep 1775 æ. 48 *DT1;* m 3 May 1750 *DV*—Elizabeth da. William & Hannah (Peck) Clark, b 24 Sep 1732 *DV*, d 11 Feb 1826 æ. 94 *DT*

I; she m (2) 14 Oct 1776 *DV*—Joseph Tomlinson; she m (3) 13 Feb 1793 *OxfC*—Joseph Osborn; m (4) James Masters. **FAM. 20.**

iii Elizabeth, b 18 Sep 1731 *DV*, d 16 Apr 1738 æ. 7 *DTI*.

iv Anna, b 9 June 1736 *DV*, bp 11 July 1736 *DC*, d 20 Aug 1776 æ. 40 *DT2;* m 10 Oct 1751 *DV*—Richard Mansfield.

3 CALEB, b 4 Feb 1695/6 *DV*, d 8 Sep 1789 *CC;* Ens.; m (1) 1 May 1724 *WV*—Mercy da. Nathan & Sarah (Beecher) Benham, b 6 Aug 1703 *NHV*, d 19 Apr 1766 *WV*, 18 Apr æ. 63 *CTI;* m (2) 2 Feb 1768 *WV*—Ruth da. John & Rebecca Merriam, wid. Josiah Robinson, b 12 Feb 1706 *Lynn, Mass., V*, d 4 July 1776 *WV*, *CC*.

(By 1): *i* Sarah, b 25 Apr 1725 *WV*, bp 7 Nov 1725 *CC*, d 19 Apr 1754 *WV*, Mar *CC*, 1 Apr æ. 29 *CTI;* m 29 Apr 1752 *WV*, *CC*—Reuben Atwater.

ii Andrew, b 23 Aug 1726 *WV*, d 21 Sep 1774 *CC*, 22 Sep æ. 49 *WV*, *CTI;* Lieut.; Census (C) 2-0-4; m 17 Oct 1750 *WV*—Lowly da. Samuel & Hannah (Lewis) Cook, b 10 May 1730 *WV*, d 15 Oct 1785 *CC*, æ. 55 *CTI*. **FAM. 21.**

iii Mary, b 27 Apr 1728 *WV*, bp June 1728 *CC;* m 3 Oct 1745 *WV*—Jotham Hitchcock.

iv Samuel, b 22 Mar 1730 *WV*, bp May 1730 *CC*, d 27 Apr 1791 (at Wallingford, Vt.); m 26 Dec 1753 *WV*—Eunice da. Samuel & Hannah (Lewis) Cook, b 29 June 1735 *WV*, d 9 May 1803 (at Wallingford, Vt.). **FAM. 22.**

v Joseph, b 29 Aug 1732 *WV*, bp Oct 1732 *CC*, d 19 Oct 1732 *WV*.

vi Abijah, b 14 Oct 1733 *WV*, bp 9 Dec 1733 *CC*, d 14 Dec 1733 *WV*.

vii Caleb, b 21 May 1735 *WV*, bp 19 May 1735 *CC*, d 8 Aug 1735 *WV*.

viii Submit, b 12 Dec 1736 *WV*, bp 23 Jan 1736/7 *CC*, d 13 Feb 1737 *WV*.

ix Joseph, b 10 June 1738 *WV*, bp June 1738 *CC*, d 4 Dec 1738 *WV*, *CC*.

x Patience, b 15 Oct 1740 *WV*, d 16 Sep 1765 *WV*, æ. 15 *CTI*.

xi Caleb, b 16 Dec 1742 *WV*, bp Dec 1742 *CC*, d 4 June 1767 *WV*, *CC*, æ. 25 *CTI;* m Mary da. John & Hannah (Hall) Street, b 4 May 1740 *WV;* she m (2) 25 June 1772 *WV*—Joseph Moss. **FAM. 23.**

4 ANDREW, b 13 Jan 1697/8 *DV*, d s. p.

5 MARY, b 13 Sep 1699 *DV;* m 2 Nov 1721 *DV*—Timothy Russell.

6 SARAH, b 13 Aug 1701 *DV*, d 1763; m (1) 1725 William Beach of St; m (2) 1761 Rev. Dr. Samuel Johnson.

7 ABIJAH, b Dec [1703] *DV*, d 10 Aug 1733 æ. 28 *DTI;* m 30 Nov

1727 *DV*—Abigail da. Ebenezer & Abigail (Tibbals) Harger; she m (2) David Wakelee of St.

i Esther, b 13 Sep 172[-] *DV;* m Zachariah Blackman of St.

ii Mercy.

8 NATHAN, b 26 Nov 17[09] *DV*, d s. p.

FAM.. 7. BENJAMIN & ELIZABETH (ANDREWS) HULL:

1 ANDREW, b 17 Aug 1694 *WV*, d s. p. 10 Dec 1717 *WV*.

2 MARY, b 31 Aug 1696 *WV*, d before 1741; m 7 Nov 1716 *WatV*—Ebenezer Bronson.

3 ELIZABETH, b 7/8 Apr 1698 *WV*, d 11 June 1767 æ. 70 *WT2;* m 12 Nov 1723 *WV*—Nathaniel Merriam.

4 DAMARIS, b 3/4 Feb 1700 *WV*, d 22 May 1787 æ. 88 *F;* m 6 Feb 1722 *WV*—Elnathan Street.

5 JOHN, b 6 Oct 1702 *WV*, d 25 May 1768 *CC*, æ. 67 *WV;* Dr.; m (1) 21 June 1727 *WV*—Sarah da. Gideon & Mary (Royce) Ives, b 9 Sep 1708 *WV*, d 29 Nov 1760 *WV*, æ. 53 *CT1;* m (2) 20 Oct 1761 *WV*—Damaris da. Samuel & Ruth (Atwater) Ives, wid. Ebenezer Frost, b 6 July 1718 *NHV*, d 19 Nov 1802 æ. 84-4 *NoHC*.

(By 1): *i* Zephaniah, b 15 Aug 1728 *WV*, d 10 Nov 1760 *Wy;* Dr.; m 28 Mar 1749 *WV*—Hannah da. Moses & Lydia (Richason) Doolittle, b 7 Nov 1732 *WV*, d 10 Nov 1760 *Wy*. FAM. 24.

ii Lois, b 25 Sep 1730 *WV*, bp Sep 1730 *CC*, d 4 June 1803 æ. 74 *CT2;* m (1) 20 Feb 1753 *WV*—Thomas Doolittle; m (2) 3 Dec 1761 *WV*—Nathaniel Royce

iii Elizabeth, b 14 Feb 1733 *WV*, bp Feb 1732/3 *CC;* m 1 Jan 1752 *WV*—Ephraim Cook.

iv Sarah, bp 1 June 1735 *CC*, "child" d 1735 *CC*.

v Sarah, b 12 Jan 1737 *WV*, bp 23 Jan 1736/7 *CC*, d 28 Jan 1740 *WV*.

vi John, b 17 Apr 1739 *WV*, bp May 1739 *CC*, d 27 May 1739 *WV*.

vii Desire, b 6 June 1740 *WV*, "child" d Aug 1740 *CC*.

viii Sarah, b 17 Sep 1741 *WV*, bp Aug (?) 1741 *CC*.

ix John, b 15 Feb 1744 *WV*, bp Feb 1743/4 *CC*, d 8 June 1781 *CC*, æ. 37 *CT1;* Dr.; m 13 Dec 1764 *WV*—Hannah da. Peter & Hannah (Smith) Hitchcock, b 23 Dec 1746 *WV*. FAM. 25.

x Amos, b 27 May 1747 (?) *WV*, bp Apr 1746 *CC*, d 1776 (in camp) *CC*, 3 Oct 1776 æ. 31 *CT1;* Dr.; m 17 Oct 1764 *WV*—Martha da. Dan & Esther (Miles) Hitchcock, b 10 Apr 1748 *WV*, d 23 Jan 1801 æ. 53 *CT1;* she m (2) 20 Nov 1778 *CC*—Dr. Gould Gift Norton. FAM. 26.

6 ABIGAIL, b 14 Jan 1704 *WV*, d 20 Jan 1774 *WV;* m 10 Dec 1719 *WV*—Eliasaph Merriman.

7 SAMUEL, b 1 Sep 1707 *WV*, d 17 Jan 1789 *CC*, æ. 82 *CT1;* Capt.; m (1) 21 Feb 1733 *WV*—Sarah da. Samuel & Love (Royce)

Hall, b 6 Dec 1713 *WV*, d 11 June 1763 *WV*, æ. 50 *CTI;* m (2) 26 Apr 1769 *CC*, *WV*—Lydia da. Samuel & Sarah (Goodsell) Parker, wid. Daniel Humiston, b c. 1726, d 1 Jan 1809 æ. 83 *CTI;* she m (3) John Atwater.

(By 1): *i* Sarah, b 26 Jan 1734 *WV*, bp 5 Feb 1734 *CC*, d 3 May 1734 *WV*.

ii Samuel, b 6 Apr 1735 *WV*, d 22 Apr 1735 *WV*.

iii Samuel, b 12 Aug 1736 *WV*, bp Aug 1736 *CC*, d 30 Apr 1780 æ. 44 *CTI;* Capt.; m (1) 22 Jan 1761 *WV*—Sarah da. Daniel & Lydia (Parker) Humiston, b 14 Dec 1744 *WV*, d 4 Sep 1775 *WV*, *CC*, æ. 31 *CTI;* m (2) 1 Jan 1777 *WV*—Hannah da. John & Hannah (Thompson) Atwater, b 17 Feb 1748/9 *WV*, d 4 Apr 1811 æ. 62 *CTI*. **FAM. 27.**

iv Sarah, b 22 Aug 1738 *WV*, bp Aug 1738 *CC*, d 17 Nov 1769 *WV;* m 22 Aug 1755 *WV*—Joseph Newton.

v Love, b 22 Aug 1738 *WV*, bp Aug 1738 *CC*, d s. p. after 1805; m Thomas Atwater.

vi Anna, b 19 June 1740 *WV*, bp June 1740 *CC*, d 17 June 1776 *WV;* m 16 Jan 1765 *WV*—Jared Newton.

vii Nathaniel, b 2 Oct 1742 *WV*, bp Oct 1742 *CC*, d s. p.

viii Jesse, b 27 Jan 1744/5 *WV*, bp Mar 1745 *CC*, d 17 Apr 1781 *CC;* m Hannah da. Jehiel & Thankful (Sedgwick) Preston, b 5 July 1748 *WV;* Census, Hannah (C) 1-1-3. **FAM. 28.**

ix Lucy, b 24 Jan 1746/7 *WV*, bp Feb 1746/7 *CC*, d 5 Oct 1831 æ. 85 *WatT2;* m (1) 5 July 1770 *WV*—Jared Hall; m (2) Isaac Benham.

x Eunice, b 23 June 1749 *WV*, bp July 1749 *CC;* m 15 Jan 1767 *WV*—Abraham Ives.

xi Levi, b 15 Oct 1751 *WV*, bp Oct 1751 *CC*, d 30 Oct 1751 *WV*.

xii Mehitabel, b 20 Oct 1752 *WV*, bp 1752 *CC;* m 1772 *WV*—David Badger.

xiii Lois, b 31 May 1755 *WV*, d 6 Sep 1825 æ. 71 *CTI;* m 19 Jan 1775 *WV*, *CC*—Asa Blakeslee.

xiv Mary, b 21 Aug 1759 *WV*, d 8 Jan 1764 æ. 5 *CTI*.

(By 2): *xv* Benjamin, b 30 June 1772 *WV*, d 3 May 1835 æ. 63 *CTI;* m Mary ———, who d 3 Nov 1838 æ. 63 *CTI*. **FAM. 29.**

8 SARAH, b 30 Mar 1710 *WV;* m 27 Dec 1732 *WV*—Samuel Hall.

9 BENJAMIN, b 6 July 1712 *WV;* Census (W) 3-0-3; m 17 Dec 1735 *WV*—Hannah Parmelee.

i Phebe, b 8 Jan 1737 *WV;* m 30 Nov 1755 *WV*—Zachariah Johnson.

ii Hannah, b 3 May 1739 *WV*, d 10 Apr 1760 *WV;* m 13 Apr 1757 *WV*—Charles Peck.

iii Benjamin, b 20 Oct 1741 *WV*, d 16 Jan 1767 (at Wtn)

WatV; Dr.; m 26 Aug 1763 *WV*—Esther da. Samuel & Elizabeth (Perkins) Merriam, b 9 May 1746 *WV*, d 1829; she m (2) 1770 Jotham Curtis; m (3) 1798 Nathaniel Barnes; m (4) Elisha Wilcox. FAM. 30.

iv Eliakim, b 1 Mar 1744 *WV*, d 18 Jan 1767 æ. 23 *WV*.

v Charles, b 1 Mar 1744 *WV*, d 1 May 1815 æ. 75 (at W) *ColR;* Census (W) 1-1-3; m 8 May 1776 *WV*—Sarah da. Joseph & Lydia (Jones) Moss, b 22 Mar 1757 *WV;* had issue.

vi Sybil, b 15 Apr 1746 *WV*, d 22 June 1758 *WV*.

vii Joel, b 6 Aug 1749 *WV*, d in Ohio; m 11 Feb 1783 *WV*—Sarah da. Joseph & Sarah (Hull) Newton, b 4 May 1758 *WV*, d 23 Aug 1816 æ. 59 *WT1;* had s. Anson.

viii Bede, b 11 Apr 1753 *WV;* m 2 Oct 1778 *WV*—Theophilus Moss.

ix Lois, b 1 Jan 1757 *WV*.

x Asahel, b 21 Aug 1759 *WV*.

FAM. 8. EBENEZER & LYDIA (MIX) HULL:

1 HANNAH, b 16 Apr 1707 *WV;* [?m 11 Jan 1743/4 *FarmV*—John Hart].

2 REBECCA, b c. 1708.

3 EBENEZER, b c. 1710, d 19 Feb 1777 *WV;* m 1 Sep 1731 *WV*—Anna da. Henry & Mary (Chatfield) Bates, b 11 Mar 1713 *WV*, d 1803.

i Dan, b 23 Feb 1732 *WV*, d 13 Mar 1732 *WV*.

ii Joseph, b 23 Feb 1732 *WV*, d 28 Mar 1732 *WV*.

iii Lydia, b 14 Apr 1734 *WV;* m 2 Sep 1759 *WV*—Nicholas Andrews.

iv Eunice, b 7 Oct 1736 *WV;* m 4 Dec 1761 *WV*—Miles Hull.

v Anna, b 13 Oct 1738 *WV;* m 13 Oct 1763 *FarmV*—Elijah Gaylord.

vi Mary, b c. 1740, d 8 Mar 1768 *WV*, *CC;* m 2 Aug 1764 *WV*—Ephraim Tuttle.

vii Joseph, b 1 Mar 1742/3 *WV*, d s. p. 11 Feb 1772 *WV*.

viii Rene, d 9 Aug 1784 *CC;* m 9 Apr 1768 *CV*—Benjamin Sperry.

ix Sarah, d 21 Aug 1775 *WV*.

x Ebenezer, b c. 1750, d 21 June 1807 æ. 57 *WT1;* Census (W) 1-2-4; m Patience ——. FAM. 31.

xi Esther, b 27 Mar 1756 *WV;* m 19 May 1773 *WV*, *CC*—Abner Hitchcock.

FAM. 9. JEREMIAH & HANNAH (COOK) HULL:

1 JOHN, b 13 Nov 1712 *WV*, d 15 Aug 1755 *WV;* Dr.; m 28 Oct 1735 *WV*—Mary da. Joseph & Abigail (Payne) Andrews, b 15 June 1714 *WV;* she m (2) Macock Ward.

i Moses, b c. 1736; m 5 May 1757 *WV*, *WC2*—Mary da. Stephen & Sarah (Hart) Ives, b 16 Apr 1735 *WV*.

FAM. 32.

ii Molly, b 12 Mar 1738 *WV;* m (1) 28 Apr 1757 *WV*—Thomas Shepard; m (2) ——— Merriam.

iii John, b 7 Mar 1741 *WV*, d 6 Oct 1828 æ. 88 *WT1;* Census (W) 1-2-3; m (1) 20 Mar 1759 *WV*—Lois da. Nathaniel & Elizabeth (Hitchcock) Beadles, b c. 1743, d 6 Sep 1802 æ. 59 *WT1;* m (2) Phebe ———, who d 3 Sep 1834 æ. 93 *WT1*. **FAM. 33.**

iv Nathaniel, b 7 Mar 1743 *WV*, d 25 Feb 1771 *WV;* Dr.; m 13 Apr 1763 *WV*—Mehitabel da. Nathaniel & Elizabeth (Hitchcock) Beadles, b 27 Aug 1745 *WV*, d 1776; she m (2) 4 June 1772 *WV*—Amos Cook. Children: (1) George, b 8 Apr 176[4] *WV*. (2) Chester, b 18 Jan 1766 *WV;* Census (Woodstock, N. Y.) 1-0-0. (3) Wyllys, b 17 Apr 1769 *WV;* m Mehitabel da. Titus & Elizabeth (McKay) Hall, b 26 July 1773 *WV*.

v Aaron, b 17 July 1745 *WV;* m 17 Nov 1769 *WV*—Sarah da. Thomas & Sarah (Perry) Marchant, b 21 Feb 1752 *WV*, d 22 Sep 1807 æ. 56 *WT2*. Children: Cornelius, b 26 Sep 1770 *WV;* Hannah, b 26 Jan 1772 *WV;* Rachel, b 10 Jan 1774 *WV;* Aaron, b 3 Feb 1776 *WV;* Zerviah, b 13 May 1778 *WV;* Sally, b 5 June 1780 *WV*.

vi Abigail, b 1 Dec 1747 *WV;* m 23 Nov 1767 *WV*—Abel Thompson.

vii Hannah, b 1 July 1750 *WV*, d 24 Feb 1828 æ. 78 *NoHT2*, *NoHC;* m Asa Bray.

2 Moses, b 26 Dec 1714 *WV*, d 3 June 1736 *WV*.

3 Tabitha, (called "Molly"), b 3 Mar 1717 *WV*, d 17 Aug 1740 *WV;* m 12 July 1737 *WV*—Timothy Bartholomew.

4 Hannah, b 18 May 1721 *WV;* m (1) 31 Aug 1742 *WV*—Jehiel Tuttle; m (2) Stephen Andrews.

5 Anna; m 3 Aug 1741 *WV*—Enos Benham.

6 Jeremiah, b 5 Jan 1729 *WV*, d 24 Aug 1790 æ. 60 *WT1;* m (1) 18 Jan 1753 *WV*—Mary da. Caleb & Ruth (Sedgwick) Merriman, b c. 1735, d 22 Aug 1775 æ. 41 *WT1;* m (2) 30 Sep 1776 *WV*—Eunice [da. Nathaniel & Lois (Curtis)] Curtis, b [12 Apr 1750 *WV*]. He had a nat. child by Ann Royce, b 1751 *NHCCt*.

(By 1): *i* Caleb, b 1 Dec 1753 *WV*.

ii Samuel, b 6 Dec 1755 *WV*, d 30 Aug 1822 æ. 68 *WT1;* m Lois [Peck], who d 30 Jan 1830 æ. 65 *WT1;* she m (2) Charles Ives. **FAM. 34.**

iii Ann, b 22 Mar 1758 *WV;* [m Jacob Royce].

iv Mary, b 7 Nov 1760 *WV*, d 29 Mar 1849; res. Jewett, Greene Co., N. Y.; m 3 Feb 1785 *WV*—Theophilus Peck.

v Jeremiah, b 18 Dec 1762 *WV*, d 10 Oct 1843 æ. 81 *WT1;* Census (W) 1-0-4; m (1) Sarah Barker da. John & Eunice (Barker) Beadles, b 6 June 1765 *WV*, d 14 Apr 1792 æ. 27 *WT1;* m (2) Phebe da. Nathaniel & Alice

(Hall) Hart, b 29 Apr 1772 *WV*, d 9 Nov 1855 æ. 84 *WT1*. **FAM. 35.**

vi Ruth, b 4 May 1765 *WV*.

vii Abigail, b 1 Sep 1767 *WV*.

viii Susanna, b 15 Jan 1770 *WV*.

(By 2): *ix* Benjamin, b 29 June 1778 *WV*.

7 JOSEPH, b 24 May 1733 *WV*, d 23 June 1777 *PC*; m 1754 Hannah [probably wid. or da. of James] Corbet; she m (2) 28 Nov 1782 *PC*—Job Bronson.

i Mary, b 20 Sep 1755 *WV*.

ii Caldwell, b 2 Jan 1759 *WV*.

iii (perhaps) Patience; m 21 Dec 1780 *PC*—Felix Curtis.

iv (perhaps) Hannah; m 13 Nov 1780 *PC*—Daniel Bronson.

v (perhaps) Lois, d 7 May 1778 *PC*.

8 PATIENCE, b 1735 *WV*.

FAM. 10. EZRA & ANNIS (JOHNSON) HULL:

1 JOHN, b 21 Feb 1772 *WatV*, d 8 Sep 1823 æ. 52 *WatT1*; m Sena ——, who d 10 Nov 1864 æ. 86 *WatT1*.

2 JANE, b 8 Feb 1774 *WatV*, d 21 Nov 1799 æ. 25 *WatT1*; m David Hoadley.

3 SARAH, b c. 1776, d 9 Aug 1794 æ. 18 *WatT1*.

4 ESTHER, b c. 1781, d 24 Jan 1810 æ. 29 *WatT1*.

FAM. 11. JAMES & MARY (BALL) HULL.

1 ELIZABETH, b c. 1767, bp 11 July 1773 *NHC2*, d 20 Sep 1812 æ. 46 *Salemx*; m Isaiah Gunn.

2 JOEL, b c. 1770, bp 11 July 1773 *NHC2*; m Mehitabel da. Jobamah & Hannah (Candee) Gunn, b 22 Mar 1777 *WatV*, d 16 June 1849 æ. 72 *Salemx*.

i Orrin, b 10 Feb 1794 *WatV*; m.

ii Alma, d 31 Aug 1796 *WatT* (*Gunntown*).

iii Alma, b 29 Aug 1797 *WatV*.

iv Henry, b 12 Jan 1804 *WatV*.

v Daniel, b 28 May 1806 *WatV*, d 15 Mar 1838 æ. 32 *Salemx*.

3 LUCY, bp 11 July 1773 *NHC2*; m 21 Dec 1788 *NHC2*—Hezekiah Bradley.

4 ABIAH, bp 10 Mar 1776 *NHC2*.

5 LYDIA, bp 19 July 1778 *NHC2*.

6 AMELIA, bp 21 July 1782 *NHC2*; m John Gunn.

7 MERCY, bp 21 July 1782 *NHC2*.

8 ASENATH, bp Mar 1785 *NHC2*.

FAM. 12. JOSEPH & ABIAH (ALLING) HULL:

1 WILLIAM, b 11 Apr 1774 *NHV*, d 22 June 1812 æ. 38 *NHT1*.

FAM. 12. JOSEPH & DAMARIS (HULL) HULL:

2 MARY; m 14 Dec 1793 *NHC1*—Newman Greenleaf.

3 ABIAH, b 3 Jan 1779 *NHV*, d 16 Feb 1847 æ. 68 *NHT1*; m Elijah Davis.

FAM. 13. DAVID & HANNAH (PUNDERSON) HULL:

1 THOMAS, b c. 1775, d Jan 1841 æ. 66 *WHD*; m Annah da Aaron

& Anna [Graham] Thomas. Children: John Thomas; Samuel; Mary, m Harvey Alling; Elizabeth, m Sylvester Colburn; Hannah P,, m William Smith; & Martha, m Sullivan M. Colburn.

2 ELISHA, b c. 1778, d 8 Apr 1842 æ. 64 *NHV;* m 22 Jan 1804 *NHC1*—Huldah da. Glover & Hannah (Hotchkiss) Ball, b 29 Apr 1779 *NHV*, d 23 Aug 1854 æ. 75-3-25 *NHV*.

3 ELIAS, b c. 1782, d 21 Jan 1862 æ. 80 *NHV;* m 14 Jan 1805 *NHx*—Sena da. Timothy & Martha (Turner) Potter.

4 ELAM, b c. 1785, d 15 July 1863 æ. 78 *NHV;* m 1811 Nancy da. Lemuel & Margaret (Green) Benham, b 17 Dec 1789 *NHV*.

5 DAVID, b c. 1788, d 5 Dec 1853 æ. 65 *NHT1*, (insane) *NHV;* m Fanny Dickerson.

6 HANNAH, b c. 1791, d 4 Aug 1864 æ. 73 *NHT2;* m Silas Ford.

FAM. 14. SAMUEL & MABEL [?BRADLEY] HULL:

1 SIDNEY, b 28 Aug 1784 *NHT1*, bp 2 Dec 1784 *NHC2*, d 21 Aug 1861 *NHT1;* m (1) 20 May 1808 Rebecca da. Amos & Amelia (Beecher) Alling, b 4 Apr 1787 *NHT1*, d 17 Feb 1819 *NHT1;* m (2) Esther da. James & Esther (Tuttle) Bradley, b 19 Feb 1785 *F*, d 18 Oct 1823 æ. 38 *NHT1;* m (3) Martha Jinks da. John L. & Phebe Abbott of Andover, Mass., who d 3 Dec 1836 æ. 37 *NHT1;* m (4) Sarah Kneeland Abbott, her sister, who d 2 Jan 1854 æ. 56 *NHT1;* m (5) Anna da. Daniel Colburn, b 26 May 1801 *NHT1*, d 31 Aug 1886 *NHT1*, æ. 85-3 *NHV*.

i Amelia, b 20 Apr 1809, d 16 June 1837; m 4 Apr 1830 William Abbott.

ii Algernon Sidney, b 28 Jan 1811, d 12 July 1873; m 24 Aug 1835 Jeannette A. Scranton.

iii Isaac, b 16 Mar 1813; m 1835 Susan Bradley.

iv Rebecca, b 24 Feb 1815, d 6 Mar 1849; m 5 Feb 1837 John Townsend.

v Samuel J.

vi Sarah Elizabeth.

vii Martha Abbott.

2 EBENEZER, bp 9 Apr 1786 *NHC2*, d 1802 æ. 16 (at Surinam) *ConnJournal*.

3 ALMIRA, bp 11 July 1790 *NHC2*, d 18 Feb 1869 æ. 78 *NHT1*.

4 HEZEKIAH, b c. 1796, d 3 Aug 1823 æ. 27 (at Alexandria, La.) *NHT1;* Rev.

FAM. 15. JOHN & MARTHA (PARDEE) HULL:

1 JOHN, b 18 Apr 1771 *F*, d 4 Sep 1864 *F;* res. Oxford, N. Y.; m Hannah Wood.

2 DAUGHTER, d 23 Oct 1773 *NoHC*.

3 SARAH, b c. 1775, d 4 Aug 1795 æ. 20 *NoHC*.

4 EBENEZER, b 15 Nov 1776 *F*, d 24 July 1849 *F;* res. Oxford, N. Y.; m 2 Jan 1803 *NoHV*—Bede da. Joseph & Lydia (Jacobs) Jacobs, b 2 July 1779 *NHV*.

5 ELI, b [12 May 1778], d 14 Sep 1854 æ. 76 *HT3*, æ. 76-4-2 *HV;*

m (1) Amelia da. Jonathan & Miriam (Bradley) Dickerman, wid. Jesse Munson, b 13 May 1779 *NHV*, d 11 Dec 1813 æ. 35 *HT3;* m (2) 1 May 1814 *OC*—Mehitabel da. Josiah & Rebecca (Thomas) Pardee, b 1777 *MV*, d 8 Dec 1831 æ. 55 *HT3;* m (3) 31 Aug 1832 *NoHV*— Anna Talmadge of Northford, who d 22 May 1839 æ. 53 *HT3.*

6 ROSANNAH, b c. 1781, d 3 Feb 1846 æ. 65 *NoHT1;* m 22 Apr 1801 *NoHC*—Thomas Smith. .

7 ELIJAH, b 14 Jan 1784 *NoHV*, d 24 Aug 1871 æ. 87 *NoHT3;* m 20 Dec 1812 *NoHV*—Nancy da. Philemon & Lydia (Brockett) Blakeslee, b 8 Nov 1787 *NoHV*, d 17 June 1872 æ. 84 *NoHT3.*

8 ELISAPH, b 30 Oct 1786 *NoHV*, d 22 Jan 1875; m 30 Dec 1811 *NoHV*—Rhoda Clark.

FAM. 16. BENJAMIN & HANNAH (HUMISTON) HULL:

1 BENJAMIN LYMAN, bp 1781 *NoHx.*

2 JESSE.

3 EZRA WHITING, b 10 Jan 1786 *NoHV*, bp 1786 *NoHx.*

4 JAMES CHAUNCEY, bp 1788 *NoHx.*

5 LAVINIA, bp 1791 *NoHx.*

6 HANNAH, bp 1793 *NoHx.*

7 ORRIN; m 13 Nov 1820 *NHV*—Hannah Botsford of D.

8 MABEL; m 27 Jan 1822 *NoHV*—Amos Bassett of H.

9 JARVIS, b 15 June 1800 *F*, d 25 June 1872 *F;* m Eliza Gay.

FAM. 17. MILES & EUNICE (HULL) HULL:

1 AMZI, b 29 May 1762 *WV*, d 3 Oct 1795 æ. 33 *WT1*, *WdC;* Dr.; Census (Wd) 1-2-2; m Mary Ann Kasson; she m (2) Gideon Leavenworth.

i Aurelius, b 31 Oct 1786 *F*, bp 28 Jan 1787 *WdC*, d 29 Oct 1794 æ. 8 *WdT1.*

ii Auretius Bevil, b 12 Oct 1788 *F*, bp 10 Oct 1788 *WdC*, d 17 May 1826 (at Worcester, Mass.); B. A. (Yale, 1807); Rev.; m 5 Mar 1817 Abigail Elizabeth da. Joseph & Aurelia (Mills) Darling, bp 30 May 1790 *NoHV*, d 9 Jan 1860 æ. 70 *NHT1.*

iii Sophia, bp 15 Mar 1791 *WdC*, d 22 Jan 1794 *WdC*, 19 Jan æ. 3 *WdT1.*

iv Amanda, bp 21 June 1793 *WdC*, d 22 Sep 1795 *WdC*, 24 Sep æ. 2-4 *WdT1.*

2 MOLLY, b 7 June 1764 *WV;* m Levi Douglas.

3 LUTHER, b 10 June 1766 *WV;* Census (C) 1-0-1.

4 EUNICE, b 30 Apr 1768 *WV*, bp 12 June 1768 *CC;* m 20 July 1789 *CC*—Nathan Baldwin.

5 MILES, b 16 Dec 1769 *WV*, bp 28 Jan 1770 *CC*, d 24 Apr 1801 æ. 31 *WT2;* m Deborah da. Joseph & Mindwell (Royce) Merriam, b 23 Oct 1776 *WV*, d 31 Oct 1802 æ. 26 *WT2.*

i Elijah G.

ii Amanda, d 1807.

6 JOSEPH, b 23 Mar 1772 *WV*, bp 26 Apr 1772 *CC.*

7 EBENEZER, b 22 Oct 1776 *WV*, bp 5 Jan 1777 *CC*.

FAM. 18. ABIJAH & RACHEL (THOMPSON) HULL (family incomplete):

1 ANER, b 21 Mar 1775 *WV*, "Anna" bp 19 Oct 1775 *CC*.

2 ROSETTA, b 4 Mar 1777 *WV*, bp 13 Apr 1777 *CC*.

3 AZUBA, b 5 July 1780 *CV*, bp 15 July 1781 *CC;* m 3 Oct 1802 *CC*—Abner Bunnell.

4 ABIJAH, b 11 Oct 1783 *CV*, bp 23 Nov 1783 *CC*.

5 ESTHER, b 10 Aug 1789 *CV*, bp 24 May 1789 *CC*.

FAM. 19. SAMUEL & ABIGAIL (HITCHCOCK) HULL:

1 EUNICE, bp 12 Mar 1769 *Dx*, d 1 Mar 1817 æ. 49 *DT2;* m William Mansfield.

2 LUCY, bp 30 Dec 1770 *Dx;* m Josiah Masters of Seatuoke (?), N. Y. [Perhaps Scaghticoke N. Y., is meant.]

3 NABBY, bp 12 Oct 1772 *Dx;* m George Riel of N. Y. State.

4 CHARITY, b c. 1775; m Munson Smith of N. Y. State.

5 SAMUEL, b c. 1777, bp 9 Mar 1783 *Dx*, d 19 Mar 1844 æ. 67 *DT2;* m (1) Lavinia da. Henry Deming of Wethersfield, who d 4 July 1804 æ. 23 *DT2;* m (2) Betsey ——, who d 19 May 1852 æ. 68 *DT2*.

6 ABIJAH, b c. 1779, bp 9 Mar 1783 *Dx;* m.

7 WILLIAM, bp 9 Mar 1783 *Dx*.

8 NANCY, bp 19 Dec 1784 *Dx*, d 31 July 1785 æ. 0-9 *DT2*.

9 KNEELAND, b c. 1786, d 1806 æ. 20 *DT2*.

10 NANCY, b c. 1790, d 1806 æ. 16 *DT2*.

FAM. 20. JOSEPH & ELIZABETH (CLARK) HULL;

1 JOSEPH, b 27 Oct 1750 *DV*, d Jan 1825; Lieut.; m (1) Sarah da. Daniel Bennett, b c. 1751, d 9 Nov 1803 æ. 50 *HuntingtonC;* m (2) Lucy da. Isaac & Lucy (Clark) Smith, wid. Joseph Wheeler, b 22 Dec 1754 *DV;* m (3) 8 Feb 1821 *DV*—Freelove, wid. Silas Nichols

(By 1): *i* Joseph, bp 20 Sep 1772 *DC*, d 1810 (N. Y. State); m 1800 Susan Barton.

ii Isaac, b 9 Mar 1773 *F*, bp 6 June 1773 *DC*, d Feb 1843; Commodore, U. S. Navy.; m Anna Hart of Saybrook.

iii Levi, bp 14 Jan 1776 *DC*, d 23 Jan 1848; m 1811 Mary Wheeler.

iv William, bp 17 Feb 1782 *DC*, d 1812 (at N. Y.).

v Daniel, bp 25 Apr 1784 *DC*, d 1817 (in Miss.).

vi Henry, b c. 1788, d 1833 (Huntington).

vii Charles, b c. 1792, d at N. Y.

2 WILLIAM, b 24 Jan 1753 *DV*, bp 24 June 1753 *Dx*, d 25 Nov 1825; B. A. (Yale, 1772); Maj. Gen.; Judge; Senator (Mass.) 1798–1805; Gov. of Mich. Territory 1805–1812; m 1781 Sarah da. Abraham Fuller of Newtown; issue, 7 das. & 1 s., Capt. Abraham Fuller, k. at Lundy's Lane 25 July 1814.

3 SAMUEL, b 5 Aug 1755 *DV;* Lieut.; m.

4 ELIZABETH, b 27 Jan 1759 *DV*, bp 25 Feb 1759 *DC*, d 1842; m Isaac Smith.

5 ISAAC, b 28 Dec 1760 *DV*, bp 8 Mar 1761 *DC*, d 1829 (at Monroe, Mich.); m Martha Clark, who d 1817 æ. 64; issue 10 children.

6 DAVID, b 27 Mar 1765 *DV*, bp 5 May 1765 *DV*, d 1834; B. A. (Yale, 1782); Dr.; res. Fairfield; m 10 Nov 1789 ——— da. Rev. Andrew Elliott of Boston.

7 SARAH, b 6 Jan 1769 *DV*, bp 5 Mar 1769 *DC*; m 11 Oct 1795 Anson Gillet.

8 LEVI, b 29 Apr 1771 *DV*, bp 5 May 1771 *DC*, d 10 Oct 1775 æ. 5 *DTI*.

FAM. 21. ANDREW & LOWLY (COOK) HULL:

1 DAMARIS, b 18 Sep 1751 *WV*, bp 3 Nov 1751 *CC*, d 4 Mar 1829 æ. 78 *NHTI*; m 14 Dec 1775 *CC*—Joseph Hull of NH.

2 LOWLY, b 16 Feb 1753 *WV*, d 10 June 1810 æ. 57 *CTI*; m Eliakim Hitchcock.

3 HANNAH, b 6 Dec 1754 *WV*, d 14 Aug 1800 æ. [42] *CTI*; m 10 Feb 1773 *CC*—Lucius Tuttle.

4 SARAH, b c. 1756.

5 ANDREW, b 6 Oct 1758 *WV*, d 24 Apr 1827 æ. 69 *CTI*; Gen.; m 21 Sep 1781 *CC*—Elizabeth Mary Ann da. Reuben & Mary (Russell) Atwater, b 7 Sep 1760 *WV*, d 25 Dec 1838 æ. 78 *CTI*.

i Eudocia, bp 20 Oct 1782 *CC*, d 12 Jan 1849; m 10 Mar 1803 *CC*—Samuel A. Foote, Gov. of Conn.

ii Son, b [5 July 1784], d 25 July 1784 æ. 0-0-20 *CTI*.

iii Son, b & d 21 May 1785 *CTI*.

iv Merab Atwater, bp 28 Jan 1787 *CC*; m 12 May 1828 *CV*—Henry Whittlesey of Catskill, N. Y.

v Betsey, bp 15 Sep 1789 *CC*, d 20 Oct 1789 æ. 0-3 *CTI*.

vi Betsey, bp 19 Dec 1790 *CC*; m 3 Oct 1821 *CV*—Rev. Ambrose Seymour Todd of Stamford.

vii Sally, bp 2 Mar 1794 *CC*; m 24 Dec 1825 *CV*—Rev. John Wurts Cloud of Jefferson Co., Miss.

viii Mary, bp 25 Sep 1796 *CC*; m 20 Oct 1819 *CV*—William R. Hitchcock.

ix Andrew, bp 29 July 1798 *CC*, d 30 Sep 1804 æ. 7 *CTI*.

x Adaline, bp 7 Apr 1802 *CC*; m Rev. ——— Mason.

6 URSULA, b 10 Nov 1760 *WV*, d 8 May 1822 æ. 61 *BristolT*; m Jason Hotchkiss.

7 MERCY, b 4 Nov 1762 *WV*, d 15 June 1790 æ. 27 *CTI*; m 11 Dec 1783 *CC*—David Royce.

8 ESTHER, b 24 Oct 1764 *WV*, d 19 Feb 1789 æ. 24 *CTI*; m 30 Dec 1785 *CC*—Merriman Hotchkiss.

9 JOSEPH, b & d 1 Dec 1766 *CTI*.

10 LOVICY.

FAM. 22. SAMUEL & EUNICE (COOK) HULL:

1 [SON, b 1 Jan 1755, d in infancy].

2 JEDEDIAH, b 26 Feb 1756 *WV*, d 28 Mar 1783 *CC*, æ. 28 *CTI*; m 17 Feb 1780 *CC*—Abigail da. John & Hannah (Thompson) Atwater; she m (2) 8 Oct 1786 *CC*—Edward Goodyear; m (3)

Solomon Alcott.

i Lois Elizabeth, b 13 Nov 1780 *CV;* m 31 Mar 1802 *CC*—Benoni Dickerman; res. Delaware Co., Ohio.

ii Abigail Alma, bp 24 Nov 1782 *CC*, d 4 Feb 1783 *CC*, 3 Feb æ. 0-5 *CTI*.

3 Son, d 2 Feb 1758 *CTI*.

4 Samuel, b 27 May 1759 *WV*, d 27 Oct 1828 æ. 70 *CTI;* Census (C) 1-1-2; m 26 May 1785 *WV*, *CC*—Abigail Ann da. Amos & Abigail (Ives) Doolittle, b 27 Jan 1766 *WV*, d 10 Oct 1835 æ. 69 *CTI*.

i Stella, b 28 Mar 1786 *CV*, bp 4 June 1786 CC, d 13 Dec 1841 æ. 56; m Jonathan Law.

ii Jedediah, b 19 Nov 1788 *CV*, d 25 Feb 1837 æ. 49 *CTI;* insane.

iii Ann, b 13 Jan 1794 *F*, bp 17 Aug 1794 CC, d 27 Aug 1818 æ. 25 *CTI*.

iv Linda, b 6 Feb 1796 *F*, d 30 Apr 1865; m David Brooks.

v Eunice, b 12 Nov 1798 *F*, bp 17 Feb 1799 *CC;* m Birdsey Booth of Cuyahoga Falls, Ohio.

vi Charlotte L., b 9 Sep 1800 *F;* m John Olmstead of Hartford.

vii Samuel Cook, b 4 Aug 1802 *F*, bp 17 Oct 1802 *CC*, d 26 Aug 1804 æ. 3 *CTI*.

viii Samuel, b 4 Feb 1805 *F;* res. Morris, Ill.

ix Julius, b 1 July 1807 *F*, bp 27 Feb 1807 *CC;* res. Ohio; m Lucy Ives.

x Andrew Franklin, b 13 Jan 1811 *F*, bp 5 May 1811 *CC*, d 1 Jan 1845 *CV;* m Adeline Munson.

5 Zephaniah, b 1 May 1761 *WV*, d 20 Feb 1840; Census (Wallingford, Vt.) 3-0-3.

6 Epaphras, b 9 Apr 1763 *WV*, d 13 Apr 1827 (at Wallingford, Vt.); Census (C) 1-1-2.

7 Eunice, b 16 Apr 1765 *WV*, d 18 Dec 1820 (at Cazenovia, N. Y.); m Sheriff Whipple.

8 Lois, b 1 Feb 1767 *WV*, d 20 Oct 1777 æ. 11 *WV*, *CTI*.

9 Caleb, b 9 Nov 1768 *WV*, d 9 Aug 1816 (at Wallingford, Vt.)

10 Elizabeth, b 28 Oct 1770 *WV*, d 13 Oct 1777 æ. 7 *WV*, *CTI*.

11 Josephus, b 24 Aug 1772 *WV*, d 18 Mar 1813 (at Wallingford, Vt.).

12 Hannah, b 11 Oct 1775 *WV;* m A. Meacham of Wallingford, Vt.

FAM. 23. Caleb & Mary (Street) Hull:

1 Ambrose, b 22 Mar 1764 *WV;* [?m Mary da. Elihu Atwater].

2 Abiathar, b 13 Jan 1766 *WV;* Census (C) 1-1-1; m Anna Hudson.

3 Mary, b 14 Aug 1767 *WV;* m David Hudson.

FAM. 24. Zephaniah & Hannah (Doolittle) Hull;

1 Lydia, b 22 Dec 1749 *WV*, bp Feb 1749/50 *CC*, d 21 Feb 1749/50

WV.

2 Titus, b 25 Mar 1750/1 *WV*, bp Mar 1751 *CC;* Dr.; Census (Bethlehem) 3-3-7; rem. to Danbury & N. Y. State; m (1) 4 Nov 1773 *Wy*—Lucy Parmelee; m (2) 1778 Olive (———) Parmelee.

3 Lydia, b 23 Jan 1753 *WyV*, d 29 July 1840 æ. 88 *CTI;* m (1) 22 Nov 1769 *Wy*—Joseph Judson; m (2) 28 Dec 1785 *CV, CC*—Amasa Clark.

4 Andrew, b 8 Dec 1754 *WyV*, d 31 Mar 1824 æ. 70 *CTI;* Census (C) 1-0-4; m 30 Nov 1774 *WV*—Naomi da. Bela & Abigail (Moss) Lewis, b c. 1754, d 28 Oct 1824 æ. 71 *CTI.*

i Naomi Hannah, b 25 June 1778 *WV*, bp 27 Sep 1789 *CC*, d 24 June 1849 æ. 71 *CTI;* m Sep 1797 *ConnJournal*—William Brown.

5 Hannah, b 28 Jan 1757 *WyV*, d 16 Nov 1760 *Wy.*

6 Sarah, b 17 May 1759 *WyV*, d 15 Nov 1760 *Wy.*

FAM. 25. John & Hannah (Hitchcock) Hull:

1 John, b 3 Oct 1765 *WV*, d 4 Feb 1768 *WV*, 1769 æ. 3 *CTI.*

2 Eliakim, b 11 Mar 1767 *WV;* res. Farm.

3 John, b 2 May 1770 *WV*, bp 10 June 1770 *CC;* res. Farm.

4 Nimrod, b 11 Feb 1773 *WV*, bp 21 Feb 1773 *CC*, d 26 Jan 1824 æ. 51 *WatT3;* Dr.; m (1) Amy Lewis, who d 1 Jan 1818 æ. 43 *WatT3;* m (2) Amelia Seeley.

5 Peter, bp 15 Oct 1775 *CC.*

6 Hannah, b 11 Apr 1778 *WV*, bp 24 May 1778 *CC.*

FAM. 26. Amos & Martha (Hitchcock) Hull:

1 Zephaniah, b 15 July 1765 *WV*, d 19 Sep 1769 *WV, CC*, 18 Sep æ. 5 *CTI.*

2 Martha, b 21 Mar 1767 *WV;* m 16 Feb 1783 *CC*—Samuel Tuttle.

3 Zephaniah, b 21 Feb 1770 *WV*, bp 23 Apr 1770 *CC*, d 17 Sep 1774 æ. 5 *CTI*, 15 Sep *WV.*

4 Amos, b 1 May 1773 *WV*, bp 9 May 1773 *CC*, d 5 Oct 1774 *WV*, æ. 2 *CTI.*

5 Amos Gift, bp 15 Oct 1775 *CC;* Dr.; m (1) c. 1797, Betsey H. da. Ira & Caroline (Shattuck) Bartholomew, b c. 1779, d 11 Sep 1798 æ. 21 *NewHartford, N. Y., T;* m (2) 3 Mar 1799 *BdC*—Elizabeth da. Timothy & Chloe Morris, bp 22 Aug 1779 *BdC*, d at Whitestown c. Oct 1802 *ConnJournal*, 1 Oct æ. 28 *NewHartford, N. Y., T;* m (3) Eunice ———, who d 5 Aug 1812 æ. 33 *NewHartford N. Y., T;* m (4) Lydia da. Aaron & Elizabeth (Taintor) Cook.

FAM. 27. Samuel & Sarah (Humiston) Hull:

1 Sarah, b 10 Nov 1761 *WV*, d 31 Aug 1766 *WV*, æ. 5 *CTI.*

FAM. 27. Samuel & Hannah (Atwater) Hull:

2 Sarah Humiston, b 21 Oct 1777 *WV*, bp 26 Oct 1777 *CC.*

3 Betsey, b 22 Feb 1779 *WV*, bp 28 Feb 1779 *CC*, d 15 May 1852 æ. 73 *CTI;* m 13 Sep 1800 *CV*—Bethuel Flagg.

4 Samuel, bp 4 Mar 1781 *CC*, d 5 May 1834 æ. 54 *CTI;* m 30 Jan

1817 *CV*—Alma da. Jesse & Lois (Doolittle) Humiston, b 8 Feb 1787 *CV*, d 14 Oct 1854 æ. 70 *CT1*.

FAM. 28. JESSE & HANNAH (PRESTON) HULL:

1 THELUS, bp 22 Nov 1778 *CC;* Census (C) 1-2-2; rem. to Ohio; m Mary da. Jared & Anna (Hull) Newton, b 9 Sep 1766 *WV*. His children Philome, Samuel, Gilbert, Mary, Anna, Lyman & Elizabeth were bp 11 May 1804 *CC*. Philome m 28 Sep 1806 *CC*—Reuben Bunnell.

2 SAMUEL, b 1769 *CV*, bp 22 Nov 1778 *CC*, d 8 Dec 1857 æ. 90 *CT1;* m 20 Feb 1810 *CC*—Rebecca Manwaring, who d 24 Apr 1884 æ. 98 *CT1*.

3 SARAH, bp 22 Nov 1778 *CC;* m c. 1796 Mark Smith of L.

4 HANNAH, bp 22 Nov 1778 *CC*.

5 LOVE, bp 22 Nov 1778 *CC*.

6 MARY ANN, bp 28 Feb 1779 *CC;* m 5 Jan 1801 *CC*—Reuel Blake.

7 RUTH, bp 10 June 1781 *CC*.

FAM. 29. BENJAMIN & MARY (———) HULL;

1 CHAUNCEY, b c. 1794, bp 16 June 1805 *CC*, d 2 Aug 1830 æ. 36 *CT1;* m Hannah Hotchkiss, who d 14 July 1878 æ. 83 *CT1*.

2 LUCY ANN, bp 16 June 1805 *CC;* m Samuel U. Beach.

3 BENJAMIN RICE, bp 16 June 1805 *CC;* res. Canada.

4 AMASA, bp 16 June 1805 *CC*.

5 DARIUS, bp 16 June 1805 *CC;* m Martha ———, who d 16 Mar 1858 æ. 53 *CT1*.

6 MARY, bp 27 Nov 1808 *CC*, d 6 Apr 1812 æ. 4 *CT1*.

7 SAMUEL LEVI, bp 7 July 1811 *CC*, d 1 June 1813 æ. 3 *CT1*.

8 ABIATHAR, b c. 1814, d 10 Oct 1839 æ. 25 *CT1*.

9 SAMUEL LEE, b c. 1818, d 5 Jan 1838 æ. 20 *CT1*.

FAM. 30. BENJAMIN & ESTHER (MERRIAM) HULL:

1 BENJAMIN (name changed from Salmon), b 11 Dec 1763 *WV*.

2 LOIS,, b 6 July 1765 *WV*, d young.

3 ESTHER, b 3 Mar 1767 *WV;* m Noah Warner.

FAM. 31. EBENEZER & PATIENCE (———) HULL:

1 JOSEPH, d Mar 1818; m Rebecca da. Josiah Mix.

2 IRA, b c. 1788, d s. p. 13 Oct 1812 æ. 24 *CT2*.

3 SARAH; m Amos Austin.

4 AMY, b c. 1791, d 22 Nov 1827 æ. 36 *CT2;* m 1 Jan 1809 *CC*—Lyman Hitchcock.

FAM. 32. MOSES & MARY (IVES) HULL (family incomplete):

1 JOHN, b 9 Oct 1757 *WV*, d 19 Sep 1772 *WV*.

2 SARAH, b 28 Oct 1758 *WV*.

3 DAVID, b 17 June 1761 *WV*.

4 SAMUEL, b 23 Aug 1763 *WV*.

5 ZEPHANIAH, b 26 Apr 1765 *WV*.

6 NATHANIEL, b 2 Mar 1771 *WV*.

7 MARY, b 10 July 1772 *WV*.

8 MOSES, b 29 Aug 1776 *WV*.

FAM. 33. JOHN & LOIS (BEADLES) HULL:

1 NATHANIEL, b 7 Sep 1759 *WV*, d 19 Jan 1762 *WV*.

2 MARY, b 30 Aug 1762 *WV*.

3 NATHANIEL, b 7 May 1764 *WV*, d 21 May 1764 *WV*.

4 SARAH, b 15 Oct 1765 *WV;* m Samuel Wolcott.

5 LOWLY, b 4 June 1767 *WV;* m 23 Sep 1787 *WV*—Reuben Ives.

6 EUNICE, b 16 Dec 1769 *WV*, d 12 Oct 1826 æ. 56 *WTI;* m Ephraim A. Humiston.

7 MATILDA, b 29 Apr 1773 *WV;* m Samuel G. Simpson.

8 DIANA, b c. 1783, d 21 Dec 1863 æ. 80 *WTI;* m Benjamin Tyler Cook.

FAM. 34. SAMUEL & LOIS (PECK) HULL:

1 WILLIAM; m Alma da. Reuben Hall.

2 BETSEY, b c. 1790, d 12 Apr 1799 æ. 9 *WTI*.

3 SYLVESTER, b c. 1794, d 16 Nov 1828 æ. 35 *WTI;* m Delilah da. Benajah Moss.

4 LOIS; m Miles Ives.

FAM. 35. JEREMIAH & SARAH B. (BEADLES) HULL:

1 ALMA; m Ira Morse.

2 JULIA; m Ira Andrews.

3 SARAH B., b c. 1789, d 9 Sep 1791 æ. 2 *WTI*.

4 SYLVESTER, b c. 1792, d 8 Feb 1792 æ. 7 wks. *WTI*.

FAM. 35. JEREMIAH & PHEBE (HART) HULL:

5 PHILO; m Betsey Cook.

6 HIRAM; m Caroline Ives.

7 MARY.

8 LUCY; m Senator Blakeslee.

9 ORRIN; m Ann Dowd.

10 JEREMIAH; m Sophronia Dudley.

HULL. FAM. 36. ENOS, b c. 1751; of W, rem. to Naugatuck; m 8 June 1775 *EHC*—Mary da. Ebenezer & Damaris (Ives) Frost, b 12 Feb 1752 *NHV*, d c. July 1809.

1 BETSEY; m 1 Nov 1801 *SalemC*—Samuel Thompson.

2 EBENEZER.

HULL. FAM. 37. SAMUEL, of "Derby Neck"; m Betty ——— .

1 ELI, b 18 Feb 1763 *DV;* m 11 Sep 1783 *WatV*—Philene Beebe.

2 DAVID, bp 6 Oct 1765 *Dx*.

3 HANNAH, bp 6 Sep 1767 *Dx*.

4 TAPHENES, bp 8 Apr 1770 *Dx*.

5 SARAH, bp 27 Sep 1772 *Dx*.

6 JOSIAH, bp 9 Oct 1774 *Dx*.

HULSE. JOSEPH, b c. 1747, d 22 Aug 1804 æ. 57 *NHx;* m (1) 31 Dec 1775 *NHCI*—Hannah Broughton; m (2) Lucy Barnes, who (as Mrs. Hulse) d 12 June 1827 æ. 53 (*NHx*) *NHV*. Family incomplete.

(By 1): 1 JOSEPH, b c. 1781, d 17 Dec 1836 æ. 56 *NHV*, 1837 *NHTI;* m 9 Oct 1803 *NHCI*—Abigail da. Elijah & Hannah (Hine) Wilmot, b c. 1782, d 1 Feb 1867 æ. 86 *NHTI*.

i Julia Ann, b c. 1808, d 24 Nov 1892 æ. 85 *NHTI;* m Merrit Macumber.

ii John W., b c. 1810, d Apr 1834 æ. 25 (at sea) *NHTI*.

iii William H., b c. 1825, d 13 Oct 1853 æ. 29 *NHTI*.

(By 2): 2 AURELIA, b [15 Mar 1801], d 22 Nov 1886 æ. 85-8-7 *WatV;* m Robert Plume.

HUMISTON. The account of this family has been amplified by records kindly furnished by Rev. Wallace Humiston of Northfield, Conn., who is compiling a genealogy and invites correspondence.

FAM. 1. HENRY, d 16 Jan 1663 *NHV;* m 28 Aug 1651 *NHV*—Joan Walker, who d after 1687: she m (2) 15 Dec 1664 *NHV*—Richard Little.

1 SAMUEL, b 7 Aug 1653 *NHV*, d 26 Jan 1690 *NHV* [1690/1]; m 21 June 1677 *NHV*—Hannah da. John & Hannah (Parmelee) Johnson, b 4 Feb 1656 *NHV*, d 1697 (?)

i Samuel, b c. 1678, bp 11 Mar 1688 *NHCI*, d 1739; m Jan 1708 *NHV*—Mary da. Lawrence & Mary (Wooden) Clinton, b c. 1681, d 2 Mar 1767 æ. 86 *NHCI;* she m (2) 4 Mar 1741/2 *NHV*—Samuel Bassett. **FAM. 2.**

ii Hannah, b 21 July 1680 *NHV*, bp 11 Mar 1688 *NHCI;* m John Tuttle.

iii Mary, b 17 Jan 1682 *NHV*, bp 11 Mar 1688 *NHCI;* m 14 Jan 1702 *NHV*—John Butler.

iv Martha, b 22 Nov 1685 *NHV*, bp 11 Mar 1688 *NHCI*, d 17 Nov 1772 æ. 86 *NoHC;* m 10 Dec 1712 *NHV*—James Payne.

v Nathaniel, b 21 Sep 1688 *NHV*, bp 12 Aug (?) 1688 *NHCI*, d young.

vi Silence, b 7 Feb 1690/1 *NHV*, bp 8 Sep 1690 *NHCI;* m 2 Oct 1719 *NHV*—Aaron Perkins.

2 NATHANIEL, b 13 Jan 1654 *NHV* [1654/5], d s. p. 1687 (at St).

3 THOMAS, b 19 Oct 1656 *NHV*, d 1715; m (1) 31 May 1694 *NHV*—Elizabeth da. Thomas & Elizabeth (Payne) Sanford, b Sep 1671 *NHV*, d before 1705; m (2) Esther da. Elnathan & Hannah (Baldwin) Botsford, wid. John How, b 18 Oct 1668 *MV*, bp 31 Mar 1669/70 *MCI*.

(By 1): *i* Ebenezer, b 14 Mar 1694/5 *NHV*, d 7 Oct 1769 æ. 74 *NHCI;* m 13 Oct 1718 *NHV*—Grace da. Ebenezer & Hannah (Lupton) Blakeslee, b 1 Jan 1693/4 *NHV*. **FAM. 3.**

ii Elizabeth, b c. 1697, d 3 May 1740 *NHV;* m 17 Dec 1723 *NHV*—Samuel Bassett.

iii Thomas, b 3 May 1699 *NHV*, d 7 Oct 1743 *NHV;* m 16 Jan 1722/3 *NHV*—Mary da. James & Abigail (Bennett) Bishop, b 11 June 1698 *NHV*, d 12 Sep 1783 æ. 83 *NoHC*. **FAM. 4.**

(By 2): *iv* Joseph, b 14 Nov 1705 *NHV*, d 22 May 1776 æ. 70 *NHCI;* m 27 Mar 1734 *NHV*—Anna da. Moses & Anna (Blakeslee) Sperry, b 19 June 1711 *NHV*, d 7 Mar 1781 æ. 70 *NHCI*. **FAM. 5.**

4 JOHN, b c. 1659, d 1696; m 10 Sep 1685 *NHV*—Sarah da. John &

Katharine (Lane) Tuttle, b 22 Jan 1661 *NHV;* she m (2) 10 Jan 1698 *WV*—Roger Tyler.

i John, b 24 Oct 1686 *NHV*, d 7 Dec 1767 æ. 82 *NoHT1*, 6 Dec æ. 80 *NoHC;* m 23 June 1711 *NHV*—Hannah Ray, b c. 1693, d 20 Nov 1786 æ. 93 *NoHC*. FAM. 6.

ii Lydia, b 1 Apr 1689 *NHV*, d 6 Apr 1742 æ. 53 *NoHT2;* m Moses Brockett.

iii Mary, "old Mrs. Ford" d 4 Jan 1773 *PC;* m 31 Dec 1723 *WV*—Barnabas Ford.

iv Sarah, b 8 Apr 1693 *NHV*, d 5 June 1766 æ. 72 *NoHC*, æ. 74 *NoHT1;* m 26 May 1714 *NHV*—James Bradley.

v James, b 7 May 1696 *NHV*, d 17 Aug 1747 *WV*, æ. 51 *WT1;* m 7 Jan 1719 *WV*—Sarah da. Ebenezer & Abigail (Heaton) Atwater, b 6 Apr 1693 *NHV*, d 28 May 1761 *WV;* she m (2) 28 June 1749 *WV*—Timothy Tuttle. FAM. 7.

5 **Abigail**, b 17 May 1661 *NHV;* she had a nat. child by John Tuttle, b 1688 *NHCCt*.

FAM. 2. **Samuel & Mary (Clinton) Humiston:**

1 **Samuel**, b 27 Oct 1709 *NHV*, bp (adult) 23 Apr 1786 *NHx*, bu. 4 Oct 1788 æ. 80 *NHx;* m 21 July 1737 *NHV*—Elizabeth da. John & Susanna (Heaton) Alcott, b 31 July 1708 *NHV*, d 23 Jan 1782 æ. 75 *NHC1*.

i Mary, b 6 July 1739 *NHV*, d s. p.

ii Susanna, b 5 May 1741 *NHV*, bp 1764 *NoHx;* m 14 Apr 1768 *NHV*, *NHC1*—Jeremiah Parmelee.

iii Samuel, b 5 May 1743 *NHV*, d 20 June 1809 æ. 66 *HT4;* Lieut.; Census (H) 1-4-5; m 15 Dec 1767 *NHV*—Mary da. John & Mary (Cooper) Gill, b 19 Feb 1750 *NHV*, d 6 June 1820 æ. 70 *HT4*. FAM. 8.

iv Elizabeth, b 13 Apr 1745 *NHV;* m (1) 3 May 1762 *NoHV*—Oliver Blakeslee; he div. her; m (2) 14 Dec 1800 *NoHV*—David Luddington.

v Sarah, bp (adult) 17 June 1770 *NHC2;* m Gurdon Turner.

vi Martha, bp 1768 *NoHx;* m 5 Mar 1776 *NHC2*—Timothy Johnson.

vii Eunice; m 11 June 1776 *NHC2*—Samuel Dayton.

2 **Abigail**, b 3 Dec 1715 *NHV;* m (1) 16 Jan 1736/7 *NHV*—Stephen Alcott; m (2) 31 Nov 1743 *NHV*—Thomas Vergison; m (3) 5 Dec 1764 *WdC*—David Barnes; perhaps m (4) Silas Hotchkiss.

3 **Mary**, b 8 Oct 1719 *NHV;* m 17 May 1739 *NHV*—Timothy Tuttle.

FAM. 3. **Ebenezer & Grace (Blakeslee) Humiston:**

1 **Lydia**, b 1 Aug 1720 *NHV*, bp 20 Dec 1720 *NHC1;* m 22 Jan 1740/1 *NHV*—Abraham Tuttle.

2 **Ebenezer**, b 1 Nov 1722 *NHV*, bp 3 Feb 1722/3 *NHC1;* m 9 June 1740 *NHV*—Mary Butler.

i John, b 2 Apr 1741 *NHV*, bp 24 May 1741 *NHC1*, d s. p.
ii Timothy, b 2 July 1743 *NHV*, bp 31 July 1743 *NHC1*, d 6 Jan 1829; Census (Harwinton) 2-2-4.
iii John, b 3 June 1745 *NHV*, bp 7 July 1745 *NHC1*.
iv Reuben, b 22 Mar 1747 *NHV*, bp 10 May 1747 *NHC1*.
v Abraham, b 13 May 1749 *NHV*, bp 18 June 1749 *NHC1;* Census (Harwinton) 1-1-4.
vi Abigail Martha, b 28 July 1751 *NHV*, bp 1 Sep 1751 *NHC1*.
vii Mary, b 4 Mar 1754 *NHV*, bp 5 May 1754 *NHC1*.
viii Lydia, bp 20 Mar 1757 *NHC2*.
ix Ebenezer, bp 28 Oct 1759 *NHC2*, d c. 1797; Census (NH) 1-3-3; m Hannah [da. Nathaniel & Desire (Taylor) Humiston, b 16 June 1757 *NHV*], d 4 Oct 1846 æ. 89. **FAM. 9.**
x Thomas, bp 13 Sep 1761 *NHC2*.
xi Jared, bp 16 Dec 1764 *NHC2*, d before 1790; m 28 Dec 1784 *NHx*—Mary Ann Gochee; Census, Mary Ann (NH) 0-2-1. Children: 1 Billy, bp 31 Aug 1788 *NHx*. 2 Jeremiah, bp 9 Mar 1789 *NHx*.

3 DANIEL, b 29 June 1727 *NHV*, bp 30 July 1727 *NHC1*, d 8 Apr 1798 æ. 70 *NHC1;* Census (Wd) 1-0-1; m (1) 19 Mar 1752 *NHV*—Desire da. Daniel & Desire (Sperry) Dorman, b 10 Sep 1729 *NHV*, bp 27 Nov 1768 *NHC1*, d 10 Oct 1793 æ. 65 *BT4;* m (2) 3 Sep 1794 *NHC1*—Abigail da. Stephen & Abigail (Bradley) Atwater, b 2 Aug 1742 *NHV*, d 20 Jan 1806 æ. 63 *HT2;* she m (2) 10 Sep 1804 William Denslow.

(By 1): *i* Abel, b c. 1753, bp 4 Dec 1768 *NHC1;* Census (Wd) 1-3-4; rem. to Farm; m 20 Dec 1775 *NHC1*—Rachel da. Daniel & Rachel (Wooding) Wooding. **FAM. 10.**
ii Patience, b c. 1755, bp 4 Dec 1768 *NHC1;* m Joel Wheeler.
iii Joel, b c. 1758, bp 4 Dec 1768 *NHC1;* Census (Wd) 1-2-2; rem. to Farm & Trumbull Co., Ohio; m Anna Wheeler. Children: 1 Isaac, b c. 1779, d 14 Aug 1861 æ. 82 *Vienna, Ohio, T;* m Abigail Alling. 2 Daniel. 3 Mary. 4 Joel.
iv Abigail, b c. 1760, bp 4 Dec 1768 *NHC1*.
v Isaac, b c. 1762, d Nov 1768 æ. 6 *NHC1*.
vi Jacob, b c. 1765, bp 4 Dec 1768 *NHC1;* m 1 Sep 1791 *Glastonbury*—Honor Hubbard.
vii Phebe, b c. 1767, bp 4 Dec 1768 *NHC1*.
viii Isaac, bp 24 Dec 1769 *NHC1*.

4 NATHANIEL, b 9 May 1730 *NHV*, bp 7 June 1730 *NHC1*, d 25 Nov 1793; Census (H) 2-0-1; m 7 Jan 1752 *NHV*—Desire da. Elnathan & Desire (Blakeslee) Taylor b 6 Sep 1732 *Wat V*, d 15 Apr 1815.

i Mary, b c. 1752, d 22 Dec 1826 æ. 75 (*NHC2*) *NHV;* m 23

Mar 1786 *NHCl*—Philip Klein.

ii Esther, b 2 Nov 1755 *NHV*, d 13 Apr 1773 æ. 17 *NHCl*.

iii Hannah, b 16 June 1757 *NHV*, [d 4 Oct 1846 æ. 89]; she had a nat. child Esther, bp 24 May 1778 *NHCl*, d 25 Feb 1872 æ. 94-10 *NHV*, æ. 95 *HTl*; m Ira Wolcott. Hannah probably m Ebenezer Humiston.

iv Ruth, b 10 Dec 1759 *NHV*, d 5 May 1773 æ. 13 *NHCl*.

v David, b 18 Apr 1764 *F*, bp 31 Aug 1764 *NHCl*, d 12 Aug 1839 *F;* Census (H) 1-2-1; m 8 Feb 1786 *NHCl*—Susanna da. Ebenezer & Susanna (Tuttle) Warner, b 1 Apr 1770 *NHV*, d 3 Oct 1838 *F*. **FAM. 11.**

vi Asa, b 15 [?July] 1766 *F*, bp 4 Aug 1766 *NHCl;* Census (Wd) 1-0-2; rem. to L; m Huldah da. Linus & Chloe (Cook) Gilbert, b 7 Mar 1769 *WdV*, d 25 July 1854 æ. 85 *LT;* she m (2) 23 June 1833 John Kilborn. **FAM. 12.**

vii Nathaniel, bp 22 Oct 1769 *NHCl*, d 15 Jan 1855 æ. 85 *F;* rem. to P; m (1) Jane ——— ; separated 1792; m (2) Mary ——— .

5 DESIRE, b 13 Oct 1733 *NHV;* m 11 Oct 1753 *NHV*—John Jocelyn.

FAM. 4. THOMAS & MARY (BISHOP) HUMISTON:

1 MARY, b 10 Oct 1723 *NHV*, d 12 Mar 1746/7 *NHV*.

2 THOMAS, b 20 June 1725 *NHV*, d 1 Apr 1802 æ. 77 *NoHTl;* Census (NoH) 1-0-2; m 19 Oct 1752 *NHV*—Abigail da. Joshua & Abigail (Barnes) Ray, b 15 Aug 1729 *NHV*, d 18 Dec 1802 æ. 74 *NoHTl*.

i Abigail, b 21 Mar 1753 *NHV*, d 1845 *NoHD;* m 7 Jan 1773 *NoHV*—David Barnes.

ii Ruth, b 21 Jan 1755 *NHV;* m 15 Jan 1777 *NoHC*—Jacob Brockett.

iii Elizabeth, b 9 Apr 1757 *NHV*, d 11 Mar 1774 æ. 17 *NoHC*.

iv Lydia, b 2 Mar 1760 *NHV*, bp 5 June 1774 *NoHC*, d Apr 1813 *NoHC;* m 19 Apr 1804 *NoHV*—Solomon Barnes.

v Esther, b 11 Mar 1762 *NHV*, bp 5 June 1774 *NoHC;* m Calvin Heaton.

vi Phebe, b 7 Dec 1764 *NHV*, bp 5 June 1774 *NoHC*, d 4 Sep 1774 *NoHC*.

vii Thomas, b 21 Oct 1767 *NHV*, bp 5 June 1774 *NoHC*, d 28 Aug 1774 æ. 7 *NoHC*.

viii Joshua, b 26 Mar 1771 *NHV*, bp 24 Mar 1774 *NoHC*, d 26 Mar 1774 æ. 3 *NoHC*.

ix Joshua, bp 5 June 1774 *NoHC*, d 9 Sep 1774 *NoHC*.

3 JAMES, b 12 Oct 1727 *NHV*, d 12 June 1812 (at Holyoke, Mass.); Census (W. Springfield, Mass.) 4-1-5; m (1) 19 July 1753 *NHV*—Dorcas da. Caleb & Lydia (Benham) Atwater, b 26 Aug 1732 *NHV*, d 15 Sep 1759 *NHV;* m (2) 11 Dec 1760 *NHV*—Abigail da. James & Elizabeth (Clinton) Bishop, b 4 Sep 1731 *NHV*.

(By 1): *i* Mary, b 19 May 1754 *NHV*, d 21 Nov 1773 *NHV*, æ. 20

NoHT1, æ. 19 *NoHC*.

ii James, b 23 Feb 1756 *NHV*, d 21 Sep 1815; Census (NoH) 1-3-4; rem. to W. Springfield, Mass., c. 1784; m 26 Feb 1777 *NoHC*—Phebe da. Samuel & Abigail (Bradley) Bassett, b 22 Nov 1759 *NHV*, d 14 Nov 1824. **FAM. 13.**

iii Caleb, b 16 May 1758 *NHV*, d 25 Sep 1759 *NHV*, æ. 2 *No HT1*.

(By 2): *iv* Caleb, b 27 May 1762 *NHV*, bp 5 Sep 1762 *NoHC*, d 5 Jan 1842; rem. to W. Springfield (Holyoke), Mass., 1784; m 14 Feb 1782 *NoHC*—Sarah da. James & Patience (Todd) Bishop, b 5 Mar 1764 *NHV*, d 7 Jan 1854. **FAM. 14.**

4 Elizabeth, b 12 May 1730 *NHV*, d 21 Nov 1731 *NHV*.

5 Elizabeth, b 25 July 1732 *NHV*, d young.

6 Esther, b 25 July 1732 *NHV*, [d 9 Mar 1774 æ. 41-7 *NoHC;* m c. 1770 Ebenezer Bradley.

7 Joy, b 14 June 1735 *NHV;* Census (Wat) 1-0-2; m 10 Aug 1758 *NHV*—Hannah da. James & Mabel (Potter) Grannis, b 6 Aug 1739 *NHV*.

i Hannah, b 11 Dec 1758 *NHV*, d Dec 1845 æ. 87 *NoHD;* m Benjamin Hull.

ii Mabel, b 19 June 1761 *NHV*, d 23 May 1844 æ. 83 *PptT;* m 3 Sep 1783 Elisha Munson.

iii Ezra, b 13 Aug 1763 *NHV*.

iv Bennett, b 8 July 1766 *NHV*, d Fall 1801 (at Butts Hollow, Washington Co., N. Y.); m 10 May 1787 *CC*—Elizabeth Benham.

v Joy, b 28 Oct 1768 *NHV*.

8 Ruth, b 27 Mar 1738 *NHV*, d 4 Oct 1743 *NHV*.

FAM. 5. Joseph & Anna (Sperry) Humiston:

1 Esther, b 9 May 1735 *NHV*, d s. p.

2 Anna, b 24 Feb 1739/40 *NHV*, bp 13 Sep 1761 *NHC1*, d Mar 1814; m 11 Nov 1761 *WV*, *NHC1*—Joseph Sperry.

3 Joseph, b 11 Apr 1744 *NHV*, d 28 Mar 1795 æ. 51 *HT2;* Census (H) 2-2-3; m Eunice da. Joseph & Jemima (Smith) Cooper, b 9 July 1753 *NHV*, d 17 July 1842 æ. 89 *HT2;* she m (2) Joel Ford.

i Ezra, bp 2 July 1786 *NHC1*.

ii Son, b [Apr 1777], d 3 Sep 1777 æ. 0-4 *NHC1*.

iii Joseph, bp 2 July 1786 *NHC1*.

iv Justus, b c. 1781, bp 2 July 1786 *NHC1*, d 8 Oct 1855 æ. 75 *HT5*, æ. 74 *HV;* m Elizabeth Harmon, who d 1 Apr 1848 æ. 62 *HT5*.

v Son, b [Apr 1781], d 15 Jan 1782 æ. 0-9 *NHC1*.

vi Anna, bp 2 July 1786 *NHC1;* m Moses Gilbert.

vii Hannah, bp 2 July 1786 *NHC1*, d 1 Sep 1866 (at Middle Haddam); m Ezra Tuttle.

viii [Child, b c. 1789, d 6 Feb 1790 æ. 0-6].

ix Jere, b 19 Mar 1790 *F*, d 29 Dec 1872 (at Fond du Lac, Wis.); m.

x Ethel, b c. 1793, d 5 Nov 1812 æ. 20 *HT2*.

FAM. 6. JOHN & HANNAH (RAY) HUMISTON:

1 JOHN, b 8 Apr 1713 *NHV*, d 25 May 1781 æ. 68 *ThomastonT;* m (1) 5 June 1738 *LV*—Mary Sanford, who d 8 Mar 1742 *LV;* m (2) 29 Dec 1742 *LV*—Ruth Culver, who d 30 Dec 1769 *PC;* m (3) 21 June 1770 *PC*—Thankful, wid. Tyler.

(By 1): *i* Mary, b 10 May 1739 *LV*, d 26 Apr 1814 æ. 75 *ThomastonT;* m 26 Oct 1762 *WatV*, *NHC2*—Asher Blakeslee.

ii John, b 25 Feb 1742 *LV*, d 30 Apr 1822 æ. 80 *LT;* Census (L) 2-1-5; m 14 Dec 1769 *LV*—Hannah Sanford.

(By 2): *iii* Thankful, b 26 Nov 1743 *LV*, d 22 Feb 1768 *WatV*, *PC;* m 25 Oct 1764 *WatV*—Amos Dutton.

iv Noah, b 20 Dec 1745 *LV*, d 2 Feb 1812 æ. 66 *LT;* Census (L) 3-2-3; m 17 Nov 1768 *WatV*, *PC*—Lucy Barnes.

v Damaris, b 10 Feb 1747 *LV*, d 20 Jan 1794 æ. 46 *ThomastonT;* m 19 Nov 1767 *WatV*, *PC*—Abel Seymour.

vi Amos, b 30 May 1749 *LV;* m 5 Nov 1771 *WatV*—Abigail Allen.

vii Titus, b 30 Nov 1751 *LV;* Census (L) 1-4-5; m 20 Dec 1775 Beulah Batchellor.

viii Ruth, b 9 June 1753 *LV;* m 25 Nov 1773 *PC*—David Allen.

ix Lois, b 30 May 1755 *LV;* [?m 9 Mar 1780 *PC*—Joseph Dunbar].

x Enos, b 27 Nov 1756 *LV*.

xi Kezia; m 8 Mar 1774 *PC*—Oliver Barnes.

xii Martha, b 9 Jan 1760 *LV*, d 10 Nov 1760 *LV*.

2 CALEB, b 20 Feb 1715/6 *NHV*, d 6 Mar 1776 *WatV*, æ. 61 *ThomastonT;* m 14 Nov 1738 *WatV*—Susanna da. Samuel & Susanna [Tuttle] Todd, b 7 Dec 1718 *NHV*, d 24 Sep 1806 æ. 88 *ThomastonT*.

i Jesse, b 12 Dec 1739 *WatV*, d soon.

ii Sarah, b 9 Dec 1742 *WatV*, d 27 July 1822 *WatV*, æ. 79 *WatT1;* m 17 May 1764 *WatV*—Stephen Bronson.

iii Hannah, b 25 June 1745 *WatV*, d 16 Dec 1785 æ. 42 *LT;* m 24 Dec 1766 *PC*—Daniel Lord.

iv Susanna, b 19 June 1747 *WatV*.

v Jesse, b 4 Dec 1749 *WatV*, d 21 Feb 1837 æ. 87 *ThomastonT;* m Abi Blakeslee.

vi Mehitabel, b 1 Jan 1752 *WatV*, d 23 Nov 1825 æ. 74 *ThomastonT;* m 7 May 1770 *WatV*, *PC*—Isaac Fenn.

vii Content, b 3 Aug 1754 *WatV*, d 3 Feb 1773 *WatV*, 12 Feb *PC*, 2 Feb æ. 19 *ThomastonT*.

viii Phebe, b 5 Dec 1756 *WatV*, d 5 Oct 1844 æ. 88 *ThomastonT;* m 29 Mar 1774 *WatV*, 30 Mar *PC*—Jesse Turner.

ix Annis, b 24 July 1759 *WatV*, d 6 June 1825 æ. 65 *ThomastonT;* m 5 July 1775 *WatV*—Samuel Sutliff.

x Martha, b 20 Dec 1762 *WatV*, d 21 Apr 1842 æ. 79 *ThomastonT;* m 25 Jan 1781 *WtnV*, *PC*—Daniel Potter.

3 **Mary**, b 30 June 1718 *NHV*, d 10 May 1806 æ. 88 *WT1;* m 23 Dec 1737 *WV*—Philip Mattoon.

4 **David**, b 30 Jan 1720/1 *NHV;* m 1 Nov 1743 *WatV*—Ruth da. Joseph & Miriam (Bradley) Bassett, b 18 Feb 1724/5 *NHV*, d 4 Nov 1776 *PC*.

i Rhoda, b 17 Jan 1744/5 *WatV*, d 13 Sep 1750 *WatV*.

ii Joel, b 14 Apr 1747 *WatV*, d 22 Sep 1750 *WatV*.

iii Lydia, b 30 July 1749 *WatV*, d 18 Sep 1750 *WatV*.

iv Rhoda, b 27 May 1751 *WatV*, d 31 Aug 1831 æ. 80 (*NHC 2*) *NHV;* m 26 Dec 1774 *PC*—Jacob Daggett.

v Joel, b 12 Nov 1753 *WatV;* Census (L) 1-0-4; rem. to Southwick, Mass.; m Lois da. Joseph & Hannah (Potter) Ball.

vi Lydia, b 1 Mar 1756 *WatV*, d June 1843; m 14 Nov 1781 *PV*, *PC*—Timothy Atwater.

vii David, b 12 Feb 1758 *WatV*, d c. 1827 (at Harwinton); m Jerusha da. John Bartholomew.

viii Ashbel, b 8 June 1760 *WatV;* rem. to Southwick, Mass.; m 10 Oct 1784 *NHC1*—Phebe Bradley, who d 18 Nov 1795.

ix Chloe, b 5 Nov 1762 *WatV;* m (1) 10 Jan 1796 *NoHC*—Edward Turner; m (2) 3 June 1805 *NoHC*—Ebenezer Darrow.

x Bede, b 8 June 1765 *WatV*, d 1 Nov 1843; m 8 May 1803 Richard Newman Atwater.

xi Hannah, b 8 June 1768 *WatV*.

5 **Sarah**, b 10 Sep 1723 *NHV*, d 13 Oct 1787 æ. 64 *NoHC;* m (1) 19 Nov 1740 *NHV*—Thomas Turner; m (2) 14 May 1752 *NHV*—Samuel Tuttle.

6 **Ephraim**, b 5 Dec 1730 *NHV*, d 3 May 1806 æ. 76 *NoHT1;* Census (NoH) 3-1-4; m 1 Dec 1757 *NHV*—Susanna da. Abraham & Mehitabel (Street) Bassett, b 18 May 1737 *NHV*, d 25 May 1813 æ. 77 *NoHT1*.

i John, b 3 Oct 1758 *NHV*.

ii Sarah, b 16 Nov 1760 *NHV*, bp 25 Jan 1761 *NoHC*, d s. p. 1818.

iii Susanna, b 5 Oct 1763 *NHV*, bp 9 Oct 1763 *NoHC*, d 16 July 1810 æ. 47 *NoHT1;* m 14 Nov 1793 *NoHC*—Samuel Mix.

iv Abram [known as Ephraim A.], b 3 Feb 1766 *NHV*, bp 9 Feb 1766 *NoHC;* m Eunice da. John & Lois (Beadles) Hull, b 16 Dec 1769 *WV*, d 12 Oct 1826 æ. 56 *WT1*.

v Joel, b 15 Aug 1768 *NHV*, bp 21 Aug 1768 *NoHC*, d 19 Feb 1847 æ. 79 *NoHT3;* m 12 Jan 1797 *NoHC*—Emilia da. Samuel & Lydia (Todd) Mix, b c. 1765, d 12 Sep 1849 æ. 84 *NoHT3*.

vi Street, b 28 June 1771 *NHV*, bp 30 June 1771 *NoHC;* rem. to Elyria, Ohio; m Mary da. Dan & Lucy (Frost) Todd.

vii Mary, bp 5 Mar 1775 *NoHC*, d young.

viii Caleb, bp 18 Aug 1781 *NoHC*, d 26 Mar 1857; rem. to Hudson, Ohio, 1833; m Polly Penfield da. Justus Lyman & Elizabeth Penfield (Goodsell) Todd, b 22 July 1789, d 1 Aug 1880. **FAM. 15.**

7 HANNAH, b 5 Dec 1730 *NHV;* m 6 Apr 1752 *NHV*—Ephraim Alling.

FAM. 7. JAMES & SARAH (ATWATER) HUMISTON:

1 STEPHEN, b 3 Oct 1719 *WV*, d 21 Feb 1722 *WV*.

2 DANIEL, b 16 Nov 1721 *WV*, d 27 July 1767 *CC*, æ. 46 *WV*, *CT1;* m Lydia da. Samuel & Sarah (Goodsell) Parker, b c. 1726, d 1 Jan 1809 æ. 83 *CT1;* she m (2) 26 Apr 1769 *CC*—Samuel Hull; m (3) John Atwater.

i Sarah, b 14 Dec 1744 *WV*, bp Sep 1747 *CC*, d 4 Sep 1775 *CC*, æ. 31 *CT1;* m 22 Jan 1761 *WV*—Samuel Hull.

ii Mary, b 17 Mar 1747 *WV*, bp Sep 1747 *CC*, d 14 Aug 1774 *CC;* m 15 Dec 1763 *WV*—Elias Hall.

iii Hannah, b 11 Feb 1748/9 *WV*, bp Apr 1749 *CC*, d 23 Aug 1767 *WV*, æ. 19 *CT1*.

iv Stephen, b 17 July 1751 *WV*, bp 25 Aug 1751 *CC*, d 7 Sep 1767 *CC*, *WV*, æ. 17 *CT1*.

v Lydia, b Mar 1754 *WV*, d 2 May 1805; m (1) Ebenezer Rowe; m (2) 16 Mar 1774 *CC*, 17 Mar *WV*—Peter Hall.

vi Patience, b 28 Nov 1756 *WV*, d 25 Apr 1793 æ. 36 *SC;* m 3 Apr 1775 *CC*—Heman Atwater.

vii Daniel, b 10 Apr 1759 *WV*, d 6 Nov 1783 *CC*, 7 Nov æ. 25 *CT1;* m Barbara ——— ; she m (2) Matthias Porter of Warwick, Pa. Child: 1 Elizabeth; res. Pennsborough, Cumberland Co., Pa., 1804.

viii John, b 30 June 1761 *WV*, d 3 June 1778 æ. 17 *CT1*.

ix Jesse, b 13 Apr 1764 *WV*, d 12 Mar 1832 æ. 68 *CT2;* Census (C) 1-1-3; m 1 May 1786 *CC*—Lois da. Amos & Abigail (Ives) Doolittle, b 13 Sep 1763 *WV*, d 8 Feb 1847 æ. 84 *CT2*.

x Katharine, b 6 Oct 1766 *WV;* m 15 Sep 1785 *WV*, *CC*—Daniel Carrington.

3 STEPHEN, b 9 Nov 1723 *WV*, d 3 Sep 1729 *WV*.

4 NOAH, d 3 Sep 1729 *WV*.

5 NOAH, b 1 Mar 1731 *WV*, d 13 June 1745 *WV*, æ. 14 *WT1*.

6 JAMES, b 28 Oct 1734 *WV*, d 18 Feb 1812 æ. 77 *WT1*, æ. 78 *WV;* m (1) 4 Feb 1756 *WV*—Abiah da. Daniel & Abiah (Parker) Ives, b 31 July 1736 *WV*, d 19 Dec 1761 *WV;* m (2) 19 May 1762 *WV*—Hannah da. Matthias & Thankful (Andrews) Hitchcock, b 9 Mar 1737 *WV*, d 5 Nov 1828 æ. 92 *WT1*.

(By 2): *i* Abiah, b 11 Feb 1763 *WV;* m 15 Jan 1783 *WV*—Daniel Johnson Hall.

ii James, b 18 Dec 1764 *WV*, d 19 Oct 1847 æ. 83 *WT1;* m Lydia da. James & Elizabeth (Hall) Peck, b 14 June 1767 *WV*, d 17 Feb 1846 æ. 79 *WT1*.

iii Giles, b 27 July 176[6] *WV*, d soon.

iv Jason b 31 May 1768 *WV*, d 21 Nov 1854 æ. 87; res. Watertown, Ohio; m (1) Amy Peck of L; m (2) Margaret (McNeal) Shaw.

v Ira, b 19 June 1770 *WV;* sailor, disappeared.

vi Sarah, b 9 Oct 1772 *WV*, d 28 Aug 1852 *F;* m 25 Jan 1794 Samuel Dibble.

vii Giles, b c. 1774, d 12 July 1836; res. Harpersfield, N. Y.

viii Linus, b 20 Feb 1778 *WV*, d Oct 1825; res. Burton, Ohio; m Rebecca Royce; she m (2) ——— Baldwin.

FAM. 8. Samuel & Mary (Gill) Humiston:

1 **Molly**, b 16 Aug 1768 *NHV*, bp 25 Nov 1770 *NHC1*, d 29 Apr 1825 æ. 57 *NoHT1;* m Alling Ives,

2 **Bede**, b 10 Apr 1770 *NHV*, bp 25 Nov 1770 *NHC1;* m 29 May 1788 *NoHC*—Ira Todd.

3 **Lowly**, b 14 July 1772 *NHV*, bp 13 Sep 1772 *NHC1*, d 5 Oct 1794 æ. 21 *NoHC*, æ. 22 *NoHT1;* m 1 July 1790 *NoHC*—Samuel Todd.

4 **Esther**, b 23 May 1774 *HV*, bp 10 July 1774 *NHC1*, d 17 Aug 1864 æ. 90 *NoHT1;* m 26 Sep 1799 *NoHV*—Daniel Pierpont.

5 **Betsey**, b 25 Mar 1776 *HV*, bp 12 May 1776 *NHC1*, d 12 Jan 1835 æ. 59 *NoHT1;* m (1) 29 Jan 1795 Benjamin Munson; m (2) 1 Sep 1825 *NoHV*—Alling Ives.

6 **Lyman**, b 27 Sep 1778 *HV*, bp 9 July 1780 *NHC1*.

7 **Phila**, b 27 Feb 1781 *HV*, *NoHT3*, d 16 Mar 1865 *NoHT3;* m 22 Oct 1801 *NoHV*, *NoHC*—Jesse Andrews.

8 **Samuel Green**, b 24 July 1783 *HV*, bp 4 Jan 1784 *NHC1;* res. Wat 1821.

9 **Silliman**, b 10 Nov 1785 *HV*, bp 19 Mar 1786 *NHC1;* rem to Meredith, N. Y.; m 7 Dec 1810 *NoHC*—Sarah da. Joel & Ann (Todd) Barnes, bp 25 Dec 1785 *NoHC*.

10 **Julia**, b 22 Aug 1788 *F*, bp 25 Jan 1789 *NHC1*, d 3 Feb 1879 æ. 90–6 *NoHT3;* m 6 Mar 1811 *NoHC*—Elam Bassett.

11 **Wyllys**, b 17 July 1790 *F*, bp 12 Oct 1790 *NoHC*.

12 **Lowly**, b 28 July 1794 *F*, d 29 Aug 1872 æ. 78 *NoHT3;* m (as "Charlotte") 27 May 1816 *NoHC*—Richard Blakeslee.

FAM. 9. Ebenezer & Hannah [Humiston] Humiston:

1 **Mary**, b c. 1781; m John Osborne Atwater.

2 **Benoni**, bp 30 Mar 1783 *NHC1*, "Benjamin" d 12 Jan 1813 æ. 30 *F*.

3 **William**, bp 1 May 1785 *NHC1*, d 22 June 1853 æ. 72 *HV*, 23 June æ. 68 *HT2;* m 16 Aug 1807 Betsey Ann da. Daniel & Thankful (Heaton) Talmadge, b 17 Aug 1789 *F*, d 25 Aug 1862 æ. 73 *HT2*.

4 **James**, b c. 1788, d 3 Dec 1810 æ. 23 (at L) *F*.

5 RUTH, bp 23 May 1790 *NHCl*; m Barney Avis.
6 RHODA, b c. 1792, d 15 July 1808 æ. 17 *F*.
7 CHARLES; m.
8 LOVINA, d 10 Sep 1798 æ. 0-5 *F*.
9 LOVISA, d 22 Sep 1798 æ. 0-6 *F*.
10 NANCY, b c. 1799, d 23 Sep 1813 æ. 14 *F*.

FAM. 10. ABEL & RACHEL (WOODING) HUMISTON:
1 ISRAEL.
2 JEREMIAH; res. Simsbury; m Rowena Barber.
3 JESSE; res. Windsor Locks; m Julia Sheldon.
4 SAMUEL.
5 RACHEL.
6 HENRY.
7 SARAH.
8 ANNA.
9 MARY; m Selden Jones.

FAM. 11. DAVID & SUSANNA (WARNER) HUMISTON:
1 ELE, b 19 June 1788 *F*, d 11 Apr 1855 *F*; m (1) Susan ——, who d 27 Dec 1829 æ. 40 *NHTl*; m (2) Hannah ——, who d 29 July 1839 æ. 34 *NHTl*.
2 JUSTUS, b 24 June 1790 *F*, d 10 Oct 1839 æ. 48 *NHV*.
3 BETSEY, b 22 Feb 1792 *F*, d 1 Feb 1835 *F*.
4 DESIRE, b 5 June 1794 *F*, d 11 Aug 1825 *F*; m Harry Beecher.
5 ROSWELL, b 22 Sep 1796 *F*, d 19 Sep 1864 *F*; m (1) Lovisa Morehouse; m (2) Aug 1831 Melinda Atwater; m (3) Lydia Hotchkiss.
6 LAURA B., b 9 Apr 1799 *F*, d 5 Sep 1871 æ. 73 *F*; m Chauncey Morehouse.
7 NATHANIEL, b 8 June 1806 *F*.
8 MERCENE, b 23 Jan 1810 *F*, d 24 Dec 1844 *F*; m (1) 9 Sep 1832 *StV*—Chauncey Lines; m (2) 29 May 1836 *F*—Aaron B. B. Downs.

FAM. 12. ASA & HULDAH (GILBERT) HUMISTON:
1 LUCINDA, b 4 Sep 1789 *F*, bp 31 Jan 1790 (at B); [?m —— Warner].
2 LEWIS G., b 10 Mar 1792 *F*, d 1877/8; m Sep 1818 Almira da. Jeremiah & Amy (Bishop) Kilborn, b 29 Sep 1795, d 28 July 1856.
i Huldah Ann, b 12 Sep 1821 *F*; m —— Barnes.
ii William Lewis, b 28 Jan 1824 *F*.
iii Lucy Maria, b 29 Apr 1827 *F*; m Capt. Alva Stone.
iv Asa, b 1 Apr 1835 *F*.
v Leonard, b 11 Oct 1836 *F*.
3 HULDAH, b 29 Aug 1794 *F*, d 29 Aug 1891 æ. 97; m James Throop.
4 RUSSELL, b 24 Oct 1796 *F*; m 12 Oct 1820 *HV*—Rachel Perkins.
5 FLORA, b 20 Feb 1799 *F*, d 27 Sep 1830; m 25 Sep 1820 Morgan Griswold of Washington.

FAM. 13. JAMES & PHEBE (BASSETT) HUMISTON:
1 ISAAC, b 1 Feb 1778, d 22 Jan 1855.
2 THOMAS, b 25 Oct 1779, d 24 June 1801 (at Leyden, N. Y.).
3 ACHSAH, b 1 Feb 1782, d 7 Mar 1868.
4 CHLOE, b 2 June 1784, d s. p. 28 Sep 1850.
5 BENJAMIN, b 19 Jan 1786, d 21 Oct 1825.
6 POLLY, b 28 Oct 1787.
7 ARTEMAS, b 26 Mar 1790, d 4 Nov 1874.
8 LURENDA, b 16 Oct 1792, d 30 Aug 1803.
9 JAMES, b 23 Jan 1796, d 20 May 1872.
10 JULIUS, b 1 Sep 1797, d 9 Sep 1821.
11 RUSSELL, b 10 Mar 1800, d 25 Aug 1803.
12 LURENDA, b 12 July 1804, d 25 June 1805.

FAM. 14. CALEB & SARAH (BISHOP) HUMISTON:
1 LOVINA, b 16 Apr 1783.
2 ABIGAIL, b 14 Jan 1787, d 6 June 1837.
3 SARAH, b 22 Sep 1789.
4 ESTHER, b 18 Oct 1792.
5 BISHOP, b 25 Jan 1796.
6 SARAH, b 26 Dec 1803.

FAM. 15. CALEB & POLLY PENFIELD (TODD) HUMISTON:
1 GEORGE LYMAN, b 3 Apr 1808.
2 JARED LAURENS, b 18 May 1810.
3 JOHN WILLIS, b 29 Sep 1812.
4 LOYAL PORTER, b 18 Mar 1814, d 25 July 1815.
5 JANE ELIZABETH, b 6 Sep 1816.
6 LOYAL FRANCIS, b 11 Feb 1819.
7 RANSOM FRANKLIN, b 29 July 1821.
8 HENRY DWIGHT, b 12 Apr 1824.
9 EDWIN RAY, b 6 May 1827.
10 EMILY SUSANNA, b 1 Aug 1830.

HUMPHREVILLE. Variant, UMBERFIELD. FAM. 1. JOHN of WH; m.
1 MARY; m (1) 26 Mar 1684 *NHV*—Thomas Mallory; m (2) 28 Nov 1694 *NHV*—Ebenezer Downs; m (3) 3 Nov 1713 *NHV*—Thomas Carnes.
2 SAMUEL, b c. 1666, d 30 Mar 1748 *NHV*, æ. 82 *WHT1*; m (1) ——— da. Jacob Gray of Fairfield; m (2) Experience da. Thomas & Mercy Pinion, b c. 1679, d 27 Aug 1753 æ. 74 *WHT1*. The maternity of younger children is doubtful.
(By 1): *i* Sarah, b 2 Apr 1695 *NHV*; m Israel Thomas.
ii Ann, b 28 Apr 1700 *NHV*, d 28 July 1758 *WV*; m 25 June 1722 *NHV*—Enos Smith.
iii John, b 15 Mar 1702 *NHV*, d 1751; m 12 Feb 1723/4 *NHV*—Rebecca da. Samuel & Rebecca (Brown) Clark, b 27 May 1698 *NHV*, d 28 Sep 1749 *NHV*, æ. 51 *WHT2*. **FAM. 2.**
iv Thomas, b 8 Feb 1704 *NHV* [1704/5], d 16 Sep 1738 *NHV*, æ. 35 *WHT1*; m (1) 27 Oct 1726 *NHV*—Sarah da.

Eliphalet & Esther (Peck) Bristol, b 15 Nov 1703 *NHV*, d 28 May 1730 *NHV*, æ. 26 *WHT1*; m (2) 28 Oct 1731 *NHV*—Rachel da. Caleb & Mehitabel (Cruttenden) Hotchkiss, wid. Ebenezer Wolcott, b 26 Oct 1709 *NHV*, bp 10 Feb 1733/4 *NHC1*, d 6 May 1774 *MV*; she m (3) 7 Nov 1745 *NHV*—Samuel Pardee. **FAM. 3.**

v Elizabeth, b 27 Oct 1708 *NHV*, d 7 Oct 1784 *WHD*; m 4 Sep 1728 *NHV*—Stephen Thompson.

vi Esther, b 12 Sep 1710 *NHV*; m 11 May 1726 *WV*—Caleb Hall.

vii Mary, b 28 Aug 1714 *NHV*; m 20 May 1736 *NHV*—Timothy Alling.

viii David, b 16 Aug 1716 *NHV*, bp 1716 *NHC1*; m 9 Dec 1745 *Edgartown, Mass.*—Parnel Butler. **FAM. 4.**

ix Benjamin, d 1764; m 28 Mar 1745 *NHV*—Sarah da. Daniel & Rebecca (Cooper) Alling, b 29 July 1722 *NHV*. **FAM. 5.**

FAM. 2. JOHN & REBECCA (CLARK) HUMPHREVILLE:

1 SAMUEL, b 6 Dec 1724 *NHV*, d 7 Nov 1790 æ. 66 *WHD*; Census (NH) 1-0-5; m 12 June 1755 *NHV*—Eunice da. Samuel & Martha (Gold) Sherman, b 11 June 1730 *NHV*, d 14 Oct 1802 æ. 76 *WHD*.

i Rebecca, b 2 Apr 1756 *NHV*, d 5 Dec 1797 æ. 41 *WHD*; m Justus Smith.

ii Abigail, b c. 1758, d 12 May 1821 æ. 63 *WHD*.

iii Samuel; Census (NH) 1-1-2; rem. to Lanesboro, Mass.

iv Eunice, b c. 1766, d 27 Jan 1849 æ. 83 *NHV*, *NHT1*; m Edward Meloy.

v Sarah; m Justus Smith.

vi Jerusha, b c. 1771, d 27 Apr 1830 æ. 59 *WHD*.

2 EBENEZER, b 29 July 1726 *NHV*, d 6 Feb 1802 æ. 76 *WHT2*, æ. 77 *WHD*; Census (NH) 1-0-2; m 25 July 1754 *NHV*—Esther da. Joseph & Hannah (Smith) Thompson, b c. 1732, d 24 Sep 1810 *WHD*, æ. 78 *WHT2*, bu. 25 Sep æ. 79 *NHx*.

i Ebenezer, b 24 Dec 1754 *NHV*, d 1800; Census (Wd) 1-3-2; m 29 Jan 1781 *NHx*—Esther da. Samuel & Sarah (Humphreville) Downs, b 18 Sep 1757 *NHV*, d 18 Sep 1791 æ. 34 *BD*, "w. of ——— Umphervile" d Sep 1791 æ. 33 (at B) *NHx*. **FAM. 6.**

ii John, b 13 Aug 1756 *NHV*, d 27 June 1817 æ. 63 *BT3*; Census (Wd) 1-4-2; m 7 June 1775 *NHx*—Esther da. Jonathan & Mehitabel (Collins) Sperry, b 19 Sep 1749 *NHV*, bp 18 Feb 1782 *NHx*, d 11 Apr 1826 æ. 76 *BT3*. **FAM. 7.**

iii Joseph, b 27 Nov 1759 *NHV*, d 8 Nov 1830 æ. 71 *WHD*; Census (NH) 1-1-1; m Bathsheba da. Daniel & Parnel (Smith) Alling, b c. 1766, d 4 Mar 1852 *OC*, 5 Mar ("of Dogman, fell in the fire & burned to death") *WHD*.

FAM. 8.

iv Moses, b c. 1763, d 13 Aug 1829 æ. 66 *WHT2*, 17 Aug *WHD;* Census (NH) 1-0-2; m Hannah da. Nathaniel & Mary (Hodge) Downs, b c. 1766, d 23 May 1845 æ. 79 *WHT2*. FAM. 9.

v Esther, b c. 1766, d 6 June 1836 æ. 70 *WHD;* m John Meloy.

vi Amy; m 18 Oct 1795 *NHx*—Richard Downs.

3 REBECCA, b 1 Mar 1727/8 *NHV;* m Stephen Miles.

4 JOHN, b 17 Dec 1729 *NHV*, d c. 1755.

5 ABIGAIL, b 9 Dec 1731 *NHV*, d 7 Nov 1753 æ. 22 *WdT2;* m 3 Jan 1753 *WdC*—Samuel Baldwin.

6 LEMUEL, b 25 June 1737 *NHV*, d 19 Apr 1798 æ. 61 *WHD*, bu. 21 Apr æ. 56 *NHx;* Census (NH) 2-1-6; m 30 July 1761 *NHC1*—Molly da. Samuel & Mary (Thomas) Beecher, b 29 Oct 1741 *NHV*.

i Anna; m 3 July 1786 *NHC1*—David Peck.

ii Lucena, b 20 Mar 1764 (at NH) *MT*, d 27 Jan 1857 æ. 93 *MT*.

iii Avis; m Caleb Alling.

iv Susan; m Pulaski King of La Porte, Ind.

v Lemuel, b 1 Sep 1770 *F*, d 13 Nov 1828 æ. 59 *LT;* m 6 Jan 1799 Ursula Preston, b [12 Feb 1780], d 26 May 1882 æ. 102-3-14 *LT*.

vi Polly; m ——— Johnson.

vii Lura, b c. 1774, d 11 June 1866 æ. 92 *MT;* m Chauncey Isbell.

viii Deborah; m Ephraim Morse of Harwinton.

ix Liberty; rem. to N. Y. State; m Milly Marsh.

x Child, d 29 Sep 1789 *WHD*.

FAM. 3. THOMAS & SARAH (BRISTOL) HUMPHREVILLE:

1 SARAH, b 8 Jan 1727/8 *NHV*, d 9 Apr 1813 æ. 86 *Bethlehem;* m 10 Dec 1746 *NHV*—Samuel Downs.

2 ESTHER, b 16 May 1730 *NHV;* m 1 Mar 1749/50 *NHV*—Moses Thomas.

FAM. 3. THOMAS & RACHEL (HOTCHKISS) HUMPHREVILLE:

3 RACHEL, b 19 Aug 1733 *NHV*, d between 1764 & 1768; m Ebenezer Chatfield of D.

4 THOMAS, b 23 Nov 1736 *NHV*, bp 11 Jan 1736/7 *NHC1*, d 1772; m 13 May 1759 *NHC2*—Elizabeth da. Benjamin & Mehitabel (Munson) Morris, b 10 Apr 1739 *NHV*.

i Lemira, b 25 Feb 1760 *NHV*, bp 5 Oct 1760 *NHC2*.

ii Thomas, b 25 Feb 1762 *NHV*, d 21 Dec 1850 *F;* rem. to Burton, Ohio, 1798; m Lydia da. Jason & Abigail (Atwater) Hotchkiss, b 22 July 1764 *WV*, d 25 Mar 1849 *F*. FAM. 10.

iii Elijah, b 2 Mar 1764 *NHV*, bp 6 May 1764 *NHC2*.

iv Elizabeth, b 10 Dec 1766 *NHV*, bp 15 Feb 1767 *NHC2*, d

9 Oct 1825 *F;* m 19 Nov 1796 *F*—Ezra Lines.

v Mehitabel, b 2 Oct 1770 *NHV*, bu. 19 Sep 1806 æ. 35 *NHx*.

5 ELIPHALET, b 20 Apr 1738 *NHV*, bp 4 June 1738 *NHC1*, bu. 19 July 1783 *Huntingtonx;* m Martha ——— ; Census, Patty (Huntington) 2-1-2; [did she m (2) Nathaniel Woodruff of L?]. Family incomplete.

i Sarah, b 1 Oct 1764 *DV*, bp 16 Dec 1764 *Dx*.

ii Nabby, b 4 Aug 1766 *DV*, bp 21 Sep 1766 *Dx*.

iii Amarillis, bp 7 June 1772 *Huntington x*.

iv David, bp 14 May 1775 *Huntingtonx*.

v Susanna, bp 11 May 1777 *Huntingtonx*.

vi Polly, bp 31 July 1783 *Huntingtonx*.

FAM. 4. DAVID & PARNEL (BUTLER) HUMPHREVILLE:

1 TIMOTHY, b 17 Sep 1746 *NHV*, d 14 Jan 1800 *Morristown, N.J., C;* [said to have m (1) 26 May 1767 Elizabeth Reed]; m (2) Rebecca Burnett, who d 20 June 1792 æ. 39; m (3) Elizabeth (Cady) Cooper. Family incomplete.

(By 1): *i* Benjamin, b 13 July 1778, d 25 Apr 1850; m 3 Apr 1802 Hannah Dalrymple, b 9 Nov 1780, d 24 Dec 1850.

(By 3): *ii* Mary.

2 PARNEL, b 24 Dec 1748 *NHV;* m 24 Dec 1772 Benjamin McVeagh of Philadelphia, Pa.

3 LYDIA, b 25 Nov 1750 *NHV*, d 12 Jan 1750/1 *NHV*, 11 Jan 1751 æ. 7 weeks *NHT1*.

4 LYDIA, b 12 Jan 1752 *NHV*, bp 19 Jan 1752 *NHC2;* m 6 Sep 1766 Henry Lewis of N. Y. City.

5 LUCRETIA, b 25 Nov 1753 *NHV*, bp 25 Nov 1753 *NHC2;* m 15 Oct 1780 *Morristown, N.J.,C*—William Shippen, "Master of Musick".

6 DAVID, bp 16 Nov 1755 *NHC2*.

7 PAMELIA, bp 3 July 1757 *NHC2*.

8 (probably) BUTLER, d 1812; res. Philadelphia, Pa.

FAM. 5. BENJAMIN & SARAH (ALLING) HUMPHREVILLE:

1 SILAS, b 16 Nov 1746 *NHV*.

2 SARAH, b 14 Sep 1749 *NHV*.

3 SAMUEL ALLING, b 28 Sep 1751 *NHV*.

4 ESTHER, b 7 May 1755 *NHV*, bp 18 May 1755 *NHC2;* m 2 Oct 1785 *NHx*—Leonard Vollume.

FAM. 6. EBENEZER & ESTHER (DOWNS) HUMPHREVILLE:

1 EBENEZER, b 11 Apr 1781 *NHV*, *WdV*, d 21 Aug 1843 æ. 62 *SeymourT;* m 24 Oct 1804 *OxfC*—Anna da. John & Elizabeth (Hawkins) Riggs, b 20 June 1784 *OxfV*, d 19 Nov 1867 *SeymourT*.

2 CLARINA, b 28 May 1783 *WdV*, d 22 Apr 1861 æ. 78 *OT;* m 10 Dec 1802 *WdC*—Asa Alling.

3 ELIPHALET, b 27 July 1785 *WdV*.

4 ANER, b 22 Jan 1788 *WdV*.

FAM. 7. JOHN & ESTHER (SPERRY) HUMPHREVILLE:

1 JOHN, b 17 Feb 1776 *F*, bp 18 Feb 1782 *NHx*, d 9 Dec 1828 æ. 53 *BT3;* m 26 Jan 1800 *F*—Martha da. Joel & Martha (Peck) Hotchkiss, b 18 Apr 1775 *F*, d 12 Oct 1856 æ. 82 *NHTI*.
The will of Martha mentioned her gr. das. Emily, Lucy Bethia, Esther, Martha Emily, & Mary Eliza.
i Harley, b 10 Apr 1801 *F*, d 20 Aug 1835 *F*.
ii Marcus, b 10 Mar 1804 *F*, d 12 July 1833 æ. 29 *BT3*.
iii Sidney, b 26 June 1806 *F*, d 12 Oct 1841 *F;* m c. 1835 Sarah Tinsley, b c. 1812, d June 1856 *F*.

2 LUCY, b c. 1778, bp 18 Feb 1782 *NHx*, d 26 Aug 1828 æ. 51 *HT3;* m Caleb Doolittle.

3 AMOS, bp 18 Feb 1782 *NHx*, d 15 Apr 1873 æ. 92-6 *WdD;* m.

4 ICHABOD, b c. 1785, d 1 Jan 1856 æ. 71 *BT3* (murdered by a maniac); m Rebecca ——, who d 25 July 1849 æ. 69 *BT3*.
i John, b c. 1804, d 11 May 1807 æ. 3 *BT3*.
ii Luritta, b c. 1806, d 15 May 1807 æ. 1 *BT3*.
iii A son.
iv Rebecca, b [Nov 1812], d 10 Mar 1885 æ. 72-3 *NHV;* imbecile.

5 TRUMAN; rem. to Pensbrook, N. Y.; m 3 June 1801 *HV*—Patty Wilmot.

FAM. 8. JOSEPH & BATHSHEBA (ALLING) HUMPHREVILLE:

1 ALLEN, b 11 Mar 1788 (at Wd) *WatV;* m 1812 *WatV*, 15 Oct 1812 *OC*—Sena Sanford, b 23 Apr 1791 (at M) *WatV*.
i Norris, b 11 July 1813 *WatV*.
ii Willis, b 26 Apr 1815 *WatV*.
iii William, b 18 Apr 1821 *WatV;* m 8 Feb 1842 *WatV*—Mary Ann Morris.

2 BELIZER WYLLYS, d 8 Sep 1865 (k. by train in O) *BAlm*.

FAM. 9. MOSES & HANNAH (DOWNS) HUMPHREVILLE:

1 ELECTA, b c. 1788, d 30 Sep 1857 æ. 69 *WHT2;* m 30 Jan 1809 *OC*—Obed Johnson.

2 HARVEY; m Grace da. Nathan & Mary (Platt) Smith.

3 ANGELINE, b c. 1797, d 3 Sep 1867 æ. 70 *WHT2*.

4 JAMES, b c. 1798, d 10 Apr 1861 æ. 63 *OC*.

FAM. 10. THOMAS & LYDIA (HOTCHKISS) HUMPHREVILLE:

1 LEMIRA, bp 4 June 1786 *CC;* m Simeon Rose.

2 HARRY.

3 STELLA; m Eleazer Hickox.

4 BETSEY; m Orson D. Johnson of Burton, Ohio.

5 MARY.

6 LYDIA; m Clark Howard.

7 ABBY.

HUMPHREVILLE. MISCELLANEOUS. ELLAMILA, b c. 1801, d 25 Apr 1853 æ. 52; m 3 Jan 1821 *WdV*—Amos Sperry......JOHN D.; m 8 Apr 1824 *WdV*—Abigail B. French......—— m Betsey da. John & Betsey (Riggs) Hotchkiss; she m (2) 16 Oct 1796 *F*—John Woodruff.

HUNNEWELL. STEPHEN, b c. 1726, bu. 11 Apr 1786 æ. 60 *NHx;* m 2 July 1751 *NHV*—Hannah da. John & Hannah (Rowe) Leek, wid. Samuel Perkins, b 2 Mar 1723/4 *NHV*, d 1806.

1 ELIZABETH, b 12/23 May 1753 *NHV;* [m (1) George Lumsden]; m (2) ——— Green of Nova Scotia.

2 HANNAH, b 2 Mar 1758 *NHV;* m 28 June 1785 *NHx*—John Graham.

3 MARY, b 25 Feb 1760 *NHV*, d before 1806; m ——— Nichols.

4 STEPHEN, b 23 Jan 1762 *NHV*.

HUNNEWELL. MISCELLANEOUS. WILLIAM s. ——— & Mary, bp 18 Mar 1786 *NHx*.

HUNT. FAM. 1. JOHN, b c. 1749, d 31 Dec 1831 æ. 83 *NHV;* came from London, Eng.; Census (EH) 2-4-6; m Elizabeth Tomline.

1 FREDERICK WILLIAM, b 16 Dec 1772 *EHR*, d young.

2 JOHN, b 10 Apr 1775 *EHR*, d young.

3 GRACE, b 20 May 1776 *NHV*, bp 9 Oct 1776 *NHx;* m 30 Jan 1797 *EHC*—Jared Thompson.

4 ANNA MARIA, b 5 Dec 1777 *NHV*, bp 19 Jan 1778 *NHx*, d 27 Dec 1853 æ. 76 *NHT1;* m (1) 5 June 1798 *EHC*—Justus Potter; m (2) 23 Feb 1819 *ColR*—Philemon Peckham.

5 SARAH, b 16 Dec 1779 *NHV, NHx*, bp 13 June 1780 *NHx*, "child" d 21 Sep 1788 æ. 9 *EHC*.

6 EMILY, b 18 Dec 1780 *NHV*, bp 5 Aug 1782 *NHx*, d s. p.

7 WILLIAM HENRY, b 13 Sep 1782 *NHV*, bp 10 Oct 1782 *NHx*.

8 ELIZABETH, b 14 Sep 1783 *EHR*.

9 JAMES RICHARD, b 29 Mar 1785 *NHV*, bp 14 Apr 1785 *NHx*, d 11 July 1857 æ. 72 *NHT3;* m (1) Hannah da. Asa & Hannah (Chidsey) Mallory, b c. 1782, d 13 Oct 1851 æ. 69 *NHT3;* m (2) Ann da. Philemon & Ann (Howell) Peckham, b c. 1799, d 25 June 1861 æ. 62 *NHT3*.

10 WOODWARD HERVEY, b 19 Jan 1787 *EHR*, d s. p.

11 CHARLES AUGUSTUS, b 27 May 1789 *EHR*, d 12 Dec 1824 æ. 36 (*NHx*) *NHV*.

12 SARAH, b 10 Nov 1790 *EHR*, bp 15 Feb 1791 (æ. 0-3) *NHx*, "child" d Jan 1791 æ. 1 *EHC*.

13 SAMUEL BRADLEY HORATIUS, b 4 Dec 1793 *NHV*.

HUNT. FAM. 2. FREDERICK, b c. 1752, d 25 Nov 1825 æ. 73 *NHT1*, 27 Nov æ. 75 (*NHx*) *NHV;* Census (NH) 2-6-2; m Elizabeth ———, b c. 1755, d 21 Jan 1826 æ. 71 *NHT1*, 25 Jan æ. 75 (*NHx*) *NHV*. The first 8 children were bp 5 July 1789 *NHx*.

1 JOHN, b 22 Aug 1772, d 9 July 1841; m (1) 12 Nov 1793 *NHC1*—Hannah da. Elias & Hannah (Sabin) Beers, b c. 1773, d 23 Feb 1794 æ. 21 *NHT1;* m (2) 8 June 1796 *NHC1*—Betsey da. Timothy & Susanna (Macumber) Atwater, b 27 Jan 1777, bp 2 Feb 1777 *NHC1*, d 28 Sep 1820 æ. 43 *NHT1*.

2 ANN; m ——— Phelps.

3 JESSE, b c. 1776, d 25 Sep 1810 æ. 34 *NHT1;* m Sally da. Timothy & Susanna (Macumber) Atwater, b 23 Nov 1778, bp 20

Dec 1778 *NHCl*, d 15 Mar 1807 æ. 28-4 *NHTl*.

4 JAMES, b c. 1778; m Harriet Cutler.

5 FREDERICK, b 26 Jan 1783 *F*, d 11 Jan 1849 æ. 66 *NHV;* m 23 Jan 1807 *NHCl*—Harriet da. Henry & Anna (Ball) Daggett, b c. 1785, d 24 Aug 1862 æ. 76 *NHV*.

6 WILLIAM HENRY, b c. 1783, d 8 Nov 1815 æ. 32 (at sea) *NHTl*.

7 THOMAS, b c. 1786, d 6 Oct 1837 æ. 51 *NHTl;* m 13 Mar 1808 *NHx*—Nancy da. Isaac & Mabel (Riggs) Watrous.

8 CHARLES, b c. 1788, d 10 Dec 1824 æ. 36 *NHTl*.

9 BETSEY, bp 12 June 1791 *NHx;* m ——— Jones.

10 SALLY MARIA, b c. 1792, d [28 Nov 1863 æ. 71] *NHTl;* m 25 Dec 1809 *NHx*—Henry Huggins.

11 THEODOSIUS, bp 4 Jan 1795 (sponsor, Theodosius Hunt the uncle), d 20 July 1828 æ. 34 *NHTl*, 18 Aug æ. 35 (*NHx*) *NHV*.

HUNTINGTON. ASA, b 22 Apr 1752 *WdV*, d 4 Feb 1825 æ. 73 (*NHC2*) *NHV*, æ. 72 *NHTl;* Census (Wd) 3-1-3; m 18 Dec 1777 *WdV*, *WdC*—Lydia da. Charles & Lydia (Sperry) Hine, b 25 Sep 1756 *WdV*, d 21 Aug 1837 æ. 80 *NHTl*.

1 POLLY, b 30 Dec 1780 *WdV;* m 30 Dec 1800 *GV*—Rev. Israel Brainard.

2 EBENEZER, b 22 July 1782 *WdV*, d 1857 (Alton, Ill.); m.

3 LOIS HARRIET, b 23 Jan 1785 *WdV*, d 19 July 1794 *WdV*, æ. 9 *WdTl*.

4 LYDIA CAROLINE, b 31 May 1792 *WdV;* m Samuel B. Woodward.

5 HARRIET, b 21 Sep 1794 *WdV;* m Elias Trowbridge of Oswego, N. Y.

6 HANNAH MARIA, b 9 Feb 1797 *WdV;* m 18 May 1823 *NHV*—John Beecher.

INCE. JONATHAN m 12 Dec 1654 *NHV*—Mary da. Richard Miles; she m (2) 22 Oct 1661 *NorwalkV*—Rev. Thomas Hanford.

1 JONATHAN, b 27 June 1656 *NHV*.

INGERSOLL. JONATHAN of M m Sarah Newton and had issue (with others): JARED (see FAM. 1): JONATHAN, who m Dorcas Moss & had a son JONATHAN (see FAM. 2): & SARAH, b 22 Oct 1726 *NHTl*, d 4 July 1769 æ. 42 *NHTl*, *NHCl;* m 7 Nov 1751 *NHV*—John Whiting.

FAM. 1. JARED INGERSOLL, s. of Jonathan & Sarah (Newton), b 3 June 1722 *M*, d 25 Aug 1781 *NHV*, æ. 60 *NHTl*, æ. 59 *NHCl;* attorney; m (1) 1 Aug 1743 *NHV*—Hannah da. Joseph & Hannah (Trowbridge) Whiting, b 21 Feb 1712 *NHV* [1712/3], d 9 Oct 1779 æ. 66 *NHTl*, 8 Oct *NHCl;* m (2) 9 Jan 1780 *NHCl*—Hannah da. Samuel & Sarah (Woodward) Miles, wid. Enos Alling, b 7 Mar 1732/3 *NHV;* she m (3) Apr 1806 Joseph Bradley.

(By 1): 1 JARED, b 21 Apr 1748 *NHV;* bp 24 Apr 1748 *NHCl*, d 7 Feb 1748/9 æ. 0-10 *NHTl*.

2 JARED, b 27 Oct 1749 *NHV*, bp 29 Oct 1749 *NHCl*, d 31 Oct 1822 (Philadelphia, Pa.); B. A. (Yale, 1766); Judge.

3 JONATHAN, b 17 June 1751 *NHV*, bp 23 June 1751 *NHCl*, d

young.

4 HANNAH, bp 17 Dec 1752*NHC1*.

FAM. 2. JONATHAN INGERSOLL, s. of Rev. Jonathan & Dorcas (Moss), b 16 Apr 1747*M*, d 12 Jan 1823 æ. 75*NHT1*, 10 Jan (*NHx*) *NHV;* B. A. (Yale, 1766); Judge; Census (NH) 2-1-5; m 1 Apr 1786*NHV*, *EHC*—Grace da. Ralph & Mary (Perit) Isaacs, bp 22 Nov 1772*NHx*, d 30 Mar 1850 æ. 79 *NHT1*.

1 GRACE, b 20 Feb 1787 *NHV*.

2 RALPH ISAACS, b 8 Feb 1789 *NHV*, *NHT1*, bp 5 Mar 1789 (sponsor, Josiah Meigs) *NHx*, d 26 Aug 1872*NHT1*, æ. 83 *NHV;* Rep. (Conn., 1819-25), Rep. (U. S., 1825-33); Minister to Russia 1846-8; m 10 Feb 1814 (at N. Y.) *ColR*—Margaret Catherine Eleanora Vandenheuvel; had issue, including Charles Roberts, Gov. of Conn.

3 MARY, b 27 Mar 1791 *NHV*, bp 7 Apr 1791 *NHx;* m 24 Oct 1813 *ColR*—Ralph I. Linzee of Boston, Mass.

4 WILLIAM ISAACS, b 25 May 1793 *NHV*, bp 21 July 1793 *NHx*.

5 CHARLES JOSEPH, bp 7 June 1795 (sponsor, Ralph Isaacs, Jr.) *NHx*, d 15 Sep 1795 æ. 0-7 *NHx*.

6 CHARLES ANTHONY, bp 1 Jan 1797 *NHx*, d 7 Feb 1860 æ. 63 *NH T1;* Judge; m Henrietta Sidell.

7 JONATHAN, bp 3 Oct 1803 *NHx*.

8 EDWARD, bp 10 Mar 1811 *NHx*.

INGRAHAM. JOHN of NH m 15 Sep 1748 *Boston, Mass, V*—Elizabeth Coit. A John, perhaps the same, d before 1754 leaving wid. Lydia & 4 children below. Perhaps Josiah was also a child.

1 (perhaps) JOSIAH, d 1760; m 7 Dec 1758 *NHC2*—Rebecca da. Samuel & Hannah (Farrington) Beecher, wid. Samuel Sherman, b 15 Dec 1718 *NHV*.

2 SARAH; m (1) 14 Jan 1747/8 *NHV*—Thomas Alcott; m (2) 17 Feb 1765 *NHC2*—Abraham Augur.

3 STEPHEN, d 1777; m 23 May 1765 *NHC2*—Sarah da. Hezekiah & Sarah (Hopson) Parmalee, wid. Joseph Talmadge, b 2 June 1732 *GV*.

i Stephen, b 15 Apr 1766 *NHV*, bp 20 Apr 1766 *NHC2*.

ii Lydia, bp 5 June 1768 *NHC2*.

4 ELIJAH.

5 REUBEN.

ISAACS. RALPH, s. of Ralph & Mary (Rumsey), of Hebraic lineage, b 4 June 1741 *Norwalk*, bu. 26 Oct 1799 (at Bd) *NHx;* B. A. (Yale 1760); loyalist; m 8 Sep 1761 *MC2*—Mary da. Peter & Abigail (Shepherd) Perit, b c. 1740, d 4 Feb 1816 æ. 76 *NHT1*.

1 (probably) MARY; m Oct 1781 *NHx*———— Malbone.

2 GRACE, d 14 Aug 1769 *NHx*.

3 RALPH, bp 6 Dec 1767 *NHx*, d 8 Aug 1815 æ. 47 (at Philadelphia) *ColR;* Col.

4 PETER, bp 15 Oct 1769 *NHx*, d 15 Oct 1769 *NHx*.

5 GRACE, bp 22 Nov 1772 *NHx*, d 30 Mar 1850 æ. 79 *NHT1;* m 1

Apr 1786 *NHV*, *EHC*—Jonathan Ingersoll.

6 **Abigail**, bp 25 Dec 1774 *NHx;* m 9 Oct 1796 *NHx*—Smith Miles of D.

7 **Sarah**, b 12 Jan 1778 *BdV*, bp 15 Apr 1778 (at Bd) *NHx;* 18 Oct 1797 George Todd.

8 **Billy**, b 7 Aug 1780 *BdV*.

9 **Sophia**, b 6 Nov 1782 *BdV;* m 9 Oct 1803 *NHx*—Thomas Trumbull Loomis.

IVES. FAM. 1. **William**, d 1648; m Hannah ——— ; she m (2) 7 Nov 1648 William Bassett.

1 **Phebe**, bp 2 Oct 1642 *NHCl;* m (1) Joseph Potter; m (2) Aug 1670 *NHV*—John Rose.

2 **John**, bp 29 Dec 1644 *NHCl*, d 1682; m 12 Nov 1668 *NHV*—Hannah da. Nathaniel & Joan Merriman; she m (2) 17 Aug 1682 *WV*—Joseph Benham.

i John, b 14 Nov 1669 *NHV*, d 15 Apr 1747 *WV;* m 6 Dec 1693 *WV*—Mary Gillet. **FAM. 2.**

ii Hannah, b c. 1672, d 29 May 1715 *WV;* m 3 Mar 1692 *WV*—Samuel Cook.

iii Joseph, b 14 Oct 1674 *WV*, d 18 May 1755 æ. 81 *CTl;* Dea.; m 11 May 1697 *WV*—Esther da. Thomas & Mary (Messenger) Benedict, b c. 1679 (at Norwalk), d 1 Jan 1752 æ. 72 *CTl*. **FAM. 3.**

iv Nathaniel, b 31 May 1677 *WV*, d 6 Nov 1711 *WV;* m 5 Apr 1699 *WV*—Mary da. Samuel & Hope (Parker) Cook, b 23 Apr 1675 *WV;* she m (2) 29 Mar 1722 *WV*—Jonathan Penfield. **FAM. 4.**

v Gideon, b c. 1680, d 6 Feb 1767 æ. 87 *WTl;* m (1) 20 Feb 1706 *WV*—Mary da. Joseph & Mary (Porter) Royce, b 12 Jan 1686 *WV*, d 15 Oct 1742 *WV*, æ. 56 *WTl:* m (2) 10 May 1743 *WV*—Elizabeth, wid. Cornwall. **FAM. 5.**

3 **Daughter**; [probably **Martha** m Azariah Beach].

4 **Joseph**, b c. 1648, d 17 Nov 1694 *NHV;* m 2 Jan 1672 *NHV*—Mary da. Thomas & Mary (Turner) Yale, b 26 Oct 1650 *NHV*, bp (adult) 27 Dec 1685 *NHCl*.

i Joseph, b 17 Oct 1673 *NHV*, bp 28 Feb 1685/6 *NHCl*, d 1 Nov 1751 æ. 79 *NoHTl;* Capt.; m 7 Jan 1700 *NHV*—Sarah da. Alling & Sarah (Thompson) Ball, b 26 Aug 1679 *NHV*. **FAM. 6.**

ii Mary, b 18 Mar 1674/5 *NHV*, d soon.

iii Mary, b 17 Mar 1675/6 *NHV*, bp 28 Feb 1685/6 *NHCl*, d 14 Apr 1712 *NHV*, æ. 36 *NHTl;* m 21 Jan 1691/2 *NHV*—John Gilbert.

iv Samuel, b 6 Nov 1677 *NHV*, bp 28 Feb 1685/6 *NHCl*, d 24 Nov 1726 *NHV*, 25 Nov æ. 49 *NoHTl;* Dea.; m 3 Jan 1705 *NHV*—Ruth da. Jonathan & Ruth (Peck) Atwater, b 31 Dec 1688 *NHV*, d 17 May 1758 æ. 69 *NoHTl*.

FAM. 7.

v Martha, b 5 Mar 1678/9 *NHV*, bp 28 Feb 1685/6 *NHC1*, d 17 Jan 1727/8 *BdV;* m 6 Jan 1713/4 *BdV*—Eleazer Stent.

vi Lazarus, b 19 Feb 1680 *NHV* [1680/1], d s. p. 1704.

vii Thomas, b 22 Aug 1683 *NHV*, bp 28 Feb 1685/6 *NHC1*, d 5 May 1767 æ. 86 *NoHC*, 10 May 1768 æ. 84 *NoHT1;* m 4 May 1711 *NHV*—Ann da. John & Rebecca (Daniel) Thompson, b 20 Mar 1682/3 *NHV*, d 12 Dec 1751 æ. near 69 *NoHT1*. **FAM 8.**

viii Abigail, b 17 Aug 1685 *NHV*, d young.

ix John, b 18 Jan 1686 *NHV* [1686/7], bp 12 Feb 1686/7 *NHC1*, "child" d 1690.

x Ebenezer, b 6 Apr 1692 *NHV*, bp 22 May 1692 *NHC1*, d 7 July 1759 æ. 67 *NoHT1;* m 17 Jan 1714/5 *NHV*—Mary da. Ebenezer & Abigail (Heaton) Atwater, b 12 Mar 1694/5 *NHV*, d 13 Feb 1772 æ. 77 *NoHT1*. **FAM. 9.**

FAM. 2. JOHN & MARY (GILLET) IVES:

1 JOHN, b 28 Sep 1694 *WV*, d 4 Aug 1745 *WV*, *WC2;* m 18 Dec 1719 *WV*—Hannah da. Joseph & Mary (Porter) Royce, b 18 June 1701 *WV*, d 5 Nov 1770 æ. 70 *WT2;* [she perhaps m (2) 9 Aug 1757 *WC2*—John Merriam].

i Eunice, b 20 Apr 1721 *WV*, d 11 Sep 1726 *WV*.

ii Anna, b 20 Apr 1725 *WV*, d 8 Sep 1809 æ. 84 *WT2;* m 2 Aug 1744 *WV*—Noah Yale.

iii Eunice, b 13 May 1727 *WV*, d 26 July 1787 æ. 61 *WT2;* m (1) 23 Feb 1748/9 *WV*—Josiah Robinson; m (2) 5 Dec 1776 *WV*—John Miles.

iv John, b 1 July 1729 *WV*, 4 (?) July 1729 *WT2*, d Feb 1816 *WT2;* Census (W) 3-2-3; m (1) 17 Jan 1759 *WC2*—Mary da. Isaac & Mary (Moss) Hall, b 5 Oct 1742 *WV*, d 15 Feb 1788 æ. 46 *WT2;* m (2) Sarah Atkins. **FAM. 10.**

v Titus, b 17 Feb 1732 [*WV*], bp 20 Feb 1732 *WC2*, d Sep 1810 æ. 78 *NorfolkC;* Capt.; m 17 Sep 1754 *WV*—Dorothy Halsey, who d Jan 1806 æ. 71 *NorfolkC*. Children: (1) Hannah, b 27 July 1755 *WV;* m 25 May 1775 *NorfolkC*—Samuel Tibbals. (2) Joseph, b 10 May 1757 *WV*. (3) Dorothy, b 18 July 1760 *WV*. (4) perhaps Rachel, who m Mar 1779 *NorfolkC*—Francis Beach. (5) Daughter, b 13 Apr 1764 *WV*, probably Sarah, who m Nov 1782 *NorfolkC*—Calvin Pease. (6) Titus Howell, bp 13 Apr 1766 *NorfolkC*. (7) George Anson, bp 6 May 1768 *NorfolkC*. (8) John, bp 15 Apr 1770 *NorfolkC*. (9) Eunice, bp 5 Mar 1772 *NorfolkC*, d Nov 1776 *NorfolkC*. (10) Erastus, bp 11 June 1775 *NorfolkC*.

vi Jesse, b 2 Apr 1735 *WV*, bp 6 Apr 1735 *WC2*, d 31 Dec 1805; B. A. (Yale 1758); m 22 Aug 1763 *WV*, 24 Aug *EHC*—Sarah da. Samuel & Mary (Jones) Bellamy, b 10

May 1746 *NHV*.

vii Joseph, b 2 Apr 1735 *WV*, bp 6 Apr 1735 *WC2*, d 17 June 1745 *WV*, 18 June *WC2*.

viii Levi, b 19 Jan 1738 *WV*, bp 26 Feb 1737/8 *WC2*, d 20 Dec 1739 *WV*, 31 Dec *WC2*.

2 SAMUEL, b 15 Jan 1696 *WV*, d 29 Aug 1734 *WV*; m 28 Jan 1720 *WV*—Phebe da. Benjamin & Rebecca (Wilcoxen) Royce, who d before 1736 *WC2*.

i Mehitabel, b 27 Mar 1724 *WV*, d 22 July 1757 *FarmV*; m 10 Nov 1743 *WC2*—David Rich.

ii Bezaleel, b 14 Dec 1726 *WV*, d 24 Nov 1798 æ. 72 *WT2*; Census (W) 2-0-2; m 14 Feb 1751 *WV*—Hannah da. Nathaniel & Elizabeth (Hull) Merriam, b 27 Aug 1731 *WV*, d 21 Mar 1815 æ. 84 *WT2*. FAM. 11.

iii Phebe, b c. 1728, d 23 Feb 1753 *WC2*; m 29 May 1751 *WV*—William Merriam.

iv Samuel, bp 19 Dec 1731 *WC2*, d before 1734 *WC2*.

v Mary, bp 19 Dec 1731 *WC2*, d before 1734 *WC2*.

vi Samuel, b 28 Jan 1733 *WV*, bp 8 Apr 1733 *WC2*, d [9 Feb 1746 *WC2*].

3 BENJAMIN, b 22 Nov 1697 *WV*, d 1754; Sgt.; res. Meriden & Goshen; m (1) 17 Jan 1723 *WV*—Rebecca da. John & Rebecca Merriam, b 26 Mar 1702 *Lynn, Mass.*, d 25 Apr 1727 *WV*; m (2) 6 May 1728 *WV*—Hannah da. John & Elizabeth (Hall) Moss, b 11 Nov 1709 *WV*; she m (2) 15 June 1768 *WV*—Phinehas Atwater.

(By 1): *i* Rebecca, b 18 Nov 1724 *WV*, d 9 Dec 1724 *WV*.

ii Rebecca, b 29 Mar 1725 *WV* [1725/6], bp 29 Apr 1731 *WC2*, d 19 Dec 1755 *WC2*; m 19 Sep 1744 *WC2*—Stephen Mix.

iii Benjamin, b 15 Apr 1727 *WV*, d 12 June 1727 *WV*.

(By 2): *iv* Benjamin, b 26 Jan 1729 *WV*, bp 29 Apr 1731 *WC2*; res. Goshen; m 6 Dec 1753 *Goshen*—Rachel Baldwin.

v Hannah, b 18 Dec 1732 *WV*, bp 19 Dec 1732 *WC2*; m 23 Mar 1752 *Goshen*—Nathaniel Baldwin.

vi Lois, b 10 Mar 1734 *WV*, bp 17 Mar 1733/4 *WC2*; m 12 Mar 1755 *Goshen*—John Beach.

vii David, b 9 July 1736 *WV*, bp 11 July 1736 *WC2*, d 20 Feb 1737 *WV*.

viii Ruth, b 31 Jan 1738 *WV*, bp 12 Mar 1737/8 *WC2*; m 2 Mar 1758 *Goshen*—Martin Wilcox.

ix David, b 15 June 1740 *WV*, bp 22 June 1740 *WC2*; m 25 Mar 1761 *Goshen*—Eunice Gillet.

x Levi, b 23 July 1743 *WV*, bp 26 July 1743 *WC2*, d 9 Sep 1745 *WV*, 10 Sep *WC2*.

xi Thankful, b 1 June 1746 *WV*, bp 29 June 1746 *WC2*.

xii Levi, b 18 Sep 1748 *WV*, bp Sep 1748 *WC2*.

4 ABIJAH, b 14 Mar 1700 *WV*, d 17 July 1762 *WV*; m (1) 31

May 1730 *WV*—Abigail da. Thomas & Deborah (Royce) Mix, b 29 Jan 1706 *WV*, d 6 May 1753 *WV*; m (2) Aug 1753 *WC2*—Abigail Porter, wid. Josiah Mix.

i Moses, b 16 Mar 1731 *WV*, d 13 Nov 1755 *WV*.

ii Mary, b 22 Sep 1732 *WV*, d 1756; m 27 Dec 1752 *WV*—Benjamin Hall.

iii Abijah, b 7 Mar 1734 *WV*, d 16 Aug 1761 *WV*.

iv Aaron, b 6 May 1736 *WV*, d 24 Nov 1742 *WV*.

v Abigail, b 14 Feb 1738 *WV*; m 21 Sep 1758 *WC2*, 20 Aug 1758 *MidV*—Joseph Higbee of Mid.

vi Phebe, b 23 Mar 1740 *WV*; m 6 Sep 1764 *WC2*—Isaac Hall.

vii Martha, b 7 May 1742 *WV*.

viii Prudence, b 19 June 1744 *WV*.

ix Aaron, b 16 Apr 1746 *WV*.

x Anna, b 21 Feb 1749/50 *WV*, d 25 June 1751 *WV*.

5 Mary, b 10 Mar 1702 *WV*, d 1 June 1731 *WV*; m 1 Oct 1726 *WV*—Elihu Yale.

6 Lazarus, b 5 Feb 1703 *WV* [1703/4], d 23 Aug 1775 *WV*; m 5 Jan 1731 *WV*—Isabel da. Timothy & Abigail Jerome, who d 12 Apr 1777 *WV*.

i Timothy, b 16 Oct 1731 [*WV*], bp 11 Apr 1736 *WC2*, d 1812; Census (W) 1-2-5; m.

ii Mamre, b 10 Feb 1733 *WV*, bp 11 Apr 1736 *WC2*; m 28 Aug 1755 *WV*—Samuel Hall.

iii Lazarus, b 2 Nov 1734 *WV*, bp 11 Apr 1736 *WC2*; Census (Rensselaerwick, N. Y.) 1-0-4.

iv Abner, b 22 May 1736 *WV*, bp (as "Ambrose") 9 May 1736 *WC2*.

v Isabel, b 19 Apr 1738 *WV*, bp 23 Apr 1738 *WC2*; m 17 Feb 1757 *WC2*—Recompence Miller of Mid.

vi Joshua, b 16 Mar 1740 *WV*, bp 23 Mar 1740 *WC2*; Census (Rensselaerwick, N. Y.) 1-1-2.

vii Amasa, bp 27 Mar 1743 *WC2*, [d 13 Dec 1817 æ. 73 *WT2*; m Rebecca ——— , who d 12 Sep 1826 æ. 71 (at Sullivan, N. Y.) *WT2*].

viii Mary, bp 9 Nov 1744 *WC2*, d young.

ix John, bp 17 May 1747 *WC2*; m 6 May 1775 *WV*—Mehitabel Rose.

x Child, bp 1749 *WC2*, d young.

xi Phebe, bp 26 Nov 1752 *WC2*, d 4 Feb 1766 *WC2*.

xii Benjamin, bp 13 Oct 1754 *WC2*, d young.

7 Daniel, b 19 Feb 1706 *WV*, *WT1*, d 21 Jan 1786 *WV*, æ. 79 *WT1*; m (1) 28 Oct 1735 *WV*—Abiah da. Samuel & Sarah (Goodsell) Parker, b 21 Aug 1716 *WV*, d 21 Sep 1767 *WV*, æ. 52 *WT1*; m (2) 18 Oct 1768 *WV*—Mary wid. Stephen Osborn.

(By 1): *i* Abiah, b 31 July 1736 *WV*, d 19 Dec 1761 *WV*; m 4 Feb 1756 *WV*—James Humiston.

ii Lydia, b 11 June 1738 *WV*, d 5 Mar 1753 *WV*.

iii Martha, b 29 Feb 1740 *WV;* m Gideon Smith of Lenox, Mass.

iv Olive, b 29 Nov 1741 *WV*, d s. p. 19 Aug 1780; m 1 Mar 1759 *WV*—Nathaniel Hitchcock.

v Daniel, b 31 Jan 1743/4 *WV*, d 27 Sep 1777 æ. 34 (Rev. soldier, late of W, at Sy) *SyT;* m (1) 3 Apr 1766 *WV*—Elizabeth ———, wid. Reuben Ives, who d 7 Nov 1767 *WV;* m (2) 7 Dec 1769 *WV*—Obedience da. Thomas & Desire (Smith) Stevens, wid. John Cook, b c. 1746, d 25 Sep 1830 æ. 84 *NoBTI;* she m (3) Rufus Hoadley. **FAM. 12.**

vi Samuel, b 9 Mar 1745/6 *WV;* Census (Woodstock, N. Y.) 1-3-4.

PAGE 2047

vii John, b 19 Feb 1747/8 *WV*, d 27 Sep 1826 æ. 79 *WV;* m Phebe ———. Children (incomplete): (1) Jerusha, b 4 Mar 1774 *WV*. (2) James, b 3 Oct 1775 *WV*.

viii Levi, b 29 Mar 1750 *WV;* m 1 May 1776 *WV*—Lois da. Ambrose & Sarah (Terrill) Hine, bp 3 Dec 1752 *WdC*.

ix Lydia, b 30 Mar 1754 *WV*, d soon.

x Jesse, b 12 Nov 1756 *WV*.

xi Lydia, b 22 May 1761 *WV;* m Samuel Wright of Stockbridge, Mass.

8 Hannah, b 10 Feb 1708 *WV*, d 13 July 1750 *WV;* m 29 May 1735 *WV*—John Stanley.

9 Abraham, b 2 Dec 1709 *WV*, d 25 Apr 1787 æ. 78 *WTI;* m (1) 13 Feb 1734 *WV*—Elizabeth Stanley, who d 4 Aug 1735 *WV;* m (2) 11 May 1736 *WV*—Barbara da. John & Sarah (Jennings) Johnson, b 5 Feb 1714 *WV*, d before 1761; m (3) 14 Oct 1761 *WV*—Lucy ———, wid. Israel Dayton & Moses Thorpe, b c. 1722, d 3 Oct 1776 *WV*, [—] Sep 1776 æ. 54 *WTI;* m (4) 8 Jan 1778 *WV*—Sabra da. Ebenezer & Lydia (Hotchkiss) Johnson, wid. William Wainwright, b 17 Jan 1721 *WV*.

(By 1): *i* Elizabeth, b 22 July 1735 *WV;* m 2 Mar 1758 *KensingtonC*—Solomon Dunham of Berlin.

(By 2): *ii* Sarah, b 23 Dec 1736 *WV*, d 8 Oct 1748 *WV*.

iii Barbara, b 9 Oct 1738 *WV*, d 5 Oct 1748 *WV*.

iv Reuben, b 11 Dec 1740 *WV*, d 20 Jan 1764 æ. 24 *WTI;* m Elizabeth ———; she m (2) 3 Apr 1766 *WV*—Daniel Ives.

v Abraham, b 8 June 1743 *WV*, 4 June *WTI*, d 22 June 1743 *WV*, *WTI*.

PAGE 2047

vi Abraham, b 8 Mar 1745/6 *WV*, d 29 July 1776 (in army) *WV;* m 15 Jan 1767 *WV*—Eunice da. Samuel & Sarah (Hall) Hull, b 23 June 1749 *WV*. **FAM. 13.**

vii Ambrose, b 30 June 1748 *WV*, d 4 Sep 1776 (in army) *WV*.

viii Sarah, b c. 1750, d 18 Sep 1776 *WV;* m 3 Mar 1774 *WV*—

Stephen Peck.

(By 3): *ix* Abijah, b 1 Nov 1762 *WV*, d 21 Oct 1830 æ. 68 *WTI;* Census (W) 1-1-3; m 21 May 1779 *WV*—Hannah da. Ephraim & Lois (Hull) Johnson, b 25 July 1763 *WV*, d 2 Mar 1827 æ. 64 *WTI.*

x Barbara, b 29 Aug 1764 *WV*, d 19 Oct 176[-] *WV.*

10 BEZALEEL, b 4 July 1712 *WV*, d 28 Oct 1714 *WV.*

FAM. 3. JOSEPH & ESTHER (BENEDICT) IVES:

1 THOMAS, b 30 May 1698 *WV*, d 13 Jan 1747/8 *WV;* m 15 Nov 1720 *WV*—Rebecca da. Daniel & Esther (Sperry) Hotchkiss, b 14 Feb 1697 *NHV*, d 25 Jan 1762 æ. 65 *CTI;* she m (2) 1 Dec 1748 *WV*—Edward Parker.

i Isaac, b 8 Nov 1721 *WV*, bp 2 May 1725 *CC*, d 29 Feb 1760 æ. 38 *CTI;* m 13 June 1744 *WV*—Lydia da. Joseph & Susanna Morgan, b c. 1719, d 8 May 1793 *CC*, 7 Mar æ. 74 *CTI;* she m (2) Henry Hotchkiss. **FAM. 14.**

ii Andrew, b 2 July 1724 *WV*, bp 2 May 1725 *CC;* Census (H) 1-0-4; m 2 Oct 1744 *WV*—Sarah da. Joel & Jemima (Benham) Prindle. **FAM. 15.**

iii Lent, b 17 May 1726 *WV*, bp May 1726 *CC*, d 11 July 1726 *WV.*

iv Enos, b 14 May 1727 *WV*, bp June 1727 *CC;* res. Rutland, Vt., 1773, Cornwall 1805; m 16 Mar 1749 *WV*—Ann da. Israel & Elizabeth (Clark) Cook, b 4 Jan 1727 *WV.* **FAM. 16.**

2 ELIZABETH, b 6 Sep 1700 *WV*, d 8 Aug 1762 *WV*, æ. 62 *CTI;* m 1 Oct 1718 *WV*—Benjamin Hitchcock.

3 HANNAH, b 13 Oct 1702 *WV*, d [1750 *CC*]; m 1 June 1725 *WV*—Abraham Sperry.

4 ABIGAIL, b 27 Aug 1704 *WV*, d 26 Feb 1762 æ. 58 *HT3;* m 5 Feb 1723/4 *NHV*—Daniel Sperry.

5 ESTHER, b 7 Jan 1706/7 *WV*, probably d 29 May 1785 *CC;* m 20 Dec 1727 *WV*—Joseph Smith.

6 JOSEPH, b 10 Dec 1709 *WV*, d 29 Mar 1766 æ. 58 *CTI;* m (1) 13 June 1733 *WV*—Mamre da. Samuel & Mary (Preston) Munson, b 16 Dec 1712 *WV*, d 24 Dec 1744 *WV;* m (2) 30 May 1745 *WV*—Mary da. Stephen & Elizabeth (Sperry) Hotchkiss, wid. Abraham Barnes, b 1 Jan 1707/8 *NHV*, d 15 Aug 1764 æ. 57 *CTI.*

(By 1): *i* Mary, b 26 May 1734 *WV*, bp June 1734 *CC*, d 18 June 1822; m 24 Jan 1753 *NHV*—Elisha Bradley; res. Stockbridge, Mass.

ii Lent, b 12 Sep 1735 *WV*, bp Sep 1735 *CC*, d young.

iii Joseph, b 17 Jan 1737 *WV*, bp Mar 1737 *CC*, d 25 Nov 1785 æ. 49 *Claremont, N.H.,T;* Lieut.; m Elizabeth ——, who d 9 Sep 1819 æ. 78 *Claremont, N. H.,T;* had issue.

PAGE1245 2047

iv Mamre, b 2 May 1738 *WV*, bp 7 May 1738 *CC*, d 17 Feb 1810 æ. 72 *Lee, Mass.;* m 19 Jan 1758 *NHV*—Jesse Bradley.

v Aner, b 13 Jan 1740 *WV;* Census (Wy) 1–2–4; m 15 June 1763 *WdC*—Rachel da. Valentine & Rachel (Johnson) Wilmot, b 11 Aug 1743 *NHV*. **FAM. 17.**

vi Asahel, b 18 June 1741 *WV*, bp June 1741 *CC*, probably d 26 July 1759 *F&IWRolls*.

vii Lydia, b 16 Feb 1742/3 *WV*, bp Jan (?) 1742/3 *CC*, d 3 May 1823 æ. 81 *CTI;* m (1) 20 Nov 1765 *WV*—Benjamin Doolittle; m (2) 6 Apr 1808 *CC*—Daniel Dutton.

viii Esther, b 29 Sep 1744 *WV*, bp Nov 1744 *CC*.

(By 2): *ix* Dinah, b 20 Mar 1746 *WV*, bp Mar 1745/6 *CC;* m 15 Dec 1775 *WV*, 14 Dec *CC*—Amasa Hall; res. Cazenovia. N. Y.

x Titus, b 11 Feb 1747 *WV*, bp Feb 1746/7 *CC*, d 2 Sep 1777 æ. 30 (at Harlem, N. Y.) *CTI*, 2 Sep 1776 *WV;* m 8 Jan 1767 *WV*—Martha da. Nathan & Thankful (Brooks) Gaylord, b 16 Mar 1745/6 *WV*, d 12 May 1815 æ. 69 *HT3;* she m (2) 27 Jan 1793 *CC*—Samuel Hitchcock. **FAM. 18.**

xi Stephen, b 27 June 1749 *WV*, bp July 1749 *CC*, d 8 Sep 1830 æ. 82 *CTI;* Census (Wat) 2–1–3; m 1 July 1773 *NHV*—Mary da. Joel & Mary (Sherman) Hotchkiss, b 25 Jan 1747/8 *NHV*, d 31 Dec 1834 æ. 87 *CTI*. Children (incomplete): 1 Mary, b 23 Mar 1774 *NHV*, d 18 Feb 1854 æ. 79 *CTI;* m Titus Ives. 2 Hannah, b 3 Dec 1776 *NHV*. 3 Lucy, b 19 Mar 1779 *WatV*.

xii Hannah, b 7 Dec 1750 *WV*, bp Aug (?) 1750 *CC*, d 14 Oct 1776 æ. 26 *CTI;* m 6 Feb 1772 *CC*—Thomas Gaylord.

7 **Phinehas**, b 8 Apr 1711 *WV*, d 17 May 1762 *WV*, æ. 52 *CTI;* m 26 Jan 1738 *WV*—Margery da. Joseph & Margery (Hitchcock) Munson, b 10 Oct 1717 *WV*, d 5 Mar 1798 *CC*.

i Phinehas, b 31 Oct 1746 *WV*, bp Jan 1746/7 *CC*, d s. p. 16 May 1804 *CC*, æ. 58 *CTI;* Census (C) 2–0–2; m (1) Lydia ——— , who d 21 Nov 1798 *CC*, 22 Nov æ. 46 *CTI;* m (2) 30 Jan 1799 *CV*—Sarah [da. Bela & Hannah (Atwater)] Hitchcock, b [1 Aug 1757 *WV*].

8 **Nathaniel**, b 15 Jan 1714 *WV*, d 23 Feb 1800 *CC;* Census (C) 1–0–1; m 1 Jan 1745/6 *WV*—Mehitabel da. Daniel & Mehitabel (Cook) Andrews, b 30 Apr 1726 *WV*.

PAGE 2047

i Abraham, b 20 Nov 1746 *WV*, bp Nov 1746 *CC*, d after 1804; res. Wallingford, Vt., 1785.

ii Nathaniel, b 17 Feb 1748 *WV*, bp 26 Mar 1749 *CC*, d after 1804; Census (Wallingford, Vt.) 2–2–6; m 20 Aug 1771 *WV*—Repentance Wise [she is called da. in the will of Esther (Pratt), w. Samuel Jones].

iii Esther, b 25 Apr 1751 *WV*, bp Apr 1751 *CC*, d 16 Dec 1833 æ. 83 *CTI;* m 10 Dec 1772 *CC*—Daniel Bradley.

iv Jotham, b 1 Oct 1753 *WV*, d 2 Aug 1816 æ. 63 *CTI;* Census (C) 1–1–4; m Lilis ——— , who d Aug 1826 æ. 65 *CT l*. Family incomplete; among the children probably were: (1) Benedict, b c. 1780, d 20 Nov 1862 æ. 83 *CT1;* m 27 Nov 1800 *CV*—Betsey da. Ezra & Elizabeth (Hotchkiss) Bristol, b 6 June 1780 *CV*, d 7 Oct 1857 æ. 77 *CT1*. (2) Rebecca, b c. 1792, d 5 Aug 1794 æ. 2 *CT1*. (3) Asa, b c. 1797, d 22 July 1816 æ. 29 *CT1*. (4) Amasa, b 6 Apr 1805 *CV*, d 4 Jan 1868 æ. 63 *CT1;* m 14 Jan 1828 *CV*—Roxanna Blakeslee, who d 2 Nov 1873 æ. 69 *CT1*.

v Asa, b 8 Apr 1756 *WV*, d 1776 (in camp) *CC*.

vi Lent, b 28 Nov 1758 *WV*, d 30 June 1838 æ. 80 *Wallingford, Vt.;* Census (Wallingford, Vt.) 2-0-3.

vii Amasa, b 7 Apr 1763 *WV*, d after 1804.

viii Mehitabel, b 16 Dec 1765 *WV*, d after 1804; m ——— Miller.

9 EPHRAIM, b 4 Jan 1717 *WV*, d 1762; m 12 Mar 1741 *WV*—Elizabeth da. John & Elizabeth (Mix) Atwater, b 17 Nov 1721 *WV*.

i Sarah, b 19/20 Nov 1741 *WV*, bp Nov 1741 *CC*, d 6 Mar 1812 æ. 70 *WatT2;* m 29 Nov [1764] *WV*—Edmund Austin.

ii Ephraim, b 7 June 1744 *WV*, bp June 1744 *CC;* d s. p.

iii Phinehas, b 12 June 1746 *WV*, bp 1746 *CC*, d 27 June 1824 æ. 78 *CT2;* Census (C) 1-5-2; m 31 Dec 1774 *WV*—Martha da. Samuel & Hannah (Royce) Moss, b 10 May 1755 *WV*, d 28 Apr 1845 æ. 90 *CT2*. **FAM. 19.**

iv Elnathan, b 21 Dec 1748 *WV*, bp 18 Dec 1748 *CC*, d 14 Dec 1841 æ. 92 *PT;* Census (Wtn) 1-3-3; m 21 Apr 1774 *PC*—Olive da. John & Olive (Curtis) Blakeslee, b 29 Mar 1758 *WatV*, d 17 May 1832 æ. 73 *PT*. **FAM. 20.**

v Elizabeth, b 6 Nov 1751 *WV*, bp 8 Dec 1751 *CC*, d 3 Sep 1826 æ. 73 *WatT1;* m 3 Aug 1775 *WatV*—Noah Baldwin.

vi Eunice, b 19 Feb 1755 *WV*, d 13 July 1831 æ. 76 *EHT;* m 11 Jan 1776 *WV*—Daniel Bradley.

vii Ephraim, b 28 May 1757 *WV*, rem. to Wtn.

viii Ichabod, b 11 Sep 1759 *WV*, d 16 Feb 1845 æ. 86 *WT1;* Census (W) 1-1-4; m Mary da. Daniel & Abigail (Horton) Clark, b c. 1760, d 9 Jan 1826 æ. 66 *WT1*.

10 DINAH, b 4 Apr 1721 *WV*.

FAM. 4. NATHANIEL & MARY (COOK) IVES:

1 CALEB, b 3 Feb 1700 *WV*, d 13 Apr 1752 *WV*, 14 Apr æ. 53 *WT1;* m (1) Mary da. William & Mary (Peck) Abernathy, b 30 Apr 1700 *WV;* m (2) 27 Feb 1733 *WV*—Elizabeth Plumb.

(By 1): *i* Nathaniel, b 12 Jan 1722 *WV;* rem. to New Hartford; m 8 Nov 1744 *WV*—Zerviah da. Samuel & Elizabeth (Doolittle) Blakeslee, b 16 Jan 1726 *WV*. **FAM. 21.**

ii Sarah, b 6 Aug 1725 *WV;* m John Andrews; rem. to New Hartford.

(By 2): *iii* Charles, b 5 Sep 1734 *WV*, d 18 June 1790 æ. 56 *WTI*; m 2 May 1755 *WV*—Sarah Butler, b c. 1737, d 11 Apr 1813 æ. 76 *WTI*. **FAM. 22.**

iv Eunice, b 13 Sep 1736 *WV*.

v Elizabeth, b 25 Dec 1738 *WV*; m 19 Nov 1759 *WV*—Aaron Parsons.

vi Olive, b 10 Aug 1742 *WV*, d young.

vii Caleb, b 19 May 1745 *WV*, d soon.

viii Caleb, b 9 Mar 1747/8 *WV*, d 20 Oct 1824 æ. 77 *WTI*; Census (W) 1-0-2; m (1) 4 Feb 1771 *WV*—Ruth Wright; m (2) Abigail ——— , who d 10 Sep 1823 æ. 68 *WTI*.

ix Amos, b 1 Aug 1750 *WV*, d 5 May 1826 *Middle Settlement, Oneida Co., N. Y., T*; Census (W) 1-2-4; m 14 May 1777 *WV*—Rebecca Collins, who d 2 Oct 1829 æ. 77 *Middle SettlementT*.

2 Stephen, b 24 Mar 1704 *WV*; m 25 Oct 1730 *WV*—Sarah da. Hawkins & Sarah (Royce) Hart, b 21 May 1710 *WV*.

i Sarah, b 29 May 1733 *WV*, d 29 July 1776 *WV*; m 26 Sep 1750 *WV*—Amasa Merriman.

ii Mary, b 16 Apr 1735 *WV*; m 5 May 1757 *WV*—Moses Hull.

iii Lois, b 9 Jan 1737 *WV*; m 1 Apr 1756 *WV*—Joseph Blakeslee.

iv Stephen, b 20 Jan 1739 *WV*; Census (Adams, Mass.) 1-2-5; m (1) 20 Nov 1766 *WV*—Susanna da. Andrew & Susanna (Blakeslee) Parker, b 10 Dec 1747 *WV*; m (2) Mary ——— . Children by 1st w., recorded *WV*: 1 [—]ier, b 27 Jan 1767. 2 Isaac, b 26 Sep 1768.

v Esther, b 13 July 1742 *WV*; m 18 Feb 1762 *WV*—Thomas Merwin.

vi Thankful, b 15 July 1744 *WV*, d 3 Feb 1792 æ. 48 *WtnD*; m 6 Nov 1768 *WatV*—Joseph Foote.

vii Amasa, b 10 Nov 1747 *WV*; Census (Adams, Mass.) 2-1-7; m Bethia ——— .

viii Asahel, b 12 May 1749 *WV*.

ix David, b 29 July 1751 *WV*; rem. to Salisbury; Census (Tinmouth, Vt.) 1-4-2; m Elizabeth ——— .

3 Thankful, b 11 Aug 1708 *WV*, d 7 July 1770 *NoHC*; m 17 Dec 1728 *NHV*—Gideon Todd.

4 Abel, b 6 May 1711 *WV*, d 31 Jan 1791 æ. 80 *WTI*; Census (W) 1-0-2; m 25 Mar 1736 *WV*—Sarah Reed, b c. 1712, d 1 Jan 1797 æ. 85 *WTI*.

i Abel, b 9 Dec 1736 *WV*, d before 1797; Census (Cornwall) 3-1-2; m 19 June 1760 *WV*—Lois Tuttle. Child b at W: 1 Ruth, 2 Apr 1761.

ii Ann, b 20 Dec 1738 *WV*, d 16 Sep 1739 *WV*.

iii Ann, b 1 Aug 1740 *WV*; m John Curtis.

iv Sarah, b 4 June 1743 *WV*, d 14 Feb 1756 *WV*.

v Elizabeth, b 30 Aug 1746 *WV;* m Amos Moss.

vi John, b 3 Apr 1749 *WV*, d 16 Apr 1814 æ. 66 *WT1;* Census (W) 1-3-2; m 29 May 1770 *WV*, *NewHartfordC*—Sarah Henderson, who d 10 Apr 1831 æ. 82 *WT1*.

vii Esther, b 4 June 1751 *WV*, d 10 June 1756 *WV*.

viii Lois, b 27 Mar 1754 *WV;* m 27 Dec 1770 *WV*—Giles Hall.

PAGE 2047 *ix* Sarah, b 12 June 1756 *WV;* m Samuel Hall.

FAM. 5. GIDEON & MARY (ROYCE) IVES:

1 **ELNATHAN**, b 22 Sep 1706 *WV*, d 1777 æ. 71 *BristolC;* m 7 May 1730 *WV*—Abigail da. Benjamin & Elizabeth (Henbury) Frisbie, b 23 June 1709 *BdV*, d 1778 æ. 69 *BristolC*.

PAGE 2047 *i* Elnathan, b 20 Mar 1731 *WV*, bp 21 Mar 1731 *WC2;* Census (W) 2-0-3; m 9 Mar 1758 *WC2*—Ann Yale.

ii Abigail, b 9 Feb 1733 *WV*, bp 11 Feb 1733 *WC2*.

iii Jerusha, b 21 Feb 1735 *WV*, bp 28 Feb 1734/5 *WC2*.

iv Josiah, b 13 Mar 1739 *WV*, bp 18 Mar 1738/9 *WC2*.

v Reuben, b 10 Mar 1743/4 *WV*, bp 11 Mar 1744 *WC2*, d 18 Aug 1823 æ. 80 *BristolT;* Census (Bristol) 2-2-2; m 24 Feb 1762 *WV*—Elizabeth Royce, who d 14 Mar 1799 æ. 53 *BristolT*.

vi Huldah, b 16 Jan 1747/8 *WV*, bp 17 Jan 1748 *WC2*.

2 **SARAH**, b 9 Sep 1708 *WV*, d 29 Nov 1760 *WV*, æ. 53 *CT1;* m 21 June 1727 *WV*—John Hull.

3 **JOTHAM**, b 26 Sep 1710 *WV*, d 2 Sep 1753 *WV*, æ. 43 *CT1;* m 28 Feb 1736 *WV*—Abigail da. Edward & Abigail (Hudson) Burroughs, b 31 May 1715 *StV*.

i Zachariah, b 31 Jan 1737 *WV*, bp Jan 1736/7 *CC*, d 9 Mar 1815 æ. 78 *CT2;* Census (C) 3-1-3; m 15 Jan 1761 *WV*—Lois da. Amos & Esther (Maltby) Harrison, bp 3 Aug 1740, d 28 Jan 1814 æ. 74 *CT2*. **FAM. 23.**

ii Abigail, b 10 Oct 1739 *WV*, d 28 July 1827 æ. 88 *CT2;* m 4 Apr 1760 *WV*—Amos Doolittle.

iii Amasa, b 7 Feb 1742/3 *WV*, bp 1742/3 *CC*.

iv Jotham, b 20 Aug 1745 *WV*, bp 1745 *CC;* res. Torrington; Census (L) 2-3-3; m (1) 10 May 1769 Anna Foster; m (2) 28 Sep 1796 *NoHC*—Lydia da. Samuel & Lydia (Todd) Mix, b 23 Apr 1753 *NHV*, d 14 Jan 1832 æ. 79 *NoHT1*.

v Abner, b 20 Aug 1745 *WV*, bp 1745 *CC;* res. Torrington; Census (L) 3-3-7; m 11 May 1768 Anna Ferguson of Haddam.

vi Chauncey, b 20 Nov 1748 *WV*, bp Dec 1748 *CC*, "child" d Dec 1748 *CC*.

vii Sarah, b 14 Apr 1752 *WV*, bp Apr 1752 *CC*.

4 **AMASA**, b 24 Aug 1712 *WV*, d 1 Sep 1715 *WV*.

5 **RHODA**, b 2 Dec 1714 *WV;* m 25 Dec 1740 *WV*—Immer Judd of S.

6 **MARTHA**, b 10 Aug 1716 *WV;* m (1) 25 Dec 1740 *WV*—Ralph Parker; m (2) 15 Nov 1759 *WV*—Jonathan Blakeslee.

7 **AMASA**, b 15 Nov 1718 *WV*, d 30 Sep 1742 *WV*, 20 Sep æ. 24 *WT*

I.

8 GIDEON, b 24 Sep 1720 *WV*, d 31 Jan 1777 æ. 57 *WT2;* m 17 Oct 1745 *WV*—Eunice da. Daniel & Ruth (How) Tuttle, b 12 July 1726 *WV*, d 6 Apr 1807 æ. 80 *BristolT;* she m (2) 18 Dec 1777 *WV*—Ebenezer Cole.

i Mary, b 5 Aug 1746 *WV*, bp 10 Aug 1746 *WC2;* m 27 Apr 1769 *WV*—Elijah Hough; res. Southwick, Mass.

ii Amasa, b 15 Apr 1748 *WV*, bp Apr 1748 *WC2*, d 24 Jan 1817 æ. 69 *BristolT;* res. Southwick, Mass.; Census (Bristol) 1-6-3; m 19 Dec 1771 *WV*—Huldah Shailer, who d 9 Sep 1810 æ. 60 *BristolT.* **FAM. 24.**

iii Eunice, b 28 Sep 1749 *WV*, bp 29 Oct 1749 *WC2;* m 1 Dec 1768 *WV*—Ebenezer Cole.

PAGE 2047 *iv* Amos, b 25 Dec 1751 *WV*, bp 5 Jan 1752 *WC2;* Census (Bristol) 1-1-2; m 23 Feb 1774 *WV*—Lucy Hall.

v Enos, b 25 Oct 1753 *WV*, bp 2 Dec 1753 *WC2*, d 1830 æ. 76 *BristolC;* Census (Bristol) 1-2-5; m Eunice da. Titus & Dinah (Andrews) Merriman, b 11 June 1757 *WV*, d 16 May 1832 æ. 75 *BristolT.* Children, recorded *Bristol V:* 1 Keturah, b (at W) 6 Aug 1778; m Asahel Barnes. 2 Eunice, b 11 Mar 1780; m Orrin Hart. 3 Charles Grandison, b 22 Oct 1781, d 7 May 1867 æ. 86 *BristolV;* m (1) 14 May 1806 *BristolV*—Parthena Rich, who d 29 Mar 1838 æ. 56 *BristolT;* m (2) Elizabeth ——, who d 24 Sep 1867 æ. 56 *BristolT.* 4 Sarah, b 24 Sep 1789; m John G. Cowles. 5 Enos, b 21 May 1793, d 13 Aug 1866 æ. 74 *BristolT.* 6 Orrin, b 1 Sep 1797.

vi Jerusha, bp 12 Oct 1755 *WC2*, "child" d 8 July 1756 *WC2.*

vii Gideon, b 13 May 1757 *WV*, bp 15 May 1757 *WC2*, d before 1777.

viii Jerusha, b 20 Feb 1759 *WV;* m 31 Aug 1780 *WV*—Nathaniel B. Johnson.

ix Sarah, b 5 June 1761 *WV;* m Ebenezer R. Hawley.

x Phebe, b 9 June 1764 *WV;* m Samuel Collins.

xi Dolly, b c. 1766, d 13 Aug 1808 æ. 42 *WT2;* m 25 Jan 1784 *WV*—Jesse Merriman.

xii Moses; m & had children recorded *BristolV:* Newton, b 29 Dec 1794; Romante, b 13 Feb 1797; Hiram, b 8 Nov 1799; & Emeline, b 1 Sep 1802.

9 JOEL, b 13 Jan 1723 *WV*, d 31 Dec 1795 æ. 73 *WT1;* Census (W) 1-0-0; m (1) 10 Feb 1747/8 *WV*—Rebecca da. Nathaniel & Elizabeth (Hull) Merriam, b 10 Feb 1729 *WV*, d 5 Nov 1750 *WV;* m (2) 27 Dec 1752 *WV*—Experience da. Jacob & Thankful (Beach) Royce, b 1 Dec 1727 *WV*, d 30 Mar 1761 *WV;* m (3) 4 Nov 1762 *WV*—Hannah da. Joseph & Hannah (Doolittle) Atwater, b 15 July 1725 *NHV*, d 6 Nov 1771 æ. 46 *WV*, æ. 47 *WT1.*

(By 1): *i* Elizabeth, b 22 July 1749 *WV*, d 21 Feb 1758 *WV.*

(By 2): *ii* Joel, d 1755 *WV*.

iii Thankful, b 1 Oct 1757 *WV*.

iv Joel, b 16 Apr 1760 *WV*, d 3 June 1807 æ. 48 *WT1;* Census (W) 1-2-3; m 22 Oct 1778 *WV*—Olive da. Charles & Sarah (Butler) Ives, b 20 Apr 1758 *WV*, d 14 Mar 1822 æ. 64 *WT1*.

10 **Mary**, b 16 Dec 1724 *WV*, d 14 May 1776 æ. 52 *WT2;* m 11 Apr 1745 *WV*—Moses Mitchell.

11 **Susanna**, b 26 May 1727 *WV;* m 26 July 1746 *WV*—Elias Roberts.

12 **Esther**, b 14 Oct 1729 *WV;* m 31 May 1748 *WV*—Ambrose Tuttle.

FAM. 6. Joseph & Sarah (Ball) Ives:

1 **John**, b 6 Nov 1701 *NHV*, d young.

2 **Joseph**, b 9 Nov 1703 *NHV*, d young.

3 **Alling**, b 23 Feb 1705/6 *NHV*, d young.

4 **Stephen**, b 27 June 1708 *NHV*, d Dec [1745] *NoHT1;* Sgt.; m 13 May 1736 *NHV*—Abigail da. Matthew & Rebecca (Mix) Rowe, b 17 Jan 1712/3 *NHV;* she m (2) Joseph Sackett.

i Mary, b 13 July 1737 *NHV*, d Oct 1813 æ. 76 (at NH) *Col R;* m Jason Cooper.

ii Rebecca, b 27 Feb 1738/9 *NHV*, d 26 Jan 1797 æ. 59 *EH C;* m William Bradley.

iii Joseph, b 26 Oct 1740 *NHV*, d 31 Jan 1768 æ. 27 *NoHC;* m (1) 5 Nov 1761 *NHV*—Elizabeth da. John & Mary (Bradley) Grannis, b 20 Dec 1741 *NHV*, d c. 1763; m (2) 6 Dec 1764 *NoHC*—Abigail da. John & Mary (Bradley) Grannis, b 26 Aug 1744 *NHV*, d 29 Jan 1773 æ. 27 *NoHC;* she m (2) Job Blakeslee. **FAM. 25.**

PAGE 1245

iv Stephen, b 16 Mar 1741/2 *NHV*, d 12 Oct 1786 æ. 44 *NoH C;* m 12 Feb 1769 *NoHC*—Sarah da. Samuel & Mary Ames, who d c. 1833; Census, Sarah (NoH) 1-0-5; she m (2) 4 Oct 1795 *NoHC*—Samuel Mix. **FAM. 26.**

v Enoch, b c. 1744, d 3 May 1762 æ. 18 *NoHC*.

5 **Enoch**, b 12 Feb 1711/2 *NHV*, d 29 Mar 1744 æ. 34 *NoHT1;* m 31 July 1735 *NHV*—Lydia da. Joseph & Abigail (Smith) Cooper, b 15 Jan 1708 *NHV* [1708/9]; she m (2) Samuel Goodsell.

i Sarah, b c. 1736, d Feb 1737 æ. 1 *NoHT1*.

ii Sarah, b 19 Apr 1738 *NHV*, d 17 Sep 1779 æ. 40 *WolT;* m Josiah Rogers of Wat.

iii Phebe, b 4 June 1740 *NHV*, d 1827/8; m 9 Oct 1760 *NHV*—Jacob Hitchcock.

6 **Elisha**, b 31 Jan 1715/6 *NHV*, d young.

7 **Sarah**, b 14 Feb 1718/9 *NHV;* m 1 Apr 1735 *NHV*—Stephen Cooper.

8 **Dan**, b 3 Jan 1721/2 *NHV*, d 27 Mar 1776 æ. 54 *NoHT1;* Capt.; m (1) Mary da. Gideon & Mary (Buckingham) Platt, b 18 Jan 1726/7 *MV*, d 17 July 1754 æ. 27 *NoHT1;* m (2) Mabel ———,

b c. 1727, d 26 June 1826 æ. 100 (at NoH) *ColR*.

(By 1): *i* Mary, b c. 1747, d 17 May 1802 æ. 55 *NoHTI*, *NoHC;* m 12 July 1770 *NoHC*—Stephen Jacobs.

ii Sarah, b c. 1749, d 25 Nov 1809 æ. 61 *HTI;* m 15 Feb 1770 *NoHC*—Hezekiah Bassett.

(By 2): *iii* Lydia, b c. 1757, d 12 Mar 1804 æ. 47 *NoHTI;* m (1) Charles Todd; m (2) Ebenezer Mansfield Gill.

iv Dan, b c. 1759, d 11 Aug 1801 æ. 42 *NoHTI;* Census (No H) 1-3-4; m 31 Dec 1783 *NoHC*—Mary Baldwin; she m (2) Hezekiah Bassett. **FAM. 27.**

v Alling, bp 3 Feb 1765 *NoHC*, d (probably s. p.) 6 May 1833 æ. 69 *NoHTI;* m (1) Molly da. Samuel & Mary (Gill) Humiston, b 16 Aug 1768 *NHV*, d 29 Apr 1825 æ. 57 *NoHTI;* m (2) 1 Sep 1825 *NoHV*—Betsey da. Samuel & Mary (Gill) Humiston, wid. Benjamin Munson, b 25 Mar 1776 *HV*, d 12 Jan 1835 æ. 59 *NoHTI*.

FAM. 7. SAMUEL & RUTH (ATWATER) IVES:

1 MARY, b 5 Dec 1706 *NHV;* m 13 Dec 1725 *NHV*—Caleb Todd.

2 LYDIA, b 7 Mar 1709 *NHV;* m 26 May 1726 *WV*—Stephen Todd.

3 SAMUEL, b 16 Sep 1711 *NHV*, d 31 Jan 1784 æ. 72 *NoHC;* m 13 June 1744 *NHV*—Mary da. Joseph & Mary (Potter) Gilbert, b 15 Jan 1716/7 *NHV*, d after 1792 (probably at Westfield, Mass.).

i Samuel, b 3 Oct 1745 *NHV;* rem. to Westfield, Mass.

ii Lois, b 27 Aug 1747 *NHV;* m William Day; res. Great Barrington, Mass.

iii Levi, b 24 May 1750 *NHV*, 4 June *F* [N. S.], d 17 Oct 1826 æ. 77 *NHTI;* Dr.; Census (NH) 2-2-5; m (1) 22 Apr 1772 *NHCI*—Lydia da. Abraham & Elizabeth (Bradley) Augur, b 30 Sep 1753 *F*, d 10 Sep 1802 æ. 49 *NHTI;* m (2) 8 Jan 1804 *F*—Margaret da. Samuel & Sarah (Prout) Bird, b 24 May 1770 *F*, d 29 Sep 1838 æ. 68 *NHTI*. **FAM. 28.**

iv Mary, b c. 1752, d 9 Jan 1757 æ. 5 *NoHTI*.

4 RUTH, b 17 Apr 1714 *NHV*, d 26 Oct 1777 *CC;* m 23 Mar 1737 *WV*—Benjamin Yale.

5 JONATHAN, b 14 Mar 1716 *NHV*, bp 8 July 1716 *NHCI*, d 2 Jan 1792 æ. 76 *HTI;* Capt.; Census (H) 1-0-1; m 19 Feb 1737/8 *NHV*—Thankful da. Joseph & Abigail (Smith) Cooper, b 11 Apr 1721 *NHV*, d after 1791.

i Jeremiah, b 19 Nov 1738 *NHV*, d c. 1825; Census (W. Springfield, Mass.) 2-0-5; m 7 June 1768 *NHV*—Hannah da. Abraham & Mehitabel (Street) Bassett, b 26 Dec 1739 *NHV*, d 14 Sep 1803. **FAM. 29.**

ii Ruth, b 28 July 1740 *NHV*, d 20 Aug 1806 æ. 66 *HTI;* m 29 May 1760 *NHV*, *NHCI*—Timothy Goodyear.

iii Mary, b 24 Apr 1744 *NHV*, d 14 Apr 1809 æ. 65 *NoHTI;* m 9 Sep 1765 *NoHC*—Seth Todd.

iv Thankful, b 14 Mar 1747 *NHV*, d 1 Aug 1834 æ. 87 *BT4;* m 5 Dec 1764 *F*—Uri Tuttle.

v Joel, b 19 May 1749 *NHV*, d 14 Aug 1825 æ. 77 (at Bd) *ColR;* Census (Bd) 2-1-4; m (1) 2 Dec 1772 *NoHC*—Mary da. Seth & Sarah (Morris) Heaton, b c. 1745, d 13 July 1784 æ. 39 *NoHT2;* m (2) 1 Nov 1785 *BdC*—Sarah da. Jonathan & Sarah (Baldwin) Harrison, b 28 Mar 1753 *BdV*, d 1835. **FAM. 30.**

vi Jonathan, b 26 Mar 1751 *NHV*, d 24 Oct 1813 æ. 63 *HT1;* Census (H) 1-1-2; m 1 May 1777 *NHV*—Sarah da. John & Sarah (Heaton) Bassett, b c. 1751, d 7 Apr 1836 æ. 85 *HT1*. **FAM. 31.**

vii Alling, b 13 Nov 1753 *NHV;* Capt.; Census (H) 1-2-2; m Rebecca da. Jonathan & Rebecca (Bassett) Dickerman, b 12 Jan 1759 *NHV*. Only child: 1 Julia, b c. 1787, d 1 July 1859 æ. 72; m Ezra Bradley.

viii Phebe, b 8 Feb 1757 *NHV;* m 4 Jan 1776 *HV*—Benjamin Gaylord.

6 Damaris, b 6 July 1718 *NHV*, bp July 1718 *NHC1*, d 19 Nov 1802 æ. 84-4 *NoHC;* m (1) 19 Apr 1739 *NHV*—Ebenezer Frost; m (2) 20 Oct 1761 *WV*—John Hull.

7 Phebe, b 20 July 1721 *NHV*, d 23 Sep 1725 æ. 4-3 *NoHT1*, d (as "Damaris") 23 Oct 1725 *NHV*.

8 David, b 7 Nov 1723 *NHV*, bp 2 Feb 1723/4 *NHC1*, d 20 May 1753 *WC2;* m 28 Feb 1744/5 *WV*, *WC2*—Elizabeth da. Nathaniel & Elizabeth (Hull) Merriam, b 28 Feb 1727 *WV*, d 30 Mar 1754 *WC2*.

i Hannah, b c. 1747.

ii David, b 13 Apr 1749 *WV;* Ens.; Census (Southwick,
PAGE 1245
Mass.) 2-4-4; m 25 Sep 1771 *WV*—Dolly da. Daniel & Violet (Benton) Hough, b 30 Jan 1755 *WV*. Child (record incomplete): 1 Matthew, b 26 June 1772 *WV*.

iii Rebecca, b 7 Mar 1752 *WV*, bp 3 May 1752 *WC2;* m 30 Sep 1772 *WV*—Thomas Hough.

9 John, b 22 Aug 1726 *NHV*, d 17 June 1812 *Barkhamsted;* res. New Hartford & Barkhamsted; Census (L) 2-2-5; m 12 Sep 1751 *NHV*—Lois da. Gershom & Mehitabel (Sanford) Barnes, b 9 Sep 1728 *NHV*, d 15 July 1814.

i Mehitabel, b 21 Jan 1754 *NHV*.

ii John, b 5 Feb 1757 *NHV*, d 10 Dec 1847 æ. 91 *Barkhamsted;* m (1) Susanna ——, who d c. 1778; m (2) 22 June 1780 Esther da. Jehiel & Charity (Dayton) Tuttle, b 14 Sep 1758 *NHV*, d 14 Feb 1836 æ. 78 *Barkhamsted*. **FAM. 32.**

iii Jesse, b 16 Aug 1759 *NHV*.

iv Lucy, b 15 Oct 1761 *NHV*, bp 22 Nov 1761 (at NoH) *NoBC2*.

v Lois, b 10 Sep 1764 *NHV*.

FAM. 8. THOMAS & ANN (THOMPSON) IVES:

1 THOMAS, b c. 1712, d 17 Nov 1752 æ. 40 *NoHT1*; m 21 May 1740 *NHV*—Ann da. Theophilus & Sarah (Earl) Heaton, b 20 Jan 1713/4 *NHV*, d 22 June 1795 æ. 81 (in Great Barrington) *NoHT1*.

i Susanna, b 26 Apr 1742 *NHV*, d 30 Oct 1793 æ. 50 (in Great Barrington) *NoHT1*; Census (NoH) 0-0-1.

ii Theophilus, b 16 Aug 1743 *NHV*, d in infancy *NoHT1*.

iii Thomas, b 4 Feb 1744/5 *NHV*, d 12 Dec 1751 æ. 7 *NoHT1*.

iv Thomas, b 2 Feb 1753 *F*, d 8 Mar 1814 æ. 61 *Great Barrington, Mass.*; Maj. Gen.; Census (Great Barrington) 4-2-5; m 2 Mar 1786 Ruth Foster of Brookfield, Mass.; 5 sons, & 7 das.

2 ANN, b 14 Apr 1717 *NHV*, bp 3 June 1717 *NHC1*, d 5 Aug 1746 æ. 30 *ThomastonT*; m 29 July 1741 *WatV*—John Sutliff.

3 REBECCA, b 14 Feb 1718/9 *NHV*, d probably s. p.

4 MABEL, b 4 Sep 1720 *NHV*; m last of Feb 1743/4 *NHV*—John Sanford.

5 ELIZABETH, b 1 Jan 1722/3 *NHV*, bp 31 Mar 1723 *NHC1*, d 18 Jan 1791 æ. 69 *ThomastonT*; m Feb 1745/6 *NHV*—Ebenezer Todd.

FAM. 9. EBENEZER & MARY (ATWATER) IVES:

1 LAZARUS, b 19 Oct 1715 *NHV*, bp 8 July 1716 *NHC1*, d 1762; m 28 Dec 1743 *NHV*—Mabel da. Thomas & Lydia (Bradley) Punderson, b 19 Mar 1725/6 *NHV*, d c. 1765; she m (2) 11 June 1764 *NHC1*—Samuel Hitchcock.

i Ezra, b 6 Nov 1744 *NHV*, bp 1745/6 *CC*, d 19 Aug 1825 æ. 81 *HT1*; Census (H) 2-3-5; m Mabel da. William & Mabel (Goodyear) Bassett, b 22 Dec 1746 *NHV*, d 24 Oct 1818 æ. 72 *HT1*. **FAM. 33.**

ii Lazarus, b 21 Apr 1747 *NHV*, bp (?Feb 1746) *CC*, d 14 May 1832 *Goshen*; Census (L) 2-4-5; m 29 Oct 1772 Chloe Beach.

iii Amos, b 14 Mar 1749/50 *NHV*, bp Apr 1750 *CC*; Census (Wallingford, Vt.) 1-2-7.

iv Jonah, b 16 June 1752 *BdV*, bp 19 July 1752 *NoBC2*, Census (Wallingford, Vt.) 1-0-0.

v Jesse, b 27 May 1755 *NHV*, bp 13 July 1755 *NoBC2*, d 30 Aug 1764 *NoHC*.

vi Asa, b 8 Mar 1758 *NHV*, bp 19 Feb (?) 1758 *BdC*, d 7 Jan 1848 *Goshen*; m Sarah Marks.

vii Ebenezer, b 21 Feb 1761 *NHV*, bp 29 Mar 1761 *NoHC*; Census (Wallingford, Vt.) 1-0-0.

2 MARTHA, b 1 May 1717 *NHV*, bp 1717 *NHC1*, d 13 July 1770 æ. 54 *WatV*; m 11 Mar 1740/1 *NHV*—Daniel Potter.

3 JAMES, b 19 Oct 1718 *NHV*, d 14 May 1804 æ. 86 *HT1*; Sgt.; Census (H) 3-0-2; m (1) 20 Nov 1750 *NHV*—Damaris da. Dan-

iel & Abigail (Tuttle) Atwater, b 30 Dec 1727 *NHV*, d 26 Oct 1751 æ. 25 *NoHT1*; m (2) 6 Nov 1753 *NHV*—Sarah da. Amos & Sarah (Mansfield) Tuttle, b 7 June 1733 *NHV*, d 21 Jan 1796 æ. 74 *HT1*.

(By 1): *i* James, b 11 Aug 1751 *NHV*, d 15 Aug 1826 æ. 74 *Great Barrington, Mass.*; Census (NoH) 2-3-3; res. Durham 1805; m (1) 15 Jan 1770 *NoHC*—Lois da. James & Lois (Todd) Turner, b 12 Oct 1748 *NHV*, d 31 Oct 1776 æ. 29 *NoHT1*; m (2) 16 June 1779 *NoHC*—Mary da. Richard & Mary (Pierpont) Brockett, b 13 Mar 1759 *NHV*, d 7 Sep 1830 æ. 71 *Great Barrington, Mass.* **FAM. 34.**

(By 2): *ii* Damaris, b 25 Dec 1754 *NHV*, d 11 Jan 1839 æ. 84 *HT3*; m 21 Sep 1775 *NHV*—Jesse Dickerman.

iii Sarah, b 16 Sep 1756 *NHV*, d 5 Apr 1790 æ. 34 *HT1*.

iv Eber, b 16 Sep 1756 *NHV*, d 12 Dec 1830 æ. 74 *HT1*; m 4 May 1793 *HV*—Esther da. Timothy & Lydia Thompson, wid. William Mowatt, b 22 Mar 1763 *HV*, d 11 Feb 1838 æ. 75 *HT1*. **FAM. 35.**

v Eunice, b 18 Aug 1758 *NHV*, d 24 Apr 1786 æ. 28 *HT1*.

vi Mary, b 10 Mar 1760 *NHV*, d 16 Sep 1842 æ. 83 *HT1*; m Joel Cooper.

vii Elam, b 16 Dec 1761 *NHV*, bp 14 Feb 1762 *NoHC*, d 24 Jan 1846 æ. 84 *HT1*; Census (H) 1-0-1; m 9 May 1790 *HV*—Sarah da. Samuel & Hannah (Bassett) Hitchcock, b 3 Jan 1771 *NHV*, d 25 Jan 1852 æ. 81 *HT1*. **FAM 36.**

viii Jason, b c. 1765, d 7 Sep 1794 æ. 29 *HT1*.

4 **Miriam**, b 28 Oct 1722 *NHV*, bp 30 Dec 1722 *NHC1*, d 11 Nov 1792 æ. 71 *HT1*; m 10 Feb 1747/8 *NHV*—Jacob Atwater.

5 **Abel**, b 17 Feb 1723/4 *NHV*, d 27 Mar 1792 æ. 69 *BD*; Census (Wd) 2-0-2; m 26 Mar 1753 *NHV*—Martha da. James & Martha (Wooding) Sperry, b 11 Sep 1726 *NHV*.

i Martha, b 29 Dec 1753 *NHV*, bp 14 Aug 1762 *NHC1*; m 22 May 1775 *NHC1*—Hezekiah Sperry.

ii Hannah, bp 14 Aug 1762 *NHC1*; m Amos Atwater.

iii Abel, bp 3 Apr 1763 *NHC1*.

iv Ira, bp 24 Mar 1771 *NHC1*, d young.

6 **Mary**, b 26 Jan 1725/6 *NHV*, d young.

7 **Ebenezer**, b 19 July 1727 *NHV*, d s. p. 1759; m 17 May 1753 *NHV*—Mary da. Stephen & Abigail (Bradley) Atwater, b 7 Mar 1735/6 *NHV*; she m (2) 10 Apr 1765 *NHV*—Gilead Gregory.

8 **Abigail**, b 25 Nov 1728 *NHV*, d 12 May 1773 æ. 45 *NoHT1*.

9 **Noah**, b 4 Dec 1730 *NHV*, d 15 Oct 1800 æ. 70 *NoHT1*; Capt.; Census (NoH) 3-2-3; m 23 Dec 1762 *NHV*—Abigail da. Joseph & Hannah (Russell) Pierpont, b 6 June 1743 *NHV*, d 13 Feb 1815 æ. 72 *NoHT1*.

i Esther, b 22 Aug 1765 *NHV*, bp 10 July 1774 *NoHC*, d 18 Sep 1805 æ. 40 *WatT2*; m 25 June 1783 *NoHC*—

Bethuel Todd.

ii Miriam, b 15 Aug 1768 *NHV*, bp 10 Oct 1773 *NoHC*, d 12 Oct 1773 æ. 5 *NoHC*.

iii Child, d 30 July 1771 æ. a few days *NoHC*.

iv Hannah, b 18 Aug 1772 *NHV*, bp 10 July 1774 *NoHC*, d 11 Dec 1838 æ. 66 *NoHT1*; m 16 July 1795 *NoHC*—Titus Mansfield.

v Giles, b 25 Apr 1774 *NHV*, bp 8 May 1774 *NoHC*, d 27 Feb 1848 æ. 74 *WatT1*; m 9 Oct 1799 *NoHC*—Abigail [da. Abraham & Abigail (Cooper)] Gilbert, b 29 Mar 1778 (at H) *WatV*, d 30 July 1861 æ. 83 *WatT1*.

vi Noah, b 18 Sep 1776 *NHV*, bp 10 Nov 1776 *NoHC*; res. Genoa, N. Y., 1817.

vii Miriam, b 3 Jan 1779 *NHV*, bp 7 Feb 1779 *NoHC*; m 3 Dec 1809 *NoHC*—Willard Frost.

viii Talcott, b 24 July 1781 *NHV*, bp 5 Aug 1781 *NoHC*, d 27 Mar 1859 æ. 76 *NoHT3*; m Hannah da. Dan & Lucy (Frost) Todd, b c. 1789, d 18 Nov 1864 æ. 75 *NoHT3*.

ix Alban, b 8 Sep 1788 *NoHV*, bp 18 Feb 1789 *NoHC*, d s. p. 28 Aug 1870 æ. 79-9 *NoHV*.

10 EUNICE, b 4 May 1732 *NHV*, d 27 Apr 1801 *NoHV*, æ. 69 *NoHT1*; m Zophar Blakeslee.

11 LYDIA, b 2 Oct 1733 *NHV*, d 15 Dec 1778 *F*; m 22 May 1755 *NHV*—John Gilbert.

FAM. 10. JOHN & MARY (HALL) IVES:

1 LUCRETIA M., b 24 Oct 1759 *WV*; m 13 Feb 1777 *WV*—Samuel Ives.

PAGE 2047 2 JOHN, b 1 May 1762 *WV*, d 1844 (Manlius, N. Y.); m Martha Merriam.

3 ISAAC, b 13 Jan 1764 *WV*, d 10 June 1845; B. A. (Yale 1788); res. N. Y. City & Danbury; m (1) 14 Mar 1792 Jerusha Benedict, who d 18 Aug 1795 æ. 23 *WT2*; m (2) 20 Dec 1796 Sarah Amelia White.

4 LEVI, b 24 Apr 1766 *WV*; Census (W) 1-1-3; m 18 June 1789 *WC2*—Fanny Silliman.

5 JOSEPH, b 26 Feb 1768 *WV*; m 4 Nov 1791 *WC2*—Clarissa Hall.

6 JOEL HALL, b 21 Jan 1770 *WV*; m Lucy Hart.

7 MARY, b 21 Nov 1771 *WV*; m John Hooker.

8 ANNA, b c. 1773, d 2 Dec 1824 æ. 51 *WT2*; m 1793 *WC2*—Noah Foster.

9 ELI.

10 OTHNIEL, d 29 Mar 1777 *WV*.

11 OTHNIEL, b 17 Aug 1779, d 22 Nov 1829 æ. 52 *WT2*; m (1) Sarah ——— ; m (2) Rosetta Yale.

12 MERIL; res. Canada; m ——— Clark.

13 TITUS, b c. 1784, d 12 Mar 1834 æ. 50 *WT2*; m Lodema Yale.

FAM. 11. BEZALEEL & HANNAH (MERRIAM) IVES:

1 SAMUEL, b 5 Jan 1752 *WV*, bp 12 Jan 1752 *WC2*, d 18 Oct 1803

æ. 52 *WT2*, 15 Oct *WC2;* Capt.; Census (W) 2-2-4; m 7 Jan 1773 *WV*—Lowly Parker.

FAM. 12. DANIEL & ELIZABETH (———) IVES:

1 JOSEPH, b 23 Dec 1766 *WV*, d 27 Sep 1845 æ. 79 *CT1;* m 5 Dec 1792 *CC*—Sarah da. Amasa & Sarah (Bradley) Hitchcock, b 29 Dec 1771 *WV*, d 10 Aug 1844 æ. 74 *CT1*.

i Marshall, b 25 Oct 1794 *CV*, d 10 Sep 1845 æ. 52 *CT1;* m 7 Jan 1814 *CV*—Laura Cook, who d 7 Apr 1863 æ. 70 *CT1*.

ii Martha, b 3 Aug 1796 *CV*.

iii Silas, b 17 June 1800 *CV*, d 16 Mar 1868 æ. 68 *CT1;* m Betsey Payne who d 19 Apr 1898 æ. 94 *CT1*.

iv Laura, b 22 Aug 1802 *CV*.

FAM. 12. DANIEL & OBEDIENCE (STEVENS) IVES:

2 ELIZABETH, b 17 Sep 1771 *WV*.

3 OLIVE, b 9 Aug 1772 *WV*.

4 JOHN, b 28 Aug 1774 *WV;* res. Woodstock, N. Y., 1796.

5 AMY, b 18 Feb 1777 *WV;* m 1797 Asahel Brockett.

FAM. 13. ABRAHAM & EUNICE (HULL) IVES: PAGE 2047

1 [——]EL, b 15 Feb 1767 *WV*.

2 EUNICE, b 1 Apr 1769 *WV*.

3 LYMAN, b 7 Sep 1771 *WV*.

FAM. 14. ISAAC & LYDIA (MORGAN) IVES:

1 REBECCA, b 3 May 1745 *NHV*, bp June 1745 *CC*, d 10 July 1752 *WV*.

2 ISAAC, b 20 Apr 1747 *NHV*, bp 1746 (?) *CC;* m 8 Dec 1771 *WV*—Sarah da. Abel & Mary (Merwin) Thompson.

3 JOHN, b 25 Dec 1748 *WV*, bp 8 Jan 1748/9 *CC*, bu. 31 July 1808 æ. 59 *NHx;* m 1 Jan 1770 *WV*—Lois da. James & Tamar (Munson) Hotchkiss. Family incomplete.

i Becca, b 27 Aug 1770 *WV*, bp 25 Oct 1772 *CC*.

ii Major, b 13 Feb 1772 *WV*, bp 25 Oct 1772 *CC*.

iii Rosalinda, b 20 Dec 1773 *WV*, bp Dec 1773 *CC*.

iv John, b 20 Dec 1775 *WV*, bp 29 Jan 1776 *CC;* m 26 Feb 1797 *NHC1*—Sarah da. Job & Rebecca (Thomas) Corey.

v [Lois, bp 26 Apr 1778 *CC*].

vi Sally, b [Mar 1792], d 27 Sep 1801 æ. 9-6 *NHT1*, "da." d 27 Sep 1801 æ. 11 *NHC1*.

vii Maria, bp 10 Aug 1794 *NHC1*, d 9 Oct 1795 æ. 0-15 *NHT1*, "da." d 9 Oct 1795 æ. 2 *NHC1*, bu. 10 Oct æ. 0-16 *NHx*.

4 REUBEN, b 3 Dec 1753 *WV;* res. Pittsford, Vt., 1792; m 23 Sep 1787 *WV*—Lowly da. John & Lois (Beadles) Hull, b 4 June 1767 *WV*.

5 REBECCA, b 3 Jan 1758 *WV*.

6 LYDIA, b 25 Aug 1760 *WV;* m 8 Apr 1779 *PV*—Timothy Jones of Wtn.

FAM. 15. ANDREW & SARAH (PRINDLE) IVES:

1 EUNICE, b 28 Apr 1745 *WV*, bp June 1745 *CC*, d s. p. c. 1810; m

——— Bishop of H.

2 THOMAS, b 18 June 1746 *WV*, bp 1746 *CC*, d after 1810.

3 SARAH, b 24 Nov 1748 *WV*, bp 8 Jan 1748/9 *CC;* m ——— Thompson.

4 JOEL, b 7 May 1751 *WV*, bp May 1751 *CC*, d 22 Aug 1833 æ. 83 *CT1;* Census (C) 1-1-2; m (1) [———] *CV*—Ann da. Joshua & Abiah (Clark) Brooks, b 25 July 1756 *WV*, d 30 May 1804 *CV*, æ. 48 *CT2;* m (2) 29 Oct 1804 *CV*—Jerusha Royce, wid. Elisha Street.

(By 1): *i* Ann Brooks, bp 27 May 1777 *HC1*, d 26 Nov 1856 æ. 80 *CT2;* m 17 Nov 1806 Moses Moss.

ii Joshua, bp 15 Nov 1778 *HC1*, d 21 Feb 1836 æ. 57 *CT2;* m 20 Oct 1808 *CV*,—Rebecca da. Moses & Esther (Hall) Moss, b 10 Dec 1773 *WV*, d 6 Jan 1851 æ. 79 *CT2*.

iii Eunice, b 5 Aug 1780 *CV*, "child murdered by its mother" 5 Feb 1781 *CC*.

iv Eunice, b 23 July 1791 *CV*, d 6 Feb 1801 *CV*.

(By 2): *v* Juliana, b 19 Apr 1806 *CV*.

5 WILLIAM, b 4 July 1753 *NHV;* Census (C) 1-0-4; m 3 June 1778 *CC*—Sarah Hotchkiss.

i Dennis, b 22 Nov 1783 *CV*.

ii Almira, b 13 Oct 1786 *CV*.

iii Fanny, b 11 Feb 1790 *CV*

iv Sally, b 13 June 1795 *CV*.

6 LENT, b 27 June 1758 *NHV;* Census (Bristol) 1-3-5; m 2 July 1776 *CC*—Hannah da. Joseph & Rebecca (Bunnell) Burr, b 18 June 1755 *WV*. Children recorded *BristolV:* Jared, b 22 Aug 1786; Thelus, b 17 Feb 1789; Belinda, b 31 Dec 1791.

7 LYDIA, b 7 Aug 1759 *NHV;* m ——— Staples.

8 LOIS; m ——— Downs.

FAM. 16. ENOS & ANN (COOK) IVES:

1 LOIS, b 16 Apr 1750 *WV*, bp Apr 1750 *CC*.

2 ELIZABETH, b 16 Nov 1752 *WV*, bp Dec 1752 *CC*.

3 REBECCA, b 9 Jan 1755 *WV*.

4 ANN, b 25 Apr 1757 *WV*.

PAGE 2047 5 ENOS, b 25 Apr 1759 *WV*.

6 JARED, b 17 Nov 1761 *WV*.

7 MARY, b 25 Apr 1766 *WV*.

8 JESSE, b 2 Jan 1771 *WV*.

FAM. 17. ABER & RACHEL (WILMOT) IVES (family incomplete):

1 ASAHEL, b 25 June 1764 (at NH) *WyV*, d 10 Aug 1830 æ. 66 *WyT;* Census (Wy) 1-2-2; m Elsey ———, who d 18 Jan 1814 æ. 57 *WyT*. Possibly he was the Asahel who m 11 Apr 1802 *NHC1*—Content Sperry.

2 ABER, d 1805; Census (Wy) 1-1-1; res. Kent; m Sybil [?Castle].

i Castle.

ii Nathaniel.

iii Reuben.
iv Harry Aner.

FAM. 18. TITUS & MARTHA (GAYLORD) IVES:

1 JOSEPH, b 3 Mar 1768 *WV*.

2 TITUS, b 30 Nov 1769 *WV*, bp 14 Jan 1770 *CC*, d 27 Nov 1815 æ. 46 *CT1*; m Mary da. Stephen & Mary (Hotchkiss) Ives, b 23 Mar 1774 *NHV*, d 18 Feb 1854 æ. 79 *CT1*.

3 BENAJAH, b 2 Feb 1772 *WV*, bp 16 Feb 1772 *CC*, d 25 Oct 1776 *WV*, 25 Oct 1777 æ. 5 *CT1*.

4 CYRUS, bp 27 Aug 1774 *CC*, d 7 Feb 1775 *WV*, æ. 3 *CT1*.

5 CHAUNCEY, b 9 Apr 1776 *CC*, bp 14 Apr 1776 *CC*, d 29 May 1869; m 24 Apr 1805 *CC*—Asenath da. Jonathan & Miriam (Bradley) Dickerman, bp 22 Oct 1786 *HC1*.

FAM. 19. PHINEHAS & MARTHA (MOSS) IVES:

1 NEHEMIAH ROYCE, b 24 Aug 1776 *WV*.

2 LOYAL MOSS, b 28 June 1779 *CV*, d Apr 1803 æ. 24 (at Crown Point, N. Y.) *CT2*.

3 PHINEHAS TRUMAN, b 5 Oct 1781 *CV*, d 1870; m (1) 4 Nov 1810 *CC*—Salome da. Reuben & Lois (Doolittle) Royce, bp 5 Mar 1780 *CC*, d 15 Dec 1820 æ. 40 *CT2*; m (2) 31 May 1821 *CV*—Baldwin, who d 17 Sep 1824 æ. 32; m (3) Julia Ann Frances ——, b 1793, d 1874.

4 NOBLE, b 23 Apr 1783 *CV*.

5 JUSTUS, b 22 Sep 1786 *CV*.

6 MARTHA MARIA, b 13 Sep 1790 *CV*, d 4 Sep 1794 æ. 4 *CT2*.

7 HANNAH K., b [Aug 1793], d 17 Nov 1796 æ. 3-3 *CT2*.

FAM. 20. ELNATHAN & OLIVE (BLAKESLEE) IVES:

1 CHAUNCEY.

2 TRUMAN, b c. 1777, d 20 Mar 1871 æ. 94 *PT*; m Eunice da. Dan & Eunice (Russell) Peck, b 14 Apr 1780 *F*, d 21 Jan 1874 æ. 94 *PT*.

i Eunice Peck, b 9 Mar 1801 *PV*.
ii Levet, b 15 Oct 1802 *PV*.
iii William, b 19 Nov 1804 *PV*.
iv Mary Ann, b 15 Dec 1806 *PV*.
v Riley, b 15 Jan 1808 *PV*.
vi Olive Adeline, b 20 Oct 1810 *PV*.
vii Betsey Anna, b 9 Dec 1812 *PV*.
viii Truman Dan, b 25 Dec 1814 *PV*.

3 BETSEY; m 12 Oct 1797 *PC*—Noah Bronson.

4 SABRA; m —— Peck.

5 MERCHANT, b c. 1785, d 13 Oct 1866 æ. 81 *PT*; m Sally ——, b c. 1785, d 27 Sep 1861 æ. 76 *PT*.

6 FRIEND.

FAM. 21. NATHANIEL & ZERVIAH (BLAKESLEE) IVES (family incomplete):

1 MARY, b 26 Sep 1746 *WV*.

2 JOSEPH, b 15 June 1749 *WV*, d 20 Apr 1832 *Colebrook*; m Rhoda ——.

3 NATHANIEL, b 23 Apr 1751 *WV*.

4 ZERVIAH, b 15 Dec 1753 *WV*.
5 SAMUEL, b 1 May 1756 *WV*.
6 ABIGAIL, b 17 Oct 1758 *WV*.

FAM. 22. CHARLES & SARAH (BUTLER) IVES:

1 SARAH, b 16 Feb 1756 *WV*; m Isaac Kirtland.
2 OLIVE, b 20 Apr 1758 *WV*, d 14 Mar 1822 æ. 64 *WT1*; m 22 Oct 1778 *WV*—Joel Ives.
3 CHARLES, b 14 Apr 1760 *WV*; Census (W) 1-1-3; m (1) 19 Dec 1783 *WV*—Mary da. Joseph & Mary (Tuttle) Francis, b 26 Apr 1765 *WV*, d 7 June 1820 æ. 55 *WT1*; m (2) Lois [Peck], wid. Samuel Hull, who d 30 Jan 1830 æ. 65 *WT1*.
4 BUTLER, b 3 May 1762 *WV*, d 15 Aug 1779 (prisoner in N. Y.) *WV*.
5 ELIHU, b 28 Feb 1764 *WV*.
6 LEVI, b 29 Apr 1766 *WV*.
7 HANNAH, b 16 May 1769 *WV* (recorded as a death, but she was living in 1790).
8 RUTH, b 26 Jan 1772 *WV*, d 25 Nov 1839 æ. 68 *WT1*; m 12 Nov 1792 John Webb Blakeslee.
9 CALEB, b 1 Jan 1774 *WV*.
10 RANSOM, b 17 Oct 1775 *WV*, d 22 Sep 1844 æ. 69 *WT1*; m Sarah ——, who d 15 Feb 1844 æ. 62 *WT1*.
11 LUCY.
12 RACHEL.

FAM. 23. ZACHARIAH & LOIS (HARRISON) IVES:

1 REUBEN, b 26 Oct 1761 *WV*, d 14 Oct 1836 æ. 75 *CT2*; B. A. (Yale 1786); Rector of St. Peter's, Cheshire; Census (C) 1-0-1; m 25 Jan 1789 *NHx*—Susanna Anna Maria Marshall, who d 24 Aug 1849 æ. 82 *CT2*.
2 CHAUNCEY, b 8 Aug 1763 *WV*, d 17 Nov 1778 *WV*, æ. 16 *CT2*.
3 LOIS, b 22 Apr 1766 *WV*, d 28 Dec 1774 *WV*, æ. 8-8 *CT2*.
4 JARED, b 23 Feb 1769 *WV*, d 26 May 1840 æ. 71 *CT1*; m (1) Achsah ——, who d 10 Mar 1827 æ. 58 *CT1*; m (2) Phebe [da. Nathan & Phebe (Thompson)] Andrews, wid. Marcus Tuttle & Wm. P. Tuttle, bp 9 July 1780 *CC*, d 5 Nov 1844 æ. 65 *CT1*.
5 AMOS HARRISON, b 14 Nov 1771 *WV*, d 24 Dec 1841 æ. 70 *CT1*; m Lucy da. Thaddeus & Sarah (Hall) Cook, b c. 1772, d 30 May 1836 æ. 64 *CT1*.
6 JESSE, b 28 Dec 1774 *WV*, d 12 Feb 1836 æ. 61 *WT2*; m Marilla ——, who d 12 Oct 1865 æ. 85 *WT2*.

FAM. 24. AMASA & HULDAH (SHAILER) IVES (family incomplete):

1 HULDAH, b c. 1772, d 3 July 1811 æ. 39 *BristolT*.
2 (probably) IRA, b c. 1775, d 19 Aug 1848 æ. 73 *BristolT*; m Cynthia ——, who d 16 Apr 1863 æ. 83 *BristolT*.
3 PHILOTHETA, b c. 1779, d 28 Aug 1785 æ. 6 *BristolT*.
4 (probably) JOSEPH, b c. 1782, d 18 Apr 1862 æ. 80 *BristolT*; m Almenia ——, who d 20 Mar 1872 æ. 89 *BristolT*.
5 SHAILER, b 4 July 1785 *BristolV*.

6 CHAUNCEY, b 28 June 1787 *BristolV*, d 25 May 1857 æ. 70 *NHV;* m Amanda ——— ; will left $1000 to wid. Mary Antoinet Mallory & residue to his children Sabrina R., Adrian C., Ellen A., Theodore A. & Celestia A.

7 PHILOTHETA, b 12 Apr 1790 *BristolV*.

8 PIERA, b 30 June 1792 *BristolV*.

FAM. 25. JOSEPH & ELIZABETH (GRANNIS) IVES: PAGE 2047

1 MARY, b 4 July 1763 *NHV*.

FAM. 25. JOSEPH & ABIGAIL (GRANNIS) IVES: PAGE 1245

2 ABIGAIL, b c. 1766, d 24 July 1844 æ. 78 *NHV;* m Archibald McNeil.

3 JOANNA; m 28 June 1786 *NoHC*—Jabez Spencer.

4 RUTH.

FAM. 26. STEPHEN & SARAH (AMES) IVES:

1 MARY, b [Oct 1769], d 4 June 1773 æ. 3-10 *NoHC*.

2 SUSANNA, b [Feb 1771], d 23 May 1773 æ. 2-3 *NoHC*.

3 SALLY, b c. 1772, d 9 Apr 1806 æ. 34 *CT2;* m Eliakim Brooks.

4 PATTY; m Asahel Barnes.

5 MARY; m Archibald Clark of W.

6 SUSAN, d 29 Dec 1843 (at Burton, Ohio); m 16 Oct 1799 *NoHC*—Ephraim Cook of C.

7 JOSEPH.

8 WILLIAM, b c. 1783, d 2 June 1858 æ. 75 *NoHT3;* m 19 Dec 1810 *NoHC*—Polly da. Asa & Hannah (Hull) Bray, b c. 1788, d 28 Sep 1852 æ. 64 *NoHT3*.

i Hoadley Bray.

ii Grace A., b c. 1818, d 24 Mar 1885 æ. 67 *NoHT3*, æ. 67-10 *NHV*.

iii Jane; m John H. Washburn.

iv Hannah Jennet.

FAM. 27. DAN & MARY (BALDWIN) IVES:

1 LEONARD, b 5 Jan 1785 *F*, bp 19 May 1793 *NoHC*, d 1 Mar 1831; m (1) 7 Aug 1806 Mabel [da. Nathaniel & Mehitabel (Beach)] Stacey, b c. 1788, d 1 Mar 1815 æ. 27 *NoHT1;* m (2) Sarah da. Eli & Sarah Sackett, b c. 1784, d 10 Mar 1864 æ. 79½ (at NoH) *BAlm*.

2 MELIA, b c. 1787, bp 19 May 1793 *NoHC*, d 1 May 1795 æ. 9 *NoHT1*.

3 SON, b [11 June 1789], d 18 June 1789 æ. 0-0-7 *NoHC*.

4 ROXANA, b c. 1791, bp 19 May 1793 *NoHC;* m Origen Atwood; res. E. H. 1816.

5 ESTHER, bp 5 Oct 1792 *NoHC;* m 18 Nov 1813 *NoHC*—Theophilus Tuttle.

FAM. 28. LEVI & LYDIA (AUGUR) IVES:

1 LEVI, b 27 Apr 1772 *F* [1773], bp 16 May 1773 *NHC2*, d s. p. 31 Jan 1811 *F*.

2 MARY, b 12 Dec 1774 *F*, bp 17 Dec 1774 *NHC2*, d 26 Oct 1776 æ. 2 *NHT1*.

3 Elihu, b 10 Aug 1777 *F*, bp 5 Oct 1777 *NHC2*, d 2 Oct 1849 æ. 72 *NHT1*, *NHV;* m (1) 16 Mar 1802 *ConnJournal*—Polly Northrop; m (2) 29 July 1804 *CC*—Lucy Whittimore, b 6 Mar 1781 *F*, d 8 Feb 1848 æ. 67 *NHT1*, (insane) *EHC*, 3 Feb (at Hartford) *NHV*.

(By 2): *i* Mary, b 2 July 1805 *F*, d 17 Sep 1806 *F*.

ii Mary Northrop, b 4 Sep 1806 *F*, d 4 Jan 1881; m Chauncey Pomeroy; res. Montgomery, Ala., 1850.

iii William Augustus, b 26 Dec 1809 *F*, d 16 July 1885 (Rubicon, Wis.); m 22 Mar 1842 *EHV*—Elizabeth M. da. Isaac Holt & Sally (Hotchkiss) Pardee, b 24 Feb 1820 *F*, d 19 Oct 1907.

iv Jane Catherine, b 21 Oct 1812 *F;* m Henry Hall; res. Columbus, Ga., 1850.

v Sophia, b 2 Sep 1814 *F;* res. Bridgeport 1850.

vi Ann Vose, b 1 Dec 1816 *F*, d 14 Sep 1838 *F*.

vii Elihu Lafayette, b 7 Oct 1818 *F*, d 27 Nov 1872; m (1) 1 June 1843 *NHV*—Grace Ann Lego, b 25 May 1820 *F*, d 8 Apr 1844 æ. 24 *NHV;* m (2) 19 May 1847 *F*—Sarah R. Bray, b 16 Mar 1820 *F*, d 8 Jan 1870 *F*.

viii Lucy Whittimore, b 13 May 1820 *F*, d s. p.

ix George Washington, b 11 May 1822 *F;* res. Bridgeport 1850.

x Lydia Augur, b 12 Apr 1824 *F;* m 5 Sep 1844 *NHV*—Abraham C. Thompson.

4 Eli, b 7 Feb 1779 *F*, bp 21 Feb 1779 *NHC2*, d 8 Oct 1861 æ. 83-8 *NHV;* Dr.; m 17 Sep 1805 Maria da. Nathan & Mary (Phelps) Beers, b c. 1786, d 14 Mar 1864 æ. 81-6 *NHV*. Children: Dr. Nathan Beers; Dr. Levi; & a da.

5 Polly, b 9 Jan 1782 *F* [1783], bp 26 Jan 1783 *NHC2*, d 13 June 1855 æ. 73 *NHT1;* m 17 Nov 1805 *NHC1*—Asaph Dunbar.

6 Nancy, b 14 Nov 1785 *F*, d s. p. 19 Apr 1836 æ. 50 *NHT1;* m 30 Oct 1825 Ezra Hotchkiss.

7 Sophia, b 1 Mar 1788 *F*, bp 19 May 1788 *NHC2*, d 31 July 1854 æ. 66 *NHT1*.

8 William, b 1 Mar 1788 *F*, bp 19 May 1788 *NHC2*, d s. p.

9 Lydia A., b 26 July 1795 *F*, d 22 Nov 1873 æ. 78 *NHT2;* m William Buddington.

FAM. 28. Levi & Margaret (Bird) Ives:

10 Samuel Bird, b 23 Jan 1805 *F*, d 21 June 1826 *F*.

11 Henry, b 21 Feb 1807 *F*, d s. p.

12 Jennet, b 8 Mar 1808 *NHT1*, 1809 *F*, d 21 Oct 1886 *NHT1;* m ——— McGill.

FAM. 29. Jeremiah & Hannah (Bassett) Ives:

1 Abraham, b c. 1769, bp 11 June 1773 *HC1*, d 16 Nov 1855 *W. Springfield, Mass.;* m 22 Jan 1795 *W. Springfield*—Eunice Day.

2 Joseph, b 2 Feb 1771 *NHV*, bp 11 June 1773 *HC1*, d 21 Dec 1830 *W. Springfield;* m 18 Mar 1801 *NHC1*—Sarah da. Isaac & Sa-

rah (Macumber) Bishop, b 3 Feb 1777 *NHV*.

3 Hannah, bp 11 June 1773 *HC1*; m 10 June 1803 *W. Springfield*—Elijah Ely.

4 Sarah, bp 23 July 1775 *HC1*; m 4 Dec 1801 *W. Springfield*—Benjamin Ely.

5 Rebecca, bp 29 Oct 1777 *HC1*.

6 Abigail, bp 17 Feb 1780 *HC1*.

FAM. 30. Joel & Mary (Heaton) Ives:

1 Sarah; m 7 Mar 1810 *BdV*—Eleazer Stent.

2 Esther.

The two children above were named in their grandfather Heaton's will. The following perhaps also belong in this family:

3 (perhaps) Enoch, b c. 1773, d 25 Mar 1817 æ. 44 *NHT1*; m Dec 1800 *NHJournal*—Sarah da. Samuel & Sarah (Lines) Gorham, b [Dec 1781], d 19 Aug 1850 æ. 68-8 *NHT1*, *NHV*.

i Truman, b [Jan 1802], d 14 Sep 1813 æ. 11-8 *NHT1*.

ii Eliza, b [July 1805], d 21 Sep 1813 æ. 8-2 *NHT1*, æ. 9 *NHx*.

iii Joel, b 11 June 1807 *NHT1*, bp 26 Sep 1813 *NHx*, d 12 Dec 1862 *NHT1*; m 15 Apr 1830 *NHV*—Jennette Bradley, who d 7 Jan 1875 æ. 68 *NHT1*.

iv Alfred, b c. 1810, bp 26 Sep 1813 *NHx*.

v Emeline, b 20 May 1813 *NHT1*, bp 26 Sep 1813 *NHx*, d 18 July 1868 *NHT1*.

vi Charles, b [Sep 1815], d 31 Dec 1880 æ. 65-3 *NHT1*; m Catherine M. da. Joel & Nancy (Hitchcock) Osborn, b [Jan 1816], d 2 May 1898 æ. 82-4 *NHT1*.

4 (perhaps) Leman, d between 1808 & 1812; m Lydia da. Titus & Lydia (Todd) Bradley, bp 27 Feb 1785 *NoHC*; she m (2) 13 Dec 1814 *NoHV*—Timothy Andrews,

i Louisa Lament, bp 22 Jan 1809 *NoHC*.

FAM. 31. Jonathan & Sarah (Bassett) Ives:

1 Leverett, b 25 Apr 1778 *NHV*, d 7 Mar 1795 æ. 17 *HT1*.

2 Sarah, b 21 May 1786 *F*, d 2 Feb 1871 æ. 85 *HT1*; m Allen Dickerman.

FAM. 32. John & Susanna (———) Ives:

1 John, b 26 Aug 1778 *HV*; "went south".

FAM. 32. John & Esther (Tuttle) Ives:

2 Lowly; m Jerry Hart.

3 Sarah; m Aranda Giddings.

4 Esther; m Warren Giddings.

5 Jesse, d s. p.; m ——— Atkins.

6 Levi; m Clara Peters.

i William.

7 David, d s. p. 10 Oct 1829; m Fanny Slade.

8 Lois, d s. p.

FAM. 33. Ezra & Mabel (Bassett) Ives:

1 Mabel, b 9 Feb 1767 *NHV*, d 4 Aug 1834 *Colebrook*; m Justus

Alling.

2 Rhoda, b 22 Jan 1770 *NHV*, bp 11 Mar 1770 *HCl*, d 27 Dec 1819 æ. 50 *HTl*; m Joshua Goodyear.

3 Betsey; b 26 May 1772 *NHV*, bp 26 July 1772 *HCl*, d 2 Apr 1858 æ. 86 *HTl*; m 13 Dec 1795 *HV*—Lyman Bradley.

4 Jesse, b 29 June 1774 *NHV*, bp 7 Aug 1774 *HCl*, d 21 Sep 1843 æ. 69 *HTl*; m (1) Apr 1798 *F*—Mabel da. Jesse & Hannah (Bradley) Goodyear, b 27 Aug 1776 *NHV*, d 31 July 1822 æ. 46 *HTl*; m (2) 20 Sep 1842 *HV*—Sukey, wid. Hall, who d 12 July 1860 æ. 84 *HTl*.

(By 1): *i* Myra, b 15 May 1799 *F*, bp 10 Jan 1802 *HCl*, d 3 Sep 1875 æ. 76 *HTl*; m Lyman Goodyear.

ii Mark, b 19 Oct 1801 *F*, bp 10 Jan 1802 *HCl*, d 6 Apr 1884 æ. 82 *HTl*; m 23 May 1822 Saritta da. Alling & Sarah (Ives) Dickerman, who d 11 Feb 1890 æ. 82-5-6 *HV*.

iii Lyman, b 24 June 1804 *F*, bp 1 Apr 1804 *HCl*.

iv Jesse Goodyear, b 1806 *HTl*, 12 Aug 1806 *F*, bp 12 Oct 1806 *HCl*, d 1874 *HTl*; m 28 Nov 1832 *HV*—Harriet L. Munson, b 1812 *HTl*, d 1873 *HTl*.

v Robert, b 31 Mar 1809 *F*, bp 14 May 1809 *HCl*.

vi Eliza, b 20 Jan 1812 *F*; [m 20 Apr 1831 *HV*—Henry Ives].

vii Maria, b 10 Nov 1814 *F*, d 6 May 1835 æ. 21 *HTl*.

viii Mabel, b 10 Jan 1817 *F*, d 23 May 1842 æ. 24 *HTl*.

ix Caroline, b 9 Feb 1821 *F*.

5 Ezra, b 18 Mar 1776 *NHV*, bp 26 May 1776 *HCl*, d 1818; M. D. (Yale 1797).

6 Lucy, b 23 Sep 1778 *NHV*, d 22 Aug 1801 æ. 23 *HTl*; m 31 Dec 1797 *HV*—Alvin Bradley.

7 Jared, b 19 Aug 1781 *NHV*, 14 Aug *HTl*, d 16 Nov 1857 *HTl*; m Sylvia da. [Chauncey] & Mary (Merrick) Bradley, b 1 Nov 1783 *HTl*, d 26 Aug 1858 *HTl*.

8 Russell, b 4 Jan 1785 *NHV*, d 19 Aug 1855 æ. 70 *HTl*; m (1) 10 Nov 1814 Abigail da. Amos & Chloe (Bradley) Dickerman, b 28 Oct 1789 *HV*, d 6 Sep 1829; m (2) 22 Jan 1834 *HV*—Emeline da. Alvin & Abigail (Hall) Bradley.

FAM. 34. James & Lois (Turner) Ives:

1 Bede, b 14 May 1770 *NHV*; m 20 Mar 1789 Jared Goodyear.

2 Amasa, b [4 Jan 1773], d 17 Oct 1776 æ 3-9-13 *NoHTl*.

3 Chloe, b [13 Dec 1774], d 17 Oct 1776 æ. 1-10-4 *NoHTl*.

FAM. 34. James & Mary (Brockett) Ives:

4 Lois, bp 24 July 1785 *NoHC*; m 19 Mar 1800 *NoHC*—Samuel Abbott.

5 Russell, bp 24 July 1785 *NoHC*.

6 Harvey, bp 24 Dec 1786 *NoHC*.

7 Polly, bp 16 Jan 1791 *NoHC*.

8 James, bp 16 June 1793 *NoHC*.

9 Chauncey, bp 23 Aug 1795 *NoHC*.

10 SON, bp 22 Apr 1798 *NoHC*.

FAM. 35. EBER & ESTHER (THOMPSON) IVES:

1 EUNICE, b 5 Aug 1795 *HV*, d 27 Sep 1801 *HV*.

2 BETSEY, b 18 Mar 1800 *HV*, d 29 Sep 1801 *HV*.

3 ESTHER, b 2 Jan 1803 *HV*, *HT1*, d 14 July 1835 *HT1*; m Loyal Francis Todd.

FAM. 36. ELAM & SARAH (HITCHCOCK) IVES:

1 PARSONS, b 29 Aug 1791 *HV*, bp 22 Sep 1799 *HC1*, d 10 Sep 1850 æ. 59 *HT1*; m Mary da. Joel & Sarah (Royce) Hough, b 25 Nov 1793 *HV*, d 29 Mar 1851.

2 BEDA, b 31 Dec 1793 *HV*, bp 22 Sep 1799 *HC1*, d 17 May 1818 æ. 24 *HT3*; m Nov 1813 *ColR*—David Bradley.

3 JASON, b 28 Apr 1795 *HV*, bp 22 Sep 1799 *HC1*, d 6 June 1879; m Phebe Freeman.

4 SARAH, b 8 Jan 1798 *HV*, d 17 Oct 1803 *HV*, æ. 6 *HT1*.

5 LYMAN, b 21 Apr 1800 *HV*, bp 29 June 1800 *HC1*, d 15 Oct 1803 *HV*, 13 Oct æ. 4 *HT1*.

6 ELAM, b 7 Jan 1802 *HV*, bp 21 Feb 1802 *HC1*, d 10 Feb 1864 æ. 63 *HT1*; m (1) Louisa da. Medad & Amanda (Bradley) Todd, bp 18 Aug 1804 *HC1*, d 30 Apr 1866 æ. 61 *HT1*.

7 WILLIAM, b 1 Jan 1804 *HV*, bp 19 Feb 1804 *HC1*, d 8 Dec 1874 æ. 71 *NoHT3*; m (1) Mary Tuttle; m (2) Susan Cutler.

8 MARY, b 28 Nov 1805 *HV*, bp 1806 *HC1*, d 16 May 1879 æ. 73-6 *HV*; m 24 Nov 1825 *HV*—Chester Dickerman.

9 HENRY, b 24 Jan 1808 *HV*, bp 13 Mar 1808 *HC1*, d 3 Feb 1859; m 20 Apr 1831 *HV*—Eliza [da. Jesse & Mabel (Goodyear)] Ives.

10 JULIA, b 24 Jan 1811 *HV*, bp 12 May 1811 *HC1*, d s. p. 17 June 1833; m 7 June 1832 *HV*—Benjamin Eastman.

11 JULIUS, b 24 Jan 1811 *HV*, bp 12 May 1811 *HC1*, d 4 Feb 1888 æ. 77 *HT1*; m Eunice Amelia Beadles, who d 21 Jan 1906 æ. 90 *HT1*.

12 LUCIUS, b 5 May 1813 *HV*, d 24 Aug 1892 æ. 79 *HT1*, æ. 79-3-20 *HV*; m Anna T. Hall, who d 11 May 1893 æ. 77-10 *HV*.

13 JAMES, b 8 Dec 1815 *HV*, d 21 Sep 1889 æ. 73-9 *HV*; m 28 Nov 1838 Lucy Ann Candee.

IVES. MISCELLANEOUS. CLARISSA m 14 Dec 1800 *NHC1*—Thaddeus Johnson...... CALEB had w. Sarah who d 15 Feb 1735 *WV*, & s. Ichabod who d 1 Mar 1715 *WV*.

JACKSON. JOHN, of NH & D, d 1 Oct 1683 æ. c. 60 *DV*; m (1) 1 Mar 1653/4 *NHV*—Mary da. Richard Hull, who d 26 Feb 1664 *NHV*; m (2) 2 July 1668 *NHV*—Sarah, wid. George Smith.

(By 1): 1 CHILD, b 8 Nov 1654 *NHV*, d 16 Nov 1654 *NHV*.

2 CHILD, b 14 Dec 1655 *NHV*, d 19 Dec 1655 *NHV*.

3 MARY, b 15 Oct 1657 *NHV*, bp 23 Nov 1657 *NHC1*, d 15 June 1724 *DV*; m Aug 1679 George Beamon of D.

4 GRACE, b 4 Feb 1658 *NHV* [1658/9], bp 6 Feb 1658 *NHC1* [1658/9], d 4 Sep 1664 *NHV*.

5 Mehitabel, b 5 Jan 1659 *NHV* [1659/60], bp 1 Apr 1660 *NHC 1*, d 23 Dec [1660] *NHV*.
6 Hannah, b 13 Mar 1662/3 *NHV*, bp 15 Mar 1663 *NHC1*, d 31 Mar 1663 *NHV*.
7 Infant, d 25 Feb 1664 *NHV*.

JACKSON. miscellaneous. Josephine. da. James H. & Hannah (Sargent) (Chamberlain) Jackson, bp by her foster-parents as Minnie Oakes Prescott, b 25 Dec 1850 (N. Y. City).

JACOBS. fam. 1. Bartholomew, of NH, d 1693; m 20 Dec 1666 (at Bd) *NHV*—Mercy da. Thomas & Mary Barnes; she m (2) 22 Nov 1694 *WV*—Joseph Thompson.

1 Daughter, b Sep [1667] *NHV*, d young.
2 Elizabeth, b 19 Oct 1668 *NHV*.
3 Samuel, b 9 Aug 1671 *NHV*, d 1742; m 6 Dec 1705 *NHV*—Margaret Old.
i Daniel, b 4 Dec 1706 *NHV*, d s. p.
ii Lydia, b Oct 1708 *NHV*, d 1 Aug 1790 *CC;* m (1) Ebenezer Fox; m (2) 22 Dec 1743 *WV*—Benjamin Bunnell.
iii Thankful, b 2 Feb 1709/10 *NHV;* m Joseph Potter of Wat.
iv Mercy, b end of Mar 1713 *NHV*.
v Susanna, b 24 Sep 1715 *NHV*, probably d Jan 1741/2 *CC*.
vi Samuel, b 16 June 1718 *NHV*, bp July 1718 *NHC1*, probably d 22 Oct 1758 *F&IWRolls*.
vii Margaret, b 3 Apr 1721 *NHV*, d 31 Dec 1798 æ. 80 *EHC*.
viii Bartholomew, b 5 Jan 1723/4 *NHV;* m 22 Apr 1751 *WatV*—Abigail da. Daniel & Lettice (Ward) Curtis, b 25 Aug 1735 *WatV*. Children, recorded *WatV:* (1) Susanna, b 13 June 1752. (2) Keziah, b 14 June 1754. (3) Daniel, b 20 Oct 1756. (4) Jonah, b 29 Mar 1759. (5) Sabra, b 8 Mar 1762. (6) Adonijah, b 3 June 1764.
ix William.
x Elizabeth, b c. 1728, d 8 Dec 1787 æ. 60 *EHC;* m 15 Dec 1756 *EHC, BdC*—Ebenezer Roberts.
4 Mercy, b 8 Sep 1674 *NHV;* m 1 Jan 1695 *NHV*—John Hull.
5 Thomas, b 14 Oct 1677 *NHV*, d 2 Apr 1740 *NHV;* m Apr 1707 *NHV*—Jemima da. Samuel & Sarah (Newman) Tuttle, b 6 Dec 1686 *NHV*, d 23 Mar 1753 *NHV*.
i Thomas, b 9 Aug 1708 *NHV*, d s. p. 1741.
ii Stephen, b 2 Dec 1710 *NHV*, d 1758; m 11 Jan 1738/9 *NHV*—Hannah da. Isaac & Elizabeth (Todd) Dayton, b 4 Aug 1718 *NHV*. **FAM. 2.**
iii Joseph, b 9 Mar 1713 *NHV*, d 6 June 1790 æ. 77 *NoHC;* m 1 June 1748 *NHV*—Elizabeth da. Stephen & Elizabeth (Bishop) Curtis, b 24 July 1724 *WV*, d 28 May 1773 *NoHC*. **FAM. 3.**
iv John, b 9 Dec 1715 *NHV*, d 16 Sep 1781 æ. 65 *NoHC;* m 18 July 1749 *NHV*—Mary da. Moses & Lydia (Humis-

ton) Brockett, b 26 Jan 1719/20 *NHV*, d 19 June 1787 æ. 67 *NoHC*. **FAM. 4.**

v David, b 19 Dec 1718 *NHV*, d 24 Mar 1809 æ. 90 *NoHT2;* Census (NoH) 1-0-1; m 11 Apr 1745 *NHV*—Hannah da. Joseph & Sarah (Hotchkiss) Turner, b 11 May 1720 *NHV*, d 20 Mar 1807 æ. 87 *NoHT2*. **FAM. 5.**

vi Amos, b c. 1721, d s. p. 13 Aug 1760 *F&IWRolls;* m Katharine ——— .

vii Abraham, b 21 Apr 1725 *NHV*, d s. p. 29 May 1760 *F&IWRolls*.

6 LYDIA, b 3 Apr 1681 *NHV*.

FAM. 2. STEPHEN & HANNAH (DAYTON) JACOBS:

1 JONAH, b 30 Nov 1739 *NHV*, d 12 Oct 1750 *NHV*.

2 THOMAS, b 2 Apr 1741 *NHV*, d 1 Jan 1818 æ. 77 *NoHT2;* m 17 Jan 1799 *NoHV*—Mary da. Caleb & Eunice (Barnes) Cooper, b c. 1769, d 5 Nov 1843 æ. 75 *NoHT2*.

i Hannah, b c. 1796, bp 16 June 1805 (æ. 9) *NHx;* if the age is correctly stated, she must have been child of a former wife.

ii Washington, b c. 1799, d 25 Sep 1839 æ. 40 *NoHT2;* m 16 Nov 1826 *NoHC*—Mary Ann da. Lemuel & Mary (Cooper) Mansfield, b 28 July 1809 *F*, d 12 Mar 1892 æ. 83 *NoHT3*.

iii Sarah.

iv Cooper, b c. 1811.

v Maria, b c. 1814.

3 STEPHEN, b 17 May 1743 *NHV*, d 26 June 1825 æ. 82 *NoHT1;* Census (NoH) 2-3-7; m (1) 22 Jan 1766 *NoHC*—Lydia da. Joseph & Lydia (Tuttle) Turner, b c. 1747, d 1 Mar 1769 æ. 21 *NoHC*, 9 Mar æ. 22 *NoHT1;* m (2) 12 July 1770 *NoHC*—Mary da. Dan & Mary (Platt) Ives, b c. 1747, d 17 May 1802 æ. 55-8 *NoHC*, *NoHT1*.

(By 1): *i* Eli, b c. 1767, d 18 May 1843 æ. 76 *NoHT1;* Census (NoH) 1-0-0; m (1) 11 Aug 1790 *NoHC*—Lydia Tyler; m (2) 16 Jan 1797 *NoHC*—Ruth da. Zuar & Mary (Mattoon) Bradley, b c. 1773, d 24 Aug 1852 æ. 79 *NoHT1*. **FAM. 6.**

ii Lydia, b c. 1769; m Daniel Merwin; res. Woodstock, N. Y., 1794.

(By 2): *iii* Stephen, b c. 1771, d 1 Oct 1814 æ. 44 *NoHC;* m 19 May 1791 *NoHV*, *NoHC*—Naomi da. John & Mary (Cooper) Gill, b c. 1771, d 21 Aug 1834 *NoHD*. **FAM. 7.**

iv Child, d 8 Dec 1772 *NoHC*.

v Polly, b c. 1774, d 29 Feb 1840 æ. 66 *NoHT1*.

vi Hannah; m ——— Merwin.

vii Sylvia, b c. 1779, d 31 Mar 1861 æ. 82 *NoHT3;* m 30 Sep 1799 *NoHV*—Ziba Shepard.

viii Leverett, b c. 1781, d 2 Mar 1800 æ. 19 *NoHT1*.

ix Lyman, b c. 1781, d 4 Apr 1860 æ. 79 *GV;* m Anna ——, who d 11 May 1860 æ. 73 *GV;* he had a nat. child (by Mary da. of Job Blakeslee): Edward L. b 18 Aug 1806 *F*, d 1878; m 31 Dec 1830 Susan H. Marks.
x Esther; m —— Keeler.
xi Sukey; m —— Miles.
xii Harvey, b c. 1787, d 10 Jan 1821 æ. 34 *NoHT1*, æ. 35 *NoHC.*

4 Isaac, b 11 Jan 1745/6 *NHV*, d 25 Oct 1750 *NHV*.

5 Enoch, b 7 Dec 1747 *NHV*, d 6 Mar 1797 *NoHC;* Census (NoH) 1-2-3; m (1) Jemima da. Joseph & Lydia (Tuttle) Turner, b c. 1749, d 12 Nov 1786 æ. 37 *NoHC;* m (2) 3 Dec 1787 *NoHV*—Lois Parker, who d 27 June 1839 æ. 78 *NoHD.*

(By 1): *i* Jemima, d 13 July 1826 æ. 84 (54?) *NoHD;* m 14 Dec 1790 *NoHV*—Richard Brockett.
ii Betsey, b [Jan 1772], d 29 July 1782 æ. 10-6 *NoHC.*
iii Eunice, b c. 1774, bp 1791 *NoHx*, d 10 Dec 1793 æ. 20 *NoHT1;* m Levi Blakeslee.
iv Sarah, b Oct 1778 *NoHV*, bp 1791 *NoHx*, d 5 Dec 1864 æ. 85 *NoHT3;* m 14 Jan 1801 *NoHC*, *NoHV*—Jesse Watrous.
v Thirza, bp 1791 *NoHx;* m Joel Mansfield; she k. him 1824.
vi Mary, bp 1791 *NoHx;* m 29 May 1797 *NoHV*—Eli Tuttle.
vii Jared, bp 1791 *NoHx*, d young.
(By 2): *viii* Randall, bp 1791 *NoHx*.
ix Betsey, bp 1791 *NoHx;* m 21 Jan 1810 *NoHC*—James Humphrey of Great Barrington, Mass.
x Lovicy, bp 1791 *NoHx;* m 20 Jan 1811 *NoHC*—John Pixley of Great Barrington, Mass.
xi Jared, bp 1793 *NoHx*.
xii Amy.

6 Daniel, b 12 Feb 1749/50 *NHV*, d 19 Oct 1750 *NHV*.

7 Hannah, b 4 Mar 1752 *NHV*, d 6 Feb 1802 æ. 49 *NoHT1*, 7 Feb æ. 50 *NoHC;* m Enos Brockett.

8 Elizabeth, b 18 Nov 1754 *NHV*.

9 Patience, b 18 Aug 1757 *NHV*, d 30 Dec 1824 æ. 67 *LT;* m 13 Oct 1777 *NoHC*—Ebenezer Todd.

FAM. 3. Joseph & Elizabeth (Curtis) Jacobs:

1 Martha, b 3 July 1749 *NHV*.

2 Jemima, b 10 July 1750 *NHV*.

3 Joseph, b 27 Feb 1752 *NHV*, d Mar 1793 æ. 41 *NoHT2;* Census (NoH) 1-2-3; m 21 June 1775 *NHV*—Lydia da. John & Mary (Brockett) Jacobs, b 30 Nov 1750 *NHV*, d 19 Dec 1844 æ. 94 *NoHT2.*

i Mary, b 9 Jan 1776 *NHV*, bp 1789 *NoHx*.
ii Bede, b 2 July 1779 *NHV*, bp 1789 *NoHx;* m 2 Jan 1803 *NoHV*—Ebenezer Hull.
iii Zophar, b 14 June 1782 *NHV*, bp 1789 *NoHx*, d 27 Mar 1870 æ. 87 *NoHV;* m 2 Jan 1804 *NoHV*—Betsey da. Jo-

siah & Susanna (Seeley) Thomas, b 31 Aug 1785 *NoHV*, d 15 July 1868 æ. 83 *NoHV*. Children: (1) Thomas, b 11 Apr 1807 *NoHV*, d 11 Sep 1813 *NoHV*, æ. 7 *NoHT1*. (2) Sina, b 1 Sep 1813 *NoHV*; m Stephen Blakeslee. (3) Maria, b 19 July 1815 *NoHV*, d 7 Dec 1824 æ. 9-4-18 *NoHT1*. (4) Betsey, b 24 July 1822 *NoHV*. (5) Bela Thomas, b 19 Sep 1829 *NoHV*.

iv Seabury, b 17 Sep 1789 *NHV*, bp 1789 *NoHx*, d 15 Feb 1870 æ. 80 *NoHT2*, *NoHV*; m 19 Jan 1848 *NoHV*—Jeannette Hannah Stilson, wid. Giles Beach, b c. 1794, d 29 May 1875 æ. 81 *NoHT2*.

4 (perhaps) ZEBULON; m 7 Apr 1781 *NoHC*—Esther da. John & Thankful (Frost) Brockett, b 7 Aug 1755 *NHV*.

i Lora; m 19 July 1802 *NoHC*—Solomon Bradley.

ii Lua.

5 (perhaps) ABEL, b c. 1758, d 21 Oct 1812 æ. 54 *NoHT2*.

6 (perhaps) ZOPHAR, d 28 Feb 1778 *NoHC*.

7 AMOS, bp 4 Nov 1764 *NoHC*.

8 ELIZABETH, bp 5 Apr 1767 *NoHC*, d 22 Apr 1850 æ. 84 *NoHT3*; m 4 Apr 1791 *NoHC*—Enos Mansfield.

FAM. 4. JOHN & MARY (BROCKETT) JACOBS:

1 LYDIA, b 30 Nov 1750 *NHV*, d 19 Dec 1844 æ. 94 *NoHT2*; m 21 June 1775 *NHV*—Joseph Jacobs.

2 JOHN, b 18 Mar 1752 *NHV*, d 15 July 1773 æ. 21-2 *NoHC*; m.

3 EZEKIEL, b 20 June 1755 *NHV*, d 11 Mar 1834 æ. 79 *NoHT2*; Census (NoH) 1-1-2; m 3 Mar 1785 *NoHC*—Eleanor da. Thomas & Mehitabel (Tuttle) Walter, b 14 Mar 1760 *NHV*, d 22 Sep 1821 æ. 61 *NoHT2*.

i Amelia, b c. 1788, d 14 Dec 1872 æ. 84 *NoHT3*; m Timothy Bassett.

ii Zeruiah, b 6 Sep 1792 *F*, d 6 Dec 1866; m 3 Dec 1821 *NoHV*, *NoHC*—John Hughes of EH.

iii Fanny; m ——— Morse.

iv William, b 1795 *NoHT3*, d 1853 *NoHT3*, 6 Nov 1853 æ. 58 *NoHD*; m 1 Jan 1822 *NoHV*—Lovisa Thorpe, b 1798 *NoHT3*, d 1872 *NoHT3*. Children: (1) George W. (2) Louisa M.; m ——— Marks. (3) Cornelia L.; m ——— Munger.

v Ammi; rem. to Grapevine Point, N. H.

vi John, b [July 1797], d 26 Feb 1800 æ. 2-7 *NoHC*, 27 Feb æ. 3 *NoHT2*

4 JOEL, bp 29 Mar 1761 *NoHC*; m 13 Feb 1782 *NoHC*—Sarah Stow.

FAM. 5. DAVID & HANNAH (TURNER) JACOBS:

1 DAVID, b 3 Jan 1745/6 *NHV*, d 28 Sep 1750 *NHV*, æ. 5 *NoHT2*.

2 SOLOMON, b 22 Mar 1747/8 *NHV*, d 8 Sep 1750 *NHV*, æ. 3 *NoHT2*.

3 HANNAH, b 26 Aug 1750 *NHV*, d [———] *NoHT2*.

4 DORCAS, b 6 Feb 1753 *NHV*, d 20 Sep 1759 æ. 7 *NoHT2*.

5 DAVID, b 1 Dec 1754 *NHV*, d 29 Aug 1759 æ. [5] *NoHT2*.

6 SARAH, b c. 1756, d 17 Sep 1759 æ. 3 *NoHT2*.

7 SOLOMON, b 1 July 1759 *NHV*, d 7 Nov 1799 æ. 40 *NoHC*, *NoHT2*; Census (NoH) 1-3-2; m 30 Dec 1779 *NoHC*—Esther da. Lawrence & Elizabeth (Todd) Clinton, b 5 Aug 1760 *NHV*, d 14 May 1842 æ. 82 *NoHT2*; she m (2) 15 June 1806 *NoHV*—James Pierpont.

i David, b 6 Jan 1781 *F*, d 17 Feb 1833 æ. 52 *NoHT2*; m Thirza da. Richard Brockett, bp 1792 *NoHx*, d 29 Apr 1834 æ. 42 *NoHT2*.

ii Clinton, b 13 Aug 1782 *F*, d 25 Dec 1836 *NoHD*; m & had a s. DeForest, whose w. d 26 Feb 1846 *NoHD*.

iii Solomon, b 9 Feb 1787 *NoHV*, d 2 Aug 1825 æ. 38 *NoHT2*; m Betsey da. Justus & Susanna (Pardee) Barnes, b 17 Jan 1790 *NoHV*, d 3 Oct 1850 æ. 60 *NoHT2*. Children: (1) Eliza; m —— Bassett. (2) Grace; m 7 Dec 1831 *NHV*—Orrin Grilley. (3) Mary; m 2 May 1846 *NHV*—Benjamin Foy. (4) Edwin.

iv Hannah, b 6 Apr 1789 *F*, d 30 Dec 1794 æ. 6 *NoHT2*.

v Linus, b 1 Sep 1791 *F*; res. Providence, R. I., 1813.

vi Anson, b 27 Sep 1793 *F*, d 27 Feb 1874 æ. 80-5 *NoHV*.

vii Silas, b 22 Mar 1796 *F*, drowned 1843 æ. 45 *NoHD*.

viii Esther, b 2 May 1800 *F*, d 31 July 1828 æ. 28 *NoHC*; m Wooden Barnes.

8 HANNAH, b 15 Sep 1762 *NHV*, bp 14 Nov 1762 *NoHC*, d 27 Oct 1773 æ. 11 *NoHC*, æ. 12 *NoHT2*.

FAM. 6. ELI & RUTH (BRADLEY) JACOBS:

1 HENRIETTA, b c. 1798, d 17 Feb 1872 æ. 74 *HT3*; m Sterling Bradley.

2 JOSEPH.

3 EUNICE JEANNETTE, b 19 Sep 1802 *NoHV*, d 7 May 1838; m 19 Sep 1821 *NoHV*—Riley Tuttle.

4 AMANDA; m George Hoadley.

5 LYDIA, b c. 1806, d 7 Sep 1871 æ. 66 *HV*; m Julius S. Tolles.

6 EMELINE MINERVA, b c. 1808, d 2 Jan 1822 æ. 13 *NoHC*, *NoHT1*.

7 RUSSELL S.; m Elizabeth Wild.

8 LORENZO DENNIS; m Harriet Blakeslee.

FAM. 7. STEPHEN & NAOMI (GILL) JACOBS:

1 ELAM, b 20 Nov 1791 *NoHV*, d 2 Dec 1813 *NoHV*, æ. 22 *NoHT1*.

2 LAURA, b 4 Aug 1794 *NoHV*, *NHT3*, d 24 Mar 1878 *NHT3*; m 9 May 1825 *NoHV*—Elmon Blakeslee.

3 ROSWELL, b 19 Jan 1800 *NoHV*, d 8 Mar 1875 æ. 75 *NoHV*; m 13 Oct 1826 *NHV*—Chloe da. Elias & Esther (Dickerman) Hotchkiss, b 18 Feb 1805, d Feb 1894 *NoHT3*.

4 MARY, b 28 Feb 1803 *NoHV*.

5 JULIA N., b 1 Aug 1810 *NoHV*, d 22 Apr 1875 æ. 64 *NHT3*.

6 NANCY.

JACOCKS. John Hill, b c. 1778 (N. Carolina), d 4 Aug 1848 æ. 70 *NHT1*; m (1) 18 Dec 1798 *NHC1*—Eunice da. Abel & Eunice (Austin) Burritt, b c. 1782, d 25 Dec 1801 æ. 20 *NHT1*; m (2) 5 Sep 1802 *NHC1*—Sally da. Abel & Eunice (Austin) Burritt, b c. 1780, d 10 Sep 1826 æ. 46 *NHT1*; m (3) Grace da. Elijah & Mabel (Alling) Thompson, wid Elijah Munson, b c. 1790, d 19 July 1864 æ. 74 *NHT1*. Family incomplete.

(By 1): 1 Elizabeth, b 10 July 1799 *NHT1*, bp 24 June 1804 *NHx*, d 8 Feb 1849 æ. 49 *NHT1*; m 10 Sep 1822 (at NH) *ConnH*—Samuel James Clark.

2 John Hill, b c. 1801, bp 24 June 1804 *NHx*, d 1828 æ. 27 *NHT1*, 19 Oct 1828 (*NHx*) *NHV*.

(By 2): 3 Eunice, bp 24 June 1804 *NHx*.

4 (probably) Abel B.

5 James Gilbert, b [July 1819], d 26 Apr 1885 æ. 65-9 *NHT1*; Rev.

JAMES. Thomas, of NH, had been an Elder in Mass. Bay; children bp *NHC1*: Nathaniel, 1 Aug 1641; Elisha, Nathaniel, Abel, & Abigail, 19 Mar 1648; Ruth, 24 Mar 1650. PAGE 1789

JANES. William, schoolteacher at NH 1651, had da. Ruth b 15 Feb 1649 *NHV*; rem. to Northampton, Mass. 1667, living there 1681. There was later a Wm. Janes at St & Jamaica, L. I.

JAUNCEY. Joseph & Susanna had a s. Joseph bp 25 May 1777 (sponsor, John Blagge) *NHx*.

JEBINE. Nicholas, Census (NH) 1-0-1; m 23 Jan 1790 *NHC1*—Mary da. Stephen & Lucy (Riley) Munson, b 23 Feb 1770 *NHV*, d 29 Dec 1823 æ. 60 (?) *NHT1*, "Widow" d 28 Dec 1823 æ. 60 (!) (*NHx*) *NHV*.

1 Mary, b [Feb 1792], bp 29 July 1793 *NHC1*, d 31 July 1793 æ. 0-17 *NHT1*, "da." æ. 2 *NHC1*.

2 John, bp 22 Sep 1794 *NHC1*.

3 Charles, bp 22 Sep 1794 *NHC1*.

JEFFRIES. Thomas, d 23 Aug 1661 *NHV*; Sgt.; had sister Sarah w. George Betty of Combe, St. Nicholas, Somerset, Eng., whose children John & Elinor were his residuary legatees; he gave legacies to Isaac s. of John Deane & to Tho. s. of Tho. North.

JEROME. Timothy, b c. 1688, d 23 Feb 1750 *WC2*, 23 Feb 1751 æ. 62 *WT2* [error for 1750, since will was proved 2 Mar 1749/50]; m Abigail ——, who m (2) 29 Mar 1752 *WC2*, *FarmV*—Jacob Deming.

1 Timothy; m 6 Aug 1736 *WV*—Ann Horton [or Norton?].

i Timothy, b 4 Oct 1738 *WV*.

ii Lydia, bp 10 Feb 1740 *WC2*.

iii Andrew, bp 7 Apr 1742 *WC2*.

2 Isabel, d 12 Apr 1777 *WV*; m 5 Jan 1731 *WV*—Lazarus Ives.

3 Zerubbabel; m (1) [Sarah da. Henry Cook] who d c. 1737; m (2) 30 Aug 1738 *WC2*—Phebe [da. Henry] Cook, bp (adult) 26 July 1741 *WC2*.

(By 1): *i* Mary, d 16 May 1737 *WC2*.

(By 2): *ii* Robert, bp 2 Aug 1741 *WC2;* m Candace ——, bp with her da. Phebe 30 Mar 1783 *Bristol x;* they had also bp there, Lois 12 Oct 1783 & Daniel 28 May 1786.

iii Thomas, bp 18 Sep 1743 *WC2*.

iv Asahel, bp 12 May 1745 *WC2*.

v (probably) Phebe, d 20 May 1776 *F;* m 30 May 1764 *F*—Moses Dunbar.

vi (probably) Chauncey; m —— ; m (2) Esther Adams, wid. Moses Dunbar. Children: Chauncey, Ana, Sybil, & Nancy, bp 6 Aug 1780 *Bristolx;* Sarah, bp 1 Sep 1784 *Bristol x;* Fanny, bp 7 Aug 1785 *Bristolx*.

4 **William**, b 28 Aug 1717 *WV*, d 20 June 1794 æ. 77 *BristolT;* m 13 Nov 1738 *WV, WC2*—Elizabeth da. Hawkins & Sarah (Royce) Hart, b c. 1716, d 12 Feb 1792 æ. 70 (76?) *BristolT*.

i Sarah, bp 19 Aug 1739 *WC2*, d 1816 æ. 77 *BristolC;* m 20 July 1759 *FarmV*—Abel Yale.

ii Abigail, bp 18 Jan 1741 *WC2;* m 8 May 1766 *FarmV*—Josiah Lewis.

iii Elizabeth, bp 21 July 1745 *WC2*.

iv Lois, bp 17 May 1747 *WC2*.

v Esther, b 174- *FarmV*.

5 **Abigail**; m 11 Jan 1742 *WC2*—Joseph Stone of Bristol.

6 **Elizabeth**; m 15 Dec 1742 *WC2*—John Atkins of Mid.

7 **Samuel**, b 3 Nov 1728 *WV*, d 1796 (Salina, N. Y.); m 19 Nov 1749 *WV*—Lucy da. Thomas & Mary (Clark) Foster, b 28 Mar 1732 *WV*. Family incomplete.

i Samuel, b 20 Aug 1750 *WV*, bp 5 May 1751 *WC2;* res. Salina, N. Y., 1791; m 17 Jan 1771 *WV*—Eunice Cole.

ii Lucy, b 9 Feb 1752 *WV*, bp 16 Feb 1752 *WC2;* m 25 May 1769 *WV*—Joseph Edwards.

iii John, bp 7 Apr 1754 *WC2*.

iv Timothy, b 6 Aug 1756 *WV*, bp 10 Aug 1755 *WC2*, d 9 May 1802 *Pompey, N. Y., T;* rem. from Stockbridge, Mass, to Fabius, N. Y., 1794; m Mary Isaacs, who d 20 July 1834 æ. 80 *Syracuse, N. Y., T;* had a da. Lucy, b 28 Feb 1779 *SyracuseT*, d 23 Nov 1857 *SyracuseT;* m Hon. James Geddes, the first chief engineer of the N. Y. state canals.

v John, b 17 Mar 1757 *WV*, bp 24 Apr 1757 *WC2*, d 1839 *Pompey Hill, N. Y., T;* m Mary St. John, b 1755, d 1836 *Pompey HillT*.

vi Chauncey; of Pompey, N. Y., 1796.

vii Levi, b c. 1761, d 11 June 1838 æ. 77 *Pompey HillT;* m Dolly Smith, who d Dec 1846 æ. 71 *Pompey HillT*.

(continued in volume V.)

ADDITIONS AND CORRECTIONS

ABBOTT. The fragmentary record which we gave of this family on page 8 can be amplified from the researches of Miss Ethel Lord Scofield. FAM. 1. The 4th child did not d soon but was apprenticed to William Lewis Sr. 28 Dec 1658 æ. 9-3-5, which makes him b 23 Sep 1649 and identifies him. The 7th child was not John, but Joseph. He is known to have been living in 1689, and despite late marriage age is probably identical with the head of FAM. 3. The 9th child Daniel, despite late marriage age, is probably identical with the head of FAM. 2. FAM. 2, 2. Joseph, b 16 Jan 1696, m 14 Apr 1730 Hannah Marks and had the following children recorded *BdV:* Samuel, b 29 Jan 1730/1; Jemima, b 13 Oct 1733; Joseph, b 28 Aug 1737 (identical with the head of FAM. 4); Lydia, b 14 Feb 1739; Hannah, b 4 Apr 1741; Rebecca, b 18 Jan 1744/5, m 23 Nov 1780 *NoBC2*—Amos Beecher; & Abigail, b 24 June 1747. FAM. 4, 1. Constant's 2d w. was Margery; his 3d w. was Thankful.

ADEE. This name may have been originally Eddy, and the first William of this family may possibly have been son of William and Hannah (Smith) Eddy of Bristol, R. I. (Page 12). FAM. 1, 1. The will of the second William made his brother Lemuel Hotchkiss, Executor. His wife Sarah was therefore da. Caleb Hotchkiss, b 12 Nov 1731 (see p. 800). The son Caleb Adee chose his father-in-law Dea. Gideon Stoddard for guardian 1 Oct 1771. This proves that William's widow m (2) Gideon Stoddard. [Contributed by Mr. Horace W. Dickerman, New Haven.]

ALLING. (Page 19). FAM. 5, 6. Samuel's 2d w. was Mary da. William & Abigail (Crampton) Ward, wid. Abijah Waterhouse. Their da.: *ii* Mary, b c. 1771, d 17 Aug 1848; m (1) 11 Nov 1790 Zerah Munson, b 20 July 1768, d 14 Sep 1822; m (2) Jesse Scovill of P.

(Page 24). FAM. 9, 7, *x*. Jesse m Sarah *Gorham*, not *Graham*. She was Sarah da. John & Susanna (Gilbert) Gorham, wid. Jared Munson. (p. 677.) *xi*. Elizabeth m Benjamin (not Thomas) Mix. The "Alling Genealogy," p. 229, erroneously states that she d unm. Proof of her marriage has recently been found among old papers of the Alling family. [Contributed by Mr. Edward B. Alling, Orange City, Fla.]

(Page 30). FAM. 14, 4. Hezekiah m Hannah Fitch; children were Fitch, b c. 1755, d 18 Nov 1777 æ. 23 *NHT1*, æ. 22 *NHC1;* Laura, m Josiah Stebbins; & Hannah, b c. 1759, d 1833, m Timothy Higgins (1755–1829) of M, My & Wol. [Not positively proved, but worked together from several family sources & believed to be correct].

BEECHER. (Page 171). FAM. 6, 4, *iv*. Justus, b 20 May 1763 (at C) *F*, d 1852 (Union, N. Y.) *F*. [Contributed by Mr. E. Stanley Welles, Newington.]

BRINTNALL. (Page 308). William m 19 Dec 1729 Zerviah Buckminster of Framingham. See Bailey's Early Mass. marriages, Book III, p. 89. They had also a da. Lucy who m Stephen Miles. [Contributed by Mr. Wm. Molthrop Stark, New London.]

BROWN. Old document, probably mostly in handwriting of Francis

Brown, gives more complete dates of FAM. 12 (p. 354) than we had from public records. The records follow (courtesy of Mr. Cleveland J. Rice, New Haven). Francis, b 6 July 1743; Hannah, b 8 Sep 1743; m 1 Jan 1767. Francis d 5 July 1810 æ. 67. (Births of children). Isaac, 24 Oct 1767; Sally, 3 Dec 1769; Francis, 9 Apr 1772; Hannah, 15 Aug 1774; Wheeler, 21 Aug 1779; Harriet, 7 Dec 1781; Nancy, 18 July 1785. "Age of grandchildren." Little Francis (of Francis) 14 Jan 1799; Maria (of Francis) 13 May 1796; Little Harriot (of Wheeler) 19 Mar 1803. (Deaths). Isaac, 21 Nov 1788; Harriot, 16 May 1794 æ. 12-6; Francis, 28 Nov 1802 æ. 30-7; Wheeler, 23 July 1803 æ. 24; Hannah, 11 Oct 1810 æ. 36.

BUNNELL. (Page 359). It was hypothetically stated in brackets that Nathaniel's da. Lydia m Ephraim Price. Various N. J. publications state that Lydia prob. m Samuel Little & that her sister Jane prob. m Ephraim Price. [Contributed by Mrs. C. W. Nichols, New Britain.]

COOK. (Page 445). FAM. 10, 8, *ii*. William enlisted in the Rev. War at age of 14 & served 6 years; became a Dr. & rem. to Durham, N. Y., where he d 25 May 1846; m Mary Whittlesey, b 9 Apr 1761, d 17 Oct 1836. Children: 1 Major, b 1790, d young. 2 Polly, b 1793. 3 William Augustus, b 1797. 4 Samuel W. D., b 1798. 5 George H., b 1801. 6 Alexander, b 1804. 7 Andrew H., b 1805. [Contributed by Mrs. M. E. Rockwell, Meriden.]

(Page 447). FAM. 14, 6. Aaron's wife was not wid. Samuel Way; it was her cousin, another Betsey Preston, who m Samuel Way.

DAYTON. (Page 529). FAM. 3, 5. Samuel b 1750, not 1751.

FORBES. (Page 610). FAM. 2, 5, *ii*. Omit John's date of marriage to second wife. The date has not been found.

FORD. (Page 616). FAM. 7, 2. Ellard had in addition to the children listed a s. Lewis Hart, b 17 May 1799, d 29 Nov 1879 at Belfast, N. Y.; m 23 Dec 1823 (at Belfast) Deborah da. Nathaniel & Margaret (MacElwayne) Reynolds, who d 1885. They had children: 1 Darius Reynolds, b Oct 1824. 2 Lucinda, b 25 Feb 1826. 3 Lewis, b 28 Oct 1827. 4 Emeline, b 27 Mar 1830. 5 Charles L., b 30 Aug 1833. 6 Sidney Allen, b 12 Nov 1837. 7 Hester, b 21 July 1840. 8 Robert Wilmer, b 21 Oct 1845. 9 Willis Ellard, b 22 Feb 1850; res. Utica, N. Y. [Contributed by Mrs. Frederick R. Ford, Utica, N. Y.]

GILBERT. (Page 646). FAM. 3, *ii*. Abraham's wid. Abigail d at Chester, Ohio Jan 1837. (Page 654). FAM. 17. Family sources give Abraham two more sons, Jared & Wyllys. Merritt d 6 Nov 1854 æ. 74 *TollandT;* his w. Phebe Ann d 9 Dec 1823 æ. 43; Aurelia his second w. d 23 Apr 1871 æ. 90. Wyllys lived in Tolland until 1837 or later. Joel, b 3 Oct 1789 *F*, d at Chester, Ohio, 27 Mar 1852; m (1) 28 Feb 1813 Lucy S. Hall, b 28 Aug 1787, d 29 Apr 1816; m (2) 16 Dec 1816 Arisilda Crocker, b 18 May 1786, d 13 Feb 1835; m (3) 25 Sep 1835 Naomi Whitmore, b 10 May 1802, d 3 July 1884. Children of Joel by 1st w.: Norton, Lucy S.; by 2nd w.: Alman, Martha J., Arisilda, Sabrina, Sarah, J. Dwight, Miles Bradley, Lauren & Warren; by 3rd w.: Clarinda R., Mary R., Abigail R., Charlotte, Darius, Martha, & Freeman. (Contributed by Homer W. Brainard, Esq., of Hartford).

GLOVER. Mr. Herbert E. Thayer, 32 Sunapee St., Springfield, Mass., kindly contributes the following from Hampden County Real Estate Records, vol. A, p. 25: a conveyance dated 8 Nov 1662 from Ensign Thomas Cooper of Springfield to "his brother Henry Glover of New Haven" of one quarter of lands at Worronoco granted by the town of Springfield to Ensign Cooper. Sarah the w. of Ens. Thomas Cooper consented to the sale ......Now who can tell us: did Thomas Cooper marry a sister of Henry Glover? And was John Cooper of New Haven brother of Thomas Ccoper of Springfield?

GOLDSMITH. (Page 663). Ephraim's w. was wid. Jonathan *Atwater*, not *Beach;* an overlooked clerical error. [Corrected by Mr. Alfred H. Beach, Casper, Wyo.]

GORHAM. (Page 675). FAM. 1, 3, *ix*. Elias d May 1811 æ. 46 *ConnH*.

(Page 677). FAM. 4, 4. Sarah m (2) Jesse Alling (see Alling above & p. 24).

GREEN. (Page 688). FAM. 2. A letter written by Miss Lucy Davis Butler, a grandaughter of Samuel Green, states that Samuel was b 4 Dec 1744, m 25 Oct 1774 Abigail Buel, b 14 June 1749; they had 4 children: 1 Abigail, b 18 Sep 1779, d 6 July 1783. 2 Elizabeth, b 20 Apr 1782, d 7 May 1794. 3 Abigail Elizabeth, b 30 June 1785, m Aaron Forbes & had a da. Abigail Green Forbes. 4 Rebecca, b 1 Oct 1788, m 7 Oct 1806 Henry Butler. [Contributed by Mrs. Elizabeth French Bartlett of Boston, Mass.] From this it appears that Abigail Hall was not w. of Samuel Green. She may have been the 2nd w. of Thomas Green, brother of Samuel; it is certain she m a Green.

HAWES. BETHIA of M had a nat. child b 1658, of whose paternity she accused John Baldwin, but he was ably defended and not convicted. Bethia m 31 Oct 1660 *MV*—Obed Seward.......ELIZABETH m 1 Apr 1675 *NHV*—Nathaniel Potter. In the printed New Haven Vital Records, Elizabeth's name is given as Howes (a variant of How), and on p. 658 we followed this by giving it as How; but we believe Hawes to be the correct reading.

HEATON. (Page 725). James, b c. 1633, not 1642. "The Street Genealogy", p. 8, states that he d 1712 æ. 70, and this erroneous statement we corrected to æ. 79, but neglected to alter the birth date to correspond. He first bought land 1654, and must then have been of age.

(Page 728). FAM. 5, 1 Jacob removed to New York, N. Y., where he had a second w. and family. By his first w., Sarah Hemingway, he was father of Samuel Eaton, b 17 May 1772, d at Madison, N. Y., 20 June 1842, m Grace (Smith) Allen, b 4 Aug 1771, d 10 Sep 1848. This was the Samuel named in the will of his grandfather Seth, and not a child of Philemon. [Contributed by Mrs. Jewett of Buffalo, only great-grandchild of Samuel].

(Page 730). FAM. 11, 1. Isaac, b 12 Nov 1793, d 10 May 1866; m (1) 18 May 1819 Jane Ann Kelly, who d Sep 1843; m (2) Eunice Bush; lived in Spencer, Owen Co., Ind., had 12 children. Charles Dennis, s. of his brother Julius, m Maria Foot and had a s. Julius who m Olivia Linsley and had 4 children. Merab Rosette m Chauncey Blakeslee, b 4 Apr 1825, d 16 Feb 1875. Susan Cirilla (p. 731) d 14 Oct 1925; m John E. (not Marshall)

Brockett, b 1828, d 1910. [Contributed by Mrs. H. Nelson Stiles, North Haven.]

HODGE. (Page 782). FAM. 2, 3. Benjamin & Eliphal had also a da. Sarah, b 13 Dec 1790; m Samuel Burwell.

HOLT. (Page 784). FAM. 1, 4. Eleazer's second w. Mary (Sanford) (Ashburn) Hotchkiss d 26 Aug 1750 *MV*. (Page 790). FAM. 7, 4, *iv*. Edward, b 17 Aug 1806 (at EH) *F*, d 12 Mar 1900 *F*; m 28 Sep 1836 *F*—Mehitabel, da. David & Martha (Hine) Clark, b 20 Oct 1818 (at M) *F*, d 24 Nov 1900 *F*. [Contributed by George C. Bryant, Esq., Ansonia.]

HOTCHKISS. (Page 800). FAM. 3, 2, *iii*. Sarah m (1) William Adee; m (2) Dea. Gideon Stoddard.

(Page 809). FAM. 9, 7, *iv*. Esther m Jacob (not Abner) Johnson.

(Page 812). FAM. 12, 3, *vi*. Cyrus m Catherine da. William & Eunice (Baldwin) Fowler, b 1 Feb 1780 *OC*.

(Page 832). FAM. 45. Some of the grandchildren of Elias are misplaced. Ransom, Lauren, & Rebecca were certainly children of Seymour, & Maria probably was. Rebecca m 14 Mar 1838 Alonzo Sperry of Bethany. Seymour also had da. Mabel Beecher (1828–1857) who m Chauncey S. Morris. Sheldon, the other s. of Elias, was father of Sophronia & Atlanta. Sophronia m 22 Nov 1826 *NHV*—Daniel Merrill; Atlanta m 18 Nov 1828 *NHV*—Dorus Clark.

[The following notes contributed by Clarence D. Smith, Rome, N. Y.] (Page 799). FAM. 2, 5, *iv*. Robert, Census (Southold, L. I.) 2–0–3, should read (Freehold, N. Y.), the former name for the present town of New Durham. This census evidently refers to Robert FAM. 19, 1 (p. 818), who was an early settler in Freehold. If this is the same Robert who appears in Census (C) 2–0–2, he must have rem. to Freehold in time to get into the census there, with one more in his family. A Samuel also appears in Freehold Census 1–2–2, identical with Samuel (p. 818) FAM. 18, 3. George (p. 818, FAM. 19, 7) res. in Freehold & had s. called Robert Jr.

(Page 827). FAM. 37, 10. Henry, b 9 Aug 1785, d 1870; m Sarah Cochran, who d 1874 æ. 87; had issue; res. Durham, N. Y.

(Page 835). FAM. 53, 7. Charles Todd Hotchkiss, according to Cortland, N. Y. Probate records d there 1812 leaving no children, his father David being the only heir. Calvin, listed as his s. who rem. to Homer, was s. of Enoch & Lois (Wolcott) Hotchkiss, (p. 845), both of whom rem. to Pontiac, Mich. Enoch appears 1796/7 in Homer, locating on Lot 76. Two other children of Enoch have been identified, viz.: Charles, b c. 1784, d 20 Oct 1868 æ. 84 (Virgil, N. Y.); had issue; & Rhoda, who m 1809 Truman Doud.

PAGE 1245

(Page 845). Henry Hotchkiss, b 24 Sep 1770, d 4 Oct 1843, s. of Amos (p. 802, FAM. 4, 1, *viii*), & Desire (Doud); m 13 Oct 1793 Eliza Tuttle da. Samuel & Hephsibah (Collins) Barnes, b 7 Mar 1770 *EHR*, d 25 Sep 1850. Children: (1) Polly, b 27 Jan 1795, d 1870; m Augustus Crittenden. (2) Henry Collins, b 16 Aug 1796, d 14 Feb 1840; m 1818 Hannah L. Richards. (3) Lyman Morris, b 14 Nov 1798, d 5 July 1875; m 15 May 1828 Ann (Shelley) Richards. (4) Eliza, b 27 Nov 1800, d 16 Mar 1878; m Simeon Leete.

(5) Henrietta, b 4 Feb 1805, d 21 Nov 1868; m Henry Benedict. (6) Sally, b 12 July 1807, d 13 Dec 1868; m Jonathan Morse. (7) Amos Samuel, b 9 Sep 1810, d 1893; m (1) 10 Apr 1831 Mary M. da. Merritt Mix of NH, b 4 July 1805, d 14 Aug 1866; m (2) 12 July 1871 Laura S. Hawkins.

Moses Hotchkiss, b "somewhere near New Haven" 1774, d 8 Dec 1838 (at Bergen, Genesee Co., N. Y.); m Lucy Griswold, b 17 Aug 1780, d 20 Dec 1836; rem. to Greene Co., N. Y., thence to Genesee Co. in 1817. Children (order uncertain) were: (1) Thomas; rem. to California. (2) Ezekiel, rem. to Homer, N. Y., thence to Pa.; had a large family. (3) Sterling, b in Conn. 1803; rem. to Bergen, N. Y., 1817; m there 27 Apr 1826 Anna da. Aaron & Polly (Allen) Jacobs. (4) Edward; rem. to Monroe, Mich. (5) George; m & rem. to Ind. (6) Hiram (youngest s.) b 9 Dec 1815, d 11 Jan 1848; m 10 Dec 1840 Lucy Sawins; res. Genesee Co., N. Y. (7) Katie. (8) Flinda. (9) Harriet. (10) Eunice; m ——— Hitchins; rem. to Michigan. (11) Sally. (12) Nancy; m (1) ——— Curtiss; m (2) ——— Drew. (13) Mary. This Moses has been confused with Moses FAM. 66, 2 (p. 840), but exhaustive research convinces us they are not identical.

James T. Hotchkiss, from Woodbridge, Ct., located on Lot 54, Homer, N. Y. in 1803. Affidavit in Cortland Co. Probate Court gives date of death 1813, in U. S. Military service, no age given. Heirs were: Mary, James P., & Erwin P. Hotchkiss.

Who can connect Enoch, Moses, & James T., with their Connecticut ancestry?

BEECHER BIBLE RECORDS

The family of Abraham Beecher, given incompletely on p. 179 (FAM. 25), is given in the family Bible, the record being furnished by his descendant, Mrs. Mignonette M. Riker, of Flanders, N. J. Abraham Beecher, b at Woodbridge, Ct., 17 Sep 1745, d at Sharon, Ct., 11 Oct 1823. Desire Tolles, b at Woodbridge, 12 Sep 1745, d at Sharon, 10 June 1812. They were m at Woodbridge, 28 Apr 1768. Children:

1 Philemon, b at Woodbridge, 19 Mar 1769, d at Oxford, 28 May 1774.

2 Abraham, b at Oxford, 20 June 1771, d at Northampton, Fulton Co., N. Y., 27 Aug 1845.

3 Amos, b at Oxford, 12 Sep 1773, d at Litchfield, 18 Dec 1819.

4 Philemon, b at Oxford, 19 Mar 1776.

5 Eli, b at Oxford, 22 Jan 1778.

6 Betsey, b at Oxford, 6 Jan 1780.

7 Fanny, b at Oxford, 22 Feb 1782, d at Sharon, 26 Apr 1803.

8 Isaac, b at Kent, 22 Nov 1783.

9 Jesse, b at Kent, 7 Jan 1785.

10 Robert Ransom, b at Kent, 12 Dec 1789,

Abraham Beecher Jr. m 23 Apr 1792 Lydia Day Fuller, b 9 July 1770. Children:

1 Leman, b 12 Feb 1793.

2 Desire, b 24 July 1794.

3 Truman, b 18 June 1796.

4 Betsey, b 1 Apr 1798.

5 Lydia Day, b 12 Sep 1800.

6 Abraham, b 2 Sep 1802, d 29 Oct 1803.

7 Abraham Fuller, b 11 Feb 1805.

8 Laura, b 11 Apr 1807.

9 Philemon Tolles, b 29 Aug 1809.

Laura Beecher, b 11 Apr 1807, d 4 Feb 1884; m 14 May 1828, Langdon Ithiel Marvin, b 20 June 1805, d 31 Jan 1869. Children: 1 Philemon Beecher, b 26 Feb 1829, d young. 2 Philemon Beecher, b 19 June 1830. 3 John Henry, b 16 Sep 1832. 4 Laura Augusta, b 5 Jan 1836. 5 Lucy Jessena, b 19 Feb 1838. 6 Frances Elizabeth, b 26 Jan 1840. 7 James Langdon, b 26 May 1842. 8 Abraham Tolles, b 11 May 1844. 9 David Truman, b 30 Mar 1847. 10 Lydia Day, b 19 Nov 1848. Of these, James Langdon Marvin m 9 May 1865 Mary Frances Force, & was father of Mrs. Riker, who sent a copy of the above records.

Leman Beecher, b 12 Feb 1793, d 13 Oct 1848; m 5 Nov 1818 Catherine Shew, b 4 May 1794. Their s.: Abraham Philemon, b 16 Jan 1834; m 1 Nov 1860 May Anna Draper. Their da. Emma May Beecher (Mrs. Clarence Wilbur Smith) furnished these dates.

OLD BRADLEY RECORD.

(From a copy printed in a newspaper, 26 Jan 1916. This record confirms the account of this family given on pages 265 to 267, and adds a few particulars.)

On the first of January, 1806, the owner of this Book thought within himself that he would inquire after the Geneoligy of his ancestors, and upon inquiry he found:

That in the Latter Part of the Sixteenth [17th] Century there was a venerable Old Gentelman Lived in the Northeasterly Part of the City of New Haven, in an old Brick house, of the name of John Bradley, who had five Sons and Three Daughters, Namely, Enos, Jason, John, Jehiel, Sarah, Elizabeth, Phineas & Susannah. His family being thus increased, he, with two of his Sons, made a Settlement about two or three miles out of town, on the Road leading to Sperries' Farm, and built two houses, a Grist Mill, Saw Mill & fulling mill. This was done the forepart of the 17th [18th] Century, and that Settlement was then called Bradley Town, which name it inherits to this day, When the said John Bradley died is not known.

The children of Enos were four sons and two Daughters, namely, Griffin, Enos, Ariel, Tibbetts, Ellen and Gamaliel. The children of Griffen were 6 sons and 6 daughters; the children of Enos were 2 sons and 2 daughters; the children of Arial were 3 sons and one daughter; the children of Tibbetts were one son and 2 daughters and the children of Ellen were thirteen in number. And Jason, second son of the first-named John, was married, but had no children, and he took his brother Enos's youngest son, named Gamaliel, and made him his Heir. And Gamaliel took a wife of the daughters of the Carmelites and she bore him 9 children. And John, the third son of the first John Bradley, had two sons and two daughters. One, Jehiel, had three sons. And Sarah, first daughter of the first-named John married John Adee, and had 2 sons, viz: John and William. And Elizabeth, second daughter, married Richard Sperry, and had 2 sons and 3 daughters. And Susanna, third daughter, married Phineas Perkins, outof a tribe that then lived in New Maddatuck, by whom she had ten children.

We shall be more fortunate respecting Phineas, the youngest son of the first named John Bradley, and his descendants, which are taken from his own record, which he kept in a large account book, Page 56.

Phineas Bradley was born 9th. October 1715. He was married to Martha Sherman, 5th. May 1750, who was born 1st of August, 1721. Their descendants were:

1. A Son, Erastus, Born 29th. April 1751.
2. A daughter, Electa, Born 31st. January, 1753.
3. A son, Phineas, Born 29th May, 1755.
4. A son, Zina, Born 3rd. January, 1758.
5. A daughter, Martha, Born 6th. November, 1750 [or 1760?].

6 A son, Aner, Born 5th. March, 1753 [or 1763?].
7 A Daughter Asenath, Born 17th. September, 1755 [or 1765?].
8 A daughter, Huldah, Born 13th. November, 1757 [or 1767?].
9 A daughter Sarah, Born 19th June, 1760 [or 1770?].
10 A daughter, stillborn, Born 14th May, 1762 [or 1772?].
11 A daughter, Molly, Born 24th. April, 1767 [1777?].

And the said Phineas, father of the 11 children, as above, died in a Fit of Appoplexy on the morning of the 30th. of December, 1780, and Martha, his widow, died 10th. of April, 1795.

Erastus, their first son, married and had 4 sons and 2 daughters. 3 of his sons died in infancy. Electa married James Storer and had 2 sons, William and James. She died 16th. November, 1768. Phineas married and had 2 sons and 2 daughters; he died 24th. of June, 1797. Zina married and had 2 sons and 2 daughters; he died 19th November, 1802. Martha married John Hubbard and had 4 sons and one daughter; she died June 6, 1812. Aner married and had 4 sons and 5 daughters. Asenath married and had 3 sons and 3 daughters; she died December 6, 1822. Huldah died 8th of December 1780. Sarah married and had 3 sons and 4 daughters. Molly married and had 2 sons and 2 daughters.

Connecticut Witches.

It was formerly the intention of the writer to prepare a book on this interesting subject, which has never been treated exhaustively, and to identify each "witch" who was ever accused or tried in Connecticut and New Haven Colonies, to identify their accusers, and to print in full the contemporary records covering each case. This plan has been indefinitely postponed because of the pressure of other labors; but since the material in a few witchcraft cases has been prepared for some time, and since the subject is one which has a certain fascination, a hold on the imagination of the general reading public, it has been decided to preserve the material which has already been collected by offering it to the readers of this publication. Two cases, those of Mary Johnson and Goodwife Bassett, are presented herewith, and the results of our research should be of special interest because so little has come down to us in the contemporary records relating to them, and in consequence fallacious conclusions have been reached by earlier writers on the subject, which here we examine and refute. To this is added the Benham case, which we believe was the last witchcraft trial in New England.

In considering each case, we reproduce first the pertinent original records, quoting them *verbatim* but not *literatim;* spelling and punctuation have been modernized, to enable the general reader to grasp more readily the sense of the passages; the spelling of personal names, however, has been retained. We reproduce next the accounts of the case, if such exist, printed by Mather and other early writers who were contemporary, or nearly so, with the events they narrated. Lastly, we add our own comments and conclusions drawn from the quoted sources and from other sources.

I. MARY JOHNSON.

Connecticut Colonial Records, volume 1, page 143; Court held 21 Aug. 1646:

Mary Johnson, for thievery, is to be presently whipped, and to be brought forth a month hence at Wethersfield, and there whipped.

Connecticut Colonial Records, volume 1, page 171; Court held 7 Dec. 1648:

The Jury finds the Bill of Indictment against Mary Jonson, that by her own confession she is guilty of familiarity with the Devil.

*Cotton Mather's "Magnalia," Sixth Book, Chapter VII, Eighth Example:**

There was one Mary Johnson try'd at Hartford in this countrey, upon an indictment of "familiarity with the devil," and was found guilty thereof, chiefly upon her own confession. Her confession was attended with such convictive circumstances, that it could not be slighted. Very ma-

---

**The same story, in similar phraseology, was first told by Mather in 1689 in his "Memorable Providences." Hale's brief notice of it in "A Modest Inquiry" (written in 1698) is drawn from Mather's account.*

terial passages relating to this matter are now lost; but so much as is well known, and can still be prov'd, shall be inserted.

She said her first familiarity with the devil came through *discontent*, and wishing the devil to take this and that, and the devil to do that and t'other thing: whereupon a devil appear'd unto her, *tendring* her what *services* might best *content* her. A devil accordingly did for her many services. Her master blam'd her for not carrying out the ashes, and a devil afterwards would clear the hearth of ashes for her. Her master sending her to drive out the hogs that sometimes broke into their field, a devil would scowre the hogs away, and make her laugh to see how he feaz'd them. She confessed that she had murder'd a child, and committed uncleanness both with *men* and with *devils*. In the time of her imprisonment, the famous Mr. Stone was at great pains to promote her conversion from the devil to God; and she was by the best observers judged very penitent, both before her execution and at it; and she went out of the world with comfortable hopes of mercy from God through the merit of our Saviour. Being ask'd what she built her hopes upon, she answer'd, "Upon these words: 'Come unto me, all ye that labour and are heavy laden, and I will give you rest;' and these: 'There is a fountain set open for sin and uncleanness.'" And she dy'd in a frame extreamly to the satisfaction of them that were spectators of it.

Comment.

This witch was an apprentice, a servant girl, of Wethersfield, and was probably of weak mentality.

Taylor, in "The Witchcraft Delusion in Colonial Connecticut," page 144, assumed that she was identical with an Elizabeth Johnson who had a child born in prison. There is no reason whatever for such an inference. To clear up this matter, the four references to the other Johnson woman need to be quoted in full (Conn. Col. Rec. I. 209, 222, 226, 232):

On 21 May 1650, "Will: Rescew's bill of charges for Elizabeth Johnson's imprisonment to the first Thursday of the next month, being 24 weeks, amounting to 6£ 10s. is allowed and approved: and the Court desires Mr. Ludlow and Mr. Warde to see the bill discharged to the said Will: Rescew out of her estate."

On 15 May 1651, "The Court grants their consent that Nathaniell Rescew should have Goodwife Johnson's child, which was born in the prison, as an apprentice to him, till he is of the age of twenty one years, and that the said Rescew shall have ten pounds with him, out of Newton's estate."

On 6 Oct 1651, "Mr. Warde and John Bankes are desired to gather up and make sale of any estate of that which was sometime Peter Johnson's of Fairfield, and that they shall therewith satisfy the charges of the nursing of the child of Goody Johnson."

On 20 May 1652, "This Court orders that Nathaniell Rescue shall be paid five pounds more with the Goody Johnson's child, according to her promise to him, he having engaged himself to maintain and well educate her son without any further demand of charges either of her or the country."

The witch Mary Johnson was condemned at the end of the year 1648, while Elizabeth was certainly living in May 1650, and she is not called deceased in any of the records quoted. It is clear she was widow of Peter Johnson of Fairfield, and Roger Ludlow, Andrew Ward, and John Banks, who were appointed to attend to certain matters in this case, were all Fairfield men.

William Ruscoe was the jail-keeper in Hartford, and Nathaniel Ruscoe, who took the child, was his son. When Nathaniel died in 1673, he left a horse and a pig to Benjamin Newton, his apprenticed servant. This, together with the fact that Nathaniel had with the boy ten pounds out of Newton's estate, indicates that the child born in prison was a bastard, and that the reputed father of the child was named Newton.

Thomas Newton of Fairfield, a man hitherto of good standing, was charged with a capital crime in 1650, but with the help of friends escaped from prison and took refuge on Long Island. Savage (Gen. Dict. III, 278) suggests that witchcraft was the charge against him, and also (*ib.* II. 556) that Elizabeth Johnson was confined for insanity. Witchcraft was not the only capital offense in Connecticut under the statute of 1642; adultery was another (Conn. Col Rec. I. 77), and Newton was a married man.

Those historians who have asked us to shed tears for the poor convicted witch who had a child born while awaiting execution, are obviously in error. The crime for which Mrs. Elizabeth Johnson served a sentence was not witchcraft. It need only be added that she was not executed, for when her son John Johnson died in 1659, the Fairfield Probate Records state that he left surviving, two brothers under age (Moses and Ebenezer), and a mother; and in 1661 Elizabeth was still living, the wife of John Fossecar.

II. GOODWIFE BASSETT.

Connecticut Colonial Records, volume 1, page 220: Court held 15 May 1651:

The Governor, Mr. Cullick and Mr. Clarke are desired to go down to Stratford to keep Court upon the trial of Goody Bassett for her life, and if the Governor cannot go, then Mr Wells is to go in his room.

New Haven Colonial Records, volume 2, pages 81 and 85:*

......Goodwife Basset, when she was condemned, said there was another witch in Fairfield that held her head full high, and then the said Goodwife Knapp stepped a little aside and told her (this deponent) Goodwife Bassett meant not her; she asked her whom she meant, and she named Goodwife Staples......

Elizabeth bid her do as the witch at the other town did, that is, discover all she knew to be witches.

****The following extracts are from the Staples suit (1653), the records of which we hope to give in a subsequent issue.***

Rev. John Hale's "A Modest Inquiry," published 1702, Chapter I, Section 8:

I have also heard of a Girl at New Haven or Stratford, that confessed her guilt.

Comment:

The records of this early case are meagre. The Magistrates who were appointed to conduct the trial at Stratford were Gov. John Haynes, Capt. John Cullick, and Mr. Henry Clarke. The references to the witch in the New Haven Staples trial two years later prove that Mrs. Bassett confessed, and that she was condemned. Hale's brief sentence undoubtedly refers to her, for there is no record of any witch at New Haven ever confessing, and she is the only Stratford witch of whom we have any account. Confession was of rare occurrence among Connecticut witches, and this helps to make the identification more certain.

No reasonable doubt of her execution can exist. In "Historical Sketches," prepared by Major W. B. Hinks and Rev. B. L. Swan and printed in 1871 (quoted in Orcutt's "History of Stratford," I. 147), we find the following tradition preserved:

"The place of her execution is pointed by tradition to this day, and would seem to be determined by the names "Gallows Brook" and "Gallows Swamp" in the first volume of Stratford town records. The former was a small stream, long since dried up or diverted into another channel, emptying into the swamp, a portion of which yet remains, a little south of the present railroad depot. A rude bridge, stoned up at the sides, crossed this brook, just where the Old Mill and the railway intersect......At that bridge, uniform tradition states the execution of the witch by hanging to have taken place. Near by where the street from the village turns off toward the depot, was, until quite recently, a small quartz boulder, with hornblende streaks like finger marks upon it, which was connected with the fate of Goody Bassett, by an ancient and superstitious tradition. The story was, that on her way to the place of execution, while struggling against the officers of the law, the witch grasped this stone and left these finger marks upon it. The stone, with its legend, came down to our day, but a few years since an unromantic individual used it in building a cellar wall, not far from the place where it had been lying."

The identity of this witch is not positively known. Some have supposed that she was the wife of John Bassett of New Haven; but in November 1653 we read "that before Margery Basset, the widow of the said John, went from New Haven to Stamford, she testified upon oath that this is a full inventory of her huaband's estate." John died in 1653, his widow Margery survived and soon moved to Stamford, and she was of Stamford when her own will, dated in June 1653, was proved in May 1656.* Obviously, she was not the witch who was executed in 1651. Their only son, Robert Bassett, was of New Haven in 1649, but appears on Stamford records as early as 1651, and was a prominent citizen of Stamford in 1653 and 1654. It is therefore most unlikely that Robert's wife was the witch, for both New Haven and Stamford were then under New Haven jurisdiction,

**New Haven Col. Rec. II. 159; New Haven Town Rec. I. 190.*

whereas Stratford, where the witch certainly lived, belonged to Connecticut, and it was the latter Colony which tried the case. Robert afterwards removed to Hempstead, L. I., but his son, Robert, Jr., later came to Stratford and was the ancestor of the Bassetts of that place; a circumstance, doubtless, which misled some investigators to identify the witch with the mother or grandmother of the younger Robert.

Hale's reference to the witch as a girl might lead to the inference that she was an unmarried woman, were it not for the contemporary and official records which designate her "Goodwife." This makes it certain that she was married. Hale wrote long after the event, but some mention of her youth may have reached him to justify his description of her as a girl. In the absence of proof to the contrary, we may assume that she was a young married woman.

Thomas Bassett came over on the ship Christian in 1635, aged 37; is said to have been a soldier in the Pequot War, 1637; was a citizen of Windsor as early as April, 1640, when he was made a freeman of Connecticut; received a homelot of 2½ acres in Fairfield in August 1653; and was of Fairfield in 1659, when he was freed from training.* His inventory was presented in Fairfield, 14 Jan. 1669/70; and he left a widow and children. It is quite possible that he lived in Stratford for a short time before receiving the homelot in the adjacent town of Fairfield in 1653. The witch may have been his wife; she could scarcely have been a daughter-in-law unless he had a wife and children before coming to this country, and of that there is no evidence. It is usually supposed that a younger Thomas, of Milford, was his son. There is no reason to doubt it, but in that case the wife of the older Thomas must have been considerably his junior in years; and the younger Thomas, who did not marry until about 1686, as well as the other children, were probably by a second wife.

Dr. Thomas Pell of Fairfield, in his will dated 21 Sept. 1669, forgave four "poor men" their debts to him. One of these was Thomas Basset, and another was Roger Knapp, and Knapp's wife is known to have been hanged as a witch. Perhaps the good doctor's compassion was especially directed to men who had lost their wives in this way.†

Unless the witch belonged to the family of Thomas, no suggestion as to her identity can be offered. It is the writer's belief that he married, after settling in Windsor, a woman considerably younger than himself. After leaving Windsor, the family may have lived in Fairfield and Stratford without a settled home until the grant of 1653. The statement of Mrs. Pell in the Staples trial, that Goodwife Bassett said "there was *another* witch in *Fairfield*," implies that the Bassetts already had Fairfield affiliations, although then living in Stratford.

This witch confessed, and was probably of weak mentality.

Orcutt's "History of Stratford," II. 1122, 1123; Conn. Col. Rec., I. 46, 336; Schenck's "History of Fairfield," I. 68.

†*Dr. Pell was more charitable than his wife and stepdaughters, judging by their affidavits in the Staples case. Pell, like Bassett, was a Pequot War veteran.*

III. WINIFRED BENHAM, MOTHER AND DAUGHTER

New Haven County Court Records, volume I, *page 202; Court held in Nov. 1692:*

Winfred Benham of Wallingford being summoned to appear at this Court for Examination upon suspicion of witchcraft, was now present, and the witnesses were called to testify what they had to say in the case, and accordingly gave in their testimonies in writing which were read in the hearing of the said Winfred. And she being called to say what she had to say for herself, her general answer was, that she knew nothing of the matters testified, and was not concerned therein. She also gave in some testimonies for herself which were read.

The Court having heard and considered all the evidence against the said Winfred Benham and not finding sufficient grounds of conviction for further prosecution (at present) of the said Winfred, do therefore at this time dismiss the business, yet advising the said Winfred Benham solemnly to reflect upon the case, and grounds of suspicion given in and alleged against her, and told her if further grounds of suspicion of witchcraft, or fuller evidences should appear against her by reason of mischief done to the bodies or estate of any by any preternatural acts proved against her she might justly fear and expect to be brought to her trial for it.

New Haven County Court Records, volume I, *page 213; Court held in June 1693:*

Winfred Benham of Wallingford, her husband Joseph Benham being bound in a bond of 20 pounds for her appearance at this Court for further examination about Witchcraft, he was now called and appeared, and the Court adjourned the case to their next session, and then upon notice given them the parties to appear, and the said bond to continue for said appearance, which said Benham consented to.

New Haven County Court Records, volume I, *page 252:*

A Special County Court by Order of the Governor held at New Haven the 31st of August 1697. Present: Robert Treat, Esq., Governor; William Jones, Esq., Deputy Governor; Major Moses Mansfield, Assistant.

Complaint being made to the Authority by Ebenezer Clark, Joseph Royce, and John Moss, Jr., all of Wallingford, against Winfred Benham, Sr., and Winfred Benham, Jr., her daughter, that Sarah Clark daughter of said Ebenezer Clark, Elizabeth Lathrop, and John Moss, son of the said John Moss, Jr., were frequently and sorely afflicted in their bodies by the said Benhams, mother and daughter, or their apparitions, and as they strongly suspect by their means or procurement by the Devil in their shapes, and therefore desire the Authority as God's Ordinance for their relief strictly to examine the said suspected persons in order to a due trial of them, that a stop may be put to their suffering and prevention of such mischiefs among them for the future.

The Court having seriously considered the accusations and informations on good testimony given in against Winfred Benham, Sr., and Winfred Benham, Jr., upon suspicion of them for witchcraft, they, or the devil in their shapes, afflicting sundry young persons above named, as formerly accused and suspected in the year 1692; and finding clear and sufficient grounds of suspicion against them after strict examination of the said persons apart and severally, see just cause to bind over the said Benhams mother and daughter to appear at the next Court of Assistants in October next at Hartford in order to their further examination and trial personally. And the husband of said Winfred Senior gave 40 pounds recognizance for their appearance accordingly, or that they be secured in prison for their said trial. And said Benham to pay the charge of this Court.

Court charges, 21 shillings. Execution granted for said 21 shillings.

Memorandum. The death of said [*blank*] young child to be inquired into, with what appeared of spots on said child and the like spots on said Benham quickly vanishing.

Robert Calef's "More Wonders," published 1700:

In *August* 1697. The Superior Court at Hartford, in the Colony of Connecticut, where one Mistress Benom was tried for Witchcraft, she had been accused by some Children that pretended to the Spectral sight; they searched her several times for Tets; they tried the Experiment of casting her into the Water, and after this she was Excommunicated by the minister of Wallinsford. Upon her Tryal nothing material appearing against her, save Spectre Evidence, she was acquitted, as also her Daughter, a Girl of Twelve or Thirteen Years old, who had been likewise Accused; but upon renewed Complaints against them, they both fled into New-York Government.

Comment:

The youthful accusers belonged to respectable families of Wallingford. John Moss (in his 15th year) was son of John and Martha (Lathrop) Moss, grandson of John Moss, for many years a deputy to the General Court and Commissioner for Wallingford, and of Samuel Lathrop, Judge of the New London Court, and great-grandson of Rev. John Lathrop. Elizabeth Lathrop (aged 19) was first cousin of John Moss, being daughter of John and Ruth (Royce) Lathrop; her father was dead and her cousin Joseph Royce may have joined in the complaint on her behalf. Sarah Clark was aged 16. She had a brother born in 1694 who did not survive, but the date of his death is not recorded. The child who had spots and died was more probably a son of Joseph Royce, who died in December 1695 aged a few months.

The accused was Winifred King of Boston who married Joseph Benham of New Haven in 1657. They were among the first settlers in Wallingford in 1670. She was probably about 57 or 58 years old at the time of the 1697 accusation. Her daughter Winifred, the youngest of her 14 children, was then aged but 13.

Calef's assertion that continued suspicions drove mother and daughter to seek refuge in New York State is doubtless true. Two of the Benham children, Joseph and James, remained in Wallingford, where the younger Joseph died in 1702. The elder Joseph appears to have died the following year, but the probate entries are meagre* and it is not certain whether his wife Winifred survived him. There is some reason to believe that the elder Joseph and his wife died on Staten Island. The Wallingford realty was divided by agreements made between the heirs in 1727 and 1728 (Wallingford Deeds, V. 453, 454). These show that the son John Benham was then resident in Kings County, N. Y., and that the three Benham daughters, Anna, Sarah, and Winifred, with their respective husbands, Lambert Johnson, Jacob Johnson, and Evert Van Namen, were then living in Richmond, N. Y. The records of the Dutch church on Staten Island contain mention of their families, and show that Lambert and Anna (Benham) Johnson had a daughter Winifred baptized in 1696. This was a year before the witchcraft accusation, and since the elder Winifred then had a married daughter living on Staten Island, it was probably to this daughter's home that she fled; and some of the younger children either accompanied or followed her thither.

Calef's account of the case seems to be trustworthy so far as it can be verified, and we need not hesitate to accept his statement that Mrs. Benham was searched for witch marks, probably at the New Haven trial. His assertion that the water test was applied is perhaps questionable. Mr. Jones, one of the examining Magistrates, is known to have held the water test in slight esteem. However, it may have been applied at Mrs. Benham's own request. Accused witches were no less superstitious than their accusers, and feeling confident of their own innocence, sometimes volunteered to undergo the water test, in the belief that it would prove them innocent.

Nothing is known against the character of Mrs. Benham, and the family was of good repute, save for the suspicions of witchcraft. Two at least of her daughters named a child for their mother, which tends to show that they were fond of her. It is pleasing to learn that the young daughter, Winifred Junior, after passing through such terrifying experiences, was married to Evert Van Namen and reared a family in Richmond, N. Y.

******The probate records perhaps all relate to the estate of the younger Joseph.*

At Ye Editor's Desk

At the end of Volume III, I explained the need of a moderate endowment for the magazine. In response, contributions to an Endowment Fund were received from the following subscribers: Mr. and Mrs. J. M. Andreini, Miss Lucy Peck Bush, Mrs. John C. Kerr, Mrs. William Maluge, Mr. E. V. D. Selden, and Mr. Henry H. Townshend. I wish to express my gratitude to those who have contributed to this undertaking. The amounts received have been deposited to the credit of the Magazine in a special account and will remain untouched until it attains an amount sufficient to carry a part of the annual deficit and to provide an index. The total is still far too small, and unless large contributions are received within the the next few months I shall be forced to abandon this publication to which I am contributing more time than I can afford and which I have carried on for four years at my personal risk and loss. If this decision is reached, I shall return the amounts which the above-named subscribers so kindly furnished; the present volume will be completed, and I shall issue a fifth volume devoted to those families whose records are now in shape for publication. The Magazine will then pass out of existence. I hope this decision need not be made, but under present conditions it is impossible for me to continue bearing the burden alone.

The need of an index is not immediate, as it can wait until the family records have all appeared. One subscriber wrote that an index was unnecessary, because the families appear in alphabetical sequence. There is some truth in this, but so many marriages bring in the names of individuals who did not belong to New Haven families that a cross index at least would prove very useful.

If the Magazine survives until the Pardee family is reached, this family will have to be omitted, because I was employed as compiler and editor of the Pardee Genealogy which has just been issued, and as I was paid for this work it would not be ethical for me to publish the same data in the magazine.

My preoccupation with the Pardee Genealogy and other research on which I have been employed, and the lack of funds for clerical assistance, have made it impossible for me to prepare the family records rapidly enough for the printer. In order not to delay the completion of the present volume unreasonably, the next issue (the fourth and last of the volume) will consist of "List of Officials Military and Civil who served from 1636 to 1665 in the Colonies of Connecticut and New Haven." This list, which took weeks of the closest application to compile, will be useful to genealogists, historians, and to all who are interested in their Connecticut ancestors. The list is alphabetical in arrangement. There is nothing like it in print and it should satisfy a long-felt want. By publishing this work, the manuscript of which was prepared some time ago, as the next issue of the Magazine, I shall gain the time to prepare more family statistics for the printer, and they will be resumed in Volume V.

THE EDITOR

POSTSCRIPT. The printer says that while I am writing to Santa Claus I might as well include a request for a linotype machine for him. Few of our subscribers realize that to the present date all issues of the Magazine have been set in type by the old hand method. More artistic, perhaps, but——more laborious!

LIST OF OFFICIALS
MILITARY AND CIVIL

Who served from March 1636 to December 1665

in the

COLONIES OF
CONNECTICUT AND NEW HAVEN

Compiled by
DONALD L. JACOBUS

NEW HAVEN, CONNECTICUT
1927

THE TUTTLE, MOREHOUSE & TAYLOR COMPANY,
NEW HAVEN, CONN.

INTRODUCTION.

All persons holding office, civil or military, by colonial authority, in Connecticut and New Haven Colonies prior to January 1, 1666, are alphabetically listed in the following pages. Non-commissioned military officers are also included, where reference to them has been found, although generally their rank was not conferred by colonial authority.

The index to the first volume of Connecticut Colonial Records does not cover the lists of Assistants and Deputies, and the index to the second volume refers only to the page where the name of each such official first occurs. The index to the New Haven Colonial Records, though it covers the lists of officials, has been proved a trifle defective. The present compilation should therefore be of use both to the historian and to those who wish to ascertain the services performed by their ancestors.

Considerable confusion has been caused by unfamiliarity with official titles as employed in colonial days, and by the fact that some titles were employed in more than a single sense. To avoid this confusion, the following terms have been adopted for use in this work:

Legislature is used for what was first called the General Court, and later the General Assembly.

Assistant designates a member of the Upper House of the General Court (Legislature). The term Magistrate was usual during this period, but the title Assistant came early into use and was employed until 1818, when the title Senator was substituted for it.

Deputy designates a member of the Lower House of the General Court (Legislature). In Connecticut, the towns originally sent "Committees" to sit with the "Magistrates," but the term "Deputy" was early substituted.

Judge designates a person appointed by colonial authority to try minor cases. In Connecticut at this period they were called Commissioners, and sometimes Magistrates or Assistants. In New Haven they were usually called Deputies, but occasionally Magistrates or Constables. Since the County Courts were not established until 1666 (following the union of the two

Colonies), all Judges mentioned in this work were of plantation (town) courts, except in a very few cases where they were given wider jurisdiction. Their duties were somewhat similar to those which later devolved upon Justices of the Peace.

By adopting this terminology, the ambiguity of the titles Magistrate and Deputy is avoided, and the clarity resulting from the use of standardized terms should compensate for the anachronisms involved.

Several persons who were early admitted as members of New Haven Court have been viewed erroneously as Deputies. They were merely made freemen of New Haven Court (the plantation), and were not Deputies to the Jurisdiction (Colony) Court. Hence they are omitted in the present work.

During this period there was great carelessness in recording the commissions of military officers, and the early Secretaries of Connecticut Colony were worse offenders in this respect than those of New Haven. The date of commission is stated herein when known; otherwise, the date when the title was first applied to a man in the colonial records. Since it was the General Court of the Colony which confirmed the choice of officers of commissioned rank, the use of the title in the colonial records should be considered positive proof of the legality of the commission, even though record of the appointment was not made.

In both Colonies, as soon as a regular system was adopted, Assistants served for a full year. Deputies were elected as a rule for each session, there being one in the Spring and one in the Autumn. Yet some towns in some instances elected their Deputies to serve for the entire year, and instances have been found where Deputies were elected to serve only at a special session. There was also a custom of electing a third man as an alternate to serve in case of the disability of either of the regular Deputies, and since special or adjourned sessions were frequent during the period covered by this compilation, cases may be found of three men actually representing the same town within the same half-year. In listing the services of Deputies herein, the dates of the two regular sessions are given, and those of interim sessions are omitted except for names which did not appear at the regular sessions. These names are those of alternates or of men elected for the special session. It should also be noted that for several years Hartford, Windsor, and Wethersfield were usually represented by four instead of two deputies.

It must be remembered by those who make use of this compilation that the records of the Colony of New Haven are missing from April, 1644, to May, 1653, except for two Courts held in 1646. The names of Assistants and Deputies for nearly the whole of this period are therefore omitted herein, except where they have been supplied from other sources. The first volume of records relates chiefly to the plantation (town) of New Haven and not to the Colony. This has not been understood by many who have used the book, with the result that Deputies (Judges) of the Town Court have often been mistaken for Deputies to the General Court of the Colony.

References to volume and page of the printed records of the Colonies are made in smaller type beneath the record of each individual, to enable the reader to verify each statement. For references to proof of service in the Pequot War, see the late James Shepard's "Connecticut Soldiers in the Pequot War" (Meriden, Conn., 1913).

The New Haven records stated what towns each Deputy represented, but the Connecticut records of this period did not do so, and often failed to state even the first names of the Deputies. This deficiency has been supplied from other sources by the editor, but the reader is asked to remember that the names of the towns are not given in the original Connecticut Colonial Records.

The greatest care has been exercised to ensure accuracy, and every reference given has been checked back and compared with the original. Many town histories have been consulted, and the editor is under special obligation to the 1922 Register of the Connecticut Society of Colonial Dames of America. It is believed that the present publication will be of great service to historians and genealogists.

ALLING, JOHN (d. 1690). Corporal, New Haven Train Band, Apr., 1661 (resigned June, 1673).

N. H. Town I. 480. II. 311.

ALLING, ROGER (d. 1674). Corporal, New Haven Train Band, June, 1652; Sergt., Apr., 1661, confirmed July, 1665 (resigned Sept., 1669). Treasurer, N. H. Col., May, 1661, May, 1662, May, 1663, May, 1664.

N. H. Town I. 131, 480. II. 250. Conn. Col. II. 23. N. H. Col. II. 403, 451, 488, 543.

ALLYN, JOHN (d. 1696). Cornet, Conn. Col. Troop, Mar., 1658; first called Lieut., Oct., 1661. Deputy (Hartford) to Conn. Leg., Oct., 1661; Assistant, Conn. Col., May, 1662, Oct., 1662, May, 1663, May, 1664, May, 1665; Secretary, Conn. Col., May, 1663, May, 1664; Commissioner to treat with New Haven Colony, Mar., 1663, Aug., 1663.

Conn. Col. I. 309, 372, 378, 384, 396, 398, 406, 407, 425. II. 13.

ALLYN, MATTHEW (d. 1671). Deputy (Windsor) to Conn. Leg., May, 1648, Oct., 1648, May, 1649, Sept., 1649, May, 1650, Sept., 1650, May, 1651, Sept., 1651, Sept., 1654, May, 1655, Oct., 1655, May, 1656, Oct., 1656, Feb., 1657, Aug., 1657, Oct., 1657; Assistant, Conn. Col., May, 1658, May, 1659, May, 1660, May, 1661, May, 1662, Oct., 1662, May, 1663, May, 1664, May, 1665; Moderator, Conn. Col., May, 1660; Patentee, Royal Charter, 1662; Commissioner to treat with New Haven Colony, Oct., 1662, Mar., 1663; Commissioner for N. Y. Boundary, Oct., 1663; Commissioner for Mass. and R. I. Boundary, Oct., 1664; Commissioner to United Colonies, May, 1664; war committee for Windsor, Oct., 1654.

Conn. Col. I. 163, 167, 185, 195, 207, 211, 218, 224, 263, 264, 274, 278, 280, 282, 288, 300, 306, 314, 334, 347, 348, 365, 378, 384, 388, 396, 398, 410, 425, 430, 435. II. 4, 13.

ALLYN, THOMAS (d. 1688). Deputy (Middletown) to Conn. Leg., May, 1656.

Conn. Col. I. 281.

ANDREWS, WILLIAM (d. 1676). Sergt., New Haven Train Band, Aug., 1642; Sergt., Artillery Co., Mar., 1645; Lieut., Artillery Co., May, 1648.

N. H. Col. I. 76, 158, 382.

ASTWOOD, JOHN (d. 1654). First called Capt., July, 1646. Deputy (Milford) to N. H. Leg., Oct., 1643, Apr., 1644; Assistant, N. H. Col., Oct., 1646, May, 1653, May, 1654; Commissioner to United Colonies, May, 1653.

N. H. Col. I. 112, 129, 263, 275. II. 1, 91.

ATWATER, JOSHUA (d. 1676). Clerk, New Haven Train Band, Aug., 1642 (resigned July, 1644). Treasurer, N. H. Col., Oct., 1646, May, 1653, May, 1654; Judge (New Haven town), June, 1652, May, 1653, May, 1654. (Removed to Boston, Mass.)

N. H. Col. I. 75, 141, 275. II. 1, 92. N. H. Town I. 131, 180, 212.

AUGUR, NICHOLAS (d. 1676). Surgeon, N. H. Col. Troop, June, 1654. (Residence, New Haven.)

N. H. Col. II. 108.

AVERY, JAMES (d. 1700). First called Ensign, Oct., 1662; Lieut., New London Train Band, May, 1665. Deputy (New London) to Conn. Leg., May, 1659, Oct., 1660, Oct., 1661, May, 1664, Oct., 1664, May, 1665; Judge (New London town), Oct., 1663, May, 1664, May, 1665.

Conn. Col. I. 334, 354, 372, 385, 412, 425, 426, 431. II. 13, 17.

BACON, ANDREW (d. 1669). Deputy (Hartford) to Conn. Leg., Nov., 1637, Apr., 1642, Aug., 1642, Apr., 1643, Sept., 1643, Apr., 1644, Apr., 1646, May, 1647, Sept., 1647, May, 1648, Sept., 1648, May, 1649, Sept., 1649, May, 1650, Sept., 1650, May, 1651, Sept., 1651, May, 1652, Sept., 1652, May, 1653, Sept., 1653, May, 1654, Sept., 1654, May, 1655, Oct., 1655, May, 1656; war committee for Hartford, May, 1653, Oct., 1654.

Conn. Col. I. 11, 71, 73, 84, 93, 103, 138, 149, 157, 163, 166, 185, 195, 207, 211, 218, 224, 231, 235, 240, 243, 246, 256, 263, 264, 274, 278, 281.

BAKER, THOMAS (d. 1700). Assistant, Conn. Col., May, 1658, May, 1659, May, 1660, May, 1661, Oct., 1662, May, 1663. (Residence, Easthampton, L. I.)

Conn. Col. I. 314, 334, 347, 365, 384, 398.

BALDWIN, RICHARD (d. 1665). Ensign, N. H. Col. Troop, June, 1654. Deputy (Milford) to N. H. Leg., May, 1662, May, 1663, Oct., 1663, Jan., 1664; Judge (Derby village), Oct., 1655.

N. H. Col. II. 108, 157, 451, 477, 488, 500, 513.

BANKS, JOHN (d. 1685). Deputy (Fairfield) to Conn. Leg., Sept., 1651, May, 1661, Oct., 1663, May, 1664, Oct., 1664, May, 1665, Oct., 1665.

Conn. Col. I. 224, 365, 410, 425, 431. II. 13, 24.

BARNES, JOSHUA. Deputy (Easthampton) to Conn. Leg., May, 1663.
Conn. Col. I. 399.

BARNES, THOMAS (d. 1689). Served in Pequot War. Sergeant, Farmington Train Band, Oct., 1651.
Conn. Col. I. 227.

BARTLETT, GEORGE (d. 1669) Sergt., N. H. Col. Troop, June, 1654; Lieut., Guilford Train Band, July, 1665. Deputy (Guilford) to N. H. Leg., May, 1663, Oct., 1663, May, 1664. Deputy (Guilford) to Conn. Leg., May, 1665.
N. H. Col. II. 108, 488, 500, 544. Conn. Col. II. 14, 22.

BASSETT, ROBERT. Chief Drummer, N. H. Col. Troop, June, 1654. (Removed to Hempstead, L. I.)
N. H. Col. II. 108.

BEARDSLEY, WILLIAM (d. 1661). Deputy (Stratford) to Conn. Leg., Sept., 1645, Sept. 1649, May, 1650, Sept., 1651, May, 1652, Oct., 1653, Feb., 1657, May, 1658.
Conn. Col. I. 130, 195, 207, 224, 231, 248, 288, 315.

BECKLEY, RICHARD (d. 1690). Sergt. of New Haven Artillery Co., May, 1648. (Removed to Wethersfield.)
N. H. Col. I. 382.

BELL, ABRAHAM. Corporal, New Haven Train Band, July, 1644 (resigned Mar., 1645).
N. H. Col. I. 141, 160.

BELL, FRANCIS (d. 1690). Lieut., Stamford Train Band, May, 1655. Deputy (Stamford) to N. H. Leg., May, 1653, May, 1654, May, 1655, May, 1656, May, 1657, May, 1658, May, 1659, May, 1661, May, 1662, May, 1663, Jan., 1664, May, 1664; Judge (Stamford town), May, 1652, May, 1654, May, 1655, May, 1656, May, 1658, May, 1659, May, 1660, May, 1661, May, 1662, May, 1663.
N. H. Col. II. 2, 92, 96, 141, 145, 148, 169, 172, 214, 232, 235, 297, 304, 369, 403, 405, 451, 453, 488, 489, 513, 544.

BENEDICT, THOMAS (d. 1690). Judge (Jamaica town), May, 1664.
Conn. Col. I. 428.

BETTS, JOHN (d. 1690). Sergt., Wethersfield Train Band, May, 1657.
Conn. Col. I. 299.

BETTS, RICHARD (d. 1713). Judge (Newtown town), May, 1664.

Conn. Col. I. 428.

BISHOP, JAMES (d. 1691). Corporal, New Haven Train Band, Aug., 1657; Sergt., confirmed July, 1665 (resigned Aug. 1665). Deputy (New Haven) to N. H. Leg., Aug., 1661, May, 1662, Nov., 1662, May, 1663, Oct., 1663, Jan., 1664; Secretary, N. H. Col., May, 1661, May, 1662, May, 1663, May, 1664; Deputy (New Haven) to Conn. Leg., Apr., 1665, May, 1665, Oct., 1665; Judge (New Haven town), May, 1661, June, 1662, May, 1663, May, 1664, May, 1665.

N. H. Col. II. 403, 418, 451, 488, 500, 513, 543. N. H. Town I. 321, 484, 485, 521, 523. II. 15, 40, 45, 89, 140, 142, 145, 155. Conn. Col. I. 439. II. 13, 18, 23.

BISSELL, JOHN, SR. (d. 1677). Deputy (Windsor) to Conn. Leg., May, 1648, Sept., 1648, May, 1650, Sept., 1650, Sept., 1651, May, 1652, Sept., 1652, May, 1653, Sept., 1653, May, 1654, Sept., 1654, May, 1655, Oct., 1655, May, 1658, Oct., 1658, May, 1664.

Conn. Col. I. 163, 166, 207, 211, 224, 231, 235, 240, 246, 256, 264, 274, 278, 315, 323, 425.

BISSELL, SAMUEL (d. 1700). Deputy (Windsor) to Conn. Leg., Mar., 1656.

Conn. Col. I. 279.

BOARDMAN, SAMUEL (d. 1673). Deputy (Wethersfield) to Conn. Leg., Oct., 1657, May, 1658, Oct., 1658, May, 1659, Oct., 1659, May, 1660, Oct., 1660, May, 1661, Oct., 1661, May, 1662, Oct., 1662, May, 1663, Oct., 1663, May, 1664, Oct., 1664, May, 1665.

Conn. Col. I. 306, 315, 323, 334, 340, 347, 354, 365, 372, 378, 384, 399, 409, 425, 431. II. 13.

BOND, ROBERT. Assistant, Conn. Col., May, 1659, May, 1660, May, 1661; Judge (Easthampton town), May, 1663, May, 1664.

Conn. Col. I. 334, 347, 365, 400, 428.

BOOSY, JAMES (d. 1649). Clerk, Wethersfield Train Band, Apr., 1645; first called Lieut., Sept., 1647. Deputy (Wethersfield) to Conn. Leg., Apr., 1639, Aug., 1639, Jan., 1640, Apr., 1640, Feb., 1641, Apr., 1641, Apr., 1642, Sept., 1643, Apr., 1644, Sept., 1644, Apr., 1645, Sept., 1645, Apr., 1646, Oct., 1646, May, 1647, Sept., 1647, May, 1648, Sept., 1648, May, 1649.

Conn. Col. I. 27, 29, 34, 41, 46, 58, 64, 71, 93, 103, 111, 124, 125, 130, 138, 145, 149, 157, 163, 166, 185.

BOTSFORD, HENRY (d. 1686). Corporal, N. H. Col. Troop, June, 1654. (Residence, Milford.)
N. H. Col. II. 109.

BOYKIN, JARVIS (d. about 1660). Corporal, New Haven Train Band, May, 1652; Corporal, N. H. Col. Troop, June, 1654; Sergt., Train Band, Aug., 1657.
N. H. Town I. 127, 321. N. H. Col. II. 109.

BREWSTER, JONATHAN (d. 1659). Deputy (New London) to Conn. Leg., Sept., 1650, May, 1655, May, 1656, May, 1657, Oct., 1657, May, 1658, Oct. 1658; Judge (New London town), May, 1657.
Conn. Col. I. 211, 274, 281, 297, 298, 306, 315, 323.

BROCKETT, JOHN (d. 1690). Surgeon, N. H. Col. Troop, June, 1654. (Residence, New Haven.)
N. H. Col. II. 108.

BRONSON, JOHN (d. 1680). Served in Pequot War. Deputy (Farmington) to Conn. Leg., May, 1651, Oct., 1655, May, 1656, Oct., 1656.
Conn. Col. I. 218, 278, 281, 283.

BROWN, FRANCIS (d. after 1686). Deputy (Stamford) to Conn. Leg., May, 1665.
Conn. Col. II. 14.

BRUEN, OBADIAH. Patentee, Royal Charter, 1662; Dep. Judge (New London town), Apr., 1660, May, 1660; Judge (New London town), May, 1662, May, 1663, Oct., 1663, May, 1664, May, 1665; Deputy (New London) to Conn. Leg., Oct., 1665. (Removed to Newark.)
Conn. Col. I. 347, 352, 382, 402, 412, 426. II. 4, 17, 24.

BRYAN, ALEXANDER (d. 1679). First called Ensign (Milford Train Band), Feb., 1650; confirmed Ensign, July, 1665.
N. H. Town I. 2. Conn. Col. II. 21. See also N. H. Col. II. 28, 486, etc.

BUCKINGHAM, DANIEL. Confirmed Sergt., Milford Train Band, July, 1665.
Conn. Col. II. 21.

BUCKINGHAM, THOMAS (d. 1657). Deputy (Milford) to N. H. Leg., May, 1656.
N. H. Col. II. 169.

BUDD, JOHN (d. about 1684). Lieut., Southold Train Band, prior to May, 1654. Deputy (Southold) to N. H. Leg., May, 1657; Judge (Southold town), May, 1657. Deputy (Hastings) to Conn. Leg., Oct., 1664; Judge (Hastings town), Oct., 1663, (Hastings and Rye), Oct., 1664.
N. H. Col. II. 97, 214, 215. Conn. Col. I. 413, 431, 436.

BULL, THOMAS (d. 1684). Served in the Pequot War. First called Lieut., Oct., 1651; Lieut., Conn. Col. Troop, May, 1653.
Conn. Col. I. 228, 230, 242.

BURCHARD, THOMAS. Deputy (Saybrook) to Conn. Leg., May, 1650, May, 1651.
Conn. Col. I. 207, 218.

BURR, JEHU* (d. before 1673). Deputy (Springfield) to Conn. Leg., Apr., 1638, Sept., 1641; Deputy (Fairfield) to Conn. Leg., Sept., 1645, Apr., 1646.
Conn. Col. I. 17, 67, 130, 138.

BURR, JEHU* (d. 1692). Deputy (Fairfield) to Conn. Leg., Oct., 1659, Oct., 1660, May, 1661, May, 1663, Oct., 1663; Judge (Fairfield town), May, 1664.
Conn. Col. I. 340, 354, 365, 399, 410, 426.

BUSHNELL, WILLIAM (d. 1683). Sergt., Saybrook Train Band, Oct., 1661.
Conn. Col. I. 375.

BUTLER, RICHARD (d. 1684). Deputy (Hartford) to Conn. Leg., Oct., 1656, May, 1657, Oct., 1657, May, 1658, Oct., 1658, May, 1659, Oct., 1659, May, 1660.
Conn. Col. I. 282, 297, 306, 315, 323, 334, 340, 347.

* Some writers have attributed all public services of Jehu Burr through the year 1670 to the father, and thereafter to the son. This may have been the fact, for the records of service do not differentiate between them, and the services of the two men cannot be separated with certainty. The elder Jehu served for two terms after settling in Fairfield, but a long break in service occurs between 1646 and 1659; thereafter the name of Jehu appears with great regularity, continuing through the period when the elder Jehu died. It is surprising if the younger Jehu had no public service until his father died and then immediately leaped into prominence. We think it more likely that the elder Jehu did not serve after 1646 and that the younger Jehu began his service in 1659, at that date being at least 35 years of age.

CALKINS, HUGH (d. 1690). Deputy (New London) to Conn. Leg., May, 1652, May, 1653, Oct., 1653, May, 1654, Sept., 1654, May, 1656, Oct., 1656, Oct., 1657, May, 1658, May, 1659, May, 1660; Deputy (Norwich) to Conn. Leg., Mar., 1663, May, 1663, May, 1664, May, 1665; war committee for New London, May, 1653, Oct., 1654.

Conn. Col. I. 231, 240, 243, 248, 256, 264, 281, 283, 306, 315, 334, 347, 392, 399, 425. II. 14.

CANFIELD, MATTHEW (d. 1673). Deputy (Norwalk) to Conn. Leg., May, 1654, May, 1655, May, 1656, May, 1657, May, 1658, May, 1659, May, 1660, May, 1661, May, 1662, Oct., 1662, Oct., 1663, May, 1664, Oct., 1664, May, 1665, Oct., 1665; Patentee, Royal Charter, 1662; Judge (Norwalk town), May, 1654, May, 1655, May, 1656, May, 1657, May, 1661. (Removed to Newark, N. J.)

Conn. Col. I. 256, 257, 274, 281, 297, 300, 315, 334, 347, 365, 379, 384, 410, 425, 432. II. 4, 14, 24.

CHAPLIN, CLEMENT. Deputy (Wethersfield) to Conn. Leg., May, 1637, Mar., 1643, Apr., 1643, Sept., 1643; Treasurer, Conn. Col., Feb., 1638.

Conn. Col. I. 9, 12, 82, 84, 93.

CHAPMAN, ROBERT (d. 1687). Served in the Pequot War. Deputy (Saybrook) to Conn. Leg., Sept., 1652, May, 1653, Sept., 1653, Sept., 1654, Feb., 1657, Aug., 1657, Oct., 1657, May, 1658, Oct., 1658, May, 1659, Oct., 1659, May, 1660, Oct., 1660, Oct., 1661, May, 1662, Oct., 1662, May, 1663, Oct., 1663, Oct., 1664, May, 1665; Judge (Saybrook town), May, 1660, May, 1661, May, 1664, May, 1665; war committee for Saybrook, May, 1653, Oct., 1654.

Conn. Col. I. 235, 240, 243, 246, 264, 300, 306, 315, 323, 334, 340, 347, 351, 354, 365, 372, 379, 384, 399, 410, 426, 431. II. 14, 17. Lyon Gardiner's *Relation of the Pequot Wars.*

CHAPMAN, THOMAS.* Deputy (Saybrook) to Conn. Leg., May, 1652.

Conn. Col. I. 231.

* Error for Robert?

CHEEVER, EZEKIEL (d. 1708). Deputy (New Haven) to N. H. Leg., Apr., 1646, Oct., 1646. (Removed to Boston.)

N. H. Col. I. 227, 274.

CHENEY, WILLIAM (d. 1705). Deputy (Middletown) to Conn. Leg., May, 1660, Oct., 1660, May, 1662, Oct., 1663, Oct., 1664.
Conn. Col. I. 347, 354, 379, 410, 431.

CHESEBROUGH, SAMUEL (d. 1673). Deputy (Stonington) to Conn. Leg., May, 1665.
Conn. Col. II. 14.

CHESEBROUGH, WILLIAM (d. 1667). Deputy (New London) to Conn. Leg., May, 1653, Sept., 1653, Sept., 1654, May, 1655, Feb., 1657; Deputy (Stonington), Oct., 1664; Judge (Stonington town), Oct., 1664.
Conn. Col. I. 240, 246, 264, 274, 288, 432, 435.

CHESTER, JOHN (d. 1698). War committee for Windsor, May, 1653.
Conn. Col. I. 243.

CHITTENDEN, WILLIAM (d. 1661). Sergt., New Haven Artillery Co., May, 1648; first called Lieut., Oct., 1653. Deputy (Guilford) to N. H. Leg., May, 1653, May, 1654, May, 1655, May, 1656, May, 1657, May, 1658, May, 1659.
N. H. Col. I. 382. II. 2, 92, 141, 169, 214, 232, 297.

CLARK, DANIEL (d. 1710). Deputy (Windsor) to Conn. Leg., Oct., 1653, Oct., 1656, Feb., 1657, Aug., 1657, Oct., 1657, May, 1658, May, 1659, Oct., 1659, May, 1661; Assistant, Conn. Col., May, 1662, Oct., 1662, May, 1663, May, 1664; Secretary, Conn. Col., May, 1658, May, 1659, May, 1660, May, 1661, May, 1662, Oct., 1662, May, 1663 (removed), May, 1665; Patentee, Royal Charter, 1662; Commissioner to treat with N. H. Col., Aug., 1663; Commissioner on N. Y. Boundary, Oct., 1663. Lieut., Conn. Col. Troop, Mar., 1658; Capt. of same, May, 1664.
Conn. Col. I. 248, 282, 288, 300, 306, 309, 315, 334, 340, 347, 365, 378, 384, 398, 407, 410, 425, 429. II. 4, 13.

CLARK, GEORGE (DEA.) (d. 1690). Deputy (Milford) to N. H. Leg., May, 1664. Deputy (Milford) to Conn. Leg., Apr., 1665.
N. H. Col. II. 544. Conn. Col. I. 439.

CLARK, HENRY (d. about 1675). Deputy (Windsor) to Conn. Leg., Sept., 1641, Apr., 1642, Aug., 1642, Mar., 1643, Sept., 1644, Oct., 1646, May, 1647, Sept., 1647, Sept., 1648, May, 1649, Sept.,

1649; Assistant, Conn. Col., May, 1650, May, 1651, May, 1652, May, 1653, May, 1654, May, 1655, May, 1656 (erroneously called John), May, 1657, May, 1658, May, 1659, May, 1660, May, 1661; Patentee, Royal Charter, 1662; war committee for Windsor, May, 1653.

Conn. Col. I. 67, 71, 73, 82, 111, 145, 149, 157, 166, 185, 195, 207, 218, 231, 240, 243, 256, 265, 274, 280, 297, 314, 334, 347, 364. II. 4.

CLARK, JOHN (d. 1649). Probably served in the Pequot War.* Sergt., New Haven Train Band, Aug., 1642 (resigned July, 1644); Clerk of same, Feb., 1648.

N. H. Col. I. 76, 141, 370.

CLARK, JOHN (d. 1673). Probably served in the Pequot War;* war committee for Saybrook, May, 1653, Oct., 1654. Deputy (Saybrook) to Conn. Leg., May, 1649, May, 1651, Sept., 1651, May, 1652, May, 1653, Sept., 1653, July, 1654, Sept., 1654, May, 1655, May, 1656, Oct., 1656, Feb., 1657, Aug., 1657, Oct., 1657, May, 1658, Oct., 1658, May, 1659, Oct., 1659, May, 1661, Oct., 1661, May, 1662, Oct., 1662, May, 1663; Deputy (Milford) to Conn. Leg., Apr., 1665, May, 1665; Patentee, Royal Charter, 1662; Judge (Saybrook town), May, 1664; Judge (Milford town), May, 1665, Oct., 1665.

Conn. Col. I. 185, 218, 224, 231, 240, 243, 246, 261, 264, 274, 281, 282, 288, 300, 306, 315, 323, 334, 340, 365, 372, 379, 384, 399, 426, 439. II. 4, 13, 17, 23.

COE, JOHN (d. about 1693). Judge (Newtown town), May, 1664; called Capt. same date.

Conn. Col. I. 428.

* It is certain that John Clark of Hartford served in the Pequot War, for he had a lot in Soldiers' Field. This man cannot be identified with the New Haven John, as he was still living in Hartford after the other man had settled in New Haven. He would have been somewhat too old to permit of identification with John of Farmington. Some have identified him with Elder John Clark of Saybrook and Milford, and this identification seems to be possible.

Stiles states that John Clark of Wethersfield served in the Pequot War. No proof of this has been found, and it is doubtful whether proof exists. The Wethersfield man left there early enough to permit us to identify him with John of New Haven, and he was probably the man who acted as interpreter in negotiating the purchase of New Haven from the Indians in 1638. The fact that he was appointed Sergt. of the New Haven Train Band as early as 1642 suggests the probability that he saw service in the Pequot War, as it was natural to give this post to one who had had active service, and several veterans were available. His knowledge of the Indian language points in the same direction.

For the research which enables us to arrive at these deductions, we are indebted to Mrs. Clarence F. Hand, of Philadelphia, Pa.

COE, ROBERT (d. 1672). Dep. Judge (Stamford town), Apr., 1643; Deputy (Stamford) to N. H. Leg., Apr., 1644; Judge (Jamaica town), May, 1664.
N. H. Col. I. 85, 129. Conn. Col. I. 428.

COLE, JOHN (d. 1685). Deputy (Farmington) to Conn. Leg., Oct., 1653, May, 1654.
Conn. Col. I. 248, 256.

COLEMAN, THOMAS (d. 1674). Deputy (Wethersfield) to Conn. Leg., Oct., 1650, May, 1651, May, 1652, Sept., 1652, May, 1653, Sept., 1653, May, 1654, Sept., 1654, Oct., 1655, May, 1656; war committee for Wethersfield, Oct., 1654.
Conn. Col. I. 212, 218, 231, 235, 240, 246, 256, 264, 278, 281.

COOKE, AARON (d. 1690). Lieut. (Commanding), Conn. Col. Troop, May, 1653; called Capt., Mar., 1658.
Conn. Col. I. 242, 309.

COOKE, THOMAS (d. 1692). Deputy (Guilford) to Conn. Leg., Apr., 1665.
Conn. Col. I. 439.

COOPER, JOHN (d. 1689). Corporal, N. H. Col. Troop, June, 1654. Deputy (New Haven) to N. H. Leg., May, 1661, Aug., 1661, May, 1662, Nov., 1662. Deputy (New Haven) to Conn. Leg., Apr., 1665, Oct., 1665. Judge (New Haven town), May, 1661.
N. H. Col. II. 109, 403, 418, 451. Conn. Col. I. 439. II. 23. N. H. Town I. 484, 485, 521. II. 15, 137, 140, 155.

CORNWALL, WILLIAM (d. 1678). Served in the Pequot War. Deputy (Middletown) to Conn. Leg., May, 1654, Oct., 1664; called Sergt. on the latter date.
Conn. Col. I. 256, 431.

COSMORE, JOHN. Assistant, Conn. Col., May, 1647, May, 1648, May, 1649, May, 1650, May, 1655, May, 1657, May, 1658.
Conn. Col. I. 149, 163, 185, 207, 274, 297, 314.

CRABBE, RICHARD (d. about 1680). Deputy (Wethersfield) to Conn. Leg., Apr., 1639, Jan., 1640, Apr., 1640, Feb., 1641, Apr., 1641.
Conn. Col. I. 27, 41, 46, 58, 64.

CRANE, JASPER (d. 1681). Deputy (New Haven) to N. H. Leg., May, 1648, May, 1649, Sept., 1649, May, 1650; Deputy (Branford) to N. H. Leg., May, 1653, May, 1654, May, 1655, May, 1656, May, 1657; Judge (New Haven town), Oct., 1645, Oct., 1646, Oct., 1647, May, 1648, May, 1649, May, 1650; Judge (Branford town), May, 1654, May, 1655, May, 1656, May, 1657; Assistant, N. H. Col., May, 1658, May, 1659, May, 1660, May, 1661, May, 1662, May, 1663, May, 1664; Assistant (provisional appointment, Conn. Col.), Oct., 1664; Assistant, Conn. Col., May, 1665.

N. H. Col. I. 173, 274, 354, 381, 456, 481. II. 2, 92, 96, 141, 148, 169, 172, 214, 215, 231, 297, 359, 402, 451, 488, 543. Conn. Col. I. 437. II. 13. N. H. Town I. 21.

CULLICK, JOHN (d. 1663). Served in the Pequot War. Deputy (Hartford) to Conn. Leg., Sept., 1644, Oct., 1646, May, 1647; Assistant, Conn. Col., May, 1648, May, 1649, May, 1650, May, 1651, May, 1652, May, 1653, May, 1654, May, 1655, May, 1656, May, 1657; Secretary, Conn. Col., May, 1648, May, 1649, May, 1650, May, 1652, May, 1654, May, 1655, May, 1656, May, 1657; Commissioner to United Colonies, May, 1652, May, 1653, June, 1654, May, 1655. First called Capt., May, 1653.

Conn. Col. I. 111, 145, 149, 163, 185, 207, 218, 231, 233, 240, 241, 256, 274, 280, 297.

DAVENPORT, JOHN, JR. (d. 1676). Judge (New Haven town), Nov., 1660, May, 1661 (declined), June 1662, May, 1663, May, 1664.

N. H. Town I. 463, 484, 523. II. 45, 89.

DEMING, JOHN (d. 1705). Deputy (Wethersfield) to Conn. Leg., Dec., 1645, Oct., 1646, Sept., 1649, May, 1650, May, 1651, Sept., 1651, May, 1652, Sept., 1652, Oct., 1653, May, 1655, Oct., 1656, Feb., 1657, May, 1657, May, 1658, Oct., 1658, May, 1659, Oct., 1659, May, 1660, Oct., 1660, May, 1661, Oct., 1661; Patentee, Royal Charter, 1662.

Conn. Col. I. 133, 145, 195, 207, 218, 224, 231, 235, 248, 274, 282, 288, 297, 315, 323, 334, 340, 347, 354, 365, 372. II. 4.

DENISON, GEORGE (d. 1694). Deputy (New London) to Conn. Leg., Sept., 1653, May, 1654, Feb., 1657. First called Capt., May, 1653; war committee for New London, May, 1653, Oct., 1654.

Conn. Col. I. 243, 246, 256, 264, 288.

DICKERMAN, ABRAHAM (d. 1711). Corporal, New Haven Train Band, July, 1665.
N. H. Town II. 144.

DICKINSON, JOHN (d. 1676). Sergt., Wethersfield Train Band, May, 1657. (Removed to Hadley.)
Conn. Col. I. 299.

DICKINSON, NATHANIEL (d. 1676). Deputy (Wethersfield) to Conn. Leg., Apr., 1646, Oct., 1646, May, 1647, Sept., 1647, May, 1648, Dec., 1648, May, 1649, Sept., 1649, May, 1650, Sept., 1650, May, 1651, Sept., 1651, May, 1652, Sept., 1652, May, 1653, Sept., 1653, Sept., 1654, May, 1655, Oct., 1655, May, 1656; war committee for Wethersfield, May, 1653, Oct., 1654. (Removed to Hadley.)
Conn. Col. I. 138, 145, 149, 157, 163, 170, 185, 195, 207, 211, 218, 224, 231, 235, 240, 243, 246, 264, 274, 278, 281.

DISBOROUGH, PETER. Deputy (Rye) to Conn. Leg., May, 1665.
Conn. Col. II. 14.

DISBOROUGH, SAMUEL (d. 1690). Deputy (Guilford) to N. H. Leg., Oct., 1643; Assistant, N. H. Col., Oct., 1646. (Returned to England.)
N. H. Col. I. 112, 275.

DOOLITTLE, ABRAHAM (d. 1690). Corporal, New Haven Train Band, Aug., 1657; Sergt. of same, July, 1665. Marshal, N. H. Col., May, 1662, May, 1663, May, 1664.
N. H. Town I. 321. II. 144. N. H. Col. II. 451, 488, 543.

DRAKE, SAMUEL (d. 1691). Deputy (Fairfield) to Conn. Leg., Oct., 1662.
Conn. Col. I. 384.

EAST, WILLIAM. Sergt., Milford Train Band, prior to May, 1654.
N. H. Col. II. 90.

EATON, SAMUEL. Assistant, N. H. Col., May, 1654, May, 1655; Judge (Southold town), May, 1655.
N. H. Col. II, 91, 140, 143.

EATON, THEOPHILUS (d. 1658). Chief Magistrate (New Haven town), Oct., 1639, Oct., 1640, Oct., 1641, Oct., 1642; Governor, N. H. Col., Oct., 1643, Oct., 1646, May, 1653, May, 1654, May, 1655, May, 1656, May, 1657; Commissioner to United Colonies, Apr., 1643, July, 1643, Oct., 1643, Oct., 1646, May, 1653, July, 1654, May, 1655, May, 1656, May, 1657. (He was Governor from 1643 until his death, Jan., 1658.)

N. H. Col. I. 21, 44, 58, 78, 87, 96, 112, 117, 275. II. 1, 91, 111, 140, 168, 213.

EDWARDS, JOHN (d. 1664). Deputy (Wethersfield) to Conn. Leg., Apr., 1643.

Conn. Col. I. 84.

ELCOCK, ANTHONY (d. 1672). Second Drummer, N. H. Col. Troop, June, 1654.

N. H. Col. II. 108.

ELY, NATHANIEL. Deputy (Norwalk) to Conn. Leg., Feb., 1657. (Removed to Springfield, Mass.)

Conn. Col. I. 288.

EVANCE, JOHN. Judge (New Haven town), Oct., 1643, Mar., 1644, Oct., 1644, Mar., 1645, Oct., 1645. (Returned to England.)

N. H. Col. I. 119, 125, 148, 156, 171.

FAIRCHILD, THOMAS (d. 1670). Deputy (Stratford) to Conn. Leg., Apr., 1646, Sept., 1654, May, 1655, Oct., 1655, Oct., 1658, May, 1659, Oct., 1659, May, 1660, May, 1664, Oct., 1664, Oct., 1665; Judge (Stratford town), May, 1664; war committee for Stratford, Oct., 1654.

Conn. Col. I. 138, 264, 274, 278, 323, 334, 340, 347, 425, 426, 431. II. 24.

FENN, BENJAMIN (d. 1672). Deputy (Milford) to N. H. Leg., May, 1653; Assistant, N. H. Col., May, 1654, May, 1655, May, 1656, May, 1657, May, 1658, May, 1661, May, 1662, May, 1663, May, 1664; Commissioner to United Colonies, May, 1661, May, 1662, May, 1663; Assistant (provisional appointment, Conn. Col.), Oct., 1664; Assistant, Conn. Col., May, 1665.

N. H. Col. II. 2, 91, 140, 168, 213, 231, 402, 451, 488, 543. Conn. Col. I. 437. II. 13.

FENWICK, GEORGE (d. 1657). Assistant, Conn. Col., Apr., 1644, Apr., 1645, May, 1647, May, 1648; Commissioner to United Colonies, July, 1643, Apr., 1644, July, 1645. (Returned to England.)

Conn. Col. I. 90 (footnote), 103, 104, 124, 128, 149, 163.

FERMAN, ROBERT. Judge (Oyster Bay town), May, 1664.
Conn. Col. I. 428.

FITCH, JOSEPH (d. 1693 or later). Deputy (Hartford) to Conn. Leg., May, 1662, Oct., 1662, May, 1663, Oct., 1663, May, 1664, Oct., 1664, May, 1665, Oct., 1665.
Conn. Col. I. 378, 384, 399, 409, 425, 431. II. 13, 23.

FITCH, SAMUEL (d. about 1656). Deputy (Hartford) to Conn. Leg., May, 1654, Sept. 1654, Oct. 1655.
Conn. Col. I. 256, 264, 278.

FITCH, THOMAS (d. 1704). Clerk, Norwalk Train Band, Feb., 1657; Ensign of same, May, 1665.
Conn. Col. I. 290. II. 14.

FLETCHER, JOHN. Deputy (Milford) to N. H. Leg., May, 1659, May, 1661.
N. H. Col. II. 297, 403.

FOOTE, NATHANIEL (d. 1644). Deputy (Wethersfield) to Conn. Leg., Sept., 1641, Nov., 1641, Apr., 1644.
Conn. Col. I. 67, 69, 103.

FORD, THOMAS (d. 1676). Deputy (Windsor) to Conn. Leg., Mar., 1638, Apr., 1638, Apr., 1639, Apr., 1640, Apr., 1641, Apr., 1644, May, 1654.
Conn. Col. I. 13, 17, 27, 46, 64, 103, 256.

FOWLER, JOHN (d. 1676). Deputy (Guilford) to N. H. Leg., May, 1661, Jan., 1664, May, 1664; to Conn. Leg., Apr., 1665, May, 1665. Sergt., Guilford Train Band, July, 1665.
N. H. Col. II. 403, 513, 544. Conn. Col. I. 439. II. 14, 22.

FOWLER, WILLIAM (d. 1661). Assistant, N. H. Col., Oct., 1643, Oct., 1646, May, 1653; Deputy (Milford) to N. H. Leg., May, 1657.
N. H. Col. I. 112, 275. II. 1, 213.

FOWLER, WILLIAM, JR. (d. 1683). Sergt., New Haven Train Band, May, 1647; Sergt., Artillery Co., May, 1648.
N. H. Col. I. 313, 382.

FOWLES, RICHARD. Deputy (Greenwich) to Conn. Leg., Oct., 1665.
Conn. Col. II. 24.

FUGILL, THOMAS. Judge (New Haven town), Oct., 1639; Secretary, N. H. Col., Oct., 1643. (Returned to England.)
N. H. Col. I. 20, 112.

FYLER, WALTER (d. 1683). Deputy (Windsor) to Conn. Leg., Oct., 1661, May, 1663, Oct., 1663; called Sergt., Oct., 1642; first called Lieut., Oct., 1661.

Conn. Col. I. 76, 372, 399, 409.

GALLOP, JOHN (d. 1675). Served in the Pequot War. Deputy (Stonington) to Conn. Leg., Oct., 1665.

Conn. Col. II. 24.

GAYLORD, WILLIAM (d. 1673). Deputy (Windsor) to Conn. Leg., Apr., 1639, Sept., 1639, Jan., 1640, Apr., 1640, Feb., 1641, Apr., 1641, Nov., 1641, Apr., 1642, Aug., 1642, Mar., 1643, Apr., 1643, Sept., 1643, Apr., 1644, Sept., 1644, Apr., 1645, Sept., 1645, Apr., 1646, Sept., 1647, May, 1649, Sept., 1649, May, 1650, May, 1651, May, 1652, Sept., 1652, May, 1653, Sept., 1653, Sept., 1654, May, 1655, May, 1656, Oct., 1656, May, 1657, Oct., 1657, May, 1658, Oct., 1658, May, 1659, Oct., 1659, May, 1660, Oct., 1660, May, 1661, Oct., 1661, May, 1662, May, 1664.

Conn. Col. I. 27, 34, 41, 46, 58, 64, 69, 71, 73, 82, 84, 93, 103, 111, 124, 130, 138, 157, 185, 195, 207, 218, 231, 235, 240, 246, 264, 274, 280, 282, 297, 306, 315, 323, 334, 340, 347, 353, 365, 372, 378, 425.

GIBBARD, WILLIAM (d. 1663). Deputy (New Haven) to N. H. Leg., May, 1652, May, 1653, May, 1654, May, 1655, May, 1656, May, 1657, May, 1658; Secretary, N. H. Col., May, 1658, May, 1659, May, 1660; Assistant, N. H. Col., May, 1661 (declined), May, 1662; Judge (New Haven town), Mar., 1645, Oct., 1645, Oct., 1646, Oct., 1647, May, 1648, May, 1649, May, 1650, May, 1651, May, 1652, May, 1653, May, 1654, May, 1655, May, 1656, May, 1657, May, 1658, May, 1659, May, 1660, Oct., 1661.

N. H. Col. I. 156, 171, 274, 354, 381, 456. II. 2, 92, 141, 169, 213, 231, 297, 360, 402, 451. N. H. Town I. 21, 72, 127, 180, 212, 240, 277, 313, 353, 402, 453, 489.

GIBBS, JOHN (d. 1690). Deputy (Wethersfield) to Conn. Leg., Mar., 1638. Judge (New Haven town), Oct., 1646, Oct., 1647.

Conn. Col. I. 13. N. H. Col. I. 274, 354.

GILBERT, JONATHAN (d. 1682). Indian Interpreter, Conn. Leg., Apr., 1646; Marshal, Conn. Col., May, 1662, May, 1663, May, 1664.

Conn. Col. I. 139, 382, 401, 430.

GILBERT, MATTHEW (d. 1680). Judge (New Haven town), Oct., 1639, Oct., 1640, May, 1641, Oct., 1641, Apr., 1642, Oct., 1642, Apr., 1643; Assistant, N. H. Col., May, 1658, May, 1659, May, 1660, May, 1664; Dep. Governor, N. H. Col., May, 1661, May, 1662, May, 1663. Assistant (provisional appointment, Conn. Col.), Oct., 1664; Judge (New Haven town), May, 1665.
N. H. Col. I. 21, 44, 51, 58, 69, 78, 85. II. 231, 297, 359, 402, 451, 488, 543. Conn. Col. I. 437. II. 18.

GILDERSLEEVE, RICHARD. Deputy (Stamford) to N. H. Leg., Apr., 1643, Oct., 1643. Judge (Hempstead town), May, 1664.
N. H. Col. I. 85, 112. Conn. Col. I. 428.

GISHOP, EDWARD. See Jessup.

GLOVER, CHARLES. Acting Lieut., Southold Train Band, May, 1654; Lieut. of same, May, 1661.
N. H. Col. II. 97, 407.

GOLD, NATHAN (d. 1694). First called Ensign, May, 1656; Lieut., Fairfield Train Band, May, 1657. Judge (Fairfield town), May, 1656, May, 1657; Assistant, Conn. Col., May, 1657, May, 1659, May, 1660, May, 1661, May, 1662, Oct., 1662, May, 1663, May, 1664, May, 1665; Patentee, Royal Charter, 1662.
Conn. Col. I. 281, 297, 299, 300, 334, 347, 364, 378, 384, 398, 425. II. 4, 13.

GOODRICH, WILLIAM (d. 1676). Served in the Pequot War; Ensign, Wethersfield Train Band, May, 1665. Deputy (Wethersfield) to Conn. Leg., May, 1660, Oct., 1660, May, 1662, Oct, 1665.
Conn. Col. I. 347, 354, 379. II. 17, 24.

GOODYEAR, STEPHEN (d. 1658). Judge (New Haven town), May, 1641; Dep. Magistrate (New Haven town), Oct., 1641, Oct., 1642; Dep. Governor, N. H. Col., Oct., 1643, Oct., 1646, May, 1653, May, 1654, May, 1655, May, 1656, May, 1657; Commissioner to United Colonies, Oct., 1646. (He was Dep. Governor from 1643 to the end of the 1657 term.)
N. H. Col. I. 51, 58, 78, 112, 275. II. 1, 91, 140, 168, 213.

GRAVES, GEORGE, JR. (d. 1692). Deputy (Middletown) to Conn. Leg., Feb., 1657, Oct., 1657, May, 1658, Oct., 1658.
Conn. Col. I. 288, 306, 315, 323.

GRAY, HENRY (d. 1658). Deputy (Fairfield) to Conn. Leg., Apr., 1643, Oct., 1656, Feb., 1657.

Conn. Col. I. 84, 282, 288.

GREGORY, JOHN (d. 1689). Deputy (Norwalk) to Conn. Leg., Oct., 1659, Oct., 1662, May, 1663, May, 1665.

Conn. Col. I. 340, 384, 399. II. 14.

GREGSON, THOMAS (d. 1647). Judge (New Haven town), Oct., 1640, May, 1641, Oct., 1641, Apr., 1642, Oct., 1642, Apr., 1643; Assistant, N. H. Col., Oct., 1643, Oct., 1646; Commissioner to United Colonies, Apr., 1643, July, 1643, Oct., 1643; Colonial Agent to Parliament, Nov., 1644.

N. H. Col. I. 44, 51, 58, 69, 78, 85, 87, 96, 112, 117, 149, 211, 275.

GRISWOLD, EDWARD (d. 1691). Deputy (Windsor) to Conn. Leg., May, 1656, May, 1658, Oct., 1658, May, 1659, Oct., 1659, May, 1660, Oct., 1660, May, 1662, Oct., 1662.

Conn. Col. I. 281, 315, 323, 334, 340, 347, 353, 378, 384.

GRISWOLD, FRANCIS (d. 1671). Deputy (Norwich) to Conn. Leg., Oct., 1664, May, 1665, Oct., 1665.

Conn. Col. I. 431. II. 14, 24.

GRISWOLD, MATTHEW (d. 1699). Deputy (Saybrook) to Conn. Leg., May, 1649, May, 1650, May, 1654, May, 1660.

Conn. Col. I. 185, 207, 256, 347.

GROVES, PHILIP (d. 1676). Deputy (Stratford) to Conn. Leg., Apr., 1642, May, 1648, May, 1651, May, 1653, May, 1654, May, 1655, Oct., 1655, Feb., 1657, May, 1660, Oct., 1660, May, 1661, Oct., 1661, Oct., 1662, May, 1663, Oct., 1663, May, 1665; Judge (Stratford), May, 1654, May, 1655, May, 1656; war committee for Stratford, May, 1653, Oct., 1654.

Conn. Col. I. 71, 163, 218, 240, 243, 256, 257, 264, 274, 278, 281, 288, 347, 354, 365, 372, 384, 399, 410. II. 13.

GUNN, JASPER (d. 1671). Deputy (Milford) to N. H. Leg., May, 1663.

N. H. Col. II. 477.

HALE, SAMUEL (d. 1691). Served in the Pequot War. Deputy (Norwalk) to Conn. Leg., Oct., 1656, Feb., 1657, Oct., 1657, May, 1660, Oct., 1660; Deputy (Wethersfield), May, 1665.

Conn. Col. I. 283, 288, 306, 347, 354. II. 13.

HALL, FRANCIS (d. 1690). Deputy (Stratford) to Conn. Leg., May, 1661.

Conn. Col. I. 365.

HALL, JOHN, JR. (d. 1695). Deputy (Middletown) to Conn. Leg., May, 1653.
Conn. Col. I. 240.

HALLETT, WILLIAM. Judge (Flushing town), May, 1664.
Conn. Col. I. 428.

HALSEY, THOMAS, SR. Deputy (Southampton) to Conn. Leg., May, 1664.
Conn. Col. I. 425.

HARRIS, GABRIEL (d. 1684). Ensign, New London Train Band, May, 1665.
Conn. Col. II. 17.

HART, JOHN (d. 1666). Deputy (Farmington) to Conn. Leg., May, 1659, Oct., 1659.
Conn. Col. I. 334, 340.

HART, STEPHEN (d. 1683). Served in the Pequot War. Deputy (Farmington) to Conn. Leg., May, 1647, May, 1648, May, 1649, Sept., 1649, May, 1650, Sept., 1650, May, 1651, Sept., 1651, Sept., 1652, May, 1653, Sept., 1653, Sept., 1654, May, 1655, May, 1660; war committee for Farmington, May, 1653.
Conn. Col. I. 149, 163, 185, 195, 207, 211, 218, 224, 235, 240, 243, 246, 264, 274, 347.

HARVEY, EDMUND (d. 1648). Deputy (Fairfield) to Conn. Leg., May, 1647.
Conn. Col. I. 149.

HAWLEY, JOSEPH (d. 1690). Deputy (Stratford) to Conn. Leg., May, 1658, Oct., 1665.
Conn. Col. I. 315. II. 24.

HAYNES, JOHN (d. 1653). Commissioner to Saybrook, Pequot War, June, 1637; Assistant, Conn. Col., Nov., 1637, Feb., 1638, Mar., 1638, Apr., 1638, Apr., 1642, May, 1648; Governor, Conn. Col., Apr., 1639, Apr., 1641, Apr., 1643, Apr., 1645, May, 1647, May, 1649, May, 1651, May, 1653; Dep. Governor, Conn. Col., Apr., 1640, Apr., 1644, Apr., 1646, May, 1650, May, 1652; Commissioner to United Colonies, Mar., 1643, Apr., 1646.
Conn. Col. I. 10, 11, 13, 17, 27, 46, 64, 71, 82, 84, 103, 124, 137, 139, 149, 163, 185, 207, 218, 230, 240.

HICKS, JOHN. Judge (Hempstead town), May, 1664.
Conn. Col. I. 428.

HILL, WILLIAM (d. 1649). Deputy (Windsor) to Conn. Leg., Aug., 1639, Sept., 1639, Jan., 1640, Feb., 1641, Sept., 1641, Nov., 1641, Apr., 1642, Aug., 1642, Mar., 1643, Sept., 1643, Apr., 1644, Sept., 1644.

Conn. Col. I. 29, 34, 41, 58, 67, 69, 71, 73, 82, 93, 103, 111.

HILL, WILLIAM (d. 1684). Deputy (Fairfield) to Conn. Leg., Sept., 1651, May, 1652, Oct., 1652, May, 1653, May, 1654, Sept., 1654, May, 1655, Oct., 1655, Oct., 1658, Oct., 1659, Oct., 1661, Oct., 1665; war committee for Fairfield, May, 1653.

Conn. Col. I. 224, 231, 235, 240, 243, 256, 264, 274, 278, 323, 340, 372. II. 24.

HOLLISTER, JOHN (d. 1665). Deputy (Wethersfield) to Conn. Leg., Sept., 1644, Apr., 1645, Sept., 1645, Dec., 1645, May, 1650, Oct., 1653, May, 1654, Sept., 1654, May, 1655, Oct., 1656, Feb., 1657, Oct., 1657, May, 1658, Oct., 1658, May, 1659, Oct., 1661. First called Lieut., Apr., 1657; war committee for Wethersfield, Oct., 1654.

Conn. Col. I. 111, 124, 130, 133, 207, 248, 256, 264, 274, 282, 288, 293, 306, 315, 323, 334, 372.

HOLLY, JOHN. Judge (Stamford town), May, 1654, May, 1655; Deputy (Stamford) to N. H. Leg., May, 1663.

N. H. Col. II. 96, 148, 477.

HOOKER, SAMUEL, REV. (d. 1697). Commissioner to treat with New Haven Colony, Oct., 1662.

Conn. Col. I. 388.

HOPKINS, EDWARD (d. 1657). Deputy (Hartford) to Conn. Leg., Mar., 1638, Apr., 1638; Assistant, Conn. Col., Apr., 1639, Apr., 1641, Apr., 1642, May, 1655, May, 1656; Secretary, Conn. Col., Apr., 1639; Governor, Conn. Col., Apr., 1640, Apr., 1644, Apr., 1646, May, 1648, May, 1650, May, 1652, May, 1654; Dep. Governor, Conn. Col., Apr., 1643, Apr., 1645, May, 1647, May, 1649, May, 1651, May, 1653; Commissioner to United Colonies, Mar., 1643, July, 1643, Apr., 1644, July, 1645, Apr., 1646, Jan., 1647, May, 1648, May, 1649, May, 1651. (Returned to England.)

Conn. Col. I. 13, 17, 27, 46, 64, 71, 82, 84, 90, 103, 104, 124, 128, 137, 139, 147, 149, 163, 164, 185, 187, 207, 218, 222, 230, 240, 256, 274, 280.

HOPKINS, WILLIAM. Assistant, Conn. Col., Apr., 1641, Apr., 1642.

Conn. Col. I. 64, 71.

HORTON, BARNABAS. Deputy (Southold) to N. H. Leg., May, 1654, May, 1656, May, 1658, May, 1659, May, 1661; Judge (Southold town), May, 1654, May, 1656, May, 1658, May, 1659, May, 1663, May, 1664.
N. H. Col. II. 92, 95, 169, 172, 232, 236, 298, 304, 403. Conn. Col. I. 402, 428.

HOSFORD, WILLIAM. Deputy (Windsor) to Conn. Leg., May, 1637, Sept., 1652. (Returned to England.)
Conn. Col. I. 9, 235.

HOWELL, EDWARD (d. 1656). Assistant, Conn. Col., May, 1647, May, 1648, May, 1649, May, 1650, May, 1651, May, 1652, May, 1653.
Conn. Col. I. 149, 163, 185, 207, 218, 231, 240.

HOWELL, JOHN (d. 1696). Deputy (Southampton) to Conn. Leg., Oct., 1662; Assistant, Conn. Col., May, 1664.
Conn. Col. I. 384, 425.

HOWKINS, ANTHONY (d. 1674). Deputy (Farmington) to Conn. Leg., Oct., 1657, May, 1658, May, 1660, Oct., 1660, May, 1661, Oct., 1661, May, 1662, Oct., 1662, May, 1663, Oct., 1663, May, 1664, Oct., 1664, May, 1665, Oct., 1665; Patentee, Royal Charter, 1662; Judge (Farmington town), May, 1663, May, 1664.
Conn. Col. I. 306, 315, 347, 354, 365, 372, 379, 384, 399, 401, 410, 425, 426, 431. II. 4, 14, 24.

HOYT, WALTER (d. 1699). Deputy (Norwalk) to Conn. Leg., Oct., 1658, Oct., 1659, Oct., 1661. Sergt., Norwalk Train Band, May, 1659.
Conn. Col. I. 323, 336, 340, 372.

HUBBARD, GEORGE (d. 1683). Deputy (Wethersfield) to Conn. Leg., Mar., 1638, Apr., 1638, Apr., 1639, Aug., 1639, Sept., 1639, Apr., 1640, Feb., 1641, Apr., 1641, Apr., 1642, Aug., 1642. Deputy (Guilford) to N. H. Leg., May, 1655, May, 1657, May, 1658, May, 1659, Aug., 1661, May, 1662; Deputy (Guilford) to Conn. Leg., Oct., 1665; Judge (Guilford town), May, 1665.
Conn. Col. I. 13, 17, 27, 29, 34, 46, 58, 64, 71, 73. II. 18, 24. N. H. Col. II. 141, 214, 232, 297, 418, 451.

HUBBARD, JAMES. Judge (Gravesend town), May, 1664.
Conn. Col. I. 429.

HULL, CORNELIUS (d. 1695). Deputy (Fairfield) to Conn. Leg., Feb., 1657, May, 1658, May, 1659, May, 1660, Oct., 1660, Oct., 1662, May, 1663, Oct., 1664.
Conn. Col. I. 288, 315, 334, 347, 354, 384, 399, 431.

HULL, GEORGE (d. 1659). Deputy (Windsor) to Conn. Leg., May, 1637, Nov., 1637, Mar., 1638, Apr., 1638, Aug., 1639, Sept., 1639, Jan., 1640, Apr., 1640, Feb., 1641, Apr., 1641, Sept., 1641, Nov., 1641, Apr., 1642, Aug., 1642, Mar., 1643, Apr., 1643, Sept., 1643, Apr., 1644, Sept., 1644, Sept., 1645, Dec., 1645, Apr., 1646; Deputy (Fairfield), May, 1649, May, 1650, May, 1651, Oct., 1655, May, 1656; Judge (Fairfield town), May, 1654.
Conn. Col. I. 9, 11, 13, 17, 29, 34, 41, 46, 58, 64, 67, 69, 71, 73, 82, 84, 93, 103, 111, 130, 133, 138, 185, 207, 218, 257, 278, 281.

HULL, JOSIAS (d. 1675). Deputy (Windsor) to Conn. Leg., May, 1659, Oct., 1659, May, 1660, Oct., 1662.
Conn. Col. I. 334, 340, 347, 384.

HUNT, THOMAS. Deputy (Rye?) to Conn. Leg., Oct., 1664.
Conn. Col. I. 431.

HURD, JOHN (d. 1682). Deputy (Stratford) to Conn. Leg., May, 1649, May, 1656, Oct., 1656, Oct., 1657.
Conn. Col. I. 185, 281, 283, 306.

HURLBUT, THOMAS (d. in or after 1682). Served in the Pequot War; Clerk, Wethersfield Train Band, June, 1649.
Conn. Col. I. 189.

JEFFREYS, THOMAS (d. 1661). Sergt., New Haven Train Band, Aug., 1642; Sergt., Artillery Co., Mar., 1645; Sergt. with Lieut. Seeley against Ninigret, Oct., 1654.
N. H. Col. I. 76, 158. II. 120.

JESSUP, EDWARD (d. 1666). Judge (Westchester town), Oct., 1663, May, 1664; Deputy (Westchester) to Conn. Leg., May, 1664.
Conn. Col. I. 412 (called Gishop), 425 (called John), 426.

JOHNSON, WILLIAM (d. 1702). Sergt., Guilford Train Band, July, 1665. Deputy (Guilford) to Conn. Leg., Oct., 1665.
Conn. Col. II. 22, 24.

JONES, WILLIAM (d. 1706). Assistant, N. H. Col., May, 1662, May, 1663; Dep. Governor, N. H. Col., May, 1664; Commissioner to United Colonies, May, 1664; Commissioner to treat with Conn. Col., May, 1664; Assistant (provisional appointment, Conn. Col.), Oct., 1664; Assistant, Conn. Col., May, 1665; Judge (New Haven town), May, 1665.
N. H. Col. II. 451, 488, 542, 543. Conn. Col. I. 437. II. 13, 18.

JORDAN, THOMAS. Deputy (Guilford) to N. H. Leg., May, 1653, May, 1654; Commissioner to Mass. Col., June, 1653, June, 1654. (Returned to England.)
N. H. Col. II. 2, 5, 92, 101.

JUDD, THOMAS (d. 1688). Deputy (Farmington) to Conn. Leg., May, 1647, May, 1648, May, 1649, Sept., 1650, Nov., 1650, Sept., 1651, Feb., 1657, Oct., 1658, Oct., 1659, May, 1661, Oct., 1661, May, 1662, Oct., 1662, May, 1663, Oct., 1663.
Conn. Col. I. 149, 163, 185, 211, 213, 224, 288, 323, 340, 365, 372, 379, 384, 399, 410.

JUDSON, JOSEPH (d. 1690). Deputy (Stratford) to Conn. Leg., Oct., 1658, May, 1659, Oct., 1659, Oct., 1661, May, 1662, Oct., 1662, May, 1663, Oct., 1663, May, 1664, May, 1665. First called Ensign, Oct., 1663.
Conn. Col. I. 323, 334, 340, 372, 379, 384, 399, 410, 425. II. 13.

KETCHUM, JOHN. Deputy (Setauket) to Conn. Leg., May, 1664; Judge (Setauket town), May, 1664.
Conn. Col. I. 425, 428.

KILBOURN, JOHN (d. 1703). Sergt., Wethersfield Train Band, May, 1657. Deputy (Wethersfield) to Conn. Leg., Oct., 1660, May, 1661, May, 1662.
Conn. Col. I. 299, 354, 365, 379.

KIMBERLY, THOMAS (d. 1672). Corporal, New Haven Train Band, Aug., 1642. Marshal, N. H. Col., Oct., 1643, Oct., 1646, May, 1653, May, 1654, May, 1655, May, 1656, May, 1657, May, 1658, May, 1659, May, 1660, May, 1661.
N. H. Col. I. 76, 112, 276. II. 1, 92, 140, 168, 213, 231, 297, 360, 403.

KITCHELL, ROBERT (d. 1672). Deputy (Guilford) to N. H. Leg., May, 1656, May, 1661, May, 1662, May, 1663, Oct., 1663; Judge (Guilford town), May, 1665. (Removed to Newark, N. J.)
N. H. Col. II. 169, 403, 451, 488, 500. Conn. Col. II. 18.

KITCHELL, SAMUEL (d. 1690). Ensign, Guilford Train Band, July, 1665. (Removed to Newark.)
Conn. Col. II. 22.

KNOWLES, ALEXANDER (d. 1663). Judge (Fairfield town), May, 1654, May, 1661; Assistant, Conn. Col., May, 1658; war committee for Fairfield, Oct., 1654.
Conn. Col. I. 257, 264, 314, 366.

LAMBERTON, GEORGE (d. 1647). Deputy (New Haven) to N. H. Leg., Oct., 1643, Oct., 1645; Judge (New Haven town), Mar., 1644.
N. H. Col. I. 111, 125, 173.

LATHAM, CARY (d. 1685). Deputy (New London) to Conn. Leg., May, 1664.
Conn. Col. I. 425.

LATHROP, SAMUEL (d. 1700). Judge (New London town), May, 1649.
Conn. Col. I. 186.

LATTIMER, JOHN (d. 1662). Deputy (Wethersfield) to Conn. Leg., May, 1654.
Conn. Col. I. 256.

LAW, RICHARD (d. 1687). Deputy (Stamford) to N. H. Leg., May, 1653, May, 1654, May, 1655, May, 1656, May, 1657, May, 1658, May, 1659, May, 1661, May, 1662, May, 1663, Oct., 1663, Jan., 1664, May, 1664; Judge (Stamford town), May, 1653, May, 1654, May, 1655, May, 1656, May, 1657, May, 1658, May, 1660, May, 1661, May, 1662, May, 1663. Assistant (provisional appointment, Conn. Col.), Oct., 1664; Judge (Stamford, Greenwich, and Rye), May, 1665; Deputy (Stamford) to Conn. Leg., Oct., 1665.
N. H. Col. II. 2, 92, 96, 141, 147, 169, 172, 214, 215, 232, 235, 297, 369, 403, 405, 451, 453, 477, 489, 500, 513, 544. Conn. Col. I. 437. II. 14, 24.

LEEK, PHILIP (d. 1676). Corporal, New Haven Train Band, Mar., 1645 (resigned May, 1652).
N. H. Col. I. 160. N. H. Town I. 127.

LEETE, WILLIAM (d. 1683). Deputy (Guilford) to N. H. Leg., Oct., 1643, Apr., 1644; Secretary, N. H. Col., Oct., 1646; Assistant, N. H. Col., May, 1653, May, 1654, May, 1655, May, 1656, May, 1657; Dep. Governor, N. H. Col., May, 1658, May, 1659, May, 1660; Governor, N. H. Col., May, 1661, May, 1662, May, 1663, May, 1664; Commissioner to Mass. Col., June, 1653, June, 1654; Commissioner to United Colonies, May, 1655, May, 1656, May, 1657, May, 1658, May, 1659, May, 1660, May, 1661, May, 1662, May, 1663, May, 1664; Judge (Southold town), May, 1655; Assistant (provisional appointment, Conn. Col.), Oct., 1664; Assistant, Conn. Col., May, 1665; Commissioner to United Colonies, May, 1665.
N. H. Col. I. 112, 129, 275. II. 1, 5, 91, 101, 140, 143, 168, 213, 231, 297, 359, 402, 450, 451, 488, 543. Conn. Col. I. 437. II. 13, 18.

LEFFINGWELL, THOMAS (d. 1714). Deputy (Norwich) to Conn. Leg., Oct., 1662, Oct., 1663, Oct., 1665.
Conn. Col. I. 384, 410. II. 24.

LEWIS, WILLIAM, JR. (d. 1690). Sergt., Farmington Train Band, May, 1649; Lieut. of same, Oct., 1651. poss ancestor
Conn. Col. I. 187, 227.

LINDON, HENRY (d. 1660). Ensign, Artillery Co., May, 1648; Ensign, New Haven Train Band, May, 1652; Deputy (New Haven) to N. H. Leg., May, 1653, May, 1654, May, 1659; Judge (New Haven town), May, 1651, May, 1652, May, 1653, May, 1654, May, 1655, May, 1656, May, 1657, May, 1658, May, 1659, May, 1660.
N. H. Col. I. 382. II. 2, 92, 297. N. H. Town I. 72, 127, 180, 212, 240, 277, 313, 353, 402, 453.

LIVERMORE, JOHN. First called Corporal (New Haven Train Band), Apr., 1646 (resigned May, 1647).
N. H. Col. I. 230, 313.

LOCKWOOD, ROBERT (d. 1658). Sergt., Fairfield Train Band, May, 1657. poss ancestor
Conn. Col. I. 299.

LORD, RICHARD (d. 1662). Deputy (Hartford) to Conn. Leg., Feb., 1657, Aug., 1657, Oct., 1657, May, 1658, Oct., 1658, May, 1659, Oct., 1659, Oct., 1660, May, 1661; Capt., Conn. Col. Troop, Mar., 1658; Patentee, Royal Charter, 1662.
Conn. Col. I. 288, 300, 306, 309, 315, 323, 334, 340, 353, 365. II. 4.

LUDLOW, ROGER (d. 1668). Commissioner appointed by Mass. to govern Conn., Mar., 1636; Assistant, Conn. Col., Apr., 1636, Sept., 1636, Mar., 1637, May, 1637, Nov., 1637, Feb., 1638, Mar., 1638, Apr., 1638, Apr., 1640, Apr., 1641, Apr., 1643, Apr., 1644, Apr., 1645, Apr., 1646, May, 1647, May, 1649, May, 1650, May, 1651, May, 1652, May, 1653; Dep. Governor, Conn. Col., Apr., 1639, Apr., 1642, May, 1648; Commissioner to Saybrook, Pequot War, June, 1637; Commissioner to United Colonies, May, 1648, May, 1651, May, 1652, May, 1653.

Hazard's State Papers I. 321. Conn. Col. I. 1, 3, 8, 9, 10, 11, 13, 17, 27, 46, 64, 71, 84, 103, 124, 137, 149, 163, 164, 185, 207, 218, 222, 231, 233, 240, 241.

MALBON, RICHARD. Judge (New Haven town), Apr., 1642, Oct., 1642, Apr., 1643, Oct., 1643, Mar., 1644, Oct., 1644, Mar., 1645, Oct., 1645 (declined); Deputy (New Haven) to N. H. Leg., Mar., 1644, Oct., 1644, Mar., 1645, Oct., 1645 (declined); Assistant, N. H. Col., Oct., 1646. Capt., Artillery Co., Mar., 1645. (Returned to England.)

N. H. Col. I. 69, 78, 85, 119, 125, 129, 147, 148, 156, 158, 171, 173, 275.

MARSHALL, SAMUEL (d. 1675). Corporal, Conn. Col. Troop, Mar., 1658.

Conn. Col. I. 309.

MARSHALL, THOMAS. Deputy (Windsor) to Conn. Leg., Mar., 1638, Apr., 1638.

Conn. Col. I. 13, 17.

MARVIN, MATTHEW (d. 1680). Deputy (Norwalk) to Conn. Leg., May, 1654.

Conn. Col. I. 256.

MARVIN, REINOLD (d. 1676). Sergt., Saybrook Train Band, Oct., 1661.

Conn. Col. I. 375.

MASON, JOHN (d. 1672). Capt. in the Pequot War; first called Major, June, 1654; war committee for Saybrook, May, 1653, Oct., 1654; Major, Conn. Col. Troop, Mar., 1658. Deputy (Windsor) to Conn. Leg., Nov., 1637, Mar., 1638, Apr., 1638, Sept., 1639, Feb., 1641, Apr., 1641, Sept., 1641; Assistant, Conn. Col., Apr., 1642, Apr., 1643, Apr., 1644, Apr., 1645, Apr., 1646, May, 1647, May, 1648, May, 1649, May, 1650, May, 1651, May, 1652, May, 1653, May, 1654, May, 1655, May, 1656, May, 1657,

May, 1658, May, 1659; Dep. Governor, Conn. Col., May, 1660, May, 1661, May, 1662, Oct., 1662, May, 1663, May, 1664, May, 1665; Patentee, Royal Charter, 1662; Commissioner to United Colonies, June, 1654, May, 1655, May, 1656, May, 1657, May, 1660, May, 1661; Commissioner to treat with N. H. Col., Mar., 1663, Aug., 1663; Commissioner for Mass. and R. I. Boundaries, Oct., 1664.

Conn. Col. I. 9, 11, 13, 17, 34, 58, 64, 67, 71, 84, 103, 124, 137, 149, 163, 185, 207, 218, 230, 241, 243, 256, 259, 264, 274, 280, 281, 297, 299, 309, 314, 334, 347, 348, 364, 365, 378, 384, 396, 398, 407, 425, 435. II. 4, 13.

MEAD, WILLIAM (d. after 1669). Deputy (New London) to Conn. Leg., Oct., 1653.

Conn. Col. I. 248.

MEIGS, JOHN (d. 1672). Clerk, New Haven Train Band, May, 1648. Judge (Guilford town), May, 1663.

N. H. Col. I. 382. Conn. Col. I. 405.

MERRIMAN, NATHANIEL (d. 1694). Served in the Pequot War; Sergt., New Haven Artillery Co. (prior to 1664); Ensign, New Haven Train Band, May, 1664; confirmed Sergt. of same, July, 1665.

N. H. Town II. 89. Conn. Col. II. 23.

MILES, RICHARD (d. 1667). Judge (New Haven town), May, 1648, May, 1649, May, 1650, May, 1651, May, 1652; Deputy (New Haven) to N. H. Leg., May, 1651; Clerk, Artillery Co., May, 1648.

N. H. Col. I. 381, 382, 456. N. H. Town I. 21, 72, 127.

MINOR, THOMAS (d. 1690). Sergt., New London Train Band, May, 1649; Chief Military Officer, Mystic Train Band, July, 1665; Deputy (New London) to Conn. Leg., Sept., 1650, May, 1651, Sept., 1651; Deputy (Stonington), May, 1665, Oct., 1665; Judge (New London town), May, 1649; Judge (Stonington town), Oct., 1664, May, 1665.

Conn. Col. I. 186, 187, 211, 218, 224, 435. II. 14, 17, 22, 24.

MITCHELL, MATTHEW (d. 1645). Deputy (Wethersfield) to Conn. Leg., May, 1637; Assistant, Conn. Col., Nov., 1637, Feb., 1638, Mar., 1638, Apr., 1638; Dep. Judge (Stamford town), Apr., 1643.

Conn. Col. I. 9, 11, 13, 17. N. H. Col. I. 85.

MOODY, JOHN (d. 1655). Lieut., Hartford Train Band, Apr., 1640.

Conn. Col. I. 48.

MOORE, ISAAC (d. after 1694). Sergt. (Chief Officer), Farmington Train Band, May, 1649; Deputy (Norwalk) to Conn. Leg., Oct., 1657.

Conn. Col. I. 187, 306, 440.

MOORE, JOHN (d. 1677). Deputy (Windsor) to Conn. Leg., Sept., 1653, May, 1661, Oct., 1661, May, 1662, Oct., 1664, May, 1665, Oct., 1665.

Conn. Col. I. 246, 365, 372, 378, 431. II. 13, 23.

MOORE, THOMAS. Deputy (Southold) to N. H. Leg., May, 1658; Judge (Southold), May, 1658.

N. H. Col. II. 232, 236.

MOREHOUSE, THOMAS (d. 1658). Deputy (Fairfield) to Conn. Leg., Sept., 1653.

Conn. Col. I. 246.

MORGAN, JAMES (d. 1685). Deputy (New London) to Conn. Leg., May, 1657, Oct., 1658, Oct., 1661, May, 1663, Oct., 1663, May, 1665, Oct., 1666.

Conn. Col. I. 297, 323, 372, 399, 410. II. 13, 24.

MOSS, JOHN (d. 1707). Corporal, New Haven Train Band, Aug., 1642 (resigned, May, 1652). Deputy to N. H. Leg., May, 1664.

N. H. Col. I. 76. II. 544. N. H. Town I. 127.

MOXON, GEORGE (REV.) (d. 1687). Deputy (Springfield) to Conn. Leg., Apr., 1638. (Returned to England.)

Conn. Col. I. 17.

MULFORD, JOHN. Assistant, Conn. Col., May, 1658; Judge (Easthampton town), May, 1664.

Conn. Col. I. 314, 428.

MUNSON, THOMAS (d. 1685). Served in the Pequot War; Sergt., New Haven Train Band, Aug., 1642; Sergt., Artillery Co., Mar., 1645; Sergt., N. H. Col. Troop, June, 1654; Ensign, New Haven Train Band, Mar., 1661 (declined, but accepted as acting Ensign); Lieut. of same, May, 1664, confirmed July, 1665. Deputy (New Haven) to N. H. Leg., May, 1663, May, 1664; Judge (New Haven town), June, 1662, May, 1663, May, 1664.

N. H. Col. I. 76, 158. II. 108, 488, 544. Conn. Col. II. 23. N. H. Town I. 474, 523. II. 45, 88, 89.

MYGATT, JOSEPH (d. 1680). Deputy (Hartford) to Conn. Leg., Oct., 1656, Feb., 1657, Aug., 1657, Oct., 1657, May, 1658, Oct., 1658, May, 1659, Oct., 1659, May, 1660, Oct. 1660, May, 1661, Oct., 1661, May, 1662.

Conn. Col. I. 282, 288, 300, 306, 315, 323, 334, 340, 347, 353, 365, 372, 378.

NASH, JOHN (d. 1687). Corporal, New Haven Train Band, Aug., 1642; Sergt. of same, July, 1644; Sergt., Artillery Co., Mar., 1645, May, 1648; Lieut., New Haven Train Band, June, 1652; Lieut. (chief military officer), Mar., 1654; Lieut., N. H. Col. Troop, June, 1654; nominated Capt., Mar., 1661 (declined); Capt., New Haven Train Band, May, 1664, confirmed July, 1665. Deputy (New Haven) to N. H. Leg., May, 1659, May, 1660, May, 1661, May, 1663, Oct., 1663, Jan., 1664; Assistant, N. H. Col., May, 1664 (declined); Judge (New Haven town), May, 1653, May, 1654, May, 1655, May, 1656, May, 1657, May, 1658, May, 1659, May, 1660, May, 1661, June, 1662, May, 1663, May, 1664, May, 1665. Deputy (New Haven) to Conn. Leg., May, 1665.

N. H. Col. I. 76, 141, 158, 382. II. 52, 108, 297, 403, 477, 500, 513, 543. N. H. Town I. 131, 180, 212, 240, 277, 313, 353, 402, 453, 474, 484, 485, 523. II. 40, 45, 89, 142. Conn. Col. II. 13, 18, 22.

NASH, JOSEPH (d. 1678). Corporal, New Haven Train Band, May, 1647.

N. H. Col. I. 313.

NEWBERRY, BENJAMIN (d. 1689). Deputy (Windsor) to Conn. Leg., May, 1656, Oct., 1656, May, 1662, May, 1663, Oct., 1663, Oct., 1664, May, 1665, Oct., 1665; Commissioner for Mass. and R. I. Boundaries, Oct., 1664. First called Captain, May, 1662.

Conn. Col. I. 281, 282, 378, 399, 409, 431, 435. II. 13, 23.

NEWMAN, FRANCIS (d. 1660). Ensign, New Haven Train Band, Aug., 1642; Lieut. (Ensign), Artillery Co., Mar., 1645; Lieut., New Haven Train Band, May, 1652 (resigned June, 1652). Judge (New Haven town), Mar., 1645, Oct., 1645, Oct., 1646, Oct., 1647, May, 1648, May, 1649, May, 1650, May, 1651, May, 1652; Deputy (New Haven) to N. H. Leg., Oct., 1647, May, 1649, Sept., 1649, May, 1650, May, 1651, May, 1652; Assistant, N. H. Col., May, 1653, May, 1654, May, 1655, May, 1656, May, 1657; Secretary, N. H. Col., May, 1653, May, 1654, May, 1655, May, 1656, May, 1657; Governor, N. H. Col., May,

1658, May, 1659, May, 1660; Commissioner to United Colonies, July, 1654, May, 1658, May, 1659, May, 1660.

N. H. Col. I. 76, 156, 158, 171, 274, 354, 381, 456, 481. II. 1, 91, 92, 111, 140, 168, 213, 231, 297, 359. N. H. Town I. 21, 72, 127, 131.

NEWMAN, ROBERT. Judge (New Haven town), Oct., 1639, Oct., 1640, May, 1641, Oct., 1641. (Returned to England.)

N. H. Col. I. 21, 44, 51, 58.

NEWTON, THOMAS (d. in or before 1683). Deputy (Fairfield) to Conn. Leg., Apr., 1645.

Conn. Col. I. 124.

NICHOLS, FRANCIS (d. 1650). Sergt., Stratford Train Band, Oct., 1639.

Conn. Col. I. 36.

NICHOLS, ISAAC (d. 1695). Deputy (Stratford) to Conn. Leg., May, 1662, Oct., 1664.

Conn. Col. I. 379, 431.

NOBLE, WILLIAM. Judge (Flushing town), May, 1664.

Conn. Col. I. 428.

NOTT, JOHN (d. 1682). Served in the Pequot War; Sergt., Wethersfield Train Band, May, 1657. Deputy (Wethersfield) to Conn. Leg., May, 1662, Oct., 1662, May, 1663, Oct., 1663, May, 1664, Oct., 1664, Oct., 1665.

Conn. Col. I. 299, 378, 384, 399, 409, 425, 431. II. 24.

OGDEN, JOHN (d. 1682). Assistant, Conn. Col., May, 1656, May, 1657, May, 1658, May, 1659, May, 1660, Oct., 1662; Patentee, Royal Charter, 1662.

Conn. Col. I. 280, 297, 314, 334, 347, 384. II. 4.

OLMSTEAD, NEHEMIAH (d. 1657). Sergt., Fairfield Train Band, May, 1657.

Conn. Col. I. 299.

OLMSTEAD, NICHOLAS (d. 1684). Served in the Pequot War; Corporal, Conn. Col. Troop, Mar., 1658.

Conn. Col. I. 309.

OLMSTEAD, RICHARD (d. 1686). Sergt., Norwalk Train Band, May, 1653; Sergt., Conn. Col. Troop, May, 1653; Lieut., Norwalk Train Band, May, 1659. Deputy (Norwalk) to Conn. Leg., May, 1653, Sept., 1654, May, 1658, Oct., 1660, May, 1661, May, 1662, May, 1663, Oct., 1663, May, 1664, Oct., 1664, Oct., 1665. Served in the Pequot War.

Conn. Col. I. 240, 242, 243, 264, 315, 336, 354, 365, 379, 399, 410, 425, 432. II. 24.

PALMES, EDWARD. Judge (New London town), May, 1664.
Conn. Col. I. 426.

PARKE, ROBERT (d. 1665). Deputy (Wethersfield) to Conn. Leg., Aug., 1642; Deputy (New London), May, 1652.
Conn. Col. I. 73, 231.

PARKER, WILLIAM (d. 1686). Served in the Pequot War. Deputy (Saybrook) to Conn. Leg., Sept., 1652.
Conn. Col. I. 235.

PEAKIN, JOHN. Deputy (Southold) to N. H. Leg., May, 1654; Judge (Southold town), May, 1654.
N. H. Col. II. 92, 95.

PELL, THOMAS (DR.) (d. 1669). Served in the Pequot War. Judge (Fairfield town), May, 1661; Deputy (Fairfield) to Conn., Leg., May, 1664, May, 1665.
Conn. Col. I. 366, 425. II. 13.

PERRY, RICHARD. Clerk, New Haven Train Band, July, 1644.
N. H. Col. I. 141.

PHELPS, WILLIAM (d. 1672). Commissioner appointed by Mass. to govern Conn., Mar., 1636; Assistant, Conn. Col., Apr., 1636, Sept., 1636, Mar., 1637, May, 1637, Nov., 1637, Mar., 1638, Apr., 1638, Apr., 1639, Apr., 1640, Apr., 1641, Apr., 1642; Deputy (Windsor) to Conn. Leg., Apr., 1645, Sept., 1645, Apr., 1646, Oct., 1646, May, 1647, Sept., 1647, May, 1648, Sept., 1648, May, 1649, Sept., 1649, Sept., 1650, May, 1651, Sept., 1651, May, 1652, Sept., 1652, May, 1653, Oct., 1653, May, 1654, Sept., 1654, May, 1655, Feb., 1657, May, 1657, Oct., 1657; Assistant, Conn. Col., May, 1658, May, 1659, May, 1660, May, 1661, May, 1662; war committee for Windsor, May, 1653, Oct., 1654.
Hazard's State Papers I. 321. Conn. Col. I. 1, 3, 8, 9, 11, 13, 17, 27, 46, 64, 71, 124, 130, 138, 145, 149, 157, 163, 166, 185, 195, 211, 218, 224, 231, 235, 240, 243, 247, 256, 263, 264, 274, 288, 297, 306, 314, 334, 347, 365, 378.

PIERCE, THOMAS. Judge (Setauket town), May, 1661.
Conn. Col. I. 366.

PIERSON, ABRAHAM (REV.) (d. 1678). Chaplain, N. H. Col. Troop, June, 1654.
N. H. Col. II. 108.

PLUMB, JOHN (d. 1648). Served in the Pequot War. Assistant, Conn. Col., Feb., 1638, Mar., 1638, Apr., 1638; Deputy (Wethersfield) to Conn. Leg., Nov., 1641, Apr., 1642, Mar., 1643.
Conn. Col. I. 11, 13, 17, 69, 71, 82.

PORTER, JOHN (d. 1648). Deputy (Windsor) to Conn. Leg., Aug., 1639, Oct., 1646, May, 1647.
Conn. Col. I. 29, 145, 149.

PRATT, JOHN (d. 1655). Deputy (Hartford) to Conn. Leg., Aug., 1639, Sept., 1639, Jan., 1640, Feb., 1641, Apr., 1641, Sept., 1641, Nov., 1641, May, 1655.
Conn. Col. I. 29, 34, 41, 58, 64, 67, 69, 274.

PRATT, WILLIAM (d. about 1678). Lieut., Saybrook Train Band, Oct., 1661.
Conn. Col. I. 375.

PURRIER, WILLIAM. Deputy (Southold) to N. H. Leg., June, 1653, May, 1656, May, 1661; Judge (Southold town), May, 1656.
N. H. Col. II. 4, 169, 172, 403.

PYNCHEON, WILLIAM (d. 1662). Commissioner appointed by Mass. to govern Conn., Mar., 1636; Assistant, Conn. Col., Nov., 1636, Mar., 1638, Apr., 1638; his shallop commandeered, Pequot War, May, 1637. (Residence, Springfield.)
Hazard's State Papers I. 321. Conn. Col. I. 5, 10, 13, 17.

RAYNER, THURSTAN (d. 1667). Deputy (Wethersfield) to Conn. Leg., Mar., 1638, Apr., 1638, Apr., 1639, Jan., 1640, Apr., 1640; Judge (Stamford town), Oct., 1641, Apr., 1643, Oct., 1643; Assistant, Conn. Col., May, 1661, May, 1663; Judge (Southampton town), May, 1664.
Conn. Col. I. 13, 17, 27, 41, 46, 365, 399, 428. N. H. Col. I. 58, 85, 112.

RICHARDS, JAMES (d. 1680). Assistant, Conn. Col., Oct., 1664, May, 1665; Lieut., Conn. Col. Troop, May, 1664. (Residence, Hartford.)
Conn. Col. I. 429, 435. II. 13.

RICHARDS, NATHANIEL (d. 1682). Deputy (Norwalk) to Conn. Leg., Oct., 1658.
Conn. Col. I. 323.

RICKBELL, JOHN. Judge (Oyster Bay town), May, 1664.
Conn. Col. I. 428.

ROBBINS, JOHN (d. 1660). Deputy (Wethersfield) to Conn. Leg., Apr., 1643, Sept., 1643, Oct., 1656, Feb., 1657, May, 1657, Oct., 1659.
Conn. Col. I. 84, 93, 282, 288, 297, 340.

ROGERS, JAMES (d. 1683). Served in the Pequot War. Deputy (New London) to Conn. Leg., May, 1661, May, 1662, Oct., 1662, May, 1663, Oct., 1663, Oct., 1664; Dep. Judge (New London town), Apr., 1660, May, 1660.
Conn. Col. I. 347, 352, 365, 379, 384, 399, 410, 432.

ROSE, ROBERT, SR. (d. 1665). Deputy (Wethersfield) to Conn. Leg., Sept., 1641, Aug., 1642, Mar., 1643, Apr., 1643.
Conn. Col. I. 67, 73, 82, 84.

ROSSITER, BRAY (DR.) (d. 1672). Ensign, Windsor Train Band, Apr., 1640; Deputy (Windsor) to Conn. Leg., Apr., 1643, Sept., 1645.
Conn. Col. I. 48, 84, 130.

ROYCE, ROBERT (d. 1676). Deputy (New London) to Conn. Leg., May, 1661.
Conn. Col. I. 365.

RUSSELL, JAMES (d. 1674). Clerk, New Haven Train Band, May, 1658.
N. H. Town I. 354.

RUSSELL, WILLIAM (d. 1665). Corporal, New Haven Train Band, May, 1652; Sergt. of same, Mar., 1661.
N. H. Town I. 127, 474.

SCRANTON, JOHN (d. 1671). Deputy (Guilford) to N. H. Leg., Jan., 1664.
N. H. Col. II. 513.

SEELEY, ROBERT (d. 1668). Lieut. (second in command under Mason), Pequot War, May, 1637; Marshal (New Haven town), Oct., 1639, to Nov., 1642; Lieut., New Haven Train Band, Aug., 1642; Lieut., Artillery Co., Mar., 1645; Capt., Artillery Co., May, 1648; Capt., N. H. Col. Troop, June, 1654; in command of N. H. Col. Troops against Ninigret, Oct., 1654; Lieut. (chief military officer), Huntington Train Band, May, 1663 (and referred to as Capt.); Judge (Huntington town), May, 1663, May, 1664; Deputy (Huntington) to Conn. Leg., May, 1664.
Conn. Col. I. 9, 401, 406, 425, 428. N. H. Col. I. 21, 44, 58, 76, 79, 80, 158, 382. II. 108, 118, 120.

SEWARD, WILLIAM (d. 1689). Sergt., Guilford Train Band, July, 1665.
Conn. Col. II. 22.

SHEAF, JACOB (d. 1659). Deputy (Guilford) to N. H. Leg., Apr., 1644. (Removed to Boston, Mass.)
N. H. Col. I. 129.

SHERMAN, JOHN (REV.) (d. 1685). Deputy (Wethersfield) to Conn. Leg., May, 1637; Deputy (Milford) to N. H. Leg., Oct., 1643.
Conn. Col. I. 9. N. H. Col. I. 112.

SHERMAN, SAMUEL (d. ~~1684~~ 1700). Served in the Pequot War. Deputy (Stratford) to Conn. Leg., Oct., 1660; Assistant, Conn. Col., Oct., 1662, May, 1663, May, 1664, May, 1665.
Conn. Col. I. 354, 384, 425. II. 13.

SHERWOOD, THOMAS (d. 1657). Deputy (Stratford) to Conn. Leg., Sept., 1645, Sept., 1649, May, 1650, Oct., 1653, Oct., 1654; war committee for Stratford, Oct., 1654.
Conn. Col. I. 130, 195, 207, 248, 261, 264 (twice called Sherratt).

SLAWSON, GEORGE (d. 1695). Judge (Stamford town), May, 1657; Dep. Judge (Stamford town), May, 1659; Deputy (Stamford) to N. H. Leg., Oct., 1663.
N. H. Col. II. 215, 304, 500.

SMITH, HENRY (REV.) (d. 1648). Commissioner appointed by Mass. to govern Conn., Mar., 1636. (Residence, Wethersfield.)
Hazard's State Papers I. 321.

SMITH, JOHN. Dep. Judge (New London town), Apr., 1660, May, 1660; Judge (same), May, 1663.
Conn. Col. I. 347, 352, 402.

SMITH, SAMUEL (d. 1680). Served in the Pequot War; Sergt., Wethersfield Train Band, prior to 1658. Deputy (Wethersfield) to Conn. Leg., Nov., 1637; Assistant, Conn. Col., Mar., 1638, Apr., 1638; Deputy again, Feb., 1641, Apr., 1641, Sept., 1641, Nov., 1641, Sept., 1643, Apr., 1644, Sept., 1644, Apr., 1645, Sept., 1645, Apr., 1646, May, 1647, Sept., 1647, May, 1648, Oct., 1648, May, 1649, Sept., 1649, Sept., 1650, Sept., 1651, May, 1653, Sept., 1653, Oct., 1655, May, 1656; war committee for Wethersfield, May, 1653. (Removed to Hadley, Mass.)
Conn. Col. I. 11, 13, 17, 58, 64, 67, 69, 93, 103, 111, 124, 130, 138, 149, 157, 163, 167, 185, 195, 211, 224, 240, 243, 246, 278, 281, 314.

SMITH, SAMUEL. Deputy (New London) to Conn. Leg., May, 1662, Oct., 1662; Dep. Judge (New London), Apr., 1660; Lieut., New London Train Band, Feb., 1657. (Removed to Virginia.)
Conn. Col. I. 292, 347, 379, 384.

SMITH, WILLIAM (d. 1669). Clerk, Wethersfield Train Band, July, 1645; Deputy (Middletown) to Conn. Leg., Sept., 1652, Aug., 1653, Sept., 1653, May, 1655, Oct., 1655. (Removed to Farmington.)
Conn. Col. I. 128, 235, 245, 246, 274, 278.

SPENCER, THOMAS (d. 1687). Served in the Pequot War. Deputy (Hartford) to Conn. Leg., Apr., 1639, Aug., 1639, Sept., 1639, Jan., 1640, Apr., 1640.
Conn. Col. I. 27, 29, 34, 41, 46.

STANLEY, JOHN (d. 1706). Served in the Pequot War; first called Sergeant, Oct., 1664. Deputy (Farmington) to Conn. Leg., May, 1659, May, 1664, Oct., 1664, May, 1665, Oct., 1665.
Conn. Col. I. 334, 425, 431. II. 14, 24.

STANTON, THOMAS (d. 1677). Served in the Pequot War. Indian Interpreter (Marshal), Conn. Col., Apr., 1638 (dismissed Apr., 1646), Jan., 1649; Deputy (Hartford) to Conn. Leg., May, 1651; Judge (Stonington town), Oct., 1664, May, 1665.
Conn. Col. I. 19, 139, 175, 218, 435. II. 17.

STAPLES, THOMAS (d. about 1687). Deputy (Fairfield) to Conn. Leg., Sept., 1649, Sept., 1650, Oct., 1661.
Conn. Col. I. 195, 211, 372.

STEBBING, EDWARD (d. 1668). Deputy (Hartford) to Conn. Leg., Apr., 1639, Apr., 1640, Feb., 1641, Apr., 1641, Sept., 1641, Nov., 1641, May, 1648, May, 1649, Sept., 1649, May, 1650, Sept., 1650, May, 1651, Sept., 1651, May, 1652, July, 1653, Sept., 1653, Sept., 1654, May, 1655, Oct., 1655, May, 1656, Oct., 1656.
Conn. Col. I. 27, 46, 58, 64, 67, 69, 163, 185, 195, 207, 211, 218, 224, 231, 245, 246, 264, 274, 278, 281, 282.

STEELE, JOHN (d. 1665). Commissioner appointed by Mass. to govern Conn., Mar., 1636; Assistant, Conn. Col., Apr., 1636, Sept., 1636, Mar., 1637, May, 1637; Deputy (Hartford) to Conn. Leg., Mar., 1638, Apr., 1638, Apr., 1639, Sept., 1639, Jan., 1640, Apr., 1640, Feb., 1641, Apr., 1641, Sept., 1641, Nov., 1641, Apr., 1642, Aug., 1642, Mar., 1643, Apr., 1643, Sept., 1643, Apr.,

1644, Sept., 1644, Apr., 1645, Sept., 1645, Dec., 1645; Deputy (Farmington), Apr., 1646, Oct., 1646, May, 1647, Sept., 1647, Sept., 1648, Jan., 1649, May, 1649, Sept., 1649, May, 1650, Sept., 1650, Oct., 1650, May, 1651, May, 1652, Sept., 1652, May, 1653, Sept., 1653, May, 1654, Sept., 1654, May, 1655, Oct., 1655, May, 1656, Oct., 1656, Feb., 1657, May, 1657, Oct., 1657, May, 1658, Oct., 1658; war committee for Farmington, May, 1653, Oct., 1654.

Hazard's State Papers I. 321. Conn. Col. I. 1, 3, 8, 9, 13, 17, 27, 34, 41, 46, 58, 64, 67, 69, 71, 73, 82, 84, 93, 103, 111, 124, 130, 133, 138, 145, 149, 157, 166, 174, 185, 195, 207, 211, 212, 218, 231, 235, 240, 243, 246, 256, 263, 264, 274, 278, 280, 282, 288, 297, 306, 315, 323.

STEELE, JOHN, JR. (d. 1653). Ensign, Farmington Train Band, Oct., 1651.

Conn. Col. I. 227.

STEVENS, THOMAS (d. 1685). Corporal, N. H. Col. Troop, June, 1654. (Residence, Guilford.)

N. H. Col. II. 109.

STICKLAND, JOHN (d. about 1672). Served in the Pequot War. Deputy (Springfield?) to Conn. Leg., Sept., 1641; first called Sergt., Nov., 1636. (Removed to Jamaica, L. I.)

Conn. Col. I. 67.

STOCKING, SAMUEL (d. 1697). Deputy (Middletown) to Conn. Leg., May, 1658, May, 1659, Oct., 1659, May, 1665, Oct., 1665.

Conn. Col. I. 315, 334, 340. II. 14, 24.

STONE, SAMUEL (REV.) (d. 1663). Commissioner to treat with New Haven Col., Oct., 1662; his widow and son received grant, Oct., 1663, for his service in Pequot War and since.

Conn. Col. I. 388, 413.

STOUGHTON, THOMAS (d. 1661). Lieut., Windsor Train Band (promoted from Ensign), Apr., 1640; Deputy (Windsor) to Conn. Leg., Apr., 1639, Aug., 1639, Jan., 1640, Apr., 1640, Apr., 1643, Sept., 1643, Dec., 1645, Oct., 1646, May, 1647, Sept., 1647, May, 1648.

Conn. Col. I. 27, 29, 41, 46, 48, 84, 93, 133, 145, 149, 157, 163.

STREAM, JOHN (d. 1685). Confirmed Ensign, Milford Train Band, July, 1665.

Conn. Col. II. 21.

SWAYNE, SAMUEL. Lieut. (chief military officer), Branford Train Band, Mar., 1654; Deputy (Branford) to N. H. Leg., May, 1653, May, 1655, May, 1656, May, 1657, May, 1658, May, 1659, May, 1661, May, 1662, May, 1663, Oct., 1663, Jan., 1664, May, 1664; Deputy (Branford) to Conn. Leg., Apr., 1665, May, 1665, Oct., 1665; Judge (Branford town), May, 1654, May, 1655, May, 1656, May, 1657, May, 1665. (Removed to Newark, N. J.)

N. H. Col. II. 2, 52, 96, 141, 148, 169, 172, 214, 215, 232, 298, 403, 451, 488, 500, 513, 544. Conn. Col. I. 439. II. 13, 18, 24.

SWAYNE, WILLIAM (d. about 1658). Commissioner appointed by Mass. to govern Conn., Mar., 1636; Assistant, Conn. Col., Sept., 1636, Mar., 1637, May, 1637, Nov., 1637; Deputy (Wethersfield) to Conn. Leg., Sept., 1641, Nov., 1641, Apr., 1642, Aug., 1642, Mar., 1643; Assistant, Conn. Col., Apr., 1643, Apr., 1644; Judge (Branford town), May, 1654, May, 1655, May, 1656, May, 1657.

Hazard's State Papers I. 321. Conn. Col. I. 3, 8, 9, 11, 67, 69, 71, 73, 82, 84, 103. N. H. Col. II. 96, 148, 172, 215.

TAINTOR, CHARLES (d. 1658). Deputy (Fairfield) to Conn. Leg., May, 1647, May, 1648.

Conn. Col. I. 149, 163.

TALCOTT, JOHN (d. 1660). Deputy (Hartford) to Conn. Leg., May, 1637, Mar., 1638, Apr., 1638, Aug., 1639, Sept., 1639, Jan., 1640, Apr., 1640, Feb., 1641, Apr., 1641, Sept., 1641, Nov., 1641, Apr., 1642, Aug., 1642, Mar., 1643, Apr., 1643, Sept., 1643, Apr., 1644, Sept., 1644, Apr., 1645, Sept., 1645, Dec., 1645, Apr., 1646, Oct., 1646, May, 1647, Sept., 1647, May, 1648, Sept., 1648, May, 1649, Sept., 1649, May, 1650, Sept., 1650, May, 1651, Sept., 1651, May, 1652, Sept., 1652, May, 1653, Sept., 1653; Treasurer, Conn. Col., May, 1652, May, 1654, May, 1655, May, 1656, May, 1659; Assistant, Conn. Col., May, 1654, May, 1655, May, 1656, May, 1657, May, 1658, May, 1659; Commissioner to United Colonies, May, 1656, May, 1657, May, 1658.

Conn. Col. I. 9, 13, 17, 29, 34, 41, 46, 58, 64, 67, 69, 71, 73, 82, 84, 93, 103, 111, 124, 130, 133, 138, 145, 149, 157, 163, 166, 185, 195, 207, 211, 218, 224, 231, 235, 240, 246, 256, 274, 280, 281, 297, 299, 314, 315, 334.

TALCOTT, JOHN, JR. (d. 1688). Ensign, Hartford Train Band, June, 1650; first called Capt., Oct., 1660. Deputy (Hartford) to Conn. Leg., May, 1660, Oct., 1660, June, 1661, Oct., 1661; Assistant, Conn. Col., May, 1662, Oct., 1662, May, 1663, May,

1664, May, 1665; Treasurer, Conn. Col., May, 1660, May, 1661, May, 1662, Oct., 1662, May, 1663, May, 1664, May, 1665; Patentee, Royal Charter, 1662; Commissioner to United Colonies, May, 1663; Commissioner to treat with N. H. Col., Mar., 1663; Commissioner on N. Y. Boundary, Oct., 1663; Commissioner on Mass. and R. I. Boundaries, Oct., 1664.

Conn. Col. I. 210, 347, 353, 365, 369, 372, 378, 384, 396, 399, 410, 425, 435. II. 4, 13.

TAPP, EDMUND (d. 1654). Assistant, N. H. Col., Oct., 1643. (Residence, Milford.)

N. H. Col. I. 112.

THOMPSON, THOMAS (d. 1655). Deputy (Farmington) to Conn. Leg., May, 1650.

Conn. Col. I. 207.

THORNTON, THOMAS. Deputy (Stratford) to Conn. Leg., May, 1651; war committee for Stratford, May, 1653.

Conn. Col. I. 218, 243.

TIBBALS, THOMAS (d. 1703). Served in the Pequot War; Sergt., N. H. Col. Troop, June, 1654; confirmed Sergt., Milford Train Band, July, 1665.

N. H. Col. II. 108. Conn. Col. II. 21.

TINKER, JOHN (d. 1662). Deputy (New London) to Conn. Leg., May, 1660, Oct., 1660; Judge (New London town), Apr., 1660, May, 1660, May, 1661.

Conn. Col. I. 347, 352, 354, 365.

TITHARTON, DANIEL (d. 1661). Deputy (Stratford) to Conn. Leg., May, 1647, May, 1649, May, 1652, May, 1654.

Conn. Col. I. 149, 185, 231, 256.

TOPPING, THOMAS (d. 1688). Deputy (Wethersfield) to Conn. Leg., Aug., 1639, Sept., 1639; Assistant, Conn. Col., May, 1651, May, 1652, May, 1653, May, 1655, May, 1656, May, 1659, May, 1660, May, 1661, Oct., 1662, May, 1663, May, 1664; Patentee, Royal Charter, 1662 (name erroneously stated as John); Judge (Southold town), Oct., 1663; first called Capt., May, 1655.

Conn. Col. I. 29, 34, 218, 231, 240, 274, 280, 334, 347, 364, 384, 399, 414, 425. II. 4.

TRACY, THOMAS (d. 1685). Served in the Pequot War; first called Ensign, Oct., 1664. Deputy (Norwich) to Conn. Leg., Oct., 1662, May, 1663, Oct., 1663.

Conn. Col. I. 384, 399, 410, 432.

TREAT, RICHARD (d. 1670). Deputy (Wethersfield) to Conn. Leg., Apr., 1644, Sept., 1644, Apr., 1645, Sept., 1645, Dec., 1645, Apr., 1646, Oct., 1646, May, 1647, Sept., 1647, May, 1648, Sept., 1648, May, 1649, Sept., 1649, May, 1650, Oct., 1650, May, 1651, Sept., 1651, May, 1652, Sept., 1652, May, 1653, Sept., 1653, May, 1654, Sept., 1654, May, 1655, Oct., 1655, May, 1656, Feb., 1657, May, 1657, Oct., 1657; Assistant, Conn. Col., May, 1658, May, 1659, May, 1660, May, 1661, May, 1662, Oct., 1662, May, 1663, May, 1664; Patentee, Royal Charter, 1662; Ensign, Wethersfield Train Band, Feb., 1653; Corporal, Conn. Col. Troop, Mar., 1658.

Conn. Col. I. 103, 111, 124, 130, 133, 138, 145, 149, 157, 163, 166, 185, 195, 207, 212, 218, 224, 231, 235, 237, 240, 246, 256, 264, 274, 278, 281, 288, 297, 306, 309, 314, 334, 347, 365, 378, 384, 398, 425. II. 4.

TREAT, ROBERT (d. 1710). Deputy (Milford) to N. H. Leg., May, 1653, May, 1654, May, 1655, May, 1656, May, 1658; Assistant, N. H. Col., May, 1659, May, 1660, May, 1661, May, 1662, May, 1663, May, 1664 (declined); Assistant (provisional appointment, Conn. Col.), Oct., 1664; Deputy (Milford) to Conn. Leg., Oct., 1665. Lieut. (chief military officer), Milford Train Band, May, 1654; Capt. of same, May, 1661, confirmed July, 1665.

N. H. Col. II. 2, 92, 99, 141, 169, 231, 297, 359, 402, 410, 451, 488, 542, 543. Conn. Col. I. 437. II. 21, 23.

TRY, MICHAEL (d. 1677). Deputy (Fairfield) to Conn. Leg., Oct., 1657.

Conn. Col. I. 306.

TURNER, NATHANIEL (d. 1647). Capt. (chief military officer), New Haven Train Band, Sept., 1640; Judge (New Haven town), Oct., 1639, Oct., 1640; Deputy (New Haven) to N. H. Leg., Oct., 1643, Mar., 1644, Oct., 1644, Mar., 1645, Oct., 1645.

N. H. Col. I. 21, 40, 44, 111, 125, 129, 147, 156, 171.

TUTTLE, JOHN. Judge (Southold town), Apr., 1642.

N. H. Col. I. 70.

UNDERHILL, JOHN (d. 1675). Served in the Pequot War; Deputy (Stamford) to N. H. Leg., Apr., 1643; Dep. Judge (Stamford town), Apr., 1643; called Capt.

N. H. Col. I. 85.

USHER, ROBERT. Deputy (Stamford) to Conn. Leg., May, 1665; Judge (Stamford town), Oct., 1662, May, 1663.

Conn. Col. I. 389, 405. II. 14.

WADSWORTH, WILLIAM (d. 1675). Deputy (Hartford) to Conn. Leg., Sept., 1652, Oct., 1656, Feb., 1657, Aug., 1657, Oct., 1657, May, 1658, Oct., 1658, May, 1659, Oct., 1659, May, 1660, Oct., 1660, May, 1661, May, 1662, Oct., 1662, May, 1663, Oct., 1663, May, 1664, Oct., 1664, May, 1665, Oct., 1665.

Conn. Col. I. 235, 282, 288, 300, 306, 315, 323, 334, 340, 347, 353, 365, 378, 384, 399, 409, 425, 431. II. 13, 23.

WAKEMAN, JOHN (d. 1661). Judge (New Haven town), Oct., 1641, Apr., 1642, Oct., 1642, Apr., 1643, Oct., 1643, Mar., 1644, Oct., 1644, May, 1655, May, 1656, May, 1657, May, 1658, May, 1659, May, 1660; Deputy (New Haven) to N. H. Leg., Apr., 1646, Oct., 1646, Oct., 1647, May, 1648, May, 1655, May, 1656, May, 1657, May, 1658, May, 1660; Treasurer, N. H. Col., May, 1655, May, 1656, May, 1657, May, 1658, May, 1659, May, 1660; Assistant, N. H. Col., May, 1661 (declined).

N. H. Col. I. 58, 69, 78, 85, 119, 125, 148, 227, 274, 354, 381. II. 140, 141, 168, 169, 213, 231, 297, 359, 402. N. H. Town I. 240, 277, 313, 353, 402, 453.

WALLER, WILLIAM. Ensign, Saybrook Train Band, Oct., 1661; Deputy (Saybrook) to Conn. Leg., Oct., 1663, Oct., 1664, May, 1665.

Conn. Col. I. 375, 410, 431. II. 14.

WARD, ANDREW (d. 1659). Commissioner appointed by Mass. to govern Conn., Mar., 1636; Assistant, Conn. Col., Apr., 1636, Sept., 1636, Mar., 1637, May, 1637; Deputy (Wethersfield) to Conn. Leg., Nov., 1637, Mar., 1638, Apr., 1638, Aug., 1639, Sept., 1639, Jan., 1640; Judge (Stamford town), Oct., 1642; Dep. Judge, Apr., 1643; Deputy (Stamford) to N. H. Leg., Apr., 1644; Assistant, N. H. Col., Oct., 1646; Deputy (Fairfield) to Conn. Leg., May, 1648, May, 1649, Sept., 1649, May, 1650, Sept., 1650, May, 1651, May, 1652, May, 1653, Sept., 1653,* May, 1654, Oct., 1654, May, 1655, May, 1656, Oct., 1656, Oct., 1658; war committee for Fairfield, May, 1653, Oct., 1654.

Hazard's State Papers I. 321. Conn. Col. I. 1, 3, 8, 9, 11, 13, 17, 29, 34, 41, 163, 185, 195, 207, 211, 218, 231, 240, 243, 256, 264, 274, 281, 282, 323. N. H. Col. I. 78, 85, 129, 275.

* The name of Andrew *Winard* is printed as a Deputy in Sept., 1653. The compiler has been unable to locate an individual of this name. The name occurs next to a Fairfield Deputy, and as Fairfield was sending two Deputies with great regularity, we are justified in assuming that a Fairfield man was intended. Andrew Ward represented Fairfield at the previous and following sessions, and we conclude that he was the man here intended.

WARD, LAWRENCE. Deputy (Branford) to N. H. Leg., May, 1654, May, 1658, May, 1659, May, 1661, May, 1662, May, 1663, Oct., 1663, Jan., 1664, May, 1664; Deputy (Branford) to Conn. Leg., May, 1665; Judge (Branford town), May, 1654, May, 1655, May, 1656, May, 1657, May, 1665. (Removed to Newark, N. J.)
N. H. Col. II. 92, 96, 148, 172, 215, 232, 298, 403, 451, 488, 500, 513, 544. Conn. Col. II. 13, 18.

WARD, NATHANIEL (d. 1664). Deputy (Hartford) to Conn. Leg., May, 1656. (Removed to Hadley, Mass.)
Conn. Col. I. 281.

WARNER, ROBERT (d. 1690). Deputy (Middletown) to Conn. Leg., May, 1660, Oct., 1660, May, 1661, Oct., 1661, Oct., 1662, May, 1663, May, 1664, Oct., 1665.
Conn. Col. I. 347, 354, 365, 372, 384, 399, 425. II. 24.

WATERBURY, JOHN (d. 1659). Judge (Stamford town), May, 1657, May, 1658.
N. H. Col. II. 215, 235.

WEBB, RICHARD (d. 1665). Deputy (Norwalk) to Conn. Leg., May, 1655.
Conn. Col. I. 274.

WEBSTER, JOHN (d. 1661). Deputy (Hartford) to Conn. Leg., May, 1637, Mar., 1638, Apr., 1638; Assistant, Conn. Col., Apr., 1639, Apr., 1640, Apr., 1641, Apr., 1642, Apr., 1643, Apr., 1644, Apr., 1645, Apr., 1646, May, 1647, May, 1648, May, 1649, May, 1650, May, 1651, May, 1652, May, 1653, May, 1654, May, 1657, May, 1658, May, 1659; Dep. Governor, Conn. Col., May, 1655; Governor, Conn. Col., May, 1656; Commissioner to United Colonies, May, 1654; war committee for Hartford, May, 1653, Oct., 1654.
Conn. Col. I. 9, 13, 17, 27, 46, 64, 71, 84, 103, 124, 137, 149, 163, 185, 207, 218, 231, 240, 243, 256, 257, 263, 273, 280, 297, 314, 334.

WEBSTER, ROBERT (d. 1676). Deputy (Middletown) to Conn. Leg., Sept., 1653, May, 1654, Sept., 1654, May, 1655, Mar., 1656, May, 1656, Oct., 1656, Feb., 1657, Oct., 1657, Aug., 1658, Oct., 1658, May, 1659; Lieut., Middletown Train Band, May, 1654; war committee for Middletown, Oct., 1654.
Conn. Col. I. 246, 256, 258, 264, 274, 279, 281, 283, 288, 306, 318, 323, 334.

WELCH, THOMAS (d. 1681). Deputy (Milford) to N. H. Leg., May, 1654, May, 1655, May, 1657, May, 1658, May, 1659, May, 1661, May, 1662, May, 1663, Oct., 1663, Jan., 1664, May, 1664; Deputy (Milford) to Conn. Leg., May, 1665; Judge (Milford town), May, 1665.

N. H. Col. II. 92, 141, 213, 231, 297, 403, 451, 488, 500, 513, 544. Conn. Col. II. 13, 17.

WELLS, HUGH. Drummer, Conn. Col. Troop, May, 1653. (Residence, Wethersfield.)

Conn. Col. I. 243.

WELLES, JOHN (d. 1659). Deputy (Stratford) to Conn. Leg., May, 1656, Oct., 1656, May, 1657, Oct., 1657; Assistant, Conn. Col., May, 1658, May, 1659.

Conn. Col. I. 281, 283, 297, 306, 314, 334.

WELLES, SAMUEL (d. 1675). Deputy (Wethersfield) to Conn. Leg., Oct., 1657, May, 1658, Oct., 1658, May, 1659, Oct., 1659, May, 1660, May, 1661, Oct., 1661; Judge (Wethersfield town), May, 1665; Ensign, Wethersfield Train Band, Mar., 1658; Lieut. of same, May, 1665.

Conn. Col. I. 306, 311, 315, 323, 334, 340, 347, 365, 372. II. 14, 17.

WELLES, THOMAS (d. 1660). Assistant, Conn. Col., Mar., 1637, May, 1637, Nov., 1637, Feb., 1638, Mar., 1638, Apr., 1638, Apr., 1639, Apr., 1640, Apr., 1641, Apr., 1642, Apr., 1643, Apr., 1644, Apr., 1645, Apr., 1646, May, 1647, May, 1648, May, 1649, May, 1650, May, 1651, May, 1652, May, 1653 (name omitted from record, but appears in later sessions of the year); Treasurer, Conn. Col., Apr., 1639, May, 1648, May, 1649, May, 1650; Secretary, Conn. Col., Apr., 1641, Apr., 1643, Apr., 1644, Apr., 1645, May, 1647; Commissioner to United Colonies, May, 1649, May, 1654, May, 1659; Moderator (in absence of Dep. Gov., the Gov. being dead), Mar., 1654; Dep. Governor, Conn. Col., May, 1654, May, 1656, May, 1657, May, 1659; Governor, Conn. Col., May, 1655, May, 1658; war committee for Wethersfield, May, 1653, Oct., 1654.

Conn. Col. I. 8, 9, 11, 13, 17, 27, 46, 64, 71, 84, 103, 124, 137, 149, 163, 185, 187, 207, 218, 231, 243, 251, 256, 257, 264, 273, 280, 297, 314, 334.

WELLES, THOMAS, JR. (d. 1668). Quartermaster, Conn. Col. Troop, Mar., 1658; Patentee, Royal Charter, 1662; Deputy (Hartford) to Conn. Leg., May, 1662.

Conn. Col. I. 309, 378. II. 4.

WELLS, WILLIAM. Deputy (Southold) to N. H. Leg., June, 1653, May, 1659; Judge (Southold town), May, 1657, May, 1659, May, 1661, May, 1662.

N. H. Col. II. 4, 215, 298, 304, 406, 456.

WESTWOOD, WILLIAM (d. 1661). Commissioner appointed by Mass. to govern Conn., Mar., 1636; Assistant, Conn. Col., Apr., 1636, Sept., 1636; Deputy (Hartford) to Conn. Leg., Apr., 1642, Aug., 1642, Mar., 1643, Apr., 1643, Sept., 1643, Apr., 1644, Sept., 1644, Apr., 1646, Oct., 1646, Sept., 1647, May, 1648, Sept., 1648, Sept., 1651, May, 1652, Sept., 1652, May, 1653, Sept., 1653, May, 1654, Sept., 1654, May, 1655, Oct., 1655, May, 1656; war committee for Hartford, May, 1653.

Hazard's State Papers I. 321. Conn. Col. I. 1, 3, 71, 73, 82, 84, 93, 103, 111, 138, 145, 157, 163, 166, 224, 231, 235, 240, 243, 246, 256, 264, 274, 278, 281.

WHEELER, JOHN (d. 1690). Deputy (Fairfield) to Conn. Leg., Oct., 1657, May, 1658, May, 1659, May, 1660.

Conn. Col. I. 306, 315, 334, 347.

WHEELER, THOMAS (d. 1654). Ensign, Conn. Col. Troop, May, 1653, having previously held title of Lieut. (Residence, Fairfield.)

Conn. Col. I. 243.

WHITE, NATHANIEL (d. 1711). Deputy (Middletown) to Conn. Leg., Oct., 1659, May, 1661, Oct., 1661, May, 1662, Oct., 1662, May, 1663, Oct., 1663, May, 1664, May, 1665.

Conn. Col. I. 340, 365, 372, 379, 384, 399, 410, 425. II. 14.

WHITEHEAD, SAMUEL (d. 1690). Served in the Pequot War; Corporal, New Haven Train Band, Aug., 1642; Sergt. of same, June, 1652, confirmed July, 1665 (resigned June, 1673); Sergt., N. H. Col. Troop, June, 1654.

N. H. Col. I. 76. II. 108. N. H. Town I. 131. II. 311. Conn. Col. II. 23.

WHITING, WILLIAM (d. 1647). Deputy (Hartford) to Conn. Leg., May, 1637, Nov., 1637; Assistant, Conn. Col., Apr., 1641, Apr., 1642, Apr., 1643, Apr., 1644, Apr., 1645, Apr., 1646, May, 1647; Treasurer, Conn. Col., Apr., 1641, Apr., 1643, Apr., 1644, Apr., 1645, May, 1647; Commissioner to United Colonies, Jan., 1647.

Conn. Col. I. 9, 11, 64, 71, 84, 103, 124, 137, 147, 149.

WHITMAN, ZACHARY (d. 1666). Deputy (Milford) to N. H. Leg., Apr., 1644.
N. H. Col. I. 129.

WHITMORE, JOHN (d. 1656). Deputy (Stamford) to N. H. Leg., Oct., 1643.
N. H. Col. I. 112.

WHITMORE, THOMAS (d. 1681). Deputy (Middletown) to Conn. Leg., Sept., 1654; war committee for Middletown, Oct., 1654.
Conn. Col. I. 264.

WILCOXSON, WILLIAM (d. 1652). Deputy (Stratford) to Conn. Leg., May, 1647.
Conn. Col. I. 149.

WILFORD, JOHN (d. 1678). Deputy (Branford) to Conn. Leg., Apr., 1665; Oct., 1665; Judge (Branford town), May, 1665.
Conn. Col. I. 439. II. 18, 24.

WILKINS, WILLIAM. Judge (Gravesend town), May, 1664.
Conn. Col. I. 429.

WILLIAMS, ROGER. Deputy (Windsor) to Conn. Leg., May, 1637. (Removed to Dorchester, Mass.)
Conn. Col. I. 9.

WILLIS. See Wyllys.

WILSON, ANTHONY (d. 1662). Deputy (Fairfield) to Conn. Leg., Apr., 1646.
Conn. Col. I. 138.

WILTON, DAVID (d. 1678). Deputy (Windsor) to Conn. Leg., Apr., 1646, May, 1650, Sept., 1650, May, 1651, Sept., 1651, May, 1652, Sept., 1652, May, 1653, Sept., 1653, May, 1654, Oct., 1655. First called Ensign, Mar., 1658; war committee for Windsor, May, 1653.
Conn. Col. I. 138, 207, 211, 218, 224, 231, 235, 240, 243, 246, 256, 278, 309.

WINARD, ANDREW. See Andrew Ward, footnote.

WINES, BARNABAS. Corporal, Southold Train Band, prior to May, 1654; Deputy (Southold) to Conn. Leg., May, 1664.
N. H. Col. II. 97. Conn. Col. I. 425.

WINSTON, JOHN (d. 1697). Corporal, New Haven Train Band, Mar., 1661; Sergt. of same, Aug., 1665.
N. H. Town I. 474. II. 145.

WINTHROP, JOHN (d. 1670). Assistant, Conn. Col., May, 1651, May, 1652, May, 1653, May, 1654, May, 1655, May, 1656; Governor, Conn. Col., May, 1657, May, 1659, May, 1660, May, 1661, May, 1662, Oct., 1662, May, 1663, May, 1664, May, 1665; Dep. Governor, Conn. Col., May, 1658; Colonial Agent to King, June, 1661; Patentee, Royal Charter, 1662; Commissioner to United Colonies, May, 1658, May, 1659, May, 1660, May, 1661, May, 1662, May, 1663, May, 1664, May, 1665.
Conn. Col. I. 218, 231, 240, 256, 274, 280, 297, 314, 315, 334, 347, 348, 364, 365, 369, 378, 379, 384, 398, 399, 425, 430. II. 4, 13, 18.

WINTHROP, WAITSTILL (d. 1717). Capt., New London Train Band, May, 1665.
Conn. Col. II. 14.

WOLCOTT, HENRY (d. 1655). Deputy (Windsor) to Conn. Leg., Apr., 1639; Assistant, Conn. Col., Apr., 1643, Apr., 1644, Apr., 1645, Apr., 1646, May, 1647, May, 1648, May, 1649, May, 1650, May, 1651, May, 1652, May, 1653, May, 1654, May, 1655; war committee for Windsor, May, 1653.
Conn. Col. I. 27, 84, 103, 124, 137, 149, 163, 185, 207, 218, 231, 240, 243, 256, 274.

WOLCOTT, HENRY, JR. (d. 1680). Deputy (Windsor) to Conn. Leg., Oct., 1655, Oct., 1660, May, 1661; Assistant, Conn. Col., May, 1662, Oct., 1662, May, 1663, May, 1664, May, 1665; Patentee, Royal Charter, 1662.
Conn. Col. I. 278, 353, 365, 378, 384, 399, 425. II. 4, 13.

WOOD, JONAS (d. 1689). Judge (Huntington town), May, 1663, May, 1664.
Conn. Col. I. 401, 428.

WOODHULL, RICHARD (d. 1690). Judge (Setauket town), May, 1661, May, 1664; Deputy (Setauket) to Conn. Leg., May, 1664.
Conn. Col. I. 366, 425, 428.

WYLLYS, GEORGE (d. 1645). Assistant, Conn. Col., Apr., 1639, Apr., 1640, Apr., 1643, Apr., 1644; Dep. Governor, Conn. Col., Apr., 1641; Governor, Conn. Col., Apr., 1642.
Conn. Col. I. 27, 46, 64, 71, 84, 103.

WYLLYS, SAMUEL (d. 1709). Assistant, May, 1654, May, 1655, May, 1656, May, 1657, May, 1658, May, 1659, May, 1660, May, 1661, May, 1662, Oct., 1662, May, 1663, May, 1664, May, 1665; Patentee, Royal Charter, 1662; Commissioner to United Colonies, May, 1662; Commissioner to treat with N. H. Col., Aug., 1663; Commissioner for Mass. and R. I. Boundaries, Oct., 1664.

Conn. Col. I. 256, 274, 280, 297, 314, 334, 347, 364, 378, 379, 384, 398, 407, 425, 435. II. 4, 13.

YOUNG, JOHN. Judge (Southold town), May, 1661, May, 1662; Deputy (Southold) to Conn. Leg., Oct., 1662; Assistant, Conn. Col., May, 1664; Judge (Southold town), Oct., 1662, May, 1663.

N. H. Col. II. 406, 457. Conn. Col. I. 386, 390, 402, 425.

DIVISION OF NEW HAVEN LANDS IN 1704

(Verbatim copy from the Proprietors' Records, labeled Vol. 4, pp. 137, 138.)

Here followeth The Claims y^t persons made & had Land laid out to them in y^e Half Deuision also allowed in y^e Sequestered Land: wch Lots was drawn Aprill 3^d 1704:

William Jones esq^r Mr Theophilus Heatons* first purchas Right

Mrs Jane gilbert M^r $Math^w$ gilberts first purchas Right

Mr James Pierpont 200^{lb} of Mr John Davenports first purchas Right

Mr Warham Mather 400^{lb} of Mr John Davenports first purchas Right

Mr Jer osborne his granfathers first purchas Right & Benhams first purchas Right: his mothers Right in 1683 half timothy gibbards Right in 1683 & two 3^{ds} of nickolas elceys 1st purchas Right & 2/3 of nicolas elceys Right in 1683

John Alling Half his fathers 1st purchas Right & 1/3 of nicolas elceys 1^s parchas & 1/3 of s^d elceys Right in 1683

Capt Nathan Andrews his fathers 1st purchas right & one half Timothy giberds Right in 1683

Capt John miles in Constables 1st purchas Right

Joseph pardee his fathers Right in 1683

Joseph Bradly 1/4 of his fathers Right in 1683

Sam^{ll} Basset 1/2 his fathers Right in 1683

John & Joseph Hull their granfather Hull 1st purchas Right & their fathers in 1683

Dan^{ll} Sperry Decon pecks 1st purchas Right also his Right s^d pecks in 1683 & one 3^d part of his father Sperries Right in 1683

John Johnson sen his uncle Thomas Johnsons 1683 Right & part of his fathers Right in 1683

Serg Benj Bradly one 3^d part of his Wives Mother in 1683 & 1/4 of his father bradly in 1683

$Nath^{ll}$ Bradly 1/4 part of his fathers Right 1683

Mr John Winston his fathers Right in 1683

Sam^{ll} Clark Sen^{or} his fathers 1st purchas Right

* The initial "H" has been crossed out.

Nath^{ll} Tharp his fathers 1st purchas Right
John Hil his fathers 1st purchas Right
Widow [Fary?]* her Husbands fathers first purchas Right
Serg^{nt} John Ball for M^{r} fugals 1^{s} purchas & 1/2 Mr Hen^{y} glouers Right in 1683
Nath Mix 1/4 of his fathers Right 1683
John Mix 1/4 of his fathers Right in 1683 & his wievs mothers Judson in 1683
Sam^{ll} Mix 1/4 of his fathers Right in 1683
Nath^{ll} Boykin his fathers 1st purchas Rig^{t}
John newman his fathers Right in 1683
Sam^{ll} Alling Jun his fathers Right in 1683
John Clark his fathers 1st purchas Right
Ben^{j} Bowden Bannisters 1st purchas Right
Serg Sam^{ll} Alling 1/2 of his fathers 1st purchase Right
Caleb Mix 1/4 of his fathers Right 1683
eben^{z} Sperry 1/3 of his fathers Right in 1683: & part of his mothers in 1702
Nath Sperry 1/3 of his fathers Right 1683 & 1/3 of his mothers in 1702
Thom^{s} Trowbridge at ye West Side 2/6 of Mr Lambertons 1st purchase Right his fathers Right in 1683 & his mothers Heads 1/3 of M^{r} trowbridg 1st purchas
Joseph becher his father Right 1683
Phillip Allcock Mr James 1st purchas Right & Jer Whitnell 1st purchas Right
John How his fathers Right in 1683
John Basset 1/2 his fathers Right in 1683
Deacon bradly 1/4 of his fathers Right in 1683 & 1/3 of his Wives mother 1683
John & Nathan Benham their fathers Right in 1683
eliaz^{r} Brown 100^{lb} of Mr Hiccocks 1st purchase Right
Ebene^{zr} Brown 100^{lb} of Mr Hiccocks 1st purchase Right
Thom^{s} panter 1/6th of Mr Lambertons 1st purchase Right
Lt Sam^{ll} Smith 3/6th of Mr Lambertons 1 purchase Right & 1/5 of his father 1st purchase Right
John ebenezer Joseph & Nathan Smith to each one 5th part of their fathers 1st purchase Right

* The transcriber is uncertain of this name, which looks most like "furs" or "fars"; possibly it should be read "fins," i.e. Fenn.

John Becher his granmother potter 1st purchase: Rt:
Peter Malary 1/2 part of his fathers Right in 1683:
John Mallary 1/2 part of his fathers Right in 1683
Ebenr frost his fathers Right in 1683
Joseph Mansfield 1/3 of his fathers Right 1683 & 1 6 part of Mr Marshals 1st purchas Right
Japhet Mansfield 1/3 of his fathers Right 1683 and one 6th part of Mr Marshals 1 purchase Right
Joseph Turner 1/4 of Capt Turners 1st purchase Right & 1/3 of his fathers Right in 1683
Mr Moses Mansfield 1/4 of Mr Marshals 1st purchase Right & 1/2 of his fathers Right in ye years 1683 and 1702
Jonathan Mansfield 1/4 of Mr Marshals 1s purchase Right & 1/2 part of his fathers Right in ye years 1683 and 1702
Nath Tharp Jun 2/4 of Richd Littels Right in 1683
Joseph Tuttle 2/3 of his fathers Right in 1683
Samll Tuttle 1/3 of his fathers Right in 1683
John Payne 1/4 of Richd Littels Right in 1683
Sergnt James Heaton Widow greens 1st purchase Right
Sergnt John Morris 200lb of Mr Hickocks 1st purchase Right & Mrs Maltbies his daughters Right 1702
John Sherman 2/6 parts of his father Thomas Right in 1683
John Thomas Jun 4/6 parts of his father Thomas Right in 1683
Wm Wooden his fathers Right 1683 Laid to him
John Pirkins 1/3 of his fathers Right in 1683
Jonathan Pirkins 1/3 of his fathers Right in 1683:
David Pirkins 1/3 of his fathers Right in 1683
Ralph Lines 1/4 of his fathers Right in 1683
Joseph Lines 1/4 of his fathers Right in 1683
Ebenr Mansfield 1/6 part of Mr Marshals 1st purchase Right & 1/3 of his fathers Right in 1683
Deacon Punderson 800lb Right pr Mr Wakeman
Sergnt Joseph Preston his fathers 1st purchase Right
Lt Thomas Talmadge 150lb 1st purchase Right & his Mothers Right in 1683
Mr Thō trowbridge 2/3 of his granfather Trowbridge Right & his fathers Right in 1683
John Todd his fathers Right in 1683
David Atwater: Mr Joshua atwaters 1st purchase Right

John Brocket Jun his mothers Right in 1683
Mr. Willm Thompson 100lb of Mr Hickcocks 1st purchase Right & 250lb of Mr Wm Davis 1st purchas
Lt John Munson 200lb of Mr Hickcocks first purchase Right
Mr John Yale Mr David Yale 1st purchase Right
Mr David atwater Right Laid next to his son David
Will Wooden Senior Laid next to his son William:
Mrs Hannah alsup hir fathers Right in 1683
Hen Bristols Right in 1683 to his Widdow:
Bartholomew Jacobs Right in 1683 Laid to his son samuell
francis Brown his fathers Right in 1683

GILBERT MORTALITY LIST

(Chiefly pertaining to Hamden)

Contributed by Mr. and Mrs. H. Nelson Stiles of North Haven, Conn.

James Gilbert (see page 654, Family 16, 4) kept a daily weather record beginning 1 Jan. 1801, and in it noted various items, chiefly deaths, but occasionally marriages and other personal references, concerning the people of the section where he lived. Since more than half of the family names which appear in this record have already appeared in the magazine, it is not possible now to make use of this private record to fill out missing dates in the proper place; and we take this opportunity to preserve this valuable record by printing it here. The earlier portion is given below, and the remainder of it will appear in the next volume. A copy of the record has also been handed down, which in a few instances gives further particulars, and where the copy adds to the original entry, note is made of it below in parentheses.

Mr. Gilbert wrote the following account of his own family:

''I James Gilbert was born August 29th 1780.

My sister Ruth Gilbert died February 26th 1795 in the 24 year of her age. If she had lived till July 4 she would have been 24 years old.

My mother Mabel Gilbert died August 25th 1807 on Tuesday at half past 4 o'clock in P.M. my mother was 63 years old the 3 day of last April.

My father, Joseph Gilbert died January 20th 1821 on Saturday half past one o'clock P.M. in the 73 year of his age.

My sister Mabel died October 21, 1823. She was 46 years old.

My sister Sarah died January 19th 1827. Friday evening. She was 43 years old the 20th day of last November. She was a kind and dutiful companion, a tender and careful mother, & an affectionate sister, & a benevolent neighbor.''

1801

Jan. 27. Died Thankful Atwater wid. Jacob Atwater in the 67th year of her age (copy says second wife)

Feb. 1. Died infant of Titus Munson living in the upper (?) yard (copy says of Isaac Munson)

Mar. 27. Died ——— Tuttle wife of Capt. Nager Tuttle of North Haven*

* Betsey (Ray), wife of Benajah Tuttle. *Editor.*

Apr. 3. Died Isaac Dickerman age 61

May 9. Died Old Widow Perkins of West Woods

17. Died Old Mr. Banjamin Galard age 79

June 2. Died Hannah Bradley age 66 wife of Maly Bradley (copy says wife of Gamaliel Bradley)

July 2. Died Jason Bradley

Aug. 8. Died ——— son of Simeon Warner

10. Died Levrit Kimberly

22. Died Lucy Bradley age 23 wife of Elvin Bradley (copy says Alvin)

Sept. 5. Died Nancy Hitchcock age 3 (copy says dau. of Samuel Jr.)

18. Died Joel Bradley

20. Died Mrs. Huff wife of Joel Huff

21. Died Eysre Eaton age 18 of North Field*

25. Died infant of Joseph Gonson Jr. (copy says Johnson)

27. Died Unis Ives age 7 dau. of Eber Ives (copy says Eunice)

29. Died Bettsy Ives age 2 dau. of Eber Ives

Oct. 18. Died Miles Bradley age 3 son of Lyman Bradley

23. Died Rucia Perecin (copy says Lucia dau. of John Perkins)†

Nov. 1. Died Patients Bradley wife of Aaron Bradley

4. Died infant son of Samuel Hitchcock Jr.

26. today Cryd of & marred Joel Huff to Thankful Rice

Dec. 4. Died Mrs. Robberds wife of Ebenezer Robberds

27. Published Mery‡ Gilbert to Phebe anny Tuttle of esth Haven

1802

Jan. 2. Died Widow Kozier Hall mother to I root (copy says Caziah Hall mother of Dr. Root)

10. Died Asaihel Tyler

13. Died Widow Thankful Ives age 81

30. Died Thommas Pardy (copy says Thomas Pardee)

* The first name is Iru on his gravestone. *Editor.*

† Jerusha Perkins is evidently intended. *Editor.*

‡ Merit. *Editor.*

Feb.(?). Published Amos Hotchkiss of Beeny* to Lois Todd of Hamden and married by Mr. Lyman

Published Semer Bradley to Olive Bradley both of Hamden†

Mar. 11. Died a child of Mr. Jes. Peck (copy says Jesse)

31. Died an infant dau. about 1½ yrs. of Elias Willots (copy says of Eldad Woolcotts)

Apr. 25. Published Alling Galard and Roxzy Dairen‡ both of Hamden

May 9. Published Hezekiah Baset to Esther Goodyear

June

July 1. Died stillborn child of Ebenezer Warner (copy says buried)

Aug. 13. Died Darius Tuttle age 12

31. Died Ruth Atwater age 19 (copy says dau. of Samuel Atwater)

Sept.

Oct.

Nov. 10. Died Rhode Goodyear age 20

Dec. 5. Died Old widow Mary Dickerman

23. Buried Enos Atwater age 53 (copy says died Dec. 22)

31. Died Old Enos Tuttle

1803

Jan. 28 or 29. Died Aged Gamaliel Bradley

Died Milly Galard (copy says Amela Galard)§

Feb. 25. Died Noah Woolcott

25. Died Widow Galard widow of old Benjamin Galard

Mar. 1. Buried infant child of Benjamin Peck

Apr.

May 18. Died Mrs. Leeke wife of old Mr. Timothy Leeke

June 10. Buried infant child of Medad Todd

July 3. Buried infant child of James Wiles

13. Died in West Indies,—Jesse Munson of this town

Aug. 11. Died Mary Woolcott wife of John Woolcott

Sept. 4. Died Widow Mary Hitchcock,—widow of S. H.

* Bethany. *Editor.*

† Married 14 Apr. 1802, by Cheshire record. *Editor.*

‡ Durand. *Editor.*

§ Child of Benjamin Gaylord. *Editor.*

Sept. 14. Died Mary Alling wife of old Mr. Nathan Alling
Oct. 6. Died Mahitable Warner age 27
11. Died Nuton Wolcott son of John Wolcott
15. Died Lyman Ives son of Elam Ives
17. Died Sally Ives dau. of Elam Ives
23. Died ——— Chatman wife of Samuel Chatman
Nov. 1. Died Dea. Stephen Goodyear age 75
5. Died ——— age 4 yrs. son of Ebenezer Warner
16 or 17. Died Bazil Munson Esq.
24. Died Theophilus Goodyear (hanged himself in East Hamden)
Dec. 12. Died Esther Bassett age 22 wife of Hezekiah Bassett

1804

Jan. 23. Died Thankful Woolcott wife of Noah Woolcott
Feb. 18. Died infant child of Alling Dickerman
20. Set out for the Jenesee*—Medad Bradley and his family
Mar.
Apr.
May 14. Died Old Mr. James Ives age 86 yrs. the oldest person then living in this Parish
June 27. Died infant age 1 yr. grandchild to old Mr. Jesse Johnson
July 28. Died Miriam Dickerman age 55 wife of Jonathan Dickerman (copy says July 24)
Aug.
Sept. — Died infant child of Obed Todd
Oct. 2. Set out for the Jenesee country Timothy Goodyear and his wife
Nov. 17. Died Betsy Bassett age 23

1805

Jan. 19. Died Mr. Nathan Alling age 46 Run over by a sleigh and died 36 hours later
23. Died Chloe Atwater age 23 consumption
Feb.
Mar.
Apr. 3 or 4. Died Capt. Caleb Cooper age 64

* The "Genesee Country," N. Y. *Editor.*

Died Phebe Kimberly age 39 wife of Ezra Kimberly

13. Died Old Mr. Reuben Perkins

May 22. Married Sarah Gilbert to Seymour Tuttle

30. Died Hannah Goodyear wife of Simeon Goodyear

June

July 13. Killed by lightning at Eber Ives House—Sarah age 17 dau. of David Warner

29. Died Isaac Cooper age 46

Aug. 12. Died infant child of Sally Davis

14. Daniel Leake age 20. In Guilford (copy says son of Timothy Leek)

Sept. 26. Married Mercy Gilbert to Ezra Bassett

Oct. 10. Died ——— son of Isaac Munson poisoned by eating toadstools.

12. Died Easter Bradley age 48 wife of Levi Bradley (copy says Esther)

21. Died ——— age 3 yrs. dau. of Alling Galard (copy says age 2)

23. Died Simeon Bristol Esq. age 67

Nov. 19. Born ——— dau. of Sarah (Gilbert) Tuttle*

20. Died Medad Todd

Dec. 20. Died Michael Talmadge† age 29. Was found dead in his own cellar. It was supposed he poisoned himself to death with Rats-Bane.

1806

Jan.

Feb. 23. Died ——— age 3 yrs. dau. of Joel Pardee

Mar.

Apr. 18. Died—A barn of Obadiah Blakeslee's burnt down & his two sons, or rather one that was his wife's before he was married to her, the two sons was burnt up in the barn. One 4 yrs. old and the other 2 yrs.

May 17. Died Widow Lydia Sugdon‡ age 60

21. Ordained in Hamden Mr. John Hide to be pastor of the Presbiterian Church

* This was the first child of the recorder's sister by her husband Seymour Tuttle. *Editor.*

† His name appears as Micajah in public records. *Editor.*

‡ Nee Cooper. *Editor.*

June
July 13. Died
27. Died Seny Bassett age 20
Aug. 8. Died Caleb Doolittle
20. Died Ruth Goodyear age 66 wife of Timothy Goodyear
Sept. 14. Buried ——— infant child of Eldad Woolcott
Oct. 11 or 13. Died Esther Bassett age 23
20. ——— age 1½ yrs. dau. of Leavit Barnes (copy says Levrit)
27. ——— age 2 yrs. son of Obed Bradley
Nov.
Dec. 26. Died Hannah Hitchcock age 29

1807

Jan. 17. Died Eliza Bradley age 4 yrs. dau. of Elam Bradley
Feb.
Mar. 26. Died Lucy Tuttle age 12 yrs. dau. of Jesse Tuttle. Drowned in Mill River
Apr.
May
June 12. Died Chester Bassett age 15 yrs. son of Capt. Hezekiah Bassett
July
Aug. 5. Buried infant child of Simeon Goodyear
25. Died Mabel Gilbert wife of Joseph Gilbert
27. Buried " " " " " "
Sept. 7. Died Justus Todd age 17 yrs. apprentice to Joel Cooper
22. Died Lucy Munson wife of Jobe Munson (copy says Job L.)
5. Died infant child of Obed Bradley
Oct.
Nov.
Dec.

1808

Jan.
Feb.
Mar.

Apr.
May 2. Died Sally Bradley age 32 wife of Medad Bradley
6. Died infant child of Mr. Stevenson (copy says Mr. Stephens)
June 2. Died ——— age 5 son of Leavit Barnes (copy says age 4, son of Levrit)
July 8. Died Mary Bradley wife of Jason Bradley
Aug.
Sept. 14. Died Lebeus Kelsey age 34 yrs.
Oct. 12 or 13. Died Joel Alling age 71 yrs.
Nov. 24. Died David Warner age 57
Dec. 5. Died ——— Goodyear wife of Deacon Asa Goodyear

1809

Jan. 15. Died ——— age 5 yrs. son of Miles Dusen (copy says Miles Duran's)
Feb. 22. Died Asa Dickerman age 36 yrs.
Mar. 2. Died ——— Kimberly age 40 yrs. wife of Ezra Kimberly (copy says, 2nd wife)
8. Died ——— age 2 yrs. son of Mr. Lee (gate-keeper Lee)
31. Eli Dickerman age 33 yrs.
Apr.
May
June
July 15. Died Rhode Humaston age 17 yrs. dau. of Ebenezer Humaston
17. Died John Bradley age 28 yrs.
Aug. 23. Died Amos Alling age 23 yrs.
27. Died ——— son of Chauncey Dickerman
Sept.
Oct. 5. Died Alven Bradley age 75 yrs.
Nov. 25. Died Sarah Bassett age 61 yrs. wife of Capt. Hezekiah Bassett
Dec. 31. Died August(?) Bradley son of Amos Bradley

1810

Jan. 8. Died ——— age 6 weeks son of Joshua Goodyear
Feb.

Mar. 24. Died Mrs. Demming one of the town poor
Apr. 13. Died Abiah Warner age 68 yrs. wife of Hezekiah Warner
May 9 or 10. Died Mrs. Eunice Bishop (copy says Widow)
24. Died ——— son of Doctor Jones
June
July 9. Buried ——— wife of Caleb Andrews of Bethany
Aug. 16. Died at Mr. Hide's, old Mrs. Wiles
18. Died Mrs. Eunice Goodyear wife of Simeon Goodyear (copy says 2nd wife)
Sept.
Oct.
Nov. 21. Died Mrs. Alling widow of Nathan Alling Jr.
Dec. 18. Died Sally Bradley widow of Jason Bradley

1811

Jan. 9. Died James Dickerman age 64 yrs.
29. Died Bettsy Stephens
Feb. 21. Died Obed Todd
23. Died Isaac Rice
Died old Mr. Ebenezer Warner
Mar. 8. Buried ——— infant of Seymour Goodyear
25. Died Dea. Asa Goodyear age 79 yrs.
Apr. 9. Died old Joseph Johnson
19. Died Joel Pardee age 5* yrs.
May
June 9. Died Lois Wiles age 15 yrs. dau. of James Wiles
12. Died ——— son of Dyman Robbards (copy says Diman)
18. Died ——— dau. of Seymour Bradley
July 14. Died ——— age 1 yr. child of John Scot
Aug.
Sept.
Oct.
Nov.
Dec. 23. Died ——— age 4 yrs. dau. of Ebenezer Warner

1812

Jan.
Feb.

* He was aged 51 years. *Editor.*

Mar.
April
May
June 1. Died old Mr. Nathan Alling
July
Aug. 18. Died Mrs. Eunice Gilbert age 80 yrs. wife of John Gilbert
19. Buried Two Babes of Amos Bradley the 3rd
Sept.
Oct. 10. Died infant child of Elipalet Gregory
19. Died " " " " " **Twins**
Nov.
Dec.

1813

Jan. 7. Died Bernice Barns age 18 yrs.
26. Died infant child of Mr. Hull
Feb. Died Hezekiah Tuttle age 69 yrs.
Mar. 4. Died Lois Dickerman age 62 yrs. widow James Dickerman
8. William Brockett age 18 yrs. son of Hezekiah Brockett
30. Phoebe Hotchkiss age 74 yrs. (copy says widow of Abraham Hotchkiss)
Apr.
May
June 20. Died Sally Done dau. of Anthony Thompson
July 31. Died Amos Bradley
Aug. 29. Buried infant child of Obed Bradley
Sept. 11. Died ——— age 3 yrs. child of William Homaston
15. Died Olive Bradley wife of Amos Bradley
20. Died ——— age 2 yrs. son of Amos Sandford
26. Died Nancy Homaston age 14 yrs. dau. of Ebinezer Homaston
27. Died John Munson son of Jesse Munson deceased
Oct. 24. Died Jonathan Ives
Nov.
Dec. 11. Died Milly Hul wife of
31. Died at Simeon Todd's,—Rheuben Perkins of Columbia

1814

Jan 2. Died Joel Todd
25. Died ——— age 3 yrs. son of Russel Galard
Feb. 22. Died John Gilbert age 85 yrs.
Mar. 3. Died Capt. Asa Atwater age 50 yrs.
17. Died Hezekiah Warner (copy says old Mr.)
Apr. 6. Died Loly Bradley age 32 yrs. wife of Elam Bradley
26. Died Mary Tyler age 59 yrs. widow of Asaihel Tyler
May 2. Died Hezekiah Dickerman age 60 yrs.
June 11. Died infant child of Russel Pierpont
12. Died Eunice Woolcott age 81 yrs.
July
Aug.
Sept.
Oct. 23. Died Polly Goodyear wife of Eli Goodyear
Nov. 17. Died Lucy Bristol dau. of Dea. Stephen Goodyear
Dec. 7. Died ——— age 2 yrs. child of Samuel Hitchcock (copy says Jr.)

1815

Jan. 2. Died old Mrs. Warner widow of Ebenezer Warner
Feb. 3. Died old Mrs. Hannah Mansfield (copy says widow)
Mar. 11. Died Deaf Brockett wife of Hezekiah Brockett
Apr. 20. Died ——— Dickerman age 57 yrs. widow of Hezekiah Dickerman
May 3. Died ——— age 4 yrs. son of Lyman Tuttle (N. H. Lyman)
11. Died Martha Hitchcock age 50 yrs. wife of Samuel Hitchcock
June
July
Aug.
Sept.
Oct.
Nov. 10. Died Hannah Dickerman wife of Chauncey Dickerman
Dec. 26. Died Simeon Goodyear age 51 yrs.

FAMILIES
of Ancient
NEW HAVEN

VOLUME V

COMPILED BY
DONALD LINES JACOBUS

PRINTER
CLARENCE D. SMITH
ROME, NEW YORK
1929

Contents

Families of Ancient New Haven

COMPILED BY DONALD LINES JACOBUS

ABBREVIATIONS

b.	born	Lieut.	Lieutenant
Bapt.	Baptist	m.	married
bp.	baptized	Maj.	Major
bu.	buried	Meth.	Methodist
c.	"circa"-about	nat.	"natural"-illegitimate
Capt.	Captain	N. S.	New Style
Col.	Colonel	O. S.	Old Style
Cpl.	Corporal	Rev.	Reverend (clergyman)
d.	died	R. W.	Revolutionary War
da.	daughter of	rem.	removed
Dea.	Deacon	res.	resided, residence
div.	divorced	s.	son of
Dr.	Doctor (physician)	s. p.	"sine prole"-without issue
Ens.	Ensign		
F. & I. W.	French & Indian Wars	Sgt.	Sergeant
Gen.	General	w.	wife of
hr.	hour	wid.	widow of
k.	killed	wk.	week

ABBREVIATIONS FOR SOURCES OF INFORMATION

These abbreviations are made up of two parts, the first signifying the town, the second, the kind of record. Thus, in *NHV*, *NH* means New Haven and *V* the vital statistics of that town. In *WdT1*, the *Wd* means Woodbridge and *T* a gravestone inscription, the figure following the *T* designating a particular graveyard. In *HC2*, the *H* stands for Hamden and *C* for a Congregational church there, the figure following the *C* specifying the particular church. *NoHx* means the Episcopal church of North Haven, *x* always standing for an Episcopal church and *NoH* for North Haven. A list of general symbols for towns and kinds of record are given below, followed by a list (arranged alphabetically by symbols) of the specific record sources.

SYMBOLS FOR TOWNS

B	Bethany	Mid	Middletown	S	Southington
Bd	Branford	My	Middlebury	St	Stratford
C	Cheshire	NH	New Haven	Sy	Southbury
D	Derby	NM	New Milford	W	Wallingford
EH	East Haven	NoB	North Branford	Wat	Waterbury
Farm	Farmington	NoH	North Haven	Wd	Woodbridge
G	Guilford	O	Orange	WH	West Haven
H	Hamden	Oxf	Oxford	Wol	Wolcott
L	Litchfield	P	Plymouth	Wtn	Watertown
M	Milford	Ppt	Prospect	Wy	Woodbury

SYMBOLS FOR KIND OF RECORD

C	Congregational Church record
CCt	County Court record
F	Family, private or Bible record (this symbol always stands alone)
SupCt	Superior Court record
T	Gravestone record
V	Vital (town) record
x	Episcopal Church record

SPECIFIC SOURCES

BAlm	Beckwith's Almanac
BD	Mortality List of Bethany, 1788-1793
BT1	"Cemetery in the Hollow", Bethany
BT2	Episcopal graveyard, Bethany
BT3	"Sperry Cemetery", Bethany
BT4	"Carrington Cemetery", Bethany
BT5	Methodist graveyard, Bethany
BV	Vital statistics, Bethany
Bx	Christ Church (Prot. Ep.), Bethany
BdV	Vital statistics, Branford
CC	Congregational Society, Cheshire
CT1	Old graveyard, Cheshire
CT2	Episcopal graveyard, Cheshire
CV	Vital statistics, Cheshire
Cx	St. Peter's Church (Prot. Ep.), Cheshire
ColR	"Columbian Register", contemporary newspaper
ConnH	"Conn. Herald", contemporary newspaper
DC	Congregational Society, Derby
DT1	Old graveyard, Derby
DT2	Episcopal graveyard, Derby
DT3	"Great Hill Cemetery", Seymour
DT4	Graveyard, Beacon Falls
DT5	Cemetery in North Derby on the Housatonic
DV	Vital statistics, Derby
Dx	St. James Church (Prot. Ep.), Derby
EHC	Congregational Society, East Haven
EHR	"East Haven Register", by Rev. Stephen Dodd
EHT	Old Graveyard, East Haven
EHV	Vital statistatics, East Haven
F	Family, Bible or private records
F&IWRolls	Muster Rolls of Conn. Troops, French and Indian Wars
FarmV	Vital statistics, Farmington
HC1	Congregational Society, Mount Carmel (in Hamden)
HC2	Congregational Society, "East Plain" or Whitneyville (in Hamden)
HT1	"Centerville Cemetery", Hamden
HT2	"Hamden Plains Cemetery", Highwood (in Hamden)

HT3	Old graveyard, Mount Carmel (in Hamden)
HT4	"State Street Cemetery", Hamden
HT5	"Whitneyville Cemetery", Hamden
HT6	"West Woods Cemetery", Hamden
HV	Vital statistics, Hamden
LT	"Litchfield and Morris Inscriptions", by Charles Thomas Payne
LV	Vital statistics, Litchfield
MC1	First Congregational Society, Milford
MC2	Second Congregational Society, Milford
MT	Old graveyard, Milford
MV	Vital statistics, Milford (including mortality lists)
MidV	Vital statistics, Middletown
MyT	Graveyard, Middlebury
NHC1	First Congregational Society, New Haven
NHC2	Second Congregational Society, New Haven
NHT1	City Burial Ground ("Grove Street Cemetery"), New Haven, including stones in Center Church crypt and those removed from the Green
NHT2	"Westville Cemetery", New Haven
NHT3	"Union Cemetery", Fair Haven (in New Haven)
NHT4	"Evergreen Cemetery", New Haven
NHV	Vital statistics, New Haven
NHx	Trinity Church (Prot. Ep.), New Haven
NMV	Vital statistics, New Milford
NoBC1	Congregational Society (1725), North Branford
NoBC2	Congregational Society (1745), Northford (in North Branford)
NoBT1	Graveyard, Northford
NoHC	Congregational Society, North Haven
NoHD	Mortality list of North Haven
NoHT1	Old graveyard, North Haven
NoHT2	Old graveyard, Montowese (in North Haven)
NoHT3	Modern graveyard, North Haven
NoHV	Vital statistics, North Haven
NoHx	St. John's Church (Prot. Ep.), North Haven
OC	Congregational Society, Orange
OT	Graveyard, Orange
OxfC	Congregational Society, Oxford
OxfT1	Two graveyards (close together), Quaker Farms (in Oxford)
OxfT2	"Zoar Bridge Cemetery", Oxford (now removed)
OxfV	Vital statistics, Oxford
PC	Congregational Society, Plymouth (formerly Northbury)
PT	Graveyard, Plymouth
PptT	Graveyard, Prospect
SC	Congregational Society, Southington
SalemC	Congregational Society, Naugatuck
Salemx	St. Michael's Church (Prot. Ep.), Naugatuck
StC	First Congregational Society, Stratford

StV	Vital statistics, Stratford
Stx	Christ Church (Prot. Ep.), Stratford
SyV	Vital statistics, Southbury
WC1	First Congregational Society, Wallingford [records not included]
WC2	First Congregational Society, Meriden
WT1	"Center Street Cemetery", Wallingford
WT2	Old graveyard, Meriden
WV	Vital statistics, Wallingford
Wx	St. Paul's Church (Prot. Ep.), Wallingford [records not included]
WatT1	City Cemetery (now destroyed), Waterbury
WatT2	"East Farms Cemetery", Waterbury
WatT3	Old graveyard and Hillside Cemetery, Naugatuck
WatV	Vital statistics, Waterbury
Watx	St. John's Church (Prot. Ep.), Waterbury
WdC	Congregational Society, Woodbridge
WdD	Mortality List, Woodbridge
WdT1	East Side ~~"Middle Cemetery~~", Woodbridge
WdT2	Graveyard, "Milford side", Woodbridge
WdT3	Graveyard (uear Seymour), Woodbridge
WdV	Vital statistics, Woodbridge
WHD	Mortality lists of Philemon Smith and "Aunt Lucena" Smith, West Haven
WHT1	Congregational graveyard, West Haven
WHT2	Episcopal graveyard, West Haven
WHT3	"Oak Grove Cemetery", West Haven
WolT	Graveyard, Wolcott
WtnD	Mortality lists (Judd and Skilton), Watertown
WtnT	Graveyard, Watertown
WyC	First Congregational Society, Woodbury
WyV	Vital statistics, Woodbury

SYMBOLS IN FRONT OF SURNAMES

*refers to a printed genealogy of the family

†refers to a magazine article on the family

†**JOHNSON.** ORIGIN. Three Johnson brothers, said to have come from Hull, Yorkshire, England, settled early in New Haven; these were JOHN, who rem. to Rowley, Mass., & d 1641 leaving issue; ROBERT (see FAM. 1): and THOMAS (see FAM. 2). A Dutchman, RICHARD JOHNSON (also called "Derrick") settled in New Haven & d 23 Mar 1679 *NHV;* his heir, probably a nephew, was WILLIAM JOHNSON (also called "Wingle", see FAM. 16). Another Dutchman, WALTER JOHNSON (see FAM. 39) settled at W.

FAM. 1. ROBERT JOHNSON, of NH, d 1661; m (1) ——— ; m (2) Adaline ———, who d Apr 1685, having m (2) 7 Jan 1662 *NHV*—Robert Hill & (3) 22 May 1666 *GV*—John Scranton.

(By 1): 1 ROBERT, B. A. (Harvard, 1645), d s. p. 1650.

2 THOMAS, d s. p. 4 Jan 1694/5 *NHV;* m Sep 1663 *NHV*—Frances, wid. John England & Edward Hitchcock.

3 JOHN, d 1687; m 30 Sep 1651 *GV*—Hannah da. John & Hannah Parmelee, who d after 1693.

i Samuel, b 25 Feb 1653 *NHV*, bp 1 Mar 1653 *NHCl;* m ———. **FAM. 3.**

ii Hannah, b 4 Feb 1656 *NHV*, bp 8 Feb 1656 *NHCl*, d [?1697]; m 21 June 1677 *NHV*—Samuel Humiston.

iii John, b 27 Aug 1661 *NHV*, d 1712/3; m 2 Mar 1684/5 *NHV*—Mabel da. Edward & Hannah (Wakefield) Grannis, b c. 1667, d 9 Dec 1745 æ. 79 *DurhamT.* **FAM. 4.**

iv Sarah, b 26 Aug 1664 *NHV*, bp 27 Aug 1664 *NHCl*, d 1 Nov 1732/3 *NHV;* m (1) 8 Feb 1683 *NHV*—John Wolcott; m (2) after 1725 Benjamin Bradley; m (3) 19 June 1729 *NHV*—David Perkins.

v Ruth, b 3 Apr 1667 *NHV;* m 10 Oct 1698 *NHV*—Benjamin Dorman.

vi Abigail, b 9 Apr 1670 *NHV;* m 30 Mar 1692 *BdV*—Joseph Foote.

vii Daniel, b 21 Feb 1671 *NHV* [1671/2], d 1759; m 23 Dec 1707 *NHV*—Mary Sanford, wid. Thomas Tuttle. Only child: (1) Lydia, b 10 Aug 1710 *NHV*, d young.

4 WILLIAM, b c. 1630, d 27 Oct 1702 at G; Dea.; Town Clerk; m 1651 Elizabeth da. Francis Bushnell; 11 children, & descendants in G & Durham; a grandson was Rev. Dr. Samuel Johnson of St, first Pres. of Columbia College.

FAM. 2. THOMAS JOHNSON, drowned in NH harbor 1640; m ———.

1 THOMAS, b c. 1631, d 5 Nov 1695 æ. 64 *Newark, N. J.;* m Ellen da. Arthur Bostwick of St.

i Joseph, b 30 Nov 1651 *NHV*, bp 8 Feb 1656 *NHCl*, d 11 Mar 1733; m Rebecca Pierson.

ii John, b 27 Apr 1654 *NHV*, bp 8 Feb 1656 *NHCl*.

iii Abigail, b 19 Jan 1657 *NHV*, bp 21 Feb 1657 *NHCl*, d c. 1661/2.

iv Saving, bp 25 Nov 1659 *NHCl*, d young.

v Abigail, b 14 June 1662 *NHV*.

vi Thomas, b 11 July 1664 *NHV;* res. Elizabeth, N. J.; m

Sarah Swayne.

vii Eliphalet, b c. 1668, d 1718; m (1) Deborah Ward; m (2) Abigail ——— . A grandson, Rev. Stephen Johnson, rem. from Newark, N. J., to NH, m 26 July 1744 *NHV*—Elizabeth da. William & Sarah (Dunbar) Diodati, had a son Diodati b 29 July 1745 *NHV*, bp 4 Aug 1745 *NHC 1*, and then rem. to Lyme.

2 JEREMIAH, d 1711/2; res. D; m Sarah da. Samuel & Elizabeth (Cleverly) Hotchkiss, bp (adult) 16 May 1675 *MC1*.

i Jeremiah, b 25 Apr 1664 *NHV*, bp 31 Jan 1674/5 *MC1*, d 11 Dec 1726 æ. 62 *DT1;* m 1692 Elizabeth da. Ebenezer & Elizabeth (Wooster) Johnson, b 20 Dec 1672 *DV*, d 1757. **FAM. 5.**

ii Child, b [1666/7] *NHV*, d young.

iii John, b 30 July 1668, bp 31 Jan 1674/5 *MC1*, d 1739; res. Wat; m 24 Sep 1694 *DV*—Mary da. Hope & Mary (Stiles) Washburn, b July 1675. **FAM. 6.**

iv Samuel, b 8 Mar 1670/1 *NHV*, bp 31 Jan 1674/5 *MC1*, d 1726 in Cape May Co., N. J., where he settled as early as 1706; left wid. Abigail & 4 children, Ebenezer, Josiah, Phebe, & Abigail.

v Moses, b 10 Apr 1674, bp 31 Jan 1674/5 *MC1*, d 1754; res. Newtown; m 15 Apr 1703 *DV*—Sarah Adams. **FAM. 7.**

vi Abigail, bp 15 Apr 1677 *MC1*.

vii Ebenezer, b 12 Sep 1679; m Hannah ——; res. Newtown; had Abraham b 19 Aug 1715 & Ichabod b June 1719.

viii Elizabeth, b Apr 1684 *DV*.

FAM. 3. SAMUEL & ——— (———) JOHNSON:

1 ABIGAIL, b 1 Nov 1687 *NHV*, d 2 Dec 1768 æ. 81 *WT1;* m 12 Dec 1710 *WV*—John Cook.

2 CHILD, d 1 Jan 1690 *NHV*.

3 ELIZABETH, b 17 June 1692 *NHV*, d s. p.

4 MARY, b 1 Jan 1694 *NHV*, d 10 May 1760 *WV;* m 30 May 1721 *NHV*, *WV*—Matthew Bellamy.

FAM. 4. JOHN & MABEL (GRANNIS) JOHNSON:

1 JOHN, b 3 Mar 1686/7 *NHV*, bp 15 Mar 1691 *NHC1*, d 17 Oct 1744 *WV;* m 12 July 1711 *WV*—Sarah Jennings, wid. Nathaniel Hitchcock, who d 24 July 1748 *WV*.

i Esther, b 4 May 1712 *WV*, d 6 Apr 1757 *WV;* m 24 Jan 1733 *WV*—Merriman Munson.

ii Barbara, b 5 Feb 1714 *WV*, d before 1761; m 11 May 1736 *WV*—Abraham Ives.

iii Damaris, b 31 Jan 1716 *WV*, d s. p. before 1745; m 23 Dec 1737 *WV*—Wait Abernathy.

iv Daniel, b 14 Dec 1717 *WV*, d 28 June 1761 *WV;* m (1) 26 Dec 1744 *WV*—Ruth da. Stephen & Lydia (Ives) Todd, b 26 Feb 1729 *WV*, d 22 Oct 1748 *WV;* m (2) 1 June 1749

WV—Ann da. Evan & Rachel (Parker) Royce, b 23 June 1727 *WV*; she m (2) 2 Mar 1762 *WV*—Stephen Hotchkiss. **FAM. 8.**

v Phebe, b 28 Apr 1720 *WV*; m 22 Dec 1743 *WV*—Didymus Parker.

vi Jennings, b 7 Jan 1722 *WV*, d 16 Dec 1782 *SC*; m 20 Oct 1748 *WV*—Sarah da. Isaac & Sarah (Osborn) Johnson, b 10 Feb 1729 *WV*, d 31 July 1819 æ. 91 *SC*. **FAM. 9.**

vii Ruth, b 1 Oct 1723 *WV*; m 12 May 1743 *WV*—Abel Hall.

viii Amos, b 4 Mar 1726 *WV*, d after 1785; res. Northford; m 24 Apr 1746 *WV*—Abigail da. Joseph & Abigail (Curtis) Holt, b 20 July 1727 *WV*, d c. 1808; she m (2) Jonah Todd. **FAM. 10.**

ix Patience, b 28 July 1728 *WV*; m 17 Dec 1746 *WV*—Daniel Culver.

2 THOMAS, b 12 Jan 1689/90 *NHV*, bp 15 Mar 1691 *NHCI*, d 22 Apr 1761 (of Mid, at W) *WV*; Capt.; m 1718 Susanna White, b 1694, d 1786.

i Thomas, b 1718, d 1774; Dea.; m 1743 Mary da. Joshua & Mary (Peck) Atwater, b 12 Feb 1727 *WV*, d 1780; she m (2) Ozias Wilcox. Children: 1 Lemuel 1746. 2 Mary 1749. 3 Thomas 1750. 4 Joshua 1753. 5 Samuel. 6 William. 7 Amos. 8 Luther.

ii Stephen, b 1720, d 1776; m 1741 Mary Sage.

iii Susanna, b 1722; m Moses Bush.

iv Hephzibah; m (1) 1744 Edward Shepherd; m (2) Aaron Roberts.

v Ruth; m 1747 John Gill.

vi Daniel, b 1729, d 1756; Capt.; m 1752 Abigail Goodwin. Children: 1 Daniel 1753. 2 Thomas 1755.

vii Amos, b 1731, d 1758; m 1753 Mary Kirby. Children: 1 James 1754. 2 Hephzibah 1756. 3 Luther 1758.

viii Desire, b 1735; m (1) 1756 Charles Burn; m (2) Noah Smith.

ix Thankful, b 1735; m 1755 Elisha Savage.

3 ANN, b Feb 1691 *NHV* [1691/2], bp Dec 1691 *NHCI*; m 20 Apr 1720 *NHV*—Willet Ranney of Mid.

4 SARAH, b 9 Apr 1694 *NHV*, bp Apr 1694 *NHCI*.

5 DANIEL, b 22 Apr 1696 *NHV*, bp 26 Apr 1696 *NHCI*, d s. p.

6 JOSEPH, b 2 Dec 1698 *NHV*, bp Nov 1698 *NHCI*; res. Durham 1732, Mid 1738, Hartford 1751; m 1725 Hannah Andrus. Children recorded at Mid: *i* Rachel 1726. *ii* Elisha, d soon. *iii* Ann 1731. *iv* Hannah 1733. *v* Phebe 1735. *vi* Elisha 1737. *vii* Esther 1739. *viii* Ruth 1741.

7 BENJAMIN, b 9 Mar 1701 *NHV*, d c. 1799; res. Durham; m Eunice Sutliff, who d c. 1784.

i Eunice, b 16 Sep 1733 *DurhamV*, bp 23 Sep 1733 *DurhamC*; m ——— Newton.

ii Mehitabel, b 23 Nov 1734 *DurhamV*, bp 24 Nov 1734 *DurhamC;* m Abiel Baldwin.

iii Submit, b 28 Sep 1736 *DurhamV*, bp 3 Oct 1736 *DurhamC*, d young.

iv Thankful, bp 14 May 1738 *DurhamC*, d young.

v John, b 28 July 1739 *DurhamV*, bp 5 Aug 1739 *DurhamC*, d young.

vi John, bp 8 Nov 1741 *DurhamC*.

vii Samuel, bp 4 Sep 1743 *DurhamC*.

8 Robert, b 5 June 1703 *NHV;* res. Mid 1732 & 1749; m 1736 Sarah Sill of Lyme, who d 1774. Children recorded at Mid: *i* Eliphalet 1737, d 1737. *ii* Robert 1739. *iii* Sarah 1742. *iv* Enoch 1746. *v* Elisha 1749. *vi* James 1752.

9 James, b 3 Sep 1705 *NHV;* res. Hopewell, N. J. 1750; m Oct 1724 *NHV*—Eunice da. Thomas & Abigail Bivins of Mid. Family incomplete. *i* Abigail, b 17 June 1726 *NHV*, 10 June 1727 *WatV*. *ii* Eunice, b 21 June 1729 *WatV*. *iii* Mehitabel, b 27 May 1731 *WatV*.

10 Mehitabel, b 29 Feb 1707/8 *NHV;* m 22 Sep 1730 *BdV*—Timothy Rose.

11 Hannah, b 23 May 1710 *NHV;* m Benjamin Hand of Mid.

FAM. 5. Jeremiah & Elizabeth (Johnson) Johnson:

1 Gideon, b 1694, d 1761; Dea.; m 6 Nov 1718 *DV*—Abigail da. John & Anna (Harger) Chatfield, b 2 Sep 1693 *DV*.

i Mabel, b 24 Aug 1719 *DV*, d 1 Dec 1806; m 20 Feb 1739/40 *DV*—Joseph Riggs.

ii Elizabeth, b 25 Aug 1722 *DV;* m 9 July 1741 *DV*—Daniel Tucker.

iii Gideon, b 3 Jan 1724/5 *DV;* m 24 Mar 1749 *DV*, 23 Mar *WdC*—Lydia da. Ebenezer & Hannah (Mix) Beecher, b 16 Mar 1725/6 *NHV*. **FAM. 11**

iv Ichabod, b 3 Mar 1726/7 *DV*, d young.

v Abigail, b 26 Jan 1730/1 *DV;* m 9 Nov 1749 *DV*—Peter Johnson.

2 Joseph, b 1696, d 1761; Lieut.; m 24 Jan 1717 *DV*—Margaret da. Samuel & Hannah (Stiles) Harger, b 6 Dec 1695 *DV*, d 1774.

i Joseph, b 29 Nov 1717 *DV*, d 15 June 1787 æ. 70 *DV;* m 5 Aug 1738 *DV*—Elizabeth da. John & Elizabeth (Bryan) Durand, b 6 Feb 1718/9 *DV*, d 1 Oct 1784 æ. 66 *DV*. **FAM. 12.**

ii Samuel, b 23 Dec 1719 *DV*, d 1788; m Mary da. John & Elizabeth (Bryan) Durand; Census, Mary (D) 0-0-1. **FAM. 13.**

iii Jeremiah, b 1 Apr 1722 *DV*, d s. p. after 1732.

iv Eliphalet, b 1 Apr 1725 *DV*, d [1741] æ. 16 *DTI*.

v Margaret, b c. 1728, d 9 Nov 1765 *DV;* m (1) Elias Frink of Windham; m (2) 15 Mar 1758 *DV*—Nathan Smith.

vi Hannah, b 16 Feb 1729/30 *DV*, d 26 July 1752 *DV;* m Ebenezer Durand.

vii Nathaniel, b 11 Feb 1731/2 *DV;* Capt.; Census (D) 3-1-2; m 30 Jan 1753 *DV*—Susanna da. Joseph & Martha (Beaman) Smith, b 23 Dec 1730 *WatV*, d 1810. **FAM. 14.**

3 ZERVIAH, b c. 1698, d 10 [——] 1734 æ. 37 *DT1;* m 22 July 1719 Timothy Baldwin.

4 ELIZABETH, b c. 1701, d 8 June 1751 *DV;* m 12 Dec 172[1] *DV*—John Chatfield.

5 BENAJAH, b 24 July 1704 *DV*, d 13 Apr 1763 æ. 59 *DV*, *DT1;* m 10 Oct 1728 *DV*—Sarah Brewster, wid. Joseph Hawkins, who d 7 May 1773 *DV*, æ. 72 *Rimmon HillT*.

i Sarah, b 16 Aug 1729 *DV*, d 31 May 1766 *WatV*, æ. 37 *WatT3;* m 13 Dec 1749 *WatV*—John Hopkins.

ii Benajah, b 20 Aug 1732 *DV;* res. Seymour.

iii Isaac, b 6 Oct 1735 *DV*, d 10 Apr 1813 æ. 78 *SeymourT* (*Meth*); res. Seymour; Census (D) 2-2-4; m 24 Jan 1758 *DV*—Lois da. Stephen & Susanna (Peck) Hopkins, b 22 June 1738 *WatV*, d 16 Oct 1814 æ. 76 *SeymourT*(*Meth*). **FAM. 15.**

iv Zerviah, b 13 Feb 1738/9 *DV*, d 29 May 1816 æ. 77 *DT4;* m 3 Sep 1761 *DV*—Abiel Fairchild.

v Amos, b 13 Aug 1743 *DV*.

6 ABNER, b 10 Apr 1709 *DV*, d 12 Nov 1780 æ. 72 *OxfC;* m 9 Aug 1738 *DV*—Abigail da. John & Elizabeth (Bryan) Durand, b 2 June 1716 *DV*, d 1805 æ. 90 *OxfV*.

i Mabel, b 23 May 1739 *DV*, d 1815 æ. 77 *OxfV;* m Apr 1760 *DV*—James Perry.

ii Timothy, b 11 June 1741 *DV*, d s. p. 1796 æ. 55 *OxfV*

iii Jeremiah, b 21 Mar 174[5] *DV;* Census (Sy) 1-2-5; m 8 Nov 1769 *SyC*—Eunice Bronson; had issue.

iv Abner, b 22 Feb 1751/2 *DV*.

v Abigail, b 13 Apr 1757 *DV;* m Noah Fulford.

FAM. 6. JOHN & MARY (WASHBURN) JOHNSON:

1 ABRAHAM, b 6 Dec 1694 *DV*, d 18 Jan 1712 *DV*.

2 MARY, b 7 Nov 1696 *DV*, d 12 May 1760 *WatV;* m 4 June 1722 *WatV*—Samuel Barnes.

3 JANE, d s. p.; m 8 June 1738 *WatV*—James Hull.

4 SILAS, b 18 July 1713 *DV;* rem. from Wat to NH; m 5 Dec 1733 *WatV*—Sarah da. John Moses of Simsbury.

i Sarah, b 5 July 1734 *WatV*, d before 1766; m 2 Apr 1760 *WdV*—Asa Sperry.

ii John, b 24 June 1736 *WatV;* Census (Tinmouth, Vt.) 1-0-3; m 11 Sep 1759 *NHV*—Mehitabel da. Jonathan & Mehitabel (Downs) Sperry, b 9 Nov 1739 *NHV*. Children (incomplete): 1 Rebecca, b 6 Feb 1760 *NHV*, bp 5 Oct 1760 *NHC1*. 2 Elihu, bp 19 June 1763 *NHC1;* Census (Tinmouth, Vt.) 1-2-1.

iii Lemuel, b 14 Nov 1739 *WatV*, d 29 Nov 1739 *WatV*.

iv Mary, b 12 June 1741 *WatV;* m 8 Apr 1762 *WdC*—Samuel

Carrington.
v Jane, b 25 Mar 1744 *WatV*.
vi Elihu, b 22 Aug 1747 *WatV*, d 28 Dec 1749 *WtnD*.

FAM. 7. MOSES & SARAH (ADAMS) JOHNSON:
1 HANNAH, b 1 Mar 1704 *DV;* m 21 May 1728 *FC*—Daniel Bulkeley of Fairfield.
2 MABEL, b 18 Oct 1707 *DV;* m 14 Dec 1730 *FV*—David Bartram.
3 JEREMIAH, b 20 Sep 1711 *DV;* m 18 Mar 1731 *StV*—Zipporah da. Peter & Elizabeth (Trowbridge) Mallory, b 15 Dec 1705 *StV*.
i Sarah, b 13 Dec 1731 *NewtownV*.
ii Charity, b 16 July 1733 *NewtownV*.
iii Abigail, b 16 Sep 1735 *NewtownV*.
iv Moses, b 30 July 1737 *NewtownV*.
v Phebe, b 13 July 1740 *NewtownV*.
vi Alice, b 2 Oct 1742 *NewtownV*.
4 RACHEL, b 13 Mar 1712 *DV* [1712/3]; m John Moger.
5 SARAH; m 19 July 1744 *FV*—Daniel Meeker.

FAM. 8. DANIEL & ANN (ROYCE) JOHNSON:
1 JOHN, b 11 Apr 1750 *WV*, d 1799; Census (W) 1-1-2; m (1) 17 Jan 1769 *WV*—Huldah [da. Gershom] Tuttle, b [21 June 1749 *FarmV*], d 20 Jan 1775 *WV;* m (2) 5 Oct 1775 *WV*—Mamre da. Dayton & Hannah (Beadles) Johnson, b 25 Aug 1752 *WV;* she div. him 1799.
(By 1): *i* Lovicy, b 6 July 1769 *WV*.
ii John (called s. of John & Mary), b 6 June 1770 *WV*.
(By 2): *iii* John Chester, b 19 July 1777 *WV*.
iv Huldah, b 26 Aug 1781 *WV*.
He had a nat. child by Miriam Newton:
v John Newton, b c. 1798.

FAM. 9. JENNINGS & SARAH (JOHNSON) JOHNSON:
1 SARAH, b 4 June 1749 *WV*.
2 DAMARIS, b 26 June 1751 *WV;* m Solomon Newell.
3 STEPHEN, b 18 Mar 1754 *WV*, d 25 June 1808 æ. 54 *SC;* Census (S) 2-4-3; m 9 June 1779 *CC*—Ruth da. Samuel Smith, who d 21 Dec 1831 æ. 78 *SC*.
i Chester, b 21 Aug 1779 *SV*.
ii Marilla, b 18 Sep 1781 *SV;* m 16 Sep 1804 *SC*—Jesse Ives of Meriden.
iii Leonard, b 15 June 1783 *SV*.
iv Ruth; m 27 July 1814 *SC*—Orrin Lee.
v Jasper; m Amanda Richards.
vi Carmi, b 31 Oct 1789; m (1) 23 Feb 1814 Urania Moss, who d 6 June 1835 *SC;* m (2) Merab (Rice) Baldwin.
vii Susanna; m ——— Merriman.
viii Memucan; m Mary Moss.
ix Cephas; res. Meriden.
4 ESTHER, b 27 Nov 1756 *WV*.
5 RACHEL, b 29 Oct 1759 *WV*.

6 BARNABAS, b 5 Dec 1762 *WV*, d soon.

7 BARNABAS, b 8 Apr 1765 *WV*, d 8 Apr 1765 *WV*.

8 BARNABAS, b 17 Jan 176[7] *WV*, d 22 Apr 1814 æ. 50 *SC;* Census (S) 1-0-1; m (1) Thankful ——, who d 25 May 1791 æ. 22 *SC;* m (2) ——.

9 RUTH, b 28 Dec 1769 *WV*, d 29 Dec 1769 *WV*.

FAM. 10. AMOS & ABIGAIL (HOLT) JOHNSON:

1 LUCY, b 11 Sep 1747 *WV*, d 21 Jan 1808 æ. 62 *F;* m 7 Sep 1769 *WV*—Samuel Preston.

2 ESTHER, b 16 Nov 1749 *WV;* m (1) Charles Tuttle; m (2) Moses Peck.

3 SYBIL, b 16 Sep 1751 *WV*, d probably s. p.

4 SIMEON; Census (Bristol) 1-7-5; m 4 Mar 1773 *WV*—Miriam da. Enos Johnson. Family incomplete.

i Ann, b 20 July 1773 *WV*.

ii Clarinda, b 20 July 1774 *WV*.

iii Benjamin, b 11 Mar 1776 *WV*.

iv Simeon, b 12 Nov 1777 *WV*.

5 AMOS; Census (Bristol) 1-3-2; m 15 Sep 1777 *WV*—Eunice Daily.

6 ABIGAIL, d after 1808; Census (Bristol) 1-0-1.

7 ELIHU, b 7 June 1773 *WV*.

FAM. 11. GIDEON & LYDIA (BEECHER) JOHNSON:

1 ANNA, b 28 Jan 1748/9 *DV*.

2 GIDEON, b 4 Feb 1749/50 *DV*, d 24 Dec 1835; Census (D) 1-0-0; m 1793 Sarah da. Hopestill & Abigail (Heaton) Crittenden, wid. Jeremiah Tuttle, b 16 Apr 1762 *NHV*.

i Hopie, b 1794 *F*, d 1869; m Henry L. Noble; rem. to Ohio.

ii Sheldon Crittenden, b 6 Nov 1797, d 13 Nov 1887; Dr.; res. Seymour; m 18 May 1828 Susan Hannah da. Dr. Abiram & Eunice (Clark) Stoddard, b 5 Aug 1809, d 30 July 1888.

3 HANNAH, b 3 Sep 1752 *DV;* m 22 Mar 1775 *DV*—John Adee.

4 LYDIA, b 31 May 1754 *DV*.

5 MABEL, b 22 Sep 1756 *DV*, bp 12 Jan 1757 *DC;* m 15 Feb 1781 Edmund Mallory.

6 LEVI, bp 14 June 1761 *DC*, d 1795; Census (D) 1-0-0; m Martha da. Hezekiah Clark, b 14 Apr 1764 *F;* she m (2) James Kellogg.

i Laura.

ii Rebecca.

7 EBENEZER BEECHER, b 24 Nov 1763 *F*, bp 27 May 1764 *DC*, d 24 July 1847 æ. 84 *SeymourT (Cong);* Census (D) 1-0-4; m 25 May 1785 Hannah P. Clark, who d 17 Sep 1846 æ. 80 *Seymour T (Cong)*.

FAM. 12. JOSEPH & ELIZABETH (DURAND) JOHNSON:

1 ASAHEL, b 15 Aug 1739 *DV*, d 14 June 1811 æ. 75 *WHD;* Census (D) 1-2-3; m (1) 19 May 1756 *DV*—Lois Williams of Fairfield,

who d 28 Jan 1783 æ. 49 *DV;* m (2) 6 Apr 1783 *DV*—Miriam da. Stephen & Miriam (Clark) Treat, wid. Abraham Ranney & William Fowler, b 30 Oct 1748 (at Mid), d 28 Aug 1822 æ. 75 *WHD.*

(By 1): *i* Esther, b 3 May 1757 *DV*, bp 14 Aug 1757 *DC.*

ii Joel, b 1 May 1759 *DV*, bp 29 July 1759 *DC*, d 23 Aug 1777 (at King's Bridge) *DV*.

iii Philena, b 5 Oct 1761 *DV*, bp Jan 1762 *DC*, d 14 Sep 1835 æ. 73 *BT3;* m Hezekiah Beecher.

iv Lucy, b 25 Aug 1763 *DV*, bp 23 Oct 1763 *DC.*

v Lois, b 11 Mar 1766 *DV*, bp 22 Mar 1766 *DC;* m 20 Sep 1788 *NHSupCt*—Nathan Smith.

vi Eunice, b 11 Mar 1766 *DV*, bp 22 Mar 1766 *DC.*

vii Elisha, b 27 Oct 1767 *DV*, bp 2 Mar 1768 *DC.*

viii Milly, b 5 Oct 1769 *DV*, bp 19 Nov 1769 *DC.*

ix Bryant, b 5 Sep 1772 *DV.*

x Joel, d s. p. 10 Aug 1800 *WHD.*

xi Olive Camp, bp 9 Aug 1778 *DC.*

(By 2): *xii* Polly, "child" bp 31 Oct 1784 *Dx*, d 10 Sep 1869 æ. 84 (at WH) *BAlm;* m Ebenezer Thompson.

xiii Fowler, d 30 Sep 1805 *WHD.*

xiv Dolly.

xv Miriam.

2 ELISHA, b 10 Apr 1741 *DV.*

3 ELIPHALET, b 22 Aug 1743 *DV.*

4 JEREMIAH, b 29 Dec 1745 *DV*, d 8 Sep 1801 æ. 50 (*sic*) *OxfV;* Census (D) 2-1-3; m 3/4 Dec 1767 *DV*—Hannah da. Samuel & Mary (Durand) Johnson, b 12 Feb 1749/50 *DV*, d 23 Sep 1781 *OxfC.*

i Ezra, b 6 Nov 1768 *DV.*

ii Hannah, b 12 Oct 1769 *DV;* m Abraham English.

iii Charity, b 24 Sep 1772 *DV.*

iv Child, d 17 Sep 1774 (infant) *OxfC.*

v Jeremiah, b 17 Nov 1775 *DV*, bp 4 Feb 1776 *OxfC.*

vi Polly, b 29 Aug 1778 *DV*, bp 18 Oct 1778 *OxfC.*

5 HEZEKIAH, b 25 Oct 1748 *DV*, d 15 Nov 1826; Census (D) 1-1-4; m 12 Dec 1784 *DV*—Rebecca Jordan, b 14 Feb 1756, d 1 May 1830.

i Elizabeth, b 6 Dec 1785 *DV*, d 6 Dec 1785 *DV.*

ii Elizabeth, b 26 Nov 1786 *DV;* m 2 Nov 1805 Bela Northrop.

iii Newell, b 22 May 1789 *DV*, d 11 June 1879; of Westville; m (1) Betsey da. Benjamin & Martha Moulthrop; m (2) 2 Sep 1810 Esther da. Elias & Content Carrington.

6 MARGARET, b 7 Dec 1750 *DV*, d 20 Feb 1751 *DV.*

7 ELIZABETH, b 4 Mar 1753 *DV;* m Jehiel Hine.

8 MARGARET, b 16 June 1756 *DV*, bp 28 June 1756 *Dx*, d 1811 æ. 55 *OxfV;* m (1) Dec 1773 *DV*—David Twitchell; m (2) Jared

Osborn.

9 JOSEPH, bp Nov 1759 *Dx*, d 25 June 1818 *DV;* m Hannah Banks, who d 21 Apr 1851 æ. 80; had issue.

FAM. 13. SAMUEL & MARY (DURAND) JOHNSON:

1 ELIZABETH, b 25 Feb 1742 *DV*, d s. p.

2 LAURANA, b 10 Dec 1744 *DV;* m 18 Sep 1765 *DV*—Jeremiah O'Kean.

3 MERCY, b 21 June 1747 *DV;* m Nehemiah Botsford.

4 HANNAH, b 12 Feb 1749/50 *DV*, d 23 Sep 1781 *OxfC;* m 3/4 Dec 1767 *DV*—Jeremiah Johnson.

5 SARAH, b 22 Aug 1752 *DV*, d soon.

6 [SAMUEL].

7 SARAH, bp 27 Nov 1757 *DC*.

8 MARY, bp 13 July 1760 *DC;* m ——— Peet.

9 ELIPHALET, b 2 Feb 1763 *DV*, bp 8 May 1763 *DC*.

10 MARGARET, b 21 Apr 1765 *DV*, bp 16 June 1765 *DC*.

FAM. 14. NATHANIEL & SUSANNA (SMITH) JOHNSON:

1 PHILO, b 4 May 1754 *DV*, d 1804; Census (D) 1-1-4; m Beath da. Abraham & Elizabeth (Bassett) Hawkins, b 25 Aug 1755 *DV*.

2 SABRA, b 12 June 1756 *DV*, bp 18 July 1756 *DC*, d 8 Oct 1763 *DV*.

3 AMOS, b 17 Jan 1759 *DV*, bp 25 Feb 1759 *DC;* Census (D) 1-0-4.

4 SUSANNA, b 15 July 1762 *DV*, bp 15 Aug 1762 *DC*, d 31 Jan 1851 æ. 88 *OT;* m John Hine.

5 SARAH, b 15 July 1762 *DV*, bp 15 Aug 1762 *DC;* m —— Pierson.

6 ANDREW, b 3 Apr 1765 *DV*, bp 5 May 1765 *DC;* m Lucy ———, who d 7 July 1821 æ. 52 *DTl*.

7 SABRA, b 8 July 1767 *DV*, bp 23 Aug 1767 *DC;* m 17 Dec 1783 *WatV*—Philo Pritchard.

8 NATHANIEL, b 21 July 1769 *DV*, bp 27 Aug 1769 *DC*, d s. p.

9 DAVID, b 21 June 1771 *DV*, bp 11 Aug 1771 *DC*, d 2 Jan 1849 æ. 77 *DTl;* m Susan ———, who d 11 Apr 1831 æ. 54 *DTl*.

10 LUCY, b 9 Sep 1774 *DV*, bp 16 Oct 1774 *DC*, d s. p.

FAM. 15. ISAAC & LOIS (HOPKINS) JOHNSON:

1 MOLLY, b 4 Apr 1759 *DV*, bp 27 May 1759 *DC*, d 13 Oct 1846 æ. 88 *DTl;* m 4 Aug 1782 Abram Smith.

2 SUSANNA, bp 12 Oct 1760 *DC;* [m 7 Aug 1780 *F*—Nathaniel Warren.]

3 SARAH BREWSTER, bp 19 Sep 1762 *DC*.

4 LOIS, b (as "Susanna") 24 Nov 1763 *DV*, bp 12 Feb 1764 *DC*.

5 RUTH, b 31 Mar 1765 *DV*, bp 12 May 1765 *DC;* m John Coe.

6 MABEL, b 27 Nov 1766 *DV*, bp 1 Mar 1767 *DC;* m 6 Oct 1784 Abraham Canfield.

7 ISAAC, b 2 July 1769 *DV*, bp 6 Aug 1769 *DC*, d 4 Dec 1774 *DV*, æ. 5-5-2 *DTl*.

8 AMOS HAWKINS, b 26 Mar 1771 *DV*, bp 12 May 1771 *DC*, d 26 Sep 1772 *DV*, æ. 0-18 *DTl*.

9 JESSE, b 28 July 1773 *DV*, bp 5 Sep 1773 *DC*, d 21 Oct 1829 æ. 56

SeymourT (*Meth*); Rev.; insane; m (1) 1795 Hephzibah da. David & Hannah (Lines) French, b 16 June 1779 *F*, d 13 Apr 1823 æ. 44 *SeymourT* (*Meth*); m (2) 10 Apr 1825 Mary ——, who d 1839.

(By 1): *i* Sally Brewster, b 6 Sep 1797 *DV*; m Jared Bassett.

ii Isaac, b 2 Apr 1799 *DV*, d 7 July 1836; m Susan White.

iii Jesse, b 28 Mar 1801 *DV*, d 9 Feb 1826 æ. 25 *SeymourT* (*Meth*); m Hannah ——.

iv Hephzibah, b 28 Jan 1803 *DV*; m 24 Apr 1820 Frederick Rowe.

v Harvey, b 30 Mar 1805 *DV*, d 28 July 1840; m 1827 Nancy Hotchkiss.

vi Polly, b 12 July 1807 *DV*; m —— Nichols.

vii Lois Emily, b 24 Feb 1810 *DV*; m Peter Varder.

viii Stiles, b 14 May 1813 *DV*; m 23 Feb 1834 Samantha Curtis.

ix Laura, b 2 June 1819 *F*.

x Chauncey, b Jan 1823 *F*.

10 Isaac, b c. 1775, d 3 July 1777 *DV*, æ. 2 *DT1*.

11 Chauncey, b 19 Apr 1777 *DV*, bp 1 June 1777 *DC*, d 26 Dec 1814 æ. 37 *SeymourT* (*Meth*); m (1) Ruth ——, who d Mar 1807 æ. 27 *SeymourT* (*Meth*); m (2) Mary da. Timothy & Mercy (Clark) White, wid. Benjamin English.

12 Ann, b 22 Mar 1779 *DV*, bp (as "Mary") 16 May 1779 *DC*, d 8 Feb 1764 æ. 85 *DT4*; m 1797 David French.

13 Stiles, b 4 Dec 1781 *DV*, bp 17 Feb 1782 *DC*, d. s. p. 4 Oct 1818; m Cynthia ——.

JOHNSON. FAM. 16. William, d 1716; m Dec 1664 *NHV*—Sarah da. John & Jane (Woolen) Hall, bp 9 Aug 1646 *NHC1*.

1 William, b 15 Sep 1665 *NHV*, d 1742; Lieut.; m (1) Elizabeth da. Joseph & Mary (Potter) Mansfield, b 20 Sep 1666 *NHV*; m (2) Sarah da. Matthew & Sarah (Peck) Gilbert, wid. Thomas Morris, b 10 Mar 1685/6 *NHV*.

(By 1): *i* Elizabeth, b 15 Mar 1692 *NHV*, bp c. Sep 1695 *NHC1*, d c. Apr 1756; m 1 Mar 1720/1 *NHV*—Josiah Thomas.

ii William, b 5 Aug 1695 *NHV*, bp c. Sep 1695 *NHC1*; m 27 Dec 1721 *NHV*—Elizabeth da. Thomas & Elizabeth (Farnes) Sperry, b 25 Nov 1695 *NHV*. **FAM. 17.**

iii Anna, b 5 Aug 1697 *NHV*, bp Aug 1697 *NHC1*; m 19 Nov 1717 *BdV*—Joseph Foote.

iv Sarah, bp 21 May 1699 *NHC1*; m 18 Mar 1724/5 *NHCCt*—Zebulon Carrington.

v Lydia, b Aug 1701 *NHV*, d young.

vi Stephen, b 28 Aug 1704 *NHV*, d 1797; Census (NH) 1-0-1; m (1) 1725 *NHCCt*—Mercy da. John & Sarah (Clark) Wilmot, b 3 Feb 1698 *NHV* [1698/9]; m (2) 25 Oct 1752 *NHC2*—Sarah da. John & Mercy (Jacobs) Hull, b 26 Jan 1707/8 *NHV*. **FAM. 18.**

vii Amos, b 29 Mar 1708 *NHV*, d 8 May 1766 *CornwallC;* m Amy da. Daniel & Elizabeth Palmer, b 8 July 1713 *BdV*. **FAM. 19.**

viii Timothy.

2 John, b 20 July 1667 *NHV*, d 1744; m (1) Abigail da. Daniel & Abiah (Street) Sherman, b 5 Sep 1665 *NHV*, d 4 Oct 1739 *NHTI;* m (2) 19 Nov 1741 *WC2*—Joanna da. Joseph & Sarah (Stanley) Gaylord, wid. Robert Royce; she m (3) 19 Dec 1745 *WC2*—Joseph Holt.

(By 1): *i* Abraham, b 7 Apr 1694 *NHV*, d 1775; m 24 Jan 1715/6 *NHV*—Sarah da. da. John & Mary (Ives) Gilbert, b 31 July 1694 *NHV*. **FAM. 20.**

ii Abigail, b 28 Sep 1695 *NHV*, d s. p. 5 Mar 1778 æ. 83 *NHTI;* m 9 May 1722 *NHV*—Thomas Holt.

iii John, b 13 Nov 1696 *NHV*, d after 1774; m (1) 20 June 1722 *NHV*—Charity da. James & Sarah (Griswold) Hill, b 4 Mar 1696 *GdV;* m (2) Lydia da. Matthew & Elizabeth (Bradley) Ford, b 29 July 1722 *NHV;* Census, Lydia (NH) 1-0-3. **FAM. 21.**

3 Abraham, b 10 Mar 1668/9 *NHV*, d young.

4 Abigail, b 6 Dec 1670 *NHV;* m 31 Mar 1692 *NHV*—Joseph Lines.

5 Isaac, b 27 Oct 1672 *NHV*, bp 10 Jan 1685/6 *NHCI*, d 23 Oct 1750 *NHV*, æ. 78 *WdTI;* Dea.; Capt.; m (1) 25 Apr 1699 *NHV*—Abigail da. John & Mary (Thompson) Cooper, b 3 Oct 1679 *NHV*, d 6 Dec 1724 æ. 45 *NHTI;* m (2) Sarah da. John & Mercy (Todd) Bassett, wid. Daniel Bradley, b 3 June 1682 *NHV*, d 1771.

(By 1): *i* Rebecca, b 7 July 1700 *NHV*, d 17 Jan 1723 æ. 23 *NHTI*.

ii Eunice, b 1 May 1703 *NHV*, d 5 Sep 1725 æ. 22 *NHTI*.

iii Isaac, b 24 Oct 1705 *NHV*, d 1758; m (1) 11 Jan 1727/8 *NHV*—Hannah da. Nathaniel & Sarah (Dickermau) Sperry, b 19 Dec 1702 *NHV;* m (2) c. 1755 Dorcas da. John & Mehitabel (Wolcott) Ford, wid. Benjamin Warner, b 5 Nov 1712 *NHV*, d c. 1788; she m (3) Joseph Mansfield. **FAM. 22.**

iv Dorcas, b 10 Aug 1707 *NHV*, d 29 Dec 1723 æ. 16 *NHTI*.

v Abigail, b 9 Feb 1709/10 *NHV*, d c. 1748; m Enos Sperry.

vi Ezra, b 29 Mar 1712 *NHV*, d 1753; m (1) 13 Feb 1734/5 *NHV*—Sarah da. Ebenezer & Rebecca (Sperry) Lines, b 28 Apr 1714 *NHV*, d c. 1735/6; m (2) Mary da. Joseph & Mary (Wilmot) Dorman, wid. Jonathan Mansfield, b 24 Oct 1711 *NHV*, d 18 July 1794 æ. 82 *WdTI*. **FAM. 23.**

vii Obed, b 27 July 1714 *NHV*, d 1760; m (1) 5 Jan 1737/8 *NHV*—Amy da. John & Sarah (Clark) Wilmot; m (2) 16 Apr 1752 *NHV*—Rebecca da. John & Rebecca (Prime) Clark, b 19 Nov 1724 *MV*, d 14 June 1795 æ. 73 *NHCI*.

FAM. 24.

viii Rachel, b 13 Apr 1716 *NHV*, bp 15 July 1716 *NHCl*; m 1735 *NHCCt*—Valentine Wilmot.

ix Lois, b 3 Dec 1719 *NHV*, bp Feb 1719/20 *NHCl*, d 23 June 1750 *NHV*, æ. 23 (?) *NHTl*; m 26 May 1743 *NHV*, *Wd C*—Ebenezer Beecher.

x David, b 27 Apr 1721 *NHV*, bp 4 June 1721 *NHCl*, d 1758; m 14 May 1744 *NHV*, *WdC*—Rachel da. Nathaniel & Sarah (Wilmot) Sperry, b 9 Feb 1722/3 *NHV*, d c. 1775; she m (2) James Peck. FAM. 25.

6 JACOB, b 25 Sep 1674 *NHV*, d 26 July 1749 *WV*, 17 July æ. 75 *W Tl*; Sgt.; m (1) 14 Dec 1693 *WV*—Abigail da. John & Abigail (Merriman) Hitchcock, b 10 Apr 1674 *NHV*, d 9 Jan 1726 *WV*; m (2) 20 June 1726 *WV*—Dorcas Phippen, wid. Jonathan Linsley, who d 1760.

(By 1): *i* Reuben, b 27 Aug 1694 *WV*, d 1778; m 11 Mar 1718 *WV*—Mary da. Isaac & Rebecca (Tuttle) Dayton. FAM. 26.

ii Isaac, b 21 Feb 1696 *WV*, d 29 Apr 1779 æ. 84 *WTl*; Dea.; m (1) 27 Nov 1723 *NHV*, 24 Nov *WV*—Sarah da. Joseph & Mary Osborn, b May 1702 *NHV*, d 16 Nov 1766 *WV*; m (2) 16 Apr 1767 *WV*—Elizabeth da. Nathaniel & Sarah (Jennings) Hitchcock, wid. Nathaniel Beadles, b 26 Jan 1707 *WV*, d 22 Nov 1773 *WV*; m (3) 6 Jan 1774 *WV*—Phebe da. Daniel & Ruth (How) Tuttle, wid. Samuel Miles, b 8 Jan 1719 *WV*, d 3 Mar 1790. FAM. 27.

iii Enos, b June 1697 *WV*, d 31 Jan 1786 æ. 88 *WTl*; m ——— . FAM. 28.

iv Abigail, b 1699 *WV*, d 4 Nov 1742 *WV*, *WTl*; m 14 Dec 1726 *WV*—Benjamin Holt.

v Abner, b 2 Aug 1702 *WV*, d 28 Dec 1757 *WV*; Capt.; m 14 Dec 1726 *WV*—Charity da. Isaac & Rebecca (Tuttle) Dayton, who d 9 Dec 1756 *WV*. FAM. 29.

vi Caleb, b 1703 *WV* [error for 1704], d s. p. 13 Oct 1777 æ. 74 *WV*, æ. 73 *WTl*; m 28 Jan 1731 *WV*—Rachel da. Samuel & Rachel (Brown) Brockett, b 23 Mar 1708 *WV*, d 25 Jan 1796 æ. 88 *WTl*.

vii Israel, b 1705 *WV* [error for 1706], d 20 Sep 1747 *WV*, æ. 41 *WTl*; m 26 Jan 1732 *WV*—Sarah da. John & Sarah (Ball) Miles, b 28 Aug 1717 *WV*, d 7 May 1773 *WV*. FAM. 30.

viii Daniel, b 1707 *WV* [error for 1708], d 14 Oct 1780 *WV*, æ. 72 *WTl*; m 24 Dec 1734 *WV*—Joanna da. Eliasaph & Rebecca (Wilcoxen) Preston, b 18 Mar 1714, d 18 Jan 1781 *WV*, æ. 67 *WTl*. FAM. 31.

ix Sarah, b 1710 *WV*; m 9 May 1734 *WV*—Daniel Bartholomew.

x Jacob, b 4 Apr 1713 *WV*, d 15 Mar 1797; Rev.; res. WilkesBarre, Pa.; m Mary Giddings, b 1730, d c. 1791; 4 children.

(By 2): *xi* Lydia, b c. 1727, d 3 June 1729 *WV*.

7 SARAH, b 6 Nov 1676 *NHV*, bp 10 Jan 1685/6 *NHC1;* m Samuel Horton.

8 SAMUEL, b 3 Sep 1678 *NHV*, bp 10 Jan 1685/6 *NHC1*, d 1755; m 13 Dec 1705 *NHCCt*—Anna da. Thomas & Sarah (Wilmot) Hotchkiss, b 12 Dec 1684 *NHV*.

i Sarah, bp (adult) 20 June 1736 *NHC1;* m Daniel Smith.

ii Amy; m ——— Pease.

iii Anna, b c. 1711, bp (adult) 22 Aug 1736 *NHC1*, d 18 May 1773 æ. 62 *OxfC;* m 24 Dec 1730 *NHV*—Moses Sperry.

iv Mary; m 20 Jan 1736/7 *NHV*—Ebenezer Peck.

v Samuel, b c. 1715, d 30 Dec 1788 æ. 73 *WdT1;* m 17 June 1742 *NHV*—Mabel da. Peter & Hannah (Ford) Perkins, b 21 Sep 1712 *NHV*, d 8 Sep 1799 æ. 88 *WdT1*. **FAM. 32.**

vi Jane, bp (adult) 22 Aug 1736 *NHC1*, d 29 Mar 1751 *NHV;* m 14 Mar 1738/9 *NHV*—John Hull.

9 MARY, b 1 Apr 1680 *NHV*, bp 10 Jan 1685/6 *NHC1;* m 18 Nov 1713 *GV*—John Bishop.

10 LYDIA, b 7 July 1681 *NHV*, bp 10 Jan 1685/6 *NHC1;* m 1699 *NHCCt*—Gideon Andrews.

11 ELIZABETH, b 11 Jan 1683 *NHV*, d 27 Feb 1683 *NHV*.

12 HOPE, b 10 May 1685 *NHV*, d 25 May 1685 *NHV*.

13 ELIZABETH, b 10 May 1685 *NHV;* m Abraham Hotchkiss.

14 EBENEZER, b 15 Apr 1688 *NHV*, bp Apr 1688 *NHC1*, d 18 Apr 1732 *WV;* m Lydia da. Thomas & Sarah (Wilmot) Hotchkiss; she m (2) 15 Apr 1736 *WV*—Nathaniel Hall.

i Eliphalet, d 3 May 1732 *WV*.

ii Rhoda, bp Aug 1736 *CC;* m 2 Oct 1739 *WV*—Zadoc Doolittle.

iii Tabitha.

iv Sabra, b 17 Jan 1721 *WV*, bp Apr 1736 *CC;* m (1) 21 Mar 1741/2 *WV*—William Wainwright; m (2) 8 Jan 1778 *WV*—Abraham Ives.

v Right, b 1 Dec 1723 *WV*.

vi Philemon, b 24 May 1726 *WV*, d 21 Mar 1777 *WV*, æ. 51 *WT1;* m 16 Oct 1760 *WC2*, 15 Oct *WV*—Sarah da. Samuel & Sarah (Hull) Hall, b 5 Dec 1737 *WV*, d 30 Apr 1797 æ. 60 *WT1*. **FAM. 33.**

vii Eunice, b 5 Sep 1728 *WV;* m 11 Feb 1762 *WV*—John Perkins. She had a nat. child by Job Brockett: (1) Sarah, b c. 1748, bp 9 July 1751 (at W) *Dx;* [m 16 Sep 1771 *NoHC*—Stephen Hitchcock].

viii Adinton, b 2 Oct 1730 *WV*, d 30 Apr 1732 *WV*.

ix Ebenezer, d 1 May 1732 *WV*.

FAM. 17. WILLIAM & ELIZABETH (SPERRY) JOHNSON:

1 THOMAS, b 21 Dec 1724 *NHV*, d s. p. 1785; m 20 Sep 1748 *WdC*—Susanna da. Nathan & Abigail (Hill) Perkins, b 13 May 1726 *NHV*, d 2 Feb 1789 *BD*.

2 WILLIAM; res. Sheffield, Mass.; had issue, Thomas, Lydia, & others.

3 ELIZABETH; m (1) 12 Aug 1762 *WdC*—John Turner; m (2) Ebenezer Bishop.

4 EDEN, b c. 1734, d 1 June 1826 æ. 92 *BT2;* Census (Wd) 1-2-3; m (1) Mary [da. Abel & Mary (Holt) Matthews, b 29 Oct 1751 *WV*], d 25 Apr 1775 æ. 22 *BT2;* m (2) Sybil da. David & Hila (Bishop) Thorpe, b 1 Aug 1757 *NHV*, d 21 Feb 1826 æ. 69 *BT2*.

(By 1): *i* Mary, b c. 1775 (at B), d 20 Aug 1856 æ. 80 *CV;* m Moses Russell.

(By 2): *ii* William, b c. 1778, d 17 Nov 1817 æ. 39 *BT2;* m.

iii Eden, b c. 1780, bu. 3 Aug 1865 æ. 85 *Bx;* m Sarah da. Eber & Abigail (Hitchcock) Downs, b c. 1787, d 9 Nov 1850 æ. 63 *BT2*.

FAM. 18. STEPHEN & MERCY (WILMOT) JOHNSON:

1 JONATHAN, b 13 Sep 1725 *NHV*, bp 16 Nov 1728 *NHC1*.

2 STEPHEN, b 28 July 1727 *NHV*, bp 16 Nov 1728 *NHC1;* m Sybil da. Abraham & Sarah (Gilbert) Johnson, b 1 Aug 1727 *NHV*, d 4 Nov 1803 *WHD;* she m (2) 13 Dec 1758 *NHC2*—Josiah Pardee.

i Lois, b c. 1750, d Sep 1813 æ. 64 *ColR;* m c. 1769 Stephen Pardee.

3 PHINEHAS, b 10 Jan 1729/30 *NHV*, bp 15 Mar 1729/30 *NHC1*, d Sep 1819 æ. 90 *OxfV;* Census (D) 1-2-4; m (1) Mary ——, who d 11 Apr 1788 *OxfC;* m (2) 9 May 1791 *OxfC*—Sarah Terrill, who d 25 Dec 1840 æ. 86 *Salemx*.

(By 1): *i* Jonathan, b c. 1752, d 16 Jan 1775 æ. 23 *OxfC*.

ii Chauncey, d 16 Feb 1792 *OxfC*.

iii Timothy, bp 19 [——] 1758 *OxfC*, d 26 Aug 1844 æ. 86 *OxfT2;* Census (D) 2-0-4; m 8 Sep 1784 *OxfC*—Olive Adams; 10 children.

iv Phinehas; m 12 Oct 1784 *OxfC*—Lois Skeels.

(By 2): *v* Susanna, b 25 June 1794 *OxfV*.

4 EUNICE, b 7 Mar 1732 *NHV*, bp 30 Apr 1732 *NHC1;* m 12 Aug 1756 *NHV*, *NHC2*—Hezekiah Bradley.

5 JABEZ, b 2 June 1734 *NHV*, bp 1 Sep 1734 *NHC1;* m 8 Nov 1764 *NHC2*—Abigail da. Ebenezer & Lydia (Bradley) Darrow, b 29 July 1745 *EHV;* she m (2) 16 Oct 1788 *NHC2*—Abraham Johnson.

i Lydia, b 4 Oct 1765 *NHV*, bp 14 Feb 1773 *NHC2*, d 6 Nov 1843 æ. 79 *WHD;* m 9 Nov 1786 Samuel Trowbridge.

ii Mercy, b 28 Aug 1767 *NHV*, bp 14 Feb 1773 *NHC2*.

iii Abigail, b 8 Aug 1770 *NHV*, d 10 June 1845 æ. 76 *NHT1;* m (1) 19 Oct 1788 *NHC2*—Jeremiah Barnett; m (2) Isaac Dickerman.

iv Eunice, b 1 Apr 1774 *NHV*, bp 15 May 1774 *NHC2.*

v Amos, b 25 Aug 1777 *NHV*, bp 5 Oct 1777 *NHC2.*

6 Ann, b 5 May 1736 *NHV*, bp 20 June 1736 *NHC1*, d 26 Dec 1825 *F*, 28 Dec 1827 æ. 92 (*Bapt*) *NHV;* m 12 Mar 1755 *NHC2*—Moses Beecher.

7 Ebenezer, b 26 Mar 1738 *NHV*, bp 14 May 1738 *NHC1;* res. Wolcott; Census (S) 1-0-3; m Hannah ——— .

i Levi, b 19 Feb 1762 *NHV*, bp 1 Nov 1767 *NHC1*, d 10 Dec 1833 æ. 72 *WolT;* Census (S) 1-0-5; m Ruth Judd, who d 18 Sep 1855 æ. 80 *WolT.*

ii Amelia, b 19 Oct 1763 *NHV*, bp 1 Nov 1767 *NHC1;* m Elijah Royce.

iii Ebenezer, b 18 June 1765 *NHV*, bp 1 Nov 1767 *NHC1;* Census (S) 1-0-4.

iv Hannah, b 24 Jan 1768 *NHV*, bp 27 Mar 1768 *NHC1.*

v Amos, b 9 Feb 1772 *NHV*, bp 12 Apr 1772 *NHC1.*

8 Lydia, b 11 Feb 1740 *NHV*, bp 20 Apr 1740 *NHC1;* m 27 May 1762 *WdC*—Abraham Payne.

9 Mercy, b 24 June 1741 *NHV*, "Wid. Baldwin" d 26 Dec 1823 æ. 84 (*NHx*) *NHV;* m 14 May 1765 *NHC1*—John Baldwin.

10 Sarah, b 30 Dec 1742 *NHV*, "Mrs. Ball" d 12 Oct 1832 æ. 89 (*Bapt*) *NHV;* m 16 Jan 1766 *NHC2*—John Ball.

11 Lois, b 15 May 1745 *NHV;* m Oliver Wright.

FAM. 19. Amos & Amy (Palmer) Johnson:

1 Amos; Census (Cornwall) 1-0-2; m 11 Sep 1755 *CornwallC*—Elizabeth Pierce.

2 Solomon; m 28 Sep 1758 *CornwallC*—Eliza(?) Pierce.

3 William; Census (Cornwall) 1-2-4; m 31 May 1759 *CornwallC*—Mercy da. Zachariah & Mary (Frisbie) How, b c. 1740; she m (2) ——— Winegar of Kent.

4 Amy; m 11 Sep 1755 *CornwallC*—Joshua Pierce.

FAM. 20. Abraham & Sarah (Gilbert) Johnson:

1 Sarah, b 1 Nov 1716 *NHV*, bp 24 Apr 1731 *NHC1*, d 24 Jan 1804 æ. 89 *PptC;* m 20 [———] 1740 *NHV*—Asa Wilmot.

2 Eliphalet, b 8 Jan 1718/9 *NHV*, bp 24 Apr 1731 *NHC1*, d 1769; m 7 July 1743 *NHV*, *WdC*—Mary da. Joseph & Hannah (Bradley) Lines, bp June 1723 *NHC1*, d 1769.

i Hannah, bp 30 Sep 1744 *WdC*, d 4 Oct 1815; m 14 Oct 1762 *WdC*—David Clark.

ii Eliphalet, bp 20 Apr 1746 *WdC*, d 2 Mar 1818 æ. 72 (at Camden, N. Y.) *F;* Census (Wd) 1-4-4; rem. to Bristol c. 1800; m Mary ——— , b c. 1753, d 26 Feb 1817 æ. 63 (at Camden, N. Y.) *F.* **FAM. 34.**

iii Hezekiah, bp 6 Mar 1748 *WdC*, d 6 Mar 1818 æ. 70 *BT4;* Census (Wd) 1-2-4; m Lorraine Linsley. Children:

Linsley, Ransom, another son, & 4 das. An infant s. d 20 Oct 1790 *BD*.

iv Mary, bp 1 July 1750 *WdC*, d soon.

v Mary, bp 6 Oct 1751 *WdC*, d 7 Apr 1799 æ. 48 *BT1;* m Phinehas Terrill.

vi Joseph, b c. 1754, d 22 Dec 1827 (Camden, N. Y.) *F;* Census (Wd) 1-4-3; rem. to P, & Camden, N. Y.; m Mary da. John & Abigail (Smith) Hotchkiss, b 23 June 1758 *WV*, d 7 Nov 1846 *F*. **FAM. 35.**

PAGE 1245

vii Rhoda.

viii Elias; Census (L) 1-2-4; rem. to Camden, N. Y.; m Chloe ——. **FAM. 36.**

ix Sarah.

3 ABRAHAM, b 15 Feb 1721 *NHV*, bp 24 Apr 1731 *NHC1;* m 8 July 1752 *NHV*—Mary da. Noah & Sarah (Tuttle) Wolcott, b 19 Feb 1726 *NHV*, d after 1790.

i Timothy, b 24 Apr 1753 *NHV;* Census (H) 1-2-4; m 5 Mar 1776 *NHC2*—Martha da. Samuel & Elizabeth (Alcock) Humiston. **FAM. 37.**

ii Sarah.

iii Eunice.

iv Abraham, d s. p. 1803; Census (NH) 1-0-3; m 16 Oct 1788 *NHC2*—Abigail da. Ebenezer & Lydia (Bradley) Darrow, wid. Jabez Johnson, b 29 July 1745 *EHV*.

v Noah; Census (H) 1-1-1; m 30 Oct 1788 *NHC2*—Sally Hill. **FAM. 38.**

4 MARY, b 1 Aug 1723 *NHV*, bp 24 Apr 1731 *NHC1*, d 11 Nov 1806 æ. 85 *HT2;* m 22 Apr 1761 *NHV*, *NHC2*—Thomas Leek.

5 ENOS, b 21 Feb 1725 *NHV*, bp 24 Apr 1731 *NHC1*, d 1 Nov 1801 æ. 77 *NHT1;* Census (NH) 2-0-3; m (1) 2 Mar 1757 *NHC2*—Abigail da. Thomas & Mary (Winston) Leek, b 9 Nov 1731 *NHV;* m (2) Mary da. John & Desire (Cooper) Wooding, wid. Hezekiah Hotchkiss, b 20 Nov 1731 *NHV*.

(By 1): *i* Rebecca, b c. 1758, d 3 Sep 1834 æ. 76 *WHT2;* m 24 July 1795 *NHC1*—Elijah Alling.

ii Esther, b c. 1760, d s. p. 21 July 1842 æ. 82 *WHT2*, 22 July *WHD*.

iii Enos, b c. 1766, d 17 Dec 1809 æ. 43 *WHT1;* m Polly ——, who d 6 Sep 1830 æ. 61 *WHT1*, *WHD*. Children (incomplete): (1) Enos L., b c. 1801, d 10 June 1839 æ. 38 *WHT2*, *WHD;* m Mary ——. (2) Sophia, b [Nov 1808], d 6 June 1809 æ. 0-6 *WHT1*.

6 SYBIL, b 1 Aug 1727 *NHV*, bp 24 Apr 1731 *NHC1*, d 4 Nov 1803 *WHD;* m (1) Stephen Johnson; m (2) 13 Dec 1758 *NHC2*—Josiah Pardee.

7 ABIGAIL, b 1 Nov 1729 *NHV*, bp 24 Apr 1731 *NHC1*, d s. p.

8 JOHN, b 17 May 1732 *NHV*, bp 16 July 1732 *NHC1*, d 29 Oct 1791 æ. 60 *WHD;* Census (NH) 2-0-1; m Mabel da. Joseph &

Hannah (Smith) Thompson, b c. 1729, d 3 July 1796 æ. 68 *WHD.*

i David, d 3 Aug 1781 (drowned) *WHD.*

ii Joseph.

iii John, b c. 1770, d s. p. 19 Oct 1827 æ. 57 *WHD*, 18 Oct *WHT1;* m Anna ——— .

iv Hannah.

v Samuel, d 3 Feb 1775 *WHD.*

vi Mabel, d 14 Nov 1777 *WHD.*

9 EUNICE, b 19 Aug 1734 *NHV*, bp 17 Nov 1734 *NHC1*, d s. p.

10 EBENEZER, b 24 May 1737 *NHV*, d 3 Nov 1818 æ. 81 *NHT1;* Census (NH) 3-3-3; m 11 Jan 1769 *WdC*—Esther da. Thomas & Mary (Miles) Punderson, b 24 Sep 1743 *NHV*, d 12 July 1824 æ. 81 *NHT1*, 13 July (*NHC2*) *NHV.*

i Mary, b 12 Jan 1770 *F*, bp 18 Mar 1770 *NHC2*, d 5 Nov 1773 *F.*

ii Nathan, b 12 Mar 1772 *F*, bp 26 Apr 1772 *NHC2*, d 20 Jan 1803 æ. 31 (by fall of a tree in Wol) *NHT1;* m 6 Nov 1798 *F*—Lucy da. Jeremiah & Mary (Smith) Smith, b c. 1777 d 9 May 1844 æ. 67 *WHT2*, 10 May *WHD;* she m (2) Dan Tolles.

iii Ebenezer, b 30 Apr 1774 *F*, bp 5 June 1774 *NHC2*, d 8 July 1863 æ. 89 *NHT1;* m (1) Hannah da. David & Grace Dougal, wid. Jonathan Mansfield, b [Mar 1778], d 15 July 1806 æ. 28-4 *NHT1;* m (2) 14 Jan 1808 *OC*—Sarah Bryan Law, b 9 Oct 1785 *F*, bp 5 Feb 1786 *MC1*, d 19 Feb 1854 æ. 68 *NHT1.* Of his children, David d 13 Nov 1802 æ. 0-10 *NHT1*, & Grace Charlotte d 15 Oct 1805 æ. 0-14-9 *NHT1.*

iv Samuel, b 2 Jan 1777 *F*, bp 23 Mar 1777 *NHC2*, d s. p. 22 June 1844; m 1 Sep 1811 Ann Buckingham.

v Mary Esther, b 12 July 1779 *F*, bp 29 Aug 1779 *NHC2*, d 3 June 1842; m 8 Mar 1803 Levi Beecher.

vi David, b 16 Dec 1782 *F*, bp 16 Feb 1783 *NHC2*, d 12 May 1802 æ. 20 *NHT1.*

vii Solomon, b 9 Feb 1786 *F*, bp 1 Apr 1786 *NHC2*, d 16 Jan 1843 æ. 57 *NHT1;* m (1) Betsey da. Chauncey Alling; m (2) Eliza T. ——— , who d 1 Feb 1840 æ. 44 *NHT1.*

FAM. 21. JOHN & LYDIA (FORD) JOHNSON:

1 SARAH.

2 CHARITY.

3 HANNAH.

4 MEHITABEL, perhaps the Miss Mabel who d May 1800 æ. 53 (at NH) *Conn Journal.*

5 LYDIA; m (1) Robert Simpson; m (2) 8 Mar 1781 *NHC1*—Josiah Merriman.

6 JOHN, b c. 1754, d 17 Feb 1837 æ. 82 *NHT1;* Census (NH) 1-2-2; res. Allingtown; m 21 Dec 1783 *NHC2*—Huldah Critten-

den, b c. 1762, d 14 Feb 1827 æ. 65 *NHT1*.*

i Sarah, bp 11 Nov 1786 *NHx*, bu. 26 Aug 1787 *NHx*.

ii John James, bp 7 Feb 1789 *NHx;* m Abigail Smith.

iii Joseph William, bp 7 Feb 1789 (sponsor, Sarah Crittenden of G) *NHx*.

iv Lydia, b c. 1790, bp 18 Feb 1807 (æ. 17) *NHx*, d 13 Apr 1867 æ. 79 *NHT1;* m 1809 Thomas Alling.

v Lyman, b c. 1791, d 8 Jan 1829 æ. 38 *NHT1;* m Betsey Buckland.

vi Huldah, b c. 1797, bp 29 Oct 1810 (æ. 13) *NHx*, d 22 Nov 1850 æ. 49 *NHT1;* m James Eaton.

vii Elizabeth, b c. 1799, bp 29 Oct 1810 (æ. 11) *NHx*, d 11 Sep 1861; m (1) ——— Crandall; m (2) 7 Feb 1831 *EHC* —Eleazer Gorham.

viii Mary, b c. 1802, bp 29 Oct 1810 (æ. 8) *NHx;* m James Eaton.

FAM. 22. ISAAC & HANNAH (SPERRY) JOHNSON:

1 ISAAC, b 5 Oct 1729 *NHV*, d s. p. 24 Nov 1792 æ. 63 *PC*, 23 Nov æ. 64 *ThomastonT;* Census (Wtn) 2-0-1; m 15 Jan 1756 *NHV* —Esther da. Ephraim & Esther (Heaton) Sanford, b 12 Mar 1736 *NHV*.

2 JESSE, b 12 Jan 1733/4 *NHV*, d 17 Mar 1822 æ. 88 *Chester Mass., C;* Dea.; Census (Chester, Mass.) 4-1-6; m 29 Nov 1759 *NHV* —Sarah da. Daniel & Abigail (Ives) Sperry, b 26 Dec 1738 *NHV*, d 5 Dec 1814 æ. 77 *Chester, Mass., T;* 11 children or more, for whom see the published Chester records.

3 EUNICE, b 27 June 1736 *NHV*, d young.

4 HANNAH, b 12 June 1741 *NHV;* m 21 Feb 1763 *NHC1*—David Ball.

FAM. 23. EZRA & SARAH (LINES) JOHNSON:

1 REBECCA, b 21 Nov 1735 *NHV*, d young.

FAM. 23. EZRA & MARY (DORMAN) JOHNSON:

2 REBECCA, bp 14 Dec 1740 *NHC1;* m 15 Nov 1756 *WdC*—Abraham Carrington.

3 NEHEMIAH, bp 16 Oct 1743 *WdC*, d (s. p?) 14 Feb 1792 *WdC*, æ. 49 *WdT1;* Census (Wd) 2-0-2.

4 LOIS, bp 12 Aug 1745 *WdC*, d young.

5 CHARLES, bp 24 May 1747 *WdC*, d young.

6 MARY, bp 18 June 1749 *WdC*, d young.

7 ELIZABETH, bp 21 July 1751 *WdC*, d young.

8 RUTH, bp 11 Aug 1753 *WdC*, d young.

FAM. 24. OBED & AMY (WILMOT) JOHNSON:

1 DORCAS, b 27 Nov 1738 *NHV*, bp 3 Nov 1751 *WdC;* m John Johnson.

---

*It is possible that this is the John who m Dorcas da. Obed Johnson. The John who m Huldah Crittenden may have been son of John of Guilford. The records are defective.

2 Abigail, b 13 Sep 1741 *NHV*, bp 3 Nov 1751 *WdC*, d 27 Feb 1793 æ. 53 *WolT;* m 2 July 1767 *WatV*, *WdC*—David Alcott.

3 Obed, b 16 Oct 1744 *NHV*, bp 3 Nov 1751 *WdC*, d 11 Dec 1789 æ. 44 *WdT1;* m 8 Nov 1764 *WdC*—Mary da. Daniel & Mary (Alcott) Lines, b 8 May 1742 *NHV*, d 1 Nov 1824 æ. 81 *WdT1*, 9 Nov *WdD.*

i Isaac, b c. 1765, d 25 July 1817 æ. 52 *WdD;* m (1) Betsey ——, who d 30 Nov 1794 æ. 27 *WdD;* m (2) 14 June 1798 *Conn Journal*—Naomi da. Nehemiah & Rebecca (Osborn) Hotchkiss; she m (2) 1819 John Thomas. Child by 2nd w: Seymour.

ii Mary, b c. 1767, d 18 Apr 1841 æ. 74 *OC;* m Samuel Pardee.

iii Thaddeus; m 14 Dec 1800 *NHC1*—Clarissa Ives.

iv Eunice, b c. 1772, d 4 July 1834 æ. 62 *WdT1;* m Asa Sperry.

v Rebecca.

vi Obed, b c. 1781, d 25 Sep 1823 æ. 42 *WdT1;* m 30 Jan 1809 *OC*—Electa da. Moses & Hannah (Downs) Humphreville, b c. 1788, d 30 Sep 1857 æ. 69 *WHT2.*

4 Amy, b 26 Oct 1746 *NHV*, bp 3 Nov 1751 *WdC;* m 22 Jan 1766 *WdC*—David Ford.

5 Eunice, b 27 Apr 1749 *NHV*, d soon.

FAM. 24. Obed & Rebecca (Clark) Johnson:

6 Eunice, b 12 Mar 1754 *NHV*, d c. 1850; m 14 Dec 1777 *NHC2*—Medad Beecher.

FAM. 25. David & Rachel (Sperry) Johnson:

1 Chloe, b 25 Nov 1744 *NHV*, bp 4 Feb 1745 *WdC*, d 13 Jan 1753 *NHV.*

2 Kezia, b 29 Mar 1747 *NHV*, bp 3 May 1747 *WdC*, d 9 Aug 1751 *NHV.*

3 Jemima, b 30 Mar 1749 *NHV*, d 30 Mar 1749 *NHV.*

4 Jemima, b 14 Jan 1749/50 *NHV*, bp 25 Mar 1750 *WdC*, d 8 Nov 1751 *NHV.*

5 Job, b 24 May 1752 *NHV*, bp 26 July 1752 *WdC;* Census (Wd) 1-5-2; m 5 Apr 1770 *WdC*—Susanna da. David & Abigail (Perkins) Sperry, b 10 May 1750 *NHV*, d 1789.

i Lois; m 1 Jan 1793 *NHC1*—William Baldwin.

ii David, b c. 1773, d Sep 1849 æ. 75 *OC;* m 24 Dec 1807 *OC*—Susanna Fowler, who d 11 Apr 1831 æ. 54 *OC.*

iii Rachel, b c. 1775, d 6 Oct 1847 æ. 73 *HT3;* m (1) Ezra Bradley; m (2) Benjamin Porter of Batavia, N. Y.

iv James.

v Abigail; m Silas Sperry.

6 Frances, b 12 Oct 1754 *NHV;* m 23 Aug 1770 *NHC1*—John Smith.

7 Chloe, b 6 May 1757 *NHV*, d 8 Dec 1787 *WdC;* m 16 Nov 1774 *WdC*—Jacob Morgan.

FAM. 26. REUBEN & MARY (DAYTON) JOHNSON:

1 JUSTUS, b 6 Apr 1720 *WV*, d 13 May 1720 *WV*.

2 JUSTUS, b 26 Mar 1721 *WV*, d 20 Jan 1748/9 æ. 28 *WT1*.

3 REBECCA, b 14 July 1723 *WV*, d 13 May 1811 æ. 88 *WT2*; m (1) 1 Aug 1745 *WV*—Wait Abernathy; m (2) 25 Mar 1747 *WC2*—Gideon Royce; m (3) 24 Feb 1763 *WC2*—Joseph Cole.

4 JERUSHA, b c. 1726, d 17 Nov 1817 æ. 92 *NoBT1*; m (1) 18 June 1745 *WV*—Eliasaph Dorchester; m (2) Samuel Munson.

5 EPHRAIM; Census (W) 3-0-3; m (1) 1 Dec 1754 *WV*—Hannah da. Macock & Hannah (Tyler) Ward, who d 22 Apr 1761 *WV*; m (2) 30 Dec 1762 *WV*—Lois da. Elihu & Lois (Whittlesey) Hall, wid. Samuel Sharp Beadles, b 11 May 1735 *WV*.

(By 1): *i* Content, b 14 July 1755 *WV*, d 9 Apr 1807 æ. 52 *ST*; m Nathaniel Jones.

ii Ward, b c. 1757, d 27 Aug 1817 æ. 60 *WT1*; Dea.; Census (W) 1-2-3; m (1) Lucy ——, who d 18 Apr 1809 æ. 48 *WT1*; m (2) Mary ——, who d 6 Apr 1856 æ. 87 *WT1*. Children by 1st w. (incomplete): (1) Macock Ward, b 28 Apr 1786 *WV*. (2) Billious, b 14 July 1789 *WV*.

iii Luther, b 25 June 1759 *WV*.

(By 2): *iv* Hannah, b 25 July 1763 *WV*, d 2 Mar 1827 æ. 64 *WT1*; m 21 May 1779 Abijah Ives.

v John Hall, b 29 May 1765 *WV*.

vi Samuel, b 1 Sep 1767 *WV*, d 29 Mar 1854 æ. 88 *WT1*; m Polly da. Jonathan & Hannah (Barnes) Tuttle, b c. 1778, d 14 May 1824 æ. 46 *WT1*.

vii Jehoiada, b 9 Feb 1770 *WV*.

viii Lucy Hall, b 20 June 1772 *WV*, d 23 Oct 1851; m Nathan Chittenden of G.

ix Chauncey, b 24 Sep 1774 *WV*.

x Sarah, b 4 May 1779 *WV*.

6 REUBEN; m (1) 30 Jan 1750 Elizabeth Brush; m (2) 20 June 1758 Susanna (——) Titus.

7 ZACHARIAH, d 1776; m 30 Nov 1755 *WV*—Phebe Hall; she m (2) 15 Feb 1778 *WV*—Nathaniel Hart. Family incomplete.

i Justus, b 6 Dec 1756 *WV*, d 1786.

ii Sybil, b 27 Jan 1759 *WV*, d 25 July 1821; m 2 June 1778 Nathan Chittenden of G.

iii Hannah, b 4 June 1761 *WV*.

iv Merab, b 14 Sep 176[-] *WV*.

8 MARY; m 27 Dec 1753 *WC2*—Amos Hall.

9 PATIENCE, b [1738/9] *WV*.

FAM. 27. ISAAC & SARAH (OSBORN) JOHNSON:

1 JOSEPH, b 1 Jan 1725 *WV*, d 1803; Census (H) 2-3-8; m Phebe ——.

i Phebe, d s. p.

ii Eunice; m Nathaniel Andrews of C.

iii Rebecca.
iv Sarah; m Ephraim Royce of Catskill, N. Y.
v Merab.
vi Elizabeth; m John Ashley of Catskill, N. Y.
vii Joseph, b c. 1764, d 23 Mar 1838 æ. 74 *HT3;* m 3 Dec 1789 *HCl*—Sarah da. Benjamin & Esther (Tuttle) Doolittle, b 20 July 1761 *NHV*, d 15 Nov 1826 æ. 65 *HT 3*.
viii Isaac; m Fanny ——. Children: 1 Chauncey. 2 Lewis Augustus. 3 Lucina. 4 Uri.
ix Rhoda; m James Gleason; res. Farm 1811, Simsbury 1816.
x Lent; res. NoH; m Esther da. Isaac & Esther Tuttle.
xi Lowly.
xii Clarissa, b c. 1784, d 22 Apr 1862 æ. 78 *HT3;* m 26 Mar 1823 *HV*—Amos Frost.

2 ABIGAIL, b 11 Feb 1727 *WV*, d 4 Nov 1759 æ. 33 *WV;* m 22 Nov 1752 *DV*—Stephen Ward of D.
3 SARAH, b 10 Feb 1729 *WV*, d 31 July 1819 æ. 91 *SC;* m 20 Oct 1748 *WV*—Jennings Johnson.
4 ISAAC, b 23 June 1731 *WV;* m Abigail ——.
i (perhaps) Abigail, d 1834; m 24 Aug 1774 *NoHC*—Daniel Doolittle.
ii David, b 24 June 1758 *WV;* Census (W) 1-4-2; m 23 Nov 1780 *WV*—Lois da. Dayton & Hannah (Beadles) Johnson, b 7 Sep 176[0] *WV*.
iii Mary, b 14 Feb 1759 *WV* [?1760].
iv Lois, b 29 Dec 1761 *WV*.
v Stephen Shipman, b 22 Oct 1763 *WV*.
vi Isaac, b 2 Jan 1766 *WV*.
vii Warren, b 9 Jan 1768 *WV*.

5 HANNAH, b 13 Sep 1733 *WV*, d 24 Nov 1760 *WV;* m 23 July 1752 *WV*—Robert Royce.
6 ESTHER, b 30 Nov 1735 *WV;* m (1) 18 Nov 1756 *WV*—Caleb Todd; m (2) 14 Apr 1773 *WV*—Benjamin Merriam.
7 LOIS, b 15 Feb 1738 *WV*, d 1807; m (1) 9 Jan 1758 *WV*—Lud Munson; m (2) Enoch Culver.
8 RACHEL, b 6 Mar 1740 *WV;* m 11 Feb 1759 *WV*—Stephen Todd.
9 RHODA, b c. 1742, d 4 July 1772; m Samuel Munson.
10 REBECCA, b 4 Aug 1744 *WV*, d 28 Feb 1774 æ. 30 *NoHC;* m Daniel Doolittle.

FAM. 28. ENOS & —— (——) JOHNSON:
1 SARAH; m 11 July 1750 *WV*—Benjamin Ford.
2 SHERBURN; m Apr 1751 *WV*—Katharine da. John & Marlow (Munson) Hitchcock, b 10 July 1731 *WV*.
i Chloe, b 15 Mar 1752 *WV*.
ii Titus, b 23 Feb 1754 *WV*.
iii Elizabeth, b 23 Feb 1756 *WV*.

iv Katharine, b 18 May 1758 *WV*, d 8 July 1842 æ. 85 *WT1*; m 14 Feb 1780 *WV*—George Merriman.
v Lyman, b 25 Mar 1760 *WV*.
vi Jonathan, b 12 May 1762 *WV*.
vii Reuben, b 28 May 1764 *WV*.
viii Miranda, b 1 July 1768 *WV*.
ix Lura, b 14 July 1771 *WV*.
x Marlow Munson, b 24 May 1774 *WV*.

3 Samuel, d 1796; res. Meriden; m (1) 20 Feb 1751 *WV*—Susanna da. Nathaniel & Elizabeth (Hitchcock) Beadles, b 17 Sep 1727 *WV*, d July 1786 *WC2*; m (2) Lucretia ——— .

(By 1): *i* Nathaniel Beadles, b 12 May 1752 *WV*, bp 25 Jan 1756 *WC2*; Census (W) 1-2-3; m (1) 6 Jan 1774 *WV*—Huldah da. Josiah & Eunice (Ives) Robinson, b 12 June 1754 *WV*, d 14 Aug 1778 *WV*; m (2) 31 Aug 1780 *WV*—Jerusha da. Gideon & Eunice (Tuttle) Ives, b 20 Feb 1759 *WV*.
ii Samuel, b 27 Apr 1754 *WV*, bp 25 Jan 1756 *WC2*; Census (W) 1-1-1.
iii Sarah, b 23 June 1757 *WV*; m 17 July 1777 *WV*—Daniel Holt.
iv Susanna, b 28 July 1762 *WV*; m 11 July 1786 *WC2*—John Merriam.

4 Elizabeth, b c. 1734, d 23 June 1777 æ. 43 *WT2*; m 20 Mar 1754 *WV*—Moses Hall.

5 Phebe.

6 Benjamin, d 21 Mar 1761 *WV*; Capt.; m 15 Aug 1759 *WV*—Esther da. Isaac & Elizabeth (Culver) Brockett, b 16 Oct 1739 *WV*; she m (2) 14 Apr 1766 *WV*—Miles Sperry.
i Benjamin, b 22 July 1761 *WV*.

7 William; m 16 Dec 1763 *WV*—Hannah da. Joseph & Susanna (Cook) Cole, b 16 Aug 1739 *WV*.
i Love, b 1 Oct 1765 *WV*, d 7 Oct 1765 *WV*.
ii Sheldon, b 20 Oct 1767 *WV*.
iii Aaron, b 27 Feb 1769 *WV*, d 2 Sep 1808 *WT2*; m 1793 Rebecca Royce.
iv Hannah, b 6 Nov 1772 *WV*, d 14 Sep 1777 *WV*.
v Joel Cole, b 13 July 1777 *WV*.
vi Titus, b 6 Apr 1780 *WV*.

8 Enos; m 19 Nov 1767 *WV*—Sarah da. Stephen & Hannah (Hotchkiss) Atwater, b 25 Nov 1751 *WV*.

9 Miriam; m 4 Mar 1773 *WV*—Simeon Johnson.

FAM. 29. Abner & Charity (Dayton) Johnson:

1 Dayton, b 8 Feb 1728 *WV*, d 19 Feb 1798 æ. 70 *WT1*; Census (W) 3-0-2; m 8 Jan 1752 *WV*—Hannah da. Nathaniel & Elizabeth (Hitchcock) Beadles, b c. 1733, d 11 Aug 1814 æ. 81 *WT1*.
i Mamre, b 25 Aug 1752 *WV*; m 5 Oct 1775 *WV*—John

Johnson; she div. him 1799.

ii Eliakim, b 31 Dec 1753 *WV;* m 21 Oct 1781 *WV*—Lydia Curtis. Children (incomplete): 1 Collins, b 10 Jan 1783 *WV*. 2 Mary, b 8 May 1785 *WV*. 3 Rice, b 21 June 1787 *WV*.

iii Hannah, b 28 Apr 1756 *WV*, d 27 Nov 1796 æ. 41 *WT1;* m Elihu Thompson.

iv Lois, b 7 Sep 176[0] *WV;* m 23 Nov 1780 *WV*—David Johnson.

v Charity, b 31 May 176[2] *WV*, d 31 Jan 1814 æ. 52 *WT1;* m 5 Sep 1784 *WV*—Beri Tuttle.

vi Benajah, b 4 Aug 176[6] *WV*, d 24 May 1836 æ. 70 *WT1;* m Mary da. Solomon & Mary (Barker) Johnson, b 26 Mar 1769, d 15 Sep 1844 æ. 75 *WT1*.

vii Abner, b 14 Oct 1768 *WV;* m Martha ——, who d 2 Jan 1822 æ. 56 *WT1*.

2 **Lydia**, b 4 Nov 1730 *WV;* m 16 May 1749 *WV*—Ebenezer Fitch.

3 **Hezekiah**, b 12 Mar 1732 *WV*, d 21 Feb 1810 æ. 77 *HT2;* Census (W) 2-1-5; m Nov 1758 *WV*—Ruth da. Caleb & Ruth (Sedgwick) Merriman, b 31 Oct 1741 *WV*, d 12 Dec 1819 æ. 77 *HT2*.

i Caleb, b 18 July 1759 *WV;* B. A. (Yale, 1785); Rev.; went south.

ii George, b 7 Nov 1760 *WV*, d 13 Nov 1760 *WV*.

iii Charles, b 2 Nov 1761 *WV*, d 1787.

iv Lucinda, b 18 July 1763 *WV*.

v Ruth, b 31 May 1765 *WV;* m Asahel Hall of Salisbury, N. Y.

vi Belcher, b 25 Dec 1767 *WV*, d 20 June 1837; res. Salisbury, N. Y.; m Hannah Cahoon.

vii Diantha, b 22 July 1770 *WV;* m Joseph Shepherd.

viii Sophia, b 3 Aug 1772 *WV*, d 17 Mar 1774 *WV*.

ix Sophia, b 31 Oct 1774 *WV*, d 27 Aug 1827 æ. 53 *NoHT1;* m 18 June 1797 *NoHV*—Bezaleel Dayton.

x Charity Betsey, b 25 Mar 1777 *WV;* m —— Kneelon.

xi Hezekiah, b 24 Dec 1779 *WV*, d 27 Jan 1845 æ. 65 *HT2;* m (1) Betsey da. Nathaniel & Elizabeth (Bassett) Tuttle, b c. 1789, d 9 Feb 1844 æ. 55 *HT2;* 9 children; m (2) Roxanna Judd.

xii Lucinda, b 3 May 1782 *WV;* m Nathan Burr of Kingsboro, N. Y.

4 **Charity**, b 19 May 1736 *WV*, d 4 Aug 1820 æ. 85 *WatT3;* m (1) 26 May 1762 *WV*—John Dickson; m (2) 10 Nov 1768 *WatV*—Samuel Hickox.

5 **Abner**, b 26 Aug 1738 *WV;* d 1817; Census (Wat) 1-0-3; m 30 June 1773 *WatV*—Lydia da. Ebenezer & Lydia (Clark) Bunnell, b 26 Jan 1753 *WV*.

i Van Julius, b 12 Apr 1774 *WatV*, d 3 Nov 1774 *WatV*.

ii Fanny, b 28 Feb 1776 *WatV;* m 19 May 1796 *WatV*—Dr. Frederick Leavenworth.

iii Narcissa, b 28 May 1778 *WatV.*

iv Chloe, b 16 June 1781 *WatV*, d 3 Feb 1782 *WatV.*

6 **Jacob**, b 21 July 1742 *WV*, d 1816; Census (L) 2-4-5; res. Torrington 1796; rem. to Johnstown, N. Y.; m Esther da. Stephen & Thankful (Cook) Hotchkiss, b 9 June 1750 *WV.*

FAM. 30. Israel & Sarah (Miles) Johnson:

1 **Eunice**, b 13 June 1734 *WV*, d 6 July 1766 *WV*, æ. 32 *WT1.*

2 **Anna**, b 18 Apr 1736 *WV*, d 2 Sep 1747 *WV*, æ. 12 *WT1.*

3 **Prudence**, b 11 July 1738 *WV*, d 9 Oct 1829 æ. 88 D*T4;* m 28 Oct 1756 *WV*—Jesse Cook.

4 **Caleb**, b 17 Sep 1739 *WV*, d 17 Mar 1760 *WV.*

5 **Miles**, b 31 Oct 1741 *WV*, d 6 Nov 1798 æ. 57 *WT1;* Capt.; Census (W) 1-3-3; m 12 Sep 1771 *WV*—Ruth da. Eliakim & Ruth (Dickerman) Hall, b 27 May 1750 *WV.*

i Eunice, b 20 July 1772 *WV;* m Phinehas Fowler.

ii Sarah Miles, b 15 May 1774 *WV.*

iii Miles H., b 21 Dec 1776 *WV;* res. Wallingford, Vt.; m Hannah Hill.

iv Eliakim, b 1779 *WV;* m Mary Denison.

v Jedediah, b 1783 *WV;* m Betsey Cooley.

6 **Warren**, b 17 Apr 1747 *WV*, d 30 May 1761 *WV.*

FAM. 31. Daniel & Joanna (Preston) Johnson:

1 **Charles**, b 13 Nov 1735 *WV*, d 13 May 1761 *WV.*

2 **Mindwell**, b 19 May 1738 *WV.*

3 **Solomon**, b 4 May 1740 *WV*, d 4 Apr 1799 æ. 59 *WT1;* Capt.; Census (W) 3-2-4; m Mary da. John & Sarah (Russell) Barker, b 10 Mar 1742/3 *WV*, d 7 Sep 1825 æ. 83 *WT1.*

i John Barker, b 11 Sep 1765 *WV*, d 25 May 1767 *WV.*

ii Charles, b 3 May 1767 *WV;* m Elizabeth Rice.

iii Mary, b 26 Mar 1769 *WV*, d 15 Sep 1844 æ. 75 *WT1;* m Benajah Johnson.

iv Lydia, b 19 May 1771 *WV*, d 30 Aug 1774 *WV.*

v Lyd a, b 6 Oct 1774 *WV;* m Benajah Brooks.

vi Sarah, b 4 Dec 1777 *WV;* m Asa Doolittle.

vii John Barker, b 7 Nov 1779 *WV*, 6 Nov *WT1*, d 15 Feb 1866 æ. 86 *WT1;* m Rachel Munson, who d 13 Sep 1863 æ. 80 *WT1.*

viii Edward, b 6 Sep 1783 *WV*, d 14 June 1803 æ. 20 (in W. Indies) *WT1.*

4 **Joanna**, b 4 Apr 1743 *WV;* m 9 Sep 1771 *WV*—Seth Lee of Farm.

5 **Dan**, b 13 Mar 1746 *WV*, d 2 Sep 1830 æ. 85 *WT1;* Census (W) 2-5-3; m (1) 19 Apr 1781 *WV*—Rebecca da. Oliver & Thankful (Parker) Hitchcock, b 18 Jan 1748/9 *WV*, d 25 July 1813 æ. 68 *WT1;* m (2) Lucy da. Seth & Hannah (Clark) Plumb, wid. Jedediah Dudley, b c. 1755, d 22 Jan 1825 æ. 69 *WT1.*

Family incomplete.

(By 1): *i* Cephas, b 8 Jan 1782 *WV*.

ii Augustus, b c. 1783, d 21 Oct 1807 æ. 25 *WT1*.

iii Dan, b c. 1787, d 20 Jan 1860 æ. 72 *WT1*; m Sarah ——, who d 11 Nov 1845 æ. 48 *WT1*.

iv Ransom, b c. 1788, d 17 May 1871 æ. 83 *WT1*; Rev.; m Esther F. ——, who d 20 Jan 1862 æ. 68 *WT1*.

6 ISRAEL, b 8 July 1748 *WV*, d 21 Mar 1820 æ. 72 *WT2*; Census (W) 1-2-3; m Huldah ——, who d 10 Jan 1850 æ. 96 *WT2*.

7 JUSTUS, b 4 Mar 1752 *WV*, bp 31 May 1752 *NoBC2*; m 14 Jan 1782 *WV*—Susa Johnson.

8 ABIGAIL, b 23 Dec 1753 *WV*, d 30 Oct 1813 *Wol*; m 31 Jan 1780 *WV*—Zenas Brockett.

9 JOSHUA, b 26 July 1757 *WV*.

10 REBECCA, b 29 Mar 1759 *WV*, d 31 Mar 1759 *WV*.

11 REBECCA, b 10 Sep 1761 *WV*, d 20 Aug 1764 *WV*.

FAM. 32. SAMUEL & MABEL (PERKINS) JOHNSON:

1 MARY, b 5 Dec 1742 *NHV*, d soon.

2 SAMUEL, b 9 Apr 1743(?) *NHV*, d soon.

3 PETER, b 16 Aug 1745 *NHV*, d 18 June 1813 æ. 68 *NHT1*; Capt.; Census (NH) 2-3-6; m (1) 26 Jan 1769 *NHV*, *NHC1*—Chloe da. Andrew & Eunice (Sherman) Tuttle, b 23 Mar 1738/9 *NHV*, d 11 Mar 1773 æ. 34 *NHT1*, *NHC1*; m (2) 22 Sep 1773 *WdC*—Comfort da. David & Hannah (Peck) Clark, bp 3 Apr 1748 *WdC*, d 25 Nov 1834 æ. 88 *NHT1*, 26 Nov (*NHC1*) *NHV*.

(By 1): *i* Daughter, d 19 Oct 1769 (just born) *NHC1*.

ii Anna, b 22 Sep 1770 *NHV*, bp 23 Sep 1770 *NHC1*, d 7 Jan 1823 æ. 52 *NHT1*, 18 Jan (*NHC1*) *NHV*; m 19 Mar 1794 *NHC1*—Simeon Newton.

iii Esther, b 30 Sep 1772 *NHV*, bp 4 Oct 1772 *NHC1*; m 22 Nov 1794 *NHC1*—John Pierson Stillman.

(By 2): *iv* Peter, bp 9 Apr 1775 *NHC1*; m Esther da. Edward & Esther Thomas, bp 2 Nov 1777 *NHx*, d 28 Feb 1848 *WHD*, 29 Feb æ. 72 (at WH) *NHV*; she m (2) 11 Aug 1811 Elihu Augur. Son: Harvey; m Elizabeth Baldwin.

v Harvey, bp 16 Feb 1777 *NHC1*, d s. p.

vi Comfort, bp 24 Jan 1779 *NHC1*, d 14 Dec 1822 æ. 44 (*NHC1*) *NHV*; m 31 Aug 1800 *NHC1*—Elisha Jones.

vii Martha, b [Jan 1781], bp 25 Mar 1781 *NHC1*, d 27 Aug 1861 æ. 80 *NHT1*, æ. 80-7 *NHV*; m (1) 2 Feb 1800 *NHC1*—John Kennedy; m (2) Frederick LeForge.

viii Chloe, bp 2 Mar 1783 *NHC1*, d 25 Jan 1810 æ. 27 *NHT1*.

ix Son, d 9 Jan 1785 æ. 1 hr. *NHC1*.

x Horace, bp 3 Sep 1786 *NHC1*; res. Compton, N. H., 1829.

4 MARY, b 9 Aug 1747 *NHV*, 7 Aug *WashingtonV*, "Wid. Baker" d 30 Sep 1822 *Washington*; m (1) 3 Nov 1768 *WdC*—Stephen Sperry; m (2) 30 Sep 1778 *Washington*—Ephraim Baker.

5 Jesse, b 9 Aug 1747 *NHV;* Census (Wd) 2-2-3; m 11 June 1772 *WdC*—Lucy da. Thomas & Rachel (Peck) Perkins.

6 Anna, b 8 June 1750 *NHV*, d 1 Jan 1833 æ. 83 *WdC;* m (1) 8 July 1772 *WdC*—Simeon Clinton; m (2) 23 Feb 1786 *WdC*—David Ford.

7 Samuel, b 16 Dec 1752 *NHV*, d 17 Mar 1791 æ. 39 *WdC*, 10 Mar æ. 38 *WdTI;* Census (Wd) 1-3-3; m 24 Mar 1776 *WdC*—Hannah da. Joseph & Elizabeth (Alling) Beecher, b c. 1754, d 17 Mar 1789 æ. (50?) *WdTI*, 10 Mar 1789 æ. 34 *WdD*.

i Samuel, b c. 1777, d s. p. 22 June 1844 æ. 68 *OT;* m 5 Sep 1811 *MCI*—Anna da. Daniel & Sybil (Bull) Buckingham, b 30 Sep 1780, d 3 May 1855 æ. 74 *OT*.

ii Hannah; m ——— Hollister.

iii Enoch, bp 16 Aug 1782 *WdC*, d soon.

iv Ann.

v Enoch, bp 14 Oct 1787 *WdC*.

vi Joseph.

FAM. 33. Philemon & Sarah (Hall) Johnson:

1 Lydia, b c. 1762, d 6 June 1785 *WV*, 5 June æ. 23 *WTI*.

2 Sarah, b c. 1764, d 6 May 1778 *WV*, æ. 14 *WTI*.

3 Lucy, b 5 Jan 1766 *WV*, d 28 Apr 1814 æ. 48 *WTI*.

4 Ebenezer, b 19 June 1768 *WV;* Census (Woodstock, N. Y.) 1-2-1; m 5 Feb 1786 *WV*—Sarah da. Samuel & Susanna (Doolittle) Peck, b 16 Oct 1761 *WV*. Children (incomplete): 1 Harvey, b 7 Aug 1786 *WV*. 2 Ira, b 27 Mar 1788 *WV*.

5 Esther, b c. 1771, d 28 May 1788 *WV*, æ. 17 *WTI*.

6 Caleb, b 25 June 1773 *WV;* res. Canaan, N. Y.

7 James Jauncey, b Dec 1776 *WV*, d 1 May 1777 *WV*, 30 Apr æ. 0-4 *WTI*.

FAM. 34. Eliphalet & Mary (———) Johnson:

1 Polly, b 13 Mar 1775 *F*.

2 Rebecca, b 7 Apr 1777 *F;* m James H. Saniord; res. 1841, Walworth Co., Wis.

3 Sally, b 8 Aug 1779 (at Wd) *F*, d 6 Sep 1856 *F;* m 9 Dec 1802 (at Bristol) *F*—Reuben Osborn.

4 Eliphalet, b 20 Sep 1781 *F;* rem. to Ohio c. 1830, & to Wis. c. 1840.

5 Isaac, b 14 Feb 1783 *F*.

6 Calvin, b 17 Nov 1785 *F;* m 11 Mar 1811 Honor da. Noah Preston. Children: Rosette; Spencer; Lorenzo; Cornelia.

7 Spencer, b 17 Feb 1788 *F;* m ——— .

i Gardner, b 12 Apr 1819, d 26 May 1885.

ii Andrew, b 30 Nov 1820.

iii E. S., b 9 Feb 1823, d 7 Sep 1825.

iv Henry, b 12 Mar 1825, d 6 May 1848.

v Elihu S., b 4 Apr 1827, d 8 Dec 1893.

vi Mariah, b 26 Jan 1829, d 14 Aug 1834.

vii Calvin, b 31 May 1831.

viii Isaac, b 20 Jan 1835, d 20 Feb 1901.
ix P. Marla, b 8 Mar 1839, d 23 June 1889.
8 DAVID, b 1 July 1790 *F.*
9 HEZEKIAH, b 31 Oct 1792 *F.*
10 LEVERETT, b 17 July 1794 *F;* rem. to Ohio.
11 LEONARD, b 8 Mar 1798 *F;* rem to Ohio.
12 AMELIA, b 11 Mar 1800 *F;* m ——— Northrop.

FAM. 35. JOSEPH & MARY (HOTCHKISS) JOHNSON (incomplete):
1 ENOS, b 17 Mar 1777 *F*, d 8 July 1864 æ. 87 *Camden, N. Y.,T;* m 1798 Patience da. Caleb & Hannah (Curtis) Grannis, b 6 Mar 1777 *F*, d 30 Apr 1865 æ. 88 *CamdenT.*
2 ANSEL, b 24 July 1785 *F*, d 11 Apr 1840 (Blossvale, N. Y.) *F;* m 1811 Susan Leonard of Taunton, Mass.
3 ALVIN.
4 ANNA, b [21 Apr 1788], d 24 May 1788 æ. 0-1-3 *BD.*
5 FANNY, b [21 Apr 1788], d 24 Mar 1788 æ. 0-1-3 *BD.*
6 SALLY; m ——— Bruce.
7 CHARRY, d 11 Aug 1854 æ. 62 *F;* m J. G. Sperry.

FAM. 36. ELIAS & CHLOE (———) JOHNSON:
1 LUCY; m Willis Brown.
2 ABRAM ELIPHALET, b 25 Feb 1793 (at L) *F*, d Aug 1866 (Richfield, Mich.) *F;* m 1818 Amanda Preston, who d 3 Oct 1865.
3 STEPHEN.
4 CHLOE.
5 LYDIA; m Asa Millington of North Bay.
6 MILES.
7 ELIAS.
8 AMY; m Daniel Seeley.
9 ANSEL.

FAM. 37. TIMOTHY & MARTHA (HUMISTON) JOHNSON (incomplete):
1 SALLY, bp 16 Jan 1780 *NHC2.*
2 HEMAN, bp 17 Feb 1782 *NHC2.*
3 "CHILD of Mr. Johnston" bp 27 July 1788 *NHC2.*

FAM. 38. NOAH & SALLY (HILL) JOHNSON:
1 LYMAN, bp 26 June 1803 (æ. 14) *NHx.*
2 BETSEY, bp 26 June 1803 (æ. 13) *NHx.*
3 BELA, bp 26 June 1803 (æ. 11) *NHx.*
4 HARVEY, bp 26 June 1803 (æ. 7) *NHx.*
5 SALLY, bp 26 June 1803 (æ. 4) *NHx.*

JOHNSON. FAM. 39. WALTER (called also Wouter Jansen), s. of Jan Wouters Van der Bosch & Arentje (Arents) of Flatbush, L. I., b c. 1666, d 6 Feb 1731 *WV;* m (1) Joanna da. Nehemiah & Hannah (Morgan) Royce, b c. 1670, d c. 1688; m (2) 5 July 1689 *Flatbush, L. I.*—Tryntie Henerig, wid. William Edwards.

(By 1): 1 JOHN, b c. 1688; rem. to Hanover, N. J.; m 2 Nov 1710 *WV*—Mary da. John & Mary (Clement) Chatterton, b 28 Apr 1692 *NHV*, d 21 Sep 1774 æ. 91 *Morristown, N. J., C.*
i John, b 12 Aug 1711 *WV*, d 4 May 1776 æ. 70 *Morristown,*

N, J.,C; m Abigail da. Caleb Ball, who d 4 Jan 1793 æ. 85 *MorristownC.*

ii Hannah, b 31 Dec 1712 *WV.*

iii Elisha, b 3 Sep 1714 *WV.*

iv Moses, b 26 July 1716 *WV.*

v Kezia, b 22 Apr 1718 *WV.*

vi Esther, b 20 Apr 1720 *WV.*

vii Alexander, b c. 1722, d 25 May 1788 æ. 66 *MorristownC;* m Lois Gregory, who d 2 Nov 1797 æ. 68 *MorristownC.*

viii Moses, b c. 1730, d 24 Jan 1803 æ. 72 *MorristownC;* m Naomi da. Ebenezer Gregory of St, who d 27 July 1797 æ. 65 *MorristownC.*

(By 2): 2 LAMBERT, b c. 1691, d 27 Nov 1726 *WV;* m 1 Mar 1716 *WV*—Rebecca da. Thomas & Mary (Merriman) Curtis, b 21 Aug 1697 *WV;* she m (2) William Munson.

i Benjamin, b 10 Dec 1716 *WV;* rem. to L; m 11 Apr 1751 *WV*—Mary da. Abraham & Mary (Lewis) Doolittle, b 23 Mar 1726 *WV.* **FAM. 40.**

ii Cornelius, b 13 Feb 1719 *WV,* d c. 1802; Census (Wat) 1-0-1; m 9 Dec 1746 *WV*—Elizabeth da. Benjamin & Esther (Matthews) Lewis, b 6 Mar 1727 *WV.* **FAM. 41.**

iii Mary, b 3 June 1721 *WV;* m 19 July 1744 *WV*—Zebulon Doolittle.

iv Anna, b c. 1724, d 15 Mar 1793 æ. 69 *BT4;* m 12 Oct 1743 *NHV*—Azariah Perkins.

v Rebecca; m (1) 3 Apr 1745 *NHV*—Benjamin Perkins; m (2) 13 Mar 1752 *NHV, WdC*—John Wilmot; m (3) 3 Aug 1756 *WdC*—Samuel Thomas; m (4) 11 Sep 1766 *WdC*—Ebenezer Morris.

3 ELEANOR; m 28 Oct 1714 *WV*—Joseph Cook.

4 (perhaps) HANNAH; m 6 Jan 1715 *WV*—Alexander Roberts.

FAM. 40. BENJAMIN & MARY (DOOLITTLE) JOHNSON (family incomplete):

1 SARAH, b 12 Jan 1752 *WV,* bp Jan 1752 *CC.*

2 ASA, b 27 May 1753 *WyV.*

3 SAMUEL, b 10 Aug 1755 *WyV.*

4 BENJAMIN, b c. 1758, d 7 Jan 1829 æ. 70 *LT;* Census (L) 1-0-2; m 1785 Lucretia Kilborn.

5 LAMBERT, b c. 1764, d 29 Nov 1842 æ. 78 *LT;* Census (L) 1-2-2; m 1785 Tilda Smith.

FAM. 41. CORNELIUS & ELIZABETH (LEWIS) JOHNSON:

1 ASA, b 17 July 1747 *WV,* bp Apr 1751 *CC,* d 13 Dec 1751 *WatV.*

2 ELIZABETH, b 22 Jan 1749/50 *WV,* bp Apr 1751 *CC,* d 12 Sep 1766 *WatV.*

3 ASA, b 24 June 1754 *WatV,* d 8 Feb 1758 *WatV.*

4 JESSE, b 27 July 1756 *WatV;* Census (Wat) 1-1-5; m 23 Aug 1780 *WatV*—Hannah da. Nathaniel Hoadley, wid. John Beach.

5 CORNELIUS, b 13 Nov 1758 *WatV,* d June 1762 *WatV.*

6 LYMAN, b 21 Jan 1761 *WatV;* Census (Wat) 1-1-3; m 6 Mar 1780 *WatV*—Mary da. Nathaniel Hoadley.

7 CORNELIUS, b c. 1764, d 17 Oct 1822 æ. 58 *WatT2;* Census (Wat) 1-1-3; m Eunice ——— .

JOHNSON. FAM. 42. ABRAHAM, b c. 1749, d 23 Sep 1844 æ. 95-6 *EHC;* Census (NH) 1-1-1; m 29 Dec 1776 *NHC1*—Experience Barnes; "wife of Abraham" d 8 Dec 1834 æ. 78 *NHV.*

1 HESTER, bp 18 Nov 1784 *NHx,* d 22 Nov 1784 *NHx.*

2 ABRAHAM WHEADON, bp 20 Aug 1789 *NHx,* "Abraham Jr." d 13 June 1830 æ. 45 *NHV;* possibly he is the Abram, b 15 Sep 1790 (at NH) *F,* d Sep 1828 (at NH) *F;* m 1 Dec 1816 (at EH) *F*—Rhoda Denslow & had issue:

i Charles Denslow, b 24 Aug 1817 *F,* d 1846 (at sea) *F.*

ii Edwin Augustus, b 8 Apr 1819 *F,* d 25 Jan 1842 *F.*

3 WILLIAM, bp 2 Nov 1796 *NHx.*

JOHNSON. FAM. 43. GEORGE, of Stratford, d 2 Jan 1714 *StV;* m 4 Jan 1695 *StV*—Hannah da. Edmund & Hannah (Hull) Dorman, b 1 Mar 1696/7 *NHV,* d 1724.

1 MARY, b 15 Oct 1695 *StV;* m 5 Sep 1717 *StV*—Thomas Stratton.

2 JOHN, b 15 Apr 1697 *StV;* d s. p. before 1767.

3 HANNAH, b 3 Apr 1699 *StV;* m 22 May 1725 *DV*—Samuel Wooster.

4 ELIZABETH, b 28 Aug 1701 *StV,* d 1797; m (1) 25 Dec 1721 *MV*—James Prichard: m (2) 28 Nov 1750 *WatV*—Stephen Upson.

5 ROBERT, b c. 1704; m 21 Mar 1727 *StV*—Sarah Chapman; 10 children b at Wat, of whom Robert Jr. settled in W. Stockbridge, Mass.

6 MARGARET, b 22 Sep 1706 *StV;* m 1 Jan 1728/9 *StV*—Gershom Bunnell.

7 JOSEPH, b 22 Jan 1709 *StV;* m Rachel ——— .

8 THANKFUL; m ——— Baldwin.

JOHNSON. MISCELLANEOUS. Children bp at *NHC1* (parents not named): Sarah, 17 Sep 1738; Stephen, 9 Aug 1741; Ezra, 7 Mar 1741/2; Ebenezer, 16 July 1738.......LYDIA m 10 Dec 1731 *NHV*—Isaac Cooper......MARY m 9 May 1750 *WV*—Jesse Merriam......MERCY m 13 July 1749 *WV*—Ebenezer Cole......JOSEPH & Sarah had da. Esther b 4 May 1712 *WV*......JOSEPH & Hannah had da. Phebe b 8 Jan 1735 *WV*......ARCHIBALD m 19 Feb 1756 *WV*—Sarah Bradley of G. Children: 1 James, b 8 July 1757 *WV.* 2 Daniel, b 6 Oct 1759 *WV*......AMOS, b c. 1777, d 30 Sep 1857 æ. 80 *NHT2;* m Sally B. ——— , who d 15 Mar 1859 æ. 69 *NHT2*......ENOS A., b c. 1787, d 16 July 1843 æ. 56 *NHT1;* m 25 Nov 1810 *NHx*—Nancy Dorman, b c. 1789, d 11 Aug 1870 æ. 81 *NHT1;* probate names 2 das., Jennet Van Wutenburg of Ill. & Sophia Hayes......SETH of C m 26 Dec 1771 *WV*—Eunice Hitchcock; had large family......MISS LUCY d 8 Mar 1788 æ. 27-6-21 *BD.*

JOLLY. CAPT. JOHN, d 17 Apr 1787 æ. 56 *CT3;* m Martha da. Ralph & Martha (Ives) Parker, b 18 Apr 1749 *WV;* d after 1794; Census, Martha (C) 0-0-2.

JONES. FAM. 1. WILLIAM, b 1624, d 17 Oct 1706 *NHV*, æ. 82 *NHTI*; Dep. Gov., NHColony 1664; Assistant, Conn. Colony 1665–1687, 1689–1691; Dep. Gov., Conn. 1691–1697; Judge of NHCtC; m (1) ——— ; m (2) 4 July 1659 (London, Eng,)—Hannah da. Theophilus & Ann (Lloyd) Eaton, b c. 1633, d 4 May 1707 *NHV*, æ. 74 *NHTI*. In 1659 he is described as Gentleman, of Martins in the Field, Middlesex Co., Eng.

(By 1): 1 WILLIAM, d 23 May 1700 *G;* m 18 Oct 1687 Abigail da. John & Annis [Chickering] Morse, wid. Israel Everett, b 1 Apr 1646 (Dedham, Mass.), d 23 Sep 1737 *G.*

i Caleb, b c. 1688, d 24 May 1754 *G;* m (1) 15 July 1723 *G*—Mary Bishop, who d 23 Jan 1724 *G;* m (2) 19 Jan 1725 *G* —Elizabeth Lucas, who d 22 Oct 1782 *G.* **FAM. 2.**

2 CALEB, d s. p. 1677.

3 NATHANIEL, d 21 Aug 1691 *NHV;* m 7 Oct 1684 *NHV*—Abigail da. David & Damaris (Sayre) Atwater, b 3 Mar 1659/60 *NHV.*

i Hannah, b 6 May 1687 *NHV*, bp May 1687 *NHCI;* m Benjamin Everest of Saybrook.

ii Theophilus, b 18 Mar 1690 *NHV*, bp 12 Jan (?) 1690 *NHC I;* m (1) 26 Dec 1711 *WV*—Hannah da. Daniel & Ruth (Rockwell) Mix, who d 26 Nov 1754 *WV;* m (2) 22 Sep 1755 *WV*—Sarah da. Edward & Mary (Thorpe) Fenn, wid. Solomon Moss, b 24 Nov 1694 *WV.* **FAM. 3.**

iii Abigail, b 26 Mar 1692 *NHV*, bp Mar 1692 *NHCI.*

(By 2): 4 HANNAH, b c. 1660, d 29 May 1717 *StV;* m (1) 2 Oct 1689 *NHV*—Patrick Falconer; m (2) James Clark; m (3) 31 Jan 1715 *StV*—John Booth.

5 THEOPHILUS, b 2 Oct 1661 *NHV*, d 5 Oct 1661 *NHV.*

6 SARAH, b 17 Aug 1662 *NHV;* m (1) 21 Oct 1687 *NHV*—Andrew Morrison; m (2) John Dudley.

7 ELIZABETH, b 28 Aug 1664 *NHV*, ["Mary" bp 23 Oct 1664 *NHC I*]; m John Morgan of New London.

8 SAMUEL, b 20 June 1666 *NHV*, bp 29 July 1666 *NHCI*, d 26 Dec 1666 *NHV.*

9 JOHN, b 4 Oct 1667 *NHV*, d 28 Jan 1718 *NHV;* m Mindwell Stebbins.

i Theophil-eaton, b 20 Mar 1706 *NHV;* rem. to Norwalk; m 17 Oct 1728 *NHV*—Sarah da. Paul & Susanna (Bowden) Cornwall, b 5 May 1707. **FAM. 4.**

ii Hannah, b 15 June 1708 *NHV*, d 16 Feb 1708/9 *NHV.*

iii Hannah, b 29 July 1710 *NHV*, d s. p. 1730.

iv Mindwell, b 22 Oct 1711 *NHV*, d soon.

v John, b 7 Feb 1712 *NHV* [1712/3]; rem. to M & Durham; m 6 Oct 1738 Hannah Bassett. **FAM. 5.**

vi Mindwell, b 14 Sep 1715 *NHV.*

vii Abigail, b 25 Jan 1717/8 *NHV.*

10 DIODATI, b 15 Mar 1669/70 *NHV*, d 5 Apr 1670 *NHV.*

11 ISAAC, b 21 June 1671 *NHV*, d 1741; m (1) 21 Nov 1692 *NHV*—Deborah da. James & Deborah (Peacock) Clark, b 1672, d 28

May 1735 *NHV*, æ. 63 *NHTI*; m (2) 1 Oct 1735 *NHV*—Abigail da. Andrew & Sarah (Gibbard) Sanford, wid. Samuel Chatterton, who d 1757.

(By 1): *i* Samuel, b 27 Sep 1693 *NHV*, bp 29 Sep 1693 *NHCI*, d 1773; m (1) 13 Mar 1719 *WV*—Sarah Hickson, who d 9 Nov 1760 *WV*; m (2) 12 Apr 1762 *WV*—Esther Pratt, who d 23 Sep 1776 *WV*. **FAM. 6.**

ii William, b 20 Jan 1694/5 *NHV*, bp c. Feb 1694/5 *NHCI*, d before 1739; rem. to Marblehead, Mass.; m & had a s. Basil.

iii Timothy, b 30 Oct 1696 *NHV*, d 24 Aug 1781 æ. 84 *NHT I*; m (1) 16 Nov 1726 *NHV*—Jane da. John & Susanna (Collins) Harris, b Sep 1705 (at Mid); m (2) Anna ——, b c. 1702, d 19 May 1783 [error for 1784] æ. 71 *NHTI*. **FAM. 7.**

iv Mary, b 6 Oct 1698 *NHV*, bp Oct 1698 *NHCI*; m 12 Oct 1720 *NHV*—Samuel Elwell; res. Fairfield 1743.

v Deborah, b 25 Sep 1700 *NHV*, bp 29 Sep 1700 *NHCI*, d 4 Sep 1751 æ. 50 *NHTI*; m (1) 4 Dec 1723 *NHV*—Nathaniel Maltby of Saybrook; m (2) John Talmadge; m (3) 14 Jan 1747/8 *FarmV*—Timothy Bronson.

vi Isaac, b 23 Dec 1702 *NHV*, d 3 Aug 1759 (Saybrook); Ens.; m Deborah da. John & Mary (Buckingham) Parker, b 12 May 1704. **FAM. 8.**

vii Hannah, b 15 Feb 1704 *NHV*, d 30 Jan 1707/8 *NHV*.

viii Jacob, b 20 Mar 1706/7 *NHV*; rem. to Ridgefield; m.

ix James, b 16 May 1709 *NHV*, d c. 1768; res. Saybrook; m Sarah Willard, who d 26 Oct 1789 *CC*. **FAM. 9.**

x Ebenezer, b 25 Feb 1712 *NHV*, d 22 Sep 1713 *NHV*.

12 Abigail, b 10 Nov 1673 *NHV*, d 15 Nov 1673 *NHV*.

13 Rebecca, b 10 Nov 1673 *NHV*, d 15 Nov 1673 *NHV*.

14 Susanna, b 18 Aug 1675 *NHV*, d 1705; m Nathaniel Wilson of Hartford.

FAM. 2. Caleb & Elizabeth (Lucas) Jones:

1 Mary, b 26 Oct 1725 *G*; m Nathaniel Foote.

2 Aaron, b 4 Apr 1727 *G*, d s. p. 30 Nov 1803 *G*; m 7 Nov 1771 *G*—Anna Fosdick, b 23 Jan 1736 *G*, d 30 Oct 1808 *G*.

3 Sybil, b 13 Jan 1729 *G*; m Samuel Hoadley.

4 Tryphena, b 2 Nov 1730 *G*; m Joseph Roberts.

5 Hannah, b 3 Jan 1735 *G*, d Feb 1740 *G*.

6 William, b 20 Aug 1737 *G*, d 29 Nov 1739 *G*.

FAM. 3. Theophilus & Hannah (Mix) Jones:

1 Caleb, b 4 Nov 1712 *WV*, d 9 Dec 1786; res. Cornwall; m 6 Oct 1741 *WV*—Mary da. Ebenezer & Mary [Harrington] Frisbie, wid. Zachariah How, bp 6 Oct 1711 *BdC*. Family incomplete.

i Ann, b 19 Aug 1742 *WV*; m 1761 *CornwallC*—Seley Abbot.

ii Zachariah How, b 3 Sep 1744 *WV*, d 31 July 1817; m 3 May 1766 *CornwallC*—Jane Dibble.

iii Hannah, b 8 June 1746 *WV*.
iv Caleb, b 29 Mar 1748 *WV*.
v Samuel, b 15 May 1752 *WV*.
vi John, b 14 Oct 1757.

2 Lydia, b 9 Nov 1714 *WV;* m 4 Feb 1735 *WV*—Joseph Moss.

3 Nathaniel, b 30 Mar 1717 *WV*, d 2 July 1801 æ. 85 *WTI;* Census (W) 1-1-2; m 8 June 1743 *WV*—Sarah da. Eliasaph & Abigail (Hull) Merriman, b 18 Nov 1723 *WV*.

i Abigail, b 26 Sep 1744 *WV*, d 11 Jan 1775 *WV*, æ. 31 *WT I;* m 12 Nov 1766 *WV*—Caleb Atwater.
ii Daniel, b 18 Mar 1745/6 *WV*, d soon.
iii John, b 25 May 1747 *WV*, d 17 Apr 1767 *WV*.
iv Daniel, b 7 Oct 1748 *WV*, d s. p. 28 Aug 1827 æ. 79 *NoB TI;* Census (Bd) 1-0-3; m (1) 25 May 1774 *WV*—Joanna da. Wait & Joanna (Beach) Chatterton, b 27 May 1753 *NHV;* m (2) Dorothy ——— , who d 29 Jan 1852 æ. 82 *NoBTI*.
v Sarah, b 16 Aug 1750 *WV*, d 9 Mar 1815 æ. 63 *WTI;* m 7 June 1773 *WV*—Samuel Doolittle.
vi Eunice, b 27 Jan 1752 *WV;* m 2 Feb 1775 *WV*—Joel Royce.
vii Nathaniel, b c. 1754, d 11 Sep 1825 æ. 72 *ST;* Census (S) 3-3-4; m (1) Content da. Ephraim & Hannah (Ward) Johnson, b 14 July 1755 *WV*, d 9 Apr 1807 æ. 52 *ST;* m (2) Mabel Crampton, who d 18 May 1848 æ. 76 *ST*. **FAM. 10.**
viii Benjamin, b 5 Feb 1757 *WV;* res. Barkhamsted 1801.
ix Amos, b 3 Aug 1758 *WV*.
x Reuben, b 11 Oct 1759 *WV*, d 6 Oct 1843 æ. 84 *WTI;* Census (W) 1-1-3; m Sarah da. Jonathan & Hannah (Barnes) Tuttle, b 18 Dec 1762 *WV*, d 12 Mar 1833 æ. 72 *WTI*. **FAM. 11.**
xi Hannah, b 25 Feb 1761 *WV;* m Isaiah Tuttle.
xii Mary; m Samuel Church of S; joined in deed with other children of Nathaniel 1801.

4 Hannah, b 4 Oct 1720 *WV*, d 26 Aug 1783 *CC;* m 5 Aug 1740 *W V*—Jehiel Merriman.

5 Theophilus, b 1 Nov 1723 *WV*, d 8 Oct 1815 æ. 91 *WTI;* Census (W) 1-1-2; m 24 May 1757 *WV*—Anna da. Elnathan & Damaris (Hull) Street, b 16 Feb 1736 *WV*, d 10 Aug 1811 æ. 76 *WTI*.

i Sarah, b 30 Mar 1758 *WV*, d 15 Sep 1836 æ. 79 *WTI;* m 8 Sep 1777 *WV*—Elisha Whittlesey.
ii Nicholas, b 25 Nov 1760 *WV*, d 25 Aug 1849 æ. 88-9 *WT I;* Census (W) 1-0-4; m Elizabeth da. Isaac & Esther (Moseley) Hall, b 28 Apr 176[4] *WV*, d 8 Feb 1845. **FAM. 12.**
iii Anna, b c. 1772, d Oct 1776 æ. 4 *WTI*.

iv Mary, b c. 1775, d s. p.; m —— Johnson of W.

6 ABIGAIL, b 28 Dec 1726 *WV*, d 13 Sep 1758 *SC, FarmV;* m 16 Mar 1747/8 *WV*—Benjamin Dutton.

7 NICHOLAS, b 17 Dec 1729 *WV*, d 24 Apr 1760 *WV;* m (1) Mary da. Ephraim & Patience (Dayton) Preston, b 8 Jan 1731 *WV*, d 27 Oct 1754 *WV*, æ. 23 *WT1;* m (2) Eunice ——, b c. 1736, d 19 Sep 1829 æ. 93 *WT1;* she m (2) 29 Apr 1761 *WV*—Charles Dutton.

(By 1): *i* Charles, b 19 May 1752 *WV;* m 14 Nov 1771 *WV*—Damaris da. Parmineas & Rachel (Curtis) Bunnell, b 30 June 1752 *WV*. Child: John, b 17 May 1772 *WV*.

ii Patience, b 27 Mar 1754 *WV*.

(By 2): *iii* Mary, b 30 Apr 1756 *WV;* m 19 Oct 1772 *WV*—John Hall.

iv Eunice, b 31 Mar 1758 *WV*, d 26 Feb 1758(?) *WV*.

v Mary [?Mercy], b 26 Feb 1760 *WV*, d 6 May 1760 *WV*.

8 DANIEL, b 28 Oct 1731 *WV*, d 1 May 1737 *WV*.

FAM. 4. THEOPHIL-EATON & SARAH (CORNWALL) JONES:

1 HEZEKIAH, b 22 Oct 1729 *NHV*, d soon.

2 HANNAH, b 1 Sep 1731 *NHV*, bp 27 Jan 1733/4 *NHC1*.

3 (probably) SARAH, bp 28 Apr 1734 *NHC1*.

4 ABIGAIL, b 29 Feb 1735/6 *NHV*, bp 8 Mar 1735/6 *NHC1*, d 14 Sep 1737 *NHV*.

5 HEZEKIAH, b 28 Jan 1737/8 *NHV*, bp 30 Jan 1737/8 *NHC1*.

6 (perhaps) ABIGAIL, bp 9 Dec 1739 *NHC1*.

FAM. 5. JOHN & HANNAH (BASSETT) JONES:

1 JOHN, b 28 Mar 1740, d 1815; res. Durham, G, H, & Reading N. Y.; m (1) 20 Sep 1768 Esther Cruttenden, b 5 Apr 1747, d 15 Feb 1803; m (2) 20 Sep 1804 Lydia A. (——) Sherman.

2 MARY, b 14 Jan 1743; m Ebenezer Smith.

3 HANNAH, b 6 Apr 1746; m Samuel Prince.

4 ISAAC, b 6 May 1748; m Mary Pond.

5 SARAH, b 23 Jan 1750, d 28 Nov 1759.

6 PHINEAS, b 4 Dec 1751; m Mary Brooks.

7 ABIGAIL, b 4 Mar 1754; m David Burr.

8 JAMES, b 15 Oct 1756, d soon.

9 JAMES, b 16 Oct 1758.

FAM. 6. SAMUEL & SARAH (HICKSON) JONES:

1 WILLIAM, b 31 May 1720 *WV*, d after 1807; Census (W) 1-0-2; m (1) 24 Nov 1759 *WV*—Sarah Pratt; m (2) Eunice da. Samuel & Sarah (Wiltshire) Merriman, wid. John Kean, b 21 Aug 1753 *WV;* [a Wm. Jones m before 1796 Hannah da. Elon & Sarah Andrews, b 1 Oct 17[66] *WV*]. Family incomplete.

(By 1): *i* William Hinkson, b 4 Dec 1761 *WV*.

(By 2): *ii* Sarah, b 16 July 1783 *WV;* m Daniel Stanton Smith.

2 MARY, b 5 Dec 1721 *WV*, d 4 Sep 1803 *HT3;* m (1) 18 Feb 1742 *WV*—Samuel Bellamy; m (2) Samuel Hitchcock.

3 DIODATI, b 15 Mar 1724 *WV*, d 18 Mar 1745/6 (at Cape Breton) *WV*.

4 HESTER, b 9 Mar 1727 *WV;* m 10 May 1758 *WV*—Dennis Covert.

5 EATON, b 26 Aug 1730 *WV;* m 5 May 1756 *LV*—Elizabeth Catlin.

i Samuel, b 15 Oct 1756 *LV*, d Dec 1759 *LV*.

ii Lucina, b 12 Sep 1758 *LV*.

iii Samuel, b 25 Oct 1760 *LV*.

iv Eaton, b 9 Nov 1762 *LV;* Census (L) 1-0-2; m 1 May 1788 *LV*—Mary McNeil.

v James, b 19 June 1765 *LV*.

vi Homer, b 29 Sep 1767 *LV*, d 1 Oct 1857.

vii Liza, b 27 Sep 1768 *LV*, d soon.

viii Liza, b 10 Mar 1771 *LV*.

ix Charles, b 20 Nov 1774 *LV*.

x Katharine, b 6 May 1777 *LV*.

FAM. 6. SAMUEL & ESTHER (PRATT) JONES:

6 DIODATI PRATT, b 16 June 176[2] *WV*, d 19 Nov 1852 æ. 90-5-3 *HV;* Census (H) 1-1-1; m (1) 12 Mar 1788 *NHC2*—Sarah da. Joseph & Lois (Perkins) Dickerman, b 30 Aug 1757 *NHV*, d 22 Sep 1828 æ. 71; m (2) ——— .

(By 1): *i* Isaac, b c. 1790, d 23 Mar 1882 æ. 92 *HV;* m (1) Betsey da. Joseph & Elizabeth (Bunnell) Benham, wid. Isaac Thomas & ———, b c. 1789, d 20 Mar 1832 æ. 53 *HT2;* m (2) Emeline Fisk, b [24 Dec 1804], d 3 Apr 1880 æ. 75-3-29 *HV;* 3 children by 1st w., of whom Rhoda Jannet, b 1814, d 20 July 1862, m Ezra Austin; 1 son, Eugene P., by 2nd. w.

ii Adah; m Benjamin Fuller.

iii Rhoda, b c. 1793, d 3 Oct 1813 æ. 20 *WdD;* m Lemuel Sperry.

iv Samuel; m (1) Abigail (Eaton) Hubbard; m (2) 13 Feb 1823 *HV*—Rhoda da. Levi & Patience (Alling) Munson, b 19 July 1795 *F*, d 29 Sep 1871 æ. 76-2 *HV;* 11 children.

v Lavinia, b c. 1796, d 14 Oct 1813 æ. 17.

vi Patty, b c. 1798, d 19 Oct 1881 æ. 83 *HT2;* m 11 Nov 1824 *HV*—Joel Goodyear Warner.

7 REUBEN, b 17 Apr 1768 *WV*.

8 CHLOE, d 29 Sep 1776 *WV*.

FAM. 7. TIMOTHY & JANE (HARRIS) JONES:

1 ELIZABETH, b 19 Nov 1728 *NHV*, bp 24 Nov 1728 *NHC1;* m ——— Roberts.

2 DEBORAH, b 4 Sep 1730 *NHV*, bp 5 Sep 1730 *NHC1*, d 18 Aug 1764; m 3 Oct 1753 *NHC2*—Samuel Gridley of Huntington.

3 SUSANNA, b 10 Aug 1732 *NHV*, bp 13 Aug 1732 *NHC1*, d 6 May 1813 æ. 81 *NHT1;* m 28 Aug 1755 *NHV*, *NHC2*—John Hotchkiss.

4 HARRIS, b 9 Sep 1734 *NHV*, bp 15 Sep 1734 *NHC1*, d 2 Sep 1824 æ. 90 (at L); m Ann da. Joseph & Sarah [Prime] Plumb.

i Mary, b 28 Nov 1760.

5 TIMOTHY, b 1 Oct 1737 *NHV*, bp 2 Oct 1737 *NHC1*, d May 1800

æ. 62 *ConnJournal;* B. A. (Yale 1757); Alderman & J. P.; Census (NH) 1-1-2; m (1) 20 June 1765 *NHC1*—Mary da. Joseph & Mary (Woodward) Trowbridge, b 10 Sep 1744 *NHV*, d 20 Sep 1789 æ. 45 *NHT1*; m (2) July 1790 Rebecca da. William Hart, wid. William Lynde, who d 26 Sep 1819.

(By 1): *i* Son, b & d 5 Apr 1767 *NHT1*.

ii Elizabeth, b c. 1769, bp 4 Mar 1784 *NHC2*, d 2 Oct 1839 æ. 70 *NHV;* m 27 June 1791 *NHC1*—Joseph Lynde.

iii William Rosewell, b c. 1774, bp 4 Mar 1784 *NHC2*, d s. p. 30 Mar 1842 æ. 68 *NHV;* deaf mute.

6 **Isaac**, b 21 Dec 1738 *NHV*, bp 24 Dec 1738 *NHC1*, bu. 22 May 1812 æ 73 *NHx;* Census (NH) 1-4-4; m (1) 5 June 1768 *NHV*, *NHC1*—Elizabeth da. Joseph & Mary (Woodward) Trowbridge, bp 15 July 1750 *NHC1*, d 4 Apr 1769 æ. 18 *NHT1;* m (2) 27 Dec 1770 *MidC*—Lucy da. Charles Goodrich of Pittsfield, Mass., who d 10 Dec 1771; m (3) 23 Jan 1774 Sybil da. John Benjamin, b c. 1755 (at St), d 19 Sep 1814.

(By 1): *i* William Trowbridge, b 25 Feb 1769 *NHV*, "child" d 7 Aug 1769 æ. 0-6 *NHT1*.

(By 3): *ii* Isaac, b 18 Feb 1775 (at NH) *LT*, bp 31 July 1791 *NHC2*, d 17 Mar 1850 æ. 75 *LT;* Rev.; m 17 Oct 1804 (at NH) *LV*—Tabitha da. Hezekiah & Chloe (Beecher) Thomas, b 18 May 1787 (at Wd) *LT*, d 9 Oct 1852 æ. 65 *LT*.

iii Mary, b c. 1777, bp 31 July 1791 *NHC2*.

iv William Henry, b 3 Nov 1778 *NHT1*, bp 31 July 1791 *NHC2*, d 27 Nov 1861 *NHT1*, 28 Nov æ. 83 *NHV;* Postmaster, NH, 1814–1842; m Sarah R. Barker, b 14 July 1788 *NHT1*, d 1 Nov 1857 *NHT1*. Child: Isaac Eaton, b 9 Oct 1825 *NHT1*, d 23 Aug 1892 *NHT1;* m Evelina da. James & Harriet (Cutler) Hunt, b 28 Mar 1825 *NHT1*, d 9 Jan 1909 *NHT1*.

v Amelia, bp 31 July 1791 *NHC2;* m 17 Sep 1797 *ConnJournal*—Charles Goodrich Jr. of Pittsfield, Mass.

vi Timothy, bp 31 July 1791 *NHC2*, d 1841.

vii Algernon Sidney, bp 31 July 1791 *NHC2*, d 1858.

viii Frances, bp 31 July 1791 *NHC2*.

ix Harriet, bp 31 July 1791 *NHC2;* m 11 Nov 1810 *NHx*—Benjamin Brooks of Providence.

7 **Jane**, b 31 Oct 1740 *NHV*, "Ann" bp 2 Nov 1740 *NHC1;* m 1 Dec 1757 *NHC2*—Thomas Ivers of Bolton.

8 **Ann**, bp 5 Sep 1742 *NHC1*, d s. p.

9 **Mary**, b 12 Dec 1743 *NHV*, bp 18 Dec 1743 *NHC1;* m 31 Oct 1764 *NHV*, *NHC2*—John Lathrop.

10 **William**, b 27 Jan 1745/6 *NHV*, bp 26 Jan 1745/6 *NHC1*, d 20 May 1783; m 1771 Elizabeth Lathrop, b c. 1753, d 13 Nov 1776.

i William, b 7 Mar 1773 *NHT1*, d 14 Mar 1773 æ. 0-0-7 *NHT1*.

ii Ann; m 25 Oct 1801 Solomon Huntington; res. Mexico, N. Y.

FAM. 8. ISAAC & DEBORAH (PARKER) JONES (record of family incomplete & perhaps not accurate; further information desired):

1 HESTER, b 11 Oct 1726.

2 ISAAC, b 7 July 1730, d 2 May 1739.

3 SON, b 7 July 1730, d 9 July 1730.

4 TEMPERANCE.

5 PARKER, b c. 1734.

6 MABEL; m Ezekiel Butler.

7 MOLLY.

8 SYBIL.

9 ISAAC.

FAM. 9. JAMES & SARAH (WILLARD) JONES:

1 WILLIAM; Census (C) 1-0-5; m (1) 14 Nov 1765 *WV*—Lois da. Amos & Obedience (Munson) Hotchkiss, who d 14 Dec 1773 *CC*, 16 Dec *WV;* m (2) 8 Apr 1774 *CC*—Lydia Hotchkiss, "wife" d 11 Feb 1800 *CC;* m (3) Olive da. Gideon & Mabel (Stiles) Hotchkiss, b 21 Nov 1769 *WatV.*

(By 1): *i* Lydia, b 31 Jan 1765 *WV*, d 10 June 1775 *WV*, "child" d *CC.*

ii Sarah, b 7 Apr 1767 *WV.*

iii Samuel, b 13 Oct 1769 *WV.*

2 DEBORAH; m Hubbell Stevens.

3 SARAH, b 27 May 1741; [?m 11 Mar 1778 *CC*—Ebenezer Howard].

4 HANNAH, b 15 Nov 1741 *F* [1742?], d 13 June 1814 *F;* m 14 May 1762 *F*—Silas Gladding.

5 JAMES, b 19 Jan 1743/4, d c. 1811; Census (C) 1-4-1; m 12 Oct 1775 *CC*—Marlow da. Amos & Obedience (Munson) Hotchkiss, wid. Titus Lines, b 20 June 1745 *WV*, d 9 Nov 1808 *CC.*

i James, b 30 Aug 1776 *CV;* m 8 Aug 1799 *CV*—Polly Stanley. Child: Sally, b 12 Aug 1799 *CV.*

ii Child, b c. 1779, d 22 Jan 1781 *CC.*

iii Titus, b 16 Apr 1782 *CV;* res. Westfield, Mass.; m 25 Apr 1805 *CC*—Rachel da. Amasa & Rachel (Lewis) Munson.

iv Samuel, b 16 Apr 1782 *CV;* res. Westfield, Mass.

v Darius, b 7 Feb 1785 *CV*, d 3 Apr 1861 æ. 76 *CTI;* m 7 July 1808 *CC*—Abigail da. Gideon & Abigail (Badger) Bristol, b 17 Apr 1788 *CV*, d 22 Feb 1867 æ. 79 *CTI.*

6 ELISHA, b c. 1747, d 21 Dec 1816 æ. 70 *NHTI;* Census (C) 1-3-3; m (1) 16 Nov 1773 *WV*, 17 Nov *CC*—Martha da. Benjamin & Martha (Brooks) Hotchkiss, b 27 Dec 1752 *NHV;* m (2) 31 Aug 1800 *NHCI*—Comfort da. Peter & Comfort (Clark) Johnson, b c. 1779, d 14 Dec 1822 æ. 44 (*NHCI*) *NHV.*

(By 1): *i* Wealthy Parmelee, b 10 Apr 1774 *WV*, bp 25 Dec 1774 *CC;* m 26 Jan 1797 *NHCI*—Abijah Wolcott of H.

ii Amaranda, b 16 Nov 1775 *WV*, bp 4 Feb 1776 *CC.*

iii Elisha Willard, b 13 Mar 1777 *WV*, bp 16 Mar 1777 *CC*, d 14 Feb 1829 æ. 52 *NHTI*, 18 Feb (*NHx*) *NHV*; m 25 Oct 1798 *NHCI*—Abigail Emeline Lewis, who d 22 Oct 1821 æ. 45 *NHTI*, 23 Oct 1820 æ. 46 (*NHx*) *NHV*. **FAM. 13.**

iv George Willis, b 9 Feb 1779 *WV*, bp 4 Apr 1779 *CC*.

v (perhaps) Amarilla, bp 22 July 1781 *CC*.

vi Simeon, bp 6 Apr 1783 *CC*; m 19 May 1805 *NHCI*—Lucy da. Zophar & Lucy (Osborn) Atwater.

vii Sylvester, bp 13 Mar 1785 *CC*, "child" d 9 Apr 1789 *CC*.

viii Sylvester, bp 16 May 1790 *CC*, d 12 May 1826 æ. 36 *NHTI*; m Elizabeth ——, who d 26 Nov 1823 æ. 35 *NHTI*.

ix David, bp 14 Apr 1792 *CC*, "child" d 14 Apr 1792 *CC*.

(By 2): *x* Betsey B.; m Henry Bacon of Camden, N. J.

xi Susan, bp 29 Mar 1804 *NHCI*.

7 Joseph.

8 Timothy, b 5 June 1755 (Saybrook), d 25 July 1810 æ. 55 *PT*; Census (Wtn) 1-1-2; m 8 Apr 1779 *CC*, *PV*—Lydia da. Isaac & Lydia (Morgan) Ives, b 25 Aug 1760 *WV*.

i Philena R., b 20 Feb 1780 *PV*, d 1 Apr 1809 *PV*.

ii Bilostee, b 8 June 1784 *PV*, d 21 May 1812 *PV*.

iii Willard, b 22 Mar 1794 *PV*, d 17 Sep 1810 *PV*.

9 George, b 14 Feb 1759.

FAM. 10. Nathaniel & Content (Johnson) Jones:

1 Luther, b 15 Oct 1783; m Betsey Porter.

2 Harriet, b 8 Jan 1786; m Abel Carter.

3 Hannah, b 13 May 1788, d 2 May 1875; m Samuel Finch.

4 Theron, b 19 Feb 1790.

5 Jehoida, b 8 Feb 1792; m Sally Merriman.

6 Theodore, b 18 Feb 1793; m 15 Jan 1817 Harriet Smith.

7 Reuben, b 22 Oct 1803; m Cornelia M. Langdon.

FAM. 10. Nathaniel & Mabel (Crampton) Jones:

8 Edward K., b 22 May 1810; m Eunice Pond.

FAM. 11. Reuben & Sarah (Tuttle) Jones:

1 Patty, b 29 Apr 1786 *WV*.

2 Polly, b 18 Jan 1789 *WV*.

3 Jeremiah.

4 Lyman, b 11 Apr 1794 *WV*, d 6 Mar 1796 æ. 2 *WTI*.

5 Hubbard.

6 Sukey, d æ. 80 *WTI*; m Roderick Hall.

7 Sarah, b c. 1801, d 11 Aug 1826 æ. 25 *WTI*; m Sherlock Avery.

FAM. 12. Nicholas & Elizabeth (Hall) Jones:

1 Anna, b 9 May 1785, d 19 Nov 1861; m Jared Doolittle.

2 Betsey Hall, b 3 May 1788, d 18 July 1855; m 8 Apr 1822 *WV*—Rufus Bradley.

3 Sally, b 10 Mar 1791, d 19 Dec 1794 æ. [4] *WTI*.

4 Esther, b 28 Dec 1793, d 9 June 1878 æ. 84 *WTI*; m 19 Feb 1817 Nathaniel Doolittle.

5 STREET, b 5 July 1801, d 31 Oct 1884 æ. 83 *WTI*; m (1) Mary Pierpont da. Peter & Mary (Trumbull) Eastman, b 11 Dec 1803 *NoHV*, d 12 Nov 1851 æ. 48 *WTI*; m (2) Elizabeth Parsons, who d 22 Dec 1875 æ. 70 *WTI*; m (3) Experience Eliza (——) Force, who d 11 June 1881; 10 children (see Dickerman Genealogy, p. 318).

6 SARAH, b 28 Oct 1806, d 27 Dec 1890; m 12 Apr 1826 Ezra Dickerman.

FAM. 13. ELISHA WILLARD & ABIGAIL EMELINE (LEWIS) JONES (incomplete):

1 ELISHA W., b c. 1802, d 18 Dec 1841 æ. 40 *NHTI*.

2 WEALTHY ANN, b c. 1804, "Jennet Abigail" bp 25 Sep 1804 *NHCI*, d 6 Jan 1824 æ. 19 (at Oxf) *NHTI*.

3 CHARLES AUGUSTUS, b c. 1807, d 9 Apr 1835 æ. 27 (at Macon, Ga.) *NHTI*.

4 EMELINE HOTCHKISS, b c 1809, d 30 Apr 1837 æ. 28 *NHTI*.

JONES. FAM. 14. BENJAMIN, s. of Benjamin & Hannah (Spencer), b 30 June 1662 *MV*, d 30 Dec 1690 *NHV*; m 30 Nov 1687 *NHV*—Hannah da. Ebenezer & Hannah (Vincent) Brown, b 1 Feb 1667 *NHV* [1668]; she m (2) 1694 Benjamin Wooding.

1 BENJAMIN, b c. 1688, d 1752; res. WH & Brookhaven, L. I.; m Anna —— .

i Benjamin, b 14 Oct 1706 *NHV*; m 19 Jan 1726/7 *NHV*—Martha da. Thomas & Judith (Bunnell) Hodge, b 18 Feb 1709/10 *NHV*. Children (incomplete): 1 Martha, b 13 Nov 1727 *NHV*, bp 13 Sep 1728 (at NH) *Stx*; 2 Benjamin, bp 23 May 1731 (at Brookhaven) *Stx*.

ii Hannah, b 14 Mar 1709 *NHV*, d 29 Mar 1769 æ. 61 *OxfC*; m (1) Ebenezer Benham; m (2) Isaac Trowbridge.

iii Ruth, b 19 Apr 1712 *NHV*.

iv Vincent, b 14 Aug 1715 *NHV*, d 1751; m Ruth Tooker; she m (2) —— Bayles. Children: 1 Dorothy; m —— Smith. 2 Jelin. 3 Penina. 4 Elizabeth.

v Martha, b 14 Sep 1718 *NHV*.

vi Ebenezer, b 5 May 1722 *NHV*.

JONES. FAM. 15. JAMES of NoH, d c. 1768; m Elizabeth da. Samuel & Ann (Payne) Thorpe, b 16 Dec 1735 *NHV*.

1 SAMUEL, b c. 1761, d 21 May 1810 æ. 49 *NoHTI*; Census (NoH) 1-2-2; m Sarah ——, who d 3 Feb 1815 æ. 52 *NoHTI*.

i Charles; res. Brookfield 1810.

ii Lucinda; m Abel J. Brown; res. Williamstown, Mass., 1815.

iii Miles; res. Savannah, Ga., 1815.

iv Samuel; res. W 1816.

v Charlotte; m Sylvester Sherman; res. W 1816.

vi Mary Ann.

vii, viii, ix. Not located.

2 MARY ANN; m —— Andrus; res. Harwinton 1810.

JONES. FAM. 16. JOHN, b c. 1737, d 7 July 1803 *WHD*, æ. 66 *WHT2;* Census (NH) 2-1-4; m Martha ——, b c. 1740, d 18 Feb 1821 æ. 81 *WHT2*, 14 Feb æ. 80 *WHD*.

1 MARTHA, b c. 1769, d 12 Jan 1806 æ. 37 *WHD*.
2 JOHN; perhaps m Sep 1804 *WdC*—Lydia (Sperry) Sherman.
3 CHRISTOPHER.
4 MARY, bp 29 Jan 1775 *NHx*.
5 CORNELIUS, bp 31 Aug 1777 *NHx*.
6 SALLY, b c. 1780, d 12 Sep 1812 æ. 32 *WHD*.
7 CHILD, d 9 Mar 1783 *WHD*.

Sarah (Downs) Jones, probably wid. of one of this family, d 17 June 1864 æ. 88 *WHT2*.

JONES. MISCELLANEOUS. JOHN, d 1657; m Joan ——, who d 5 Nov 1675 *NHV*. Her will gave bulk of property to the Austins, to whom she was was probably related.......SARAH w. James d 23 July 1820 æ. 64 *WT1*. ......JACOB d 28 Oct 1675 *NHV*.

JORDAN. TILLOTSON & Rebecca of Wd had a s. Miles bp 25 Aug 1776 (at house of Charles Prindle) *NHx*.

JOSLIN. Variant, JOCELYN. FAM. 1. Nathaniel of EH m 15 Mar 1719/20 *NHV*—Abigail da. Joseph Abbot, b 15 Aug 1700 *EHV*.

1 NATHANIEL, b 19 Sep 1721 *NHV*, d 1794; res. G; Census (NH) 1-0-1; m (1) 1 Dec 1743 *BdV*—Ann Wade of Lyme; m (2) 13 Apr 1789 *NHC2*—Sarah, wid. Stephen Bristol.

(By 1): *i* Amaziah, b 1 Sep 1744; rem. to Wilmington, N. C.; m 25 Oct 1763 *GV*—Elizabeth Stevens. **FAM. 2.**

ii Simeon, b 22 Oct 1746, d 5 June 1823 æ. 77 (*NHC2*) *NHV;* Census (NH) 1-0-2: m (1) Hannah ——, who d 20 July 1786 *NHV;* m (2) 17 June 1789 *NHV, SC*—Luceana Smith, who d 12 Oct 1843 æ. 79 *NHV*. **FAM. 3.**

iii Pember, b c. 1750, d 27 Sep 1832 æ. 83 (*Meth*) *NHV;* Census (NH) 2-2-4; m 6 Feb 1771 *NHV*—Elizabeth da. Josiah & Silence (Dowd) Dudley, b July 1740 (at G). **FAM. 4.**

iv Jared, b 13 June 1753 *GV*, d 1 Oct 1797 æ. 44 *GV*.

2 ABRAHAM, b 29 Sep 1723 *EHV*, d 8 Oct 1758 *F&IWRolls;* m Esther ——; she m (2) 6 Aug 1767 *NoHC*—Samuel Wooding.

i Desire, bp (as da. of Wid. Esther) 31 Aug 1766 *NHC1*.

ii (probably) Kezia of H m 29 Mar 1796 *NHC1*—Daniel Wooding.

3 ABIGAIL, b 23 July 1725 *EHV;* m 16 Apr 1746 *Wy*—Nathaniel Porter of Wy.

4 JOSEPH, b 31 May 1726 *EHV;* m 3 Apr 1753 *NHC2*—Sarah da. Abel & Mary (Beecher) Parmelee, b 28 Nov 1732 *NHV*, d 29 Nov 1757 *GV*.

i Reuben, b 9 Aug 1755 *NHV*.

ii Sarah, b 10 Nov 1757 *GV;* m 24 June 1778 *GV*—Samuel Cruttenden.

5 ANNA, b 29 Juue 1729 *EHV;* m Elijah Atwood of Wy.
6 JOHN, b 22 May 1733, bu. 7 Aug 1786 æ. 60 *NHx;* m 11 Oct 1753

NHV—Desire da. Ebenezer & Grace (Blakeslee) Humiston, b 13 Oct 1733 *NHV*.

i Susanna, b 19 Aug 1754 *NHV;* m 14 Oct 1777 *NHx*—John [?Niles or Jiles].

ii Moses, b 16 Jan 1756 *NHV*.

iii (probably) Abigail m 10 Jan 1783 *NHx*—John Coyle.

iv David, bp 14 Sep 1769 *NHx*.

v Lois, bp 14 Sep 1769 *NHx;* m 13 June 1785 *NHx*—Arthur Keefe.

vi Joseph, bp 14 Sep 1769 *NHx*.

vii Mary, bp 14 Sep 1769 *NHx*, d 25 Sep 1769 *NHx*.

viii Abraham, bp 24 Mar 1774 (sponsors, Abraham & Martha Turner) *NHx*.

ix Isaac, bp 24 Mar 1774 *NHx*.

(John s. of Abraham bp 17 Apr 1792 *NHx;* David s. of John bp 17 Apr 1792 *NHx*, d 17 Apr 1792 *NHx;* perhaps belong to this branch of the family).

7 SARAH, b 5 Nov 1746, d 29 May 1827 æ. 80 *EHC;* m 6 Feb 1766 *EHC*—George Lancraft.

FAM. 2. AMAZIAH & ELIZABETH (STEVENS) JOSLIN:

1 SAMUEL RUSSELL, b 19 Oct 1764 *GV*.

2 ELIZABETH, b 16 Aug 1766 *GV*.

3 HENRIETTA, b 28 Feb 1768 *GV*, d 26 Oct 1768 æ. 0-8 *GV*.

4 NANCY, b 13 Feb 1770 *GV*.

5 CLARISSA, b 3 June 1772 *GV*.

6 FREDERICK JARED, b 10 Sep 1779 *GV*, d 1802 (Wilmington, N. C.) *Conn Journal*.

7 HENRY, b 20 Mar 1782 *NHV*.

FAM. 3. SIMEON & HANNAH (———) JOSLIN:

1 HANNAH, b 6 July 1786 *NHV*, bp 14 July 1786 *NHC1*, d 15 July 1786 *NHV*.

FAM. 3. SIMEON & LUCEANA (SMITH) JOSLIN:

2 NATHANIEL, b 31 Jan 1796 *NHV*, *NHT1*, bp 18 Sep 1796 *NHC2*, d 13 Jan 1881 *NHT1*, æ. 84-11-13 *NHV;* artist; m Sarah Atwater Plant, b 4 Dec 1800 *NHT1*, d 16 June 1880 *NHT1*.

3 SIMEON SMITH, b 21 Nov 1799 *NHV;* Rev.; m 18 Nov 1822 (at Mid) *Conn H*—Harriet Starr.

FAM. 4. PEMBER & ELIZABETH (DUDLEY) JOSLIN (family incomplete):

1 AUGUSTUS, b 18 Feb 1772 *NHV*, bp 18 Oct 1772 *NHC1;* m 21 Feb 1791 *NHC1*—Hannah Byington.

2 WILLIAM, b 4 Feb 1774 *NHV*, bp 6 Feb 1774 *NHC1*, d 28 Nov 1852 æ. 78-10 *NHV;* Capt.; m (1) 16 Feb 1797 *NHC1*—Lucretia Byington; m (2) 15 Oct 1828 (at N. Y.)—Nancy, wid. Joseph Culver; a "wife of William" d 8 June 1845 æ. 63 *NHV*.

3 ANNA, bp 28 June 1784 *NHC1*.

4 HANNAH, bp 5 Apr 1789 *NHC1*.

5 JOSEPH DUDLEY, bp 5 Feb 1792 *NHC1*, "son" d 8 June 1793 æ. 2 *NHC1*.

JUDD. FAM. 1. THOMAS, s. of Thomas, d 1724; m 11 Apr 1688 *WatV*—Sarah da. Joseph & Sarah (Stanley) Gaylord, b 11 July 1671 *Windsor*, d 28 Sep 1738 æ. 69 *WatT1*.

1 THOMAS, b 28 Mar 1690 *WatV*.
2 JOSEPH, b 2 Feb 1692/3 *WatV*, d 10 Feb 1692/3 *WatV*.
3 SARAH, b 2 Feb 1692/3 *WatV;* m (1) 29 Dec 1715 *WatV*—James Williams; m (2) ——— Weed.
4 ELIZABETH, b 18 Oct 1695 *WatV;* m 7 July 1730 *WatV*—Joshua How.
5 JOANNA, b 12 Sep 1698 *WatV*, d 25 Jan 1771 *WatV;* m 30 Nov 1727 *WatV*—William Scott.
6 JOSEPH, b 21 Apr 1701 *WatV*, d 16 Feb 1750 *WatV;* m 10 Nov 1726 *WatV*—Elizabeth da. Robert & Abigail (Benedict) Royce, b c. 1709, d 14 May 1770 *WatV*.
7 EBENEZER, b 30 Mar 1702/3 *WatV*.
8 MARY, b 2 Apr 1706 *WatV*, d 28 Jan 1747/8 *WV;* m 28 Oct 1734 *WV*—Samuel Moss.
9 RACHEL, b 4 Oct 1708 *WatV*.
10 ABIGAIL, b c. 1712, d 31 July 1751 æ. 39 *CT1;* m 16 June 1737 *WV*—Joseph Hall.

JUDD. FAM. 2. NATHANIEL d 20 Feb 1742 *WV;* m 24 Mar 1708 *WV*—Lydia da. John & Mary (Parker) Hall, b 21 Jan 1683 *WV*.

1 MARY, b 11 Dec 1708 *WV*.
2 ETHEL, b 8 Dec 1710 *WV*, d 24 Feb 1742; m 4 July 1737 Mary Judd.
3 NATHANIEL, b 1 Feb 1713 *WV*, d 30 June 1785 æ. 72 *SC;* m Eunice ——— .
4 LYDIA, b 8 Mar 1715 *WV*, m 1 Jan 1735/6 *WatV*—Nathan Hubbard of Wat.
5 IMMER, b 20 Feb 1717 *WV*, d 30 July 1801 æ. 84 *SC;* m (1) 25 Dec 1743 *WV*—Rhoda da. Gideon & Mary (Royce) Ives, b 2 Dec 1714 *WV;* m (2) Margaret Scott, wid. Titus Atwater.
6 MINDWELL, b 10 Apr 1719 *WV*, d 21 Mar 1741/2 *WV;* m 20 Jan 1741 *WV*—Daniel Hough.
7 ICHABOD, b 30 Sep 1721 *WV*, d 28 Feb 1725 *WV*.
8 ELIZABETH, b 18 Aug 1724 *WV*, d 23 Jan 1796; m 12 Feb 1744/5 *WV*—Joseph Dutton.
9 SARAH, b 25 Dec 1727 *WV*.

JUDSON. WILLIAM d 29 July 1662 *NHV;* m (1) Grace ——— , who d 29 Sep 1662 *NHV;* m (2) 8 Feb 1659 *NHV* [1660]—Elizabeth, wid. ——— Heaton & Benjamin Wilmot, who d 1685. Sons by 1st w., Joseph, Jeremiah, & Joshua. This family settled in St.

KEEFE. ARTHUR, Census (NH) 1-1-4; m 13 June 1785 *NHx*—Lois da. John & Desire (Humiston) Joslin.

1 MARY, bp 11 July 1787 (as child of "Lois Joslin that was") *NHx*.
2 CHILD, bp 11 July 1787 *NHx*.

KELLOGG. BENJAMIN, s. Daniel & Elizabeth (Preston), b c. 1704, d Dec 1748 *CC;* m Elizabeth da. Samuel & Elizabeth (Frederick) Curtis, b 11 Jan 1707/8 *WV;* she m (2) 20 Mar 1749 Thomas Andrews.

1 DANIEL, b 16 Aug 1729 *WV*, bp Aug 1729 *CC*, d s. p. c. 1753.

2 SAMUEL, b 15 Oct 1731 *WV*, bp Oct 1731 *CC*, d s. p. 13 Sep 1758 *F&IWRolls*.

3 JUSTUS, b 13 Apr 1733 *WV*, bp 15 Apr 1733 *CC*, d 17 Nov 1755 (in camp at Lake George) *WV*, 18 Nov *F&IWRolls*.

4 BENJAMIN, b 18 Dec 1734 *WV*, bp Dec 1734 *CC*, d 1 Feb 1737 *WV*.

5 LOIS, b 29 Oct 1736 *WV*, bp Nov 1736 *CC;* m 7 Sep 1752 *WV*—Josiah Smith.

6 ELIZABETH, b 21 May 1738 *WV*, bp 7 (?)May 1738 *CC;* m 8 June 1758 *WV*—Elijah Hotchkiss.

7 BENJAMIN, b 21 Dec 1741 *WV*, bp Dec 1741 *CC*, d 13 Oct 1790 *CC*.

8 SARAH, b 28 Jan 1745/6 *WV*, bp Feb 1745/6 *CC*, d 5 Jan 1770 *CC*, *WV;* m 9 Jan 1765 *WV*—Job Winchell.

KELLOGG. MISCELLANEOUS. LOIS m 7 Sep 1770 *WV*—Titus Rice.

KENNEDY. JOHN had children: Peleb(?) Johnson & Nathaniel bp 26 Jan 1804 *NHC1;* John, bp 14 July 1805 *NHC1*.

KIBBE. NEHEMIAH m Rebecca ——— .

1 REBECCA, bp 7 Apr 1754 *NHC2*.

KILBY. CHRISTOPHER, d 27 Feb 1774 *NHx;* Capt.; m Mary ——— , b c. 1728, d 1 Apr 1805 æ. 77 *NHx*.

1 CHARLES; res. Wastford, Herts., Eng.

2 SARAH, b c. 1759, d 27 Oct 1821 æ. 62 *NHT1;* m (1) Titus Butler; m (2) Elias Shipman.

3 JOHN, d s. p. 1787.

4 CHRISTOPHER, b 7 May 1762 *NHV*.

5 WILLIAM ALLING, b 25 Dec 1763 *NHV;* he had a child by Abigail Cooper: *i* William, bp 13 Sep 1789 *NHx*.

6 THOMAS TYLER, b 14 Oct 1765 *NHV;* m 17 Apr 1791 *NHC1*—Abigail Parmelee.

7 ELIZABETH MARY, bp 8 Dec 1768 (sponsors, Stephen Mansfield & Catherine Mills) *NHx*, d Sep 1769 *NHx*.

8 GEORGE SEARL, bp 22 Sep 1771 (sponsors, Stephen Mansfield & Abiather Camp) *NHx*, d s. p.

KILLAM. MISCELLANEOUS. Susanna had a nat. da. Katharine bp 4 Nov 1770 *NHC1;* Susanna m 7 Mar 1773 *NHx*—Philip Maighan...... PHILENA m 16 Jan 1752 *NHV*, *WdC*—Dan Carrington.

KIMBERLY. FAM. 1. THOMAS, of NH & St; d Jan 1672; m (1) Alice ——— , who d 10 Oct 1659 *NHV;* m (2) Mary da. Robert Seabrook, wid. William Preston.

(By 1): 1 THOMAS, d s. p. Feb 1705; m Hannah da. James & Mary (Ball) Russell, who d 28 Nov 1714 *NHV*.

2 ABRAHAM, d before 1680; of St; m Hannah ——— ; she m (2) John Curtis. Family incomplete.

(By 1): *i* Hannah, b 11 Jan 1655 *NHV*.
ii Mary, bp 25 July 1659 *NHCl*.
iii Mary, b 4 May 1668; m John Blakeman.
iv Abigail, b 1670; m Ebenezer Blakeman.
v Sarah, b 1 Aug 1672; m Benjamin Hurd of Wy.
vi Abraham, b 4 Mar 1674/5, d 1728; res. Newtown; m 11 May 1696 Abigail Fitch. Children: (1) Hannah, m James Hard. (2) Abigail; m John Lake. (3) Abraham; m Abigail Adams. (4) Gideon; res. Wilton; m Mary Osborn. (5) Sarah; m Joseph Prindle. (6) Mary; m Thomas Leavenworth of Newtown. (7) Abiah; m John Curtis of Wy. (8) Prudence; m Joseph Smith of St. (9) Thomas; res. Roxbury & S. Britain; m 28 Jan 1742 *Wy*—Lois Tuttle.

3 **Mary**; m Nathaniel Hayes of Norwalk.

4 **Nathaniel**, d 1705; res. WH; m.
i Sarah; m 20 Nov 1684 *NHV*—Samuel Blakeslee.
ii Elizabeth; m (1) 30 Dec 1686 *NHV*—John Mallory; m (2) Benjamin Barnes of Wat.
iii Nathaniel, d 1720; Lieut.; m 22 Sep 1692 *NHV*—Hannah da. John Downs, b 19 Jan 1670 *NHV* [1670/1]. **FAM. 2.**
iv Abiah, d 28 Apr 1704 *NHV;* m Joseph Kirby.
v Mary; m Joseph Chittenden of G.

(Child b 4 Jan 1667 *NHV*, & da. b Apr 1671 *NHV*, perhaps identical with some of above children).

5 **Eleazer**, b 1639 (first male child b at NH) *GlastonburyT*, bp 17 Nov 1639 *NHCl*, d 3 Feb 1709 æ. 70 *GlastonburyT;* m Ruth Robbins; left issue.

6 **Abiah**, bp 19 Dec 1641 *NHCl;* m Israel Boardman.

FAM. 2. Nathaniel & Hannah (Downs) Kimberly:

1 **Hannah**, b 13 Apr 1694 *NHV;* m (1) John Lyon of Fairfield; m (2) Thomas Pike of Fairfield.

2 **Abigail**, b 28 July 1696 *NHV*, d 28 Nov 1763 *G;* m 19 Sep 1716 *G*—Joseph Parmalee.

3 **Mary**, b 24 July 1698 *NHV;* m Benjamin Treadwell of Fairfield.

4 **Nathaniel**, b 11 Mar 1700 *NHV*, d 15 Aug 1780 æ. 80 *WHTl*, 5 Aug æ. 81 *WHD;* m 22 Apr 1724 *NHV*—Hannah da. Samuel & Abigail (Pinion) Candee, b 1703 *NHV*, d 13 Jan 1781 æ. 77 *WHTl*, 12 Jan *WHD*.
i Israel, b c. 1724, d 1768; Capt.; Census, Mary (NH) 0-0-2; m (1) 10 Sep 1744 *NHV*—Esther da. Joseph & Esther (Morris) Smith, b 8 July 1729 *NHV*, d 30 Nov 1744 æ. 16 *WHTl;* m (2) 7 Dec 1749 *NHV*—Mary da. Henry & Mary (Goodsell) Tolles, b 29 Oct 1729 *NHV*, d 28 Aug 1807 æ. 78 *WHD*. **FAM. 3.**
ii Abigail, b c. 1726, d 12 Sep 1789 æ. 63 *WHTl;* m 11 Mar

1757 *F*—Lamberton Smith.

iii Silas, b c. 1743, d 17 Jan 1803 æ. 60 *WHT1;* Capt.; Census (NH) 2-5-6; m (1) Sarah da. Jonathan & Mary (Catlin) Smith, b 24 Oct 1750 *NHV*, d 30 Apr 1793 æ. 43 *WHT1*, æ. 42 *WHD;* m (2) Martha da. Joseph & Martha Merwin, wid. Abraham Tolles, b 26 May 1754 *NHV*. **FAM. 4.**

5 BATHSHUA, b 28 Feb 1703 *NHV;* m Samuel Wilson.

6 ZURIEL, b 25 Nov 1706 *NHV;* m (1) 26 Nov 1730 *NHV*—Hannah da. John & Hannah Hill, b Dec 1702 *NHV*, d 8 June 1766 æ. 64 *NHC1;* m (2) 17 Dec 1766 *NHV*, 15 Dec *NHC2*—Martha, wid. John Hitchcock.

(By 1): *i* Sarah, b 16 Aug 1731 *NHV*, bp 15 Aug 1731 *NHC1*, d 8 Nov 1780 æ. 49 *NHC1*.

ii Nathaniel, b 21 Jan 1734/5 *NHV*, bp 25 Jan 1734 *NHC1* [1734/5], d 28 Oct 1739 æ. 4 *NHT1*.

iii John, b 6 Sep 1738 *NHV*, bp 10 Sep 1738 *NHC1*, d before 1767; m 21 May 1761 *NHC1*—Lydia Wise, b c. 1746, d 13 May 1797 æ. 51 *NHC1;* she m (2) 26 Nov 1780 *NHC1*—Isaac Bishop. **FAM. 5.**

iv Hannah, b 8 May 1741 *NHV*.

v Nathaniel, b 12 May 1743 *NHV*, bp 22 May 1743 *NHC1;* Census (NH) 1-3-3; m Mabel da. John & Elizabeth (Bradley) Thompson, b 5 Nov 1745 *NHV*, d Apr 1808 æ. 63 *Conn H*. **FAM. 6.**

vi Susanna, b 8 Sep 1746 *NHV*, bp 14 Sep 1746 *NHC1*, d 28 Oct 1798 æ. 51 *NHT1*, æ. 52 *NHC1;* m 15 May 1771 *NHC1*—Eli Beecher.

7 ABRAHAM, b 22 Mar 1709 *NHV*, d 19 Feb 1797 *G;* m (1) 7 Mar 1732 Mary Sherman; m (2) ——— .

FAM. 3. ISRAEL & ESTHER (SMITH) KIMBERLY:

1 ESTHER, b 24 Nov 1744 *NHV*, d 26 May 1764 æ. 20 *WHT1*.

FAM. 3. ISRAEL & MARY (TOLLES) KIMBERLY:

2 AZEL, b c. 1752, d 25 May 1802 æ. 50 *NHT1*, 28 May *NHC1;* Census (NH) 1-3-3; m Amy da. George & Abigail (Mallory) Smith, b c. 1752, d 17 Aug 1831 æ. 79 *NHT1*.

i Leverett, b c. 1772, d 10 Aug 1801 æ. 29 *HT3;* m Lucy da. Zaccheus & Rebecca (Smith) Candee, b c. 1775, d 5 Aug 1833 æ. 58 *HT1;* she m (2) Samuel Goodyear. **FAM. 7.**

ii Linus, d 21 Sep 1775 *WHD*.

iii Linus, b c. 1777, d 18 June 1837 æ. 60 *NHT1*, æ. 61 *NHV;* m Sarah Elizabeth da. Joel & Elizabeth (Bradley) Gilbert, bp 10 Sep 1780 *NHC2*, d 5 Jan 1836 æ. 55 *NHT1*, *NHV*. **FAM. 8.**

iv David, b 4 Oct 1778 *F*, d 6 July 1856 æ. 78 *NHV;* m 23 Nov 1799 *F*—Polly [da. Caleb & Martha (Talmadge)] Ford, b 3 Sep 1778 *F*, d 25 Feb 1862 *F*. **FAM. 9.**

v Polly; m Amos White.
vi Gratia; m William F. Simpson of Bethlehem.
vii George, probably s. p.
viii Jerre, probably s. p.

3 MARY, b c. 1753, d 13 Sep 1833 æ. 80 *WHT1;* m (1) Seth Thomas; m (2) James B. Reynolds.

4 GILEAD, b c. 1755, d 12 Feb 1831 æ. 76 *WHT1*, 11 Feb *WHD;* Census (NH) 1-1-3; m (1) Mary da. Hezekiah & Mary (Beecher) Brockett, b 7 Aug 1765 *F*, d 22 Feb 1804 æ. 38 *WHT1*, 23 Feb *WHD;* m (2) Mary da. Barnabas & Ellis (Bangs) Merrick, wid. —— Bradley & Ebenezer M. Gill, b 12 Oct 1760, d 5 Sep 1830 æ. 69 *WHT1*, æ. 70 *WHD.*

(By 1): *i* William, d 1839 *WHD;* m Ruth Ann Nichols. **FAM. 10.**
ii Maria, b c. 1787, d 25 Nov 1865 æ. 78 *WHT2;* m Eliakim Kimberly.
iii Elizabeth; m Francis B. Davis.
iv Hannah, b c. 1791, d 24 Sep 1806 æ. 15 *WHT1*, Oct 1896 *WHD.*
v Child, d 21 Oct 1795 *WHD.*
vi Lydia, b [Sep 1796], d 21 May 1887 æ. 90-8 *NHV*, *WHT3;* m John Neagle.

5 SARAH, b c. 1759, d 7 June 1830 æ. 71 *WT1;* m (1) Benjamin Smith; m (2) Lewis Hubbell of Newtown; m (3) 2 Apr 1803 Andrew Bartholomew of W.

6 NATHANIEL, b c. 1759, d 3 Sep 1804 æ. 45 *WHD;* Census (NH) 1-2-3; m Elizabeth da. Nehemiah & Eunice (Smith) Smith, b c. 1757, d 24 Sep 1812 æ. 55 *WHD.*

i Horace, b c. 1780, d 20 Jan 1825 æ. 45 *WHD;* m Huldah da. Silas & Sarah (Smith) Kimberly. **FAM. 11.**
ii John, d Nov 1782 *WHD.*
iii John, d 5 Sep 1784 *WHD.*
iv Nehemiah, b 27 May 1786 *WHT2*, d s. p. 20 Oct 1856 *WHT2;* m Mary Graves.
v Betsey; m —— Hitchcock.
vi Lucretia; m —— Wright.
vii Lovisa; m Simeon Smith.
viii Eunice; m Edwin Nimus(?)

7 HANNAH, b c. 1761, d 3 Sep 1854 æ. 93 (at WH) *BAlm.*

8 EZRA, b c. 1763, d 28 Aug 1844 æ. 82 *BT2;* Census (H) 3-2 3; m (1) Phebe da. Joel & Abigail (Tuttle) Bradley, b 7 May 1766, d 7 Apr 1805 æ. 39 *HT3;* m (2) 27 Apr 1806 Phebe da. Stephen & Elizabeth (Phipps) Brown, wid. Noah Barber, b 13 July 1769 *NHV*, d 3 Mar 1809 æ. 40 *HT3;* m (3) Lucy [da. Timothy & Abigail] Ball, wid. Calvin Beecher, b c. 1777, d 29 Dec 1871 æ. 95 *BT2.*

(By 1): *i* Cynthia, b c. 1783, d 14 Aug 1871 æ. 88 *HT3;* m Amos Bradley.
ii Morris, b c. 1785, d 2 June 1869 æ. 85 *DT2;* m 30 Nov

1809 *CC*—Smarla da. Samuel & Susanna (Hitchcock) Durand, b 30 Dec 1787 *CV*, d 16 Sep 1850 æ. 63 *DT2*.

iii Roderick, b [18 Sep 1787], d 9 Mar 1865 æ. 77 *HT3*, æ. 77-5-27 *HV*; m Bede da. Jared & Mary (Dickerman) Cooper, b c. 1792, d 12 Sep 1866 æ. 74 *HT3*.

iv Electa, b 11 Aug 1789 *F*, d 30 Dec 1874 æ. 85 *HV*; m Leverett Tuttle.

v Sophia, b 9 Oct 1791 *F*, d 29 Apr 1873; m c. 1812 Amos Munson.

vi Ezra, b 26 Apr 1794 *F*, d 19 June 1867; m 1 Dec 1819 Mary da. Ebenezer & Mary (Lewis) Mansfield, b 30 Jan 1800 *F*, d 1870.

vii Mary; m 15 Aug 1822 *HV*—Beecher Porter of Meriden.

viii Julia Angeline, b c. 1803, d 11 Dec 1842 æ. 39 *BT2*; m 18 Sep 1824 *WdV*—Andrew Castle.

(By 2): *ix* George; m 15 Apr 1832 Sarietta da. James Seymour & Sarah (Gilbert) Tuttle.

(By 3): *x* DeWitt; m 24 Nov 1839 *SeymourV*—Eliza da. Abel & Content (Ford) Lines.

xi Charles, d 1844; m Harriet da. Enos Sperry. Children: (1) Enos S.; m Sarah Chatfield. (2) Charles; m Sarah Hull.

xii Phebe, b c. 1815, d 7 Sep 1909 æ. 94 *BT2*; m Andrew Castle.

xiii Jane, b c. 1817, d 4 May 1848 æ. 31 *BT2*.

xiv Lucretia, d s. p.

9 GIDEON, b c. 1765, d s. p. 13 Jan 1815 æ. 50 *WHD*.

10 LIBERTY, b c. 1767, d 17 June 1827 æ. 60 *DT1*; Dr.; Census (D) 1-1-1; m (1) Elizabeth da. Elisha & Susanna (Hall) Whittlesey, b 4 Apr 1763 *WV*, d 17 Mar 1801 æ. 38 (at D) *WT1*; m (2) Mary Pease.

(By 1): *i* Elisha.

ii Eliza.

iii Susan.

iv Gideon.

v John Liberty; m Eliza ——— .

(By 2): *vi* Marion; m Henry Atwater.

vii Jennet; m ——— Cronin.

11 ISRAEL; res. Onondaga, N. Y.; m (1) Desire da. Jesse & Elizabeth (Sherman) Stevens, b c. 1766, d 31 Aug 1794 æ. 28 *WHD*, *DT1*; m (2) Charity da. Oliver & Hannah (Clark) Curtis, bp June 1768 *Dx*.

(By 1): *i* Harry; m Sally Johnson. Children: (1) Harry; m Mary Hill. (2) Thomas J.; m Almira Stevens. (3) Eliza; m George Plumb. (4) Sheldon; m Mary Potter.

ii Israel.

iii Henrietta; m Jacob Ward.

iv Philomela, d young.

(By 2): *v* George.
vi Louisa; m ——— Brockway.
vii Catherine; m ——— Webber.
viii John.
[*ix* James].
12 HULDAH, d 19 June 1819 *WHD;* m Lemuel Nichols of Wat.

FAM. 4. SILAS & SARAH (SMITH) KIMBERLY:
1 HETTY, b c. 1771, d 21 May 1825 æ. 55 *WHD;* m Samuel Clark.
2 ELIAKIM, b c. 1772, d 25 July 1854 æ. 72 *WHT2*, Aug *WHD;* m Maria da. Gilead & Mary (Brockett) Kimberly, b c. 1787, d 25 Nov 1865 æ. 78 *WHT2*.
i Mary; m Asahel Thomas.
ii Lester; m Augusta Lum.
iii Louisa; m David A. Benjamin.
iv Dennis, d young.
v Elizabeth; m Lucius Stevens.
vi Nathaniel; m Mary Jones.
vii Sarah Maria; m Edmond Dickerman.
3 ABIGAIL; m ——— Bardwell.
4 LOUISA, b c. 1777, d 5 Oct 1794 æ. 17 *WHT1*, æ. 16 *WHD*.
5 SILAS; res. Conway, Mass., 1829; m Clara da. Justus & Rebecca (Humphreville) Smith.
6 HULDAH; m Horace Kimberly.
7 SARAH, b c. 1784, d 19 June 1794 æ. 10 *WHT1*, 20 June æ. 9 *WHD*.
8 LESTER, b 20 Jan 1787 *NHT1*, d 13 Oct 1811 *NHT1*.
9 DENNIS, b 23 Oct 1790 *NHT1*, d s. p. 14 Dec 1862 *NHT1*, æ. 73 *NHV*.
10 FRANCIS, b c. 1792, d Aug 1827 æ. 37 (at sea) *WHD*, æ. 35 *WHT3;* Capt.; m Adáh da. John & Eunice (Richards) Ward, b c. 1794, d 8 Feb 1876 æ. 82 *WHT3*.

FAM. 5. JOHN & LYDIA (WISE) KIMBERLY:
1 JOHN, b 24 Aug 1762 *NHV*, bp 25 Oct 1767 *NHC1*.
2 SARAH, b 10 Feb 1765 *NHV*, bp 25 Oct 1767 *NHC1*, d 6 Sep 1807 æ. 41 *NHC1;* m 23 Apr 1791 *NHC1*—Solomon Mudge.

FAM. 6. NATHANIEL & MABEL (THOMPSON) KIMBERLY:
1 WILLIAM, bp 6 Mar 1774 *NHC2*.
2 ESTHER, bp 6 Mar 1774 *NHC2*.
3 SAMUEL, bp 6 Mar 1774 *NHC2*.
4 NATHANIEL, b 23 Jan 1775 *F*, bp 22 Jan 1775 *NHC2*, d 19 Feb 1846 *F;* m Ann Tittle, b 5 Nov 1787 *F*, d 26 Feb 1872 *F*.
5 HENRY, bp 19 July 1778 *NHC2*, d s. p.
6 SARAH, bp 4 Mar 1781 *NHC2*.
7 JOHN, bp 1 Oct 1784 *NHC2*.
8 THOMPSON.

FAM. 7. LEVERETT & LUCY (CANDEE) KIMBERLY:
1 NANCY, b c. 1796, bp 16 Aug 1801 *HC1*, d 10 June 1870 æ. 74 *HT3;* m 3 Jan 1816 Amos Dickerman.

2 ELIZA, b c. 1799, bp 16 Aug 1801 *HC1*, d 22 Jan 1837 æ. 38 *HT1*; m Jesse Fowler Goodyear.

FAM. 8. LINUS & SARAH E. (GILBERT) KIMBERLY:

1 ELIZA, b [28 Mar 1800], d 1 Apr 1882 æ. 82-0-3 *NHV*.

2 GRACE; m John McLagon.

3 MARY E., b [Apr 1807], d 23 Aug 1880 æ. 73-4 *NHV*; m (1) 25 Nov 1830 *NHV*—Miles P. Barber; m (2) —— Darrow.

4 LEVERETT, b c. 1813, d 4 Mar 1840 æ. 37 *NHT1*.

5 WILLIAM S., b c. 1815, d 30 June 1837 æ. 22 (at Hawkinsville, Ga.) *NHT1*.

FAM. 9. DAVID & POLLY (FORD) KIMBERLY:

1 CHILD, b 5 Dec 1800 *NHT1*, d 6 Dec 1800 *NHT1*.

2 FRANCES, b 26 Nov 1801 *F*, d 2 Aug 1803 *F*.

3 FRANCES ANN, b 25 Sep 1803 *F*, d 10 May 1808 æ. 4-7 *NHT1*.

4 CHARLES JEREMIAH, b 25 Aug 1805 *F*, d 11 Jan 1824 (at sea) æ. 18-5 *NHT1*.

5 MARTHA FORD, b 2 Sep 1807 *F*; m 26 Apr 1832 *F*—Merrit W. Barnes of Oswego, N. Y.

6 DAVID, b 29 Sep 1809 *F*, d 19 Oct 1841 æ. 32 *F*.

7 DAUGHTER, b & d 20 Aug 1810 *F*.

8 SON, stillborn 11 Aug 1811 *F*.

9 GRACE, b 13 Aug 1812 *F*, d 23 Sep 1813 *F*.

10 HORACE, b 23 July 1814 *F*, d 5 Sep 1864 æ. 50 *F*.

11 JAMES HENRY, b 5 Nov 1815 *F*, d 6 Aug 1846 æ. 30-9 *F*.

12 DAUGHTER, stillborn 20 Jan 1817 *F*.

13 JOHN FORD, b 16 June 1818 *F*, d 20 Nov 1818 *F*.

FAM. 10. WILLIAM & RUTH ANN (NICHOLS) KIMBERLY:

1 WILLIAM HENRY; m Mehitabel Coggeshall.

2 ELIZA ANNA.

3 JAMES.

4 MARTHA; m 5 Aug 1852 *NHV*—Augustus Lines.

5 GILEAD; m Abigail Baldwin.

6 DENNIS.

7 FRANCIS, d s. p.; m Jane Platt.

8 HARRIET NEWEL; m Charles Gates Bostwick.

9 EDWIN.

10 ELIZA; m 1 Dec 1852 *NHV*—Cornelius Starr Morehouse.

11 JAMES; m Margaret E. Clark.

12 GEORGE DWIGHT; m Mary L. Hurlbut.

FAM. 11. HORACE & HULDAH (KIMBERLY) KIMBERLY:

1 ABIGAIL; m Elisha Benham.

2 SALLY.

3 SOPHIA; m Newton Platt.

KING. FAM. 1. GEORGE of EH; Census (Brookhaven, N. Y.) 2-1-1, still living there 1802; m 27 Dec 1756 *EHC*—Patience Conklin.

1 GEORGE; m 30 May 1776 *EHC*—Elizabeth da. Timothy & Anna (Washburn) Tuttle, who d 17 Dec 1786 æ. 22 (*sic*) *EHC*.

i Patience, b c. 1778, "child" d Jan 1786 æ. 8 *EHC*.

ii John, b 12 Oct 1780 *EHV*.
iii Rebecca, b c. 1783, "child" d 26 Jan 1786 æ. 2 *EHC*.
iv Elizabeth, b 14 Sep 1785 *EHV*.
2 EDWARD; res. Brookhaven, N. Y., 1802.

KING. FAM. 2. WALTER, s. of Wm. & Jemima (Bliss), b Nov 1758 (Wilbraham, Mass.), d 1 Dec 1815 æ. 57 (Williamstown, Mass.); Rev.; m (1) 17 Feb 1784 *NHC2*—Sarah da. David & Mary (Mix) Austin, b 24 July 1763 *NHV*, d 17 May 1791 æ. 28 *NorwichT;* m (2) Emilia da. Nathaniel Porter, b (Lebanon), d 8 Mar 1799 æ. 34 *NorwichT;* m (3) 21 Dec 1803 *NorwichV*—Catherine Peabody.

(By 1): 1 WALTER, b 6 Jan 1785 *NHV*, bp 19 Feb 1786 *NHC2*.
2 CHARLES BACCHUS, b 27 Feb 1788 *NorwichV*.
3 SARAH, b 5 Dec 1789 *NorwichV*, d 18 Apr 1791 æ. 0–16 *NorwichT*.
(By 2): 4 SARAH AUSTIN, b 8 Jan 1796 *NorwichV;* m Ezra Williams of W.
5 GEORGE PORTER, b 18 Jan 1797 *NorwichV*.

KING. MISCELLANEOUS. SIMON, "a poor old man," bu. 15 Mar 1787 *NHx*.

KINGSLEY. SAMUEL, d 24 Nov 1789 *BD;* m 19 Jan 1774 *WV*—Sarah da. Roger & Mary Perkins, b 7 Oct 1748 *DV*.

1 SALLY, b 2 Nov 1774 *WV*, d 14 Apr 1858 æ. 81 *BT1*, 3 Apr æ. 83 (b at C) *BV*.
2 SAMUEL BENNET, b 30 Oct 1776 *WV*, d 26 Mar 1832 æ. 55 *HT3;* m (1) Esther ——, who d 17 Jan 1798 æ. 21 *BT4;* m (2) 18 May 1806 *CC*—Mehitabel Munson, who d 29 Aug 1872 æ. 93 *HT3*.
(By 2): *i* Esther, b [Feb 1807], d 21 Aug 1880 æ. 73–6 *NHV;* m —— Osborn.
3 EUNICE, b c. 1779, d 14 Dec 1863 æ. 84 *BT1*.
4 HANNAH, b 25 Apr 1784 *WdV*, d 10 Dec 1863 æ. 82 *BT1*.

KINGSLEY. ADONIJAH, b c. 1780, d 3 Oct 1816 æ. 37 *NHT1;* m Lovina da. Joseph & Abigail (Horton) Hotchkin.

KIRBY. JOSEPH, s. of John & Elizabeth, b 17 July 1656, d 2 Dec 1711; res. Mid, Fairfield, WH, & Mid; m (1) 10 Nov 1681 Sarah Markham; m (2) Abiah da. Nathaniel Kimberly, who d 28 Apr 1704 *NHV;* m (3) 17 Oct 1704 *NHV*—Mary da. John & Elizabeth (Norton) Plumb, b 15 May 1673 *MV*.

(By 1): 1 ELIZABETH, b 20 Feb 1683; m 31 Oct 1704 *NHV*—James Brown.
2 SARAH, b 10 Aug 1685; m 9 Apr 1712 Samuel Baldwin.
3 DEBORAH, b 27 Mar 1688, d soon.
4 JOHN, b 16 Feb 1691, d 25 Apr 1760; m 3 Mar 1718 Hannah Stow.
5 MARY, b 10 June 1693, d 17 Feb 1771; m 10 Dec 1717 Benoni Stebbins of NM.
6 JOSEPH, bp 9 June 1695, d soon
7 BETHIA, bp 10 July 1698 *FairfieldC;* m Nathaniel Sanford of NM.
8 DEBORAH, bp 29 Sep 1700 *NHC1;* she had nat. child, Lois, b c. 1726; m subsequently John Pierson.
(By 2): 9 ROGER, b 14 Apr 1705 *NHV* [error for 1704], d 12 June 1793 æ. 95 *LT;* res. Washington; m Martha —— .
(By 3): 10 JOSEPH, b 14 May 1705 *NHV*, d Dec 1725.

11 SUSANNA, bp 29 Dec 1706, d s. p. 1733.

12 MARGARET, b 2 Sep 1709, d 1780; m Nathaniel Wooster of Oxf.

KIRTLAND. CONSTANT, s. of John & Lydia (Belden), b 24 Dec 1727, d 3 Feb 1792 æ. 65 *WTI*; m 19 Apr 1753 *WV*—Rachel da. Isaac & Mary (Sedgwick) Brockett, b 23 May 1732 *WV*, d 17 Feb 1812 æ. 80 *WTI*.

1 ISAAC, b 30 Mar 1754 *WV*, d 29 Sep 1807 æ. 54 *WTI*; m Sarah da. Charles & Sarah (Butler) Ives, b 16 Feb 1756 *WV*.

2 TURHAND, b 16 Nov 1755 *WV*, d 16 Aug 1844 (Poland, Ohio); m (1) Mary da. Moses & Phebe (Preston) Beach, b 14 Feb 1758 *WV*, s. p. 24 Nov 1792; m (2) Mary da. Jared & Sarah (Forbes) Potter, b 10 Feb 1772, d 21 Mar 1850.

3 MARY, b 23 Dec 1757 *WV*, d 10 Mar 1839 æ. 82 *WTI*; m 28 May 1778 Samuel Cook.

4 JOHN, b 20 Dec 1759 *WV*; m (1) 10 Apr 1788 Lucy A. Burbank; m (2) 7 June 1829 Mary (Tyler) Benham.

5 BILLIOUS, b 9 June 1762 *WV*, *WTI*, d 23 Oct 1805 æ. 44 *WTI*; m Sarah da. Jared & Sarah (Forbes) Potter, b 5 Oct 1767, d 4 Nov 1805 æ. 39 *WTI*.

6 RACHEL, b 9 July 1764 *WV*, d 13 June 1823 æ. 60 *WTI*; m Edward Barker.

7 JARED, b 8 Aug 176[6] *WV*; m (1) Lois Yale; m (2) ——— .

8 GEORGE, b 2 July 1769 *WV*, d 10 Apr 1793 æ. 25 *WTI*.

9 LYDIA, b 27 Feb 1772 *WV*, d 16 Aug 1850 (Poland, Ohio); m Jonathan Fowler of G.

10 SARAH, b 19 Mar 1778, d 28 Nov 1842 æ. 65 *NoBTI*; m (1) Wm. Douglas; m (2) John Maltby.

KITCHELL. SAMUEL, s. of Robert & Margaret (Sheaffe), m 11 Mar 1656/7 *NHV*—Elizabeth Wakeman; children: 1 Sarah, b 9 Dec 1657 *NHV*, d 5 Jan 1657 *NHV* [1658]. 2 Elizabeth, b 1 Feb 1658 *NHV* [1659], bp 13 Mar 1659 *NHCI*. 3 Abigail, b 10 Aug 1661 *NHV*, bp 11 Aug 1661 *NHCI*; returned to G & had others.

LAMBERT. DAVID, s. of David & Martha (Northrop), b 28 Dec 1758, d 10 Mar 1837; Census (M) 1-1-2; res. WH, rem. to Sharon 1806; m 7 Apr 1784 *NHx*—Lois da. Joseph & Lois (Clark) Prindle, b 1 Feb 1761, d 28 Dec 1842.

1 DAVID, bp 21 Nov 1784 (sponsors, Joseph Prindle & wife) *NHx*, "child" d Nov 1784 *WHD*.

2 MARY, b c. 1786, d 28 May 1856.

3 ENOCH, b 19 Sep 1789; m 26 Dec 1819 Azuba Richards.

4 DAVID, b 4 Mar 1792, bp 20 May 1792 *NHx*, d s. p. 8 Jan 1840.

5 LOIS, b 9 Jan 1795, bp 25 Jan 1795 *NHx*, d 23 June 1856; m 16 Aug 1818 George White.

6 SARAH, b c. 1798, d 25 Aug 1872.

7 ELIZABETH, b c. 1801, d 13 Jan 1872.

8 MARTHA NORTHROP, b 4 Sep 1804, d 10 Mar 1812.

LAMBERTON. GEORGE, d 1646; Capt.; m 6 Jan 1629 (in London, being of St. Mary's Whitechapel) Margaret Lewen; she m (2) Stephen Goodyear.

1 ELIZABETH, b c. 1632, d 1716; m (1) 17 Oct 1654 *NHV*—Daniel

Sellivant; m (2) 9 Mar 1656/7 *NHV*—William Trowbridge.

2 HANNAH, b c. 1634; m (1) Samuel Welles of Weth; m (2) John Allyn.

3 HOPE, b c. 1636; m (1) Samuel Ambrose; div.; m (2) —— Herbert; m (3) William Cheney.

4 DELIVERANCE, b c. 1638, d s. p. after 1664.

5 MERCY, bp 17 Jan 1640 *NHC1*, d before 1677; m Shubael Painter.

6 DESIRE, bp 14 Mar 1642 *NHC1;* m Aug 1667 (Springfield)—Thomas Cooper.

7 OBEDIENCE, bp 9 Feb 1644 *NHC1*, d 29 Mar 1734 æ. 93 *WHT1;* m 13 Jan 1675 *NHV*—Samuel Smith.

LAMPSON. THOMAS, d 28 Dec 1663 *NHV;* m (1) ——— ; m (2) Feb 1650 ——— , wid. Paul Williamson of Ipswich, Mass.; m (3) 6 Nov 1663 *NHV*—Elizabeth da. Richard Harrison, wid. Henry Lines; she m (3) 29 Mar 1666 *NHV*—John Morris.

(By 1): 1 AZUBA, d bef. 1687; m 5 May 1670 *Windsor*—Joshua Wells.

2 JONATHAN, bp 2 Mar 1645 *NHC1*, d s. p. c. 1687.

(By 2): 3 ELEAZER, b 14 Aug 1664 *NHV;* rem. to Newark, N. J.; m Abigail Swayne.

LANCRAFT. GEORGE, b c. 1725, d 17 Sep 1807 æ. 83 *EHR;* Census (EH) 1-3-1; m 6 Feb 1766 *EHC*—Sarah da. Nathaniel & Abigail (Abbott) Joslin, b 5 Nov 1746, d 29 May 1827 æ. 80 *EHC.*

1 MARY; m 5 Aug 1792 *NHC1*—Joseph Hill.

2 GEORGE, b c. 1771, d 16 Dec 1840 æ. 69-8 *EHC;* m Mary Day.

i Sarah, b c. 1796, d 27 Oct 1887 æ. 91 *NHV;* m Joseph Shepard

3 NATHANIEL.

4 CHILD, d young.

5 ABIGAIL; m John St. John.

6 JOSEPH, d s. p.

7 SIMEON; m 14 Jan 1813 *EHC*—Hannah Curtis (p. 475).

8 THOMAS; m Lois da. John & Mary (Grannis) Hughes, b 12 Sep 1782 *EHV*, d 15 June 1832 æ. 48 *EHC.*

9 JOSEPH, b c. 1785, d 19 Sep 1863 æ. 78 *EHT;* m 24 Dec 1812 *EHC* —Dorcas da. Timothy & Hannah (Shepard) Way, wid. Nathan Snow, b c. 1785, d 1 Apr 1863 æ. 78 *EHT.*

10 AMAZIAH, b c. 1788, d 1 Oct 1836 *EHC*, æ. 48 *NHV.*

LANCRAFT. MISCELLANEOUS. NATHANIEL, b c. 1794, d 15 Jan 1870 æ. 75 *NHT3;* m Mary A. M. ——— , who d 11 Sep 1855 æ. 52 *NHT3*...... WILLIAM T., b c. 1800, d 9 Feb 1876 æ. 75 *NHT3;* m Amanda da. Samuel & Ruth (Merriman) Frost, who d 3 Feb 1888 æ. 85 *NHT3*......ALMIRA, b c. 1809, d 9 Apr 1860 æ. 53 *NHT3;* m Ai Russell.

LANDON. JOHN had Samuel bp 13 Mar 1796 *NHC1*......EZEKIEL & Elizabeth had Oliver bp 26 June 1785 *NHx.*

LANE. JOHN of M, will 10 Sep 1669, proved Sep 1669, named sons-in-law Jobamah Gunn, Samuel Camp & Edward Camp; dau-in-law Mary Camp; w. Mary; s. Isaac Lane; dau-in-law Mercy Baldwin; brother Wm. East......ISAAC of Mid, inventory 30 Aug 1711; eldest s. John; Isaac;

Hannah w. Benj. Smith; heirs of Elizabeth dec'd; Eleanor w. Samuel Blaksly; Sarah w. Zaccheus Candee. Elizabeth m May 1693 *NHV*—Joseph Clark. Eleanor m (1) 11 Feb 1695/6 *NHV*—Ebenezer Brown; m (2) 2 Jan 1709/10 *NHV*—Samuel Blakeslee. Sarah m 19 Nov 1702 *NHV*—Zaccheus Candee......KATHARINE m 8 Nov 1653 *NHV*—John Tuttle...... KATHARINE m 29 Dec 1662 *NHV*—George Pardee......Wife of JAMES d 14 Jan 1790 æ. 54 *NHC1*.

LANFAIR. RUSSELL, b 8 July 1775 *EHV*, bp (s. of Mehitabel Russell) 24 Aug 1777 *EHC*, d 25 Apr 1840 æ. 65 *EHC;* m Mehitabel da. Edward & Lydia (Luddington) Goodsell, b 20 Mar 1774 *EHV*.

1 SALLY AMANDA, b 2 July 1799 *EHV*.

2 MARY ANN, b 29 Mar 1801 *EHV;* m 18 Apr 1830 *EHV*—Alfred G. Mallory.

3 JOHN RUSSELL, b 15 July 1806 *EHV*, *NHT3*, d 6 June 1889 *NHT3;* Capt.; m Abby Lancraft, b 30 Nov 1808 *NHT3*, d 15 May 1881 *NHT3*.

4 (probably) HORACE S., b c. 1808, d 3 Feb 1889 æ. 81 *NHT3;* m Esther R. Sanford, who d 8 Sep 1884 æ. 72 *NHT3*.

5 (probably) NANCY LEMIRA; m 8 Aug 1830 *EHV*—Hezekiah Tuttle.

LANGDON. THOMAS, d c. 1666; from Lynn, Mass., of NH & D; rem. to Hempstead, L. I., 1655; "brother" of Edward Wooster of D; his w. had a "son" Wm. Osborn in 1678; had s. Joseph, b 23 Mar 1649 *NHV*......SAMUEL, b 17 June 1776 *NHT1*, d 13 Apr 1846 æ. 70 *NHT1;* m (1) Lavinia ——, who d 11 Sep 1816 æ. 32 *NHT1;* m (2) Nancy ——— , who d 7 Mar 1871 æ. 78 *NHT1*. Child by 1st w.: Mary Ann, b 16 Feb 1805 *NHT1*, d 16 Oct 1870 *NHT1*. Child by 2nd w.: Samuel W., b 17 July 1823 *NHT1*, d 6 Aug 1899 *NHT1;* m (1) Mary J. Holcolm, who d 2 Jan 1884 æ. 53-5 *NHT1;* m (2) Lillie A. Way, b 1859, d 1918 *NHT1*.

LANGMUIR. ALEXANDER, b c. 1757 (Hamilton, Scotland), d 12 Apr 1823 æ. 66 *NHT1*, 28 Oct æ. 66 (*NHx*) *NHV;* Census (NH) 1-0-0; m (1) Hannah da. John & Sarah (Ingersoll) Whiting, b 15 Aug 1765 *NHV*, d 8 Feb 1794 æ. 28 *NHx;* m (2) 26 Sep 1795 *NHx*—Mary wid. Jacob Brown, who d 5 Jan 1830 æ. 79 *NHT1*.

LANGRILL. MRS. (stranger from Hartford) d 16 Dec 1766 æ. 34 *NHC1*.

LARABEE. DAVID, d c. 1801; res. WH; Census (NH) 1-0-4; m Esther [prob. da. Jonathan & Margaret (Smith?) Thompson], b [20 Aug 1766], d 23 Sep 1853 æ. 87 *NHT1*, æ. 87-1-3 *NHV*. Family incomplete.

1 SARAH, b c. 1786, "da." bp 3 July 1791 *NHx*, d 4 May 1852 æ. 66 *NHT1;* m 30 Nov 1809 *NHx*—Ezekiel Hotchkiss.

2 PERSIS, b c. 1788, "da." bp 3 July 1791 *NHx*, d 1862 æ. 74; m 5 June 1822 *NHV*—John Gilbert [called Gillet *NHC2*].

3 ESTHER, b 9 May 1791 *F*, "da." bp 3 July 1791 *NHx*, d 15 July 1867 æ. 77 *NHT1;* m 3 Jan 1814 *F*—Stephen Hine, of Buffalo, N. Y., & Erie, Pa.

4 SAMUEL, b c. 1794, d 4 Jan 1799 æ. 4 *WHT1*.

5 CHILD, bp 22 Apr 1798 *NHx*.

6 SAMUEL, b c. 1800, d 1 Jan 1882 æ. 81 *WHT3;* m Caroline D.

——— , who d 7 Mar 1875 æ. 73 *WHT3.*

LARABEE. Miscellaneous. Charles m 10 Mar 1806 *NHCl*—Desire Huldah Hotchkiss.

LATHROP. Variant, Lothrop. Rev. John & Hannah (House) had Samuel of Norwich who m Elizabeth Scudder & had several children, of whom the following settled in W: John (see fam. 1); Elizabeth, b Mar 1648 *NorwichV;* m (1) 15 Dec 1669 Isaac Royce; m (2) Joseph Thompson; Sarah, b Oct 1655; m 21 Apr 1681 *WV*—Nathaniel Royce; Martha, b Jan 1657; m 12 Dec 1676 *WV*—John Moss.

Fam. 1. John, b Dec 1646 *NorwichV*, bp 7 Dec 1645 *BostonC*, d 26 Aug 1688 æ. 44 *WV;* m 15 Dec 1669 *New London*—Ruth da. Robert & Mary Royce; she m (2) 12 Feb 1689 *WV*—Abraham Doolittle.

1 Ruth, d 10 Aug 1750; m 17 Mar 1697/8 Samuel Post of Norwich.

2 Mary, d 14 Mar 1754 *WV;* m 3 June 1692 *DV*—William Tyler.

3 Samuel, d c. 1745; m (1) 3 Feb 1703/4 *WV*—Ruth da. John & Mary (Moss) Peck, b 20 July 1679 *WV*, d 8 Jan 1738 *WV;* m (2) 27 Sep 1738 *WV*—Lydia da. Thomas & Martha (Munson) Elcock, wid. Benjamin Brockett, b 17 Dec 1700 *NHV*.

(By 1): *i* Barnabas, b 6 May 1705 *WV*, d s. p.

(By 2): *ii* John, b 12 Nov 1739 *WV*, d 13 Nov 1739 *WV*.

iii Ruth, b 15 Mar 1741 *WV*, bp 7 Feb 1751 *WC2*, d 9 Feb 1752 *WV*, *WC2*.

4 Elizabeth, b 15 Apr 1678 *WV;* m Bowley Arnold of Mansfield.

5 John, b 19 May 1680 *WV;* m (1) Hannah da. Samuel & Mary (Bate) Hough, who d s. p.; m (2) 12 Oct 1706 *WV*—Abiah Saunders.

6 Bethia, b 27 Dec 1682 *WV*, d 8 Dec 1716 *WV*.

7 Barnabas, b 14 June 1685 *WV*, d s. p.

8 Hannah, b 31 Jan 1686 *WV* [1686/7]; m (1) Samuel Thompson of Farm; m (2) Samuel Parker.

LATHROP. Miscellaneous. John m (1) 31 Oct 1764 *NHV*, *NHC2*—Mary da. Timothy & Jane (Harris) Jones, b 12 Dec 1743 *NHV;* m (2) 13 Jan 1774 *NoHC*—Mary da. Timothy & Mary (Goodrich) Bonticou. Children: Fanny, b 24 July 1765 *NHV*, d 6 July 1767 *NHV;* Polly, b 25 Mar 1767 *NHV*......Widow Eunice, Census (NH) 0-0-5; had children Frances, Eunice & Julia bp 31 July 1791 *NHC2*, & Henry bp 5 Feb 1792 *NHC2*.

LAXEN. Benjamin, lived with Matthew Moulthrop, b 20 Aug 1675 *NHV*.

***LEAVENWORTH.** Jesse, s. of Rev. Mark & Ruth (Peck), b 20 Nov 1740 *WatV*, d 1824; Col.; m (1) 1 July 1761 *WatV*—Catharine da. John Conkling, wid. Culpepper Frisbie of Bd, who d 29 June 1824 æ. 87; div.; m (2) Eunice Sperry.

(By 1): 1 Melines Conkling, b 4 May 1762 *WatV*.

2 Ruth, b 25 Feb 1764 *WatV*.

3 Frederick, b 14 Sep 1766 *WatV*.

4 Catharine, b 1769 m (1) Samuel Dennis; m (2) Thomas Peck.

5 Jesse, b Aug 1771.

6 Mark, b 30 Aug 1774 (at NH); m 1795 *WatV*—Anna da. Moses

Cook.

LEAVENWORTH. Eli m Sarah da. John & Lydia (Atwater) Eliot, b 30 Nov 1750 *NHV*. Children bp *NHC2:* Sally, 13 Feb 1780, Fanny, 9 Mar 1783.

LEAVIT. David, b c. 1690, d 19 Oct 1754 æ. 64 *BdT;* m Mary ——— .

1 Samuel, b c. 1716, d s. p. 29 Dec 1803 æ. 87 *WC2*, 30 Dec æ. 93 *WT2;* Census (W) 1-0-1; m Adah da. Samuel & Elizabeth (Frederick) Curtis, b 26 Jan 1721 *WV*, d 9 Feb 1801 æ. 79 *WT 2.*

2 David, bp 25 Mar 1722 *DurhamC*, d 19 Mar 1808 æ. 86 *Bethlehem C;* m 27 Apr 1748 *NHV*—Rebecca da. Hezekiah & Lydia (Clark) Camp, who d 3 May 1816 *BethlehemC.*

i Sarah, b 27 Feb 1748/9 *NHV;* m ——— Bartholomew.

ii Rebecca, b c. 1751, d 9 Oct 1828 æ. 78 *BethlehemC;* m 3 Dec 1772 *BethlehemC*—Levi Thompson.

iii (probably) Silence, b c. 1753, d 4 July 1814 æ. 61 *BethlehemC;* m July 1772 *BethlehemC*—David Bellamy.

iv Irene; m ——— Hull.

v David, b c. 1757, d 16 Jan 1807 æ. 50 *BethlehemC;* m Lucy Clark.

vi Samuel, b c. 1761, d 22 July 1831 æ. 70 *WashingtonT;* m 8 June 1785 *Washington*—Lydia Wheeler.

3 Mary, b 24 Sep 1725 *WV*, d 12 Oct 1783 æ. c. 57 *EHC;* m 12 Apr 1750 *BdC*—Isaac Pardee.

4 Kezia, b 5 Mar 1728 *WV;* m (1) 27 Aug 1752 *EHV*, *BdC*—Gideon Potter; m (2) 6 Sep 1768 *EHC*—Abner Bean.

Perhaps other children. A Jacob Leavit m 18 Oct 1742 *FairfieldC*—Catee Gold, & had bp there, David, Nathan, Mary, Catee, Elizabeth & Joanna.

LEEK. fam. 1. Philip, Cpl., d May 1676 *NHV;* m ——— .

1 Philip, b 26 Aug 1646 *NHC1*, bp 1646 *NHC1*.

2 Ebenezer, bp 12 Sep 1647 *NHC1;* rem. to Easthampton, L. I.; m Hannah Baker.

3 Thomas, bp 21 Jan 1648 *NHC1* [1648/9], d 1719; m Sarah Hitcheson, who d 11 May 1729 *NHV.*

i Sarah, b 9 Nov 1679 *NHV;* m c. 1704 Thomas Lucas of Mid.

ii Abigail, b 17 Oct 1683 *NHV;* m 11 Feb 1707 *MidV*—Daniel Johnson.

iii Mary, b 9 Oct 1685 *NHV*, d 28 Oct 1766 æ. 80 *NoHC;* m 18 May 1709 *NHV*—Thomas Barnes.

iv Thomas, b 22 Mar 1688 *NHV*, d 9 Aug 1752 *NHV;* m 1 June 1716 *NHV*—Mary da. John & Elizabeth (Daniel) Winston, b 12 Mar 1688 *NHV*. **FAM. 2.**

v John, b 14 Apr 1692 *NHV*, d 16 Aug 1724 *NHV;* m 1 Sep 1720 *NHV*—Hannah da. John & Abigail (Alsop) Rowe, b 11 Feb 1691 *NHV*, d 16 May 1770 æ. 78 *NHC1;* she m (2) 10 July 1729 *NHV*—James Peck. **FAM. 3.**

vi Elizabeth, b 11 Feb 1694 *NHV*, bp Mar 1719 *NHC1*, d 2

Nov 1729 *NHV*.

vii Lydia, b 5 July 1699 *NHV;* m 14 Sep 1727 *NHV*—John Matthews

4 MARY, b 16 June 1652 *NHV*, bp 16 June 1651(?) *NHCl;* m 9 Mar 1674/5 *NHV*—John Davis.

5 JOANNA, b 22 Jan 1657 *NHV*, bp 28 Mar 1658 *NHCl;* m (1) 6 Feb 1677 *NHV*—Henry Stevens; m (2) Joseph Preston.

FAM. 2. THOMAS & MARY (WINSTON) LEEK:

1 DANIEL, b 1 Apr or June 1717 *NHV*, bp Dec 1721 *NHCl;* Census (H) 1-0-2; m 23 Jan 1750/1 *NHV, BdC*—Rebecca da. Nathaniel & Rebecca (Morris) Hitchcock, b 28 Mar 1718 *NHV*.

2 ELIZABETH, b Jan 1719 *NHV*, bp Dec 1721 *NHCl*, d 24 Apr 1791 æ. 72 *HT3;* m 19 Jan 1741/2 *NHV*—Amos Peck.

3 MARY, b Aug 1721 *NHV*, bp Dec 1721 *NHCl;* m 17 June 1752 *NHV*—Samuel Alling.

4 THOMAS, b Nov 1723 *NHV*, bp 2 Feb 1723/4 *NHCl*, d 18 Nov 1791 æ. 69 *HT2;* Census (H) 1-0-1; m 22 Apr 1761 *NHV*—Mary da. Abraham & Sarah (Gilbert) Johnson, b 1 Aug 1723 *NHV*, d 11 Nov 1806 æ. 85 *HT2*.

i Thomas, b 29 May 1762 *NHV*, d 28 Oct 1821 æ. 60 *HT2;* Census (H) 1-1-3; m 1 Jan 1787 *NHCl*—Rhoda da. David & Patience (Sanford) Alling, b 14 Feb 1764 *NHV*, d 19 Feb 1838 æ. 74 *HT2*. **FAM. 4.**

ii Sarah Mary, b 18 June 1765 *NHV*, d 12 Sep 1789 æ. 25 *HT2*.

5 SARAH, b Oct 1725 *NHV*, bp 21 Apr 1726 *NHCl;* m 9 Feb 1748/9 *NHV*—Stephen Hitchcock.

6 PHEBE, b Oct 1727 *NHV*, bp 7 Jan 1727/8 *NHCl;* m 11 Oct 1753 *NHV*—James Hitchcock.

7 ABIGAIL, b 9 Nov 1731 *NHV*, bp 6 Feb 1731/2 *NHCl;* m 2 Mar 1757 *NHC2*—Enos Johnson.

8 TIMOTHY, bp 29 July 1733 *NHCl*, d 1820; Census (H) 2-0-1; m 18 Oct 1758 *NHV*—Martha da. Jacob & Elizabeth (Dickerman) Hotchkiss, b 26 June 1735 *NHV*.

i Timothy, b 24 Sep 1762 *NHV;* Census (H) 1-2-2; m 8 Jan 1784 *HCl*—Elizabeth da. Zadoc & Desire (Warner) Alling, b 15 Dec 1766 *NHV*. **FAM. 5.**

ii Elisha, b 14 Oct 1764 *NHV;* m 15 May 1808 *HV*—Hannah da. Samuel & Esther (Bradley) Gilbert, bp 17 Feb 1782 *NHx*. **FAM. 6.**

FAM. 3. JOHN & HANNAH (ROWE) LEEK:

1 JOHN, b 18 Dec 1721 *NHV*, bp July 1751 (at NH) *Dx;* m 7 Aug 1743 *NHV*—Penelope [?da. Josiah & Elizabeth (Miles)] Thompson,, bp July 1751 (at NH) *Dx*, "wife" bu. 25 Nov 1770 *NHx*.

i John, bp July 1751 (at NH) *Dx;* Census (NH) 1-2-3; m Anna ——— & had a child bp 12 Feb 1786 *NHx*, bu. 15 Nov 1786 *NHx*.

ii Hannah, bp July 1751 (at NH) *Dx;* m Edmund French.

2 HANNAH, b 2 Mar 1723/4 *NHV;* m (1) 17 Feb 1742/3 *NHV*—Samuel Perkins; m (2) 2 July 1751 *NHV*—Stephen Hunnewell.

FAM. 4. THOMAS & RHODA (ALLING) LEEK:

1 ABIGAIL, b 13 May 1757 *F,* d 10 Feb 1864 æ. 77 *HT2.*

2 CHARLOTTE, b 4 Mar 1789 *F,* d 2 June 1825 æ. 37 *HT2;* m 26 Aug 1807 Daniel Gilbert.

3 MICHAEL, b 23 Dec 1790 *F,* d Mar 1881; m Amanda da. Ezra & Abigail (Crittenden) Sperry.

i Alonzo; m Lavinia Cable.

ii Mary, b [Mar 1825], d 19 Jan 1828 æ. 2-10 *HT2.*

iii Thomas, b [Feb 1829], d 7 Oct 1831 æ. 2-8 *HT2.*

iv Betsey; m J. B. Quillinas.

v Amanda, b c. 1831, d 26 Aug 1861 æ. 30 *HT2;* m Lauren Hotchkiss.

4 THOMAS, b 29 Nov 1792 *F,* d s. p. 19 Apr 1851 æ. 58 *HT2.*

5 DAVID, b 12 Feb 1795 *F,* d 20 Sep 1825 æ. 31 *HT2;* Capt.; m 26 Sep 1822 *HV*—Julia Maria da. Jesse & Kezia (Stiles) Mansfield, b 26 Sep 1797 *F,* d 26 May 1885 æ. 87-8 *NHV;* she m (2) 21 Jan 1830 George Atwater.

i Daughter, d 30 Apr 1823 æ. 3 wks. *HT2.*

ii Julia Maria, b 12 Feb 1825 *F.*

6 RUSSELL, b 26 Apr 1797 *F,* d 7 July 1872 æ. 75 *HV;* m (1) 2 Nov 1823 *HV*—Minerva Bradley; m (2) Nancy Beecher.

(By 1): *i* Eliza, b 2 Sep 1824, d 1872; m 24 Apr 1870 Silas C. Lewis.

ii Minerva, b 17 Sep 1826.

(By 2): *iii* J. Beecher, b 9 May 1830.

7 ASA, b 7 May 1799 *F,* d s. p. 4 July 1857; rem. to Mich. & Iowa; m Jan 1830 (Ann Arbor, Mich.) *ColR*—Maria Brown.

8 RHODA, b 28 Apr 1801 *HT2,* d 17 Sep 1866 *HT2;* m 10 May 1829 Eneas Wooding.

9 HORACE, b 10 Sep 1803 *F;* rem. to Washtenaw Co., Mich.; m 1 Feb 1826 *HV*—Louisa Ann Goodyear.

10 ENOS, b 25 Sep 1805 *F,* d 20 Feb 1881; rem. to Oakland Co., Mich.; m Rebecca Stratton.

11 DANA WINSTON, b 14 Jan 1810 *F,* d 31 Jan 1893; m 11 Nov 1832 *HV*—Abigail Goodyear; had 10 children.

FAM. 5. TIMOTHY & ELIZABETH (ALLING) LEEK:

1 PHEBE; m 26 May 1833 *HV*—Amasa Hitchcock.

2 CHARLES, b c. 1791, d 10 Jan 1858 æ. 66 *NHV;* m.

3 REBECCA.

4 HARVEY, b [Apr 1800], d 31 Dec 1883 æ. 83-8 *HT5;* m Martha da. Frederick Beecher, who d 4 Oct 1858 æ. 62 *NHV, HT5.*

5 ZADOC ALLING, b c. 1805, d 31 May 1864 æ. 59 *HV.*

FAM. 6. ELISHA & HANNAH (GILBERT) LEEK:

1 HENRY, b 24 May 1809 *HV;* m 30 Apr 1840 *HV*—Abiah da. Ira

& Esther (Humiston) Wolcott, b c. 1803, d 1 Nov 1881 æ. 78 *HT1*.

2 MARTHA, b 30 Oct 1811 *HV;* m 25 Feb 1838 *HV*—James Warner.

LEETE. MISCELLANEOUS. GOV. WILLIAM of G m (2) 7 Apr 1670 *NHV*—Sarah wid. Henry Rutherford, who d 3 Feb 1673 *NHV;* m (3) Mary wid. Gov. Francis Newman & Rev. Nicholas Street......ANN, b 10 Mar 1661 *G*, d 2 Aug 1747 æ. 87 *NHT1;* m (1) 19 Nov 1683 *NHV*—John Trowbridge; m (2) 9 May 1696 *NHV*—Ebenezer Collins.

LEFFINGWELL. WILLIAM C., b at Norwich, Sep 1765, d 23 Oct 1834 æ. 69 *NHT1;* m 1786 Sally Maria da. Isaac & Mary (Mansfield) Beers, bp 12 Feb 1786 *NHx*, d 25 Aug 1830 æ. 65 *NHT1;* had 7 children.

LE FORGE. HENRY, b c. 1740, d 14 Aug 1839 æ. 100 *HT2;* m Betsey Hunt, who d 12 May 1833 æ. 87 *HT2*. Family incomplete. PAGE 1245

1 PATTY; m 8 Nov 1796 *NHC1*—Merritt Baldwin.

2 ANNA, b c. 1780, d 28 Dec 1860 æ. 80 *HT2;* m Moses Ford.

3 FREDERICK H., b c. 1786, d 1 Aug 1833 æ. 47 *NHT1;* m Martha da Peter & Comfort (Clark) Johnson, bp 25 Mar 1781 *NHC1*, d 27 Aug 1861 æ. 80 *NHT1*.

LERAKE. LEWIS d Feb 1763 æ. c. 60 *NHC1*......THOMAS bp (adult, sick) 19 Sep 1772 *NHx*.

LETORT. FRANCIS d 3 Sep 1769 *NHC1*.

LEWIS. FAM. 1. EBENEZER of W, s. of William Jr. of Farm, d 1709; m 2 Dec 1685 *WV*—Elizabeth da. Nathaniel & Joan Merriman, b 14 Sep 1669 *NHV*, d 2 Feb 1749 æ. 81 *CT1*, Feb 1749/50 *CC;* she m (2) William Frederick.

1 HEZEKIAH, b 12 Oct 1686 *WV*, d. p. 1711.

2 MARY, b c. 1689, d Aug 1749 *CC;* m 10 Aug 1710 *WV*—Abraham Doolittle.

3 CALEB, b 15 Oct 1691 *WV*, d 1749; m (1) 25 Nov 1713 *WV*—Sarah da. Isaac & Mary (Foote) Curtis, wid. Isaac Cook, b 11 June 1685 *WV;* m (2) 13 Mar 1748/9 *WV*—Lucy da. Joseph & Abigail (Curtis) Holt, b 12 Dec 1722 *WV*.

(By 1): *i* Ichabod, b 18 Apr 1714 *WV*, d 24 Dec 1778 æ. 61 *WT1;* m Esther da. Caleb & Esther (Humphreville) Hall, b 24 Apr 1729 *WV*. **FAM. 2.**

ii Ebenezer, b 4 Aug 1715 *WV*, d 16 Apr 1776 *Goshen;* m 12 June 1735 *WV*—Sarah Avery, b July 1716 (at G). **FAM. 3.**

iii Caleb, b 28 Feb 1717 *WV*.

iv Hezekiah, b 14 Oct 1720 *WV*, d 5 July 1764 *WV;* m 25 Apr 1744 *WV*—Abigail Chamberlin. **FAM. 4.**

4 FELIX, b 25 Oct 1693 *WV;* m Thomas Andrews.

5 ELIZABETH, b 15 Oct 1695 *WV;* m Ephraim Bidwell of Glastonbury.

6 BARNABAS, b 4 Nov 1697 *WV*, d 1 Oct 1729 *WV;* m Elizabeth ——, b c. 1703, d 26 July 1766 æ. 63 *WV;* she m (2) 4 Mar 1730 *WV*—Daniel Merwin; she m (3) 9 Feb 1762 *WC1*—Joseph Holt.

i Lent [see FAM. 10].
ii Lucy, b 23 Mar 1724 *WV*, d 18 Sep 1789 æ. 66 *BristolT;* m 2 Apr 1740 *WV*—Zebulon Frisbie.
iii Lowly.
iv Lois, b 26 May 1728 *WV*.

7 HANNAH, b 10 Oct 1699 *WV*, d June 1757 *CC;* m 8 Feb 1721 *WV* —Samuel Cook.

8 BENJAMIN, b 21 Sep 1701 *WV*, d 31 Jan 1789 æ. 88 *CT2;* Dr.; m (1) 3 Nov 1724 *WV*—Esther da. Caleb & Elizabeth (Hotchkiss) Matthews, b 1 Aug 1708 *WV*, d 19 Apr 1773 æ. 65 *CT2;* m (2) 3 Apr 1775 *WV*—Mary, wid. Maltbie.

(By 1): *i* Bela, b 10 Jan 1725 *WV*, bp Nov 1727 *CC*, d 15 May 1763 *WatV;* m (2) Abigail da. Solomon & Ruth (Peck) Moss, b c. 1727; m (2) 15 May 1760 *WatV*—Damaris da. Jonathan & Elizabeth (Thompson) Prindle, b 17 Dec 1738 *WV*, d 24 Oct 1808 æ. 71 *PptC;* she m (2) 15 May 1764 *WatV*—Oliver Terrell. **FAM. 5.**
ii Elizabeth, b 6 Mar 1727 *WV*, bp Nov 1727 *CC;* m 9 Dec 1746 *WV*—Cornelius Johnson.
iii Benjamin, b 11 June 1729 *WV*, bp June 1729 *CC;* rem. to Stockbridge, Mass.
iv Barnabas, b 17 Aug 1731 *WV*, bp Aug 1731 *CC;* Census (C) 2-1-5; res. Wells, Vt., 1807; m (1) 10 Mar 1752 *WatV*—Jerusha da. Ebenezer & Lydia (Warner) Doolittle b 26 Feb 1731 *WV*, d 24 May 1754 *WatV;* m (2) 15 Dec 1756 *WatV*—Deborah da. Thomas & Desire (Bristol) Brooks, b 15 Feb 1732 *WV*, d 11 Feb 1759 *WatV;* m (3) 24 Feb 1762 *WV*—Rachel da. Enoch & Rachel (Plumb) Curtis, b c. 1741, d 6 Oct 1817 æ. 76 *F*. **FAM. 6.**
v Jesse, b 29 June 1734 *WV*, bp Mar 1734 *CC*, d 20 Oct 1758 (in camp at Lake George) *WV;* Dr.
vi Caleb, b 22 May 1736 *WV*, bp May 1736 *CC;* m 13 Mar 1760 *WV*—Abigail da. Benjamin & Abigail (Cole) Moss, b 30 Sep 1740 *WV*. Children recorded *WV:* Jesse, b 30 Dec 1760; Martha, b 3 Nov 1762; Gaius, b 15 July 1765.
vii Esther, b 23 Oct 1738 *WV*, bp 5 Nov 1738 *CC*, d 1837; m 21 May 176[2] *WV*—Joseph Moss.
viii Hannah, b 8 Mar 1741 *WV*, bp Apr 1741 *CC;* m 1 Feb 1759 *WV*—Nathaniel Douglas.
ix Mary, b 10 Oct 1743 *WV*, bp 1 Oct 1743 *CC*, "child" d Jan 1743/4 *CC*.
x Amasa, b 17 Feb 1744/5 *WV*, bp Feb 1744/5 *CC*, d 20 Dec 1815 æ. 71 *CT1;* Census (C) 3-1-3; m (1) 21 May 1772 *WV*—Miriam da. Isaiah & Phebe (Doolittle) Moss, b 29 Sep 1744 *WV*, d 28 July 1812 æ. 68 *CT1;* m (2) Mary ——— .
xi Mary, b 11 June 1747 *WV;* m 20 Nov 1764 *WV*—Titus Doolittle.

xii Levi, b 23 May 1750 *WV*, bp Apr (?) 1750 *CC*, d 17 Nov 1750 *WV*.
xiii Levi, b 19 Oct 1751 *WV*, bp 8 Dec 1751 *CC*, d 31 Dec 1775 *WV*, æ. 25 *CT2*.
9 MALACHI, b 4 Oct 1703 *WV;* rem. to Mid.
10 AGAPE, b 10 Jan 1705 *WV;* m c. 1727 Jonathan Munger of G.

FAM. 2. ICHABOD & ESTHER (HALL) LEWIS:
1 SAMUEL, b 7 Oct 1748 *WV*, *WT1*, d 8 Feb 1824 *WT1;* Census (W) 3-1-4; m 3 Dec 1772 *WV*—Esther da. Charles & Martha (Miles) Sperry, b 6 Mar 1748/9 *WV*, d 17 July 1805 æ. 57 *WT1*.
i Sarah, b 8 Sep 1773 *WV*, d 10 Dec 1849; m Ephraim Cook.
ii Eunice, b 8 May 1775 *WV*.
iii Esther, b 15 July 1776 *WV*.
iv Elihu, b 5 Nov 1778 *WV*.
2 ELIHU, b 10 June 1752 *WV*, d 12 Feb 1777 (in army) *WV*.
3 SARAH, b 11 July 1756 *WV*, d 12 Sep 1826 æ. 70 *WT1;* m (1) 17 Dec 1778 *WV*—Charles Hall; m (2) 11 Dec 1820 Aaron Hall.
4 JARED, b 10 May 1761 *WV*, d 14 May 1826 æ. 65 *WT1;* m 16 June 1780 *WV*—Rhoda da. Lud & Lois (Johnson) Munson, b 24 Jan 17[59] *WV*, d 19 Jan 1827 æ. 68 *WT1*.
i Isaac, d 1823; m Esther Beaumont.
ii Chauncey, b 13 Jan 1784 *WV*, d 6 May 1806 æ. 23 (at Is. St. Crowe) *WT1*.
iii Samuel, b 22 Jan 1786 *WV*, d 8 Mar 1806 æ. 21 *WT1*.
iv Amelia.
v Julia, b c. 1790, d 27 Oct 1804 æ. 15 *WT1*.
vi Frederick; m Sinai Hall.

FAM. 3. EBENEZER & SARAH (AVERY) LEWIS (family incomplete):
1 HANNAH, b 9 Oct 1736 *WV*.
2 ANN, b 2 Feb 1739 *WyV*.
3 MINDWELL, b 4 May 1741 *WyV*.
4 ELIZABETH, b 22 Sep 1743 *WyV*.
5 ESTHER, b 27 Nov 1747 *WyV*.

FAM. 4. HEZEKIAH & ABIGAIL (CHAMBERLIN) LEWIS:
1 JOHN, b 22 May 1745 *WV*, d 25 Oct 1782 *CC;* m 15 May 1766 *WV*—Thankful da. Oliver & Thankful (Parker) Hitchcock, b 13 May 1747 *WV;* Census, Thankful (C) 0-0-3.
i Martha, b 14 Dec 176[7] *WV;* m 20 Dec 1792 *CC*—Abner Johnson.
ii Mary, b 21 May 1769 *WV*.
iii Thankful, b 15 Jan 1771 *WV*.
iv John, b 7 Feb 1773 *WV*.
v Abigail, b 17 Aug 1775 *WV*.
vi Oliver, b 30 Aug 1777 *WV*.
2 EBENEZER, b 14 Oct 1746 *WV*, bp 25 June 1786 *CC;* Census (C) 1-1-4; m 8 Jan 1769 *CC*—Elizabeth da. Enoch & Rachel

(Plumb) Curtis, b 16 Oct 1751 *FarmV*, d 2 Aug 1786 *CC*.
i Elizabeth, bp 6 Aug 1786 *CC*.
ii Enoch, bp 6 Aug 1786 *CC*.
iii Molly, bp 6 Aug 1786 *CC;* m 15 Feb 1791 *WatV*—Josiah Terrill.
iv Eunice, bp 6 Aug 1786 *CC*.
v Ichabod Ensign, bp 6 Aug 1786 *CC*.
vi (probably) Sylvester. bp 8 Nov 1789 *CC*.
3 CHAMBERLIN, b 7 Oct 1748 *WV*, d 27 Oct 1749 *WV*.
4 JOSEPH, b 7 Dec 1750 *WV*, bp Aug (?) 1750 *CC*.
5 ABIGAIL, b 8 Dec 1752 *WV*.
6 HEZEKIAH, b 27 Apr 1755 *WV*.
7 MARY, b 27 Apr 1755 *WV*.
8 BENJAMIN, b 18 Nov 1757 *WV*.
9 ABEL, b 25 Dec 1760 *WV*.

FAM. 5. BELA & ABIGAIL (MOSS) LEWIS:
1 SARAH, b 12 Jan 1746/7 *WV*.
2 JOSEPH, b 6 May 1748 *WV*, d s. p.
3 ABIGAIL.
4 RUTH.
5 NAOMI, b c. 1754, d 28 Oct 1824 æ. 71 *CTI;* m Andrew Hull.

FAM. 6. BARNABAS & JERUSHA (DOOLITTLE) LEWIS:
1 SON, b & d 7 June 1752 *WatV*.
2 BENONI, b 30 Apr 1754 *WatV*, d s. p.

FAM. 6. BARNABAS & DEBORAH (BROOKS) LEWIS:
3 DAVID, b 29 Apr 1757 *WatV*, d 3 Mar 1845 (at Wells, Vt.); [a David in 1778 was husband of Elizabeth da. Ebenezer Benham]; m [(2)] 24 Nov 1785 Rebecca da. John & Phebe (Gillam) Hotchkiss.

FAM. 6. BARNABAS & RACHEL (CURTIS) LEWIS:
4 JERUSHA, b 1 Nov 1762 *WV*, d 16 July 1786 æ. 24 *CTI;* m 3 Mar 1785 *CC*—Andrew Durand.
5 ZURIEL, b 30 Sep 1764 *WV*, d 12 Jan 1854 æ. 90 (at Harbor Creek, near Erie, Pa.); m 18 Jan 1787 *CC*—Lucy da. Abner & Elizabeth (Preston) Bunnell, b 27 Jan [1768] *WV*, d 3 Feb 1843.
6 DEBORAH, b 3 Sep 1766 *WV;* m Robert Curtis.
7 RACHEL, b 20 Mar 1768 *WV;* m c. 1784 Amasa Munson.
8 SARAH, b 15 Sep 1770 *WV;* m 12 Feb 1795 *CC*—Eliakim Hough.
9 ESTHER, b 13 Nov 1772 *WV;* m Azariah Lathrop.
10 BENJAMIN, b 13 Nov 1772 *WV;* d 1847; m 7 Apr 1799 *CC*—Abigail Hitchcock, who d 1862.
11 LEVI, b 5 Mar 1775 *WV*, d 1811 (Wells, Vt.); m Bethia Lumbard.
12 MIRIAM, b 14 Feb 1777 *WV;* m 9 July 1795 *CV*—Titus Andrews.
13 AMARILLIS; m Aaron B. Tyler.
14 BARNABAS; res. near Port Colburn, Canada; m (1) Amy Bradley; m (2) Mary Perry.

LEWIS. FAM. 7. BENJAMIN of W, rem. to St; had children recorded *WV*, —John, b 30 Sep 1672, & Mary, b 9 Nov 1674.

LEWIS. FAM. 8. CALEB, b c. 1701, d 30 Sep 1775 *CC*, æ. 74 *WV;* m 13 Jan 1736 *WV*, 10 Jan *WatV*—Eunice da. Stephen & Mary (Gaylord) Welton, b 19 Apr 1707 *WatV*, d 11 Nov 1771 *CC*, *CT1*, æ. 65 *WV*.

1 JACOB, b 7 Sep 1736 *WV;* (?rem. to Wells, Vt.); m 22 June 1775 *WV*, *CC*—Mary Martin.

i Jacob, b 10 Mar 1776 *WV*.

ii Ezekiel, b 6 July 1777 *WV*.

2 EUNICE, b 6 Apr 1738 *WV*.

3 ABNER, b 21 Aug 1741 *WyV;* m Azuba Williams.

i Asahel, b 3 Oct 1762 *WatV*.

ii Mary, b 19 Apr 176[7] *WV*.

4 CALEB, d 15 July 1749 *WV*.

5 AMY, b 31 Jan 1745/6 *WV*, bp Feb 1745/6 *CC;* m 15 June 1765 *WV*—Caleb Preston.

6 CALEB, b 15 Apr 1752 *WV*, bp Apr 1752 *CC;* Census (C) 1-1-4; m 13 June 1782 *CC*—Phebe da. Isaiah & Kezia (Prindle) Moss, b 20 Mar 1764 *WV*.

LEWIS. FAM. 9. ISAAC, b c. 1718, d 12 Oct 1784 æ. 66 *WT1;* Dr.; m Kezia ——— .

1 ISAAC, b 30 June 1747 *WV*, d 9 May 1772 æ. 25 *WV*, *WT1*.

2 REUBEN, b 31 Jan 1748/9 *WV*.

3 "JOHN", b 11 Sep 1750 *WV*, "Charles" d 8 May 1772 æ. 21 *WV*.

4 KEZIA, b 27 Nov 1753 *WV*, d 29 May 1772 æ. 19 *WV*, *WT1*.

5 ANNA, b 22 Apr 1756 *WV*.

6 JOHN, b 26 May 1758 *WV*.

7 [C]LEAR, b 4 Sep 176[2] *WV;* m Mary Ives.

i Pauline; m Dr. Augustus Bristol of Chili, N. Y.

LEWIS. FAM. 10. LEONARD [can he be Lent, s. of Barnabas, FAM. 1, 6?] m 10 Oct 1753 *NH* —Hannah da. Isaac & Hannah (Miles) Gorham; she m (2) 19 July 1767 *NHC1*—Stephen Bradley.

1 BETTY, b 31 July 1754 *NHV*, d 20 Aug 1754 *NHV*.

2 HANNAH, b 7 Feb 1764 *NHV*.

3 BARNABAS.

4 HANNAH, b [Dec 1756], d 19 Sep 1764 æ. 0-9 *NHC1*.

LEWIS. FAM. 11. JOHN m Rachel da. Israel & Rachel Dodge of New London.

1 RACHEL, b 19 May 1763 *NH V*.

2 MARY, b 7 Nov 1765 *NHV;* m 23 Sep 1784 *NHC1*—Ebenezer Mansfield.

3 ELIZABETH, b 27 May 1768 *NHV;* m 1 Oct 1786 *NHC1*—Simeon Cooper.

LEWIS. FAM. 12. NEHEMIAH, d 1757; m Lois da. Job & Esther (Dorman) Bishop, b 13 Sep 1734 *NHV*, d 4 Apr 1813 *F;* she m (2) 7 Apr 1763 *NHC2* —Isaac Bradley.

1 JOSEPH, b 20 Aug 1755 *NHV*, d young.

2 HANNAH, b c. 1757, d 1 May 1840 æ. 84 *NHT1;* m 22 Feb 1783

NHCl—Henry Peck.

3 MARY, b c. 1760, d 9 Apr 1833 æ. 73 *NHTl*; m 26 Oct 1788 *NHCl*—John Peck.

LEWIS. FAM. 13. NEHEMIAH, b c. 1739, d 30 July 1810 æ. 71 *NHTl*, bu. 1 Aug *NHx*.

1 BENJAMIN, b c. 1773, d 19 May 1830 æ. 57 *NHTl*; m Mary ——. (The first 3 children called grandchildren of Nehemiah Lewis at baptism).

i Sally Miles, b c. 1803, bp 24 July 1810 (æ. 8) *NHx*, d 9 Sep 1851 æ. 48 *NHTl*; m Oliver Sage, who d 29 Apr 1835 æ. 33 *NHTl*.

ii Charles, b c. 1805, bp 24 July 1810 (æ. 5) *NHx*, d 26 Sep 1829 æ. 24 *NHTl*.

iii Charlotte, b c. 1807, bp 24 July 1810 (æ. 3) *NHx*.

iv George Benjamin, d Feb 1833 (at sea) *NHTl*.

v Roxana, b c. 1816, d 8 Aug 1832 æ. 16 *NHTl*.

LEWIS. MISCELLANEOUS. SAMUEL d 19 Feb 1776 æ. 71 *NHCl*; WIDOW d 20 Nov 1779 æ. 75 *NHCl*; perhaps parents of some of the stray New Haven Lewises above......SUSANNA d 14 Dec 1802 æ. 82 *NHCl*......SOLOMON m 29 Oct 1759 *NHV*—Rhoda da. John & Desire (Cooper) Wooding, b 23 Dec 1733 *NHV*, d 28 May 1760 *NHV*; child Samuel b 10 Apr 1760 *NHV*...... ELISHA, b c. 1768, d 25 Feb 1829 æ. 61 *NHTl*; m (1) Sarah [?Phelps], who d 27 Dec 1803 æ. 29 *NHTl*, *NHx*; m (2) Esther da. John & Elizabeth Phelps, wid. Elijah Austin & Peleg Sanford, who d 9 Aug 1829 æ. 72 *NHTl*. A child, Dudley Saltonstall, bp 12 Jan 1804 *NHx*.

LINDON. Variant, LINDALL. JOHN d [1667] *NHV*......HENRY d 29 Sep 1660 *NHV*; Dea.; m Rosamond —— ; she m (2) 15 Mar 1663/4 *NHV*—Nathaniel Richards. Children: 1 Mary, bp 19 July 1646 *NHCl*. 2 Sarah, bp 29 Oct 1648 *NHCl*. 3 Hannah, b 7 Jan 1650 *NHV*, bp 12 Jan 1650 *NHCl*. 4 Rebecca, b 20 Oct 1653 *NHV*, bp 20 Oct 1653 *NHCl*. 5 Grace, b 31 Mar 1656 *NHV*, bp 5 Apr 1656 *NHCl*. 6 Mary, b 18 Dec 1658 *NHV*, bp 30 Jan 1658 *NHCl* [1658/9]. Family rem. to Norwalk.

†LINES. FAM. 1. HENRY, s. of John of Badby, Co. Northampton, Eng., d 13/14 Jan 1662 *NHV*; m Elizabeth Harrison; she m (2) 6 Nov 1663 *NHV*—Thomas Lampson; m (3) 29 Mar 1666 *NHV*—John Morris.

1 JOHN, b 7 Aug 1656 *NHV*, d 14 Dec 1656 *NHV*.

2 JOANNA, b 20 Oct 1658 *NHV*, bp 24 Oct 1658 *NHCl*, d young.

3 SAMUEL, b 16 Jan 1659 *NHV* [1660], bp 4 Mar 1659/60 *NHCl*, d Apr 1660 *NHV*.

4 HOPESTILL, b 6 Nov 1661 *NHV*, bp 9 Nov 1661 *NHCl*.

FAM. 2. RALPH, probably brother or cousin of Henry, was nephew of Lt. John Budd; d 7 Sep 1689 *NHV*; m Alice —— .

1 SAMUEL, b Apr 1649 *NHV*, bp (adult) 28 Aug 1687 *NHCl*, d 1692; m Nov 1674 *NHV*—Mary da. John & Ellen (Harrison) Thompson, b 24 Apr 1652 *NHV*; she m (2) John Hitchcock; she m (3) 18 Apr 1717 *NHV*—Samuel Clark.

i John, b 18 Apr 1676 *NHV*, bp 25 Sep 1687 *NHCl*, d 1718; m 27 Dec 1700 *NHV*—Hannah da. John & Mary

(Thompson) Cooper, b 10 Aug 1681 *NHV*, d 11 Nov 1772 æ. 94 *WdTI*. **FAM. 3.**

ii Samuel, b c. 1677, bp 25 Sep 1687 *NHCI*, d s. p. 22 Oct 1709 *NHV*, 23 Oct æ. 33 *NHTI*.

iii Mary, b 29 Jan 1679 *NHV* [1680], bp 25 Sep 1687 *NHCI*, d before 1721; m 27 June 1705 *NHV*—Thomas Wilmot.

iv Lydia, b 17 Feb 1681 *NHV* [1682], d 28 May 1683 *NHV*.

v Ebenezer, b 18 Aug 1684 *NHV*, bp 25 Sep 1687 *NHCI*. d Dec 1740; m 30 July 1713 *NHV*—Rebecca da. Nathaniel & Sarah (Dickerman) Sperry, b 28 Mar 1690 *NHV*. **FAM. 4.**

vi Daniel, b 24 Dec 1686 *NHV*, bp 25 Sep 1687 *NHCI*; d 20 Jan 1710 æ. 24 *WTI*,

vii Ruth, b 27 Feb 1689/90 *NHV*, bp c. Mar 1690 *NHCI*, d young.

2 Ralph, b 18 July 1652 *NHV*, bp (adult) 27 May 1694 *NHCI*, d Jan 1712; m 27 Apr 1681 *NHV*—Abiah da. William Bassett, bp 7 Feb 1657 *NHCI* [1658].

i Rebecca, b 22 Jan 1681 *NHTI* [1682], d 20 Apr 1696 æ. 15 *NHTI*.

ii Ralph, d 8 May 1688 *NHV*.

iii Hannah, b 28 July 1684 *NHV*, bp 27 May 1694 *NHCI*; m c. 1713 John Thomas.

iv Joseph, b 20 Feb 1685 *NHV* [1686], bp 27 May 1694 *NHCI*, d 1749; m 3 Feb 1708/9 *NHV*—Hannah da. Benjamin & Elizabeth (Thompson) Bradley, b 18 Apr 1682. *NHV*. **FAM. 5.**

v Phebe, b 18 June 1687 *NHV*, bp 27 May 1694 *NHCI*; m (1) 27 May 1709 *NHV*—Nathan Clark; m (2) Joshua Tuttle.

vi Alice, b 27 Feb 1688/9 *NHV*, d 18 Nov 1689 *NHV*.

vii Ralph, b 23 Sep 1690 *NHV*, d 7 Dec 1693 *NHV*.

viii Child, d 7 Dec 1693 *NHV*.

ix Benjamin, b 1 Jan 1693/4 *NHV*, bp 27 May 1694 *NHCI*, d 1755; m 2 Feb 1719/20 *NHV*—Dorcas da. Joseph & Abigail (Preston) Thomas, bp 18 Feb 1693/4 *NHCI*. **FAM. 6.**

x Abiah, b 7 Feb 1695/6 *NHV*, bp 15 Mar 1696 *NHCI*; m Sylvanus Clark.

xi Rebecca, b Feb 1697/8 *NHV*, bp 27 Mar 1698 *NHCI*, d 12 Mar 1780 æ. 82 *NHTI*; m 31 Aug 1732 *NHV*—Nathaniel Mix.

xii Alice, b 1 Mar 1702 *NHV*, d 1726.

3 John, b Nov 1655 *NHV*, bp 27 June 1661 *NHCI*, d s. p.

4 Joseph, b Jan 1657 *NHV* [1658], bp 27 June 1661 *NHCI*, d 1736; m 30/31 Mar 1692 *NHV*—Abigail da. William & Sarah (Hall) Johnson, b 6 Dec 1670 *NHV*.

i Abigail, b 14 Jan 1692/3 *NHV*; m 11 June 1713 *NHV*—

John Pease.

ii Sarah, b 26 Oct 1694 *NHV*, d 1771; m 24 Feb 1719/20 *NHV*—Joseph Dorman.

iii Lydia, b 14 Dec 1696 *NHV*, d s. p.

iv Elizabeth, b 16 June 1703 *NHV;* m Ephraim Terrell.

v Hannah, b 8 May 1706 *NHV;* m (1) 6 Oct 1731 *NHV*—Joseph Chatterton; m (2) 17 Oct 1743 *WdC*—Israel Baldwin.

vi Thankful, b 8 May 1706 *NHV;* m Stephen Hine.

5 BENJAMIN, b Dec 1659 *NHV*, bp 27 June 1661 *NHC1*, d 26 July 1689 *NHV;* m Anna da. William & Sarah (Thomas) Wilmot, b 26 Feb 1669/70 *NHV*, d after 1727; she m (2) Peter Carrington.

i Benjamin, b 8 Nov 1689 *NHV*, d 21 Feb 1732 æ. 44 *FairfieldT;* m Esther da. Joseph & Mary (Hill) Sturges, bp 2 Mar 1700/1 *FairfieldC;* she m (2) William Hill. **FAM. 7.**

6 HANNAH, b 21 Nov 1665 *NHV*, bp 27 Jan 1665 *NHC1* [1666], d c. 1688; m 28 Mar 1683 *WV*—John Merriman.

FAM. 3. JOHN & HANNAH (COOPER) LINES:

1 RUTH, b 27 Oct 1701 *NHV*, d 3 Apr 1788 æ. 85-5-9 *BD;* m 7 May 1724 *NHV*—Josiah Lounsbury.

2 MARY, b c. 1703, d 25 Oct 1790 æ. 90 *WdT2;* m 21 May 1724 Alexander Hine.

3 HELENA, b 3 Mar 1706 *NHV*, bp (adult) 20 June 1736 *NHC1;* m 22 Dec 1742 *WdC*—Caleb Wheeler.

4 SAMUEL, b 17 Jan 1708 *NHV*, d 1735; m 16 Aug 1733 *NHV*—Dorcas da. Richard & Elizabeth (Wilmot) Sperry, b 22 July 1713 *NHV;* she m (2) 28 Mar 1745 *NHV*—John Sherman.

i Samuel, b 20 Sep 1733 *NHV*, bp 22 Aug 1736 *NHC1*, d Feb 1810 *F;* Census (Wd) 2-1-2; m 13 June 1755 *WdC*—Mercy da. Zebulon & Sarah (Johnson) Carrington, b c. 1734, d 28 Dec 1817 æ. 83 *F.* **FAM. 8.**

ii Jabez, bp 22 Aug 1736 *NHC1*, d soon.

5 DANIEL, b 6 May 1712 *NHV*, bp (adult) 6 Mar 1736/7 *NHC1*, d 28 June 1793 æ. 83 *WdT1;* Census (Wd) 1-1-1; m 11 Nov 1736 *NHV*—Mary da. John & Susanna (Heaton) Alcock, b 10 Aug 1717 *NHV.*

i Hannah, b 11 Jan 1737/8 *NHV*, bp 5 Mar 1738 *NHC1*, d soon.

ii Susanna, b 2 Jan 1739/40 *NHV*, bp 24 Feb 1739/40 *NHC1*, d 24 Nov 1817 æ. 78 *WdT1;* m (1) 5 Oct 1763 *WdC*—Amos Sperry; m (2) 6 July 1774 *WdC*—Samuel Carrington.

iii Mary, b 8 May 1742 *NHV*, bp 13 June 1742 *NHC1*, d 1 Nov 1824 æ. 81 *WdT1;* m 8 Nov 1764 *WdC*—Obed Johnson.

iv Sarah, b 29 Apr 1744 *NHV*, bp 3 June 1744 *WdC*, d young.

v Kezia, b 30 Nov 1747 *NHV*, bp 24 Jan 1748 *WdC;* m 2

July 1767 *WdC, DV*—Abraham Pierson.

vi Daniel, bp 20 May 1750 *WdC*, d young.

vii Hannah, bp 26 July 1752 *WdC*, d 29 Jan 1829 æ. 77 *WdT I;* m 11 Nov 1773 *WdC*—Samuel Sperry.

6 **Kezia**, b 5 Apr 1715 *NHV*, bp 20 June 1736 *NHCI*, d 12 Jan 1782 æ. 67 *WdTI;* m c. 1737 Samuel Alling.

FAM. 4. Ebenezer & Rebecca (Sperry) Lines:

1 **Sarah**, b 28 Apr 1714 *NHV*, bp 25 Dec 1726 *NHCI*, d c. 1735/6; m 13 Feb 1734/5 *NHV*—Ezra Johnson.

2 **Ralph**, b 23 May 1716 *NHV*, bp 25 Dec 1726 *NHCI*, d 27 Feb 1781 æ. 65 *CTI;* m (1) ——, who d July 1745 *CC;* m (2) ——, who d Nov 1749 *CC;* m (3) Bathsheba da. Stephen & Elizabeth (Sperry) Hotchkiss, b 1 Sep 1726 *WV*, d 8 Aug 1813 æ. 87 *SyT.*

(By 1): *i* Titus, b 19 Mar 1740/1 *NHV*, bp Mar 1740/1 *CC*, d 11 June 1769 *CC;* m 13 Nov 1764 *WV*—Marlow da. Amos & Obedience (Munson) Hotchkiss, b 20 June 1745 *WV*, d 9 Nov 1808 *CC;* she m (2) 12 Oct 1775 *CC*—James Jones. Child: Samuel, b 30 Mar 1765 *WV*, "child" d 18 Oct 1768 *CC.*

ii Erastus, bp Nov 1743 *CC*, "child" d Aug 1744 *CC.*

(By 2): *iii* Dinah, b 18 Jan 1746/7 *NHV*, bp Feb 1746 *CC;* [m —— Andrews].

iv Child, d Dec 1748 *CC.*

(By 3): *v* Erastus, b 24 Nov 1751 *WV*, bp 8 Dec 1751 *CC*, d 15 Nov 1815 æ. 64 *DT4;* Census (C) 1-2-4; m 15 Jan 1778 *CC, WV*—Sarah da. Caleb & Tamar (Thompson) Doolittle, b 5 July 1748 *WV*, d 26 Nov 1815 æ. 67 *DT4.* **FAM. 9.**

vi Abraham, b 25 Sep 1753 *WV*, d s. p. 3 June 1815 æ. 62 *SyT;* m 26 Apr 1784 *Sy*—Sarah da. Edward & Sarah Spencer, b 5 Dec 1761 (at Bolton) *SyT*, d 5 Apr 1845 *SyT.*

vii Joseph, b 29 Feb 1756 *WV*, d s. p. 16 Nov 1804 æ. 49 *DT 4;* Census (D) 1-1-2; m (1) Lois da. Samuel & Lois (Fairchild) Wheeler, b 24 Mar 1764 *DV*, d 12 May 1798 æ. 35 *DT4;* m (2) Ruth da. Ezra & Ruth (Sperry) Sperry, b 22 Aug 1762 *NHV*, d 1843.

viii Ralph, b 2 Oct 1758 *WV*, d 21 Dec 1776 æ. 19 (a prisoner in N. Y.) *CTI.*

ix Rufus, b 18 Nov 1763 *WV;* Census (C) 2-2-3; rem. to Franklin, Pa.; m 23 May 1784 *CV*—Tamar da. Andrew & Eunice (Hotchkiss) Durand, b [31 May 1764 *WV*]. **FAM. 10.**

x Sarah, b 8 Mar 1768 *WV*, d 1833; m 15 Feb 1791 Theophilus Merriman.

3 **Ebenezer**, b 26 Apr 1718 *NHV*, bp 25 Dec 1726 *NHCI*, d Sep 1798 æ. 81 *Conn Journal;* Census (NH) 1-0-1; m (1) [a Burrill?]; m (2) Mary da. Israel & Rachel Dodge.

(By 1): *i* Sarah.

ii Rebecca; she had a nat. child by Jared Sherman b 1772; m 13 Feb 1774 *NHC1*—Timothy Clark.

iii Laban, bp 14 Oct 1744 *WdC*, d soon.

iv Rufus, bp 16 Mar 1746 *WdC*, d young.

v Major, b 14 Oct 1747 *F*, bp 29 Nov 1747 *WdC*, d 2 Mar 1814 æ. 66 *NHT1*; Capt.; Census (NH) 1-3-6; m 12 Aug 1775 *NHC1*—Susanna da. Nathan & Deborah (Dayton) Mansfield, b 23 Sep 1756 *F*, d 2 Aug 1824 æ. 68 *NHT1*. **FAM. 11.**

vi Laban, bp 11 June 1749 *WdC*, d young.

4 JOHN, b 13 Mar 1719/20 *NHV*, bp 25 Dec 1726 *NHC1*; Capt.; Census (Wd) 1-0-1; m 29 Mar 1743 *NHV*—Deborah da. Abraham & Deborah (Thomas) Hotchkiss, b c. 1723.

i Zenas, bp 14 Aug 1743 *WdC*.

ii Lucas, bp 28 July 1745 *WdC*; loyalist; Census (Wd) 1-1-3; m ——— . **FAM. 12.**

iii Hannah, bp 15 Apr 1748 *WdC*, d 19 Aug 1823 æ. 76 *BT2*; m David French.

iv John, bp 6 May 1750 *WdC*.

v Deborah, bp 1 Apr 1753 *WdC*; m 10 Apr 1776 *GV*—John Morse; rem. to Homer, N. Y.

vi Eber, b c. 1755, d 20 Feb 1844 æ. 89 *BT2*; Census (Wd) 1-1-3; m Hannah da. Dan & Ann (Brewster) Welton, b 12 May 1757 *WatV*, d 2 June 1828. **FAM. 13.**

vii Abel b c. 1757, d 28 Apr 1823 æ. 66 *BT2*; Census (Wd) 1-1-4; m Arma da. Ebenezer & Rachel (Humphreville) Chatfield, b [Nov 1758], d 4 Oct 1854 æ. 96 *BT2*. **FAM. 14.**

viii Ebenezer, b c. 1759, d 23 Nov 1812 æ. 53 *BT1*; Census (Wd) 1-0-2; m Mercy ———, b c. 1766, d 20 Apr 1845 æ. 79 *BT1*. **FAM. 15.**

5 TITUS, b 6 Aug 1731 *NHV*, bp 27 Sep 1731 *NHC1*, d young.

FAM. 5. JOSEPH & HANNAH (BRADLEY) LINES:

1 ESTHER, b c. 1710, bp 3 May 1719 *NHC1*, d 21 Dec 1773 æ. 64 *HT4*; m 4 Feb 1730/1 *NHV*—John Potter.

2 LYDIA, b c. 1714, bp 3 May 1719 *NHC1*, d 1796; m 23 Sep 1736 *NHV*—Timothy Peck.

3 HANNAH, b c. 1716, bp 3 May 1719 *NHC1*, d before 1749; m Stephen Gilbert.

4 RACHEL, b c. 1718, bp 3 May 1719 *NHC1*, d c. 1783; m (1) 7 June 1738 *NHV*—Aaron Gilbert; m (2) 1 Dec 1748 *NHV*—Benjamin Wooding.

5 JOSEPH, bp Dec 1720 *NHC1*, d s. p.

6 MARY, bp June 1723 *NHC1*, d 1769; m 7 July 1742 *NHV*, *WdC*—Eliphalet Johnson.

FAM. 6. BENJAMIN & DORCAS (THOMAS) LINES:

1 BENJAMIN, b 1 Sep 1720 *NHV*, bp 9 Oct 1737 *NHC1*; m 3 Mar

1746 *WdC*—Sarah [da. Zebulon & Sarah (Johnson)] Carrington; she probably m (2) by 1792 Reuben Thomas. Family incomplete.

i Dorcas, bp 7 Dec 1746 *WdC;* m 25 Jan 1779 *WdC*—Martin Ford.

ii Rachel, bp 15 May 1748 *WdC;* m (1) 27 Dec 1771 *WV*—Thomas Jaynes; m (2) 19 Apr 1787 *WV*—Isaac Royce.

iii Alice, bp 13 July 1749 *WdC,* d 11 Jan 1828 æ. 82 *WdD.*

iv Sarah, bp 11 Aug 1751 *WdC,* d 9 Oct 1825 æ. 73 *NHT1;* m 8 Dec 1776 *NHC2*—Samuel Gorham.

v Cleopatra, bp Sep 1753 *WdC,* d 20 Dec 1819 æ. 66 *WdC;* m 25 Nov 1773 *WdC*—Francis Martin.

vi Peter, d s. p. 1784.

vii (probably) Zebulon; m 25 Jan 1795 *OxfC*—Lois Andrus. **FAM. 16.**

2 JAMES, bp 9 Oct 1737 *NHC1*, d 18 Oct 1792 *WdD;* Census (NH) 2-0-1; m 7 Jan 1745/6 *NHV*—Thankful da. John & Sarah (Perkins) Sperry, b 7 July 1725 *NHV,* d 17 Aug 1811 æ. 88 *WdC.*

i John, b 22 Aug 1746 *NHV,* bp 4 June 1749 *NHC2,* d 30 Dec 1831 æ. 87 *NHV.*

ii James, b 30 Nov 1748 *NHV,* bp 4 June 1749 *NHC2,* d 5 Aug 1816 æ. 68 *WdT1;* Census (Wd) 1-1-2; m 1 Jan 1772 *NHV, WdC*—Susanna da. John & Sarah (Alcott) Alling, b 28 Oct 1753 *NHV,* d 6 Mar 1834 æ. 80 *WdT1.* **FAM. 17.**

iii Ashbel, b 9 Apr 1751 *NHV,* d 11 May 1823 æ. 72 *NHV;* Census (NH) 1-3-5; m Eunice da. Joseph & Hannah (Patterson) Murray, bp 27 Aug 1749 *NMC,* d 1 Oct 1840 æ. 91 *NHV.* **FAM. 18.**

iv Ezra, b 22 Nov 1753 *F,* bp 25 Nov 1753 *NHC2,* d 18 Apr 1756 *F.*

v Pamelia, b 15 Apr 1756 *NHV,* d 3 Aug 1815 *F;* m 15 Oct 1773 *F*—Levi Potter.

vi Ezra, b 24 Sep 1760 *NHV,* bp 20 Sep (?) 1760 *NHC2,* d 15 Sep 1820 *F;* Census (NH) 1-1-4; m (1) 4 June 1782 *NHC1*, 3 June *F*—Lue da. Thomas & Mary (Page) Wheaton, who d 5 Sep 1794 *F,* bu. 5 Sep *NHx;* m (2) 14 Jan 1795 *F,* 24 Jan *NHx*—Abigail da. Joshua & Martha (Minor) Ray, wid. Richard Hood, b 20 July 1763 *NHV,* d 15 June 1796 *F,* bu. 16 June æ. 33 *NHx;* m (3) 19 Nov 1796 *F*—Elizabeth da. Thomas & Elizabeth (Morris) Umberfield [i. e. Humphreville], b 10 Dec 1766 *NHV,* d 9 Oct 1825 *F.* **FAM. 19.**

vii Benjamin, b 16 Aug 1762 *NHV,* bp 29 Aug 1762 *NHC2,* d 22 Oct 1840 æ. 78 *NHV;* m 26 July 1784 *BdC*—Sarah Brown. [His nephew's Bible says he m —— Malery at EH; but she was prob. sister of Abigail Brown who m Amos Mallory.] FAM. 20.

viii Sarah, b 31 Dec 1764 *NHV*, bp 20 Jan 1765 *NHC2;* m 24 Jan 1785 *NHC1*—Stacey Potter.

ix Ebenezer, b 25 June 1767 *NHV*, bp 19 July 1767 *NHC2*, d s. p.

3 DORCAS, bp 9 Oct 1737 *NHC1*.

4 ALICE, bp 9 Oct 1737 *NHC1*.

5 MABEL, bp 9 Oct 1737 *NHC1;* m 31 Oct 1747 *WdC*, 31 Dec *MV*—John Clark.

6 JOSEPH, b c. 1732, bp 9 Oct 1737 *NHC1*, d 29 July 1792 æ. 60 *NMT;* m 12 Sep 1758 *NMC*—Phebe da. Ebenezer Baldwin, b 21 June 1738 *NMV*, d 23 Aug 1823 æ. 85 *NMT*.

i Clarissa, b 12 Mar 1759 *NMV;* m Noah D. Mygatt.

ii Reuben, b 21 Jan 1761 *NMV;* m 11 Apr 1784 *NHC1*—Rebecca Brown. He had Polly bp Apr 1800 & Samuel bp 1 July 1803 *SharonC.*

iii Aminta, b 9 June 1763 *NMV;* she had a child: Isaac L. Hunt.

iv Daniel, b c. 1766, d 24 June 1837 æ. 71 *NMT;* m 20 Nov 1791 *NMC*—Hannah Todd, "Mrs. Lines" d 13 July 1817 *NMC.* FAM. 21.

v Philo, b 11 Jan 1769 *NMV;* m (1) Phebe da. John Marchant, who d 20 Aug 1797 æ. 18 *NMT;* m (2) ——— . FAM. 22.

vi Benjamin, b [3 Feb 1774], d 8 July 1846 æ. 72-5-5 *SharonT;* m (1) Lucy ——— , who d 30 Mar 1825 æ. 47 *SharonT;* m (2) 4 Dec 1825 *Sharon*—Sophia Platt, who d 4 Nov 1868 æ. 83 *SharonT.* FAM. 23.

FAM. 7. BENJAMIN & ESTHER (STURGES) LINES:

1 BENJAMIN, b c. 1717, d c. 1755; res. F; m 30 May 1742 *GreenfieldC*—Grace da. Samuel & Elizabeth (Rumsey) Barlow, bp 24 May 1724 *FC.*

Esther, b c. 1743; m 19 Nov 1761 *GreenfieldC*—Reuel Thorp.

ii Ruhamah, b c. 1745; m 3 May 1762 *FV*—John Robinson.

2 ESTHER, b [10 June 1719], d 22 May 1722 æ. 2-11-12 *NorwalkT.*

3 DAVID, b c. 1722; m 14 Jan 1748 *StamfordV*—Mary Cheson.

i Mary, b 9 Apr 1749 *StamfordV.*

ii Polly, b 21 Jan 1752 *StamfordV*, d 1804; m 10 Nov 1772 *St John's x, Stamford*—Silas Hamlin of Amenia, N. Y., & Prescott, Ont.

iii Esther, b 12 Jan 1755 *StamfordV;* m 15 Aug 1782 Richard Nash of Ridgefield.

iv Nancy, b 28 Feb 1757 *StamfordV.*

v (probably) Benjamin, b 1760, d 1845; res. Ridgefield; m 23 Nov 1786 Sarah Coley. Family incomplete Children: 1 Stephen Coley, b 1787, d 1872 (N. Y. City); m Hannah Maltbie of F. 2 (probably) Daniel, d 1831

(Ridgefield); m Rachel ——. 3 Samuel, b 16 Feb 1798; m Elizabeth Hoyt Isaacs.

vi (probably) David, d 1812; res. Wilton; m Patience Bunnell; she m (2) Elijah Seeley. Children: 1 Sally; m Hiram Nash. 2 Synderella, b 11 Jan 1800, d 27 Oct 1821. 3 David. 4 Nathaniel; res. Newburgh, N. Y. 5 Dennis W., b 22 Feb 1805, d 14 Aug 1825. 6 Mary Ann, b c. 1807, d 5 Dec 1848; m c. 1828 Charles Edward Britto.

4 SAMUEL, b c. 1726, d c. 1765; m 28 Feb 1749 *StamfordV*—Mercy Holly.

i Rebecca, b 11 Apr 1750 *StamfordV;* m 9 Feb 1774 *ReddingC*—Levi Dikeman.

ii Holly, b 1751, d 1841; res. Stamford, & Oyster Bay, N. Y.; m 22 Oct 1782 Martha Pierce. Births of children: Samuel 4 Mar 1783; Abigail 17 Sep 1784; Mercy 19 Jan 1786; Elizabeth 2 Nov 1787; Esther 22 June 1789; Martha 11 Feb 1791; Mary 20 Dec 1792 (m 10 Oct 1826 Ebenezer Selleck); Rebecca 27 May 1796; Benjamin 11 June 1798; Phebe 4 July 1800.

iii (probably) John, d before 1824; m 18 Mar 1779 *ReddingC*—Mary Hendrick.

iv Sturges.

v David, b 20 June 1764 *F*, d 29 Aug 1856 *F;* res. Cairo, Greene Co., N. Y.; m 31 Mar 1796 *F*—Polly Bradley, b 10 Apr 1774 *F*, d 31 Mar 1847 (?) *F*. **FAM. 24.**

5 DAUGHTER.

FAM. 8. SAMUEL & MERCY (CARRINGTON) LINES:

1 ALVIN, b c. 1756, d 10 Apr 1827 æ. 76 *WdT1*, *WdC;* Census (Wd) 1-1-3; m Phebe ——, b c. 1752, d 12 Dec 1822 æ. 70 *WdT1*.

i Anna, b 13 Apr 1785 *F*, d 26 July 1852 æ. 67 *F;* m (1) Ezekiel Ball; div.; m (2) 1 Nov 1838 *F*—Nathaniel Camp.

ii Polly; m Jan 1812 *WdC*—Charles Willoughby.

iii George, b c. 1792, d 16 Mar 1852 æ. 68 *WdD;* m Aug 1816 *WdC*—Susan da. David Morris. Children: 1 William, b c. 1816, d 20 Jan 1824 æ. 5 *WdD*. 2 Edwin, b c. 1820, d 11 Nov 1885; res. WH; m 5 Apr 1846 Frances A. Smith, who d 10 Mar 1901. 3 Jane, d s. p.; m Austin Smith. 4 David Wallace, b c. 1824; m (1) 5 Nov 1848 Adeline Louisa Johnson: div.; m (2) 7 July 1854 Susan A. Brown.

He had also a nat. child by Anna [Morris or Thomas]:

iv Leverett, b c. 1783, d 26 Dec 1826 æ. 44 (*NHC1*) *NHV;* m 27 Jan 1802 *OxfC*—Sarah da. David & Lucy (Marchant) Blake. **FAM. 25.**

2 PHILENA; m —— Wilcox.

3 LINUS, b c. 1760, d 27 Mar 1814 æ. 54 *WdT1*, æ. c. 52 *WdC;* Census (Wd) 1-0-3; m Keturah da. Joseph & Eunice (Thomas)

Smith, wid. —— Hotchkiss, b 12 Apr 1764 *NHV*.

i Huldah, b c. 1788, d 30 Apr 1841 æ. 53 *WdT1;* m Philo Alling.

ii Lewis, b c. 1792, d 16 Sep 1849 æ. 57 *BT2;* m Thirza da. Elijah & Eunice (Bradley) Wooding, b c. 1791, d 6 Dec 1855 æ. 64 *BT2*. Children: 1 Edwin, b c. 1815, d 20 Nov 1846 æ. 31 *BT2;* m 13 Sep 1840 Mary A. Castle. 2 Lucretia, d s. p.; m 18 Nov 1849 *HV*—Eneas Gorham.

iii Nancy; m (1) Feb 1813 *WdC*—Seymour Sperry; m (2) John Gorham.

iv Keturah; m Mar 1822 (at Sy) *ConnH*—Obadiah Wheeler.

v Linus; res. Barrington, Ill.; m ——. Children: 1 Edwin. 2 Linus. 3 Charles. 4 Fred E. 5 Pearl.

vi Julia Ann; m Hiram Downs.

vii Joseph Willard; res. Naugatuck; m 13 Oct 1825 *WatV*—Lydia M. da. Enoch Russell.

4 REBECCA, b c. 1762, d 27 Feb 1826 æ. 64 *WdC*.

5 SELEY, d s. p. June 1803 *WdC*.

6 LUTHER, b c. 1768, d 28 Mar 1847 æ. 79 *WdT1;* Capt.; m Susanna da. Amos & Susanna (Lines) Sperry, b c. 1773.

i Child, d Jan 1792 *WdD*.

ii Sophia, b c. 1793, d 2 Jan 1823 æ. 29 *WdD;* m 1813 *WdC*—Zenas Peck.

iii Emily, b c. 1797, d 8 Mar 1841 æ. 44 *WdT1;* m 3 Apr 1823 Truman Hotchkiss.

iv Sally Maria, b c. 1802, d 15 Feb 1874; m 2 May 1830 *NHV*—Miles Camp.

7 CORNELIUS, b c. 1771, d after 1835; Census (Wd) 1-1-1; m Lois da. John & Sarah (Johnson) Ball.

i Chauncey, b c. 1790, d 26 May 1847 æ. 57 *NHT3;* m 1819 Hannah Bradley, who d 27 Aug 1848 æ. 48 *NHT3*. See MISCELLANEOUS.

ii Alvin, d 1845.

iii Levi; m Julia Ann Newton, who d May 1849 æ. 37 *NHT3*.

iv Elias, b c. 1811, d s. p. 8 Aug 1849 æ. 38 *NHT3*.

8 SAMUEL, b c. 1774, d 23 Feb 1848 æ. 74 *WdD;* m 18 June 1795 *WdC*—Polly da. Samuel & Susanna (Lines) Carrington, b c. 1775, d 14 Feb 1844 æ. 69 *WdT1*.

i Amadeus, b c. 1796, d 11 Apr 1812.

ii Merrit, b c. 1798, d 27 Jan 1840.

iii Jeremiah, b c. 1801, d 7 May 1882; m 27 Nov 1823 *WdC*—Nancy Richardson. Children: 1 Betsey, b 1824, m 1849 George P. Morgan. 2 Albert, b & d 1826.

iv Eunice, b c. 1804; m 24 Oct 1825 William Mintonye.

v Sally, b c. 1806, d 10 Sep 1877; m 27 Mar 1826 Caleb Andrus Finch.

vi Harriet; m 5 Feb 1826 Silas Alling.

vii John, b c. 1812, d 15 Nov 1815.

viii John J., b c. 1818, d 2 Apr 1860; m 29 Apr 1842 Eliza Riggs.

FAM. 9. ERASTUS & SARAH (DOOLITTLE) LINES:

1 ZIPPORAH, b 17 Nov 1778 *WV*, d 3 Jan 1864 æ. 85 *NoHD;* m 1 Mar 1798 *NoHC*—Sebe Thorpe.

2 RANSOM, b 21 Jan 1780 *CV*, bp 19 Mar 1780 *CC*, d 6 Nov 1815 æ. 36 *NHT1;* m 21 Sep 1801 *NHC1*—Elizabeth da. Isaac & Anna (Mix) Gilbert, b 27 Dec 1778 *F*, d 19 May 1839 æ. 60 *NHT1*.

i Jairus Gilbert, b c. 1802; res. Whitesboro, N. Y.; m 21 Feb 1823 *NHV*—Sally Prudencia da. Abner & Elizabeth (Gilbert) Sperry, b 4 Apr 1804, d 14 Dec 1893. Children: Dr. Jairus F., b 30 July 1834, & Elizabeth G.

ii Charles Mix, b c. 1803, d 12 June 1877; res. Thompsonville, N. C.; m & had: Charles, George & Loyal J.

iii Harriet Elizabeth, b 6 June 1805 *NHT1*, d 17 Mar 1826 *NHT1;* m John Warner Barber.

iv Grace M., b c. 1809, d s. p. 1 Oct 1860 æ. 52 *NHT1*.

v George L., b c. 1811; m & had: Mary (m Sidney Fairchild) & Virginia.

vi Henry, b c. 1813; res. Bristol, Wis., 1843, Kenosha, Wis., 1853; m Susan D. ——— ; child: Henry of Washington, D. C.

vii Son, b c. 1815, d 29 Sep 1815 æ. 1 *NHT1*.

3 RALPH, b 28 May 1782 *CV*, bp 27 July 1782 *CC;* res. Oxf; m Lois ———, who d 8 June 1865 æ. 87 (at Wat) *BAlm.*

i Anna, b 21 Feb 1804 (at Oxf) *WatV;* m 15 Apr 1834 *WatV*—John Mix.

ii Augustus.

iii (perhaps) Melinda, b c. 1808, d 11 July 1864 æ. 56 (at Wat) *BAlm.*

iv Joseph; m 11 June 1831 *WatV*—Eliza Gaylord, wid. Alfred Stevens.

v Caleb.

vi David.

4 CALEB, b 27 Sep 1783 *CV*, d 28 Dec 1784 *CV*.

5 BETSEY, b 17 Nov 1785 *CV*, d 29 June 1812 æ. 27 *DT4;* she had a nat. child: Lyman Jacobs, b c. 1804, d 18 July 1818 æ. 14 *DT4*.

6 SARAH, b 29 May 1788 *CV*, d 15 May 1847 æ. 59 *DT4;* m Josiah Lounsbury.

FAM. 10. RUFUS & TAMAR (DURAND) LINES (incomplete):

1 EUNICE, b 5 Nov 1784 *CV;* m 21 May 1804 Friend Tuttle.

2 SHUBAEL, b 6 July 1787 *CV*, bp 2 Sep 1787 *CC*.

3 BILLOSTA, b 17 Aug 1789 *CV*, bp 18 Oct 1789 *CC*.

4 ESTHER, b 8 Nov 1792 *CV*, bp 27 Jan 1793 *CC*.

5 RUFUS, bp 21 May 1797 *CC;* res. Franklin, Pa.; m 1 Dec 1820 Lucy Ann Smith.

i Caroline E., b 16 July 1822; m 24 May 1843 Harmon Ensign.
ii Lewis E., b 2 June 1832.
iii Flavy A., b 19 Sep 1836.
iv James R., b June 1838, d 1 Dec 1839.

6 JOSEPH, b 6 June 1798 *F*, bp 20 Aug 1798 *CC*, d 28 Dec 1874 *F;* m 19 Oct 1821 Elizabeth Mack, b 14 Sep 1800, d 25 Mar 1887.
i Mary Elizabeth, b 15 Aug 1822, d 25 Jan 1879; m 19 Dec 1850 Conger Tiffany of Brooklyn, Pa.
ii Joseph, b 15 Aug 1824, d 10 Dec 1882; m 19 Mar 1849 Lydia Caswell.

7 LAURA, b Jan 1806; m 1 Oct 1822 Billosta Smith.

FAM. 11. MAJOR & SUSANNA (MANSFIELD) LINES:*

1 STEPHEN, b 31 Jan 1777 *F*, bp 29 Sep 1782 *NHC2*, d 25 Dec 1816 æ. 40 *NHT1;* m 11 June 1796 *NHC1*—Elizabeth Gourley.

2 CHARLES BURRILL, b 29 July 1779 *F*, bp 29 Sep 1782 *NHC2*, d 1 Mar 1833 æ. 53 *NHT1*, 2 Mar æ. 54 (*NHC2*), *NHV;* m 25 Dec 1803 *NHC1*—Laura Frost.

3 WILLIAM, b 18 Mar 1781 *F*, bp 29 Sep 1782 *NHC2*, d 10 Oct 1822 æ. 41 (at Charleston, S. C.) *ColR;* Capt.; m 20 July 1802 *NHC1*—Elizabeth Osborn.

4 ELIZABETH, b 5 July 1783 *F*, bp 24 Aug 1783 *NHC2*, d 20 Mar 1852 æ. 69 *NHT1*, 19 Mar æ. 68-8-15 *NHV;* m 13 May 1810 John Chatterton.

5 SUSANNA, b 31 May 1785 *F*, bp 6 Oct 1785 *NHC2*, d 21 Jan 1871 æ. 86 *NHT1*.

6 MARY, b 31 Mar 1788 *F*, bp 1 June 1788 *NHC2*, d 27 Dec 1854; m 6 May 1840 David Daggett.

7 FRANCES, b 21 May 1790 *F*, bp 27 June 1790 *NHC2*, d 8 Feb 1869 æ. 79 *NHT1*.

8 MAJOR, b 11 July 1792 *F*, bp 9 Sep 1792 *NHC2*, d 10 June 1870 æ. 78 *NHT1;* m 11 July 1843 Martha Truesdel.

FAM. 12. LUCAS & ——— (———) LINES:

1 MARCUS, b c. 1774, d s. p. Apr 1798 æ. 24 (at sea) *ConnJournal*.

2 ZENAS, b 17 Oct 1778 *F*, d 9 Aug 1849 (Jefferson, N. Y.) *F;* m Sally ———, b 25 July 1783 *F*, d 19 Feb 1863 *F*.
i Marcus, b 25 May 1806, d 19 July 1880; m 17 June 1827 Charlotte Eggleston, b 25 Mar 1807, d 25 June 1888. Children: 1 Milo Miles, b 29 May 1835. 2 Samuel Delos, b 9 Feb 1837. 3 Eliza Ette, b 11 June 1844. Katherine, Philena & a son d young.
ii Angeline T., b 9 Mar 1808; m 30 Apr 1828 Ephraim Wilbur Potter, b 3 Dec 1801.
iii Ovid, b 2 Apr 1810; res. Otego, N. Y.; m Katherine Eg-

---

*For later descendants of this branch, see "Tuttle Family", p. 207, or "Mansfield Genealogy."

gleston. Children: 1 Wellington. 2 Howard Willis. 3 Lena.

iv Sally Emeline, b 3 Aug 1812, d 11 Dec 1899; m (1) —— Bailey; m (2) —— Moon.

v Lueyette, b 25 Jan 1815, d 3 June 1889; m James Hubbard.

vi Roxana, b 25 May 1818, d s. p. 4 Jan 1894.

vii Lucas, b 8 July 1822, d 7 June 1860; m 10 Feb 1847 Mary A. Howe, b 5 July 1826. Children: 1 Charles Z., b 27 Oct 1848. 2 Harriet A., b 24 Dec 1851.

3 MARGARET; m Chilion Sperry.

4 SARAH, b c. 1785, d 18 Dec 1848 æ. 63 *BT3;* m Jesse Beecher.

FAM. 13. EBER & HANNAH (WELTON) LINES:

1 PHILENA, b 1777 *DT4*, d 1862 *DT4;* m Moses Sanford.

2 CALVIN, b 8 Jan 1780 *F*, d 21 Sep 1818 æ. 40 *WdT1;* m 13 Oct 1808 Sally Newton da. Walter & Mary (Newton) Booth, b c. 1790, d 26 Feb 1876 æ. 86 (at Meriden) *WdD;* she m (2) Oct 1819 *WdC*—David Smith.

i Edwin Lyman, b 1810; m Elizabeth Curtis of Meriden, b 1810. Children settled in Peoria, Ill.

ii Henry Willis, b 5 Dec 1812, d 30 Jan 1863; m 2 June 1835 Harriet Bunnell, who d 24 Feb 1898. Children: 1 H. Wales, of Meriden. 2 Mary E. 3 Rt. Rev. Edwin Stevens, Bishop of N. J.

iii Mary Elizabeth; m Philo Chatfield.

3 ALMA, b c. 1782, d 2 May 1823 æ. 42 *DT4;* m John Sanford.

4 HANNAH, b c. 1790, d 19 Nov 1866; m (1) Truman Terrill; m (2) Aveil Peck.

5 EBER, b c. 1792, d 2 Oct 1836 æ. 43 *BT2;* m Mary da. Benjamin & Lois (Williams) Farrel, b 11 Jan 1797 *F*, d 2 May 1886. Children: 1 Calvin. 2 Minerva. 3 Rebecca. 4 Hannah. 5 Eliza. 6 Goodell. 7 Catherine Cordelia. 8 Calvin. 9 Eber. 10 Andrew E.

FAM. 14. ABEL & ARMA (CHATFIELD) LINES:

1 PATTY, b c. 1783, d 10 Mar 1864 æ. 81 *BT4;* m Philo Hotchkiss.

2 FANNY; m —— Dingee.

3 ABEL, b c. 1788, bu. 9 Mar 1864 æ. 76 *Bx;* m 16 Apr 1812 *WdC*—Content da. Ellard & Esther (Russell) Ford, b 9 Mar 1786 *WdV*, d 31 Aug 1854 æ. 68 *BT2*.

i Lavinia, d s. p.

ii Eliza; m 24 Nov 1839 DeWitt Kimberly.

4 LAURA; m Sheldon Church of Seymour.

FAM. 15. EBENEZER & MERCY (——) LINES:

1 HULDAH, b 20 July 1793 *F*, d 20 Apr 1875; m 23 Jan 1817 Jared Alling.

2 EBENEZER, d 1847; m Amaryllis Payne, b 1795, d 1875 *NHT4*, she m (2) —— Beecher.

i (perhaps) S. DeForest; m 2 July 1852 *NHV*—Hannah M.

Porter of Stamford.

ii Harriet, bp 13 Mar 1825 *WatC.*

iii Jane, b 1827 *NHT4*, d 1913 *NHT4;* m (1) Lyman J. Lane, b 1827, d 1863 *NHT4;* m (2) Wm. Beach.

iv James B., b 1837 *NHT4*, d 1864 *NHT4;* m Catherine E. ——, b 1840, d 1860 *NHT4.*

3 DEBORAH; m —— Baldwin; "went west."

4 ISAAC; rem. to Pike, Pa.; m.

i Commodore P., b 1820, d 8 May 1901; res. Leraysville, Pa., & NH; m 19 July 1849 Eunice Wood.

FAM. 16. ZEBULON & LOIS (ANDRUS) LINES:

1 BENJAMIN VINCEN, bp 25 Sep 1798 *OxfC;* m (1) Hannah da. Abraham & Hannah English, b 23 Sep 1800 *DV*, d 3 Apr 1834 æ. 34 *DT3;* m (2) 4 Sep 1842 Polly Johnson.

(By 1): *i* Clark b 22 Nov 1821; m Nancy Cornelia ——, b c. 1828, d 10 Nov 1850 æ. 22 *DT3.*

ii Marshall, b 9 June 1824, d 16 Dec 1864 æ. 39 (in prison at Salisbury, N. C.: Co. I, 2nd Conn. Art.) *DT3.*

iii Harriet, b 2 Feb 1827.

iv Washington Irving, b 3 June 1830; m 1852 Maria Roswell.

v Benjamin F., b 9 Sep 1832, d 20 Mar 1907; m (1) 2 Jan 1853 Mary Ann Burke; m (2) 30 Mar 1856 Nancy P. Griffen, b c. 1824, d 30 Mar 1878.

2 ALVIN AUSTIN, bp 25 Sep 1798 *OxfC.*

3 SHERMAN, b 12 Nov 1798 *OxfV*, bp 10 Mar 1799 *OxfC*, d 31 Aug 1876 æ. 78 *ThomastonT;* m Harriet ——, who d 13 Mar 1871 æ. 66 *ThomastonT.*

4 THIRZA, b 3 Oct 1800 *OxfV*, bp 11 Jan 1801 *OxfC.*

5 ZEBULON MARSHALL, bp 3 Mar 1803 *OxfC*, d 23 Nov 1804 *OxfC.*

6 MARCIA, bp 2 Dec 1804 *OxfC*, d May 1805 *OxfC.*

FAM. 17. JAMES & SUSANNA (ALLING) LINES:

1 SARAH, b 4 Feb 1775 *NHV;* m James Landon.

2 JOHN, b 31 Apr 1777 *NHV*, d 19 May 1847 æ. 70 *WdD;* m 8 Jan 1800 Betsey da. David & Anna (Beecher) Perkins, b c. 1780, d 6 June 1851 æ. 71 *WdD.*

i Charles, b 15 Nov 1800 *F*, d 11 July 1857 æ. 57 *WdD;* m Asenath da. Marshall & Abigail (Brockett) Alling, bp 10 June 1792 *WdC*, d 11 Oct 1862. Child: 1 John Marshall, b 15 Sep 1830, d 28 Mar 1894; m 21 July 1854 Adeline Curley.

ii David, b 1 July 1803 *F*, d 2 June 1862 æ. 60 (at Niagara Falls) *WdD;* Capt.

iii Anna, b 27 Oct 1805 *F*, d 10 Mar 1880 æ. 74-5 *NHV;* m 19 Aug 1821 *WdV*—Elihu Sperry.

iv Betsey, b c. 1809, d 7 Mar 1824 æ. 15 *WdD.*

3 ALLING, b 2 Nov 1791 *F*, d 9 Mar 1792 æ. 0-4-7 *WdT1.*

FAM. 18. ASHBEL & EUNICE (MURRAY) LINES:

1 TYRUS, b c. 1774, d 5 Nov 1832 æ. 58 *WyV;* m Mar 1796 *WdC*—

Martha da. Joseph & Jemima (Smith) Potter, b c. 1778, d 8 Jan 1866 æ. 87 *HV;* he div. her 1801; m (2) Irene ——— .

(By 1): *i* Truman; m 7 Dec 1820 *NHSupCt*—Susan ——— ; she div. him 1833.

(By 2): *ii* Thomas; m (1) Marcia ——— , who d 19 June 1826 æ. 21; m (2) 31 May 1828 *NHV*—Betsey Baldwin.

iii Betsey, b c. 1810, d 7 Nov 1836 *Wy;* m 2 Mar 1831 *Wy*—Chauncey Allen.

iv Irene.

2 ASHBEL, b c. 1780, d s. p. 13 Dec 1864 æ. 84 *SeymourV.*

3 EUNICE, b c. 1784, d 3 Oct 1816 æ. 32 *NHT1;* m Aner Thomas.

4 MARTHA, b c. 1786, d 19 Sep 1870 æ. 85 *NHT1;* m (1) ——— Palmer; m (2) James McHoggan.

5 ASENATH, b c. 1789, d 11 Apr 1857 æ. 68 *DT1;* m (1) Jan 1808 (at D) *ConnH*—John Canfield; m (2) Samuel Carrington.

6 TRUMAN, d s. p.

7 PHILEMON, b 1794 *NHT2*, d 1854 *NHT2;* m Abigail Watrous, b 1800 *NHT2*, d 1871 *NHT2*. Children: Clark (m Elizabeth Cooper), Jane, Eunice, Eliza B. (m George H. LaForge), Lucinda, Henriette, Kate, Grace, Emily (m Loyal B. Todd), Adeline (m Loyal B. Todd), Frederick (d. y.).

FAM. 19. EZRA & LUE (WHEATON) LINES:

1 POLLY, b 28 Mar 1783 *F*, d 12 June 1791 *F.*

2 HENRY, b 2 Sep 1784 *F*, bp 4 Aug 1794 (æ. 10) *NHx*, d 19 Dec 1835 *F*, 19 Dec 1836 æ. 52 *NHT1;* Rev.; m 6 Feb 1806 *NHx*, 1805 *F*—Amelia P. Tooker, who d 17 Jan 1861 æ. 76 *NHT1.*

i Henry Shelden, b 15 June 1806 *F*, d 11 Mar 1834 *F.*

ii Amelia Elizabeth, b 1 Feb 1812 *F*, d 18 Apr 1813 *F.*

iii Luther Rice, b 27 June 1815 *F*, d 31 Mar 1846 *F.*

iv Amelia Elizabeth, b 3 Feb 1823 *F*, d 11 Nov 1829 *F.*

3 BETSEY, b 21 Feb 1788 *F*, bp 4 Aug 1794 (æ. 6) *NHx*, d 10 July 1828 (at Cincinnati, Ohio) *F;* m 10 Aug 1806 *NHx*—Jacob Wolf.

4 POLLY, b 12 June 1791 *F*, d 1 Oct 1791 *F.*

5 LUE WHEATON, b 28 Sep 1792 *F*, bp 4 Aug 1794 (æ. 1½) *NHx*, d 25 Jan 1858; m 16 Nov 1809 Eli Trowbridge.

FAM. 19. EZRA & ABIGAIL (RAY) LINES:

6 MARTHA, b 17 Oct 1795 *F*, bp 18 Mar 1796 (æ. 0-5) *NHx*, d 11 Apr 1796 *NHx.*

FAM. 19. EZRA & ELIZABETH (UMBERFIELD) LINES:

7 EZRA AUGUSTUS, b 13 Sep 1797 *F*, "child" bp 24 Jan 1798 *NHx*, d 31 Dec 1887 æ. 90 *NHT1;* m (1) 11 June 1820 *NHV*—Lucy Ann Ritter, b 5 Mar 1803, d 16 June 1851; m (2) Martha Kimberly, b c. 1819, d 29 Oct 1902. Children by 1st w.: Augustus, b 4 Nov 1822 *F;* George P., b 23 Nov 1824 *F;* Jane E., b 2 Aug 1830 *F;* by 2d w.: Martha, b 14 May 1853, Maria, b 5 Mar 1859.

8 FREDERICK, b 8 Sep 1799 *F*, bp 24 Nov 1799 *NHx*, d s. p. 1 Dec 1875 æ. 76 *NHT1;* m Nancy Bradley.

9 JAMES, b 6 Nov 1801 *F*, d 3 July 1806 *F*.
10 WILLIAM, b 6 Jan 1804 *F*, bp 30 May 1804 *NHx*.
11 JAMES UMBERFIELD, b 9 Oct 1806 *F*, bp 22 Feb 1807 (æ. 0-5) *N Hx*, d 16 Sep 1829 *F*.
12 MEHITABEL H., b 30 Sep 1808 *F*, d 1 Jan 1832 *F*.

FAM. 20. BENJAMIN & SARAH (BROWN) LINES:
1 NANCY, b 11 Dec 1784 *F*, b 1784 d 1832 *NHT3*; m George Fries, b 1777 d 1854 *NHT3*.
2 GRACE, b 21 Aug 1786 *F*; m 12 May 1806 *NHC2*—John Jones.
3 ONOMEL (?), b 5 Aug 1788 *F*
4 SALLY, b 15 Oct 1790 *F*.
5 BENJAMIN, b 2 Nov 1792 *F*, d 23 Mar 1811 (at Albany, N. Y.) *F*.
6 AMOS, b 14 May 1794 *F*.
7 JAMES, b 6 Apr 1796 *F*, d 16 Oct 1796 (at G) *F*.
8 THERESA, b 6 Aug 1797 *F*; m 18 Nov 1821 Robert Sutton.
9 JAMES, b 27 Oct 1799 *F*, d 21 Nov 1824 (at Boston, Mass.) *F*.
10 ALANSON, b 11 Feb 1804 *F*, d 23 Aug 1824 (at Rye, N. Y.) *F*.

FAM. 21. DANIEL & HANNAH (TODD) LINES:
1 MABEL, b 13 Apr 1795 *NMV*; res. Great Bend, Pa.
2 CHARLOTTE, b 21 Mar 1797 *NMV*, bp (with next 3 children) 4 July 1813 *NMC*; m Gerardus Roberts.
3 LUCY, b 19 Jan 1801 *NMV*, d 18 Apr 1846; m Wm. Albert Knapp.
4 MERCY, b 30 June 1806 *NMV*; m Alanson Canfield.
5 RICHARD DANIEL, b 25 Mar 1809 *NMV*, d 5 Jan 1845.
6 OLIVER TODD, b 11 Oct 1813 *NMV*, bp 10 July 1814 *NMC*; m Aurelia Wickes.

FAM. 22. PHILO & ——— (———) LINES:
1 HENRY.
2 WILLIAM A., b 1809, d 1885; m Betsey Ann Sullivan.
3 GEORGE.

FAM. 23. BENJAMIN & LUCY (———) LINES:
1 (probably) WILLIAM M., b 30 May 1798, d 15 Aug 1869.
2 (probably) SARAH; m 25 Jan 1821 *Sharon*—Charles Leonard Prindle.
3 (probably) CHESTER G., b c. 1803, d 15 Jan 1836 æ. 32 *Sharon*; m Sarah ——— .
4 (probably) ELIZA ANN; m 9 Sep 1829 *Sharon*—Alfred Petton.
5 LUCY, b [Nov 1810], d 12 Feb 1824 æ. 13-3 *Sharon*.

FAM. 24. DAVID & POLLY (BRADLEY) LYNES:
1 JOSEPH BRADLEY, b 21 Nov 1797, d 13 May 1873; res. Catskill, N. Y.; m (1) 21 Dec 1818 Maria ——— ; m (2) Amanda Shurman.
2 STURGES, b 25 Feb 1799, d 22 Mar 1869; res. Avon, Ohio; m 2 Jan 1821 Betsey Lindsley, b 12 Jan 1800, d 13 Oct 1849. Children: 1 Betsey Ann, b 25 Sep 1821. 2 Mary, b 25 Mar 1824. 3 Benjamin Sturges, b 15 June 1826. 4 Mary Matilda, b 24 Dec 1829. 5 Samuel David, b 27 Apr 1835. 6 Cla-

rissa Arinda, b 12 May 1837. 7 Ada Antoinette, b 9 Dec 1839.

3 RHODA, b 9 June 1801, d 8 Feb 1872; m 20 Apr 1817 John Sawyer.

4 DAVID, b 6 Apr 1806; m 3 Jan 1826 Jane ——. Child: 1 Washington.

5 POLLY, b 19 Apr 1808; m 31 Dec 1828 George A. Smith.

6 SALLY, b 1812, d 10 June 1853; m 1 Jan 1829 Harry Ryder.

7 SAMUEL, b 1812, d c. 1882; res. Middleburgh, N. Y., m (1) 28 Jan 1834 Maria ——, who d 15 Nov 1863; m (2) c. 1864 ——. Children: George, Polly Catharine, Arindy, David & 2 others.

FAM. 25. LEVERETT & SARAH (BLAKE) LINES:

1 LEVERETT H., b [Dec 1802], d 19 June 1853 æ. 49-6 *NHV*, 21 June æ. 50 *NHT1*; m Harriet [da. Frederick & Jane (Benton) Beecher], b c. 1791 (at Wethersfield), d 26 Sep 1853 æ. 62 *NHV*, 25 Sep *NHT1*. Children: 1 Leverett, m twice, d in Fla. 2 Harriet M., m Charles P. Brockett. 3 Jane, m (1) —— Houston, m (2) Wm. H. Snediker. 4 Mary E.

2 DAVID HARPIN, b c. 1805, d 14 Aug 1871; res. Delphi, N. Y.; m (1) 17 Jun 1824 *WV*—Julia Ann da. Street Hall & Martha (Bartholomew) Morse, b c. 1808, d 28 Sep 1846 *F*; m (2) c. Jan 1847 Electa Mahala (Aldrich) Hill. Children by 1st w.: 1 Henry, b 7 May 1825. 2 Augustus, b 21 June 1826. 3 David Josiah, b 19 Jan 1829. 4 James Elizur, b 17 Dec 1833. 5 Thomas Duane, b 4 Mar 1837. 6 Francis Newton, b 20 Dec 1842. 7 Helen, b 8 Nov 1845, d y. Children by 2nd w.: 8 Oscar, b 13 Mar 1848, d y. 9 Charles Arthur, b 23 Aug 1851. 10 Kate, b 14 May 1854, d y. 11 Orrin Judson, b 10 Sep 1857. 12 Fred, b 23 Dec 1862.

3 ORRIN J., b 23 Mar 1810, d 22 Mar 1889 (Painesville, O.); m (1) 29 Apr 1832 Grace Ann Sabin; m (2) Anna ——; had issue.

4 SARAH M., b 13 Feb 1813, d 12 May 1885 æ. 72 *NHV*; m Elizur H. Clark.

5 LUCY JANE, b c. 1815, d 26 July 1854 æ. 39 *NHV*.

LINES. MISCELLANEOUS. CHAUNCEY d 18 Jan 1836; m 9 Sep 1832 Mercene Humiston & had 2 das. who d young. See FAM. 8, 7, *i*. The other Chauncey (which one was s. of Cornelius?) m Hannah Bradley & had: 1 Louisa Bradley, b 1820, m John M. Finch. 2 Jerome, b 1822, d 5 Dec 1843 æ. 22 *NHT3*. 3 Lavinia Ann, b 1824, d young. 4 Caroline A., m —— Rebair. 5 Horace V. B., b 10 Mar 1828. 6 Marion I., b c. 1832. 7 Henry, b 21 Mar 1835.

LING. BENJAMIN, d s. p. 27 Apr 1673 *NHV*; m Joanna ——, who m (2) 3 Nov 1673 *NHV*—John Dixwell & d soon after. Benjamin was uncle of Ellis Mew, & of Sarah w. of John Cooper of Southampton, L. I.

LITTLE. FAM. 1. RICHARD, of NH, d 1689; m 15 Dec 1664 *NHV*—Joan, wid. Henry Humiston, who d 1692.

1 ELIZABETH, b 4 Apr 1666 *NHV*, d 23 Apr 1735 *NHV*, æ. 70 *NoH*

T1; m Nathaniel Thorpe.

2 Hannah, b 21 Oct 1667 *NHV*, d Aug 1669 *NHV*.

3 Mary, b 28 July 1669 *NHV*, bp (adult) c. Apr 1694 *NHC1*; m John Payne.

4 Hannah, b 30 Nov 1671 *NHV*, d 1726; m c. 1695 Samuel Gilbert.

5 Martha, b 29 Mar 1677 *NHV*; m Daniel Clark of New London County.

Constance who m 7 Dec 1658 *NHV*—George Ross, was perhaps sister of Richard. John, an apprentice youth, was perhaps a brother. John & Constance rem. to Elizabeth, N. J.

LITTLE. fam. 2. Edward of NoH & w. Mary [possibly da. Daniel Atwater]; their children in 1774 were Samuel & Lucy Little of NH, Thomas Little of L, Edward Little of Simsbury, Elizabeth Wallace & Mary w. Thomas Ranney of Mid, & Rebecca w. Matthew Gregory of Danbury [*NH CCt* 8:80].

1 Samuel, bp 1759 *NoHx*, d 1792; Census (NH) 1-0-0; m 11 Sep 1774 *NHx*—Martha Gray; he div. her.

i Benjamin, b 10 Mar 1776 *NHProFiles*, bp 21 Apr 1776 *NHx*; m 6 May 1800 *NHC1*—Amelia da. Stephen & Desire (Shattuck) Osborn, b 14 Mar 1780 *WV*.

A son d 22 June 1801 *NHC1*.

ii William, b 7 Apr 1778 *NHProFiles*, bp 12 July 1778 *NHx*; res. Meriden; m Susan da. Timothy & Martha (Talmadge?) Thompson.

PAGE 1528

iii Polly, bp 29 Oct 1780 *NHx*, d (as Mary) 20 Jan 1863 æ. 83 *F*; m 2 Aug 1815 (at Meriden) *F*—Divan Butler of Southwick, Mass.

iv Martha, b c. 1782, perhaps the "da." bp Mar 1787 *NHx*, d 25 Sep 1871 æ. 90 (Southwick, Mass.); m 18 Oct 1812 *F*—Gaius Vining of Simsbury.

2 Lucy, b c. 1746, bp 1759 *NoHx*, d 13 June 1832 æ. 86 *WT2*; m 30 Nov 1783 *WV*—Moses Andrews.

3 (probably) William, d 5 Aug 1759 *F&IWRolls*.

LITTLE. fam. 3. Alexander m Elizabeth da. Daniel & Elizabeth Collis, b 18 Oct 1769 (Gloucester, Mass.), d 16 Feb 1824; she m (2) 18 Oct 1807 *NHx*—William Munson.

1 Jennet, b c. 1793, d 11 Sep 1795 æ. 2 *NHT1*.

2 Jennet, b [5 Oct 1796], d 27 Oct 1802 æ. 6-0-22 *NHT1*.

LIVERMORE. John had bp *NHC1*: Samuel 15 Aug 1641, Daniel 7 Oct 1643, Daughter 1 June 1645, Mary 12 Sep 1647.

LIVINGSTON. John m Martha ———, who d 1768 *WC2*.

1 James, b 23 May 1741 (at Mid) *WV*.

2 Jane, b 5 Oct 1742 *WV*, bp 17 Oct 1742 *WC2*.

3 Mary, b 19 Apr 1744 *WV*.

4 Martha, b 5 Dec 1745 *WV*, bp 8 Dec 1745 *WC2*.

5 Agnes, b 22 June 1748 *WV*, d 7 May 1770 *WatV*; m 2 Aug 1769 *WatV*—Samuel Smith.

6 ABIGAIL, b 17 Mar 1749/50 *WV*.

7 DANIEL, b 22 June 1752 *WV*, bp 22 Oct 1752 *WC2*.

8 ISAAC, b 27 Jan 1755 *WV*, "child" bp 20 Apr 1754 *WC2*.

LONDON. AMBROSE m 9 Nov 1752 *WV*—Ann da. John & Jemima (Abernathy) Curtis, b 26 May 1728 *WV*.

1 SARAH, b 12 Apr 1754 *WV*.

2 GILES, b 5 Feb 1758 *WV*.

3 AMBROSE, b 25 June 1759 *WV;* Census (W) 1-1-2.

4 CHARLES, b 20 Sep 1762 *WV;* Census (W) 1-1-2.

5 ELEANOR, b 27 Apr 1768 *WV*.

6 JEMIMA, b 22 Apr 1770 *WV*.

LORD. JABEZ, s. of Samuel & Katharine (Ransom), b 16 Apr 1745 (Lyme), d 2 Apr 1794 *WHD;* m 14 Nov 1765 *F*—Elizabeth da. Daniel & Lydia (Thomas) Clark, b c. 1745, d 18 Feb 1826 æ. 81 *WHD*.

1 ELIZABETH, b 10 Feb 1767 *F;* m (1) Christopher Willoughby; m (2) Thomas Russell of Virgil, N. Y.

2 DORCAS, b 7 Jan 1769 *F*, d 5 Jan 1855 æ. 86 *NHV;* m Moses Beecher.

3 LYDIA, b 13 Mar 1771 *F*, d 19 Nov 1776 *F*, 2 Nov 1776 *WHD*.

4 JABEZ, b 30 Oct 1773 *F*, d 17 May 1816 *F;* m Betsey Beecher.

5 LUCY, b 5 Dec 1775 *F;* m (1) Ebenezer Johnson; m (2) Anson Clinton.

6 LYDIA, b 17 Mar 1778 *F*, d 2 June 1811; m Beecher Parmalee.

7 NATHAN, b 8 Apr 1780 *F*, d 18 Sep 1825 æ. 45 (*Methodist*) *NHV;* m 22 Apr 1804 *CC*—Roxanna Bradley.

8 CATHERINE, b 30 Apr 1784 *F*, d 31 Aug 1871 æ. 87 *NHV;* m Jabez Brown.

9 SARAH, b 8 Sep 1786 *F*, d 6 Feb 1883; m (1) Samuel Noyes; m (2) Joseph Coates.

10 RANSOM CLARK, b 2 Sep 1788 *F*, d 1 June 1835 *F*, 3 June æ. 45 *WdC;* m Charity Sperry.

LOUNSBURY. FAM. 1. JOHN of [Kingstown,] N. Y.; m Abigail da. John & Lydia (Parker) Thomas, [wid. Samuel Preston], b 21 Nov 1674 *NHV*. Family incomplete.

1 RICHARD; res. Kingstown, N. Y., 1733.

2 JOSIAH, d 1782; res. B; m 7 May 1724 *NHV*—Ruth da. John & Hannah (Cooper) Lines, b 27 Oct 1701 *NHV*, bp (adult) 5 Jan 1728/9 *NHC1*, d 3 Apr 1788 æ. 85-5-9 *BD*.

i John, b 18 Jan 1724/5 *NHV*, bp 13 Apr 1729 *NHC1*, d 20 July 1811 æ. 86 *WatV;* Census (Wat) 1-1-2; m (1) 4 Apr 1751 *NHV*, *WdC*—Ruth da. John & Elizabeth (Hayward) Perkins, b 30 May 1726 *NHV*, d 31 Oct 1763 æ. 37 *BT1;* m (2) ——, who d 24 Mar 1811 æ. 73 *WatV*. **FAM. 2**

ii Mary, b 12 Feb 1727/8 *NHV*, bp 13 Apr 1729 *NHC1*, d s. p.

iii Josiah, b 5 Aug 1729 *NHV*, bp 12 Oct 1729 *NHC1*, d before 1782; res. Salisbury; m 26 Oct 1749 *WdC*—Martha da. Isaac & Rachel (Carnes) Hotchkiss. **FAM. 3.**

iv Stephen; res. B; Census (Wd) 1-1-3; m 26 Oct 1761 *WdC*—Hannah da. Isaac & Hannah (Perkins) Sperry, b 27 May 1743 *NHV*. **FAM. 4.**

v Samuel, bp 22 Apr 1739 *NHCI*; Census (Bristol) 1-0-3; m 1763 *WdC*—Ruth da. Ebenezer & Elizabeth Tibbals; had issue, including David, Census (Bristol) 1-0-3.

vi Ruth, bp 5 July 1741 *NHCI*, d 16 Apr 1835; m (1) 20 Sep 1759 *WdC*—Nehemiah Tolles; m (2) Dan Hine.

vii Timothy, bp 1 May 1743 *WdC*, d 1828; Census (Wd) 2-0-2; m Hannah da Nathan & Hannah (Tibbals) Smith, who d c. 1828. **FAM. 5.**

viii Daniel, bp 31 Jan 1748 *WdC*; m Betty da. Isaac & Katharine (Cook) Smith, b 20 Mar 1755 *NHV*.

ix Esther, bp 19 Aug 1750 *WdC*; m c. 1783 Daniel Strong of Wy.

FAM. 2. JOHN & RUTH (PERKINS) LOUNSBURY:

1 JAIRUS, b 14 Jan 1752 *NHV*, bp 3 May 1752 *WdC*, d c. 1848; Census (Maidstone, Vt.) 2-2-3; m Amelia Chapman.

i Collins, b 19 July 1783 *F*. d 1863; res. Vt.

ii Clarissa, b 11 Feb 1791 *F*; m John Gamsby.

iii Betsey, b 11 Aug 1794 *F*; m Harvey Finch.

iv Victory, b 8 Sep 1795 *F*, d 25 Nov 1868.

v Sally, b 13 Apr 1800 *F*; m Russell Moulton.

vi Crownage, b 20 May 1803 *F*; m 14 Feb 1831 *F*—Eliza Samantha Hotchkiss of Wd.

vii David, b 15 Aug 1805 *F*, d 1 Apr 1877.

2 BENJAMIN, b 11 Apr 1753 *NHV*, bp 10 June 1753 *WdC*.

3 RICHARD, b 20 Aug 1754 *NHV*, d 2 Sep 1782 ("of Wallingford") *RevWRolls*.

4 ITHIEL, b 15 July 1756 (?) *F*; "went west"; m 10 Apr 1796 *OxfC*—Betsey da. Joseph & Ann (Canfield) Riggs, b 26 Jan 1777 *DV*. Family incomplete.

i Joseph, bp 15 Oct 1797 *OxfC*.

ii Edmund, bp 16 Apr 1802 *OxfC*, "child" d 23 Oct 1805 *OxfC*.

iii David, bp 24 June 1804 *OxfC*.

iv Edmund, bp 31 Aug 1806 *OxfC*.

5 (probably) JOSIAH, d 24 Feb 1776 (apprentice of Asa Leavenworth, in camp at Boston) *WtnD*.

6 ETHAN, b 10 Sep 1760 (?) *F*, d s. p.

7 RUTH; m James Cooper of L.

FAM. 3. JOSIAH & MARTHA (HOTCHKISS) LOUNSBURY:

1 LINUS, bp 3 Mar 1751 *WdC*, "Mr. Lounsbury of D" d 3 Sep 1832 æ. 83 (*Meth*) *NHV*; Census (Wd) 1-3-1; res. Beacon Falls; m 1783 *F*—Prudence Scott.

i Josiah, b 1785 *F*; m Sarah da. Erastus & Sarah (Doolittle) Lines, b 29 May 1788 *CV*, d 15 May 1847 æ. 59 *DT4*.

Children: (1) Harriet, b c. 1817, d 26 May 1853 æ. 36 *DT4;* m Willis Umberfield. (2) Caroline, b c. 1821; m Jesse Hotchkiss. (3) Ransom, b 30 Jan 1828 *F;* m 25 Aug 1847 Mary Joyce.

ii Calvin, b 1786 *F.*

iii Amelia, b 1788 *F;* m Daniel Davis.

iv Ansel, b 1790 *F.*

v Lyman, b 1791 *F.*

vi Esther, b 1793 *F;* m Edmund Mallory.

vii Martha, b 1795 *F;* m Titus Smith.

2 MARY, b 31 Mar 1753 *SalisburyV;* m Jedediah Atwood.

3 RACHEL, b 3 Sep 1755 *SalisburyV,* d (at Lee, Oneida Co., N. Y.); m Nicholas Porter; had 16 children.

FAM. 4. STEPHEN & HANNAH (SPERRY) LOUNSBURY:

1 ELIAS; Census (Wd) 1-2-1; m (1) Appalina Judd; m (2) Mary da. Edward & Mary (Thomas) Perkins, b 13 Jan 1771 *NHV,* d 5 Jan 1859 æ. 88 *BT4.* Family incomplete.

(By 1): *i* Elias, b c. 1784, d 1 Jan 1869 æ. 84 *NHT2;* m Harriet da. Felix & Phebe (Downs) Downs, b c. 1792; d 16 July 1866 æ. 74 *NHT2.*

(By 2): *ii* Major, b c. 1793, d 1 May 1863 æ. 70 *BT2;* m Hannah Beeecher, who d 5 Mar 1876 æ. 77 *BT2.*

iii (perhaps) Obadiah, b c. 1795, d 18 Mar 1837 æ. 42 *BT4;* m Rebecca, da. John & Anna (Sperry) Wooding, b c. 1794, bu. 6 Oct 1876 æ. 82 *Bx;* she m (2) Harmon Alling.

2 HEZEKIAH, b c. 1771, d 1841 æ. 70 *NHV;* m Mary nat. da. Damaris Punderson, bp 5 June 1774 *NHC2.*

3 PENE, b c. 1774, d 29 May 1842 æ. 62 *Bx.*

4 IRENE.

FAM. 5. TIMOTHY & HANNAH (SMITH) LOUNSBURY:

1 LUCY; m James Hotchkiss.

2 HANNAH F.; m Robert R. Russell.

3 TIMOTHY, b 24 Jan 1770 *BT2,* d 6 Jan 1856 *BT2;* Census (Wd) 1-0-2; m (1) Hannah da. David & Hannah (Lines) French, b 16 Jan 1770 *BT2,* d 23 Apr 1839 *BT2;* m (2) Sally da. Asa & Esther (Tuttle) Sperry, wid. Aner Sperry & Joel Hine, b 11 Apr 1770 *WdV,* d 29 Apr 1847 æ. 77 *BT2.*

(By 1): *i* Dorcas, b July 1788 *F;* m Jabez Wilcox.

ii Timothy, b 25 Mar 1791 *F;* m Mary Ann Clark.

iii Lewis, b 1793 *F;* m Charity da. Amos Clark.

iv Daniel, b 1795 *F;* m Sarah da. David & Sarah Wooding.

v Jesse, b Dec 1796 *F;* m Bede da. Jesse & Mary (Peck) Bradley.

vi Hannah, b 1799 *F;* m Herschel Sanford of Ppt.

vii Smith; m 11 Feb 1824 Jennett Tomlinson.

viii Allen, b 1803 *F;* m Maria da. Elam Cook.

ix Eunice, b 14 Jan 1805 *BT2,* d 12 Aug 1897 *BT2;* m (1) Vincent Brown; m (2) McDonald Fisher.

x Mary, b 14 Mar 1807 *F;* m Burrit Hitchcock.

xi John, b 16 Aug 1809 *BT2*, d 6 Apr 1895 *BT2;* M. D. (Yale 1837); m Mary Church, b 11 Oct 1810 *BT2*, d 23 Sep 1889 *BT2*.

xii George, b 23 Nov 1812 *BT2*, d 27 Jan 1887 *BT2;* m Mary Austin of Ppt.

4 Eri, b c. 1772, d 11 Aug 1836 æ. 64 *BT2;* m Sarah da. Abraham & Rebecca (Johnson) Carrington, bp 31 Jan 1776 *NHx*, d 23 Dec 1841 æ. 67 *BT2*,

i Sally, b c. 1797, d 1 Aug 1872 æ. 75 *DT4;* m Lyman Wheeler.

PAGE 1247

ii Abraham, b c. 1799, d 27 Apr 1860 æ. 61 *BV;* m Emily da. David & Polly B. (Peck) Perkins.

iii Rebecca, b c. 1800, d 11 Jan 1880 æ. 79 *HT3;* m Asa Bradley.

iv Lucy, b c. 1803, d 30 June 1837 æ. 34 *BT2*.

v Isaac; res. Meriden; m Lodema ——— .

vi Lucretia; b 29 June 1807 *F*, d 26 Nov 1874 (at Naugatuck); m 15 Dec 1827 Selden Hoadley.

vii Polly; m Miles Horton.

viii Harriet; m William Todd.

ix William H., b 30 Dec 1815 *F*, d 14 Nov 1900 æ. 85 *BT5;* m (1) Charity Buckingham, who d 21 Oct 1865 æ. 52 *BT5;* m (2) 8 Sep 1873 Susan Beard.

5 Eunice, b c. 1781, d 3 Sep 1804 æ. 23 *BT1;* m Truman Prince.

6 Micah, b [b Feb 1786], d 4 June 1788, æ. 2-3-29 *BD*.

PAGE 1247

LOVE. FAM. 1. William, b c. 1765, d 15 Nov 1831 æ. 66 *NHT1*, 18 Nov (*NHC1*) *NHV;* m Abi, wid. Zenas Brace, b c. 1763, d 20 Oct 1841 æ. 78 *NHV* & *NHT1*. Abi's will named da. Huldah w. Bazel Munson, da. Abi Slade & s. Wm. Love.

1 William, b c. 1793, d 4 May 1859 æ. 66 *NHT1;* m Charlotte ———, who d 18 Feb 1848 æ. 55 *NHT1*.

2 Adam, bp 4 June 1797 *NHC1*, d 19 June 1819 æ. 22 (drowned) *NHT1*.

LOVE. FAM. 2. Joseph, bp (adult) 17 Aug 1803 *NHx;* m 23 Feb 1794 *NHC1*—Martha da. Hezekiah & Martha (Bradley) Tuttle, b 7 July 1764 *NHV*, d 23 Sep 1823.

1 Hepsibah Smith, b c. 1794, bp 17 Aug 1803 (æ. 11) *NHx*.

2 Daughter, b [Mar 1795], d 7 Aug 1795 æ. 0-4 *NHC1*.

3 Son, b c. 1797, d 18 Aug 1803 æ. 6 *NHC1*.

4 Charles, b c. 1799, bp 17 Aug 1803 (æ. 4) *NHx*, perhaps identical with above.

5 Daughter, b c. 1801, d 3 Aug 1803 æ. 2 *NHC1*.

6 Elizabeth, b [Mar 1802], bp 17 Aug 1803 (æ. 0-17) *NHx*.

LOW. Andrew, d 14 Apr 1670 *NHV;* m (1) ———, by whom he had a s. Andrew in Eng.; m (2) Joan, wid. Henry Peck.

LUCAS. MISCELLANEOUS. Augustus, b c. 1707, d Aug 1737 æ. 30 (in W. I.) *NHT1;* m 10 Mar 1734/5 (at NH) *Stx*—Mary da. Henry & Abigail

(Flagg) Canner, b c. 1715, d 8 Mar 1797 æ. 83 *NHx*, 8 Mar 1798 æ. 85 *NHT I*. Children: 1 Mary, b 8 Dec 1735 *NHV*, bp 22 Jan 1736 *Stx*, d 20 June 1822 æ. 89 *NHT1*; m James Abraham Hillhouse. 2 Augustus, b [Nov 1737], d 27 Sep 1738 æ. 0-10 *NHT1*......EBENEZER m Sarah da. John & Jerusha (Hall) Mattoon, b 3 Oct 1707 *WV*......WILLIAM m 21 Aug 1764 *NHC2*—Huldah Ranney of Mid.

LUDDINGTON. FAM. 1. WILLIAM, b c. 1607, d 1661; res. Malden, Mass., & EH; m Ellen sister of Matthew Moulthrop, b c. 1619; she m (2) 1663 *NHV*—John Rose, Sr.

1 THOMAS, b c. 1637; rem. to Newark, N. J.; see FAM. 11.

2 JOHN, b c. 1640.

3 MARY, b 6 Feb 1643.

4 HENRY, d s. p. 1676.

5 HANNAH; m George Tyler of Bd.

6 WILLIAM, b c. 1655, d 1736 *EHV* (Feb 1736/7); m (1) Martha [da. John Rose]; m (2) June 1690 Mercy Whitehead, who d 23 Nov 1743 *EHV*.

(By 1): *i* Henry, b c. 1679, d 1727; m 20 Aug 1700 *NHV*—Sarah da. William & Sarah (Morrell) Collins, b 31 Dec 1679 *NHV*, d 31 Mar 1743 *EHV*. **FAM. 2.**

ii Eleanor, d 31 May 1748; m 13 May 1714 Nathaniel Bailey.

iii William, b 25 Sep 1686 *NHV*; rem. to Wat; m 28 Feb 1710/1 *NHV*, 1 Mar 1711 *EHV*—Anna [sister of Charles?] Hodges. **FAM. 3.**

iv Mercy; m 17 Mar 1707 Ebenezer Deanes of Norwich.

(By 2): *v* Mary, b last May 1691 *EHV*; m 1715 John Dawson.

vi Hannah, b 13 Mar 1693 *EHV*, d 11 June 1719 æ. 27 *EHT*; m Isaac Penfield.

vii John, b 31 Jan 1694 *EHV* [1694/5], d 30 Oct 1726 *EHV*; m Elizabeth da. John & Elizabeth (Holt) Potter b 24 Sep 1697 *NHV*, d 3 Sep 1746 *EHV*; she m (2) 7 Oct 1734 *NHV*—Thomas Wheaton of Bd. **FAM. 4.**

viii Eliphalet, b 28 Apr 1697 *EHV*. d 26 Jan 1761 æ. 64 *EHT*; m 20 Aug 1721(?) Abigail da. Daniel & Abigail (Thompson) Collins, b 14 Sep 1700 *NHV*, d 12 Dec 1790 æ. 91 *EHC*. **FAM. 5.**

ix Elizabeth, d 28 July 1707 *EHV*.

x Dorothy, b 16 July 1702 *EHV*, d 19 Sep 1742 *EHV*; m Benjamin Mallory.

xi Dorcas, b 16 July 1702 *EHV*; m 1722 James Way.

7 MATTHEW, b 16 Dec 1657, d 12 Jan 1657/8.

FAM. 2. HENRY & SARAH (COLLINS) LUDDINGTON:

1 DANIEL, b 21 June 1701 *NHV*, *EHV*; rem. to W; m (1) 28 Dec 1726 *NHV*—Hannah da. John & [Mary (Little)?] Payne, b 10 Nov 1708 *NHV*, d 17 Sep 1739 *NHV*; m (2) 14 Oct 1741 *NHV*, *WC2*—Susanna da. Ebenezer & Elizabeth (Parker) Clark, b 30 Sep 1717 *WV*.

(By 1): *i* Daniel, b 22 Feb 1726/7 *NHV*, d 1736 æ. 9 *EHV*.

ii Ezra, b 21 Dec 1728 *NHV*, d 9 Dec 1755 *WV;* m 18 Jan 1753 *WV*—Mary da. Daniel & Esther McKay. Child: 1 Eunice, b 31 Dec 1753 *WV;* m 4 Oct 1787 *EHC*—William Sanford Bailey.

iii Solomon, b 3 Nov 1732 *NNV;* rem. to Southampton, Pa.

iv Hannah, b 4 Nov 1734 *NHV;* m 5 Feb 1755 *WV*—Abraham Morgan.

(By 2): *v* Phebe, b 19 Nov 1742 *NHV;* m 6 Feb 1766 *WV*—David Sturges of Danbury.

vi Daniel, b 9 May 1744 *NHV;* m 26 Apr 1773 *FarmV*—Mabel Lee.

vii Titus, b 13 Sep 1747 *NHV*, d after 1805; rem. to Manchester, Nova Scotia; m 15 July 1772 *WV*—Miriam da. Arnon & Abigail (Doolittle) Parker, b 20 Oct 1747 *WV*, d between 1800 & 1805. Children: 1 Sena, b 20 July 1773 *WV;* m Alexander Henderson. 2 Jared, b 11 Dec 1775 *WV*. 3 Miriam, b 8 June 1778 *WV*, d s. p. 4 Bede, b 13 Sep 1780 *WV;* m John Conrad Demas. 5 Miriam, b 30 Jan 1783 *WV;* m ——— McIntosh.

viii Collins, b 9 June 1750 *WV*, d 3 Jan 1750/1 *WV*.

ix Collins, b 19 Mar 1752 *WV*, d 1821 (Candor, N. Y.); rem. to Oswego, N. Y.; m 9 Feb 1775 *FarmV*—Sarah Smith.

x John, b 13 June 1754 *WV*, d 26 July 1756 *WV*.

xi John, b 17 Aug 1756 *WV*.

xii Susanna, b 13 Jan 1763 *WV*, d 27 Oct 1772 *WV*.

2 WILLIAM, b 6 Sep 1702 *EHV*, 6 Sep 1703 *NHV;* res. Bd; m (1) 5 Nov 1730 *BdV*—Mary da. Nathaniel & Mary (Hunt) Knowles, b Sep 1713 *WindhamV*, d 16 Apr 1759; m (2) 17 Apr 1760 Mary Wilkinson.

(By 1): *i* Submit, b 10 Feb 1732/3 *BdV;* m 28 June 1754 *BdV*—Stephen Johnson.

ii Mary, b 20 May 1736 *BdV*.

iii Henry, b 25 May 1739 *BdV*, d 24 Jan 1817 æ. 78 *Patterson, Putnam Co., N. Y., T;* m Abigail [?da. Elisha Luddington], who d 3 Aug 1825 æ. 80-3 *Patterson T*.

iv Lydia, b 25 July 1741 *BdV;* m 20 Oct 1761 *EHC*—William Buckley ("Aaron" in record).

v Samuel, b 30 Apr 1744 *BdV;* m 5 Mar 1766 *Wy*—Ruth Galpin. Child: William, b 23 Nov 1766 *Wy*.

vi Rebecca, b 10 May 1747 *BdV*, d 20 May 1754 *BdV*.

vii Ann, b 20 June 1750 *BdV*, d 20 May 1754 *BdV*.

viii Stephen, b 18 Oct 1753 *BdV*.

3 SARAH, b 3 Feb 1703 *EHV* [1703/4], d 27 Mar 1709 *EHV*.

4 DINAH, b 16 Jan 1704/5 *EHV*, d c. 1743; m 5 Oct 1725 *NHV*—Isaac Thorpe.

5 LYDIA, b 9 Feb 1706/7 *EHV*, d 27 July 1794 æ. 88 *NoHC;* m 5 Dec 1732 *NHV*—Moses Thorpe.

6 NATHANIEL, b 20 Apr 1708 *EHV;* m (1) Mary da. John & Mary Foote, wid. John Chidsey, b c. 1696, d 7 May 1758 æ. 62 *EHT;* m (2) Eunice da. Samuel & Mary (Hemingway) Russell, wid. Thomas Smith.

(By 1): *i* Lucy, b 31 Jan 1731/2 *EHV*, d 22 Dec 1803 æ. 71 *EHC;* m Russell Grannis.

(By 2): *ii* Eunice, bp 19 Aug 1759 *EHC*, d 13 Apr 1838 æ. 79 *NHT3;* m 4 Oct 1781 *EHV*—Matthew Rowe.

iii Nathaniel, bp 29 Nov 1761 *EHC.*

iv Mary, bp 13 Nov 1763 *EHC.*

v Stephen, bp 30 Mar 1766 *EHC.*

7 MOSES, b 8 Oct 1709 *EHV*, d 30 July 1758 *F&IWRolls;* m Sarah da. John & Mary (Foote) Chidsey, b 6 Dec 1716 *EHV*, d 4 Oct 1777 *PC.*

i David, b 28 Aug 1733 *EHV*, d 31 Oct 1821 æ. 89 *PT;* m (1) 4 Dec 1755 *WatV*—Lois da. Samuel & Elizabeth (Humiston) Bassett, b 9 Dec 1724 *NHV*, d 7 July 1799 æ. 75 *PC;* m (2) 14 Dec 1800 *NoHV*—Elizabeth da. Samuel & Elizabeth (Alcott) Humiston, div. w. Oliver Blakeslee, b 13 Apr 1745 *NHV.* **FAM. 6.**

ii Jerusha, b 23 Aug 1735 *EHV*, d s. p.

iii Comfort.

iv Aaron, b 19 Apr 1739 *EHV;* rem. to Dutchess Co., N. Y.; m (1) 19 Feb 1761 *WatV*—Sarah da. John How, wid. Cephas Ford; m (2) 21 Nov 1791 *PC*—Sarah Loomis, wid. Lemuel Fancher. Children (incomplete): 1 Polly, b 19 Apr 1762 *WatV.* 2 Content, b 9 Apr 1769 *WatV.* 3 (perhaps) Huldah, m 13 Feb 1794 *WtnV*—Edward Kellogg.

v Nathaniel, b c. 1741, d 4 Feb 1772 (killed) *PC;* m 1 Dec 176[-] *WV*—Elizabeth da. Daniel & Esther McKay, who d 12 Sep 1777 *WV;* she m (2) 8 July 1774 *WV*—Asa Brown. Child: 1 Rebecca, b 9 Oct 1764 *WV.*

vi Mary, b 27 May 1744 *WatV;* [m 26 Sep 1779 *PC*—Ephraim Camp].

vii Jerusha, b 4 Oct 1746 *WatV;* m Wm. Wetmore.

viii Sarah, b 27 June 1748 *WatV*, d 19 Apr 1777 *PC;* she had a nat. child: 1 Molly, b 16 Apr 1766 *WatV.*

ix Moses, b 4 Aug 1750 *WatV.*

x Lucy, b 15 Jan 1753 *WatV;* she had a nat. child 1773 *NHCCt.*

xi Luman, b 20 Mar 1757 *WatV.*

xii Eunice, b 22 Feb 1759 *WatV.*

8 AARON, b 16 Jan 1710 *EHV* [1710/1], d s. p. before 1755.

9 ELISHA, b 29 Aug 1712 *EHV*, d 27 Mar 1714 *EHV.*

10 SARAH, b 6 Mar 1714 *EHV.*

11 ELISHA, b 7 Jan 1715/6 *EHV;* rem. to Phillip's Precinct, N. Y.; Census (Fishkill, N. Y.) 2-0-4.

12 THOMAS, b c. 1718, d 30 May 1743 (drowned) *EHV.*

FAM. 3. WILLIAM & ANNA (HODGES) LUDDINGTON:

1 MATTHEW, b 23 Apr 1712 *EHV*, d c. 1752; m Lydia da. William & Mary (Collins) Smith, b 4 Feb 1711/2 *EHV*, d 6 Feb 1794 æ. 84 *EHC.*

i Mabel, b c. 1734, d 12 Sep 1791 æ. 57 *EHC;* m Isaac Mallory.

ii Joseph, b c. 1736, d 20 Feb 1801 æ. 65 (fell from tree) *WtnD;* m 3 Mar 1754 *WatV*—Mercy (Northrop) Peck. Child: 1 Rachel, b 8 Feb 1759 *WatV.*

iii Timothy, "of G, k. iu battle at EH" 5 July 1779 *EHC;* m 13 Oct 1762 *GC*—Ruth Spencer.

iv Samuel, b [May 1741], d 13 Jan 1832 æ. 90-8 *EHC;* m 4 Dec 1787 *EHC*—Desire Barnes. A child d 3 Dec 1791 *EHC.*

2 RUTH, b 7 June 1713 *EHV;* m 15 June 1735 *WatV*—Jonathan Cook.

3 NAOMI, b 15 Dec 1716 *EHV;* m (1) 26 June 1740 *WatV*—Josiah Tuttle; m (2) 6 Dec 1751 *WatV*—Gideon Allen; m (3) ——— Blakeslee.

4 ELIZABETH, b 9 Feb 1719/20 *EHV;* m 5 Apr 1755 *WatV*—Wm. Fancher.

5 ABRAHAM, b 30 Nov 1721 *EHV*, d 20 Oct 1758 *WatV;* m 23 July 1747 *WatV*—Catherine da. Ebenezer Elwell; she m (2) 18 July 1761 *WatV*—Jonathan Preston.

i Ann, b 2 July 1748 *WatV.*

ii Asa, b 6 Mar 1749/50 *WatV.*

iii Ruth, b 27 Feb 1752 *WatV;* m 10 May 1781 *PC*—Josiah Curtis.

iv Mehitabel, b 27 Sep 1754 *WatV*, d 17 Oct 1756 *WatV.*

v Mehitabel, b 23 Nov 1757 *WatV.*

6 SAMUEL, b 10 Aug 1723 *EHV.*

7 JOSEPH, b 3 Apr 1726 *EHV.*

FAM. 4. JOHN & ELIZABETH (POTTER) LUDDINGTON:

1 JOHN, b 8 Feb 1720/1 *EHV*, d 7 Nov 1753 *EHV.*

2 ELIZABETH, b 26 June 1723 *EHV;* m 15 Mar 1739 John Rose.

3 JUDE, b 23 July 1725 *EHV;* Census (West Springfield, Mass.) 2-1-3; m (1) Martha da. Daniel & Hannah (Johnson) Page; m (2) Mary (Wade) Frisbie.

FAM. 5. ELIPHALET & ABIGAIL (COLLINS) LUDDINGTON:

1 JESSE, b c. 1722, d 8 Feb 1799 æ. 77 *EHC;* Census (EH) 2-1-3; m (1) c. 1749 Mehitabel da. John & Martha (Tuttle) Smith, b 17 Apr 1726 *NHV*, d 19 Oct 1793 æ. 69 *EHC;* m (2) Thankful ———, b c. 1727, d 1 Oct 1817 æ. 90 *EHC.*

(By 1): *i* Lydia, b c. 1751, d 1813 *EHC*, 23 Aug 1813 æ. 67(?) *EHR;* m (1) 4 Oct 1770 *EHC*—Edward Goodsell; m (2) 24 Feb 1783 *EHC*—Thomas Shepard.

ii Elam, b c. 1754, d 1784 æ. c. 30 *EHC;* m 8 Dec 1774 *EHC*

—Rachel da. Timothy & Anna (Washburn) Tuttle, b c. 1756, bp (adult) 13 Feb 1785 *EHC*, d 1 Oct 1827 æ. 71 *BT3;* she m (2) 12 Apr 1792 *EHC*—David Burnham. "Naomi Smith da. Rachel Ludinton" b 3 Mar 1787 *EHV;* "Naomi da. Wid. Rachel Tuttle" bp 6 Sep 1789 *EHC*. **FAM. 7.**

iii Eliphalet, b c. 1756, d 4 Oct 1838 æ. 84 *Bethlehem;* m (1) 9 June 1777 *EHC*—Sarah da. Israel & Mary (Dawson) Potter; he div. her 1786, calling himself late of L now of EH; Census (L) 1-1-3, m (2) ——— , who d 3 Nov 1835 æ. 72 *Bethlehem*. Children: 1 Jairus, b c. 1777, d 20 May 1822 æ. 46 *Bethlehem;* m Anna ——— . 2 Sarah. 3 Eunice & 4 Lois, twins. 5 Eliphalet.

iv Jesse, bp 23 Apr 1758 *EHC*, d 1 Jan 1841 æ. 83-11 *EHC;* Census (EH) 1-0-3; m (1) 10 Aug 1779 *EHC*—Thankful da. Caleb & Mabel (Moulthrop) Chidsey, b 20 May 1760 *EHV*, bp (adult) 11 Aug 1782 *EHC*, d 25 Oct 1796 æ. 37 *EHC;* m (2) Sarah da. Samuel & Sarah (Denison) Moulthrop, b 13 Jan 1764 *EHR*, d 22 Oct 1845 æ. 81-9 *EHC*. **FAM. 8.**

v Mehitabel, bp 14 Dec 1760 *EHC*, d 16 Feb 1854 æ. 94; m 1781 *EHC*—Stephen Bradley.

vi Abigail, bp [c. Feb] 1764 *EHC* d 10 Nov 1813 *EHC*, æ. 49 *EHT;* m Sep 1786 *EHC*—Christopher Tuttle.

vii Amos, bp 29 June 1766 *EHC*, d 16 Jan 1836 æ. 71 *NHV*,
PAGE 2048 1772-1836 *NHT3;* m 12 Feb 1791 *EHC*—Huldah Chid-
1770-1825 *NHT3*. **FAM. 9.**

2 **Elam**; m 5 May 1748 *NHV*—Anna da. Daniel Finch, b 3 Mar 1727/8 *NHV;* she m (2) 28 Feb 1754 *BdC*—Daniel Olds.

i Anna, b 6 Oct 1751 *NHV*, d 6 Aug 1821 æ. 70 *EHT;* m 8 Mar 1770 *EHC*—John Chidsey.

3 **Hannah**, b c. 1726, d 18 Feb 1789 æ. c. 63 *EHC*.

4 **Abigail**, b c. 1729, d 8 June 1768 æ. 39 *LT;* m 3 Dec 1746 *EHV* —Enos Barnes.

5 **Olive**, b c. 1731, d 7 May 1788 æ. 57 *EHC;* m Joseph Grannis.

6 **Amos**; m 7 June 1757 *EHC*—Mercy Thompson; she m (2) Philip Barnes of Kent.

i Sybil; m Joel Dawson; res. Schodack, N. Y., 1785.

ii Amy; m Ephraim Brockway; res. Schodack 1785; Census (Mohawk, N. Y.) 1-2-3.

7 **Mary**; m Amos Frisbie.

8 **Asa**, d 6 Nov 1760 (at Albany, N. Y.) *F&IWRolls*.

9 **Isaac**, b c. 1740, d 10 Jan 1782 æ. over 40 *EHC;* m Mary da. Samuel & Mary (Hotchkiss) Goodsell, b 13 Feb 1740, d 12 Nov 1820 æ. 81 *EHC;* Census, Mary (EH) 2-0-5.

i Mary, b c. 1761, bp 12 June 1774 *EHC*, d 21 Aug 1837 æ. 76 *NHT3;* m (1) Isaac Grannis; she had a da. Huldah b c. 1786; m (2) Seth Barnes.

ii Martha, bp 12 June 1774 *EHC;* m 25 July 1786 *NoHV*—Jared Grannis.

iii Isaac, b 12 Aug 1768 *F*, bp 12 June 1774 *EHC*, d 26 July 1854 æ. 86 *F;* m 9 Apr 1795 (at Bd, at house of Thomas Frisbie *NHx*—Sarah Frisbie, b 18 Sep 1774 *F*, d 4 Apr 1852 æ. 78 *F*. **FAM 10.**

iv Asa, bp 12 June 1774 *EHC*, d 1811 (in W. I.) *EHC;* m 29 Nov 1799 *EHC*—Betsey da. Jesse & Thankful (Chidsey) Luddington, b 22 Mar 1780. Children: 1 Jared, b c. 1800, "son" drowned 7 June 1803 æ. 3 *EHC*. 2 Henry, b c. 1802, "child" d 14 Mar 1803 æ. 1 *EHC*. 3 Eliza. 4 Lorinda. 5 Betsey.

v Sarah; m 2 Mar 1796 *EHC*—Josiah Howd.

vi Anna, bp 15 June 1777 *EHC;* m Jacob Hitchcock.

vii Jared; m 7 June 1798 *EHC*—Sarah Goodsell.

viii Amy.

10 AMY, d s. p.

FAM. 6. DAVID & LOIS (BASSETT) LUDDINGTON:

1 SUSANNA, b 22 Jan 1757 *WatV*.

2 LOIS, b 11 Nov 1759 *WatV*.

3 JOTHAM, b 11 July 1763 *WatV*, d 8 July 1848 æ. 85 *PT;* m (1) 27 Apr 1794 Abigail Anna Lattin, who d 13 Sep 1796 æ. 37 *PT;* m (2) 1 Feb 1798 Beulah Fairchild. Child by 1st w.: 1 Polly, b 9 Mar 1795; m 13 Mar 1816 Sherman Potter.

4 ZERAH, b 11 Aug 1768 *WatV*.

5 PATIENCE, b 27 Mar 1770 *WatV*.

FAM. 7. ELAM & RACHEL (TUTTLE) LUDDINGTON:

1 JOHN, b 26 May 1775 *EHV*, d 1 Sep 1776 *EHV*, "child" d Sep 1776 æ. 0-15 *EHC*.

2 ELAM, b 2 Nov 1777 *EHV*, bp 20 Feb 1785 *EHC;* res. Bethlehem 1818.

3 RACHEL, b 4 Sep 1780 *EHV*, 20 Feb 1785 *EHC*, d 14 Sep 1864 æ. 82 *NHT3;* m John Rowe.

4 MEHITABEL, b 21 Apr 1783 *EHV*, bp 20 Feb 1785 *EHC*, d s. p. 13 Oct 1865 æ. 82 *BT3*.

FAM. 8. JESSE & THANKFUL (CHIDSEY) LUDDINGTON:

1 BETSEY, b 22 Mar 1780; m 29 Oct 1799 *EHC*—Asa Luddington.

2 CHILD, d 1782 *EHC*.

3 CALEB, bp 9 Mar 1783 *EHC*, "only son" d 12 Dec 1788 æ. 6 *EHC*.

4 CHILD, d 9 Dec 1784 æ. 6 wks. *EHC*.

5 CHILD, d Aug 1786 æ. 1 wk. *EHC*.

6 CHILD, d Nov 1787 æ. a few days *EHC*.

7 CALEB CHIDSEY, b 22 Aug 1790 *EHV*, bp 26 Sep 1790 *EHC;* m 2 Mar 1814 *EHC*—Lucy Andrews.

8 CHILD, stillb Jan 1793 *EHC*.

9 LUCY, b 22 July 1794, bp 31 Aug 1794 *EHC*, d 12 Aug 1859 æ. 65 *EHT;* m Joseph Grannis.

10 JUSTIN, b 22 Aug 1796 *EHV*, bp 30 Oct 1796 *EHC*, d 5 Mar 1871

æ. 74 *NHT3;* m (1) Olive Grannis; m (2) 24 Aug 1820 *EHV*—Harriet Grannis, b 23 June 1800 *NHT3*, d 16 Mar 1876 *NHT 3*.

FAM. 8. JESSE & SARAH (MOULTHROP) LUDDINGTON:

11 ROXANA, b 13 Apr 1798 *F*, d 4 Apr 1883 æ. 86 *NHV;* m (1) Alfred Works; m (2) 1 May 1825 *EHV*—Roswell Augur.

12 WYLLYS.

13 SARAH.

14 NANCY.

15 LEWIS, b c. 1809, d 15 Feb 1861 æ. 51 (at EH) *NHV*.

FAM. 9. AMOS & HULDAH (CHIDSEY) LUDDINGTON:

1 HULDAH, b c. 1792, d 3 Feb 1811 æ. 19 *EHC*.

2 FANNY, b c. 1793, d 12 Apr 1844 æ. 51 *EHC;* m 23 Nov 1813 *EHC*—Matthew Rowe.

3 POLLY.

4 AMOS.

5 LEVI, b 1800 *NHT3*, d 1889 *NHT3;* m Betsey ——, b 1801, d 1849 *NHT3*.

6 SARAH; m 25 Aug 1824 *EHV*—Alfred Goodsell.

7 JESSE, b c. 1805, d 14 Sep 1886 æ. 81 *NHT3;* m Julia A. Story, who d 26 Nov 1900 æ. 90 *NHT3*.

8 ALMIRA; m 17 Sep 1823 *EHV*—John Turner.

9 ELAM.

10 MEHITABEL.

11 HULDAH.

FAM. 10. ISAAC & SARAH (FRISBIE) LUDDINGTON (from Bible record):

1 POLLY, b 11 Jan 1797, bp 17 May 1798 (æ. 1) *NHx*, d 5 Feb 1838 æ. 42; m Frederick W. Frisbie.

2 HARRIET, b 14 Jan 1799, d 3 July 1844 æ. 45 *EHC*.

3 LEVI G., b 10 Oct 1800, d 30 Nov 1833 æ. 33 *EHC;* m Oct 1828 Esther H. Pardee, b 1807, 1865.

4 ALMENA, b 15 Apr 1803, d 13 July 1841 æ. 48 *NHT3;* m 27 May 1824 *EHV*—Tyrus Bradley.

5 WILLIAM S., b 14 Dec 1805, d 5 Oct 1844 æ. 39; m 29 Aug 1835 *EHV*—Charlotte Pardee, b Feb 1812, d 1840 (at Savannah, Ga.).

6 ISAAC, b 9 May 1809, d 2 Oct 1832 æ. 23 *EHC*.

7 SARAH, b 9 May 1809, d 20 May 1887 æ. 78 *NHV;* m 26 Oct 1828 *EHV*—Reuben Tuttle.

8 ASA, b 1 Jan 1813, d 8 Nov 1835 æ. 23 *EHC*.

FAM. 11. JOHN, said to be s. of Thomas (FAM, 1, 1), d c. 1730; res. EH; m Rebecca, prob. Rebecca Clark from Island of St. Christophers.

1 JAMES, b 8 Aug 1703 *EHV*, d 3 Sep 1756 *F&IWRolls;* m 2 Jan 1734/5 *NHV*—Eleanor da. Ebenezer & Mercy (Luddington) Deanes, b 4 Feb 1709/10; she m (2) —— Parmeter & res. 1789 in Brookfield, Vt.

i Elizabeth, b 23 Apr 1737; m 18 June 1760 Zachariah Deanes of Windham; Census (Bethel, Vt.) 3-3-4.

ii David, b 19 Mar 1739, d 13 Sep 1756 *F&IWRolls.*
iii Anna, b 19 Mar 1744 *WatV.*
iv Lemuel, b c. 1748; Census (Bethel, Vt.) 1-1-2; m Hopestill ——— .
v Eunice, b 11 May 1751 *EHV.*

2 REBECCA, b 23 Aug 1707 *EHV.*

3 ABIGAIL, b 23 Aug 1707 *EHV*, d 9 Oct 1742 *EHV;* she had a nat. child b 1729 *NHCCt;* m 19 July 1736 *BdC*—Edward Canodise.

4 ELIZABETH, b 25 Sep 1710 *EHV*, d 13 Dec 1713 *EHV.*

LUFF. SARAH Jr. bp 11 Jan 1713 *StratfieldC;* m (1) 12 May 1725 *NHV*—John Elcock; m (2) 9 June 1735 (Divorce record)—Peter Brown; he deserted her 1735/6 & she div. him 1739.

LUMSDON. GEORGE m Elizabeth [prob. da. Stephen & Hannah (Leek) Hunnewell, b 23 May 1753 *NHV*]; she m (2) ——— Green.

1 ELIZABETH, bp 25 Dec 1774 (sponsors, Wm. & Sarah Harrison & Elizabeth Cables) *NHx*, d 26 May 1794 æ. 20 *NHx.*

2 GEORGE, bp 21 Apr 1776 (sponsors, Moses Ventrus & Rebecca Rebecca Cables) *NHx.*

3 SAMUEL PERKINS, bp 30 Aug 1778 (sponsors, Abiatha & Rebecca Camp) *NHx.*

LUPTON. THOMAS of Norwalk, d 1684; m [1662] *NHV*—Hannah da. Thomas & Elizabeth Morris, b 14 Mar 1641 *NHV.*

1 HANNAH, b 27 May 1665 *NHV;* m Ebenezer Blakeslee.

2 THOMAS, b 10 Apr 1670 *Fairfield Probate;* m 23 Jan 1715/6 *NHV*—Elizabeth ——— (perhaps a second marriage, or it may pertain to a younger Thomas).

***LYMAN.** MISCELLANEOUS. DOROTHY m 20 Nov 1691 *WV*—Jabez Brockett......MARY m 8 Dec 1692 *WV*—John Hall......THANKFUL m 15 Mar 1693 *WV*—Daniel Hall......EXPERIENCE m [*WV*] Henry Cook.

LYMAN. FAM. 1. DANIEL, s. of Benjamin & Thankful (Pomeroy), b Apr 1718 (Northampton, Mass.), d 16 Oct 1788 æ. 71 *NHT1;* Dea.; B. A. (Yale 1745); m (1) 6 June 1748 *NHV*—Sarah da. Joseph & Hannah (Trowbridge) Whiting, b 15 Apr 1725 *NHV*, d 1 Aug 1751 *NHV*, æ. 27 *NHT1;* m (2) 25 June 1752 *NHV*—Sarah da. Samuel & Sarah (Woodward) Miles, b 6 Aug 1731 *NHV*, d 14 Oct 1768 æ. 37 *NHT1;* m (3) Ellen da. Jonathan Fairchild, wid. Seth Benedict; she m (3) Dr. Thaddeus Betts of Norwalk & d 23 Mar 1825 æ. 95.

(By 1): 1 SARAH, b 17 Mar 1748/9 *NHV*, bp 19 Mar 1748/9 *NHC1*, d 18 Apr 1749 *NHV*, æ. 0-1 *NHT1.*

2 SARAH, b 3 May 1750 *NHV*, bp 6 May 1750 *NHC1*, d 16 Aug 1751 *NHV*, æ. 1-3 *NHT1.*

(By 2): 3 DANIEL, b 13 July 1753 *NHV*, bp 15 July 1753 *NHC1;* B. A. (Yale 1770); Maj. (British Army); m 15 Aug 1773 *NHx*—Statira da. Abiathar Camp, who d æ. 45 at St. John, N. B., formerly of NH (reported 13 Nov 1800 *ConnJournal*).

4 ROSWELL, b 9 July 1755 *NHV*, bp 13 June 1755 *NHC1*, d s. p.

5 SARAH, b 21 Dec 1757 *NHV*, bp 25 Dec 1757 *NHC2;* m Peter Colt of Hartford; res. Rome, N. Y., 1800.

6 ELIHU, b 24 Aug 1760 *NHV*, bp 24 Aug 1760 *NHC2*, d 9 Oct 1800 æ. 40 (at Rome, N. Y.) *ConnJournal;* m 26 Dec 1789 *NHx*—Polly Forbes.

i Mary, b [Dec 1790], bp 2 Oct 1791 *NHx*.

ii James Rice, bp 1 Apr 1794 (sponsors, James & Mary Rice) *NHx*.

7 HANNAH, b 9 Oct 1762 *NHV*, bp 17 Oct 1762 *NHC2*.

LYMAN. FAM. 2. MEDAD (brother of Daniel above), b 20 Mar 1722 (Northampton, Mass.), d 1776; m 8 Jan 1750/1 *NHV*—Mary da. Nehemiah & Mary (Griffen) Bassett, b 4 Feb 1732, d Nov 1802 at advanced age (at NH) *ConnJournal;* Census, Mary (NH) 0-0-3.

1 MARY, b 16 Dec 1751 *NHV*, bp 22 Dec 1751 *NHC1*, d 26 Nov 1828 æ. 77 *NHV*.

2 MEDAD, b 4 May 1754 *NHV*, bp 5 May 1754 *NHC1*, d 29 May 1757 æ. 3-0-25 *NHT1*.

3 MARTHA, b c. 1756, d 1 Feb 1829 æ. 72 *NHT1;* m 27 Nov 1784 *NHC1*—Wm. Joseph Whiting.

4 ESTHER, bp 5 June 1760 *NHC2*.

LYMAN. FAM. 3. AARON, b [8 Nov 1707], d 15 Nov 1801 æ. 94 (wanting 4 days) *WC2*, æ. 94 *WT2;* Capt.; Census (W) 1-0-1; m (1) 13 Nov 1730 *WV*—Rebecca Norton, who d 8 Nov 1748 *WV*, æ. 44 *WT2*, 9 Nov *WC2;* m (2) 6 Dec 1749 *WV*—Susanna Andrus, who d July 1786 *WC2;* m (3) 22 June 1788 *WC2*—Rebecca da. Thomas & Mary (Benham) Yale, wid. Thomas Berry & ——— Hough, who d 19 Dec 1806 æ. 90 *WC2*.

(By 1): 1 AARON, b 7 Mar 1737 *WV*, bp 13 Mar 1736/7 *WC2*, d 15 Sep 1757 *WV*, 14 Sep æ. 21 *NHT1;* B. A. (Yale).

(By 2): 2 SUSANNA, b 10 Sep 1754 *WV*, bp 15 Sep 1754 *WC2*, d 14 Oct 1821 æ. 67 *WT2;* m 17 May 1774 *WV*—Dan Collins.

LYMAN. FAM. 4. MOSES of W & S, m (1) 10 Jan 1733 *WV*—Ruth Hickox, who d 19 Aug 1734 *WV*, by whom he had Moses, b 20 Jan 1734 *WV*, d 17 Mar 1734 *WV;* m (2) June 1735 *WV*—Ruth Gaylord, by whom he had Ruth, b 23 Mar 1736 *WV*, m 2 Feb 1758 *SC*—Samuel Woodruff; m (3) 5 Feb 1739/40 *SC*—Sarah Gridley, by whom he had 7 children bp *SC*.

LYNUS. NATHANIEL, s. of Nathaniel of N. Y. City, was early in NH, settled in St; m Anna ——— .

1 NATHANIEL, b 1 Jan 1741 *LV*, d 20 Jan 1741 *LV*.

2 FREELOVE, b 23 May 1742 *LV*, d 6 Jan 1826 æ. 84 *DT3;* m (1) 18 Oct 1769 *DV*—John Lum; m (2) 18 July 1776 *DV*—Josiah Nettleton.

3 EUNICE, b 11 Aug 1744 *LV*.

4 ROBERT.

5 LOIS; m ——— French.

6 REBECCA WILCOXSON, b 5 Nov 1751 *StV*.

7 ANNA, b c. 1753, d 26 Jan 1834 æ. 80 *WdT2;* m Benajah Beach.

LYON. FAM. 1. WILLIAM, b c. 1687 (Buckinghamshire, Eng.), d Mar 1726 æ. 39 (at Barbadoes) *NHT1;* m 9 Dec 1714 *BostonV*—Experience da. John Hayward, b c. 1687, d 17 Sep 1751 æ. 64 *NHT1*.

1 WILLIAM, b 10 Apr 1716 *BostonV*, *NHT1*, d 31 Jan 1767 æ. 51

NHTI; m 9 Oct 1746 *NHV*—Elizabeth Maltbie, b 4 Sep 1724 (at Saybrook) *NHTI*, d 16 Oct 1810 æ. 87 *NHTI*.

i William, b 23 Feb 1747/8 *NHV*, bp 28 Feb 1747/8 *NHCI*, d 12 Oct 1830; Census (NH) 2-0-7; m 13 Jan 1772 *NHCI*—Lois da. Nathan & Deborah (Dayton) Mansfield, b 13 Apr 1747 *NHV*, d 28 Aug 1821 æ. 74 (*NHCI*) *NHV*. **FAM. 2.**

ii Mary, bp 23 Nov 1755 *NHCI*, d 11 Sep 1817; m 27 May 1779 *NHCI*—John Beecher.

iii Elizabeth, bp May 1757 *NHCI*, d 18 Oct 1817; m 5 Dec 1776 *NHCI*—William Mansfield.

iv John Howard, bp 31 Dec 1758 *NHCI*.

v Anna, bp 30 Nov 1760 *NHCI*, d 25 Oct 1838 æ. 78 *NHTI*; m 26 May 1787 *NHCI*—John Cook.

vi Nathaniel, b 13 Nov 1762 *NHTI*, bp 14 Oct 1762 *NHCI*, d 8 Sep 1836 æ. 74 *NHTI*; Census (NH) 2-0-4; m Sep 1788 *NHx*—Lucy da. Alexander & Sybil (Baldwin) Booth, b c. 1768, d 1 Mar 1813 æ. 45 *NHTI*. **FAM. 3.**

vii Sarah, bp 22 Sep 1765 *NHCI*; m 19 Dec 1795 *NHCI*—Eli C. Sherman.

2 Mary, b 16 Dec 1717 *BostonV*, d 16 Sep 1742 æ. 24 *NHTI*.

3 Experience, b 8 Mar 1719 *BostonV*, d 17 Sep 1757 æ. 35 (at Brunswick, N. J.) *NHTI*; m 1 Nov 1752 Rev. John Brainard.

FAM. 2. William & Lois (Mansfield) Lyon:

1 William, b 12 July 1772 *F*, bp 27 Apr 1777 *NHCI*, d 26 Oct 1841 æ. 69 *NHV*.

2 Sarah, b c. 1775, bp 27 Apr 1777 *NHCI*; m Samuel A. Law of Meredith, Vt.

3 Elizabeth, b 2 July 1777 *F*, bp 14 Sep 1777 *NHCI*, d 26 Nov 1851 æ. 74 *NHV*.

4 Mary, b 7 Oct 1780 *F*, bp 17 Dec 1780 *NHCI*, d 11 Sep 1817 (at Charleston, S. C.) *F*.

5 Sophia Barnard, b 17 Mar 1782 *F*, bp 12 May 1782 *NHCI*, d 31 Jan 1866 *F*; m Rev. James Harvey Linsley.

6 Amelia, bp 20 May 1787 *NHCI*; m Joseph Bennett.

FAM. 3. Nathaniel & Lucy (Booth) Lyon:

1 Nancy, bp 7 Oct 1789 *NHCI*, d 12 Mar 1872 *NHTI*; m John M. Garfield, who d 10 Mar 1872 æ. 81 *NHTI*.

2 Sarah B., b c. 1790, d 18 Sep 1871 æ. 81 *NHTI*; m Abiel Holmes Maltby, who d 26 May 1853 æ. 61 *NHTI*.

3 John, b [Jan 1792], d 4 Sep 1795 æ. 3-8 *NHTI*, "son" æ. 2 *NHCI*.

***MACOMBER.** FAM. 1. Abiel, s. of Wm. & Mary, b 12 Jan 1685 *Dartmouth, Mass.*, d before 1720; m Susanna da. Jeremiah & Martha Childs, b c. 1679, d 10 Mar 1758 æ. 79; she m (2) Samuel Darling.

1 Jeremiah, b c. 1711, d 20 Sep 1795 æ. 84 *NHTI*, *NHx;* Census (NH) 2-0-0; m (1) Sarah da. Samuel & Elizabeth (Smith) Cooper, b 13 Oct 1716 *NHV*, d 8 Apr 1778 æ. 62 *NHCI*, æ. 63

NHT1; m (2) 18 Jan 1794 *NHC1*—Sarah Pardee [perhaps da. Thomas & Sarah (Mansfield) Wilmot, wid. Moses Pardee, b 6 Feb 1746/7 *NHV*.]

(By 1): *i* Abiel, bp 28 Sep 1740 *NHC1;* Census (NH) 1-1-1; m Abigail Sherwood, b c. 1754, d 28 June 1816 æ. 62. **FAM. 2.**

ii Sarah, bp 8 Feb 1740/1 *NHC1*, d 30 Apr 1780 æ. 39 *NHC1;* m 21 Jan 1762 *NHV, NHC1*—Isaac Bishop.

iii Abiah, bp 13 Nov 1743 *NHC1*.

iv Thomas, bp 2 Feb 1745/6 *NHC1*, d 17 Feb 1831 æ. 85 *Col R*, 18 Feb æ. 85 (*NHC2*) *NHV*.

v Mary, bp 24 Apr 1748 *NHC1*, d 1811; m (1) 28 Dec 1769 *NHC1*—Thomas Trowbridge; m (2) John Morris.

vi Esther, bp 2 Sep 1750 *NHC1*, d 14 Aug 1829 æ. 79 *NHT1;* m 24 Oct 1771 *NHC1*—Leverett Stevens.

vii Margaret, bp 4 Feb 1752/3 *NHC1*, d 2 Apr 1834 æ. 82 *NHT1;* m 28 May 1772 *NHV*—Thomas Atwater.

viii Susanna, bp 7 Sep 1755 *NHC1*, d 11 Jan 1831 æ. 75 *NHT1;* m 27 Aug 1776 *NHC1*—Timothy Atwater.

2 Abiah, b c. 1712, d 13 Nov 1798 æ. 86 *NHC1;* m 19 Feb 1734/5 *NHV*—John Hall.

FAM. 2. Abiel & Abigail (Sherwood) Macomber:

1 Sherwood, b c. 1774, d 19 Apr 1779 æ. 5 (shot) *NHC1*.

2 (probably) Nancy; m Alanson Bartholomew.

3 Esther, b c. 1779, bp 19 July 1795 (æ. 16) *NHx;* Christopher Law.

4 Thomas, b c. 1783, d Feb 1835 æ. 52 *NHV;* m (1) 19 Dec 1804 Mehitabel Alling; m (2) 23 June 1835 Sarah Kiffe.

(By 1): *i* Merit, b 2 Nov 1805 *F*, d 12 Aug 1849 æ. 43 *NHT1;* m 11 June 1826 Julia Hulse, who d 24 Nov 1892 æ. 85 *NHT1*.

ii Henry, b 3 Nov 1807 *F*, d Mar 1851.

iii Harriet, b 3 Nov 1807 *F*, d 4 Oct 1842.

iv Wyllys, b 10 Apr 1810 *F*, d 8 Nov 1854.

v Allen, b 30 July 1813 *F*, d 2 Feb 1851.

vi Thomas, b 30 July 1817 *F*, d 19 Feb 1820 *F*.

vii Sarah, b 15 Dec 1819 *F;* m 15 July 1838 Marcus B. Foster.

viii Mehitabel, b 31 May 1822 *F;* m 29 Oct 1843 Daniel Sackett Glenny.

ix Julia Ann, b 1 Mar 1825 *F*.

5 Sherwood; m 16 Mar 1809 Comfort Somers.

6 (probably) Elizabeth, m c. 1810 John Hunt.

MAHAN. Variant, maighan. Philip, Census (NH) 1-0-0; m 7 Mar 1773 *NHx*—Susanna Killam.

MALBON. Richard, an original proprietor of NH, Magistrate, Capt. of Artillery, etc. Returned to Eng.

MALBONE. ——— m Oct 1781 *NHx*—Mary Isaacs.

MALLORY. Variant, mallery. Mr. E. B. McConnell of Newark, N. J. has collected Mallory data, and has contributed some of the items in the following record. FAM. 1. PETER MALLORY of NH, d 1698/9; m Mary [da. William & Elizabeth (Sale) Preston, bp 13 Dec 1629 Chesham, Bucks, Eng.], d Dec 1690 *NHV*.

1 REBECCA, b 18 Mar 1649 *NHV* [1649/50]; m Benjamin Bunnell.

2 PETER, b 27 July 1653 *NHV*, d 1720; rem. to St; m (1) 28 May 1678 *NHV*—Elizabeth da. William & Elizabeth (Lamberton) Trowbridge, b 5 Jan 1661 *NHV* [1661/2]; m (2) Abigail ——.

(By 1): *i* Peter, b 22 Apr 1679 *NHV*, d soon.

ii Caleb, b 3 Nov 1681 *NHV*, d 20 Aug 1716 *NMV;* m 13 Feb 1706/7 *NHV*—Miriam da. Samuel & Sarah (Kimberly) Blakeslee, b 2 May 1688 *NHV*, d 23 June 1776 *NMV;* she m (2) 13 Dec 1716 *NMV*—Thomas Pickett. **FAM. 2.**

iii Peter, b 2 Aug 1684 *NHV*, d young.

iv Elizabeth, b 27 Apr 1687 *NHV;* m 10 Dec 1712 *StV*—George Welton.

v Judith, b 2 Sep 1689 *NHV;* m 24 July 1711 *MV*—Jeremiah Canfield.

vi Benjamin, b 3 Apr 1692 *NHV;* res. Huntington; m 22 Dec 1715 *StV*—Eunice Butler. **FAM. 3.**

vii Stephen, b 12 Oct 1694 *NHV;* res. Huntington; m Mary ——. **FAM. 4.**

viii Ebenezer, b 29 Nov 1696 *NHV*.

ix Zaccheus, b 22 May 1699 *NHV*, bp 25 June 1699 *NHCl;* m 17 Apr 1722 *StV*—Sarah Rise. **FAM. 5.**

x Abigail, b 5 Aug 1701 *NHV*.

xi Achsah; m 2 Feb 1720/1 *StV*—Charles Lane.

xii Zipporah, b 15 Dec 1705 *NHV;* m 18 Mar 1731 Jeremiah Johnson.

xiii Peter, b 1 Mar 1708 *NHV;* m Mary da. Thomas & Sarah (Denman) Beardsley. It is not certain that she was mother of all the children. **FAM. 6.**

3 MARY, b 28 Oct 1655 *NHV*, d soon.

4 MARY, b 28 Nov 1656 *NHV*, bp 11 July 1663 *NHCl*, d 17 Sep 1752 æ. 96 *CTl;* m (1) Eli Roberts; m (2) 14 July 1696 *WV*—Samuel Cook; m (3) 9 Apr 1705 *WV*—Jeremiah How.

5 THOMAS, b 15 Apr 1659 *NHV*, bp 11 July 1663 *NHCl*, d 15 Feb 1690/1 *NHV;* m 26 Mar 1684 *NHV*—Mary da. John Humphreville; she m (2) 28 Nov 1694 *NHV*—Ebenezer Downs; she m (3) 3 Nov 1713 *NHV*—Thomas Carnes.

i Thomas, b 11 Jan 1685 *NHV*, d 21 July 1783 æ. 101 *Wy;* m (1) 13 Jan 1706/7 *StV*—Elizabeth da. John Bartlett, who d 5 Nov 1719 *WyV;* m (2) 10 Aug 1720 *WyV*—Hannah Minor, who d 20 Aug 1749 *WyV;* m (3) Abigail, wid. David Hurd, who d 1787. **FAM. 7.**

ii Daniel, b 2 Jan 1687 *NHV*, d 24 Apr 1760 æ. 72 *WHTl;* m c. 1715 Abigail da. Thomas & Abigail (Beardsley) Trowbridge, b 8 Apr 1695 *NHV*, d Oct 1780 (at Wy) *W*

HD; she m (2) c. 1761 Nathaniel Beecher. **FAM. 8.**

iii Aaron, b 10 Mar 1689/90 *NHV*, d 12 July 1710 (in NH) *WyV*.

6 Daniel, b 25 Nov 1661 *NHV*, bp 11 July 1663 *NHCl*, d after 1685.

7 John, b 10 May 1664 *NHV*, bp 17 May 1664 *NHCl;* m 30 Dec 1686 *NHV*—Elizabeth da. Nathaniel Kimberly, bp (adult) 19 Jan 1695/6 *NHCl;* she m (2) Benjamin Barnes of Wat.

i John, b 6 Sep 1687 *NHV*, bp 7 Oct 1695 *NHCl*, d soon.

ii Elizabeth, b 1 May 1691 *NHV*, bp 7 Oct 1695 *NHCl;* m 9 Jan 1717/8 *StV*—John Booth.

iii Rebecca, b 15 Sep 1693 *NHV*, d 23 Sep 1767; m 22 Nov 1715 *GV*—Nathaniel Hall.

iv Mehitabel, b 19 Dec 1695 *NHV*, bp 19 Jan 1695/6 *NHCl*, d 23 Oct 1794 æ. 104 *OxfC;* m 16 May 1717 *NHV*—Jonathan Griffin.

v Silence, b 13 Oct 1698 *NHV*, bp Oct 1698 *NHCl;* m 6 Aug 1719 *StV*—Nathan Hawley.

vi John, b 1 Mar 1700/1 *NHV*, d (in Indian War) *F*.

vii Obedience, b 11 Apr 1704 *NHV*, living 1785; m (1) 12 Dec 1723 *StV*—Edmund Curtis; m (2) 14 Feb 1728 *StV*—Nathan Fairchild; m (3) 20 Nov 1740 *StV*—Benjamin Sherman; m (4) 25 Dec 1763 Robert Bassett.

8 Joseph, b 1666 *NHV;* res. EH; m (1) Mercy da. Thomas & Mercy Pinion, bp (adult) 27 Sep 1696 *NHCl;* m (2) Joanna da. Peter & Hannah (Wilcoxen) Farnum, wid. Thomas Barnes, b 1687, d 13 Sep 1742 *EHV*.

(By 1): *i* Mary, b 1690 *NHV*.

ii Thankful, b Aug 1694 *NHV;* [m 7 July 172[7] *GV*—John Chamberlin, mariner].

iii Abigail, b Aug 1696 *NHV*, bp 27 Sep 1696 *NHCl*.

iv Joseph, b 5 Nov 1698 *NHV*, bp 30 July 1699 *NHCl*.

v Benjamin, b 5 Nov 1701 *NHV*, d 1763; m (1) Dorothy da. William & Mercy (Whitehead) Luddington, b 16 July 1702 *NHV*, d 19 Sep 1742 *EHV;* m (2) Mary [da. Henry & Abigail (Hodges)] Nails. Perhaps Mary d 15 Feb 1781 æ. 38 (?58) *EHC*. **FAM. 9.**

vi Hannah, b 1 Sep 1709 *EHV;* m 5 Dec 1733 *BdV*—Jonathan Byington.

9 Benjamin, b 4 Jan 1668 *NHV* [1668/9], disappeared 1690.

10 Samuel, b 10 Mar 1672/3 *NHV*, d s. p. 1711; m Mary da. Azariah & Martha Beach; she m (2) ——— Reynolds of Bd.

11 William, b 2 Sep 1675 *NHV*, bp 18 June 1676 *MCl*, d 1738; res. Fairfield; m Anna ——— ; she m (2) Nathaniel Fitch. Children bp *FairfieldC:*

i Jonathan, bp 17 Dec 1699; res. Redding; m (1) Abigail da. John & Rachel Hide, b 20 May 1702 *GreenfieldC;* m (2) 22 Sep 1755 *WestportC*—Elizabeth [?da. Stephen &

Mehitabel (Canfield) Pierson, b 12 Jan 1699 *DV*], wid. Edmund Bennett. **FAM. 10.**

ii Mary, bp 22 Aug 1703.

iii Rebecca, bp 24 Feb 1705/6; m Benjamin Williams of Fairfield.

iv Sarah, bp 11 July 1708.

v John, bp 3 Dec 1710, d 1785; res. Redding; m 10 Apr 1735 *ReddingC*—Elizabeth Adams. Children, b *FairfieldV:* 1 John, b 7 Jan 1736; Census (Redding) 1-0-3. 2 Elizabeth, b 11 Dec 1738; m ——— Hull. 3 Jonathan, b 12 Oct 1744; Census (Redding) 2-3-4.

vi Anna, bp 17 May 1713.

vii William, bp 22 Apr 1716, d 1770; res. Danbury; m Eunice da. Jacob & Hannah Gray. Children bp *Greenfield Hill C*, Fairfield: 1 Eunice, bp 13 Oct 1736; m 7 July 1760 *ReddingC*—John Clugstone. 2 David, bp 19 Mar 1737/8. 3 Deborah, bp 15 May 1743. 4 Rhoda, bp 1 Sep 1745.

viii Peter, bp 30 Nov 1718, d 1761; res. Redding; m 28 Jan 1737 Joanna Hall. **FAM. 11.**

ix Ebenezer, bp 14 May 1721, d 1762; res. Fairfield; m (1) 6 Feb 1744 Hannah Keys; m (2) Joanna ———. Children by 1st w.: 1 Anna. 2 Levi; Census (Fairfield) 1-1-4; m 3 Aug 1772 *FairfieldV*—Sarah da. Anthony Annibil & had Ebenezer b 11 Feb 1773 & Priscilla b 6 Sep 1774.

x Lydia, bp 20 Oct 1723; d young.

xi Deborah, bp 22 May 1726 *GreenfieldC;* d young.

FAM. 2. CALEB & MIRIAM (BLAKESLEE) MALLORY:

1 MIRIAM, b 23 May 1708 *NHV;* m 16 Oct 1728 *NMV*—Jonathan Hitchcock.

2 DEBORAH, b 11 May 1710 *NHV;* m 23 Apr 1730 *NMV*—Samuel Hitchcock.

3 CALEB, b 3 Aug 1712 *NHV*, d 1784; res. Roxbury & Washington; m (1) 3 Dec 1734 *NMV*—Elizabeth DeForest; m (2) 12 Sep 1755 *Wy*—Jane Weller.

(By 1): *i* Lois, b 10 Dec 1735 *NMV*, d soon.

ii Lois, b 5 Apr 1738 *NMV*, bp 9 Apr 1738 *NMC;* m 5 Apr 1764 Solomon Northrop.

iii Elizabeth, b 7 May 1743 *NMV*, bp 19 June 1743 *NMC*.

iv Eunice, b 7 Sep 1746 *NMV;* m 18 Dec 1766 *Wy*—Richard Guernsey.

v Caleb, b 23 Oct 1749 *NMV;* probably of St. John, New Brunswick, 1783; m 17 Mar 1768 *Wy*—Mary Terry.

vi Jonathan Noble, b 22 June 1752 *NMV;* rem. to Albany, N. Y.

(By 2): *vii* Miriam, b 27 May 1756 *Wy;* m 14 June 1780 *RoxburyC*—James Armstrong.

4 JOHN, b 7 Apr 1715 *NHV*, d 1793; res. Roxbury; m (1) 7 May 1740 *NMV*—Ann Woodruff of Kensington, who d 8 Aug 1778 *Wy;* m (2) 27 Apr 1779 *WashingtonC*—Elizabeth Penfield, wid. Isaac Goodsell.

(By 1): *i* Simmons, b 29 July 1741 *NMV*, d 12 Apr 1753 *RoxburyC.*

ii Sarah b 29 Dec 1742 *NMV*, bp 2 Jan 1742 *NMC* [1742/3], d 15 Apr 1753 *RoxburyC.*

iii Miriam, b 24 Sep 1744 *WyV*, bp 4 Nov 1744 *RoxburyC*, d 22 Apr 1753 *RoxburyC.*

iv Deborah, b 6 June 1746 *WyV*, bp 17 Aug 1746 *RoxburyC*, d 3 Apr 1753 *RoxburyC.*

v Hannah, b 5 Apr 1748 *WyV*, "child" bp 8 May 1748 *RoxburyC;* m 8 Feb 1764 *RoxburyC*—Jedediah Elderkin.

vi John, b 5 Oct 1750 *WyV*, bp 16 Dec 1750 *RoxburyC;* m 11 Jan 1769 *RoxburyC*—Beulah da. Abraham & Mary (Baker) Thomas, bp 24 June 1753 *RoxburyC.*

vii David, b 18 July 1752 *WyV*, "child" bp 24 Sep 1752 *RoxburyC;* m (1) 28 Dec 1773 *RoxburyC*—Lydia da. Noah & Margery (Post) Frisbie, b 17 Feb 1756 *WyV*, d 28 Nov 1793 *RoxburyC;* m (2) 20 May 1794 *NMC*—Dinah Welton, wid. David Punderson.

viii Sarah, b 4 May 1754 *WyV*, bp 7 July 1754 *RoxburyC;* m 23 Aug 1775 *RoxburyC*—Thomas Canfield.

FAM. 3. BENJAMIN & EUNICE (BUTLER) MALLORY:

1 BENJAMIN, b 5 Jan 1716 *StV*, d 1767; Dea.; res. Newtown, Washington & Kent; m Hannah ——— . [Probably she was Hannah (Burton) Beach, & his 2nd wife, not mother of his children.] Family incomplefe.

i (probably) Samuel, d 1775; m 18 Nov 1762 *KentV*—Sarah Tracy. Children, recorded *KentV:* 1 Benjamin, b 26 Apr 1764. 2 Kezia, b 23 Aug 1766; m 9 Jan 1783 *New PrestonC*—Abram Guthrie. 3 Sarah, b 11 Sep 1769. 4 Ashbel, b 5 Jan 1773.

PAGE 1247

ii Isaac, bp (without feet & but one hand) 23 Sep 1750 *NewtownC;* m 2 Aug 1775 *New PrestonC*—Silena Hurd.

iii Ithamar, bp 27 Oct 1754 *NewtownC;* Census (Washington) 1-2-3.

iv Merida, bp 15 Aug 1756 *WashingtonC.*

v Medina, b 17 Dec 1758 *F;* m Joseph Bosworth.

2 HANNAH, b 16 Sep 1718 *StV.*

3 LOIS, b 28 Feb 1720 *StV.*

4 NATHANIEL, b 14 Mar 1722 *StV*, d 6 Apr 1722 *StV.*

5 BUTLER, b 24 Feb 1723 *StV*, d 1789; res. Warren; m ——— .

i Grace.

ii Hannah.

iii Child, d 20 Sep 1751 *RoxburyC.*

iv Nathaniel.

v George, bp 15 Dec 1765 *RoxburyC*, d young.

vi Patience, bp 7 Oct 1770 *New PrestonC.*
vii Eunice, bp 29 Aug 1773 *New PrestonC.*

6 CALEB, b 19 Dec 1725 *StV*, d Mar 1816 *HuntingtonC;* Census (Huntington) 1-0-1; m 28 Feb 1753 *NewtownC*—Ann da. Ephraim & Sarah (Ford) Peck, b 3 Sep 1731, d 2 Apr 1810 æ. 78 *HuntingtonC.* Family incomplete.

i Truman, bp 2 Dec 1753 *NewtownC.*
ii Gideon; Census (Huntington) 1-2-2; m 1 Sep 1784 *HuntingtonC*—Ann Laborie.
iii (perhaps) Truman, b [20 Sep 1758], d 3 Jan 1830 æ. 71-3-14 *T;* Census (Montgomery, Mass.) 1-1-3; m 1783 Olive Hubbell.
iv Ebenezer, d 4 June 1795 *HuntingtonC;* [Census (Newtown) 2-2-3; m 20 Feb 1782 *NewtownV*—Eunice Judson. Children, recorded *NewtownV:* 1 Sarah, b 27 May 1784. 2 Clarina, b 3 Aug 1785. 3 Ebenezer, b 26 Apr 1787. 4 Laurin, b 7 Mar 1789].
v (perhaps) Lyman.
vi (perhaps) Lemuel.
vii Cyrenius [or Caleb Cyrene]; m (1) 21 Dec 1796 *SyC*—Catherine Baldwin; m (2) Dec 1806 *RoxburyC*—Anna Clark.
viii Eli, bp 9 Apr 1775 *HuntingtonC*, d 8 Nov 1856 æ. 82 *So. BritainT;* m 11 Feb 1795 *SyC*—Eunice Green, who d 24 Sep 1843 æ. 70 *So. BritainT.*

7 EUNICE, b 11 June 1729 *StV.*

8 BETTY, b 19 Nov 1731 *StV.*

9 EBENEZER, b 12 July 1734 *StV.*

10 RUTH, b 12 Aug 1736 *StV.*

11 ELIJAH, [called Elle], b 22 Jan 1738 *StV;* res. Southbury; m 23 Feb 1776 *SyC*—Sarah Ward.

i Eunice, b 6 Oct 1776 *SyV.*
ii Anna, b 24 July 1778 *SyV*, d 9 June 1788 *SyV.*
iii Mary, b 14 Oct 1780 *SyV.*
iv Ezra, b 23 Jan 1785 *SyV.*
v Bethia, b 13 Jan 1788 *SyV*, d 14 Feb 1790 *SyV.*
vi Lucy, b 25 Apr 1790 *SyV.*
vii Sally, b 3 Aug 1792 *SyV.*
viii Charles, b 2 Sep 1794 *SyV.*
ix Betsey, b 31 Jan 1797 *SyV.*

12 JOHN, b 28 May 1739 *StV*, d 28 Mar 1824 æ. 85 *Roxbury;* Census (Wy) 1-0-1; m (1) Esther Barnes, who d May 1770 *So. BritainC;* m (2) 1771 Hannah Moulthrop, "wife of John" d 27 Mar 1822 æ. 75 *Roxbury.*

(By 1): *i* Aner, b c. 1764, d 18 May 1813 æ. 49 *RoxburyC.*
ii Adna, b c. 1767, d 1848; rem. to Hamden, Delaware Co., N. Y.; m (1) 26 Nov 1788 Hamutal Ward, b 30 Sep 1764, d 2 Jan 1813 æ. 48 *RoxburyC;* m (2) Lois Beardsley of

Warren; had 10 children.

(By 2): *iii* Daniel, b 23 Dec 1774; res. Roxbury, Warren & N. Y. State; m 19 Aug 1794 *RoxburyC*—Sybil Allen.

iv John G.; m Deborah Warner.

v Elizabeth; m 13 Sep 1798 *RoxburyC*—Abel Bronson.

vi Sarah, b c. 1777, d 10 Sep 1849 æ. 72 *Roxbury*.

vii Esther, b c. 1782, d 3 Oct 1799 æ. 17 *RoxburyC*.

viii Ann; m Ashur Ward.

FAM. 4. STEPHEN & MARY (———) MALLORY:

1 MARY, b 15 Dec 1719 *StV;* m 14 Feb 1738 *StV*—Joseph Pulford.

2 BENAJAH, b 4 Jan 1722 *StV*, d 30 July 1793 æ. 71 *HuntingtonC;* Census (Huntington) 1–0–2; m 20 Jan 1743 *StV*—Elizabeth da. Henry & Sarah (Frost) Wakelee, wid. Elijah Crane, bp 11 May 1712 *StratfieldC*, d 29 Oct 1800 æ. 88 *HuntingtonC*.

i Enoch, b 8 July 1744 *StV;* m Huldah ——— & had children bp at Huntington: Elisha, 26 Nov 1769 & Jeremiah, 6 Oct 1771.

ii Eunice, b 7 Jan 1747 *StV*.

iii Sarah, b Feb 1749 *StV*, [d 28 Apr 1827 æ. 80 *HuntingtonC;* m 13 Apr 1794 *HuntingtonC*—Isaac Durand].

iv (perhaps) Daniel of M; Capt.; m Ann Green, b c. 1753, d 7 Feb 1800.

3 MOSES, b 10 Mar 1724 *StV*, d 7 Dec 1793 æ. 70 *MD;* Census (M) 2–0–1; m 19 Aug 1744 *MV*—Frances da. Samuel & Rebecca (Prichard) Oviatt, b 17 Jan 1725 *MV*.

i Moses, b 23 Feb 1744/5 (at Ripton) *MV*, d 1826 *MD;* Census (M) 1–3–4; m ———, who d 1811 æ. 70 *MD*. Had issue, doubtless including Moses 3rd, Census (M) 1–1–1.

ii Aaron, b 11 Nov 1746 *MV*, d 11 Nov 1749 æ. 3 *MT*.

iii Frances, b 29 Sep 1748 *MV*.

iv Benjamin, b 20 Nov 1750 *MV;* Census (M) 1–0–1.

v Aaron, b 23 Mar 1753 *MV;* Census (M) 1–3–3; m Margaret da. Humphrey & Margaret Colebreath.

vi Rebecca, b 12 June 1755 *MV*.

vii Annis, b 24 Jan 1758 *MV*.

viii David, b 18 Oct 1760 *MV*, d 1838 (Waterford); Census (New London Co.) 1–2–4; m 23 Feb 1778 *New London*—Amy Crooker, b 8 July 1760.

ix Samuel, b 27 Oct 1762 *MV*, d 14 Sep 1818 æ. 55 *OC*, 1818 æ. 60 *MD;* Census (M) 2–0–5; m Esther da. John & Susanna (?Gibson) Fenn, who d 24 Feb 1813 *MC2*.

x Benajah, b 22 Dec 1765 *MV*, d 2 Mar 1837 *F;* m (1) Hannah [Welch], who d 23 Oct 1808 æ. 42 *MT;* m (2) 9 Sep 1810 *MC1*—Lucy Fowler.

4 PHEBE, b 7 Mar 1726 *StV*, d 5 May 1752 *WatV;* m 6 Nov 1750 *WatV*—John Thomas.

5 OGDEN, b 18 Nov 1731 *StV*, d 1811; rem. to Wells, Vt.; m Sarah

da. Zaccheus & Sarah (Rise) Mallory, bp 5 Aug 1733 *Stx.*

i Silas; Census (Middletown, Vt.) 1-4-2.

ii Gill; Census (Wells, Vt.) 1-2-3; d 1841æ. 86 (Elbridge, N. Y.)

iii Stephen.

iv Justin.

6 AGNES, b 1 Oct 1734 *StV;* m 20 Mar 1755 *SyC*—Alexander Pettigrew.

7 AMY, b 9 June 1737 *StV.*

8 CHARITY, b Nov 1740 *StV.*

9 (perhaps) JACOB, who by w. Helena had children bp at Huntington: Abigail Helena, 20 May 1764 & Obedience, 20 May 1770.

FAM. 5. ZACCHEUS & SARAH (RISE) MALLORY:

1 NATHAN, bp 27 Sep 1724 *Stx;* res. Norwalk 1745; had w. Sarah 1786; conveyed to Lewis, John & Samuel Mallery 1803.

2 EPHRAIM, bp 27 Sep 1724 *Stx;* Census (Bennington, Vt.) 1-0-1; loyalist. Ephraim Jr., Census (Bennington, Vt.) 1-0-1.

3 JOSIAH, bp Aug 1726 *Stx.*

4 ZACCHEUS, bp 30 June 1728 *Stx;* Census (Orwell, Vt.) 1-0-1; m ——— .

i David.

ii Nathaniel; rem. to Troupsburg, Steuben Co. N. Y.

iii Sarah.

iv Amos Northrop.

v Betty.

5 DAVID, bp June 1731 *Stx*, d 1775; m Mercy ——— , who d 7 Sep 1830 æ. 99 *Berkshire, NewtownT.*

i Thomas Lattin.

ii Mercy Rachel.

6 SARAH, bp 5 Aug 1733 *Stx;* m Ogden Mallory.

7 VIOLETTA, bp 9 Nov 1735 *Stx.*

8 (probably) RACHEL; m 2 Mar 1758 *NorwalkV*—Joseph Lockwood 3rd & had s. Josiah Mallery b 23 Dec 1758.

FAM. 6. PETER & [MARY (BEARDSLEY)] MALLORY:

1 PETER, d 1769; res. H; m 17 Feb 1756 *NHV*—Mary da. Joel & Mary (Morris) Munson, b 2 Jan 1736/7 *NHV;* she m (2) Matthew Johnson of Lanesborough, Mass.

i Luther, b 25 Sep 1756 *NHV;* Census (Milton, Vt.) 1-1-2.

ii Daniel, b 25 June 1758 *NHV;* Census (C) 2-2-1; rem. 1794 to Poultney, Vt.; m 6 Oct 1783 *CV*—Martha da. Daniel & Phebe (Atwater) Dutton. **FAM. 12.**

iii Esther, b 4 Aug 1760 *NHV.*

iv Calvin, b 13 Aug 1762 *NHV;* Census (Poultney, Vt.) 1-1-2; m (1) Miriam da. Jacob & Miriam (Ives) Atwater, b 2 Sep 1768 *NHV*, d 7 Nov 1787 æ. 19 *HT3;* m (2) —— . Child by 1st w.: 1 Miriam.

v James; Census (Poultney, Vt.) 2-1-1.

2 (probably) MARY, d 19 Apr 1762 *NHV;* m 2 Jan 1757 *NHV*—Lemuel Hotchkiss.

3 CHARITY; m 2 Oct 1759 *WatV*—Jesse Hotchkiss.

4 ELISHA, b [Feb 1736], d 23 Mar 1812 (at Winchester); res. H & Winchester; Census (L) 1-2-6; m 13 Jan 1762 *NHV*—Esther da. Wait & Esther (Punderson) Chatterton, b 14 June 1742 *NHV*, d 27 Aug 1828.

i Amasa, b 20 Feb 1763 *NHV*, d 9 Nov 1855; m Salome Smith.

ii Samuel, b 1 May 1765 *NHV*.

iii Lowly, b 20 Nov 1767 *NHV;* m Benjamin Wheeler, of Wayne Co., Pa.

iv Lue, b 21 Apr 1770, d 20 Aug 1835; m John Hawkins.

v Elisha, b 7 July 1772, bp 26 July 1772 *HCl*, d 8 Nov 1853; m 13 Feb 1794 Sarah Smith.

vi Esther, b 10 Nov 1774, bp 8 Jan 1775 *HCl*, d 21 Aug 1858; m Salmon Treat.

vii Lydia, b 19 July 1777; m 26 Nov 1801 Jesse Clark.

viii Peter, b 19 Sep 1779, d 10 May 1780.

ix Chloe, b 16 Mar 1781; m Reynold Wilson.

x Mary, b 24 May 1784, d 10 Jan 1851; m 1 May 1806 Lorrin Whiting.

xi Asa, b 7 Dec 1786; rem. to Concord, Ohio; m 8 Dec 1807 Fanny North.

5 JONAH; Census (Westfield, Mass.) 3-2-4; m Hannah da. Daniel & Abigail (Alling) Smith, b 20 Nov 1738 *WV*.

i Mary Ann b 20 Dec 1765 *WV*.

ii Hannah, b 5 May 1767 *WatV*.

iii Allen, b 18 Apr 1769 *WatV*.

iv Abigail, b 20 Nov 1771 *WatV*.

v Jonah, b 29 Sep 1773 *WatV*.

vi Peter, b 9 Oct 1775 *WatV*.

vii Sylvia, b 7 Feb 1778 *WatV*.

viii Lydia, b 20 Aug 1781 *WatV*.

ix Levi, b 20 Aug 1781 *WatV*.

x Lucy, b 20 Aug 1781 *WatV*.

6 SAMUEL.

7 ANDREW, b 13 Apr 1743 *StV*.

8 URANE; m 5 Jan 1767 *WatV*—Elemuel Hoadley.

9 ELIAKIM, b c. 1748, d 5 Nov 1817 æ. 69 *CornwallT;* Census (Cornwall) 3-3-4; m (1) 13 Oct 1771 *NHV*—Sarah da. Elisha & Mary (Ives) Bradley, b 25 Feb 1754 *NHV*, d 22 June 1785 æ. 32 *CornwallT;* m (2) Olive (Douglas) Johnson, who d 26 Jan 1820 æ. 75 *CornwallT*. Family incomplete.

(By 1): *i* Philomelia, b 31 May 1772 *NHV*.

ii Sarah, b 17 May 1774 *NHV*, bp 7 Aug 1774 *HCl*.

iii Mary Ann, b 25 June 1776 *NHV;* m 1795 Miner Pratt.

iv Eliakim, b 24 Feb 1778 *NHV*, d 6 June 1856; res. Salisbury; m Esther ——— .

v Elisha B.

FAM. 7. THOMAS & ELIZABETH (BARTLETT) MALLORY:

1 MARY, b 4 Dec 1707 *WyV*, bp Dec 1707 *WyC*, d 30 Dec 1715 æ. 9 *Wy*.

2 BARTLETT, b 23 Mar 1710 *WyV*, d 11 Mar 1711 *Wy*.

3 AARON, b 16 Feb 1712 *WyV*, bp Feb 1711/2 *WyC*, d 15 Oct 1783 æ. 72 *Wy;* m (1) 1 Aug 1739 *Wy*—Elizabeth Squire, who d 31 Jan 1741 *Wy;* m (2) June 1744 *Wy*—Joanna Mitchell, who d 17 Apr 1791.

(By 1): *i* Samuel, b 22 June 1740, d 23 Apr 1744.

(By 2): *ii* Samuel, b 24 Apr 1745, d young [?13 Jan 1777].

iii Reuben, b 7 Apr 1747, d 1776; m 11 July 1769 Elizabeth Masters. Children) 1 Elizabeth, bp 17 Mar 1771. 2 James, bp 6 Dec 1772.

iv Elizabeth, bp 30 Apr 1749, d young.

v Joanna, bp 14 July 1751, d s. p.

vi Simeon, b 6 Dec 1753, d young.

vii Eunice, bp 28 Mar 1756; m Comfort Hoyt.

viii Anna, bp 16 July 1758, d s. p.

ix Aaron, bp 13 Apr 1760; rem. to Canada; m Olive Terrill.

4 JOHN, b 25 Aug 1714 *WyV*, bp Aug 1714 *WyC*, d c. 1760; m Mary ——— ; she m (2) Capt. Matthew Minor.

i Mary, b 23 June 1745, d soon.

ii Mary, bp 25 June 1749; m Simeon Minor.

iii Nathan, b 12 Aug 1751, d 1791.

iv David, bp 5 May 1754, d 1 June 1841 æ. 87 *Cornwall;* m 3 Sep 1778 *SyC*—Ruth da. Joseph & Trial (Morehouse) Trowbridge.

v Isaiah, bp 26 Dec 1756, d 1775.

vi Samuel, bp 26 Aug 1759.

5 JESSE, b 5 Apr 1717 *WyV*, bp Apr 1717 *WyC*, d 4 Nov 1719 *WyV*.

6 ELIZABETH, bp 8 Nov 1719 *WyC;* m 7 June 1749 *Wy*—Thomas Thompson.

FAM. 7. THOMAS & HANNAH (MINOR) MALLORY:

7 SON, b & d 27 Mar 1721 *WyV*.

8 ABNER, b 18 July 1723 *WyV*, bp 21 July 1723 *WyC*, d Dec 1804 æ. 81 *Wy;* Capt.; m 25 Jan 1747 *Wy*—Susanna Walker, who d 3 June 1802 æ. 77 *Wy*.

i Electa, b 19 Apr 1748, d 3 Nov 1765; m 10 Apr 1765 Delucena Baskus.

ii Hannah, b 16 Feb 1750, d 4 Aug 1751.

iii Hannah, b 17 Jan 1752.

iv Walker, b 25 Feb 1754, d 1 Apr 1813; m 12 Oct 1776 Martha Minor.

v Jemima, b 3 Mar 1756; [m 25 Sep 1782 Nathan Dudley].

vi Abner, b 18 Feb 1758, d 15 Sep 1775.

vii Susanna, b 25 Sep 1760; m 6 Sep 1784 Ebenezer Moody.

viii Charlotte, b 7 Feb 1763; m 27 Nov 1778 Israel Judson.
ix John, b 18 Feb 1765; m 14 June 1789 Harriet Dubois.
x Electa, b 22 Sep 1767.
xi Love, b 23 Mar 1772.

9 EUNICE, b 26 June 1725 *WyV*, bp 27 June 1725 *WyC;* m 9 July 1747 *Wy*—John Crissy.

10 GIDEON, bp 9 June 1728 *WyC*, d 17 Nov 1780 *WyV;* m Olive ——, who d 1809.
i Abigail, bp 5 Apr 1752, d soon.
ii Amos, b 2 Sep 1755.
iii Simeon, b 12 July 1758.
iv Jemima, bp 30 Nov 1760; m —— Munn.
v Gideon, b 17 Sep 1763; m 14 Feb 1788 Sarah Brown of Mid.
vi Abigail, b 2 July 1766; m —— Walker.
vii Thomas, bp 29 May 1768, d soon.
viii Molly, b 31 July 1770; m 11 Feb 1789 Job Wheeler.
ix Thomas Burr, b 20 Jan 1773.
x Ruth, b 16 Mar 1775.
xi Reuben, b 25 June 1777, d 21 Oct 1800.

11 MARY, b 14 Dec 1730 *WyV*, bp 30 Dec 1730 *WyC;* m Nathan Munn.

12 JEMIMA, bp 20 May 1733 *WyC*, d s. p.

13 SIMEON, b 18 Feb 1737 *WyV*, bp 21 Feb 1737 *WyC*, d s. p.

FAM. 8. DANIEL & ABIGAIL (TROWBRIDGE) MALLORY:

1 ABIGAIL, b 29 May 1716 *NHV*, d 15 Nov 1797 æ. 82 *WHD;* m George Smith.

2 ESTHER, b 18 June 1718 *NHV*, d 21 Mar 1769 æ. 51 *OxfC;* m 11 Nov 1742 *WatV*—Daniel Osborn.

3 DANIEL, b 4 Feb 1719/20 *NHV*, d c. 1790; res. Wy, & Washington, N. Y.; m Mary da. Deliverance & Mary (Smith) Painter, b 14 Jan 1727/8 *NHV*.
i Abigail, b 18 Jan 1748 *WyV;* [?m Titus Doolittle].
ii Mary, b 17 Oct 1749 *WyV*.
iii Freelove Amy, b 21 Apr 1752 *WyV*, d 27 Oct 1794 *OxfC*, æ. 40 *Jack's HillT;* m 30 June 1777 *OxfC*—Jared Osborn.
iv Edmund, b 17 June 1754 *WyV;* Census (Washington, N. Y.) 1-3-4; m 15 Feb 1781 *OxfC*—Mabel Johnson.
v Lois, b 21 Mar 1756 *WyV;* m 5 Aug 1778 *DV*—Eli Chatfield.
vi Azariah, b 3 Apr 1758 *WyV*, d 10 Sep 1759 *WyV*.
vii Daniel, b 27 Apr 1760 *WyV*.
viii Adah, b 8 May 1762 *Wy V*.
ix Rebecca, b 5 Feb 1764 *WyV*.
x Mabel, b 17 Nov 1765 *WyV*.
xi Pene, b 9 Sep 1767 *WyV*.

4 LOIS, b 30 Nov 1721 *NHV*, d 1 Mar 1790 *OxfC*, 31 Mar æ. 68 *Jack's HillT;* m Caleb Candee.

5 **Thomas**, b 12 Aug 1723 *NHV*, d 14 Apr 1805 æ. 82 *WHT1*, 15 Apr (of My) *WHD;* m (1) Elizabeth da. John & Jemima (Allen) Catlin, b 31 Mar 1726 *Deerfield, Mass.*, d 26 May 1795 æ. 70 *MyT;* m (2) c. 1796 Persenath ——, wid. John Smith of WH & Thomas Bolter of Boston.

(By 1): *i* Eunice, b c. 1754, d s. p. 15 Apr 1792 *WatV;* m 31 Oct 1783 *WatV*—James Brown.

ii David, b 6 Mar 1756 *WatV*, d 5 Aug 1833 æ. 78 *WHT1*, 6 Aug æ. 77 *WHD;* m 30 Sep 1783 *SyC*—Hannah Curtis, who d 1 June 1831 æ. 66 *MyT.*

iii Elizabeth, b 11 Apr 1758 *WatV;* m 22 Jan 1784 *SyC*—James Ratford.

iv Sarah, b 25 June 1760 *WatV;* m —— Bradley.

v Esther, b 20 Feb 1762 *WatV;* m 25 Aug 1784 *SyC*—Reuben Hale.

vi Ann, b 5 Nov 1763 *WatV;* m —— Smith.

vii Thomas, b 27 July 1765 *WatV*, d 30 Jan 1849 æ. 84 *MyT;* m Esther ——, who d 16 Mar 1857 æ. 84 *MyT.*

viii Enos, b 24 May 1768 *WatV*, d s. p.

6 **Eunice**, b 8 Aug 1725 *NHV;* m Ebenezer Clark.

7 **Sarah**; m Israel Bunnell.

8 **Hannah**; m 21 Aug 1753 *DV*—Joseph Smith of Oxf.

FAM. 9. **Benjamin & Dorothy (Luddington) Mallory:**

1 **Joseph**, b c. 1730, bp 15 [Mar] 1775 *EHC*, d 9 June 1791 *Wol;* Census (Wat) 1-2-3; m (1) Thankful da. Jonathan & Bridget (Hunnewell) Roberts, b 24 Mar 1729 *WV*, d 30 July 1773 æ. 43 *EHV;* m (2) 23 Feb 1774 *EHC*—Eunice Barnes, b c. 1738, d 22 Nov 1793 æ. 56 *SC.*

(By 1): *i* Benjamin, b c. 1751, bp 23 May 1756 *EHC*, d 11 Jan 1819 æ. 68 *EHC;* Census (EH) 2-2-4; m 19 Dec 1774 *EHC*—Eunice da. Hezekiah & Thankful (Prout) Talmadge, b 17 Nov 1750 *NHV*, d 6 Mar 1816 æ. 65 *EHC.* **FAM. 13.**

ii Elizabeth, bp 23 May 1756 *EHC*, d young.

iii Amos, bp 25 Oct 1757 *EHC*, d 16 Aug 1803 æ. 46 *EHT*, 17 Aug *EHC;* Census (EH) 1-0-2; m 4 June 1777 *EHC*—Abigail Brown, bp (adult) 24 May 1789 *EHC.* Children: 1 Amos, b [Aug 1778], "child" d 29 Oct 1778 æ. 0-2 *EHC.* 2 Emily, b c. 1781, "child" d 7 Sep 1783 æ. 2 *EHC.*

iv Abigail, bp 6 Mar 1760 *EHC*, d 4 Nov 1851 æ. 91; m Samuel Cook of W.

v Thankful, bp 18 July 1762 *EHC;* m (1) Samuel Shepard of S; m (2) Clark Royce of S.

vi Joseph, d s. p. 1796.

vii Ezra, bp 1 Mar 1767 *EHC;* res. Wol 1794.

(By 2): *viii* Noah Woodruff, bp 15 [Mar] 1775 *EHC.*

ix Eunice, bp [May 1777] *EHC*, [d 24 May 1777].

x Elizabeth, bp 4 July 1779 *EHC.*

2 ISAAC, b c. 1732, d 20 Dec 1786 æ. c. 55 *EHC;* m Mabel da. Matthew & Lydia (Smith) Luddington, b c. 1734, bp 20 Feb 1757 *EHC*, d 12 Sep 1791 æ. 57 *EHC;* Census, (Mabel) 0-0-2.

i Asa, b c. 1754, d 9 Oct 1832 æ. 78 *EHC*, æ. 79 *NHV;* Census (EH) 1-0-4; m 26 Feb 1778 *EHC*—Hannah da. Samuel & Hannah (Grannis) Chidsey, b 6 May 1749 *F*, d 15 Dec 1815 æ. 67 *EHC*, *NHT3*. **FAM. 14.**

ii Jared.

iii Lorana, bp 30 Sep 1759 *EHC;* m 3 May 1782 *EHC*—Lemuel Shepard.

iv Amy, bp 30 Sep 1759 *EHC;* m Moses Matthews.

v Jesse, b c. 1762, d 27 Nov 1825 æ. 63 *EHC, NHT3;* Census (EH) 1-2-2; m 1781 *EHC*—Hannah da. John & Hannah (Smith) Rowe, b 9 June 1762 *NHV*, d 10 Jan 1826 æ. 63 *EHC*, 19 Jan *NHT3*. **FAM. 15.**

vi Adah, bp 29 [Jan] 1764 *EHC;* m 23 Dec 1784 *CC*—Caleb Hitchcock.

vii Jacob, b c. 1766, d 13 Mar 1834 æ. 68 *EHC;* [Census (Wtn) 1-2-2]; m Hannah Foote, b c. 1765, d 27 Mar 1830 æ. 65 *EHC*. **FAM. 16.**

viii Mercy, bp 2 Apr 1769 *EHC;* m Jones Curtis.

ix Lydia, bp 2 Feb 1772 *EHC;* m Joshua Baker.

x Lorinda, bp 2 Jan 1774 *EHC;* m Timothy Way.

xi Hannah, bp 10 Aug 1777 *EHC*, "child" d 19 July 1778 æ. 0-10 *EHC*.

3 DAVID, b c. 1734, d 1736 æ. 2 *EHV*.

4 MERCY, b c. 1736, "child" d 19 Sep 1742 *EHV*.

FAM. 9. BENJAMIN & MARY (NAILS) MALLORY:

5 DAVID, b c. 1745, bp 2 Jan 1757 *EHC*, d 17 May 1785 (drowned) *EHC;* m 16 Aug 1769 *BdC*—Mary Wardell, who d 21 June 1799 æ. 52 *EHC;* Census (EH) 1-1-2. The 6 children were all bp 5 Apr 1789 *EHC*.

i Sarah; m 7 Mar 1790 *EHC*—Adoniram Bickford.

ii David.

iii Samuel.

iv Polly.

v Irene.

vi Culpepper.

6 MERCY, b c. 1747, bp 2 Jan 1757 *EHC*.

7 LEVI, b c. 1749, bp 2 Jan 1757 *EHC*, d (probably s. p.) 14 Mar 1799 æ. 50 *EHC;* Census (EH) 1-0-1; [m Eleanor da. Timothy & Susanna (Prout) Bontecou, b 25 Dec 1749 *NHV*, d 13 Dec 1819 æ. 70 *EHC*].

8 DOROTHY, b c. 1751, bp 2 Jan 1757 *EHC;* m (1) 7 Dec 1769 *EHC*—Thomas Alling; m (2) 15 Mar 1790 *NHC1*—Moses Brockett.

9 JOHN, b c. 1753, bp 2 Jan 1757 *EHC*, d 5 May 1777 æ. 24 *EHC;* m 20 June 1775 *BdC*—Miriam Stokes; she m (2) 25 Jan 1778 *NHC2*—Edmund Smith.

10 MARY, bp 20 Feb 1757 *EHC*.
11 SIMEON, bp 26 Feb 1758 *EHC*; Census (Northfield, Mass.) 1-2-3; m Sarah Dickinson.

FAM. 10. JONATHAN & ABIGAIL (HIDE) MALLORY (family incomplete):
1 GRIZZEL; m 29 Oct 1744 *ReddingC*—Lemuel Wood.
2 DANIEL, b [29 May 1725], d 18 July 1805 æ. 80-1-19; Dea.; Census (Redding) 2-0-2; m 30 Nov 1748 *ReddingC*—Sarah Lee, b [12 Oct 1730], d 4 July 1819 æ. 88-9-22.
i Daniel, b 13 Oct 1750; Census (Redding) 2-1-3; m Rachel ——. His gr. son was Stephen Mallory, U. S. Sen. & Sec. Confederate Navy.
ii Samuel, b 21 June 1752, d 22 July 1834 æ. 82-0-20; Census (Redding) 1-2-3; [?m 14 Sep 1777 *Redding*—Hannah (Hull) Nichols].
iii Nathan, b 16 Aug 1754.
iv Abigail, b 12 Mar 1757; m James Dunning.
v Sarah, bp 8 May 1763; m Billy Morehouse.
vi Joseph, b 1767.
3 DEBORAH; m 11 Feb 1758 *FV*, 1759 *ReddingC*—Samuel Clugstone.

FAM. 11. PETER & JOANNA (HALL) MALLORY:
1 REBECCA, bp 5 Feb 1738 *ReddingC*, d Mar 1738 æ. 0-4 *ReddingC*.
2 REBECCA, bp 13 Jan 1739 *ReddingC*.
3 WILLIAM, b c. 1742; Census (Hillsdale, N. Y,) 2-3-5; m Mary ——.
4 SAMUEL, b c. 1744, d 1802; Census (Hillsdale, N. Y.) 1-4-4; m Mary Carley.
5 OLIVER, b c. 1746; Census (Hillsdale, N. Y) 2-2-2; m Margaret ——.
6 (perhaps) URIAH; Census (New Ashford, Mass.) 2-3-3; m Patience Lewis.
7 PETER; Census (New Ashford, Mass.) 1-2-2; m (1) Lucy ——; m (2) 5 Aug 1787 *New Ashford*—Anna Dorman.
(By 1): *i* Patience, bp 3 Oct 1779 (at Lanesboro') *Gt. Barrington, Mass., x*; also Peter & William at the same time.
ii Peter.
iii William.
iv Lucy, bp 15 July 1787.

FAM. 12. DANIEL & MARTHA (DUTTON) MALLORY:
1 ROLLIN CAROLUS, b 27 May 1784 *CV*, bp 15 July 1787 *CC*, d 16 Apr 1831; U. S. Rep.; m Ruth Stanley.
2, 3 TWINS, d 15 Feb 1786 *CV*.
4 HORACE, b 15 Nov 1787 *CV*, bp 5 Nov 1787 *CC*.
5 DANIEL, b 23 Feb 1789 *CV*, bp 17 Apr 1791 *CC*; m (1) Sarah Stanley; m (2) Fanny Adams.
6 MARTHA, b 3 Mar 1795 *F*, bp 21 June 1795 *CC*, d Aug 1796.
7 HENRY, b c. 1798, d 1804.
8 CHARLES DUTTON, b 23 Jan 1801 *F*, d 31 July 1864; Rev.; m (1) 1825 Sarah Mary Evans; m (2) 1840 Mary E. (——) Welch.

9 PHEBE, b 14 Nov 1807 *F;* m Henry J. Ruggles.

FAM. 13. BENJAMIN & EUNICE (TALMADGE) MALLORY:

1 AMMI, b c. 1780, bp 11 Nov 1787 *EHC*, d 27 Oct 1851 æ. 71 *NHT3;* m Polly da. Thomas & Dorothy (Mallory) Alling, wid. Amos Broughton, b c. 1774, d 24 Feb 1843 æ. 68 *NHT3.*

i Amos, b c. 1805, d 21 Oct 1815 æ. 11 *EHC.*

2 ELIZABETH, b c. 1784, bp 11 Nov 1787 *EHC*, d 10 Feb 1836 æ. 52 *NHT3;* m 30 Sep 1811 *EHC*—Isaac Mallory.

3 PATTY, bp 9 Mar 1788 *EHC.*

4 ZINA, bp 6 Mar 1791 *EHC*, d s. p.

FAM. 14. ASA & HANNAH (CHIDSEY) MALLORY:

1 JARED, b c. 1778, "only son" d 28 Aug 1788 æ. 10 *EHC.*

2 ANNIS, b c. 1779, d 5 Apr 1801 æ. 22 *EHT*, 6 Apr *EHC.*

3 HANNAH, b c. 1782, d 13 Oct 1851 æ. 69 *NHT3;* m James R. Hunt.

4 HULDAH, bp 17 Feb 1785 *EHC*, "child" d Dec 1786 æ. 2 *EHC.*

5 HULDAH, bp 9 Sep 1787 *EHC;* m 9 Sep 1807 *NHx*—James Wetmore.

6 JARED, d young.

FAM. 15. JESSE & HANNAH (ROWE) MALLORY:

1 JAMES, b 26 Mar 1782 *EHV*, d 15 Nov 1863 æ. 82 *NHT3*, (at EH) *NHV;* m Polly ——— , b c. 1788, d 25 Mar 1845 æ. 57 *NHT3.*

i Jared, b c. 1806, d 5 Jan 1885 æ. 78 *NHV*, *NHT3;* m Mary Hemingway, who d 29 Aug 1888 æ. 82 *NHT3.*

ii Polly, b c. 1816, d 13 Jan 1851 æ. 34 *NHT3.*

2 LOWLY, b 3 Oct 1784 *EHV*, d 1 Aug 1855 æ. 71 *EHT;* m 17 July 1805 *CC*—Aner Pardee.

3 HEMAN, b 12 Apr 1787 *EHV*, d 5 Sep 1848 æ. 61 *EHC;* m 29 Nov 1810 *EHC*—Sally Grannis.

i Harry, b c. 1812, d 31 July 1827 æ. 15 (drowned) *EHC.*

ii Willis, b c. 1819, d 31 July 1827 æ, 8 (drowned) *EHC.*

4 SALLY, b c. 1791, d 7 Aug 1870 æ. 79 (at Staatsburgh, N. Y.) *NHT3.*

5 WILLIS, b 6 Apr 1793 *EHV*, "son" d 2 Sep 1799 æ. 6 (drowned) *EHC.*

6 JESSE, b 27 Mar 1796 *EHV*, d 9 Jan 1859 æ. 66 *NHT3;* m 27 Nov 1813 *EHC*—Wealthy Grannis.

7 WILLIS, b c. 1800, d 4 Dec 1868 æ. 68 (at Baltimore) *NHT3;* m (1) 18 Oct 1821 *EHV*—Leuramah Barnes, who d 10 Feb 1830 æ. 25 *NHT3;* m (2) 30 Jan 1831 *NHV*—Betsey Rowe, who d 26 Feb 1878 æ. 70 *NHT3.*

FAM. 16. JACOB & HANNAH (FOOTE) MALLORY:

1 ISAAC, b c. 1787, d 9 Jan 1869 æ. 82 *NHT3;* m (1) 7 Nov 1805 *NHC1*—Martha da. Nathaniel & Martha (Smith) Grannis, b c. 1784, d 3 Feb 1811 æ. 27 *NHT3;* m (2) 30 Sep 1811 *EHC*—Elizabeth da. Benjamin & Eunice (Talmadge) Mallory, b c. 1784, d 10 Feb 1836 æ. 52 *NHT3.*

2 SARAH; m 29 Nov 1807 *NoHC*—John Larkin.

3 JESSE.
4 CHILD, d infant.
5 FANNY.
6 EMILY.
7 JACOB, bp 26 Nov 1803 *NHx*.

MALLORY. MISCELLANEOUS. Married at *New PrestonC:* Betty m 4 May 1786 Gillet Jones; Truman m 21 Oct 1790 Amy Sharp.....JOHN d Nov 1829 æ. 29 *NHT3;* his w. Polly d June 1883 æ. 89 *NHT3*.

MALONE. JOHN of NH; m Phebe ——. Family incomplete.

1 SARAH, b Jan 1757 *NHV*.
2 DANIEL, b 23 Nov 1758 *NHV;* Census (NH) 1-3-2; m 27 May 1784 *NHC1*—Hannah da. John & Mary (Sackett) Gordon, b c. 1766, "Wid." d Sep 1806 *NHC1*.
   i John, b c. 1784, bp 17 July 1795 (æ. 11) *NHx*.
   ii James, b c. 1787, bp 17 July 1795 (æ. 8) *NHx*, d 21 July 1795 æ. 8 *NHx*.
   iii Elizabeth, b c. 1791, bp 17 July 1795 (æ. 4) *NHx*, d 22 July 1795 æ. 4 *NHx*.
   iv Daniel, b c. 1793, bp 17 July 1795 (æ. 2) *NHx*.
   v Sarah, bp 17 July 1795 (æ. 5 or 6 mos.) *NHx*.
3 DAUGHTER, b c. 1766, d 25 Dec 1769 æ. 3 *NHC1*.

MALTBY. Baptized *NHC1:* William, 1 June 1700; Elizabeth, 27 Mar 1726; John, 30 July 1727; William, 6 Apr 1729; Sarah, 26 July 1730; William, 20 June 1731.

MANCHESTER. —— & Lydia (adults) bp 26 Dec 1784 (witnesses, Benjamin & Mary Sanford) *NHx*.

MANROSS. NEHEMIAH, of W (Meriden) & Farm (Bristol), d 1761; m (1) ——; m (2) 3 Jan 1745 *WC2*—Thankful Roberts, wid. Ebenezer Cooper.

(By 1): 1 ESTHER; m 5 Apr 1736 *WV*—Asa Yale.
• 2 RUTH; m 5 Apr 1736 *WV*—Thomas Mix.
3 NEHEMIAH; m 5 May 1742 *WV*, 12 May *WC2*—Sarah da. Robert & Joanna (Gaylord) Royce.
4 ELIJAH, m twice; family incomplete.
   (By 1): *i* Elijah, b 1761, d 1832; Col.; Census (Bristol) 1-1-1; m Martha da. Elisha Manross & had: Elisha, b 11 May 1792.
   (By 2): *ii* (perhaps) Jesse; Census (Essex, Vt.) 2-1-2.
5 ELISHA, b c. 1727, d 17 Jan 1810 æ. 83 *BristolT;* Census (Bristol) 2-1-4; m (1) Martha ——, who d 29 Apr 1789 æ. 55 *BristolT;* m (2) Abigail Chalker.
   i Ruth; m 21 May 1806 Noah Byington.
   ii Martha; m Elijah Manross.
   iii Anna; m Sep 1811 Dana Carrington.
   iv Hannah.
   v Jerusha.
6 BISHOP, d 1774 (Burlington); res. S; m.
   i John, b 20 Feb 1757.
   ii Theodore, b 6 Jan 1760, d Aug 1825 (Clinton, N. Y.); m

Martha White.

iii Sybil.

7 SAMUEL; m.

i Samuel, bp 1753 *Bristol x.*

ii Timothy, bp 1753 *Bristol x.*

***MANSFIELD.** FAM. 1. RICHARD, d 1655; m 10 Aug 1636 *Exeter, Co. Devon, Eng.*—Gillian Drake, who d 1669; she m (2) Alexander Field.

1 JOSEPH, b c. 1637, d 15 Nov 1692 *NHPro;* m Mary da. William & Frances Potter, who d c. 1701.

i Mary, b 6 Apr 1658 *NHV*, d 1712; m (1) Henry Wise; m (2) c. 1686 Thomas Turhand; m (3) John Hill.

ii Martha, b 18 Apr 1660 *NHV;* m 16 Dec 1680 *NHV*—Richard Sperry.

iii Mercy, b 26 July 1662 *NHV;* m John Bristol.

iv Silence, b 24 Oct 1664 *NHV;* m (1) Obadiah Wilcoxen of G; m (2) ——— Chatfield of Killingworth.

v Elizabeth, b 20 Sep 1666 *NHV;* m Wm. Johnson.

vi Comfort, b 6 Dec 1668 *NHV;* m John Benham.

vii John, b 8 Apr 1671 *NHV*, d 22 Dec 1690 *NHV*.

viii Joseph, b 27 Dec 1673 *NHV*, d 8 Oct 1739 *NHV*, æ. 64 *NHT1;* m Elizabeth da. John & Lydia (Parker) Thomas, b c. 1677, bp 16 Dec 1688 *NHC1*, d 4 Mar 1763 æ. 86 *NoHT1*, 10 Mar æ. 84 *NoHC*. **FAM. 2**

ix Ebenezer, b 6 Feb 1677 (name changed from Ichabod) *NHV*, d 3 Aug 1745 æ. 73 *NHT1;* m 20 Apr 1710 *NHV*—Hannah da. John & Mercy (Todd) Bassett, b 3 Oct 1679 *NHV*, bp 2 Apr 1721 *NHC1*, d 22 Jan 1766 æ. 87 *NHC1*. **FAM. 3.**

x Japhet, b 8 July 1681 *NHV*, d 1745; m 14 Jan 1703 *NHV*—Hannah da. Abraham & Hannah (Thompson) Bradley, b 8 Nov 1682 *NHV*, d 27 Oct 1768 æ. 86 *NHC1*. **FAM. 4.**

2 MOSES, b c. 1640, d 3 Oct 1703 *NHV*, æ. 67 (?64) *NHT1;* Major; Judge; m (1) 5 May 1664 *NHV*—Mercy & Henry & Helena Glover, bp 16 Aug 1643 *NHC1;* m (2) Abigail da. Thomas & Mary (Turner) Yale, b 5 May 1660 *NHV*, d 28 Feb 1708/9 *NHV*, æ. 49 *NHT1*.

By 1): *i* Abigail, b 7 Feb 1664 *NHV* [1664/5], d 24 Sep 1717 *WV;* m 13 Sep 1682 *NHV*—John Atwater.

ii Mercy, b 2 Apr 1667 *NHV*, d 9 Jan 1743 [1743/4] æ. 77 *EHT;* m (1) John Thompson; m (2) Nathaniel Bradley.

iii Hannah, b 11 Mar 1668/9 *NHV*, d 1 Nov 1726 æ. 57 *NHT1;* m Gershom Brown.

iv Samuel, b 31 Dec 1671 *NHV*, d s. p. 1701.

v Moses, b 15 Aug 1674 *NHV*, d 15 Feb 1740/1 æ. 67 *NHT1;* m 3 Nov 1702 *NHV*—Margaret da. John & Mary (Rutherford) Prout, b 7 June 1682 *NHV*. **FAM. 5.**

vi Sarah, b 14 June 1677 *NHV;* m 1 June 1698 *NHV*—William Rhodes.

vii Richard, b 20 July 1680 *NHV*, d 7 Aug 1681 *NHV*.

viii Bathshua, b 1 Jan 1682 *NHV* [1682/3]; m 22 Jan 1705 *NHV*—Joseph Chapman of Newport, R. I.

ix Jonathan, 15 Feb 1685 *NHV* [1685/6], bp 21 Mar 1685/6 *NHC1*, d 10 Jan 1775 æ. 89 *NHT1*; Dea.; m (1) 1 June 1708 *NHV*—Sarah da. John & Susanna (Coe) Alling, b 29 Aug 1685 *NHV*, d 4 May 1765 æ. 80 *NHT1*, 3 May æ. 79 *NHC1*; m (2) 13 May 1766 *NHC1*—Abigail da. James & Abigail (Bennett) Bishop, wid. Ebenezer Dorman, b 1 Sep 1707 *NHV*, d 25 Jan 1798 æ. 91 *HT2*. **FAM. 6.**

FAM. 2. JOSEPH & ELIZABETH (THOMAS) MANSFIELD:

1 MARY, b Apr 1701 *NHV*, d 15 Feb 1779 æ. 78 *NoHC*; m 26 Apr 1726 *NHV*—Daniel Tuttle.

2 LYDIA, b 25 Dec 1702 *NHV*, bp 7 May 1727 *NHC1*, d 18 Sep 1781 æ. 79 *NoHT1*; m 10 Apr 1730 *NHV*—Thomas Cooper.

3 JOHN, b 2 Jan 1704 *NHV* [1704/5], d June 1751; m (1) 1730 *NHCt*—Sarah da. Samuel & Rachel (Brown) Brockett, b 26 Aug 1702 *WV*; m (2) Lydia da. John & Hannah (Humiston) Tuttle, b 15 Mar 1707 *NHV*. Family incomplete.

(By 1): *i* Lydia, b c. 1730, d 15 Dec 1814 æ. 84 *NoHT1*; m James Pierpont.

ii Sarah; b c. 1733; m James Thomas.

iii Elizabeth, b c. 1736, d 28 Feb 1821 æ. 85 (*NHC2*) *NHV*; m (1) 24 Apr 1754 *NHV*—Amos Thorpe; m (2) 15 Mar 1757 *NHV*—John Hill.

(By 2): *iv* Eunice, b 1 Apr 1740 *NHV*, bp 5 July 1741 *NHC1*.

v David, b 3 July 1741 *NHV*, bp 28 Nov 1742 *NHC1*, d 1833 (at Harwinton); m (1) 20 Oct 1770 *PC*—Eunice da. Jeremiah & Mercy (Northrop) Peck, b 23 Feb 1745 (at P); m (2) 27 Nov 1788 Abigail (———) Copley.

vi Rebecca, b 17 May 1745 *NHV*, bp 11 June 1749 *NHC2*; m 17 Nov 1763 *NoHC*—Benjamin Bishop.

4 ELIZABETH, b 23 Oct 1706 *NHV*, d 11 Sep 1807; m 14 Feb 1727/8 *NHV*—Nathaniel Hitchcock.

5 JOSEPH, b 17 Aug 1708 *NHV*, d c. 1762; m (1) 10 Oct 1732 *NHV*—Phebe da. Samuel & Mary (Hitchcock) Bassett, b 12 May 1713 *NHV*; m (2) Dorcas da. John & Mehitabel (Wolcott) Ford, wid. Joseph Warner & Isaac Johnson, b 5 Nov 1712 *NHV*, d c. 1788.

(By 1): *i* Dan, b 29 Jan 1732/3 *NHV*, d 1773; res. NH; m Sarah ———. **FAM. 7.**

ii Titus, b 5 Nov 1734 *NHV*, d c. 1808; Census (H) 3-0-1; m Mabel da. Gershom & Hannah (Mansfield) Todd, b c. 1738, d 12 Sep 1783 æ. 45 *NoHC*. **FAM. 8.**

iii Joseph, b 16 Apr 1737 *F*, d 6 June 1821 æ. 84 *MorrisT*; m 27 May 1761 *NHV*, 28 May *NHC2*—Hannah da. David & Thankfu (Todd) Punderson, b 21 Oct 1740 *NHV*, d

22 Aug 1826 æ. 86 *MorrisT.* **FAM. 9.**

iv Phebe, b c. 1740, d 2 May 1809 æ. 69 *HT4;* m 13 Aug 1761 *NHC1*—Philemon Potter.

v (possibly) Lois; m 13 Aug 1761 *NHV*, *NHC1*—Daniel Atwater.

6 ABIGAIL, b c. 1711, bp (adult) 25 Nov 1733 *NHC1*, d Sep 1740 *NHV;* m 20 Jan 1733/4 *NHV*—Jacob Turner.

7 THOMAS, b c. 1713, bp (adult) 25 Nov 1733 *NHC1*, d 4 Nov 1798 æ. 85 *NoHT1;* Census (NoH) 2-0-2; m Dec 1738 *NHV*—Hannah da. Nathaniel & Sarah (Wooding) Goodyear, b 14 Aug 1718 *NHV*, d 24 Nov 1798 æ. 81 *NoHT1*.

i Samuel, b Aug 1740 *NHV*, d 10 Nov 1813 æ. 73 *NoHT1*, *NoHC*.

ii Mabel, b 13 Mar 1742/3 *NHV*, d 20 Feb 1789 æ. 46 *NoHT1;* m 19 June 1760 *NHV*—Walter Munson.

iii Bede, b 21 Nov 1746 *NHV*, d 24 May 1811 æ. 66 *NoHT1;* m (1) 8 Nov 1767 *NoHC*—Philip Daggett; m (2) 24 Oct 1785 *NoHC*—Thomas Cooper.

iv Polly, b 14 June 1756 *NHV*, d 3 June 1775 æ. 18 (wanting 11 days) *NoHT1*.

8 AMOS, bp (adult) 25 Nov 1733; was he perhaps father of the Lois listed in his brother's family above? And of Amos who m 5 July 1776 *NHV*—Mary da. Amos & Deborah (Tuttle) Clark, b 2 Nov 1753 *NHV*, & had Ephraim b 3 Aug 1778 *NHV*?

9 JOSIAH, d before 1757; m Abigail da. Joseph & Abigail (Smith) Cooper, b 22 May 1719 *NHV*,

i Abigail, b 5 June 1738 *NHV;* m 22 June 1757 *NHV*—Seth Barnes.

ii Timothy, b 4 Mar 1739/40 *NHV*.

iii Lemuel, b 25 Dec 1741 *NHV*.

iv Uzal, b 6 Nov 1744 *NHV*, d Dec 1817 æ. 73 *BethlehemC;* m (1) 1 Oct 1770 *NHV*—Rachel da. Israel & Elizabeth (Tallman) Sperry, b 16 Feb 1747/8 *NHV*, d 28 Sep 1806 æ. 60 *BethlehemC;* probably m (2) Abigail [Hitchcock?], who d 5 Nov 1819 æ. 63 *BethlehemC.* **FAM. 10.**

v Josiah, d 1777; m 7 Feb 1769 *NHV*—Hannah da. Joseph & Jemima (Smith) Cooper, b 7 Sep 1740 *NHV;* Census, Hannah (H) 1-1-2. **FAM. 11.**

10 EBENEZER, bp (adult) 25 Nov 1733 *NHC1*, d s. p. 1745.

FAM. 3. EBENEZER & HANNAH (BASSETT) MANSFIELD:

1 SAMUEL, b 28 Jan 1710/1 *NHV*, bp 2 Apr 1721 *NHC1*, d 1750; m 23 Dec 1736 *NHV*—Susanna da. Jonathan & Sarah (Alling) Mansfield, b 9 Dec 1712 *NHV;* she m (2) John Stone of M.

i Hannah, b 16 May 1739 *NHV*, d young.

FAM. 4. JAPHET & HANNAH (BRADLEY) MANSFIELD:

1 HANNAH, b 6 Jan 1703/4 *NHV*, d 29 Dec 1772 æ. 69 *NoHT1;* m Gershom Todd.

2 SARAH, b 8 Apr 1706 *NHV;* m Amos Tuttle.

3 JAPHET, b 5 Jan 1708 *NHV* [1708/9], d s. p. 25 Mar 1741 æ. 33 *NHT1;* m 18 Jan 1737/8 *NHV*—Ruth Tuttle.

4 MERCY, b 18 Nov 1711 *NHV*, d s. p.

5 RACHEL, b 3 Apr 1714 *NHV;* m Stephen Tuttle.

6 ESTHER, bp 1717 *NHC1;* m Joseph Beach of St.

7 COMFORT, bp July 1720 *NHC1;* m 19 Oct 1741 *StV*—Samuel Nichols.

8 MARTHA, bp 17 June 1724 *NHC1*, d 26 Aug 1804 æ. 81 *WdC;* m Thomas Sperry.

9 MARY, bp 29 Jan 1726/7 *NHC1;* m 3 Feb 1745/6 *NHV*—Elihu Sperry.

FAM. 5. MOSES & MARGARET (PROUT) MANSFIELD:

1 SAMUEL, b 23 Aug 1705 *NHV*, d 12 Dec 1705 æ. 16 wks. *NHT1*.

2 MARY, b 23 Feb 1706/7 *NHV;* m (1) 7 Oct 1725 *NHV*—FitzJohn Allyn; m (2) 17 Mar 1739/40 *NHV*—Alexander Wolcott.

3 MARGARET, b 7 Oct 1708 *NHV*, d before 1757; m 27 Sep 1744 *NHV*—Israel Munson.

4 DANIEL, b 23 Mar 1711 *NHV*, d s. p. 1788.

5 SUSANNA, b 16 Feb 1713 *NHV*, d 1789; m 5 Nov 1735 *NHV*—Samuel Cooke.

6 SAMUEL, b 23 Nov 1717 *NHV*, bp Nov 1717 *NHC1*, d 22 June 1775 æ. 57 *NHT1;* m 4 Oct 1742 *NHV*—Esther Hall of Mid, who d 21 Oct 1795 æ. 77 *NHT1;* Census, Esther (NH) 0-0-2.

- *i* Esther, b 6 Jan 174[3/4] *NHV*, bp 8 Jan 1743/4 *NHC1*, d 14 Jan 1743/4 *NHV*, 1744 æ. 0-0-8 *NHT1*.
- PAGE 1528 *ii* Margaret, b 24 Apr 1745 *NHV* bp 28 Apr 1745 *NHC1*, d 19 June 1775 æ. 30 *NHC1*, æ. 31 *NHT1*.
- *iii* Esther, b 2 Nov 1746 *NHV*, bp 9 Nov 1746 *NHC1*, d 25 July 1828 æ. 82 *NHT1;* m 30 Aug 1773 *NHC1*—Jacob Thompson.
- *iv* Mary, b 3 July 1748 *NHV*, bp 3 July 1748 *NHC1*, d 26 Apr 1817 æ. 69 *NHT1;* m 25 Jan 1780 *NHC2*—John Prout Sloan.
- *v* Elizabeth, b 26 Feb 1749/50 *NHV*, bp 4 Mar 1749/50 *NHC1*, d 29 Aug 1751 æ. 1-6 *NHT1*.
- *vi* Moses Samuel, b 6 Dec 1751 *NHV*, d soon.
- *vii* Giles Daniel, b 14 Nov 1753 *NHV*, bp 15 Nov 1753 *NHC2;* Census, Daniel (NH) 1-0-1.
- *viii* Elizabeth, bp 10 Aug 1755 *NHC2*, d 24 Sep 1794 æ. 39 *NHT1*.
- *ix* Moses Samuel bp 29 May 1757 *NHC2*, d 15 Jan 1835 æ. 75 *NHT1;* m Hannah ——, who d 30 Aug 1848 æ. 99 *NHT1*, 28 Aug 1847 æ. 98 *NHV*.
- *x* Susanna, bp 14 Jan 1759 *NHC2*.

PAGE 1248 7 MERCY, b 3 Mar 1718/9 *NHV*, bp Mar 1719 *NHC1*, d 7 July 1793 æ. 75 *NHC1*.

8 SARAH, b 25 July 1720 *NHV*, bp July 1720 *NHC1*, d 18 Feb 1720

/1 *NHV*.

FAM. 6. JONATHAN & SARAH (ALLING) MANSFIELD:

1 MOSES, b 5 May 1709 *NHV*, d 1754; m (1) 17 May 1734 *NHV*—Ann Mary Kierstead, b c. 1709, d 5 July 1742 *NHV*, æ. 33 *NHT1*; m (2) 17 Feb 1747/8 *NHV*—Rachel da. Joseph & Mary (Wilmot) Dorman, wid. Ambrose Ward, b 15 Feb 1707/8 *NHV*, d Oct 1794 æ. 87 *NHJournal*.

(By 1): *i* John, b 18 Aug 1734 *NHV*; see MISCELLANEOUS.

ii Sarah, b 7 July 1736 *NHV*, bu 21 Feb 1775 *NHx*; m 13 July 1758 *NHV*—John Danielson.

iii Jonathan, b 8 Mar 1739 *NHV*, d 2 Sep 1769 *NHV*, æ. 30 *NHC1*; Capt.; m 10 Nov 1761 *NHV*—Mary [da. Benjamin & Sarah (Bradley)] Dorchester, b c. 1739, d 25 Sep 1830 æ. 92 (*NHC2*) *NHV*; she m (2) Edmund Burke. **FAM. 12.**

(By 2): *iv* Moses, b 25 Sep 1749 *NHV*, bp Nov 1749 (at NH) *Dx*, d s. p. 14 Dec 1831 æ. 84 *NHV*; Census (NH) 1-0-1.

v James Kierstead, b 15 Feb 1750/1 *NHV*, bp 10 Apr 1751 (at NH) *Dx*, d 1804; Census (NH) 1-1-6; m 2 Feb 1774 *NHC1*—Mary da. Joseph & Hannah (Ball) Hitchcock, b 4 Dec 1751 *NHV*. **FAM. 13.**

2 JONATHAN, b 27 Jan 1710/1 *NHV*; m Mary da. Joseph & Mary (Wilmot) Dorman, b 24 Oct 1711 *NHV*, bp 28 Sep 1735 (adult) *NHC1*, d 18 July 1794 æ. 82 *WdT1*; she m (2) Ezra Johnson.

i Sarah, b 14 Jan 1735/6 *NHV*, bp 18 Jan 1736 *NHC1*; m 25 Jan 1757 *WdC*—Benajah Peck.

3 SUSANNA, b 9 Dec 1712 *NHV*; m (1) 23 Dec 1736 *NHV*—Samuel Mansfield; m (2) John Stone.

4 SARAH, b 2 May 1715 *NHV*; m 21 Feb 1738/9 *NHV*—Thomas Wilmot.

5 STEPHEN, b 14 Nov 1716 *NHV*, bp 1716 *NHC1*, d 15 July 1774 *NHx*; Capt.; m 31 Dec 1746 *NHV*—Hannah Beach, b c. 1728, d 20 Sep 1795 æ. 67 *NHT1*, bu. 21 Sep *NHx*.

i Hannah, b 17 Nov 1747 *F*, d 22 May 1825 æ. 77 *NoBT1*; m 5 July 1767 William Douglas.

ii Stephen, b [Sep 1750], d 25 Aug 1751 æ. 0-11 *NHT1*.

iii Stephen, b 31 July 1753 *NHV*, d 14 Aug 1756 æ. 3 *NHT1*.

iv John, b 11 Apr 1756 *NHV*, d 5 Nov 1766 æ. 11 *NHT1*.

v Jared, b 23 May 1759 *NHV*, *NHT1*, d 3 Feb 1830 *NHT1*, 4 Feb æ. 71 (*NHx*) *NHV*; Col.; Census (NH) 1-0-1; rem. to Cincinnati, Ohio; m 2 Mar 1800 Elizabeth Phipps.

vi Henry, b 1 Feb 1762 *NHV*; Census (NH) 1-1-2; m 3 Aug 1785 *NHSupCt*—Mary Fenno of Mid; she div. him 1804. **FAM. 14.**

vii Sarah, b c. 1765; m 21 Aug 1784 *NoHC*—James Sisson of Newport, R. I.

viii Child, stillborn 1768 *NHx*.

ix Grace, bp 16 Sep 1770 *NHx*, d 12 July 1792 æ. 22 *NHT1;* m 15 Oct 1785 *NHV*, *NHx*—Peter Totten.

6 NATHAN, b 15 Nov 1718 *NHV*, bp Nov 1718 *NHC1*, d 13 Mar 1783 æ. 65 *NHT1;* Lieut.; m 5 Dec 1745 *NHV*—Deborah da. Isaac & Elizabeth (Todd) Dayton, b 8 Aug 1724 *NHV*, d 29 May 1817 æ. 93 *NHT1;* Census, Deborah (NH) 0-0-1.

i Mary, b 14 Dec 1745 *NHV*, bp 18 Feb 1748/9 (at NH) *Dx*, d 16 Aug 1805 æ. 60 *NHT1;* m 29 Dec 1766 *NHC2*—Isaac Beers.

ii Lois, b 13 Apr 1747 *NHV*, bp 18 Feb 1748/9 (at NH) *Dx*, d 28 Aug 1821 æ. 74 (*NHC1*) *NHV;* m 13 Jan 1772 *NHC1*—Wm. Lyon.

iii Nathan, b 30 Nov 1748 *NHV*, bp 18 Feb 1748/9 (at NH) *Dx*, d 5 Nov 1835 æ. 87 *DT5;* Census (D) 2-1-4; m 5 Mar 1775 *DV*—Anna da. Henry & Patience (Tomlinson) Tomlinson, b c. 1756, d 10 Dec 1838 æ. 82 *DT5*. **FAM. 15.**

iv William, b 21 Mar 1749/50 *NHV*, d 28 May 1842; Census (NH) 1-2-4; m (1) 5 Dec 1776 *NHC1*—Elizabeth da. Wm. & Elizabeth (Maltby) Lyon, bp May 1757 *NHC1*, d 18 Oct 1817; m (2) 1 Dec 1818 *WC1*—Lucy da. Abner & Sarah [Cook] Peck, wid. Ambrose Culver, b 6 Dec 1781 *WV*, d 30 Apr 1842 æ. 60 *NHV*. **FAM. 16.**

v Achilles, bp 17 Nov 1751 (at NH) *Dx*, d 22 July 1814; Rev.; res. Killingworth; m 10 Mar 1779 Sarah (Eliot) Huntington; had issue.

vi Susanna, b 23 Sep 1756 *F*, bp 18 Oct 1761 (at NH) *Dx*, d 2 Aug 1824 æ. 68 *NHT1*, 4 Aug æ. 62 (*NHC2*) *NHV*.

vii Elisha, b c. 1761, bp 19 Apr 1772 *NHC1*.

viii Glover, b 20 Dec 1767 *F*, bp 19 Apr 1772 *NHC1*, d 26 Oct 1849 æ. 82 *NHT1;* m 5 Apr 1792 Mary Aikens, who d 18 Nov 1858 æ. 83 *NHT1*. Mary w. Glover bp 14 Apr 1799 *NHC1;* children bp *NHC1*—Giles, Wm., & Eli, 12 May 1799; Mary, 11 Aug 1799; Elias, 12 Apr 1801; Harriet, 3 Apr 1803; Andrew, 19 Aug 1804.

7 LOIS, b 27 Apr 1721 *NHV*, bp 7 May 1721 *NHC1*, d 16 Mar 1806 æ. 85 *NHC1;* m (1) 9 Jan 1745/6 *NHV*—Abraham Bradley; m (2) Josiah Woodhouse; m (3) 13 July 1766 *NHC1*—John Watts.

8 RICHARD, b 1 Oct 1723 *NHV*, bp c. Oct 1723 *NHC1*, d 12 Apr 1820 æ. 96 *DT2;* Rev.; Rector of St. James, Derby, 72 yrs.; Census (D) 2-1-4; m 10 Oct 1751 *DV*—Anna da. Joseph & Sarah Hull, b 9 June 1736 *DV*, d 20 Aug 1776 æ. 40 *DT2*.

i Richard, b 23 Aug 1752 [O. S.] or 3 Sep 1752 [N. S.] *Dx*, bp 30 Aug 1752 [O. S.] or 11 Sep 1752 [N. S.] *Dx;* Census (D) 2-1-4; m Abiah Shelton.

ii Elizabeth, b 15 Sep 1754 *DV*, bp 29 Sep 1754 *Dx*, d 22 Feb 1826 æ. 70 *DT2*.

iii Anna, bp 2 May 1756 *Dx*, d 11 Apr 1841 æ. 85 *DT2;* m 22 Oct 1774 *DV*—Elijah Humphrey.

iv Sarah, b 9 Aug 1758 *Dx*, bp 17 Sep 1758 *Dx*, d 23 Dec 1790 æ. 32 *DT2;* m Edward Blakeslee.

v Henrietta, b 3 Oct 1760 *Dx*, bp 16 Nov 1760 *Dx*, d 3 Feb 1761 *DT2*.

vi Joseph, b 24 Feb 1762 *Dx*, bp 13 Mar 1762 *Dx*, d 19 Dec 1782 æ. 20 *DT2*, bu. 22 Dec *NHx*.

vii William, bp 12 Jan 1764 *Dx*, d 1 Oct 1816 æ. 53 *DT2;* Census (D) 1-0-1; m Eunice Hull.

viii Stephen, b 12 Sep 1765 *Dx*, bp 15 Sep 1765 *Dx*, d s. p. 9 Aug 1819; Census (D) 1-1-0.

ix Jonathan, bp 21 Jan 1768 *Dx*, d soon.

x Jonathan, bp 12 Nov 1769 *Dx*, d 10 Dec 1770 *DT2*.

xi Lucretia, b 12 Jan 1772 *Dx*, bp 2 Feb 1772 *Dx*, d 10 Feb 1849; m 10 Aug 1796 Abel Allis.

xii Mary Louisa, bp 12 June 1774 *Dx*, d 6 May 1863; m Giles Mardenbrough.

xiii Grace, b 15 Aug 1776 *Dx*, bp 25 Aug 1776 *Dx*, d 14 Oct 1776 *DT2*.

FAM. 7. DAN & SARAH (———) MANSFIELD:

1 AHIMAAZ, d s. p. 1797.

2 MARY; m 4 Sep 1783 *NHC2*—Asa Potter.

3 TIMOTHY, d s. p. 1782.

FAM. 8. TITUS & MABEL (TODD) MANSFIELD:

1 EBENEZER, b 16 July 1757 *NHV*, d 8 Oct 1819 æ. 63 *ColR;* Census (H) 2-0-4; m 23 Sep 1784 *NHC1*—Mary da. John Lewis.

i Rhoda, b c. 1785; m 12 Aug 1802 *NHC1*—Darius Cooper.

ii Sally, b c. 1787, d 17 Oct 1864 æ. 78; m 18 Nov 1804 *NHC1*—Ransley Hall.

iii Mabel, b 13 Nov 1788 *F*, d 19 June 1867; m Stephen Babcock.

iv Ebenezer, b 23 Jan 1791 *F*, d 10 Feb 1865 æ. 74 *NoHT3;* m 26 Dec 1814 Laura Stiles.

v John Lewis; m 11 Nov 1819 Martha da. David Burnham. "Mrs. Martha" of H m 18 Nov 1846 *HV*—Robert Knight of Portland, Me.

vi Mary, b 30 Jan 1800 *F*, d 1870; m 1 Dec 1819 Ezra Kimberly.

2 ENOS, b 12 Dec 1758 *NHV*, d 20 Feb 1814 æ. 55 *NoHT3;* m 4 Apr 1791 *NoHC*—Elizabeth da. Joseph & Elizabeth (Curtis) Jacobs, b c. 1767, d 22 Apr 1850 æ. 84 *NoHT3*.

i Child, b 16 Aug 1791 *F*, d 16 Aug 1791 *F*.

ii Child, b 16 Aug 1791 *F*, d 19 Aug 1791 *F*.

iii Lyman, b 29 Jan 1793 *NoHV*, d 20 Sep 1869; m (1) Abiah Cooper; m (2) Lucy Hubbell.

iv Seymour, b 1 July 1794 *NoHV*, d 21 Jan 1868 æ. 74 *NoHT3;* m 28 Dec 1826 Almera Bassett.

v Melinda, b 8 July 1797 *NoHV*, d 15 Aug 1866 æ. 69 *NoHT2;* m 10 Apr 1823 *NoHC*—John Frost.

vi Bede, b 7 Dec 1800 *HV*, d 27 Apr 1856 æ. 55 *NoHT3.*

vii Eliza, b 14 Aug 1802 *HV;* m 1829 John Henry Mansfield.

3 Hannah, b 12 Feb 1761 *NHV*, bp 19 Apr 1761 *NoHC;* m 6 Oct 1789 *NoHC*—Daniel Tuttle.

4 Richard, b 24 May 1763 *NHV*, bp 3 July 1763 *NoHC;* Census (NoH) 2-2-1; m 23 June 1785 *NoHC*—Mary da. Isaac & Mabel (Clark) Stiles, b 22 Feb 1763, d 13 Mar 1828 æ. 65 *NoHT1.*

i Leverett, b Nov 1786, d 22 Dec 1868 (at Esperance, N. Y.); m 23 Feb 1806 Sally Sanford.

ii Richard, b 1 Feb 1790, d 19 Feb 1850 æ. 60 *NoHT3;* m Charlotte Potter.

iii Stiles; res. Little Falls, N. Y.; m.

5 Lemuel, bp 5 Jan 1766 *NoHC*, d 26 Sep 1826 æ. 61 *NoHT1;* m 24 Dec 1800 *NHC1*—Mary da. Jason & Mary (Ives) Cooper, b 23 May 1771 *NHV*, d 3 Feb 1858 æ. 83 *NoHT3.*

i Delana; m Zenas Bassett.

ii Eunice m Alfred Thorpe.

iii John, b c. 1808, d 12 July 1849 æ. 41 *NoHT3.*

iv Mary Ann, b 28 July 1809 *F*, d 12 Mar 1892 æ. 83 *NoHT3;* m 16 Nov 1826 *NoHC*—Washington Jacobs.

6 Mabel, bp Oct 1767 *NoHC*, d 5 Mar 1773 *NoHC*, æ. 6 *NoHT1.*

7 Titus, bp 4 Mar 1770 *NoHC*, d 19 Jan 1829 æ. 59 *NoHT1;* m 16 July 1795 *NoHC*—Hannah da. Noah & Abigail (Pierpont) Ives, b 18 Aug 1772 *NHV*, d 11 Dec 1838 æ. 66 *NoHT1.*

i Charlotte, b Jan 1796, d 20 Sep 1871; m 13 May 1824 *NoHC*—Elias Bassett.

8 Jesse, b 11 Aug 1772 *F*, d 21 July 1825 æ. 53 *HT4;* m 28 June 1795 *NoHC*—Kezia da. Isaac & Mabel (Clark) Stiles, bp 15 Nov 1772 *NoHC*. d 4 July 1854 æ. 82 *HT4.*

i Elias, b 25 Nov 1795 *F*, d Feb 1883; res. Sandersfield, Mass.; m 23 May 1817 *NoHC*—Mary Todd.

ii Julia Maria, b 26 Sep 1797 *F*, d 26 May 1885 æ. 87-8 *NHV;* m (1) 26 Sep 1822 *HV*—David Leek; m (2) 21 Jan 1830 George Atwater.

iii Jesse Merrick, b 11 July 1801 *F*, d 23 Mar 1878; m (1) 23 Oct 1825 *HV*—Charlotte Heaton, who d 19 June 1844; m (2) 19 June 1845 *HV*—Julia Tuttle, who d 16 July 1849; m (3) 4 Nov 1850 *HV*—Catherine B. Warner.

9 Mabel, b c. 1774, d 12 Sep 1857 æ. 83 *NoHT1;* m 14 Nov 1793 *NoHV*—Joel Todd.

10 Joel, b c. 1778, d 25 July 1824 æ. 46 *NoHT1;* m Thirza da. Enoch & Jemima (Turner) Jacobs; she k. him with an axe & was living 1827 in Granby.

i Jared, b 29 Sep 1801 *NoHV*, d 7 May 1849; m Sally B. Bradley.

ii John Henry, b 6 June 1806 *NoHV*, d 2 Dec 1881; m 1829

Eliza da. Enos & Elizabeth (Jacobs) Mansfield, b 14 Aug 1802 *HV*.

iii Liverus, b 28 Nov 1808 *NoHV;* res. Livingston, N. Y.; m (1) Esther Jane Osborne; m (2) Charlotte Amanda Latham.

iv Orrin, b 22 Oct 1812 *NoHV;* res. Sherwood, Wis.; m 25 Nov 1838 Betsey A. Bishop.

v Joel Leverett, b 7 Apr 1816 *NoHV*, d s. p. 21 May 1837.

11 MARY, b c. 1781, d 2 Oct 1849 æ. 68 *NoHT3;* m Lyman Smith.

FAM. 9. JOSEPH & HANNAH (PUNDERSON) MANSFIELD:

1 CHARLES, b 14 Dec 1762 *NHV*, d 12 Jan 1830; res. Winchester, N. H.; m (1) Molly Howard; m (2) Elizabeth Howard.

2 ELISHA, b 12 Dec 1764, d 27 Apr 1840; res. Canaan; m Rebecca Camp.

3 JOSEPH, b 17 June 1767, d Aug 1837 æ. 71 *CanaanC;* m 6 Apr 1791 Mary Ann Harrison.

4 SALLY, b 27 Dec 1769, d 8 May 1773.

5 DAVID, b 11 Feb 1772, d 4 Mar 1866 æ. 96 *Westmoreland, N. Y., T;* m (1) 1797 Louisa Harmon; m (2) 1808 Melinda Harmon. A s. David Jr. d 23 Jan 1886 æ. 69-4 *WestmorelandT.*

6 WILLIAM PUNDERSON, b 6 Sep 1774, d 16 Mar 1855; res. Kent, & Waterford, N. Y.; m 1807 Sarah Mills.

7 JOHN TODD, b 31 Dec 1776, d 25 Oct 1860; res. 1830 Macdonough, Chenango Co., N. Y.; m 1798 Dolly Steele.

8 SALLY, b 13 June 1779, d s. p. 18 May 1857.

9 TIMOTHY, b 1 May 1782, d 2 Apr 1845; res. Salisbury; m 11 Mar 1809 Annie Carter.

FAM. 10. UZAL & RACHEL (SPERRY) MANSFIELD:

1 ABIGAIL, b 7 Aug 1771 *NHV*, bp 14 Sep 1774 *HCI*.

2 URI, b 30 May 1773 *NHV*, bp 14 Sep 1774 *HCI*, d 5 Jan 1813 æ. 40 *BethlehemC;* m Eunice Atwater.

3 TIMOTHY, b 17 May 1775 *NHV*, bp 20 Aug 1775 *HCI*.

4 MABEL, b 1 June 1777 *NHV*, bp 16 Aug 1777 *HCI*.

5 ELIZABETH, b 24 June 1779 *NHV*, d 10 Dec 1786 æ. 7 *HTI*.

6 JOSIAH, b 20 Oct 1781 *NHV*.

7 LEMUEL, bp Oct 1784 *HCI*.

8 EBENEZER, bp 14 Jan 1787 *HCI*.

9 ELIZABETH, bp 5 July 1789 *HCI*, d 8 Nov 1808 æ. 19 *BethlehemC.*

10 JAMES, bp 25 Mar 1792 *HCI*.

FAM. 11. JOSIAH & HANNAH (COOPER) MANSFIELD:

1 JOSEPH.

2 JOSIAH, b c. 1773, d 28 June 1826 æ. 53 *HT3;* m 18 Mar 1796 *NHCI*—Anna Dickerman.

3 JERE.

FAM. 12. JONATHAN & MARY (DORCHESTER) MANSFIELD:

1 MARY, b 22 June 1762 *NHV*, d 31 Mar 1792 æ. 30 *BD;* m 18 Apr 1781 *WdC*—Wheeler Beecher.

2 JOHN, b 28 Dec 1764 *NHV*, d probably s. p.

3 Sarah, b c. 1768, d 26 Apr 1856 æ. 88 *NHT1;* m 1786 John Benedict.

FAM. 13. James Kierstead & Mary (Hitchcock) Mansfield:

1 Jonathan, b c. 1775, bp 26 June 1778 *NHC1*, d 1801; m 9 Jan 1796 *NHx*—Hannah Dougal; she m (2) Ebenezer Johnson.
i Lucy Maria, b c. 1797, d 19 May 1847 æ. 50 *NHV.*

2 Kierstead, b c. 1777, bp 26 June 1778 *NHC1*, d 16 Jan 1805 æ. 28 *NHT1;* m 15 Mar 1797 *NHC1*—Anna Thompson, who d 6 Oct 1849 æ. 70-9 *NHT1;* she m (2) Dec 1818 *ColR*—Eli Osborn.
i Eliza A., b 28 Jan 1800, d 14 Apr 1861; m 19 Sep 1821 Samuel Rowland.
ii George K., b 10 May 1802, d 21 July 1815.

3 Mary, bp 12 Sep 1779 *NHC1;* m 4 Mar 1800 *NHC1*—Leman Hall.

4 Sarah, bp 17 Mar 1782 *NHC1;* m Stephen Porter.

5 Julia, b 1 Nov 1784 *F*, bp 9 Jan 1785 *NHC1*, d 9 Oct 1850 æ. 66 *NHT1;* m 21 Mar 1821 David Ritter.

6 Rachel, b 14 Mar 1787 *F*, bp 20 May 1787 *NHC1*, d 26 Feb 1855; m James Webster Townsend.

FAM. 14. Henry & Mary (Fenno) Mansfield:

1 Henry Stephen, b 26 May 1786 *F*, bp 4 June 1786 *NHx*, d 26 Mar 1851; res. Slatersville, R. I.; m 10 Nov 1811 Elizabeth Buffwin.

2 John Fenno, b 9 Jan 1788 *F*, bp 18 Oct 1788 *NHx*, d 12 Sep 1812.

3 Mary Grace Caroline, b 4 June 1792 *F*, d 16 Apr 1825; m Daniel Wade of Cincinnati.

4 Grace Totten, b 13 Feb 1799 *F*, d 10 Mar 1878; m 15 June 1816 E ias Parker.

5 Hannah Fenno, b 24 Feb 1801 *F*, d s. p. c. 1873.

6 Joseph King Fenno, b 22 Dec 1803 *F*, d 18 Sep 1862; m 25 Sep 1838 Louisa Maria Mather.

FAM. 15. Nathan & Anna (Tomlinson) Mansfield:

1 Jared, b 11 July 1775 *DV*, bp 14 Aug 1774 *Dx*, d 28 May 1828 æ. 54 *DT5;* m 4 Mar 1807 Eunice (Jennings) Lum.

2 Betsey, b 1 Dec 1777 *DV*, bp 7 Dec 1777 *Dx*, d 31 Jan 1863 æ. 85 *DT3;* m Anson Gillet.

3 Sally, bp 18 Mar 1781 *Dx*, d 4 Apr 1855 æ. 74 *DT5;* m Cyrus Holbrook.

4 Isaac, bp 28 Jan 1787 *Dx.*

5 Anna, "child" bp 14 June 1789 *Dx*, d 10 Apr 1870; m Wm. Dyer of Berlin.

FAM. 16. William & Elizabeth (Lyon) Mansfield:

1 William, b 23 Oct 1777 *F*, bp 16 Apr 1780 *NHC1*, d 27 Aug 1861 æ. 84 *NHV;* m 25 Feb 1799 *NHC1*—Sally da. Nathan & Esther (Peck) Oakes, bp 10 June 1781 *NHC2*, d 14 June 1840 æ. 52 (?) *NHV.*

2 Elizabeth, b 27 Jan 1780 *F*, bp 16 Apr 1780 *NHC1*, d 23 May

1818; m 31 Mar 1811 *NHx*—Richard Everit.

3 ANNA, b 3 Sep 1782 *NHT1*, bp 29 Sep 1782 *NHC1*, d 25 Mar 1863 *NHT1*; m 4 Mar 1810 *NHx*—Henry Eld.

4 ISAAC, b 28 May 1786 *F*, bp 13 Aug 1786 *NHC1* .

5 MARY, b 28 Apr 1789*F* , bp 20 Aug 1789 *NHC1*, "child" d 22 Aug 1789 æ. 0-4 *NHC1*.

6 SARAH, b 4 Apr 1791 *F*, bp 18 Sep 1791 *NHC1*, d 23 July 1875; m 6 Feb 1820 Richard Everit.

7 SUSANNA, b 19 Jan 1795 *F*, bp 24 May 1795 *NHC1*, d s. p. 5 June 1871.

8 LUCIUS, b 26 Feb 1798 *F*, bp 27 July 1798 *NHC1*, d 13 Apr 1873 (at Lumpkin, Ga.): m (1) 1824 ——— Winter; m (2) 15 Aug 1838 Elizabeth Bryan.

9 LOIS, b 15 May 1803 *F*, bp 13 Nov 1803 *NHC1*, d 9 Feb 1804.

10 LOUISA, b 10 Dec 1806 *F*, d 1835; m 1833 Peter Mettaner of Va.

FAM. 16. WILLIAM & LUCY (PECK) MANSFIELD:

11 BENJAMIN FRANKLIN, b 14 Mar 1820 *F*; m 16 Apr 1843 Harriet Janet da. Elisha & Jane (Baldwin) Clark of M.

12 FREDERICK, b 28 Feb 1825 *F*; m 20 Sep 1846 Emily da. Jared & Sally Barnes of NoH.

MANSFIELD. MISCELLANEOUS. JOHN of W, d 1823; Capt.; was he FAM. 6, 1, *i*?; m (1) Sybil ———, who d 13 Jan 1779 æ. 46 *WT1*; m (2) Eunice ———. Children: 1 Abel, b 29 Dec 1772 *WV*. 2 Ira, b 16 Oct 1776 *WV*, d 16 June 1849 (at Atwater, Ohio); m Sukey Kirtland. 3 Sybil; m John Hiddleston......CALVIN, d 13 Jan 1851 æ. 78 *NoBT1*; m Polly ——. Children: Celina, d 11 Sep 1805 æ. 5-10 *NoBT1*; Nathan, d Sep 1828 æ. 27 (at St. Kitts, W. I.) *NoBT1*; Emily Celina, d 12 May 1833 æ 19 *NoBT1*. ......HANNAH, bp 24 June 1739 *NHC1*......TIMOTHY, bp 21 July 1723 *NHC1*.

MANSOR. WILLIAM of Medford, Mass., m 2 Feb 1714/5 Lydia Swan, b 10 Nov 1689, & had a da. Lydia, b 10 Apr 1716, d 20 Aug 1717; he & family warned from Medford 1723; may be identical with WILLIAM, b c. 1694, d 31 May 1768 æ. 74 *NHC1*; m Rebecca da. William & Jane (Holmes) Wooding, wid. Joseph Smith, b 1707, d after 1779, probably the "Widow Mansor" who d 1795 (*HT2 list*).

1 WILLIAM, b 1 Feb 1739/40 *NHV*; m 30 May 1758 *NHC2*—Lois Potter. Lorain w. Wm. d 13 Apr 1774 *WtnD*; child of Wm. bu. 12 Mar 1766 *WtnD*; infant child & s. of Wm. d 22 Mar 1770 *WtnD*. A Wm. res. Wtn 1814. Rebecca d 14 Oct 1866 æ. 75 *NHT2*. The above perhaps are members of this family.

2 JOHN, b 8 Jan 1741/2 *NHV*, d 9 July 1812 æ. 71 *WV*; Census (H) 1-1-2; m (1) 26 Mar 1765 *WV*—Rachel da. Aaron & Rachel (Lines) Gilbert, b 22 June 1746 *NHV*, d before 1782; m (2) 16 Oct 1783 *NHC2*—Elizabeth da. Thomas & Mary (Miles) Punderson, wid. Samuel Wooding, b 2 Sep 1747 *NHV*, d 29 Jan 1837 æ. 90 (*HT2 list*); he div. her; m (3) Eunice ——— .

(By 1): *i* Huldah, b 6 Apr 176[6] *WV*; m John Hendrick.

ii Javan, b c. 1767; m 1 Nov 1789 *WC*—Lydia Parker.
iii William, b 20 Sep 1769 *F*, d 7 Feb 1855; Census (H) 1-1-1; rem. to Great Barrington & Tyringham, Mass.; m 1789 Phebe Munson.
iv Rachel; m Ephraim Manchester.
v Esther; m 16 Apr 1796 *NHx*—Jonathan Manchester.
vi John; m 2 Sep 1799 *NHC1*—Sarah Barney; she m (2) Sep 1808 *ConnH*—John Groom of Lexington, Ky.
vii Aaron; res. Great Barrington, Mass., 1812.
viii Hannah; m Daniel Twiss.
(By 2): *ix* Samuel, b c. 1785, d 18 Dec 1871 æ. 87 *HV;* m Sarah Alling.
(By 3?): *x* Miles.
xi Betsey; m 5 Nov 1818 *NoHC*—Russell Thorpe.

3 RICHARD, b 18 Apr 1745 *NHV*, d s. p. 27 Apr 1814 æ. 70 (*HT2 list*).

MARCHANT. Variant, MERCHANT. FAM. 1. THOMAS, s. of Joseph & Abigail (Wheeler), b 9 June 1727 *MV*, d 17 Aug 1799 æ. 73 *WtnD;* Census (Wtn) 2-0-3; m (1) 19 July 1751 *WV*—Sarah Perry, b c. 1731, d 22 Jan 1794 æ. 63 *PC;* m (2) Asenath ——— .

(By 1): 1 SARAH, b 21 Feb 1752 *WV*, d 22 Sep 1807 æ. 56 *WT2;* m 17 Nov 1769 *WV*—Aaron Hull.
2 ELIZABETH, b 7 June 1754 *WV*, d 8 Dec 1756 *WV*.
3 THOMAS, b 4 Aug 1756 *WV;* Census (Wtn) 1-1-3; m.
4 JOEL, b 8 Sep 1758 *WV*, d s. p.
5 ZERUIAH, b 17 Nov 1760 *WV*, d 26 May 1842 æ. 81 *MorrisT;* m Joel Hubbard.
6 ESTHER, b 1 Jan 1763 *WV;* m Thomas Fenn.
7 REUBEN, b 3 Mar 1765 *WV*.
8 ANNA, b 30 Apr 1767 *WV;* m July 1791 Thomas Turner of L.
9 ELIZABETH, b c. 1769; m Reuben Hine.
10 MARY, b 8 Feb 1771 *WV;* m Seba Blakeslee.
11 SAMUEL, b 3 Aug 1773 *WV*, d 11 Aug 1829 æ. 56 *LT;* m Jemima ——— .

MARCHANT. FAM. 2. JOHN, of Wat, d 1782; adm'n granted to David Royce of Washington; distrbution 1789 to wid. Sarah; Charlotte Merchant; eldest s. Joseph; youngest s. David.

MARKS. FAM. 1. JONATHAN, s. of Wm. & Mary of Mid; res. W; m 6 Nov 1735 *WV*—Deborah da. Jabez & Dorothy (Lyman) Brockett, b 1703, d 25 Aug 1770 *WV*. Family incomplete?

1 JAMES, b c. 1738, d 16 Mar 1824 æ. 86 *WT1;* Census (W) 1-2-3; m 23 Dec 1762 *WV*—Hannah Blakeslee, who d 16 May 1814 æ. 73 *WT1*.
i Sarah, b 6 Oct 1763 *WV*.
ii Levi, b 17 July 1765 *WV;* Census (W) 1-2-1; m 8 Oct 1786 *WV*, *NHSupCt*—Hope Treadwell of Haddam; she div. him 1799.
iii Eunice, b 23 Aug 176[7] *WV*, d 13 June 1831 æ. 64 *WT1;* m 23 Mar 1790 *WV*—Jared Brockett.

iv Hannah, b 22 Dec 1769 *WV*, d 11 Jan 1771 *WV*.
v Nathan, b 1 Dec 1771 *WV*, d 11 May 1828 æ. 56 *NoHT1*; Capt.; m 25 Nov 1796 *NoHV*—Susanna da. James & Lydia (Mansfield) Pierpont, b c. 1771, d 2 Nov 1858 æ. 88 *NoHT1*. **FAM. 2.**
vi Abigail, b 13 Nov 1773 *WV*.
vii James, b 19 Apr 1776 *WV*, d 22 Feb 1856 æ. 80 *WT1*; m
PAGE 1789 (1) Esther H. ——, who d 6 Oct 1831 æ. 48 *WT1*; m (2) Catherine ——, who d 27 Sep 1841 æ. 60 *WT1*.
viii William, b 3 Mar 1778 *WV*, d 15 Nov 1840 æ. 63 *WT1*; Col.; m Hannah ——, who d 26 Aug 1851 æ. 73 *WT1*.
ix Hannah, b 22 Apr 1781 *WV*.

2 Nathan, b 29 May 1744 *WV*, d 5 Sep 1751 *WV*.

FAM. 2. Nathan & Susanna (Pierpont) Marks:

1 Electa, b 1 Feb 1797 *NoHV*, bp 15 Dec 1799 *NoHC*; m 18 Dec 1816 *NoHC*—Hoadley Bray.
2 Amanda, b 2 Feb 1800 *NoHV*, bp 2 Feb 1800 *NoHC*, d 12 Feb 1800 *NoHV*, æ. 0-0-10 *NoHC*.
3 Thomas, b 30 Mar 1802 *NoHV*, bp May 1802 *NoHC*, d 11 Aug 1841 æ. 39 *NoHT3*.
4 Lodema, b 13 Dec 1804 *NoHV*, *NoHT3*, d 11 Apr 1895 *NoHT3*.
5 George Riley, b 9 Jan 1808 *NoHV*.
6 Susan Amanda, b 14 Sep 1811 *NoHV*, d 4 Oct 1872 æ. 61 *NoHT 3*.
7 William Henry, b 31 Mar 1814 *NoHV*, d 11 Feb 1865 æ. 51 (at Wilmington, N. C.) *NoHT3*.
8 Justin, b 3 June 1818 *NoHV*, d 10 Oct 1848 æ. 30 *NoHT3*.

MARKS. Joseph (bro. of Jonathan, fam. 1) m 8 Jan 1736 *WV*—Dorcas da. Jabez & Dorothy (Lyman) Brockett; Sarah (their sister) m 19 Feb 1736 *WV*—Nathan Brockett.

MARSH. Jonathan & Samuel, early settlers in NH, had a sister Hannah who m (1) Launcelot Fuller & (2) —— Finch. Jonathan & Mary had: Sarah, Deborah, Mary & Dorothy, bp Oct 1653 *MC1*; John, b Feb 1653/4 *MV*, bp 14 May 1654 *MC1*; & Jonathan, b 29 Sep 1657 *MV*. Samuel had:

1 Mary, b 1648 *NHC1*, bp 20 Mar 1653 *NHC1*.
2 Samuel, b 12 Feb 1649 *NHV*, bp 20 Mar 1653 *NHC1*.
3 Comfort, b 22 Aug 1652 *NHV*, bp 20 Mar 1653 *NHC1*.
4 Hannah, b 22 July 1655 *NHV*, bp Aug 1655 *NHC1*.
5 Elizabeth, b 27 Dec 1657 *NHV*, bp 11 Feb 1657 *NHC1* [1657/8].
6 John, b 2 May 1661 *NHV*, bp 2 May 1661 *NHC1*.
7 Joseph, b 1 Apr 1663 *NHV*, "child" bp 1663 *NHC1*.

MARSH. Robert, Census (NH) 1-2-1; m Abigail ——.

1 Robert, bp 11 July 1787 *NHx*.
2 Abigail, bp 22 Nov 1789 *NHx*, bu. 9 Dec 1789 (æ. 0-3) *NHx*.

MARSHALL. Samuel Bryan, of M, D & NH, 19 Feb 1826 æ. 69 *NHT1*; his w. Mary d 19 June 1843 æ. 77 *NHT1*.

1 Sarah; m Josiah Hitchcock.

2 Maria; m Isaac Pinto.

3 Augusta M.

4 Julia, b 13 Sep 1791 *NHTI*, d 21 Jan 1866 *NHTI*; m (1) Enos Bassett; m (2) 21 Apr 1824 *NHV*—Luther Hall of W.

5 Eliphal; m 28 Sep 1823 *NHV*—Edward Bement of Charleston, S. C.

MARTIN. Robert of NH had children: Mary, bp 26 May 1646 *NHCI*; John, bp 28 May 1648 *NHCI*; & Stephen, bp 15 May 1652 *NHCI*......John m 15 Jan 1684 *WV*—Elizabeth da Nathaniel & Elizabeth How, b 27 July 1666 *NHV*. Perhaps Robert (fam. 1) belonged to this family.

fam. 1. Robert, d 1 June 1758 *F&IWRolls*; m 15 July 1734 *WV*—Abigail da. John & Mary (Kibbe) Parker, b 3 Mar 1710 *WV*.

1 James, b 3 Mar 1735 *WV*; m 8 Mar 1758 *WV*—Agnes Crawford.

i Mary, b 28 Dec 1758 *WV*.

ii Samuel Crawford, b 28 Oct 1760 *WV*.

iii James, b 10 Nov 1761 *WV*.

2 Sarah, b 27 Mar 1737 *WV*; m 11 Mar 1756 *WV*—Aaron Parker.

3 Robert, b 11 July 1739 *WV*; m 15 July 1762 *WV*—Elizabeth Tyler; Census, Elizabeth (C) 0-0-2.

4 Lydia, b 27 Oct 1740 *WV*; m 23 May 176[0] *WV*—Joshua Curtis.

5 Elizabeth, b 23 Sep 1742 *WV*; m (1) 8 Dec 1762 *WV*—Moses Bellamy; m (2) 3 Oct 1771 *CC*—Abel Wolcott.

6 Samuel, b 1 May 1744 *WV*, d 1779; res. NH; m Freelove da. Enoch & Rebecca Thomas.

7 Abigail, b 9 Dec 1745 *WV*; m Ephraim Beebe.

8 Isaac, b 25 Apr 1748 *WV*; m 21 May 1767 *CC*—Lois Ives.

i Obed, b 28 Mar 1768 *WV*.

ii Lucinda, b 3 Dec 1772 *WV*.

9 Mary, b 30 Aug 1750 *WV*; m 22 June 1775 *WV*, *CC*—Jacob Lewis.

10 John, b 27 Sep 1754 *WV*; Census (C) 1-2-3; m 16 Oct 1777 *WV*—Jerusha Doolittle.

i Eli, b 19 Oct 1778 *CV*.

ii Chauncey, b 26 Aug 1780 *CV*.

iii David, b 19 Feb 1786 *CV*.

iv Lotty, b 24 Aug 1788 *CV*.

v Eudocia, b 12 Mar 1798 *CV*.

fam. 2. Francis, b c. 1748, d 9 Jan 1838 æ. 90 (?) *WdC*, æ. 100 (a Frenchman) *WdD*; m 25 Nov 1773 *WdC*—Cleopatra da. Benjamin & Sarah (Carrington) Lines, bp 1753 *WdC*, d 20 Dec 1819 æ. 66 *WdC*. Family incomplete.

1 William, b c. 1776, d 12 Apr 1795 æ. 19 *WdC*.

2 Jesse, b c. 1778, d 14 Sep 1806 æ. 28 *WdC*.

3 (possibly) Chloe, b [30 Nov 1787], d 15 Mar 1875 æ. 87-3-15 *WdV* (called da. Samuel & Chloe); m Eliakim Terrell.

4 Joseph, bp 21 July 1793 *WdC*; m Sally ——, who d 21 Feb 1865 æ. 75 *WdD*.

5 WILLIAM, bp 26 June 1796 *WdC*, d Feb 1803 *WdD*.

MARTIN. MISCELLANEOUS. JOHN m 6 Mar 1760 *WdC*—Mary Sanford. ......ANNA d 13 June 1815 æ. 50 *WdC*......RICHARD d 12 Dec 1790 æ. 65 *NHC1*; Kate w. Richard d 3 June 1791 æ. 62 *NHC1*......WIDOW d 27 Feb 1799 æ. 65 *NHC1*......ANTHONY of Mid, d 16 Nov 1673, had John, b c. 1662; Mary, b c. 1666, m Nathan Andrews of W; Elizabeth, b c. 1671.

MATHER. ALLYN had children: Allyn, bp 19 Mar 1775 *NHC2*; Elizabeth, bp 21 Feb 1779 *NHC2*; Thankful Sophia, bp 20 Jan 1782 *NHC2*; Increase, bp 23 Nov 1783 *NHC2*......WARHAM m Dec 1700 *NHV*—Elizabeth da. John & Abigail (Pierson) Davenport, b 7 Oct 1666 *NHV*, d 23 July 1744 *NHV*.

MATTHEWS. FAM. 1. WILLIAM, d 1684; res. NH & Bd; m [?Jane ——].

1 ELIZABETH, b 27 Dec 1672 *NHV*; she had a nat. child by Thomas Biggs, b 1700.

2 CALEB, b [24 Apr 1675], d 23 Aug 1755 *WV*, æ. 81 *CT1*; Sgt.; m (1) 13 Jan 1702 *NHV*—Elizabeth da. Daniel & Esther (Sperry) Hotchkiss, b 30 Aug 1684 *NHV*, d Jan 1735/6 *CC*, 11 Jan 1736 æ. 62(?) *CT1*; m (2) 22 July 1736 *WV*—Elizabeth da. Arthur & ——— (Hill) Henbury, wid. Benjamin Frisbie.

(By 1): *i* Caleb, b 18 Dec 1703 *NHV*, d 7 Apr 1786; Capt.; res. Bristol; m (1) 7 Mar 1727 *WV*—Hannah da Nathaniel & Sarah (Jennings) Hitchcock, b 11 Jan 1709 *WV*, d Dec 1731 *CC*, 5 Dec *WV*; m (2) 9 May 1733 *WV*—Ruth da. William & Ruth Merriam, b 2 Nov 1713 *Lynn, Mass.*, d 3 Nov 1785. **FAM. 2.**

ii Elizabeth, b 6 Oct 1705 *NHV*, d 17 Sep 1731 æ. 26 *CT1*; m 25 Feb 1731 *WV*—Amos Hotchkiss.

iii Esther, b 1 Aug 1708 *WV*, d 19 Apr 1773 æ. 65 *CT2*; m 3 Nov 1724 *WV*—Benjamin Lewis.

iv Abel, b 26 Feb 1710 *WV*, d 29 July 1789 *CC*; m 17 June 1735 *NHV*—Mary da. Joseph & Abigail (Curtis) Holt, b 9 Feb 1714 *WV*. **FAM. 3.**

v Abner, b 22 July 1712 *WV*; res. Bristol; m 20 July 1735 *WV*—Lois da. Obadiah & Eunice (Beach) Hotchkiss, b 11 Jan 1717 *WV*. **FAM. 4.**

vi Jesse, b 20 Sep 1716 *WV*, d 26 Sep 1729 *WV*.

vii Aaron, b 19 Nov 1721 *WV*, d 24 Apr 1806 æ. 84 *PV*; Ens.; m 14 Jan 1742 *WV*—Huldah da. John & Susanna (Henbury) Frisbis, b 15 Nov 1715, d 27 Apr 1797 æ. 81 *PV*. **FAM. 5.**

3 THOMAS, d 5 Sep 1762 *WV*; m 23 May 1700 *WV*—Abiah da. John & Hannah (Bassett) Parker, b 26 Mar 1677 *NHV*.

i Thomas, b 14 Feb 1701 *WV*, bp (as Jr.) 31 Oct 1725 *CC*, d 6 Sep 1798 æ. 98 *WtnD*; m (1) 14 July 1724 *WV*—Eunice da. William & Atheldred (Berry) Merriam, b 18 May 1704 *Lynn, Mass.*, d 2 May 1783 æ. 79 *WtnT*, æ. 78 *WtnD*; m (2) 26 Mar 1784 *WtnV*—Hannah Scott. **FAM. 6.**

ii Joseph, b 5 May 1703 *WV*, d 21 Feb 1785 *CC*; m 4 Oct 1726 *WV*—Hannah da. Nathaniel & Sarah (How) Curtis, b 19 Feb 1705 *WV*. **FAM. 7.**

iii Deborah, b 8 July 1704 *WV*, d 1754; m 17 Oct 1727 *WV*—John Parker.

iv Abigail, b 30 July 1707 *WV*; m 1 Jan 1740 *WV*—John Andrews.

v Moses, b 16 Aug 1710 *WV*, d 23 Oct 1806 æ. 75 *SC*; m 21 Aug 1753 Huldah ——— .

vi Amos, b 6 Apr 1714 *WV*; Census (C) 1-0-1; m 3 May 1739 *WV*—Elizabeth da. John & Elizabeth (Hall) Moss, b 6 Dec 1741 *WV*.

vii Benjamin, b 14 May 1720 *WV*; rem. to S; res. 1763 Westfield, Mass.; m 3 Dec 1740 *WV*, *WC2*—Lucy da. Joseph & Mary (Parker) Clark, b 28 June 1721 *NHV*. Children recorded *FarmV*: Abiah, b 8 Apr 1750; daughter, b 21 June 1752.

4 WILLIAM.

FAM. 2. CALEB & HANNAH (HITCHCOCK) MATTHEWS:

1 NATHANIEL, b 29 Nov 1727 *WV*, bp Dec 1727 *CC*, d 15 Feb 1806; m (1) Sarah ———, who d 1764 æ. 32 *BristolC*; m (2) Martha ———, who before marriage had a da. Martha Harden.

(By 1): *i* Phebe, b 5 Jan 1749/50 *FarmV*; m ——— Roberts.

ii Elizabeth, b 8 Mar 1752 *FarmV*; m ——— Hungerford.

iii Sarah, bp 27 Nov 1758 *Bristol x*; m ——— Rich.

iv Hannah, bp 28 Sep 1760 *Bristol x*, d young.

(By 2): *v* Nathaniel, bp 12 Jan 1766 *Bristol x*.

vi Hannah, bp 13 Sep 1767 *Bristol x*, d young.

vii Mary Ann, bp 9 Dec 1770 *Bristol x*; m ——— Woodruff.

viii Asahel.

ix Hannah, bp 18 Aug 1776 *Bristol x*; m ——— Mitchell.

x Margot, bp 15 Oct 1780 *Bristol x*.

2 MAMRE, b 15 Apr 1730 *WV*, bp Apr 1730 *CC*, d Apr 1732 *CC*.

FAM. 2. CALEB & RUTH (MERRIAM) MATTHEWS:

3 MAMRE, b 18 Aug 1734 *WV*, bp Sep 1734 *CC*, d 12 Sep 1734 *WV*, "child" d Sep 1734 *CC*.

4 RUTH, bp 12 Oct 1735 *CC*.

5 HANNAH, b 31 Jan 1737 *WV*, bp 23(?) Jan 1736/7 *CC*.

6 JERUSHA, b 8 May 1739 *WV*, bp May 1739 *CC*, "child" d Mar 1740/1 *CC*.

7 JERUSHA, b 30 May 1741 *WV*, bp June 1741 *CC*.

8 CALEB, b 16 Dec 1743 *WV*, bp Dec 1743 *CC*; m 1 Jan 1766 *FarmV*—Anna Carrington. Family incomplete.

i Caleb, b 16 Oct 1767 *FarmV*, bp 6 Nov 1767 *Bristol x*, d 8 Apr 1840 æ. 72 *BristolT*; m 22 Jan 1794 *Bristol x*—Sarah da. David Newell, who d 17 Jan 1851 æ. 87 *BristolT*.

ii Simeon, b 20 May 1769 *FarmV*, bp 25 June 1769 *Bristol x*.

iii Nancy, b 21 June 1771 *FarmV*, bp 23 June 1771 *Bristol x*.

iv Atheldred; m 1 Feb 1790 *WtnV*—John Fancher.

9 MAMRE, b 19 Feb 1745/6 *FarmV*, bp 6 Apr 1746 *CC*, d 25 Apr 1759.

10 ATHELDRED, b 17 May 1748 *FarmV*, bp 16 July 1748 *Bristolx*, d soon.

11 ATHELDRED, b 11 Jan 1754 *FarmV*, bp 8 Sep 1754 *Bristolx*, d 10 Dec 1811 æ. 58 *BristolT;* m Lemuel Carrington.

FAM. 3. ABEL & MARY (HOLT) MATTHEWS:

1 ELIZABETH, b 17 Mar 1735/6 *NHV*, bp Mar 1736 *CC*.

2 ESTHER, b 27 Dec 1738 *NHV*, bp Dec 1738 *CC*, d 20 Nov 1741 *WV*, "child" d 1 Nov 1741 *CC*.

3 ABIGAIL, b 23 Aug 1741 *WV*, bp Oct 1741 *CC*, d 12 Dec 1819 æ. 78 *HT1;* m 10 Feb 1773 *CC*—Samuel Warner.

4 ESTHER, b 21 May 1744 *WV*, bp May 1744 *CC*, d 8 Sep 1807 *CC;* Census, "Hester" (C) 0-0-1.

5 ABEL, b 25 Feb 1746/7 *WV*, bp Feb 1746/7 *CC;* m 24 July 1777 *WV*—Eunice Pardee.

i John, b 4 Mar 1778 *WV*.

ii Hannah, b 19 Dec 1779 *WV*.

6 JOHN, b 24 Oct 1749 *WV*, d in Camp 1776 *CC*.

7 MARY, b 29 Oct 1751 *WV*, bp 3 Nov 1751 *CC;* m [Eden] Johnson.

8 EPHRAIM, b 23 Sep 1754 *WV;* Census (C) 1-1-2.

9 SUSANNA, b 23 July 1756 *WV*, b 1756 d 1829 *CT1;* m 3 Nov 1784 *CC*—Roswell Bradley.

FAM. 4. ABNER & LOIS (HOTCHKISS) MATTHEWS:

1 JESSE, b 14 May 1736 *WV*, bp May 1736 *CC*.

2 ABNER, b 23 Jan 1738 *WV*, bp 29 Jan 1737/8 *CC;* m (1) Sarah ——, who d 1765 æ. 32 *BristolC;* m (2) Eunice da. Gershom & Lois Tuttle, b 23 Apr 1743 *FarmV*. Children recorded *FarmV:* Mamre 14 July 1760, Lucretia 14 Apr 1762, Sarah 2 Mar 1764, Thomas 14 June 1766, Lois 14 Dec 1767, Levi 10 Aug 1769.

3 EUNICE, b 3 Mar 1740 *WV*, bp Mar 1739/40 *CC*.

4 LOIS, b 6 Aug 1742 *WV*, bp 1 (?) Aug 1742 *CC*.

5 DAVID, b 27 Oct 1744 *FarmV*.

6 OBADIAH, b 15 Feb 1746/7 *FarmV*, bp 21 June 1747 *CC*.

7 AMOS, b 17 Nov 1755 *FarmV*.

8 WILLIAM, b 17 Apr 1757 *FarmV*.

9 EBENEZER, b 28 May 1759 *FarmV*.

FAM. 5. AARON & HULDAH (FRISBIE) MATTHEWS:

1 REUBEN, b 29 Mar 1743 *WV*, bp 3 Apr 1743 *CC*, d 22 Feb 1777 *CC;* m 31 Oct 1765 *WV*—Elizabeth McKean, who d 9 Feb 1790 *CC;* Census, Elizabeth (C) 0-0-2.

i Sarah, b 21 Sep 1767 *WV*, bp 18 Sep 1768 *CC*.

ii Ruth, b 25 May 1769 *WV*, bp 9 July 1769 *CC*.

iii William, b 17 Jan 1772 *WV*, bp 15 Feb 1772 *CC*.

iv Reuben, b 24 Jan 1774 *WV*.

v Ruth Elizabeth, b 29 May 1776 *WV*, bp 28 July 1776 *CC*.

PAGE 1248

2 AARON, b 23 Mar 1744/5 *WV*, bp Mar 1745 *CC;* m 17 Jan 1765 *WV*—Hannah Tuttle.
3 LYDIA, b 22 Nov 1747 *WV*, bp 18 Oct (?) 1747 *CC*.
4 HULDAH, b 9 July 1750 *WV*, bp June 1750 *CC*.
5 REBECCA, b 19 Nov 1754 *WV*.
6 SARAH, b 10 Feb 1758 *WV*, d 11 May 1786 *CC*.
7 SAMUEL, b 23 Feb 1761 *WV*, d 1812; m Mamre Catlin.
A "child" d July 1753 *CC*.

FAM. 6. THOMAS & EUNICE (MERRIAM) MATTHEWS:
1 STEPHEN, b 1 May 1725 *WV*. bp 22 Aug 17[25] *CC;* Census (Wtn) 2-0-3; m 5 Dec 1750 *WatV*—Hannah Parker.
2 PHINEAS, b 18 Dec 1726 *WV*, bp Feb 1726/7 *CC*, d 26 Dec 1763 *WtnD;* m 23 Mar 1747/8 *WatV*—Elsie Tompkins.
3 GIDEON, b 8 Apr 1729 *WV*, bp May 1729 *CC*, d 29 May 1740 *WatV*.

FAM. 7. JOSEPH & HANNAH (CURTIS) MATTHEWS:
1 EDMUND, b 7 Feb 1727 *WV*, bp Apr 1735 *CC*.
2 SAMUEL, b 4 Oct 1728 *WV*, bp Apr 1735 *CC;* m 17 Jan 1754 *WV*—Abigail Smith.
3 REUBEN, b 6 Jan 1731 *WV*, bp Apr 1735 *CC*, d 24 June 1737 *WV*, "child" d June 1737 *CC*.
4 SARAH, b 22 Oct 1732 *WV*, bp Apr 1735 *CC*, d 6 Dec 1742 *WV*, "child" d Dec 1742 *CC*.
5 JOSEPH, bp Aug 1735 *CC*.
6 EUNICE, b 25 Nov 1737 *WV*, bp 8 Jan 1737/8 *CC*, d 4 Dec 1742 *WV*, "da." d Dec 1742 *CC*.
7 HANNAH, b 16 Jan 1741 *WV*, bp Mar 1740/1 *CC*, d 8 Dec 1742 *WV*, "da." d Dec 1742 *CC*.
8 REUBEN, b 10 Feb 1743/4 *WV*, bp Apr 1744 *CC;* rem. to Wat; m 24 July 1768 *CC*—Adah da. Enoch & Rachel (Plumb) Curtis, b 12 Mar 1753 *FarmV*.
i Hannah, b 9 Oct 1769 *Chester, Mass., V*.
ii Lucas, b 24 Aug 1772 *WatV*.
iii Samuel, b 15 Dec 1774 *WatV*. d Feb 1776 *WatV*.
iv Samuel, b 13 Oct 1776 *WatV*.
9 ELIADA, b 15 Nov 1746 *WV*, bp Jan 1746/7 *CC*, d 15 Oct 1749 *WV*, "child" Oct 1749 *CC*.
10 ELIADA, b 5 Sep 1749 *WV*, bp 6 Sep 1749 *CC;* m 28 July 1768 *WV*—Lucy da. Gideon & Miriam (Hotchkiss) Curtis, b 29 Mar 1747/8 *WV*, d 1 Mar 1821 æ. 73 *Wells, Vt., T;* she m (2) Robert Hotchkiss.

MATTHEWS. MISCELLANEOUS. JOHN of Mid & NH, d before 1745; m 14 Sep 1727 *NHV*—Lydia da. Thomas & Sarah (Hitcheson) Leek, b 5 July 1699 *NHV*. Children: 1 John, b 10 June 1728 *NHV*, bp 11 Apr 1736 *NHC1*. 2 Lydia, b 25 Oct 1730 *NHV*. 3 Hannah, bp 11 Apr 1736 *NHC1*....... ISAAC m 2 Dec 1734 *NHV*—Susanna da. Paul & Susanna (Bowden) Cornwall, b 20 Jan 1713 *NHV* [1713/4]; she m (2) Hachaliah Thomas...... BENJAMIN, b 23 June 1754 *F*, d 7 Feb 1788 *F*, bu. 9 Feb æ. 34 *NHx;* m 27 Apr

1783 *NHx*—Sarah da. Joseph & Prudence (Alling) Brown, wid. Samuel Perkins, b 13 July 1754 *F*, d 19 Aug 1834; had da. Hannah...... WILLIAM m 7 Mar 1802 *NHCl*—Lucy da. Silas & Hannah (Upson) Merriman, b c. 1777, "Wid." d 31 Oct 1805 æ. 28 *NHCl*. Child of Widow d 19 Sep 1805 *NHCl*....... WIDOW d 30 Mar 1805 æ. 67 *NHCl*.

MATTOON. FAM. 1. JOHN, b 12 Oct 1682 *Deerfield, Mass.*, d 19 Feb 1754 *WV*, æ. 71 *WTl;* Sgt.; m 20 Oct 1706 *WV*—Jerusha da. David & Sarah (Rockwell) Hall, b 28 Oct 1687 *WV*, d 28 Sep 1760 æ. 72 *WTl*.

1 SARAH, b 3 Oct 1707 *WV;* m Ebenezer Lucas.

2 JERUSHA, b 27 Dec 1709 *WV*, d 15 Aug 1741 *WV*, bu. 17 Aug *CC;* m Cornelius Brooks.

3 PHILIP, b 24 Sep 1711 *WV*, d 21 Jan 1782 æ. 71 *WTl;* m 23 Dec 1737 *WV*—Mary da. John & Hannah (Ray) Humiston, b 30 June 1718 *NHV*, d 10 May 1806 æ. 88 *WTl*.

(By 1): *i* Ebenezer, b 17 Sep 1738 *WV*, d 27 May 1814 æ. 77 *WTl;* Census (W) 1-0-2; m 16 Nov 1773 *WCl*—Martha da. Samuel & Sarah (Clark) Merriman, b 23 Apr 1733 *NHV*, d 10 Nov 1802 æ. 69 *WTl*. FAM. 2.

ii Mary, b 14 June 1740 *WV*, d 7 Oct 1784 æ. 44 *NoHTl;* m 13 Jan 1762 *NHV*, *WCl*—Zuar Bradley.

iii Jerusha, b 25 Mar 1742 *WV*, d 22 Nov 1827 æ. 86 *WTl;* m 13 Jan 1762 *WV*—Eliasaph Merriman.

iv John, b 11 May 1744 *WV*, d s. p.

v Hannah, b 16 Aug 1746 *WV*, d s. p.

vi Sarah, b 1 Feb 1749/50 *WV*, bp 31 May 1752 *NoBC2;* m 8 Dec 1777 *WV*, *WCl*—John Culver.

vii John, b 20 Jan 1750/1 *WV*, d s. p. 18 Jan 1808 æ. 57 *WTl;* Census (W) 1-1-1; m 8 Feb 1783 *WV*—Lydia Abbott.

viii Hannah, b 19 Oct 1753 *WV;* m 4 Oct 1781 *WCl*—Ambrose Avery.

ix Caleb; Census (W) 1-0-5; rem. to Deerfield or Atwater, Portage Co., Ohio; m 16 July 1781 *WV*, *WCl*—Hannah Spencer of Haddam.

4 MARY, b 19 Sep 1713 *WV*.

5 DAVID, b 26 July 1715 *WV*, d 6 Apr 1775 *WtnD;* m 5 Oct 1741 *WV*—Phebe da. James & Hannah Curtis, b 4 Oct 1719 *DurhamV*, d 28 Sep 1776 *WtnD*.

i Esther, b 20 Nov 1742 *WV*, d 10 Mar 1769 *WatV;* m 25 July 1764 *WatV*—John Foote.

ii Charles, b 12 Dec 1744 *WV*.

iii David, b 30 Jan 1746/7 *WV*, d 4 June 1768 *WtnD*.

iv Phebe, b 15 Jan 1748/9 *WV*.

v Eunice, b 19 Mar 1751 *WV*, d 18 July 1777 *WtnD*.

vi Seth, b 21 Mar 1753 *WV;* m Thankful ——.

vii Amasa, bp 22 June 1755 *NoBC2;* Census (Wtn) 1-3-2; m 25 May 1780 *WtnV*—Elizabeth Dayton.

viii John; Census (Wtn) 1-0-3.

6 EBENEZER, b 21 July 1718 *WV*, d 4 Apr 1735 *WV*.

7 John, b 18 Jan 1721 *WV*, d s. p.

8 Isaac, d 1792; Census (W) 2-0-3; m 29 Oct 1767 *WV*—Martha, wid. Foster.

i Jerusha, b 30 Sep 1768 *WV*.

ii Esther, b 22 May 1770 *WV*.

9 Nathaniel, b 13 July 1725 *WV*, d c. 1761; m 17 Feb 1745/6 *WV*—Mary da. John & Jemima (Abernathy) Curtis, b 20 Nov 1724 *WV*; she m (2) 21 Dec 1770 *WV*—Philip Curtis.

i Samuel, b 8 Oct 1746 *WV*; res. Harwinton 1789; Census (W) 1-1-3; res. W 1800; m 10 Sep 1770 *WV*—Martha Moss. **FAM. 3.**

ii Joel, b 5 Sep 1748 *WV*; m 15 Nov 1778 *WV*—Esther Culver; Census, "Hester" (W) 0-0-2.

iii Mary, b 24 June 1750 *WV*, d soon.

iv Mary, b 26 July 1758 *WV*; m Jonathan Clark of Granville, Mass.

v Sarah, b 5 Sep 1760 *WV*; m 14 Sep 1778 *WV*—John Booth.

10 Eleazer, b 18 Dec 1727 *WV*.

11 Gershom, b 18 Aug 1730 *WV*; m 5 Dec 1776 *WV*—Ruth Parker.

i David Hall, b 7 Oct 1777 *WV*.

ii John, b 24 May 1779 *WV*.

FAM. 2. Ebenezer & Martha (Merriman) Mattoon:

1 Martha, b 10 July 1775 *WV*; [?m ——— Young].

FAM. 3. Samuel & Martha (Moss) Mattoon:

1 Margery, b 6 Dec 1771 *WV*.

2 Nathaniel, b 22 July 1773 *WV*.

3 Isaiah, b 4 Feb 1775 *WV*, d 26 Dec 1844 æ. 76 *WTI*; m Abigail ———, who d 16 Apr 1867 æ. 86 *WTI*.

4 David, b 8 Sep 1776 *WV*.

5 Polly, b 20 June 1778 *WV*.

6 Aaron, b 14 Feb 1780 *WV*.

FAM. 4. Samuel & Lydia (———) Mattoon (are these children of the same Samuel?):

1 Lydia, b 22 Jan 1788 *WV*.

2 Samuel, b 11 Jan 1790 *WV*.

3 Isaac, b 8 Feb 1792 *WV*.

4 Salome, b 15 Apr 1794 *WV*.

5 Daniel Smith, b 18 Nov 1796 *WV*.

6 Marcus Columbus, b 4 Mar 1801 *WV*.

McBANE. Alexander & Elizabeth had: Ruth bp 26 June 1785 *NHx*.

McCLEAVE. John d [———] *WTI*; m (1) 14 Sep 1762 *WV*—Mabel da. Samuel & Phebe (Tuttle) Miles, b 1 Oct 1741 *WV*, d 29 Dec 1775 *NHV*, æ. 34 *NHTI*, *NHCI*; m (2) 18 Jan 1781 Thankful da. Jehiel & Thankful (Sedgwick) Preston, wid. Andrew Hall, b 10 Dec 1752 *WV*, d 24 May 1817 æ. 65 *WTI*.

(By 1): 1 Miles, b 9 Aug 1763 *WV*, d 1 Aug 1776 (at camp) æ. 17 (?) *NHTI*, 2 Aug æ. 13 *NHCI*.

2 Eunice, b 2 Sep 1765 *WV*.

3 PHEBE, b 10 Aug 1767 *NHV*, d after 1830; m 6 Dec 1789 *NHC1*—Nathaniel Hubbard.

4 POLLY, b 26 June 1770 *NHV*, d 2 Oct 1773 æ. 4 *NHT1*, æ. 3 *NHC1*.

5 PATTY, b 26 Jan 1773 *NHV*, d 12 Mar 1836 æ. 64 *WT1;* m 26 Jan 1794 James Carrington.

6 THANKFUL, b 4 Aug 1776 *WT1*, d 19 Dec 1811 æ. 36 *WT1;* m 16 Feb 1800 *WV*—Liverus Carrington.

JAMES & Sarah had Molly b 7 June 1752 *WV*.

McCONNELLY. PATRICK, b c. 1726, d 1 Jan 1797 æ. 71 *NHx;* Census, Patrick Collony (NH) 1-1-3; m 30 Oct 1775 *NHx*—Margaret, wid. Joseph Yeomans, b c. 1735, d 7 June 1822 æ. 87 (*NHx*) *NHV*.

1 THOMAS, bp 1 Sep 1776 (sponsor, Fred'k Chappel) *NHx*, d 10 June 1793 æ. 17 *NHx*.

2 MARY, bp 11 Apr 1779 (sponsor, Martha Little) *NHx;* m 15 Feb 1798 *NHC1*—Asahel Tuttle.

McCOY. WILLIAM m 25 Mar 1796 *NHC1*—Lois da. Isaac & Lois (Bishop) Bradley, b 20 Sep 1768 *NHV*, d 24 Sep 1848 æ. 80 *NHT2;* she m (2) Dec 1818 *ColR*—Lemuel Bradley. Family incomplete.

1 WILLIAM, b c. 1797, d 8 Oct 1864 æ. 68 *NHT2;* m Spring 1819 *ColR*—Betsey da. Lemuel & Eunice (Durand) Bradley, b c. 1798, d 21 Sep 1854 æ. 56 *NHV*.

2 (probably) BETSEY; m 13 Dec 1820 *NHV*—Philemon Smith Jr. of Oxford.

McCRACKAN. JOHN, d 19 Sep 1757 æ. 32 *NHT1*, *NHC1*. His younger brother WILLIAM, b c. 1735 (at Glencoe, Galloway, Scotland) d 3 July 1809 æ. 74 *NHT1;* Census (NH) 1-4-5; lived 42 yrs. in NH (*NHT1*); m 8 Oct 1772 *NHC1*—Sarah da. James & Phebe (Thompson) Miles, b 20 May 1749 *WV*, d 26 Dec 1809 æ. 61 *NHT1*.

1 DAUGHTER, stillborn 7 Dec 1773 *NHT1*.

2 JOHN, "son" bp 5 Mar 1775 *NHx*.

3 SARAH, bp 23 Feb 1777 (sponsor, Abigail Miles) *NHx*, d 8 Nov 1849 æ. 73 *NHT1;* m 28 Dec 1796 *NHx*—Nathan Smith.

4 POLLY, bp 20 Dec 1778 (sponsor, Abigail Miles) *NHx;* m 4 Nov 1797 *NHx*—Samuel Lathrop of Springfield, Mass.

5 WILLIAM, b 17 May 1780 (sponsor, Edmund French) *NHx*, d 15 Feb 1845 *NHT1;* m Mary Godfrey Jenkins of Providence, R. I.

6 NANCY, bp 21 Mar 1784 (sponsor, Ann Hubbard) *NHx*.

7 HENRIETTA, bp 19 Mar 1786 (sponsor, Esther Austin) *NHx*, d 6 July 1816 æ. 30 *NHT1;* m 22 Mar 1807 *NHx*—Abel Burritt.

8 JAMES, b 23 June 1788 (sponsor, Thomas Green) *NHx*, d 24 Nov 1849 *NHT1*, bu. 26 Nov 1849 æ. 62 *Cx*.

9 GEORGE, b [Mar 1790], bp 6 June 1790 (sponsor, Josiah Burr) *NHx*, d 9 Nov 1790 æ. 0-8 *NHx*.

10 ELIZABETH, bp 11 Dec 1791 *NHx;* m 17 Nov 1813 *NHx*—John Clark.

11 GEORGE MILES, bp 23 Nov 1794 (sponsor, Russell Clark) *NHx*,

bu. 12 Sep 1795 *NHx*.

McDONALD. ALLING, m Abigail ——— ; Census, Abigail (H) 0-1-1.

1 MARY, b 8 Aug 1784 *HV*.

2 SARAH, b 27 Nov 1785 *HV*.

3 ALLAN, b 31 Aug 1787 *HV*.

McKAY. Variant, MACKEY. FAM. 1. JOHN of Wethersfield, b c. 1640. d 13 Nov 1712; m 6 May 1692 *NHV*—Mary da. Nathaniel & Mary (Ford) Thorpe, b 1 Feb 1667 *NHV* [1667/8].

1 JOHN, b c. 1694, d s. p. 15 June 1756 *WV;* m 23 May 1725 *WV*—Mary da. John & Hannah (Thorpe) Cook, b c. 1702, d 1763.

2 MARY, b 16 June 1696 *WethV*, d 3 July 1757 æ. 63 *NMT;* m 2 Dec 1718 *WV*—Eli Roberts.

3 SAMUEL, b 25 June 1698 *WethV*, d 7 Apr 1699 *WethV*.

4 ELIZABETH, b 20 Mar 1700 *WethV*, d 9 June 1764 *WV;* m 25 Mar 1729 *WV*—William Hendrick.

5 ANNA, b 13 Nov 1702 *WethV*, d 6 Mar 1763 *WV;* m 21 July 1730 *WV*—Thomas Royce.

6 DANIEL, b 11 Nov 1705 *WethV*, d 19 July 1761 *WV*, *WC2;* m (1) Esther ——— , who d 4 Sep 1751 *WV;* m (2) Jan 1753 *WV*—Hannah da. John & Sarah (Payne) Yale, b 12 Feb 1712 *WV*.

(By 1): *i* Daniel, Census (W) 2-0-2; m 19 Nov 1761 *WV*—Sarah da. Nash & Sarah (Emerton) Yale, b 7 Sep 1741 *WV*. FAM. 2.

ii Mary; m 18 Jan 1753 *WV*—Ezra Luddington.

iii Deborah.

iv Esther.

v Elizabeth, d 12 Sep 1777 *WV;* m (1) 1 Dec 176[-] *WV*—Nathaniel Luddington; m (2) 8 July 1774 *WV*—Asa Brown.

vi Rachel; m 22 Nov 1770 *WatV*—Isaac Camp.

7 SAMUEL, bp 14 Dec 1707 *WethC*.

FAM. 2. DANIEL & SARAH (YALE) McKAY (incomplete):

1 WYLLYS, b 30 June 1763 *WV*, d 9 May 1782 *WV*.

2 BARNABAS, b 10 Mar 176[5?] *WV*.

3 DANIEL, b 19 Sep 1766 *WV*, d 26 Oct 1770 *WV*.

4 LOIS, b 11 Apr 1768 *WV*, d 2 June 1777 *WV*.

5 DANIEL, b 2 Oct 1770 *WV*.

6 SARAH, b 2 Oct 1770 *WV*, d 18 Jan 1787 *WV*.

7 LUCY, b 1 Jan 1773 *WV*, d 1 May 1777 *WV*.

8 ESTHER, d 30 Apr 1776 *WV*.

McKAY. FAM. 3. SAMUEL & Abigail had children recorded *WV:*

1 ANNA, b 16 July 1764.

2 ABIGAIL, b 25 Sep 1766.

3 ELIHU, b 16 Oct 1768.

4 SAMUEL, b 25 Apr 1771.

5 JOSIAH, b 19 Jan 1774.

6 SETH, b 27 Mar 1777.

McKAY. MISCELLANEOUS. ELIZABETH m (1) 23 Aug 1763 *WV*—Titus

Hall; m (2) 12 June 1777 *WV*—Samuel Page; she was of Pittstown, N. Y., 1797.

McKEE. WILLIAM m May 1769 *DV*—Anna da. Joseph & Ann (Tomlinson) Durand, b 3 Dec 1742 *DV*, d 1 Mar 1773 *DV*.

1 WILLIAM, b 1770 *DV*.

2 SAMUEL, b 31 July 1772 *DV*.

McKENZIE. "Mary Ann presented by Makinzy" bp 20 Nov 1784 *NHx*.

McLANE. JOHN & Elizabeth had: 1 Polly Ann, bp 31 Jan 1776 *NHx*. 2 Elizabeth Juliana, bp (at NH Goal) 2 Sep 1777 *NHx*......The wife of —— Macklean of B bp Dec 1775 *Dx*......DANIEL had 3 children bp 9 Nov 1786 *NHx*, & 2 bu. Nov 1786 *NHx*. (Was his w. Mary da. Robert & Mary (Prout) Sloan?)

McNEIL. FAM. 1. ARCHIBALD of Bd & NH, d 1753; m Mary da. Samuel & Abigail (Whiting) Russell, wid. Benjamin Fenn.

1 ARCHIBALD, b 20 Sep 1736 *BdV*, d 1779; m 2 May 1758 *NHV*—Sarah da. William & Hannah (Peck) Clark, b 22 Jan 1742 *DV*, d Mar 1821 æ. 78 *OxfV*.

i William, b 13 May 1759 *NHV*, d before 1808; B. A. (Yale 1777); m 25 Sep 1779 *NHC2*—Huldah da. Abraham & Elizabeth (Bradley) Augur, b c. 1758. **FAM. 2.**

ii Archibald, b c. 1761, bp 7 July 1794 (æ. 33) *NHx*, d 8 July 1794 *NHx*; Census (NH) 1-3-1; m Abigail da. Joseph & Abigail (Grannis) Ives, b c. 1766, bp 7 July 1794 *NHx*, d 24 July 1844 æ. 78 *NHV*. **FAM. 3.**

iii Mary; m Samuel Bassett of Oxf.

2 CHARLES, bp 18 Jan 1739 *BdC*, d soon.

3 CHARLES, bp 1 Nov 1741 *BdC*, d young.

4 JOHN, b 2 Aug 1745 *BdV*, bp 4 Aug 1745 *BdC*; rem. to Amenia, N. Y.

5 SAMUEL, b 15 Oct 1748 *F*, bp 9 (?) Oct 1748 *BdC*; rem. to L.

FAM. 2. WILLIAM & HULDAH (AUGUR) McNEIL:

1 (perhaps) SARAH, b c. 1780, d 26 Sep 1802 æ. 23 *WdT1*; m 7 Feb 1800 *WdC*—Hezekiah Beecher.

2 NANCY, b 4 June 1783 *F*, d 9 Feb 1833 *F*; m 25 Feb 1805 Raphael Dickinson.

3 WILLIAM, b c. 1785, d 24 June 1852 æ. 67 *NHT1*; m Nancy ——, who d 23 Dec 1854 æ. 68 *NHT1*.

4 (perhaps) POLLY, b c. 1788, d July 1809 æ. 21 *ConnH*; m 27 Nov 1806 *NHx*—Alexander Coburn.

5 JOHN, b c. 1790, d Nov 1818 æ. 28 (at NH) *ColR*; m Maria da. John & Mary (Talmadge) Miles. Child: Elizabeth, m John E. Wylie.

6 MARIA; m 12 Sep 1824 *NHV*—Russell Bradley.

7 HENRY.

8 ABRAHAM ARCHIBALD, b 21 July 1802 *F*.

FAM. 3. ARCHIBALD & ABIGAIL (IVES) McNEIL:

1 JOSEPH IVES, b c. 1784, bp 7 July 1794 *NHx*, d 17 Aug 1836 æ. 52 *NHV*; m 7 Oct 1806 *NHC2*—Polly Beard.

2 SAMUEL, b c. 1786, bp 27 July 1794 (æ. 7) *NHx*.
3 ASA, bp 7 July 1794 *NHx*.
4 ARCHIBALD, bp 7 July 1794 *NHx*.
5 ABIGAIL, bp 7 July 1794 *NHx;* m 13 Sep 1812 *NHx*—George Johnson.

MECOM. BENJAMIN & Elizabeth had: 1 Jane, bp 24 June 1764 *NHC2*. 2 Elizabeth, bp 13 Oct 1765 *NHC2*.

MEEKER. ROBERT, rem. to Fairfield, d 1684; m 16 Sep 16 1651 *NHV*—Susan Turberfield, who survived him.

1 JOHN, d 1727; m Elizabeth ——— .
2 DANIEL, d 1716; m Elizabeth da. Richard Ogden.
3 MARY; m 15 July 167[-] *FdV*—Samuel Adams.

WILLIAM, probably brother of Robert, rem. to Newark, N. J.; m [———] *NHV*—Sarah da. William & Elizabeth (Sale) Preston, bp 18 Jan 1623 *Chesham, Co. Bucks, Eng.*

1 BENJAMIN, b 17 Mar 1649 *NHV*.
2 SARAH, b 7 Feb 1653 *NHV*.
3 MARY, b 6 Oct 1656 *NHV*.
4 CHILD, b Dec [1663] *NHV*, d [1663] *NHV*.
5 JOHN, b 7 Sep 1666 *NHV*.

MELOY. EDWARD, b c. 1734, d 14 Sep 1790 æ. 56 *NHT1;* Census (NH) 3-2-1; m 7 Feb 1758 *NHV*—Mary da. Abel & Mary (Beecher) Parmalee, bp 20 Oct 1739 *NHC1*, d c. 1800.

1 EDWARD, b 27 Apr 1760 *NHV*, d 29 Apr 1760 *NHV*.
2 JOHN, b 27 Apr 1760 *NHV*, d 29 Apr 1760 *NHV*.
3 ROSANNA, b 6 Feb 1761 *NHV*, bp 24 Nov 1771 *NHC2;* m Joseph Baldwin of Bd.
4 EDWARD, b 21 May 1763 *F*, bp 24 Nov 1771 *NHC2;* Census (NH) 1-1-2; m Eunice da. Samuel & Eunice (Sherman) Humphreville, b c. 1766, d 27 Jan 1849 æ. 83 *NHV*, *NHT1*. Family incomplete.
  i (probably) Julia; m Sep 1809 *ConnH*—Capt. John Stevens.
5 JOHN, b 5 Dec 1766 *NHV*, bp 24 Nov 1771 *NHC2*, d 23 Aug 1841 æ. 75 (drowned) *WHD;* Census (NH) 1-1-2; m Esther da. Ebenezer & Esther (Thompson) Humphreville, b c. 1766, d 6 June 1836 æ. 70 *WHD*.
  i Falame; m Amarilla Richards.
  ii Child, b c. 1794, d 15 Dec 1795 æ. 1 *WHD*.
  iii Betsey; m Philemon Smith.
  iv Merrit, b c. 1798, d 9 Aug 1848 æ. c. 50 *WHD*, æ. 49 *WHT2;* m Catherine ——— , who d 26 Aug 1846 æ. 45 *WHT2*.
  v David, b c. 1802, d Feb 1825 æ. 23 (in West Indies) *WHD*.
  vi Mary, b 10 Sep 1804 *WHT3*, d 28 Aug 1858 *WHT3;* m Nathan Platt.
  vii Cynthia R.
6 WILLIAM, b 10 Feb 1771 *F*, bp 24 Nov 1771 *NHC2*, d s. p. 1795.
7 PHILEMON, b 10 May 1773 *F*, bp 27 June 1773 *NHC2*, d s. p.

8 DAVID, b 19 Nov 1775 *F*, bp 14 Jan 1776 *NHC2*, d s. p. between 1790 & 1800.

9 HENRY STARK, b 25 Mar 1778 *BdV*, bp 24 May 1778 *NoBC1*, d 8 Mar 1860 (at Union, N. Y.); m 25 Mar 1798 Anna da. Timothy & Abigail (Winston) Dawson, b 7 Aug 1779 *F*, d 26 Feb 1858 (at Union, N. Y,).

10 POLLY, b 21 June 1781 *F*, bp 26 Aug 1781 *NHC2*.

MELYN. CORNELIUS, d 1674; res. Staten Island, N. Y.; m Janneken ——.

1 JACOB, d Dec 1706; res. Elizabeth, N. J., & Boston, Mass.; m 1662 Hannah da. George & Mary Hubbard.

2 CORNELIUS.

3 ISAAC.

4 MARIA; m (1) —— Pardice; m (2) 25 Aug 1664 *NHV*—Matthias Hitfield.

5 SUSANNA; m (1) 25 Aug [1664] *NHV*—John Winus; m (2) Jacob Schillinger of N. Y.

6 MAGDALEN; m Jacob Loper of N. Y. & had Janneken & Jacob.

MERRIAM. FAM. 1. WILLIAM, s. of Wm. & Elizabeth (Breed), b 8 Mar 1668 *Lynn, Mass.*, d 26 Feb 1752 æ. 85 *BristolT;* m (1) 3 June 1690 *Lynn*—Hannah Daggle, who d 18 Aug 1693 *Lynn;* m (2) 20 Dec 1695 *Lynn*—Ætheldred Berry; m (3) 30 Oct 1709 *Lynn*—Abigail Mower, who d 26 Feb 1711 *Lynn;* m (4) 7 Nov 1711 *Lynn*—Ruth, wid. John Webb, b c. 1683, d 12 Nov 1755 æ. 72 *WT2*, "Capt. Webb's mother Merriam" d 15 Nov 1754 *WC2*. All children except last two b at Lynn.

(By 1): 1 HANNAH, b 1 Mar 1691, d s. p. 29 Nov 1728 *WV*.

(By 2): 2 WILLIAM, b 9 Sep 1696, d 20 Sep 1696.

3 JERUSHA, b 21 Feb 1698, d 27 Dec 1745 *WV;* m (intention 4 Aug 1716) *Lynn*—Edward Parker.

4 ICHABOD, b 20 Nov 1700, d 2 June 1750 *WV*, æ. 50 *CT1*, June 1750 *CC;* m 19 Oct 1725 *WV*—Abigail da. Joseph & Margery (Hitchcock) Munson, b 2 Apr 1704 *WV*, d 17 Sep 1792 *CC*.

i Ichabod, b 11 Jan 1728 *WV*, bp July 1728 *CC*, d 15 Jan 1757 *WV*, æ. 30 *CT1*, 15 Apr 1756 (?) *CC;* m 14 Aug 1751 *WV*—Elizabeth da. Nathaniel & Elizabeth (Hitchcock) Beadles, b 12 Dec 1731 *WV;* she m (2) 6 Apr 1758 *WV*—Amos Hotchkiss. **FAM. 3.**

ii Munson, b 19 Aug 1730 *WV*, d 26 Nov 1793 *CC;* Census (C) 3-0-4; m 26 Dec 1764 *WV*—Rebecca da. Isaac & Martha (Barnes) Bartholomew, b 1 Aug 1736, d 28 Sep 1801 *CC*. **FAM. 4.**

5 EUNICE, b 18 May 1704, d 2 May 1783 æ. 78 *WlnD;* m 14 July 1724 *WV*—Thomas Matthews.

6 WILLIAM, b 31 Mar 1708.

(By 4): 7 RUTH, b 2 Nov 1713, d 3 Nov 1785; m 9 May 1733 *WV*—Caleb Matthews.

8 SAMUEL, b 20 May 1716, d 16 Sep 1783 *CC*, æ. 67 *CT1;* m 21 Mar 1739 *WV*—Elizabeth da. John & Elizabeth (Hayward) Perkins, b 12 Aug 1713 *NHV*, d 2 Feb 1806 *CC*, æ. 92 *SC*.

i Eunice, 14 Feb 1740 *WV*, bp 23 Mar 1739/40 *CC*, d 6 Dec 1742 *WV*, "child" Dec 1742 *CC*.

ii Elizabeth, b 13 July 1741 *WV;* m 2 Apr 1761 *WV*—William Hendrick.

iii Eunice, b 17 Mar 1743/4 *WV*, bp Mar 1744 *CC*.

iv Esther, b 9 May 1746 *WV*, bp Apr 1746 *CC*, d 1829; m (1) 26 Aug 1763 *WV*—Benjamin Hull; m (2) 1770 Jotham Curtis; m (3) 1798 Nathaniel Barnes; m (4) Elisha Wilcox.

v Samuel, b 26 Apr 1748 *WV*, bp Apr 1748 *CC;* Census (C) 1-1-3; m 24 July 1768 *CC*, 28 June 1768 *WV*—Martha da. John & Mary (Cook) Smith, b 23 Sep 1748 *WV*. FAM. 5.

vi Rebecca, b 9 Dec 1750 *WV*, bp Aug 1750 *CC*, d 21 Dec 1751 *WV*.

vii William, b 5 Nov 1754 *WV*, d 1776 (k. in battle) *CC*, 16 Sep 1776 (at battle, N. Y.) *WV*.

9 EBENEZER, b 26 Mar 1718 *WV*, d 8 Aug 1752 *CC;* m 6 June 1739 *WV*—Hannah da. Ebenezer & Mary (Ford) Blakeslee, b [17 Jan 1720/1 *NHV*]; she m (2) Daniel Blakeslee.

i Joseph, b 28 Sep 1740 *WV*, d 16 Oct 1740 *WV*.

ii Hannah, b [1742] *WV*.

iii Joseph, b 8 Mar 1744 *WV*.

iv Ebenezer, b 13 Apr 1746 *WV;* m 9 Oct 1767 *WV*—Rebecca da. Joseph & Abigail (Beecher) Rowe, b 29 June 1750 *NHV*. Children (incomplete): 1 Joseph, bp 31 Mar 1771 *BristolC*. 2 Rebecca, bp 8 May 1774 *BristolC*. 3 Rispah, bp 13 Oct 1776 *BristolC*. 4 Anson, bp 17 Aug 1783 *BristolC*.

v Ruth, b 4 Feb 1747/8 *WV*.

vi William, b 5 July 1750 *NHV*, 15 June 1750 *WV;* rem. to Bedford, Mass.; m Esther da. Samuel & Mary (Jones) Bellamy, b 9 June 1751 *NHV*. A William, Census (Harwinton) 2-3-4, d 28 Mar 1800 æ. 50 *HarwintonT*, & his wid. Deborah d 24 Sep 1843 æ. 89 *HarwintonT*.

10 JOSEPH LENTO, b 14 July 1724 *WV*, d 17 July 1733 (bit by snake) *WV*.

FAM. 2. JOHN, s. of Wm. & Elizabeth (Breed), b 25 Apr 1671 *Lynn*, d 11 Oct 1754 *WC2;* m 1693 Rebecca da. Nathaniel & Rebecca (Marshall) Sharp, b 1671, d 30 Apr 1751 *WC2*. Children all b at Lynn.

1 CHILD, b 25 Mar 1695, d 25 Mar 1695.

2 NATHANIEL, b 26 Mar 1696, d 1774 *Pro*, 1775 æ. 81 *WT2;* Capt.; m 12 Nov 1723 *WV*—Elizabeth da. Benjamin & Elizabeth (Andrews) Hull, b 8 Apr 1698 *WV*, d 11 June 1767 æ. 70 *WT2*.

i Elizabeth, b 28 Feb 1727 *WV*, d 30 Mar 1754 *WC2;* m 28 Feb 1744/5 *WV*—David Ives.

ii Rebecca, b 10 Feb 1729 *WV*, d 5 Nov 1750 *WV;* m 10 Feb 1747/8 *WV*—Joel Ives.

iii Hannah, b 27 Aug 1731 *WV*, d 21 Mar 1815 æ. 84 *WT2;* m 14 Feb 1751 *WV*—Bezaleel Ives.

iv Lois, d Apr 1735 *WV*.

v Nathaniel, b 5 Jan 1734 *WV*, 16 Jan 1734 [N. S.] (at Meriden) *WT2*, bp 6 Jan 1733/4 *WC2*, d 5 Aug 1807 *WT2;* Census (W) 2-1-3; m 19 Feb 1756 *WV*—Martha da. Thomas & Rebecca (Ballard) Berry, b 9 Dec 1736 *Lynn*, d 28 Dec 1797 æ. 61 *WT2*, *WC2*. **FAM. 6.**

vi Matthew, b 25 Jan 1738 *WV*, bp 29 Jan 1737/8 *WC2;* rem. to Berwick, Mass.

vii Lois, b 28 July 1740 *WV*, bp 3 Aug 1740 *WC2;* m 10 Jan 1760 *WV*, *WC2*—John Hough.

3 JOHN, b 26 Oct 1697, d 26 May 1772 æ. 75 *WT2;* m (1) 21 Apr 1725 *WV*—Mary da. John & Elizabeth (Peck) Merriman, b 15 Mar 1705 *WV*, d 23 May 1732 *WV;* m (2) (intention 8 Oct 1732 *Lynn*), 22 Nov 1732 *WV*—Mary Burrage, b c. 1700, d 5 Dec 1756 *WV*, *WC2*, 6 Dec æ. 56 *WT2;* m (3) 9 Aug 1757 *WC 2*—Hannah [da. Joseph & Mary (Porter) Royce, wid. John] Ives.

(By 1): *i* Sarah, b 9 Apr 1726 *WV;* m (intention 5 May 1745) *Lynn* —Ignatius Rhodes.

ii Jesse, b 21 Jan 1728 *WV*, d Sep 1791 *WC2;* Census (W) 1-0-1; m 9 May 1750 *WV*—Mary Johnson, who d 6 Mar 1790 *WC2*. **FAM. 7.**

iii John, b 8 May 1730 *WV*, bp 10 May 1730 *WC2*, d 6 Aug 1732 *WV*.

(By 2): *iv* Mary, bp 14 Sep 1735 *WC2*, "child" d 1735/6 *WC2*.

v John, b 7 Sep 1737 *WV*, bp 11 Sep 1737 *WC2*, d 28 June 1738 *WC2*.

vi Burrage, b 27 Oct 1739 *WV*, bp 8 Oct 1739 *WC2*, d 30 Nov 1776 æ. 38 *WethersfieldT;* Rev.; m 12 Sep 1765 *WC2*—Hannah da. Ebenezer & Abigail (Root) Royce, b 5 Jan 1743 *WV*, d 9 Jan 1816 æ. 72 *Weth.T;* she m (2) ——— Seldon.

vii Susanna, bp 26 Sep 1742 *WC2*, d 25 Oct 1742 *WC2*.

4 WILLIAM, b 9 Apr 1700, d 4 Oct 1751 *WC2*, æ. 52 *WT2;* Lieut.; m 24 Mar 1726 *WV*—Ruth da. Hawkins & Sarah (Royce) Hart, b 13 Aug 1704 (at Farm) *WV*, d 4 Nov 1784 æ. 81 *WT2;* she m (2) 30 Sep 1762 *WV*—Edward Parker.

i William. b 12 Feb 1728 *WV*, d Sep 1791 æ. 63 *WC2;* Census (W) 2-0-1; m (1) 29 May 1751 *WV*—Phebe da. Samuel & Phebe (Royce) Ives, b c. 1729, d 23 Feb 1753 *WC 2*, æ. 23 *WT2;* m (2) 24 Sep 1755 *WV*—Mary da. John & Mary (Royce) Austin, b 17 Apr 1733 *WV*. **FAM. 8.**

ii Thomas, b 20 Oct 1731 *WV*, bp 24 Oct 1731 *WC2*, d 1 Apr 1811 æ. 80 *WT2;* Census (Wtn) 2-0-2; m (1) 22 Jan 1756 *WatV*—Ann da. John & Elizabeth (Hall) Moss, b Aug 1738 *WV*, d 15 Jan 1782 *WatV;* m (2) 10 July 1783

WtnV—Sarah Parker; m (3) Ruth da. Stephen & Elizabeth (Yale) Atwater, wid. John Miles, b 6 June 1740 *WV*, d 6 Apr 1827 æ. 87 *WT2*.

iii Esther, b 24 Nov 1733 *WV*, bp 25 Nov 1733 *WC2;* m Benjamin Whiting.

iv Mary, b 20 Apr 1735 *WV*, bp 20 Apr 1735 *WC2*, d 7 June 1735 *WV*.

v Ruth, b 2 Oct 1736 *WV*, bp 3 Oct 1736 *WC2*.

vi Susanna, b 10 Nov 1738 *WV*, bp 12 Nov 1738 *WC2*, d 31 Mar 1740 *WV*, *WC2*.

vii John, b 10 May 1740 *WV*, bp 11 Apr (?) 1740 *WC2;* m 12 July 1764 *WatV*—Hannah da. Thomas & Lydia (Hackley) Fenn, b 24 Mar 1741 *WV*.

viii Sarah; m 6 Nov 1769 *CC*—Samuel Culver.

ix Asael, b 21 Dec 1745 *WV*, bp 22 Dec 1745 *WC2*.

5 Rebecca, b 26 Mar 1702, d 25 Apr 1727 *WV;* m 17 Jan 1723 *WV*—Benjamin Ives.

6 Joseph, b 29 Mar 1704, d 24 Aug 1752 *WC2*, æ. 49 *WT2;* Sgt.; m 6 July 1729 *WV*—Deborah da. Samuel & Hannah (Benedict) Royce, b 30 July 1709 *WV*, d 12 Aug 1761 *WC2*, æ. 52 *WT2*.

i Benjamin, b 24 Dec 1730 *WV*, bp 27 Dec 1730 *WC2*, d 14 Feb 1807 æ. 76 *WT2;* Census (W) 2-1-2; m (1) 19 Dec 1753 *WV*—Mary da. Ephraim & Mary (Johnson) Berry, who d 14 Mar 1772 æ. 30 (?) *WT2;* m (2) 14 Apr 1773 *WV*—Esther da. Isaac & Sarah (Osborn) Johnson, wid, Caleb Todd, b 30 Nov 1735 *WV*. **FAM. 9.**

ii Joseph, b 20 Nov 1732 *WV*, d 30 Apr 1807 æ. 75 *WT2;* Census (W) 3-1-4; m (1) 15 Nov 1759 *WV*, *WC2*—Sarah da. John & Mary (Royce) Austin, b 22 Nov 1734 *WV*, d 14 Apr 1767 *WV;* m (2) 29 Dec 1767 *WV*—Mindwell da. Ephraim & Eunice (Harris) Royce, b 12 Aug 1740 *WV*, d 15 Oct 1839 æ. 100 *WT2*. **FAM. 10.**

iii Anna, b 27 Dec 1734 *WV*, bp 29 Dec 1734 *WC2;* m 10 Mar 1757 *WV*—Thomas Berry.

iv Isaac, b 27 Mar 1737 *WV*, bp 27 Mar 1737 *WC2*, d 1825; Ens.; Census (Wtn) 3-1-4; m 21 Feb 1760 *WatV*—Sarah Scovill.

v Deborah, b 29 Mar 1739 *WV*, bp Apr 1738 (?) *WC2*, d 12 May 1740 *WV*, *WC2*.

vi Samuel, b 17 Oct 1741 *WV*, bp 18 Oct 1741 *WC2;* Census (W) 1-1-2; m 10 May 1770 *WV*—Huldah Beckwith. Children: (1) Amy, b 7 Apr 1771 *WV*. (2) Silas, b 8 Sep 1780 *WV*.

vii Deborah, b 18 Oct 1743 *WV*, bp 23 Oct 1743 *WC2*, d 18 Aug 1780 *WV;* m (1) 15 Mar 1770 *WV*—Alling Royce; m (2) 6 Nov 1777 *WV*—James Hough.

viii Susanna, b 9 Sep 1745 *WV*, bp 15 Sep 1745 *WC2*.

ix Mehitabel, b 10 Sep 1747 *WV*, bp 13 Sep 1747 *WC2;* m 9 June 1768 *WV*—Elisha Perkins.

x Marshal, b 21 June 1749 *WV;* Census (Wtn) 1-2-4; m 4 Dec 1777 *WV*—Mary da. Stephen & Elizabeth (Yale) Atwater, b 25 Jan 1749/50 *WV*, d 20 Feb 1780 æ. 30 *WT2*.

xi Christopher, b 31 Dec 1751 *WV*, bp 23 Feb 1752 *WC2;* Census (Wtn) 3-2-3; m 23 Mar 1778 *WatV*—Rebecca Guernsey.

7 Ruth, b 12 Feb 1706, d 4 July 1776 *CC;* m (1) 29 Mar 1725 *WV*—Josiah Robinson; m (2) 2 Feb 1768 *WV*—Caleb Hull.

8 Abigail, b 14 Aug 1708; m 6 May 1729 *WV*—Thomas Dutton.

9 Susanna, b 10 Nov 1710; m 30 Nov 1730 *WV*—Hawkins Hart.

FAM. 3. Ichabod & Elizabeth (Beadles) Merriam:

1 Ichabod, b 11 June 1752 *WV*, d 18 May 1754 *WV*, 19 May æ. 1-11 *CTI*, "child" May 1754 *CC*.

2 Abigail, b 27 Nov 1753 *WV;* m 26 Dec 1771 *WV*—David Hotchkiss.

3 Ichabod, b 28 Mar 1755 *WV*, d 29 Feb 1756 æ. 0-11 *CTI*.

4 Ichabod, b 7 Jan 1757 *WV;* Census (C) 1-1-4; res. 1792 Lott Ara (?), N. Y.; m 24 Feb 1778 *WV*—Desire da. Ebenezer & Lydia (Clark) Bunnell, b 7 June 1759 *WV*.

FAM. 4. Munson & Rebecca (Bartholomew) Merriam:

1 Rebecca, b 6 Oct 1765 *WV*.

2 Munson, b 11 Apr 1767 *WV*, bp 31 May 1767 *CC;* Census (C) 1-0-2; m 26 Oct 1789 *CC*—Eunice da. Waitstill & Eunice (Bradley) Hotchkiss, b 25 Mar 1768 *WV*. Child: Abigail, b 10 June 1790 *CV*, bp 10 Jan 1802 *CC*.

3 Isaac, b 9 Feb 1770 *WV*, bp 1 Apr 1770 *CC*, d 12 Aug 1830 (at W. Hartland); m 11 Feb 1802 *CC*—Mary Lois da. Uri & Lois (Doolittle) Benham, b 27 Oct 1775 *WV*. Probable children: Wm., Eunice & Munson, bp 26 July 1807 *CC;* Laura, bp 15 Jan 1809 *CC;* Cornelia, bp 7 July 1811 *CC*.

4 Rufus, b 8 Jan 1772 *WV*, bp 8 Mar 1772 *CC*, d 1821; m 14 Jan 1798 *CC*—Lucy da. Samuel & Lucy (Johnson) Preston, b 7 July 1776 *WV*, d Jan 1810 æ 36 *F*.

5 Rebecca, bp 27 Feb 1774 *CC;* m 5 Jan 1792 *CC*—Thomas Brooks.

6 Eunice, b 19 Mar 1776 *WV*, bp 31 Mar 1776 *CC*, "child" d 27 Oct 1777 *CC*.

7 Eunice, b 24 Nov 1781 *CV*, bp 10 Mar 1782 *CC*.

FAM. 5. Samuel & Martha (Smith) Merriam:

1 Elizabeth Mary, b 13 Nov 1768 *WV*, bp 24 June 1770 *CC*, d 21 July 1774 *WV*.

2 John Smith, b 2 Feb 1770 *WV*, bp 24 June 1770 *CC*, d 26 July 1774 *WV*.

3 Ezra, b 21 Feb 1772 *WV*, bp 12 Apr 1772 *CC*.

4 Rebecca, b 14 Jan 1774 *WV*.

5 Elizabeth Mary, b 7 Sep 1775 *WV*, bp 15 Oct 1775 *CC*.

6 WILLIAM, b 12 Feb 1777 *WV*, bp 30 Mar 1777 *CC*.
7 JOHN, b 24 Oct 1778 *WV*, bp 10 Dec 1778 *CC*.
8 (probably) SAMUEL, bp 17 Sep 1780 *CC*.
9 (probably) CLARISSA, bp 5 Nov 1786 *CC*.

FAM. 6. NATHANIEL & MARTHA (BERRY) MERRIAM:
1 REBECCA, b 29 Mar 1757 *WV*, d 15 Aug 1785 æ. 30 *WT2;* m 28 Dec 1773 *WV*—Elisha Cole.
2 DAMARIS, b 17 June 1759 *WV*.
3 EDMUND, b 28 Mar 1761 *WV*, d 25 Jan 1791 æ. 30 *WT2;* Census (W) 1-2-3; m 23 Dec 1784 *KensingtonC*—Huldah Peck.
4 ELIZABETH, b 13 Aug 176[3] *WV*.
5 MARTHA, b 1 Jan 176[6?] *WV*.
6 NATHANIEL, b 3 June 1769 *WV*.
7 LOIS, b 22 Oct 1771 *WV*.
8 LUCRETIA, b 11 Jan 1775 *WV*.

FAM. 7. JESSE & MERCY (JOHNSON) MERRIAM:
1 MARY, b 28 Feb 1751 *WV*.
2 JOHN, b 26 June 1752 *WV;* Census (W) 1-2-5: m 4 Sep 1777 *WV* —Huldah da. Ebenezer & Abigail (Root) Royce, wid. Phineas Hough, b 10 May 1749 *WV*.
3 JAMES, b 2 Apr 1754 *WV*, d young.
4 SARAH, b 26 Jan 1757 *WV;* m.
5 ELIZABETH, b 18 Feb 1759 *WV*, d 5 Dec 1841 æ. 83 *WT2;* m 24 Feb 1777 *WV*—Jared Benham.
6 SYLVIA, b 10 Dec 1761 *WV;* m Daniel Crane.
7 HANNAH, b 24 Nov 1763 *WV*.
8 JESSE, b 23 Dec 1765 *WV;* m Sarah Andrews.
9 ELEANOR, b 19 May 1769 *WV;* m Joel Mix.
10 JAMES JOHNSON, b 20 June 1772 *WV*.

FAM. 8. WILLIAM & MARY (AUSTIN) MERRIAM:
1 PHEBE, b 29 May 1756 *WV;* m 1 Feb 1781 *WV*—Daniel Yale.
2 AMASA, b 27 Sep 1757 *WV*.
3 ASAPH, b 14 Mar 1759 *WV*, d 27 July 1836 æ. 77 *WT2;* Census (W) 1-4-2; m Damaris ——.
4 CHLOE, b 12 July 1761 *WV;* m 25 Dec 1782 *WV*—Elisha Merriman.
5 ESTHER, b 7 July 1763 *WV;* m Aaron Merriam.
6 JOEL, b 20 June 1766 *WV*, d s. p.
7 WILLIAM, b 8 June 1768 *WV;* [?m Anna da. Solomon Hotchkiss].

FAM. 9. BENJAMIN & MARY (BERRY) MERRIAM:
1 RACHEL, b 27 Nov 1755 *WV*.
2 EPHRAIM, b 31 July 1758 *WV*, d 22 Mar 1834 æ. 77 *WT2;* Census (W) 1-2-4; m 12 Feb 1784 *WV*—Beulah Galpin, who d 18 Feb 1827 æ. 68 *WT2*.
3 AARON, b 9 June 1762 *WV;* Census (W) 1-1-3; m Esther da. Wm. & Mary (Austin) Merriam, b 7 July 1763 *WV*.
4 MARY, b 12 Oct 1766 *WV*.

5 Benjamin, b 22 Apr 1770 *WV*.

FAM. 10. Joseph & Sarah (Austin) Merriam:

1 Eunice, b 20 Dec 1760 *WV*.

2 Lucy, b 6 Sep 1762 *WV*, d 25 Apr 1849 (Bristol); m 22 Aug 1782 *WV*—Isaac Atwater.

3 Sarah, b 18 Mar 1764 *WV*, d 3 May 1765 *WV*.

FAM. 10. Joseph & Mindwell (Royce) Merriam:

4 Sarah, b 12 Dec 1768 *WV*.

5 Joseph, b 16 July 1770 *WV*,

6 Ira, b 15 June 1772 *WV*, d 25 Aug 1774 *WV*.

7 Ira, b 24 Aug 1774 *WV*.

8 Deborah, b 23 Oct 1776 *WV*, d 31 Oct 1802 æ. 26 *WT2;* m Miles Hull.

9 Asahel, b 21 Oct 1778 *WV*.

***MERRIMAN.** FAM. 1. Nathaniel, s. of George of London, b c. 1614, d 13 Feb 1693/4 æ. 80 *WV;* Capt.; m Joan ——— , b c. 1628, d 8 Dec 1709 æ. 81 *WV*. No basis of fact has been found for oft-repeated statements that he m (1) Abigail Olney.

1 Nathaniel, d s. p. 19 Dec 1675 (in K. Philip's War).

2 John, d 26 Sep 1651 *NHV*.

3 Hannah, b 16 May 1651 *NHV;* m (1) 12 Nov 1668 *NHV*—John Ives; m (2) 17 Aug 1682 *WV*—Joseph Benham.

4 Abigail, b 18 Apr 1654 *NHV*, bp 27 June 1661 *NHC1;* m 18 Jan 1670 *NHV*—John Hitchcock.

5 Mary, b 12 July 1657 *NHV*, bp 27 June 1661 *NHC1;* m 9 June 1674 *WV*—Thomas Curtis.

6 John, b last of Feb 1659 *NHV* [1659/60], bp 27 June 1661 *NHC1*, d 1741; Capt.; m (1) 28 Mar 1683 *WV*—Hannah da. Ralph & Alice Lines, b 21 Nov 1665 *NHV*, d c. 1688; m (2) 20 Nov 1690 *WV*—Elizabeth da. John & Mary (Moss) Peck, b 29 Dec 1673 *WV*, d c. 1709; m (3) Hannah Dewey, wid. Benjamin Newberry of Windsor; he div. her 1716; m (4) after 1720 Elizabeth da. Eleazer & Sarah (Bulkeley) Brown, wid. Michael Todd & Samuel Street.

(By 1): *i* Esther, b 24 Jan 1683 *WV* [1683/4], d young.

ii Abigail, b 1 Feb 1685 *WV*, d young.

iii George, b 14 July 1688 *WV*, d 1736; m 8 Jan 1713 *WV*—Susanna da. William & Sarah (Doolittle) Abernathy, b 18 July 1689 *WV*. **FAM. 2.**

(By 2): *iv* John, b 16 Oct 1691 *WV*, d 17 Feb 1784 (at S); Rev. (Bapt.); m 24 Feb 1726 *WV*—Jemima da. Obadiah & Silence (Mansfield) Wilcoxson, b 30 Oct 1699 *GV*, d 11 Oct 1764 (at S). **FAM. 3.**

v Israel, b 23 Jan 1693/4 *WV*, d after 1753; m 23 June 1714 Comfort da. John & Comfort (Mansfield) Benham, b 15 Aug 1692 *NHV*. **FAM. 4.**

vi Sarah, b 17 Feb 1702 *WV*, d 3 Feb 1733 *WV*, m 28 Dec 1722 *WV*—Moses Atwater.

vii Elizabeth, b 2 July 1703 *WV*, d between 1732 & 1735; m Gershom Todd.

viii Mary, b 15 Mar 1705 *WV*, d 23 May 1732 *WV;* m 21 Apr 1725 *WV*—John Merriam.

ix Caleb, b 2 Apr 1707 *WV*, d 2 June 1770 æ. 63 *WTI*, æ. 64 *WV;* Dea.; m 31 Aug 1732 *WV*—Ruth da. Samuel & Ruth (Peck) Sedgwick, b 22 Jan 1712 *HartfordV*, d 1799. **FAM. 5.**

x Susanna, b 20 July 1709 *WV;* m 21 Apr 1729 *NHV*—Ezekiel Tuttle.

7 Samuel, b 29 Sep 1662 *NHV*, d 25 Sep 1694 *Pro;* m Anna [da. Samuel & Anna (Miles) Street, b 17 Aug 1665 *NHV*], d 1705; she m (2) Bartholomew Crossman.

i Nathaniel, b 27 May 1687 *WV*, d young.

ii Nathaniel, b 16 Mar 1690 *WV*, d 9 June 1767 *WV;* m Mehitabel da. David & Sarah (Rockwell) Hall, b 15 Aug 1691 *WV*, d 1772. **FAM. 6.**

iii Theophilus, b 28 Apr 1693 *WV*, d 21 Aug 1723 (at Northfield, Mass.); m 9 Sep 1714 *WV*—Mary Mattoon, who d 6 Jan 1782 æ. 84; she m (2) Benjamin Miller. **FAM. 7.**

iv Samuel, b 19 Dec 1694 *WV*, d before 1783; m 9 Nov 1727 *WV*—Sarah da. Thomas & Sarah (Abernathy) Wiltshire, b 16 May 1707 *WV*. **FAM. 8.**

8 Caleb, b May 1665 *NHV*, d 19 July 1703 *WV;* Cpl.; m 9 July 1690 *WV*—Mary da. Eliasaph & Mary Preston, b 12 Apr 1674 *StV*, d 28 Nov 1755; she m (2) 18 Mar 1708 *WV*—Samuel Munson.

i Moses, b 31 Oct 1691 *WV*, d 4 Feb 1743/4 *WV;* Sgt.; m 6 Feb 1713 *WV*—Martha da. Azariah & Martha [Ives] Beach, b c. 1690. **FAM 9.**

ii Elizabeth, b 4 May 1693 *WV*, d 24 Dec 1775 æ. 83 *WTI;* m (1) 4 Nov 1712 *WV*—Henry Turhand; m (2) Joseph Royce.

iii Eliasaph, b 20 May 1695 *WV*, d 19 Aug 1758 *WV;* Capt.; m 10 Dec 1719 *WV*—Abigail da. Benjamin & Elizabeth (Andrews) Hull, b 14 Jan 1704 *WV*, d 20 Jan 1774 *WV*. **FAM. 10.**

iv Hannah, b 10 Sep 1697 *WV*, d 27 Sep 1738 *WV;* m 19 July 1714 *WV*—John Andrews.

v Phebe, b 11 Sep 1699 *WV*, d Dec 1772; m 10 Dec 1719 *WV*—Waitstill Munson.

vi Lydia, b 8 Sep 1701 *WV*, d soon.

vii Lydia, b 12 Nov 1702 *WV*, d 25 Dec 1785 æ. 84 *CTI;* m Ephraim Cook.

9 & 10 Sons, b [1667] *NHV*, d 1667.

11 Elizabeth, b 14 Sep 1669 *NHV*, d 2 Feb 1749 æ. 81 *CTI*, Feb 1749/50 *CC;* m (1) 2 Dec 1685 *WV*—Ebenezer Lewis; m (2) William Frederick.

FAM. 2. GEORGE & SUSANNA (ABERNATHY) MERRIMAN:

1 NATHAN, b 30 Nov 1713 *WV*, d soon.

2 HANNAH, b c. 1715, d 19 Oct 1751 *WV;* m 15 May 1734 *WV*—Samuel Thorpe.

3 NATHAN, b 16 July 1717 *WV*, d 1755; m 3 Aug 1741 *WV*—Sarah da. John & Mary (Harrington) Bartholomew.

i Lois, b 11 June 1742 *WV;* m before 1771 Benjamin Randall of Rumboot, Dutchess Co., N. Y.; she had Benjamin Randle Bragg, b 17 Feb 176[-] *WV*, d 20 Aug 1768 *WV*, & John, b 23 Oct 176[-] *WV*.

ii George, b 12 Jan 1743/4 *WV*, d 6 Oct 1759 *F&IWRolls*.

iii Joel, b 16 July 1745 *WV*, d 30 Aug 1760 (in hospital) *F&IWRolls*.

iv Titus, b 5 Apr 1747 *WV;* rem. to Cornwall.

v Susanna, b 10 Aug 1752 *WV*.

vi Ichabod, b 23 Jan 1755 *WV;* rem. to Torrington; Census (L) 1-3-3; m 12 Dec 1777 *WV*—Rebecca da. Moses & Sybil (Thomas) Tuttle, b 21 Feb 1752 *WV*. Family incomplete. Children: (1) George, b 24 Sep 1778 *WV*. (2) Samuel, b 16 Apr 1780 *CV*. (3) Charles, b 17 Mar 1782 *TorringtonV;* rem. to Camden, N. Y.; m Electa Thorpe. (4) Reuben, b c. 1784, d 22 Sep 1866 æ. 83 *LT:* m Melia Byington.

4 LOIS, b 10 Nov 1720 *WV*.

5 SUSANNA, b 13 Sep 1723 *WV;* m 31 Dec 1739 *WV*—Benjamin Thorpe.

6 DANIEL, b 22 Feb 1727 *WV*, d s. p. after 1751.

7 MOLLY, b 6 Jan 1730 *WV;* m Abner Thorpe.

FAM. 3. JOHN & JEMIMA (WILCOXSON) MERRIMAN:

1 JOHN, b 12 Sep 1728 *WV*, d 13 Apr 1801; m Mabel da. Samuel & Hannah (Thompson) Thorpe, b 12 Jan 1724 *WV*.

i Mansfield, b 3 May 1752 *FarmV*, d c. 1790; m —— ; Census, Widow (S) 0-0-5. Children: (1) Mary, b 5 Jan 1778. (2) Patience, b 3 Feb 1780. (3) Wadsworth, b 1 June 1784, d s. p. (4) Dervilla, b 9 July 1786. (5) Anna, b 18 Mar 1788. (6) Jemima Mansfield, b 7 Aug 1790; probably m 10 Nov 1820 *SV*—William Hills.

ii Chauncey, b c. 1755; Census (S) 1-3-4; m 13 Feb 1777 Sarah Ives.

iii Jemima, b 30 June 1764 *FarmV;* m Daniel Carter.

iv Caleb, b 8 June 1768 *FarmV*, d 14 Oct 1838; m (1) 1 June 1801 Elizabeth Allen; m (2) 10 Oct 1814 Sarah Allen.

2 THANKFUL, b 2 Aug 1731 *WV*, d s. p.

3 SILAS, b 3 Jan 1734 *WV*, d 8 May 1805 æ. 71 *NHT1;* Census (NH) 3-0-2; m 15 Oct 1760 *WV*—Hannah Upson, who d 28 Apr 1820 æ. 84 *NHT1*.

i James, b 18 July 1761 *WV*, d 20 June 1813 æ. 52 *NHT1;* Brig. Gen.; m 7 Mar 1802 *NHC1*—Frances da. Stephen

& Lucy (Riley) Munson, b 31 Oct 1765 *NHC1*, d 8 Sep 1831 æ. 65 *NHT1*. **FAM. 11.**

ii Marcus, b 31 Oct 1762 *WV*, d 20 Feb 1850 æ. 87 *NHT1*; Maj.; Census (NH) 1-1-3; m (1) 13 Nov 1783 Sally Betty da. Hezekiah & Elizabeth (Cook) Parmelee, b 21 Dec 1766 *NHV*, d 16 May 1793 æ. 27 *NHT1*; m (2) 1 Dec 1793 *NHC1*—Susanna da. Timothy & Susan (Gordon) Bonticou, bp 18 Oct 1775 *NHx*, d 11 Jan 1807 æ. 32 *NHT1*; m (3) 22 Dec 1807 Lydia Wilcox, b c. 1767, d 5 Feb 1822 æ. 55 *NHT1*; m (4) 29 Nov 1822 *HuntingtonC*—Betsey, wid. Othniel DeForest. **FAM. 12.**

iii Silas, b 12 Feb 1769 *WV*, d [——] 1789 *NHT1*.

iv Samuel, b 9 Sep 1771 *NHT1*, d 13 Oct 1805 *NHT1*; m (1) Mary da. Nathaniel & Mary (Thompson) Fitch, b 20 July 1774 *NHV*, d 15 July 1796 æ. 22 *NHC1*; m (2) Nancy ——, who rem. to Windham before 1807. Child by first wife: (1) Samuel Fitch, b 3 July 1794 *NHV*. Child by second w.: (2) Mary.

v Lucy, b c. 1777, d 31 Oct 1805 æ. 28 *NHC1*; m 7 Mar 1802 *NHC1*—William Matthews.

4 EBER, b 26 Feb 1736 *WV*, d 2 June 1808; Census (S) 3-5-3; m (1) Sarah Hastings, who d 17 Apr 1782; m (2) Hannah Rogers, d 22 Oct 1833.

(By 1): *i* Peleg, b 1763, d 5 Nov 1773.

ii Perez, b 17 Oct 1765, d 23 Oct 1833; m Lucy Barnes.

iii Harmon, b 17 Mar 1768, d 3 Sep 1836; m 10 Feb 1794 Lovisa Tuttle.

iv Ezra, b 1770, d 7 Nov 1773.

v Stillman, b 6 Jan 1772, d 15 Nov 1808; m 10 Nov 1801 Sarah Hall.

vi Albert, b 6 Sep 1774, d 2 Aug 1827; m 22 Nov 1803 Roxanna Hart.

vii Doctor, b 8 July 1776, d 6 Nov 1841 (Westfield, Mass.); Dr.; m 11 Jan 1803 Sabrina Atkins, who d 10 May 1856.

viii Olcott, b 13 Jan 1779, d 23 Nov 1820; m Sophronia Hitchcock.

(By 2): *ix* Rogers, b 9 Nov 1783.

x Mehitabel, b 24 June 1785, d Aug 1855; m Jesse Hall of W.

xi Sarah, b 1787, d 17 Mar 1788.

xii Seabury, b 14 Oct 1789, d 2 Aug 1822.

xiii Hannah; m (1) 3 July 1813 Stoddard Neal; m (2) Samuel Bartholomew.

xiv James, b 1797, d 17 Jan 1800.

FAM. 4. ISRAEL & COMFORT (BENHAM) MERRIMAN:

1 JOSEPH, b 28 Aug 1716 *WV*, d 1768; res. Harwinton; m (1) 9 May 1745 Mary Phelps of Simsbury; m (2) 6 Aug 1754 Mary Wheeler.

(By 1): *i* Joseph, b 19 May 1746, d 1775; res. L; m Rachel Culver. Children: (1) Joseph, b 1772, m & had issue. (2) Silas, b 1774, m Sarah Moss; had Harlow 1799, John Adams 1801, & Lucy 1805.
ii Lydia, b 5 Feb 1748.
iii Esther, b 15 Mar 1750.
iv Ebenezer, b 26 Dec 1751.
(By 2): *v* Eunice, b 17 Oct 1756.
vi George, b 15 Aug 1757; m 29 Apr 1783 Rachel Matthews. Children recorded at Harwinton: Rachel, 21 Sep 1785; Laura, 21 Oct 1788; George, 18 Dec 1791; Loyal, 13 Dec 1793; Roswell, 5 May 1798.
vii William, b 13 Sep 1760.
2 COMFORT, b 3 Oct 1720 *WV*.
3 JELIN, b 16 Feb 1724 *WV*.
4 ELIZABETH, b 11 Mar 1727 *WV*.
5 SARAH, b 16 Dec 1729 *WV*.
6 ISRAEL, b 30 Nov 1732 *WV;* m (1) Prudence ——— ; m (2) 17 Apr 1782 Abigail Bradley of Farm; had a child Mary by 1st. w. & probably others.
7 ELPHAS, b 20 Aug 1737; m Esther ——— .
i Nathaniel, b 10 Mar 1787.

FAM. 5. CALEB & RUTH (SEDGWICK) MERRIMAN:
1 SARAH, b 25 May 1733 *WV;* m 18 Jan 1753 *WV*—Titus Cook.
2 MARY, b c. 1735, d 22 Aug 1775 æ 41 *WT1;* m 18 Jan 1753 *WV*—Jeremiah Hull.
3 GEORGE, b c. 1737, d 26 Apr 1757 *WV*, 24 Apr æ. 20 *WT1*.
4 ELIZABETH, b 24 Nov 1739 *WV*, d before 1797; m 9 Mar 1756 *WV*—Abel Merriman.
5 RUTH, b 30/31 Oct 1741 *WV*, d 12 Dec 1819 æ. 77 *HT2;* m Nov 1758 *WV*—Hezekiah Johnson.
6 JERUSHA, d 5 July 1751 *WV*.
7 ABIGAIL, d 3 Apr 1761 *WV*.
8 ANN, b 29 Apr 1749 *WV*, d 4 July 1751 *WV*.
9 CALEB, b 26 Feb 1751 *WV*, d 9 Oct 1751 *WV*.
10 CALEB, b 30 Sep 1754, d 7 Apr 1816 æ. 67 (62?) *WT1;* Census (W) 1-3-2; m (1) 18 Jan 1778 *WV*—Mary Peck, b c. 1746, d 15 Dec 1779 *WV*, æ. 33 *WT1;* m (2) 14 Dec 1780 *WV*—Amy da. Caleb & Eunice (Welton) Lewis, b 31 Jan 1745/6 *WV*, d c. 1783; m (3) 20 Oct 1785 *WV*—Statira da. Benjamin & Susanna (Peck) Hall, b 20 Mar 1766 *WV;* m (4) 5 Feb 1800 *CC*—Hannah da. Stephen & Hannah (Hotchkiss) Atwater, wid. John Hall, b 27 Nov 1754 *WV*, d 1825.
(By 2): *i* Isaac L., b 22 Nov 1781 *WV*, d July 1813 (at Pittsfield) *ColR*. He had a child by Polly Dunscomb: (1) Eunice Atwater, b 1 Nov 1805.
ii Caleb, b c. 1783; m (1) 6 Dec 1807 *WV*—Eunice Hall; she div. him 1823; m (2) 1 Oct 1823 *WV*—Charity

Clark.

(By 3): *iii* Benjamin Hall, b 21 Aug 1787 *WV;* m 26 Dec 1813 *WV* —Laura Parker.

FAM. 6. NATHANIEL & MEHITABEL (HALL) MERRIMAN:

1 SAMUEL, b 3 May 1712 *WV*, d c. 1758; m (1) Sarah da. Stephen & Sarah (Hill) Clark, b 28 Aug 1707 *NHV;* m (2) Mary wid. Henry King.

(By 1): *i* Martha, b 23 Apr 1733 *NHV*, d 10 Nov 1802 æ. 69 *WT1;* m 18 Nov 1773 *WV*—Ebenezer Mattoon.

ii Sarah, b 29 Apr 1735 *NHV;* m 9 Sep 1756 *WV*—Thomas Beach.

iii (probably) Mehitabel; m 5 Aug 1762 *MidC*—James Hopkins.

iv John, d s. p. 1778.

v Thankful, b 5 Nov 1743 *MidV;* m 27 May 1762 Daniel Dimock of Durham.

vi (probably) Lucy; m 3 June 1773 *MidC*—Samuel Tuells.

vii (probably) Abigail; m 12 May 1776 *MidC*—Benjamin Birdseye.

2 DAVID, b 11 Feb 1715 *WV*, d 13 Oct 1771 *WV*, æ. 57 *WT1;* Lt.; m Elizabeth da. Joseph & Hope (Cook) Benham, b c. 1721, d 24 May 1784 æ. 63 *WT1;* she m (2) 5 May 1774 *WV*—Benjamin Atwater.

i Thankful, b 17 Mar 1749/50 *WV*, d 14 July 1796 æ. 47 *WT1;* m 24 Dec 1772 *WV*—Giles Hall.

ii Elizabeth, b c. 1752, d 21 Nov 1801; m 30 Oct 1769 *WV*—Hezekiah Hall.

3 THANKFUL, b 31 May 1717 *WV*, d 9 Oct 1749 æ. 33 *PT;* m 15 Nov 1743 *WatV*—Phinehas Royce.

4 NATHANIEL, b 31 May 1720 *WV*, d 10 July 1765 *WV*, æ. [—] *WT1;* m 19 Dec 1743 *WV*—Prudence da. John & Prudence (Royce) Austin, b 10 Nov 1723 *WV*, d 1806.

i Phineas, d s. p. before 1777.

ii Prudence, b c. 1746, d 29 Nov 1807 æ. 61 *WT2;* m 27 Mar 1775 *WV*—Archelaus Alling.

iii Mehitabel; m Theophilus Page.

iv Mary, d s. p. after 1807.

v Nathaniel, b c. 1760, d 7 July 1808 æ. 48 *WT1;* Census (W) 1-1-4; m 27 Dec 1781 *WV*—Lucy da. Jonathan & Esther (Curtis) Moss, b 1 Jan 1765 *WV*. **FAM. 13.**

5 THOPHILUS, b c. 1729, d 2 Aug 1807 æ. 78 *WT1;* m 16 Oct 1772 *WV*—Margery da. Abial & Mary (Leete) Eliot, b 19 Mar 1742 *NoHT2*, d 15 May 1823 *NoHT2*.

i Ruth, b 18 July 1773 *WV*, d 4 Mar 1864 æ. 93 *NoHT2;* m 24 Nov 1794 Samuel Frost.

ii Eliot Hall, b 8 Jan 1775 *WV*, "Eliot" d 26 Oct 1774 *WV*.

iii Mary, b c. 1777, d 31 May 1843 æ. 66 (in Fair Haven) *WT1;* m 27 Dec 1798 *NoHC*—John Hunt.

iv Sarah, b 6 Apr 1780 *WV*.

6 ABEL, Capt. (Rev. soldier); Census (Wells, Vt.) 1-0-1; m 9 Mar 1756 *WV*—Elizabeth da. Caleb & Ruth (Sedgwick) Merriman, b 24 Nov 1739 *WV*, d before 1797.

i Caleb, b 22 Feb 1757 *WV;* res. Wells, Vt.

ii George, b 26 Aug 1759 *WV*, d 21 May 1836 æ. 77 *WTI;* Census (W) 2-1-6; m 17 Feb 1780 *WV*—Katharine da. Sherburn & Katharine (Hitchcock) Johnson, b 18 May 1758 *WV*, d 8 July 1842 æ. 85 *WTI*. Children: (1) Martha, b 6 May 1781 *WV*. d 20 Sep 1862 æ. 82 *WTI;* m Erastus Alling. (2) Mary, b 25 July 1782 *WV*, d 18 Mar 1858 æ. 77 *WTI;* m (1) 25 Jan 1801 Jeremiah Tuttle; m (2) 10 Nov 1823 Caleb Ives; m (3) Nov 1826 John Earl Dudley. (3) Nancy, b 14 Apr 1787 *WV;* m ——— Hotchkiss.

iii Samuel Sedgwick, b 2 Apr 1762 *WV*, d 19 Sep 1847 (Wells, Vt.); Census (Wells) 1-1-2; m Polly Cross.

iv Abel.

v Abigail, b 12 Apr 1770 *WV;* m Timothy Hebard of Orwell, Vt.

FAM. 7. THEOPHILUS & MARY (MATTOON) MERRIMAN:

1 ANNA, b 1 Sep 1715 *WV*, d 7 July 1778; m (1) 1733 Ephraim Chamberlain; m (2) 29 May 1750 *WV*—Benjamin Royce.

2 THEOPHILUS, b 28 Aug 1717 *WV;* d s. p. 25 Sep 1792 *Northfield;* deaf & dumb.

3 SARAH, b 11 Aug 1719 *Northfield*, d 21 Aug 1719 *Northfield*.

4 SARAH, b 5 Dec 1720 *Northfield*, d before 1755; m c. 1739 Thomas Taylor.

5 SAMUEL, b 13 Feb 1722/3 *Northfield*, d 22 June 1803 *Northfield;* m (1) 3 Mar 1747 Mary Hawks; m (2) 21 Dec 1759 Lydia (Harwood) Stebbins.

FAM. 8. SAMUEL & SARAH (WILTSHIRE) MERRIMAN:

1 SAMUEL, b 24 Aug 1728 *WV*, d soon.

2 NICHOLAS, d 17 Feb 1737 *WV*.

3 ANNA, d 10 Mar 1737 *WV*.

4 SAMUEL, b 14 Oct 1734 *WV*, d 28 Feb 1737 *WV*.

5 KATHARINE, b 28 Dec 1736 *WV;* m c. 1784 James Kemp.

6 SARAH, b 28 Jan 1742 *WV;* m 29 June 1783 *WV*—Elihu Yale.

7 MILES, b 11 June 1744 *WV*, d s. p.

8 STEPHEN, b 25 May 1747 *WV*, d s. p.

9 HANNAH, b 1 Dec 1750 *WV*, d s. p.

10 EUNICE, b21 Aug 1753 *WV;* m (1) 19 May 1773 *WV*—John Kean; m (2) William Jones.

FAM. 9. MOSES & MARTHA (BEACH) MERRIMAN:

1 JEHIEL, b 28 Oct 1713 *WV*, d 25 July 1772 *CC;* m 5 Aug 1740 *WV*—Hannah da. Theophilus & Hannah (Mix) Jones, b 4 Oct 1720 *WV*, d 26 Aug 1783 *CC*.

i Hester, bp Feb 1742 *CC*, d after 1773.

ii Daniel, bp Jan 1743 *CC*, d 19 Feb 1825 *Dalton, Mass.,T;* m 3 Oct 1764 *WV, NHCl*—Damaris da. Elnathan & Hannah (Hitchcock) Andrews, b 23 May 1745 *WV*, d 6 Mar 1835 *DaltonC*. **FAM. 14.**

iii Hannah, b c. 1745, d after 1773.

iv Lydia, bp 18 Oct 1747 *CC*, d after 1773.

v Jehiel, bp Jan 1750 *CC*, d 12 May 1806 *CC*, æ. 52 *CTl;* Census (C) 1-1-3; m 11 June 1788 *CV*—Eunice da. Ephraim & Eunice (Merriman) Preston. Child: Elizabeth, b 12 Oct 1789 *WV;* m Daniel S. Ives.

vi Thankful, bp Dec 1751 *CC*, bu. 17 Jan 1839 æ. 88 *Bx;* m 3 May 1787 *CC*—Jesse Terrill.

vii Phebe, b c. 1759, d 13 Sep 1829 æ. 71 *SalemC;* m 17 June 1794 *WatV, CC*—Asahel Hotchkiss.

viii Abigail, b c. 1762, d 2 Oct 1835 æ. 74 *WTl;* m 31 Dec 1787 *CC*—Titus Preston.

ix Theophilus, b c. 1764, d 2 Mar 1832; Census (C) 1-0-2; rem. to Franklin, Pa.; m 15 Feb 1791 Sarah da. Ralph & Bathsheba (Hotchkiss) Lines, b 8 Mar 1768 *WV*, d 1833.

2 Esther, b 11 Nov 1716 *WV*, d 3 Apr 1734 *WV*.

3 Phebe, b 27 Mar 1720 *WV;* m (1) 18 July 1739 *WV*—Moses Munson; m (2) 9 Apr 1752 *NoBCl*—Josiah Bartholomew.

4 Benjamin, b 21 Jan 1722 *WV*, d 8 Aug 1813 æ. 91 *Richmond, Mass.,V;* m 2 Jan 1744/5 *WV*—Susanna da. Abraham & Sarah (Sutliff) Crittenden, b 5 Sep 1720. Family incomplete.

i Amos, b 20 Oct 1745 *WV*.

ii Abraham, b 17 Oct 1747 *FarmV*, d 17 May 1825 *Richmond;* m Ruth ——— .

5 Martha, b 20 Dec 1723 *WV;* m 16 Nov 1775 *WV*—Daniel Doolittle.

6 Mary, b 26 Feb 1726 *WV;* m 7 Jan 1745/6 *WV*—Joseph Royce.

7 Moses, b 14 Feb 1728 *WV*, d 20 Sep 1758 *F&IWRolls;* m c. 1752 Joanna da. Daniel & Lydia (Avery) Mix, b 12 Nov 1727 *WV;* she m (2) 14 Mar 1761 *WV*—Jacob Teal.

i Thankful, bp 14 July 1754 *SC*.

8 Lent, b 25 May 1731 *WV*, d 3 Sep 1800 æ. 72 *SC;* Census (C) 2-1-4; m 30 Jan 1754 *WV*—Katharine Wright, who d 11 Jan 1797 *CC*.

i Lucy, b 14 Feb 1755 *WV;* m 5 Dec 1776 *CC, WatV*—Caleb Barnes.

ii Joel, b 11 Sep 1756 *WV*, d 19 Apr 1811 *CC;* m 13 Feb 1775 *CC*—Lue da. Benjamin & Rhoda (Cook) Hitchcock, b 24 Mar 1755 *WV*, d 2 July 1819 æ. 64 *CTl*. **FAM. 15.**

iii Mamre, b 30 June 1758 *WV;* m 3 Feb 1783 *CC*—Asahel Tillotson.

iv Katharine, b 23 May 1760 *WV;* m 16 Mar 1780 *CC, SV*—

Amos Bunnell.

v Moses, 30 Oct 1761 *WV*, d 17 Mar 1814 æ. 52 *HT2 list;* Census (Wd) 1-1-2;; m Nov 1787 *NHC2*—Lois Wantwood, who d 4 Nov 1843 æ. 83 *HT2 list.* **FAM. 16.**

vi Benjamin, b 1 Nov 1763 *WV;* m Mary da. William & Isabel (Holbrook) Everton, b 23 Apr 1762 *EHV.* Child: William, of Terre Haute, Ind.

vii Esther, b 19 Jan 1766 *WV.*

viii Lent, b 6 Nov 1768 *WV*, bp 5 Feb 1769 *CC*, d 1 Apr 1817 æ. 48 *SC.*

ix Martha, b 5 Nov 1770 *WV*, bp 6 Jan 1771 *CC.*

x Eunice, b 23 Feb 1773 *WV*, bp 6 June 1773 *CC;* m 8 Jan 1794 *NHC1*—William Trowbridge; she div. him 1805.

FAM. 10. ELIASAPH & ABIGAIL (HULL) MERRIMAN:

1 EUNICE, b 7 Oct 1720 *WV*, d 12 Jan 1721 *WV.*

2 EUNICE, b 24 Nov 1721 *WV;* m (1) 9 Dec 1747 *WV*—Samuel Doolittle; m (2) 25 Mar 1754 *WV*—Ephraim Preston.

3 SARAH, b 18 Nov 1723 *WV;* m 8 June 1743 *WV*—Nathaniel Jones.

4 CALEB, b 3 Sep 1725 *WV*, d 6 Aug 1797 æ. 72 *WC2;* Census (W) 2-0-2; m 12 May 1747 *WV*—Margaret da. Josiah & Ruth (Merriam) Robinson, b 26 June 1729 *WV*, d July 1795.

i Josiah, b 25 Mar 1748 *WV;* Census (W) 1-3-1; m 8 Mar 1781 *WV*, *NHC1*—Lydia da. John & Lydia (Ford) Johnson, wid. Robert Simpson.

ii Rebecca, b 7 Nov 1750 *WV;* m Edward Collins.

iii Jesse, b 25 Dec 1752 *WV*, "child" d 13 Sep 1756 *WC2.*

iv Caleb, b 4 Apr 1754 *WV*, d 14 Feb 1817 æ. 63 *GranbyT;* Census (W) 2-3-2; m 12 Dec 1775 *CC*—Sarah Royce.

v Enoch, b 7 Dec 1755 *WV;* m 31 Dec 1781 *WV*—Abigail da. Yale & Sarah (Talmadge) Bishop, bp 18 Nov 1759 *NHC2.*

vi Jesse, b 5 Oct 1759 *WV*, d 8 May 1827 æ. 68 *WT2;* Census (W) 1-2-2; m 25 Jan 1784 *WV*—Dolly da. Gideon & Eunice (Tuttle) Ives, b c. 1766, d 13 Aug 1808.

vii Ruth; m John Wade.

viii Christopher; m 26 Nov 1789 Polly Bronson.

ix Howell, b c. 1768/9, d 29 Oct 1805 æ. 33 *WT2*, æ. 37 *WC2.*

5 TITUS, b 28 Aug 1727 *WV*, d 24 Dec 1806 æ. 80 *WT2*, *WC2;* Census (W) 2-0-3; m 20 Feb 1748/9 *WV*—Dinah da. Elisha & Mabel (Andrews) Andrews, b 23 Mar 1729 *WV*, d 1 Sep 1813 æ. 85 *WT2.* PAGE 1528

i Elisha, b 21 Sep 1749 *WV*, d 1814; Census (W) 1-2-3; m (1) 3 June 1773 *WV*—Mary da. Abel & Mary (Gridley) Hawley, b Aug 1755, d 15 Nov 1774 *WV*, æ. 20 *WT2;* m (2) Damaris —— who d 7 Aug 1781 *WV;* m (3) 25 Dec 1782 *WV*—Chloe da. Wm. & Mary (Austin) Merriam, b 12 July 1761 *WV*.

ii Charles, b 31 Oct 1751 *WV*, d 28 May 1823 (Otisco, N. Y.); res. 1800 Manlius, N. Y.; m 10 Aug 1775 Rachel Cole.

iii Eunice, bp 14 Oct 1753 *WC2*, d 11 Sep 1756 *WV*, æ. 2 *WT2*.

iv Eunice, b 11 June 1757 *WV*, "child" bp 1757 *WC2*, d 16 May 1832 æ. 75 *BristolT;* m Enos Ives.

v Joel, b 10 May 1760 *WV*, d 1832; Census (W) 1-0-0; m Anna ——— .

vi Abigail, b 8 Nov 1762 *WV;* m 10 June 1784 *WV*—Zenas Mitchell.

vii Sally, b 21 Mar 1764 *WV;* m 24 May 1786 *WV*—Asahel Yale.

viii Titus, b c. 1768, d 1 Apr 1848 æ. 80 *BristolT;* Dr.; m (1) Polly ———, who d 28 Mar 1823 æ. 50 *BristolT;* m (2) Catherine ———, who d 17 Jan 1849 æ. 68 *BristolT*.

ix Elizabeth, b c. 1771; m Aaron Holt.

6 AMASA, b 17 June 1729 *WV*, d 1794; Census (W) 2-3-2; m (1) 26 Sep 1750 *WV*—Sarah da. Stephen & Sarah (Hart) Ives, b 29 May 1733 *WV*, d 29 July 1776 *WV;* m (2) 18 Feb 1778 *WV*—Tabitha da. Gershom & Hannah (Pease) Sexton, wid. Joseph Atkins, b 9 Apr 1729 *EnfieldV*.

(By 1): *i* Hannah, b 14 July 1751 *WV*, d 29 Sep 1751 *WV*.

ii Phebe, b 25 Dec 1752 *WV*, d 20 Oct 1755 *WV*.

iii Mary, b 19 Nov 1754 *WV*, d 17 Oct 1755 *WV*.

iv Amasa, b 10 Oct 1757 *WV*, d 25 Feb 1758 *WV*.

v Sarah, b 11 May 1759 *WV*.

vi Charles, b 29 Aug 1762 *WV*, d 26 Aug 1829; m 16 May 1784 Anna Punderson.

vii Phebe, b 24 June 1765 *WV*.

viii Amasa, b 2 June 1767 *WV*, d 7 June 1843 *F;* res. Hatley, Quebec; m 17 Mar 1792 *Guildhall, Vt.*—Ann Hall.

ix Joseph, b 17 Jan 1769 *WV*.

x Benjamin, b 17 Oct 1771 *WV*, d 18 May 1774 *WV*.

7 ENOCH, b 1 May 1731 *WV*, d 14 June 1731 *WV*.

8 ELIZABETH, b 27 July 1732 *WV;* m 25 May 1756 *WV*—Reuben Preston.

9 ESTHER, b 2 Dec 1734 *WV*, d 25 May 1787; m 5 Aug 1762 *WV*—Ephraim Preston.

10 ELIASAPH, b 9 Nov 1736 *WV*, d 1 May 1815 æ 79 *WT1;* m 13 Jan 1762 *WV*—Jerusha da. Philip & Mary (Humiston) Mattoon, b 25 Mar 1742 *WV*, d 22 Nov 1827 æ. 86 *WT1*.

i Amos, b 1 Dec 1762 *WV;* Census (C) 1-0-3; rem. to Scott Co., Ky.; m Abigail Williams.

ii Abigail, b 6 July 1764 *WV*, d 19 Mar 1843 æ. 78 *WT1;* m Willoughby Williams.

iii Eunice, b 11 May 1766 *WV*.

iv Eliakim, b 2 July 1769 *WV*, d 15 Aug 1780 *WV*, 13 Aug æ. 19 *WTl*.
v Polly, b 10 Sep 1773 *WV*.
vi Reuben, b 9 Sep 1775 *WV*, d 18 June 1790 *WV*, æ. 15 *WTl*.
vii Asaph, b 1 July 1778 *WV*, d 13 Sep 1830 æ, 56 (at W, suicide) *ColR;* m Eunice da. Bartholomew Andrews.
viii Eliakim, b 7 Oct 1780 *WV*.
ix Esther; m 20 Jan 1803 *WV*—Isaac Merriman.

11 ENOCH, b 26 May 1739 *WV*, d s. p.
12 EBENEZER, b 26 May 1739 *WV*, d s. p.
13 TURHAND, b 24 May 1741 *WV*, d s. p.
14 CHARLES, b 2 Sep 1744 *WV*, d s. p.
15 ABIGAIL, b 17 June 1749 *WV*, d 4 Aug 1758 *WV*, æ. 10 *WTl*.

FAM. 11. JAMES & FRANCES (MUNSON) MERRIMAN:
1 LUCY.
2 JOHN, b 1806, d 1855; m (1) 16 Oct 1827 Jane Elizabeth Daggett, who d 11 Apr 1842 æ. 36 *NHTl;* m (2) 10 Feb 1844 Caroline Lewis.
3 FRANCES; m 6 Aug 1834 Jeremiah D. G. Manning.

FAM. 12. MARCUS & SALLY BETTY (PARMELEE) MERRIMAN:
1 CHILD, d *NHTl*.
2 ELIZABETH, b c. 1787, d 9 Apr 1833 æ. 46 (*Meth*) *NHV;* m Nov 1808 *ConnH*—Joseph H. Josselyn of Bridgewater, Mass.
3 CHILD, d *NHTl*.
4 HANNAH; m (1) Apr 1814 *ColR*—Nathan Sherman Read; m (2) Sidney Wells of Cambridge, N. Y.
5 MARCUS, b 1792, d 11 Dec 1864; m (1) 12 Sep 1813 Mary Hotchkiss; m (2) Nancy Hood.

FAM. 12. MARCUS & SUSANNA (BONTICOU) MERRIMAN:
6 JOHN, d æ. 0-3 *NHTl*.
7 SALLY, d æ. 0–18 *NHTl*.
8 SARAH PARMELEE, b 27 Apr 1799, d 12 Aug 1869; m 27 Aug 1817 Eben Norton Thomson of Goshen & NH.
9 CHILD, d *NHTl*.
10 CHILD, d *NHTl*.

FAM. 13. NATHANIEL & LUCY (MOSS) MERRIMAN:
1 ISAAC; m 20 Jan 1803 *WV*—Esther da. Eliasaph & Jerusha (Mattoon) Merriman.
2 LUCY, b 27 Feb 1786 *WV;* m 6 Sep 1802 *WV*—William Ward.
3 NANCY, b 3 Nov 1788 *WV;* m 11 June 1807 *WV*—Noah Pomeroy of P.
4 NATHANIEL, b 25 Feb 1792 *WV*.
5 EDWARD, b 4 Nov 1794 *WV*.
6 HIRAM, b 18 Apr 1799 *WV*.
7 HENRY, b 1801 *WV*.
8 MABEL, b 31 May 1803 *WV*.
9 ARTEMISIA, b 31 Dec 1807 *WV*.

FAM. 14. DANIEL & DAMARIS (ANDREWS) MERRIMAN:

1 CHLOE, b 13 July 1765 *WV*.

2 JESSE, b 29 Jan 1767 *WV;* m (1) (intention) 29 Apr 1792 *DaltonV*—Rhoda Fox, who d 11 Apr 1811 æ. 37 *DaltonT;* m (2) Susan ——, who d 21 Sep 1829 æ. 60 *DaltonT.*

3 NATHANIEL, b 28 Mar 1770 *WV*, d 2 Oct 1828 æ. 58 *DaltonT;* m (intention) 6 Sep 1795 *DaltonV*—Clarissa Fox.

4 MARTHA, b 8 Apr 1772 *WV;* m 9 Feb 1792 *DaltonC*—Azariah Haskin of Pittsfield, Mass.

5 AMELIA, bp 17 Sep 1775 (at Lanesboro) *Gt. Barrington x;* m (intention) 29 Jan 1797 *DaltonV*—William Hall of Pownal, Vt.

6 DANIEL; m 19 Jan 1800 *DaltonV*—Sally Taggart.

7 BETSEY, b c. 1780, d 15 Feb 1800 æ. 20 *DaltonT.*

FAM. 15. JOEL & LUE (HITCHCOCK) MERRIMAN:

1 JOEL, bp 22 Feb 1778 *CC;* m 22 Mar 1803 Clementina Tuttle.

2 RHODA COOK, bp 3 Oct 1779 *CC.*

3 MARY, bp 4 Mar 1781 *CC;* m —— Barnes.

4 EZRA, bp 18 Aug 1782 *CC.*

FAM. 16. MOSES & LOIS (WANTWOOD) MERRIMAN:

1 BETSEY, b 22 Feb 1787 *HT1*, bp 18 Aug 1795 *HC2*, d 1 Apr 1869 æ. 82 *HT1*, æ. 82-1-8 *HV;* m Elam Warner.

2 HENRY, bp 18 Aug 1795 *HC2;* m Caroline Downs.

3 HARVEY, bp 18 Aug 1795 *HC2.*

4 WEALTHY bp 18 Aug 1795 *HC2.*

5 ELIZA, b 27 Feb 1795 *F*, bp 18 Aug 1795 *HC2*, d 17 Aug 1835 æ. 40 *HT2;* m 25 Oct 1818 *F*—Harvey Bradley.

6 LEWIS, bp 1800 *HC2;* m Julia da. Mansfield & Asenath (Sperry) Sperry, who d May 1881 æ. 79 (at H) *WdD.*

7 WEALTHY MARIA, bp 1802 *HC2*, d 1841 (Painesville, Ohio) *F;* m 25 July 1827 *NHV*—Orrin Smith.

8 MARCUS, b 16 Apr 1804 *F*, bp 1804 *HC2;* res. Batavia, Genesee Co., N. Y.; m 16 June 1828 *F*—Charlotte da. Ezra Bradley.

PAGE 1248 **MERWIN.** FAM. 1. SAMUEL, s. of Miles, b 21 Aug 1656 *MV*, d 22 Jan 1706; m (1) 13 Dec 1682 *NHV*—Sarah da. William & Sarah (Clark) Wooding, b 13 Sep 1654 *NHV*, d 9 Mar 1690 *MC1* [1690/1]; m (2) Hannah ——, who d 1741; she m (2) c. 1707 Isaac Beecher.

(By 1): 1 SAMUEL, b c. 1685; m 7 May 1707 Mary Burwell.

2 ABIGAIL, bp 22 Jan 1687 *MC1*, d 1707.

3 SARAH, bp 3 Nov 1689 *MC1;* m 25 Aug 1708 Zachariah Baldwin.

4 DANIEL, bp 15 Mar 1691 *MC1*, d 1761; m (1) Joanna da. Henry & Joanna (Leek) Stevens, b 9 Feb 1685 *NHV*, d 1 Jan 1730 æ. 44 *WT1;* m (2) 4 Mar 1730 *WV*—Elizabeth, wid. Barnabas Lewis, b c. 1703, d 26 July 1766 æ. 63 *WV;* she m (3) 9 Feb 1762 *WC1*—Joseph Holt.

(By 1): *i* Daniel, b 9 Nov 1713 *WV*, d c. 1790; m 22 Apr 1736 *WV*—Mehitabel da. Thomas & Abigail (How) Twiss, b 4 Jan 1714 *WV*, d 5 Jan 1753 æ. c. 40 *WT1.* **FAM. 2.**

ii Henry, b 28 Dec 1715 *WV;* m 2 Jan 1742 *WV*—Sarah

Mott. **FAM. 3.**

iii Abigail, b 6 Aug 1718 *WV*.

iv Stephen, b 12 Aug 1720 *WV;* m 12 Apr 1743 *WV*—Mehitabel da. Stephen & Sarah (Hill) Clark, wid. Joseph Tyler, b 5 Feb 1718/9 *NHV*. **FAM. 4.**

v Ebenezer, b 2 Apr 1724 *WV*, d 26 Aug 1745 (at Woodstock, returning from Cape Breton) *WV*.

(By 2): *vi* Joanna, b 5 Apr 1732 *WV;* m 9 Jan 1750 *WV*—Timothy Page.

vii Deborah.

5 Deborah, bp 15 Mar 1691 *MCl;* m 2 Jan 1717 *WV*—Eliasaph Preston.

(By 2): 6 Hannah, b 1702, d 20 Dec 1725 *WV;* m 25 Apr 1723 *WV*—Ezekiel Royce.

7 Justina, b 1704; m 30 Oct 1734 *NHV*—John Bristol. PAGE 1248

FAM. 2. Daniel & Mehitabel (Twiss) Merwin:

1 Thomas, b 22 June 1737 *WV;* Census (Woodstock, N. Y.) 3-0-0; m 18 Feb 1762 *WV*—Esther da. Stephen & Sarah (Hart) Ives, b 13 July 1742 *WV*.

i Daniel, b 9 Nov 17[62?] *WV*.

ii Denny, b 3 June 1765 *WV*.

iii Samuel, b 22 Mar 1767 *WV*.

iv Mehitabel, b 26 Mar 1769 *WV*, d 29 Oct 1769 *WV*.

v Thomas, b 16 Feb 1771 *WV*.

vi Esther, b 28 Apr 1773 *WV*.

vii Mary. b 2 Mar 1775 *WV*.

viii Archibald, b 11 Feb 1777 *WV*, d 23 Apr 1777 *WV*.

ix Lucy, b 22 May 1778 *WV*.

2 Samuel, b 18 May 1740 *WV*, d before 1790; m 18 Nov 1764 *WV*—Jerusha da. Samuel & Mary (Parmelee) Peck, b 29 July 1747.

i Samuel, bp 21 July 1770 *NHCl*, d 22 July 1770 æ. 5 wks. *NHCl*.

ii Samuel, b 23 Dec 1771 *WV*, bp 8 Mar 1772 *NHCl*.

3 Stephen, b 18 Mar 1741/2 *WV*, d 4 Oct 1748 *WV*.

4 Mehitabel, b 6 Jan 1743/4 *WV;* m 5 Jan 1769 *WV*—James Swift.

5 Stephen, b 19 Sep 1748 *WV;* m 3 June 1773 *WV*—Sarah Bestow.

FAM. 3. Henry & Sarah (Mott) Merwin:

1 Jesse, b 27 Oct 1742 *WV;* res. Cornwall 1786; m 14 June 176[-] *WV*—Hannah da. Seth & Hannah (Clark) Plumb, b 19 Aug 1743 *NHV*.

2 Ebenezer, b 3 Apr 1744 *WV;* res. Pittsfield, Mass., 1786; m 1 May 1766 *WV*—Jemima da. Seth & Hannah (Clark) Plumb, b 14 Nov 1745 *NHV*. A child, Lois, b 19 July 176[-] *WV*.

3 Sarah, b 28 Feb 1752 *WV;* [?m 23 June 1766 *WV*—Asahel Coley].

4 Moses, b 10 Aug 1755 *WV*.

FAM. 4. Stephen & Mehitabel (Clark) Merwin:

1 Thankful, b 1 Feb 1743/4 *WV*, d 3 Jan 1813 æ. 67 *SC;* m 8 Nov 1764 Silas Clark of Farm.

2 Joseph, b 27 Nov 1747 *WV*.

3 Joanna, b 30 May 1750 *WV*.

4 Sarah, b 23 Oct 1757 *WV*.

MERWIN. FAM. 5. Joseph, b c. 1712, d 7 Jan 1782 *WHD*, "Mr." bu. 6 Feb 1782 æ. 70 *NHx;* m Margaret Fowler, b c. 1714, d 28 Oct 1790 æ. 76 *WHT1*, 29 Oct *WHD;* Census, Margaret (NH) 0-0-3.

1 Joseph, b 28 May 1739; Census (NH) 2-0-2; m 18 Dec 1766 Phebe da. Isaac & Phebe (Smith) Platt, b 13 Aug 1744.

i Joseph, b 17 June 1768, d 22 Aug 1850; Dea.; m 3 Nov 1783 Gratia da. Samuel Candee, b 8 Jan 1769, d 5 Oct 1839.

ii Phebe Abigail, b 4 Oct 1782.

PAGE 1248 2 Fowler, b 15 July 1740.

3 Susanna, b 10 May 1742; m Epenetus Platt of NM.

4 David, b 11 Oct 1746; res. NM; m Tamasin da. John & Deborah (Welch) Comstock.

5 Jonas, b 1 Aug 1748, bp 11 Sep 1748 *MC1*, d 23 Jan 1834 æ. 85 *WHD, WHT2;* m Phebe da. Samuel Miles, b c. 1755, d 27 Sep 1833 æ. 78 *WHT2*, æ. 79 *WHD*.

i Samuel Miles, bp 19 Aug 1779 (sponsors, Thaddeus & Ann Clark) *NHx*.

ii Phebe, bp 19 Aug 1779 *NHx*, d 23 Jan 1861 æ. 81 *WHT2;* m James Ward.

iii Jonas Fowler, bp 1 May 1785 *NHx*, d 11 Sep 1841 æ. 56 *WHT2;* m (1) Sarah ——, who d 4 Dec 1817 æ. 25 *WHT2;* m (2) 7 Oct 1818 *WdC*—Polly da. Samuel & Lucy Newton, who d 8 Jan 1823 æ. 29 *WHT2;* m (3) Anna C. ——, who d 19 Apr 1864 æ. 73 *WHT2*.

6 Margaret, b 31 Aug 1751.

7 Hannah, b 13 May 1761; [?m Nehemiah Platt].

MERWIN. FAM. 6. Miles, 2d, brother of Samuel (FAM. 1), m 20 Sep 1681 *NHV*—Hannah da. Benjamin & Elizabeth Wilmot, wid. Samuel Miles, & had a da. Ann b 17 Jan 1681 *NHV* [1681/2]...... Miles, 3d, m (1) Ann da. Joseph & Frances (Bryan) Treat, b 30 Jan 1696 *MV*, bp 31 Mar 1700 *MC1*, d 3 Dec 1723 æ. 28 *MT;* m (2) 11 Nov 1730 *NHV*—Mary da. Thomas & Mary (Winston) Trowbridge, wid. Stephen Alling, b 9 Apr 1691 *NHV*.

(By 1): 1 Miles, b 29 Nov 1719 *MV*, d 14 May 1764 æ. 45 *MT;* w. Mary d 27 Dec 1797 æ 75 *MT*.

2 Joseph, b c. 1721, d 1 May 1799 æ. 77 *WdC*, æ. 78 *WdT1;* Census (Wd) 1-1-2; m Martha da. Fletcher & Hannah (Platt) Newton, b c. 1726, d 31 July 1809 æ. 83 *WdC*.

i Joseph, b 16 Apr 1751 *NHV*, d Sep 1803 *WdD;* Census (Wd) 1-0-4; m 13 Mar 1774 *WdV*, *WdC*—Eunice da.

John & Obedience (Sperry) Horton, bp 1 Apr 1748 *Wd C.* **FAM. 7.**

ii Martha, b 26 May 1754 *NHV*, d 28 Oct 1834 æ. 80 *WHT 1;* m (1) Oct 1792 *WdC*—Abraham Tolles; m (2) Silas Kimberly.

iii Fletcher, b 13 Aug 1757 *NHV*, d 28 May 1809 æ. 52 *Wd T1;* Census (Wd) 1-1-3; m (1) 1 May 1783 *WdV*—Mercy Osborn, b c. 1756, d 27 Oct 1806 *WdV*, æ. 50 *WdT1;* m (2) 22 Feb 1807 *WdD*—Sarah da. Simeon & Patience (Smith) Sperry, b c. 1776, d 8 Feb 1861 æ. 85 *WdD;* she m (2) Mar 1818 (at Wd) *ColR*—David Perkins. **FAM. 8.**

iv Miles, b 9 May 1760 *NHV*, d s. p.

3 STEPHEN, b 22 Oct 1722 *MV*, d 23 Dec 1722 *MV.*

4 ANN, b 23 Dec 1723 *MV.*

(By 2): 5 MARY, b 10 Mar 1734 *MV*, bp 12 May 1734 *MC1;* m Lewis Mallett.

FAM. 7. JOSEPH & EUNICE (HORTON) MERWIN:

1 BEZALEEL, b 19 June 1775 *WdV;* res. Cornwall 1810; m 7 Jan 1800 *WdV*—Anna Beach.

2 EUNICE, b 19 Apr 1777 *WdV*, d 27 Apr 1809 (at Winchester) *WatV;* m 12 Jan 1796 *WatV*—Benjamin Hoadley.

3 RUANNA, b 30 Mar 1779 *WdV;* m Lyman Thomas of Cornwall.

4 LUCINDA, b 14 Dec 1781 *WdV*, d 20 July 1804 æ. 24 *WdD.*

5 ALVIRA, b 4 Jan 1786 *WdV*, *WtnV;* res. Cornwall 1810.

6 WILLARD, b 6 May 1788 *WdV*, *WtnV*, d 30 Apr 1790 *WdV.*

FAM. 8. FLETCHER & MERCY (OSBORN) MERWIN:

1 POLLY, b 16 Jan 1784 *WdV*, d 5 Aug 1794 *WdV*, æ. 11 *WdT1.*

2 ANN, b 14 Nov 1785 *WdV*, d 26 Apr 1812 æ. 27 *WdT1.*

3 FLETCHER NEWTON, b 21 May 1788 *WdV*, d 5 Feb 1846 æ. 58 *WdD;* m Charlotte da. Abel & Susannah Smith, who d 14 Jan 1864 æ. 77 *WdD.*

4 JOHN, b 4 Feb 1793 *WdV*, d 8 Aug 1794 *WdV*, æ. 2 *WdT1.*

5 POLLY, b 25 June 1795 *WdV*, d 30 Sep 1820 æ. 25 *WdD;* m John Smith.

6 PATTY, b 3 Oct 1799 *WdV*, d 9 June 1862 æ. 62-8 *WdD;* m Isaac Nettleton.

FAM. 8. FLETCHER & SARAH (SPERRY) MERWIN:

7 JOHN MILES, b 10 Jan 1809 *WdV*, d 14 July 1875 æ. 66 *WdD;* m (1) Mary da. Camp & Elizabeth Newton, who d 26 June 1844 æ. 33 *WdD;* m (2) Eliza Ann da. Lewis & Elizabeth Ann (Beecher) Peck, b 25 Dec 1826 *F*, d 22 Aug 1912 *F.*

MESIER. ABRAHAM & Cornelia had: James White, bp 13 Apr 1783 *NHx.*

MESSENGER. DANIEL, b c. 1683, d c. 1751; Capt.; from Norwalk to W 1702; res. Hartford 1715, Harwinton 1730; m 28 Jan 1703/4 *WV*—Lydia da. Nehemiah & Hannah (Morgan) Royce, b 28 May 1680 *WV;* they had Susanna, b 30 Nov 1704 *WV*, Nehemiah, & others.

MEW. ELLIS, d 1681; nephew of Benjamin Ling; his sister Hannah m

John Cooper of Southampton, L. I.; m Ann da. William Gibbons, who d Feb 1703/4.

1 ANN, d 1681.

MILES. FAM. 1. RICHARD, from Wormley, Co. Herts, Eng., d 7 Jan 1666 *NHV;* Dea.; m (1) ——— ; m (2) Katharine, wid. Constable, who d 27 Jan 1687 [1687/8] æ. 95 *WV*.

(By 1): 1 MARTHA, b c. 1633, d before 1662; m 20 Oct 1650 *NHV*—George Pardee.

2 MARY, b c. 1635, d 12 Sep 1730 æ. 100; m (1) 12 Dec 1654 *NHV* Jonathan Ince; m (2) 22 Oct 1661 *NorwalkV*—Rev. Thomas Hanford of Norwalk.

3 RICHARD, b c. 1637; res. Boston, Mass.; m Experience Callicot.

i Elizabeth, b 22 Dec 1664 *Boston, Mass.,V*.

ii Richard, b 18 Oct 1667 *Boston, Mass.,V*.

4 SAMUEL, bp 22 Apr 1640 *MCI*, d 24 Dec 1678 *NHV;* m (1) [perhaps he was the Samuel who m 16 Oct 1659 *BostonV*—Elizabeth Dows; divorced?]; m (2) Hannah da. Benjamin & Elizabeth Wilmot, bp 21 May 1648 *NHCI;* she m (2) 20Sep 1681 *NHV*—Miles Merwin.

(By 1): *i* [Samuel, b 27 Apr 1662 *BostonV*].

ii John, b 29 Jan 1663 *NHV* [1663/4].

(By 2) *iii* Samuel, b 1668 *NHV*, d [1668].

iv Abigail, b 3 Jan 1669 *NHV* [1669/70]; m Samuel Hine of Milford.

v Samuel, b 15 July 1672 *NHV*, d 1730; res. M; m Sarah da. Jobamah & Sarah (Lane) Gunn, b 30 Mar 1674 *MV*, bp 5 Apr 1674 *MCI*. **FAM. 2.**

vi Stephen, b 5 Dec 1674 *NHV*, d 27 Mar 1713 *DV;* res M & D; m (1) 1697 *MV*—Mary da. Israel & Mary (Welch) Holbrook, b 7 Apr 1679 *MV;* m (2) Patience da. Joseph & Patience (Holbrook) Wheeler, b 7 June 1679 *MV;* she m (2) 27 Aug 1717 *NMV*—Benjamin Bunnell. **FAM. 3.**

vii Theophilus, b 17 Mar 1676/7 *NHV*, d 1701; res. D; m Bethia [?da. John Pettit]; she m (2) 24 Oct 1705 *MV* Josiah Tibbals. **FAM. 4.**

PAGE 1248

5 ANNA, bp 7 Oct 1642 *NHCI*, d 19 July 1730 *WV;* m 3 Nov 1664 *NHV*—Samuel Street.

6 JOHN, bp Oct 1644 *NHCI*, d 7 Nov 1704 *NHV;* Capt.; m (1) 11 Apr 1665 *NHV*—Elizabeth da. John & Elizabeth Harriman, bp 22 July 1648 *NHCI*, d 3 Dec 1675 *NHV;* m (2) 2 Nov 1680 *NHV*—Mary da. Joseph & Elizabeth (Preston) Alsop, b 3 Oct 1654 *NHV*, bp 26 Apr 1657 *NHCI*, d 16 Oct 1705 *NHV*.

(By 1): *i* Elizabeth, b 21 Dec 1666 *NHV;* m 21 Jan 1686 *NHV*—Nathan Andrews.

ii John, b 9 Jan 1667 *NHV* [1667/8], d 10 Feb 1709/10 æ. 42 *NHTI;* Capt.; res. EH, New London, W & NH; m (1) [?Hannah da. William & Mary (Desborough)

Prindle]; m (2) Abigail da. John & Dorothy Thompson, wid. Joseph Alsop, b 26 Jan 1651 *NHV*, d Apr 1727. **FAM. 5.**

iii Mary, b 10 Mar 1669/70 *NHV;* m ——— Keeney.

iv Richard, b 21 Mar 1671/2 *NHV*, d 5 July 1756 æ. 86 *NHT1;* Lieut.; m (1) Hannah da. Joseph Easton of Hartford, b c. 1673, d 28 Sep 1714 æ. 41 *NHT1;* m (2) 10 Apr 1716 *StratfieldC*—Elizabeth Sherwood, wid. Charles Chauncey; m (3) 22 Nov 1721 *NHV*—Abigail da. John & Elizabeth (Booth) Minor, wid. John Treadwell, b 6 Feb 1680/1. **FAM. 6.**

v Samuel, b 6 Apr 1674 *NHV*, bp 21 June 1674 *MC1*, d s. p.

(By 2): *vi* Hannah, b 20 Aug 1681 *NHV*, bp 1694 *NHC1*, d 18 Aug 1741 æ. 60 *NHT1;* m Richard Hall,

vii Daniel, b 20 Sep 1683 *NHV*, bp 1694 *NHC1*, d 25 Dec 1711 æ. 27 *NHT1;* m Sarah da. Samuel & Martha (Fenn) Newton, bp 26 Sep 1686 *MC1*, d 22 Apr 1748 æ. 62 *MT;* she m (2) 12 Mar 1712 Jonathan Ingersoll. **FAM. 7.**

viii Joseph, b 25 Oct 1690 *NHV*, bp 1694 *NHC1*, d 1750; m 20 Mar 1717/8 *NHV*—Elizabeth da. Thomas & Mary (Winston) Trowbridge, b 29 Mar 1693 *NHV*, d 23 Jan 1783 æ. almost 90 *NHC1;* she m (2) 21 Aug 1758 *NHC1* —Stephen Howell. **FAM. 8.**

FAM. 2. SAMUEL & SARAH (GUNN) MILES:

1 SAMUEL, bp 18 June 1699 *MC1*, d young.

2 SARAH, bp 28 Jan 1699/1700 *MC1*, d s. p. before 1728; m 29 July 1728 *MV* [*sic*, error for 1724?]—Jonathan Arnold of WH.

3 THEOPHILUS, b 1 Dec 1703 *MV*, d 1767; Lieut.; m Katharine ———, probably niece of Louis Liron of M.

PAGE 1267

i Samuel, d 1775; res. M; m ———. Children: (1) Phebe, b c. 1755, d 27 Sep 1833 æ. 78 *WHT2;* m Jonas Merwin. (2) Theophilus, d 1833; Census (M) 1-1-3; m (1) Sarah Prince da. Benjamin & Mary (Peck) Fenn, b c. 1763, d 15 May 1790 æ. 27 *MT;* m (2) 15 Sep 1791 *MC1*—Martha da. Thomas & Sybil (Smith) Clark. (3) Sarah. (4) Eliphal. (5) Mary Ann.

ii Sarah, b c. 1729, d 13 Sep 1750 æ. 21 *MT.*

iii Katharine, b c. 1732, d 19 July 1784 æ. 52 *MV;* m 23 Apr 1752 Nathaniel Smith.

iv Eliphal, d 1805 *MV;* m Isaac Smith.

v Ann; m Jehiel Baldwin.

vi Theophilus, b c. 1741, d 3 Sep 1750 æ. 9 *MT.*

vii Susanna, b c. 1743, d 2 Sep 1798 æ. 55 *MT;* m 14 July 1761 *MC2*—Nathan Fowler.

FAM. 3. STEPHEN & MARY (HOLBROOK) MILES:

1 MARY, b 24 Aug 1697 *DV;* m 15 June 1725 *Durham*—David Fowler.

2 Stephen, b 20 Jan 1701 *MV*, 20 Feb *DV*, d c. 1738; res. M; m (1) Susanna Baldwin, wid. John Burwell, bp 15 Nov 1696 *MCl*, d 16 June 1733 *MV;* m (2) 5 May 1734 *MV*—Frances Bryan, wid. Jeremiah Gillet, bp 24 Sep 1704 *MCl*, d c. 1771.

(By 1): *i* Stephen, bp 2 Oct 1726 *MCl;* Census (Cornwall) 1-0-1; m 6 Dec 1751 *MV*—Rebecca da. John & Rebecca (Clark) Humphreville, b 1 Mar 1727/8 *NHV*. Children: (1) Rebecca, b 21 Oct 1751 *MV* [?1753]. (2) Abigail, b 5 May 1755 *WatV*. (3) John, b 1 Mar 1757 *WatV*. (4) Timon, b 22 Apr 1759 *WatV*, d 21 May 1833 *WatV;* Census (Wat) 1-0-1; m 5 Apr 1785 *WatV*—Mercy Judd. (5) Sarah, b 22 Apr 1761 *WatV*. (6) Isaac, b 11 July 1763 *WatV*.

ii Isaac, b 8 May 1728 *MV*, bp 16 June 1728 *MCl*, d 15 Nov 1780 æ. 55 *MT;* m Katharine da. Phinehas & Rebecca (Baldwin) Baldwin, b 5 Nov 1731 *MV;* she m (2) John Harpin. Children: (1) Susanna, b c. 1752, d 16 Jan 1788 æ. 36 *MT*. (2) Mary; m Silvanus Dickinson. (3) Katharine; m Samuel Wales.

iii Susanna, b 7 June 1730 *MV*, d s. p.

iv David, b 25 Dec 1731 *MV*, bp 12 Mar 1732 *MCl*, d 1772; res. Wy; m (1) Hannah da. Nathaniel & Sarah (Wheeler) Gunn, b 2 Aug 1743 *WatV;* m (2) Concurrence da. Ezekiel & Tabitha (Hickox) Tuttle, bp 15 Mar 1747; she m (2) Daniel Tuttle. Child by 1st w.: (1) Hannah; m 13 June 1782 *WatV*—Joseph Beach. Children: by 2nd w.: (2) Sarah, b c. 1769, d 14 Jan 1850 æ. 80 *WyV*. (3) Concurrence, b c. 1771, d 19 Apr 1848 æ. 77 *MyT;* m Samuel Fenn. (4) Catherine, b c. 1771, d 30 Mar 1849 æ. 78 *WyV*.

(By 2): *v* Mary, b 17 Feb 1734/5 *MV;* m John Newton.

3 Joseph, b 24 Jan 1703 *DV*, d 1762; res. NM, Norwalk & Ridgefield; m 25 Apr 1732 Deborah Ferris, wid. John Welch.

i Mary, b 14 Oct 1733 *NMV*, bp 21 Oct 1733 *NMC;* m Emerson Cogswell.

ii Mercy, b 5 Jan 1736 *NMV*, bp 11 Jan 1735/6 *NMC*.

iii Joseph, b 4 July 1737 *NMV*, bp 10 July 1737 *NMC;* d s. p.

iv Eunice, b 3 Aug 1739 *NMV*, bp 2 Sep 1739 *NMC*, d 1770; m c. 1759 Eli Taylor.

v Sarah, b 23 July 1742 *NMV*.

vi Patience, b 6 May 1745 *NMV*.

4 Patience, b 20 Sep 1704 *DV;* m 29 June 1721 *NMV*—Ebenezer Washburn.

5 Eunice, b 11 Apr 1707 *DV;* m 29 Sep 1730 *NMV*—Moses Buck.

FAM. 3. Stephen & Patience (Wheeler) Miles:

6 Justus, b 27 July 1711 *DV*, d 2 Apr 1795 æ. 83 *NMT;* Census (NM) 4-0-1; m Hannah da. Nathan & Mercy (Comstock) Olmsted, b 1713 (Norwalk), d 11 Dec 1796 æ. 83 *NMT*.

i Justus, b 3 Aug 1740 *NMV*, d s. p. 19 Aug 1760 *F&IW Rolls.*

ii Samuel, b 21 Oct 1743 *NMV;* loyalist; rem. to St. John's, New Brunswick; m (1) Molly Pickett, who d 17 June 1774 æ. 31 *NMT;* m (2) ——— .

iii Stephen, b 19 Feb 1746/7 *NMV*, d 31 Jan 1825; Census (NM) 3-3-4; m (1) Mary da. Abner & Mary Gunn, who d 18 May 1782 æ. 35 *NMT;* m (2) Phebe ———, who d 4 Feb 1827 æ. 64 *NMT.* Children: John: Anna (m Ingersoll): Sarah (m Riggs): Mary (m Hungerford): Hannah, b c. 1779, d 12 Sep 1805; m Josiah Hungerford: Betsey (m Cushman): Stephen: Justus, b c. 1791, d 17 Apr 1842; Capt.; m Maria E. Blackney, who d 14 Dec 1826 æ. 27.

iv Elijah, b 16 Jan 1753 *NMV;* m Harriet da. Abel & Martha (Trion) Gunn.

v Hannah, b 13 Dec 1758 *NMV;* m ——— Averill.

FAM. 4. THEOPHILUS & BETHIA (———) MILES:

1 JONATHAN, b c. 1700, d 21 Feb 1784 æ. 84 *DT2;* m 4 Apr 1723 *DV*—Zerviah da. Thomas & Phebe (Tomlinson) Wooster, b c. 1699, d 15 Nov 1753 æ. [—] *DT2.*

i Bethia, b 1 Feb 1723/4 *DV*, d soon.

ii Theophilus, b 12 Feb 1729/30 *DV*, d soon.

iii Phebe, b 3 Sep 1732; m Abraham Bassett.

iv Hannah, bp 27 Jan 1735 *Stx*, d young.

v Theophilus, bp 1740 *Stx*, d 11 Dec 1822 æ. 83 *SeymourT (Ep.);* Census (D) 1-2-7; m (1) Mary Meeker of Bethlehem, who d 19 Oct 1795 æ. 44; m (2) 29 Sep 1802 *EHC*—Lucinda da. Nicholas & Desire (Thompson) Street, wid. Darius Hickox & Titus Alling, b 17 July 1763 *EHV*, d 7 Oct 1843 æ. 80 *EHT.* **FAM. 9.**

vi Bethia, bp 15 Aug 1742 *Dx*, d 20 Apr 1824 æ. 82 *EHT;* m 6 Sep 1761 Samuel Tuttle.

vii Zerviah, d s. p. 23 Sep 1826 æ. 89 *NoHD;* m 30 May 1764 *NHV*—Stephen Mix.

viii Jonathan, b 1745, d 25 Feb 1830 æ. 85 *SeymourT (Ep.);* Census (D) 2-0-6; m 17 Feb 1768 *DV*—Lucy Smith of Glastonbury, whe d 4 Oct 1822 æ. 77 *SeymourT (Ep.).* Children: (1) Manoah Smith, b 22 Mar 1769 *DV*, bp (as "Benoni") 26 Mar 1769 *Dx;* Rev.; m 8 Oct 1796 *NHx*—Abigail da. Ralph & Mary (Perit) Isaacs, bp 25 Dec 1774 *NHx.* (2) Sarah, b 6 Nov 1771 *DV*, bp 8 Nov 1771 *Dx;* m Luther French. (3) Betsey, b 17 Feb 1774 *DV;* m ——— Platt. (4) Child, bp 4 Aug 1776 *Dx*, probably identical with one of the following. (5) Lucy, b c. 1778, d 7 Oct 1849 æ. 72 *SeymourT (Union).* (6) Daughter; m ——— Botsford. (7) Nancy, b c. 1788, d 16 Sep 1862 æ. 74 *SeymourT (Union).*

FAM. 5. JOHN & [HANNAH (PRINDLE)] MILES:

1 THOMAS, b c. 1688, d 5 Oct 1741 *WV;* Maj.; m 7 Sep 1709 *WV*—Abigail da. John & Elizabeth (Wilmot) Mix, b 17 Apr 1687 *NHV*, d 19 Aug 1770 *WV*.

i John, b 14 Jan 1711 *WV*, d young.

ii James, b 18 Dec 1713 *WV*, d 17 Jan 1766 æ. 52-7-29 *WV;* Capt.; m 10 Jan 1733 *WV*—Phebe da. John & Sarah (Culver) Thompson, b 21 Sep 1712 *WV*, d 23 Oct 1756 *WV*. **FAM. 10.**

iii Elizabeth, b 18 Sep 1718 *WV*, d 17 Apr 1755 *WV;* m 17 Sep 1741 *WV*—Daniel Clark.

iv Mary, b 19 June 1721 *WV;* m 14 Mar 1739 *WV*—Josiah Stanley.

v Martha, b 5 Nov 1723 *WV;* m Charles Sperry.

vi Eunice, b 6 Dec 1725 *WV*, d 14 Nov 1809 æ. 84 *WatT2;* m 12 Feb 1745/6 *WV*—Stephen Culver.

vii Abigail, b 2 Apr 1727 *WV*, d 20 Nov 1747 æ. 22 *CT1*, 22 Nov *WV;* m 8 Jan 1746/7 *WV*—Timothy Hall.

2 JOHN, b c. 1690, d 18 Nov 1760 *WV;* m 2 Aug 1710 *NHV*—Sarah da. John & Sarah (Glover) Ball, b 26 Sep 1687 *NHV*, d 25 Nov 1760 *WV*.

i Susanna, b c. 1712, d 25 Jan 1760 *WV*, 1759 æ. 48 *CT1;* m 22 Nov 1732 *WV*—Isaac Tyler.

ii Samuel, b 18 Dec 1714 *WV*, d 19 Apr 1761 *WV;* m 29 Nov 1736 *WV*—Phebe da. Daniel & Ruth (How) Tuttle, b 8 Jan 1719 *WV*, d 3 Mar 1790; she m (2) 6 Jan 1774 *WV*—Isaac Johnson. **FAM. 11.**

iii Sarah, b 9 May 1717 *WV*, d 7 May 1773 *WV;* m 26 Jan 1732 *WV*—Israel Johnson.

iv Daniel, b c. 1719, d 12 Dec 1756 *WV;* m Ann da. Owen & Mary Daly, b 25 Jan 1726 *WV*. **FAM. 12.**

v Hannah, b c. 1721, d 1775 *Goshen;* m 9 June 1741 *WV*—Adna Beach.

vi John, b 4 Oct 1723, *WV*, d Oct 1796 æ. 73 *WC2;* Census (W) 1-0-1; m (1) 14 Nov 1743 *WV*—Martha da. Joseph & Martha (Collins) Curtis, b 29 Jan 1725 *WV;* m (2) 5 Dec 1776 *WV*—Eunice da. John & Hannah (Royce) Ives, wid. Josiah Robinson, b 13 May 1727 *WV*, d 26 July 1787 æ. 61 *WT2*, æ. 60 *WC2*. **FAM. 13.**

vii Esther, b 28 Aug 1726 *WV;* m 17 Aug 1743 *WV*—Dan Hitchcock.

viii Mehitabel, d 2 May 1741 *WV*.

3 JOSEPH, b c. 1692; rem. to Newtown; m 19 Nov 1718 *Newtown V*—Jane Bowden.

4 SON, living 1710.

FAM. 6. RICHARD & HANNAH (EASTON) MILES:

1 ELIZABETH, b 10 Sep 1695 *NHV*, d 1 Mar 1771 æ. 75 *NHC1;* m Josiah Thompson.

2 HANNAH, b 27 Oct 1697 *NHV;* m 6 Aug 1717 *NHV*—Isaac Gorham.

3 SAMUEL, b 4 Aug 1701 *NHV*, bp 17 May 1702 *HartfordC2*, d Apr [1761] *NHT1;* m Sarah da. John & Sarah (Rosewell) Woodward, b c. 1704, d 16 Aug 1769 æ. 65 *NHT1*.

i Sarah, b 6 Aug 1731 *NHV*, bp 1 Mar 1751/2 *NHC1*, d 14 Oct 1768 æ. 37 *NHT1;* m 25 June 1752 *NHV*—Daniel Lyman.

ii Hannah, b 7 Mar 1732/3 *NHV*, bp 1 Mar 1751/2 *NHC1*, d 3 Dec 1786 æ. 54 *NHT1*, *NHC1;* m (1) 26 July 1753 *NHV*—Enos Alling; m (2) 9 Jan 1780 *NHC1*—Jared Ingersoll; m (3) Apr 1786 Joseph Bradley.

iii Roswell, b c. 1735, bp 1 Mar 1751/2 *NHC1*, d 16 Dec 1753 æ. 19 *NHT1*.

iv Samuel, b c. 1738, bp 1 Mar 1751/2 *NHC1*, d s. p. 1764.

v Mary, b c. 1741, bp 1 Mar 1751/2 *NHC1*, d 21 Dec 1831 æ. 91 *NHT1;* m (1) 21 June 1759 *NHC1*—James Rice; m (2) 14 Sep 1798 James Dana.

4 TIMOTHY, b 24 Dec 1703 *NHV*, d after 1761; rem. to Providence, R. I.; m (1) 13 Mar 1721/2 *NHV*—Mabel da. Samuel & Elizabeth (Smith) Cooper, b 13 Nov 1700 *NHV*, d 1777; apparently they were div., since she m (2) before 1736 Timothy Baldwin. He probably m (2) ——— .

(By 1): *i* Hannah, b 10 May 1722 *NHV*, bp 2 May 1724 *NHC1*, d 12 Nov 1801 æ. 81 *NHC1;* m 15 Jan 1748/9 *NHV*—Thomas Mix.

5 MARY, b 19 Mar 1707 *NHV*, d 18 Aug 1783 æ. 77 *NHT1;* m (1) 1 Sep 1729 *NHV*—Stephen Whitehead; m (2) Jehiel Thomas; m (3) David Gilbert.

6 JAMES, b 20 Apr 1709 *NHV*, d 1 Feb 1715 æ. 6 *NHT1*.

7 JOSEPH, b 24 Apr 1712 *NHV*, d 9 Dec 1768 æ. 56 *NHC1;* m 17 Jan 1737/8 *NHV*—Elsie da. Stephen & Lydia (Bassett) Munson, b 12 July 1716 *NHV*, d 2 Mar 1792 æ. 75 *NHC1*.

i Lucy, b 26 Feb 1738/9 *NHV*, bp 14 Mar 1738/9 *NHC1*, "Wid. Peck" d 19 Feb 1795 æ. 57 *NHC1;* m 26 Jan 1764 *NHV*, *NHC1*—Stephen Peck.

ii Abigail, b 24 Oct 1741 *NHV*, bp 25 Oct 1741 *NHC1*, d 3 May 1787 æ. 46 *NHC1;* m Christopher Hughes.

iii James, b 31 Jan 1745/6 *NHV*, bp 2 Feb 1745/6 *NHC1*, d 25 Oct 1781 æ. 36 *NHC1;* m 19 Jan 1768 *NHC1*—Elizabeth da. Jeremiah & Elizabeth (Sperry) Osborn, b 29 Apr 1750 *NHV*, d 14 Feb 1820; she m (2) 15 Nov 1789 *NHC1*—Stephen Hotchkiss; m (3) Thomas Rogers of Northford. **FAM. 14.**

iv Richard, b 25 Nov 1748 *NHV*, bp 27 Nov 1748 *NHC1*, d 6 May 1794 æ. 46 *WtnD;* Census (Wtn) 1-3-4; m (1) Margaret ——— , who d 24 Oct 1793 æ. 46 *WtnD;* m (2) Prudence ——— . Children by 1st w.: (1) Joseph.

(2) James. (3) Eri. (4) Leve; m ——— Eggleston. (5) Charlotte. (6) Aurelia. Child by 2nd w.: (7) Richard, b 26 Nov 1794.

v Joseph, b 28 June 1751 *NHV*, bp 30 June 1751 *NHCl*, d s. p.

vi Hannah, b 2 Sep 1752 *NHV*, bp 30 Aug (?) 1752 *NHCl*; m 19 Jan 1774 *NHCl*—Jedediah Cook.

vii Mary, b 1 June 1757 *NHV*, bp 26 June 1757 *NHCl*.

FAM. 6. RICHARD & ABIGAIL (MINOR) MILES:

8 KATHARINE, b 22 Mar 1722/3 *NHV*, bp 24 Mar 1723 *NHCl*, d 29 Apr 1723 *NHV*, *NHTl*.

FAM. 7. DANIEL & SARAH (NEWTON) MILES:

1 JOHN, b 2 May 1708 *NHV*, d 1755; m 3 Nov 1737 *MV*—Martha da. Joseph & Martha (Bryan) Smith, bp 13 Apr 1718 *MCl*, d 26 Apr 1797 æ. 85 *MT*.

PAGE 1248

i John, b 3 Aug 1738 *MV*, d 1815; Census (M) 4-0-5.

ii Martha, b 26 Apr 1740 *MV*, d 1797; m 1767 Charles Pond.

iii Daniel, b [6 July 1742], bp 11 July 1742 *MC*, d 16 June 1746 æ. 3-11-10 *MT*.

iv David, b 20 May 1745 *MV*, d 10 Jan 1800 æ. 55 *MV*; Census (M) 1-2-3; m (1) Siana Moore, who d 22 Apr 1791 *MV*; m (2) Ann ———.

v Daniel, b 11 Oct 1747 *MV*, d 1808 *MV*; Capt.; Census (M) 2-2-3; m Mary Mallett, who d 1 Nov 1799 *MV*.

vi Jared, b 3 Sep 1750 *MV*, d 1780.

2 DANIEL, b 12 July 1709 *NHV*, d 1 Feb 1785 *MV*; m Elizabeth ———.

PAGE 1248

i Sarah, b 15 July 1751 *MV*.

ii Tyley, b 27 Apr 1755 *MV*, d 1829; Census (M) 1-1-1.

FAM. 8. JOSEPH & ELIZABETH (TROWBRIDGE) MILES:

1 MARY, b 18 Dec 1719 *NHV*, bp Sep 1720 *NHCl*, d 9 Sep 1795 æ. 78 *NHTl*; m Thomas Punderson.

2 ELIZABETH, b 26 Oct 1720 *NHV*; m 7 Sep 1743 *NHV*—Daniel Perkins.

3 SARAH, b 6 Oct 1722 *NHV*, bp Oct 1722 *NHCl*; m 21 Sep 1747 *NHV*—Joshua Chandler.

4 JOSEPH, b 27 Mar 1725 *NHV*, bp 28 Mar 1725 *NHCl*, d 19 Jan 1795 æ. 70 *NHCl*; Census (NH) 1-0-1; m 24 Jan 1748/9 *NHV*—Ann da. Samuel & Abigail (Atwater) Bishop, b 6 Mar 1730/1 *NHV*, d 12 Nov 1789 æ. 59 *NHCl*.

i Sarah, b 19 Nov 1749 *NHV*, bp 15 Apr 1750 *NHCl*, d soon.

ii Joseph, b 19 Oct 1752 *NHV*, bp 22 Oct 1752 *NHCl*, d 3 Dec 1778 *NHCl*; m 1 June 1778 *NHCl*—Mary da. John & Hannah Wise, bp Feb 1758 *NHCl*. Child: (1) Sarah.

iii Sarah, b 22 Nov 1754 *NHV*, bp 24 Nov 1754 *NHCl*, d 24 Dec 1831 æ. 76 *NHTl*; m 11 Apr 1775 *NHV*, *NHCl*—Samuel Huggins.

iv Anna, b 8 Mar 1757 *NHV*, d 20 Oct 1851 æ. 94-7 *NHV;* m Joshua Sears.

v Isaac, b 21 Nov 1759 *NHV*, bp Nov 1759 *NHCl*, d soon.

vi Molly, b 6 May 1762 *NHV*, bp 9 May 1762 *NHCl;* "Mary" m Feb 1806 *ConnH*—Stephen Miles.

vii Isaac, bp 20 Sep 1767 *NHCl*, d 30 Aug 1768 æ. 1 *NHCl*.

5 JOHN, b 21 May 1727 *NHV*, bp 4 June 1727 *NHCl*, d 6 Mar 1803 æ. 76 *NHTl;* Census (NH) 3-0-4; m 1 Jan 1752 *NHV*—Henrietta da. Richardson & Elizabeth (Munson) Minor, b 5 July 1728 *TrumbullC*, d 15 Mar 1794 æ. 63 *NHTl*, 17 Mar æ. 66 *NHx*.

i John, b 1 Sep 1752 *NHV*, d 2 Apr 1830 æ. 78 (*NHx*) *NHV;* Capt.; Census (NH) 1-3-2; m (1) 30 Aug 1778 *NHCl*—Mary da. Thomas & Mary (Thomas) Bills, b 18 Jan 1756 *NHV*, d 28 Apr 1795 æ. 39 *NHTl*, æ. 40 *NHCl;* m (2) 6 Feb 1796 *NHCl*—her sister Sarah Bills, b c. 1773, d 10 Sep 1807 æ. 34 *NHTl*, *NHCl;* m (3) her sister Elizabeth Bills, b 1 July 1754 *NHV*. **FAM. 15.**

ii William, b 22 Dec 1753 *NHV*, d 1796; Capt.; Census (NH) 1-2-5; m 12 Apr 1778 *NHCl*—Mary da. Amos & Dorcas (Foote) Hitchcock, b 6 Mar 1758 *NHV*, bp 4 Nov 1789 (æ. 31) *NHx*, d 12 Apr 1798 æ. 41 *NHx*. **FAM. 16.**

iii Elizabeth, b 1 June 1755 *NHV*; d 30 Nov 1756 *NHV*.

iv Minor, b 10 Jan 1757 *NHV*, d s. p. 6 May 1795 æ. 37 *NHx*.

v Elnathan, b 22 Dec 1758 *NHV*, d 1790.

vi Stephen, b 2 Nov 1761 *NHV* d 30 May 1762 *NHV*.

vii Stephen, b 23 Oct 1763 *NHV*, d 23 Feb 1810 æ. 47 *NHx;* Census (NH) 1-0-1; m (1) Lucy da. Buckminster & Abigail (Waterhouse) Brintnall, b c. 1768, d Oct 1805 *ConnH;* m (2) Feb 1806 *ConnH*—Mary da. Joseph & Ann (Bishop) Miles, b 6 May 1762 *NHV*. **FAM. 17.**

6 HANNAH, b 15 Nov 1731 *NHV*, bp 20 Nov 1731 *NHCl*, d 25 Oct 1738 æ. 7 *NHTl*.

FAM. 9. THEOPHILUS & MARY (MEEKER) MILES:

1 DAVID, b 6 Aug 1771 *F*, bp 15 Sep 1771 *Dx*, d 5 Nov 1773 *F*.

2 HANNAH, b 24 Feb 1773 *F*, bp 28 Feb 1773 *Dx*, d before 1806; m Ebenezer Hurd.

3 MARY, b 25 July 1775 *F*, bp 12 Feb 1783 *Dx;* m Isaac Botsford.

4 DAVID, b 30 Apr 1777 *F*, bp 22 June 1777 *Dx*, d 13 Dec 1777 *F*.

5 THEOPHILUS, b 27 Nov 1778 *F*, d 15 Mar 1849 æ. 70 *SeymourT* (*Union*); m Freelove da. Josiah & Freelove (Lynus) Nettleton, b 6 May 1779 *DV*.

6 CHARLOTTE, b 29 Aug 1780 *F*, bp 17 Oct 1780 *Dx;* m Josiah Nettleton.

7 CHARITY, b 29 Dec 1782 *F*, bp 12 Feb 1783 *Dx;* m Nathan Vose.

8 LUCRETIA, b 27 July 1784 *F*, bp Oct 1784 *Dx;* m 12 Oct 1804 Isaac Beach of Wd.

9 SHELDON, b 13 Feb 1786 *F*, bp 16 May 1786 *Dx*, d 2 Oct 1795 *F*.

FAM. 9. THEOPHILUS & LUCINDA (STREET) MILES:

10 HANNAH MARIA, b 19 Apr 1805 *F*, d 22 Aug 1822 *F*.

FAM. 10. JAMES & PHEBE (THOMPSON) MILES:

1 THOMAS, b 14 Oct 1733 *WV*.

2 ANN, b 24 Mar 1735 *WV*; m [Samuel Culver].

3 JOSEPH, b 9 Mar 1737 *WV*.

4 JOHN, b 24 Nov 1739 *WV*, d 14 Nov 1817 æ. 78 *NHT1*; Census (NH) 2-1-1; m 24 Mar 1768 *NHV*—Mehitabel da. Enos & Tamar (Wooster) Brooks, bp July 1740 *CC*, d 3 Nov 1816 æ. 77 *NHT1*.

i Philomela, b 2 Mar 1769 *NHV*, *NHT1*, bp 12 Mar 1769 *NHC2*, d 14 Oct 1844 *NHT1*; m 10 Nov 1792 *NHx*—Samuel Hughes.

ii Marcus, b 21 May 1771 *NHV*, bp 9 June 1771 *NHC2*, d 22 Feb 1817 æ. 47 *NHT1*; m 9 Nov 1800 *ConnJournal*—Betty da. Benjamin & Naomi (Davis) Davis, bp 20 Aug 1780 *Dx*, d 9 May 1827 æ. 47 *DT2*. Children: (1) Philomela, bp 18 Mar 1804 *NHx*. (2) Enos Brooks, b c. 1807, d 6 Apr 1846 æ. 39 *NHT1*; m Jane ——, who d 5 Nov 1849 æ. 38 *NHT1*. (3) Henry B., b 25 Oct 1809 *NHT1*, d 20 Aug 1841 æ. 31-9-25 *NHT1*. (4) John D. (5) Lucy.

iii Enos Brooks, b 20 July 1773 *NHV*, bp 1 Aug 1773 *NHC2*, d 8 Mar 1795 æ. 22 *NHT1*.

5 KATHARINE, b 23 Nov 1741 *WV*.

6 JAMES, b 19 Feb 1743/4 *WV*.

7 ABIGAIL, b 9 Mar 1746/7 *WV*, d Feb 1814 æ. 67 *NHT1*; m 21 Mar 1782 *NHx*—Thomas Green.

8 SARAH, b 20 May 1749 *WV*, d 26 Dec 1809 æ. 61 *NHT1*; m 8 Oct 1772 *NHC1*—William McCracken.

9 GEORGE, b 22 Apr 1752 *WV*, d 13 Feb 1838 æ. 86 *WT1*; res. NH 1814; m 9 Aug 1784 *Boston, Mass., V*, 10 Nov 1784 (at Boston) *NHSupCt*—Mary Walker; he div. her 1814.

i George; res. Hingham, Mass.; m 13 June 1809 *Boston, Mass., V*—Sarah Brown Blagge. Children: (1) Mary. (2) Sarah H. B. (3) Susan W. (4) Margaret B.

ii Henry; res. Florence, Italy.

iii William; res. St. Louis, Mo.

iv James; res. Cincinnati, Ohio.

FAM. 11. SAMUEL & PHEBE (TUTTLE) MILES:

1 AMOS, b 6 Sep 1737 *WV*.

2 RUTH, b 24 May 1739 *WV*; m 21 Apr 1762 *WV*—Stephen Hall.

3 MABEL, b 1 Oct 1741 *WV*, d 29 Dec 1775 æ. 34 *NHT1*; m 14 Sep 1762 *WV*—John McCleave.

4 MARTHA, b 28 June 1743 *WV*; m Ebenezer Peck.

5 DANIEL, b 15 Mar 1747/8 *WV*; Census (W) 1-2-4; m 6 Dec 1770 *WV*—Olive da. James & Hannah (Cook) Hall, b 20 May 1745 *WV*.

i Obedience, b 28 July 1771 *WV*.

ii Betsey, b 3 Mar 1774 *WV*.
iii Wyllys, b 25 Nov 1775 *WV*.
iv George, b 16 May 1778 *WV*.
v Sarah, b 23 Mar 1780 *WV*.

6 JOEL, b 18 Nov 1749 *WV*, d c. 1752.

7 ISAAC, b 25 Aug 1752 *WV;* Census (L) 1-3-4; res. Goshen, & Homer, N. Y.; m Mary Beach.
i Sylvester.
ii Mabel.
iii Manley.
iv Isaac.
v Edmund.
vi Polly.
vii Erastus.

8 SAMUEL, b 12 Aug 1757 *WV*, d 16 May 1848; Census (L) 2-2-3; res. Goshen; m 18 Mar 1781 *WV*—Sylvia Merwin.
i Polly, b 26 Dec 1781; m Jesse Ives of Homer, N. Y.
ii Samuel, b 1784; m ——— .
iii Nancy, b 1786; m Zachariah Spencer of Cornwall.
iv Augustus, b 1788, d 1864; m 1811 Roxa Norton.
v William, b 1790, d 1849; m 1821 Harriet Collins.
vi Harriet, b 1793; m Daniel Glover of Homer, N. Y.
vii George, b 1796, d 1875; m 1825 Charlotte Baldwin.

9 CALEB, b 8 Apr 1760 *WV*.

FAM. 12. DANIEL & ANN (DALY) MILES:

1 DANIEL; res. Goshen, & Amsterdam, N. Y.; m 1771 Ruth Baldwin.

2 SAMUEL, b 9 Oct 1746 *WV*.

3 CHARLES, b 9 Feb 1748/9 *WV;* m Ruth Thompson.
i Daniel.
ii Thompson.
iii Charles.
iv Susanna.

4 SUSANNA, b 6 Sep 1750 *WV*.

5 MOLLY, b 19 Oct 1753 *WV;* m 27 June 1771 *WatV*—Stephen Hopkins.

6 ANNA, b 4 Apr 1756 *WV*, d 27 Dec 1761 *WV*.

FAM. 13. JOHN & MARTHA (CURTIS) MILES:

1 JOHN, b 31 Aug 1745 *WV*, d 1818; Lt.; Census (C) 2-2-6; m 23 Jan 1766 *WC2*—Abigail da. Elisha & Dinah (Sperry) Perkins, b 13 June 1746 *NHV;* [?m (2) Ruth da. Stephen & Elizabeth (Yale) Atwater, b 6 June 1740 *WV*, d 6 Apr 1827 æ. 87 *WT2;* she m (2) Thomas Merriam].
(By 1): *i* Burrage, b 5 Nov 1766 *WV;* Census (C) 1-0-1.
ii Eunice, b 3 July 1768.
iii Simeon, b 13 Apr 1770.
iv Moses, b 18 Apr 1772; m 18 Dec 1794 *CC*—Hannah Hall.
v Martha, b 22 Apr 1774.
vi Abigail, b 16 Mar 1776.

vii John, b 13 Sep 1778, d 11 July 1853 æ. 74-9-30 *CT3;* m Laurinda P. White, who d 18 Aug 1871 æ. 89-3-26 *CT 3.*

viii Russell, b 17 June 1780, d 13 May 1863 æ. 83 *GV;* m (1) 9 June 1810 Rachel J. Bradley, b 4 May 1787, d 29 May 1828 æ. 41 *CT3;* m (2) Maria Payne, who d 24 Sep 1871 æ. 71 *CT3.*

2 SIMEON, b 30 Sep 1746 *WV*, d 28 Nov 1769 *CC;* he had a nat. child by Sybil da. Elisha & Eunice (Perkins) Perkins:

i Simeon, b 1 Mar 1764 *WV;* Census (H) 1-0-4; m Lois da. Moses & Elizabeth (Johnson) Hall.

3 SARAH, b 4 Apr 1749 *WV;* m 11 Feb 1773 *WV*—Moses Way.

4 EUNICE, b 26 July 1751 *FarmV;* m 5 Jan 1769 *WV*—Solomon Royce.

5 RUSSELL, b 16 Mar 1756 *FarmV.*

6 ESTHER, b 17 Sep 1757 *FarmV.*

7 SUSANNA, b 18 May 1760 *WV.*

8 HANNAH, b 24 Feb 1764 *WV.*

9 PHEBE, b 10 Apr 1766 *WV;* m 1788 *WC2*—Ozias Foster.

Children (unnamed) d Sep 1744 & June 1757 *CC.*

FAM. 14. JAMES & ELIZABETH (OSBORN) MILES:

1 (perhaps) JOHN; res. NH; m Mary da. Timothy & Martha (Thompson) Talmadge, wid. David Osborn, b 25 Jan 1753 *F*, d 6 Mar 1814 æ. 61 *NHT1.*

i James.

ii Maria, b c. 1797, d 1831; m (1) John McNeil; m (2) William Townsend.

2 ELIZABETH, b c. 1775, bp 1 Sep 1782 *NHC1;* [?m Stephen Rowe].

3 MARY, b c. 1777, bp 1 Sep 1782 *NHC1*, d 23 Mar 1830 æ. 53 *HT 3;* m 23 Jan 1800 *HV*—Jeremiah Peck.

4 SAMUEL, b c. 1779, bp 1 Sep 1782 *NHC1.*

5 HANNAH, b c. 1782 (posthumous), bp 1 Sep 1782 *NHC1.*

FAM. 15. JOHN & MARY (BILLS) MILES:

1 JOHN, b c. 1779, bp 3 June 1787 *NHC1*, d 20 Aug 1809 æ. 30 (at Charleston, S. C.) *NHT1*, probably s. p., but possibly he was the John who m Mary (Talmadge) Osborn (see FAM. 14, 1).

2 THOMAS, b c. 1781, bp 3 June 1787 *NHC1*, d 28 Feb 1830 æ. 49 (*NHx*) *NHV;* Capt.

3 GEORGE, b c. 1783, bp 3 June 1787 *NHC1;* m 15 July 1807 *NHx*—Polly da. Nathaniel & Polly Augusta (Bonticou) Storer, b 1 July 1789 *NHV.* Family incomplete.

i John William, bp 7 June 1812 *NHx.*

ii Thomas Henry.

FAM. 15. JOHN & SARAH (BILLS) MILES:

4 WILLIAM BILLS, bp 11 Dec 1796 *NHC1*, d s. p.

5 ELIZABETH MARY, bp 10 Aug 1800 *NHC1*, d 24 Apr 1816 æ. 17

NHT1.

6 HENRIETTA MINOR, bp 26 Sep 1802 *NHC1*, d 24 Sep 1832 æ. 30 *NHT1*; m 5 Jan 1823 *NHV*—Jacob Brown.

FAM. 16. WILLIAM & MARY (HITCHCOCK) MILES:

1 WILLIAM, b 12 July 1779 *NHV*, bp 4 Nov 1789 (æ. 10-9) *NHx*; disappeared "beyond seas".

2 MARY, b 1 Sep 1780 *NHV*, bp 4 Nov 1789 (æ. 9-2) *NHx*, d 3 Mar 1866 (at Racine, Wis.): m 1803 John T. Trowbridge.

3 PATTY, b 17 Dec 1781 *NHV*, bp 4 Nov 1789 (æ. 8) *NHx*.

4 HENRIETTA, b 6 Jan 1784 *NHV*, bp 4 Nov 1789 (æ. 5-3) *NHx*; m 1 Dec 1808 *NHx*—Charles Peterson.

5 HARRIET, b 13 Sep 1785 *NHV*, bp 4 Nov 1789 (æ. 4-10) *NHx*, d 23 July 1841 æ. 56 *NHT1*; m 7 Feb 1808 *NHx*—William Chapman.

6 ELNATHAN, b 15 July 1787 *NHV*, bp 4 Nov 1789 (æ. 2-4) *NHx*, d young.

7 SAMUEL, b 6 Apr 1789 *NHV*, bp 4 Nov 1789 (æ. 0-6) *NHx*, d 5 Nov 1789 *NHx*.

8 SAMUEL, bp 15 May 1791 (sponsor, grandfather John Miles) *NHx*, d 28 June 1848 æ. 57 *NHT1*; m Mary Ann Burr, b c 1800, d 24 Jan 1845 æ. 44 *NHT1*.

9 CHILD, bp 20 Jan 1793 *NHx*, d young.

FAM. 17. STEPHEN & LUCY (BRINTNALL) MILES (family incomplete):

1 ABIGAIL, bp 13 Mar 1791 *NHx*, d 22 Sep 1793 æ. 3 *NHx*.

2 NANCY, bp 7 July 1793 *NHx*, d 3 Dec 1808 æ. 16 *NHx*.

3 SAMUEL BRINTNALL, bp 28 Feb 1796 *NHx*, "son" bu. 15 Sep 1798 æ. 3 *NHx*.

4 HENRIETTA ELIZA, bp 24 June 1798 *NHx*.

5 GRACE.

6 LUCY, b c. 1804, bp 27 Nov 1808 (æ. 4) *NHx*.

MILES. MISCELLANEOUS. Child of Molly d 1 Sep 1795 æ. 0-6 *NHC1*.

MILLER. MISCELLANEOUS. JOHN m 7 July 1766 *NHV*—Eleanor, wid. William More. He is probably the John of New London who d 10 Feb 1770 æ. 47 *NHT1*, & perhaps (by a prior marriage) was father of the John & Caleb following......JOHN, d June 1802 æ. 48 *ConnJournal;* Capt.; Census (NH) 1-0-2; m 26 Nov 1777 *NHC1*—Lydia da. Stephen & Lydia (Burroughs) Trowbridge, b 23 Dec 1757 *NHV*. Children: (1) Lydia, bp 26 Aug 1778 *NHx*; m 4 Oct 1801 *NHx*—Henry Waggaman Edwards. (2) John, bp 27 Feb 1791 (æ. 1 wk.) *NHx*, d 28 Feb 1791 *NHx*.......CALEB, b c. 1758, d 7 Aug 1837 æ. 79 *NHV*; Census (NH) 1-0-1; m 3 Aug 1788 *NHC2*—Phebe da. Israel & Lydia (Bassett) Wooding, b 19 Aug 1758 *NHV*, bp (adult) 24 Dec 1794 *NHC1*, d Apr 1819. Children: (1) Nancy, bp 24 Dec 1794 *NHC1*; m Chauncey Bradley. (2) Joseph, bp 12 July 1798 *NHx*, d "soon" *NHx*. (3) Horace, bp 26 Sep 1802 *NHC1*, perhaps the "son" who d 10 Jan 1803 æ. 1 (?day or year) *NHC1*.

MINOR. RICHARDSON, s. of Elnathan, d 1744; Rev.; res. Trumbull; m 16 May 1728 *NHV*—Elizabeth da. Theophilus & Esther (Mix) Munson, b 26 Sep 1697 *NHV*, d 19 Aug 1751 *NHV*. Children, births recorded at Trumbull.

1 HENRIETTA, b 5 July 1728, bp 11 Aug 1728 *NHC1*, d 15 Mar 1794 æ. 63 *NHT1*, 17 Mar æ. 66 *NHx;* m 1 Jan 1752 *NHV*—John Miles.

2 PRUDENCE, b 18 Nov 1729; m 1752 Philip Benjamin of St.

3 ESTHER, b 4 Mar 1730/1.

4 ISABELLA, b 1 Jan 1732/3; m 13 Aug 1760 Brewster Dayton.

5 ELIZABETH, b 7 Mar 1733/4; m Jeremiah Curtis of St.

6 MARTHA, b 7 Mar 1734/5, d 12 Mar 1734/5.

7 RICHARDSON, b 5 Mar 1735/6; m 23 Jan 1764 Tabitha Curtis.

8 MARTHA, b 13 Feb 1736/7, d 27 Sep 1793 æ. 56 *NHx;* m 4 Oct 1757 *NHV*—Joshua Ray.

9 REBECCA, b 16 Oct 1738.

10 WILLIAM, b 24 Nov 1739.

MINOT. JAMES, s. of James & Martha (Lane), b c. 1724 (Concord, Mass.), d 2 Aug 1773 æ. 49 *NHT1;* Capt.; m (1) Rebecca Stow, b c. 1730 (at Merrimac, Mass.), d 9 Feb 1767 æ. 37 *NHT1;* m (2) Betty ——— .

(By 1): 1 JOSEPH.

2 RACHEL.

3 ELIZABETH.

4 JAMES.

5 MARTHA, bp 10 Apr 1768 *NHC2*.

6 SARAH, bp 10 Apr 1768 *NHC2*.

7 HANNAH, bp 10 Apr 1768 *NHC2*.

(By 2): 8 SHERMAN, bp 10 Feb 1771 *NHC2*.

MINOT. MISCELLANEOUS. REBECCA m 10 Jan 1770 *NHC1*—Isaac Newton of Wd & Goshen......SUSAN, d before 1777 s. p.; m Hezekiah Augur.

MITCHELL. FAM. 1. THOMAS of NH, d 1660; m Elizabeth ——— , who d 6 Oct 1683 *NHV*—Jeremy Whitnell.

1 HANNAH, perhaps m (1) Robert Coe, (2) Nicholas Elsey, but that Hannah is also given as da. Matthew Mitchell of Stam; no proof either way found.

2 ELIZABETH, b 6 Aug 1651 *NHC1*, bp 22 Feb 1651 *NHC1* [1651/2]; m 5 Dec 1672 *NHV*—Philip Alcott.

MITCHELL. FAM. 2. MICHAEL of W; m Sarah ——— .

1 JOHN, b 22 Jan 1695 *WV;* m 27 Oct 1720 *WV*—Katharine da. Samuel & Martha (Fernes) Munson, b 3 June 1704 *WV*.

i (probably) James; m 7 Mar 1743 *WV*—Jane Stracken. Children (incomplete): (1) Mary, b 10 Jan 1743/4 *WV*. (2) Elizabeth, b 25 Jan 1745/6 *WV*, d 29 Aug 1751 *WV*. (3) Martha, b 15 Mar 1747/8 *WV*, d 30 Aug 1751 *WV*. (4) John, b 6 June 1750 *WV*, bp June 1750 *CC*.

ii (probably) Moses, b c. 1723, d 8 Nov 1797 æ. 74 *WC2*, 7 Nov æ. 75 *WT2;* Census (W) 1-0-2; m (1) 11 Apr 1745 *WV*—Mary da. Gideon & Mary (Royce) Ives, b 16 Dec 1724 *WV*, d 14 May 1776 æ. 52 *WT2;* m (2) 11 Dec 1775 *CC* [?1776]—Patience da. Nathan & Mary Benham. **FAM. 3.**

iii (probably) John; m 8 Feb 1750 *WV*—Lydia [da. Joseph

& Lydia (Munson)] Sperry. Children: (1) Lydia, b 24 Oct 1750 *WV*, bp Aug (?) 1750 *CC*. (2) Damaris, b 16 Dec 1754 *NHV*.

2 (probably) SARAH; m 9 July 1718 *WV*—James Hough.

3 (probably) MICHAEL; m Mary ——— .

i Katharine, b 22 Jan 1725 *WV*.

4 (probably) Samuel; m 5 Jan 1738 *WV*—Abigail Cook.

i Michael, b 26 Feb 1739 *WV*.

ii Oliver, b 14 Apr 1741 *WV*.

iii Samuel, b 17 Aug 1743 *WV;* m 20 Oct 1763 *WV*—Elizabeth Stark. Children: (1) Elizabeth, b 24 July 1764 *WV*. (2) [Me]dad, b 2 Dec [1765] *WV*. (3) [Sa]muel, b 9 Nov 1767 *WV*.

iv Abigail, b 26 Apr 1746 *WV*.

v Rebecca, b 3 Feb 1748/9 *WV*, bp Feb 1749 *WC2*.

FAM. 3. MOSES & MARY (IVES) MITCHELL:

1 KATHARINE, b 4 Apr 1746 *WV*, bp 27 Apr 1746 *WC2*, d 12 May 1746 *WV*, *WC2*.

2 ASAPH, b 24 June 1748 *WV*, bp 24 July 1748 *WC2;* Census (W) 1-1-2; m (1) 30 Jan 1771 *WV*—Phebe Shailor; m (2) Susanna da. Joseph & Susanna (Cook) Cole, b 1 May 1748 *WV*.

3 MOSES, bp June 1750 *WC2*.

4 MARY, bp 2 Aug 1752 *WC2*, d 5 June 1756 *WV*.

5 JOTHAM, b 1 Apr 1754 *WV*, bp 7 Apr 1754 *WC2*, d 2 Nov 1825 æ. 71-7-1 *WT2;* Census (Bristol) 1-1-3; m 14 Mar 1782 *WV*—Rebecca da. Gideon & Rebecca (Johnson) Royce, b 16 Apr 1758 *WV*, d 15 May 1811 æ. 54 *WT2*.

i Betsey, b [18 Oct 1783], d 26 Nov 1784 æ. 0-13-8 *WT2*.

ii Moses, b c. 1786, d s. p. 4 July 1811 æ. 25 *WT2*.

iii Sally.

iv Betsey; m Christopher Atwater.

v Laura; m Walter Booth.

vi Aaron, b c. 1793, d 11 June 1811 æ. 18 *WT2*.

6 MARY, b 26 Mar 1757 *WV*, bp 8 May 1757 *WC2*, d 12 Mar 1806 æ. 49 *WT2*, *WC2*.

7 ROTHER (?), b 4 Aug 1760 *WV*.

8 ZENAS, b 10 Apr 1762 *WV;* Census (W) 2-1-4; m 10 June 1784 *WV*, 9 Jan *CC*—Abigail da. Titus & Dinah (Andrews) Merriman, b 8 Nov 1762 *WV*. Children, unknown except Titus who m Maria Barnes.

MIX. FAM. 1. THOMAS of NH, d 1691; m Rebecca da. Nathaniel Turner.

1 JOHN, b 1649 *NHCCt*, d 21 Jan 1711/2 *NHV*, æ. 62 *NHT1;* m Elizabeth da. Benjamin & Elizabeth Wilmot, bp 23 Sep 1649 *NHC1*, d 20 Aug 1711 *NHV*, 21 Aug æ. 61 *NHT1*.

i John, b 25 Aug 1676 *NHV*, bp 12 Aug 1688 *NHC1*, d 20 Dec 1721 *NHV*, 10 Dec 1722 æ. 47 *NHT1;* m (1) 25 Nov 1702 *NHV*—Sarah da. John & Ann (Vicars) Thompson, b 16 Jan 1671 *NHV* [1671/2], d 21 Nov 1711 *NHV;* m

(2) 12 Nov 1712 *NHV*——Elizabeth Booth, who d May 1716 *NHV;* m (3) 14 Feb 1716/7 *NHV*—Esther da. Joseph & Esther (Winston) Morris, wid. John Peck, b 3 Sep 1684 *NHV*, d 19 Aug 1751 æ. 65 *NHTl;* she m (3) Joseph Smith. **FAM. 2.**

ii Esther, b 25 Dec 1678 *NHV*, bp 12 Aug 1688 *NHCl*, d 16 Sep 1746 *NHV*, æ. 68 *NHTl;* m Theophilus Munson.

iii Elizabeth, b 18 Feb 1681 *NHV*, bp 12 Aug 1688 *NHCl*, d 26 Feb 1758 æ. 76 *CTl;* m 4 Aug 1713 *WV*—John At water.

iv Joseph, b 18 Dec 1684 *NHV*, bp 12 Aug 1688 *NHCl*, d 12 Feb 1757 æ. 72 *NHTl;* Lieut.; m (1) 24 Mar 1709 *NHV*—Hannah da. John & Sarah (Glover) Ball, b 12 Jan 1689/90 *NHV*, d 20 Jan 1752 æ. 62 *NHTl;* m (2) Rebecca ——, who d 30 Apr 1774 *WV;* she m (2) Samuel Hall of W. **FAM. 3.**

v Stephen, b 24 Mar 1686/7 *NHV*.

vi Abigail, b 17 Apr 1687 *NHV* [?1688], bp 12 Aug 1688 *NHCl*, d 19 Aug 1770 *WV;* m 7 Sep 1709 *WV*—Thomas Miles.

vii Mercy, b 16 Apr 1692 *NHV*, bp 18 Apr 1692 *NHCl;* m (1) 5 Jan 1715/6 *NHV*—Ebenezer Alling; m (2) 5 July 1744 *NHV*—James Talmadge.

2 Nathaniel, b 14 Sep 1651 *NHV*, bp 23 May 1658 *NHCl*, d 14 Oct 1725 *NHV*, æ. 74 *NHTl;* m Mary da. John & Hannah (Tuttle) Pantry, b c. 1654, d Mar 1724 *NHV*, 25 Mar 1723 æ. 69 *NHTl*.

i Mary, b 18 Nov 1682 *NHV*, d s. p?

ii Rebecca, b 23 Nov 1684 *NHV*, d 6 Dec 1760 æ. 76 *EHT;* m 1 Feb 1710/1 *NHV*—Matthew Rowe.

iii Hannah.

iv Sarah, b 12 Jan 1690/1 *NHV*, d s. p?

v Nathaniel, b c. 1693, bp (adult) 24 July 1737 *NHCl*, d 24 Oct 1756 *NHV*, æ. 64 *NHTl;* m (1) 2 Jan 1723/4 *NHV*—Anna da. Benjamin & Elizabeth (Post) Bunnell, b 11 Oct 1695 *NHV*, d 15 Sep 1731 *NHV*, æ. 35 *NHTl;* m (2) 31 Aug 1732 *NHV*—Rebecca da. Ralph & Abiah (Bassett) Lines, b Feb 1697/8 *NHV*, d 12 Mar 1780 æ. 82 *NHTl*, *NHCl*. **FAM. 4.**

3 Daniel, b 8 Sep 1653 *NHV*, bp 23 May 1658 *NHCl*, d 1720; m 2 May 1678 *WV*—Ruth Rockwell, b 5 Mar 1655, d 1739.

i Thomas, b 25 Mar 1678/9 *WV;* m 21 Mar 1705 *WV*—Deborah da. Samuel & Hannah (Churchill) Royce, b 8 Sep 1683 *WV*, d 15 Dec 1738 *WV*. **FAM. 5.**

ii Lydia, b end of July 1682 *WV*, d 1710; m 7 Mar 1706 *WV*—Ebenezer Hull.

PAGE 1789

iii Daniel, b 1 June 1685 *WV;* m 28 May 1712 *WV*—Lydia Avery. **FAM. 6.**

iv Ruth.

v Hannah, d 26 Nov 1754 *WV;* m 26 Dec 1711 *WV*—Theophilus Jones.

vi Theophilus, b c. 1697, d 1 July 1750 *WC2*, 3 July æ. 53 *WT2;* m 17 Jan 1729 *WV*—Damaris Olmstead, who d 5 Oct 1775 *WV.* **FAM. 7.**

4 THOMAS, b 30 Aug 1655 *NHV*, bp 23 May 1658 *NHC1;* res. Norwich; m 30 June 1677 Hannah Fitch.

5 REBECCA, b 4 Jan 1657 *NHV*, bp 23 May 1658 *NHC1*, d 17 Oct 1734 æ. 78 *NoHT1;* m John Yale.

6 ABIGAIL, b [1659] *NHV*, bp 22 Jan 1659 *NHC1;* m John Pantry.

7 CALEB, bp 15 Dec 1661 *NHC1*, d 12 Aug 1708 *NHT1;* m (1) Hannah da. John & Elizabeth Chidsey, b 9 Jan 1663 *NHV*, d 11 Dec 1693 *NHV;* m (2) Mary da. Nathan & Hester Bradley, b 1672; she m (2) 26 Feb 1710 *NHV*—Joshua Tuttle.

(By 1): *i* Thomas, b 18 Dec 1685 *NHV*, d s. p. 15 Mar 1721/2 *NHV*, 14 Mar æ. 36 *NHT1*.

ii Caleb, b 27 Sep 1687 *NHV*, d 30 Jan 1765 æ. 77 *NHT1*, *NHC1;* m 20 Dec 1716 *NHV*—Rebecca da. John & Rebecca (Daniel) Thompson, bp 24 Aug 1689 *NHC1*, d 3 Dec 1760 æ. 71 *NHT1*. **FAM. 8.**

iii Hannah, b c. 1691, d 15 Feb 1739/40 æ. 48 *NHT1;* m Ebenezer Beecher.

(By 2): *iv* Thankful, b 3 Oct 1695 *NHV*, d before 1745; m 8 Feb 1721/2 *NHV*—Caleb Alling.

v Rachel, b 15 Dec 1697 *NHV*, bp Dec 1697 *NHC1*, d 23 Nov 1760; m 26 Apr 1716 *GV*—John Collins of G.

vi Patience, b 23 Mar 1699 *NHV* [1699/1700], bp 29 Mar 1700 *NHC1*, d 23 May 1786 æ. 86 *NHC1;* m 26 Dec 1723/4 *NHV*—John Alling.

vii Esther, b 31 Dec 1702 *NHV;* m 5 Mar 1721/2 *NHV*—Nathaniel Hubbell of Stratfield.

8 SAMUEL, b 11 Jan 1663 *NHV*, bp 21 Feb 1663 *NHC1*, d 10 Apr 1730 *NHV*, æ. 67 *NHT1;* m 26 July 1699 *NHV*—Rebecca da. George & Katharine (Lane) Pardee, b 18 Apr 1666 *NHV*, d 14 June 1731 *NHV*, æ. 65 *NoHT1*.

i Samuel, b 20 May 1700 *NHV*, d 15 Oct 1755 *NHV*, æ. 56 *NHT1;* B. A. (Yale 1720); M. A.; m 1 Jan 1727/8 *NHV*—Abigail da. David & Abigail (Flagg) Cutler, b 21 Feb 1706 *Boston, Mass.,V* [1706/7], d 16 Oct 1797 æ. 91 *NHx;* she m (2) William Greenough. **FAM. 9.**

ii George, b 24 Mar 1702 *NHV*, bp (adult) 6 May 1724 *NHC1;* res. NoH; m 14 Feb 1724/5 *NHV*—Katharine da. Joseph & Elizabeth (Sanford) Tuttle, b 25 Nov 1699 *NHV*. **FAM. 10.**

iii Stephen, b 12 Aug 1705 *NHV*, d s. p.

9 HANNAH, b 30 June 1666 *NHV*, bp 12 Aug 1666 *NHC1;* m 25 June 1691 Thomas Olmstead of Hartford.

10 ESTHER, b 30 Nov 1668 *NHV*, d 1670 *NHV*.

11 STEPHEN, b 1 Nov 1672 *NHV*, d 28 Aug 1738; Rev.; res. Wethersfield; m 1 Dec 1696 Mary Stoddard; had issue.

FAM. 2. JOHN & SARAH (THOMPSON) MIX:

1 MEHITABEL, b 19 Aug 1706 *NHV;* m (1) 9 Nov 1726 *NHV*, 10 Nov *WV*—Caleb Atwater; m (2) 18 Mar 1739 *WV*—John Peck.

FAM. 2. JOHN & ELIZABETH (BOOTH) MIX:

2 ELIZABETH, b 9 Nov 1713 *NHV;* m 7 Oct 1730 *FairfieldV*—Ephraim Sanford of Redding.

3 EBENEZER, b 18 Apr 1716 *NHV*, bp 15 July 1716 *NHC1*, d 4 Aug 1766; res. W. Hartford; m Mary (Sedgwick) Merrill.

FAM. 2. JOHN & ESTHER (MORRIS) MIX:

4 ESTHER, b 14 Apr 1718 *NHV;* m Thomas Painter.

5 JOHN, b 30 Mar 1720 *NHV*, bp Apr 1720 *NHC1*, d 24 Jan 1796 æ. 76 *NHT1;* Capt.; Census (NH) 5-1-3; m (1) 20 Nov 1743 *NHV*—Lois da. Samuel & Abigail (Pinion) Candee, b c. 1719, d 26 Aug 1758 æ. 39 *NHT1;* m (2) Sarah da. Deodate & Lydia (Woodward) Davenport, b 7 July 1731 *NHV*, d 18 Dec 1806 æ. 76 *NHT1*.

(By 2): *i* John, b [25 Dec 1759], bp 30 Dec 1759 *NHC2*, d 4 Jan 1760 æ. 0-0-10 *NHT1*.

ii John, b [2 Nov 1760], d 3 Nov 1760 æ. 15 hrs. *NHT1*.

iii John, b 22 Oct 1761 *NHV*, bp 25 Oct 1761 *NHC2*, d 1 Apr 1844 æ. 83 *NHV*.

iv Samuel, b 22 Aug 1763 *NHV*, bp 28 Aug 1763 *NHC2*, d before 1789; m ——. Only child: (1) Samuel; Samuel Punderson was his conservator, 1808; perhaps the Samuel Mix who d 9 Dec 1843 æ. 61 *NHV*.

v Deodate, b 31 July 1765 *NHV*, bp 4 Aug 1765 *NHC2;* res. Wol. 1807.

vi Amos, bp 4 Oct 1767 *NHC2*, d 6 Sep 1846 æ. 79 *Camden, N. Y., T.*

vii Hezekiah, bp 3 June 1770 *NHC2*, d 29 Sep 1828 æ. 58 *Camden, N. Y., T.*

FAM. 3. JOSEPH & HANNAH (BALL) MIX:

1 TIMOTHY, b 24 Sep 1711 *NHV*, d 15 Dec 1779; B. A. (Yale, 1731); Dr.; m (1) 19 July 1733 *NHV*—Mary Cooper, b c. 1715 (St. George's Manor, L. I.), d 15 Dec 1761 *NHV*, æ. 46 *NHT1;* m (2) Ann ——, b c. 1722, d Oct 1815 æ. 93 (at NH) *ColR;* Census, Anna (NH) 0-0-1.

(By 1): *i* Mary, b 18 May 1734 *NHV*, bp 19 May 1734 *NHC1*, d 3 Sep 1781 æ. 48 *NHT1;* m 14 Dec 1752 *NHV*—David Austin.

ii Hannah, b 27 Nov 1735 *NHV*, bp 30 Nov 1735 *NHC1;* m 17 Feb 1760 *NHC2*—Elihu Crane of Norwalk.

iii John, b [21 Oct 1737], bp 23 Oct 1737 *NHC1*, d 5 Nov 1738 æ. 1-0-15 *NHT1*.

iv Timothy, b 20 Jan 1739/40 *NHV*, 1740 *NHT1*, bp 24 Feb 1739/40 *NHC1*, d 11 June 1824 *NHT1*, 9 June æ. 85 (*N*

HC2) *NHV;* Lieut., Rev. soldier *NHT1;* Census (NH) 1-0-4; m 30 Sep 1762 *NHC2*—Margaret [da. John & Mary (Griffin)] Storer, b c. 1744, d 23 July 1815 æ. 72 *NHT1*. **FAM. 11.**

v Anna, b 1 Sep 1741 *NHV*, bp 1 Oct 1741 (at NH) *BdC*, d 25 June 1742 æ. 0-9 *NHT1*.

vi Ann, b 13 May 1743 *NHV* (called "Permit Ann" in later records); m 28 Oct 1762 *NHC2*—John Austin.

vii Sarah, b 11 Oct 1748 *NHV*, bp 2 Apr 1749 *GC4;* m 11 Nov 1767 *NHC2*—Jabez Colt.

2 **John**, b 15 Nov 1713 *NHV*, d 7 Apr 1734 æ. 21 *NHT1*.

3 **Joseph**, b 29 Oct 1715 *NHV*, bp 8 July 1716 *NHC1*, d July 1789; m (1) 9 June 1737 *NHV*—Damaris da. Thomas & Lydia (Bradley) Punderson, b 12 July 1719 *NHV*, d 9 Sep 1742 *NHV;* m (2) 15 Dec 1743 *NHV*—Anna da. Thomas & Abigail (Peck) Alcott, b 20 Nov 1717 *NHV*, d 6 Nov 1751 *NHV;* m (3) 21 May 1752 *NHV*, *NHC2*—Sarah da. Thomas & Sarah (Gilbert) Morris, b 20 Dec 1723 *NHV*.

(By 1): *i* Abel, b 17 Jan 1737/8 *NHV*, bp 5 Mar 1737/8 *NHC1;* Census (Wy) 2-0-6; m 23 Feb 1761 *NHC2*—Ruth Hawley of Farm; had issue.

ii Joseph, b 28 July 1740 *NHV*, d 5 Feb 1813 æ. 72 *NHT1*, 19 Feb 1814 *NHV;* Census (NH) 2-3-5; m 15 Oct 1764 *NHC1*—Patience da. Joseph & Anna (Wilmot) Sperry, b 4 Feb 1738/9 *NHV*, d 9 July 1811 æ. 72 *NHT1*. **FAM. 12.**

(By 2): *iii* David, b 25 Sep 1744 *NHV*, d 20 Aug 1790 æ. 46 *NHC1;* m 7 Mar 1771 *NHV*, *NHC1*—Elizabeth da. James & Elizabeth (Alling) Atwater, b 3 Nov 1745 *NHV*. Children: (1) Elizabeth Polly, b 23 Dec 1771 *NHV*, bp 29 Dec 1771 *NHC1*, d 13 June 1793 æ. 23 *NHC1*. (2) Abiather, bp 15 Aug 1773 *NHC1*. (3) Alling, bp 25 Apr 1779 *NoHC*. (4) Anna; m ——— Sherman. (5) Sally; m ——— Oakley. (6) Ebenezer, bp 9 Nov 1788 *NHC1;* m Jemima Debow.

iv Ezra, bp 4 June 1749 *NHC2*, d soon.

v Anna, b 28 Oct 1751 *NHV;* m 5 Dec 1771 *WV*—Prindle Hall.

(By 3): *vi* Ezra, b 21 Mar 1753 *NHV*, bp 6 May 1753 *NHC2*.

vii Hannah, b 19 Sep 1754 *NHV*, bp 3 Nov 1754 *NHC2*.

viii Esther, bp 18 Sep 1757 *NHC2*.

ix Eli, bp 9 Apr 1760 *NHC2*, d c. 1796, probably s. p.

x Amos, bp 29 May 1763 *NHC2*.

xi Sarah, bp 29 Dec 1765 *NHC2*.

xii Joel, bp 15 Jan 1769 *NHC2;* Census (W) 1-0-1.

4 **Stephen**, b 2 Dec 1717 *NHV*, d 3 Dec 1717 *NHV*.

5 **Stephen**, b 4 Dec 1718 *NHV*, bp Dec 1718 *NHC1*.

6 [**Abel**, bp Dec 1720 *NHC1*, d young].

7 [ABRAM, bp 13 May 1722 *NHC1*, d young].

8 [DANIEL, bp c. Oct 1723 *NHC1*, d young].

9 HANNAH, b 7 Mar 1725/6 *NHV*, bp 27 Mar 1726 *NHC1*.

10 MABEL, b 16 Dec 1727 *NHV*, bp 31 Dec 1727 *NHC1*.

11 JONATHAN, b 7 Nov 1729 *NHV*, bp 9 Nov 1729 *NHC1*, d 7 June 1779 [error for 1778] æ. 48 *NHT1*; m (1) 8 Dec 1748 *NHV*—Mary da. Joseph & Deborah [Ward] Peck; m (2) 22 Apr 1756 *NHV*—Patience da. John & Patience (Mix) Alling, b 27 Feb 1729/30 *NHV*.

(By 1): *i* William, b 3 Nov 1749 *NHV*, bp 27 Jan 1750/1 *NHC1*; [m ——— Eels].

• *ii* John, b 19 June 1751 *NHV*, bp 23 June 1751 *NHC1*, d 28 Jan 1820 æ. 68 (*NHC2*) *NHV*; m (1) Elizabeth [?Farrand]; m (2) c. 1784 Rebecca da. Ezekiel & Rebecca (Russell) Hayes, div. w. Abel Frisbie, b 30 Oct 1750, d 9 Dec 1827 (Romulus, N. Y.); her first husband returned, the div. was set aside & Rebecca was reunited with Frisbie. **FAM. 13.**

iii Jonathan, b 19 Apr 1753 *F*, bp 15 Apr 1753 *NHC2*, d 18 Jan 1817 æ. 64 *NHT1*; Census (NH) 2–4–3; m (1) 6 Aug 1776 Nancy da. Joshua Sears, b 28 Sep 1758 *F*, d 23 June 1799 æ. 40 *NHT1*; m (2) 5 Aug 1800 *F*—Mary Elizabeth da. Solomon & Elizabeth (Todd) Phipps, div. w. Webster Brown, b 27 Nov 1776 *F*, d 15 Apr 1849 æ. 72 *NHT1*, *HV*. **FAM. 14.**

iv Elijah, bp 12 Jan 1755 *NHC2*, d 1780; m.

(By 2): *v* Eldad, b 23 May 1757 *NHV*, bp 29 May 1757 *NHC2*; Census (NH) 1–2–4; m 15 July 1780 *NHC2*—Mary da. James & Phebe (Leek) Hitchcock, b c. 1754, bp (adult) Oct 1784 *NHC2*, d 5 Sep 1837 æ. 83 *NHV*. **FAM. 15.**

vi Mary, b 20 Nov 1759 *NHV*, bp 25 Nov 1759 *NHC2*, d 25 July 1760 *NHV*.

vii Joseph; res. Suffield; 11 Mar 1797 *NHC1*—Sally da. David & Mary (English) Phipps, b 26 Nov 1774 *NHV*.

viii Medad, bp 3 July 1763 *NHC1*.

ix Rebecca, bp 23 Aug 1767 *NHC1*.

x Elizabeth, bp 16 July 1769 *NHC1*.

12 [EZRA, bp 11 Sep 1731 *NHC1*, d young].

FAM. 4. NATHANIEL & ANNA (BUNNELL) MIX:

1 NATHANIEL, b 11 Mar 1724/5 *NHV*, bp 24 July 1737 *NHC1*, b 20 Sep 1749 *NHV*, æ. 25 *NHT1*; m 9 Feb 1748/9 *NHV*—Sarah da. Abner & Abigail (Gilbert) Bradley, b 14 Sep 1724 *NHV*, d 1806; Census, Sarah (NH) 0–0–1.

i Nathaniel, b 17 Nov 1749 *NHV*, bp 6 May 1750 *NHC1*, d 29 Nov 1781 æ. 32 *NHT1*, *NHC1*; m 9 Feb 1773 *NHV*, 1774 *NHC1*—Thankful da. John & Abiah (Hitchcock) Alling, b c. 1755, d 8 Aug 1831; Census, Thankful (NH) 0–1–3; she m (2) 1 Jan 1794 Rutherford Trowbridge. **FAM. 16.**

2 STEPHEN, b 10 Dec 1728 *NHV*, d 21 May 1736 æ. 9 *NHT1*.

3 JABEZ, b 12 Sep 1728 *NHV*, bp 24 July 1737 *NHC1*, d 1762 *NHC1*, 5 Oct 1762 æ. 31 *NHT1*; B. A. (Yale, 1751); m 12 Feb 1759 *NHV*, *NHC1*—Jemima Brown, bp 3 Sep 1738 *NHC1*; she m (2) 12 Feb 1764 *NHC1*—Jeremiah Barnett; m (3) 14 Nov 1775 *NHC2*—Charles Sabin.

i Mary, b 17 June 1760 *NHV*, bp 23 June 1760 *NHC1*, d 23 Nov 1825 æ. 69 (*NHC2*) *NHV*; m William Noyes.

ii Anna, b 6 Feb 1762 *F*, bp 14 Jan 1762 *NHC1*, d 13 Feb 1800 *F*; m 31 May 1778 *NHC1*—Isaac Gilbert.

FAM. 4. NATHANIEL & REBECCA (LINES) MIX:

4 MARY, b 9 June 1733 *NHV*, d 11 June 1736 æ. 4 *NHT1*.

5 ANNA, b 2 Apr 1735 *NHV*, bp 24 July 1737 *NHC1*, d 23 Dec 1778 æ. 44 *NHT1*; m 20 Apr 1757 *NHV*—Jeremiah Atwater.

6 STEPHEN, b [?1737], d 4 Sep 1737 æ. 3 (?) *NHT1*.

7 STEPHEN, b 18 Apr 1739 *NHV*, bp 22 Apr 1739 *NHC1*.

FAM. 5. THOMAS & DEBORAH (ROYCE) MIX:

1 ABIGAIL, b 29 Jan 1706 *WV*, d 6 May 1753 *WV*; m 31 May 1730 *WV*—Abijah Ives.

2 JOSIAH, b 20 Nov 1707 *WV*, d 1752; m (1) 5 Aug 1730 *WV*—Sybil da. Joseph & Abigail (Curtis) Holt, b 16 Mar 1710 *WV*, d 5 Aug 1738 *WV*; m (2) 23 Dec 1742 *WV*—Abigail Porter; she m (2) Aug 1753 *WC2*—Abijah Ives.

(By 1): *i* Jesse, b 22 Oct 1731 *WV*; m 22 Nov 1753 *WV*—Deborah da. John & Deborah (Matthews) Parker, b 4 May 1734 *WV*; Census, Deborah (Granville, N. Y.) 0-0-1. Children: (1) Ruth, b 5 Sep 1754 *WV*. (2) Josiah, b 22 Aug 1757 *WV*; Census (Granville, N. Y.) 1-2-2; but who then was Josiah, Census (W) 2-3-5?; m 17 Aug 1777 *WV*—Mindwell Royce. (3) Phebe, b 14 May 1759 *WV*. (4) Zenas, b 3 Apr 1763 *WV*. (5) Jesse, b 28 June 1765 *WV*. (6) Martha, b 17 Sep 1767 *WV*. (7) Deborah, b 7 June 1773 *WV*. The 5 younger children of Jesse were bp in 1777 and 1779 *CC*.

ii Eldad, b 20 Oct 1733 *WV*, bp 25 Nov 1733 *CC*, d 30 Oct 1806 æ. 73 *WatV*; Census (Wat) 2-0-2; m 25 June 1756 *WatV*—Lydia da. Joseph & Experience (Beecher) Beach, b 13 Sep 1735 *WV*. **FAM. 17.**

iii Titus, b 4 Dec 1735 *WV*, bp Jan 1735/6 *CC*.

iv Sybil, b 5 Apr 1738 *WV*, "child" bp Apr 1738 *CC*, "child" d Aug 1738 *CC*.

3 THOMAS, b 27 Nov 1709 *WV*, d 1794; Census (W) 1-0-0; m 5 Apr 1736 *WV*—Ruth da. Nehemiah Manross.

i Samuel, b 13 Feb 1740 *WV*, d s. p.

ii Martha, b 13 Dec 1742 *WV*; m (1) 20 Jan 1763 *WV*—Jacob Francis; m (2) Isaac Hall.

iii Thomas, b 12 Aug 1745 *WV*; Census (Wallingford, Vt.) 1-4-4; m (1) 11 Dec 1766 *WV*—Lois da. Jonathan &

Agnes (Lynn) Collins, b 1 Mar 1748 *WV;* m (2) 12 Aug 1783 *WV*—Comfort da. Philip & Hannah Curtis, wid. Thomas Davis; had issue.

iv Enos, b 2 Feb 1747/8 *WV;* m 10 May 1781 *WV*—Hannah da. Daniel & Mercy (Heaton) Baldwin, b 5 Mar 1752 *WV.*

v John, b 23 Aug 1750 *WV*, d 3 Oct 1824 æ. 75 *WT1;* Census (W) 3-3-3; m 10 Dec 1781 *WV*—Elizabeth [da. Daniel & Sarah (Atwater)] Hall, b [21 June 1764 *WV*], d 7 Sep 1845 æ. 81 *WT1.*

vi Amos, b 2 Dec 1753 *WV;* m 1 Feb 1776 *WV*—Anna Yale.

4 DANIEL, b 27 Apr 1712 *WV.*

5 DEBORAH, b 17 Mar 1714 *WV;* m 4 Feb 1736 *WV*—Jonathan Curtis.

6 HANNAH, b 20 Jan 1716 *WV.*

7 STEPHEN, b 8 May 1718 *WV;* m (1) 19 Sep 1744 *WC2*—Rebecca da. Benjamin & Rebecca (Merriam) Ives, b 29 Mar 1725 *WV* [1726], d 19 Dec 1755 *WC2;* m (2) 17 Sep 1760 *KensingtonC*—Ann Porter.

i Theophilus, b 18 Dec 1745 *WV*, bp 9 Feb 1746 *WC2.*

ii Rebecca, b 13 May 1747 *WV*, bp 12 July 1747 *WC2.*

iii Stephen, b 2 Nov 1748 *WV*, bp Dec 1748 *WC2.*

iv Sarah, b 31 Dec 1749 *WV*, "child" bp 25 Mar 1750 *WC2.*

v Child, bp 1752 *WC2.*

8 ENOS, b 29 May 1720 *WV*, d 20 Dec 1737 *WV.*

9 SARAH, b 1 Apr 1723 *WV.*

10 MARTHA, b 18 July 1725 *WV.*

11 TIMOTHY, b 28 Dec 1727 *WV*, d 23 Jan 1800 æ. 75 *BristolT;* Census (Bristol) 2-1-3; m Elizabeth ———, who d 20 June 1804 æ. 70 *BristolT.*

FAM. 6. DANIEL & LYDIA (AVERY) MIX:

1 BENJAMIN, b 16 Aug 1713 *WV*, d soon.

2 LYDIA, b 21 Sep 1716 *WV*, "Lydia, town poor, drowned at Westfield" 11 July 1784 *WV.*

3 RUTH, b 5 Oct 1718 *WV;* m 1 Dec 1737 *WV*—John Hendrick.

4 BENJAMIN, b 11 Dec 1720 *WV.*

5 ISAAC, b 7 June 1723 *WV*, d soon.

6 ISAAC, b 5 Nov 1725 *WV.*

7 JOANNA, b 12 Nov 1727 *WV;* she had a nat. child, Jacob Parker, bp 17 June 1750 *SC;* m (1) c. 1752 Moses Merriman; m (2) 14 May 1761 *WV*—Jacob Teal of S.

8 DANIEL, b 31 Mar 1730 *WV.*

FAM. 7. THEOPHILUS & DAMARIS (OLMSTEAD) MIX:

1 MOSES, b 3 Jan 1730 *WV*, d 14 Feb 1730 *WV.*

2 MARY, b 3 Apr 1731 *WV*, bp 1 May 1731 *WC2*, d 22 June 1732 *WV.*

3 SARAH, b 26 Aug 1732 *WV*, bp 27 Aug 1732 *WC2;* m (1) 14 Apr 1757 *WV*—Christopher Robinson; m (2) 21 Nov 1766 *WV*—

Yale Bishop.

4 MARY, b 4 Aug 1734 *WV*, bp 11 Aug 1734 *WC2*, d 3 July 1735 *WV*.

FAM. 8. CALEB & REBECCA (THOMPSON) MIX:

1 DOROTHY, b 27 Oct 1718 *NHV*, bp Nov 1718 *NHC1*, d 11 Aug 1767 æ. 49 *NHT1*; m 9 Dec 1742 *NHV*—Isaac Atwater.

2 SARAH, b 17 Nov or 16 Dec 1722 *NHV*, bp Dec 1722 *NHC1*, d 4 Feb 1762 *F*; m 29 May 1750 Isaac Bradley.

3 THOMAS, b 16 June 1725 *NHV*, bp 20 June 1725 *NHC1*, d 10 Aug 1759 *NHC1*, æ. 34 *NHT1*; m 18 Jan 1748/9 *NHV*—Hannah da. Timothy & Mabel (Cooper) Miles, b 10 May 1722 *NHV*, d 12 Nov 1801 æ. 81 *NHC1*; Census, Hannah (NH) 0-0-1.

i Caleb, b c. 1750, d 26 Mar 1802 æ. 52 *NHT1*, (at H) *Conn Journal;* Capt.; Census (H) 2-1-3; m (1) 14 Aug 1769 *NHC1*—Peggy Perkins; m (2) 5 Oct 1790 *NHC1*—Phila Potter, who d Oct 1804 *NHT1*. **FAM. 18.**

ii Elisha, b c. 1752, d 11 Dec 1813 æ. 62 *NHT1*; Census (NH) 1-1-4; m 10 Nov 1774 *NHC1*—Mehitabel da. John & Mary (Wilmot) Beecher, b c. 1755, bp (adult) 27 Aug 1780 *NHC1*, d 24 Feb 1825 æ. 69 *NHT1*, 29 Feb (*NHC1*) *NHV*. **FAM 19.**

iii Stephen, b c. 1753, d 1784; m 19 Nov 1777 *NHC2*—Esther Read, b c. 1754, d 7 Mar 1807 æ. 53 *NHC1*; Census, Esther (NH) 0-3-1. Children: (1) Merrit. (2) Miles.

iv Thomas, b 3 May 1755 *NHV*, d 4 Sep 1810 æ. 55 *HT2*; Census (H) 1 2-3; m 17 Jan 1776 *NHC1*—Rebecca da. Benjamin & Rachel (Lines) Wooding, b 17 May 1755 *NHV*, d 19 Sep 1825 æ. 71 *HT2*. **FAM. 20.**

v Samuel, b c. 1757, d 25 Aug 1805 æ. 47 *NHT1*, 19 Aug 1804 æ. 48 *NHC1*; Census (NH) 1-2-4; m 5 Apr 1778 *NHC2*—Martha Burrit. Children unknown except: (1) Samuel, b c. 1787, d 12 Apr 1808 æ. 21 *NHT1*. (2) Burrit, b[Mar 1799], d 18 Sep 1803 æ. 4-6 *NHT1*, "son" d 17 Sep æ. 5 *NHC1*.

4 REBECCA, b 3 Dec 1727 *NHV*, bp 10 Dec 1727 *NHC1*, d 3 June 1767 æ. 39 *NHT1*, *NHC1*.

5 HANNAH, b 5 Dec 1730 *NHV*, bp 1 Oct 1732 *NHC1*, d 14 Apr 1769 æ. 39 *NHT1*, æ. 38 *NHC1*.

FAM. 9. SAMUEL & ABIGAIL (CUTLER) MIX:

1 REBECCA, b 19 Jan 1728/9 *NHV*, bp 26 Jan 1728/9 *NHC1*, d 17 Aug 1739 *NHV*, æ. 11 *NHT1*.

2 ELIZABETH, b 29 Nov 1730 *NHV*, bp 6 Dec 1730 *NHC1*, d 15 Aug 1739 *NHV*, *NHT1*.

3 MARY, b 3 Nov 1732 *NHV*, bp 5 Nov 1732 *NHC1*, d 17 Aug 1739 *NHV*.

4 WILLIAM, b 8 Dec 1735 *NHV*, d 12 Aug 1739 *NHV*.

5 ABIGAIL, bp 24 Dec 1737 *NHC1*, d 7 Aug 1739 *NHV*, æ. 2 *NHT1*.

6 REBECCA ABIGAIL, b 2 Oct 1741 *NHV*, bp 4 Oct 1741 *NHC1*, d 11 Aug 1764 æ. 23 *NHT1*; m 2 May 1762 *NHV*, *NHC1*—Richard Woodhull.

7 ELIZABETH MARY, b 30 Sep 1746 *NHV*, bp 5 Oct 1746 *NHC1*, d 3 Jan 1810; m 15 May 1766 *NHV*, *NHC1*—Jonathan Fitch.

FAM. 10. GEORGE & KATHARINE (TUTTLE) MIX:

1 SON, b 4 Sep 1725 *NHV*, d 7 Sep 1725 *NHV*.

2 SYBIL, b 10 Sep 1726 *NHV*, bp Sep 1726 *NHC1*; m 10 Aug 1744 *NHV*—John Wolcott.

3 KATHARINE, b 22 Jan 1728/9 *NHV*, bp 26 Jan 1728/9 *NHC1*, d 26 Aug 1818; m 24 Jan 1750/1 *NHV*—Gershom Todd.

4 SAMUEL, b 25 Dec 1730 *NHV*, d 26 Jan 1813 æ. 82 *NoHT1*; Census (NoH) 3-0-5; m (1) 3 Jan 1753 *NHV*—Lydia da. Benjamin & Lydia (Alling) Todd, b 1 Apr 1732 *NHV*, d 23 June 1794 æ. 63 *NoHT1*; m (2) 4 Oct 1795 *NoHC*—Sarah da. Samuel & Mary Ames, wid. Stephen Ives, who d c. 1833.

(By 1): *i* Lydia, b 23 Apr 1753 *NHV*, d s. p. 14 Jan 1832 æ. 79 *NoHT1*; m 28 Sep 1796 *NoHC*—Jotham Ives of Torrington.

ii Samuel, b 25 Jan 1756 *NoHV*, d 6 Nov 1827 æ. 72 *NoHT1*; m 14 Nov 1793 *NoHC*—Susanna da. Ephraim & Susanna (Bassett) Humiston, b 5 Oct 1763 *NHV*, d 16 July 1810 *NoHV*, æ. 47 *NoHT1*. **FAM. 21.**

iii Lucretia, b c. 1758, d 9 Oct 1813 æ. 55 *CT2*; m Abijah Brooks.

iv Rebecca; m Isaac Wooding.

v Emilia, b c. 1765, d 12 Sep 1849 æ. 84 *NoHT3*; m 12 Jan 1797 *NoHC*—Joel Humiston.

vi Katharine, b c. 1773, d 9 Aug 1851 æ. 78 *NoHT3*; m 26 Dec 1801 *NoHV*—Theophilus Todd.

5 ESTHER, b 22 Nov 1732 *NHV*, d before 1767; m 15 Feb 1756 *NHV*—Timothy Potter.

6 ISAAC, b 13 June 1735 *NHV*, d 30 Nov 1739 *NHV*.

7 STEPHEN, b 11 May 1739 *NHV*, d after 1802, apparently s. p.; Census (NoH) 1-0-1; m 30 May 1764 *NHV*—Zerviah da. Jonathan & Zerviah (Wooster) Miles, who d 23 Sep 1826 æ. 89 *NoHD*.

FAM. 11. TIMOTHY & MARGARET (STORER) MIX (family incomplete):

1 TIMOTHY, bp 27 Nov 1763 *NHC2*, d 1778 (on prison ship, N. Y.) *NHT1*.

2 (probably) ELIZABETH, b c. 1765, d 25 Feb 1854 æ. 89 *NHT1*; m 5 June 1783 *NHC2*—Abner Tuttle.

3 ELIHU; m Margaret Stevens.

4 WILLIAM, b [Aug 1773], d 29 Apr 1845 æ. 71-8 *NHT1*, æ. 72 *NHV*; m (1) 23 Mar 1794 *NHC1*—Elizabeth Plant; m (2) 14 Oct 1797 *NHC1*—Lucy da. Lemuel & Margaret (Green) Benham, b 7 Nov 1776 *NHV*, d 26 June 1818 æ. 42 *NHT1*.

5 POLLY ANN, bp 27 Oct 1776 *NHC2*.

6 MEHITABEL, bp 21 Feb 1779 *NHC2*, d 3 Sep 1842 æ. 64 *NHT1*; m 30 Dec 1804 *NoHC*—Uri Ames.

7 ISAAC, bp 11 Nov 1781 *NHC2*, d 12 Dec 1866 æ. 86 *NHT1*; m 12 Sep 1803 *NHC1*—Mary da. John & Hannah Dodd, b [Oct 1784], d 4 Apr 1866 æ. 82-5 *NHV*.

FAM. 12. JOSEPH & PATIENCE (SPERRY) MIX:

1 ANNA, [b c. 1766, d 5 Mar 1848 æ. 78 *NHV*].

2 REBECCA, b c. 1768, d 16 Aug 1841 æ. 73 *Great Barrington, Mass.*; m 13 Oct 1786 *NHx*—Elijah Turner.

3 PUNDERSON; m 17 May 1800 *NHC1*—Sally da. Robert & Mary (Law) Brown.

4 ELIAS, b c. 1772, bp 22 Oct 1796 (æ. 24) *NHx*, d 11 June 1806 æ. 34 *NHT1*; m 15 Oct 1800 *NHC1*—Mary da. Robert & Mary (Law) Brown, bp 19 Apr 1778 *NHC1*.

i Elias Carpenter, b 24 Oct 1801 *F*, d 11 Nov 1883 æ. 82-1 *NHV*; m 23 Dec 1834 (at Madison)—Louisa Tryon.

ii Henry, b 15 Sep 1803 *NHT1*, d 17 Feb 1885 *NHT1*, æ. 81-5 *NHV*; m Azuba K. Tryon, b 22 Sep 1816 *NHT1*, d 15 July 1881 *NHT1*,

5 LOIS, b 17 May 1774 *F*, bp 22 Oct 1796 (æ. 22) *NHx*, d 8 Aug 1863 æ. 89 *NHT1*; m 27 Oct 1796 *NHx*—Joseph Trowbridge.

6 EUNICE, b [17 May 1774], d 11 Oct 1869 æ. 95-5 *NHT1*; m (1) William Harwood; m (2) 28 July 1798 *NHC1*—Robert Brown.

7 PATTY.

8 JOSEPH, b 24 Jan 1779 *NHV*, bp 14 Sep 1803 *NHx*, d 19 Feb 1814 æ. 35 *ColR*; m 30 Oct 1799 *NHV*—Sally da. Nehemiah & Polly Higgins, bp 14 Sep 1803 *NHx*.

i Elias Howard, b 27 Mar 1800 *NHV*, d 27 July 1800 *NHV*.

ii Rebecca, b 19 Aug 1802 *NHV*, bp 14 Sep 1803 (æ. 0-14) *NHx*.

iii Horace, b 29 July 1804 *NHV*, d 18 Apr 1881 æ. 76-8-17 *NHV*; m.

iv Jeremiah Townsend, b 12 Nov 1806 *NHV*.

v John Joseph, b Sep 1809 *NHV*.

9 JAIRUS BRADLEY, b c. 1781, bp 22 Oct 1796 (æ. 16) *NHx*.

10 ELI, b 11 Apr 1784 *F*, d 21 Nov 1848 æ. 65 *NHT1*; m 5 June 1808 *NHV*—Grace da. Henry & Hannah (Lewis) Peck, b 2 Dec 1786 *F*, d 6 Jan 1865; 10 children, of whom:

i Charles E., b 4 Feb 1810 *NHV*; res. Washington, D. C.

ii Elisha Peck, b 19 Nov 1811 *NHV*, d 5 Oct 1836 æ. 25 (at Barbadoes, W. I.) *NHT1*.

iii Hannah, b [Jan 1820], d 1 June 1820 æ. 0-4 *NHT1*.

iv Lewis, b 2 Oct 1821 *F*; m 1848 Mary E. Lee.

v Virginia; m William Pettit of Redlands, Calif.

FAM. 13. JOHN & ELIZABETH [?FARRAND] MIX:

1 WILLIAM, bp 6 Oct 1782 *NHC2*.

2 NATHANIEL FARRAND, bp 6 Oct 1782 *NHC2*; m 27 Oct 1796 *N*

HSupCt—Ann —— of Philadelphia, Pa.; she div. him 1805.

3 FRANCIS, bp 6 Oct 1782 *NHC2*.

4 ANNA, b 14 June 1781 *F*, bp 6 Oct 1782 *NHC2*, d 26 Dec 1821 *F*, 28 Dec æ. 44 (*NHC1*) *NHV*; m 24 Sep 1800 Ezra Hotchkiss.

FAM. 13. JOHN & REBECCA (HAYES) MIX:

5 ELIZABETH, d 1844; m William Reed of Belle Isle, N. Y.

FAM. 14. JONATHAN & NANCY (SEARS) MIX:

1 JAMES PECK, b 2 Aug 1778 *F*, bp 30 July 1780 *NHC2*; rem. to South America.

2 ELIJAH, b 17 June 1780 *F*, bp 30 July 1780 *NHC2*; m Maria Cooper of Virginia.

3 CLARISSA, b 8 Sep 1782 *F*, bp 15 Sep 1782 *NHC2*, d 1812; m 25 June 1800 *NHC1*—Ebenezer Townsend.

4 JONATHAN MARVIN, b 28 Sep 1784 *F*, d 11 July 1785 æ. 0-10 *NHT1*.

5 MARVIN PECK, b 9 June 1786 *F*, d 8 Feb 1839; m.

6 NANCY MARIA, b 13 Sep 1788 *F*, bp 7 Dec 1788 *NHC2*, d 5 Oct 1789 *F*, 4 Oct æ. 1-0-10 *NHT1*.

7 JONATHAN LUCIUS, b 1 June 1790 *F*, bp 1 Aug 1790 *NHC2*, d May 1805 æ. 15 (at Guadeloupe, W. I.) *NHT1*.

8 MARY ELIZA, b 16 Mar 1793 *F*, bp 9 June 1793 *NHC2*.

9 WILLIAM AUGUSTUS, b 6 Apr 1795 *F*, bp 2 Aug 1795 *NHC2*.

10 JULIA ANN, b 23 June 1797 *F*, d 1849; m 20 June 1817 Gustavus Loomis.

FAM. 14. JONATHAN & MARY ELIZABETH (PHIPPS) MIX:

11 ADELINE NANCY, b 18 Apr 1805 *NHT1*, d 20 Jan 1883 *NHT1*, æ. 77-9-2 *HV*; m Elihu Blake.

FAM. 15. ELDAD & MARY (HITCHCOCK) MIX:

1 JAMES HITCHCOCK, b c. 1782, bp 1 Oct 1784 *NHC2*.

2 MARY, bp 1 Oct 1784 *NHC2*.

3 MEDAD, bp 30 Dec 1787 *NHC2*.

4 PHEBE, bp 28 Mar 1790 *NHC2*.

5 MEDAD, bp 18 Mar 1792 *NHC2*.

6 HARRIET, bp 15 Sep 1793 *NHC2*.

FAM. 16. NATHANIEL & THANKFUL (ALLING) MIX:

1 JESSE BRADLEY, b 23 Dec 1774 *NHV*, bp 1 Jan 1775 *NHC1*; m 9 Apr 1796 *NoBC2*—Rebecca da. Amos & Elizabeth (Alling) Gilbert, who d 1852.

2 LOIS, b 22 Aug 1776 *NHV*, bp 1 Sep 1776 *NHC1*, d 29 June 1842 æ. 65 *NHT1*; m 25 Sep 1796 *NHx*—Joseph Trowbridge.

3 ELI, b 7 Sep 1778 *NHV*, bp 13 Sep 1778 *NHC1*, d 23 Sep 1842 æ. 64 *NHT1*, 24 Sep (insane, suicide) *NHV*; m Nancy da. Amos & Elizabeth Ann (Alling) Gilbert, bp 27 May 1781 *NHC2*, d 7 Jan 1839 æ. 57 *NHT1*, (insane) *NHV*.

4 SARAH, b 23 Dec 1779 *NHV*, bp 29 Oct 1780 *NHC1*, d 11 June 1825 æ. 45 *NHT1*.

FAM. 17. ELDAD & LYDIA (BEACH) MIX:

1 TITUS, b 14 Feb 1757 *WatV*, k. in batttle of Harlem, 18 Sep 1776 *WatV*.

2 AMOS, b 2 Feb 1759 *WatV;* m 4 Jan 1784 *CC*—Clarinda Barnes.

3 SAMUEL, b 17 Jan 1761 *WatV;* Census (Wat) 1-3-1; m 13 Dec 1781 *WatV*, *CC*—Mary da. Henry & Esther (Smith) Hotchkiss, b 29 Sep 1760 *WV;* had issue.

4 LEVI, b 15 Sep 1763 *WatV;* Census (Wat) 1-0-1; m 7 Sep 1789 *WatV*—Eunice da. Asahel & Sarah (Burr) Andrews, b 17 May 1768 *WV*.

5 SYBIL, b 13 Apr 1767 *WatV;* m 15 Dec 1783 *WatV*—Gershom Olds.

6 URI, b 23 July 1769 *WatV*.

7 PHILO, b 28 Oct 1773 *WatV;* m 30 Nov 1797 *WatV*—Anna da. Prindle & Ann (Mix) Hall.

8 LYDIA, b 13 Apr 1777 *WatV*.

9 SARAH, b 2 Jan 1782 *WatV*.

FAM. 18. CALEB & PEGGY (PERKINS) MIX (family incomplete):

1 LEVERETT, b c. 1770, d 13 July 1816 æ. 46 (*HT2 list*); Capt.; m 22 Oct 1793 *NHC1*—Sarah da. Moses & Eunice (Potter) Ford, bp 17 Dec 1774 *NHC2*.

2 GATES, b c. 1779, d 5 May 1804 æ. 25 (*HT2 list*).

3 SALLY, b [Jan 1786], d 12 May 1786 æ. 0-4 *NHC1*.

FAM. 18. CALEB & PHILA (POTTER) MIX:

4 CALEB, b 8 Nov 1791 *NHT1*, d 13 Dec 1768 *NHT1;* m 21 Sep 1815 *NHV*—Ann Sophia Pinto.

5 JAMES, b c. 1793.

FAM. 19. ELISHA & MEHITABEL (BEECHER) MIX:

1 ELIHU, b c. 1776, bp 27 Aug 1780 *NHC1*, d 16 Jan 1807 æ. 31 (at Honolulu) *NHT1*; 15 Jan 1808 æ. 32 *ConnH;* m 8 July 1801 *NHC1*—Nancy da. Thomas & Margaret (Macumber) Atwater, b 15 Jan 1783 *F*, d 19 Apr 1837 æ. 53 *NHT1;* she m (2) John Richards.

i Edward Augustus, b [29 May 1802], d 6 June 1882 æ. 80-0-8 *HV;* m Emily Townsend.

ii Elihu Leonard, b 14 May 1807 *NHT1*, d 24 Dec 1892 *NHT1;* m Ann Maria Barney.

2 LOIS, b c. 1779, bp 27 Aug 1780 *NHC1*, d 1817 æ. 38; m 20 May 1799 *NHC1*—Caleb Brintnall.

3 MEHITABEL, bp 26 Oct 1783 *NHC1*, d 5 Dec 1841 æ. 57 *NHT1;* m 28 Apr 1803 *NHC1*—Miles Gorham.

4 CONTENT, bp 1 Mar 1789 *NHC1*, d 5 Nov 1865 æ. 76 *NHT1;* m (1) Francis Bulkeley; m (2) 1821 Caleb Brintnall.

5 ELISHA, bp 3 Nov 1793 *NHC1*, d 1813 æ. 19 (at sea) *NHT1*.

6 HENRY, b c. 1797, bp 4 Feb 1803 *NHC1*, d 12 Aug 1821 æ. 24 (at W. Indies) *NHT1*.

7 MARY ANN, b [18 Jan 1800], bp 4 Feb 1803 *NHC1*, d 22 May 1870 æ. 70-4-4 *NHV;* m Leverett Pardee.

FAM. 20. THOMAS & REBECCA (WOODING) MIX:

1 **Mabel**, b c. 1778, bp 24Aug 1783 *NHC2;* m (1) 5 Jan 1796 *NHC1*—Jonathan Booth; m (2) 3 July 1842 *HV*—William Shares.
2 **Sene** [Asenath], b c. 1780, bp 24 Aug 1783 *NHC2;* m 13 Apr 1796 *NHC1*—Ezra Cooper.
3 **Zina**, b c. 1780, bp 24 Aug 1783 *NHC2*, d 18 June 1823 æ. 43 *HT2;* m Lois da. David & Sarah (Wooding) Warner, wid. Phinehas Austin, bp 1 Oct 1780 *NHC2*, d 3 July 1852 æ. 72 *HT2.*
i Jane, b [16 May 1814], d 12 June 1902 æ. 88-0-27 *HV;* m 17 Apr 1836 *HV*—William H. Turner,
ii Charles, d 17 Nov [———] æ. 58 *HT2;* m Catherine L Alling, who d 22 June 1850 æ. 23 *HT2.*
4 **Benjamin**, b 10 Aug 1782 *F*, bp 24 Aug 1783 *NHC2*, d 30 Aug 1862 æ. 80 *HV*, *HT2;* m (1) Elizabeth da. Caleb & Lois (Dorman) Alling, b c. 1789, d 11 Jan 1810 *F;* m (2) 12 Apr 1810 *F*—Betsey da. Ithiel & Rebecca (Bradley) Potter, b c. 1791, d 30 Jan 1871 æ. 79 *HT2.*
(By 1): *i* Rebecca Elizabeth, b 1 Jan 1810 *F*, d 14 Mar 1890 *F;* m 28 Oct 1833 Walter Nichols.
(By 2): *ii* Ithiel Potter, b 4 Feb 1811 *F.*
iii Grace, b 31 Aug 1812 *HV*, d 5 Mar 1907 æ. 94-6-5 *HV;* m Alfred Howarth.
iv Eliza, b 1816 *HT2*, 27 Aug 1816 *F*, d 1908 *HT2;* m George W. Bradley.
v Benjamin, b 10 Sep 1818 *F.*
vi Henry, b 8 July 1821, d 24 June 1895 æ. 74 *HT2;* m 9 Nov 1842 *HV*—Louisa Warner.
vii James Perry, b 9 Feb 1824; m Hannah da. Minot & Rebecca (Hotchkiss) Collins, b 16 Aug 1830 (at B) *HV*, d 16 Mar 1909 æ. 78-7-0 *HV.*
viii Norris Bennett, b 3 Feb 1826 *F*, d 28 Mar 1903 æ. 77-1-25 *HV;* m Maria Hendrick.
ix Frances Betsey, b 26 Dec 1829 *HV*, d 23 Jan 1917 *HV;* m William Potter.
x Dwight Walter, b 1834 *HT2*, 19 Dec 1834 *F*, d 1915 *HT2.*
5 **Stephen**, b c. 1784, d s. p. 28 June 1823 æ. 39 *HT2.*
6 **Thomas**, b 1786 *F*, d 1826 *F;* m 1811 *F*—Thankful da. Jonah & Mary [Ford] Ford, b c. 1789, d 9 July 1868 æ. 79 *HV.*
i Major, b 1812 *F*, bp 1819 *HC2.*
ii Mary Amelia, b 1814 *F*, bp 1819 *HC2*, d 10 Apr 1889; m Edward Hall.
iii Albert, b 26 Jan 1816 *F*, bp 1819 *HC2*, d 9 Apr 1887: res. Macon, Ga.; m 24 Jan 1852 *NHx*—Maria da. William & Maria (Miles) Townsend.
iv Juliette Maria, b 1818 *F*, bp 1823 *HC2*, d 1896; m Edward Ensign.
v Thomas William, b 1820 *F*, bp 1819 *HC2*, d 9 Apr 1856 (at Macon, Ga.) *F.*

Fam. 21. Samuel & Susanna (Humiston) Mix:

1 BENJAMIN, b 14 Aug 1796 *NoHV*, d 11 Feb 1844 *NoHD*.

2 SAMUEL, b 11 Oct 1798 *NoHV*, d 15 May 1854 æ. 56 *NoHT3*; m 4 June 1823 *NoHC*—Melinda da. William & Thankful (Wolcott) Shares, bp 1803 *HC2*, d 7 Jan 1887 æ. 84 *NoHT3*.

3 LYDIA, b 1 Feb 1801 *NoHV*, d 24 May 1833 æ. 32 *NoHT1*; m Leverett Hotchkiss.

MIX. MISCELLANEOUS. HANNAH bp (adult) 2 Feb 1784 *NHC2*...... GRACE, b 12 Mar 1786 *F*, d 6 Sep 1813 *F*; m Sep 1808 *F*—James Gilbert.... CHESTER d 20 Jan 1821 æ. 40 (*NHx*) *NHV*......JOSEPH d 14 Apr 1820 æ. 66 (*NHC2*) *NHV*......WID. RUTH d 3 Dec 1820 æ. 61 (*NHC2*) *NHV*.

MOFFAT. ALEXANDER & Rachel had a da. Elizabeth bp 13 Oct 1771 (sponsor, Jacob Barney) *NHx*.

MONTCALM. MOSES, Census (NH) 1-3-4; m Amy da. Moses & Ann (Johnson) Beecher, bp (adult) 20 Nov 1785 *NHx*.

1 POLLY, bp 18 Sep 1784 *NHx*.

2 SALLY, bp 18 Sep 1784 *NHx*.

3 JOHN, bp 18 Sep 1784 *NHx*; m 22 July 1807 *RoxburyC*—Betsey da. David & Dinah (Welton) Punderson, b c. 1786, d 8 June 1829 æ. 43 *Roxbury*.

4 MOSES, bp 20 Nov 1785 *NHx*, d before 1827; m Sally ——— .

5 FRANCIS, bp 3 Aug 1788 *NHx*; m 11 Dec 1807 *NHC1*—Polly Ord.

6 AMY; m 25 June 1807 *NHx*—William Buchanan.

7 ANTHONY, bp 13 Apr 1794 *NHx*.

MONTCALM. MISCELLANEOUS. AMELIA m 31 May 1801 *NHC1*—David Ewen.

MORE. MISCELLANEOUS. WILLIAM m Eleanor ———, who m (2) 7 July 1766 *NHV*—John Miller. Child: Mary Ann, b 13 Sep 1764 *NHV*...... FRANCIS, b c. 1756, bu. 11 June 1797 æ. 41 *NHx*; Census (NH) 1-0-5; m 3 Apr 1782 *WdC*—Eliphal da. William & Eliphal (Hine) Hotchkiss.

MORGAN. FAM. 1. JOSEPH, d 8 Aug 1752 *CC*; m (1) Susanna ———, who d 27 Sep 1728 *WV*; m (2) 9 Jan 1729 *WV*—Jemima da. Nathan & Sarah (Beecher) Benham, wid. Joel Prindle, b 21 Sep 1700 *NHV*, d 8 Aug 1752 *CC*.

(By 1): 1 SUSANNA; m 27 July 1741 *WV*—Benjamin Andrews.

2 LYDIA, b c. 1719, d 8 May 1793 *CC*, 7 Mar æ. 74 *CT1*; m (1) 13 June 1744 *WV*—Isaac Ives; m (2) Henry Hotchkiss.

(By 2): 3 CONTENT, b 1 Sep 1730 *WV*, d 13 Feb 1776 *CC*; m 3 Apr 1750 *WV*—Amos Andrews.

4 ABRAHAM, b 9 Sep 1732 *WV*; Census (Hampton, N. Y.) 2-0-4; m 5 Feb 1755 *WV*—Hannah da. Daniel & Hannah (Payne) Luddington, b 4 Nov 1734 *WV*.

i David, b 28 Jan 1756 *WV*; Census (Hampton, N. Y.) 1-1-3; m 23 Sep 1779 *WV*, *CC*—Mary da. Joseph & Abigail (Beecher) Rowe, b 28 Jan 1753 *WV*. A child, Ezra Randall, bp 23 Feb 1783 *CC*.

ii Joseph, b Dec [——] *WV*; Census (Hampton, N. Y.) 1-1-4; m 25 Nov 1779 *WV*, *CC*—Eunice da. Ambrose & Martha (Munson) Doolittle, b 21 June 1758 *WV*. A

child, Eliab, b 19 Dec 1780 *CV*.
iii Hannah, b 31 Mar [——] *WV*.
iv Esther, b 2 Dec [——] *WV*, d 4 Jan 1766 *WV*.
v Abraham, b 12 Feb 1770 *WV*, bp 24 Feb 1770 *CC*.
vi Esther, b 25 Apr 1773 *WV*, bp 2 May 1773 *CC*.
vii Lydia, b 21 Nov 1775 *WV*, bp 26 Nov 1775 *CC*.
5 DAVID, b 12 May 1734 *WV*, d 27 Sep 1755 *F&IWRolls*.
6 CHARLES, b 13 July 1743 *WV*.

MORGAN. FAM. 2. JACOB, b c. 1750, bu. 1 June 1811 æ. 62 (at WH) *NHx;* Census (NH) 1-1-2; m (1) 16 Nov 1774 *WdC*—Chloe da. David & Rachel (Sperry) Johnson, b 6 May 1757 *NHV*, d 8 Dec 1787 *WdC;* m (2) 23 May 1789 *NHx*—Elizabeth Upson, wid. Timothy Prout Bonticou.

1 GEORGE W., b c. 1777, d 5 Apr 1827 æ. 50 *WdT1;* m Patty ——, bp (as widow) 1828 *WdC*, d 4 Jan 1849 æ. 66 *WdT1*.
i Almira, b c. 1803, d 13 June 1867 æ. 64 *WdD;* m Joel Perkins.
ii John, b c. 1811, d 10 Nov 1847 æ. 36 *WdD*.
iii Samuel O., b c. 1815, d 12 Mar 1859 æ. 44 *WdD;* m Louisa ——.
2 (perhaps) WEALTHY ANN, bp (as da. of John) 29 Aug 1784 (sponsors, Elias Shipman & —— Fish) *NHx;* probably the "Nancy" who m 9 Apr 1806 *WdC*—Thomas Bevins of Bridgeport.

MORGAN. MISCELLANEOUS. OWEN m 9 Apr 1650 *NHV*—Wid. Joan Bryan; rem. to Norwalk......MARGERY d 28 Apr 1690 æ. 88 *WV*......JERUSHA m 22 Apr 1707 *WV*—Nicholas Street......JOHN & Anna had children, recorded *WV:* 1 Anna, b 9 Oct 1763; perhaps m May 1794 or 1784 David Roberts. 2 Asahel, b 9 Jan 1765. 3 Deborah, b 3 Feb 1767. 4 Sarah, b 2 Jan 1769......ISAAC of Wd m 26 Dec 1807 *OC*—Sarah Downs of WH.

MORRILL. HENRY, of NH, d 1665; m Blanche ——.
1 ELIZABETH; m 3 Jan 1665 *NHV*—John Butler.
2 SARAH, b 17 Nov 1650 *NHV;* m 1 Jan 1667 *NHV*—William Collins.

MORRILL. TIMOTHY & Anna had a s. William, bp 29 Apr 1778 *NHx*.

†**MORRIS.** FAM. 1. THOMAS, d 21 July 1673 *NHV;* m Elizabeth ——, who d 1681.

1 HANNAH, b 14 Mar 1641 *NHC1* [1641/2]; m [1662] *NHV*—Thomas Lupton.
2 ELIZABETH, bp 20 Dec 1643 *NHC1*.
3 JOHN, bp 12 Mar 1645 *NHC1*, d soon.
4 JOHN, bp 8 Mar 1646 *NHC1*, d 10 Dec 1711 æ. 65 *NHT1;* Sgt.; m 12 Aug 1669 *NHV*—Hannah da. James & Mary [Lewen] Bishop, b 29 May 1651 *NHV*, bp 1 June 1651 *NHC1*, d 12 June 1710 æ. 59 *NHT1*.
i Mary, b 19 June 1670 *NHV*, d [1670] *NHV*.
ii Hannah, b 10 Aug 1671 *NHV;* m (1) Joseph Smith; m (2) 26 Feb 1717/8 *NHV*—Joseph Sackett.

iii Mary, b 9 Sep 1673 *NHV*, d 8 Sep 1743 æ. 70 *EHT;* m John Hemingway.

iv Elizabeth, b 1675 *NHV;* m (1) William Maltby; m (2) John Davenport.

v Thomas, b 26 Apr 1679 *NHV*, d young.

vi Abigail, b 22 Aug 1683 *NHV*, d before 1729; m 14 Feb 1705/6 *NHV*—James Peck.

vii Desire, b 29 Mar 1687 *NHV*, bp 12 Feb 1686/7 *NHCl;* m 4 Mar 1707/8 *NHV*—Stephen Howell.

5 Eleazer, bp 29 Oct 1648 *NHCl*, d after 1717, before 1725; m Ann da. Jeremiah & Mary Osborn, b 6 Apr 1663 *NHV*, d 10 Dec 1726 *NHV*.

i Rebecca, b 20 June 1682 *NHV*, bp 27 May 1694 *NHCl*, d 1729; m 23 Dec 1702 *NHV*—Nathaniel Hitchcock,

ii John, b 8 Oct 1684 *NHV*, bp 27 May 1694 *NHCl*, d s. p. 19 Nov 1744 *NHV*, æ. 60 *EHT;* m 24 Dec 1713 *NHV*—Elizabeth da Samuel & Sarah (Chidsey) Alling, b Nov 1691 *NHV*, d 5 Apr 1767 æ. 77 *NHT;* she m (2) 12 June 1754 Isaac Dickerman.

iii Anna, b c. 1686, bp 27 May 1694 *NHCl*, d 19 Oct 1743 æ. 57 *EHT;* m 30 Dec 1708 *NHV*—Samuel Smith.

iv James, b c. 1689, bp 27 May 1694 *NHCl*, d June 1725 *NH Pro;* m 24 Feb 1714/5 *NHV*—Abigail da. John & Abigail (Alsop) Rowe, b 13 Aug 1689 *NHV*. **FAM. 3.**

v Eleazer, b c. 1691, bp 27 May 1694 *NHCl*, d Dec 1740; m Mercy da. Alling & Sarah (Thompson) Ball, b c. 1693; she m (2) 10 Jan 1760 *EHC*—Deodate Davenport. **FAM. 4.**

vi Jemima, b c. 1694, bp 27 May 1694 *NHCl*, d s. p.

vii Adonijah, bp 14 Dec 1696 *NHCl*, d c. 1751; res. Durham; m Sarah da. John & Abigail (Bradley) Moulthrop, b 10 Oct 1701 *NHV;* she m (2) Simeon Coe. **FAM. 5.**

6 Thomas, b 3 Oct 1651 *NHV*, bp 5 Oct 1651 *NHCl*, d young.

7 Ephraim, b 3 Oct 1651 *NHV*, bp 5 Oct 1651 *NHCl*, d 6 Oct 1651 *NHV*.

8 Joseph, b 25 Mar 1656 *NHV*, bp 25 Mar 1656 *NHCl;* m 2 June 1680 *NHV*—Esther da. John & Elizabeth Winston, b 11 Nov 1662 *NHV*, d after 1747; she m (2) Nathaniel Sperry.

i Thomas, b 23 Mar 1681/2 *NHV*, d 17 Apr 1726 *NHV;* m 25 May 1708 *NHV*—Sarah da. Matthew & Sarah (Peck) Gilbert, b 10 Mar 1685/6 *NHV;* she m (2) William Johnson. **FAM. 6.**

ii Esther, b 3 Sep 1684 *NHV*, d 19 Aug 1751 æ. 65 *NHTl;* m (1) 30 Jan 1706/7 *NHV*—John Peck; m (2) 14 Feb 1716/7 *NHV*—John Mix; m (3) Joseph Smith.

iii Sarah, b c. 1686; m 3 Aug 1710 *NHV*—Joseph Beecher.

iv Joseph, b c. 1688; m (1) 4 Mar 1713 *BdV*—Lydia da. Thomas & Margaret Harrison; m (2) Elizabeth, da.

Edward & Esther (Wheadon) Johnson. **FAM. 7.**

v Ephraim, b Jan 1694 *NHV*, d 15 Feb 1778 æ. 84 *NHC1*; m 24 Jan 1716/7 *NHV*—Ruth da. Ebenezer & Abigail (Dickerman) Sperry, b 30 May 1695 *NHV*, d 10 Feb 1773 æ. 77 *NHC1*. **FAM. 8.**

vi Dorothy, b Sep 1695 *NHV*, d 1751; m James Denison.

vii Benjamin, b Apr 1699 *NHV*, d before 1779; m 17 Nov 1731 *NHV*—Mehitabel da. John & Sarah (Cooper) Munson, b 17 Oct 1709 *NHV*, d 26 Feb 1779 æ. 70 *NHC1*. **FAM. 9.**

viii Mary. b June 1702 *NHV*, bp 6 June 1725 *NHC1*; m 9 May 1727 *NHV*—Joel Munson.

ix Samuel, b May 1705 *NHV*, bp 18 Jan 1736 *DC*; rem. to Warren; m c. 1729 Margaret Smith. **FAM. 10.**

FAM. 2. JOHN MORRIS, perhaps nephew of Thomas (FAM. 1); rem. to Newark, N. J.; d 1675; m (1) Ann ——— , who d 4 Dec 1664 *NHV*; m (2) 29 Mar 1666 *NHV*—Elizabeth da. Richard Harrison, wid. Henry Lines & Thomas Lampson, who d between 22 Oct 1689 & 24 Feb 1692/3.

(By 2): 1 JOHN, b 16 Dec 1666 *NHV*, d 22 Oct 1749 in 83 yr. *NewarkT*; m (1) Sarah [?Crane], b c. 1665, d 3 Sep 1739 æ. c. 74; m (2) Mary [da. Samuel & Mary (Ward) Harrison, wid. Peter Condit], b c. 1677, d 10 Dec 1761.

2 PHILIP.

FAM. 3. JAMES & ABIGAIL (ROWE) MORRIS:

1 JEMIMA, b 27 Dec 1715 *NHV*, bp 1716 *NHC1*, d s. p?

2 DANIEL, b 4 June 1718 *NHV*, bp c. June 1718 *NHC1*; res. Salisbury, Ct., & Gt. Barrington, Mass.; m 15 Oct 1742 *NHV*—Elizabeth da. Thomas & Abigail (Potter) Smith.

i Abigail, b 13 Aug 1742 *NHV*; m (intention) 23 Feb 1762 *Gt. Barrington*—Eliathah Rew.

ii Elizabeth, b 19 Oct 1743 *NHV*.

iii John, b 12 Oct 1745 *NHV*.

iv Jemima, b 25 Aug 1747 *NHV*, d Dec 1800 *NorfolkC*.

v Eleazer, b 25 May 1749 *NHV*.

vi Anna, b c. 1752, d 25 Nov 1802; m William Elton of Burlington.

vii Daniel, b 1754 *SalisburyV*.

viii Lois, b 11 Mar 1756 *SalisburyV*.

ix Sarah, b 14 Sep 1758 *SalisburyV*.

x Mary, b c. 1760, d 1831; m 1779 James Dickson of Erie Co., Pa.

xi Esther; m Benjamin Dickson of Ripley, N. Y.

xii Levi.

3 ABIGAIL, b 10 Jan 1719/20 *NHV*, bp Feb 1719/20 *NHC1*; m David Gaylord of Farm.

4 JAMES, bp 21 Jan 1721/2 *DurhamC*, d 6 June 1789 æ. 68 *LV*; m 8 Apr 1751 *LT*—Phebe (Barnes) Barnes. Descendants in Morris, Ct.

5 AMOS, bp c. Oct 1723 *NHCI*, d 30 Dec 1801 æ. 79 *EHT*, æ. 78 *EHC;* Dea.; Capt.; Census (EH) 1-1-2; m (1) 27 June 1745 *NHV*, 26 June *BdC*—Lydia da. Hezekiah & Lydia (Clark) Camp, b c. 1727, d 1 Sep 1777 æ. 50 *EHT;* m (2) 4 Mar 1778 *EHC*—Lois da. Silas & Eunice (Cook) Clark, wid. Joel Clark, b 20 Nov 1730 *WV*, d 5 Aug 1781 æ. 48 *EHC;* m (3) 8 Mar 1784 *EHC*—Esther, wid. Benjamin Smith, b c. 1736, d 4 Oct 1813 æ. 77 *EHC.*

(By 1): *i* Lydia, b June 1746 *F*, bp 2 Sep 1764 *EHC*, d c. 1773; m 15 May 1771 *EHC*—David Beecher.

ii Amy, b 19 Feb 1747/8 *NHV*, bp 2 Sep 1764 *EHC;* m (1) 12 May 1768 *EHC*—Asa Bradley; m (2) Apr 1783 *EHC*—Eliphalet Fuller.

iii Amos, b 13 Mar 1749 *NHV* [1749/50], bp 2 Sep 1764 *EHC*, d 11 Oct 1823 æ. 74 *EHT;* Census (EH) 1-2-8; m 20 Dec 1778 *EHV*—Betsey da. Richard & Susan (Deluce) Woodward, b c. 1748, d 30 Oct 1824 æ. 76 *EHT*, 31 Oct *EHC.* **FAM. 11.**

iv Sarah, b 18 Mar 1752 *NHV*, bp 2 Sep 1764 *EHC;* m (1) 6 Nov 1771 *EHC*—Gershom Scott; m (2) 1782 *EHC*—Edward Brockway.

v John, b 22 July 1754 *NHV*, d 21 Sep 1756 *NHV*, 27 Sep æ. 3 *EHT.*

vi Elizabeth, b 6 Mar 1757 *NHV*, d 25 July 1760 *NHV*, æ. 4 *EHT.*

vii John, b 2 Sep 1759 *NHV*, bp 2 Sep 1764 *EHC*, d 22 June 1844; Census (EH) 1-3-3; m 8 Aug 1779 *EHC*—Desire da. Nicholas & Desire (Thompson) Street, b 15 Aug 1761 *NHV.* **FAM. 12.**

viii Elizabeth, b 13 Oct 1761 *NHV*, bp 2 Sep 1764 *EHC*, d 20 Aug 1849 æ. 88 *EHT;* m 20 Jan 1780 *EHC*—Stephen Woodward.

ix Esther, b 24 Oct 1763 *NHV*, bp 2 Sep 1764 *EHC;* m 10 Feb 1783 *EHC*—William Collins.

x Asahel, b 14 Feb 1766 *NHV*, bp 21 May 1766 *EHC;* d July 1830; rem. to Washington Co., N. Y.; m 14 Feb 1795 Catherine Van Ness.

xi Lorinda, b 4 June 1768 *NHV*, bp 31 July 1768 *EHC;* m 11 Nov 1788 *EHC*—Samuel Hathaway.

xii Anna, b c. 1773; m 13 Nov 1797 *EHC*—Bela Farnham.

FAM. 4. ELEAZER & MERCY (BALL) MORRIS:

1 STEPHEN, b c. 1718, d 28 Oct 1775 æ. 57 *EHT*, æ. c. 60 *EHC;* m 18 June 1741 *NHV*—Esther da. Thomas & Esther (Tuttle) Robinson, b 7 July 1720 *EHV*, d 17 Feb 1790 æ. 69 *EHT*, *EHC.*

i William, d s. p.

ii Hannah, b 1 Jan 1745/6 *NHV*, d 6 Aug 1751 æ. 6 *EHT.*

iii Samuel, d s. p.

iv Hannah, b c. 1751, d 17 Feb 1787 æ. 34 *EHT;* m 1 Jan 1771 *EHC*—Samuel Hemingway.

2 **Sarah**, b c. 1720; m 19 Dec 1739 *NHV*—Seth Heaton.

3 **Mercy**, b c. 1725, d Oct 1801 æ. 77 *NorfolkC;* m Isaac Holt.

4 **Mary**, b c. 1725, d 1736 æ. 11 *EHV*, 5 July 1737 æ. 12 *EHT*.

5 **Jacob**, b c. 1730, d 12 Mar 1734 æ. 4 *EHT*.

6 **Mabel**, b c. 1734, d 20 July 1825 æ. 92 *EHT;* m 2 Nov 1757 *EHC*—Jehiel Forbes.

7 **Mary**, b c. 1740, d s. p. 15 July 1765 æ. 25 *EHT;* m Samuel Davenport.

FAM. 5. Adonijah & Sarah (Moulthrop) Morris:

1 **Adonijah**, b 26 Oct 1723 *DurhamV*, bp 29 Dec 1723 *DurhamC*.

2 **John**, b 15 Nov 1725 *DurhamV*, bp 12 Dec 1725 *DurhamC*.

3 **Anna**, b 24 Feb 1728 *DurhamV*, bp 7 Apr 1728 *DurhamC*, d 15 Feb 1813; m 16 Jan 1746 Simeon Coe.

4 **Timothy**, b 27 Jan 1730 *DurhamV*, bp 8 Mar 1729/30 *DurhamC*.

FAM. 6. Thomas & Sarah (Gilbert) Morris:

1 **Esther**, b c. 1709, bp 23 Apr 1721 *NHCI*, d 12 Jan 1788 æ. 80 *HTI;* m 20 Aug 1743 *NHV*—Andrew Goodyear.

2 **Thomas**, b Mar 1712 *NHV*, bp 23 Apr 1721 *NHCI*, d after 1790; res. Kent; m Ruth. Family incomplete.

i Phebe, bp 7 Aug 1748 *KentC*.

ii Sarah, bp 7 Aug 1748 *KentC*.

iii Ruth, bp 5 Nov 1749 *KentC*.

iv Thomas, bp 28 July 1751 *KentC;* m 15 Nov 1774 Rachel Budd.

v Elizabeth, bp 5 Aug 1753 *KentC;* m 20 Dec 1770 *KentV*—Caleb Merin [?Morgan].

3 **Daniel**, b Apr 1715 *NHV*, bp 23 Apr 1721 *NHCI*, d 1 Mar 1792; res. Fairfield & Newtown; m (1) 19 July 1741 *FV*—Sarah da. Benjamin Fairweather, wid. Matthew Mackhard, who d 16 Apr 1761 *FV;* m (2) 29 Dec 1761 *FV*—Prudence Summers, wid. Curtis; m (3) Elizabeth ——— .

(By 1): *i* Mary, b 1 Dec 1742 *FV*, d 30 Nov 1776.

ii Sarah, b 1 Sep 1745 *FV*, d 21 Nov 1771.

iii Amos, b 30 Nov 1747 *F*, d 7 Dec 1747 *F*.

iv Daniel, b 8 Mar 1749 *F*, d 7 May 1749 *F*.

v Daniel, b 13 Dec 1750 *FV*, d 28 Mar 1828; res. Newtown; m 12 June 1774 Elizabeth Burritt.

vi James, b 14 June 1753 *FV;* m 19 Feb 1781 *Sup Ct*—Eunice ——— ; she div. him 1787.

vii Matthew McHard, b 25 July 1757 *FV*, d 3 Feb 1825; res. Wy; m Mehitabel Judson.

(By 2): *viii* Amos, b 28 Sep 1762 *FV*, d 2 Apr 1841; res. Bridgewater; m Eunice Clark.

4 **Amos**, b 26 Feb 1717/8 *NHV*, bp 23 Apr 1721 *NHCI*, d s. p. 1741.

5 **Asa**, b 20 Feb 1720/1 *NHV*, bp 23 Apr 1721 *NHCI*, d 1760; Lt.;

m 1 Mar 1758 *NHV*—Hannah da. Eleazer & Sarah (Rowe) Brown, b 19 June 1735 *NHV*, d 1 May 1824 æ. 93 *BT3;* she m (2) Daniel Tolles.

i Elizabeth, b [14 June 1758], d 14 Feb 1788 æ 29 *BT1*, æ. 29-7-29 *BD;* m Abraham Tolles.

ii Asa, b June 1760 *NHV*, d 11 July 1828 æ. 68 *BT3;* m Mary ——. **FAM. 13.**

6 SARAH, b 20 Dec 1723 *NHV*, bp 16 Feb 1723/4 *NHC1;* m 21 May 1752 *NHV*, *NHC2*—Joseph Mix.

7 ELIZABETH, b 9 Feb 1725/6 *NHV*, bp 21 Apr 1726 *NHC1*.

FAM. 7. JOSEPH & LYDIA (HARRISON) MORRIS:

1 JOSEPH, b 1 Jan 1714 *BdV*, d s. p. after 1736.

2 LYDIA, b 15 Oct 1715 *BdV;* m 27 Nov 1740 *BdV*—Samuel Linsley.

3 AARON, b 13 Mar 1718 *BdV*, d 1784; m 29 Nov 1744 *BdV*—Elizabeth Munroe.

4 MARY; m 20 Nov 1755 *BdV*—Nathaniel Wheadon.

FAM. 7. JOSEPH & ELIZABETH (JOHNSON) MORRIS:

5 ELIZABETH, d s. p.

6 TIMOTHY, bp 8 June 1735 *BdC;* m Chloe ——.

FAM. 8. EPHRAIM & RUTH (SPERRY) MORRIS:

1 ABIGAIL, b 31 Oct 1717 *NHV*, bp 7 Apr 1723 *NHC1*.

2 RUTH, b 27 Nov 1718 *NHV*, bp 7 Apr 1723 *NHC1*, d 23 Aug 1769 æ. 50 *NHC1*.

3 EPHRAIM, b 23 May 1721 *NHV*, bp 7 Apr 1723 *NHC1*, d 1792; Census (Danbury) 1-0-2; m Eunice ——, who d after 1803.

i Samuel, d 1792; Census (Danbury) 3-2-4; m Jerusha ——; had children: (1) Bethel, of Danbury; (2) Chauncey, of Canaan; (3) Edmund, of Poughkeepsie, N. Y.; (4) Amos, of Danbury; (5) Rebecca, m 1793 Levi Andrus; (6) Lucy, m Miles Hoyt; (7) Anna, m Benjamin Stiles.

ii Shadrach, b c. 1744, d 12 July 1831 æ. 87 *DanburyT;* Census (Danbury) 2-1-3; m Rachel ——, who d 17 Nov 1823 æ. 78-7 *DanburyT.* Children (incomplete): (1) Asher, d 1811; m Hannah da. Eliphalet & Abigail (Gray) Stevens, b 1774; (2) Elijah, b [5 Sep 1778], d 19 May 1831 æ. 52-8-14; m 8 Apr 1798 *DanburyV*—Olive da. Eliphalet & Abigail (Gray) Stevens, b 1776, d before 11 Apr 1834.

iii Jachin; res. 1802 Boston, Mass.

iv Ruth, m Dec 1791 *DanburyC*—Joseph Mead.

v Eunice, m Nathan Stewart of Litchfield.

vi Lydia, m 13 Dec 1774 *DanburyC*—Matthew Judd of Kent.

vii Rachel, m Mar 1789 *DanburyC*—Timothy Preston of Dover, N. Y.

4 EBENEZER, bp 1 Aug 1725 *NHC1*, d c. 1798; m (1) 28 Nov 1750 *NHV*, *WdC*—Mabel da. Zebulon & Sarah (Johnson) Carring-

ton; m (2) 11 Sep 1766 *WdC*—Rebecca [da. Lambert & Rebecca (Curtis) Johnson, wid. Benjamin Perkins, John Wilmot & Samuel] Thomas.

(By 1): *i* Major, b 16 Oct 1751 *NHV*, bp 24 Nov 1751 *WdC*, d 5 Sep 1811; Census (Wat) 1-4-4; m Elizabeth da. John & Sarah (Sanford) Hine, b c. 1754, d 9 Sep 1834. **FAM. 14.**

ii Hester, b 28 Feb 1753 *NHV*, bp 15 Apr 1753 *WdC*.

iii Abigail, b 1 Sep 1754 *NHV*, d Apr 1835 æ. 80 (*NHC1*) *NHV;* m 20 Mar 1776 *NHC1*—Miles Gorham.

iv Sarah, b 17 May 1756 *NHV*.

v Lydia, b 1 June 1757 *NHV*, d 4 Aug 1765 æ. 8 *NHC1*.

vi Amos, b 7 Oct 1759 *NHV;* Census (Wtn) 1-1-2.

5 Isaac, bp 3 Jan 1730/1 *NHC1;* m Hannah da. Jonathan & Mary (Chidsey) Gilbert, b 4 Sep 1733 *NHV*, d 28 Aug 1769 æ. 36 *NHC1*.

i Mary, bp 18 Feb 1759 *NHC1*.

ii Adonijah, bp 7 Mar 1762 *NHC1*.

iii Mabel, bp 13 May 1764 *NHC1*.

iv Isaac, bp 21 Sep 1766 *NHC1;* Census (Wtn) 1-0-0; m Phebe ——— . A child Hannah, b c. 1806 (P), d 7 Sep 1887 æ. 81 *NHV;* m Linus Preston.

v Lydia, bp 25 Sep 1768 *NHC1*.

FAM. 9. Benjamin & Mehitabel (Munson) Morris:

1 (perhaps) Peter, served in F&IW 1759; m 28 Jan 1759 *NHC1*—Ann Cooke.

2 Sarah, b 15 Mar 1737 *NHV;* m 14 Feb 1759 *NHC2*—Judah Thompson.

3 Elizabeth, b 10 Apr 1739 *NHV;* m 13 May 1759 *NHC2*—Thomas Humphreville.

4 John, b 9 Mar 1741/2 *NHV*, bp 9 May 1742 *NHC1*, d 24 Oct 1820 æ. 79 (*NHC1*) *NHV;* Census (NH) 2-1-3; (1) m Mary da. Jeremiah & Sarah (Cooper) Macumber, wid. Thomas Trowbridge, b c. 1748, d 1811; m (2) Chloe ——— , b c. 1766, d 18 Oct 1824 æ. 58 *NHT1*.

(By 1): *i* Mehitabel, b c. 1786, d 14 Feb 1849 æ. 63 *NHT1;* m John Gilbert.

ii Daughter, b c. 1790, d 21 Aug 1795 æ. 5 *NHC1*.

5 (perhaps) Benjamin, d after 1813; Census (Wd) 1-0-3; m Elizabeth ——— , who d after 1813. Children: (1) Sally; (2) Juliana. A Benjamin m 1 May 1783 *SupCt*—Abigail Ashburn of M & div. her 1786, she then being of Colebrook. A Benjaminn of Wtn m 27 Nov 1799 *HuntingtonC*—Rachel Frasier of Huntington.

FAM. 10. Samuel & Margaret (Smith) Morris (family incomplete):

1 Ann, bp 20 Feb 1737 *DC;* m Sep 1755 *WdC*—Eliphalet Beecher; res. Kent 1756.

2 Samuel, bp 13 Jan 1745 *WdC*.

3 (perhaps) EUNICE, m 12 Dec 1771 *KentV*—Philip Judd.

FAM. 11. AMOS & BETSEY (WOODWARD) MORRIS:

1 AMOS, b 27 July 1780 *EHV*, bp 20 July 1780 *EHC*; m Charlotte ———, who d 11 Dec 1815 æ. 32 *EHC*.

2 BETSEY, b 2 Nov 1781 *EHV*, d 11 June 1849; m 6 Sep 1801 *EHC* —Nicholas Street.

3 CLARISSA, b 6 July 1783 *EHV*; m 12 Nov 1802 *EHC*—Elnathan Street.

4 SUSAN, b 17 Oct 1784 *EHV*, *NHT1*, bp 31 Oct 1784 *EHC*, d 17 Feb 1854 *NHT1*; m (1) 17 Mar 1805 *EHC*—Willet Bradley; m (2) Eli Barnes: m (3) Jeremiah Atwater.

5 HARRIET, b 6 Apr 1786 *EHV*; m 27 Nov 1811 *EHC*—Lucas Hart of Burlington.

6 LYDIA C., b 18 June 1787 *EHV*.

7 LUCY, b 12 Apr 1789 *EHV*.

8 HEZEKIAH CAMP, b 15 Aug 1790 *EHV*, bp 29 Aug 1790 *EHC*, d 31 Oct 1791 *EHV*, "child" 1 Nov 1791 æ. 0-18 *EHC*.

FAM. 12. JOHN & DESIRE (STREET) MORRIS:

1 SALLY, b 20 Feb 1780 *EHV*, d 15 July 1793 æ. 14 *EHV*, æ. 13 *EHC*, 15 July 1792 (?) æ. 14 *EHT*.

2 JAMES, b 5 Jan 1782 *EHV*, bp 6 Jan 1782 *EHC*, d 26 Mar 1789 *EHV*, æ. 7 *EHC*, 27 Mar æ. 9 *EHT*.

3 JOHN, b 7 Nov 1783 *EHV*, bp 9 Nov 1783 æ. 0-0-3 *EHC*, d s. p.

4 WILLIAM, b 3 Oct 1785 *EHV*, bp [Oct 1785] *EHC*, d 17 Mar 1823 (Sackett's Harbor, N. Y.); m 4 Jan 1804 Sarah Durham.

5 STEPHEN, b 13 June 1787 *EHV*, bp 29 July 1787 *EHC*.

6 NANCY, b 28 May 1789 *EHV*, bp 7 June 1789 *EHC*; m 17 Sep 1812 (Deerfield, Mass.) Rodney Burt.

7 JAMES, b 25 June 1791 *EHR*, bp 24 July 1791 *EHC*; m (1) 20 June 1818 Rebecca Ludden; m (2) 11 July 1824 Elizabeth C. Judd.

8 SARAH, b 24 Feb 1793, bp 30 Mar 1794 *EHC*, d 4 Apr 1828; m 11 Mar 1819 Oliver Ackley.

9 HEZEKIAH, b 25 July 1796, bp 31 July 1796 *EHC*; rem. to Calif.

10 LORINDA, b 29 Aug 1798, bp 2 [Sep] 1798 *EHC*, d 24 June 1834; m 16 Jan 1822 Joseph Strong Kinsley.

11 ANSON, b 8 Oct 1802.

FAM. 13. ASA & MARY (———) MORRIS:

1 ELIZABETH; m Nathan Nettleton.

2 ASA, b c. 1785, d Sep 1852 æ. 67 (at Bastrop, Tex.) *WdD*; m 20 Mar 1818 Ann Riggs, who d 21 Feb 1845 æ. 56 (at Hartford) *WdD*.

3 ALANSON, b c. 1789, d 10 Aug 1812 (at Antigua, W. I.) æ. 23 *BT3*.

4 NATHAN RUEL, b c. 1792, d 9 Dec 1848 æ. 56 *BT3*; m 27 Dec 1820 *WdV*—Lucy da. David & Sarah (Andrews) Wooding, b c. 1796. d 9 Aug 1860 æ. 64 *BT3*.

5 ARVIL, d c. 1866: res. Wat; m Dec 1826 Caroline Castle.

FAM. 14. MAJOR & ELIZABETH (HINE) MORRIS:

1 BETSEY, b c. 1781, d 10 Dec 1803.

2 SHELDON, b c. 1783, d 6 Feb 1858; res. Sy; m Olive Hickox.

3 MILES, b 27 Apr 1785, d 26 Feb 1861; m (1) 1815 Katie Scott; m (2) Aug 1845 Mary (Cady) Riggs.

4 NEWTON, b 27 Apr 1785; m 27 Apr 1807 Molly da. Thelus Hotchkiss.

5 MEHITABEL, d 1862; m William Morgan.

6 AMOS, d 1872; m (1) 29 May 1816 Mary Atkins; m (2) 27 Nov 1833 Anna (Andrews) Hine.

MORRIS. MISCELLANEOUS. BENONI d 18 Feb 1777 *HuntingtonC*......RICHARD of M d Apr 1759; m 24 May 1721 *Newport x*—Jean da. John Eddy, who d 1767. Among their children were: (1) Margaret, b c. 1722, d 1 Sep 1785 æ. 63 *MD;* m Job Marchant; (2) Susanna, m Samuel Bassett; (3) John res. Ridgefield, m 12 Nov 1750 *WdC*—Sybil Newton; (4) George, b c. 1731, d 10 Mar 1776 æ. 45 *MD;* m Eunice Plumb; (5) Joseph, probably d 3 Jan 1778, *MD;* (6) Mercy, d 25 Mar 1778 *MD;* (7) probably Thomas who d 21 Apr 1777 *WV*, 22 Apr *CC*, "once of M" 4 May 1777 *MD*.

MORRISON. FAM. 1. ANDREW, d c. 1703; m 21 Oct 1687 *NHV*—Sarah da. William & Hannah (Eaton) Jones; she m (2) John Dudley.

1 SARAH, b 7 July 1689 *NHV*, bp 22 July 1689 *NHC1*, d 29 Apr 1753 *G;* m (1) 19 Apr 1711 *NHV*—Jonathan Todd; m (2) 1735 Benjamin Stone.

2 MARGARET, b 16 Aug 1691 *NHV*, bp Aug 1691 *NHC1*, d 5 Nov 1691 *NHV*.

3 ANNA, b 4 Nov 1693 *NHV*, bp 5 Nov 1693 *NHC1*, d 4 Oct 1773; m 17 June 1714 Ebenezer Tallman of G.

4 THEOPHILUS, b 6 Jan 1695/6 *NHV*, bp 19 Jan 1695/6 *NHC1;* m Elizabeth ——, probably the "Wid. Morrison" who d 27 Apr 1771 æ. 74 *NHC1*.

i Theophilus, bp 22 June 1725 *DurhamC*, d soon.

ii Sarah, bp 22 June 1725 *DurhamC*, d soon.

iii Theophilus, b 12 July 1726 (at Durham) *WV*, bp 10 July 1726 *DurhamC*.

iv Sarah, b 16 Oct 1727 (at Durham) *WV*, bp 22 Oct 1727 *DurhamC*.

v Margaret, b 9 Mar 1729 (at Durham) *WV*, bp 16 Mar 1728/9 *DurhamC*.

vi William, b 11 July 1730 *WV*.

vii Anna, b 27 June 1733 *WV;* m 31 Jan 1765 *NHC1*—John Wilson.

viii Andrew, b 4 Sep 1735 *NHV*, bp 6 Sep 1735 *NHC1*.

ix (probably) Amos, bp 21 May 1738 *NHC1*, d before 1791; m (1) Katharine ——; m (2) Elizabeth ——; Census, Widow Morrison (NH) 0-1-1. **FAM. 2.**

5 MARGARET, b 12 Aug 1699 *NHV*, bp 13 Aug 1699 *NHC1*.

6 ANDREW, b 1 Oct 1701 *NHV*, d c. 24 Apr 1728 *NHV;* m 11 Mar 1726/7 *NHV*—Elizabeth Davis.

i Margaret, b 15 Jan 1727/8 *NHV*, d 4 Feb 1809 æ. 81 *Washington;* m Robert Lemon, who d 4 Feb 1806 æ. 91 *Washington.*

FAM. 2. AMOS & KATHARINE (———) MORRISON:

1 MARGARET, b 5 Feb 1767 *F*, d 17 Oct 1813 æ. 46 *NHx;* m Jan 1793 *NHx*—Uri Tuttle.

2 ELIZABETH, bp 27 Nov 1768 *NHx;* m 24 Oct 1789 *NHx*—Eneas Alling.

3 KATHARINE, bp 23 Sep 1776 *NHx*, bu. 25 Sep 1776 *NHx.*

4 WILLIAM AMOS, bp 23 Sep 1776 *NHx.*

FAM. 2. AMOS & ELIZABETH (———) MORRISON:

5 JOHN, bp 10 Sep 1791 (æ. 14) *NHx;* res. Harwinton; m Desire da. Benjamin & Rhoda (Munson) Wooding. Child: Maria, m Chester Bradley.

6 SAMUEL, bp 10 Sep 1791 (æ. 10) *NHx.*

MOSS. Variant, MORSE. JOHN, b c. 1604, d 1707 æ. 103 *WTI;* Cpl; m ———.

1 JOHN, bp 11 Jan 1639 *NHCI*, d soon.

2 SAMUEL, bp 4 Apr 1641 *NHCI.*

3 ABIGAIL, bp 10 Apr 1642 *NHCI*, d 5 Nov 1710 æ. 68 *WV;* m 2 July 1663 *NHV*—Abraham Doolittle.

4 JOSEPH, bp 6 Nov 1643 *NHCI*, d 1727; m (1) 11 Apr 1667 *NHV*—Mary da. Roger & Mary (Nash) Alling, bp 26 Nov 1643 *NHCI*, d 18 Mar 1715/6 *NHV*, 26 Mar 1716 æ. 72 *NHTI;* m (2) 11 July 1717 *NHV*—Sarah da. Joseph & Sarah (Parker) Peck, wid. Matthew Gilbert, b 4 Aug 1663 *LymeV*, d 4 Apr 1730 æ. 67 *NHTI.*

(By 1): *i* Samuel, b 27 Jan 1675 *NHV*, d 26 Apr 1676 *NHV.*

ii Joseph, b 7 Apr 1679 *NHV*, d 23 Jan 1731 æ. 53 *DTI* [1731/2]; Rev.; m (1) 19 Nov 1701 *NHV*—Mary da. Edward Barker, who d 28 Feb 1714 *DV*, 23 Feb 1714 æ. 42 *DTI;* m (2) 10 Feb 1714/5 *NHV*, 20 Feb 1714 *DV*—Dorcas da. Richard & Lydia (Trowbridge) Rosewell, b 21 Dec 1684 *NHV*, d 2 Sep 1715 *DV*, æ. 30 *DTI;* m (3) 3 Oct 1716 *DV*—Abigail da. Samuel & Abigail (Whiting) Russell, b 16 Aug 1690 *BdV;* she m (2) 6 Aug 1733 Samuel Cooke. **FAM. 2.**

iii Samuel, b 18 Mar 1680/1 *NHV*, d 8 June 1721 *DV;* m 1 Dec 1713 *DV*—Barbara da. John & Bridget (Thompson) Bowers, who d 8 Sep 1745 *DV.* **FAM. 3.**

5 EPHRAIM, bp 16 Nov 1645 *NHCI*, d young.

6 MARY, bp 11 Apr 1647 *NHCI*, d 16 Nov 1725 *WV;* m 3 Nov 1664 *NHV*—John Peck.

7 MERCY, bp 1 Apr 1649 *NHCI*, d 1685; m Elizabeth da. William Curtis, b 13 Sep 1654 *StV;* she m (2) before 1687 John Rose of Bd.

i John, b 7 Jan 1677 *WV* [1677/8], d c. 1723; res. Jamaica, L. I., & St; m 22 Dec 1707 *NHV*—Jane da. William &

Joanna (Daniel) Thompson, b 29 Oct 1683 *NHV*, d 28 Sep 1743 *StV*. **FAM. 4.**

ii William, b 28 June 1682 *NHV*, d 26 Aug 1749 æ. 69 *DV;* Sgt.; m (1) ——— ; m (2) 18 Mar 1714 *DV*—Abigail da. Isaac Nichols, wid. Edward Riggs. **FAM. 5.**

8 JOHN, b 12 Oct 1650 *NHV*, bp 20 Oct 1650 *NHC1*, d 31 Mar 1717 *WV;* m 12 Dec 1676 *WV*—Martha da. Samuel & Elizabeth (Scudder) Lathrop, b Jan 1657 *NLV*, d 21 Sep 1719 *WV*.

i Esther, b 5 Jan 1678 *WV* [1678/9], d after 1742; m (1) 27 Oct 1702 *BdV*—Daniel Maltby, b 19 May 1679, d 26 Dec 1731; m (2) 10 June 1739 *NHV*—Samuel Todd; m (3) ——— Frary.

ii Samuel, b 10 Nov 1680 *WV*, d 29 July 1765 æ. 85 *WV*, *WT1;* Dea.; m 15 Dec 1703 *WV*—Susanna [da. Samuel & Hannah (Walker)] Hall, b c. 1683, d 4 Mar 1766 *WV*, æ. 83 *WT1*. **FAM. 6.**

iii John, b 10 Nov 1682 *WV*, d 14 May 1755 *WV*, æ. 73 *WT1;* m (1) 25 Feb 1708 *WV*—Elizabeth da. Samuel & Hannah (Walker) Hall, b 6 Mar 1690/1 *WV*, d 17 Jan 1754 *WV;* m (2) Dec 1754 *WC2*—Martha da. Daniel & Hannah (Cornwall) Doolittle, wid. Theophilus Fenn, b 16 Apr 1703, d 1760. **FAM. 7.**

iv Martha, b 22 Dec 1684 *WV*, d 25 May 1771 æ. 87 *WT1;* m (1) 27 Nov 1706 *BdV*—Samuel Stent; m (2) 24 May 1738 *WV*—John Peck.

v Solomon, b 9 July 1690 *WV*, d 10 Oct 1752 *WV;* m (1) 28 Jan 1714 *WV*—Ruth da. Joseph & Ruth (Atkins) Peck, bp 3 May 1696 *HartfordC*, d 29 Mar 1728 *WV;* m (2) 1 Aug 1728 *WV*—Sarah da. Edward & Mary (Thorpe) Fenn, b 24 Nov 1694 *WV;* she m (2) 22 Sep 1755 *WV*—Theophilus Jones. **FAM. 8.**

vi Isaac, b 6 July 1692 *WV*, d 31 Oct 1750 *WV*, 2 Oct *CC;* Sgt.; m (1) 2 May 1717 *WV*—Hannah da. Samuel & Hannah (Benedict) Royce, b 19 Feb 1698 *WV*, d 1 Mar 1736 *WV*, Mar 1736 *CC*, last day of Mar 1737 æ. 40 *CT1;* m (2) 14 Oct 1736 *WV*—Kezia da. Samuel & Lydia (French) Bowers, b 2 Mar 1698/9 *DV*, d 19 Nov 1770 *CC*. **FAM. 9.**

vii Mary, b 25 July 1694 *WV*, d probably c. 1720; m 28 June 1714 *WV*—Solomon Munson.

viii Israel, b 31 Dec 1696 *WV;* m 31 Dec 1717 *DV*—Lydia da. Samuel & Lydia (French) Bowers, b 1 Aug 1692 *DV*, d 9 Dec 1772 æ. 81 *WV*. **FAM. 10.**

ix Benjamin, b 10 Feb 1702 *WV*, d 10 June 1761 *WV*, æ. 59 *CT1;* Lieut.; m 28 May 1728 *WV*—Abigail da. Joseph & Abigail (Royce) Cole, b 18 Jan 1702/3 *WV*, d 11 Feb 1794 æ. 91 *CT1;* Census, Abigail (C) 0-0-3. **FAM. 11.**

9 ELIZABETH, b 3 Oct 1652 *NHV*, bp 7 Oct 1652 *NHC1;* m 18 Jan

1670 *NHV*—Nathaniel Hitchcock.

10 Esther, b 2 Jan 1653 *NHV* [1653/4], bp 2 Jan 1653 *NHCl*, d [19 June 1677 *WV;* m 27 Oct 1673 *WV*—Nathaniel Royce; the marriage record does not state the bride's surname].

11 Isaac, b 27 Nov 1655 *NHV*, bp 30 Nov 1655 *NHCl*, d [1659] *NHV*.

FAM. 2. Joseph & Abigail (Russell) Moss:

1 Abigail b 8 Sep [1717] *DV;* m 3 Apr [1732] *DV*—Rev. Elisha Kent.

2 Mary, b 28 Aug 1721 *DV;* m 20 Oct 1736 *DanburyV*—Rev. Ebenezer White,

3 Dorcas; m 10 Nov 1740 Jonathan Ingersoll.

FAM. 3. Samuel & Barbara (Bowers) Moss:

1 Mary, b 20 Nov 1715 *DV;* m 26 Nov [1734] *DV*—Jonah Tomlinson.

2 Jonathan, b 10 May 1718 *DV*.

FAM. 4. John & Jane (Thompson) Moss:

1 Mary, b 5 Dec 1708 *NHV*, d 30 Oct 1749; m (1) Dec 1729 *StV*—Daniel Holmes; m (2) Zachariah Tomlinson.

2 John, b c. 1710, d 3 Feb 1789 æ. 79 *MonroeT;* Lieut.; m [(1) —— Sabine; m (2)] Sarah da. Thomas & Sarah (Janes) Salmon, b c. 1719, d 29 Apr 1788 æ. 68 *MonroeT*.

i William, b c. 1736, d 18 Sep 1815 æ. 79 *TrumbullT;* m Mercy da. Ephraim & Sarah (Everit) Lewis, b c. 1745, d 22 Aug 1825 æ. 80 *TrumbullT*.

ii John, m Rhoda da. Daniel & Mary (Bennett) Beardsley, wid. David Beach.

iii Daniel, d 3 Jan 1822; Rev.; res. Dorset, Vt.; m 27 June 1776 Rebecca da. Samuel & Abigail (Hollingsworth) Munson, b 22 June 1752, d 1 Mar 1844.

iv Sarah, b Sep 1742, d 13 Dec 1840; m (1) Robert Lewis; m (2) 15 Sep 1779 Elihu Curtis.

v Nancy, b c. 1744, d Feb 1826; m Wells Curtis.

vi Joseph; m Elizabeth Booth.

vii Jane, b 1750, d 1831; m Elijah Curtis.

viii Mabel, m Samuel Booth.

ix Elizabeth, b 1 Apr 1756; m Isaac Booth.

x Isaac, b 1 Apr 1756, d 24 May 1849 (Canandaigua, N. Y.); m 15 Nov 1787 Charlotte Grant.

xi Elihu, b 22 Jan 1759, d 13 Jan 1845 Bristol, N. Y.; m (1) Eunice Riggs da. Andrew & Eunice (Bassett) Scott; m (2) —— (——) Richmond.

3 Elizabeth, d 6 Sep 1743 *StV*.

4 Joanna; m 21 Dec 1738 *StV*—Samuel Ufford.

5 Mehitabel, d 4 Oct 1743 *StV*.

6 Joseph, b 13 Apr 1720 *StV*, d 14 Nov 1795 æ. 75 *MonroeT;* Capt.; m Mehitabel ——, who d 10 Nov 1795 æ. 77 *MonroeT*.

7 Jane, b 22 May 1722 *StV;* m 17 Nov 1743 *StV*—Ebenezer Ufford.

FAM. 5. WILLIAM & —— (——) MOSS:

1 ANN, b c. 1710, d 14 Sep 1791 æ. 81 *OxfT;* m 28 Oct 1731 *DV*—Samuel Wooster.

FAM. 5. WILLIAM & ABIGAIL (NICHOLS) MOSS:

2 DEBORAH, b 10 Feb 1714/5 *DV*, d 1 Jan 1746 *WyV;* m John Leavenworth.

3 NICHOLS, b 28 Apr 1716 *DV*, d 24 Nov 1759 æ. 44 *DTl;* m 25 Mar 1740 *DV*—Hannah da. Thomas & Mary (Dorman) Leavenworth, b c. 1719, d 15 Oct 1789 æ. 70 *HT3;* she m (2) Jonathan Dickerman.

i Nehemiah, b 18 Aug 1741 *DV*, d 3 Jan 1762.

ii Nichols.

iii Joseph, b 22 Apr 1758 *F*, bp 28 May 1758 *DC*, d Sep 1827 (Volney, Vt.); Census (D) 1-4-3; m Eunice da. Isaac & Lucy (Clark) Smith, who d 30 Oct 1815 (Volney, Vt.).

4 ELIZABETH, b 23 June 1718 *DV*, d soon.

5 ELIZABETH, b 30 Apr 1721 *DV*.

6 MERCY.

7 WILLIAM, b 19 Mar 1725/6 *DV*, d 1797; Census (D) 4-0-4; m (1) 30 May 1751 *DV*—Prudence da. James & Hannah Hard who d 6 Apr 1754 *DV;* m (2) 20 Sep 1759 *DV*—Rachel da. Daniel & Mary (Bennett) Beardsley.

(By 1): *i* Sarah, b 2 May 1752 *DV;* m Isaac Hawkins.

ii Prudence, b 27 Mar 1754 *DV*.

(By 2): *iii* Isaac Nichols, b 30 June 1761 *DV;* "Rachel" bp 29 Nov 1761 *Dx*, d 22 Aug 1840; m 27 Dec 1800 Mercy da. Elijah & Mary (Osborn) Wooster, b 28 Dec 1771, d 21 Aug 1865.

iv Edward, b 26 Apr 1765 *DV*, bp 6 May 1764 *Dx;* res. Cazenovia, N. Y.; m (1) Lois Fairchild; m (2) Mary Atwater.

v William, b 31 July 1766 *DV*, bp 2 Nov 1766 *Dx*, d s. p. 1791.

vi Rhoda, bp 15 July 1770 *Dx;* m Benjamin Hall.

vii Rachel, b 19 Oct 1771 *F;* m Daniel Tomlinson.

FAM. 6. SAMUEL & SUSANNA (HALL) MOSS:

1 THEOPHILUS, b 24 Oct 1704 *WV*, d 19 Jan 1786 *WV;* m 13 Apr 1738 *WV*—Ruth Ranney, b c. 1706, d 3 Aug 1775 æ. 69 *WV*.

i Ebenezer, b 25 Nov 1740 *WV*, d 4 Sep 1799 æ. 59 *WTl;* Census (W) 3-1-4; m 27 Apr 1762 *WV*—Esther da. Jehiel & Thankful (Sedgwick) Preston, b 1 Apr 1744 *WV*, d 23 July 1822 æ. 80 *WTl*. **FAM. 12.**

ii Esther, b 10 June 1744 *WV*, d 25 Aug 1744 *WV*.

iii Ruth, b 17 Apr 1746 *WV;* probably m (1) 1 May 1765 *WV*—Jesse Vorce; m (2) 3 Jan 1771 *WV*—Abel Hall.

2 MARTHA, b 7 June 1706 *WV*, d 18 Nov 1791 æ. 85 *CTl;* m 25 Dec 1728 *WV*—Samuel Royce.

3 SUSANNA, b 5 Dec 1708 *WV*, d 16 Mar 1738 *WV;* m 10 Oct 1736

WV—Theophilus Doolittle.

4 SAMUEL, b 4 Apr 1711 *WV*, d 11 Sep 1791 æ. 81 *CT2;* Census (C) 1-0-4; m (1) 28 Oct 1734 *WV*—Mary da. Thomas & Sarah (Gaylord) Judd, b 2 Apr 1706 *WatV*, d 28 Jan 1747/8 *WV*, Jan 1747/8 *CC*, 28 Jan 1748 *CT1;* m (2) 1 Nov 1748 *WV*—Hannah da. Nehemiah & Kezia (Hall) Royce, wid. John Doolittle, b 15 May 1720 *WV*, d 30 Nov 1797 æ. 78 *CT2.*

(By 1): *i* Susanna, b 20 Oct 1735 *WV*, bp Nov 1735 *CC;* m —— Stanton.

ii Hannah, b 31 Dec 1737 (?) "Mary" bp 21 Dec 1737 *CC*, "child" d 21 Dec 1737 *CC*.

iii Samuel, b 31 Mar 1739 *WV*, bp May 1739 *CC*, "child" d Mar (?) 1739 *CC*.

iv Son, bp May 1741 *CC*, d 8 Aug 1752 *CC*.

v Joshua, b 18 Jan 1742/3 *WV*, bp Mar 1742/3 *CC*.

vi Sarah, b 30 Apr 1745 *WV;* m Jonas Martin.

vii Thomas, b 19 Jan 1747/8 *WV*, bp 20 Dec 1747 *CC*, d 1 Feb 1747/8 *WV*, Jan 1747/8 *CC*.

(By 2): *viii* Theophilus, b 17 Nov 1749 *WV*, bp 25 Dec 1749 *CC;* rem. to Crown Point, N. Y.; m 2 Oct 1778 *WV*—Bede da. Benjamin & Hannah (Parmelee) Hull, b 11 Apr 1753 *WV*. Children: (1) Bede, b 8 July 1779 *WV*, bp 17 Oct 1779 *CC*, d 16 Dec 1796 *CC*. (2) Eliakim Hull, bp 8 July 1781 *CC*. (3) Gift, b 13 June 1783 *CV*, bp 23 July 1783 *CC*. (4) Elias, b 5 Oct 1796 *CV*, bp 6 Apr 1797 *CC*.

ix Thomas, b 27 July 1751 *WV*. bp Sep 1751 *CC*, d 5 Feb 1831 æ. 79 *CT1;* Census (C) 2-1-3; m 16 Jan 1777 *CC*—Lucy da. Thomas & Lois (Hull) Doolittle, b 9 Apr 1757 *WV*, d 28 Mar 1839 æ. 82 *CT1*. FAM. 13.

x Mary, b 9 Apr 1753 *WV*, d s. p. 15 Dec 1836.

xi Martha, b 10 May 1755 *WV*, d 28 Apr 1845 æ. 90 *CT2;* m 31 Dec 1774 *WV*—Phineas Ives.

xii Bethia, b 21 May 1757 *WV*.

xiii Kezia, b 21 Dec 1762 *WV*, d s. p. 25 Aug 1824.

5 ESTHER, b 30 July 1713 *WV*; m 1 Dec 1735 *WV*—Joel Canfield.

PAGE 2048

6 ISAIAH, b 5 Dec 1715 *WV*, d before 1776; m (1) 11 Apr 1738 *WV*—Phebe da. John & Mary (Frederick) Doolittle, b 26 Nov 1713 *WV*, d 10 May 1758 *WV*, Mar 1758 *CC;* m (2) 19 Mar 1758 *WV*—Kezia da. Jonathan & Elizabeth (Thompson) Prindle, b 14 Mar 1733 *WV*.

(By 1): *i* Phebe, b 3 June 1739 *WV*, bp 15 July 1739 *CC*, d soon (perhaps the "child" who d Oct 1750 *CC*).

ii Hezekiah, b 20 Jan 1741 *WV*, bp Mar 1740/1 *CC*, d 18 Jan 1742 *WV*, "child" 1741/2 *CC*.

iii Mehitabel, b 15 Nov 1743 *WV*, bp Dec 1742 (?) *CC*.

iv Miriam, b 29 Sep 1744 *WV*, bp Nov 1744 *CC*, d 28 July 1812 æ. 68 *CT1;* m 21 May 1772 *WV*.

v Kezia, b 3 Nov 1746 *WV*, "Phebe" bp Nov 1746 *CC*, "child" d 1747 *CC*.
vi Isaiah, bp 18 Dec 1748 *CC*, "child" d Dec 1748 *CC*.
vii Lemuel (parentage proved by W Deeds, 20:543); m 22 Dec 1774 *WV*—Ann da. John Hall. Children recorded *WV*: Nabby, b 23 Sep 1775; John, b 24 Feb 1777.
viii Phebe, b 18 Aug 1753 *WV*, "child" d June 1757 *CC*.
(By 2): *ix* Isaiah, b 18 Dec 1759, d 27 Oct 1831; res. Paterson, N. J.; m Beulah Page.
x Linus, b 2 Mar 1761 *WV*.
xi Enos, b 1 Oct 1762 *WV*; m (1) 24 Feb 1789 *CC*—Sarah da. Nathaniel & Mary (Dorchester) Moss, b 19 Aug 1762, d 25 Jan 1802 *CC*; m (2) 26 Jan 1804 *CC*—Lydia da. Hezekiah & Lydia (Frost) Todd, wid. Joel Sackett, bp 13 Aug 1769 *NoHC*.
xii Phebe, b 20 Mar 1764 *WV*; m 13 June 1782 *CC*—Caleb Lewis.

7 Sarah, b 10 Feb 1718 *WV*, d 15 Aug 1800 æ. 83 (Springfield, Mass.); m (intention 10 June 1745) Jonathan Chapin.
8 Kezia, b 16 Oct 1720 *WV*; m Isaac Lewis.
9 Bethia, b 2 Mar 1723 *WV*; m 19 Jan 1748/9 *DurhamV*—John Canfield.
10 Ebenezer, b 15 June 1725 *WV*, d 26 July 1740 *WV*, 25 July 1740 æ. 16 *WT1*.
11 Jesse, b 10 Mar 1728, d s. p.
12 Lois, b 7 Jan 1730 *WV*; m 3 July 1749 *WV*—David Cook.

FAM. 7. John & Elizabeth (Hall) Moss:
1 Hannah, b 11 Nov 1709 *WV*, d 20 Jan 1787 *CC*; m (1) 6 May 1728 *WV*—Benjamin Ives; m (2) 15 June 1768 *WV*—Phineas Atwater.
2 Elizabeth, b 6 Dec 1711 *WV*; m 3 May 1739 *WV*—Amos Matthews.
3 Joseph, b 9 Feb 1714 *WV*, d 10 July 1775 æ. 62 *CT2*; m 4 Feb 1735 *WV*—Lydia da. Theophilus & Hannah (Mix) Jones.
i Phebe, b 9 Jan 1736 *WV*, d 1 Mar 1799 æ. 64 *CT1*; m 19 June 1755 *WV*—Benjamin Atwater.
ii Moses, b 18 Mar 1738 *WV*, bp 7 May 1738 *CC*, d 27 Sep 1809 æ. 72 *CT2*; Census (C) 3-3-4; m (1) 5 Nov 1760 *WV*—Abiah da. Benjamin & Abiah (Chauncey) Hall, b 1 May 1737 *WV*, d 13 Jan 1767 *WV*; m (2) 17 Mar 1768 *WV*—Esther da. Samuel & Sarah (Hull) Hall, b 21 Jan 1740 *WV*, d 15 Aug 1820. **FAM. 14.**
iii Lydia, b 18 Aug 1740 *WV*, bp Sep 1740 *CC*; m 10 Jan 1765 *WV*—Josiah Hart.
iv Eunice, b 5 Mar 1742/3 *WV*, bp Mar 1742/3 *CC*; m 29 May 1769 *WV*—Eliakim Hall.
v Hannah, b 9 Apr 1745 *WV*, bp Apr 1745 *CC*, "child" d 15 Apr 1756 *CC*.

vi Joseph, b 21 Mar 1747/8 *WV*, bp Apr 1748 *CC*, d s. p. 6 Oct 1777 *WV;* m 25 June 1772 *WV*—Mary da. John & Hannah (Hall) Street, wid. Caleb Hull, b 4 May 1740 *WV*.

vii Elizabeth, b 31 May 1750 *WV*, bp June 1750 *CC;* m 28 Dec 1769 *NHV*—Azariah Perkins.

viii Isaac, b 29 Mar 1754 *WV*, d 15 Dec 1839 æ. 86 *CT2;* Census (C) 1-5-3; m 15 June 1774 *WV*—Sarah da. Moses & Sybil (Thomas) Tuttle, b 19 Aug 1750 *WV*, d 1 Jan 1836 æ. 84 *CT2*. **FAM. 15.**

ix Sarah, b 22 Mar 1757 *WV;* m 8 May 1776 *WV*—Charles Hull.

x Amos, b 2 Oct 1760 *WV;* m Mary da. Elihu & Mary (Mansfield) Sperry.

4 Mary, b 22 Apr 1716 *WV*, d 9 Oct 1791 æ. 75 *WT2;* m 5 Nov 1739 *WV*—Isaac Hall.

5 Kezia, b c. 1718, d 3 Oct 1770 æ. 53 *WT1;* m 18 Nov 1736 *WV*—Reuben Royce.

6 John, b 14 Nov 1720 *WV*, d 5 Oct 1770 *WV*, æ. 50 *WT1;* m 1 May 1749 *WV*—Sarah da. John & Sarah (Culver) Thompson, b 5 Oct 1724 *WV*, d 9 Jan 1777 æ. 53 *WT1*.

i Eunice, b 30 Oct 1750 *WV*, d 18 July 1789 æ 39 *WT1;* m 29 May 1769 *WV*—Eliakim Hall.

ii Joel, d 12 June 1756 *WV*.

iii John, b 7 Apr 1753 *WV*, d 11 Jan 1813 (Peru, N. Y.): rem. to Sandy Hill, N. Y.; m Rhoda Everest.

iv Sarah, b 22 Nov 1755 *WV*, d 1 Aug 1847 æ 91 *CT1;* m 18 Jan 1775 *WV*—Ezra Doolittle.

v Joel, b 7 July 1757 *WV*, d 28 July 1796 æ. 38 *WT1;* Census (W) 1-3-1; m 19 Mar 1778 *WV*—Hannah da. Street & Hannah (Fowler) Hall, b 3 July 1751 *WV*, d 9 Feb 1828 æ. 78 *WT1*. Children: (1) Street Hall, b 9 Dec 1778 *WV*, d 9 Sep 1836; res, Delphi & Union, N. Y.; m 6 Sep 1802 Martha da. Isaac & Martha (Moss) Bartholomew. (2) Joel Fowler, b 10 Feb 1781; m 6 Sep 1802 Lucretia da. Samuel & Thankful (Hall) Hough, b 20 Dec 1778. (3) Lyman Hall, b 29 Sep 1784, d Feb 1879; m 7 May 1805 Sarah da. Amos & Sarah (Curtis) Francis, b Aug 1788, d 16 Mar 1862.

vi Phebe, b 6 May 1760 *WV*, d 14 Dec 1776 æ. 17 *WT1*.

vii Anna, b 27 Dec 1765 *WV*, d 3 Nov 1766 *WV*.

7 Levi, b 31 Dec 1722 *WV*, d 16 Sep 1802 æ. 80 *WT1;* Census (W) 2-1-2; m 19 Jan 1743/4 *WV*—Martha da. Theophilus & Martha (Doolittle) Fenn, b 23 Sep 1725 *WV*, d 6 Sep 1818 æ. 93 *WT1*.

i Amos, b 17 Nov 1744 *WV*, d Dec 1819; Census (L) 4-2-6; m (1) Betsey da. Abel & Sarah (Reed) Ives, b 30 Aug 1746 *WV;* m (2) 13 Dec 1777 Rachel da. Zebulon & Eleanor

(Taylor) Culver, wid. Joseph Merriman, who survived him.

ii Levi, b 16 Nov 1746 *WV*, d 6 May 1825 æ. 78 *LT;* Census (L) 2-2-6; m 14 June 1773 Martha da. John Sherman, b c. 1750, d 26 Aug 1843 æ. 94 *LT*.

iii Elizabeth, b 3 Dec 1748 *WV;* m 18 Nov 1773 *WV*—Aaron Hackley.

iv John, b 14 Feb 1750/1 *WV*, d 17 Aug 1820 æ. 69 *LT;* Census (L) 1-3-5; m 14 May 1773 Mehitabel Hall, who d 22 June 1840 æ. 87 *LT*.

v Martha, b 18 Aug 1753 *WV*, d soon.

vi Mary, b 28 Nov 1755 *WV*, d 9 Feb 1847 (Sheffield, Mass.); m Andrew Andrews.

vii Martha, b 28 Nov 1755 *WV*, d 22 Feb 1784 æ. 30 *WT1;* m Isaac Bartholomew.

viii Stephen, b 6 Feb 1758 *WV*, d 5 Apr 1777 *WV*.

ix Hannah, b 24 July 1760 *WV;* m 15 Mar 1781 Abel Thorpe.

x Benajah, b 11 Jan 1763 *WV*, d 12 July 1841 æ. 79 *WT1;* Capt.; Census (W) 1-0-3; m Lois [da. David & Ruth (Francis) Hall, b 24 Sep 1768 *WV*], d 2 Nov 1841 æ. 71 *WT1*.

xi Thankful, b 13 Mar 1766 *WV*, d 24 Sep 1826 æ. 61 *WT1;* m 22 Sep 1790 David Hall.

xii Philo Thaddeus, b 7 July 1769 *WV*, d 3 Sep 1769 *WV*, æ. 1 *WT1*.

8 Eunice, b 6 Feb 1726 *WV*.

9 Thankful, b 26 Apr 1728 *WV;* m 19 Mar 1744/5 *WatV*—Abel Doolittle.

10 Ann, b 18 Aug 1730 *WV*, d soon.

11 Martha, b Sep 1733 *WV*, d 1804 æ. 71 (Goshen); m (1) 17 June 1752 *WatV*—Ebenezer Foot of Wat; m (2) John Hart of Cornwall; m (3) John Thompson of Goshen.

12 Ann, b Aug 1738 *WV*, d 15 Jan 1782 *WatV;* m 22 Jan 1756 *WatV*—Thomas Merriam.

FAM. 8. Solomon & Ruth (Peck) Moss:

1 Daniel, b 28 Oct 1714 *WV;* res. Kent; m 13 Oct 1737 *WV*—Mary Watts.

2 David, b 15 May 1716 *WV*, d 16 May 1766 æ. 50 *WV;* m 7 Oct 1737 Mindwell da. Samuel & Mehitabel Doolittle, b 11 June 1715 *WV*.

i Chloe, b 6 Dec 1739 *WV;* m 13 Oct 1763 *WV*—Ephraim Hall.

ii Simeon, b 16 Oct 1740 *WV;* res. L & Broome Co., N. Y.; m Nov [1764] *WV*—Eunice da. Richard & Eunice (How) Hackley, b 11 Mar 1740/1 *WV*. Children recorded *WV:* Sarah, b 19 July 176[6]; Jesse, b 9 July 1768; Elizabeth, b 14 Apr 1772; Joseph, b 3 Sep 1776.

iii Amos, b 30 Sep 1742 *WV*, d 19 Mar 1813; rem. to Shutesbury, Mass.; m (1) Eleanor da. Zebulon & Eleanor (Taylor) Culver, b 3 June 1747; m (2) 10 Jan 1798 Eunice Lock.

iv David, b 26 Dec 1746 *WV*, d 1813; Col.; res. Harwinton & Shutesbury, Mass.; m (1) 17 Sep 1767 *WV*—Eunice da. Ephraim & Eunice Hall; m (2) Statira Baldwin.

v Solomon, b 18 Feb 1749 *WV*, d 4 June 1820; Ens.; m 23 Mar 1770 *WV*—Mary da. Samuel Spellman. Children recorded *WV:* Huldah, b 30 Sep 1771; Elihu, b 16 July 1774; Solomon, b 19 Dec 1777; Samuel Spellman, b 14 Feb 1780.

vi Chauncey, b 14 Mar 1751 *WV;* res. Camden, N. Y.; m 24 Jan 1771 *WV*—Tryphena [da. Wm. & Tryphena (Cook)] Barstow.

vii Abel, b 13 Dec 1753 *WV;* m Annis ——— .

viii Naomi, b 1 Oct 1755 *WV;* m 22 Feb 1776 *WV*—Simeon Hopson.

ix Joseph, b 6 Aug 1757 *WV*.

x Jesse.

3 Abigail, b 7 Mar 1718 *WV*, d soon.

4 Solomon, b 31 Oct 1719 *WV*, d 1755; res. Nine Partners, N. Y.; m 30 Nov 1742 *WV*—Elizabeth da. Theophilus & Martha (Doolittle) Fenn, b 30 Mar 1723 *WV*.

i Elizabeth, b 28 Aug 1744 *WV;* m 1 Sep 1763 *WV*—Josiah Hart of S & Rutland, Vt.

ii Eunice; m Amasa Holcomb of Canaan.

iii Sarah; m Israel Harris of Cornwall.

iv Solomon, b c. 1749, d 13 Apr 1822; Dea.; rem. to Poultney, Vt., Canaan, Conn., & Troy, Pa; m (1) 11 Nov 1773 Huldah Coleman, who d 1786; m (2) 13 Mar 1789 Jemima Parker, who d 4 Apr 1829.

v Moses, b 15 Aug 1751, d 7 May 1847; res. Farm; m 20 Nov 1775 Mary Dutton, who d 3 Jan 1832.

vi Benjamin.

vii Joseph, b 6 Sep 1756, d 28 Sep 1833; res. Poultney, Vt.; m 18 Jan 1780 Anna Coleman, who d 1856.

5 Ruth, b 5 Aug 1721 *WV*, d 13 Apr 1743 *WatV;* m 20 Nov 1741 *WatV*—Ebenezer Elwell.

6 Martha, b 30 Sep 1723 *WV*.

7 Abigail, b 10 Sep 1725 *WV*, d 11 Sep 1725 *WV*.

8 Abigail, b c. 1727; m Bela Lewis.

FAM. 8. Solomon & Sarah (Fenn) Moss:

9 Sarah, b 2 May 1729 *WV*, d 9 July 1729 *WV*.

10 Jonathan, b 8 Feb 1731 *WV*, d 1801; Census (W) 2-3-6; m 23 Apr 1761 *WV*—Esther Curtis.

i Lois, b 30 Apr 1762 *WV;* [m 11 Feb 1790 *WV*—Benjamin Baldwin].

ii Lucy, b 1 Jan 1765 *WV;* m 27 Dec 1781 *WV*—Nathaniel Merriman.

iii Amos, b 14 Feb 176[7] *WV;* m.

iv Jonathan, b 26 Mar 1769 *WV*, d 12 Mar 1817; Census (W) 1–0–0; m 4 Nov 1790 *WV*—Thankful Blakeslee, b 16 May 1771, d 13 Aug 1839; she m (2) Nathaniel Andrews.

v Esther, b 16 Apr 1771 *WV.*

vi Polly, b 13 June 1774 *WV;* m Erastus Hall.

vii Stephen, b 20 Oct 1776 *WV.*

viii Sarah, b 25 Mar 1779 *WV*, d soon.

ix Asahel, b 15 Dec 1780 *WV.*

x Ira, b 12 May 1783 *WV;* res. Ohio; m 1804 Laura Alma Hull.

xi Sarah, b 10 May 1785 *WV.*

xii Dema, b 4 Apr 1789 *WV.*

11 SARAH, b 28 Nov 1734 *WV*, d 13 Dec 1808 æ. 75 *HT3;* m (1) 17 Jan 1754 Amos Royce; m (2) John Couch.

FAM. 9. ISAAC & HANNAH (ROYCE) MOSS:

1 HEMAN, b 21 July 1718 *WV*, d 9 May 1720 *WV.*

2 HANNAH, b 7 Mar 1722 *WV*, d 27 Feb 1787 *CC*, æ. 65 *CTI;* m 9 July 1741 *WV*—Enos Atwater.

3 ISAAC, b 5 Nov 1724 *WV*, d 9 June 1807; Lieut.; m 29 May 1746 *WV*—Anna da. Eli & Mary (McKay) Roberts, b 31 Dec 1727 *WV*, d 8 June 1792. He was admitted to *NMC* 1753 from Cornwall.

i Kezia, b 18 Mar 1746/7, bp Feb 1746 (?) *CC.*

ii Anna.

iii Mehitabel, b 12 Mar 1753 *NMV*, bp 22 Apr 1753 *NMC.*

iv Isaac, b 2 Jan 1755 *NMV*, bp 16 Feb 1755 *NMC.*

v Simeon, bp 7 Nov 1756 *NMC*, d 21 Dec 1847; res. Sandy Hill, N. Y.; m Dec 1779 Elizabeth (Pitcher) Carter.

vi Esther, bp 6 Aug 1758 *NMC.*

vii Mary, b 27 Aug 1760 *NMV*, bp 23 Nov 1760 *NMC.*

viii Hannah, bp 4 Apr 1762 *NMC.*

ix Solomon.

x Lois; m ——— Norris of Sodus, N. Y.

xi Eunice; m Burton Phillips.

4 HEMAN, b 12 Jan 1727 *WV*, bp Feb 1726/7 *CC*, d May 1740 *CC.*

5 JESSE, b 10 Mar 1729 *WV*, bp Apr 1729 *CC*, d 20 Mar 1793 *CC*, æ. 64 *CTI;* Capt.; Rev. soldier; Census (C) 4–1–3; m 25 Jan 1753 *WV*—Mary da. Benjamin & Abigail Cole) Moss, b 23 Oct 1731 *WV*, d 19 Aug 1819 æ. 88 *CTI.*

i Hannah, b 16 Jan 1754 *WV;* m 3 Aug 1774 *WV*, *CC*—Thomas Hitchcock.

ii Joel, b 17 Dec 1755 *WV*, d 22 Nov 1756 *WV.*

iii Jesse, b 10 Sep 1757 *WV*, d 7 Feb 1778 *CC.*

iv Reuben, b 11 June 1759 *WV*, d 17 Feb 1809 (Ware,

Mass.); Rev.; m 15 Oct 1795 (Stonington) Esther Chesborough.

v Job, b 25 Sep 1761 *WV*, d 26 Sep 1761 *WV*.

vi Mary, b 25 Feb 176[3] *WV*, d 9 May 1776 *CC*.

vii Isaac Bowers, b 16 Mar 1765 *WV*, d 18 Apr 1838 æ. 73 *CT1*; Census (C) 1-0-1; m 12 Feb 1789 *CC*, *CV*—Esther da. Abraham & Mary (Ball) Atwater, b 10 Dec 1763 *WV*, d 26 Sep 1840 æ. 77 *CT1*.

viii Lothrop, b 8 Feb 1768 *WV*, bp 10 Apr 1768 *CC*, d 2 Nov 1769 *WV*.

ix Clarina, b 13 Apr 1770 *WV*, bp 10 June 1770 *CC*, d 5 June 1771 *WV*.

x Rufus, b 1 July 1772 *WV*, bp 5 July 1772 *CC*; rem. to Syracuse, N. Y.; m Sarah Thomas.

xi Emaluel, b 2 June 1774 *CV*, bp 7 Aug 1774 *CC*; res. Middlebury; m (1) 8 May 1799 Lydia da. Moses & Esther (Hall) Moss, b 29 Feb 1776, d 1 Sep 1826 *CV*.

xii Mary Clarinda, b 4 Apr 1777 *CV*, bp 22 June 1777 *CC*, d 29 Sep 1848; m John Moss.

6 Elihu, b 25 May 1731 *WV*, bp 11 July 1731 *CC*, d 12 Feb 1778 *S*; m 23 Feb 1758 Esther Clark.

7 Mehitabel, bp Apr 1734 *CC*, d 9 May 1735 *WV*, "child" d May 1735 *CC*.

FAM. 9. Isaac & Kezia (Bowers) Moss:

8 Ebenezer, b 9 Aug 1737, bp 2 Oct 1737 *CC*, d 23 Aug 1823; res. Harwinton & East Dorset, Vt.; m Elizabeth Kent.

9 Mehitabel, bp 20 Jan 1738/9 *CC*, "child" d Aug 1740 *CC*.

10 Jabez, b 23 Jan 1741 *WV*, bp Apr 1741 *CC*.

FAM. 10. Israel & Lydia (Bowers) Moss:

1 Rachel, b 13 Jan 1719 *DV*; m 5 Feb 1739/40 *DV*—John Harris.

2 John, b 10 May 1721 *DV*, d before 1752; m 31 July 1744 *WV*—Lydia da. Eli & Mary (McKay) Roberts, b 30 Mar 1726 *WV*; wid. Lydia admitted to *NMC* 1752; she m (2) James Bradshaw.

i Amasa, b 22 Apr 1746 *WV*, bp 11 July 1752 *CC*; rem. to Williamstown, Mass; m 3 Nov 1768 *NMV*—Ruth Clark. They had Lydia b 8 May 1769 *NMV*.

ii John, b 3 Sep 1747 *WV*, bp 29 Aug 1752 *NMC*, prob. d s. p.

iii Lemuel, bp 29 Aug 1752 *NMC*.

iv Sarah, b 5 July 1751 *NMV*, bp 29 Aug 1752 *NMC*.

3 Nathaniel, b 14 Dec 1722 *DV*, *WV*, d 21 Aug 1804 æ. 82 *CT1*; Lt.; Census (C) 4-1-3; m (1) 20 Jan 1746/7 *WV*—Kezia da. Nehemiah & Kezia (Hall) Royce, b 16 Mar 1726 *WV*, d 5 Feb 1750/1 *WV*, Feb 1750/1 *CC*; m (2) 19 Dec 1751 *WV*—Mary [da. James & Lydia (Preston)] Dorchester, who d 19 Feb 1808.

(By 1): *i* Kezia, b 12 Dec 1749 *WV*, d 3 Oct 1750 *WV*, "child" 2

Oct *CC*.

(By 2): *ii* Stephen, b 6 Oct 1752 *WV*, bp 11 July (?) 1752 *CC*, d 2 June 1812 æ. 60 *CTI*.

iii Nathaniel, b 15 Apr 1754 *WV*, d 17 July 1787; m 3 Nov 1785 *CC*—Lucy Hall Beach.

iv Kezia, b 13 May 1756 *WV*, d 7 Mar 1821; m 24 Feb 1780 *CC*—Solomon Morris.

v Mary, b 19 July 1758 *WV*, d 24 Oct 1796 æ. 38 *CTI*; m 19 Apr 1786 *CC*—Amos Atwater.

vi Lydia, b 26 Aug 1760 *WV*, d 28 Jan 1808; m Ebenezer Hotchkiss.

vii Sarah, b 19 Aug 1762, d 25 Jan 1802 *CC*; m 24 Feb 1789 *CC*—Enos Moss.

viii Asenath, b 2 Aug 1765 *WV*; m 24 Jan 1788 *CC*—Aaron Newton.

ix Asahel, b 16 Nov 1767 *WV*, bp 24 Jan 1768 *CC*; m (1) Eunice Doolittle; m (2) 25 Apr 1805 *CC*—Amy Hitchcock.

x Jared, b 17 July 1770 *WV*, bp 16 Sep 1770 *CC*, d 20 July 1845 æ. 75 *CTI*; m (1) 8 Nov 1795 *CV*—Sarah Hitchcock; m (2) Nov 1820 Clarissa Smith.

4 Israel, b 10 Apr 1725 *WV*, bp 30 May 1725 *CC*, "child" d Dec 1727 *CC*.

5 Lydia, b 17 Mar 1727 *WV*, bp Apr 1729 [?1727] *CC*.

6 Kezia, bp Nov 1729 *CC*, "child" d 1 Oct 1731 *CC*.

7 Israel, b 15 Dec 1731 *WV*, bp 13 Feb 1731/2 *CC*.

8 Kezia, b 9 Dec 1734 *WV*, bp Feb 1734/5 *CC*, d 20 July 1737 *WV*, "child" July 1737 *CC*.

9 Asael, b 22 Feb 1737 *WV*, bp Apr 1737 *CC*.

FAM. 11. Benjamin & Abigail (Cole) Moss:

1 Abigail, b 28 Dec 1728 *WV*, bp 25 Jan 1728/9 *CC*, d 6 Jan 1729 *WV*, "child" d 1729 *CC*.

2 Benjamin, b 27 Nov 1729 *WV*, bp 4 Jan 1729/30 *CC*, d 17 Dec 1797 *CC*, æ. 69 *CTI*; Census (C) 1-0-2; m 5 Jan 1763 *WV*—Mehitabel Beach.

3 Mary, b 23 Oct 1731 *WV*, bp Nov 1731 *CC*, d 19 Aug 1819 æ. 88 *CTI*; m 25 Jan 1753 *WV*—Jesse Moss,

4 Barnabas, b 27 Dec 1733 *WV*, bp 3 Feb 1733/4 *CC*; m 1 Sep 1755 *WV*—Anna Hollingworth.

i John, b 17 May 1756 *WV*.

ii Anna, b 29 Nov 1757 *WV*; [?m 23 Mar 1780 *CC*—Stephen Atwater].

iii Abigail, b 25 Jan 1760 *WV*.

iv Richard, b 19 Jan 1762 *WV*.

v Rachel, b 13 Mar 1764 *WV*.

vi Margery, b 20 Apr 1766 *WV*.

vii Barnabas, b 21 Nov 1768 *WV*.

viii Eunice, b 4 Apr 1770 *WV*, bp 10 June 1770 *CC*.

ix Ichabod, b 4 June 1773 *WV*, bp 13 June 1773 *CC*.

x Pitt, b 20 Mar 1775 *WV*, bp 30 Apr 1775 *CC*.

xi Claranze, b 8 June 1778 *WV*, "Clarenza" bp 12 July 1778 *CC*.

5 TIMOTHY, b 17 Mar 1736 *WV*, d 1828; res. Wells, Vt.; m (1) 10 Jan 1759 *WV*—Esther da. Abraham & Mary (Ball) Atwater, b 1 Dec 1738 *WV*, d 29 June 1763 *WV*; m (2) 1 Feb 1764 *WV*, *AvonC*—Mary Owen.

(By 1): *i* Chloe, b 23 Mar 1760 *WV*.

ii Martha, b [———] *WV*, d 3 Feb 1764 *WV*.

6 TITUS, b 16 May 1738 *WV*, d 23 Dec 1818 æ. 81 *CT1*; Capt.; Census (C) 2-2-3; m 13 May 1761 *WV*—Mary da. Abraham & Mary (Ball) Atwater, b 28 Apr 1740 *WV*.

i Merab, b 13 Feb 1762 *WV*, d 15 Feb 1835; m 22 Feb 1786 *CC*—"Joel" [John] Peck.

ii Miriam, b 14 Aug 1764 *WV*, d 13 May 1832 æ. 68 *CT2*; m 26 Jan 1786 *CV*, *CC*—Joel Brooks.

iii Joel, b 7 July 176[6] *WV*, d 6 Mar 1847 æ. 81 *CT2*; Census (C) 1-1-1; m 4 Dec 1788 *CC*—Abigail Hotchkiss.

iv Heman, b 8 May 1768 *WV*, bp 12 June 1768 *CC*, d 19 May 1822 æ. 54 *CT2*; m Phebe da. Nathaniel Royce, who d 31 Jan 1846 æ. 75 *CT2*.

v Mary, b 6 Mar 1772 *WV*, bp 8 Mar 1772 *CC*; m 24 Dec 1792 *CC*—Joel Johnson.

vi Lois, b 25 Nov 1773 *WV*, bp 28 Nov 1773 *CC*, "child" d 10 June 1775 *CC*.

vii Lois, b 3 Oct 1776 *WV*, bp 17 Nov 1776 *CC*; m 23 Jan 1800 *CC*—Samuel Bixby.

7 ABIGAIL, b 30 Sep 1740 *WV*, bp Nov 1740 *CC*; m 13 Mar 1760 *WV*—Caleb Lewis.

8 JOSEPH, b 17 Dec 1742 *WV*, d 1819 (Augusta, N. Y.); m 21 May 1762 *WV*—Esther da. Benjamin & Esther (Matthews) Lewis, b 23 Oct 1738 *WV*, d 1837.

i Obed, b 13 Sep 1762 *WV*, d 14 Oct 1832 æ. 71 *CT1*; m 22 Jan 1786 *CC*—Sarah Bunnell, who d 2 May 1814 æ. 47 *CT1*. They had Chloe, bp 17 July 1796 *CC*, d 5 Feb 1797 æ. 1 *CT1*; Anson, bp 16 Dec 1799 *CC*, d 3 May 1801 æ. 2 *CT1*; & others.

ii Amy, b 20 May 1764 *WV*; m 16 Feb 1792 *WdC*—Thomas Clinton.

iii Asahel, b 1 Feb 1766 *WV*.

iv Esther, b 1768.

v Elizabeth, b 1768; [m ——— Parmelee].

vi Sarah; [m ——— Loss].

vii Jared, b 10 Jan 1771, d 1839; res. Augusta, N. Y.; m 2 Feb 1794 *CC*—Patience da. Valentine & Sarah (Hotchkiss) Hitchcock, who d 29 Nov 1820.

viii Martha.

ix Joseph, b Sep 1775, d 29 Oct 1856 (Marshall, Mich.); res.

New Berlin, N. Y.; m 1797 Rhoda da. Daniel & Rhoda Griffith, b 28 July 1780 (Ward, Mass.), d 29 Sep 1851 (Sandusky, Ohio).

9 MARTHA, b 27 Jan 1744/5 *WV*, bp Mar 1745 *CC*, d 1765 *NHPro*.

10 EUNICE, b 12 Aug 1747 *WV*, bp Sep 1747 *CC;* m 15 Jan 1761 *WV*—Ebenezer Tuttle.

11 ESTHER, b 10 Feb 1753 *WV*, d 19 July 1806 æ. 51 *CT1*.

FAM. 12. EBENEZER & ESTHER (PRESTON) MOSS:

1 SAMUEL, b 27 Mar 1763 *WV*, d s. p. 2 Feb 1802.

2 ESTHER, b [25] Dec 176[4] *WV;* m Ichabod Munger of C & Salisbury, N. Y.

3 THEOPHILUS, b 25 Jan 1767 *WV*, d 24 Jan 1845; m (1) 8 Apr 1795 Christiana Horton; m (2) 20 Apr 1809 Betsey Byington.

4 THANKFUL SEDGWICK, b 31 Oct 1768 *WV;* m John Carter of Salisbury, N. Y.

5 RUTH; m ——— Nickerson of Salisbury, N. Y.

6 EBENEZER, b 8 Nov 1773 *WV;* res. Salisbury, N. Y.

7 LOIS, b 4 Nov 1778 *WV;* m Henry Handy of Salisbury, N. Y.

FAM. 13. THOMAS & LUCY (DOOLITTLE) MOSS:

1 LOWLY, b 13 Sep 1777 *WV*, bp 9 Nov 1777 *CC*, d 20 Dec 1846 æ. 69 *CT1;* m 22 May 1800 *CC*—Leonard Beecher.

2 LUCY LOUISA, b 1 Jan 1781 *CV*, bp 18 Mar 1781 *CC*, d 12 Aug 1794 æ. 14 *CT1*.

3 THOMAS DOOLITTLE, b 10 Dec 1783 *CV*, d 23 Dec 1867 æ. 84 *CT1;* m 15 Jan 1807 *CC*, *CV*—Ruth Hale.

FAM. 14. MOSES & ABIAH (HALL) MOSS:

1 ABIAH, b 25 Aug 1761 *WV;* m ——— Johnson.

2 MOSES, b 5 Apr 1763 *WV*, d 16 Jan 1840 æ. 77 *CT2;* m 17 Nov 1806 Ann Brooks Ives.

3 ICHABOD, d 9 Jan 1766 *WV*.

FAM. 14. MOSES & ESTHER (HALL) MOSS:

4 ESTHER, b 25 Aug 1769 *WV*, d 4 July 1848 æ. 79 *NHV;* m 13 Nov 1825 *CV*—Amos Doolittle of NH.

5 JOHN, b Aug 1771, d 25 Aug 1816 (Onondaga, N. Y.); m Mary Clarinda da. Jesse & Mary (Moss) Moss, b 4 Apr 1777 *CV*, d 29 Sep 1848.

6 REBECCA, b 10 Dec 1773, d 6 Jan 1851 æ. 79 *CT2;* m 20 Oct 1808 *CV*—Joshua Ives.

7 LYDIA, b 29 Feb 1776, d 1 Sep 1826 *CV;* m 8 May 1799 Emaluel Moss.

8 JOSEPH, b 5 Apr 1778, d s. p. 19 May 1802 æ. 25 *CT2*.

9 WILLIAM, b 3 Aug 1780; res. Georgia; m Huldah Beecher.

10 SECKER, b 10 Feb 1783; res. Auburn, N. Y.; m (1) ——— ; m (2) Polly Beecher.

FAM. 15. ISAAC & SARAH (TUTTLE) MOSS:

1 JOSEPH, b 17 June 1775 *WV*, d 9 Oct 1843; m 6 Jan 1800 *CV*, 16 Jan *CC*—Ruth da. Amasa & Sarah (Bradley) Hitchcock, b 1 Oct 1775, d 21 Dec 1872.

2 FREELOVE, b 23 Feb 1778 *WV*, d 26 June 1859 æ. 81 *CT2;* m Allen Bishop.

3 LENT, b 30 Mar 1780, d 22 Oct 1845 (Prospect); m (1) 17 Nov 1802 *CV*—Lotta Doolittle, who d 30 Nov 1826; m (2) Chloe da. Elisha & Mabel (Humiston) Munson, wid. Riley Tuttle, b 9 Apr 1790.

4 AARON, d 5 July 1782.

5 JEDEDIAH, b 27 Jan 1784, d 1865 (Walworth, Wayne Co., N. Y.); m 12 Nov 1809 *CC*—Charlotte da. Jonathan G. & Desire (Brooks) Bristol.

6 MASON, b 1787, d 13 Jan 1867 æ. 80; m Sarah Sackett.

7 SARAH; m 17 Apr 1811 *CC*—Russell Page; rem. to Mich.

8 ISAAC, d bef. 1841; res. Hartland?, Mich.; m 26 Nov 1812 *CC*—Eunice da. Benjamin & Leva Doolittle.

MOSS. MISCELLANEOUS. MARTHA m 10 Sep 1770 *WV*—Samuel Mattoon. ......MOLLY m 26 Oct 1767 *WV*—Jonathan Beck......MARGARET had da. Lorena Mix, b 4 Feb 1775 *WV*.

MORSE. ABEL, b c. 1746, d 10 Mar 1795 æ. 49 *NHT1*, æ. 48 *Conn Courant;* Census (NH) 4-3-2; m Mehitabel Fabian, b c. 1762, d 29 Mar 1821 æ. 58 *NHT1*.

1 SAMUEL LANGDON, b [Sep 1778], d 22 June 1795 æ. 16-9 *NHT1*.

2 WILLIAM WALKER, bp 26 Nov 1780 *WethC*.

3 EZEKIEL WILLIAMS, b 25 Sep 1782 *NHT1*, bp 6 Oct 1782 *NHC2*, d 21 June 1840 *NHT1;* m Mary Allen, b 4 Sep 1781 *NHT1*, d 11 Sep 1836 *NHT1*.

i Theodore Allen, b 1 July 1808 *NHT1*, d 22 Nov 1809 *NHT1*.

ii Mary, b [Sep 1811], d 10 Nov 1813 æ. 2-2 *NHT1*.

iii Cushing Allen, d 27 Oct 1817 [æ. —] *NHT1*.

iv Theodosia, d 23 Dec 1823 [æ. —] *NHT1*.

4 MEHITABEL EMERY FABIAN, bp 7 Dec 1788 *NHC2*.

5 DEBBY WALKER, b [Feb 1791], bp 10 July 1791 *NHC2*, d 10 Apr 1793 æ. 2-2 *NHT1*.

6 JOHN FABIAN, b [Apr 1793], bp 30 June 1793 *NHC2*, d 6 Sep 1795 æ. 2-5 *NHT1*.

MOTT. JEREMIAH of Westerly, R. I., & W; m Margaret da. Shubael & Mercy (Lamberton) Painter, prob. wid. ——— Morris & Lawrence Clinton. Other Motts early in W were prob. his children or gr.ch. by a former marriage......HANNAH m 22 Nov 1726 *WV*—Eliasaph Preston...... SARAH m 2 Jan 1742 *WV*—Henry Merwin.

FAM. 1. ADAM m 28 Aug 1717 *WV*—Elizabeth da. Henry & Mary (Hall) Cook.

1 MARY, b 18 May 1718 *WV;* m 17 May 1745 [1741?] *WV*—Lewis Wilkinson.

2 ELIZABETH, b 3 Jan 1721 *WV*, d soon.

3 JONATHAN, b 19 Apr 1723 *WV*, d 1818; rem. to Winchester; m 10 Nov 1743 *WV*—Hannah Bailey, who d 1820.

i Simeon, b 7 Oct 1744 *WV*

4 Samuel, b 16 Apr 1726 *WV*.

5 Elizabeth, b 20 Sep 1728 *WV*.

6 Eunice, b 5 May 1732 *WV;* m Aaron Neal of Farm.

7 Adam, b 24 Apr 1736 *WV*, d c. 1836; rem. to Winchester & Vernon, N. Y.; m (1) 3 Jan 1760 Abiah Filley; m (2) 14 Feb 1786 Anna Cyrena Filley.

8 Lent, b 5 Aug 1738 *WV;* rem. to Winchester; m (1) ——— ; m (2) 1 Jan 1766 Mary Filley.

FAM. 2. Samuel, d 5 Mar 1745/6 (at Cape Breton) *WV;* m 18 Aug 1735 *WV*—Sarah Gie (?)

1 Abel, b 22 Feb 1736 *WV;* rem. to NM; m 11 May 1756 Rachel Pierce.

2 Ezekiel, b 18 Feb 1838 *WV*.

3 Comfort, b 7 Nov 1740 *WV;* m 12 Sep 1765 *WV*—Peter Richards.

MOULTHROP. FAM. 1. Matthew, d 22 Dec 1668 *NHV;* m Jane ———, who d May 1672 *NHV*, 13 May *NHPro.* Matthew's sister Ellen m William Luddington.

1 Matthew, d 1 Feb 1690/1 *NHV;* m 26 June 1662 *NHV*—Hannah da. John & Dorothy Thompson, who d 17 Jan 1712/3 *EHV;* she m (2) Samuel Hotchkiss.

i Hannah, b 2 Nov 1663 *NHV*, d 2 Jan 1663 *NHV* [1663/4].

ii Hannah, b 20 Apr 1665 *NHV;* m 19 Aug 1687 *NHV*—John Russell.

iii John, b 5 Feb 1667 *NHV* [1667/8], d 14 Feb 1712/3 *EHV;* Sgt.; m 29 June 1692 *NHV*—Abigail da. Joseph & Silence (Brockett) Bradley, b 9 Sep 1671 *NHV*, d 3 Sep 1743 *EHV*. **FAM. 2.**

iv Matthew, b 18 July 1670 *NHV*, d 12 May 1740 *EHV;* m Mary da. Benjamin & Elizabeth (Barnes) Brockett, b 6 May 1675 *NHV*, d 15 Aug 1745 *EHV*. **FAM. 3.**

v Child, b 1673 *NHV*, d soon.

vi Lydia, b 8 Aug 1674 *NHV*.

vii Samuel, b 24 June 1677 *NHV*, d 14 Oct 1677 *NHV*.

viii Samuel, b 13 Apr 1679 *NHV*, d 30 Jan 1712/3 *EHV;* m Sarah da. Thomas & Mary (Hubbard) Barnes, b 17 Feb 1681 *NHV;* she m (2) 24 May 1721 *NHV*—Thomas Wilmot. **FAM. 4.**

ix Kezia, b 13 Apr 1682 *NHV*, d c. 1757/8; m 24 Aug 1701 (at NH) *BdV*—Daniel Barker.

2 Elizabeth, b 1638 *NHCl*, bp 1642 *NHCl;* m 18 Oct 1663 *NHV*—John Gregory.

3 Mary, b 1641 *NHCl*, bp 1642 *NHCl*.

FAM. 2. John & Abigail (Bradley) Moulthrop:

1 Abigail, b 12 Aug 1693 *NHV*, bp 18 Aug 1700 *NHCl*, d after 1758; rem. to Durham.

2 John, b 17 Mar 1695/6 *NHV*, bp 18 Aug 1700 *NHCl*, d c. 1757;

m Sarah da. Samuel & Sarah (Newman) Tuttle, b 27 Jan 1698/9 *NHV*, d 3 Nov 1734 æ. 36 *EHT*.

i John; m Abigail da. Daniel & Anna (Smith) Holt, b 22 Nov 1736 *NHV*, d 3 May 1828 æ. 91-5 *EHC*; she m (2) 17 Nov 1785 *EHC*—Samuel Shepard. **FAM. 5.**

ii Stephen; m ——— & had a child b c. 1767, d 27 Sep 1773 æ. 6 *EHC*.

iii Mary; m John Dawson.

iv Sarah, b [Aug 1725], d 26 Feb 1816 æ. 90-6 *NoHC*; m (1) Timothy Russell; m (2) John Pardee.

v Abigail, b c. 1727, d 10 May 1792 æ. 65 *EHC*; m 30 June 1748 *EHV*—Dan Goodsell.

3 Mary, b 5 Apr 1699 *NHV*, d c. 1 July 1708 *EHV*.

4 Sarah, b 10 Oct 1701 *NHV*; m (1) Adonijah Morris; m (2) Simeon Coe.

5 Daniel, b 1 Dec 1703 *NHV*, d 29 Jan 1759 æ. 56 *EHR*; m (1) Hannah Belcher; m (2) Lydia da. John & Hannah (Hemingway) How, b 19 Dec 1711 *EHV*, d 12 Feb 1760 æ. 43 (48?) *EHR*.

(By 1): *i* Child, d 1736 *EHV*.

ii Enoch, b c. 1737, d 9 Feb 1737/8 æ. 1 *EHT*.

iii Daniel, d s. p. 1765.

(By 2): *iv* Charles, d s. p. 1765; lost at sea *EHR*.

v Timothy; Census (W) 1-0-0.

vi Hannah, b c. 1746; m 15 Sep 1763 *EHC*—Israel Linsley.

vii Enoch, b c. 1748, d Apr 1802 æ. 54 (at NH) *ConnJournal*; Census (NH) 1-0-3; m 17 Mar 1768 *NHC1*—Mary da. Nehemiah & Mary (Rexford) Hotchkiss, b 2 Jan 1746/7 *NHV*, d 17 Feb 1826 æ. 79 *NHT1*. **FAM. 6.**

viii Sarah, b [Dec 1750], d 16 Aug 1838 æ. 89 *EHT*, æ. 87-8 *EHC*; m 31 Aug 1769 *EHC*—Elisha Andrews.

ix Eli, b c. 1752, d 16 Sep 1813 æ. 61 *EHC*; Census (EH) 1-0-2; m Jan 1787 *EHC*—Mary da. Asher & Anna (Grannis) Moulthrop, b 8 May 1749 *EHR*, d 3 Mar 1826 æ. 77 *EHC*.

x Lydia, bp 15 Dec 1754 *NoBC2*, d 1760.

xi Mabel, bp 9 Oct 1757 *EHC*, d 1760.

6 Israel, b 7 June 1706 *NHV*, d 15 Oct 1788 æ. 82 *EHC*; m Lydia Page.

i Samuel, b c. 1730, d 1 May 1790 æ. 60 *EHC*; m Sarah da. James & Dorothy (Morris) Denison, b c. 1733, d 1 Oct 1819 æ. 86 *EHC*. **FAM. 7.**

ii Jacob, d s. p.

iii Timothy, b c. 1736, d 22 Sep 1742 *EHV*, æ. 6 *EHT*.

iv Lydia; m 13 Mar 1766 *EHC*—John Fuller.

v Lois, b 26 Mar 1745 (at NH) *BdV*; m (1) 31 Oct 1765 *EHC*—Charles Page, who drowned 3 Dec 1769 æ. 25 at sea *BdV*; m (2) ——— Baldwin.

7 JOSEPH, b 18 June 170[8] *EHV*, d 1771; m Mary Wheadon, b c. 1717, d 13 Oct 1776 æ. 59 *NoHTI;* she m (2) 23 Feb 1774 *NoHC*—James Bishop.

i Adonijah, d 11 Nov 1760 (at Albany) *F&IWRolls.*

ii Rhoda; m 25 Mar 1762 *DurhamC*—Solomon Rose of Granville.

iii Joseph; Census (Bd) 1-1-4; m 6 Feb 1766 *EHC*—Lucretia da. Caleb & Sarah (Russell) Bradley. **FAM. 8.**

iv Elihu, b c. 1747, d 1782 æ. c. 35 (at sea) *EHC;* m 21 Nov 1770 *EHC*—Mary da. Joseph & Esther (Russell) Hotchkiss, b 24 June 1750, d 30 Mar 1826 æ. 76 *WolT;* she m (2) 24 Nov 1784 Charles Upson. **FAM. 9.**

v Hannah; perhaps m c. 1771 John Mallory of Roxbury.

vi Mary; perhaps m 30 Dec 1771 *EHC*—Ebenezer Burrinton.

vii Abigail; m 10 Jan 1776 *NoHC*—Jonathan Carter of S.

viii Jude, bp 16 [July] 1758 *EHC;* m 30 July 1777 *Sy*—Betsey Wheeler.

ix Lucretia; m John Talmadge of Wat.

8 TIMOTHY.

FAM. 3. MATTHEW & MARY (BROCKETT) MOULTHROP:

1 JANE, b 13 Dec 1694 *NHV;* m Thomas Hodges.

2 MATTHEW, b 1 Sep 1696 *NHV*, d soon.

3 JOSEPH, b 12 Oct 1698 *NHV*, d 28 Apr 1716 æ. 17-6 *EHV*.

4 MARY, b 4 June 1701 *NHV*, d Nov 1786 æ. 85 *EHC;* m (1) 24 Oct 1723 *EHV*—Gideon Potter; m (2) 7 Apr 1767 *EHC*—Samuel Thompson.

5 MARTHA, b 18 Feb 1703 *EHV* [1703/4], d Mar/Apr 1785 (New Fairfield) *F;* m Ebenezer Pardee.

6 MATTHEW, b 1 Feb 1705 *EHV* [1705/6], d 15 Dec 1795 æ. 90 *EHC;* m (1) Sarah da. Joseph & Hannah (Russell) Grannis, who d 22 June 1745 *EHV;* m (2) Hannah da. Thomas & Ann Way, b c. 1707, d 23 Dec 1781 æ. 74 *EHV*.

(By 1): *i* Thankful, b 6 Nov 1728 *EHV*, d 12 Sep 1742 *EHV*.

ii Joseph, b 11 Dec 1730 *EHV*, d young.

iii Sarah, b 10 Jan 1732[/3] *EHV*, d young.

iv Mabel, b 6 Sep 1735 *EHV;* m (1) 3 Sep 1759 *EHC*—Caleb Chidsey; m (2) 23 Sep 1762 *EHC*—Isaac Smith.

v Matthew, b c. 1738, d 12 Sep 1742 *EHV*.

vi Mary, b c. 1740, d 13 Sep 1742 *EHV*.

vii Matthew, b 9 Nov 1743 *EHV*, d 3 Aug 1745 *EHV*.

(By 2): *viii* David, b 23 Mar 1746/7 *EHV*, d 26 Dec 1826 æ. 79-9 *EHC;* Census (EH) 1-2-4; m Rachel Swayne, b c. 1746, d 2 May 1830 æ. 85 *NoHD*. **FAM. 10.**

7 BENJAMIN, b 2 Mar 1707 *EHV* [1707/8], d 1736 *EHV;* m Elizabeth ——— . Perhaps she m (2) Joseph Rundle of New Fairfield, or she may have been his sister,

i Benjamin, b 20 July 1735 *EHV*, d 2 Sep 1815 æ. 85 *DT2;*

Census (D) 2-0-2; m [July] 1761 *EHC*—Thankful da. William & Thankful (Ailing) Grannis. **FAM. 11.**

8 ASHER, b 28 Jan 1709/10 *EHV*, d 25 Nov 1780 æ. c. 71 *EHC;* m Anna da. Joseph & Hannah (Russell) Grannis, b c. 1713, d 16 June 1797 æ. 84 *EHC.*

i Desire, b 13 Apr 1737 *EHV*, d 31 Dec 1814 æ. 78 *EHC;* m 12 Sep 1759 *EHC*—Samuel Thompson.

ii Isaac, b 5 Feb 1738/9 *EHV;* Census (L) 2-3-3; m 11 Nov 1761 *EHC*—Jemima da. Thomas & Mehitabel (Thompson) Grannis. **FAM. 12.**

iii William, b 5 Mar 1740/1 *EHV*, d 1766 (at sea).

iv Levi, b 18 Oct 1743 *EHV*, d at sea.

v Solomon, b 3 Oct 1745 *EHV*, d bef. 1774 (at sea); m 10 Oct 1765 *EHC*—Lois da. John & Hannah (Smith) Rowe, b 21 Mar 1746 *NHV*, d 8 Sep 1791 æ. 45 *EHC.* **FAM. 13.**

vi Mary, b 8 May 1749 *EHR*, d 3 Mar 1826 æ. 77 *EHC;* m Jan 1787 *EHC*—Eli Moulthrop.

vii Thankful, b 1 June 1750 *EHV*, d 28 Sep 1826; m (1) John Crawford; m (2) Thomas Shepard.

viii Anna, b 25 Mar 1752 *EHV*, d 30 Apr 1845 æ. 93-0-35 *EHC;* m 9 Mar 1775 *EHC*—Samuel Smith.

ix Joseph, b c. 1754, d 24 Dec 1800 æ. 47 *EHC;* Census (EH) 1-3-3; m 26 May 1774 *EHC*—Lorana da. Isaac & Kezia (Moulthrop) Grannis, b c. 1751, bp 17 May 1798 (æ. 47) *NHx*, d c. 1811. **FAM. 14.**

x Asher, bp 5 Mar 1758 *EHC*, d 29 Mar 1832 æ. 74 *EHC*, 1832 æ. 75 *NHV;* Census (EH) 1-1-2; m 13 Oct 1783 *EHC*—Mary da. Ebenezer & Elizabeth (Grannis) Chidsey, b c. 1763, bp 17 May 1798 (æ. 34) *NHx*, d 2 Sep 1827 æ. 64 *EHC.* Child: (1) Isaac, b c. 1783, bp 17 May 1798 *NHx*, d 20 May 1839 æ. 57 *EHC;* m Lydia ———, who d 21 Mar 1824 æ. 31 *EHC.*

9 DOROTHY, b 1 Dec 1712 *EHV*, d 31 Dec 1793 æ. 82 *ThomastonT;* m 1 June 1738 *BdV*—Samuel Potter.

10 KEZIA, b 6 Jan 1714/5 *EHV*, d 3 Jan 1793 æ. 78 *EHC;* m Isaac Grannis.

FAM. 4. SAMUEL & SARAH (BARNES) MOULTHROP:

1 SARAH, b 24 Feb 1704/5 *NHV;* m Job Smith.

2 LYDIA, b 5 May 1707 *EHV*, d 1760; m (1) Eliakim Robinson; m (2) Roger Tyler of Bd.

3 HANNAH, b 10 Apr 1709 *EHV;* m Noadiah Carrington.

4 PHEBE, b 15 Oct 1711 *EHV;* m 23 Feb 1728/9 *NHV*—Joseph Perkins.

FAM. 5. JOHN & ABIGAIL (HOLT) MOULTHROP:

1 DAVID, b c. 1755, d c. 1779 (on prison ship, N. Y.); m 1 Jan 1777 *NHC2*—Hephzibah da. Lemuel & Mary (Mallory) Hotchkiss, b 14 Mar 1760 *NHV;* she m (2) 14 Nov 1780 *NHC*

2—Phineas Andrus.

i David, bp 6 Sep 1778 *NHC2;* m 5 Sep 1796 *NHC1*—Lydia da. Eleazer & Elizabeth (Cook) Brown, bp 17 Nov 1776 *NHC1*. Their 3 children James Henry, Lydia Emeline, & Charles Peck, bp 20 Aug 1811 *NHx*, of whom the last d 22 Aug 1811 *NHx*.

2 John, bp 24 July 1757 *EHC*.

3 Reuben, bp 9 July 1759 *EHC*, d soon.

4 Rosanna, b [Mar 1761], d 27 Sep 1844 æ. 83-[-] *EHC;* m 9 Dec 1777 *EHC*—Abijah Pardee.

5 Reuben, bp 24 July 1763 *EHC*, d 29 July 1814 æ. 51 *EHT*, 28 July *EHC;* m 18 Nov 1792 *EHC*—Hannah da. Nicholas & Hannah (Austin) Street, b 7 Mar 1767 *NHV*, 8 Mar *EHV*, d 9 June 1848 æ. 81-3 (at WH) *EHC*, æ. 81 *WHD*.

i Daniel Bowen, bp 19 Oct 1794 *EHC*, "only child" d 3 Oct 1795 æ. 1 *EHC*.

ii Hannah Maria, bp 21 Aug 1796 *EHC*.

iii Clarissa, bp 10 June 1798 *EHC*, d 29 Oct 1842 æ. 43 (at NH) *EHC*.

iv Daniel, b 11 Feb 1800 *WHT2*, bp 23 Mar 1800 *EHC*, d 25 Sep 1852 *WHT2*, æ. 52 *WHD;* Dea.; m Sarah ——— .

v Sidney, bp Oct 1802 *EHC*.

vi Deba.

vii Reuben Street, b c. 1808, d 10 June 1841 æ. 33 *EHC*.

FAM. 6. Enoch & Mary (Hotchkiss) Moulthrop:

1 Charles, b c. 1769, bp 18 Sep 1790 (æ. 22) *NHx;* Census (NH) 1-0-3; m Rachel ——— , who d 23 Aug 1846 æ. 80 *NHV*.

i Sally, bp 18 Sep 1790 *NHx*.

ii Betsey, b c. 1791, bp 19 July 1795 (æ. 4) *NHx*.

iii Maria, b c. 1793, bp 19 July 1795 (æ. 2) *NHx*.

iv Charlotte, b [Nov 1794], bp 19 July 1795 (æ. 0-8) *NHx*, d 29 Jan 1797 æ. 2 *NHx*.

2 Lydia, b c. 1772, bp 18 Sep 1790 (æ. 19) *NHx*, d 26 Jan 1813 æ. 41 *NHT1*.

3 Dan, d soon.

4 Dan.

5 Polly, b c. 1778, bp 18 Sep 1790 (æ. 12) *NHx*, "Mary" d 6 May 1867 æ. 89 *NHT1*.

i Grace Moulthrop, b c. 1803; d 10 May 1867 æ. 64 *NHT1;* m James Fordham, b c. 1800, d 28 Mar 1892 æ. 92 *NHT1*.

6 Betsey.

7 Silas.

8 Timothy, b c. 1786, bp 18 Sep 1790 (æ. 4) *NHx*.

FAM. 7. Samuel & Sarah (Denison) Moulthrop:

1 Josiah, b 30 May 1754 *EHR*, d 7 Nov 1823 æ. 70 *EHC;* Census (EH) 2-1-3; m (1) 4 July 1792 *EHC*—Lydia da. Samuel & Lydia (Dawson) Grannis, wid. Joseph Smith, b c. 1756, d

23 May 1797 æ. 41 *EHC;* m (2) Esther da. Caleb & Eunice (Barnes) Cooper, b c. 1764, d 30 May 1822 æ. 58 *EHC.*

(By 1): *i* Desire, b 16 Apr 1793 *EHR*, d 10 May 1824 æ. 31 *EHC.*

ii Jared, b 9 Mar 1795 *EHR*, d 12 June 1854 æ. 59 *NoHT2;* m Anna ——, who d 10 Apr 1874 æ. 94 *NoHT2.*

iii Samuel Russell, b 5 May 1797 *EHR*, d 26 Dec 1876 æ. 80 *NHT3;* m 30 Sep 1821 *EHV*—Polly Bradley, who d 7 Nov 1882 æ. 86 *NHT3.*

2 Desire, b 16 Nov 1756 *EHR*, d 10 Apr 1833 æ. 76 *EHC;* m 23 May 1775 *EHC*—Moses Thompson.

3 Jared, b 20 Jan 1759 *EHR.*

4 Jacob, b 29 Aug 1762 *EHR;* m (1) 22 Dec 1785 *NoHC*—Abigail da. Eliphalet & Mary (Blakeslee) Pardee, b c. 1762, d 30 July 1788 æ. 26 *EHC;* m (2) 30 Mar 1791 *BdC*—Elizabeth Goodrich.

(By 1): *i* Abigail.

ii Child, b [July 1788], d 30 July 1788 *EHC.*

(By 2): *iii* Betsey.

iv & *v* Twins, b [27 July 1795], d [29 July] 1795 *EHC.*

vi Eunice, bp 12 July 1798 *NHx.*

vii Leonard, bp 12 July 1798 *NHx.*

viii Bela.

ix Sarah.

x Damaris, bp Aug 1801 (with her twin sister) *NHx.*

5 Sarah, b 13 Jan 1764 *EHR*, d 22 Oct 1845 æ. 81-9 *EHC;* m Jesse Luddington.

6 Mercy, b 9 Sep 1767 *EHR.*

7 Lydia, b 7 Aug 1769 *EHR.*

8 Samuel, b 1 Sep 1773 *EHR*, d 26 Feb 1846 æ. 72 *NoHT3;* m Sarah da. Samuel & Abigail (Blakeslee) Sackett, b 15 Apr 1776 *NoHV*, d 11 Oct 1841 æ. 56 [66?] *NoHT3.*

i Sackett; m 25 Sep 1828 *NHV*—Charlotte L. Barnes of Northford.

ii Lavinia; m 23 Dec 1818 Jacob Foote.

iii Philena, b c. 1798, d 21 May 1876 æ. 78 *NoHT3.*

9 James, b 14 Oct 1776 *EHR.*

10 Israel, b Sep 1779 *EHR*, "son" d Dec 1786 æ. 7 *EHC.*

FAM. 8. Joseph & Lucretia (Bradley) Moulthrop:

1 Irene, b c. 1767, d Mar 1788 æ. 21 *NoB.*

2 Abijah.

3 Joseph, b c. 1775.

4 Jared.

5 Rhoda.

6 Chauncey.

FAM. 9. Elihu & Mary (Hotchkiss) Moulthrop:

1 Jerry; m Hester ——, who d 9 Mar 1795 æ. 21 *WolT.*

2 Polly, b [July 1776], d 9 Nov 1862 æ. 86-4 *NHT3;* m c. 1798 Elijah Rowe.

3 Adonijah.

4 ELIHU, b c. 1780, d 25 Oct 1853 æ. 74 *WolT;* m 8 Sep 1807 Wealthy Minor.

5 ESTHER; m Rollin Harrison of Wol.

FAM. 10. DAVID & RACHEL (SWAYNE) MOULTHROP:

1 JOHN, b c. 1770, "child" d 28 Feb 1773 æ. 3 *EHC.*

2 CALEB, b c. 1773, d 21 Sep 1796 æ. 23 *EHC.*

3 JOHN, b c. 1776, bp 2 Apr 1797 *EHC*, d 1811 (at sea) *EHC*, 1810 æ. 34 *EHR;* m 19 May 1807 *NoHV*—Hannah Cook da. Jonathan & Rhoda (Hall) Heaton, b 31 Oct 1788 *NoHV*, d 26 Sep 1841 æ. 53 *NoHT2.*

i Albert E., b 11 Feb 1808 *NoHV*, d 19 Nov 1856 æ. 48 *NoHT3;* m (1) Mahala ——— , who d 15 Dec 1851 æ. 44 *NoHT3;* m (2) Cynthia H., who d 23 Mar 1861 æ. 39 *NoHT3.*

ii Emery H., b 23 Oct 1809 *NoHV.*

iii John, b 20 May 1811 *NoHV*, d Oct [1811] *NoHV.*

4 MAJOR, b c. 1778, bp 2 Apr 1797 *EHC;* m 28 June 1801 *NoHC*—Bede da. Jacob & Eunice (Bishop) Thorpe, b c. 1776, d 1867; she m (2) 2 Apr 1818 *NoHV*, *NoHC*—John Barnes.

5 POLLY, b c. 1781, bp 2 Apr 1797 *EHC;* m 6 Sep 1800 *NoHV*—Billy Thorpe.

6 MARTIN, b c. 1783, bp 2 Apr 1797 *EHC*, d 14 Aug 1860 æ. 77 *NoHT3;* m 26 Jan 1804 *NoHC*—Amelia Phelps, who d 21 Mar 1865 æ. 81 *NoHT3.*

7 SWAYNE, bp 2 Apr 1797 *EHC*, d Aug 1815 *EHC;* m Mary da. John & Sarah (Mattoon) Culver.

FAM. 11. BENJAMIN & THANKFUL (GRANNIS) MOULTHROP:

1 BENJAMIN, bp 13 Mar 1763 *EHC*, d 1801; Census (D) 1-0-2; m Martha da. Abraham & Mary (Clinton) Harger, bp 11 Feb 1770 *Dx*, d 25 Nov 1809 æ. 44 *DT2.* A child, Betsey, d 6 Feb 1810 æ. 22 *DT2.*

2 SEBA, bp 24 Mar 1771 *EHC*, d 8 July 1831 æ. 61 *SeymourT;* m Katharine Fowler, who d 22 May 1859 æ. 79 *SeymourT.*

FAM. 12. ISAAC & JEMIMA (GRANNIS) MOULTHROP:

1 LEVI.

2 DESIRE.

3 WILLIAM, b c. 1770, d 6 Feb 1850 æ. 80 *LT;* m 27 Nov 1793 *LV*—Mary Page, who d 15 May 1850 æ. 76 *LT.*

4 SALMON, b c. 1772, d 30 Dec 1859 æ. 88 *LT;* m 11 July 1797 *LV*—Polly Stone, who d 25 Oct 1846 æ. 70 *LT.*

5 IRA.

6 ABRAHAM.

7 JACOB.

8 POLLY.

9 ANNA.

10 RACHEL.

11 CHILD.

12 CHILD.

FAM. 13. SOLOMON & LOIS (ROWE) MOULTHROP:

1 POLLY ROWE, b [Nov 1766], bp 24 Oct 1784 *EHC*, d 31 May 1844 æ. 77-6 *NHT3;* m 6 Oct 1785 *EHC*—William Bradley.

2 LOIS, b c. 1770, "child of Wid. Lois" d 16 Sep 1774 æ. 4 *EHC.*

FAM. 14. JOSEPH & LORANA (GRANNIS) MOULTHROP:

1 JOSEPH, b c. 1775, d Nov 1793 æ. 18 (at sea) *EHC.*

2 CHILD, b c, 1777, d 24 May 1777 *EHC.*

3 LORANA, b c. 1779, bp 17 May 1798 (æ. 19) *NHx*, d 13 Oct 1823 æ. 45 *EHC.*

4 ANNA, b c. 1781, bp 17 May 1798 (æ. 17) *NHx.*

5 LEVI, b c. 1783, bp 17 May 1798 (æ. 15) *NHx;* m 4 Nov 1811 *EHC*—Abigail da. Ebenezer & Elizabeth (Grannis) Chidsey, wid. ——— Baldwin. Childern: (1) Edward, b c. 1816; (2) Charlotte, b c. 1818; (3) Elizabeth, b c. 1820.

6 ELIHU, b c. 1786, bp 17 May 1798 (æ. 12) *NHx*, d 22 June 1847 æ. 61 *NHV.*

7 WILLIAM, b c. 1789, bp 17 May 1798 (æ. 9) *NHx.*

8 HERVEY, b c. 1793, bp 17 May 1798 (æ. 5) *NHx.*

9 POLLY, b c. 1797, bp 17 May 1798 (æ. 1) *NHx.*

MOULTHROP. MISCELLANEOUS. AMY, b 8 Oct 1777 (at EH) *BdV;* m 7 June 1799 *BdV*—Samuel N. Williams, b 5 Feb 1776 (at Susquehanna, N. Y.) *BdV.*

MOWATT. JAMES, d 1798; from Berwick, co. Northumberland, Eng.; left estate to w. Lydia...... WILLIAM m 27 Nov 1786 *NHx*—Esther [da. Timothy & Lydia] Thompson, b 22 Mar 1763 *HV*, d 11 Feb 1838 æ. 75 *HT1;* she m (2) 4 May 1793 *HV*—Eber Ives.

(CONTINUED IN VOLUME VI)

ADDITIONS AND CORRECTIONS

ANDREWS. (Pages 41, 45, 46). Nathan (father of FAM. 4) m (1) Elizabeth Miles, by whom he had Elizabeth & Daniel; m (2) Mary da. Anthony Martin of Mid, b c. 1666, by whom he had Mary, Jonathan & Abigail; divorced, since Mary was living 1723; m (3) Hannah ——, by whom he had William. Lack of mention of the second wife in NH records led us to attribute her children to the first wife; but Hartford Pro. proves the above statement.

AUSTIN. (Page 95). David m Mary da. Isaac & Rebecca (Williams) Shepard. [Contributed by Mr. G. F. Shepard, New Haven.]

BALDWIN. (Page 101). FAM. 1, 5. Theophilus did not m Dorothy Munson, as suggested in brackets to indicate doubt. He m Dorothy da. Thomas & Dorothy (Bulkeley) Treat, b 28 Aug 1704. She d 10 Oct 1790 æ. 86 *WdD*, which is more accurate than her gravestone; d 19 Oct 1790 æ. 80 *WdT2*, unless misread.

BENHAM. (Page 188). FAM. 2, 6, *i*. John, b 27 Sep 1736 *NHV*, d Aug 1821 æ. 87 *AmeniaT*. Of his children (page 192), John, b c. 1761, d 8 Nov 1805 æ. 44 *AmeniaT;* David, b [30 June 1765], d 5 Oct 1846 æ. 81-2-5 *AmeniaT;* m Mabel Smith, who d 14 Mar 1850 æ. 85-7-14 *AmeniaT*.

[The following contributed by Mrs. L. H. Headstrom, Stromsburg, Neb.]

FAM. 9. (p. 192). EBENEZER & DESIRE (BEECHER) BENHAM:

1 HANNAH, b 15 Jan 1757 *WatV;* m Mar 1779 *NorfolkC*—Heman Smith.

2 MARTHA, b 24 Aug 1758 *WatV;* m 1 Aug 1780 *NorfolkC*—Zebina Smith.

3 ISAAC, b 21 Oct 1760 *WatV*, d 1853 (Jericho, Vt.); Census (Amenia, N. Y.) 1-2-2; served in 5th Conn. Regt. & was a pensioner; m Thankful Reed. A son, Silas, d 29 Apr 1865, m Elizabeth Humphrey, who d 2 Jan 1837, & had children: Henry, Amy, Wm., Laura, Nancy, Smith, Mary & Adelbert.

4 ESTHER, b 23 Sep 1762 *WatV;* m 26 July 1789 *Sharon*—Joel Smith.

5 ANNA, b 11 July 1764 *WatV*.

6 EBENEZER, b 21 July 1766 *WatV;* rem. 1806 to Hopewell, N. Y.; m (1) 8 Jan 1792 Rebecca Smith; m (2) 30 Nov 1796 Ruth Clement.

CLARK. (Page 413). FAM. 11, 6, *v*. Edmund, b 11 Oct 1750, d 17 Sep 1828 in 78th year (Peru, N. Y.); rem. from Wallingford, Vt., to Peru, c. 1804; m Lois ——. [Contributed by Frederick Arnold, Esq., Plattsburgh, N. Y.]

COLE. (Page 428, bottom line.) This Sarah did not m Nathaniel Peck, whose wife was Sarah Hopkins, wid. Ichabod Cole of Mid, b 21 Aug 1687 *Hartford*. This agrees with her age at death. [Contributed by Timothy Hopkins, Esq., San Francisco.] What then became of Sarah da. Wm. Cole?

COOK. (Page 445). FAM. 10, 8, *ii*. William, b 13 Feb 1763, Rev. soldier, enlisting at W 1777, served 6 yrs; Dr.; res. Durham, N. Y., where he d 25 May 1846; m Mary Whittlesey, b 9 Apr 1761, d 17 Oct 1836. Children: Major, b 1790, d soon; Polly, b 1793; William Augustus, b 1797; Samuel W. D., b 1798; George H., b 1801; Alexander, b 1804; Andrew H., b 1805. [Contributed by Mrs. M. E. Rockwell, Meriden, Conn.]

COOPER. (Page 459). FAM. 11, *iii*. James Ford m Cornelia Wakelee. [Contributed by Horace W. Dickerman, Esq., New Haven.]

DARROW. (Page 520). It was Sarah w. of the first Richard, not of his son, who d 12 Mar 1774 æ. 84 *EHC*. The record calls her "wife of aged Richard" without specifying her first name. [Corrected by Mr. G. F. Shepard, New Haven.]

DENSLOW. (Page 534). FAM. 1, 3. William's 1st w. Sarah (Dorman) d 30 Mar 1801 *NoBC2*. (Page 535). FAM. 2, 9. William, b 1807, d 1 Mar 1858; rem. to Tioga Co., N, Y.; m Abigail Crosly; children: Elizabeth, Wm. Herbert, Sarah, George R. FAM. 2, 5. The town record of the death of Temperance calls her Roberts, but family papers make a second marriage seem impossible, and grave doubt of the accuracy of the public record is felt. [Contributed by George McK. Roberts, Esq., New York City.] Mr. Roberts retracts his correction printed on p. 765 regarding James s. of William (FAM. 1), having found in Stamford Pro. Rec. the order for distribution of the estate of John Denslow (28 Jan 1757) to the brothers and sisters *James*, William, Charles, and Ann Denslow.

DORMAN. (Page 569). FAM. 9. The youngest child of Daniel & Phebe (Warner) Dorman was inadvertently omitted; she was 7 Phebe, b c. 1796, d 13 Sep 1838 æ. 42 *HT2;* m Chester Alling.

FENN. (Page 600). FAM. 2, 2. Austin removed to Ludlow, later to Weston, Vt., where his w. Hannah Ives d 20 May 1829 æ. 59; he m (2) 2 June 1836 Bina (——) Chamberlain. Children (record incomplete):

1 AUSTIN, of Landgrove, Vt.; m Mary Gilman Utley. Children: Henry; Horace, d unm; Helen, d unm; Joseph, m Ella Woodward & had only s. Minor.

2 CALEB, b at Ludlow, d 20 Dec 1884 æ. 83-11-20 (Weston); m 1 July 1830 (Weston)—Persis da. David & Rhoda (Holt) Rideout, b 29 Jan 1801. Children: Joseph, d s. p., m Hannah Pease; Seymour, m 23 Mar 1856 Lydia Jane Austin, & had Mary, unm; Winfield, d at Westminster, Vt., m Gertrude Peters; Carrie, m —— Nutting of Westminster; Minnie.

3 IRA, b 9 Aug 1803 (Ludlow), d 18 Feb 1885 (Weston); m 6 May 1827 (Weston)—Lydia da. Thomas & Hannah (Spofford) Richardson, b 17 June 1806. Children: Artemas Ira, b 8 Jan 1828, res. Boston, m Fannie —— ; William Wallace, b 6 Mar 1831, d 30 Mar 1862, m & had William Wallace, D. D., Dean of Harvard Divinity School; Mary Utley, b 29 Aug 1832; Cynthia Delilah, b 1 Sep 1834; Hannah, m Henry Buss; Charles H., b 1841, d 1857; George Harvey, b 17 Aug

1845, d 8 Jan 1857. [Contributed by Raymond Taylor, Esq., Weston, Vt.]

FORBES. (Page 607). FAM. 1, 5. The wid. of Elias m (3) Jonathan *Goodsell*, not *Goodrich;* the error was copied from Hist. of Wethersfield.

GLOVER. (Page 661). FAM. 1, 4, *iv.* Mehitabel m (2) Rev. Joseph *Webb*, whose name by overlooked clerical or typographical error was misprinted. (Page 661, line 2). For *Richard* Hubbell, read *John.*

GRANNIS. (Page 681). FAM. 2, 1. Elizabeth did not die before 1764, which we supposed as her sister Abigail m Joseph Ives that year. Two sisters m Joseph Ives,-but they were different Josephs. See Ives correction in this issue. FAM. 2, 4. It was a Lydia of the Southington branch who was b 1750 & m Darius Scovill. This Lydia m ——— Candee.
(Page 684). FAM. 6, 4. DAVID's w. was Mary da. John & Sarah (Russell) Shepard, b 30 Sep 1746 *EHV*, d 9 Feb 1838 æ. 91-4-9. The other Mary was her cousin & m Thomas Cooper (see p. 452). (Page 685). FAM. 8, 6, *ii.* Amy m 3 Feb 1813 *EHC*—Elias Shepard, instead of Amy (FAM. 12, 6) on p. 686; proved by deed of Amy & her husband of land distributed to mother Martha Grannis from her father Isaac Luddington. [Corrections by Mr. G. F. Shepard, New Haven.]

HALL. (Page 714). FAM. 25, 2. George, bp 20 May 1770, settled in Onondaga Co., N. Y., where he was prominent in public life; m 30 Nov 1802 (Onondaga Hollow, N. Y.) Theodocia da. Daniel Keeler. Children: 1 George, b 1804, d 1816. 2 Daniel Keeler, b 1806, d 1849. 3 Lucien, b 1808. 4 Theodocia Emeline, b 1810. 5 Frederick, b 1813, d 1816. 6 George, b 1819. [Contributed by Charles H. Hall, Esq., Baldwinsville, N. Y.]
(Page 698). FAM. 4, 2, *vii.* Eunice, b 6 Feb 1751 *WV*, d 31 Jan 1819 æ. 68 *CT1;* m (1) 31 Jan 1771 *WV*—Levi Royce; m (2) 28 Apr 1791 *CV*—Rev. John Foote.

HEATON. (Page 730). FAM. 10, 5. Austin d æ. 86-11-23 *HV;* m 5 Nov 1837 *HV*—Marian Bassett, who d 5 Apr 1890 æ. 77 *HT2.*

HEMINGWAY. (Page 731). FAM. 1. Samuel b 1636, not 1736.

HOLBROOK. (This family accidentally omitted in proper place.) DANIEL, s. of Peletiah & Martha (Sanford), bp 20 May 1705 *MC1*, d c. 1755; m Priscilla da. Daniel & Abigail (Thompson) Collins, b 1 Mar 1708 *EHV*, d 14 Nov 1793 æ. 86 *EHC.*

1 LYDIA, b 25 Dec 1729 *EHV*, *NHV;* m 25 Dec 1753 *NHV*—Jonah Atwater.

2 MABEL, b 22 Oct 1731 *NHV*, d 7 July 1823 æ. 92 *EHT.*

3 ISABEL, b 10 Sep 1734 *NHV*, d 12 May 1801 æ. 67 *EHC;* m 1755 *EHV*, 14 Nov 1755 *EHC*—William Everton.

4 ABIGAIL, b 3 June 1737 *NHV;* m 19 June 1766 *EHC*—Timothy Cooper.

5 DAVID, b 15 Dec 1739 *NHV*, living 1755.

6 DANIEL, b 12 Nov 1742 *NHV*, living 1757.

7 HANNAH, b 23 Jan 1744/5 *NHV*, d 5 July 1827 æ 81 (*NHC2*) *N*

HV; m 7 Nov 1764 *EHC*—John Wooding.

HOTCHKISS. (Page 819). FAM. 21, 2. Robert & Jerusha (Cook) had 4 das.: Hannah, m —— Castle; Lola; Pamela, m —— Bronson; & Narsha, m c. 1814 Elisha Platt. Children of Elisha & Narsha (Hotchkiss) Platt: George Cook, b 1816; Robert Hotchkiss, b 1820; & Julia Ann, b 1824. [Contributed by Mrs. S. M. Macneil, Wauwatosa, Wis.]

(Page 801). FAM. 3, 2, *viii.* The editor has never felt satisfied that this Caleb left issue. Perhaps a more accurate account states that Rosetta Owen, b 25 Aug 1742, m (1) 10 Aug 1760 Elisha Phelps, & m (2) 31 Mar 1778 Caleb Hotchkiss; by Phelps she had 6 children, one being Helpah Rosella, b 7 Oct 1763, m Caleb Hotchkiss; and another, Rosanna Clorinda, b 16 Sep 1770, m —— Fabridge of Boston. This is evidently the da. Lorinda wrongfully attributed on p. 801 to Rosetta by Caleb, but actually belonging to her first husband. What Caleb m the da. Helpah is uncertain; but see p. 822 for a Caleb of proper age.

(Page 840). FAM. 65, 1, *iii.* Hiram m Rebecca *sister* of Clark & da. of Isaac as appears correctly on p. 839.

(Page 840). FAM. 65, 6. On family monument in Maple Grove Cemetery, Ravenna, Ohio, may be found the following death & marriage records. Lyman Hotchkiss, b 29 Mar 1777 Bethany, Conn., d 12 Mar 1852 æ. 75; m 6 Nov 1799 Lois Sperry b 19 Apr 1776 Bethany, Conn., d Feb 1849 æ. 73; their children: (1) Mark, d 11 Mar 1849 æ. 47. (2) Julius, d 26 Nov 1847 æ. 44. (3) George, d 17 Aug 1825 æ. 22. (4) Harvey, d 17 Nov 1871 æ. 67.

(Page 841). FAM. 66, 8. Hephzibah m c. 1800 Caleb Keep of Homer, N. Y. (Page 946). Two more children of Enoch & Lois (Wolcott) Hotchkiss have been identified, viz.: Benjamin S. & Lois. [Last 3 items contributed by Clarence D. Smith, Rome, N. Y.

HOW. (Page 857). FAM. 4, 1. Thankful m 24 Jan 1722/3 *BdV*—John *Palmer*, not *Parmelee.*

IVES. (Page 923). FAM. 7, 8, *ii.* David & Dolly (Hough) had also a s. Chauucey who m Orpha Pelton & a da. Fanny who m Samuel s. Samuel & Olive (Warren) Hayes. [Contributed by Mr. George McK. Roberts, New York City.]

(Page 915). FAM. 3, 6, *iii.* Joseph m 5 Nov 1761 *NHV*—Elizabeth da. John & Mary (Bradley) Grannis, b 20 Dec 1741 *NHV*......(Page 921). FAM. 6, 4, *iii.* This Joseph had but one wife, Abigail Grannis; Elizabeth was w. of a different Joseph (see above)...... (Page 931). FAM. 25. Mary da. Joseph & Elizabeth (Grannis) belongs to the other Joseph (see p. 915), and not to this family.

JOHNSON. (Page 1044). FAM. 20, 2, *vii.* Rhoda, b 21 May 1756 *F*, d 12 July 1847; m 1 Feb 1774 *CC*—Elisha Sanford.

LEFORGE. The record of this family on p. 1085 was incomplete. A descendant, Mrs. Burton A. Davis, has kindly contributed the following record of descendants, compiled by Mrs. Addison Sandford, a granddaughter of Henry Leforge.

I

Henry Leforge married Elizabeth Hunt.

II

Their children:

Anne married Moses Ford.
Susanna m Reuben Hills.
Patty m Merritt Baldwin.
Frederick m Martha (Johnson) Kennedy.
Theodosius lost at sea.
Henry better known as Harry.
Rebecca m Major Goodsell.
Betsey m Ebenezer Fisher.
Charlotte m William Love.

III

Children of Anne and Moses Ford.

Almira m James Augur.
Elias m (1) Mary Ann Bradley, m (2) Sally Rosetta Pierpont.
Caroline m (1) Abiel Leonard, m (2) Jere Gilbert.
Merritt m (1) Alethea Brockett, m (2) Jeannette Goodyear.

Children of Susanna and Reuben Hills.

Henry m Esther Doolittle.
Jeannette m Lorenzo Lee.
Vallorous died young.
James m Melissa(?) D. Willey.
Theresa m Henry W. Bassett.
Susan m Henry Gunn.

Children of Frederick Leforge and Martha Kennedy.

James m Martha Lewellyn.
Martha m —— Parkerson.
Theodosius unm.
Major m Augusta —— .

Children of Henry or Harry Leforge.

Anne m Peleg Bronson.
Theodosius.
George [m Eliza B. Lines, p. 1103.]

Children of Rebecca Leforge and Major Goodsell.

James Augur died young.
Elizabeth Leforge m Addison Sandford.

Children of Betsey Leforge and Ebenezer Fisher.

James m Charlotte Newcomb.
Elizabeth m D. O. Benjamin.

Hart m Eliza Shares.
Esther m William Bowe.
Maria m Cyrus Lee.

Children of Charlotte Leforge and William Love.
Charlotte m twice Sperry and Bishop.
Caroline m Isaac Hopkins.
Abi m Robert Sizer.

IV

Children of Almira Ford and James Augur.
Adeline m Sherman Warner.
Minot m Esther Morrell.
Betsey m Edward Davis.
George m Jane Chambers.
Almyra m George Lines.
Charles m Esther Murray.
Lydia m Edward Burgess.

Children of Merritt Ford and Alethea Brockett.
Burton m Jane Danks.
Mary m (1) Bailey Hawkins, m (2) Frank Bliss.
Emily m Austin Mansfield.
Henry unm.

Children of James Hills.
Ella unm.
Ada unm.
James Willey unm.
Caroline m L. D. Richards.
Mary m T. W. Lyman.

Children of Elizabeth Goodsell and Addison Sandford.
Sarah died young.
James died young.
Martha m E. B. Barney.
Mary unm.
Joseph m Marcia Lawton.
Jane died young.

LOUNSBURY. (Page 1110). FAM. 5, 4, *ii*. Abraham m Emily da. David & *Lowly* (*Todd*) Perkins. His brother Isaac m Lodema Delight da. Obed & Mary (Parker) Todd.

LOVE. (Page 1110). FAM. 1, 1. William m Charlotte Leforge.

MALLORY. (Page 1125). FAM. 3, 1, *i*, 4. Ashbel, b 5 Jan 1773, d 1 Feb 1856 æ. 83; Mary his w. d 23 Nov 1854 æ. 74; they were early settlers of the town of New Hartford, Oneida Co., N. Y., and are buried in the old cemetery in that village. [Contributed by Clarence D. Smith, Rome, N. Y.]

MANSFIELD. FAM. 5, 7. Mercy m Rev. William Throop.

MATTHEWS. (Page 1154). FAM. 5, 2. Aaron & w. Hannah were early residents of the town of Camden, Oneida Co., N. Y., where both died & are buried. Their tombstones in the old cemetery on Mexico street are broken so that dates cannot be read; he was a Rev. soldier & had s. Lyman & other issue. [Contributed by Clarence D. Smith, Rome, N. Y.]

MERWIN. (Page 1178). FAM. 1, 1. Samuel, bp 20 Feb 1686/7 *MCI*. (Page 1179). Justina, b 16 Oct 1704 *MV*. (Page 1180). FAM. 5, 2. Fowler, b 25 July 1740 [by Hist. of Goshen], d 9 Feb 1823 æ. 83 [Hist. of Cornwall]; m 23 Oct 1764 Amy da. Sylvanus & Mary (Whitmore) Nettleton, b 28 June 1743 [O. S], 10 July [N. S.], d 9 Mar 1823 æ. 80. His sister Susanna d 7 Aug 1825 æ. 83 *NMT*. FAM. 6, 1. Miles, b 1719, m Mary da. Samuel & Ruth (Rogers) Tibbals, b 26 Feb 1722/3. His sister Ann (page 1181) d 7 Sep 1758 æ. 35 *WdT;* m 23 May 1753 Andrew Baldwin. Mary, b 1734, d 27 May 1802 æ. 68-0-6 *MT*. [Contributed by George C. Bryant, Esq., Ansonia.]

MILES. (Page 1182). Bethia, wid. Theophilus (FAM. 1, 4, *vii*), d 21 Mar 1714/5 *MV*. (Page 1188). FAM. 7, 2. Daniel d 1 Feb 1786, not 1785. FAM. 7, 1, *i*. John m Jane Green [D. A. R. Lineage Books, 14:46]. His sister Martha d 29 May 1797 æ. 57 *MT*. Their bro. David m Diana (not Siana) da. Abijah & Anna Moore. [Contributed by George C. Bryant, Esq., Ansonia.]

Gilbert Mortality List

(Concluded from Volume 4, page 1024)

1816

January 1 Died Timothy Goodyear age 80 years.

January 15 Died Ebenezer Rice.

January 16 Died ——— age 5 months child of Thomas Gill.

February 1 or 2 Died old widow Beda Cooper age 86 years.

February 18 Died old Mr. Asa Bradley.

March

April 15 Died Samuel Ford age 80 years. (copy says one of town poor)

May

June 9 Died Abraham Chatterton.

July 5 Died Rebekah Gil age 37 years, wife of Thomas Gil.

July 12 Died Whiting Dickerman.

July 26 Died Roxy Hitchcock age 33 years, wife of Ichabod Hitchcock.

July 26 Died Dan Kelsey age 13 years, grandson to Chauncey Dickerman.

August

September 5 Died Samuel Hitchcock age 73 years.

October 19 Died ——— infant child of Jared Atwater.

November

December

1817

January 16 Died old widow Abagail Hitchcock age 87 years

January 23 Died Ruth Cooper age 72 years, widow Alling Cooper.

February

March

April

May 24 Died Capt. Jesse Goodyear age 82 years.

June

July 31 Died Enos Atwater age about 60 years.

August

September 3 Died Mercy Goodyear age 47 years, wife of Jese Goodyear.

October

November 16 Died Joshua Goodyear.
December

1818
January
February
March
April 6 Died ——— age 8 months, daughter of Elizur Caldwell.
April 7 Died Anthony Thompson.
April 10 Died at Doct. Andrew's, Triphene Cooper one of the town poor.
May 17 Died Beda Bradley wife of David Bradley & daughter of Elam Ives.
May 24 Died Sally Goodyear age 23 years, daughter of Jese Goodyear.
June
July
August 11 Died Sarah Thompson, widow of Anthony Thompson.
September
October 25 Died Mabel Ives age 72 years, wife of Ezra Ives.
November
December 3 Died at Doct. Andrew's, Betty Doolittle, wife of Titus Doolittle.

1819
January
February 26 Died at Ebenezer Warner's, old widow Andrews age 78 years, one of the town poor.
March 25 Died Lorry Dickerman wife of Jason Dickerman.
April 23 Died old Mrs. Chatterton age 82 years, widow of Abraham Chatterton.
May 1 Died Jason Bradley age 77 years.
June
July
August
September 16 Died Amos Bradley age 73 years.
September 26 Died Sylvia Bradley daughter of Amos Bradley deceased.

October 16 Died Andrew Goodyear age 36 years.
October 24 Died infant child.
November 18 Buried Amos Thompson Jr. age 22 years.
November 28 Buried Maryan Thompson (copy says daughter of Amos Thompson)
December 12 Died widow Abagail Warner.
December 27 Died Rhode Goodyear age 50 years, widow of Joshua Goodyear.

1820

January 18 Buried widow Eunice Atwater, one of the town poor.
January 27 Died ——— age 1 year, 8 months, daughter of Lewis Goodyear.
February 4 Died Benjamin Trumbel D. D. age 84 years, of North Haven.
March
April 28 Died Chauncey Dickerman.
May
June
July 21 Died ——— age 60 years, wife of Timothy Bassett
August 27 Died Manly Dickerman.
September
October 2 Died Ruth Atwater, wife of Samuel Atwater.
October 18 Died Vashti Woolcott age 19 years, daughter of Ira Woolcott.
October 18 Buried John Thompson age 36 years.
October 19 Died ——— Bradley, wife of Asa Bradley.
November 16 Died Timothy Leake age 87.
December 5 Died Luther Roper, M. D. age 26.
December 21 Died Joseph Scranton, killed by a fall at Job Munson's mill from shutting down the gate.

1821

January 20 Died Joseph Gilbert age 73 years.
January 22 Died Timothy Bassett age 62 years.
January 30 Died Dea. Daniel Bradley age 93 years.
February 21 Died Esther Bradley wife of Dea. Aaron Bradley (copy says 2nd wife)
March
April 2 Died at Jason Atwater's, Widow Damaris Sanford

age 75 years, formerly of Woodbridge.

April 15 Died Patty Goodyear age 39 years, widow of Asa Goodyear.

May 22 Died Dea. Jesse Dickerman.

May 27 Died Jonathan Dickerman.

June 19 Died Seymour Bradley age 41 years.

July

August

September

October 4 Buried Enos Bassett age 37 years.

October 6 Died Samuel Hitchcock.

November

December

1822

January

February

March

April 3 Died Hannah Goodyear age 82 years, widow of Capt. Jesse Goodyear.

May

June

July 6 Died Amos Dickerman age 63 years.

July 31 Died Mabel Ives age 46 years, wife of Jesse Ives.

August (Copy says, died Anna Bradley 3rd wife of Asa Bradley)

September

October 15 Died at Job Munsons, Zenus Munson grandson of Job Munson (copy says age 11 years)

November 12 Died Frances L. Goodyear age 16 months, son of Lewis Goodyear.

November 12 Died Lois Dickerman age 41 years wife of Samuel Dickerman.

November 13 Died Mabel Bradley age 87 years, widow of Alven Bradley.

December

1823

January

February 21 Died old ——— Bradley widow Dea. Daniel

Bradley.

March 15 Died Levi Bradley age 6 years.

March 31 Died Lorry Woolcott age 9 years, daughter of Ira Woolcott.

April 21 Died Joseph Dorman of the Plains.

April 25 Died Ebenezer Hitchcock age 26 years.

May 13 Married Sally Bradley to Julius Brooks.

June 18 Died Zina Mix.

July

August

September

October 8 Died Capt. Hezekiah Bassett age 78 years.

October 21 Died Mabel Gilbert age 46 years.

October 25 Died Joel Heaton age 61 years, of North Haven.

November 23 Died Joel Goodyear.

December

1824

January 9 Died Samuel Linsley age 28.

January 24 Died infant 4 days old, child of Eldad Bassett.

February 26 Died Phebe Galard age 68 years, wife of Benjamin Galard.

March 31 Died Lucy Bradley 3rd wife of Asa Bradley.

April

May 17 Died ———, wife of John Perkins.

June 1 Died ———, wife of Eli Alling.

July

August

September 1 or 2 Died Stiles Hitchcock age 17.

September 9 Died Ichabod Hitchcock age 48 years. (copy says 45 years)

September 27 Died Hannah Hitchcock, daughter of Ichabod Hitchcock.

October

November

December 8 Died at Norwalk, Polly Cooper wife of Capt. Jared Cooper.

December 15 Died Mrs. Woods, wife of (?)

1825

January 8 Died in New Haven, Eli Whitney Esq.

February 24 Died Alling Galard age 46 years. Killed by falling a tree.
March 26 Died Benjamin Galard.
April
May 23 Died ——— age 10 months, child of Dr. John Cornwell.
June
July 2 Died Elam Dickerman.
July 8 Died ——— age 17 months, son of Arba Dickerman.
July 23 Died Lenny Bradley, daughter of old Mr. Amos Bradley.
August 3 Died Rhode Barns age 13 years, daughter of Leverit Barnes.
August 5 Died Dr. John Cornwell.
August 19 Died Ezra Ives age 81 years.
September 23 Died Mrs. Cloe Barns, wife of Leverit Barnes.
October 4 Died ——— age 2 years, daughter of Amos Dickerman.
November 15 Died Alvira Rouly age 3 years, daughter of (?)
December 7 Married by Mr. Boardman, James Gilbert to Betzy Todd.

1826

January
February
March 3 Died Sarah Woods age 7 years, daughter of (?)
March 10 Died ——— age 3 years, son of Titus Doolittle (copy says Jr))
March 25 Died Jesse Goodyear age 60 years. Drowned himself by jumping into the river.
March 27 Died ———, child of Capt. Kingsley.
April 9 Died Capt. Jared Cooper age 60 years.
May
June
July 2 Died Josiah Mansfield.
August
September 2 Died Polly Blakeslee, daughter of Obed Blakeslee.

September 6 Died Dr. T. Brunson of Cheshire (copy says age 60 years)
September 23 Died in North Haven, Serviah Mix age 90 years, widow of Stephen Mix. (copy says Zuviah Mix)
September 28 Died Polly Brunson, age 57, wife of Dr. T. Brunson of Cheshire.
October 7 Died ———, wife of Eldad Woolcott.
October 17 Died Minerva Leek age 22 years, wife of Russel Leek.
October 29 Died ——— age 6, son of Elisha Woolcott.
October 29 Died ———, infant child of Mrs. Porter. (copy says Mrs. Polly Porter)
November 1 Died Esther Hotchkiss age 47, wife of Elias Hotchkiss.
November 7 Died ——— age 5, son of Russel Ives.
December 7 Died Alvin Bradley age 52. Killed under Ezra Kimberly's shed by a stone flung by a blast.

1827
January 6 Died Capt. Amasa Bradley, Esq.
January 19 Died Sarah (Gilbert) Tuttle age 43, wife of Seymour Tuttle.
January 26 Died in New Haven, Obed Bradley and buried in our burying ground.
February 22 Died wife of Matthew Gillet, one of the canal men.
March
April
May 1 Died an Irishman at Shepherd's Brook. One of the canal men.
May 30 Died Rebecca Leek age 24. (copy says age 25)
June 10 Died Loly Tuttle age 50, wife of Lyman Tuttle.
July
August 4 Died in Berlin, Dea. Elijah Hart, by the sting of a bumble bee.
August 5 Died at Mr. Gillet's an Irishman to work on the canal.
August 26 Died Samuel Goodyear age 49.
September 20 Died child of Ichabod Hitchcock deceased.
September Died child of Lushanous Munson.
September 24 Died daughter of John Perkins.

September 27 Died Lucy Tuttle, daughter of Eli Tuttle .
October 5 Died Olive Goodyear age 40, wife of Capt. Seymour Goodyear.
October 12 Died widow Cloe Galard age 30.
October 14 Died Jason Goodyear, son of the late Samuel Goodyear.
October 29 Died Milly Warner age 42. (copy says Amela Warner)
November 6 Died Simeon Warner.
November 21 Died Zadock Alling age 53.
December

1828
January
February 5 Died Deac. Aaron Bradley age 71.
March 16 Died Eliakim Brooks age 60.
April 29 Died Elizur Cadwell age 42. (copy says Caldwell)
May 29 Died widow of Joel Bradley age 87.
June 10 Died Job L. Munson age 76.
July
August 23 Died in North Haven, Theophilus Bradley. Hanged himself.
September 27 Died age 4 months, child of Alfred Bassett.
October 7 Died a transcient man at Levrit Barns.
November
December 3 Died Caroline Goodyear age 16, daughter of Lewis Goodyear.
December 22 Died Lousina Goodyear age 14, daughter of Lewis Goodyear.

1829
January
February
March 21 Died Samuel Atwater age 74.
April
May
June
July 22 Died Lois Tuttle, widow of Hezekiah Tuttle.
August
September 5 Died Abigail Ives age 40, wife of Russel Ives.

October 14 Died old widow Sarah Hitchcock.
October 24 Died Sally Hough age 40.
November
December

1830
January
February 7 Died David Brockett age 55.
February 10 Died Sally Munson age 41, wife of J. Lushanus Munson.
February 18 Buried Julia Bradley, daughter of Obed Bradley, deceased.
March 19 Died Serilla Brooks age 21, daughter of Enos Brooks.
March 23 Died Polly Peck, wife of Jeremiah Peck.
April
May 19 Ordained Mr. Hubbil.
June
July 7 Died Elias Hotchkiss age 58.
July 26 Died Burr Perkins, son of Amasa Perkins, drowned
August
September
October
November 29 Died at Jeremiah Peck's, Anjuline Todd, daughter of Linus Todd deceased of North Haven.
December 12 Died Eber Ives age 74.

1831
January
February
March
April
May
June 5 Died widow Laura Sherry age 34, daughter of Josiah Mansfield deceased.
July
August
September
October
November

December 8 Died Mehitibel Hull age 53, wife of Eli Hull.

1832

January 17 Died at Austin Munson's, Joel Walter.

February 8 Died Sarah Cooper age 77, by many called Aunt Sarah Leek.

March 26 Died Capt. Kingsley age 55.

April 2 Died John Pardee age 4, son of John Pardee. (copy says age 5)

May 15 Died Cordealia Goodyear age 22, daughter of Samuel Goodyear deceased.

May 26 Died at Levi Alling's, Levi Alling's wife's mother.

June

July

August

September 23 Buried wife of Amos Thompson.

September 27 Died Levina Dickerman, wife of Seymour Dickerman.

October 8 Died John Perkins age 82.

October 27 Died Obed Moss.

October 29 Died, old Mrs. Goodyear age 85, widow of Dea. Stephen Goodyear. (copy says Mary)

November

December

1833

January

February 24 Died infant child of Edward Dickerman.

March

April 11 Died in the Jenesee Country, Joseph Goodyear formerly a neighbor of mine.

April 14 Died Loundso Spencer put up at Sterling Bradleys and in the morning was found dead.

April 20 Died Ezra Warner age 49.

May

June

July 31 Died Hannah Leek age 54, wife of Elisha Leek.

August 5 Died Lucy Goodyear age 58, widow of Samuel Goodyear.

August 14 The bell for Hamden Church was cast in New Haven by Mr. Bradley, and brought up today and

raised into Hamden Church.
September
October 7 Died Mary Woolcott age 22.
(Copy says October 3 Died William Todd age 17, drowned in Arba Dickerman's lock)
November 12 Died wife of Dr. Joseph Foot of (?)
November 29 Died Simeon Todd.
December 17 Died Mary Ann Ford age 25, wife of Elias Ford. Her former name was Mary Ann Bradley. (copy says daughter of Levi Bradley deceased)

1834
January 25 Died widow of Mr. Joel Todd.
January 25 Kelsey began to ring the bel for a year at $15.00.
February 18 Buried Titus Goodyear age 23. (copy says Feb. 14)
March
April
May
June
July Died Brackett Todd dropped down dead amowing.
July 16 Died Asa Churchel choaked to death eating a clam.
August 23 Died Mary Preston age 17, daughter of Chauncey Preston.
September 28 Died Widow Beda Dorman.
October 27 Died Elisha Leek age 70.
October 28 Died infant child of Almirene Sandford.
November
December

1835
January
February 1 Died child of Ezra Dickerman age 1 year. PAGE 1529
March 13 Died Albert Dickerman age 28.
April
May 6 Died Maria Ives age 20, daughter of Jesse Ives.
May 31 Married Ann Thomas to Ruben Doolittle.
June 22 Died child of Shanus Munson age 2 years. (copy says Lushanus)
June 29 Died Sylvia Dickerman age 15, daughter of Widow

Suphroney Dickerman.
July 3 Died Edward Todd age 9 years, son of Uriah Todd.
July 14 Died Esther Todd age 32 years, wife of Loyal Todd
July 29 Died infant child of Julius Ives.
August 4 Died at Harvey Leek's, Amos Potter, town poor.
August 23 Died Stephen Hitchcock age 58.
September 6 Died Eunice Tuttle age 74, wife of Jese Tuttle
September 9 Died at Dr. C. B. Foot's, infant child of Mr. Hassey late of New Haven.
October
November 15 Died at Harvey Leek's, widow Hannah Ford age 92.
December

1836

January
February 4 Died at Harvey Leek's, Ezra Talmage age 76.
March 8 Died Widow Abigail Goodyear age 86.
March 31 Died Levi Alling age 66.
April 3 Died Ely Alling age 79.
April 7 Died Widow Sarah Ives age 85.
April 17 Died at Harvey Leek's, Mrs. Murry age 80, town pauper.
April 24 Died Dr. Joseph Foote of North Haven.
May 6 Died at Harvey Leek's, Mrs. Woodin, widow of Daniel Woodin.
May 10 Died daughter of Carline Prichard age 2 years, sister of Timothy. (copy says Carline Prichard age 2)
May 25 Died James Cooper of North Haven.
June
July
August 21 This day church was opened and prayers read by Mr. Collins.
September
October
November
December

1837

January 4 Died Mrs. Ruth Huff age 69 years, 3rd wife of Joel Huff.

January 23 Died Eliza Goodyear age 38 years, wife of Fowler Goodyear.
January 14 Died Titus Doolittle age 88 years.
February 3 Buried Betsy Atwater age 79, widow Capt. Asa Atwater.
February 13 Died at Ebenezer Warner's, old Lydia Melone age 86, town poor.
February 23 Died Benjamin Peck.
March
April 17 Died Friend Goodyear age 21.
April 21 Died Sally Bassett age 16, daughter of Hezekiah Bassett.
May
June 8 Died Jesse Barnes age 40.
July 1 Died Emuline Munson age 30.
July 2 Died daughter of Miles Durin.
July 4 Died Daniel Chatterton age 71.
July 6 They begin to ring the bell noon and night.
July 16 Our church was opened today and first for this year Mr. Bradley preached.
July 24 Died in Plains Society, Rev. Abraham Alling age 83.
August 5 Died at Mr. Joel Cooper's, Lambert Stephens.
August 18 Died infant child of Zealous Warner.
August 25 Died Cloey Bull age 92.
August 27 Died Roxy Preston age 45, wife of Chauncey Preston. (copy says Roseny)
September 22 Died William F. Bradley age 28.
September 26 Died Abigail Bishop.
October 22 or 28 Died Mrs. Cornelia Cook age 28, wife of Hobart Cook late of Cheshire.
November 28 Died Maria Wiles age 35.
December

1838
(Omission here?)
June 23 Merie Ives age 23.
July 9 Mary Dickerman age 5, daughter of Jared Dickerman.
July 24 ——— Hart.
August 31 Polly Todd age 43, wife of Roswell Todd.

September
October 23 Amos Peck age 89.
December 2 Mary Kelsey age 55, wife of Ansel Kelsey.
December 3 Infant child at Harvey Leeks. Town poor.

1839

January 11 Damaris Dickerman age 84, widow of Deacon Jesse Dickerman.
February 27 Delight Bradley age 27, daughter of Sterling Bradley.
March 11 Albert Bradley age 27. (copy says son of late Alvin Bradley)
March 12 George Thompson age 23.
March 20 At Harvey Leek's, Mrs. Way, age about 50. Town poor.
April 4 Patty Bradley age 72, widow of Capt. Amasa Bradley.
April 11 Mrs. Doolittle age 64, wife of Ruben Doolittle.
May 16 Loly Bassett age 61, wife of Hezekiah Bassett.
May 22 Mrs. Hull, age 53, third wife of Eli Hull.
June
July 26 Olive Peck age 75, wife of Joseph Peck.
August 24 Lyman Tuttle Jr., or 3rd, age 28.
September
October
November
December

1840

January 7 Polly Tuttle age 55, wife of Ambrose Tuttle Esq.
January 10 Betsy Dickerman.
February 29 Up under the blue hills, John Lines. (copy says a transient man)
March 16 Zealous Warner age 41.
April
May
June
July
August
September 21 Densa Tuttle age 38, wife of Jese Tuttle. (copy says Dantha)

October 10 Lewis Goodyear age 52.
November 21 Mrs. Brockett wife of Hezekiah Brockett. (copy says Mehitable, age 65)
December 10 Lieut. Joel Cooper. (copy says age 91)

1841
January 22 Widow Elizabeth Leek.
February 6 Julia Goodyear age 20, daughter of Lyman Goodyear.
February 25 Infant child of George Bradley.
March
April 4 General Harrison, President of the United States.
May 14 Emily Ives age 10, granddaughter of Jared Ives.
May 28 Widow Abigail Chatterton.
June
July 20 Mrs. Doolittle, 2nd wife Reuben Doolittle.
August 25 Sally Pierpont age 72, widow of Russell Pierpont.
September 29 Abigail Wolcott age 58, 2nd wife of Eldad Wolcott.
October 6 Hubbard Bradley Bury'd, age 52.
October 25 Sarah Caldwell age 26.
November 12 Jese Cooper age 66.

1842
January
February
March 9 Levi Dickerman age 68.
March 16 Lusina Warner age 67, widow of Simeon Warner.
March 17 Eldad Woolcott.
March 31 Buryd in our burying ground, James Slade age 29. (copy says he was drowned in Farmington)
April 8 Lyman Tuttle age 63.
April 15 An infant child of William Dickermans.
May 13 Grace Hubbil age 5.
May 23 Mabel Ives age 26, daughter of Jese Ives.
May 25 Drowned in canal, Mary Jane Bradley age 5 years, daughter of Ives Bradley.
June 5 Drowned in canal, Robbart Henry 3 years. (copy says, Hobart Henry)
June 9 Capt. Aaron Chatterton age 51.

July 1 Emmy Goodyear age 20, daughter of Lyman Goodyear.
August 18 James Wiles age 70.
September 16 Mary Cooper age 83, widow of Joel Cooper.
September 20 Mary Bradley age 69.
October 13 Elam Warner age 62.
November
December

1843
January
February
March 1 Eliza Potter age 5, daughter of Bill Potter.
March 5 A son, 2 years old, of Vanhortons.
March 5 Infant child of Mrs. Taylors.
March 25 Ira Woolcott age 72.
April 3 Robert Stephens age 16.
May 20 Esther Dunbar, wife of Giles Dunbar.
June 29 Sarah Loisa Averyst age 24, wife of Mr. Averyst, Minister.
July
August
September 10 Joel Hough age 87. (copy says Jr.)
September 11 Mr. Courrier age 34.
September 21 Jese Ives age 69.
October 9 A child, age 18 months, of Henry Pecks.
November
December

1844
January 27 Anna Cooper Hinman age 6.
February 3 An infant child of Henry Dickermans.
February 8 Mary Dickerman age 66, wife of Capt. Enos Dickerman.
February 11 Died at Mr. Kelseys, Edward Hills of Cheshire age 41.
February 19 Maryan Downs, daughter of Laban Downs.
March 2 Widow Amy Mansfield.
March 11 Sally Peck age 59.
April 21 Eli Tuttle 62 years.

(Taken from copy; original sheets for these two

months missing)

May

June 1 Jeremiah Gilbert. (copy says aged 65).

June 22 A son of Goodyear Ives. (copy says 1 year old)

July

August

September 23 Elias Tirrel. (copy says age 67)

October 26 Ezra Potter. (copy says town pauper)

November

December 12 Russel Pierpont Esq. age 82 years.

1845

January 3 Loisa Dickerman wife of William B. Dickerman.

February 5 An infant child of Joseph Grannis.

March 9 Margaret Vanhorton age 27, daughter of Levirit Dickerman.

April 4 Drowned, a son age 2 years, of Orchard Warners.

April 21 Lucy Thompson age 67, widow of Joel Thompson.

May 3 Grace Alling age 72, widow of Levi Alling.

May 12 or 13 Sybil Blakeslee age 62. (copy says wife of Obed Blakeslee)

June 11 Chester Scovel age 45.

June 25 or 27 Infant of Ezra Dickermans. PAGE 1529

July 21 Giles Dunbar age 60.

August 9 Joseph Peck age 83.

September Died at Henry Ives, Loisa Gorham (of New Haven)

October 29 Died at Ives factory, James Combs, age 27.

November

December

1846

January 21 Mary, wife of Bennet Peck.

January 25 Elam Ives Esq. age 84.

January 26 Died at Amasa Hitchcocks, Samuel Hitchcock.

February

March

April 24 Buryd in our burying ground, John Warner age 73.

April 16 Ann Doolittle age 32, wife Reuben Doolittle.

April 17 David Andrews age 21 years.
July 20 Andrew P. Potter was hanged in New Haven for killing a man.
———— George Scranton's daughter age 5 years.
August 24 Amasa Hitchcock age 66.
September 18 Levi Perkins age 53.
September 22 A son, 5 years old, of Joseph Grannis.
October 4 Widow Esther Homaston, age 89.
November 8 A child, 18 months old, of Hiram Smiths.

1847

January 4 Ezra Bassett, 66 or 76 years old.
March 7 Widow Ford.
March 12 Mrs. Julia Andrews 34 years old, wife of Ziba Andrews.

This completes the Gilbert Mortality List, contributed by Mr. and Mrs. H. Nelson Stiles of North Haven, Conn.

MILES, TYLEY, ATKINS, STRATTON

By Mrs. Frances Harrison Corbin

On page 1183 it was stated that Theophilus Miles, b at Milford 1 Dec 1703, married Katharine ——, probably niece of Louis Liron. This statement was based on Liron's will, which referred to Katharine Miles as his kinswoman. My investigations show that she was actually grandniece of Liron's wife, and establish a distinguished ancestry for her.

Bartholomew Stratton, bapt. in London, Eng., 12 Jan 1627/8, d in Boston, Mass., 9 Jan 1686; m Eliphal Sanford, b 9 Dec 1636, d 19 Jan 1724, da. of John Sanford of Portsmouth, R. I., by his second wife Bridget Hutchinson, da. of William and Ann (Marbury) Hutchinson. The Thomas Sanford Genealogy, p 1387, erroneously states that Eliphal was by Sanford's first wife. Children:

1 William, b 30 Jan 1658/9.

2 Katharine, b 1661 (no record), d at Milford 26 Nov 1727 in 58th yr.; m (1) —— Cuthbert; m (2) at Boston, 3 Oct 1706, Louis Liron, who d at Milford 18 Sep 1738 in 88th yr.

3 Ann, b 19 Feb 1662/3; see below.

4 Bridget, b 28 Jan 1664/5; m Robert Ladd.

Ann Stratton, b at Boston, 19 Feb 1662/3, m Tobias Atkins, and had:

Eliphal Atkins, b at Boston, 4 Dec 1688, m c. 1709 Samuel Tyley, b at Boston 19 July 1689, son of Samuel and grandson of Thomas Tyley. He m (2) Elizabeth Foster. Samuel and Eliphal lived for a time in Milford, where their da. Katharine was b 15 Apr 1710; she m Theophilus Miles. The Tyleys returned to Boston.

References: Thomas Sanford Gen.; Book of the Strattons; York Deeds, vol. 11, p. 100, and vol. 12, p. 37; Boston Births, Marriages and Deaths; Essex Institute Coll. vol. 42, p. 205; Suffolk Deeds, vol. 14, p. 252.

Enoch Culver, Sr.

REVOLUTIONARY SOLDIER

This is the story of a pair of stockings, and how they proved service in the Revolutionary War.

Enoch Culver was born in Wallingford, Conn., 30 Jan., 1725, and died there 22 Sept., 1812 in the 88th year of his age. He came of vigorous stock. His great-grandfather, Edward Culver, a veteran of the Pequot War of 1637, was robust enough to serve in his old age as a scout in King Philip's War in 1675. His grandfather, Joshua Culver, settled in New Haven, removing from there about 1680 to Wallingford, where he died at the age of 70. Enoch was son of Samuel Culver by his first wife, Ruth Tyler. His maternal grandparents were William Tyler and Mary Lathrop, the latter being a great-granddaughter of the Rev. John Lathrop.

The Colver-Culver Genealogy, page 76, says of Enoch: "It is stated by some authorities that he was a Revolutionary soldier, and that with his brother Samuel, he was taken prisoner at Fort Washington, but the compiler of this genealogy has been unable to verify this statement." The book quoted is quite incomplete and contains many inaccuracies, but it is probable that the above statement was based on family tradition. Such muster rolls of Connecticut soldiers in the Revolutionary War as have been preserved do not contain the name of Enoch Culver, Sr. This negative evidence is inconclusive, because the extant muster rolls are very incomplete. It can be proved from muster rolls and official documents that Samuel Culver, Enoch's younger half-brother, who was born 25 Sept., 1728, served as Ensign in Col. Hooker's regiment, that he was held a prisoner from 29 June, 1779 to 2 Jan., 1781, and that he died at Wallingford, 22 March, 1781, shortly after his release, as a result of the privations he had undergone. Enoch Culver, Sr., who settled his brother's estate, presented a claim to the Conn. Legislature for wages due to his deceased brother Samuel, on behalf of the latter's family.

Hence it is certain that Enoch Culver, Sr., was in sympathy with the patriotic cause, for had there been the slightest question of his loyalty, he would not have been chosen to present this petition on behalf of his brother's family. This fact also suggests that there may have been some truth in the family tradition preserved in the Colver-Culver Genealogy, though it cannot be proved now.

In the Revolutionary Archives at the Conn. State Library, vol. 12, document 439a, is an account against the State presented by the town of Wallingford. It is headed "Wallingford, Jan.[a] 1, 1778 . . . . . . A Count of the Clothing bought for the Continental Army by sd Army," and the following item appears thereunder: "1. Pare of Stockings to Enoch Culver——0. 9. 0." Taking these words in their usual significance, the implication of this item is that Enoch Culver was serving in the Continental Army prior to Jan. 1, 1778, most likely during the preceding year, and that these stockings having been bought and supplied to him, the town of Wallingford was billing the State for their value. The question is whether the reference pertains to Enoch, Sr., or to his son Enoch.

The following references to the family of Enoch, Sr., are found in the Wallingford Vital Records, which are scattered through the early volumes of deeds. These entries are in vol. 15, the margins of which are frayed, making portions of the entries illegible. The missing portions have been supplied in parentheses from the History of Wallingford (published 1870), page 722, the children named in Enoch's will, and other sources. On page 680: "Enoch Culver Married Lois Benham P. Saml[l] Hall Esq[r]. (8 Feb., 1749)." On the following page are entered the births of the following children to Enoch and Lois Culver:

Ebenezer, born 30 Aug., 1749.
(E)sther, born 24 July, 1751.
(John), born 28 Dec., 1753.
(L)ois, born 4 June, 1756.
(E)noch, born 24 Oct., 1763.

On page 682 are entered the deaths of Enoch and William, sons of Enoch (Sr.) and Lois Culver, but the year of death in both instances has been lost from the margin of the page. The births of these two sons are not found on record, but presumably they were born between Lois in 1756 and Enoch in 1763.

Enoch Culver, Jr., married Lucy Hall on 19 Oct., 1786 (Wallingford Deeds, vol. 22, page 222). The files of the Bureau of Pensions at Washington contain documents relating to the service in the Revolutionary War of Enoch, Jr. A letter from the Acting Commissioner of the Bureau, dated 16 April, 1924, gives the following information:

"I have to advise you that from the papers in the Revolutionary War petition claim, W. 25464, it appears that Enoch Culver (Jr.) was born October 24, 1761, at Wallingford, New Haven County, Connecticut.

"While residing in Wallingford, Connecticut, he enlisted and served in the Connecticut Militia as follows;

"From August 1778 two months in Captain Lusk's Company.

"From July 1779 two months in Captain Dan Collins' Company.

"From September 1780 two months in Captain Oliver Stanley's Company.

"From August 1781 two months in Captain John Hough's Company.

"He was allowed pension on his application executed January 23, 1838, while residing in Burlington, Hartford County, Connecticut. He died March 1, 1838.

"He married October 19, 1786, at Wallingford, Connecticut, Lucy Hall. She was allowed pension on her application executed December 27, 1838, while residing in Burlington, Connecticut, aged sixty-six years."

As Enoch, Sr., died before the passage of the first general pension act, he never applied for a pension, and would not have been likely to do so unless totally incapacitated as a result of his service. It is extremely probable that Enoch, Jr., claimed in his application for pension ALL the military service he performed. It is important that the earliest service claimed by him started in August 1778, over seven months after the date of the Wallingford account dated 1 Jan., 1778, which included the item of stockings to Enoch Culver. The latter document did not specify Sr. or Jr., and in the lack of specification, it is more reasonable to infer that the father was intended, rather than a young boy of not quite fifteen.

Apparently the only objection to the conclusion that the service prior to 1 Jan., 1778, belonged to Enoch, Sr., is his age at the time of service, which was fifty-two years. It has been shown above that Enoch's half-brother Samuel was in active service when over fifty years old; in fact, both Samuel and his son of the same name served in the army, the father being an officer and the son a private. Enoch, Sr., lived to be eighty-eight, and the family in that generation seems to have been robust and hardy. What his brother Samuel did, it was possible for Enoch to do.

Largely on the strength of the pair of stockings, Enoch Culver, Sr., has been accepted by the General Society, Daughters of the Revolution, and by the National Society, Daughters of Founders and Patriots, as an eligible ancestor with active war service.

It will be noted that Enoch Culver, Jr., in his application stated his date of birth as 24 Oct., 1761, whereas the entry of his birth in Wallingford records stated it as 24 Oct. 1763. The present writer read the date as 1763 in the Wallingford records, but after learning from the Pension Office that the man himself had stated the year as 1761, and realizing the damaged condition of the page on which the birth was entered, modestly assumed that he had misread the date, and therefore printed it as 1761 in volume II., page 469, of the present work. Another examination of the Wallingford record has verified the original reading of the date as 1763. Whether the Wallingford entry or the man's own knowledge of his age is at fault, cannot be determined with certainty. If 1763 was correct, he was not quite fifteen at the date of his first enlistment, August 1778, and like many youths eager to play their part in war times, may have overstated his age deliberately at his first enlistment. In that event, he may have set back the date of his birth two years when filing his pension application, in order to make it correspond with his alleged age at the time of his enlistment. This is the most probable explanation of the discrepancy, and if true, makes it all the more unlikely that he was in active service earlier than August 1778, and confirms our conclusion that the service rendered prior to 1 Jan., 1778 was the service of his father Enoch, Sr.

DONALD LINES JACOBUS.

Bethany Mortality List

Contributed by Rev. Wallace Humiston, Northfield, Conn.

This list of deaths was kept for five years in a book in which appear the words "Denzel Hitchcock's book". It relates to people who lived in Bethany parish, and since scarcely one of these entries is to be found in the public records, the list is of great value. It should be noted that this private recorder, while usually stating ages in years, months, and days, in several instances overstated the age by an exact year.

	Yrs.	Mos.	D's
1788			
February 11 Mrs. Elizabeth Tolles wife of Ens. Abraham Tolles	29	7	29
February 13 Infant son of Medad Hotchkiss	0	0	1
February 15 Infant son of Winard Mitchell	0	1	12
February 21 Mrs. Hannah Buckingham wife of Abijah Buckingham	51	5	4
March 8 Miss Lucy Johnson	27	6	21
March 15 Stillborn infants (twins) of Lieut. Jesse Beecher			
March 20 Miles son of Simeon Wheeler	2	11	5
March 29 Infant son of Ebenezer Bishop	0	1	18
April 3 Widow Ruth Lounsbury	85	5	9
April 21 Lieut. Jonathan Mansfield Peck			
May 18 Lemuel Wooding	44	11	13
May 24 Infant twin daughters of Joseph Johnson (Anna and Fanny)	0	1	3
June 4 Micah, son of Timothy Lounsbury	2	3	29
July 9 Anna, wife of Elijah Clark	26	11	16
July 19 Stillborn son of John Huggs			
December 17 Catherine wife of Joseph Hitchcock	22	7	1
December 24 Thankful Perkins, about	82		
1789			
February 2 Widow Susanna Johnson			
April 23 Sarah wife of Cyrus Wooding	27	10	24
June 12 Mary wife of Samuel Beach	56	7	
June 24 Daniel Tyler	51	2	27
August 1 John Andrew	29	7	

September 12 or 15	Thankful, wife of John Alsop Talmadge	40	4	3
September 19	Infant son of Daniel Tolles	0	0	4
November 24	Samuel Kingsley			

1790

January 5	Widow Deborah Carrington	96	6	(28)
March 21	Widow Dorcas Thomas	89	3	19
April 5	Joel son of Samuel Brisco	0	2	17
April 23	William son of William Purdee	0	5	17
May 31	Nathan Nettleton	31	3	21
July 10	Isaac son of Polycarp Smith	0	3	10
July 26	Infant son of Ezra Sperry Jr.	0	0	1
October 20	Son of Hezekiah Johnson			

1791

March 15	Sarah Bellamy Tolles, daughter of Capt. Lazarus Tolles			
March 25	Samuel Brisco	33	4	21
July 9	Isaac Beecher 2d (Jr.)			
August 11	Rebecca Wooding, wife of Cyrus Wooding			
September 18	Esther, wife of Ebenezer Humfreville	34		
October 13	Phinehas Tirrel	66	4	13

1792

February 15	Silas Nelson			
March 27	Abel Ives	69		
March 31	Wife of Wheeler Beecher	30		
April 13	Ens. Gershom Thomas			
July 10	Joanna Smith			
October 9	Abel Ward			
November	Capt. Amos Hitchcock	68	5	
December 23	Esther wife of Ama(sa) Tuttle			

1793

February 3	Ezekiel Smith stillborn infant			
March 15	Anna wife of Azariah Perkins			
April	Mary, wife of Rev. S. Hawley	( )		

Book Reviews

This department of the New Haven Genealogical Magazine offers to compilers and publishers of genealogical books the opportunity to secure fair and honest reviews of their productions. The reviewer will do his utmost to point out the good features of every book which is presented for review, but in fairness to those who read the reviews will mention striking deficiencies, such as the lack of an index, unusually poor arrangement of material, or gross inaccuracies. All genealogical books, even the poorest, have some value, insofar as they present material not to be found elsewhere in print, and it is our aim to say the best that can be said of each book. Those who wish books reviewed should send them to the address below.

Donald L. Jacobus, Editor
554 Central Avenue
Westville, Conn.

BLACKMAN Blackman and Allied Families. Compiled for Nathan Lincoln Blackman by Alfred L. Holman. Privately printed, Chicago, 1928. 8°, cloth, 1 chart, 258 pp. Address: Nathan L. Blackman, 6930 South Shore Drive, Chicago, Ill.

The first twenty-one pages are devoted to a record of the family of John Blackman (of Dorchester 1640), one branch of which is brought down for eight generations. A very full account is given of the families of James Adams (of Westerly 1698), of Thomas Joslin (of Hingham 1635), and of John Keigwin (of Stonington 1702).

The remainder of the volume deals less exhaustively with other families from whom Mr. Blackman traces his descent. A great deal of information is compressed into small compass, and descendants of the following *Connecticut* settlers will find much of interest in the book: Robert Allen or Allyn (of New London 1651); William Billings (of New London by 1670); Richard Birge (of Windsor 1640); Robert Campbell (of New London 1714); Stephen Gates (of Preston 1708, son of Stephen of Hingham 1638); William Gaylord (of Windsor 1638); George Geer (of New London 1659); Jonathan Gillett (of Windsor 1635); Thomas Holcombe (of Windsor 1635); Robert Howard (of Windsor by 1643); John Ingersoll (of Hartford by 1651); William Kennedy (of Preston before 1727); Thomas Kilbourne (of Wethersfield by 1640); Joseph Loomis (of Windsor 1639); Thomas Lord (of Hartford 1636); Daniel McMains of Plainfield 1734); John Marsh (of Hartford 1636); John Packer (of New London by 1651); Walter Palmer (of Stonington); Robert Parke (of Stonington); George Phelps (of Windsor 1635); Stephen Randall (of Stonington, son of John of Westerly); Thomas Rose (of New London); Ephraim Sawyer (of Windham 1717, grandson of Thomas of Lancaster); Gerard Spencer (of Haddam 1660); Josiah Standish (of Norwich 1686, son of Myles of Plymouth); Roger Sterry (of Stonington 1671));

and Gov. John Webster (of Hartford 1636).

Other New England families, of the following names, are also considered: Allen, Blogget, Brooks, Brown, Church, Collins, Edmands, Farrar, Gardner, George, Hall, Hayward, Heywood, King, Linton, Mason, Newhall, Pelton, Potter, Prescott, Richards, Sabin, Scott, Shaw, Smith, Tucker, Warren, Waters, Wheeler, Whitcomb, Wilder, and Woodward.

The matter is well arranged, and an index provided. References to printed sources are given, and on many of the families much original research has been done. Many documents are quoted, and the illustrations add to the value of the book. The fact that Mr. Holman is the compiler gives assurance that the research was carefully done and that the information found in the book is dependable. It ranks with the best pedigree books of this type, and is recommended to genealogical students and libraries.

DODGE Dodge Genealogy Colonial Ancestry: The Nicholls-Upham Line: The Nicholls-Bruce Line. Compiled by Olive E. Dodge. Published by Melvin Gilbert Dodge, Utica, N. Y., 1925. 15 p. 8°.

This pamphlet states the ancestry of Lydia Nicholls, wife of William Dodge, through her father Benjamin Nicholls of Mansfield, Conn., and her mother Lydia Upham. It follows "Sergeant Francis Nicholls and Descendants of his Son, Caleb", by Walter Nicholls, in stating that Francis Nicholls of Stratford, the first settler, was son of Francis & Margaret (Bruce) Nicholls and hence brother of Gov. Richard Nicolls of New York. This statement of the parentage of Francis of Stratford is erroneous. Francis the brother of Richard was a Royalist Captain, who followed the King into exile, and died on the Continent; since the Civil War in England did not break out until 1642, and our American Francis was in Strafford in 1639 and died there in 1650, the identification is impossible. On page 13 it is stated that Benjamin Nicholls who was born at Stratford 15 June 1729, married at Mansfield, Conn., 20 June 1745, Lydia Upham. No proof is given, and although it is not impossible that a youth of sixteen was married at that age in a town far removed from his place of residence, the circumstances are unusual and descendants of the Mansfield Benjamin should seek record proof of these statements before accepting them.

HARMON The Ancestry of Lydia Harmon 1755-1836, wife of Joseph Waterhouse of Standish, Maine. By Walter Goodwin Davis. Published by Stanhope Press, Boston, Mass., 1924. 122 p. 8°

This is a model volume, evidencing careful and thorough research in original record sources. The material is well arranged and presented, and there is an adequate index. A very full account is given of the early Harmons of New England, and other families treated are those of William

Roberts of Oyster River, N. H., Robert Goodale of Salem and Wells, Isaac Cousins of Wells, John Hoyt of Amesbury, Newington and Scarborough, George Brown of Salisbury, Robert Taprill and George Walton of Great Island, N. H., and Daniel Hasty of Scarborough. This volume also contains a reprint of a curious tract entitled "Lithobolia: or, the Stone-Throwing Devil", originally printed in London in 1698, which narrates the supernatural events that harassed George Walton's family at Great Island, N. H.

HOSMER Hosmer Genealogy. Descendants of James Hosmer who Emigrated to America in 1635 and Settled in Concord, Mass. By George Leonard Hosmer. Pub. Cambridge, Mass., 1928. 271 p. 8°. Order from George L. Hosmer, Room 1-239, Mass. Institute of Technology, Cambridge, Mass. Price, $10.00.

The family name is traced to Saxon times, and the ancestry of the American Hosmers is authentically traced to James Hosmer (died 1605) of Ticehurst, co. Sussex, the grandfather of Thomas Hosmer, founder of the Hartford, Conn., branch and of his brother James Hosmer, founder of the Concord, Mass., branch. The old difficulty regarding the identity of the mother of the emigrants is carefully analysed, and her real identity established.

The book, which is attractively bound in cloth, with gilt top, traces the Concord branch, and lists over 3400 individuals who were related by descent or marriage to the emigrant James. The arrangement of the genealogical matter is clear and workmanlike, and there is an adequate index (27 pages). The compiler in his preface modestly disclaims any pretense that his Hosmer history is complete. However, completeness is an ideal impossible of attainment in this kind of work, and Mr. Hosmer has merited the gratitude of Hosmer descendants and genealogical students in general, for preserving the valuable material he has collected by publication in a form which makes it accessible to all.

There are pictures of the churches at Ticehurst, co. Sussex, and at Hawkhurst, co. Kent, with which the grandparents and parents of the emigrants were associated, and other illustrations. We recommend the volume to genealogical libraries.

SEAMAN The Seaman Family in America as descended from Captain John Seaman of Hempstead, Long Island. By Mary Thomas Seaman. New York, 1928. 338 p. 8°. Order from the author, Miss Mary T. Seaman, 2 Montague Terrace, Brooklyn, N. Y. Price, $20.00.

This volume, recently issued from the press of Tobias A Wright, Inc., presents an attractive appearance, with red cloth binding, gilt top, a high grade of laid paper, and excellent typography.

It contains a wealth of material on the descendants of Capt. John Seaman, who after a brief sojourn in Massachusetts and Connecticut, became an original proprietor of Hempstead, L. I., in 1647, and was appointed Captain of Queens County Troop in 1665. Miss Seaman's courage in undertaking to record the history of so prolific a family is worthy of applause; for Captain John is credited with sixteen children, and the Hempstead Census of 1698 lists forty Seamans. A simple numbering system is employed; descendants in the male line are traced, and the children of Seaman daughters given, when known.

Great praise should be bestowed on the choice of the twenty-two illustrations. Of these, the coat-of-arms (in black and white)may be purchased separately for $1.00, and the reproductions of the 1657 deed from the Indians to Seaman and others, and the autographed deed of John Seaman to his sons, as well as three pictures of Seaman homesteads, and a unique map, are sold separately at fifty ceuts each. Other original documents, deeds, marriage certificates, etc., are reproduced in the book, which as a whole and in detail should be of absorbing interest to Seaman descendants. The book is well indexed (45 pages).

The difficulties that beset the searcher who attempts to trace Long Islan l families are only too well known to the reviewer, and where deficiencies occur in the present volume, we are more disposed to sympathize than to criticise. However, the possibilities of research on the early generations have not been exhausted, and a few inaccuracies strike the eye. On page 14 we find the statement: "In 1646 John Seaman and his brother Caleb are recorded in New Haven, Conn. At this period came the Pequod Indian War, and Captain John Mason was given chief command (as Major) of the Connecticut Troops. To John Seaman he gave command of one of the Companies", etc. Actually, the name of John Seaman was not mentioned in New Haven records in 1646, when Caleb Seaman, quite possibly his brother, was recorded as about to return to England. The Pequot War was fought in 1637, before New Haven was in existence. John Mason led the Connecticut Colony troops as Captain, and was called by that title in the colonial records as late as 1653, the title Major being first applied to him in May 1654. We have been unable to find in any contemporary source the statement that John Seaman served under Mason in the Pequot War. No muster roll of Connecticut troops serving under Mason has ever been found or published, and the most accurate list obtainable is the one painstakingly compiled by the late James Shepard in his pamphlet, "Connecticut Soldiers in the Pequot War of 1637"-a work which, incidentally, does not mention the name of John Seaman.

We have called attention, in the interest of historical accuracy, to what we can only consider an unproved (and probably unprovable) statement in "The Seaman Family", and we believe that Miss Seaman was led into error by following secondary instead of primary sources of historical information respecting the career of Capt. John Seaman. We in no sense intend to impugn her general accuracy, or the value of the genealogical statistics which she has preserved in her sumptuous volume, which we cordially recommend to genealogical libraries.

STORK The Genealogy of the Descendants of Moses Stork, Scarborough, Yorkshire, Old England. Compiled and published by Charles A. Storke of Santa Barbara, Calif., 1925. 21 p. 12°.

The founder of this family was Moses Stork, who by 1746 had come from Scarborough, co. York, England, to New London, Conn., removing a few years later to Branford, Conn. From there the family removed to Chenango County, N. Y. The descendants are traced and listed with exactness. This pamphlet was issued and distributed in the hope of eliciting additional information for a more complete history of the family. On the early generations, unpublished vital, probate and census records are quoted, adding to the value of the booklet.

Accurate; not indexed.

STOWE Ancestry and some of the descendants of Capt. Stephen Stowe of Milford, Conn. Compiled and published by Nathan Stowe of Milford, Conn., 1924. 24 p. 8°

This interesting pamphlet traces one branch of the John Stowe family of Roxbury, Mass., through his son Thomas of Middletown, Conn., and Thomas, Jr., and Dea. Samuel, both of Middletown, to the latter's son Stephen Stowe (1726–1777) of Milford, who had four sons in active service in the Revolutionary War, and lost his own life nursing the sick American soldiers. The line is traced to the grandfather of the emigrant, based on the research in England of Mrs. Elizabeth (French) Bartlett. A full record of brothers and sisters is given in each generation; also biographical notes of ancestors in the direct line; the ancestry of Freelove Baldwin, wife of Capt. Stephen Stowe; and a partial record of their descendants.

Accurate; complete within self-imposed limits; not indexed.

TOWNE The Ancestry of Lieut. Amos Towne 1737-1793 of Arundel (Kennebunkport), Maine. By Walter Goodwin Davis. Published by The Southworth Press, Portland, Me., 1927. 81 p. 8°

Like the Harmon book noticed above, this is a splendid piece of work, based on original research both here and abroad. It treats of the families of William Towne of Topsfield and Arundel, whose antecedents in England are traced, Thomas Browning of Salem and Topsfield, Robert Smith of Boxford, Ens. Thomas French of Ipswich, Zacheus Curtis of Boxford and Topsfield, and Thomas Looke of Lynn and Boxford. Mr. Davis, in issuing monographs on the families of early settlers, such as are contained in this volume and the Harmon book, has set a high standard of excellence, and we hope he will continue to publish the results of his researches.

At Ye Editor's Desk

In sending out renewal forms for Volume VI, it gives the editor the greatest pleasure to announce that the magazine has at last been placed on a solid foundation, and to thank those subscribers and friends whose interest and generosity made this possible.

Within the past two years a total of $419 was donated to the Endowment Fund, the individual gifts ranging from $1 to $100. This has made it possible for the editor to employ the the needed clerical assistance, and since the establishment of this fund the manuscript of the New Haven families has been prepared for the printer, from the letter M to the end of the alphabet.

In addition to the cash endowment, the magazine has been greatly assisted by the action of several subscribers in subscribing for an extra copy, and particularly the liberality of the Society of the Colonial Wars in the State of Connecticut in purchasing five complete sets of the magazine.

The raising of the advance subscription price from $5 to $6, beginning with Volume V., enabled the magazine for the first time in its history to pay current printing expenses out of current income.

The pre paration of the manuscript for the printer to the end of the alphabet, although it will nearly exhaust the Endowment Fund, guarantees the continued publication of the magazine until the record of New Haven families is completed. It is estimated that Volumes VI., VII. and VIII. will take care of this material. It is the editor's intention, as the sale of back issues gradually produces profit, to replace the amount that has been expended out of the Endowment Fund, and to hold it towards the preparation of an index after the eight volumes are completed.

Contributors to the Endowment Fund were:

J. M. Andreini
Mrs. J. M. Andreini
Mrs. Noyes D. Baldwin
Lucius B. Barbour
H. Prescott Beach
George C. Bryant
Miss Lucy Peck Bush
Leonard M. Daggett
John Clapperton Kerr
Mrs. John Clapperton Kerr
Mrs. William Malnge
John C. Pearson
William H. Peck
George McK. Roberts
E. V. D. Selden
George Dudley Seymour
Henry H. Townshend
Francis B. Trowbridge
Albert M. Turner
Society of Colonial Wars in the State of Connecticut

To all of these good friends, as well as to the other subscribers, many of whom expressed their regret at not feeling able to contribute, the editor is grateful for the assistance and encouragement he has received.

The New Haven Genealogical Magazine is the only publication in Connecticut which is devoted solely to genealogy. It was begun with the object of publishing the material which the editor had collected during many years of research on the old families of New Haven. After this work is completed, we hope to continue the magazine and make it state-wide in scope. With this in view, we have from time to time added occasional features in line with the new policy. In the present issue, we have started a new section for the purpose of reviewing genealogical books. Very few periodicals in the country, and none in Connecticut, offer to compilers and publishers of this type of book a forum for a fair and honest review. We hope that many will take advantage of it. In order that subscribers may lose nothing by the addition of the book review and advertising features, we have increased the size of this issue to the extent of several pages.

In closing, we feel moved to say a word in appreciation of our printer's work, and to thank him for the keen interest he has always shown in the Magazine and its success, for his patience when we have been (at times) impatient, and for his moderation in charges for his services. Without the last named, the Magazine could not have survived its first two years, which financially were the hardest. Mr. Smith is himself a genealogical student, with a wide knowledge of the early families of Central New York, and not infrequently he has added items to our manuscript which have increased its value, and which we have not heretofore acknowledged as they were incorporated in the body of the work.

Others, non-subscribers as well as subscribers, have furnished many items relating to New Haven families, which we are glad to be able to print at the end of each volume under the heading, "Additions and Corrections". It is always our intention to make acknowledgement, when printing these items, to those who contributed them.

YE EDITOR

FAMILIES
OF
ANCIENT NEW HAVEN

VOLUME VI

Compiled by
DONALD LINES JACOBUS, M.A.

Gratefully dedicated to the
SOCIETY OF COLONIAL WARS
IN THE STATE OF CONNECTICUT

DONALD L. JACOBUS
NEW HAVEN, CONN.
1930

CONTENTS

Families of Ancient New Haven

Compiled by Donald Lines Jacobus

ABBREVIATIONS

b.	born	Lieut.	Lieutenant
Bapt.	Baptist	m.	married
bp.	baptized	Maj.	Major
bu.	buried	Meth.	Methodist
c.	"circa"—about	nat.	"natural"—illegitimate
Capt.	Captain	N. S.	New Style
Col.	Colonel	O. S.	Old Style
Cpl.	Corporal	Rev.	Reverend (clergyman)
d.	died	rem.	removed
da.	daughter of	R. W.	Revolutionary War
Dea.	Deacon	res.	resided, residence
div.	divorced	s.	son of
Dr.	Doctor (physician)	s. p.	"sine prole"—without issue
Ens.	Ensign		
F & I W.	French & Indian Wars	Sgt.	Sergeant
Gen.	General	w.	wife of
k.	killed	wid.	widow of
		wk.	week

ABBREVIATIONS FOR SOURCES OF INFORMATION

These abbreviations are made up of two parts, the first signifying the town, the second, the kind of record. Thus, in *NHV*, *NH* means New Haven and *V* the vital statistics of that town. In *WdT1*, the *Wd* means Woodbridge and *T* a gravestone inscription, the figure following the *T* designating a particular graveyard. In *HC2*, the *H* stands for *Hamden* and *C* for a Congregational church there, the figure following the *C* specifying the particular church. *NoHx* means the Episcopal church of North Haven, *x* always standing for an Episcopal church and *NoH* for North Haven. A list of general symbols for towns and kinds of record are given below, followed by a list (arranged alphabetically by symbols) of the specific record sources.

SYMBOLS FOR TOWNS

B	Bethany	Mid	Middletown	S	Southington
Bd	Branford	My	Middlebury	St	Stratford
C	Cheshire	NH	New Haven	Sy	Southbury
D	Derby	NM	New Milford	W	Wallingford
EH	East Haven	NoB	North Branford	Wat	Waterbury
Farm	Farmington	NoH	North Haven	Wd	Woodbridge
G	Guilford	O	Orange	WH	West Haven
H	Hamden	Oxf	Oxford	Wol	Wolcott
L	Litchfield	P	Plymouth	Wtn	Watertown
M	Milford	Ppt	Prospect	Wy	Woodbury

SYMBOLS FOR KIND OF RECORD

C	Congregational Church record
CCt	County Court record
F	Family, private or Bible record (this symbol always stands alone)
SupCt	Superior Court record
T	Gravestone record
V	Vital (town) record
x	Episcopal Church record

SPECIFIC SOURCES

BAlm	Beckwith's Almanac
BD	Mortality List of Bethany, 1788-1793
BT1	''Cemetery in the Hollow,'' Bethany
BT2	Episcopal graveyard, Bethany
BT3	''Sperry Cemetery,'' Bethany
BT4	''Carrington Cemetery,'' Bethany
BT5	Methodist graveyard, Bethany
BV	Vital statistics, Bethany
Bx	Christ Church (Prot. Ep.), Bethany
BdV	Vital statistics, Branford
CC	Congregational Society, Cheshire
CT1	Old graveyard, Cheshire
CT2	Episcopal graveyard, Cheshire
CV	Vital statistics, Cheshire
Cx	St. Peter's Church (Prot. Ep.), Cheshire
ColR	''Columbian Register,'' contemporary newspaper
ConnH	''Conn. Herald,'' contemporary newspaper
DC	Congregational Society, Derby
DT1	Old Graveyard, Derby
DT2	Episcopal graveyard, Derby
DT3	''Great Hill Cemetery,'' Seymour
DT4	Graveyard, Beacon Falls
DT5	Cemetery in North Derby on the Housatonic
DV	Vital statistics, Derby
Dx	St. James Church (Prot. Ep.), Derby
EHC	Congregational Society, East Haven
EHR	''East Haven Register,'' by Rev. Stephen Dodd
EHT	Old graveyard, East Haven
EHV	Vital statistics, East Haven
F	Family, Bible or private records
F&IWRolls	Muster Rolls of Conn. Troops, French and Indian Wars
FarmV	Vital statistics, Farmington
HC1	Congregational Society, Mount Carmel (in Hamden)
HC2	Congregational Society, ''East Plain'' or Whitneyville (in Hamden)

HT1	"Centerville Cemetery," Hamden
HT2	"Hamden Plains Cemetery," Highwood (in Hamden)
HT3	Old graveyard, Mount Carmel (in Hamden)
HT4	"State Street Cemetery," Hamden
HT5	"Whitneyville Cemetery," Hamden
HT6	"West Woods Cemetery," Hamden
HV	Vital statistics, Hamden
LT	"Litchfield and Morris Inscriptions," by Charles Thomas Payne
LV	Vital statistics, Litchfield
MC1	First Congregational Society, Milford
MC2	Second Congregational Society, Milford
MT	Old graveyard, Milford
MV	Vital statistics, Milford (including mortality lists)
MidV	Vital statistics, Middletown
MyT	Graveyard, Middlebury
NHC1	First Congregational Society, New Haven
NHC2	Second Congregational Society, New Haven
NHT1	City Burial Ground ("Grove Street Cemetery"), New Haven, including stones in Center Church crypt and those removed from the Green
NHT2	"Westville Cemetery," New Haven
NHT3	"Union Cemetery," Fair Haven (in New Haven)
NHT4	"Evergreen Cemetery," New Haven
NHV	Vital statistics, New Haven
NHx	Trinity Church (Prot. Ep.), New Haven
NMV	Vital statistics, New Milford
NoBC1	Congregational Society (1725), North Branford
NoBC2	Congregational Society (1745), Northford (in North Branford)
NoBT1	Graveyard, Northford
NoHC	Congregational Society, North Haven
NoHD	Mortality list of North Haven
NoHT1	Old graveyard, North Haven
NoHT2	Old graveyard, Montowese (in North Haven)
NoHT3	Modern graveyard, North Haven
NoHV	Vital statistics, North Haven
NoHx	St. John's Church (Prot. Ep.), North Haven
OC	Congregational Society, Orange
OT	Graveyard, Orange
OxfC	Congregational Society, Oxford
OxfT1	Two graveyards (close together), Quaker Farms (in Oxford)
OxfT2	"Zoar Bridge Cemetery," Oxford (now removed)
OxfV	Vital statistics, Oxford
PC	Congregational Society, Plymouth (formerly Northbury)
PT	Graveyard, Plymouth
PptT	Graveyard, Prospect

SC	Congregational Society, Southington
SalemC	Congregational Society, Naugatuck
Salem x	St. Michael's Church (Prot. Ep.), Naugatuck
StC	First Congregational Society, Stratford
StV	Vital statistics, Stratford
Stx	Christ Church (Prot. Ep.), Stratford
SyV	Vital statistics, Southbury
WC1	First Congregational Society, Wallingford [records not included]
WC2	First Congregational Society, Meriden
WT1	"Center Street Cemetery," Wallingford
WT2	Old graveyard, Meriden
WV	Vital statistics, Wallingford
Wx	St. Paul's Church (Prot. Ep.), Wallingford [records not included]
WatT1	City Cemetery (now destroyed), Waterbury
WatT2	"East Farms Cemetery," Waterbury
WatT3	Old graveyard and Hillside Cemetery, Naugatuck
WatV	Vital statistics, Waterbury
Watx	St. John's Church (Prot. Ep.), Waterbury
WdC	Congregational Society, Woodbridge
WdD	Mortality List, Woodbridge
WdT1	"Middle Cemetery," Woodbridge
WdT2	Graveyard, "Milford side," Woodbridge
WdT3	Graveyard (near Seymour), Woodbridge
WdV	Vital statistics, Woodbridge
WHD	Mortality lists of Philemon Smith and "Aunt Lucena" Smith, West Haven
WHT1	Congregational graveyard, West Haven
WHT2	Episcopal graveyard, West Haven
WHT3	"Oak Grove Cemetery," West Haven
WolT	Graveyard, Wolcott
WtnD	Mortality lists (Judd and Skilton), Watertown
WtnT	Graveyard, Watertown
WyC	First Congregational Society, Woodbury
WyV	Vital statistics, Woodbury

SYMBOLS IN FRONT OF SURNAMES

* refers to a printed genealogy of the family
† refers to a magazine article on the family

MUDGE. SOLOMON, b c. 1766, d 30 June 1794 *NHV*, æ. 28 *NHx;* m 23 Apr 1791 *NHC1*—Sarah da. John & Lydia (Wise) Kimberly, b 10 Feb 1765 *NHV*, d 6 Sep 1807 æ. 41 *NHC1.* (Adm'n on estate of Oliver Sacket of NH granted 25 June 1794 to Solomon Mudge, Lucy Mudge mother of dec'd refusing adm'n.)

1 JENNET BROOM, b 28 Jan 1795 *NHV*, bp 15 Feb 1795 (æ. 3 wks.) *NHx*, bu. 2 July 1811 æ. 16 (fell on scissors in a fit) *NHx.*

MUIRSON. GEORGE, b c. 1708, bu. 25 Feb 1786 æ. 78 *NHx;* Dr.; loyalist; res. Brookhaven, L. I., & NH; m Anna Smith.

1 JAMES DELANCEY; res. N. Y. City.

2 GLORIANA; m Thomas Rice.

MULFORD. BARNABAS, s. of Barnabas & Hannah (Petty), b 13 Feb 1745 *BdV*, d 19 Aug 1827 æ. 82-6 *NHT1;* Census (NH) 2-2-3; m 10 Nov 1771 *NHV*, *NHC1*—Mehitabel da. Timothy & Mary (Punchard) Gorham, b 21 Dec 1747 *NHV*, d 26 Apr 1835 æ. 89-4-1 *NHT1.*

1 MARY, b 24 June 1775, bp 12 Jan 1777 *NHC2*, d 22 Dec 1787 æ. 12 *NHT1.*

2 HERVEY, b 7 July 1777, d 16 Feb 1847; m Nancy Bradley.

3 MEHITABEL, b 25 Jan 1780, d Sep 1854; m Chauncey Daggett.

4 ELIZABETH, b 14 Apr 1782, d 11 Jan 1868; m Benjamin Thompson.

5 BARNABAS, b 29 Apr 1784, d 22 June 1807; m Elizabeth Forbes.

MULFORD. MISCELLANEOUS. DAVID & Jerusha had: Lucretia, bp 15 Apr 1781 *NHC2*.......JOHN m May 1663 *NHV*————, wid. [William] Osborn.

MULLINOR. THOMAS, s. of Thomas; m Martha Brown of Debach, Suffolk.

1 MARTHA, b 4 July 1656 *NHV.*

2 ELIZABETH, b 10 June 1658 *NHV.*

MUNN. ANNA of M m (1) 29 Nov 1733 *NHV*—Roger Alling; m (2) 21 Sep 1771 *MV*—Nathan Platt of Wd.

MUNROE. JONATHAN & Elizabeth had:

1 ELIZABETH, b 29 Apr 1756 *WV.*

2 CALEB, b 24 Oct 1757 *WV.*

3 JONATHAN, b 8 Oct 1759 *WV*, d 21 Mar 1760 *WV.*

*MUNSON. Variant, MONSON. FAM. 1. THOMAS, bp 13 Sep 1612 *Rattlesden, co. Suffolk*, d 7 Mar 1685 æ. 73 *NHT1* [1685/6]; Capt.; m Joanna ———, b c. 1611, d 13 Dec 1678 æ. 68 *NHT1.*

1 ELIZABETH; m (1) 19 Oct 1664 *Springfield*—Timothy Cooper; m (2) Richard Higginbotham.

2 SAMUEL, bp 7 Aug 1643 *NHC1,* d [1692] *NHV;* Ens.; m 26 Oct 1665 *NHV*—Martha da. William & Alice (Pritchard) Bradley, bp Oct 1648 *NHC1;* she m (2) c. 1694 Eliasaph Preston & (3) Matthew Sherman.

i Martha, b 6 May 1667 *NHV,* d 24 Apr 1728 *NHV;* m Thomas Elcock.

ii Samuel, b 28 Feb 1668 *NHV* [1668/9], d 23 Nov 1741 æ. 74 *WV;* Sgt.; m (1) Martha da. Samuel Farnes, b c. 1670, d 7 Jan 1707 *WV* [1707/8]; m (2) 10 Mar 1708 *WV* [1708/9]—Mary da. Eliasaph & Mary Preston, wid. Caleb Merriman, b 12 Apr 1674 *StV,* probably d 28 Nov 1755 *WV.* FAM. 2.

iii Thomas, b 12 Mar 1670/1 *NHV,* d 28 Sep 1746 æ. 76 *CT1;* m 15 Sep 1694 *NHV*—Mary da. Obadiah & Lydia (Alling) Wilcoxson, b 11 Dec 1676 *GV.* FAM. 3.

iv John, b 28 Jan 1672 *NHV* [1672/3], d before 1752; Capt.; m (1) 10 Nov 1692 *NHV*—Sarah da. John & Mary (Thompson) Cooper, b 26 Apr 1673 *NHV;* m (2) c. 1736 Elizabeth, wid. Joseph Talmadge. FAM. 4.

v Theophilus, b 1 Sep 1675 *NHV,* d 28 Nov 1747 *NHV,* æ. 72 *NHT1;* Capt.; m Esther da. John & Elizabeth (Wilmot) Mix, b 25 Dec 1678 *NHV,* bp 12 Aug 1688 *NHC1,* d 16 Sep 1746 *NHV,* æ. 68 *NHT1.* FAM. 5.

vi Joseph, b 1 Nov 1677 *WV,* d 30 Oct 1725 *WV;* Ens.; m 10 Mar 1699 *WV*—Margery da. John & Abigail (Merriman) Hitchcock, b 9 Sep 1681 *WV,* d before 1764; she m (2) 8 May 1727 *WV*—Stephen Peck. FAM. 6.

vii Stephen, b 5 Dec 1679 *WV,* d c. 1768; m (1) 23 Dec 1703 *NHV*—Lydia da. John & Mercy (Todd) Bassett, b 10 Aug 1685 *NHV,* d 4 Jan 1738/9 *NHV;* m (2) Ruth da. Philip Lewis, wid. Richard Hollingsworth, who d 14 Feb 1772. FAM. 7.

viii Caleb, b 19 Nov 1682 *NHV,* d 23 Aug 1765; m (1) 26 Mar 1706 *WV*—Elizabeth Harmon, who d 11 Feb 1739 *WV* [1739/40]; m (2) 10 Jan 1740 *WV* [1740/1]—Hannah Porter. FAM. 8.

ix Joshua, b 7 Feb 1684 *NHV* [1684/5], bp 19 July 1685 *NHC1,* d 9 Dec 1711 *WV;* m 20 Dec 1710 *WV*—Katharine da. Samuel & Anna (Miles) Street, b 19 Nov 1679 *WV;* she m. 11

Mar. 1714 *WV*—Joshua Culver. Child: Mary, b 2 Mar 1712 *WV*, d c. 1713.

x Israel, b 6 Mar 1686 *NHV* [1686/7], bp 17 Apr 1687 *NHC1*, d bef. 1697.

3 HANNAH, bp 11 June 1648 *NHC1*, d 30 Nov 1695 *GV;* m (1) 2 May 1667 *NHV*—Joseph Tuttle; m (2) 21 Aug 1694 *GV*—Nathan Bradley.

FAM. 2. SAMUEL & MARTHA (FARNES) MUNSON:

1 SOLOMON, b 18 Feb 1689 *WV* [1689/90], d 1773; rem. to Morristown, N. J.; m (1) 28 June 1714 *WV*—Mary da. John & Martha (Lathrop) Moss, b 25 July 1694 *WV*, d [c. 1720]; m (2) Tamar ———, b c. 1701, d 17 Jan 1779 æ. 77.

(By 1): *i* Martha, b 14 Sep 1715 *WV;* m 6 Jan 1731/2 *BdV*—Uzal Barker of Bd & Wtn.

ii Samuel, b 15 Sep 1717 *WV;* m (1) 9 Nov 1743 *Morristown*—Elizabeth Potter; m (2) 9 Oct 1745 *Morristown*—Mary Allen; m (3) 1 May 1751 Sarah (———) Prudden.

iii Eliasaph, b 17 Nov 1719 *WV*, d 1 Feb 1745/6 (at Cape Breton) *WV*.

(By 2): *iv* Moses; Capt.; res. Morristown; m Martha ———.

v Solomon, b c. 1725, d 8 Feb 1803 æ. 78 *Morristown;* m 16 Oct 1750 *Morristown*—Mary da. Benjamin Pierson, who d 1820 æ. 98.

vi Waitstill, b c. 1730, d 26 Feb 1777 æ. 47 *Morristown;* m 19 Mar 1755 *Morristown*—Mary Wade.

vii Stephen, b c. 1733, d 8 Nov 1805 æ. 72 *Whippany T;* Dea.; Capt.; m (1) 8 Feb 1755 *Morristown*—Letitia Ludlam; m (2) Kezia ———, who d 5 Apr 1817 æ. 75.

viii Caleb, b c. 1735, d 25 Feb 1815 æ. 80 New Vernon, N. J.; m 22 June 1758 *Morristown*—Susanna Ludlum.

2 SAMUEL, b 25 Aug 1691 *WV*, d at Port Royal in 20 yr. *WV*.

3 MARLOW, b 15 Feb 1693/4 *WV*, d 1 July 1739 *WV;* m 21 Nov 1712 *WV*—John Hitchcock.

4 WILLIAM, b 13 Oct 1695 *WV*, d 21 July 1773; m Rebecca da. Thomas & Mary (Merriman) Curtis, wid. Lambert Johnson, b 21 Aug 1697 *WV*.

i Martha, b 2 Apr 1729 *WV;* m Ambrose Doolittle.

ii William, b 5 July 1731 *WV*, bp 11 July 1731 *CC*, d 26 May 1815; Census (Wtn) 1-1-4; m

28 Feb 1753 *WatV*—Sarah da. Isaac & Mary (Clinton) Griggs, b 26 June 1734 *WV*, d 7 Aug 1806 æ. 74 *PptC*.

iii Eunice, b 15 Aug 1733 *WV*, bp Sep 1733 *CC*.

iv Peter, b 22 Nov 1735 *WV*, bp Jan 1735/6 *CC*, d 3 Feb 1830 ; Census (C) 2-3-1; m 6 Oct 1762 *WV*—Elizabeth da. [John & Abigail] Hall, b [28 Sep 1745 *WV*], d 31 Oct 1822. FAM. 9.

v Hannah, b 6 Sep 1737 *WV*, bp Sep 1737 *CC;* m 30 July 1759 *WV*—Titus Hitchcock.

vi "George," b 7 Oct 1739 *WV*, "Samuel" bp 9 Dec 1739 *CC;* name apparently was Samuel; res. C, Wat, & Vienna, O.; m 3 Aug 1764 *WV*—Susanna da. Isaac & Susanna (Miles) Tyler, b 8 Apr 1745 *WV;* had 12 children of whom Calvin bp 10 June 1770 *CC* & Jesse bp 12 July 1772 *CC*.

vii Amasa, b 27 Jan 1741/2 *WV*, bp Feb 1741/2 *CC*; Census (C) 1-1-3; m 23 Feb 1769 *WV*—Hannah Chapman; m (2) Rachel Lewis.

5 WAITSTILL, b 12 Dec 1697 *WV*, d 6 Mar 1789 ; m 10 Dec 1719 *WV*—Phebe da. Caleb & Mary (Preston) Merriman, b 16 Sep 1699 *WV*, d Dec 1772.

i Reuben, b 9 May 1721 *WV*, d 7 June 1780 ; res. S.; m 29 Dec 1741 *WV*—Mary da. Abraham Crittenden, who d 15 Jan 1801 æ. 78 (at Whitestown, N. Y.) *F*. FAM. 10.

ii Hannah, b 20 Feb 1723 *WV;* m 20 Jan 1741 *WV*—Benjamin Cook.

iii Samuel, b 7 Dec 1724 *WV*, d 11 Oct 1801 æ. 77 *NoBT1;* m (1) 14 May 1747 *WV*—Rachel da. David & Rebecca (Wilson) Cook, b 19 Nov 1724 *WV*, d 22 Dec 1748 æ. 24 *WT1;* m (2) Jerusha da. Reuben & Mary (Dayton) Johnson, wid. Eliasaph Dorchester, b c. 1725, d 17 Nov 1817 æ. 92 *NoBT1;* had issue.

iv Phebe, b 14 June 1726 *WV*, d 25 Jan 1745/6 *WV;* m 25 Dec 1744 *WV*—Phineas Peck.

v Solomon, b 19 Mar 1728 *WV*, d 15 Oct 1802 (Windham, N. Y.); m (1) 14 June 1753 *WV*—Sarah da. Jonathan & Thankful (Benham) Peck, b 16 Nov 1733 *WV;* m (2) 11 Oct 1759 *NoBC2*—Sarah da. Abel & Sarah (Peck) Munson, b 6 Sep 1740 *WV*, d 1 Jan 1761; m (3) 19 Nov 1761 *NoBC2*—Hannah Baldwin, b 8 June 1739, d 1831. FAM. 11.

vi Waitstill, b 24 Nov 1729 *WV*, d 1786; res. S; m (1) Ann ———, who d 18 Apr 1772 æ. 41; m (2) Esther Bronson, wid. Rufus Blakeslee, who d 9 July 1828 æ. 84.

vii Medad, b 31 Aug 1731 *WV*, d 14 May 1777 *WV;* m 15 Oct 1761 *WV*—Desire da. John & Deborah (Hunn) Carrington, b 13 Sep 1738 *FarmV*, d 10 Sep 1822 æ. 83. Children: (1) Hunn, b 25 Apr 1762 *WV;* (2) Zerah, b 20 July 1768 *WV*.

viii Mamre, b 20 Jan 1734 *WV*, d 5 July 1787 æ. 54 *WT1;* m 26 Sep 1751 *WV*—Timothy Carrington.

ix Martha, b 11 June 1738 *WV*, d 27 Jan 1738/9 *WV*.

x Martha, b 16 Jan 1740 *WV*, d 26 Jan 1740 *WV*.

6 Eunice, b 13 Sep 1700 *WV;* m 29 Dec 1720 Stephen Hart.

7 Obedience, b 13 Oct 1702 *WV*; m Amos Hotchkiss.

8 Katharine, b 3 June 1704 *WV;* m 27 Oct 1720 *WV*—John Mitchell.

9 Tamar, b 5 Dec 1707 *WV*, d 2 Oct 1788 *CC;* m 23 July 1728 *WV*—James Hotchkiss.

FAM. 2. Samuel & Mary (Preston) Munson:

10 Lemuel, b 5 Feb 1709 *WV* [1709/10], d 1 July 1741 æ. 32 *WV*.

11 Merriman, b 30 Nov 1710 *WV*, d 9 Sep 1782 æ. 72 *NoBT1;* Dea.; m (1) 24 Jan 1733 *WV*—Esther da. John & Sarah (Jennings) Johnson, b 4 May 1712 *WV*, d 6 Apr 1757 *WV*, æ. 46 *NoBT1;* m (2) 23 Jan 1758 *WV*—Thankful da. Joseph & Hope (Cook) Benham, wid. Jonathan Peck, b 14 Feb 1716 *WV*, d 23 May 1790 æ. 75 *NoBT1*.

(By 1): *i* Sarah, b 16 Dec 1734 *WV*, d soon.

ii Esther, b 25 Mar 1740 *WV;* m 30 June 1768 *NoBC2*—Isaac Linsley.

iii Samuel, b 8 Dec 1741 *WV*, d 18 Aug 1791 æ. 50 *NoBT1;* m (1) Rhoda da. Isaac & Sarah (Osborn) Johnson, b c. 1742, d 4 July 1772 æ. 31 *NoBT1;* m (2) 7 Oct 1772 *WV*—Kezia Frisbie, who d 31 Jan 1821 æ. 72 *NoBT1;* she m (2) Uriah Collins.

iv Mamre, b 12 Aug 1745 *WV*, d 17 Sep 1745 *WV*.

(By 2): *v* Sarah, b 7 Oct 1758 *WV*; m 20 Feb 1782 Isaac Munson.

12 Mamre, b 16 Dec 1712 *WV*, d 24 Dec 1744 *WV;* m 13 June 1733 *WV*—Joseph Ives.

13 Lent, b 16 Nov 1714 WV, d 19 Nov 1771 *S;* m 29 Oct 1740 *WV*—Mary [da. "Mr." & Mary] Cooley, b c. 1715, d 21 Oct 1777 æ. 62.

i Mamre, b 9 Dec 1749 *WV,* d 31 Aug 1751 *WV,* æ. 1-8-21 *WT1.*

ii John, b 26 Aug 1754 *WV,* d c. 1777.

iii Mary, b 29 Sep 1756 *WV,* d 23 Oct 1726; m 17 Apr 1780 Samuel Hitchcock.

iv Child, d Apr 1772.

FAM. 3. Thomas & Mary (Wilcoxson) Munson:

1 Lydia, b 5 May 1696 *NHV,* bp 6 Jan 1698 *NHC1;* m 27 Apr 1717 *NHV*—Joseph Sperry.

2 Thomas, b 18 Aug 1698 *NHV,* bp Aug. 1698 *NHC1,* d bef. 1793; m Sarah da. Moses & Sarah (Benton) Blakeslee, b 31 Mar 1708 *NHV.*

i Sarah, b 27 June 1744 *NHV;* m 13 Nov 1760 *NHV*—Jacob Brockett.

3 Mary, b 25 Aug 1700 *NHV,* bp 29 Sep 1700 *NHC1;* m 6 Feb 1723/4 *NHV*—Aaron Tuttle.

4 Obadiah, b 3 Apr 1703 *NHV,* d 29 Apr 1773 æ. 71 *NoHT1;* m (1) 27 Mar 1729 *NHV*—Hannah da. Alexander & Mary (Norris) Wilmot, wid. Elisha Booth, b 10 Dec 1699 *NHV,* d 1754 *CC;* m (2) 15 Oct 1755 *WV*—Mary Williams.

(By 1): *i* Mary, b 6 Feb 1729/30 *NHV,* bp 19 Apr 1730 *NHC1;* m 11 Mar 1756 *WV*—Joseph Doolittle.

ii Obadiah, b 27 Aug 1731 *NHV,* bp 31 Oct 1731 *NHC1,* d 26 May 1805 (Harwinton); m (1) 28 Feb 1753 *WV*—Rachel da. Nathan & Rachel (Tuttle) Tyler, b 24 Nov 1736 *WV,* d 1778; m (2) 25 Jan 1779 Eunice Bradley of Wol, who d after 1816; she m (2) John Frisbie. FAM. 12.

iii Walter, b 25 Dec 1733 *NHV,* bp 10 Feb 1733/4 *NHC1,* d 27 Dec 1802, bu. 29 Dec æ. 68 *NHx;* Dr.; Census (NoH) 2-0-3; m (1) 19 June 1760 *NHV*—Mabel da. Thomas & Hannah (Goodyear) Mansfield, b 13 Mar 1742/3 *NHV,* d 20 Feb 1789 æ. 46 *NoHT1;* m (2) Elizabeth Barnes, b c. 1754, d 7 Jan 1816 æ. 62 *NHT1.* FAM. 13.

(By 2): *iv* Sybil, b 11 Aug 1756 *WV,* d 5 Feb 1794; m 28 Jan 1778 Samuel Porter.

5 Hannah, b 27 Sep 1705 *NHV.*

6 Joanna; m 28 Mar 1729 *NHV,* 27 Mar *WV*—Benjamin Curtis.

7 Rachel, b 18 Nov 1709 *NHV*.
8 Eunice, b 28 Jan 1712/3 *NHV;* m 16 Dec 1732 *NHV* —Samuel Bradley.
9 Thankful, b 3 Feb 1714/5 *NHV,* bp 8 July 1716 *NHC1.*
10 Ebenezer, b 16 June 1717 *NHV,* bp Apr 1718 *NHC1;* res. Ppt & Danbury; m 20 Sep 1737 *NHV*—Abigail da. Abraham & Elizabeth (Johnson) Hotchkiss, who d 1792.

i Ebenezer, b 19 Aug 1738 *NHV,* bp 24 Sep 1738 *NHC1,* d 8 Aug 1818 *Bethel;* m (1) 6 Oct 1757 Thankful Gregory; m (2) Sarah da. Benoni & Lydia (Ferry) Bailey, wid. Ebenezer Ferry.
ii Abigail, b 6 Nov 1739 *NHV,* bp 23 Dec 1739 *NHC1.*
iii Thomas, b 24 Oct 1741 *WV,* bp Nov 1741 *CC.*
iv Huldah, b 4 Aug 1743 *WV,* bp Sep 1743 *CC.*
v Lydia, b 30 Jan 1745 *WV,* bp Apr 1745 *CC.*
vi Elizabeth, b 13 Jan 1746/7 *WV;* m 7 June 1775 *DanburyV*—Asa Curtis.
vii Patience, b 31 Aug 1749 *WV,* bp 6 Sep 1749 *CC,* d 2 Apr 1774.
viii Jesse, b 5 July 1751 *WV,* d bef. 1777; m 7 May 1775 *DanburyV*—Abigail Ketchum, who d 1775.
ix John, b 30 Dec 1752 *WV,* [d 2 Mar 1850; res. NM, Washington, & Oppenheim, N. Y.; m Damaris Martin, b Dec 1753, d Sep 1844].
x Mary, b 20 Sep 17[54] *WV,* d 4 Sep 1775.
xi Rachel; m 15 Apr 1783 Stephen Ambler.

FAM. 4. John & Sarah (Cooper) Munson:

1 John, b 7 July 1693 *NHV,* d 1745/6; m 28 Jan 1711/2 *NHV*—Esther da. Samuel & Hannah (Tuttle) Clark, b 2 Jan 1692/3 *NHV,* d c. 1747.

i Samuel, b 11 June 1713 *NHV,* d 11 Oct 1714 *NHV.*
ii Dorothy, b 7 June 1715 *NHV,* bp 29 June 1718 *NHC1.*
iii David, b 8 Oct 1718 *NHV,* bp 12 Oct 1718 *NHC1,* d 3 Sep 1811 æ. 93 *NHT3;* Census (NH) 1-1-3; m (1) 3 Apr 1740 *NHV*—Abigail da. Samuel & Abigail (Hill) Potter, b 28 Aug 1719 *NHV;* m (2) 15 Oct 1780 *EHC*—Huldah da. Thomas & Mary (Clark) Foster, wid. Nathaniel Yale & ——— Ives, b 10 May 1744 *WV,* d 29 Aug 1833 æ. 86 *NHT3.* FAM. 14.

iv Dorcas, b 18 Nov 1720 *NHV*, bp 20 Dec 1720 *NHC1*, d 22 Sep 1761 *NHV*; m 3 Apr 1740 *NHV*—Aaron Potter.

v [? John, bp 16 Feb 1723/4 *NHC1*, d soon].

vi [? Hannah, bp 18 Dec 1726 *NHC1*, d soon].

vii John, b 27 Nov 1731 *NHV*, bp 28 Nov 1731 *NHC1*, d 22 July 1808 (Hebron, N. Y.); m 2 Feb 1748/9 *NHV*—Esther da. Nathaniel & Sarah (Hotchkiss) Turner, b 21 Jan 1732/3 *NHV*. FAM. 15.

viii Timothy, b 1 July 1734 *NHV*, bp 7 July 1734 *NHC1*, d 29 Oct 1826; res. Brookfield 1763 & Pownal, Vt., 1782; m (1) 17 July 1754 *NHC2*—Sarah da. Willet & Elizabeth (Sturdevant) Bishop, bp 18 July 1736 *NHC1*, d 5 Feb 1806 æ. 60(?); m (2) Sarah ———, who d 2 Mar 1819 æ. 71. FAM. 16.

ix [? Temperance, bp 6 Aug 1738 *NHC1*, d soon].

2 ELIZABETH, b 15 May 1695 *NHV;* m (1) 28 Feb 1716/7 *NHV*—Seth Perkins; m (2) 7 June 1733 *NHV*—Nicholas Russell.

3 HANNAH, b 9 Feb 1697/8 *NHV;* m Gideon Andrews.

4 JOEL, b 18 Aug 1702 *NHV*, d after 1775; m 9 May 1727 *NHV*—Mary da. Joseph & Esther (Winston) Morris, b June 1702 *NHV*.

i Austin, b 20 Mar 1727/8 *NHV*, bp 24 Mar 1727/8 *NHC1*, d c. 1776; rem. to Claverack, N. Y.; m Annetje Osterhout.

ii Basil, b 23 Jan 1729/30 *NHV*, bp 25 Jan 1729/30 *NHC1*, d 17 Nov 1803 æ. 73 *HT3;* Census (H) 2-0-3; m (1) 2 May 1751 *NHV*—Kezia da. Isaac & Esther (Hooker) Stiles, b 6 Aug 1731 *NHV*, d 16 Oct 1768 *NHV*, æ. 38 *HT3;* m (2) 22 Oct 1771 *NHV*—Abigail da. John & Elizabeth (Thompson) Bassett, b 10 Dec 1732 *NHV*, d 20 July 1772 *NHV*, æ. 38 *HT3;* m (3) 4 May 1773 *BdC*—Mary Munroe, b c. 1731, d 5 Oct 1817 æ. 86 *HT3*. FAM. 17.

iii Sarah, b 18 Mar 1731/2 *NHV*, d 1 Dec 1775 ae. 43 *HT1;* m Theophilus Goodyear.

iv Joel, b 14 July 1734 *NHV*, d c. 1774; m 4 Feb 1761 *NHV*, *NHC2*—Sarah da. Samuel & Mary (Alling) Dickerman, b 29 Dec 1741 *NHV*. FAM. 18.

v Mary, b 2 Jan 1736/7 *NHV;* m (1) 17 Feb 1756 *NHV*—Peter Mallory; m (2) Matthew Johnson of Lanesboro, Mass.

vi Mehitabel, b 14 Nov 1739 *NHV;* m 8 Apr 1762 *NoHC*—Phineas Castle.

vii Sybil, b 25 Oct 1743 *NHV,* d 24 Oct 1795 æ. 53 *WatT1*; m 1 Aug 1764 *NHV*—Charles Cook.

5 AMY, b 18 Sep 1704 *NHV;* m 1727 *NHCCt*—Joshua Sperry.

6 RUTH, b 30 Jan 1707/8 *NHV,* d 21 May 1785 æ. 81 *NHT1;* m 19 Dec 1728 *NHV*—Caleb Hotchkiss.

7 MEHITABEL, b 17 Oct 1709 *NHV,* d 26 Feb 1779 æ. 70 *NHC1;* m 17 Nov 1731 *NHV*—Benjamin Morris.

8 SARAH, b 27 Sep 1713 *NHV;* m 17 Nov 1731 *NHV*—Enos Stone.

FAM. 5. THEOPHILUS & ESTHER (MIX) MUNSON:

1 ELIZABETH, b 26 Sep 1697 *NHV,* bp 5 Apr 1719 *NHC1,* d 19 Aug 1751 *NHV;* m 16 May 1728 *NHV*—Richardson Minor.

2 ESTHER, b 8 Nov 1699 *NHV,* bp 5 Apr 1719 *NHC1,* d 26 Sep 1730 *NHV;* m 21 July 1720 *NHV*—John Talmadge.

3 ISRAEL, b 11 Dec 1701 *NHV,* bp 5 Apr 1719 *NHC1,* d 28 July [1754 æ.—] *NHT1;* Capt.; m (1) 1 Feb 1726/7 *NHV*—Elizabeth da. Samuel & Hannah (Yale) Bishop, b 16 Apr 1704 *NHV,* d 17 Nov 1734 *NHV,* æ. 30 *NHT1;* m (2) 28 Oct 1736 *NHV*—Mary da. Daniel & Mercy Brinsmade, b 12 May 1716 *StV,* d 30 Oct 1742 *NHV,* 28 Oct æ. 26 *NHT1*; m (3) 27 Sep 1744 *NHV*—Margaret da. Moses & Margaret (Prout) Mansfield, b 7 Oct 1708 *NHV,* d bef. 1757.

(By 1): *i* Joseph, b 8 Oct 1727 *NHV,* bp 15 Oct 1727 *NHC1,* d 9 Jan 1793 æ. 66 *NHT1;* Capt.; Census (NH) 4-2-6; m 2 Feb 1757 *NHV*—Sarah da. Samuel & Abigail (Atwater) Bishop, b 6 Feb 1732/3 *NHV,* d Nov 1790 æ. 58 *NHT1,* 10 Nov *NHC1.* FAM. 19.

ii Elisha, bp 23 Nov 1729 *NHC1.*

iii Esther, b 11 Feb 1731/2 *NHV,* bp 13 Feb 1731/2 *NHC1;* m 3 Apr 1753 *NHV*—Stephen Peck.

iv Ichabod, b 17 Nov 1734 *NHV,* bp 17 Nov 1734 *NHC1,* d 29 Aug 1739 *NHV.*

(By 2): *v* Israel, bp 9 Oct 1737 *NHC1,* d 27 Dec 1806; Census (NH) 5-0-3; m 11 Apr 1765 *NHV*—Anna Griswold. FAM. 20.

vi Elizabeth, b 12 Aug 1739 *NHV,* bp 12 Aug 1739 *NHC1;* m 30 Mar 1757 *StV*—Ephraim Middlebrook.

vii Mary, b 21 Aug 1741 *NHV,* bp 23 Aug 1741 *NHC1,* d 17 Dec 1742 *NHV.*

(By 3): *viii* William, b 20 May 1747 *NHV*, bp 31 May 1747 *NHC1*, d 26 Feb 1826 ; Maj.; Census (NH) 1-3-4; m (1) 8 May 1770 *NHV*—Martha da. John & Abiah (Macomber) Hall, b 25 Apr 1749 *NHV*, d 10 Apr 1806 æ. 55 *NHC1;* m (2) 18 Oct 1807 *NHx*—Elizabeth Collis, wid. Alexander Little, b 18 Oct 1769 (Gloucester, Mass.), d 16 Feb 1824 ; m (3) 1 May 1825 *NHV*—Mary Groves, who d 15 Mar 1835 æ. 67. FAM. 21.

ix Margaret, b 10 Mar 1749/50 *NHV*, 1750 *NHT1*, d 11 Mar 1825 æ. 75 *NHT1;* m 5 July 1770 *NHC1*—Benjamin Gillet.

4 MARTHA, b 8 Aug 1704 *NHV*, bp 5 Apr 1719 *NHC1;* m ——— Jennings.

5 DANIEL, b 12 Jan 1708/9 *NHV*, bp 5 Apr 1719 *NHC1*, d 21 June 1746 ; Dr.; B.A. (Yale 1726); m 27 Apr 1730 *NHV*—Mary da. Joseph & Sarah Gorham; she m (2) 9 Nov 1747 *StV*—Benjamin Arnold.

i Joseph Kirk, bp 1 Aug 1731 *NHC1;* res. Huntington; m Margaret da. Elihu Chapin; had issue.

ii [George, bp 7 Jan 1732/3 *NHC1*, d soon.]

iii [Sarah, bp 14 July 1734 *NHC1*, d soon.]

iv [Daniel, bp 31 Oct 1736 *NHC1*, d soon.]

v George, b 21 July 1740 *StV*.

vi Sarah, b 21 Nov 1742 *StV*.

vii Daniel, b 4 Apr 1745 *StV*, bp 7 Apr 1745 *Stx*, d 27 Oct 1827; res. M; m 22 May 1766 Mary Sears, who d Oct 1833 æ. 85. FAM. 22.

6 BENJAMIN, b 28 Mar 1711 *NHV*, bp 5 Apr 1719 *NHC1;* m 6 June 1732 *NHV*—Abigail da. John & Abigail (Alling) Punderson, b 3 Dec 1700 *NHV*.

i Eneas, b 13 June 1734 *NHV*, bp 24 Nov 1734 *NHC1*, d 16 June 1826 æ. 92 *NHT1;* Dr.; B.A. (Yale 1753); Census (NH) 3-3-2; m (1) 15 Mar 1761 *NHC1*—Susanna da. Stephen & Susanna (Cooper) Howell, b 7 Jan 1738/9 *NHV*, d 21 Apr 1803 æ. 64 *NHT1*, 23 Apr *NHC1;* m (2) 24 Nov 1804 Sarah da. Benjamin & Mary (Brown) Sanford, wid. Job Perit, b c. 1760, d 25 July 1829 æ. 69 *NHT1*. FAM. 23.

ii Abigail, b 28 Sep 1735 *NHV*, bp 28 Sep 1735 *NHC1*, d 27 Dec 1789 ; m 3 June 1762 *NHV*, *NHC1*—Adonijah Sherman.

iii Benjamin, b 28 Feb 1738/9 *NHV,* bp 5 Mar 1737/8 *NHC1,* d 9 June 1746 æ. 8 *NHT1.*
iv Susanna, b 28 Feb 1741 *NHV,* bp 28 Feb 1741/2 *NHC1,* d 21 Sep 1742 æ. 6 mos. 3 wks. *NHT1.*
v Susanna, b c. 1745, "Hannah" bp 3 Feb 1744/5 *NHC1,* d 15 Dec 1770 æ. 25 *NHC1;* m 13 Nov 1766 *NHC1*—Nathan Howell.

7 Theophilus, b 25 June 1713 *NHV,* bp 5 Apr 1719 *NHC1,* d 13 Dec 1793 æ. 80 *NHT1;* Census (NH) 1-0-2; m 27 Sep 1739 *NHV*—Abigail da. James & Hannah (Harrison) Talmadge, b 14 Aug 1714 *NHV,* d 16 Mar 1795 æ. 80 (at Wat) *NHT1.*
i Ann, b 14 July 1740 *NHV,* bp 20 July 1740 *NHC1;* m 24 Oct 1765 *NHC2*—Jeremiah Osborn.
ii Philemon, b 18 Aug 1741 *NHV,* bp 23 Aug 1741 *NHC1,* d 8 Sep 1741 *NHV.*
iii Sybil, b 9 Nov 1742 *NHV,* bp 11 Nov 1742 *NHC1.*
iv Hannah, b 17 May 1744 *NHV,* bp 4 June 1749 *NHC2;* m (1) 14 June 1762 *NHC2*—Charles Munson; m (2) 2 Oct 1770 *NHC1*—Elijah Hills.
v Theophilus, b 4 Jan 1747 *F,* bp 4 June 1749 *NHC2,* d 30 Mar 1795 *Redding;* B.A. (Yale 1768); Maj.; m 26 Feb 1782 *Redding*—Sarah da. John Read, wid. Jabez Hill; had issue.
vi Esther, bp 12 July 1752 *NHC2,* d soon.
vii James, bp 16 Dec 1753 *NHC2.*
viii Esther, bp 10 Oct 1756 *NHC2.*

8 James, b 1 Oct 1715 *NHV,* bp 5 Apr 1719 *NHC1,* d 20 Oct 1742 æ. 27 *NHT1.*

9 Ann, b 4 Jan 1717/8 *NHV,* bp 5 Apr 1719 *NHC1,* d 18 Oct 1739 *NHV;* m 27 Apr 1738 *NHV*—John Punderson.

10 Sybil, b 22 Mar 1719/20 *NHV,* bp c. Mar 1719/20 *NHC1,* d s.p. 31 Oct 1742 *NHV;* m 3 Sep 1741 *NHV*—Aaron Day.

11 Lois, b 7 June 1722 *NHV,* bp 10 June 1722 *NHC1.*

FAM. 6. Joseph & Margery (Hitchcock) Munson:

1 Abel, b 10 Jan 1701 *WV,* d 13 Feb 1779 *WV;* Dea.; m 7 Nov 1728 *WV*—Sarah da. Nathaniel & Sarah (Hopkins) Peck, b 21 Mar 1713 *WV,* d 22 Sep 1775 æ. 63.
i Mabel, b 2 June 1730 *WV,* d 8 Jan 1793; m 29 Aug 1750 Dan Pond.

ii Mary, b 2 May 1732 *WV,* d 16 Jan 1763; m 20 June 1751 *NoBC2*—Timothy Pond.

iii Titus, b 5 July 1734 *WV,* d 12 Apr 1776 æ. 42 *NoBC2;* m 22 Sep 1757 *WV, NoBC2*—Lydia Linsley, who d 23 Jan 1776 *WV.* FAM. 24.

iv Lud, b 5 May 1736 *WV,* d 28 Mar 1779 ; Sgt.; m 9 Jan 1758 *WV*—Lois da. Isaac & Sarah (Osborn) Johnson, b 15 Feb 1738 *WV,* d 1807; she m (2) Enoch Culver. FAM. 25.

v Levi, b 29 Aug 1738 *WV,* d 1815; rem. to Windham & Camden, N. Y.; m 27 Nov 1760 *WV*—Mary da. Asahel & Mary (Benham) Coley, b 20 Nov 1740 *SomersV,* d 1827 Camden, N. Y. Children rec. *WV:* Orange, b 19 Nov 1763; Mary, b 14 Feb 1766; Lent, b 3 Mar 1768; Ephraim, b 22 Sep 1770; Levi, b 23 Aug 1772.

vi Sarah, b 6 Sep 1740 *WV,* d 1 Jan 1761; m 11 Oct 1759 *NoBC2*—Solomon Munson.

vii Nathaniel, b 20 Oct 1742 *WV,* d 25 Feb 1830; res. Goshen; m 19 May 1768 *NoBC2*—Avis Hopson.

viii Abigail, b 2 Sep 1744 *WV,* d 11 Sep 1796 æ. 52 Whately, Mass.; m 22 Jan 1767 Moses Munson.

ix Margery, b 3 Nov 1746 *WV*; m Charles Culver.

x Lydia, b 1 Oct 1748 *WV,* d 6 Jan 1748/9 *WV.*

xi Abel, b 3 Jan 1749/50 *WV,* d 21 Dec 1778 (in Army); m & had da. Jerusha.

xii Joseph, b 16 Nov 1751 *WV,* d 29 June 1830; res. Salisbury, N. Y.; m (1) 11 Nov. 1773 *WV*—Elizabeth Hart; m (2).

xiii Lydia, b 12 Oct 1753 *WV,* bp 2 Dec 1753 *NoBC2;* m Erwin Ives.

xiv Adah, bp 19 Nov 1758 *NoBC2;* m 14 Apr 1779 Abraham Bunnell.

2 Abigail, b 2 Apr 1704 *WV,* d 17 Sep 1792 *CC;* m 19 Oct 1725 *WV*—Ichabod Merriam.

3 Joseph, b 25 Dec 1705 *WV,* d 4 Aug 1765 æ. 60 *WV,* æ. 65(?) *WT1;* m 2 Mar 17[58] *WV*—Ruth ———, wid. John Rexford; she m (2) 3 Oct 1766 *WV*—Job Clark.

i Jemima, b 15 May 1758 *WV,* d 2 Oct 1773.

ii Joseph, b 2 July 1760 *WV,* d 30 July 1772 æ. 12 (suicide) *WC1.*

iii Charles, b 31 May 1762 *WV,* d 29 Nov 1786; cripple.

iv Ruth, b 24 July 1764 *WV;* m 26 Nov 1801 John Beadles.

4 Desire, b Feb 1707/8 *WV*, d 8 Nov 1791 *WV;* m 28 Mar 1734 *WV*—Stephen Peck.

5 Thankful, b 17 Jan 1710 *WV;* m 19 Aug 1729 *WV*—Samuel Gaylord.

6 Ephraim, b 5 Nov 1714 *WV*, d 21 Sep 1770; res. Bd, & Granville, Mass.; m 6 Feb 1739 *WC2*—Comfort da. Nathaniel & Sarah (How) Curtis, b 30 Oct 1716 *WV;* had 9 children.

7 Margery, b 10 Oct 1717 *WV*, d 5 Mar 1798 *CC;* m 26 Jan 1738 *WV*—Phineas Ives.

8 Jemima, b 27 Mar 1720 *WV;* m 27 Oct 1742 *WV*—Waitstill Parker.

9 Agur, b 7 Apr 1725 *WV*, d 17 Dec 1726 *WV*.

FAM. 7. Stephen & Lydia (Bassett) Munson:

1 Stephen, b 15 Nov 1704 *NHV*, bp 4 Aug 1717 *NHC1*, d May 1730 *Greenwich;* B.A. (Yale 1725); Rev.; m Susanna da. John & Abigail (Alling) Punderson, b 29 July 1703 *NHV*, d 14 Dec 1741 æ. 38 *NHT1*.

i Stephen, b 14 Dec 1730 *NHV*, bp 20 Dec 1730 *NHC1*, d 31 Aug 1800 æ. 69 *NHC1;* B.A. (Yale 1751); Census (NH) 1-0-3; m 16 Oct 1756 *NHV*—Lucy da. Isaac & Jemima (Sage) Riley, b 27 Mar 1732 *WethV*, d 15 May 1790 æ. 59 *NHC1, NHT1*. FAM. 26.

2 Lydia, b 22 Nov 1707 *NHV*, bp 4 Aug 1717 *NHC1*, d 12 Sep 1769 ; m 13 Jan 1725/6 *NHV*—Joseph Burroughs.

3 Phebe, b 5 Feb 1709/10 *NHV*, bp 4 Aug 1717 *NHC1;* m 25 Dec 1734 *NHV*—John Brown.

4 Rebecca, b 9 Dec 1713 *NHV*, bp 4 Aug 1717 *NHC1;* m 9 Aug 1738 Charles Norton of Farm.

5 Elsie, b 12 July 1716 *NHV*, bp 4 Aug 1717 *NHC1*, d 2 Mar 1792 æ. 75 *NHC1;* m 12 Jan 1737/8 *NHV*—Joseph Miles.

6 Amos, b 9 Apr 1719 *NHV*, bp Apr 1719 *NHC1*, d s. p. 1748.

7 Samuel, b 4 Aug 1722 *NHV*, bp c. Aug 1722 *NHC1*, d 1 Aug 1804 æ. 82 *NHT1;* Census (NH) 1-1-1; m 21 May 1741 *NHV*—Abigail da. Richard & Ruth (Lewis) Hollingsworth, bp 2 June 1723 *FairfieldC*, d 23 Feb 1793 æ. 70 *NHT1*.

i Lydia, b 8 Mar 1742/3 *NHV*, d 31 Mar 1785 æ. 42 *MonroeT;* m 30 June 1765 *NHC2*—Elisha Rexford.

ii Samuel, b 31 Aug 1745 *NHV*, d 14 May 1814; res. Lenox, Mass.; m Mary Morse.

iii Abigail, b 23 Feb 1748 *NHV*, 26 Feb *NHT1*, d 19 Dec 1819 æ. 72 *NHT1;* m William Brintnall.

iv Rebecca, b 3 Oct 1750 *NHV,* d 29 Aug 1751 *NHV.*

v Rebecca, b 22 June 1752 *NHV,* bp 28 June 1752 *NHC2;* m Daniel Morse of Fairfield, Vt.

vi Sarah, b 8 Oct 1755 *NHV,* bp 12 Oct 1755 *NHC2;* m 4 Nov 1776 *NHV*—Hezekiah Sabin.

vii Elizabeth, bp 19 July 1767 *NHC2.*

8 JABEZ, b 17 Dec 1728 *NHV,* bp 22 Dec 1728 *NHC1,* d c. 1778; m Eunice da. Joshua & Anna (Bradley) Atwater, b 7 Aug 1730 *NHV;* Census, Eunice (H) 1-0-2.

i Amos, b 18 Feb 1753 *NHV,* d 1783; m Hannah da. John & Abiah (Macomber) Hall, b c. 1751, d 30 Aug 1832 *NHV;* she m (2) c. 1800 Stephen Trowbridge. Children: (1) Elizabeth, b c. 1781, bp 18 June 1783 *NHC2;* (2) Sarah, bp 31 Aug 1783 *NHC2,* d c. 1790.

ii Jabez, b 20 Jan 1755 *NHV,* d 14 July 1805 æ. 51 *HT2;* Census (H) 1-3-2; m Desire da. Benjamin & Rachel (Lines) Wooding, b c. 1757, d 14 Dec 1828 æ. 74*HT2.* FAM. 27.

iii Eunice, b 10 Apr 1757 *NHV,* d s. p.

iv Stephen, b 1759 *NHV,* d 11 Mar 1830 æ. 70 *NoHT1;* Capt.; m 16 Aug 1781 *NHC2*—Mary da. Asa & Mehitabel (Sackett) Goodyear, b 23 Mar 1760 *NHV,* d 18 Aug 1837 æ. 77 *NoHT1.* FAM. 28.

v Isaac, b 24 Nov 1716 *NHV,* d c. 1816; Census (H) 1-2-3; m 30 Oct 1781 *NHC2*—Elizabeth da. Roger Dearing & Phebe (Brown) Phipps, b 18 Feb 1763 *NHV.* FAM. 29.

vi Levi, b 1 May 1764 *NHV,* d 22 Jan 1826 æ. 62 *HT2;* Census (H) 1-1-1; m Patience da. David & Patience (Sanford) Alling, b 21 July 1766 *NHV,* d 7 July 1851 æ. 85 *HT2.* FAM. 30.

vii Joshua, b 17 Aug 1765 *NHV,* d 19 Aug. 1844; Census (H) 1-0-1; rem. to Canaan; m (1) 9 June 1790 Sarah da. Jonathan & Rebecca (Cooper) Booth, b 25 Dec 1772 *F,* d 14 Dec 1806; m (2) 14 Dec 1807 Eunice da. Caleb & Lois (Dorman) Alling, b 12 Oct 1779, d. 30 Apr 1866 (Millerton, N. Y.); had issue.

viii Jared, b 13 Mar 1769 *NHV,* d 7 Nov 1819 æ. 50 *HT2;* m (1) Lucy da. John & Susanna (Gilbert) Gorham, b c. 1781, d 22 Oct 1801 æ. 20 *HT2 (list)*; m (2) Sarah da. John & Susanna

(Gilbert) Gorham, b [Sep] 1787, d 9 May 1876 æ. 88-8 *HT2*; she m (2) Jesse Alling.
FAM. 31.

ix Anna, b 14 Mar 1772 *NHV*.

FAM. 8. CALEB & ELIZABETH (HARMON) MUNSON:

1 KEZIA, b 13 Jan 1706 *WV* [1706/7]; m 12 Nov 1734 *WV*—Samuel Street.

2 CALEB, b 19 Aug 1709 *WV*, d 25 July 1747 *WV;* m 23 Apr 1735 *WV*—Abigail da. Samuel & Rachel (Brown) Brockett, b 11 Feb 1711 *WV*, d 17 Nov 1800 ; she m (2) 22 Nov 1750 *WatV*—Isaac Bronson.

i Abner, b 2 Mar 1736 *WV*, d 12 Dec 1807; res. My; m 24 Sep 1764 Azuba Bronson.

ii Hermon, b 28 Oct 1738 *WV*, d 12 Feb 1829 æ. 91; m 21 July 1769 Anna Bronson.

iii Cornelius, b 16 Apr 1742 *WV*, d (in British Army).

iv Benjamin, b 23 Aug 1744 *WV*, d 30 Apr 1813; rem. to Paris, Oneida Co., N. Y.; m 6 June 1775 Rosanna (———) Burges.

v Caleb, b 13 Mar 1747 *WV*, d July 1826; res. My; m 10 May 1781 Lucy Roberts.

3 JOSHUA, b 30 Jan 1712 *WV*, d 3 Aug 1772 ; m Anne da. Daniel & Abigail (Tuttle) Atwater, b 4 June 1726 *NHV*, d 16 Jan 1804 ; she m (2) 29 Sep 1773 Oliver Hitchcock.

i Joshua, b 4 Feb 1750 *WV*, d soon.

ii Elizabeth, b 29 Feb 1752 *WV*, d 25 June 1833 æ. 82 *WT1;* m 2 May 1773 *WV*—Thomas Royce.

iii Joshua, b 2 Aug 1754 *WV*, d 7 June 1838 æ. 84 *WT1;* m 18 Apr 1774 Miriam da. Michael & Mehitabel (Doolittle) Dayton, b 26 Jan 1751 *WatV*, d 2 Jan 1833 æ. 81 *WT1*.

iv Lucy, b 3 Feb 1757 *WV*, d 29 Sep 1795 ; m 17 Apr 1782 *BdV*, 1 Apr *NoBC1*—Amaziah Rose.

v Anna, b 28 June 1760 *WV*, d 1829; m 10 May 1785 Samuel Street.

vi Miriam, b 22 Oct 1763 *WV;* m 17 Oct 1808 George Street of Springfield.

vii Mary, b 26 Feb 1766 *WV*.

viii Abigail, b 17 July 1770 *WV;* m 23 Dec 1795 *BdV*—Amaziah Rose.

4 MOSES, b c. 1715, d c. 1750; m 18 July 1739 *WV*—Phebe da. Moses & Martha (Beach) Merriman, b 27

Mar 1720 *WV;* she m (2) 9 Apr 1752 Josiah Bartholomew.

i John, b 2 Aug 1740 *WV,* d 1828; res. Lee, Mass.; m 2 July 1761 *WV*—Lydia da. Stephen & Lydia (Ives) Todd, b 21 Nov 1744 *WV,* d c. 1834.

ii Thomas Ensign, b 5 Apr 1742 *WV,* d 20 Jan 1820; res. Goshen; m 22 Apr 1766 *WV*—Ruth, da. Isaac & Elizabeth (Culver) Brockett, b 26 Oct 1744 *WV,* d 1 Oct 1798 æ. 54 *GoshenT.*

iii Margaret, b 14 Apr 1744 *WV;* m 22 Dec 1763 David Maltby.

iv Caleb, b 22 May 1746 *WV,* d 1 Dec 1802; m 19 Mar 1767 Mary Lee.

v Hannah, b 17 May 1748 *WV.*

vi Moses, b 13 Aug 1750 *WV,* d 1751.

5 ELIZABETH, b 31 Mar 1717 *WV;* m 10 May 1743 Jedediah Frisbie.

6 MIRIAM, b 22 Apr 1720 *WV,* d 20 Aug 1757; m 18 Feb 1741/2 *WV*—James Royce.

FAM. 9. PETER & ELIZABETH (HALL) MUNSON:

1 LYDIA, b 27 Apr 1763 *WV;* m 27 Nov 1781 *CV*—Zealous Bristol.

2 EUNICE, b 20 Oct 1764 *WV,* perhaps the "child" who d 23 Oct 1777 *CC.*

3 WAIT, b 20 Sep 1766 *WV,* d 23 Dec 1846 (N. Y. City); m 25 Jan 1795 Mary Elizabeth Davies, who d 2 June 1842.

4 JOEL, b 5 Nov 1768 *WV,* bp 18 Dec 1768 *CC,* d 3 Sep 1803 (Portsmouth, Va.).

5 REUBEN, b 28 Sep 1770 *WV,* d 29 Sep 1846 (Flushing, L. I.); m Abigail Wilsey, b 21 July 1781, d 23 Apr 1865.

6 (Probably) ELIZABETH, bp 12 Oct 1772 *CC,* "child" d 22 Oct 1777 *CC.*

7 AMOS, bp 7 Aug 1744 *CC,* "child" d 12 Oct 1777 *CC.*

8 ASA, bp 21 Apr 1776 *CC,* "child" d 13 Oct 1777 *CC.*

9 AMOS, bp 31 May 1778 *CC,* d 5 Jan 1810 (N. Y. City).

10 ASA, bp 8 Apr 1781 *CC,* "child" d 28 June 1788 *CC.*

11 LEVI, b 9 Apr 1783 *F,* bp 8 June 1783 *CC,* d 25 Dec 1844; res. C; m 5 Jan 1810 Tenna Brooks, who d 3 Jan 1862.

12 PETER HALL; res. N. Y. City; m.

13 CHILD, d 20 Feb 1789 *CC.*

FAM. 10. REUBEN & MARY (CRITTENDEN) MUNSON:

1 STEPHEN, b 23 Sep 1742 ; rem. to Byron, N. Y.; m 8 July 1762 Ann Cogswell.

2 Moses, b 24 Sep 1744 *WV*, d 13 July 1837 (Whately, Mass.); m (1) 22 Jan 1767 Abigail da. Abel & Sarah (Peck) Munson, b 2 Sep 1744 *WV*, d 11 Sep 1796 æ. 52 (Whately); m (2) 1797 Lucy Morton; m (3) Oct 1810 Mary Truesdale.

3 Reuben, b 22 Dec 1746 *WV*, d 20 Mar 1837 (Whately, Mass.); m 16 July 1769 Sybil Smith of Bristol.

4 Phebe, bp 19 Mar 1748/9 *SC;* m Isaac Smith.

5 Mary, bp 14 Apr 1751 *SC*, d 28 Oct 1786; m 9 July 1767 Jehudi Hart.

6 Sarah, bp 18 Mar 1753 *SC;* m 19 Jan 1769 Ebenezer Evans.

7 Joel, bp 30 Mar 1755 *SC*, d 19 Sep 1776 (in Army, at Stamford).

8 Benjamin, bp 8 May 1757 *SC*, d 1777.

9 Martha, bp 12 Oct 1760 *SC*, d 20 Aug 1799 æ. 39 *F;* m 26 June 1782 Ezekiel Andrews.

10 Samuel, b 9 July 1762 *F*, bp 5 Sep 1762 *SC*, d 27 Feb 1841 (Whitestown, N. Y.); m 3 Feb 1785 Martha Barnes.

FAM. 11. Solomon & Sarah (Peck) Munson:

1 Eunice, b 19 Nov 1754 *WV;* m 28 Oct 1772 Timothy Barnes of L.

2 Jonathan, b 30 June 1756 *WV*, d 24 Mar 1847 æ. 91 *NoBT1;* Capt.; m (1) 16 July 1778 Mary Taintor, who d 4 Sep 1822 æ. 67 *NoBT1;* m (2) Sarah (———) Johnson.

FAM. 11. Solomon & Sarah (Munson) Munson:

3 Sarah, b 11 Dec 1760 *WV*, d 11 Oct 1845 (Hatfield, Mass.); m 4 Apr 1785 Isaac Frary.

FAM. 11. Solomon & Hannah (Baldwin) Munson:

4 Bede, b Aug 1762 *WV*, d s. p. (at Hartford); m (1) 11 Dec 1783 Joseph Wheeler of S; m (2) ——— Camp.

5 Phebe, b 1 July 1764 *WV*, d 14 Oct 1857 (Greenfield); m Moses Munson.

6 Jairus, b 6 Feb 1767 *WV*, d 7 Oct 1862 (Windham, N. Y.); m 11 Feb 1790 Anna Hart.

7 Hannah, b Oct 1772, d 5 Mar 1853 (Whately, Mass.); m (1) 31 Mar 1791 Frederick Bunce; m (2) 29 Sep 1803 Dexter Morton.

8 Lucy, b 3 July 1775; m Michael Mitchell of Salem, Pa.

FAM. 12. Obadiah & Rachel (Tyler) Munson:

1 Barnabas, b 24 Sep 1754 *WV*, d s. p. 1 Mar 1792 in 29 [39] yr. *CT2*.

2 Wilmot, b 23 July 1755 *WV*, d Oct 1845 (Westfield, O.); m Patience Cooper; had issue.

3 Hannah, b 12 Jan 1757 *WV*, d bef. 1792. She had children:

i Jubal; res. Harwinton 1798.

ii John; res. S; supposed dead 1798.

4 Stephen, b 10 Feb 1759 *WV*, d 9 July 1824 (Huntington, Mass.); m 13 Mar 1783 Elizabeth da. William & Submit (Frost) Andrus, b c. 1767, d 3 Mar 1847 æ. 80; had issue.

5 Daniel, b 1 Aug 1761 *WV*, d (in Rev. W.).

6 Ephraim, b 30 Apr 1763 *WV*, d 27 Nov 1834 (Bethlehem); m c. 1786 Deborah Scott, b 14 Aug 1766, d 28 Feb 1842; had issue.

7 Rachel, b 5 Mar 1765 *WV*, d young.

8 Sarah, b 7 Apr 1767 *Farm*; m Benjamin Elton of Wtn & Harwinton.

9 Obadiah, b 7 Apr 1769 *Farm*, d 23 Sep 1834; res. Harwinton & C; m Sally Atwood, who d 1 Sep 1850 æ. 84.

10 Walter, b 6 May 1771 *Farm*, d 5 Nov 1836 (Orange, Pa.); m c. 1794 Mehitabel Trowbridge, b 28 Nov 1777, d 26 Oct 1855.

11 Irene; m Daniel Cheney of Cattaraugus Co., N. Y.

12 Benoni, d young.

FAM. 13. Walter & Mabel (Mansfield) Munson:

1 John, b 1 Mar 1761 *NHV*, bp 3 Mar 1761 *NoHC*, d 3 Mar 1761 *NHV*, 4 Mar æ. 0-0-2 *NoHC*.

2 Mansfield, bp 5 Sep 1762 *NoHC*, d c. 1820 (Harmony, Champaign Co., O.); m 13 Jan 1785 *WC1*—Lua da. Benjamin & Thankful (Hickox) Brooks, bp 29 Jan 1764 *Bristol x*, d after 1820.

3 Wilmot, b 4 July 1764 *NHV*, bp 28 June 1764 *NoHC*, d 7 July 1764 *NHV*, 30 June *NoHC* (dates in *NHV* must be about 9 days too late).

4 Betty, b 7 Nov 1765 *NHV*, bp 17 Nov 1765 *NoHC;* m Abner Andrews of Meriden.

5 Purlina, b 2 Apr 1770 *NHV*, bp 6 May 1770 *NoHC*, d s. p. after 1814.

6 Jared, b 18 Sep 1772 *F*, bp 1772 *NoHx*, d 26 Oct 1822 (Harmony, O.); m 12 July 1797 *WdC*—Elizabeth da. Phineas & Elizabeth (Hine) Peck, b 11 Feb 1774 *F*, d 3 Sep 1820; had 9 children.

7 Polly; m Abraham Decker of Athens, Pa.

FAM. 14. David & Abigail (Potter) Munson:

1 Charles, b 22 Aug 1741 *NHV*, d bef. 1770; m 14 June 1763 *NHC2*—Hannah da. Theophilus & Abigail

(Talmadge) Munson, b 17 May 1744 *NHV;* she m (2) 2 Oct 1770 *NHC1*—Elijah Hills.

i Mary, bp 12 May 1771 *NHC1.*

2 Dorothy, b 18 Nov 1743 *NHV,* d 8 Sep 1811 æ. 71 *HT4;* m 27 Aug 1761 *NHV, NHC2*—Joseph Gilbert.

3 David, b 4 July 1746 *NHV,* d 18 Oct 1821 (Tyringham, Mass.); Census (H) 1-2-2; m Elizabeth da. Joseph & Phebe (Dorman) Dorman, b 6 Apr 1751 *NHV,* d 26 Oct 1827 (Exeter, N. Y.).

i Phebe, b 13 July 1770, d 17 July 1850; m 1789 William Mansor.

ii Charles, b 2 June 1773, d 9 Dec 1844; res. Oxf. & Exeter, N. Y.; m 6 May 1795 *F*—Lorana da. David & Lorana (Trowbridge) Wooding, b 14 Oct 1773 *F,* d 11 July 1850.

iii Jared, b 17 Dec 1775, bp 3 Mar 1776 *NHC2,* d 11 Oct 1847 (Richfield, N. Y.); m 3 Jan 1805 Eunice da. Joseph Curtis.

iv Isaac, bp 17 June 1781 *NHC2,* d soon.

v Isaac, b 26 Feb 1786, d Feb 1855 (Virgil, N. Y.); m Althana Lewis, who d 14 Apr 1873.

vi Betsey, b 5 May 1790; m John Dilley of New Berlin, N. Y.

vii David, b 10 Jan 1795, d 5 Nov 1851 (New Marlborough, Mass.); m 13 Apr 1820 Alta Huggins.

4 Jared, b 25 June 1749 *NHV.*

5 Rhoda, b 9 Oct 1751 *NHV,* d 15 Aug 1819 æ. 67 *HT2;* m Benjamin Wooding.

FAM. 14. David & Huldah (Foster) Munson:

6 John, b 22 Jan 1782 *NHV,* bp 31 Mar 1782 *NHC1.*

7 Abigail, bp 28 Mar 1784 *NHC1,* d 28 Dec 1879 æ. 95 *NHT3;* m Robert Talmadge.

FAM. 15. John & Esther (Turner) Munson:

1 Moses Turner, b 2 Oct 1749 *NHV;* res. Hebron, N. Y.; m Abigail Ruggles.

2 John, b 30 Jan 1752 *NHV;* res. Hebron, N. Y.; m Mary [Mansfield].

3 Nathaniel, b 17 Mar 1755 *NHV,* d 17 Nov 1828; res. Hebron, N. Y.; m Edatha da. Reuben Noble.

4 Thomas, b 31 Jan 1758 *NHV,* d 3 Oct 1759 *NHV.*

5 Anna, b 2 Oct 1760 *NHV;* m Stephen Smith of Rupert, Vt.

6 Thomas, b 1 Nov 1763 *NHV.*

7 Esther; m Calvin Smith of Herkimer Co., N. Y.

FAM. 16. Timothy & Sarah (Bishop) Munson:

1 Sarah, b c. 1756, bp 15 Oct 1758 *NHC2,* d Sep 1846; m William Oviatt of Pownal, Vt.

2 Huldah, bp 15 Oct 1758 *NHC2;* m Ephraim Tanner of Warren.
3 Lucena; m Adonijah Carter of Warren.
4 Dorcas; m Joseph Carter of Warren, & St. Albans, Vt.
5 Electa, b 26 Sep 1765, d 14 Jan 1848; m 17 Mar 1787 James Bushnell of Bennington, Vt.
6 Timothy, b c. 1767, d. 25 Aug 1845 (Harrisville, O.); m (1) Abigail ——; m (2) Amelia ——.
7 Ruth, b c. 1768, d 11 Jan 1858 æ. 93; m David Stannard of Pownal, Vt.
8 Temperance; m —— Scranton.
9 John Clarke, b July 1774, d 1858 (Erie Co., Pa.); m 12 Nov 1801 Elizabeth Folsom, who d c. 1866 æ. 85.
10 Martha, b 29 Oct 1777, d 23 Aug 1869 (Ballston, N. Y.); m 28 Jan 1796 John Stanton.

fam. 17. Basil & Kezia (Stiles). Munson:
1 Job Lucianus, b 26 Sep 1752 *NHV,* d 10 June 1828 æ. 76 *HT3;* Census (H) 1-3-4; m (1) 2 Oct 1775 *HV*—Lucy da. Ebenezer & Mary (Bradley) Beach, b 29 Oct 1758 *NHV,* d 22 Sep 1807 æ. 49 *HT3;* m (2) 10 Apr 1808/9 Nancy Thompson, b 21 Jan 1779 (Farm), d c. 1862.
(By 1): *i* Ebenezer Beach, b 14 Sep 1777 (Stockbridge, Mass.) *HV,* bp May 1783 *HC1,* d 17 Oct 1834 (Broadalbin, N. Y.); m 6 Feb 1799 Rebecca da. Jonathan & Miriam (Bradley) Dickerman, b 21 Feb 1781 *F,* d 22 Aug 1858.
ii Mehitabel, b 14 Dec 1779 *HV,* bp May 1783 *HC1,* d 29 Aug 1872 æ. 93 *HT3;* m 18 May 1806 *CC*—Samuel B. Kingsley.
iii Bazel, b 30 Dec 1781 *HV,* bp May 1783 *HC1,* d 7 Jan 1854 æ. [—] *NHT1;* m 12 Apr 1804 Huldah Brace.
iv Sarah, b 1 Mar 1785 *HV,* bp 1 May 1785 *HC1;* m Asahel Strong of Durham.
v Lucy, b 19 Oct 1787 *HV,* d 18 June 1881 (Greenville, N. Y.); m 1 Feb 1813 Asahel Dickerman.
vi Job Lucianus, b 23 Nov 1789 *HV,* bp 10 Jan 1790 *HC1,* d 28 June 1864 æ. 75 *HT3;* m (1) Sally Moss; m (2) 17 June 1830 Adelia Tuttle; m (3) 30 Dec 1850 Lodema (Morse) Watson.
2 Titus, b 31 Jan 1755 *NHV,* 9 Oct 1757 *HT3,* d 15 Oct 1809 (Pittsford, N. Y.) *HT3;* m (1) 12 June 1775 *CC*—Mary da. Joel & Abigail (Tuttle) Bradley, b

11 Nov 1760 *NHV,* d 25 Mar 1797 æ. 36 *HT3;* m (2) 26 Jan 1800 Ruth (Lyon) Seeley.

3 Ezra, b 15 May 1757 *NHV,* d c. 1800; Census (H) 1-0-4; m 1 Mar 1784 *HC1*—Mabel da. John & Eunice (Todd) Gilbert, bp 10 May 1767 *NoHC.*

i Lydia, b 21 Mar 1786 *HV,* bp 25 Jan 1795 *HC1;* m Leonard Curtis of Great Barrington, Mass.

ii Harriet, b 21 Feb 1788 *HV,* bp 25 Jan 1795 *HC1,* d young.

iii Austin, b 12 July 1790 *HV,* bp 25 Jan 1795 *HC1,* d 4 Nov 1859; res. Bridgeport; m Rhoda Silliman.

iv Chauncey, b 6 June 1792 *HV,* bp 25 Jan 1795 *HC1,* d (in South).

v Justus Gilbert, b 7 Mar 1795 *HV,* bp 5 Apr 1795 *HC1,* d 7 July 1875 (Gt. Barrington); m (1) Esther (Stanton) Vosburgh; m (2) 29 Jan 1862 Bede (———) Dorman.

vi Kezia, b 31 Jan 1798 *HV,* bp 22 Apr 1798 *HC1,* d 1829; m Jared Seeley of Gt. Barrington.

4 Isaac Stiles, b 13 Sep 1761 *NHV* [1760], bp 28 Dec 1760 *NoHC;* res. Boyle, N. Y.; m Eleanor ———.

5 Kezia, b 1 Mar 1763 *NHV,* d 2 Aug 1799 æ. 37 *HT3;* m 4 Dec 1780 Jotham Tuttle.

6 Mehitabel, bp 6 Sep 1766.

FAM. 17. Basil & Abigail (Bassett) Munson:

7 Abigail Bassett, b 20 July 1772 *NHV,* bp 26 July 1772 *HC1,* d 1852; m (1) 6 Oct 1791 *NoHC*—George A. Bristol; m (2) 9 Jan 1822 *SC*—Aaron Bradley.

FAM. 18. Joel & Sarah (Dickerman) Munson:

1 Samuel Dickerman, b 29 Jan 1763 *NHV,* d 25 Mar 1814; res. Truro, Mass., & New Sharon, Me.; m 21 May 1790 Elizabeth Lombard.

2 Mary, b 30 Sep 1766 *NHV,* d 10 Dec 1859; m 25 Dec 1788 Henry Mead of Rutland, Vt.

3 Joel, b 25 Jan 1769 *NHV;* rem. to Baltimore?

4 Jesse, b 30 May 1771 *NHV,* d 1803; m Amelia da. Jonathan & Miriam (Bradley) Dickerman, b 13 May 1779 *NHV,* d 11 Dec 1813 æ. 35 *HT3;* she m (2) Eli Hull.

FAM. 19. Joseph & Sarah (Bishop) Munson:

1 Mary, b 23 Nov 1757 *NHV,* bp 25 Mar 1759 *NHC1,* d 29 Sep 1828.

2 Elizabeth, b 7 Aug 1759 *NHV,* bp 12 Aug 1759 *NHC1,* d 1 Aug 1825.

3 Elisha, b 7 Apr 1761 *NHV,* bp 12 Apr 1761 *NHC1,* d 31 Aug 1841 æ. 80 *NHV.*

4 SARAH, bp 20 Feb 1763 *NHC1,* d 13 Sep 1838 æ. 75 *NHV.*

5 ESTHER, bp 20 Jan 1765 *NHC1,* d 14 Jan 1847.

6 HANNAH, bp 7 Sep 1766 *NHC1,* d 4 Feb 1833, "Mrs. Munson" 6 Feb æ. 65 *NHV.*

7 JOSEPH, b 4 May 1768 *F,* bp 29 May 1768 *NHC1,* d 23 Sep 1769 æ. 0-16 *NHT1.*

8 JOSEPH, b 19 Sep 1770 *F,* bp 23 Sep 1770 *NHC1,* d 2 Dec 1842 æ. 72 *NHV;* m 18 Feb 1796 *NHC1*—Hannah da. Nehemiah & Mary (Dodd) Higgins, b c. 1777, d 4 Sep 1860 (at Cincinnati, O.).

9 JAMES, b 30 Apr 1772 *F,* bp 3 May 1772 *NHC1,* d 16 May 1839 æ. 67 *NHV;* m 16 June 1802 Sarah Trowbridge.

FAM. 20. ISRAEL & ANNA (GRISWOLD) MUNSON:

1 ISRAEL, b 3 Feb 1767 *NHV,* bp 8 Feb 1767 *NHC2,* d s. p. 2 Feb 1844.

2 ISAAC, b 5 Apr 1771 *F,* bp 7 Apr 1771 *NHC2,* d 11 Feb 1835; rem. to Wallingford, Vt.; m Sarah Bradley.

3 ANNA, bp 28 Feb 1773 *NHC2,* d c. 1807; m William Thacher.

4 LOIS, bp 31 Aug 1783 *NHC2,* d 21 Jan 1851; m Joel Hill of Wallingford, Vt.

FAM. 21. WILLIAM & MARTHA (HALL) MUNSON:

1 RICHARD HALL, b 16 Jan 1771 *F,* d 23 July 1773 æ. 2 *NHC1.*

2 WILLIAM, b 26 July 1772 *NHV,* d 5 Apr 1781 æ. 9 *NHC1.*

3 MARTHA, b 26 June 1774 *F,* bp 7 July 1782 *NHC1,* d 7 Apr 1820 (N. Y. City); m 3 June 1797 *NHx*—William Boyer.

4 MARGARET, b 4 Mar 1778 *F,* bp 7 July 1782 *NHC1,* d 25 May 1811.

5 JOHN, b 16 May 1780 *F,* bp 7 July 1782 *NHC1,* d 28 Apr 1812 (N. Y. City).

6 HARRIET, b 4 Jan 1784 *F,* bp 11 Apr 1784 *NHC1,* d 8 Dec 1831; m (1) 14 Nov 1804 Oliver Dyer of Providence, R. I.; m (2) Henry Lockwood of N. Y. City.

7 WILLIAM, b 21 Jan 1787 *F,* bp 18 Mar 1787 *NHC1,* d 2 Aug 1859 (Sandy Creek, N. Y.); m Gytly ———.

8 RICHARD HALL, b 12 July 1789 *F,* bp 28 Mar 1790 *NHC1,* d 1816 (at sea).

9 GRACE, b 14 Aug 1792 *F,* bp 18 Nov 1792 *NHC1,* d 18 Feb 1892; m 14 Dec 1811 Stephen Wheeler.

FAM. 21. WILLIAM & ELIZABETH (COLLIS) MUNSON:

10 ALEXANDER LITTLE, b 20 July 1808 *F,* bp 2 Oct 1808 *NHx,* d 27 Mar 1837.

11 DANIEL COLLIS, b 28 May 1810 *F*, d Nov 1825 (at Martinique).

12 GEORGE HOTCHKISS, b 7 Jan 1816 *F*, bp 5 May 1816 *NHx*, d 16 Sep 1861 (N. Y. City).

FAM. 22. DANIEL & MARY (SEARS) MUNSON:

1 WILLIAM, b 26 Feb 1767 *MV*, d 29 June 1847 æ. 80 *SheltonT;* m 29 Jan 1789 *MC1*—Sarah Beardsley, who d 2 Oct 1845 æ. 80 *SheltonT*.

2 SARAH, b 3 Sep 1769.

3 MARY, b 11 Aug 1771.

4 DANIEL, b 20 Sep 1773; m (1) ———, who d 3 Jan 1797; m (2) 19 Mar 1798 *MC1*—Fanny Tolles. He had a da. Sarah b c. 1797 who ran away from home (at P) 1814.

5 ELIZABETH, b 30 July 1775; m ——— Griswold.

6 JOHN, b 27 Jan 1778; m 2 Sep 1801 *NHC1*—Mehitabel Herrick.

7 FANNY, b 27 Dec 1780; m 29 Nov 1798 Harvey Bronson of Wat.

8 ISAAC, b 27 Apr 1782, d c. 1848; res. H; m Polly Prichard.

9 PATTY, b 20 May 1784; m (1) Caleb C. Northrop; m (2) ——— Lines.

10 GORHAM, b 31 May 1786; res. NH; m.

11 RANSOM, b 8 June 1789, d 8 Feb 1830 *NHV*; m 24 Nov 1810 Charlotte Jennet da. Joab Way.

12 LEWIS, b 1 Feb 1792, d 25 Dec 1881; res. M; m 2 Mar 1814 *MV*—Sybil Ford, who d 18 Oct 1868 æ. 72.

FAM. 23. ENEAS & SUSANNA (HOWELL) MUNSON:

1 CLARINDA, b 30 Dec 1761 *F*, bp 24 Jan 1762 *NHC1*, d 17 Aug 1841 æ. 80 *NHV*.

2 ÆNEAS, b 11 Sep 1763 *F*, bp 18 Sep 1763 *NHC1*, d 22 Aug 1852; m 3 May 1794 *NHC1*—Mary Shepherd, b 28 Apr 1772, d 6 Feb 1848.

3 ELIJAH, b 8 Mar 1765 *F*, bp 31 Mar 1765 *NHC1*, d 10 Oct 1838 æ. 74 *NHV;* Dr.; m (1) Martha Curtis of Sy, who d 28 May 1827 æ. 53; m (2) 21 Oct 1827 Grace da. Elijah & Mabel (Alling) Thompson, b c. 1790, bp 18 June 1803 (æ. 14) *NHx*, d 19 July 1864 æ. 74 *NHT1;* she m (2) John H. Jacocks.

4 WEALTHY ANN, b 3 Mar 1767 *NHT1*, bp 8 Mar 1767 *NHC1*, d 9 July 1839 *NHT1*, æ. 72 *NHV*; m 10 Sep 1786 *NHV*, *NHC1*—David Daggett.

5 SUSANNA, b 29 July 1768 *F*, bp 31 July 1768 *NHC1*, d 24 Aug 1769 æ. 0-13 *NHC1*.

6 GEORGE, b 25 May 1771 *F*, bp 9 June 1771 *NHC1*, d 17 Nov 1840 æ. 70 *NHV;* m 23 Sep 1804 Mary Daggett, who d 9 Aug 1861 (Boston, Mass.); div.

7 ELIHU, b 4 Dec 1774 *F,* bp 25 Dec 1774 *NHC1,* d 23 Aug 1852; m (1) 17 Jan 1798 *NHC1*—Silence da. Hanover & Phebe (Wolcott) Barney, bp 14 Feb 1779 *NHC1,* d 10 Nov 1805 æ. 26 *NHT1;* m (2) 27 Apr 1806 Elizabeth Sanford da. Job & Sarah (Sanford) Perit, bp 14 Aug 1785 *NHx,* d 8 Jan 1858 æ. 72.

8 HENRY, b 10 Feb 1777 *F,* bp 16 Feb 1777 *NHC1,* d 14 Mar 1856; m (1) 8 Jan 1804 *NHC1*—Hannah Talmadge, b c. 1780, d 27 July 1806 æ. 26 ; m (2) 21 Sep 1806 Jehila Johnson, b 16 Sep 1784 (at B) *F,* d 12 Aug 1859.

9 FREDERICK, b 15 Feb 1779 *F,* bp 28 Feb 1779 *NHC1,* d 12 Nov 1795.

FAM. 24. TITUS & LYDIA (LINSLEY) MUNSON:

1 IRENE, b 9 Mar 1758 *WV;* m 14 May 1776 Samuel Bartholomew.

2 ITHIEL, b 11 Dec 1760 *WV,* d 17 Dec 1835; m Sarah Ann Finch.

3 JACOB, b 23 May 1763 *WV,* d 28 Jan 1766.

4 MARY, b 15 June 1766 *WV,* d 28 Jan 1844; m 6 Dec 1786 Jared Bishop of N. Guilford.

5 JACOB, b 25 Oct 1768 *WV,* d 13 Oct 1776.

6 TITUS, b 10 June 1771 *WV;* res. Lyme 1792.

7 REBECCA, b 6 May 1775 *WV,* d 5 Mar 1776 *WV.*

FAM. 25. LUD & LOIS (JOHNSON) MUNSON:

1 RHODA, b 24 Jan 17[59] *WV,* d 19 Jan 1827 æ. 68 *WT1;* m 16 June 1780 *WV*—Jared Lewis.

2 ISAAC, b 9 Dec 17[60] *WV,* d bef. 1807; res. Palestine, N. Y., 1797; m 20 Feb 1782 *WV*—Sarah Munson.

3 AMZI, b 13 Feb 17[63] *WV,* d 13 Apr 1789.

4 ABIGAIL, b 28 Nov 17[65] *WV,* d c. 1820; m 5 Dec 1782 Timothy Bartholomew.

5 LOIS, b 14 Feb 1768 *WV,* d bef. 1807; m ——— Tibbals.

6 BENJAMIN, b 19 Dec 1771 *WV,* d 28 May 1815; m 29 Jan 1795 Betsey da. Samuel & Mary (Gill) Humiston, b 25 Mar 1776 *HV,* d 12 Jan 1835 æ. 59 *NoHT1;* she m (2) 1 Sep 1825 *NoHV*—Alling Ives.

i Mary, b 8 Dec 1795 (in Northford) *NoHV,* d 10 Jan 1839 æ. 43 *NoHT1;* "deaf & dumb."

ii Henrietta, b 8 Mar 1798 (in Northford) *NoHV,* d 28 July 1890 (Worcester, Mass.); m 21 June 1835 Horace Bartlett.

iii Betsey, b 10 Mar 1800 (in Northford) *NoHV,* d 24 Jan 1886; m 12 June 1825 Israel Wooding.

iv Benjamin Green, b 20 Feb 1803 (in Northford) *NoHV,* d 6 July 1825.

v Julius, b 15 Sep 1805 *NoHV,* d 19 Sep 1821 (at sea).

vi Lois Jennet, b 31 Aug 1809 *NoHV,* d 17 Oct 1886; m 31(*sic*) June 1830 Bela Bassett.

7 EUNICE, b 30 June 1775 *WV;* m 6 Nov 1796 *NoBC2*—Bela Peck.

FAM. 26. STEPHEN & LUCY (RILEY) MUNSON:

1 LUCY, b 16 Oct 1756 *NHV,* bp c. Apr 1757 *NHC1,* d 24 Sep 1785 æ. 29 *NHC1;* m 21 Sep 1783 *NHC1*—Samuel Russell.

2 STEPHEN, b 20 Feb 1758 *NHV,* bp 26 Feb 1758 *NHC1,* d 16 Aug 1759 *NHV, NHC1.*

3 SUSANNA, b 3 Nov 1759 *NHV,* bp 4 Nov 1759 *NHC1;* m 8 Feb 1792 *NHC1*—Norman Griswold of Torringford.

4 HANNAH, b 7 Dec 1762 *NHV,* bp 12 Dec 1762 *NHC1.*

5 FANNY, b 31 Oct 1765 *NHV,* d 10 Sep 1831 æ. 65 *(NHC2) NHV,* 8 Sep *NHT1.*

6 POLLY, b 23 Feb 1770 *NHV,* bp 25 Feb 1770 *NHC1,* "Wid." d 28 Dec 1823 æ. 60(!) *(NHx) NHV;* m 23 Jan 1790 *NHC1*—Nicholas Jebine.

FAM. 27. JABEZ & DESIRE (WOODING) MUNSON:

1 ANNA, b c. 1775, d 7 Feb 1863 æ. 88 *HV, HT1;* m Hezekiah John Warner.

2 JOSEPH, b c. 1777, d 22 Dec 1817 ae. 41 *HT2.*

3 JABEZ, b c. 1780, d 21 July 1854 æ. 73 *HV;* m c. 1806 Patience da. Noah & Thankful (Hitchcock) Wolcott, b c. 1782.

4 LYMAN, b 20 Aug 1781 *F,* d 20 Feb 1849 ; m c. 1803 Comfort da. Eliada & Esther (Warner) Hitchcock, b 24 July 1786 *F,* d 30 Apr 1849.

FAM. 28. STEPHEN & MARY (GOODYEAR) MUNSON:

1 MEHITABEL, bp 28 Sep 1783 *NHC2,* d 19 July 1860 ; m 24 Dec 1801 *NoHC*—Stephen Ford.

2 MARY, b c. 1785, d 19 Aug 1861 æ. 76 *NoHT3;* m 6 Feb 1805 *NoHV*—Titus Bradley.

3 AMOS, b 20 June 1787 *F,* "child" bp 16 Nov 1787 *NHC2,* d 25 June 1827 æ. 40 *NoHT1;* m (1) Polly da. Samuel & Lowly (Pardee) Dickerman, b 17 July 1785 *HV,* d 8 May 1811; m (2) Sophia da. Ezra & Phebe (Bradley) Kimberly, b 9 Oct 1791, d 29 Apr 1873.

4 MILES, bp 8 July 1798 *NoHC,* d s. p. 25 June 1841 æ. 43 *NoHT1;* m 31 Dec 1820 Lois da. M. & Polly Robinson, b [Sep 1792], d 7 Dec 1872 æ. 80-2 *NHV.*

5 MARIA, bp 5 Oct 1800 *NoHC.*

FAM. 29. ISAAC & ELIZABETH (PHIPPS) MUNSON:

1 LUCY J., b c. 1782, d 19 Feb 1855 æ. 74 *HT2;* she had a nat. child: Henry, b 29 June 1807, d 21 Mar 1893; m 29 Jan 1834 Jane Ford.

2 SUSANNA.

3 DEARING, b c. 1788, d 13 Apr 1860 æ. 72.

4 ELIZABETH, b c. 1790, d 27 Sep 1842 æ. 52 *HT2;* m Alva Keep.

5 ISAAC; m 1 Jan 1823 *HV*—Esther Maria Barnes.

6 HARVEY, b c. 1799, d 17 Apr 1879 æ. 80; res. Canaan; m Maria Judd, who d 2 Apr 1831 æ. 24.

7 LEWIS, d after 1830.

8 ALVA, b 4 May 1803 *F,* d 4 Apr 1882 æ. 78-11 *HT2;* m 4 May 1825 *HV*—Patty Malinda da. Ezekiel & Ruth (Warner) Dorman, b 7 Jan 1805, d 26 Nov 1885 æ. 79 *HT2.*

FAM. 30. LEVI & PATIENCE (ALLING) MUNSON:

1 RUSSELL, b 28 May 1789 *F,* d 11 Nov 1823 æ. 35 *HT2;* m Hephzibah da. John Foot, who d 12 Dec 1847 æ. 57.

2 LEVI, b 22 Dec 1791 *F,* d 5 Feb 1826 æ. 36 *HT2;* m Huldah da. Samuel & Lydia (Hitchcock) Warner, b c. 1791, d 20 Oct 1835 æ. 42 *HT2.*

3 LUCINDA CAROLINE, b 6 Feb 1793 *F,* d 25 Feb 1877 æ. 85 *HT2;* m 11 Oct 1812 Samuel Alling.

4 RHODA, b 19 July 1795 *F,* d 29 Sep 1871 ae. 76-2 *HV;* m 13 Feb 1823 Samuel Jones.

5 HULDAH, b 11 Jan 1798 *F,* d 21 Dec 1850 æ. 53 *HT2;* m Dearing Dorman.

6 HARRIET, b 22 Nov 1809 *F,* d 18 Feb 1833 æ. 23 *HT2.*

7 WILLIAM, d c. 1840.

FAM. 31. JARED & LUCY (GORHAM) MUNSON:

1 LUCY, b c. 1801, d 1884; m (1) Hubbard Bradley; m (2) Harvey Bradley.

FAM. 31. JARED & SARAH (GORHAM) MUNSON:

2 SYLVIA, b 11 Jan 1805 *F,* d 22 Feb 1889 æ. 84 *HT2;* m 17 Nov 1823 Lewis Heaton.

MURRAY. FAM. 1. JOSEPH, adopted child of Jonathan Booth, bp (at Newtown) 28 Dec 1712 *StratfieldC;* res. Newtown & NM; m 16 Apr 1724 *NewtownV*—Hannah da. Andrew & Elizabeth (Peat) Patterson, b 18 Apr 1703 *StV.*

1 ELIZABETH, b 24 Jan 1724/5 *NewtownV;* m 5 May 1743 *NMV*—John Henry Nearing.

2 JAMES, b 19 May 1727 *NewtownV.*

3 JOHN, b 2 July 1729 *NewtownV.*

4 MARY.

5 ELISHA.

6 HANNAH, bp 5 Sep 1736 *NMC;* m Samuel Lum.

7 Ruby, bp 29 Apr 1739 *NMC.*
8 Parthena, bp 16 June 1741 *NMC;* m 6 Mar 1765 *NHV*—Lemuel Hotchkiss.
9 Joseph.
10 Philemon, b c. 1745, d 25 Jan 1791 æ. 45 *LT;* m Esther da. Caleb & Ruth (Munson) Hotchkiss, b 5 Aug 1745 *NHV,* d 6 Oct 1831 æ. 86 *LT.*
11 Eunice, bp 27 Aug 1749 *NMV,* d 1 Oct 1840 æ. 91 *NHV;* m Ashbel Lines.

MURRAY. fam. 2. James, Census (NH) 1-2-4; m 28 May 1777 *NHC2*—Katharine [? da. Dennis] Scovit.
1 Sally, bp 21 June 1778 *NHC2,* d 19 Jan 1839 æ. 60; m (1) Joel Pardee; m (2) Eli Goodyear.
2 Nancy, bp 24 June 1781 *NHC2.*
3 John, bp 10 Aug 1783 *NHC2.*

MURRAY. miscellaneous. Daniel m Mary da. Richard & Martha (Mansfield) Sperry, bp 22 June 1690 *NHC1;* she m (2) 27 Jan 1725/6 *NHV*—James Vandermark. Child: Mary, b 19 Nov 1716 *NHV.*

NAILS. Variants, Neal, O'Neal. Henry of EH; m 29 July 1713 *NHV*—Abigail [da. Charles & Ann] Hodges, who d Apr 1786 æ. 100 *EHC.*
1 Patience, b 24 Aug 1713 *EHV,* bp 28 Sep 1735 (adult) *NHC1,* d 17 Nov 1794; m 13 Nov 1737 Ebenezer Plumb of G.
2 Henry, b 23 Aug 1715 *EHV.*
3 Abraham, b 21 Sep 1717 *EHV,* d 8 Oct 1798 æ. 82 *EHC;* Census (EH) 1-0-3; m Sarah Conklin, b c. 1724, d 27 Oct 1809 æ. 85 *EHC.*
i Charles.
ii Henry.
iii John.
iv Archer.
v Hannah; m 13 Dec 1776 *BdC*—Solomon Tompkins.
vi Sarah, b c. 1761, d 7 July 1781 æ. 20 *EHC.*
vii Esther, b c. 1761, d 25 Sep 1832 æ. 72 (called "Esther O'Neal") *EHC;* m June 1786 *EHC*—John Mitchell "of ye World."
viii Pamela; m Sep 1787 *EHC*—George Oswell.

Abraham Nails & w. Sarah of NH conveyed 1754 land in Bd from Est. of their gr. gr. father Tho. Whedon.
4 Charles, b 21 Jan 1719/20 *EHV.*
5 (prob.) Mary; m Benjamin Mallory.
6 (prob.) Phebe; m 4 July 1756 *EHC*—John Mulloon. She had a nat. child by Wm. Oakes, b Sep 1750 *NHCCt.*
7 (prob.) Martha, b c. 1731, d 22 Oct 1774 æ. c. 43

EHC; m 16 Feb 1758 *EHC*—David Slaughter. She had a nat. child:

i Ambrose Bradley, b 19 June 1749 *EHV.*

8 ABIGAIL, b 27 May 1733 *EHV;* m James Adkins Broton.

NASH. THOMAS, d 12 May 1658 *NHV;* m Margery da. Nicholas & Mary (Hodgett) Baker, who d after 11 Feb 1655/6 & bef. 1 Aug 1657.

1 JOHN, b c. 1615, d 3 July 1687 *NHV,* æ. 72 *NHT1;* Maj.; m Elizabeth da. Edmund Tapp, who d 1 May 1676 *NHV.*

i Elizabeth, bp 3 Jan 1646 *NHC1* [1646/7]; m 2 Dec 1676 *NHV*—Aaron Cook of Northampton, Mass.

ii Sarah, bp 29 July 1649 *NHC1,* d 27 May 1716 *WV;* m 8 Feb 1688/9 *NHV*—Thomas Yale of W.

iii Mary, b 13 Dec 1652 *NHV,* bp 14 Jan 1652 *NHC1* [1652/3]; m 1 Jan 1679 *NHV*—Philip Payne of Northampton.

iv Hannah, b 24 July 1655 *NHV,* bp 29 July 1655 *NHC1,* d 3 Feb 1707/8 *NHV;* m (1) 13 Feb 1672 *NHV*—Eliphalet Ball; m (2) 2 Apr 1689 *NHV*—Thomas Trowbridge.

2 JOSEPH, d 1678; Cpl.; res. Hartford; m (1) Mary ———, who d 25 Dec 1654 *NHV;* m (2) Margaret ———, wid. Arthur Smith, who d 1693/4; she m (3) Stephen Hart.

(By 1): *i* John, b 12 July 1650 *NHV,* bp 14 July 1650 *NHC1,* d young.

ii Hannah, b 21 Jan 1651 *NHV* [1651/2], bp 23 Jan 1651 *NHC1* [1651/2], "da." d 18 June 1654 *NHV.*

(By 2?): *iii* Sarah; m Noah Cooke.

PAGE 1528 3 MARY, d 16 Aug 1683 *NHV.*

4 SARAH; m Robert Talmadge.

5 TIMOTHY, b c. 1626, d 13 Mar 1699 æ. 73 (Hadley, Mass.); m [1657] *NHV*—Rebecca da. Rev. Samuel Stone, who d Mar/Apr 1709. Children recorded *NHV:* Rebecca, b 12 Mar 1657/8; Samuel, b 3 Feb 1659.

NASH. JOHN, blacksmith, of Bd 1651, d 1683; m 22 Aug 1677 *BdV*—Elizabeth Hitchcock, wid. Anthony Howd.

i Joseph, b 1 Aug 1678 *BdV,* d young.

ii Thomas, b 28 Jan 1679 *BdV* [1679/80]; res. F.

iii Elizabeth, b 15 Aug 1681 *BdV;* m Stephen Foote.

NESBIT. ALLEN, d 1746; res. NH; m c. 1731 Susanna da. Ebenezer & Abigail (Wooding) Hill, b c. 1696.

1 JOHN, b 4 Oct 1731 *NHV*.

NESBITT. SAMUEL & Mehitabel had:

1 MARGARET, bp 21 Oct 1772 *NHx*.

2 ELIZABETH, bp 2 Oct 1774 (sponsor, Sarah Henshaw) *NHx*.

3 MEHITABEL, bp 8 Dec 1776 (sponsor, Rebecca Camp) *NHx*.

4 RALPH, bp 2 Sep 1781 (sponsor, Wm. McCracken) *NHx*.

5 JAMES BURR, bp 20 June 1784 *NHx*.

6 MARY, bp 18 June 1786 (sponsor, Sarah Perit; child's mother called Margaret, prob. error for Mehitabel) *NHx*.

NEWELL. SAMUEL d Mar 1796 (at sea) *WHD*.

NEWHALL. [Contributed by Mrs. Frank A. Corbin.] JOSHUA, s. of Joshua & Elizabeth (Hodgman), bp 8 Dec 1765 *Salem, Mass.*, æ. 14 in 1767 when guardian was appointed; m 25 Sep 1777 *NHC1*—Comfort da. Dan & Philena (Killam) Carrington, b 31 July 1756 *NHV*.

NEWMAN. FAM. 1. FRANCIS, d 18 Nov 1660 *NHV;* Lt.; Sec.; Magistrate & Gov., NH Colony; m Mary ———, who d 13 Dec 1683; she m (2) Rev. Nicholas Street & (3) Gov. Wm. Leete. No known issue; he was not father of Elizabeth w. (1) of Thomas Knowles & (2) of Nicholas Knell, as often erroneously stated.......ROBERT, brother of Francis; Dea.; returned to Eng., near Stratford, co. Warwick. Children: 1 Bethia, bp 2 Oct 1642 *NHC1;* 2 Grace, bp 24 Oct 1646 *NHC1*, d 26 Aug 1650 *NHV*. ......Possibly Sarah w. Henry Rutherford was sister of Francis & Robert Newman, a conjecture based on the appearance of Newman as a Christian name among Rutherford's descendants.

NEWMAN. FAM. 2. RICHARD, of NH 1641, d after 1680; m ———. Probably he was not related to the above family, but possibly was connected with Wm. Newman of Stamford.

1 SAMUEL, b 1 July 1656 *NHV*, d s. p. 1689; m 15 Feb 1687/8 *NHV*—Elizabeth da. John Rose, who d 1690.

2 JOHN, bp 1665 *NHC1*, d s. p. 30 Jan 1712 *NHV;* m Abigail ———, who d 20 Nov 1742 *EHV*.

3 SARAH, bp 1665 *NHC1;* m June 1684 *NHV*—Samuel Tuttle.

4 MERCY, b 7 Dec 1665 *NHV*, bp 27 Jan 1665 *NHC1* [1665/6], d s. p.

NEWTON. FAM. 1. SAMUEL, s. of Samuel & Phebe (Platt), b c. 1710, d 21 Oct 1769 æ. 59 *WdT2;* m Deborah da. Thomas & Jerusha (Clark) Baldwin, b 25 Jan 1716.

1 Samuel, b 7 Dec 1737, bp 18 Apr 1742 *MC1,* d 31 Dec 1814 æ. 77 *WdT1;* Lt.; m (1) 13 May 1762 *WdV*—Mary Camp, b [19 Feb 1742 N. S.], d 26 Feb 1809 æ. 67-0-7 *WdT1;* m (2) 9 Jan 1811 *WdC*—Hannah da. Joseph Treat, wid. Enoch Clark & Zenas Peck, bp 12 Aug 1750 *MC1,* d 12 Feb 1840 æ. 89 *WdC.*

(By 1): *i* Mary, b 6 Feb 1763 *WdV,* d 7 Apr 1798 *WdV,* æ. 36 *WdT2;* m Dec 1781 *WdC*—Walter Booth.

ii Samuel, b 2 Feb 1765 *WdV,* d 22 Feb 1818 æ. 53 *WdC;* m 2 June 1790 *WdV*—Lucy da. David & Huldah (Beecher) Smith, b c. 1772, d 10 July 1848 æ. 76 *WdD.* FAM. 2.

iii Phebe, b 11 Aug 1766 *WdV,* d 31 Dec 1830 æ. 64 *WdT2.*

iv Martha, b 27 July 1768 *WdV,* d 26 Aug 1826 æ. 56 *WdT1;* m Ephraim Baldwin.

v Camp, b 14 Aug 1771 *WdV, WdT1,* d 23 Dec 1773 *WdV,* æ. 3 *WdT1.*

vi Joseph, b 19 July 1773 *WdV,* d 15 Mar 1830 æ. 57 *WdT2;* Capt.; m (1) May 1795 *WdV,* 25 May *WdC*—Elizabeth da. Jonathan Rogers, who d 22 Mar 1807 æ. 33 *WdT2;* m (2) 30 Oct 1808 *OC*—Rhoda da. Daniel & Lucena (Sperry) Russell, b c. 1783, d 2 Jan 1863 æ. 80 *WdT2,* æ. 81 (at O) *WdD;* she m (2) Isaac Bronson. FAM. 3.

vii Camp, b 7 Sep 1776 *WdV,* d 3 Apr 1847 æ. 72 *WdT1;* m Oct 1798 *WdC*—Elizabeth da. Samuel Fiske & Elizabeth (Platt) Peck, b 5 Aug 1774 *F,* d 28 July 1858 æ. 84 *WdD.* Children: (1) Amadeus, b [Sep 1799], d 9 Feb 1885 æ. 85-5 *WdD;* m Abigail da. John & Sarah (Gilbert) Thomas, b c. 1803, d 22 May 1877 æ. 74 *WdD;* (2) Mary, b 27 Dec 1811 *WdT,* d 26 June 1844 *WdT;* m John Miles Merwin; others.

viii Deborah, b 18 Dec 1778 *WdV,* d 10 Oct 1807 æ. 29 *PptC;* m 3 Apr 1797 *WdC*—Lyman Sperry.

ix Amadeus, b 29 Sep 1781 *WdV,* d 20 Nov 1799 *WdV,* æ. 19 *WdT1.*

2 Enoch, b c. 1740, bp 18 Apr 1742 *MC1,* d 5 Mar 1817 æ. 77 *WdT1;* Capt.; m (1) 7 Sep 1761 *WdC*—Experience da. Joseph & Elizabeth (Alling) Beecher, b c. 1743, d 8 Dec 1810 æ. 67 *WdT1;* m (2) 10 June 1811 *OC*—Mary, wid. Woodruff.

(By 1): *i* Enoch, b 26 Nov 1761 *WdT1,* d 6 Dec 1772 *WdT1.*

ii Joseph, b 18 Apr 1765 *WdT1,* d 10 Dec 1772 *WdT1.*

iii Roger, b c. 1766, d 16 May 1838 æ. 72 *WdC,* æ. 83 (!) *WdT1;* m (1) 16 Nov 1788 *WdC*—Elizabeth Mary da. Benajah & Sarah (Mansfield) Peck, b c. 1772, d 27 Dec 1819 æ. 47 *WdT1,* æ. 48 *WdC;* m (2) Lucy ——, b c. 1771, d 10 Apr 1860 æ. 89 *WdD.* FAM. 4.

iv Experience, b 17 Dec 1768 *WdT1,* d 14 Dec 1772 *WdT1.*

v Jonah, b 11 Nov 1771 *WdT1,* d 4 Dec 1772 *WdT1.*

vi Enoch, b c. 1772, d 20 Sep 1837 æ. 65 *WdT1;* m (1) 22 May 1791 *WdC*—Anna da. Simeon & Anna (Johnson) Clinton, bp 1 Aug 1775 *BethlehemC,* d 10 June 1834 æ. 63 *WdT1;* m (2) Sally ——. FAM. 5.

vii Experience, b c. 1776, d 16 Aug 1856 æ. 80 *WdD;* m 1 Sep 1796 *WdV*—Robert Clark.

viii Jonah, b c. 1779, d 3 Feb 1820 æ. 41 *WdC;* m 3 Oct 1799 *WdC*—Polly da. Zenas & Hannah (Treat) Peck, b c. 1780, "Wid. Mary" d 9 Feb 1870 æ. 92 *WdV.* FAM 6

ix Child, d 27 Nov 1786 *WdC.*

3 JOSEPH, bp 5 Dec 1742 *WdC,* d young.

4 ISAAC, bp 2 Sep 1744 *WdC,* d 1832 (Goshen); m 10 Jan 1770 *NHC1*—Rebecca Minott. Children, Rebecca & Isaac, bp 1772 *WdC.*

5 EUNICE, bp 18 June 1749 *WdC.*

6 DEBORAH.

FAM. 2. SAMUEL & LUCY (SMITH) NEWTON:

1 SAMUEL, b 1 Jan 1792 *WdV,* bp 17 Nov 1793 *WdC,* d 28 May 1865 (San Antonio, Tex.); Rev.; m (1) 4 Jan 1813 *WdC*—Betsey da. Silas & Mary (Smith) Baldwin, b 18 June 1795 *F,* d 6 May 1821 (Shawneetown, Ill.); m thrice more.

2 POLLY, b 5 Mar 1793 *WdV,* bp 17 Nov 1793 *WdC,* d 8 Jan 1823 æ. 29 *OT3;* m 7 Oct 1818 *WdC*—Jonas F. Merwin.

3 LUCY, b 23 Dec 1794 *WdV,* bp 29 Mar 1795 *WdC,* d 12 Sep 1874 æ. 79 *WdD;* m 4 June 1817 *WdC*—Thomas Darling.

4 HULDAH, b 29 Dec 1798 *WdV,* bp Dec 1798 *WdC,* d 19 Mar 1874 æ. 75-6 *WdD;* m 25 Nov 1818 *WdC*—Elihu Beecher.

5 OLIVIA, b 9 July 1801 *WdV,* bp 18 Oct 1801 *WdC,* d 22 Feb 1883 æ. 81 *NHV;* m Isaac Leavenworth.

6 SON, d 25 Mar 1810 *WdD.*

FAM. 3. JOSEPH & ELIZABETH (ROGERS) NEWTON:

1 JOSEPH ROGERS, b 5 Jan 1797 *WdV*, bp Dec. 1798 *WdC*, d 10 Oct 1813 æ. 17 *WdC*, *WdT2*.

2 LEWIS CAMP, b 6 Feb 1800 *WdV*, bp 1 June 1800 *WdC*, d 6 Feb 1866 æ. 66 *WdT2;* m 4 Oct 1820 *WdC*—Lucinda Higgins, who d 12 Apr 1877 æ. 74 *WdT2*, 22 May *WdV*.

FAM. 3. JOSEPH & RHODA (RUSSELL) NEWTON:

3 SAMUEL WYLLYS, bp 24 Nov 1811 *WdC*, d 25 Sep 1813 æ. 2 *WdC*, *WdT2*.

4 ELIZABETH ROGERS, bp 4 June 1815 *WdC*, d 21 Oct 1815 æ. 1 *WdC*, 22 Oct æ. 0-9 *WdT2*.

5 ELIZABETH ROGERS, bp 1 June 1817 *WdC*.

FAM. 4. ROGER & ELIZABETH MARY (PECK) NEWTON:

1 POLLY, b c. 1790, d 28 Sep 1826 æ. 37 *WdT1;* m 7 May 1806 *WdC*—Tubal Sanford.

2 SALLY, b c. 1793, d 7 May 1813 æ. 20 *WdD;* m David R. Baldwin.

3 LUCRETIA, b c. 1797, d 9 Dec 1819 æ. 22 *WdT1*, æ. 22 or 23 *WdC*.

4 HENRY, b c. 1799, d 3 Nov 1819 æ. 20 *WdT1*, *WdC;* m 2 July 1818 *WdC*—Anna Parmalee da. Truman & Rhoda (Peck) Clinton, b 10 Oct 1799 *LV*, d 27 July 1818 æ. 19 *WdC*.

i Child, d 23 July 1818 æ. 0-0-1 *WdC*.

5 [? BETSEY, b c. 1801, d 21 Oct 1887 æ. 86 *WdD*.]

6 JEREMIAH, b c. 1803, d 17 July 1854 æ. 51 (at NH) *WdD;* m Esther ———, who d 13 Oct 1866 æ. 63-7 (at NH) *WdD*.

7 SOPHIA, b c. 1804, d 23 Feb 1872 æ. 68 *WdD;* m 1815 *WdC*—Lyman Law.

8 ELIZA, b [Feb 1805], d 16 June 1805 æ. 0-4 *WdT1*, "infant" d 15 June *WdC*.

9 NELSON, b c. 1808, d 11 Mar 1871 æ. 63 *WdD;* m Betsey R. ———, wid. John P. Newton.

10 JULIA, b [Sep 1810], d 16 Feb 1815 æ. 4-5 *WdT1*.

FAM. 5. ENOCH & ANNA (CLINTON) NEWTON:

1 MERRIT, bp 1 May 1794 *WdC*, d 13 Dec 1812 æ. 19 *WdT1;* m 23 Apr 1812 *WdC*—Hannah da. Samuel Sperry.

i Julia; m Levi Lines.

2 MARY, bp 3 Nov 1798 *WdC*, d 20 Nov 1798 æ. 4 wks. *WdT1*.

3 ANN MARIA, bp 16 June 1800 *WdC*, d 4 Sep 1824 æ. 24 *WdT1*, *WdC;* m 24 June 1818 *WdC*—Newton Baldwin.

4 SHERMAN CHAUNCEY, bp May 1802 *WdC*, d 22 Nov 1845 æ. 43 *WdT1;* m (1) Lenora Emeline ———, who d 17 Apr 1832 æ. 29 *WdT1;* m (2) Hannah da. Truman & Rhoda (Peck) Clinton, who d 10 Oct 1886 æ. 76 *WdD.*

5 JULIA A., b c. 1805, d 29 Jan 1809 æ. 4 *WdT1.*

6 SON, d 16 July 1811 (infant) *WdT1.*

FAM. 6. JONAH & POLLY (PECK) NEWTON (family incomplete?):

1 PENE, b 9 July 1800 *WdT1*, d 26 Apr 1877 *WdT1;* m 20 May 1822 *WdC*—Abiel Fairchild.

2 HENRIETTA, b c. 1802, d 20 Jan 1852 æ. 49 *WdD;* m Joseph W. Davis.

3 ELIZA ANN, b c. 1805, d June 1882 æ. 77 (at NH) *WdD;* m Silas Irvin Baldwin.

4. JONAH SIDNEY, b c. 1810, d 25 Mar 1862 æ. 52 *WdD.*

5 JOHN P., b c. 1816, d 10 Sep 1850 æ. 34 *WdD;* m Betsey R. ———, who m (2) Nelson Newton.

NEWTON. FAM. 7. THOMAS, s. of Thomas & Mary (Baldwin), b 8 Feb 1706/7 *MV*, d 28 Apr 1783 *CT1, CC;* Cpl.; m 13 Jan 1729/30 *MV*—Sarah Leete, who d 14 Sep 1782 *CT1, CC.*

1 JOSEPH, b 14 Sep 1730 *MV*, d 28 Aug 1797 *CC;* Census (C) 1-0-3; m (1) 22 Aug 1755 *WV*—Sarah da. Samuel & Sarah (Hall) Hull, b 22 Aug 1738 *WV*, d 17 Nov 1769 *WV*, 18 Nov *CC;* m (2) 13 June 1770 *CC, WV*—Esther da. Daniel & Abigail (Ives) Sperry, b 8 Feb 1734/5 *NHV*, d 8 Apr 1797 *CC.*

(By 1): *i* Joel, b 3 Nov 1755 *WV*, "child" d 13 Apr 1771 *CC.*

ii Sarah, b 4 May 1758 *WV*, d 23 Aug 1816 æ. 59 *WT1;* m 11 Feb 1783 *WV*—Joel Hull.

iii Sybil, b 8 Feb 1760 *WV*, d 29 Sep 1801 *CC.*

iv Aaron, b 22 Feb 1762 *WV.*

v Abner, b 28 May 1764 *WV;* Census (C) 1-0-1; m 24 Jan 1788 *CV*—Asenath Moss.

vi Miriam, b 17 Apr 1769 *WV*, bp 18 June 1769 *CC;* she had a nat. child by John Johnson: John [Newton], b c. 1798.

(By 2): *vii* Esther, b 18 Apr 1773 *WV*, bp 6 June 1773 *CC.*

2 [? EUNICE, d 7 Mar 1801 *CC;* m 18 Dec 1754 *WV*—Moses Atwater.]

3 THOMAS, b 18 Nov 1734 *WV*, bp 1 Dec 1734 *CC*, d 20 Mar. 1779 æ. 45 *CT1* (incorrect), 14 Mar 1788 *CC* (correct); m 24 Mar 1763 *WV*—Chloe da. Abraham & Mary (Ball) Atwater, b 27 Oct 1742 *WV*, d 17 Mar 1823 æ. 77 *CT1;* Census, Chloe (C) 1-2-3.

i Thomas, b 2 May 1764 *WV.*

ii Simeon, b 29 Oct 1765 *WV*, d 22 Nov 1765 *WV.*

iii Eunice, b 22 Oct 1766 *WV.*

iv Silas, b 21 Sep 1768 *WV,* d 23 Sep 1828 æ. 58 *CT1;* m (1) 24 Dec 1795 *CV*—Lucinda da. Daniel & Miriam (Curtis) Parker, b 24 July 1771 *WV,* d 3 Apr 1808 æ. 36 *CT1;* m (2) 16 Dec 1819 *CV*—Isabella da. James & Mary (Smith) Pardee, b 17 July 1785 *NoHV,* d [c. 1861] æ. 76 *CT1.*

v Simeon, b 3 Jan 1770 *WV,* bp 25 Feb 1770 *CC,* d 30 Sep 1818 æ. 49 *NHT1;* m Anna da. Peter & Chloe (Tuttle) Johnson, b 22 Sep 1770 *NHV,* d 7 Jan 1823 æ. 52 *NHT1.* They had: Julia Ann, bp 3 Sep 1797 *NHC1,* d 5 Oct 1823 æ. 25 (in Ga.) *NHT1;* m Dr. Lewis French; & Sidney Johnson, bp 25 Jan 1804 *NHC1,* d 15 Feb 1824 æ. 20 (drowned at Wilmington Bar) *NHT1.*

vi Billious Ball, b 2 Feb 1771 *WV,* bp 12 Apr 1772 *CC;* m Olive da. Nicholas & Dinah (Howd) Peck, b 9 Aug 1773 *WV,* d 19 Oct 1854 (Pittsburgh, Pa.).

vii Abraham, b 9 Jan 1774 *WV,* bp 16 Jan 1774 *CC,* d 2 Jan 1775 *WV.*

viii John, b 3 Feb 1776 *WV,* bp 11 Feb 1776 *CC.*

ix Chloe, b 10 Jan 1778 *WV,* bp 8 Mar 1778 *CC,* d 10 Oct 1854 æ. 77 *NHT1;* m 17 Nov 1800 *CC*—Nehemiah Bradley.

x Amos, b 14 Mar 1780 *CV.*

xi Sarah, b 14 Feb 1782 *CV.*

xii Lemuel, b 29 Nov 1783 *CV;* m 8 Nov 1807 *CC*—Eunice Linsley.

4 JARED, b 4 Jan 1738 *WV,* bp 29 Jan 1737/8 *CC,* d 15 Nov 1811 *CC;* Census (C) 2-2-2; m (1) 16 Jan 1765 *WV*—Anna da. Samuel & Sarah (Hall) Hull, b 19 June 1740 *WV,* d 17 June 1776 *WV;* m (2) 15 Jan 1778 *CC*—Mary da. Parmineas & Rachel (Curtis) Bunnell, b 6 Jan 1744/5 *WV.*

(By 1): *i* Mary, b 9 Sep 1766 *WV;* m Thelus Hull.

ii Jared, b 26 May 1768 *WV;* m 22 Dec 1791 *CC*—Esther Parsons.

iii Anna, bp 6 Oct 1771 *CC;* m 27 Jan 1794 *CC*—William Clark.

NEWTON. MISCELLANEOUS. SARAH m 4 July 1683 *NHV*—John Wilson.......SUSANNA of M m 13 Mar 1728/9 *NHV*—Daniel Smith.......ANN of M m 27 July 1737 *NHV*—Daniel Smith.......MARY of M m 14 May 1747 *NHV*—Josiah Platt. ......MOSES & Eunice had Lyman, b 8 Apr 1759 *WV.*

NICHOLS. MISCELLANEOUS. ADAM m Ann da. Francis & Ann (Goode) Wakeman, bp 3 July 1614 (Bewdley, co. Worcester, Eng.). Children: 1 John, bp 11 Aug 1645 *NHC1*. 2 Barakiah, bp 14 Feb 1646 *NHC1* [1646/7]. 3 Chloe, b 8 Mar 1649 *NHV* [1649/50], "Hester" bp 10 Mar 1650 *NHC1*. 4 Lydia, b 28 Feb 1651 *NHV* [1651/2].......SARAH of St m 13 Nov 1751 *NHV*—Ebenezer Beecher.......RUTH of St m 19 Oct 1752 *NHV*—John Hatch.......NOAH d 23 Aug 1799 æ. 27 *NHT1*.

NICOLL. JOHN, b c. 1756, d 8 Oct 1831 æ. 75 *(NHx)NHV;* Census (NH)2-1-4; m Jane da. Samuel Deal, b c. 1759, d 25 Oct 1829 æ. 70 *(NHx)NHV*.

1 EDWARD, b c. 1779, d 18 Sep 1780 æ. 1 *NHT1*.

2 ELIZABETH DEAL, b c. 1781 (N. Y. City), d 10 Oct 1863 æ. 82 *NHV;* m (1) ——— Lynde; m (2) Jan 1819 *ColR*—Abraham Bishop.

3 JANE, b c. 1782, d 1 July 1783 æ. 1 *NHT1*.

4 AUGUSTUS, b c. 1784, d 24 Mar 1789 æ. 5 *NHT1*.

5 CHARLOTTE, bp 18 Oct 1788 (sponsor, Eunice Todd) *NHx,* d 30 May 1798 æ. 12 *NHT1*.

6 JANE DEAL, bp 18 Oct 1788 *NHx;* "Jennet" m Dec 1806 *NHx*—John Shepherd.

7 EDWARD, bp 12 June 1791 *NHx,* d [20 Apr 1831 æ. 26 (?) *(NHx) NHV*.]

8 AUGUSTA MARIA, bp 27 Oct 1793 (sponsors, Frances Bolling & Lydia Miller) *NHx;* m 3 Jan 1810 *NHx*—Watson Effingham Lawrence.

9 JOHN, b c. 1795, d 20 Nov 1797 æ. 3 *NHx*.

10 CHARLES; m 6 Apr 1828 *NHV*—Caroline Bishop.

NILES. JOHN m 14 Oct 1777 *NHx*—Susanna da. John & Desire (Humiston) Joslin, b 19 Aug 1754 *NHV*. [Possibly surname should be Jiles.]

1 JOHN; bp 1 Nov 1778 (sponsors, Moses & Abigail Joslin) *NHx*.

NOBLES. MARK had children:

1 CHILD, d 1767-1769 (unbaptized) *NHx*.

2 JOHN, bp 9 Apr 1775 *NHx*.

3 DAUGHTER, bp 9 Apr 1775 *NHx*.

NORTH. THOMAS m Mary da. Walter Price, wid. Philip Petersfield of Holborn, Eng.; she m (3) Thomas Dunk of Saybrook.

1 THOMAS, b 30 June 1650 *NHV*.

2 JOHN, b 13 Mar 1651/2 *NHV*.

3 BATHSHUA, b 25 Dec 1654 *NHV*. PAGE 2048

NORTHROP. JOEL, s. of Amos & Ann (Baldwin), b 27 July 1753 *NMV;* Dr.; Census (NH) 1-5-3; m 17 May 1777 *NHC2*—Mabel Sarah da. Samuel & Sarah (Prout) Bird, b c. 1757.

1 JOHN PROUT, b c. 1778, bp 15 Aug 1794 (æ. 16) *NHx*.

2 Mary, b c. 1780, bp 15 Aug 1794 (æ. 15) *NHx*, d bef. 1804; m 16 Mar 1802 *Conn Journal*—Elihu Ives.
3 William Bird, b c. 1782, bp 15 Aug 1794 (æ. 13) *NHx*.
4 Amos, b c. 1784, bp 15 Aug 1794 (æ. 10) *NHx*.
5 Samuel Bird, b c. 1786, bp 15 Aug 1794 (æ. 8) *NHx*.
6 Joel, b c. 1788, bp 15 Aug 1794 (æ. 6) *NHx*.

NORTON. Abraham, Census (Bd) 1-1-2; had da. Chloe bp 11 July 1773 *NHC1*.

NOTT. Epaphras m Isabel ———.
1 Polly, b 28 Apr 17[—] *WV*.
2 Lovisa, b 28 Oct 17[—] *WV*.
3 Hannah, b 22 Oct 17[—] *WV*.
4 Abraham, b 29 Aug 1765 *WV*.
5 Lucy, b 29 June 1767 *WV*.
6 Samuel, b 27 May 1769 *WV*.

NOTT. John, b c. 1750, d 12 Feb 1816 æ. 66 *NHT1*; m 16 Apr 1788 *NHC2*—Esther da. Isaac & Dorothy (Mix) Atwater, b 16 July 1759 *F*, d 16 Aug 1836 æ. 77 *NHT1*.
1 Isaac, b c. 1789, d 12 Dec 1846 æ. 57 *NHT1*.
2 Riley, b 15 Jan 1792 *NHT1*, d 16 Dec 1847 *NHT1*; m 13 Mar 1823 *EHV*—Almira da. Stephen & Elizabeth (Morris) Woodward, bp 4 Feb 1799 *EHC*, d 21 Sep 1835 æ. 37 *NHT1*.

NOYES. fam. 1. Joseph, s. of James & Dorothy (Stanton), b 16 Oct 1688 (Stonington), d 14 June 1761 *NHV*, æ. 73 *NHT1*, *NHC1*; Rev.; m 6 Nov 1716 *NHV*—Abigail da. James & Sarah (Haynes) Pierpont, b 19 Sep 1696 *NHV*, d 10 Oct 1768 *NHV*, æ. 73 *NHT1*.
1 Joseph Haynes, b 6 Aug 1718 *NHV*, bp 10 Aug 1718 *NHC1*, d 6 Oct 1718 *NHV*, *NHT1*.
2 Sarah, b 19 Mar 1721/2 *NHV*, bp Mar 1722 *NHC1*, d 25 Jan 1797 æ. 75 *WethersfieldT*; m 19 Nov 1747 John Chester.
3 Abigail, b 20 Mar 1722/3 *NHV* [1723/4], bp 22 Mar 1723/4 *NHC1*, d 19 July 1797 æ. 74 *NHC1*; m 23 July 1745 *NHV*—Thomas Darling.
4 Joseph, b 25 Sep 1726 *NHV*, bp 25 Sep 1726 *NHC1*, d 29 Jan 1726/7 *NHV*.
5 Joseph, b 29 Feb 1727/8 *NHV*, bp 3 Mar 1727/8 *NHC1*, d 23 Apr 1728 æ. 8 wks. *NHT1*.
6 Dorothy, b 3 Jan 1729/30 *NHV*, bp 4 Jan 1729/30 *NHC1*, d 14 Mar 1734/5 *NHV*, 14 Mar 1736 æ. 5-1-2 *NHT1*.
7 Ann, b 14 Nov 1731 *NHV*, bp 14 Nov 1731 *NHC1*, d 22 Sep 1739 æ. 8 *NHT1*.
8 James, b 13 Dec 1733 *NHV*, bp 15 Dec 1733 *NHC1*, d 23 Sep 1739 æ. 6 *NHT1*.

9 JOHN, b 15 Dec 1735 *NHV,* bp 20 Dec 1735 *NHC1,* d 5 Nov 1767 æ. 32 *NHC1, NHT1;* m 16 Nov 1758 *NHV*—Mary da. Joseph & Rebecca (Peabody) Fish, b c. 1736 (Stonington), d 2 July 1818 æ. 82 *WT1;* she m (2) 21 May 1775 Gold Selleck Silliman of F, & (3) 1804 John Dickinson of Mid.

i Rebecca, b 22 Nov 1759 *NHV,* "Elizabeth" bp Nov 1759 *NHC1,* d May 1760 *NHC1,* 14 May *NHV.*

ii Joseph, b 14 Feb 1761 *NHV,* bp 15 Feb 1761 *NHC1,* d 1817; m (1) 1783 Amelia Burr; m (2) 1804 Lucy Morton.

iii John, b 27 Aug 1762 *NHV,* bp 29 Aug 1762 *NHC1,* d 1846; m (1) 1786 Eunice Sherwood; m (2) 1827 Fanny Swan.

iv James, b 4 Aug 1764 *NHV,* d 18 Feb 1844 æ. 80 *WT1;* Rev.; m Anna da. John & Esther (Nichols) Holbrook, b 22 Jan 1769 *DV,* d 1 Jan 1838 æ. 69 *WT1.*

v Mary, b 21 June 1766 *NHV,* bp 22 June 1766 *NHC1,* d 11 Aug 1770 æ. 4 *NHT1.*

NOYES. FAM. 2. PAUL, Census (NH) 1-1-3; m 11 July 1771 *NHC1*—Rebecca da. Stephen & Susanna (Cooper) Howell, b 27 Mar 1746 *NHV,* d 17 Dec 1786 æ. 41 *NHC1.*

1 SAMUEL, b 6 Oct 1772 *NHV,* bp 11 Oct 1772 *NHC1,* d soon.

2 REBECCA, b 17 Oct 1773 *NHV,* bp 24 Oct 1773 *NHC1.*

3 DESIRE, b. 23 Sep 1775 *NHV,* bp 24 Sep 1775 *NHC1,* d 1 Aug 1776 æ. 0-10 *NHC1.*

4 DESIRE HOWELL, bp 15 Dec 1776 *NHC1.*

5 SAMUEL, bp 9 Aug 1778 *NHC1,* d soon.

6 SUSANNA, bp 27 May 1781 *NHC1,* d 7 Sep 1834 æ. 53 *NHT1;* m Samuel Barnett.

7 NATHANIEL, bp 15 Oct 1785 *NHC1.*

8 HANNAH, bp 15 July 1786 *NHC1,* d 5 Sep 1786 æ. 7 wks. *NHC1.*

9 SAMUEL, bp 10 Sep 1786 *NHC1.*

NOYES. FAM. 3. WILLIAM, b c. 1746, d 1812; Census (NH) 2-2-2; m (1) 23 June 1778 *NHC2*—Rebecca da. Silas & Dorcas (Baldwin) Alling, b c. 1760, d 29 Mar 1780 æ. 21 *DV;* m (2) Mary da. Jabez & Jemima (Brown) Mix, b 17 June 1760 *NHV,* d 23 Nov 1825 æ. 69 *(NHC2) NHV.*

(By1) :1 WILLIAM, bp 16 July 1780 *NHC2,* d 23 Oct 1823 æ. 43 *(NHC2) NHV;* m 25 June 1796 *NHC1*—Temperance [da. Hezekiah & Elizabeth (Cook)] Parmelee, b 8 Dec 1778, d 8 Dec 1857.

OAKES. NATHAN, b c. 1747, d 10 Jan 1796 æ. 49 (at St. Johns, Nova Scotia) *NHT1*; Census (NH) 6-1-7; m 15 May 1776 *NHC1*—Esther da. Stephen & Esther (Munson) Peck, b 1 July 1753 *NHV*, d 9 Apr 1850 æ. 97 *NHT1*. Family incomplete.

1 ESTHER, bp 9 Feb 1777 *NHC2*, d 25 Dec 1824 æ. 49 *NHT1;* m 5 Apr 1796 *NHC1*—Samuel Burroughs.

2 NATHAN, bp 21 Mar 1779 *NHC2*, d 13 Jan 1830 æ. 51 *NHT1;* m Julia Ann da. Wm. Bowditch of Shelter Island, who d 27 May 1812 æ. 23 *NHT1*.

3 SALLY, bp 10 June 1781 *NHC2*, d 14 June 1840 æ. 52 (?) *NHV;* m 25 Feb 1799 *NHC1*—William Mansfield.

4 LAVINIA, bp 9 Nov 1783 *NHC2*, d Sep 1816; m Samuel Langdon.

5 POLLY, b Feb 1786, bp 14 May 1786 *NHC2*, d 22 Mar 1834 æ. 48 *NHV;* m Russell Hotchkiss.

6 HENRY, b c. 1792, d 8 Apr 1841 æ. 49 (at sea) *NHT1;* m (1) Polly da. Joseph & Temperance (Andrews) Hotchkiss, b 15 May 1793 *EHR*, d 9 Nov 1826 æ. 33 *NHT1;* m (2) Minerva Atwood of Bethlehem.

O'HARA. TIMOTHY m 26 Feb 1775 *NHC2*—Eleanor Pattlebie(?).

1 ELEANOR, bp 3 Oct 1776 *NHx*.

OLDS. DAVID, d bef. 1764; m Hannah ———. Child: David. Perhaps another child was TAMAR, who had a nat. child, Silas Marsh, b c. 1763, living 1778, & a nat. da. b c. 1768, d 5 Jan 1773 æ. 4 *NHC1*......MARGARET m 6 Dec 1705 *NHV*—Samuel Jacobs.

ORSHALL. JOHN, d 1793; Census (NH) 1-1-4; m 20 Oct 1785 *NHC1*—Sarah da. George & Rachel (Bradley) Peckham, b c. 1767, "Mrs. Elizabeth" d 27 Nov 1820 æ. 54 *(NHx) NHV*.

1 WILLIAM, bp 27 May 1787 *NHx*, d 28 Jan 1827 æ. 40 *(Bapt) NHV*. His only heir was his sister.

2 ELIZABETH, bp 15 Mar 1789 *NHx;* m 19 Apr 1807 (at house of her uncle Geo. Peckham) *NHx*—Elijah Tripp of P.

OSBILL. JOHN, d 1690 *NHV*.

OSBORN. Variant, OSBORNE. RICHARD of NH, rem. to F & Westchester, N. Y.......WILLIAM, d 30 Sep 1661 *NHV;* m Fridswide ———, who as "Mrs." Osborn m (2) May 1663 *NHV*—John Mulford of Easthampton, L. I. Children: 1 Recompence, b 26 May [1644] *Dorchester, Mass., V;* B.A. (Harvard, 1661). 2 Joseph, b 6 Apr 1652 *BostonV*. 3 Jonathan, b 16 Nov 1656 *BostonV*.......The following children bp *NHC1*, usually attributed to Jeremiah (FAM. 1), but paternity uncertain: Rebecca, 23 Oct 1642; Increase, 5 Feb 1642 [1642/3]; Benjamin, 3 Jan 1646.......THOMAS of NH, rem. to Easthampton, L. I., was father of Jeremiah (FAM. 1).

FAM. 1. JEREMIAH, d 26 Apr 1676 *NHV;* m Mary ———, who d 1695.

1 JEREMIAH, b 3 May 1652 *NHV,* d 16 May 1652 *NHV.*

2 (probably) MARY, b 29 Mar 1653 *NHC1,* bp 21 Oct 1655 *NHC1,* d 28 Nov 1726 in 73 yr. *StratfieldT;* m (1) 9 June 1675 *NHV*—Ephraim Booth; m (2) James Bennett.

3 ELIZABETH, b 7 Jan 1654 *NHV,* 5 Jan *NHC1* [1654/5], bp 21 Oct 1655 *NHC1,* d soon.

4 JEREMIAH, b 28 Nov 1656 *NHV,* bp 30 Nov 1656 *NHC1,* d 4 Jan 1712 *NHV* [1712/3]; m Sarah da. Robert & Hannah (Mitchell) Coe, wid. Timothy Gibbard, b 1656.

i Sarah, b 19 May 1689 *NHV,* bp May 1689 *NHC1,* d [1750].

ii Jonathan, b 29 Mar 1692 *NHV,* bp 22 Mar 1692 *NHC1,* d 1750; m (1) 9 Sep 1723 *NHV*—Ann da. Andrew & Sarah (Gibbard) Sanford, b 1691 , d 27 July 1734 *NHV;* m (2) 28 July 1748 *WdC*—Beulah, wid. Ezekiel Wilmot; she m (3) ——— Collier & (4) Daniel McNamara. FAM. 2.

5 JOANNA, b 8 Dec 1658 *NHV,* bp 30 Jan 1658 *NHC1* [1658/9], d 1 Mar 1668/9 *NHV.*

6 THOMAS, b 6 Oct 1660 *NHV.*

7 ANNA, b 6 Apr 1663 *NHV,* d 10 Dec 1726 *NHV;* m Eleazer Morris.

8 ELIZABETH, b 9 Dec 1665 *NHV,* bp 14 Jan 1665 *NHC1* [1665/6]; m Samuel Thomas.

9 JOSEPH, b 15 Dec 1667 *NHV,* d 19 Nov 1735 æ. 68 *NHT1;* m Mary da. James & Mary (Joy) Bennett, who d 1737.

i Thomas, b 23 July 1692 *NHV,* bp 18 Feb 1693/4 *NHC1,* d soon.

ii Joseph, bp 18 Feb 1693/4 *NHC1,* d Dec 1724 æ. 32 *NHT1;* m Experience da. Henry & Dorothy (Thomas) Tolles; she m (2) 1731 Nathaniel Beecher. FAM. 3.

iii Mary, b 18 June 1696 *NHV,* bp June 1696 *NHC1;* m Oct 1711 *NHV* Ephraim Osborn.

iv Jeremiah, b 8 Apr 1699 *NHV,* bp 9 Apr 1699 *NHC1,* d 18 Jan 1789 æ. 91 *NHC1;* Ens.; m (1) Elizabeth ———, b c. 1701, d 22 Sep 1744 æ. 43 *NHT1;* m (2) 18 Apr 1745 *NHV*—Elizabeth da. Richard & Elizabeth (Wilmot) Sperry, b 11 Nov 1716 *NHV,* d 18 Dec 1799 æ. 84 *NHC1.* FAM. 4.

PAGE 1789

v Sarah, b May 1702 *NHV,* d 16 Nov 1766 æ. [—] *WT1;* m 27 Nov 1723 *NHV,* 24 Nov *WV* —Isaac Johnson.
vi Thomas, b 27 Aug 1706 *NHV,* d s. p.
vii Anna, b 6 Jan 1708/9 *NHV;* m 10 Feb 1731/2 *NHV*—Nathaniel Bradley.
10 REBECCA, b 11 July 1673 *NHV.*

FAM. 2. JONATHAN & ANN (SANFORD) OSBORN:

1 SARAH, b 4 Oct 1724 *NHV;* m 12 Nov 1770 *WdC*—Jonathan Griswold.
2 JEREMIAH, b 23 Sep 1726 *NHV,* d s. p. 1748.
3 JONATHAN, b 20 July 1729 *NHV,* d 22 May 1777 æ. 48 *NHT1;* m 30 Jan 1755 *NHV*—Mehitabel da. William Maltby, b c. 1734, d 31 Jan 1821 æ. 87 *NHT1,* 4 Feb æ. 88 *(NHC2) NHV;* Census, Mehitabel (NH) 1-0-2.
i Lois, b 19 Jan 1757 *NHV,* bp 13 Dec 1767 *NHC2,* d 15 Mar 1845 æ. 88 *NHV;* m 12 Mar 1780 *NHC2*—John Peck.
ii Abigail, b 28 Sep 1758 *NHV,* bp 13 Dec 1767 *NHC2,* d [c. 1787] æ. 29 *NHT1;* m Titus Atwater.
iii Mehitabel, b 1 Oct 1760 *NHV,* bp 13 Dec 1767 *NHC2,* d 4 Dec 1794 æ. 32 *NHT1.*
iv Anna, b 4 Sep 1762 *NHV,* bp 13 Dec 1767 *NHC2,* d 8 Mar 1851 æ. 87 *NHT1.*
v Mary, bp 13 Dec 1767 *NHC2.*
vi Elizabeth, bp 28 Jan 1769 *NHC2.*
vii Jonathan, b c. 1771, d 4 Nov 1796 æ. 26 *NHT1;* B.A. (Yale, 1789).
viii Elizabeth, bp 13 June 1773 *NHC2.*
4 EZEKIEL, b 18 Oct 1733 *NHV;* rem. to Stamford.
5 OBEDIENCE, b 18 Oct 1733 *NHV,* d 30 Apr 1734 *NHV.*

FAM. 3. JOSEPH & EXPERIENCE (TOLLES) OSBORN:

1 DANIEL, b 18 Oct 1715 *NHV;* m (1) 12 Jan 1736/7 *NHV*—Obedience da. Ebenezer & Hannah (Smith) Smith, b 1 Nov 1719 *NHV,* d 18 Apr 1760 *WatV;* m (2) 18 Feb 1762 *WatV*—Sarah, wid. Smith of Lyme, b c. 1725, d 17 Dec 1812 æ. 87 *Salem x.*
(By 1): *i* Abraham, b 5 Sep 1737 *NHV,* d 13 Oct 1813 æ. 76 *Salem x;* m 21 Oct 1762 *WatV*—Eunice da. Peter & Mary (Baldwin) Johnson, b c. 1740, d 18 Jan 1825 æ. 85 *Salem x.*
ii Daniel, b 13 May 1739 *NHV;* m 5 Sep 1764 *WatV, OxfC*—Mary Pickett.
iii Obedience, b 1 Nov 1740 *NHV,* d 25 Feb 1813 æ. 72 *WatT3.*

iv Mary, b 26 Sep 1742 *NHV;* m 4 Apr 1764 *WatV*—Elijah Wooster.
v Ebenezer, b 26 Sep 1742 *NHV;* m 12 Apr 1769 *OxfC*—Mamre Ward.
vi Abigail, b 26 Oct 1744 *NHV,* d 13 Sep 1751 æ. 7 *WHT1.*
vii Rachel, b 6 Oct 1746 *NHV;* m 8 Sep 1768 *WatV, OxfC*—Samuel Fenn.
viii David, b 18 Sep 1748 *NHV;* res. Granby 1793; m 26 May 1774 *WatV*—Barsheba da. Matthew Griffin.
ix Martha, b 13 Sep 1750 *NHV;* m Jonah Loomis.
x Abigail, b 26 Aug 1752 *NHV,* d 5 June 1768 æ. 16 *OxfC.*
xi Sarah, b 22 Oct 1754 *WatV,* bp 8 Dec 1754 *OxfC;* m 2 Dec 1784 *WatV*—Richard Pitts. She had a nat. child: Lemuel Osborn Smith, b 26 Jan 1779 *WatV,* d 22 July 1852 æ. 73 (Naugatuck).
xii Lydia, b 27 Feb 1757 *WatV,* d 22 July 1841 æ. 85 *LT;* m 9 Jan 1783 *OxfC*—George Clark.
xiii Eli, b 1 May 1759 *WatV,* bp 3 May 1759 *OxfC.*
xiv Ruth, b 1 May 1759 *WatV,* bp 3 May 1759 *OxfC,* d 19 May 1759 *WatV.*
xv Lois, b 1 May 1759 *WatV,* bp 3 May 1759 *OxfC,* d 5 May 1759 *WatV.*
(By 2): *xvi* Ashbel, b 3 Nov 1762 *WatV;* m 9 June 1785 *WatV*—Ruth da. Nathaniel & Phebe (Bronson) Richardson, b 15 Dec 1761 *WatV.*
xvii Ruth, b 16 Apr 1764 *WatV;* m Jacob Talmadge.
xviii Philo Thompson, b 4 May 1766 *WatV,* d 27 Mar 1838 æ. 72 *SalemC.*

2 THOMAS, b 1 June 1717 *NHV,* d 1 Aug 1807 æ. 91-1-20 *Salem x;* Dea.; Census (D) 1-0-1; m (1) 12 June 1735 *NHV*—Elizabeth da. John & Mehitabel (Talmadge) Smith, b 21 July 1716 *NHV;* m (2) 20 Feb 1778 *NHx*—Comfort da. Nathan & Elizabeth (Rogers) Baldwin, wid. Elijah Alling, b 26 Dec 1729 *MV,* d 1 July 1798 æ. 68 *SalemT.*

(By 1): *i* Experience, b 15 Oct 1737 *NHV,* d 10 Aug 1783 *DT2;* m John Washburn.
ii Lois, b 23 Feb 1744 *DV,* d 16 Apr 1782 *OxfC;* m 17 May 1759 *DV*—Edward Riggs.
iii Elizabeth, b 18 Dec 1748 *DV,* bp 12 Mar 1749 *Dx.*
iv Child, d s. p.
v Thomas, b 1 Aug 1757 *WatV,* d 22 Apr 1813 æ.

56 *Salem x;* m 7 May 1777 *WatV*—Hannah da. Israel & Elizabeth (Wakelee) Johnson, b 26 Oct 1750 *DV,* d 30 Nov 1814 æ. 64 *Salem x.*

3 JOSEPH, b 7 Dec 1718 *NHV,* d 21 Mar 1797 *OxfC,* æ. 79 *OxfV;* Capt.; Census (D) 3-1-2; m (1) 11 Nov 1742 *WatV*—Esther da. Daniel & Abigail (Trowbridge) Mallory, b 18 June 1718 *NHV,* d 21 Mar 1769 æ. 51 *OxfC;* m (2) 26 Oct 1769 *OxfC*—Abigail da. Timothy & Mary (Hull) Russell, wid. Jonathan Lyman, b 29 Sep 1722 *DV,* d 28 May 1791 *OxfC;* m (3) 13 Feb 1793 *OxfC*—Elizabeth da. William & Hannah (Peck) Clark, wid. Joseph Hull & Joseph Tomlinson, b 24 Sep 1732 *LymeV,* d 11 Feb 1826; she m (4) James Masters.

(By 1): *i* Esther, b 10 Dec 1743 *WatV,* d Dec 1813 æ. 70 *OxfC,* 22 Dec *Jack's HillT;* m 6 Mar 1760 *OxfC*—Nathan Buckingham.

ii Jared, b 24 Sep 1745 *WatV,* bp Nov 1745 *OxfC,* d 24 Nov 1832 æ. 87 *Jack's HillT;* Census (D) 1-3-3; m (1) 30 June 1777 *OxfC*—Freelove Amy da. Daniel & Mary (Painter) Mallory, b 21 Apr 1752 *WyV,* d 27 Oct 1794 *OxfC,* æ. 40 *Jack's HillT;* m (2) Margaret da. Joseph & Elizabeth (Durand) Johnson, wid. David Twitchell, b 16 June 1756 *DV,* d 1811 æ. 55 *OxfV.* Children (incomplete): Laura, b c. 1790, d 14 Oct 1817 æ. 27 *Jack's HillT;* Electa, b [Apr 1793], d 5 Oct 1794 æ. 0-17 *Jack's HillT;* & perhaps Gilbert, b [8 May 1782], d 23 July 1825 æ. 43-2-15 *Jack's HillT.*

iii Joseph, b 7 Dec 1747 *WatV,* bp 20 Mar 1748 *OxfC,* d 16 Sep 1794 *OxfC,* æ. 46 *Jack's HillT;* Census (D) 1-5-1; m 10 Mar 1783 *OxfC*—Sarah da. John & Abigail (Gunn) Smith, b 29 Jan 1762 *DV,* d 26 Feb 1837 æ. 75 *Jack's HillT.* FAM. 5.

iv Samuel, bp 27 May 1750 *OxfC,* d soon.

v Samuel, bp 3 Dec 1752 *OxfC;* [m 20 Apr 1786 *WdC*—Lucy da. Oliver & Hannah (Peat) Pierson, bp 21 Aug 1768 *DC*].

vi Naboth, bp 27 July 1755 *OxfC;* Lt.; Census (D) 1-0-0; m Susanna ———. FAM. 6.

vii Edward, d 5 Mar 1792 *OxfC.*

4 AMOS, b 6 June 1722 *NHV,* d 1 Nov 1790 æ. 69 *WatT3;* Lt.; m (1) 15 Nov 1743 *NHV*—Joanna da. John & Mary (Beamon) Weed, b 22 Apr 1724 *DV;* m (2) 25 Mar 1758 *WatV*—Elizabeth da. Joshua & Mary

(Hotchkiss) Hotchkiss, wid. Ebenezer Benham, b 30 Mar 1735 *WV*.

(By 1): *i* Sarah, b 6 Dec 1744 *NHV;* m 11 Sep 1769 *OxfC*—Jabez Riggs.

ii Lucy, b 6 July 1746 *WatV*.

iii [Amos, d soon.]

iv Amos, b 13 Sep 1750 *WatV;* m 14 May 1776 *WatV*—Lorana da. Isaac & Anna (Terrill) Hotchkiss, bp 30 Aug 1752 *WdC*. Children rec. *WatV:* Phebe, b 14 Apr 1777; Isaac, b 12 Jan 1781.

v Elijah, b 15 Sep 1752 *WatV;* Census (Wat) 1-3-3; m 2 Feb 1773 *NHV*—Phebe da. Enos & Deborah (Payne) Tuttle, b 22 Nov 1747 *NHV,* d 2 Oct 1803 æ. 56 *SalemC*. FAM. 7.

vi Reuben, b 8 Apr 1755 *WatV,* d 23 Feb 1830 æ. 75 *F;* res. Harwinton; m Miriam da. Jonathan & Miriam (Canfield) Atwater, b c. 1755, d 5 Mar 1813 æ. 58 *F*. FAM. 8.

(By 2): *vii* Joshua, b 18 Feb 1759 *WatV,* d 27 Sep 1837 (Southington, O.) *F;* Census (D) 1-3-3; m Diana da. Stephen & Phebe (Baldwin) Warner, b 4 Jan 1764 *WatV,* d 9 Mar 1857 *F*. A son, Leonard, b 21 Feb 1796, d 10 Sep 1862; res. Bloomfield, O.; m 6 Sep 1821 Amanda da. Aaron & Miriam (Howard) Smith, b 20 Nov 1804, d 16 Jan 1888.

viii Thaddeus, b 28 Jan 1761 *WatV*.

ix Asahel, b Apr 1763 *WatV;* m 1 Feb 1787 *WatV*—Molly da. Elemuel & Urana (Mallory) Hoadley, b 1 Nov 1767 *WatV*.

x Amy, b 3 Jan 1765 *WatV;* m Simeon Andrews of D.

xi Samuel, b 4 Feb 1768 *WatV;* m 25 Jan 1797 *WatV*—Sally da. Benjamin & Sarah (Downs) Hotchkiss, b 16 Aug 1778 *NHV,* d Oct 1817 *SalemC*.

FAM. 4. JEREMIAH & ELIZABETH (———) OSBORN:

1 JEHIEL, b c. 1728, bp 23 Nov 1735 *NHC1;* m Rebecca da. Joshua & Amy (Munson) Sperry, b 10 June 1730 *NHV*.

i Amy, b 4 Mar 1750/1 *NHV,* bp Nov 1761 *NHC1*.

ii Medad, b 31 May 1753 *NHV,* bp Nov 1761 *NHC1,* d 24 Sep 1814 æ. 61 *NHT1;* Capt.; Census (NH) 2-2-5; m Rachel da. Joel & Mary (Sherman) Hotchkiss, b 21 Feb 1754 *NHV,* d 19 Nov 1828 æ. 75 *NHT1*. FAM. 9.

iii Rachel, b 14 Oct 1755 *NHV,* bp Nov 1761 *NHC1.* [A Rachel had a nat. child Sally bp 16 July 1786 *NHx;* Rachel m 1 Dec 1789 *NHx* Michael Kenny of Ireland & their s. Daniel was bp same date æ. 0-9.]

iv Lucy, b 4 Mar 1758 *NHV,* bp Nov 1761 *NHC1;* m 27 Apr 1780 *NHC2*—Zophar Atwater.

v Elisha, b 22 June 1761 *NHV,* bp Nov 1761 *NHC1,* d 23 Oct 1808 æ. 48 *WdT3;* m 20 Feb 1782 *WdC*—Elizabeth da. Benjamin & Thankful (Russell) Peck, b 25 Jan 1763 *NHV,* d 1 Sep 1843 æ. 81 *WdT3.* FAM. 10.

vi Rebecca, bp 23 Sep 1764 *NHC1,* d Dec 1842 æ. 79 *NHT2;* m 3 Mar 1782 *NHC2*—Elijah Hotchkiss.

vii Elizabeth, bp 1 Mar 1772 *NHC1;* m 21 Dec 1795 *NHC1*—Herman Payne.

2 REBECCA, b c. 1730, bp 23 Nov 1735 *NHC1,* d 27 Aug 1738 æ. [—] *NHT1.*

3 JOHN, b c. 1732, bp 23 Nov 1735 *NHC1,* d 7 June 1803 æ. 71 *WdD;* Census (*Wd*) 1-0-2; m 14 Feb 1754 *WdC*—Elizabeth da. John & Ann (Hitchcock) Russell, b 9 Feb 1736/7 *NHV,* d 25 Nov 1813 æ. 80 *WdD.* Family incomplete.

i Elijah, [? d Jan 1814 *WHD*]; Census (Wd) 1-1-3; m 20 Feb 1782 *WdC*—Abiah [da. Abraham & Elizabeth (Holbrook)] Downs, b [22 Nov 1761 *DV*], d 20 Mar 1794 *WdD.* Children (incomplete): (1) Betsey, bp 24 May 1789 *WdC.* (2) Irena, bp 24 May 1789 *WdC;* m Dec 1805 (at NH) *NHJournal*—Isaac Sisson. (3) Lyman, bp 7 Oct 1792 *WdC.*

ii Russell; m 18 Sep 1796 *NHC1*—Polly Ball.

4 SAMUEL, b c. 1734, bp 23 Nov 1735 *NHC1,* d 28 June 1813 æ. 80 *WdT1;* m Rhoda ———, b c. 1734, d 17 July 1814 æ. 80 *WdT1.*

5 JOSEPH, bp 30 May 1736 *NHC1,* d young.

6 JEREMIAH, bp 21 May 1738 *NHC1,* d Mar 1813 æ. 73 (at NH) *ColR;* Census (NH) 1-0-1; m 24 Oct 1765 *NHC2*—Ann da. Theophilus & Abigail (Talmadge) Munson, b 14 July 1740 *NHV.*

7 ELIZABETH, bp 1 June 1740 *NHC1,* d young.

8 DAVID, bp 20 June 1741 *NHC1,* d young.

9 REBECCA, bp 14 Aug 1743 *NHC1,* d 3 Dec 1781 æ. 38 *NHC1;* m 25 Jan 1768 *NHC1*—Nehemiah Hotchkiss.

FAM 4. JEREMIAH & ELIZABETH (SPERRY) OSBORN:

10 DAVID, b 26 Apr 1746 *NHV,* d 26 May 1786 æ. 40

NHC1; m 14 Oct 1769 *NHV,* 12 Oct *NHC1*—Mary [da. Timothy & Martha] Talmadge, b 25 Jan 1753 ***F,*** d 6 Mar 1814 æ. 61 *NHT1;* Census, Mary (NH) 0-0-3; she m (2) John Miles.

i Nehemiah, b 25 Aug 1770 *NHV;* rem. to Albany, N. Y.; m & had Eli, Nehemiah & others.

ii Polly, b 18 Dec 1772 *NHV, NHT1,* d 10 Aug 1849 *NHT1.*

iii David, b 6 Apr 1775 *NHV,* d 18 July 1807 æ. 33 *NHT1;* m [Mary Thompson]; had David, Eli, Nehemiah, Mary & Sarah.

iv Eli, b 4 Nov 1777 *NHV, NHT1,* d 9 Sep 1844 æ. 67 *NHT1;* m (1) 18 Mar 1805 *NHV*—Elizabeth da. Hezekiah & Lydia (Atwater) Augur, b 4 Oct 1779 *NHV,* d 18 Jan 1817 æ. 37-3 *NHT1;* m (2) Dec 1818 *ColR*—Anna da. Isaac & Elizabeth (Thompson) Thompson, wid. Kierstead Mansfield, bp 17 Jan 1779 *NHC2,* d 6 Oct 1849 æ. 70-9 *NHT1.* Children by 1st w.: (1) Walter, b 21 Dec 1805 *NHV.* (2) Elizabeth Susan, b 8 Jan 1809 *NHV.* (3) Minot Augur, b 28 Apr 1811 *NHV,* d 22 Oct 1877; m (1) 4 Nov 1834 Caroline da. Wm. & Nancy (Prindle) McNeil, who d 1 Feb 1839; m (2) 31 May 1841 Catherine da. Ezekiel & Sarah (Hurd) Gilbert, b 19 Nov 1821, d 24 Dec 1899.

v Leverett, b 4 Feb 1780 *NHV,* d 30 June 1780 æ. 0-5 *NHC1.*

vi Walter, b [June 1781], d 9 May 1782 æ. 0-11 *NHC1.*

vii Sarah, b 27 July 1783 *NHV;* m (1) 1 Jan 1809 Minott Augur; m (2) 21 Mar 1813 John W. Kelsh.

viii Fanny; m 4 Feb 1805 *ConnH*—Augustus Stevens.

11 Benjamin, b 9 Apr 1747 *NHV;* Census (NH) 1-1-3; m (1) 28 Apr 1771 *NHC1*—Chloe Wheaton, b c. 1750, d 30 Oct 1772 æ. 22 *NHC1;* m (2) 21 Dec 1774 *NHC1*—Elizabeth Hurd, wid. Jonathan Bradley, b c. 1747, d 3 Apr 1804 æ. 57 (at NH) *ConnH.*

(By 2): *i* Jonathan, bp 4 Feb 1776 *NHC1.*

ii Esther, bp 25 Oct 1778 *NHC1.*

iii Rebecca, bp 31 Mar 1782 *NHC1.*

iv Amos, b 28 July 1787 *NHV.*

12 Thomas, b 14 May 1748 *NHV.*

13 Elizabeth, b 29 Apr 1750 *NHV,* d 14 Feb 1820 ;

m (1) 19 Jan 1768 *NHC1*—James Miles; m (2) 15 Nov 1789 *NHC1*—Stephen Hotchkiss; m (3) Thomas Rogers.

14 MARY, b 24 Jan 1752 *NHV*, d 6 Apr 1807 æ. 55 *NHC1;* m 16 Nov 1773 *NHC1*—John Scott.

15 NEHEMIAH, b 5 Mar 1754 *NHV*, bp 19 May 1754 *NHC1*, d 2 Aug 1765 æ. 12 *NHC1*.

16 JABESH, b 23 June 1757 *NHV*, bp 31 July 1757 *NHC1*.

17 JOSEPH, bp 6 Apr 1760 *NHC1*.

18 RHODA, bp 21 June 1761 *NHC1*, d bef. 1792; m 16 Jan 1781 *NHC1*—Eli Forbes.

FAM. 5. JOSEPH & SARAH (SMITH) OSBORN:

1 AMBROSE; m Rebecca da. William & Rebecca Wooding.

2 JOSEPH, bp 8 Apr 1787 *OxfC*.

3 LEVERETT, bp 17 Nov 1788 *OxfC*.

4 RANSOM, b 5 Apr 1790 *OxfC;* m Sarah da. Ebenezer & Hannah (Miles) Hurd.

FAM. 6. NABOTH & SUSANNA (———) OSBORN:

1 LOVICE, bp 22 Apr 1787 *OxfC*, d 16 Nov 1863 æ. 77 *New Preston T;* m Joseph Blake.

2 LORINDA, bp 26 Oct 1788 *OxfC*.

3 LEWIS, b 2 Jan 1791 *OxfV*, bp 16 Jan 1791 *OxfC*.

4 LEMAN STONE, b 4 June 1793 *OxfV*, bp 14 July 1793 *OxfC*.

5 LUTHENA, b Nov 1795 *OxfV*, bp 14 Feb 1796 *OxfC*.

6 SALLY, b Apr 1798 *OxfV*, bp 3 June 1798 *OxfC*.

7 DANIEL, b Oct 1801 *OxfV*.

8 ELETAS, b Dec 1813 (?) *OxfV*.

FAM. 7. ELIJAH & PHEBE (TUTTLE) OSBORN:

1 ELI, b 24 Nov 1773 *NHV*, bp 22 Jan 1775 *NHC2;* m 10 June 1793 *WatV*—Lydia da. Eleazer Finch.

2 JOANNA, bp 17 Feb 1777 *NHC2*.

3 ENOS, b 12 July 1779 *NHV*, bp 5 Sep 1779 *NHC2*.

4. ELIPHALET, b 17 Dec 1782 *WatV*.

FAM. 8. REUBEN & MIRIAM (ATWATER) OSBORN:

1 THOMAS CANFIELD, b 12 Sep 1776 *F*, d 21 Apr 1854 æ. 77; res. Harwinton; m Susannah Hotchkiss of C.

i Sheldon; res. Harwinton; m Julia Bartholomew; had: (1) David S. of New Britain; m Catharine Hopkins. (2) Henry C. (3) Julia. (4) Maria; m Almon N. Wood. (5) Adaline C., d æ. 20.

ii Cynthia; m Lewis Smith of Harwinton.

iii Susan; m Sherman Osborn of Camden, N. Y.

iv Emily; m Orson Barber of Harwinton.

v Sarah, unm.

vi Reuben Canfield; res. Newington; m Olive Barber.

2 Reuben, b 4 Nov 1778 (in Wd) *F*, d 24 Mar 1860 æ. 81; rem. to Camden, N. Y., 1803, & to Cleveland, O., 1811; m 9 Dec 1802 (at Bristol) *F*—Sally da. Eliphalet & Mary Johnson, b 8 Aug 1779 (in Wd) *F*, d 6 Sep 1856.

i Polly, b 27 Feb 1804 (Camden).

ii Selden, b 9 June 1809 (Camden), d 23 Sep 1867 (Dover, O.); m.

iii Julia, b 3 Apr 1813 (Dover, O.), d 18 Apr 1833 æ. 20-0-15.

3 Polly, b 11 Aug 1780 *F*, d 25 Mar 1781 æ. 0-7-14 *F*.

4 David, b 13 Jan 1782 *F*, d 25 Mar 1859 æ. 77; Dea.; res. Camden, N. Y.; m Esther da. Eliakim Potter of P, who d 9 Mar 18[—] æ. 84 (Camden).

i Sherman; m Susan Osborn.

ii David.

iii Elam Potter, d 22 Aug 18[—] at New Britain.

iv Esther; m Isaiah Barber Loomis.

5 Miles, b 17 Apr 1785 *F*, d 23 Aug 1788 æ. 3-4-6.

6 Clarissa, b 3 Dec 1789 *F*, d 4 Nov 1831; m Chauncey Potter.

7 Amos, b 20 Mar 1792 *F*, d 25 Apr 1859; m Laura Marsh.

i Sidney.

ii Ursula; m ——— Burnell.

iii Mary A.

iv Laura; m ——— Fenn.

8 Miriam, b 31 Mar 1796 *F*, d 9 June 1859; m Isaiah Barber Loomis.

FAM. 9. Medad & Rachel (Hotchkiss) Osborn:

1 Joel, bp 18 June 1780 *NHC2*, d 14 Aug 1824 æ. 45 *NHT1*, 16 Aug æ. 44 *(NHC2) NHV;* m Nancy da. William & Phebe (Hotchkiss) Hitchcock, b 4 May 1788 *F*, d 27 Dec 1863 æ. 76 *NHT1*.

i Curtis Edwin, b [Jan 1809], bp 29 May 1810 *NHx*, d 17 Aug 1833 æ. 24 (at Tampico, Mex.) *NHT1*.

ii Robert Hitchcock, b 20 Dec 1810 *NHT1*, bp 5 July 1811 (æ. 0-6) *NHx*, d 11 Feb 1882 *NHT1*, 13 Feb æ. 71-2 *NHV*.

iii Charles H., b c. 1812, d 3 June 1867 æ. 55 *NHT1;* m Eliza J. Stock, who d 25 Jan 1889 æ. 66 *NHT1*.

iv Lewis M., b [Jan 1814], d 30 July 1820 æ. 6-6 *NHT1*.

v Catherine M., b [Jan 1816], d 2 May 1898 æ. 82-4 *NHT1;* m Charles Ives.

vi John Joel, b 18 Dec 1817 *NHT1,* d 25 June 1887 *NHT1;* m Charlotte A. Gilbert, b 29 Jan 1827, d 21 Dec 1914 *NHT1.*

2 Mary, bp 6 Oct 1782 *NHC2;* m Jared Leavenworth.

3 Rebecca, b c. 1785, d 30 June 1862 æ. 77 *NHT1;* m Clement s. of Reuben & Abigail Goodell, who d 2 Mar 1843 æ. 64 *NHT1.*

PAGE 1528 4 Emma Maria, bp 29 May 1810 *NHx;* m David Forest Smith.

5 Julia Ann, b c. 1791, bp 29 May 1810 *NHx,* d 7 Apr 1844 æ. 53 ; m Stephen Dickerman.

6 Frances Louisa, b 20 Aug 1796 *NHT1,* bp 29 May 1810 *NHx,* d 20 Oct 1882 *NHT1,* æ. 86-2 *NHV;* m (1) Eleazer Hotchkiss; m (2) ——— Crandall.

fam. 10. Elisha & Elizabeth (Peck) Osborn:

1 Clarissa, b c. 1782, d 20 June 1857 æ. 75 *WdT2;* m 1809 Benajah Beach.

2 Alanson; res. DeWitt, N. Y.

3 Amelia, b [13 Mar 1787], d 29 Nov 1885 æ. 98-8-16 *NHV;* m Jonathan Clark.

4 William Merrit, b c. 1789, d 1 Oct 1852 æ. 63 (at NH) *WdD;* m Amanda da. Jedediah Northrup, who d 23 June 1869 æ. 70 *WdD.*

5 Lucinda.

6 Maria.

7 Elihu, b c. 1797, d 23 Oct 1859 æ. 62 *NHV, NHT1;* m Esther Strong, who d 15 Mar 1889 æ. 86 *NHT1.*

8 Elizur, d young.

PAGE 1789 OSBORN. fam. 11. Ephraim, res. NH, Newtown, C & Sy; m Oct 1711 *NHV*—Mary da. Joseph & Mary (Bennett) Osborn, b 18 June 1696 *NHV.*

1 Stephen, b 23 July 1713 (at NH) *NewtownV.*

2 Mary, b 14 Dec 1715 (at Newtown) *NewtownV;* m 10 July 1740 *WatV*—James Bellamy.

PAGE 1789 3 John, b last Aug 1718 (at NH) *NewtownV,* bp 31 Aug 1718 *NHC1.*

4 Timothy, b 28 Aug 1720 *NewtownV,* d 3 Feb 1807 æ. 87 *SyT;* m 19 July 1744 *Sy*—Rachel Judd. Their s. Shadrach m 16 Oct 1783 *NHx*—Aletta Blagge.

PAGE 1789 5 Nathan, b 14 May 1723 *NewtownV.*

6 [Benjamin, bp 20 June 1725 *NHC1.*]

7 [Eunice, bp 8 Dec 1728 *NHC1.*]

8 Ephraim, bp 11 July 1731 *CC.*

9 Daniel, bp July 1733 *CC.*

10 Phineas, bp Sep 1735 *CC.*

11 Joseph, bp 11 Sep 1737 *WyC;* res. Oxf 1764; rem. to West Britain 1783; Census (Lanesboro', Mass.)

1-4-3; rem. to Batavia, N. Y.; m Rebecca da. John & Sarah (Wildman) Towner, b 8 Jan 1742 *DV*.

i Isaac Wildman, bp 4 Feb 1776 *OxfC*.

ii Sally Towner
iii Loisa
iv Nathan
v Richard
vi Joseph
} bp 3 Nov 1788 (at Lanesboro') *Gt. Barrington x.*

12 Sarah, bp 29 June 1740 *WyC*.

OSBORN. FAM. 12. Stephen m Mary ———, who m (2) 18 Oct 1768 *WV*—Daniel Ives. PAGE 1789

1 Joseph, b 16 June 1742 *WV;* m 24 Nov 1762 *WV*—Dorcas Savage.

2 Samuel, b 15 Feb 1745 *WV;* m (1) 1 Feb 1770 *WV*—Mary Green, who d 1 Oct 1773 *WV;* m (2) 1 Feb 1775 *WV*—Sarah Yale.

3 Stephen, b 26 Sep 1747 *WV,* d 26 Nov 1824 æ. 77 *DT2;* Capt.; Census (NH) 5-5-4; m (1) 12 Feb 1767 *WV*—Desire Shattuck, b c. 1748, d 20 Dec 1806 æ. 58 *NHC1;* m (2) Apame da. George & Sarah (Stevens) Gorham, wid. Abel Thompson, bp 17 July 1768 *Huntington x,* d 1 Oct 1855 æ. 87 *DT2*.

(By 1): *i* Asenath, b 1 Feb 1768 *WV,* d 13 Dec 1823 æ. 55 *Meadville, Pa.,T;* m 6 Feb 1787 *NHV, NHC1*—Gad Peck.

ii Billious Ward, b 20 Mar 1772 *WV,* d 4 May 1798 æ. 27 *NHT1*.

iii Samuel b 27 Mar 1775 *WV*.

iv Stephen, b 1 Mar 1778 *WV,* d 12 Apr 1797 æ. 19 (at St. Croix) *Conn Journal*.

v Amelia, b 14 Mar 1780 *WV;* m 6 May 1800 *NHC1*—Benjamin Little.

vi Henry, b 7 Mar 1782 *WV;* m 22 May 1804 *NHC1*—Esther Stevens.

vii Hubbard, b 19 July 1785 *NHV,* bp 31 July 1785 *NHC1,* d 3 July 1852 æ. 75 *NHT1,* æ. 76 *NHV;* m 28 Mar 1808 *NHx*—Phebe Edwards, who d 25 Apr 1862 æ. 72 *NHT1,* 26 Apr æ. 72-6 (b at St) *NHV*. Children: Amelia, Charlotte, Shattuck, & Henry, bp 24 Oct 1813 *NHx,* of whom a "da." d 7 Nov 1813 æ. 3 *NHx*.

viii Daniel; d [———] 1806 æ. [—] *NHT1* (stone nearly illegible; should name have been read Samuel?).

(By 2): *ix* Charles Chauncey, bp 17 Apr 1808 *NHx*.

x Harriet Jane, bp 17 Apr 1808 *NHx*.

xi John White, b 26 June 1810 *F,* bp 2 Sep 1810 *NHx,* d 6 Mar 1895 *F;* m (1) Susan Durand; & twice thereafter.

4 Mary, b 21 Mar 1750 *WV,* d 20 May 1832 æ. 83; m 2 May 1768 *WV*—Merriman Cook.

5 John, b 4 Oct 1752 *WV,* d 25 Apr 1833 æ. 81 *PT;* Census (Wtn) 1-0-5; m 21 Jan 1776 *WV*—Rhoda Atkins, who d 7 Apr 1838 æ. 84 *PT.* They had Lucy, b 14 Dec 1776 *WV.*

6 Esther, b 10 Mar 1756 *WV;* m 25 Oct 1775 *WV*—Joseph Bartholomew.

7 White, b 9 June 1759 *WV;* Census (Wtn) 1-1-3.

Henry d 9 May 1717 *WV.*

OSWALD. Eleazer, Col.; his w. Elizabeth d 18 Sep 1797 (Philadelphia). His da. Mary Hillhouse, bp 2 Sep 1774 *NHx,* d 27 Mar 1778 æ. 3-9 *NHT1,* bu. 28 Mar æ. 4 *NHx.*

OTTEE. Variant, Auter. William, Census (NH) 1-0-3; m 9 Dec 1784 *EHC*—Eleanor da. Isaac & Mabel (Moulthrop) Smith, b 29 Nov 1767 *EHV,* d 6 May 1838 æ. 70 *EHC;* she div. him 1800 & m (2) Eli Forbes.

1 Polly, bp 3 Aug 1788 *NHx.*

2 William, bp 3 Aug 1788 *NHx,* bu. 28 Feb 1789 æ. 0-7 or 8 *NHx.*

3 Nancy, bp 1 July 1791 (æ. 1) *NHx.*

4 Daughter, b & d Apr 1792 *NHx.*

PAGE. fam. 1. George, d 1689; res. Bd; m Sarah da. John & Ellen Linsley, who d 1695.

1 John, b 12 Mar 1664 *BdV,* d s.p. before 1695.

2 Sarah, b 18 May 1666 *BdV;* m Francis Tyler.

3 Samuel, b 1 Mar 1670/1 *BdV;* m Mindwell ———. For his s. Timothy, see fam. 2.

4 George, b 2 Feb 1672 *BdV* [1672/3]; m Mary da. John & Mary (Parker) Hall, b 28 June 1675 *WV.* For his s. Moses, see fam. 3.

5 Jonathan, b 15 Sep 1675 *BdV,* d s. p. 8 Feb 1707 *BdV* [1707/8].

6 Hannah, b 17 Dec 1677 *BdV;* m 21 Apr 1703 *BdV*—Ebenezer Frisbie.

7 Nathaniel, b 18 Jan 1679 *BdV,* d 1742; m May 1710 *BdV*—Abigail Wheadon.

8 Daniel, b 2 May 1683 *BdV,* d 7 Apr 1766 æ. 83 *BdV;* Dea.; m 3 Jan 1710 *BdV*—Hannah Johnson.

fam. 2. Timothy Page, b 7 Sep 1700 *BdV,* d 1759; m 27 Nov 1722 *WV*—Thankful da. Theophilus & Thankful (Hall) Doolittle, b 8 May 1700 *WV.*

1 Enos, b 15 Sep 1723 *WV;* m 18 Apr 1750 *WV*—Bethia da. Theophilus & Martha (Doolittle) Fenn, b 18 Feb 1728 *WV.*

i Ann, b 6 May 1751 *WV,* d 22 Dec 1798 æ. 48 *PC;* m Amos Avery.
ii Isaac, b 6 Mar 1753 *WV,* d 10 Nov 1757 *WV.*
iii Enos, b 1 June 1755 *WV.*
iv Sarah, b 12 Feb 1758 *WV.*
v Bethia, b 6 Mar 1760 *WV.*
vi Adah, b 1 June 1763 *WV.*
vii Bethia, b 4 Feb 1766 *WV,* d 26 Dec 1851 æ. 86 *NoHT3;* m 25 Dec 1787 *WV*—Joseph Austin.
viii Isaac, b 31 July 1768 *WV.*
ix Ruth, b 12 Nov 1771 *WV.*

2 Timothy, b 29 June 1728 *WV;* m 9 Jan 1750 *WV*—Joanna da. Daniel & Elizabeth Merwin, b 5 Apr 1732 *WV.*
i Samuel, b 14 July 1753 *WV;* [perhaps m 12 June 1777 *WV*—Elizabeth McKay, wid. Titus Hall].
ii Jared, b 19 Jan 1756 *WV;* Census (C) 2-5-3; m 26 Nov 1778 *WV*—Lydia da. Amos & Joanna (Parker) Bristol, b 15 Sep 1757 *WV.* Children recorded *CV:* Sherman, b 9 May 1779; Betsey, b 14 Dec 1780; Jared, b 29 Oct 1782; Luman, b 4 Sep 1784; Nancy, b 18 Sep 1786; Rufus & Ransom, b 8 Mar 1789; Charlotte, b 9 Mar 1798.
iii Titus, b 4 Apr 1758 *WV.*
iv Lucy, b 10 Sep 1760 *WV.*
v Deborah, b 12 Aug 1763 *WV.*
vi Elizabeth, b 24 June 1766 *WV.*
vii Joanna, b 3 Dec 1767 *WV.*

3 Thankful, b 29 Mar 1730 *WV;* m 10 Dec 1751 *WV*—Asher Thorpe.

4 Sarah, b 6 Mar 1732 *WV,* d 27 Nov 1757 *WatV;* m 24 Aug 1754 *WatV*—John Cole.

5 Susanna, b 4 May 1734 *WV,* d s. p.

6 Asa, b 21 Dec 1735 *WV;* m 7 May 1759 *WV*—Eunice Page of Durham. A child, Asa, b 7 May 1761 *WV.*

7 David, b 11 May 1738 *WV,* d 2 Feb 1820 æ. 84 *LT;* m 31 Oct 1765 *WV*—Ann da. Elisha & Mabel (Foster) Andrews, b 15 Dec 1738 *WV,* d 6 Aug 1813 æ. 74 LT.

8 Theophilus, b 18 Aug 1740 *WV;* m Mehitabel da. Nathaniel & Prudence (Austin) Merriman. They had sons: Joel of W; Phinehas of Hansley, Hampshire Co., Mass.; Levi of Conway, Hampshire Co., Mass.; & Nathaniel of Meriden.

9 Jonathan, b 27 Aug 1742 *WV;* res. L 1786; m 1764

WV—Rachel da. Seth & Hannah (Clark) Plumb, b 19 Aug 1743 *NHV*.

FAM. 3. MOSES PAGE, b 1 Mar 1704/5 *BdV*, d 26 Jan 1788 æ. 84 *EHC;* m (1) 20 Oct 1731 *BdV*—Thankful da. Joseph & Margaret (Wilcoxson) Graves, b 18 Feb 1706 *GV;* m (2) Lydia Fields, wid. John Smith.

(By 1): 1 MOSES, b 1 Sep 1732 *BdV*.

2 AARON, Census (L) 1-1-1, living at L 1802; m 22 May 1758 *EHC*—Desire da. William & Thankful (Alling) Grannis, b c. 1740, d 6 June 1819 æ. 79 *LT*. Family incomplete:

i Josiah, bp 27 Oct 1771 *EHC*.

ii Huldah, bp 27 Oct 1771 *EHC*.

iii Thankful, bp 27 Oct 1771 *EHC*.

iv William, bp 27 Oct 1771 *EHC;* Census (L) 1-0-1.

v Desire, bp 27 Oct 1771 *EHC*.

vi (probably) Mary, b c. 1774, d 15 May 1850 æ. 76 *LT;* m 27 Nov 1793 *LV*—William Moulthrop.

vii Aaron Grannis, bp 21 Jan 1779 *S. Britain C*.

3 SARAH.

(By 2): 4 ICHABOD, Census (NH) 1-1-2; res. Sherburn, N. Y., 1806; m 15 Nov 1763 *NHC2*—Ruth da. Caleb & Ruth (Munson) Hotchkiss, b 3 June 1740 *NHV*, d 1835.

i Pamela, bp 5 Dec 1774 *NHC2;* m 17 Dec 1787 *NHC2*—Eber Sperry.

ii Sena, bp 5 Dec 1774 *NHC2;* m 26 May 1786 *NHC1*—Moses Hawkins Woodward.

iii George, bp 5 Dec 1774 *NHC2;* m (1) Thankful Starr; m (2) ———.

iv Caleb, bp 19 Feb 1775 *NHC2*.

v John Munson, bp 14 June 1778 *NHC2*.

FAM. 4. SAMUEL PAGE, s. of Samuel & Mary (Rose), b 7 July 1740 *BdV;* m 3 Apr 1766 *BdV*—Sarah da. William & Mabel (Chidsey) Woodward.

1 ALICE, b 25 Oct 1766 *EHV*, Oct 1766 (at NH) *BdV*.

2 ANN, b c. 1770, bp 16 Nov 1789 (æ. 19) *NHx*, d 1845; m 12 Oct 1788 *NHx*—John Bromham.

3 BETSEY, b c. 1772, bp 16 Nov 1789 (æ. 17) *NHx*.

4 POLLY, b c. 1780, bp 16 Nov 1789 (æ. 9) *NHx*.

PAINTER. FAM. 1. THOMAS, s. of Shubael & Mercy (Lamberton), b c. 1670, d 1747; m Rebecca da. Zaccheus & Rebecca (Bristol) Candee, b 29 Dec 1671 *NHV*, d 1 June 1739 æ. 56(?) *WHT1*.

1 REBECCA, b 28 June 1695 *NHV*, bp 3 Mar 1694/5

NHC1, d 10 Sep 1740 æ. 46 *WHT1;* m Jonathan Smith.

2 THOMAS, b 31 Aug 1696 *NHV,* d 1760; m (1) Esther da. John & Esther (Morris) Mix; m (2) Desire da. Samuel & Mary (Cooper) Smith, wid. Thomas Stevens, b 30 Sep 1712 *NHV,* d 5 Mar 1799 æ. 86 *WHD;* she m (3) Jahleel Law of C.

i Esther, b 20 May 1738 *NHV;* m John Chandler of Woodstock.

ii Thomas, b 10 Dec 1740 *NHV,* d 18 Feb 1747/8 æ. 8 *WHT1.*

iii Elkanah, b c. 1742, d 14 Feb 1747/8 æ. 5 *WHT1.*

3 SHUBAEL, b 23 Apr 1697 *NHV,* bp Apr or May 1697 *NHC1,* d 9 Oct 1785 æ. 88 *WHD;* m (1) 12 Mar 1730 *NHV*—Elizabeth da. John & Elizabeth (Beecher) Dunbar, b 27 Mar 1701 *NHV,* d before 1758; m (2) Abiah ———, who d 23 Mar 1777 *WHD.*

(By 1): *i* Joseph, b 26 Apr 1731 *NHV,* d 1766 (at sea); Capt.; m 25 Dec 1755 *NHV*—Amy da. Thomas & Desire (Smith) Stevens, b 30 Sep 1737 *NHV,* d 23 Oct 1774 *WHD.* FAM. 2.

ii Rebecca, b 19 May 1734 *NHV,* bp 19 May 1734 *BdC,* d 4 May 1807 *WHD;* m William Trowbridge.

iii Elisha, b 29 July 1736 *NHV,* d s. p. 12 Jan 1781 *WHD;* Maj.; m 7 Mar 1770 *Hartford*—Hannah da. Thomas Seymour.

iv Lydia, b 1 June 1739 *NHV,* d 18 Nov 1814 æ. 76 *WHT1;* m Gamaliel Benham.

v Sarah, b 4 Oct 1742 *NHV,* d 25 Oct 1825 æ. 85 *WHD;* m Jotham Williams.

vi Gamaliel, b 22 May 1743 *NHV,* d 21 May 1819 æ. 76 Salisbury, *Vt.,T;* Judge; res. Salisbury, Ct., & Salisbury, Vt.; m (1) 20 Aug 1767 *SalisburyV*—Abigail Chipman, who d 21 Apr 1790 æ. 40 *Salisbury, Vt.,T;* m (2) Victoria Ball, who d 9 June 1806 æ. 46; m (3) Ursula da. Isaac & Eunice (Gillet) Bull, wid. ——— Philips & William Bull, who d 28 Feb 1824 æ. 77. FAM. 3.

4 MARY, b 1 Nov 1699 *NHV,* bp 10 Dec 1699 *NHC1,* d 20 May 1752 æ. 54 *SheltonT;* m 2 Mar 1724/5 *NHV*—John Stevens.

5 DELIVERANCE, b 31 May 1701 *NHV,* d 3 Aug 1781 (drowned) *WHD;* m 23 June 1725 *NHV*—Mary da. Samuel & Mary (Cooper) Smith, b 7 Mar 1707 *NHV,* d 29 May 1786 *RoxburyC.*

i Samuel, b 7 Mar 1725/6 *NHV,* d Dec 1748 æ. 22 *WHT1.*
ii Mary, b 14 Jan 1727/8 *NHV;* m Daniel Mallory.
iii Amy, b c. 1730, d 2 Sep 1751 æ. 21 *WHT1.*
iv Thomas, b 2 May 1733 *NHV,* d 13 Feb 1755 æ. 22 *WHT1.*
v Abigail, b c. 1738, d 26 Jan 1755 æ. 16 *WHT1.*
vi Lamberton, b c. 1741, d 22 Dec 1795 æ. 55 *WHT1,* 23 Dec æ. 54 (called of Roxbury) *WHD;* Lt.; Census (Wy) 3-1-7; m Mabel da. Andrew & Mercy (Painter) Smith, b c. 1738, d 26 Apr 1808 æ. 70 *RoxburyT.* FAM. 4.
vii Rebecca; m John Sherman.
viii Freelove, b c. 1749, d 26 Aug 1751 æ. 2 *WHT1.*

6 MERCY, b Aug 1703 *NHV,* d 20 May 1785 *WHD;* m Andrew Smith.
7 ELIZABETH, b 23 May 1706 *NHV,* d 17 Feb 1792 æ. 86 *WHD;* she had a nat. child by George Clinton, q. v.
8 RACHEL, b 19 July 1708 *NHV;* m Nathan Smith.
9 MARGARET, b 4 May 1715 *NHV,* d 1 Feb 1802 æ. 87 *WHD;* m 29 Aug 1744 *NHV*—John Catlin.

FAM. 2. JOSEPH & AMY (STEVENS) PAINTER:

1 AMY, b c. 1757, d c.1832; m (1) David Clinton; m (2) Thomas Benham of Amenia, N. Y.
2 THOMAS, b 24 Jan 1760 *F,* d 28 Oct 1847 æ. 88 *WHT1, WHD;* Capt.; Census (NH) 1-1-2; m (1) 1783 *F*—Hannah da. Samuel & Lydia (Sherman) Candee, b c. 1761, d 19 Nov 1830 æ. 69 *WHT1, WHD;* m (2) Dec 1831 Elizabeth W., wid. Buddington, of Hartford, who d 11 July 1849 æ. 76 *WHT1,* 15 July *WHD.*

(By 1): *i* Angelina, b 8 Aug 1784 *F,* d 24 July 1856 æ. 72 (in NH) *F;* m 7 May 1806 *F*—Samuel Rich.
ii Joseph, b 21 Mar 1787 *F,* d 3 Jan 1788 æ. 0-9 *WHT1,* æ. 1 *WHD.*
iii Joseph Alexis, b 16 Apr 1789 *F,* d 12 June 1793 æ. 4 *WHT1, WHD.*
iv Cynthia, b 20 Aug 1791 *F,* d 28 Apr 1880; m 15 May 1815 Simeon Collins of Westfield, Mass.
v Alexis, b 24 Nov 1794 *F,* d 14 Oct 1867; m 23 Apr 1826 Thalia Maria MacMahon.
vi Samuel, b 7 Apr 1797 *F,* d 27 Jan 1845 æ. 47 *WHT1;* m.
vii Sidney, b 3 Oct 1799 *F,* d s. p. 8 June 1873.

viii Amelia, b 26 Feb 1802 *F,* d 14 Jan 1803 æ. 0-10 *WHT1,* "child" d 13 Jan *WHD.*

ix Lucius, b 21 May 1804 *F,* d 18 Sep 1813 æ. 9 *WHT1, WHD.*

3 Elizabeth, d 17 Sep 1774 *WHD.*

4 Child, d infancy *F.*

5 Shubael, d 9 May 1787 (at sea) *WHD.*

fam. 3. Gamaliel & Abigail (Chipman) Painter:

1 Joseph, b 22 Oct 1770 *SalisburyV,* d 10 Oct 1804 æ. 34 *Salisbury, Vt.,T.*

2 Samuel, b 3 Mar 1772 *SalisburyV,* d 28 June 1797 æ. 25 *Salisbury, Vt.,T.*

fam. 3. Gamaliel & Victoria (Ball) Painter:

3 Abby Victoria, b c. 1797, d 9 Dec 1818 æ. 22 *Salisbury, Vt.,T.*

fam. 4. Lamberton & Mabel (Smith) Painter:

1 Abigail; m.

2 Amy, d 17 Oct 1793 *RoxburyC.*

3 Deliverance Lamberton, b c. 1764, d 5 Sep 1841 æ. 77 *RoxburyT;* m 13 Jan 1802 Urania Hine.

4 Thomas; m.

5 Azariah, b 176—; Census (Vergennes, Vt.) 3-0-0; Census 1810 (Vergennes), 1 male 26 to 45, 2 males 16 to 26; 1 female over 45; 4 females 26 to 45; 2 females 10 to 16.

6 Polly, b c. 1770, d 29 Apr 1856 æ. 86 *Sy;* m 21 Feb 1793 Bethuel Treat.

7 Samuel.

8 Zillah; m 27 July 1794 *RoxburyC*—Levi Downs.

9 Lyman, b c. 1774, d 11 Sep 1843 æ. 69 *RoxburyT;* m 9 May 1820 Flora Hurd.

10 Freelove; m 15 Jan 1809 Timothy Castle of Wilmington, Vt.

11 Mabel, b c. 1777, d 7 June 1828 æ. 51 *RoxburyC.*

12. Hannah.

13 Child, d 3 May 1783 *WHD.*

14 Child, d 3 May 1783 *WHD.*

PAINTER. fam. 5. John, b c. 1719, d 27 July 1796 æ. 76 *PT,* æ. 87 (Episcopalian) *PC;* m 27 Mar 1738 *WV*—Deborah da Thomas & Sarah (Abernathy) Wiltshire, b 8 Mar 1718 *WV,* d 26 Mar 1794 æ. 76 *PT.*

1 Johanna, b 31 Jan 1739 *WV,* bp 4 Mar 1738/9 *WC2.*

2 Sarah, b 2 Apr 1741 *WV;* m 8 Apr 1762 *WatV*—Benjamin Williams.

3 John, b 29 May 1743 *WV,* bp 5 June 1743 *WC2,* d 16 Nov 1761 *F&IWRolls,* Nov 1761 (Camp at Crown Point) *WtnD.*

4 Edward, b 5 Oct 1745 *WV*, bp 13 Oct 1745 *WC2*.
5 Susanna, b 12 Aug 1748 *WV*, bp 14 Aug 1748 *WC2*.
6 Eunice, b 16 Mar 1751/2 (at Mid) *WatV;* m Nathan Woodward.
7 Lot, b 9 Feb 1755 *WatV*, d 21 Feb 1757 *WtnD*.
8 Elizabeth, b 7 Sep 1757 *WatV*.
9 Thomas Wiltshire, b 25 Sep 1760 *WatV*, d 27 Mar 1817 æ. 57 *PT;* m 28 Mar 1784 *PV*—Lucina Dunbar, b c. 1769, d 4 July 1854 æ. 85 *PT*.

i Chester, b 19 Nov 1787 *PV*, 19 Nov 1788 *PT*, d 11 Jan 1838 *PT;* m (1) 10 Apr 1816 *PV*—Eunice da. Thomas & Olive (Dunbar) Fancher, b c. 1790, d 19 Dec 1817 æ. 27 *PT;* m (2) 25 Nov 1818 *PV*—Orrel da. Hezekiah & Mabel Bunnell, who d 20 Aug 1819 æ. 32 *PT;* m (3) 27 Jan 1820 *PV*—Laura Maria da. Walter & Hannah (Johnson) Wilmot, who d 16 Mar 1823 æ. 24 *PT;* m (4) 31 Mar 1824 *PV*—Polly Barnes, who d 9 May 1857 æ. 65 *PT*. Child by 2d w.: Orrel, b 16 Aug 1819 *PV*. Child by 3d w.: William Walter, b 15 Feb 1821 *PV*.
ii Sarah, b 22 Oct 1789 *PV;* m Silas Hoadley.
iii Lucina, b 20 Mar 1792 *PV;* m Butler Dunbar.
iv William, b 29 Mar 1794 *PV;* res. Ohio; m Polly Barnes.
v Chloe, b 10 Jan 1796 *PV*, d 27 Dec 1861; m 7 Feb 1822 *PV*—Ephraim Downs.
vi Edward, b 29 July 1798 *PV*, d 22 Feb 1801 *PV*.
vii Laura, b 6 Nov 1801 *PV*, d 1884; m 17 Oct 1827 *PV*—Joseph W. Byington.
viii Edward, b 14 Mar 1803 *PV*, d 13 Apr 1863 æ. 60 *PT;* m 4 Apr 1832 *PV*—Clarinda Palmer of L.

10 John, b 25 Dec 1763 *WatV;* m 13 Aug 1786 *PV*—Sally Watrous.

i Betsey, b 19 July 1787 *PV*.
ii Roxey, b 11 Feb 1789 *PV;* m ——— Barnes.
iii Harry, b 12 Apr 1791 *PV*, d 4 Apr 1846 æ. 55 *PT;* m Sally Nichols, who d 21 Aug 1886 æ. 90 *PT*.
iv Martin, b 3 May 1793 *PV*.

(*Continued on page 1345*)

BOOK REVIEWS

This department of the New Haven Genealogical Magazine offers to compilers and publishers of genealogical books the opportunity to secure fair and honest reviews of their productions. The reviewer will do his utmost to point out the good features of every book which is presented for review, but in fairness to readers will mention striking deficiencies, such as the lack of an index, usually poor arrangement of material, or gross inaccuracies. Those who wish books reviewed should send one copy to the address below.

Donald L. Jacobus, Editor,
554 Central Avenue,
Westville, Conn.

KELSEY A Genealogy of the Descendants of William Kelsey, Volume I. From data collected by many, and concluded by Earl Leland Kelsey. Coat-of-arms in color. 295 p. 8°. Pub. 1928 by a committee of the Kelsey Family. Order from Dwight C. Kelsey, 53 Hillcrest Ave., Hamden, Conn. Price, $5.25, postpaid.

This attractively printed and bound volume from the press of Tuttle, Morehouse and Taylor, New Haven, Conn., presents through the births of the fifth generation the descendants of William Kelsey, who settled at Cambridge in 1632, at Hartford in 1636, and at Killingworth in 1663. Female lines are carried down to a considerable extent, so that this first volume is really a history of a related group of Connecticut families, making it a valuable addition to genealogical libraries both public and private. Among the Killingworth family names to which considerable space is devoted are Chatfield, Hull, Nettleton, Parmelee, Stevens, and Wilcox.

It is apparent that much research has been done; authorities are stated; and a full index is provided. The tone of the book is judicial, and even though the reader may not in every instance accept the suggested solutions of the more difficult problems, these problems are always stated fairly and the editors are not dogmatic in expressing their opinions.

The preface, which is well worth reading, tells what patience and self-sacrificing labor during the course of many years were required to compile this work and prepare it for publication. The demand for this type of book is necessarily limited, and printing costs are high. The backers of such a publication cannot hope to get back a tithe of the money and labor that have gone into it, but they deserve sufficient support from those of the family name and blood to refund at least the printing costs and enable them to proceed with the publication of the data relating to subsequent generations. The very moderate price at which this first volume is offered should make it possible for every Kelsey to purchase a copy,—until the edition is exhausted.

LEWIS Randall Lewis of Hopkinton, Rhode Island and Delaware County, New York and some of his Descendants. By Frank Pardee Lewis and Edward Chester Lewis. Seattle, 1929. 200 p. 12°. Price $5.00; order from Mr. Frank P. Lewis, Seattle, Wash.

This is an intimate, friendly sort of book, with much genealogy, considerable biography, a few pages of verse and other matter of interest to the compilers and their family. The binding is attractive and substantial, a heavy glazed paper is used, suitable for the frequent illustrations, the indexes occupy fourteen pages, and at the end are sixteen ruled blank pages for the use of the owner in writing additions.

Randall Lewis of Hopkinton, R. I., married in 1765, and his birth may be placed hypothetically at about 1740. There are strong genealogical reasons for believing that he was son of Amos Lewis, a great-grandson of the first John Lewis of Westerly, R. I., and the present reviewer is convinced that such was the fact. The compiler conscientiously refrains from making positive statements unless he has valid legal evidence, and therefore, after presenting what is known concerning Randall's probable connection with the earlier generations, begins the genealogy at that point, and traces Randall's descendants.

Genealogical tables are inserted here and there, giving the ancestry of some of the Lewis wives, thus aiding the descendants in tracing their other ancestral lines. The arrangement of material, though easy enough to follow, is more complex than the systems which to-day are more generally employed in genealogies.

The compiler has been engaged on Lewis research for many years, and in 1887 founded the Lewis Letter, a monthly family magazine, which later was published for many years under the name Lewisiana by Mr. Carll A. Lewis now of North Branford, Conn. The present book will be welcomed by all the members of this branch of the Lewis family.

CLARENCE D. SMITH

It is with real grief we announce the death of our friend and printer, Clarence D. Smith, on May 6th, after a brief illness, at his home near Elmer Hill, Lake Delta, a suburb of Rome, N. Y.

Mr. Smith was keenly interested in historical and genealogical subjects, and had correspondents all over the country, many of whom he generously aided in their researches. He visited all the cemeteries of his section, copying stones, and in particular establishing the burial places of the veterans of the Revolutionary War. Many headstones in memory of these have been placed as a result of his untiring efforts.

In 1921 he was appointed official historian for the town of Western, a position for which he was well qualified. He was compiling a record of the descendants of Henry Peck of New Haven, and had collected over 22,000 names. He also compiled the descendants of Lieut. Jonathan Rudd, of Saybrook, and of John Smith (miller), of Providence, R. I. He planned to issue his Peck Genealogy in parts after completing the labor of printing the Families of Ancient New Haven in our magazine. Perhaps in the years to come, he will be longest remembered by genealogical students for his share in the production of the last-named work, five volumes of which he printed, a total of over 1280 pages.

Mr. Smith was an honorary member of Fort Stanwix Camp, No. 58, S. O. V., and a member of the Connecticut Society, S. A. R. In addition to his other interests, he was an enthusiastic collector of postage stamps.

In spite of severe physical handicaps, Mr. Smith was an indefatigable worker. He was a man of cheerful and optimistic temperament, and in the face of misfortunes and discouragements maintained his equanimity and continued to build for the future. Immediately after the first issue of the magazine was published, his house was destroyed by fire, but he loyally insisted on carrying on the printing of the magazine as soon as he could replenish the type and machinery which had been destroyed. His kindness and good nature were manifest to all who had the pleasure of knowing him or dealing with him.

AT YE EDITOR'S DESK

The death of the printer who has "stood by" us in the publication of the first five volumes of the magazine occurred just as we were getting under way on Volume VI, with renewal blanks already issued, and the renewals coming in. The necessity of finding a new printer at once is responsible for the changes which subscribers will observe in the current issue.

We have always known that we could not secure as favorable a rate from a large metropolitan printing house, as Mr. Smith of Rome, N. Y., gave us. There are sound business reasons why that is so, and it does no good to bewail the facts; it is more to the point to face them, and to arrive at the best solution possible. We are bitterly opposed to raising the price of the magazine again, and shall not do so under any circumstances. We are also opposed to reducing the number of pages in each issue. The only other way to bring the cost of producing the magazine within the sum received from annual subscriptions is to employ a larger size of type.

Of course this reduces somewhat the amount of material printed in each issue, but we have adopted this solution as the most practical one. To tell the truth, we have regretted that we did not begin the magazine with the larger type, for proof-reading the smaller type is hard on the editor's eyes, and some typographical errors have escaped notice which should have been caught had larger type been employed. No doubt some of our subscribers will welcome the larger type for the same reason, that it is easier on the eyes of the reader. But welcome or not, the change had to be made, and we have confidence that our subscribers will accept the inevitable in the same spirit in which we have met it.

Four pages will be reserved at the end of each issue for book reviews and necessary announcements. If the financial condition of the magazine permits, we shall print 80 pages instead of 64 in the final issue of each volume.

YE EDITOR.

Families of Ancient New Haven

(*Continued from page 1340*)

PAINTER (concluded).

v Abijah, b 7 June 1795 *PV;* m Polly Reynolds.

vi Allen, b 3 July 1797 *PV,* d 19 Dec 1854 æ. 58 *PT;* m 16 Feb 1824 *PV*—Hannah Hall, who d 20 Dec 1843 *PT.*

vii John, b 4 May 1800 *PV.*

viii Austin, b 14 Sep 1804 *PV.*

*PARDEE. The announcement that this family would be omitted brought so many requests for a reconsideration of this decision, that we are including the local New Haven branches; but refer the reader to The Pardee Genealogy (1927)for omitted branches and much additional history.

FAM. 1. GEORGE, s. of Rev. Anthony & Anstice (Cox), bp 19 Feb 1623/4 (Pitminster, co. Somerset, Eng.), d Apr 1700; m (1) 20 Oct 1650 *NHV*—Martha da. Richard Miles; m (2) 29 Dec 1662 *NHV*—Katherine Lane; m (3) Rebecca ———.

(By 1): 1 JOHN, b 20 Aug 1651 *NHV,* d c. 28 June 1653 *NHV.*

2 JOHN, b 2 Dec 1653 *NHV,* d s. p. 1683.

3 GEORGE, b 15 Jan 1655 *NHV* [1655/6], bp 13 May 1662 *NHC1,* d 22 Nov 1723 æ. 66 *EHT;* m (1) 10 Feb 1675 *NHV*—Mercy da. Alling & Dorothy Ball, b c. 1654, d 13 Aug 1684 *NHV;* m (2) 11 Feb 1685 *NHV*—Mercy da. James & Bethia (Boykin) Denison, b 26 July 1668 *NHV,* d 1757.

(By 1): *i* Mercy, b 16 Jan 1676 *NHV,* bp 8 July 1688 *NHC1.*

ii Eliphalet, b 26 Dec 1678 *NHV,* bp 8 July 1688 *NHC1,* d 3 Sep 1723 æ. 45 *EHT;* m Hannah da. Samuel & Sarah (Boykin) Edwards, who d 1761; she m (2) 5 Jan 1724/5 *NHV*—Peter Woodward. FAM. 2.

iii Martha, b 18 Mar 1680/1 *NHV,* bp 8 July 1688 *NHC1;* m 30 Dec 1702 *BdV*—Edward Frisbie.

iv John, b 4 Nov 1683 *NHV,* bp 8 July 1688 *NHC1,* d 1760; m (1) 9 July 1712 *NHV*—Abigail da. John & Elizabeth (Doolittle) Brockett, b 31 Mar 1683 *NHV,* d 2 Aug 1752 æ. 71 *NoHT2;* m (2) bef. 1756 Mary da. Elijah & Mary (Bushnell) Brainerd, wid. Moses Pond, b 20 June 1700 *HaddamV,* d 21 Nov 1770 *NoBC2.* FAM. 3.

(By 2): *v* James, b c. 1687, d s. p. 1731.
vi George, b [1690] *NHV,* bp 12 Jan 1690 *NHC1,* d c. Oct 1763; m Sarah da. Isaac & Elizabeth Bradley. FAM. 4.
vii Stephen, bp 6 Dec 1692 *NHC1,* d 1736 *EHV;* m Mary da. John & Hannah (Hemingway) How, b 9 Mar 1697/8 *NHV.* FAM. 5.
viii Sarah, bp c. Feb 1695/6 *NHC1,* d 9 Jan 1749 æ. 54 *EHT;* m (1) John Thompson; m (2) Samuel Smith.
ix Ebenezer, bp c. Apr 1699 *NHC1,* d 1756; Dea.; res. New Fairfield; m Martha da. Matthew & Mary (Brockett) Moulthrop, b 18 Feb 1703 *EHV* [1703/4], d Mar or Apr 1785. FAM. 6.
x Elizabeth; m Benjamin Frisbie.
xi Mary, b c. 1712, d 23 Dec 1789 æ. 77 *EHC;* m Isaac Chidsey.

4 MARY, b 18 Apr 1658 *NHV,* bp 13 May 1662 *NHC1,* d c. 1684; m 29 Nov 1677 *NHV*—Joshua Hotchkiss.

5 ELIZABETH, b 10 June 1660 *NHV,* bp 13 May 1662 *NHC1;* m (1) 25 Dec 1679 *NorwalkV*—Thomas Gregory; m (2) John Olmstead.

(By 2): 6 JOSEPH, b 27 Apr 1664 *NHV,* d after 1742; m (1) 30 Jan 1688/9 *NHV*—Elizabeth da. Thomas & Mary (Turner) Yale, b 29 Jan 1667 *NHV,* d 19 Sep 1702 *NHV;* m (2) 23 Dec 1703 *NHV*—Elizabeth da. John & Abigail (Brockett) Payne, b 2 Oct 1677 *NHV,* d after 1750.

(By 1): *i* John, b 20 Oct 1689 *NHV,* d c. 27 Oct 1689 *NHV.*
ii Enos, b c. 1691, bp (adult) 23 Nov 1718 *NHC1,* d 27 Sep 1771 æ. 82 *NoBT1;* m Abigail da. Eleazer & Tabitha (Thomas) Holt, b 17 Nov 1686 *NHV,* d 1760. FAM. 7.
iii Joseph, b 9 Aug 1693 *NHV,* d 1762; m 25 Dec 1723 *StamfordV*—Elizabeth da. Joseph & Mary (Smith) Ferris, b 19 Mar 1699, d 11 Dec 1776 (Salem, Westchester Co., N. Y.); had 9 children.
iv Thomas, b 26 Oct 1695 *NHV,* d soon.
v John, b 6 Feb 1697 *NHV* [1697/8], d 13 July 1766 æ. 69 *SharonT;* m (1) Betsey Horn, b c. 1699, d 8 Jan 1762; m (2) Hopestill da. Ebenezer & Sarah (Lewis) Hamlin, wid. Jonathan Hunter, b 23 July 1702 (Barnstable, Mass.); had 11 children.
vi Mary, b 9 Apr 1700 *NHV,* d 6 Jan 1758; m 4 Dec 1722 *NHV*—Nathaniel Peck of Greenwich.

(By 2) : *vii* Elizabeth, b 16 Sep 1704 *NHV;* m 5 Sep 1727 *NHV*—Benjamin Ruggles.
viii Abigail, b 1 Sep 1705 *NHV.*
ix Daniel, b 28 Nov 1706 *NHV,* d 1764; m 19 Dec 1734 *NHV*—Lydia da. Richard & Mary Porter, b c. 1716, d after 1795. FAM. 8.
x Rebecca, b 26 Mar 1708 *NHV.*
xi Josiah, b 14 Sep 1711 *NHV,* d 1766; m (1) 13 Sep 1737 *NHV*—Abigail da. Eliphalet & Esther (Peck) Bristol, b 11 Aug 1709 *NHV;* m (2) 13 Dec 1758 *NHC2*—Sybil da. Abraham & Sarah (Gilbert) Johnson, wid. Stephen Johnson, b 1 Aug 1727 *NHV,* d 4 Nov 1803 *WHD;* Census, Sybil (NH) 2-0-3. FAM. 9.
xii Ebenezer, b 4 Nov 1714 *NHV,* bp July 1716 *NHC1,* living 1747.
xiii Dorothy, b 14 Oct 1715 *NHV,* bp 8 July 1716 *NHC1,* d 15 Feb 1811 æ. 95 *WHD;* m 7 Apr 1736 *NHV*—John Benham.
xiv Samuel, b 3 Aug 1718 *NHV,* bp 31 Aug 1718 *NHC1,* d 13 Jan 1791 *WdC;* Census (Wd) 1-3-4; m (1) 7 Nov 1745 *NHV*—Rachel da. Caleb & Mehitabel (Cruttenden) Hotchkiss, wid. Ebenezer Wolcott & Thomas Humphreville, b 26 Oct 1709 *NHV,* d 6 May 1774 *MV;* m (2) 21 Aug 1775 *WdC*—Lydia da. Dow & Kezia (Barker) Smith, b 1 Jan 1743 *BdV,* d 4 Nov 1793 *WdC.* FAM. 10.
xv Hannah, b 29 Oct 1719 *NHV,* bp Feb 1719/20 *NHC1.*
xvi Sarah, b 21 Aug 1721 *NHV;* m 6 May 1751 *WiltonC*—John Keeler.

7 REBECCA, b 18 Apr 1666 *NHV,* bp 23 Apr 1666 *NHC1,* d 14 June 1731 æ. 65 *NoHT1;* m 26 July 1699 *NHV* —Samuel Mix.

8 SARAH, b 2 Feb 1667 *NHV* [1667/8], d s. p. 1756; m [Francis] Sayre of Elizabeth, N. J. She had a nat. child by Samuel Bullard of Charleston, b c. 1699.

9 HANNAH, b 7 July 1672 *NHV;* m [Philip] Vicars of Fairfield, N. J.

FAM. 2. ELIPHALET & HANNAH (EDWARDS) PARDEE:

1 SAMUEL, b 7 Jan 1705/6 *NHV,* d s. p.

2 EBENEZER, b 5 Apr 1710 *NHV,* d [1763?]; m 22 Nov 1739 *NHV*—Eunice Smith of Kensington.
i Hannah, b 18 Jan 1741/2 *NHV;* m 7 Jan 1762 *NHC2*—Aaron Hayes of Simsbury.

ii Sarah, b 3 Apr 1744 *WyV;* m 29 Aug 1770 *NHV* —David Beach.
iii Eliphalet, b 6 May 1746 *WyV,* d 15 Aug 1752 *NHV,* æ. 7 *EHT.*
iv Eunice, bp 2 Apr 1748 *WashingtonC;* m 24 July 1777 *WV*—Abel Matthews.
v Ruth, b 14 Feb 1753 *NHV.*

3 ELIPHALET, b 13 Sep 1712 *NHV,* d 4 Dec 1725 *NHV.*

4 BENJAMIN, b 9 Dec 1714 *NHV,* d 4 July 1782 æ. 69 *EHC;* m 17 June 1740 *NHV*—Mary da. Daniel & Mehitabel (Hemingway) Bradley, b 2 Apr 1720 *NHV,* d 11 Nov 1799 æ. 82 *EHC.*

i Levi, b 14 Jan 1741/2 *NHV,* d 21 Nov 1813 æ. 72 *EHT, EHC;* Dea.; Census (EH) 2-1-3; m 3 Jan 1771 *EHC*—Sarah da. Isaac & Sarah (Bradley) Chidsey, b 28 Jan 1753 *EHV,* d 25 Dec 1830 æ. 78 *EHC.* FAM. 11.
ii Moses, b 24 July 1744 *F,* d bef. 1787; m 2 May 1765 *NHC2*—Sarah da. Thomas & Sarah (Mansfield) Wilmot, b 6 Feb 1746/7 *NHV;* Census, Sarah (NH) 1-2-3; she m (2) 18 Jan 1794 *NHC1*—Jeremiah Macomber. FAM. 12.
iii Hannah, b 13 Dec 1746 *F,* d 20 May 1830 æ. 83-5 *EHC.*
iv Jared, b 28 Sep 1748 *F,* d 7 Feb 1825 æ. 76 *EHC;* Census (EH) 1-2-2; m 19 June 1784 *EHV,* 19 July *EHC*—Rebecca da. Stephen & Mabel (Bradley) Brown, b 28 May 1756 *NHV,* d 20 July 1796 æ. 40 *EHC.* FAM. 13.
v Lois, b 18 May 1751 *F,* d 9 Nov 1832 æ. 82 *EHT;* m 12 Feb 1776 *EHC*—Isaac Barnes.
vi Benoni, b 18 Feb 1754 *F,* d 18 Aug 1782 æ. 28 *EHC.*
vii Noah, b 12 Jan 1757 *F,* bp 17 Apr 1757 *EHC,* d 22 Apr 1787 æ. c. 30 *EHC;* m Mary da. Phinehas & Sarah (Dunham) Woodruff, b 31 Mar 1763, d 8 Jan 1826 *SC;* she m (2) 2 Sep 1790 Elkanah Smith of S. FAM. 14.
viii Desire, b 7 July 1759 *F,* bp 30 Sep 1759 *EHC,* d 22 May 1785 æ. c. 23 *EHC.*
ix Mehitabel, b 11 Jan 1763 *F,* bp 24 Apr 1763 *EHC,* d 12 Nov 1774 æ. 11 *EHC.*

5 HANNAH, b 5 Mar 1716/7 *NHV,* d 4 Apr 1720 *NHV.*

6 SARAH, b 5 Nov 1719 *NHV,* d s. p. 17 May 1806 æ. 90 *EHC;* m 20 July 1758 *EHC*—Anthony Thompson.

7 NOAH, b 30 Dec 1721 *NHV,* d 21 May 1754 æ. 33 *EHT.*

FAM. 3. JOHN & ABIGAIL (BROCKETT) PARDEE:

1 JOHN, b 27 June 1713 *NHV,* d 11 Mar 1789 æ. 76

NoHC; m (1) 12 Dec 1744 *NHV*—Sarah da. Ebenezer & Mary (Tuttle) Frost, b 22 Feb 1712 *NHV* [1712/3]; m (2) 18 Feb 1761 *NHV,* 18 Aug *EHC* —Sarah da. John & Sarah (Tuttle) Moulthrop, wid. Timothy Russell, b [Aug 1725], d 26 Feb 1816 æ. 90-6 *NoHC.*

(By 1): *i* James, b 25 Mar 1746 *NHV,* d 7 Dec 1827 æ. 80 *CT1;* Census (NoH) 1-1-4; m 2 Nov 1772 *NoHV, NoHC*—Mary da. James & Lydia (Todd) Smith, b 22 Dec 1747 *NHV,* d 1 Sep 1796 æ. 49 *NoHT1.* FAM. 15.

ii Martha, b 6 July 1747 *NHV,* d 28 Feb 1815 æ. 68 *NoHT1;* m 9 Feb 1769 *NoHC*—John Hull.

iii John, b 10 Dec 1750 *NHV,* d young.

iv Sarah, b 31 July 1753 *NHV;* m 1 Jan 1777 *NoHC*—Joseph Hull.

v Ebenezer, b 27 Jan 1755 *NHV;* Census (Bd) 1-3-2; m 22 Mar 1781 *NoHC,* 23 Mar *NoHV*—Jemima da. Daniel & Sarah (Sackett) Barnes, bp 8 Nov 1761 *NoHC.* FAM. 16.

(By 2): *vi* Susanna, b 13 Oct 1762 *NHV,* bp 19 Dec 1762 *NoHC,* d 22 Sep 1828 æ. 66 *NoHT2;* m 6 Mar 1783 *NoHC*—Justus Barnes.

vii Rosanna, b 13 Oct 1762 *NHV,* bp 19 Dec 1762 *NoHC,* d 21 Dec 1842 æ. 80 *NoHT1;* m 12 Feb 1787 *NoHC*—Isaac Bassett.

viii John, b 24 Oct 1764 *NHV,* bp 14 Apr 1765 *NoHC,* d 20 May 1838 *NoHD;* Census (NoH) 1-1-3; m 8 Oct 1789 *NoHV*—Elizabeth da. John & Thankful (Frost) Brockett, b 13 Oct 1760 *NHV,* d 8 Sep 1837 *NoHD.* FAM. 17.

ix Lydia, b 22 July 1766 *NHV,* bp 31 Aug 1766 *NoHC,* d 30 Mar 1815 æ. 49 *NoHT1;* m 4 Feb 1789 *NoHV*—Asa Thorpe.

2 ABIGAIL, b 15 Apr 1717 *NHV;* m Ebenezer Barnes of Bd.

3 MARTHA, b 30 Nov 1723 *NHV,* d 10 Oct 1796 æ. 73 *NoHT2;* m 15 Jan 1745/6 *NHV*—John Frost.

4 ELIPHALET, b 4 May 1726 *NHV,* d 1804; Census (NoH) 2-1-2; m (1) 8 Apr 1756 *NHV*—Mary da. Isaac & Mary (Frost) Blakeslee, b 13 Oct 1735 *NHV,* d 4 Mar 1780 *NoHC;* m (2) 24 Oct 1782 *EHC*—Abigail da. Joseph & Esther (Russell) Hotchkiss, wid. Benjamin Bishop, b 6 May 1748 *EHV,* d 16 Nov 1816 æ. 69 *WolT.*

(By 1): *i* Jesse, b 3 June 1757 *NHV,* d 25 Jan 1768 æ. 10-7 *NoHC.*

ii David, b 8 Aug 1759 *NHV*, bp 3 Nov 1771 *NoHC*, d 5 Feb 1844 (Wol); m (1) 19 May 1785 *NoHC*—Polly Spencer, who d 15 Apr 1802 æ. 38 *WolT;* m (2) 1805 Philetta, wid. Timothy Neal, who d 20 Aug 1826 æ. 62 *WolT;* had 6 children.

iii Abigail, b c. 1762, bp 3 Nov 1771 *NoHC*, d 30 July 1788 æ. 26 *EHC;* m 22 Dec 1785 *NoHC*—Jacob Moulthrop.

iv Mary, b c. 1766, bp 3 Nov 1771 *NoHC;* m 29 May 1788 *NoHC*—Solomon Barnes.

v Hannah, b 1 Nov 1769 *NoHV*, bp 3 Nov 1771 *NoHC*, d Mar 1843 æ. 74 *NoHT1;* m 14 July 1785 *NoHV, NoHC*—John Cooper.

vi Jesse, b 12 Apr 1771 *NHV*, bp 3 Nov 1771 *NoHC*, d s. p. 8 Dec 1801 æ. 31 *WolT;* m 12 June 1799 *SC*—Clarissa da. Amos & Mary (Dunham) Hart, b 28 Apr 1773, d 28 Aug 1854.

FAM. 4. GEORGE & SARAH (BRADLEY) PARDEE:

1 ISAAC, b 30 Nov 1723 *EHV*, d 27 Jan 1761 æ. 37 *EHR;* m 12 Apr 1750 *BdC*—Mary da. David & Mary Leavit, b 24 Sep 1725 *WV*, d 12 Oct 1783 æ. c. 57 *EHC*.

i Jemima, b c. 1751, d 4 Nov 1784 æ. c. 34 *EHC*.

ii Mary, b c. 1753, d s. p.

iii Isaac, bp 25 Apr 1756 *EHC*, d 5 July 1779 (k. by cannonball) æ. 22 *EHC*.

iv Joseph, bp 25 Apr 1756 *EHC*, d 22 Nov 1836 æ. 80 *EHC;* m 5 Feb 1783 *EHC*—Sarah da. Ezra & Sarah (Chidsey) Fields, b c. 1761, d 18 Oct 1837 æ. 76 *EHC*. FAM. 18.

v Leavit, bp 14 May 1758 *EHC*, d 1831; Census (EH) 1-2-2; rem. 1797 to Harwinton; m (1) 18 Nov 1782 *EHC*—Elizabeth da. Abraham & Mercy (Tuttle) Hemingway, b 1 May 1760 *EHV*, d 18 Aug 1813 *HarwintonC;* m (2) Nancy ———. FAM. 19.

vi Amy, bp 19 Oct 1760 *EHC*.

2 MERCY, b 10 Jan 1724/5 *EHV*, d s. p. 3 May 1790 æ. c. 60 *EHC*.

3 JACOB, b c. 1727, d 10 Aug 1807 æ. 80 *EHR;* Census (EH) 2-1-4; m Mary da. Samuel & Mehitabel (Denison) Hemingway, b 19 Apr 1737 *NHV*, d 19 May 1802 æ. 63 *EHC*.

i Abijah, b [Jan 1753], d 10 Sep 1832 æ. 79-8 *EHC;* Census (EH) 1-2-4; m 9 Dec 1777 *EHC*—Rosanna da. John & Abigail (Holt)

Moulthrop, b c. 1761, d 27 Sep 1844 æ. 83-[—] *EHC.* FAM. 20.

ii Sarah, b c. 1755, d soon.

iii Jacob, bp 17 Apr 1757 *EHC,* d 1779 (prison ship, N. Y.) *EHC;* m 30 Nov 1777 *EHC*—Lydia da. John & Mary (Tuttle) Hemingway, b 22 May 1759 *EHV,* d 2 Sep 1840; she m (2) 16 Feb 1789 *EHC*—Eli Gilbert. Child: 1 Jacob, b c. 1779; m 6 Sep 1810 *HuntingtonC*—Anna Wheeler, b c. 1773, d 10 Dec 1851.

iv Chandler, bp 9 Dec 1759 *EHC,* d 9 Mar 1829 æ. 69 *EHC,* 14 Mar *EHT;* Capt.; Census (EH) 1-1-2; m (1) 4 Feb 1790 *EHC*—Lydia da. Ezra & Sarah (Chidsey) Fields, wid. Isaac Hotchkiss, b c. 1757, d 24 May 1812 æ. 55 *EHC;* m (2) 7 Mar 1813 *EHC*—Mary da. James & Abigail Walker, div. w. Alling Frost, b 29 Jan 1770 *EHV,* d 2 Aug 1842 æ. 72 *EHC.* FAM. 21.

v Sarah, bp 4 Apr 1762 *EHC,* d 2 July 1837 æ. 76 *WT2;* m 5 Sep 1787 *EHC*—Daniel Austin.

vi Mary, bp 26 Apr 1765 *EHC,* d 26 Apr 1814; m (1) 10 Oct 1785 *EHC*—Stephen Foote; m (2) 23 Oct 1800 Timothy Johnson.

vii John, b c. 1768, d s. p. May 1796 æ. 27 (at sea) *EHC;* m 6 Aug 1795 *NHx*—Anna da. Levi & Sarah (Tuttle) Forbes, b 23 Mar 1770 *EHV,* d 31 Aug 1837 æ. 67 *EHT;* she m (2) Truman Colt.

viii Eunecia, b c. 1770, d 15 Aug 1825 æ. 55 *EHC;* m Timothy Thompson.

ix Abraham, b [Jan 1772], bp 1 Mar 1772 *EHC,* "child" d 12 Mar 1773 æ. 0-14 *EHC.*

x Elizabeth, bp 8 May 1774 *EHC,* d 16 Feb 1809 æ. 34 *EHC.*

xi Lovisa, "Vicca" bp July 1776 *EHC,* d 14 Oct 1824 æ. 46 *EHC;* m 13 Apr 1807 Rosewell Augur.

xii Abraham, bp 16 Aug 1778 *EHC,* d 7 Feb 1826 æ. 47 *EHC;* m 4 June 1806 *EHC*—Anna da. Joseph & Temperance (Andrews) Hotchkiss, b 22 Sep 1780 *EHR,* d 4 Dec 1852 æ. 72 *EHT.*

4 LYDIA, b c. 1730, d s. p. 31 Oct 1794 æ. 64 *EHC;* Census (EH) 0-0-1.

FAM. 5. STEPHEN & MARY (HOW) PARDEE:

1 STEPHEN, b 30 Mar 1725 *EHV,* d 30 Mar 1788 æ. 63 *EHT, EHC,* bu. 31 Mar *NHx;* m Mabel da. John & Mary (Forbes) Russell, b 7 May 1729 *EHV,* bp 1 Aug 1779 *NHx,* d 1807; Census, Mabel (EH) 0-0-2; she m (2) Joshua Porter of S.

i Stephen, b c. 1748, bp 11 Aug 1779 *NHx,* d 9 Dec 1816 æ. 69 *PT;* Census (Wtn) 2-1-3; m 1 Dec 1768 *EHC*—Abigail da. Thomas & Eunice (Russell) Smith, b 3 Feb 1747 *EHV,* d 3 Aug 1816 æ. 70 *PT.* FAM. 22.

ii James, b c. 1750, d æ. 7 *EHT.*

iii Samuel, b c. 1752, bp 11 Aug 1779 *NHx,* d 19 Mar 1829 æ. 77 *SC;* Capt.; Census (S) 1-0-4; m (1) 20 Nov 1777 *SC*—Mercy da. Joshua & Mercy Porter, b 6 Mar 1755 , d 28 Dec 1806 *SC;* m (2) Clarina da. Eliakim & Esther (Beach) Hitchcock, wid. Silas Doolittle, b 18 Oct 1767 *WV,* d 24 Dec 1831 æ. 64 *CT1.* No surviving issue.

iv Eli, b 3 Mar 1756 [pension application], bp 11 Aug 1779 *NHx,* d 1835 (Hartland); Census (L) 1-3-2; m (1) 24 Apr 1781 *LV*—Martha da. John Lyman, wid. Isaac Marsh; m (2) 24 Feb 1791 *LV*—Sarah da. John Lyman; had 11 children.

v James, b 2 June 1758 *F,* bp 11 Aug 1779 *NHx,* d 5 Mar 1831 æ. 73 (at Madison) *ColR;* m 10 Aug 1780 *CC*—Sarah Pardee, b 25 Nov 1760 *F,* bp 1 Apr 1781 *NHx,* d 22 Nov 1844 *GV;* had 12 children, of whom Chloe, bp 6 June 1784 *NHx,* & Sally, bp 6 Aug 1786 *NHx.*

vi Amos, d æ. 9 *EHT.*

vii [Asahel, d young *EHR.*]

viii Mercy, bp 11 Aug 1779 *NHx;* m 3 May 1791 *NoHV*—James Frisbie; res. Winchester 1794, Norfolk 1797.

ix Mary; m Moses Thompson.

x Elizabeth, d æ. 4 *EHT.*

xi John, d æ. 2 *EHT.*

xii Amos, b c. 1770, bp 11 Aug 1779 (æ. 9) *NHx,* d 2 Dec 1849 (Caldwell, N. Y.); B.A. (Yale 1793); Rev.; m Eunice ———, b c. 1776, d 14 Apr 1861 (Lanesborough, Mass.); had 3 children.

2 MARY, b c. 1732, d 13 Nov 1821 æ. 90 *EHC;* m Edward Russell.

3 ELIZABETH, b c. 1735, d 2 Apr 1783 æ. 48 *EHT;* m Samuel Shepard.

FAM. 6. EBENEZER & MARTHA (MOULTHROP) PARDEE:

1 HANNAH, b 28 Mar 1728 *EHV;* m Zaccheus Brush of New Fairfield.

2 JAMES, b 27 Dec 1729 *EHV,* d 1805 (New Paltz, N. Y.); m 5 Feb 1756 *New Fairfield C*—Ann da. Samuel & Abigail Wheeler; had 7 children.

3 Ebenezer, b c. 1732, d 1776 (in Rev. War); m Anna da. Jedediah & Amy (Thrall) Richards, b 19 Feb 1740 (Hartford); had issue.

4 Stephen, b c. 1737, d 31 Jan 1795 (New Fairfield); Capt.; Census (N. Fd) 1-2-2; m 10 Mar 1762 *F*—Ellen da. Abel & Ruth (Bronson) Barnum, b c. 1744, d 6 Feb 1805; had 8 children.

5 Mercy; m 28 Mar 1763 *New Fairfield C*—Zadoc Barnum.

6 Dorothy; m Stephen Baker.

7 Mary; m John Baker.

8 Martha, b c. 1744, d 29 Nov 1804; m (1) Charles Knapp; m (2) Zebulon Crane; m (3) Samuel Hendrick.

FAM. 7. Enos & Abigail (Holt) Pardee:

1 Susanna, b 12 Nov 1715 *NHV*, bp 23 Nov 1718 *NHC1*, d 15 Nov 1799 æ. 85 *NoBT1;* m 23 Aug 1748 *BdV*—Joseph Rogers.

2 Benjamin, b 5 Jan 1718/9 *NHV*, bp Mar 1719 *NHC1*, d 29 Aug 1776 æ. 60 *HT1;* m (1) 24 Dec 1747 *NHV*—Hannah da. Samuel & Hannah (Farrington) Beecher, bp 5 Nov 1727 *NHC1*, d 5 July 1767 æ. 40 *HT1;* m (2) Abigail ———, b c. 1730, d 13 Jan 1817 æ. 87 *HT1;* she m (2) 5 Nov 1778 *NoHC*—Stephen Hitchcock.

(By 1): *i* Lowly, b 1 Nov 1748 *NHV*, d 15 Jan 1749/50 *NHV*, 5 July 1749 æ. 2 *HT1*.

ii Lowly, b 30 Aug 1750 , d 5 Oct 1796 æ. 46 *HT3;* m 11 Feb 1773 *NHV*—Samuel Dickerman.

iii Levi, b 25 May 1752 *NHV;* rem. to Claremont, N. H.; m Jerusha da. Asa Jones, b 28 July 1767 (Colchester), d 18 July 1825; had issue.

iv Rebecca, b 2 Mar 1754 *NHV*, d 5 Apr 1839 æ. 85 *ClaremontT;* m Ichabod Hitchcock.

v Hannah, b c. 1756, d 25 July 1828 æ. 72 *ClaremontT;* m Ebenezer Sperry.

vi Mary, b 10 July 1759 *NHV*, bp 7 Oct 1759 *NHC2*, d 17 May 1833 æ. 76 *ClaremontT;* m 20 Jan 1783 *F*—Asa Jones.

vii Abigail, bp 7 June 1761 *NoHC*, d 18 Mar 1814 æ. 53 *ClaremontT;* m 17 May 1781 *F*—Ephraim Tyler.

viii Benjamin, b 23 Mar 1763 *NHV*, bp 3 July 1763 *NoHC*, d 22 May 1764 æ. 2 *HT1*.

ix Amy, b 30 Dec 1765 *NHV*, d 9 Aug 1818 æ. 53 *ClaremontT;* m Josiah Jones.

x Benjamin Holt, b [May 1767], d 28 July 1767 æ. 0-2 *HT1*.

3 ENOS, b 12 Sep 1720 *NHV,* bp Dec 1720 *NHC1,* d before 1792; m 7 May 1752 *NHV*—Hannah da. William & Hannah (Brown) Punchard, wid. Hezekiah Beecher, b 2 Oct 1711 *NHV.*

i Hannah, b 5 June 1753 *NHV;* m 5 June 1774 *F* —Timothy Sperry of Burlington.

4 ELIZABETH, b 14 Aug 1722 *NHV,* bp 14 Oct 1722 *NHC1,* d 20 Apr 1805 æ. 82 *Roxbury;* m 18 Feb 1752 *NoBC2*—Ezekiel Frisbie.

5 THOMAS, b 12 June 1725 *NHV,* bp 1 Aug 1725 *NHC1,* d 29 Jan 1802 æ. 77 *HT1;* Census (H) 1-0-1; m 28 Nov 1754 *NoBC2*—Lois da. Joseph & Miriam (Gilbert) Bradley, b 4 Oct 1732 *NHV,* d 30 Oct 1798 æ. 67 *HT1.*

i Joseph, b 11 July 1755 *NHV,* d 1798; Census (H) 1-0-2; m Elizabeth da. John & Mary (Cooper) Gill, b 23 Apr 1763 *NHV,* d 22 Mar 1855 æ. 93 *HT1.* Children: 1 Esther, b c. 1786, bp 18 May 1800 *HC1,* d 22 May 1856 æ. 69 *HT1;* m Elizur Cadwell. 2 John, b c. 1791, bp 18 May 1800 *HC1,* d 5 Dec 1862 æ. 71 *HT1;* m 3 Jan 1815 *NoHC*—Harriet Todd, b c. 1795, d 13 Mar 1878.

ii Susanna, b 11 Feb 1760 *NHV;* m 29 Apr 1790 *NoHC*—Austin Goodyear.

iii Joel, b 11 Feb 1760 *NHV,* d 19 Apr 1811 *Gilbert list;* m (1) c. 1789 Eunice da. Ebenezer & Susanna (Brockett) Heaton; div.; m (2) Sally da. James & Katharine (Covert) Murray, bp 21 June 1778 *NHC2,* d 19 Jan 1839; she m (2) Eli Goodyear. FAM. 23.

iv Thomas, b c. 1767, d 13 Sep 1775 æ. 8 *HT1.*

6 ABIGAIL, b 28 Aug 1727 *NHV;* m 25 Dec 1753 *WV*—Joseph Thompson.

7 NATHANIEL, b 3 May 1731 *NHV,* d 1760 (in Camp) *SC,* 17 Sep 1760 *F&IWRolls;* m 20 May 1755 *SC*—Rebecca Wheadon; she m (2) Mar 1764 *SC*—Ithiel Dean.

i Jemima, bp 30 May 1756 *SC;* res. Lenox, Mass., 1778.

ii Deborah, b c. 1758; m Apollos Allen of Greenfield, Mass.

FAM. 8. DANIEL & LYDIA (PORTER) PARDEE:

1 LYDIA, b 27 Oct 1736 *NHV;* m (1) 27 Feb 1758 *NHV,* 22 Feb *NHC2*—Joseph Peck; [m (2) 1 Jan 1784 *WatV*—Samuel Chatfield].

2 DANIEL, b 30 Dec 1738 *NHV,* d s. p. bef. 1764.

3 DAVID, b 17 May 1741 *NHV,* d 31 May 1821 æ. 80 *CromwellT;* m 1 Jan 1761 *SC*—Phebe da. Samuel & Esther (Bird) Woodruff, bp 12 July 1741 *SC,* d 30 Nov 1822 æ. 81 *CromwellT;* had issue.

4 JONATHAN, b 8 May 1744 *NHV,* d c. 1789 (Wat); m Tryphena da. Samuel & Mary (Thomas) Beecher, b 5 Feb 1745 *NHV;* had issue.

5 STEPHEN, b 4 July 1747 *NHV,* d Aug 1796 (at sea) *F;* Census (H) 2-2-3; m Lois da. Stephen & Sybil (Johnson) Johnson, b c. 1750, bp 22 Sep 1807 (æ. 58) *NHx,* d Sep 1813 æ. 64 (at NH) *ColR.*

i Ezekiel, b 2 Sep 1770 *NHV.*

ii Jesse, b 1 July 1772 *F,* d Jan 1817 æ. 44 (at sea) *NHT1;* m 17 June 1802 *NHC1*—Abigail da. Stephen & Eunice (Tuttle) Dickerman, b 15 Jan 1776 *F,* d 22 Apr 1859 æ. 83 *NHT1;* had 6 children.

iii Lois, b c. 1777, d 15 Sep 1827 æ. 50 *NHT1;* m 29 Nov 1801 *NHC1*—William Gorham.

iv Philinda, b c. 1779; m 9 Feb 1804 *NHC1*—Parsons Gorham.

v Stephen, b c. 1782.

6 ABIGAIL, b 3 July 1750 *NHV,* d 21 Feb 1839 (West Avon); m 19 Feb 1776 *NHV*—Elisha Alling.

7 ISAAC, b 17 Aug 1755 *NHV,* living 1777.

8 MARY, b 22 Dec 1761 *NHV,* d 11 Mar 1821 (W. Avon).

FAM. 9. JOSIAH & ABIGAIL (BRISTOL) PARDEE:

1 JOSIAH, b 1 July 1738 *NHV,* d 6 Mar 1803 æ. 65 *MT;* Census (M) 1-2-7; m 10 Aug 1763 *NHC2*—Rebecca da. Samuel & Mary (Thomas) Beecher, b 24 Dec 1743 *NHV,* 2 Jan 1746 *OC,* d 6 Aug 1826 æ. 81 *OT.*

i Lucy, b Feb 1764 *F;* m Jere Burwell.

ii Abigail; m 16 Sep 1784 *MC1*—Daniel Burwell.

iii Sarah, b 7 Oct 1766 *MV;* m 15 Jan 1792 *MC1*—Israel Isbel. She had a child by Elijah Bryan, b 1781/2 *NHCCt.*

iv Rebecca, b 9 Apr 1768 *MV,* d 17 Oct 1835 æ. 68 *HT3;* m 26 Apr 1817 *OC*—Jonathan Dickerman.

v Content, b 22 Nov 1769 *MV,* d 2 Aug 1841; m 1 Oct 1815 *OC*—Samuel Bryan Smith.

vi Ann, b 16 Mar 1771 *MV;* m 28 Mar 1801 *OC*—William Smith.

PAGE 2048

vii Mabel, b 18 Jan 1773 *MV;* m 21 Oct 1793 *MC*—John Jones of Sy; rem. to Seatacook, N. Y.

viii Josiah, b 10 Apr 1775 *MV,* d 16 Apr 1822 æ. 45 *OC;* m Comfort da. Zachariah & Mary (Bryan) Marks, b c. 1774, d 28 Jan 1868.

ix Mehitabel, b 1777 *MV,* 24 Nov 1777 *OC,* d 8 Dec 1831 æ. 55 *HT3;* m 1 May 1814 *OC*—Eli Hull.

2 MOSES, b 16 July 1741 *NHV,* d Nov 1790 *WHD;* Census (NH) 2-0-5; m Mary da. Joseph & Hannah (Smith) Thompson.

i Silas, b c. 1766, d Apr 1832 æ. 66 *WHD;* m 18 Nov 1789 *NHC1*—Betsey da. John & Lydia (Hull) Alling, b c. 1771, d 18 Apr 1840 æ. 69 *WHD.* FAM. 24.

ii Lois, b c. 1768, d 20 May 1793 æ. 25 *WHD.*

iii Hannah, b c. 1770; m c. 1790 Nathan Oviatt of M.

iv Huldah; m 10 Sep 1809 *MC1*—Matthew Mallory.

v Sybil, b c. 1777, d 7 Nov 1778 *WHD.*

vi Child, d 7 Nov 1778 *WHD.*

vii Molly, res. M 1790; "Mary" m 22 Dec 1808 Elisha Sanford.

3 ELIPHALET, b 20 July 1744 *NHV,* d 4 May 1830 (Herkimer Co., N. Y.); m Rebecca da. Stephen & Ann (Prichard) Bradley, b 19 Feb 1747/8 *MV,* d 17 June 1829 *F;* had 10 children.

4 JOSEPH, b 2 Jan 1747/8 *NHV,* d 16 Mar 1824 æ. 77 *OC;* Census (M) 1-1-3; m Abigail Bryan, b c. 1742, d 25 Jan 1833 æ. 91 *OC.*

i Abigail, b c. 1775, d 13 Oct 1834 æ. 59 *MT;* m 23 Sep 1799 *MC1*—Isaac Bristol.

ii Sybil; m Fitch Welch.

iii Joseph, b 20 Sep 1780 *F,* d 1 Nov 1863 æ. 83 *OT1,* 2 Nov *OC;* m 1800 Sarah da. John & Comfort (Baldwin) Hine, b 31 Oct 1780 *DV,* d 28 Dec 1865 æ. 85 *OC;* had 6 children.

FAM. 9. JOSIAH & SYBIL (JOHNSON) PARDEE:

5 JOHN, b c. 1760, d s. p. 12 Mar 1822 æ. 62 *OT1;* m 18 Jan 1808 *MC1*—Sarah da. Moses & Elizabeth (Baldwin) Northrop, wid. Jonah Clark, b 30 July 1769, d 27 Dec 1824 æ. 55-4-27 *MT.*

6 SAMUEL, b 26 July 1762 *NHV,* d 20 Nov 1818 æ. 56 *WHD;* Capt.; m Mary da. Obed & Mary (Lines) Johnson, b c. 1767, d 18 Apr 1841 æ. 74.

i Samuel Lewis, b c. 1791, d 5 Dec 1863; m Julia Downs, b c. 1798, d 5 Mar 1850.

ii Jesse Seymour, d Apr 1865; m 2 Nov 1826 Eliza Ann da. John & Betsey (Riggs) Hotchkiss, b c. 1807, d 15 Feb 1844.

7 EUNICE, b c. 1764; [m (1) ——— Smith]; m 15 Mar 1802 *NHC1*—Theophilus Alling.

8 JOEL, b c. 1766, d c. 1811; m Mary ———, b c. 1776, d 26 July 1845 æ. 69 *NHV*, 25 July æ. 70 *NHT1;* had issue.

FAM. 10. SAMUEL & RACHEL (HOTCHKISS) PARDEE:

1 ELIZABETH, b 24 July 1746 *NHV*, bp 25 Aug 1746 *NHC1*, d 6 Aug 1833 æ. 87 *WtnT;* m 27 Oct 1773 *WdC*—Jonas Hungerford.

2 PHILENA, b 6 Jan 1747/8 *NHV*, bp 20 Mar 1747/8 *NHC1*, d July 1826; m 24 Dec 1766 *WdC*—Isaac Baldwin of D.

FAM. 10. SAMUEL & LYDIA (SMITH) PARDEE:

3 SAMUEL, b c. 1776, d after 1793.

4 LYDIA, b 1 Jan 1778 *OC;* m 23 Nov 1800 *OC*—David Treat.

5 DANIEL, b c. 1780.

6 ISAAC, b 15 June 1784 *F* [error for 1782], d 31 Aug 1850 (Berrien Co., Mich.); m c. 1815 Lucy da. Isaac & Hannah (Ball) Dickerman, wid. John Hooker, b 20 May 1782 *NHV*, d 4 Sep 1850 (Delaware, Ohio).

7 SARAH, b c. 1784, d 20 Mar 1846 æ. 60 *WdC*.

8 RACHEL, b c. 1786, d 1838 æ. 53 *MV;* m 20 Oct 1803 *MC1*—Hezekiah Porter.

9 EBENEZER, b [July 1789], bp 2 Oct 1791 *WdC*.

FAM. 11. LEVI & SARAH (CHIDSEY) PARDEE:

1 GURDON, b 20 June 1771 *EHV*, bp 20 Aug 1780 *EHC*, d 5 June 1843 æ. 72 *EHT*, 5 May *EHC;* m (1) 3 Nov 1799 *EHV*, *SC*—Phebe da. Immer & Rhoda (Atwater) Judd, b 16 Apr 1779 , d 1 Jan 1822 æ. 42 *EHC;* m (2) 30 Apr 1826 *EHV*—Lydia da. Thaddeus & Peninah (Brockett) Todd, wid. John Beers, b 1796, d 16 June 1866; had 6 children.

2 HULDAH, b 3 Nov 1773 *EHV*, d 12 Nov 1775 æ. 1 *EHT*, 10 Nov 1774 æ. 0-12 *EHC*.

3 HULDAH, b 29 Nov 1775 *EHV*, bp 20 Aug 1780 *EHC*, d Dec 1834 æ. 60 (at S) *EHC;* m 31 Dec 1795 *EHC* —Abiud Hemingway.

4 MEHITABEL, b 7 Feb 1779 *EHV*, "child" d 29 June 1779 æ. 0-5 *EHC*.

5 ANER, b 29 Dec 1782 *EHV*, bp 23 [Feb] 1783 *EHC*, d 21 Apr 1845 æ. 62 *EHT*, æ. 62-4 *EHC;* m 17 July 1805 *CC*—Lowly da. Jesse & Hannah (Rowe) Mallory, b 3 Oct 1784 *EHV*, d 1 Aug 1855 æ. 71 *EHT*.

6 REUEL, bp 16 [Sep] 1785 *EHC*, "child" d 28 Aug 1786 æ. ½ *EHC*.

FAM. 12. MOSES & SARAH (WILMOT) PARDEE:

1 POLLY, b c. 1767, d after 1802.

2 SARAH, b c. 1769; m Curtis Lewis.

3 Thomas, b c. 1771, d 19 Apr 1848 æ. 76 *NHV*.
4 William, b [July 1773], d 2 Dec 1774 æ. 0-16 *NHT1*.
5 William, b c. 1775, d 27 Jan 1832 æ. 57 *(Meth)NHV;* m c. 1799 Rebecca da. Samuel & Rhoda (Alling) Andrews; had issue.
6 Elizabeth, b 26 Dec 1777 *F,* d 25 July 1871; m 27 Dec 1805 *F*—Elijah Gilbert.
7 Mehitabel, b c. 1780; m 6 Oct 1799 *NHC1*—Nathan Andrews.
8 Julia, b c. 1783, d 29 Sep 1805 æ. 22 *NHT1;* m 19 June 1804 *NHC1*—William Gilbert.
9 Moses, b c. 1786, d after 1801.

fam. 13. Jared & Rebecca (Brown) Pardee:
1 Benjamin, b 6 June 1785 *EHV,* bp 31 July 1785 *EHC,* d 5 June 1863 æ. 78 *NHT3;* m 28 Oct 1811 *EHC*—Sarah da. Isaac & Mary (Fields) Bradley, b c. 1788, d 13 Jan 1835 æ. 47 *EHC;* had 4 children.
2 Stephen Brown, b 10 Jan 1787 *EHV,* bp 11 Mar 1787 *EHC,* d s. p. 5 Aug 1819 æ. 33 *EHC*.
3 Polly, b 26 June 1789 *EHV,* d 8 Aug 1809 æ. 20 *EHC*.
4 Mabel, b c. 1791, "child" d 15 Nov 1795 æ. 5 *EHC*.
5 Sarah, bp 27 Mar 1792 *EHC;* m 30 May 1822 *EHV*—Harvey Johnson.

fam. 14. Noah & Mary (Woodruff) Pardee:
1 Mehitabel, b c. 1780, d 21 July 1805 æ. 25 *SC;* m 22 Dec 1800 *SC*—William Davis; res. Wtn 1801.
2 Phineas, b 13 Dec 1781 *F,* d 6 Nov 1853; Dea.; m 7 Jan 1808 *SC*—Emma da. Seth & Rhoda (Cole) Lewis, b 17 Jan 1789 (S), d 5 Sep 1861 (NH).
3 Benoni, b c. 1785, d 25 Oct 1808 æ. 22 *SC*.

fam. 15. James & Mary (Smith) Pardee:
1 Polly, b c. 1774, d 18 Nov 1778 æ. 5 *NoHT2,* æ. 3-10 *NoHC*.
2 Sarah, b 5 July 1776 *NoHV,* bp 18 July 1779 *NoHC,* d 24 Dec 1861 *CV;* m Jeremiah Bradley.
3 Mabel, b 16 June 1778 *NoHV,* bp 18 July 1779 *NoHC,* d 15 Feb 1834 æ. 55 *NoHT2;* m 7 Nov 1805 *NoHC*—Samuel Hemingway.
4 Polly, b 30 Nov 1780 *NoHV,* bp 18 Mar 1781 *NoHC,* d 23 Oct 1863 æ. 83 *NoHT3;* m 10 June 1807 *NoHC*—Oliver Smith.
5 Martha, b 17 Dec 1782 *NoHV,* bp 16 Mar 1783 *NoHC,* d 13 Mar 1802 æ. 18 *NoHC,* 13 Apr. æ. 20 *NoHT2*.
6 Isabel, b 17 July 1785 *NoHV,* bp 23 Apr 1786 *NoHC,* d [1861?] æ. 76 *CT1;* m 16 Dec 1819 *CV*—Silas Newton.

7 John, b [7 Sep 1786], d 8 Sep 1786 æ. 0-0-1 *NoHT2.*
8 James Smith, b 1 July 1789 *NoHV,* bp 27 Sep 1789 *NoHC,* d 8 Feb 1880 æ. 90 *CT1;* m (1) 23 Nov 1812 *CV*—Anna Foote da. Jude & Olive (Foote) Smith, b c. 1793, d 18 Nov 1846 æ. 53 *CT1;* m (2) 23 Mar 1847 *CV*—Eudocia da. Gideon & Abigail (Badger) Bristol, b 4 Feb 1791 *CV,* d 10 Nov 1870 æ. 80 *CT1.*

FAM. 16. Ebenezer & Jemima (Barnes) Pardee:
1 Lyman, b 9 Nov 1781 *NoHV.*
2 Samuel, b 6 July 1783 *NoHV.*
3 Elizabeth, b 21 July 1785 *NoHV.*
4 Ebenezer, b 13 Sep 1787 *NoHV;* rem. to Scott, N. Y.; m 8 May 1810 *SC*—Thankful [da. Barnabas & Thankful] Johnson, b c. 1791.
5 Lucinda; m Samuel Hart of S; rem. to Tallmadge, Ohio.
6 Abigail.
7 Jairus, b 23 Dec 1795 *F,* d 14 Dec 1833 æ. 38 *EHC;* m 17 Nov 1819 Sarah Bradley da. Samuel & Betsey (Holt) Chidsey, b 15 Dec 1800 , d 27 Aug 1868.
8 Hannah, b 28 Feb 1800 *F;* m 6 Nov 1823 *SC*—Jude Hart.
9 Nancy.

FAM. 17. John & Elizabeth (Brockett) Pardee:
1 Rhoda, b 17 Feb 1790 *NoHV,* bp 23 Aug 1795 *NoHC,* d 12 Sep 1837 *NoHD;* m 20 Oct 1818 *NoHC*—Jeffrey Fitch.
2 Esther, b 20 Sep 1791 *NoHV,* d 19 Nov 1794 æ. 3-2-3 *NoHV.*
3 John, b 5 Sep 1793 *NoHV,* d 22 Nov 1794 æ. 1-2-17 *NoHV.*
4 Esther, b 24 June 1796 *NoHV,* "child" bp June 1796 *NoHC,* d 17 Dec 1871.
5 John, b 27 July 1798 *NoHV,* bp 2 Sep 1798 *NoHC,* d 3 Apr 1874 æ. 75-8 *NoHT2;* m Deborah da. Oliver & Betsey (Smith) Todd, wid. Thomas Heaton, b 28 July 1791 *NoHV,* d 28 July 1855 æ. 64 *NoHT2.*
6 Harriet, b 6 Dec 1800 *NoHV,* bp 29 Mar 1801 *NoHC,* d 25 June 1828 æ. 27 *NoHC,* 24 June *NoHT2.*
7 Betsey, b 23 July 1804 *NoHV,* bp 2 Sep 1804 *NoHC,* d 12 June 1837 æ. 33 *NoHT3;* m Jesse Thorpe.

FAM. 18. Joseph & Sarah (Fields) Pardee:
1 Isaac, b 18 Apr 1784 *F,* bp 6 June 1784 *EHC,* d 29 Mar 1870; m 14 Mar 1811 *EHC*—Adah da. Edmund & Lydia (Chidsey) Bradley, b 11 Dec 1790 *F,* d 25 May 1836 æ. 45 *EHC.*
2 Betsey, b 22 Dec 1786 *F,* d 16 Feb 1873 æ. 86 *NHT3;* m [5 June] 1806 *EHC*—Ezra Rowe.

3 Laban, b 4 Nov 1790 *F*, d 23 May 1859 æ. 68 *EHT*, æ. 68-6 *NHV;* m (1) 31 Dec 1820 *EHV*—Lucy da. Samuel & Sarah (Bradley) Bradley, b 17 Jan 1801 *F*, d 14 Oct 1821 æ. 20 *EHC;* m (2) 1 June 1824 *EHV*—Mary da. James & Lydia (Chidsey) Thompson, b [2 Oct 1799], d 1 May 1882 æ. 82-6-28 *NHV*.

4 Hezekiah, b c. 1793, d 24 Sep 1825 æ. 32 (in Miss.) *EHC*.

5 Almira, b 21 Oct 1806 *F*, d 27 Aug 1869 (EH).

FAM. 19. Leavit & Elizabeth (Hemingway) Pardee:

1 Samuel, b c. 1784, bp 10 June 1787 *EHC*, d Dec 1804 ("at a distance") *HarwintonC;* m Laura Ann Ward, b 13 Apr 1786 *F*, d 4 May 1871 (Binghamton, N. Y.); she m (2) c. 1812 David Carrington.

i Samuel, b 2 May 1803 *F*, d 26 June 1873 (Conklin, N. Y.); m 15 June 1825 *Bristol V*—Julina H. Jerome, b c. 1806, d 1891.

2 Sarah, b c. 1786, bp 10 June 1787 *EHC*, d 11 Dec 1803 *HarwintonC*.

3 Leavit, b c. 1788, d 12 Nov 1795 æ. 8 *EHC*.

4 Child, b [June 1790], d July 1790 æ. 3 wks. *EHC*.

5 Jared Whitfield, b 2 Jan 1792 *F*, d 7 Jan 1867 (Bristol); B.A. (Yale 1816), M.D. (1818); m 8 June 1818 *Bristol*—Ruth Norton Upson, b 1 Jan 1795, d 13 Aug 1874.

6 Amy, bp 12 Oct 1794 *EHC*.

7 Leavit, b 22 Jan 1797 *F*, bp 10 Mar 1797 *EHC*, d 9 Sep 1849 *Harwinton;* m 19 Dec 1821 *P*—Eunice Linsley, b 21 Dec 1799, d 5 Oct 1860.

8 Sally, b 5 Feb 1805 *F*, d 2 Jan 1895; m 23 Nov 1825 Lawson Wooding.

9 Nancy [more prob. child of her father's 2d w.].

FAM. 20. Abijah & Rosanna (Moulthrop) Pardee:

1 Abigail, b 4 Nov 1779 *F*, bp Apr 1795 *EHC*, d 24 Mar 1852 (EH); m 17 Apr 1806 *EHC*—Seba Munson.

2 Isaac Holt, b c. 1781, d 31 July 1822 æ. 41 *EHC;* m 5 June 1806 *EHC*—Sally da. Isaac & Lydia (Fields) Hotchkiss, b 19 Mar 1781 *EHR*, d 15 Dec 1838 æ. 57 *EHC*.

3 Polly, b c. 1783, d 27 Jan 1873; m (1) Charles Thompson; m (2) ——— Bradley.

4 Clarissa, b c. 1786, bp Apr 1795 *EHC*, d 23 Oct 1802 æ. 17 *EHC*.

5 Abijah, b c. 1788, bp Apr 1795 *EHC*, d 26 Jan 1843 æ. 54 *EHC;* m 14 Jan 1824 *EHC*—Sarah da. Moses & Delight (Upson) Todd, b 23 Feb 1795 (Wol), d 1 Oct 1885 (Vermillion, Ohio).

6 Maria, b 2 Dec 1791 *F*, bp Apr 1795 *EHC*, d 2 Dec 1867; m 5 Sep 1813 *EHC*—Solomon Dewey.
7 Sarah, b c. 1793, d soon.
8 George, bp 24 Jan 1796 *EHC*, "child" d 11 Sep 1803 *EHC*.
9 Anna, bp 29 Apr 1798 *EHC*, "child" d 30 Jan 1806 æ. 7 *EHC*.
10 Sarah, bp 1 Feb 1801 *EHC*; m (1) 3 Sep 1826 Selah Upson; m (2) ——— Schoonmaker.

FAM. 21. Chandler & Lydia (Fields) Pardee:
1 Reuel, bp 23 Jan 1791 *EHC*, "child" d 16 Apr 1791 æ. 0-4 *EHC*.
2 Reuel, b 4 Sep 1792 *EHV*, bp 1792 *EHC*, d 6 Nov 1825 æ. 33 *EHC*.
3 Eunecia, b 20 Aug 1794 *EHV*, bp 12 Oct 1794 *EHC*; m (1) 1 Jan 1812 *EHC*—Luman Cowles of Berlin; m (2) 23 Nov 1828 *EHV*—Linas Cowles.

FAM. 22. Stephen & Abigail (Smith) Pardee:
1 Samuel, bp 4 Jan 1778 *EHC*; res. Camden, N. Y., 1809.
2 Mary, bp 4 Jan 1778 *EHC*; [Polly m Jan 1818 Eliphalet Barnes].
3 Child, b [May 1774], d 3 Dec 1775 æ. 0-18 *EHC*.
4 Mabel; m 24 May 1801 *PV*—Ephraim Camp.
5 Asahel, bp 31 Dec 1782 *PC*; m 22 July 1811 *PC*—Rhoda Fenn, b c. 1790, d 16 Oct 1876 æ. 86 *PT*.
6 Elizabeth, b c. 1789, d 2 Mar 1806 æ. 17 *PT*.

FAM. 23. Joel & Eunice (Heaton) Pardee:
1 Philo; supposed deceased by 1842.
2 Laura; m 28 Feb 1822 *HarwintonV*—Noadiah Cotton.
3 Ebenezer Heaton, d 1860 (Avon); m Laura Maria Robinson.

FAM. 23. Joel & Sally (Murray) Pardee:
4 Lois, b c. 1801, d 22 Oct 1854 æ. 53 *NHV*; m Kneeland Ramsdell.
5 Nancy, b [17 Mar 1803], d 18 Feb 1883 æ. 79-11-1 *NHV*; m (1) Hezekiah Winchell; m (2) Kelly Smith.
6 Susan, b c. 1805; m Sherman West of Hartford.
7 Leonard, b 24 July 1807 *F*, d 11 June 1869 *NHV*; m Sarah W. da. Ralph & Mary (Morehouse) Burns, b 15 May 1808 (at M), d 11 May 1880 *NHV*.
8 Mary Ann, b c. 1810; res. Hartford 1842.

FAM. 24. Silas & Betsey (Alling) Pardee (first 8 bp 21 May 1809 *NHC1*):
1 Elizabeth, b 24 Dec 1790 *F*, d 21 Feb 1833; m 21 Mar 1813 *NHx*—Isaac Trowbridge.

2 Julia Ann, b 20 Jan 1792 *NHT1,* d 7 July 1857 *NHT1;* m James C. Parker.
3 Willis, b [Feb 1794], d 1871; m Isabella da. Benjamin & Rachel (Clark) Brockett, b July 1801, d 21 Nov 1878.
4 Louisa; m ——— Bradley.
5 Angelina, b c. 1801, d 23 Dec 1831; m Lyman Brockett.
6 William, b c. 1803, d 14 May 1838 *WHD;* m (1) 2 Nov 1831 *NHV*—Jane da. Dan & Amy (Smith) Tolles, b c. 1803, d 6 Sep 1832; m (2) 24 Apr 1833 Lucy N. da. Jared & Content Downes, b [Sep 1814], d 22 June 1894.
7 Laura, b 7 Apr 1805, d 30 May 1897 *NHV.*
8 John Alling, b [Aug 1807], d 20 Nov 1883 *NHV;* m 12 Oct 1836 *NHV*—Jennet R. da. Eleazer & Fanny L. (Osborn) Hotchkiss, b c. 1817, d 4 Oct 1881.
9 Jerusha, bp 20 Aug 1809 *NHC1,* d 5 Oct 1875; m 6 June 1819 Medad C. Munson of W.
10 Mary Ann, b c. 1810, d 11 Dec 1844 æ. 34 *NHV;* m Alexander Oviatt.
11 Silas, b [Sep 1812], d 10 Mar 1901; m (1) 20 Sep 1840 Catherine B. da. David & Martha (Gillett) Merwin, b c. 1818, d 9 Feb 1878; m (2) 21 June 1881 *WHV*—Ellen Maria da. John L. & Marietta A. (Ingraham) Whittlesey, b 5 June 1844, d 24 June 1909.

PARKER. fam. 1. Edward, d 1662; m Elizabeth, wid. John Potter, who d 28 July 1677 *NHV;* she m (3) Robert Rose.

1 Mary, bp 27 Apr 1648 *NHC1,* d 23 Sep 1725 *WV;* m 6 Dec 1666 *NHV*—John Hall.
2 John, bp 8 Oct 1648 *NHC1,* d 1711; m 8 Nov 1670 *NHV*—Hannah da. William Bassett, b 13 Sep 1650 *NHV,* bp 15 Sep 1650 *NHC1,* d 7 June 1726 *WV.*
i Hannah, b 20 Aug 1671 *NHV,* d 1758; m (1) 12 Jan 1692 *WV*—William Andrews; m (2) Bartholomew Foster.
ii Elizabeth, b c. 1673, d 10 Sep 1751 *WV;* m (1) 24 Mar 1693 *WV*—Josiah Royce; m (2) 22 Dec 1696 *WV*—Ebenezer Clark; m (3) 16 Oct 1721 *WV*—Nathaniel Andrews.
iii John, b 26 Mar 1675 *NHV,* d 1745; m 1 Nov 1699 *WV*—Mary Kibbe, b c. 1679, d 23 June 1769 æ. 90 *WV.* fam. 2.
iv Abiah, b 26 Mar 1677 *NHV,* d æ. over 90 *WC1;* m 23 May 1700 *WV*—Thomas Matthews.

v Rachel, b 16 June 1680 *WV*, d 8 Sep 1763 *WV;* m 1700 *WV*—Thomas Richardson.

vi Joseph, b c. 1682, d 1758; m 7 June 1705 *WV*—Sarah da. Thomas & Mary (Merriman) Curtis, b 1 Oct 1687 *WV*, d 6 Mar 1760 *WV*. FAM. 3.

vii Mary, b c. 1685, d æ. 85 *WC1;* m 27 Nov 1707 *NHV*—Joseph Clark.

viii Eliphalet, b c. 1687, d 1758 *WV;* Sgt.; m (1) 5 Aug 1708 *WV*—Hannah da. John & Mary (Royce) Beach, b 17 Mar 1683/4 *WV*, d 21 Dec 1749 *WV;* m (2) 26 Dec 1751 *WV*—Damaris da. Samuel & Sarah (Alling) Atwater, wid. Henry Bristol, b 21 May 1700 *NHV*, d 27 Dec 1770 *WV*, æ. 71 *WT1*. FAM. 4.

ix Samuel, b c. 1690, d 1750; m 16 July 1713 *WV*—Sarah da. Thomas & Sarah (Hemingway) Goodsell, b 14 Sep 1689 *BdV*, 20 Sep 1688 *NHV*. FAM. 5.

x Edward, b c. 1692, d 22 Oct 1776 *CC*, 21 Oct in 84 yr. *CT3;* Ens.; Dea.; m (1) (intention 4 Aug 1716) *Lynn, Mass.*—Jerusha da. William & Atheldred (Berry) Merriam, b 21 Feb 1698, d 27 Dec 1745 *WV*, 28 Dec æ. 48 *CT1;* m (2) 1 Dec 1748 *WV*—Rebecca da. Daniel & Esther (Sperry) Hotchkiss, wid. Thomas Ives, b 14 Feb 1697 *NHV*, d 23 Feb 1762 *WV*, 25 Jan (?) 1762 æ. 65 *CT1;* m (3) 30 Sep 1762 *WV*—Ruth da. Hawkins & Sarah (Royce) Hart, wid. William Merriam, b 13 Aug 1704 (at Farm) *WV*, d before 1785. FAM. 6.

xi Abigail, b c. 1694, d c. May 1732 *WV;* m 8 Dec 1715 *WV*—Josiah Hotchkiss.

3 HOPE, b 26 Apr 1650 *NHV*, bp 26 May 1650 *NHC1*, d between 1686 & 1691; m 2 May 1667 *NHV*—Samuel Cook.

4 LYDIA, b 14 Apr 1652 *NHV*, bp 14 Apr 1652 *NHC1*, d after 1740; m 12 Jan 1671 *NHV*—John Thomas.

FAM. 2. JOHN & MARY (KIBBE) PARKER:

1 RACHEL, b 6 Jan 1701/2 *WV*, d 27 Sep 1767 *CC;* m (1) 20 May 1724 *WV*—Evan Royce; m (2) Daniel Andrews.

2 JOHN, b Oct 1703 *WV*, d 28 Mar 1749 *WV;* m 17 Oct 1727 *WV*—Deborah da. Thomas & Abiah (Parker) Matthews, b 8 July 1704 *WV*, d 1754.

i Abiah, b 13 July 1728 *WV*, d 14 Aug 1728 *WV*.

ii John, b 25 Dec 1730 *WV*, d 1757; m 16 June 1752 *WV*—Eunice [da. Samuel & Hannah (Benham)] Beach, [b 27 June 1735 *WV*]. Child: John, b 8 Dec 1755 *WV*.

iii Deborah, b 4 May 1734 *WV;* m 22 Nov 1753 *WV* —Jesse Mix.

iv Jesse, b 16 Mar 1736 *WV;* m 16 Feb 1758 *WV*— Dorothy Spencer. Children recorded *WV:* Jesse, b 30 May 1759; Lucy, b 17 Sep 1761; Jared; b 31 Jan 1764; Jotham, b 2 Feb 1767; & Dorothy, b 5 Aug 1770.

v Reuben, b 12 Mar 1738 *WV;* m 10 Dec 1764 Hannah Chapman.

vi Gideon, b 5 July 1740 *WV;* m 17 Aug 1763 *NHC1*—Elizabeth da. Hachaliah & Elizabeth (Clark) Thomas.

vii Elizabeth, b 11 Nov 1743 *WV.*

viii Isaiah, b 14 June 1746 *WV;* m 14 Feb 1771 Susanna Yale.

3 Aaron, b 8 July 1704, d 12 Jan 1727 *WV.*

4 Mary, b 8 Feb 1706 *WV,* d between 1746 & 1752; imbecile; had children:

i Moses Tuttle, b 29 Dec 1726 *WV,* d s. p. 1756.

ii Ephraim, b 30 Sep 1737 *WV.*

iii Job, b 13 June 1746 *WV,* d Nov 1799 æ. 53 *KensingtonC;* Census (C) 1-4-3; m 18 Dec 1765 *WV*—Olive da. Jehiel & Rebecca (Brown) Royce, b 6 July 1747 *WV.* Children recorded *WV:* Daughter, b 18 May 17[66]; Jarus, b 27 Aug 1769 [1768?]; Amos Matthews, b 10 June 1770; Clark Rice, b 7 July 1772; Salmon, b 30 Aug 1774; Selah, b 27 Nov 1776.

5 Elisha, b 23 Oct 1708 *WV,* d Sep 1748 *CC;* m 7 Feb 1728 *WV*—Susanna da. William & Mary (Abernathy) Tuttle, b 10 Nov 1708 *NHV.*

i Ruth, b 8 Feb 1728 *WV.*

ii Aaron, b 9 Apr 1730 *WV;* m 11 Mar 1756 *WV*— Sarah da. Robert & Abigail (Parker) Martin, b 27 Mar 1737 *WV.* Children recorded *WV:* Mamre, b 14 Feb 1757; Robert, b 12 Feb 1759; Susanna, b 20 Feb 1762; Abigail, b 1 Apr 1764; Sally, b 20 Mar 1766; Lyman, b 17 Apr 1768; Eunice, b 11 Jan 1771; Ruth, b 1 Feb 1774.

iii Dan.

iv Elisha, b 25 July 1735 *WV;* m 10 Aug 1759 *WV* —Esther Spencer. Children recorded *WV:* Elisha, b 28 Apr 1761; Katharine, b 30 Mar 1763; Chloe, b 2[8] Dec 176[5]; Asahel, b 2 Apr 1768; Esther, b 28 Mar 1771; Polly, b 20 Mar 1773; Shailor, b 28 Aug 1775; Polly, b 13 Sep 1778.

v John, b 17 Sep 1739 *WV*.
vi Damaris, b 16 July 1743 *WV;* m 2 Dec 1761 *WV*—Enos Parker.
vii Susanna, b 7 Dec 1745 *WV,* bp Feb 1745/6 *CC*.
viii Israel, bp Aug 1750 *CC*.

6 Abigail, b 3 Mar 1710 *WV;* m 15 July 1734 *WV*—Robert Martin. She had a child:
i Zuba, b 1 Nov 1731 *WV*.

7 Elizabeth, b 3 June 1716 *WV*.

8 Lois, b 20 July 1718 *WV,* d 3 July 1749 *WV;* m 5 Nov 1740 *WV*—Thomas Beach.

9 Isaac, b 1720 *WV;* m (1) 11 Aug 1742 *WV*—Hannah da. Timothy & Hannah (Cook) Beach, b 21 Apr 1722 *WV,* d 23 June 1773 *WV;* m (2) 27 Apr 1775 *WV, WC1*—Lois, wid. Royce.
(By 1): *i* Kezia, b 12 Feb 1743/4 *WV,* d bef. 1776.
ii Lois, b 30 Apr 1746 *WV*.
iii Ruth, b 11 July 1750 *WV;* [m 5 Dec 1776 *WC1*—Gershom Mattoon].
iv Isaac, b 14 Sep 1754 *WV;* m 19 Mar 1778 *WV, WC1*—Ann [da. Gamaliel & Elizabeth (Blakeslee)] Parker, [b 8 Feb 1759 *WV*].
v Mary, b 14 Aug 1755 *WV*.
vi Timothy, b 14 Aug 1757 *WV*.
vii John, b 21 Feb 1762 *WV*.
viii Phineas, b 14 Jan 1765 *WV*.
(By 2): *ix* Kezia, b 16 Oct 1776 *WV*.

FAM. 3. Joseph & Sarah (Curtis) Parker:

1 Joseph, b 6 Aug 1706 *WV,* d 25 July 1707 *WV*.

2 Thomas, b 7 June 1708 *WV,* d young.

3 Hannah, b 30 Aug 1710 *WV,* d 29 Dec 1739 *NHV;* m 1 Jan 1729/30 *NHV*—Samuel Barnes.

4 Ebenezer, b 5 Mar 1713 *WV,* d 23 Jan 1797 *CC;* m 1 Apr 1735 *WV*—Lydia da. Thomas & Mary (Leek) Barnes, b 10 Dec 1716 *NHV*.
i Desire, b 7 June 1735 *WV,* d 10 Feb 1806 æ. 70 *CT1;* m 20 Dec 1753 *WV*—Aaron Bellamy.
ii Ebenezer, b 6 July 1737 *WV;* Census (C) 2-0-2; m Ann da. Thomas & Sarah (Abernathy) Doolittle, b 20 Dec 1730 *WV*. FAM. 7.
iii Caleb, b 30 Mar 1739 *WV,* d soon.
iv Joshua, b 17 Apr 1741 *WV;* m 30 Oct 1765 *WV*—Mary da. Oliver & Thankful (Parker) Hitchcock, b 13 July 1745 *WV*. Children recorded *WV:* Stephen, b 1 Apr 1766; Lydia, b 23 May 1769; Hannah, b 21 Apr or June 1773; Chestina, b 20 June 1777; Jared, b 22 Mar 1781.

v Jared, b 16 Nov 1743 *WV.*

vi Lydia, b 8 Mar 1744/5 *WV;* m 23 Aug 1762 *WV*—Abel Parker.

vii Stephen, b 27 Oct 1747 *WV.*

viii Eliakim, b 10 July 1751 *WV;* m (1) 20 Feb 1775 *WV*—Phebe Carrington, & had a s. Eliakim, b 13 Mar 1777 *WV;* m (2) 17 Nov 1777 *WV*—Lois da. Ambrose & Sarah (Terrill) Hine, wid. Levi Ives, bp 3 Dec 1752 *WdC,* & had: Phebe, b 18 Aug 1778 *WV,* & Levi, b 8 July 1780 *WV.*

ix Caleb, b 2 Nov 1759 *WV,* d 31 Dec 1800 *CC,* æ. 42 *CT1;* Census (C) 1-2-4; m 1 Nov 1783 *CC*—Dorothy da. Charles & Dorothy (Hall) Peck, b 16 Mar 1763 *WV,* d 12 May 1806 æ. 42 *CT1.* FAM. 8.

5 JOSEPH, b 3 Apr 1716 *WV;* m 23 Feb 1742/3 *WV*—Lucy Parmalee.

i Esther, b 11 Jan 1743/4 *WV,* d 8 Feb 1744/5 *WV.*

ii Joseph, b 5 Nov 1746 *WV;* m 29 June 1769 *WV*—Patience da. Eliada & Sarah (Curtis) Parker, b 18 Aug 1748 *WV.* Children recorded *WV:* Jehiel, b 26 Sep 1770; Sena, b 23 Feb 1773; Lucy, b 20 Nov 1775; Sarah, b 23 Mar 1778; Amy, b 16 Oct 1780.

iii Lucy, b 13 Mar 1748/9 *WV;* m 10 Dec 1764 *WV*—Oliver Parker.

iv Esther, b 27 Mar 1754 *WV;* [m Nathaniel Curtis].

v Charles, b 26 Feb 1756 *WV;* m 21 Oct 1784 *WV*—Charity Dibble of Saybrook.

6 ANDREW, b c. 1718; rem. to Adams, Mass.; m 27 Apr 1737 *WV*—Susanna da. Samuel & Elizabeth (Doolittle) Blakeslee, b 15 Mar 1719 *WV.*

i Ambrose, b 6 Mar 1738 *WV;* Census (Granville, N. Y.) 2-0-2; m 22 Mar 1758 *WV*—Comfort da. Eliada & Sarah (Curtis) Parker, b 16 Sep 1738 *WV.* Children recorded *WV:* Andrew, b 15 Jan 1759, Census (Granville, N. Y.) 1-2-2; Giles, b 15 Sep 1760; Lydia, b 26 May 1763; Comfort, b 23 May 1766.

ii Grace, b 10 Dec 1739 *WV,* d 11 Dec 1739 *WV.*

iii Patience, b 10 Dec 1739 *WV,* d 13 Dec 1739 *WV.*

iv Zerviah, b 28 Nov 1741 *WV;* m 3 Jan 176[5] *WV*—David Miller; Census, Zerviah Miller (Adams, Mass.) 0-0-2.

v Oliver, b 20 Nov 1743 *WV;* Census (Adams, Mass.) 2-1-3; m 10 Dec 1764 *WV*—Lucy da. Joseph & Lucy (Parmelee) Parker, b 13 Mar 1748/9 *WV*.

PAGE 2049 *vi* Ezra, b 2 Dec 1745 *WV;* Census (Adams, Mass.) 3-5-5.

vii Susanna, b 10 Dec 1747 *WV;* m 20 Nov 1766 *WV*—Stephen Ives.

viii Rachel, b 28 Dec 1749 *WV;* m Ebenezer Atwater.

ix Sybil, b 9 Feb 1753 *WV*.

x Jason, b 17 Aug 1764 *WV*.

7 Waitstill, b 24 July 1721 *WV;* m (1) 27 Oct 1742 *WV*—Jemima da. Joseph & Margery (Hitchcock) Munson, b 27 Mar 1720 *WV;* m (2) 19 Nov 1751 *WV*—Jemima da. Nathan & Jemima (Curtis) Beach, b 11 May 1732 *WV;* m (3) 13 Dec 1759 *WV*—Martha da. Daniel & Martha (Doolittle) Hall, b 14 June 1729 *WV*.

(By 1): *i* Margery, b 20 Mar 1743/4 *WV,* d 1 Oct 1744 *WV*.

ii Justus, b 1 Jan 1747/8 *WV*.

iii Margery, b 5 Feb 1749/50 *WV;* m (1) 10 May 1770 *WV*—Eliada Parker; m (2) 25 Feb 1778 *WV*—Stephen Peck.

(By 2): *iv* Jemima, b 2 June 1753 *WV*.

v Rhoda, b 25 Mar 1755 *WV,* bp 22 June 1755 *NoBC2*.

(By 3): *vi* Charles, b 21 Aug 1760 *WV*.

vii Eunice, b 9 Aug 1762 *WV*.

viii Justus, b 23 May 176[4] *WV*.

ix Martha, b 17 Apr 176[6] *WV*.

x Abigail, b 10 June 1768 *WV,* d 22 Jan 1836 æ. 68 *PptT;* m 5 Feb 1795 *CC*—Abel Austin.

xi Sarah, b 2 Apr 1771 *WV*.

8 Sarah, b 18 Oct 1725 *WV,* d c. 1818; m 15 Jan 1744/5 *WV*—Asaph Cook.

9 Thomas, b 29 Mar 1728 *WV,* d 15 Feb 1788 æ. 60 *WashingtonT;* rem. to Wy 1756; m 30 Aug 1748 *WV*—Abigail da. Thomas & Abigail (Merriam) Dutton, b 8 July 1732 *WV*.

i Thomas, b 3 Apr 1749 *WV,* bp 29 Oct 1758 *WashingtonC,* d 15 Apr 1822 æ. 73 *WashT;* m 21 Mar 1770 *WyV*—Jerusha Clark, who d 14 July 1808 æ. 56 *WashT*.

ii Amasa, b 28 Feb 1751 *WV,* bp 29 Oct 1758 *WashC;* m 30 Nov 1771 *WyV*—Diadama Parmelee.

iii Peter, b 11 Mar 1753 *WV*, bp 29 Oct 1758 *WashC;* res. Washington Co., N. Y.; m 24 Nov 1774 Esther Clark.

iv Abigail, b 28 Aug 1755 *WV*, bp 29 Oct 1758 *WashC;* m 29 Sep 1773 *Wash*—David Root.

v Justus, b 6 Mar 1758 *WyV*, bp 29 Oct 1758 *WashC;* m.

vi Joseph, b 21 Apr 1760 *WyV*, d 6 Feb 1830 æ. 70 *LT;* Dr.; m (1) Lydia Harrison; m (2) Sarah Moss, wid. Jerry Blackman.

vii Sarah, b 10 Oct 1762 *WyV*, bp 28 Nov 1762 *WashC;* m 17 Apr 1782 *Wash*—Daniel Richards of Milton.

viii Abner, bp 14 Apr 1765 *WashC.*

ix Rebecca, bp 21 June 1767 *WashC;* m 20 Mar 1785 Joseph Smith of Newburg, N. Y.

x David, bp 5 May 1770 *WashC.*

FAM. 4. ELIPHALET & HANNAH (BEACH) PARKER:

1 ELIADA, b 2 Apr 1710 *WV*, d 24 Mar 1712 *WV.*

2 ELIADA, b 22 June 1712 *WV*, d 7 Feb 1802 æ. 90 *WT1;* m 21 Dec 1732 *WV*—Sarah da. Nathaniel & Sarah (How) Curtis, b 30 Mar 1712 *WV*, d 1 Nov 1799 æ. 87 *WT1.*

i Martha, b 8 July 1734 *WV;* [perhaps m Titus Parker].

ii Lettice, b 18 Sep 1736 *WV*, d after 1810; m Ebenezer Hitchcock.

iii Comfort, b 16 Sep 1738 *WV;* m 22 Mar 1758 *WV*—Ambrose Parker.

iv Eliada, b 24 Nov 1740 *WV*, d 23 Nov 1742 *WV.*

v Sarah, b 23 Jan 1743/4 *WV;* [m 10 May 1770 *WC1*—Simeon Stedman of Farm].

vi Hannah, b 23 Sep 1746 *WV.*

vii Patience, b 18 Aug 1748 *WV;* m 29 June 1769 *WV*—Joseph Parker.

viii Eliada, b 14 Jan 1750/1 *WV*, d 12 Sep 1776 *WV;* m 10 May 1770 *WV*—Margery da. Waitstill & Jemima (Munson) Parker, b 5 Feb 1749/50 *WV;* she m (2) 25 Feb 1778 *WV*—Stephen Peck. Children: Munson, b 18 Feb 1771 *WV;* Chester, b 20 Oct 1773 *WV;* Linus, b 18 Dec 1775 *WV*, d soon.

ix Phebe, b 31 Oct 1752 *WV.*

x Levi, b 8 June 1757 *WV*, d 6 Oct 1833 æ. 76 *WT1;* m 22 July 1779 Lydia Bradley.

3 JUSTINA ("Chestina"), b 18 Apr 1714 *WV*, d 15 Feb 1777 (Simsbury); m (1) 22 Nov 1732 *WV*—Peter Curtis; m (2) 18 Feb 1767 Sylvanus Woodruff.

4 Arnon, b 17 Feb 1716 *WV;* m 7 Feb 1737 *WV*—Abigail da. Daniel & Hannah (Cornwall) Doolittle, b 6 May 1712 *WV,* d 16 Nov 1785 æ. 74 *WT1.*

i Esther, b 24 Nov 1737 *WV,* bp 29 Jan 1737/8 *CC.*

ii Daniel, b 2 Aug 1740 *WV,* bp Nov 1740 *CC,* d 22 Mar 1814 æ. 72 *WT1;* m 18 Nov 1762 *WV*—Miriam da. Benjamin & Miriam (Cook) Curtis, b 30 Aug 1737 *WV,* d 14 Oct 1813 æ. 75 *WT1.* FAM. 9.

iii Abigail, b 30 Jan 1742/3 *WV,* bp 3 Feb 1743 *CC;* m ——— Bradley.

iv Miriam, bp Nov 1744 *CC,* "child" d Dec 1745 *CC.*

v Bethia; m 3 Nov 1773 *WC1*—Jonathan Gaylord of Wat.

vi Miriam, b 20 Oct 1747 *WV;* m 15 July 1772 *WV*—Titus Luddington.

vii Hannah, d s. p. 1800; m ——— Clark.

5 Gamaliel, b 6 June 1718 *WV,* d 18 Sep 1770 æ. 53 *WV;* m Elizabeth da. Samuel & Elizabeth (Doolittle) Blakeslee, b 8 July 1721 *WV,* d 1782.

i Abel, b 4 Jan 1741 *WV;* rem. to Washington, Ct., & Greenfield, Vt.; m 23 Aug 1762 *WV*—Lydia da. Ebenezer & Lydia (Barnes) Parker, b 8 Mar 1744/5 *WV.*

ii Elizabeth, b 7 Jan 1742/3 *WV;* m 25 Dec 1771 *WV*—Timothy Ward.

iii Eunice, b 6 Jan 1744/5 *WV,* d 15 Sep 1825 æ. 81 *CT1;* m 19 May 1763 *WV*—Thomas Bristol.

iv Gamaliel, b 9 Dec 1746 *WV,* d 29 Oct 1755 *WV.*

v Amos, b 20 Jan 1748/9 *WV,* d soon.

vi Ephraim, b 25 June 1751 *WV,* d 14 Sep 1794 æ. 43 *WT1;* m 14 May 1772 *WV*—Miriam da. Gideon & Miriam (Hotchkiss) Curtis, b 28 June 1753 *WV,* d 24 Apr 1815 æ. [—] *WT1.* Children recorded *WV:* John Merriam, b 28 Mar 1774; George Wyllys, b 21 Jan 1776.

vii Miriam, b 26 Jan 1753 *WV,* d 25 Jan 1823 æ. 70 *WT1;* m 22 Dec 1774 *WV*—Stephen Beach.

viii Gamaliel, b 22 Oct 1755 *WV,* d 8 Nov 1755 *WV.*

ix Gamaliel, b 2 Nov 1756 *WV,* d 3 Dec 1799 æ. 43 *WT1;* res. Wy; m 2 May 1782 *WV*—Martha Parker.

x Ann, b 8 Feb 1759 *WV;* [m 19 Mar 1778 *WV*—Isaac Parker].

xi Amos, b 11 Dec 1761 *WV;* m 5 Dec 1785 *WV*—Mary Curtis.

xii Merab, b 15 Aug 1770 *WV.*

6 Didymus, b 29 Jan 1721 *WV;* Lt.; Census (Granville, N. Y.) 1-0-1; m 22 Dec 1743 *WV*—Phebe da. John & Sarah (Jennings) Johnson, b 28 Apr 1720 *WV.*

i Enos, b 12 Nov 1744 *WV;* Census (Granville, N. Y.) 1-1-3; m 2 Dec 1761 *WV*—Damaris da. Elisha & Susanna (Tuttle) Parker, b 16 July 1743 *WV.*

i Dorcas, b 17 Dec 1761 (?) *WV.*

ii Dan, b 18 Mar 176[4] *WV.*

ii Ichabod, b 2 Jan 1748/9 *WV;* Census (Granville, N. Y.) 2-1-1; m 3 Dec 1769 *WV*—Susanna da. Asaph & Sarah (Parker) Cook, b 13 Apr 1750 *WV.*

7 Eliphalet, b 29 Jan 1721 *WV,* d 19 May 17[60] *WV;* m 21 May 1745 *WV*—Thankful da. Matthias & Thankful (Andrews) Hitchcock, b 29 Mar 1725 *WV,* d 28 Nov 17[63] *WV.*

i Valentine, b 5 Mar 1745/6 *WV,* d 14 Dec 17[60] *WV.*

ii Matthias, b 24 Sep 1747 *WV.*

iii Nathaniel, b 29 Oct 1750 *WV;* Census (Granville, N. Y.) 1-1-4.

iv Eliphalet, b 22 Jan 1754 *WV;* rem. to Hartland; Census (Granville, N. Y.) 3-5-3.

v Thankful, b 3 Apr 1756 *WV.*

vi Michael, b 15 Oct 1758 *WV;* Census (Granville, N. Y.) 1-1-4.

8 Joanna, b 8 July 1723 *WV,* d 15 Nov 1776 *CC;* m 1 Jan 1740 *WV*—Amos Bristol.

9 Thankful, b c. 1725, d 5 June 1772; m 19 Oct 1744 *WV*—Oliver Hitchcock.

10 Bethuel, b 2 Apr 1727 *WV,* d 13 Mar 1778 *WV;* m 19 July 1749 *WV*—Tabitha da. Matthias & Thankful (Andrews) Hitchcock, b 26 Feb 1730 *WV,* d 1786.

i Jerusha, b 6 Apr 1750 *WV;* m 10 July 1777 *WV*—William Smith.

ii David, b 9 Mar 1752 *WV,* bp Apr 1752 *CC,* d 6 Sep 1753 *WV.*

iii Olive, b 9 Mar 1754 *WV;* m 27 Feb 1777 *WV*—Joseph Distance.

iv David, b 18 Mar 1756 *WV,* d 9 Oct 1776 *WV.*

v Martha, b 12 Dec 1757 *WV,* d s. p. 1787; m 26 June 1780 *WV*—John Glover.

vi Joanna, b 18 June 1760 *WV,* d 1 July 1836 æ. 77 *WT1;* m Thaddeus Royce.

vii Tabitha, b 16 Nov 1762 *WV,* d 25 Aug 1844 æ. 82 *WT1;* m James Beard.
viii Bethuel, b 21 Feb 1765 *WV;* m Eunice ——.
ix Simeon, b 15 Apr 1767 *WV,* d 13 Sep 1773 *WV.*
x Thankful, b 15 June 1769 *WV.*
xi Asa, b 4 Dec 1771 *WV,* d 18 Oct 1827 æ. 57 *WT1;* m Kezia ——, who d 22 Apr 1843 æ. 66 *WT1.*
xii Mary, b 29 Sep 1776 *WV,* d 15 Dec 1777 *WV.*

11 BENJAMIN, b 12 Feb 1729 *WV.* PAGE 1529

FAM. 5. SAMUEL & SARAH (GOODSELL) PARKER:

1 SARAH, b 17 May 1714 *WV;* m 26 Aug 1735 *NHV*—David Barnes.

2 ABIAH, b 21 Aug 1716 *WV,* d 21 Sep 1767 æ. 52 *WT1;* m 28 Oct 1735 *WV*—Daniel Ives.

3 SAMUEL, b c. 1718; m 9 Jan 1744 *WV*—Mary Chamberlin. Family incomplete.
i Thankful, b 8 Oct 1745 *WV.*
ii Martha, b 12 Sep 1749 *WV.*
iii Lent, b 8 July 1752 *WV;* m 9 Nov 1774 *WtnV*—Sarah da. Edward & Hannah (Curtis) Dunbar, b 9 June 1756 *WatV.*
iv (possibly) Eldad, bp 2 May 1762 *Bristol x.*

4 ABRAHAM, b 24 Mar 1720 *WV,* d 26 July 1775 *WV;* m 9 Sep 1747 *WV*—Damaris da. William & Mary (Peck) Abernathy, b 30 Aug 1720 *WV,* d 20 Dec 1775 *WV.*
i Sarah, b 16 July 1748 *WV.*
ii Damaris, b 28 Jan 1751 *WV.*
iii Abraham, b 20 July 1753 *WV,* d 1 May 1754 *WV.*
iv Benjamin, b 27 May 1755 *WV;* m 25 June 1778 *WV*—Lurinda Curtis.
v Abraham, b 22 Aug 1757 *WV.*
vi William, b 19 Dec 1759 *WV;* Census (Woodstock, N. Y.) 3-1-1.
vii Mehitabel, b 30 June 1762 *WV.*

5 JACOB, b 24 Apr 1722 *WV,* d 24 Sep 1767 *WV;* m 26 Apr 1749 *WV*—Elizabeth da. John & Elizabeth (Barnes) Beecher, b 13 Sep 1729 *WV,* d 9 June 1826 æ. 102-8-17 *Claremont,N.H.,T.*
i Samuel, b 10 Jan 1749/50 *WV;* Census (C) 1-1-5; m 11 July 1776 *WV, CC*—Hannah da. Ebenezer & Lydia (Clark) Bunnell, b 11 Apr 1756 *WV.* Child: Jared, b 22 Apr 1777 *WV,* bp 25 May 1777 *CC,* "child" d 28 Feb 1779 *CC.* Possibly Hannah, bp 6 Sep 1778 *CC,* & Jared, bp 30 July 1780 *CC* (names of parents not stated) were other children.

ii Solitary, b 7 Jan 1752 *WV*, bp Dec 1751(?) *CC*, d 31 Aug 1754 *WV*.
iii Elizabeth, b 18 May 1754 *WV*, d 8 Nov 1821 æ. 67 *Claremont,N.H.,T;* m 19 Feb 1778 *WdC*—John Vergison.
iv Jacob, b 13 Jan 1756 *WV*, d 17 Sep 1756 *WV*.
v Jacob, b 1 July 1757 *WV*, d 6 Mar 1836 æ. 79 *ClaremontT*.
vi Rebecca, b 27 Feb 1759 *WV*, d 15 Mar 1759 *WV*.
vii James, b 3 Mar 1760 *WV*.
viii Solomon, b 12 Apr 1762 *WV*.
ix Adah, b 23 Feb 1765 *WV*.
x Abiah, b 8 Mar 1767 *WV*, d 1 May 1834 æ. 67 *ClaremontT*.

6 Lydia, b c. 1725, d 1 Jan 1809 æ. 83 *CT1;* m (1) Daniel Humiston; m (2) 26 Apr 1769 *WV*—Samuel Hull; m (3) John Atwater.

7 Titus, b 23 Feb 1728 *WV*, d 25 June 1811 (Paris, N. Y.); rem. to Lenox, Mass.; m Martha [perhaps da. Eliada & Sarah (Curtis) Parker, b 8 July 1734 *WV*].
i Rufus.
ii Titus.
iii Hannah.
iv Linus.
v Eliada, b 18 June 1766 *BdV*.
vi Sarah, b 19 July 1769 *BdV*.
vii Martha.

8 Hannah, b 5 Dec 1730 *WV;* m 5 Dec 1750 Stephen Matthews.

9 Martha, b 3 Sep 1733 *WV*, d young.

fam. 6. Edward & Jerusha (Merriam) Parker:

1 Ralph, b 9 Jan 1718 *WV*, d Oct 1748 *CC*, 15 Oct *WV*, æ. 31 *CT1;* m 25 Dec 1740 *WV*—Martha da. Gideon & Mary (Royce) Ives, b 10 Aug 1716 *WV;* she m (2) 15 Nov 1759 *WV*—Jonathan Blakeslee.
i Jerusha, b 1 Nov 1741 *WV*, bp Nov 1741 *CC*, d after 1795 (Berlin); m 27 May 1762 *WV*, *WC2*—Robert Royce.
ii Ralph, b 8 Feb 1743/4 *WV*, bp Feb 1743 *CC;* m 6 Oct 1768 *CC*—Ruth Hawley.
iii Medad, b 29 Mar 1746 *WV*.
iv Martha, b 18 Apr 1749 *WV*, bp May 1749 *CC*, d after 1794; m Capt. John Jolly.

2 Etheldred, b 1 July 1719 *WV;* m 10 Jan 1748/9 WV—Timothy Hall.

3 Edward, b 11 Mar 1721 *WV*, d 4 July 1792 æ. 72 *CT3;* Census (C) 1-0-1; m 24 Aug 1744 *WV*—

Sarah da. Edward & Abigail (Chauncey) Burroughs.

i Sarah, b 28 Aug 1745 *WV*, bp Sep 1745 *CC.*

ii Elizabeth, b 7 June 1748 *WV*, bp 27 June 1748 *CC.*

iii William, b 18 June 1752 *WV*, bp 11 July 1752 *CC*, d 18 Mar 1826 æ. 74 *CT3;* Census (C) 2-2-6; m 25 Feb 1779 *WV, CC*—Desire da. Parmineas & Rachel (Curtis) Bunnell, b 7 Nov 1750 *WV*, d 24 Sep 1836 æ. 86 *CT3.* Children recorded *CV:* William, b 2 June 1781; Nancy, b 8 Feb 1783.

iv Abigail, b 7 July 1755 *WV*, d 15 Feb 1779 *WV;* m 17 Dec 1777 *WV, CC*—Benjamin Yale.

v Edward, b 21 Apr 1760 *WV;* Census (C) 2-2-2; rem. to Cazenovia, N. Y.; m Rebecca da. William & Elizabeth (Merriam) Hendrick, b 15 Feb 1762 *WV.* FAM. 10.

4 JOEL, b 24 Feb 1723 *WV*, d 27 Dec 1761 *WV;* m 25 Dec 1746 *WV*—Susanna Hotchkiss.

i Etheldred, b 7 Sep 1747 *WV*, bp 18 Oct 1747 *CC;* m 5 Feb 1772 *WV, CC*—Asa Bronson.

ii Amos, b 22 Oct 1749 *WV*, bp 6 Sep (?) 1749 *CC;* Census (C) 2-1-6; m & had Merab & Joel bp 25 Dec 1774 *CC.*

iii Susanna, b 8 Mar 1752 *WV*, bp Apr 1752 *CC;* m 17 Feb 1774 *CC*—Ebenezer Alling Bronson.

iv Joel, b 17 June 1754 *WV*, d 1776 (in Camp) *CC.*

v Levi.

vi Stephen, b 5 Aug 1759 *WV*, d 2 July 1846 æ. 87 *CT3;* Census (C) 1-1-1; m (1) 27 May 1787 Sally da. Joseph & Mehitabel (Burr) Twiss, b 19 Mar 1759 *WV*, d 5 Dec 1803 æ. 45 *CT3;* m (2) Rebecca da. Joshua & Martha (Minor) Ray, wid. ——— Stone, b 19 Aug 1765 *NHV*, d 13 Nov 1836 æ. 72 *CT3.*

5 EPHRAIM, b 23 Apr 1725 *WV;* res. S & Norfolk; m 11 Nov 1747 *WV*—Bathsheba da. Abraham & Sarah Pierson, b 1 Dec 1726 *DV.* Family incomplete.

i Eunice, b 28 Sep 1748 *WV*, bp 20 Nov 1748 *CC;* m 6 Aug 1767 *CC*, 8 Aug *WV*—Bailey Blakeslee.

ii Amasa, bp 26 May 1751 *SC;* m 28 Aug 1771 *WV*—Thankful Andrews. Children bp *NorfolkC:* Mark, 26 Mar 1774; Abraham Pierson, 28 May 1775; Adah, 30 Jan 1780.

iii Jotham, bp 16 June 1754 *SC.*

iv Olive, bp 17 May 1772 *NorfolkC.*

6 AMOS, b 10 Nov 1726 *WV*, d 30 Aug 1748 *WV*, æ. 22 *CT1*, Sep 1748 *CC*.
7 WILLIAM, b 12 Oct 1728 *WV*, d 2 May 1752 æ. 24 *WV*, *CT1*.
8 ELDAD, b 14 Sep 1731 *WV*, bp Sep 1731 *CC*, d 6 July 1779 (k. by enemy at NH) *CC*; m 24 Apr 1755 *WV*—Thankful da. Matthew & Rachel (Clark) Bellamy, b 23 Nov 1734 *WV*, d bef. 1796; Census, Thankful (C) 1-1-2.
i Phebe, b 23 July 1756 *WV*; m Elisha Cole.
ii Thankful, b 6 Oct 1757 *WV*, d 25 May 1760 *WV*.
iii Ann, b 1 Jan 1760 *WV*; m Luman Frisbie.
iv Thankful, b 8 Mar 1762 *WV*.
v Eldad, b 27 Sep 1763 *WV*.
vi Levi, b 28 Sep 1765 *WV*, d soon.
vii Levi, b 19 Mar 1767 *WV*; Census (C) 1-0-1; m Phebe da. James & Hannah (Hough) Scovill, b 16 Apr 1770 *WV*.
viii Thankful, b 12 May 1769 *WV*, bp 24 June 1769 *CC*.
ix Oliver, b 19 Mar 1771 *WV*, bp 20 June 1771 *CC*; m 2 Jan 1793 *CC*—Abigail Lewis.
x Rebecca, b 16 Mar 1773 *WV*, bp 6 June 1773 *CC*; m 2 Jan 1793 *CC*—William Stork.
9 JOSEPH MERRIAM, b 2 Feb 1734 *WV*, bp Mar 1733/4 *CC*, d 21 Mar 1734 *WV*, "child" d Mar 1734 *CC*.
PAGE 2049 10 JOSEPH, b 9 Oct 1735 *WV*, bp Nov 1735 *CC*; m 30 Mar 1758 *WV*—Mary da. William & Mary (Foster) Andrews, b 21 Aug 1740 *WV*.
i Rebecca, b 29 Mar 1760 *WV*.
ii Joseph Merriam, b 10 Oct 1762 *WV*.
iii Eldad.
iv Mary, b 24 Jan 1767.
v Zephaniah, b 26 Feb 1769 *WV*.
11 TIMOTHY, d s. p. 1782.

FAM. 7. EBENEZER & ANN (DOOLITTLE) PARKER:
1 EBENEZER, b 4 June 1762 *WV*, d 11 Dec 1762 *WV*.
2 JABEZ, b 18 July 176[3] *WV*; Census (C) 1-1-2; m 25 Mar 1786 *WV*—Mary Comstock.
3 JEMIMA DOOLITTLE, b 16 Nov 1764 *WV*, d bef. 1804; she had a nat. child, Anna.
4 THOMAS, b 8 Mar 1767 *WV*, bp 20 July 1767 *CC*; Census (C) 1-0-2.
5 EBENEZER, b 7 May 1771 *WV*, bp 28 Apr 1771 *CC*; res. Wd 1804.

FAM. 8. CALEB & DOROTHY (PECK) PARKER:
1 AUGUSTUS, b 10 Sep 1784 *CV*, d 13 May 1794 æ. 10 *CT1*.
2 CALEB, b 30 Jan 1787 *CV*.

3 Paulina, b 30 Dec 1789 *CV*, bp 14 Mar 1790 *CC*, d 13 May 1794 æ. 5 *CT1*.
4 Nancy, b 5 July 1792 *CV*, bp 9 Sep 1792 *CC*.
5 Juliana, b 2 Nov 1794 *CV*, bp 15 Feb 1795 *CC*, d [——] *CT1*.
6 George, bp 28 May 1797 *CC*.
7 Charles, bp 30 Sep 1799 *CC*.

fam. 9. Daniel & Miriam (Curtis) Parker:
1 Ruth, b 3 Feb 1764 *WV*, d 10 Dec 1774 *WV*.
2 Denison, b 28 Sep 176[6] *WV*.
3 Leman, b 21 Dec 1768 *WV*, d 2 Oct 1838 æ. 70 *CT1*; m (1) Ruth ———, who d 21 July 1803 æ. 31 *CT1*; m (2) Lois ———, who d 7 Oct 1861 æ. 79 *CT1*.
4 Lucinda, b 24 July 1771 , d 3 Apr 1808 æ. 36 *CT1*; m 24 Dec 1795 *CV*—Silas Newton.
5 Daniel, b 24 May 1775 *WV*.
6 Ruth, b 27 Dec 1777 *WV*.
7 Betsey, b 16 July 1780 *WV*.

fam. 10. Edward & Rebecca (Hendrick) Parker:
1 Chauncey, b 9 Oct 1786 *CV*.
2 Elizabeth, b 21 Jan 1788 *CV*, d 7 June 1794 æ. 6-5 *CT3*.
3 Oren, b 9 Mar 1790 *CV*, d 4 Aug 1790 *CV*, æ. [—] *CT3*.
4 Oren, b 11 July 1791 *CV*.
5 Edward, b 22 Sep 1793 *CV*, d 8 June 1794 æ. 0-8-14 *CT3*.
6 Edward, b 15 Mar 1795 *CV*.
7 Don Carlos, b 27 Apr 1797 *CV*.
8 Louisa, b 18 June 1799 CV.
9 William Hendrick, b 9 Aug 1801 *CV*.

PARKER. fam. 11. James m 4 Jan 1721/2 *NHV*—Lydia da. Thomas & Abigail (Beardsley) Trowbridge, b 16 Dec 1697 *NHV*.
1 Lydia, b 28 Mar 1723 *NHV*, [d 22 Aug 1776 æ. 53 *NoHC*; m Isaac Thorpe].
2 John, b 26 May 1725 *NHV*, d 18 Feb 1811 æ. 85 *NoHC*; Census (NoH) 1-1-4; m 8 Feb 1749 *NHV*—Mary da. Isaac & Dinah (Luddington) Thorpe, b 9 May 1726 *NHV*, d 31 July 1814 æ. 89-2 *NoHC*.
i John, b 23 Oct 1750 *NHV*, d soon.
ii John, b 29 Nov 1751 *NHV*.
iii Edmund, b 21 Mar 1753 *NHV*, d 18 Mar 1822 æ. 68 *NoHC*; Census (NoH) 1-2-3; m Lydia ——. Children recorded *NoHC*: Clara, bp 21 Nov 1784; Jonathan, bp 21 Nov 1784; Susa, bp 21 Nov 1784; David, bp 16 Mar 1788; Lois, bp 8 Sep 1793; Polly, bp 17 June 1798; Edward, bp 3 Mar 1799.

iv Mary, b 13 Apr 1755 *NHV*, d soon.
v Sarah, bp 28 Dec 1760 *NoHC*.
vi Mary, bp 29 Sep 1762 *NoHC*.
vii Joseph, bp 25 Nov 1764 *NoHC*.
viii Anna, bp 12 June 1768 *NoHC;* m 1 May 1794 *NoHV*—Reuben Batchelor of L.
ix James, bp 24 Feb 1771 *NoHC*, d 2 Dec 1859 æ. 89 *NHV, NHT1;* m Ama Crumb.

3 JAMES, b 10 June 1729 *NHV*.
4 MERCY, b 16 Aug 1731 *NHV*, d 21 Apr 1795 æ. 63 *NoHC*.

Records of this family are meagre. John Parker was appointed guardian of a son of James Parker 1751. Mary Parker of Woodbridge, N. J., wid. of James who by will left his Est. in NH to Jane, conveyed her interest to da. Jane w. Gunning Bedford, 1774 (NH Deeds, 34:177).

PARKER. MISCELLANEOUS. JOSEPH of Saybrook, m 1673 *NHV*—Hannah da. Matthew & Jane (Baker) Gilbert, bp Apr 1653 *NHC1*.......DAVID m 4 Mar 1689/90 *NHV*—Jane Maltby. ......LOWLY m 7 Jan 1773 *WV*—Samuel Ives.......LOIS m 3 Dec 1787 *NoHV*—Enoch Jacobs.......SIMEON, bp 7 Jan 1776; AARON, bp 18 Oct 1778; & Moriah, bp 16 May 1790; names of parents not stated, *CC*.

PARMELEE. Variant, PARMALEE. FAM. 1. ABEL, s. of Job & Betty (Edwards), b 20 May 1703 *GV;* living 1766; m (1) 28 May 1729 *NHV*—Sarah Doolittle; m (2) 23 Dec 1731 *NHV*—Mary da. Joseph & Lydia (Roberts) Beecher, who d 22 May 1766 *NHV*.

(By 1): 1 SARAH, b 4 Apr 1729/30 *NHV*, d soon.
(By 2): 2 SARAH, b 28 Nov 1732 *NHV*, bp 17 Dec 1732 *NHC1*, d 29 Nov 1757 *GV;* m 3 Apr 1753 *NHV, NHC2*—Joseph Joslin.
3 MARY, b 21 Oct 1734 *NHV*, bp 27 Oct 1734 *NHC1*, d soon.
4 JEREMIAH, b 5 Sep 1736 *NHV*, bp 5 Sep 1736 *NHC1;* Census (NH) 2-2-3; m 14 Apr 1768 *NHV, NHC1*—Susanna da. Samuel & Elizabeth (Alcock) Humiston, b 5 May 1741 *NHV*. Family incomplete.
i Mary, b 28 Mar 1769 *NHV;* m 22 Feb 1792 *NHC1*—William Lacy.
ii Sarah Amelia, b 3 Sep 1770 *NHV*.
5 ACHSAH, b 23 Sep 1737 *NHV*, bp 25 Sep 1737 *NHC1;* m (1) 6 Dec 1757 *NHC2*—Nathaniel Hatch; m (2) 10 Jan 1791 *NHx*—Stephen Chatterton.
6 MARY, bp 20 Oct 1739 *NHC1*, d c. 1800; m 7 Feb 1758 *NHV, NHC2*—Edward Meloy.
7 LYDIA, bp 6 Nov 1743 *NHC1*.
8 ELIZABETH, bp 2 July 1749 *NHC1*.

FAM. 2. HEZEKIAH PARMELEE, bro. of Abel (above), b 11 Mar 1700 *GV;* m Sarah Hopson, b 14 Apr 1705 *GV.*

1 SARAH, b 2 June 1732 *GV;* m (1) 2 Nov 1752 *NHV, NHC2*—Joseph Talmadge; m (2) 23 May 1765 *NHC2*—Stephen Ingraham.

2 JEMIMA, b 10 Feb 1734 *GV,* d prob. young.

3 DOROTHY, b 7 Feb 1735 *GV;* m 17 June 1756 *NHC2*—Zebulon Cruttenden of G.

4 HEZEKIAH, b 20 Apr 1737 *GV,* d 3 Dec 1794 æ. 57 *NHT1;* m 6 Dec 1764 *NHV, NHC2*—Elizabeth da. Jedediah & Sarah (Rexford) Cook, bp 17 Feb 1739/40 *NHC1,* d 30 Apr 1816 æ. 77 *NHT1.* Family incomplete.

i Elias, b 26 Sep 1765 *NHV;* m Elizabeth ———, who d 2 Feb 1794 æ. 22 *NHT1.*

ii Sally Betty, b 21 Dec 1766 *NHV,* d 16 May 1793 æ. 27 *NHT1;* m 13 Nov 1783 Marcus Merriman.

iii Hezekiah, b c. 1776, d Mar 1807 æ. 31 *NHT1.*

[*iv* Temperance, b 8 Dec 1778 *F;* m William A. Noyes.]

v Polly, b 5 Mar 1781 *NHT1,* d 13 July 1843 *NHT1;* m 25 Sep 1799 *NHC1*—William A. Thompson (proof, NH Deeds, 51 : 314).

[*vi* Henry, b 9 Dec 1784 *NHT1,* d 12 Dec 1824 *NHT1;* m 26 Apr 1807 *NHx*—Rachel da. George & Azuba Peckham, b 22 Sep 1790 *NHT1,* d 25 Feb 1857 *NHT1,* æ. 67 *NHV.*]

5 BENJAMIN, b 10 Jan 1739 *GV,* d 25 Oct 1760 *F&IW Rolls.*

6 TEMPERANCE, b 25 Nov 1741 *GV,* d prob. young.

7 JEREMIAH, b 10 Feb 1744 *GV,* d 24 Mar 1778 æ. 34 *NHT1;* Rev. soldier; Capt.; m (1) 14 Jan 1767 *NHV, WdC*—Abigail da. Daniel & Abigail (Collins) Russell, b 19 Apr 1744 *NHV,* d 24 Nov 1767 *NHV,* æ. 25 *NHT1;* m (2) 21 Nov 1768 *NHx*——Sarah da. Isaac & Sarah (Todd) Doolittle, b 29 June 1747 *NHV,* d 21 July 1832 æ. 85 *NHT1,* 22 July *(NHC1) NHV;* Census, Sarah (NH) 0-0-2.

(By 1): *i* Abigail, b 3 Nov 1767 *NHV;* m 17 Apr 1791 *NHC1*—Thomas Kilby.

(By 2): *ii* William, bp 19 Jan 1772 *NHx,* d 1 Nov 1794 æ. 24 *NHC1,* 2 Nov æ. 23 *NHT1, NHx.*

iii Sarah, bp 10 Sep 1773 *NHx,* d 10 Sep 1773 *NHx.*

iv Wealthy, b 23 Feb 1775 *NHT1,* bp 15 Apr 1775 *NHx,* d 21 Aug 1863 *NHT1;* m 13 Nov 1794 *NHC1*—Benjamin Beecher.

v Lucy, b 13 Dec 1775 *NHV.*

8 SIMEON, bp 11 May 1746 *NHC1;* m 29 Nov 1773 *NHC1*—Katharine Gordon.

FAM. 3. EBENEZER PARMELEE, b c. 1738, d 3 Feb 1802 æ. 64 *NHT1;* Census (NH) 1-0-4; m Rebecca ———, who d 4 Sep 1809 æ. 64 *NHT1.*

1 REBECCA, b c. 1765, d 14 July 1842 æ. 77 *NHT1;* m 16 Dec 1786 *NHx*—Ambrose Ward.

2 WEALTHY ANN, b c. 1772, d 6 June 1861 æ. 89 *NHT1;* m 11 Sep 1799 *NHx*—Andrew Kidston.

3 RUTH CAROLINE, b [21 Nov 1774(G)], bp 12 Aug 1793 (adult) *NHx,* d 11 Oct 1853 æ. 78-10-20 *NHV;* m 21 May 1796 *NHx*—Elnathan Atwater.

4 PHEBE MARIA, b [May 1777], bp 12 Aug 1793 (adult) *NHx,* d 12 Mar 1874 æ. 96-10 *NHV;* m Abraham Heaton.

PARMELEE. MISCELLANEOUS. REBECCA m 30 May 1723 *WV*—Benjamin Whiting.......HANNAH m 22 Jan 1733 *WV*—Benjamin Hull.......HANNAH m 17 Dec 1735 *WV*—Benjamin Hull.......MARY m 18 Jan 1727 *WV*—Samuel Peck....... SARAH m 10 Sep 1738 *WV*—Asahel Hall.......LUCY m 23 Feb 1742/3 *WV*—Joseph Parker.......WID. RACHEL d 10 June 1780 æ. 76 *NHC1.*

PARRIS. ELIZABETH m 11 Nov 1662 *NHV*—Samuel Van Goodenhousen.

PARROT. MARTIN, b c. 1754 (at Lynn, Mass.), d 30 Apr 1833 æ. 79 *NHT1,* 1 May *(NHC1) NHV;* Census (NH) 1-2-4; m Sarah da. Samuel & Sarah (Dickerman) Horton, b 13 Sep 1751 *NHV,* d 17 Feb 1832 æ. 80 *(NHC2) NHV,* 15 Feb *NHT1.*

1 NAOMI, b c. 1781, bp 24 Sep 1786 *NHC2,* d 15 Nov 1850 æ. 70 *NHV, NHT1;* m Joseph Beecher.

2 SARAH, b c. 1785, bp 24 Sep 1786 *NHC2,* d 5 Dec 1860 æ. 76 *NHT1;* m 18 Dec 1806 *NHC2*—Elam C. Brown.

3 LEVI, bp 15 Feb 1789 *NHC2,* d 10 Jan 1832 æ. 43 *NHT1,* 12 Jan *(NHC2) NHV.*

PARSONS. AARON m 19 Nov 1759 *WV*—Elizabeth da. Caleb & Elizabeth (Plumb) Ives, b 25 Dec 1738 *WV,* d 3 Sep 1783 *WV.*

1 SAMUEL, b 1 Apr 1761 *WV,* d 4 Mar 1848 æ. 89 *MT;* m Martha da. Jared Clark.

2 BETSEY, b 8 Feb 176[5] *WV.*

3 EUNICE, b 19 Aug 1768 *WV,* d soon.

4 ESTHER, b 20 July 1770 *WV.*

5 CALEB, b 11 Feb 1776 *WV.*

6 EUNICE, b 29 July 1778 *WV.*

PATCHEN. MARTIN, b c. 1758, d 6 Mar 1785 æ. 27 *NHC1;* m Jemima ———, who m (2) 3 June 1787 *NHC1*—James Sales. A son d 26 Sep 1782 æ. 1 *NHC1*.......ELIZABETH d 14 Apr 1793 æ. 15 *NHx*.......JAMES, Census (D) 1-0-1.

PATTEN. ROBERT m 10 May 176[—] *WV*—Eunice da. Abner & Mary (Chapman) Curtis, b 2 Apr 1746 *WV*. Children recorded *WV:* Huldah, b 21 May 1765; Margaret, b 26 Oct 1766; & Robert, b 30 Apr 1768.

PATTERSON. EDWARD, b c. 1601, d 31 Oct 1670 *NHV;* m.

1 JOHN, bp Jan 1644 *NHC1,* d young.

2 ELIZABETH, bp 12 July 1644 *NHC1,* d 24 Dec 1727 *NHV;* m Thomas Smith.

PAYNE. Variant, PAINE. FAM. 1. WILLIAM, d 1684; res. NH; m (1) ———; m (2) Mary Edwards, wid. Francis Brown, who d 7 Dec 1693 *NHV*. Family incomplete.

(By 1): 1 MERCY; m 9 June 1664 *NHV*—John Frost.

2 [ELIZABETH; m 11 Oct 1666 *NHV*—Thomas Sanford.]

3 JOHN, b c. 1649, bp (adult) 27 Sep 1685 *NHC1;* testified 1724 æ. 75, d 4 June 1729 *NHV*, 4 July æ. 80 *NHT1;* m (1) 22 Jan 1673 *NHV*—Abigail da. John Brockett, b 10 Mar 1649/50 *NHV;* m (2) Mary da. Richard & Joan (Walker) Little, b 28 July 1669 *NHV*.

(By 1): *i* John, b 15 Oct 1674 *NHV*, bp 27 Dec 1685 *NHC1;* living 1744 incapable, bro. Wm. conservator.

ii Abigail, b 17 Mar 1675/6 *NHV*, bp 27 Dec 1685 *NHC1,* d s. p. after 1746.

iii Elizabeth, b 2 Oct 1677 *NHV*, bp 27 Dec 1685 *NHC1;* m 23 Dec 1703 *NHV*—Joseph Pardee.

iv Josiah, b 21 Sep 1679 *NHV*, d 16 Sep 1680 *NHV*.

v William, b 24 Feb 1680 *NHV* [1680/1], d soon.

vi Samuel, b 27 Feb 1682 *NHV* [1682/3], bp 27 Dec 1685 *NHC1,* d 3 May 1761 æ. c. 80 *NoHC*.

vii Mary, b 18 Sep 1685 *NHV*, bp 27 Dec 1685 *NHC1,* d 6 Oct 1703 *NHV*.

viii James, b 6 Apr 1687 *NHV*, bp 12 June 1687 *NHC1,* d 25 Sep 1751 *NHV;* m 10 Dec 1712 *NHV*—Martha da. Samuel & Hannah (Johnson) Humiston, b 22 Nov 1685 *NHV*, d 17 Nov 1772 æ. 86 *NoHC*. FAM. 2.

ix [Israel, bp 7 Apr 1689 *NHC1,* d soon.]

(By 2): *x* William, b 5 Nov 1695 *NHV*, d 1784; res. Wd; m 21 Sep 1720 *NHV*—Esther da. Thomas & Anna Carnes. FAM. 3.

xi Ann, b 16 Feb 1697 *NHV*, d 24 Feb 1697 *NHV*.

xii Nathaniel, b 4 May 1699 *NHV*, bp May 1699 *NHC1,* d 16 Mar 1766 æ. 61 *NHC1;* m 17 Feb 1725/6 *NHV*—Experience da. Nathaniel & Sarah (Brooks) Thorpe, b 4 Mar 1698 *NHV*, d 7 Sep 1768 æ. 70 *NHC1*. Child: 1 Sarah, b

9 Oct 1733 *NHV*, bp 21 Nov 1733 *NHC1*, d bef. 1791; m 10 June 1750 *NHV*—Stephen Chatterton.

xiii Ann, b 6 Jan 1700 *NHV* [1700/1]; m 28 Dec 1727 *NHV*—Samuel Thorpe.

xiv Hannah, b 2 Apr 1703 *NHV*, d soon.

xv Mary, b 31 Jan 1705 *NHV* [1705/6], d 8 Oct 1727 *NHV*.

xvi Hannah, b 10 Nov 1708 *NHV*, d 17 Sep 1739 *NHV*; m 28 Dec 1726 *NHV*—Daniel Luddington.

xvii Joanna.

xviii Deborah, b 24 June 1712 *NHV*, d 10 Mar 1798 æ. 86 (at Wat, formerly of NH) *ConnJournal*; m 16 Dec 1736 *NHV*—Enos Tuttle.

FAM. 2. JAMES & MARTHA (HUMISTON) PAYNE:

1 JAMES, b 28 Feb 1714 *NHV* [1714/5], bp 29 July 1716 *NHC1*, d 18 Dec 1782 æ. 67 *NoHC*; m 20 Mar 1739/40 *NHV*—Lydia da. Benjamin & Sarah (Elcock) Ford, b 17 Mar 1717/8 *NHV*, d 5 Mar 1782 *NoHC*.

i Benjamin, b 17 Jan 1740/1 *NHV*, d 1777; m Elizabeth da. Israel & Elizabeth (Tallman) Sperry, b 5 May 1744 *NHV*. FAM. 4.

ii James, b 16 Dec 1743 *NHV*.

iii Samuel, b 15 May 1745 *NHV*.

iv Ruth, b 15 May 1745 *NHV*, d 3 Aug 1834 æ. 91 *NoHD*.

v Jesse, b 14 Feb 1748 *NHV*.

vi Lydia, b 4 Mar 1751 *NHV*.

vii Abigail, b 8 Nov 1752 *NHV*.

viii Sarah, b 4 Dec 1754 *NHV*, d 11 Dec 1829 æ. 72 *WolT*; m 2 July 1776 *CC*—Zealous Blakeslee.

ix Lois, b 20 May 1757 *NHV*; m 5 Sep 1774 *NoHC*—Samuel Orell.

2 ABIGAIL, b 11 Dec 1717 *NHV*, d 21 Feb 1717/8 *NHV*.

3 ABIGAIL, b 8 Sep 1719 *NHV*, d 4 June 1725 *NHV*.

4 JOHN, b 6 Feb 1721/2 *NHV*, d 24 Mar 1721/2 *NHV*.

5 MARTHA, b 4 June 1723 *NHV*, bp 7 July 1723 *NHC1*; m 11 Feb 1761 *NoHC*—Elihu Sperry.

6 JOHN, b 29 Dec 1726 *NHV*, drowned 22 July 1762 *NoHC*.

FAM. 3. WILLIAM & ESTHER (CARNES) PAYNE:

1 DAVID, b 24 July 1721 *NHV*, bp 28 Sep 1735 *NHC1*, d s. p. 1746.

2 PHEBE, b 10 May 1724 *NHV*, bp 28 Sep 1735 *NHC1*, d 14 Feb 1768 *NoHC*; m 28 June 1749 *NHV*—Ebenezer Bradley.

3 THOMAS, b 18 May 1726 *NHV*, bp 28 Sep 1735 *NHC1*, d 1769; Sgt.; m Joanna Naughty, niece of David Naughty of G.

i David, b c. 1749, d 18 Mar 1825 æ. 76 *PptT;* m 15 June 1775 *WatV*—Submit da. Gideon & Ann (Brockett) Hotchkiss, b 2 June 1753 *WatV*, d 10 Dec 1844 æ. 91-6 *PptT;* had large family, of whom Clarissa m 21 Mar 1799 *WatV* —Amos Neal; & David Miles & Anna bp 7 Nov 1802 *PptC*.

ii Joseph, b 14 Nov 1751 *F*, d 25 Apr 1805 æ. 54 *WatT1;* m (1) 8 Apr 1773 *WatV*—Huldah da. Gideon & Ann (Brockett) Hotchkiss, b 27 June 1747 *WatV*, d 28 Mar 1774 *F;* m (2) 21 Nov 1774 *WatV*—Esther da. Silas & Lois (Richards) Hotchkiss, b 2 Jan 1750/1 *WatV*, d 23 Feb 1787 æ. 37 *WatT1;* m (3) 26 Sep 1787 *F*—Abigail Alcock, b c. 1764, d 29 Jan 1795 æ. 31 *WatT1;* m (4) 1 June 1795 *F*—Lois da. Abraham & Hannah (Weed) Hotchkiss, b 2 June 1773 *WatV*, d Nov 1842 *F*. FAM. 5.

iii Thomas; m (1) 10 Oct 1779 *NewHartfordC*—Elizabeth [da. William] Payne; m (2) ———.

4 WILLIAM, b 10 Sep 1728 *NHV*, bp 28 Sep 1735 *NHC1*, d 1805; res. New Hartford; m.

i Abraham.

ii Eber.

iii Ezra.

iv Phebe; m Bezewith Hopkins.

v [Elizabeth; m 10 Oct 1779 *New HartfordC*—Thomas Payne.]

5 TIMOTHY, b c. 1731, bp 28 Sep 1735 *NHC1;* m 31 Jan 1760 *WdC*—Deborah Oatman.

6 SAMUEL, b 25 May 1733 (at NH) *F*, bp 28 Sep 1735 *NHC1*, d 21 June 1813 *F;* Census (Panton, Vt.) 4-2-2; m 15 Dec 1757 *Goshen*—Abigail da. Christopher & Abigail (Williams) Grimes [Graham], b 18 July 1735 (at Weth) *F* [N. S.], 7 July 1734 *WethV* [O. S.], d 19 July 1824 *F*.

i Loveana, b 9 Nov 1759 *F*.

ii Zerah, b 26 Sep 1761 *F*, d 1778 (in Rev War).

iii Jared, b 13 Oct 1763 *F*.

iv Huldah, b 20 May 1765 *F*.

v Asenath, b 15 July 1768 *F;* m Ralph Rodolphus Phelps.

vi Chloe, b 26 May 1770 *F*.

vii Amasa, b 28 Apr 1772 *F*.

viii Solomon, b 5 May 1774 *F*.

ix Almon, b 5 May 1774 *F*.
x Olive, b 6 July 1776, d æ. 1 *F*.
xi Zerah, b Sep 1778 *F;* m ——— Bird.

7 Abraham, bp 28 Sep 1735 *NHC1;* Census (Wd) 1-1-2; m 27 May 1762 *WdC*—Lydia da. Stephen & Mercy (Wilmot) Johnson, b 11 Feb 1740 *NHV*. Family incomplete.
i Philemon, b bef. 1765; Census (Wat) 1-1-1; res. Ppt; m (1) c. 1789 Abigail da. Gideon & Jane (Colbreath) Sanford of M; m (2) Roxana Doolittle of Durham.

8 Isaac, bp 8 May 1737 *NHC1*.
9 Esther, bp 18 May 1740 *NHC1;* she had a child b c. 1771; perhaps m Samuel Dorman.
10 Mary, bp 30 May 1742 *NHC1*.
11 Lydia, bp 17 Feb 1744/5 *NHC1*.

FAM. 4. Benjamin & Elizabeth (Sperry) Payne:
1 Elizabeth, bp 6 Mar 1768 *NoHC;* m 9 Aug 1787 *NHC2*—Nicholas Tuttle.
2 Solomon, bp 29 Jan 1769 *NoHC*, d 2 Feb 1769 *NoHC*.
3 Thina, bp 18 Feb 1770 *HC1*.
4 Benjamin.
5 Jared, bp 26 May 1776 *HC1*.

FAM. 5. Joseph & Huldah (Hotchkiss) Payne:
1 Harmon, b 9 Dec 1773 *WatV*, d 3 Nov 1816 æ. 43 *WatT1;* m 21 Dec 1795 *NHC1*—Elizabeth da. Jehiel & Rebecca (Sperry) Osborn, bp 1 Mar 1772 *NHC1*.

FAM. 5. Joseph & Esther (Hotchkiss) Payne:
2 Joseph, b 13 Oct 1776 *WatV*, d 17 Nov 1855 æ. 79-1-4 *PptT;* m (1) 16 Jan 1798 *F*—Ruth da. Hezekiah & Lydia (Hotchkiss) Beecher, b 28 Aug 1777 *CV*, d 3 Aug 1822 æ. 45 *PptT;* m (2) 23 Nov 1823 *F*—Rebecca Barnes, who d 17 Nov 1875 æ. 84 *PptT*.
3 Peter, b 12 June 1779 *WatV;* m ——— Hitchcock.

FAM. 5. Joseph & Abigail (Alcock) Payne:
4 Esther, b 23 July 1788 *F*.
5 Susanna, b 25 June 1790 *F*, d 13 Sep 1804 æ. 14 *WatT1*.
6 Huldah, b 6 Dec 1792 *F*.

FAM. 5. Joseph & Lois (Hotchkiss) Payne:
7 Silas, b 19 Apr 1796 *F*, d [——] *PptT*.
8 Olcott Hotchkiss, b 12 Mar 1798 *F*, d 9 Oct 1841 æ. 44 *PptT;* m Sally da. Benjamin & Esther (Barrett) Beecher, bp 28 Aug 1796 *CC*, d 9 July 1837 æ. 41 *PptT*.
9 Herrick, b 12 June 1802 *F;* m Patty Frost.

10 EDWARD MERRIT, b 21 Oct 1804 *F;* m 19 Sep 1827 *WatV*—Sally Hickox.

PAYNE. MISCELLANEOUS. JOHN of Southold, L. I., m 24 Mar 1691/2 *NHV*—Jemima da. Joseph & Elizabeth (Preston) Alsop, b 10 Feb 1670 *NHV*.......PHILIP m 1 Jan 1679 *NHV*—Mary da. John & Elizabeth (Tapp) Nash, b 13 Dec 1652 *NHV;* had Martha, b 24 Oct 1681 *NHV,* d 15 Nov 1681 *NHV*.......PHILIP d 21 Apr 1733 *WV*.......ABIGAIL m 10 Nov 1704 *WV*—Joseph Andrews.......SARAH m 22 Feb 1710 *WV*—John Yale.

PAYNE. WILLIAM of W, nephew of Shadrack Seegar from R. I.; m Sarah ———, "wid." d 13 Oct 1793 *CC.*

1 [SARAH; m 24 Sep 1775 *WV*—Jesse Sharp.]

2 ALICE, b 3 Sep 1754 *WV,* "Elsa" d 24 Feb 1813 *CC.*

i Sarah, b 28 Dec 1777 *WV.*

3 ELIZABETH, b 14 Feb 1756 *WV.*

i Ebenezer, b 7 Apr 1776 *WV,* d 20 Dec 1777 *WV.*

4 ELEANOR, b 25 Oct 1757 *WV,* d 24 May 1799 æ. 44 *WC2.*

i Eunice, b 11 Apr 1777 *WV.*

5 PRISCILLA, b 25 Dec 1763 *WV.*

6 RACHEL, b 14 Jan 1766 *WV;* m 1787 Isaac Royce.

PEASE. JOHN m 11 June 1713 *NHV*—Abigail da. Joseph & Abigail (Johnson) Lines, b 14 Jan 1692/3 *NHV.*

1 LYDIA, b 16 Dec 1714 *NHV.*

2 JOHN, b 5 May 1717 *NHV,* d 18 Apr 1787 *WdD;* [m Mary ———, Census (Wd) 0-0-2].

i Job.

ii [Dorcas; m 21 Aug 1766 *WdC*—Lemuel Wooding.]

3 ABIGAIL, b 11 Aug 1720 *NHV,* [d 5 Nov 1801 æ. 84 *WdD*].

4 JOSEPH, b 18 Oct 1729 *NHV,* d bef. 1792; res. D; m.

i Isaac, b c. 1773, d 27 Nov 1825 æ. 52 *DT1;* m Sarah da. Jabez & Hannah (Curtis) Thompson, b c. 1782, d 3 Jan 1830 æ. 48 *DT1.* Children: William; Sheldon; John; Betsey, m ——— Beach; Jane, m Daniel B. Van Vosburgh; Sarah Ann; & Catherine.

5 LYDIA, b 18 Oct 1729 *NHV.*

Records of above family are meagre. JEMIMA, b 1 Jan 1757 *OC;* m 25 Sep 1775 *WdC*—Richard Clark.......MARY m Liberty Kimberly.......JOHN, d 1796; m 18 Dec 1775 *NHC1*—Eunice Atwater.

*PECK. The line of Henry begins with FAM. 10; that of Joseph with FAM. 38.

FAM. 1. WILLIAM, b c. 1604, d 14 Oct 1694 æ. 90 *NHV,* æ. 93 *NHT1;* Dea.; m (1) Elizabeth ———, who d 5 Dec 1683 *LymeV;* m (2) Sarah, wid. William Holt, who d 1717.

1 JEREMIAH, d 7 June 1699 *WatV;* Rev.; res. G 1656-60, NH 1660, Saybrook 1661, Newark 1667, Elizabeth 1674, Greenwich 1678, Wat 1689; m 12 Nov 1656 Joanna da. Robert & Margaret (Sheaffe) Kitchell, who d 1711.

i Samuel, b 18 Jan 1659 *GV,* d 28 Apr 1746; res. Greenwich; his s. Nathaniel m 4 Dec 1722 *NHV*—Mary da. Joseph & Elizabeth (Yale) Pardee, b 9 Apr 1700 *NHV.*

ii Ruth, b 3 Apr 1661 *NHV;* m 1 June 1681 *NHV* —Jonathan Atwater.

iii Caleb, b 1663, d young.

iv Anna, b 1665; m 1690 Thomas Stanley.

v Jeremiah, b c. 1667, d 1752; Dea.; m 14 June 1704 *WatV*—Rachel da. Obadiah & Hannah (Barnes) Richards, bp 6 May 1683. FAM. 2.

vi Joshua, b c. 1673, d s. p. 14 Feb 1736.

2 JOHN, b c. 1638, d 1724; m 3 Nov 1664 *NHV*—Mary da. John Moss, bp 11 Apr 1647 *NHC1,* d 16 Nov 1725 *WV.*

i Mary, b 4 Mar 1665/6 *NHV,* d 1 Sep 1710 *WV;* m 13 Feb 1682 *WV*—John Doolittle.

ii Elizabeth, b [1668] *NHV,* d Jan 1668 *NHV.*

iii John, b 16 Mar 1669/70 *NHV,* d 22 Mar 1669/70 *NHV.*

iv John, b Aug 1671 *NHV,* d 28 June 1768 *WV,* æ. 99 *WT1;* Dea.; m (1) 23 May 1694 *WV*—Susanna da. Samuel & Anna (Miles) Street, b 15 June 1675 *WV,* d 2 Apr 1704 æ. 28 *WV;* m (2) 2 July 1706 *WV*—Mary [perhaps da. Joseph & Silence (Brockett)] Bradley, b [6 Dec 1674 *NHV*], d 12 June 1737 *WV;* m (3) 24 May 1738 *WV*—Martha da. John & Martha (Lathrop) Moss, wid. Samuel Stent, b 22 Dec 1684 *WV,* d 25 May 1771 *WV,* æ. 87 *WT1.* FAM. 3.

v Elizabeth, b 29 Dec 1673 *WV,* d c. 1709; m 20 Nov 1690 *WV*—John Merriman.

vi Lydia, b 1 May 1677 *WV.*

vii Ruth, b 20 July 1679 *WV,* d 8 Jan 1738 *WV;* m 3 Feb 1703/4 *WV*—Samuel Lathrop.

viii Abigail, b 16 Mar 1682 *WV,* [d 31 May 1741 æ. [58] *EHT;* m (1) David Austin; m (2) 11 Jan 1715/6 *NHV*—Thomas Alcott].

ix Anna, b 3 Nov 1684 *WV,* d soon.

x Anna, b Mar 1686 *WV,* d 26 Feb 1716 *WV;* m (1) 11 Feb 1703 *WV*—Nathaniel Yale; m (2) 1 Apr 1715 *WV*—Joseph Cole.

3 JOSEPH, bp 17 Jan 1640 *NHC1* [1640/1], d 25 Nov 1718 *LymeV*, æ. 78 *Lyme T*; Dea.; m. Sarah da. William & Margery Parker, b Oct 1637, d 14 Sep 1726 æ. 90 *LymeT*.

i Sarah, b 4 Aug 1663 *LymeV*, d 4 Apr 1730 æ. 67 *NHT1*; m (1) 2 May 1684 *LymeV*—Matthew Gilbert; m (2) 11 July 1717 *NHV*—Joseph Moss.

ii Joseph, b 12 Mar 1667 *LymeV*, d 10 Oct 1667 *LymeV*.

iii Elizabeth, b 9 Sep 1669 *LymeV*.

iv Deborah, b 31 July 1672 *LymeV*, d 16 Dec 1711 *NHV*; m 3 Apr 1694 *NHV*—Daniel Sperry.

v Hannah, b 14 Sep 1674 *LymeV*; m 25 June 1696 *LymeV*—Thomas Anderson.

vi Ruth, b 19 Aug 1676 *LymeV*.

vii Samuel, b 29 July 1678 *LymeV*, d 28 Jan 1734 æ. 56 *LymeT*; m 28 Dec 1699 *LymeV*—Elizabeth Lee, who d 29 Aug 1731 æ. 49 *LymeT*.

viii Joseph, b 20 Mar 1680 *LymeV*, d 12 Aug 1757 æ. 78 *LymeT*; m 3 Oct 1704 *LymeV*—Susanna ———, who d 18 Apr 1760 æ. 78 *LymeT*.

FAM. 4.

4 ELIZABETH, bp 6 May 1643 *NHC1*; m Samuel Andrews.

FAM. 2. JEREMIAH & RACHEL (RICHARDS) PECK:

1 JOANNA, b 12 Apr 1705 *WatV*; m Joseph Galpin.

2 JEREMIAH, b 19 Nov 1706 *WatV*, d 1750; m 14 June 1739/40 *WatV*—Mercy da. Samuel Northrop, b 7 Sep 1715 *MV*; she had a nat. child (in her widowhood), Abel Clark, b 1752 *WatV*; she m (2) 3 Mar 1754 *WatV*—Joseph Luddington.

i Esther, b 3 Nov 1740 *WatV*, d s. p.

ii Ruth, b 28 Nov 1742 *WatV*, d 27 Nov 1767 *PC*.

iii Eunice, b 23 Feb 1744/5 *WatV*; m 20 Oct 1770 *PC*—David Mansfield.

iv Rachel, b 4 Jan 1746/7 *WatV*, d s. p.

v Lemuel, b 27 Nov 1748 *WatV*, d 1758.

3 RACHEL, b 10 May 1709 *WatV*, d 12 June 1785 *OxfC*; m 5 July 1733 *DV*—Ebenezer Riggs.

4 ANNA, b 10 Mar 1713 *WatV*; m 28 Nov 1733 *WatV*—John Guernsey.

5 MARY, b 1 Oct 1715 *WatV*, d s. p. 1753.

6 PHEBE, b 26 Jan 1716/7 *WatV*; m Jonas Weed.

7 RUTH, b 18 Feb 1718/9 *WatV*, d 8 Aug 1750 *WatV*; m 6 Feb 1739/40 *WatV*—Mark Leavenworth.

8 ESTHER, b 22 June 1721 *WatV*.

9 Martha, b 4 May 1725 *WatV;* m 7 July 1742 *WatV*—Caleb Weed.

FAM. 3. John & Susanna (Street) Peck:

1 Mary, b 3 Feb 1695 *WV*, d 26 Feb 1740 æ. 46 *WT1;* m 17 Jan 1723 *WV*—Joshua Atwater.

2 Susanna, b 26 Apr 1697 *WV*, d last Dec 1755 *WatV;* m 20 Aug 1718 *WatV*—Stephen Hopkins.

3 Samuel, b 19 Apr 1704 *WV*, d 20 May 1755 *WV*, æ. 51 *WT1;* Lt.; m 18 Jan 1727 *WV*—Mary Parmelee, who d 14 Oct 1781 æ. [—] *WT1.*

i John, b 5 Nov 1727 *WV*, d 15 Jan 1799 *CC*, æ. 72 *CT1;* Census (C) 2-2-3; m (1) 16 Nov 1752 *WV*—Patience da. John & Mary (Frederick) Doolittle, b 17 July 1732 *WV*, d 14 Sep 1755 *WV;* m (2) 10 July 1755 *WV*—Jerusha da. Peter & Rebecca (Bartholomew) Hall, b c. 1733, d 19 Aug 1817 æ. 85 *CT1.* FAM. 5.

ii Mary, b 24 Mar 1729 *WV*, d 24 Mar 1729 *WV.*

iii Mary, b 1 Feb 1730 *WV*, d 23 Feb 1737 *WV.*

iv Susanna, b 26 Feb 1732 *WV.*

v Samuel, b 4 June 1734 *WV*, d 28 Sep 1815 æ. 82 *WT1;* m 10 Dec 1760 *WV*—Susanna da. Theophilus & Sarah (Dorchester) Doolittle, b 2 Sep 1739 *WV*, d 3 July 1812 æ. 72 *WT1.* FAM. 6.

vi Charles, b 12 Mar 1736 *WV*, d 7 Aug 1780 æ. 45 *WV;* m (1) 13 Apr 1757 *WV*—Hannah da. Benjamin & Hannah (Parmelee) Hull, b 3 May 1739 *WV*, d 10 Apr 1760 *WV;* m (2) 30 Apr 1761 *WV*—Dorothy da. Benjamin & Abiah (Chauncey) Hall, b c. 1739, d 4 Oct 1829 æ. 93 (at C) *Col R.* FAM. 7.

vii Mary, b 25 Sep 1738 *WV*, d 23 May 1745 *WV.*

viii Abigail, b 21 Feb 1740 *WV;* m 12 Apr 1759 *WV*—Tyrannus Collins.

ix Jesse, b 8 May 1741 *WV*, d Sep 1758 æ. 17 *WT1*, 28 Sep *F&IWRolls.*

x Nicholas, b 11 Feb 1744/5 *WV*, d 30 Dec 1820 æ. 77 *WT1;* m 31 Oct 1765 *WV*—Dinah Howd of Goshen. FAM. 8.

xi Jerusha, b 29 July 1747 *WV;* m 18 Nov 176[—] *WV*—Samuel Merwin.

xii Joel, b 23 Apr 1750 *WV*, d 26 May 1842; res. Farm; m (1) 25 Mar 1773 Mary Brooks; m (2) Lucy (Moss?) Merriman; m (3) 28 Jan 1824 *HV*—Mary, wid. Bassett.

FAM. 4. JOSEPH & SUSANNA (———) PECK:

1 JOSEPH, b 13 Aug 1705 *LymeV*, d 1755; m Deborah da. Andrew & Deborah (Joy) Ward, b 17 Jan 1698 *GV*. Family incomplete.

i Augustus, b [3 Feb 1729], d 26 Aug 1729 æ. 0-6-23 *LymeT*.

ii Mary, b c. 1730; m 8 Dec 1748 *NHV*—Jonathan Mix.

iii Joseph, b c. 1734, d 7 Apr 1775 *NHV;* m 27 Feb 1758 *NHV*, 22 Feb *NHC2*—Lydia da. Daniel & Lydia (Porter) Pardee, b 27 Oct 1736 *NHV*, bp (adult) 1 Aug 1773 *NHC2;* she m (2) 1 Jan 1784 *WatV*—Samuel Chatfield. FAM. 9.

iv Augustus, b c. 1736, d (presumably 1757, when will was proved).

2 JASPER, b 3 Feb 1708 *LymeV*, d 21 Oct 1788 æ. 82 *LymeT;* m 24 Nov 1731 Sarah Clark, who d 26 Aug 1785 æ. 80 *LymeT*.

3 SARAH, b 17 Mar 1710 *LymeV;* m ——— Cleveland.

4 HANNAH, b 10 Mar 1712 *LymeV*, d Sep 1801 æ. 91 *DT2;* m 30 Nov 1731 William Clark.

5 DEBORAH; m ——— Hazen.

6 JOHN, b 21 Apr 1716 *LymeV*, d 27 Apr 1785 *LymeV;* m Katherine Lay.

7 LYDIA, d bef. 1757; m Nathaniel Clark.

8 DAVID, b 15 Feb 1721 *LymeV;* m Abigail Southworth.

9 NATHANIEL, b 14 Mar 1723 *LymeV*, d 8 July 1780 æ. 58 *LymeT;* m 27 May 1744 Lucy Mather.

FAM. 5. JOHN & PATIENCE (DOOLITTLE) PECK:

1 SAMUEL, b 10 Apr 1755 *WV*, d 13 Oct 1776 *WV*, *CC*, æ. 21 *CT1*.

FAM. 5. JOHN & JERUSHA (HALL) PECK:

2 PATIENCE, b 28 Mar 1758 *WV*, d 22 Jan 1837 æ. 79 *CT1;* m 6 Dec 1781 *CC*—Samuel Atwater.

3 JERUSHA, b 8 June 1760 *WV;* m 23 Feb 1786 *CC*—Warren Benham.

4 JOHN, b 9 Apr 1762 *WV*, d 12 Mar 1813 æ. 52 *CT1;* Census (C) 1-1-3; m 22 Feb 1786 *CC*—Merab da. Titus & Mary (Atwater) Moss, b 13 Feb 1762 *WV*, d 15 Feb 1835 æ. 73 *CT1*.

5 MARY, b 13 July 1764 *WV*, d 1 Dec 1825 æ. 62 *CT1;* m Jesse Thompson.

6 ASA, b 10 Mar 1767 *WV*, bp 17 May 1767 *CC*, d 9 Aug 1839 æ. 72 *CT1;* Census (C) 1-0-1; m 4 Feb 1789 *CV*, 1790 *CC*—Elizabeth da. Charles Chauncey & Lydia (Holt) Hall, b 10 Aug 176[6] *WV*, d 28 May 1851 æ. 84 *CT1*.

7 Levi, b 21 Feb 1770 *WV*, bp 15 Apr 1770 *CC*, d 16 Feb 1813 æ. 43 *CT1;* m 27 May 1799 *CV*—Esther L. Ives, who d 22 Nov 1847 æ. 71 *CT1.*

8 Roxana, b 1 Feb 1774 *WV*, bp 13 Feb 1774 *CC*, d 15 Jan 1775 *WV*, æ. 0-11 *CT1*, "child" d 14 Jan *CC.*

9 Samuel, b 23 May 1777 *WV*, bp 25 May 1777 *CC*, d 21 Apr 1848 (E. Bloomfield, N. Y.); m (1) 22 Feb 1801 *CV*—Elizabeth da. David & Elizabeth (Doolittle) Brooks, b 17 Dec 1777 *WV*, d 2 Sep 1807 æ. 30 *CT1;* m (2) 1 Feb 1809 Lydia Tyler, who d 17 Jan 1821; m (3) 13 Nov 1822 Harriet Brockett.

FAM. 6. Samuel & Susanna (Doolittle) Peck:

1 Sarah, b 16 Oct 1761 *WV;* m 5 Feb 1786 *WV*—Ebenezer Johnson of G.

2 Lucy, b 26 Feb [1763] *WV.*

3 Theophilus, b 2 Sep [1764] *WV;* Census (Woodstock, N. Y.) 2-1-2; m 3 Feb 1785 *WV*—Mary da. Jeremiah & Mary (Merriman) Hull, b 7 Nov 1760 *WV*, d 29 Mar 1849.

4 Samuel, b 20 July [1766] *WV.*

5 John, b 23 Aug 1768 *WV.*

6 Isaac, b 15 Jan 1771 *WV*, d 24 Feb 1847 æ. 77 *WT1;* m 22 Dec 1799 *WV*—Miriam da. James & Mary (Tyler) Royce, b 14 Nov 1771 *WV.*

7 Patty, b 7 May 1773 *WV;* m Jesse Peck of Farm.

8 Sena, b 8 Jan 1775 *WV.*

9 Amos, b 27 July 1777 *WV;* m 22 Sep 1799 *WV*—Sybil Parker.

FAM. 7. Charles & Hannah (Hull) Peck:

1 [——]el, b 24 Dec 1757 *WV.*

2 Hannah, b 5 Apr 1760 *WV.*

FAM. 7. Charles & Dorothy (Hall) Peck:

3 [———], b 21 Nov 1761 *WV.*

4 Dorothy, b 16 Mar 1763 *WV*, d 12 May 1806 æ. 42 *CT1;* m 1 Nov 1783 *WV*—Caleb Parker.

5 Abigail, b 10 Nov 1764 *WV.*

6 Charles, b 10 July 1766 *WV*, d Mar. 1767 *WV.*

7 Abiah, b 16 Mar 1768 *WV*, d 25 Sep 1773 *WV.*

8 Charles, b 14 Aug 1772 *WV.*

9 Joel, b 15 Oct 1774 *WV*, bp 20 Nov 1774 *CC.*

10 Eunice, b 5 Oct 1776 *WV*, bp 5 Sep 1777 *CC.*

11 John, b 28 Sep 1780 *WV*, bp 26 Nov 1780 *CC.*

FAM. 8. Nicholas & Dinah (Howd) Peck:

1 Olive, b 29 Oct 1766 *WV*, d 8 Aug 1770 *WV.*

2 Jesse Street, b 15 Apr 1769 *WV*, d 3 Mar 1845 (Buffalo, N. Y.); m Sally Barnes.

3 MILES, b 15 May 1771 *WV*, d 27 Mar 1832; m Eunice Hall.
4 OLIVE, b 9 Aug 1773 *WV*, d 19 Oct 1854 (Pittsburgh, Pa.); m Billious Ball Newton.

FAM. 9. JOSEPH & LYDIA (PARDEE) PECK (all but youngest bp 1 Aug 1773 *NHC2*):
1 JOSEPH, b 4 Feb 1759 *NHV*, d s. p.
2 AUGUSTUS, b 9 Dec 1760 *NHV*, d s. p. 3 June 1812 æ. 52 *MyT*; m (1) Lucy da. Timothy & Mary (Baldwin) Porter, b 8 June 1753 *WatV*; m (2) Elizabeth ———, who d 17 Feb 1838 æ. 64 *MyT*.
3 WARD, b 7 Oct 1762 *NHV*, d 8 Apr 1842; m 22 Jan 1784 *WatV*—Dorcas da. James & Lucy (Bronson) Porter, b 10 June 1766 *WatV*, d 12 May 1847.
4 MERCY, b 22 Apr 1765 *NHV*.
5 DEBORAH, b 31 Aug 1767 *NHV*, d 8 Sep 1775 *NHV*.
6 LYDIA, b 15 Feb 1770 *NHV*.
7 SARAH, b 3 Jan 1773 *NHV*.
8 PATIENCE, b 25 Feb 1775 *NHV*; m Herman Byington of Camden, N. Y.

PECK. FAM. 10. HENRY, d 1651; res. NH; m Joan ———; she m (2) Andrew Low.
1 ELEAZER, bp 12 Mar 1643 *NHC1*; m (1) 31 Oct 1671 *NHV*—Mary da. William & Ann (Wilmot) Bunnell, b 4 May 1650 *NHV*, d 20 July 1724 *WV*; m (2) 31 Oct 1726 WV—Elizabeth da. Timothy Ford, wid. Joshua Culver.
(By 1): *i* Samuel, b 3 Mar 1672/3 *WV*, d 12 Mar 1672/3 *WV*.
ii Abigail, b 6 Mar 1673/4 *WV*; m James Alling.
iii Mary, b 14 July 1677 *WV*, d 1 Jan 1757 *WV*; m William Abernathy.
iv Martha, b 2 July 1679 *WV*.
v Stephen, b 4 Aug 1681 *WV*; m (1) 10 Apr 1706 *WV*—Susanna da. Joseph Collier; m (2) 8 May 1727 *WV*—Margery da. John & Abigail (Merriman) Hitchcock, wid. Joseph Munson, b 9 Sep 1681 *WV*. FAM. 11.
vi Eleazer, b 19 Feb 1683 *WV*, d June 1685 *WV*.
vii Eleazer, res. W & S; m (1) Ann da. Bartholomew & Hannah Foster; m (2) 29 Nov 1737 *WC2*—Ann Andrews, wid. Amos Camp of Durham. FAM. 12.
viii Nathaniel, d 26 Mar 1752 *WV*; m 10 Jan 1712 *WV*—Sarah Hopkins, wid. Ichabod Cole of Mid, bp 21 Aug 1687 *HartfordC*, d 14 Feb 1780 æ. 93 *WV*; she was of Courtland, N. Y., 1764. FAM. 13.

ix Elizabeth, d 8 June 1740 *WV;* m (1) 21 Nov 1711 *WV*—Samuel Abernathy; m (2) 14 Dec 1726 *WV*—William Hough.

2 JOSEPH, bp 5 Sep 1647 *NHC1,* d 15 Apr 1720 *NHV;* m 28 Nov 1672 *NHV*—Sarah da. Roger & Mary (Nash) Alling, bp 12 Oct 1649 *NHC1,* d 1743.

i Sarah, b 11 Sep 1673 *NHV,* bp 13 Dec 1685 *NHC1,* d 2 Oct 1724 *NHV;* m 31 Mar 1698 *NHV*—Thomas Gilbert.

ii Joseph, b 9 Oct 1675 *NHV,* bp 13 Dec 1685 *NHC1,* d 9 Jan 1746 [1746/7] æ. 71-3 *Newark, N.J.,T;* m Lydia da. Edward Ball of Bd & Newark, who d 1742; descendants in N. J.

iii Samuel, b 29 Dec 1677 *NHV,* bp 13 Dec 1685 *NHC1,* d 1739; Sgt.; m 30 Dec 1703 *NHV*—Abigail da. Nathaniel & Elizabeth (Moss) Hitchcock, b 26 Oct 1680 *NHV.* FAM. 14.

iv James, b 17 Feb 1679 *NHV,* bp 13 Dec 1685 *NHC1,* d 1760 *NHC1;* m (1) 14 Feb 1705/6 *NHV*—Abigail da. John & Hannah (Bishop) Morris, b 22 Aug 1683 *NHV;* m (2) 10 July 1729 *NHV*—Hannah da. John & Abigail (Alsop) Rowe, wid. John Leek, b 11 Feb 1691 *NHV,* d 16 May 1770 æ. 78 *NHC1.* FAM. 15.

v John, b 6 Oct 1682 *NHV,* bp 13 Dec 1685 *NHC1;* m 30 Jan 1706/7 *NHV*—Esther da. Joseph & Esther (Winston) Morris, b 3 Sep 1684 *NHV,* d 19 Aug 1751 æ. 65 *NHT1;* she m (2) 14 Feb 1716/7 *NHV*—John Mix; m (3) Joseph Smith. FAM. 16.

vi Eliphalet, b 12 May 1685 *NHV,* d s. p.

vii Abigail, b 2 May 1686 *NHV,* bp 27 June 1686 *NHC1,* d 21 Oct 1782 æ. 97 *NHC1;* m Robert Talmadge.

viii Mary, b 6 Oct 1689 *NHV,* bp 6 Oct 1689 *NHC1,* d 22 Jan 1747/8 *WV;* m (1) Stephen Rowe; m (2) 9 June 1729 *NHV*—Timothy Tuttle.

ix Ebenezer, b 2 May 1693 *NHV,* bp 23 Apr(?) 1693 *NHC1,* d s. p.

3 BENJAMIN, bp 5 Sep 1647 *NHC1,* d Mar 1730; m 29 Mar 1670 *NHV*—Mary da. Richard & Dennis Sperry, b 14 Mar 1650 *NHV,* bp (adult) 25 Sep 1687 *NHC1.*

PAGE 2049

i Benjamin, b 4 Jan 1670 *NHV* [1670/1], d 3 Mar 1722; res. Norwich; m 2 May 1700 *DV*—Mary da. John & Elizabeth (Post) Sperry, b 16 Jan 1679 *NHV,* d 31 May 1742. FAM. 17.

ii Mary, b 23 Sep 1672 *NHV*, bp 12 Sep 1686 *NHC1*, d after 1749; m (1) John Chatterton; m (2) 17 Apr 1709 *FarmV*—John Bronson.

iii John, b c. 1674/5, bp 12 Sep 1686 *NHC1*.

iv Joseph, b 26 Feb 1676 *NHV* [1676/7], bp 12 Sep 1686 *NHC1*, d s. p. c. 1704.

v Esther, b 1679 *NHV*, bp 12 Sep 1686 *NHC1*; m Eliphalet Bristol.

vi Ebenezer, b 24 Apr 1681 *NHV*, d soon.

vii Lydia, b c. 1683, bp 12 Sep 1686 *NHC1*; m 7 Feb 1704/5 *Springfield, Mass.*—Solomon Ferry; res. Danbury.

viii Ebenezer, b 5 Jan 1684 *NHV*, bp 12 Sep 1686 *NHC1*, d 20 Mar 1768 æ. 84 *WdT1*; m (1) 10 May 1709 *NHV*—Hannah da. Joshua & Hannah (Tuttle) Hotchkiss, b c. 1686, d 3 Aug 1723 *NHV*; m (2) 8 Dec 1724 *NHV*—Elizabeth da. John & Sarah (Clark) Wilmot, b 20 Apr 1703 *NHV*, d 9 Sep 1785. FAM. 18.

ix Desire, b 26 Aug 1687 *NHV*, bp 25 Sep 1687 *NHC1*, d 1724 *WV*; m 10 May 1709 *NHV*—Nathaniel Bunnell.

x Mehitabel, bp 6 Oct 1689 *NHC1*; m Ebenezer Stevens of Danbury.

4 ELIZABETH, b 16 Mar 1649 *NHV* [1649/50], bp 24 Mar 1650 *NHC1*, d bef. 1732; m 4 Dec 1672 *NHV*—John Hotchkiss.

FAM. 11. STEPHEN & SUSANNA (COLLIER) PECK:

1 JONATHAN, b 14 Sep 1706 *WV*, d 18 Oct 1752 *WV*, 6 Oct æ. 46 *WT1*; Sgt.; m 31 Jan 1733 *WV*—Thankful da. Joseph & Hope (Cook) Benham, b 14 Feb 1716 *WV*, d 23 May 1790 æ. 75 *NoBT1*; she m (2) 23 Jan 1758 *WV*, *NoBC2*—Merriman Munson.

i Sarah, b 16 Nov 1733 *WV*, d bef. 1759; m 14 June 1753 *WV*—Solomon Munson.

ii Susanna, b 8 Nov 1735 *WV*, d 12 Dec 1779 æ. 44 *WT1*; m 24 June 1754 *WV*—Benjamin Hall.

iii Eunice, b 13 Jan 1739 *WV*, d 2 Oct 1752 æ. 14 *WT1*, 12 Oct *WV*.

iv Martha, b 2 Feb 1741 *WV*; m 1 Jan 1761 *BdV*, *NoBC2*—Phineas Baldwin.

v Thankful, b 15 Aug 1743 *WV*; m 17 Dec 1761 *NoBC2*—Wilkinson Howd.

vi Ruth, b 22 Dec 1745 *WV*, d 28 Dec 1787 æ. 42 *NoBT1*; m 28 May 1767 *NoBC2*—Rufus Hoadley.

vii Samuel, b Apr 1752 *WV*, d 20 Nov 1824; rem. to Salisbury, N. Y.; m 10 June 1772 *WV*—Anna da. Peter & Rebecca (Bartholomew) Hall, b 30 May 1753 *WV*. Children: 1 Eunice, b 26 Sep 1772 *WV;* 2 Jonathan, b 16 May 1774 *WV;* 3 Elihu, b 6 May 1776 *WV;* 4 Ann, b 5 Sep 1780 *WV*.

2 ABEL, b 25 Feb 1709 WV, d 18 June 1771 *WV;* m Lydia da. James & Esther (Preston) Benham, b 9 Jan 1717 *WV*.

i Peter, b 27 May 1739 *WV*, d 17 Dec 1790 *WV;* m 11 Oct 1767 *WV*—Esther da. Benjamin & Abigail (Smith) Smith, b c. 1746. FAM. 19.

ii James, b 25 Nov 1742 *WV;* Capt.; m 21 June 176[3] *WV*—Elizabeth [da. Abel & Ruth (Johnson)] Hall, b [12 Feb 1743/4 *WV*]. FAM. 20.

iii Esther, b 28 Sep 1744 *WV;* m 25 Sep 1765 *WV*—Ambrose Cook.

iv Abel, b 29 Dec 1749 *WV*, d s. p. bef. 1773.

3 STEPHEN, b 20 Mar 1711 *WV*, d 26 Apr 1769 *WV;* m 28 Mar 1734 *WV*—Desire da. Joseph & Margery (Hitchcock) Munson, b Feb 1707/8 *WV*, d 8 Nov 1791 *WV*.

i Dan, b 3 Dec 1734 *WV*, d 2 Jan 1736 *WV*.

ii Dan, b c. 1736, d s. p. 27 Sep 1807 *WV*, æ. 72 *WT1;* m 28 July 1768 *WV*—Abigail da. Joshua & Hannah (Hall) Hall, b 25 Apr 1745 *WV*, d 31 Aug 1814 æ. 60 *WT1*.

iii Titus, b 2 Jan 1738 *WV*, d 22 Sep 1778 *WV*.

iv Collier, b 3 Nov 1739 *WV*, d s. p.

v Abner, b 8 Mar 1741/2 *WV;* m Sarah [da. Titus & Sarah (Merriman) Cook, b 14 Nov 1753 *WV*]. FAM. 21.

vi Stephen, b 18 Mar 1744 *WV*, d 28 Mar 1812 æ. 68 (on his birthday) *WV;* m (1) 3 Mar 1774 *WV*—Sarah da. Abraham & Barbara (Johnson) Ives, who d 18 Sep 1776 *WV;* m (2) 25 Feb 1778 *WV*—Margery da. Waitstill & Jemima (Munson) Parker, wid. Eliada Parker, b 5 Feb 1749/50 *WV;* m (3) Lois da. Joseph & Em (Curtis) Benham, wid. Isaac Beecher, b 13 July 1750 *WV*, d 15 May 1825 æ. 75 *CT1;* she m (3) Giles Hall. FAM. 22.

vii Desire, b 31 Jan 1746 *WV;* m Ashbel Hopson.

viii Phebe, b 30 Apr 1749 *WV*, d s. p. after 1793.

4 JOHN, b 16 Sep 1713 *WV*, d 21 Jan 1754 *WV;* m 18 Mar 1739 *WV*—Mehitabel da. John & Sarah (Thompson) Mix, wid. Caleb Atwater, b 19 Aug 1706 *NHV*.
i Susanna, b 18 Oct 1739 *WV*.
ii Elizabeth, b 9 May 1741 *WV*.
iii Giles, b 29 Apr 1743 *WV*, d 29 Dec 1745 *WV*.
5 SUSANNA, b 3 Sep 1717 *WV*, d 17 Dec 1770 *WV;* m 29 Aug 1738 *WV*—Edward Collins.

FAM. 12. ELEAZER & ANN (FOSTER) PECK (first 6 bp 9 Feb 1728/9 *SC*):
1 HANNAH, b 20 Jan 1717 *WV;* m 26 Apr 1737 James Bronson.
2 MEHITABEL, b 19 July 1719 *WV*.
3 ELIAKIM, b 24 Oct 1721 *WV*, d 7 May 1801 æ. 79 *SC;* m 10 Nov 1748 *SC*—Abigail Woodruff, "wid. of Eliakim" d 28 Sep 1809 æ. 80 *SC*.
4 BENAJAH, b 8 or 22 Feb 1724 *WV*, d 11 Jan 1777 *PC;* res. Roxbury; m Lydia da. Thomas & Christian Fenn; they had a child bp 5 Oct 1760 *RoxburyC* & Samuel bp 26 June 1763 *RoxburyC*.
5 GIDEON, d 14 June 1781 *HarwintonT;* m (1) 5 Nov 1744 *SC*—Mary da. John & Mary (Peck) Bronson, b 20 Jan 1711/2 *FarmV*, d 1 Jan 1751 *SC;* m (2) 12 Aug 1752 *SC*—Esther ———.
(By 1): *i* Ruth, bp 15 Sep 1745 *SC*, "eldest da." d 2 May 1765 *WtnD*.
ii Mary, bp 8 Mar 1746/7 *SC;* m 20 July 1769 *WatV*—John Foote.
iii Ann, bp 23 May 1748 *SC*.
iv Solomon, bp 3 Feb 1750/1 *SC*, d young.
(By 2): *v* Solomon, b 17 Sep 1753 *WatV;* Census (Harwinton) 1-1-3.
vi Annis, b 1 Nov 1755 *WatV*.
vii Sarah, b 24 Mar 1758 *WatV*.
viii Eunice, b 15 July 1760 *WatV*.
ix Gideon, b 25 Feb 1763 *WatV;* Census (Harwinton) 1-3-1.
x Olive, b 5 Nov 1764 *WatV*.
xi Samuel, b 5 Jan 1767 *WatV*.
xii Lorene, b 5 Mar 1769 *WatV*.
6 CHARLES, b 8 Nov 1727.
7 ELEAZER, b 2 July 1730, bp 9 Aug 1730 *SC;* m 6 Dec 1755 Elizabeth Woodruff.
8 ZEBULON, b 9 Dec 1733, bp 10 Feb 1734 *SC*.

FAM. 13. NATHANIEL & SARAH (HOPKINS) PECK:
1 SARAH, b 21 Mar 1713 *WV*, d 22 Sep 1775 æ. 63; m 7 Nov 1728 *WV*—Abel Munson.

2 JOSEPH, b 19 July 1716 *WV;* rem. to Saybrook; m 2 Feb 1737 *WV*—Lydia da. Samuel & Hannah (Thompson) Thorpe, b 31 Oct 1714 *WV*.

3 PHINEAS, b 4 Aug 1719 *WV;* rem. to Bateman's Precinct, N. Y.; m (1) 25 Dec 1744 *WV*—Phebe da. Waitstill & Phebe (Merriman) Munson, b 14 June 1726 *WV*, d 25 Jan 1745/6 *WV*~~; m (2)~~ 4 June 1747 *WV*—Leah da. David & Rebecca (Wilson) Cook, bp 21 Mar 1726 *CC*.

(By 1): *i* Lydia, b 13 Oct 1745 *WV*, d 20 Dec 1745 *WV*.

(By 2): *ii* Susanna, b 28 Sep 1748 *WV*, d Nov 1750 *WV*.

iii Rebecca, b 4 Mar 1751 *WV*.

iv Nathaniel, b 2 May 1753 *WV*.

v Phineas C., b 9 Jan 1756 *WV*, d 15 Aug 1809 æ. 56 *PptT;* Census (C) 1-3-3; m Elizabeth Doolittle. A child, Benjamin Doolittle, b 12 Jan 1777 *WV*.

vi Barnabas, b 25 Sep 1758 *WV*.

vii Joseph, b 4 Oct 1761 *WV*.

viii Lydia, b 2 June 1764 *WV*.

ix Daniel, b 28 June 1769 *WV*.

4 BARNABAS, b 2 Dec 1722 *WV*, d 20 July 1745 *WV*.

5 MARY, b 1 June 1725 *WV*, d 4 Jan 1749 *WV;* m 10 Nov 1743 *WV*—John Thorpe.

6 DANIEL, b 30 Apr 1730 *WV*, d 25 or 26 July 1751 *WV*.

FAM. 14. SAMUEL & ABIGAIL (HITCHCOCK) PECK:

1 SARAH, b 21 Mar 1705 *NHV*, d bef. 1758; m 20 Apr 1727 *NHV*—Anthony Thompson.

2 SAMUEL, b 9 Oct 1708 *NHV*, d after 1784; rem. to Wtn; m (1) 26 Jan 1731/2 *NHV*—Elizabeth da. Daniel & Deborah (Peck) Sperry, b c. 1707, d 27 Sep 1774 æ. 68 *WatV;* m (2) 5 Jan 1775 *PC*—Mary, wid. Timothy Crosby.

i Joseph, b 26 Feb 1732/3 *NHV*, bp 29 Apr 1733 *NHC1*, prob. d s. p.

ii Elizabeth, bp 30 Mar 1735 *NHC1;* m 27 Feb 1754 *WatV*—Ambrose Dutton.

iii Thankful, bp 11 July 1737 *NHC1*, d 15 Dec 1785 *WatV;* m 25 Sep 1755 *WatV*—Abner Blakeslee.

iv Sarah; m 11 Apr 1759 *WatV*—Titus Barnes.

v Deborah; m 23 Apr 1766 *WatV*—Reuel Upson.

3 TIMOTHY, b 6 Apr 1711 *NHV*, d 2 Jan 1784 æ. 73 *BT1;* Dea.; m 23 Sep 1736 *NHV*—Lydia da. Joseph & Hannah (Bradley) Lines, b c. 1714, d 1796.

i Timothy, b 5 July 1737 *NHV*, bp 14 Aug 1737 *NHC1*, d 5 Sep 1807 æ. 71 *BT4;* loyalist; was in N. Y. 1778; m Anna da. Joseph & Esther

(Ives) Smith, b 10 May 1735 *WV*, d 3 Oct 1812 æ. 77 *BT4*. Child: Timothy. Others?

ii Lydia, b 13 Mar 1738/9 *NHV*, bp 15 Apr 1739 *NHC1*, d c. 1804; m 23 Dec 1762 *NHV*, *WdC*—Samuel Hotchkiss.

iii Penina, b 5 Aug 1740 *NHV*, bp 14 Sep 1740 *NHC1;* m (1) 16 Aug 1764 *NHV*—Charles Todd; m (2) 5 July 1775 *WatV*—David Hotchkiss.

iv Titus, b 7 Apr 1742 *NHV*, bp 6 June 1742 *NHC1*, d 20 Oct 1776 æ. 35 *BT1;* Lt.; m Rebecca da. Ebenezer & Rebecca (Thomas) Hitchcock; she m (2) David Sperry. FAM. 23.

v Mary, bp 25 Dec 1743 *WdC*, d c. 1769; m 22 Dec 1767 *WdC*—Timothy White.

vi Roger, bp 8 June 1746 *WdC*, d 17 Sep 1808 æ. 62 *WatT1;* m (1) 19 May 1773 *WdC*—Philena da. Stephen & Elizabeth (Carrington) Hine, b 30 July 1749; [m (2) Mary Atwater]. FAM. 24.

vii Martha, "Mary" bp 10 Apr 1748 *WdC*, d c. 1815; m Joel Hotchkiss.

viii Samuel, "child" bp 11 Feb 1753 *WdC*, d 9 Aug 1795 æ. 43 *BT1;* Census (Wd) 1-5-3; m Mary da. Samuel & Mary (Nettleton) Beach, b 18 Oct 1754 *MV*, d 19 May 1847 *Homer, N.Y.,T;* she m (2) Josiah Heath.

ix Caleb; m (1) Amia ———, who d 7 Dec 1795 æ. 35 *BristolV;* m (2) Hannah da. Samuel & Mary (Nettleton) Beach, b 27 July 1771 *MV*. Children rec. *BristolV:* 1 Sally, b 1 Apr 1782 (at B); 2 Miles, b 17 June 1784 (at B); 3 Lanson, b 1 May 1787; 4 Annah, b 14 Sep 1789; m Leverett Hungerford; 5 Amia, b 28 Feb 1792.

4 AMOS, b 29 Jan 1712 *NHV* [1712/3], d 28 Jan 1783 æ. 69 *HT3;* Dea.; m 19 Jan 1741/2 *NHV*—Elizabeth da. Thomas & Mary (Winston) Leek, b Jan 1719 *NHV*, d 24 Apr 1791 æ. 72 *HT3*.

i Abigail, b 30 Oct 1742 *NHV*, d 24 Mar 1817 æ. 74 *CT2;* m 16 Mar 1765 *WV*—Bela Andrews.

ii Elizabeth, b 22 June 1744 *NHV*, d 26 Dec 1833 æ. 91 *HT3;* m 30 Oct 1765 *NoHC*—Joel Todd.

iii Sarah, b 21 Feb 1745/6 *NHV*, d soon.

iv Sarah, b 30 Sep 1747 *NHV*, bp 11 June 1749 *NHC2*, d 10 Jan 1784 æ. 38 *HT3;* m 3 Dec 1766 *NHV*—David Sperry.

v Mary, bp (with Sarah) 11 June 1749 *NHC2,* d 29 Oct 1832 æ. 85 *HT1;* m 3 Dec 1777 *NHV, NHC1*—Stephen Goodyear.

vi Amos, b 29 July 1749 *NHV,* d 23 Oct 1838 *HT3;* Census (H) 3-0-4; m 2 Jan 1772 *NHV*—Lois da. Wait & Joanna (Beach) Chatterton, b 19 Jan 1752 *NHV,* d 22 Sep 1852 æ. 100-8-6 *HT3.* FAM. 25.

vii Phebe, b 13 May 1751 *NHV;* m Lemuel Alling.

viii Moses, b 13 Mar 1753 *NHV,* bp 13 May 1753 *NHC2,* d c. 1837; Census (H) 1-1-4; m Abigail Esther da. Amos & Abigail (Holt) Johnson, wid. Charles Tuttle, b 16 Nov 1749 *WV.* FAM. 26.

ix Elijah, b 12 Apr 1755 *NHV,* bp 15 June 1755 *NHC2;* Census (C) 1-3-2; m 10 Apr 1781 *CC*—Sarah da. Jabez & Esther (Beach) Bradley, b 29 Nov 1760 *NHV.* FAM. 27.

x Hannah, b 20 May 1757 *NHV,* bp 24 July 1757 *NHC2,* d 1 June 1824 æ. 67 *HT3;* m Eli Alling.

xi Jesse, b 29 Sep 1760 *NHV,* bp 2 Nov 1760 *NHC2,* d 30 Dec 1805 æ. 47 *BT4;* Census (H) 1-1-1; m Huldah [? da. Jonah & Rachel Atwater, b 20 Oct 1768], d 21 Apr 1830 æ. 61 *NHT1,* 20 Apr (formerly of Wd) *ColR,* "Rachel" d 20 Apr æ. 61 *NHV.* FAM. 28.

xii Joseph, b 5 July 1762 *NHV,* d 9 Aug 1845 æ. 83 *HT3;* Census (H) 1-0-3; m 2 Oct 1784 *HC1*—Olive da. Wait & Joanna (Beach) Chatterton, b c. 1762, d 26 July 1839 æ. 77 *HT3.* FAM. 29.

5 ELIZABETH, b 27 Oct 1714 *NHV.*

6 MARY, b 2 Feb 1715 *NHV* [1715/6], bp 8 July 1716 *NHC1.*

7 MOSES, b 19 Nov 1717 *NHV,* bp c. Nov 1717 *NHC1,* d c. 1800; m 4 July 1743 *BostonV*—Elizabeth Williston. Children recorded *BostonV:* 1 Abigail, b 17 Oct 1744; 2 Sarah, b 11 Mar 1749; 3 Elijah, b 24 Nov 1752; 4 Samuel, b 30 Oct 1758; 5 Elizabeth, b 24 Jan 1760; 6 Hannah, b 25 July 1761; 7 Moses, b 4 July 1766; 8 Samuel, b 21 Sep 1768; 9 Elizabeth, b 24 June 1771.

8 ABIGAIL, b 2 Nov 1719 *NHV,* bp Nov 1719 *NHC1.*

9 ROGER, b 13 June 1721 *NHV,* bp June 1721 *NHC1;* disappeared c. 1742.

FAM. 15. JAMES & ABIGAIL (MORRIS) PECK:

1 EBENEZER, b 20 Jan 1706/7 *NHV,* d s. p.

2 JAMES, b 11 Aug 1708 *NHV,* d 2 Mar 1794 æ. 86 *NHT1, NHC1;* Capt.; Census (NH) 1-0-1; m (1)

18 Feb 1730/1 *NHV*—Mary da. John & Abiah (Bassett) Hitchcock, b 16 Mar 1711/2 *NHV;* m (2) c. 1760 Rachel da. Nathaniel & Sarah (Wilmot) Sperry, wid. David Johnson, b 9 Feb 1722/3 *NHV,* d c. 1775; m (3) 16 July 1776 *WdC*—Abigail da. Samuel & Abigail (Atwater) Bishop, wid. Joseph Hitchcock, b 13 Jan 1726/7 *NHV,* d 6 Aug 1793 æ. 67 *NHC1.*

(By 1): *i* Eunice, b 14 Feb 1731/2 *NHV,* bp 20 Feb 1731/2 *NHC1,* d 13 Nov 1765 æ. 34 *NHC1;* m 10 Aug 1749 *NHV*—Michael Todd.

ii Ebenezer, b 16 Jan 1733/4 *NHV,* bp 20 Jan 1733/4 *NHC1,* d young.

iii William, b 12 July 1736 *NHV,* bp 18 July 1736 *NHC1,* d 1784; Capt.; m 1 Oct 1761 *NHC1*—Elizabeth da. John & Abiah (Macumber) Hall, b 9 Oct 1738 *NHV.* Children: 1 Eunice; 2 Son, b [31 July 1776], d 1 Aug 1776 æ. 0-0-1 *NHC1.*

iv Abiah, b 22 Nov 1738 *NHV,* bp 26 Nov 1738 *NHC1.*

v Thankful, b 6/9 Apr 1741 *NHV,* bp 19 Apr 1741 *NHC1,* d 28 July 1768 æ. 28 *NHT1;* m Jacob Pinto.

vi James, b 14 Jan 1742/3 *NHV,* bp 20 Mar 1742/3 *NHC1;* Capt.; res. H & Canaan; m 30 Oct 1783 *NHC2*—Sybil da. Joel & Thankful (Potter) Ford, b 22 May 1764 *NHV,* d 8 Jan 1842 æ. 78 *HT5.* Children: 1 William, b c. 1787, d 2 July 1845 æ. 58 *HT5;* res. Canaan 1824. 2 Sheldon.

vii Mary, b 25 Feb 1744/5 *NHV,* bp Feb 1744/5 *NHC1.*

viii Hannah, b 15 Feb 1746/7 *NHV,* bp 1 Mar 1746/7 *NHC1,* d 13 May 1797 æ. 50 *NHT1;* m 15 Sep 1766 *NHV, EHC*—Israel Bishop.

ix Abigail, b 6 Mar 1748/9 *NHV,* bp 12 Mar 1748/9 *NHC1,* d 9 Mar 1798 æ. 49 *NHT1;* m Jacob Pinto.

x Ebenezer, b 14 Jan 1750/1 *NHV,* bp 27 Jan 1750/1 *NHC1,* d 8 Apr 1818; Capt.; Census (NH) 4-2-2; m 20 Nov 1790 *NHC1*—Rebecca da. Stephen & Eunice (Tuttle) Dickerman, bp 29 Dec 1765 *NHC1,* d 28 Oct 1846 æ. 81 *NHV.* FAM. 30.

(By 2): *xi* David, bp 7 Nov 1762 *NHC1,* d 3 May 1841 æ. 80 *OxfV;* m 3 July 1786 *NHC1*—Anna da. Lemuel & Molly (Beecher) Humphreville. Children (incomplete): 1 Child, d 13 Dec 1786

WHD. 2 Anna Maria, b c. 1797, d 12 Feb 1820 æ. 23 *Salem x*, 1820 æ. 22 *OxfV*.

3 Hannah, b 10 Aug 1710 *NHV;* m 29 Oct 1730 *NHV*—James Heaton.

4 Abigail, b 1 July 1713 *NHV;* m Thomas Potter.

5 John, b 30 June 1718 *NHV*, bp July 1718 *NHC1*, d s. p.

6 Morris, b 30 June 1718 *NHV*, bp July 1718 *NHC1*, d s. p.

7 Eunice, b 2 June 1721 *NHV*, bp 4 June 1721 *NHC1*, d s. p.

FAM. 15. James & Hannah (Rowe) Peck:

8 Stephen, b 5 June 1730 *NHV*, bp 7 June 1730 *NHC1*, d 23 Aug 1778 æ. 48 *NHC1;* m (1) 3 Apr 1753 *NHV*—Esther da. Israel & Elizabeth (Bishop) Munson, b 11 Feb 1731/2 *NHV;* m (2) 26 Jan 1764 *NHV*—Lucy da. Joseph & Elsie (Munson) Miles, b 26 Feb 1738/9 *NHV*, "wid." d 19 Feb 1795 æ. 57 *NHC1*.

(By 1): *i* Esther, b 1 July 1753 *NHV*, bp 8 Feb 1761 *NHC1*, d 9 Apr 1850 æ. 97 *NHT1;* m 15 May 1776 *NHC1*—Nathan Oakes.

ii Henry, b 20 Aug 1755 *NHV*, bp 8 Feb 1761 *NHC1*, d 16 Aug 1802 æ. 47 *NHT1*, 17 Aug *NHC1;* Census (NH) 1-1-5; m 22 Feb 1783 *NHC1*—Hannah da. Nehemiah & Lois (Bishop) Lewis, b c. 1757, d 1 May 1840 æ. 84 *NHT1*, *NHV*. FAM. 31.

iii Elisha, b 11 Oct 1757 *NHV*, bp 8 Feb 1761 *NHC1*, d 18 July 1778 æ. 21 *NHC1*.

iv John, b 12 Dec 1759 *NHV*, bp 8 Feb 1761 *NHC1*, d 12 Oct 1805 æ. 47 *NHT1*, 13 Oct *NHC1;* Census (NH) 1-1-1; m 26 Oct 1788 *NHC1*—Mary da. Nehemiah & Lois (Bishop) Lewis, b c. 1760, d 9 Apr 1833 æ. 73 *NHT1*, 12 Apr *(NHC1) NHV*. FAM. 32.

(By 2): *v* Stephen, b 2 Feb 1765 *NHV*, d s. p. 7 Aug 1807 æ. 43 (at St. Croix) *NHT1*.

vi Sarah, b 24 Apr 1766 *NHV*, 25 Apr *LT*, d 25 Apr 1841 *LT;* m 27 Dec 1785 *NHC1*—Thomas Trowbridge.

vii Lucy, b 20 July 1768 *NHV*, bp 26 July 1768 *NHC1*, d 2 Sep 1810 æ. 52 *NHT1;* m 27 July 1788 William Trowbridge.

viii Hannah, bp 18 Mar 1770 *NHC1*, d 31 July 1770 æ. 0-4 *NHC1*.

9 Sarah, bp 31 Dec 1732 *NHC1*, d 1758 *NHC1;* m 7 Aug 1755 *NHV*—Timothy Howell.

10 John, d s. p. c. 1757.

FAM. 16. JOHN & ESTHER (MORRIS) PECK:

1 JOSEPH, b 27 Jan 1707/8 *NHV;* res. Norwalk & Bethel; m.

2 ELIPHALET, b 4 Mar 1710 *NHV;* res. Danbury; m Rebecca da. John Hoyt.

3 JOHN, b 30 Aug 1712 *NHV,* d s. p. after 1721.

FAM. 17. BENJAMIN & MARY (SPERRY) PECK:

1 DINAH, b 30 Nov 1700 *NHV,* d s. p.?

2 ELIZABETH, b 16 Aug 1704 *NorwichV,* d 4 Aug 1720 *NorwichV.*

3 JOSEPH, b 14 Nov 1706 *NorwichV,* d 9 Sep 1776; m (1) 25 Mar 1729 Hannah Carrier; m (2) 19 Oct 1742 Elizabeth Edgarton; m (3) 22 Dec 1754 Elizabeth Carpenter.

4 MARY, b 19 Feb 1709 *NorwichV.*

5 BENJAMIN, b 4 Dec 1710 *NorwichV;* m 3 Nov 1736 Martha Carrier.

6 JOHN, b 7 Mar 1713 *NorwchV,* d 1743; m.

7 EBENEZER, b 15 Feb 1716 *NorwichV,* d 14 Oct 1788; m Elizabeth ———.

8 JONATHAN, b 1 Mar 1718 *NorwichV,* d c. 1780; m 14 Jan 1741/2 Bethia Bingham. Their s. John, b 14 Nov 1756 *Norwich,* lost at sea, m (1) c. 1785 Rebecca da. Joel & Abiah (Baldwin) Atwater, b 21 Mar 1766 *NHV,* d 25 Apr 1788 æ. 22 *NHT1;* m (2) Rebecca da. Stephen & Ann (Prichard) Bradley.

9 DANIEL, b 9 May 1719 *NorwichV,* d (at Scipio, N. Y.); m (1) 18 Apr 1743 Hannah Dodge; m (2) 15 Sep 1763 Jerusha Tracy, wid. Rev. Jedediah Hyde; m (3) 7 Oct 1765 Mary, wid. Chapman.

10 SUBMIT, b 1 Aug 1722 *NorwichV;* m (1) 1739 Aaron Cook; m (2) 1742 Dr. Wm. Wheatley of Boston.

FAM. 18. EBENEZER & HANNAH (HOTCHKISS) PECK:

1 EBENEZER, b 12 Mar 1710 *NHV,* bp 5 July 1719 *NHC1,* d c. 1768; m 20 Jan 1736/7 *NHV*—Mary da. Samuel & Anna (Hotchkiss) Johnson; Census, Molly (Wd) 0-0-3.

i Hannah, b 18 Jan 1737/8 *NHV,* d soon.

ii Mary, b 24 Sep 1739 *NHV,* d Feb 1799 "rising 60" *WdC.*

iii Ebenezer, b 27 Sep 1741 *NHV,* d 1814; Census (D) 1-0-3; m 5 Mar 1764 *WdC*—Dorcas da. Aaron & Dorcas (Munson) Potter, b 4 Apr 1743 *NHV,* d 6 May 1790 æ. 47 *NHC1.*

iv Noah, b 3 Dec 1743 *NHV.*

v Hannah, b 7 Dec 1745 *NHV;* m George Sutton.

vi Rachel, b 10 June 1748 *NHV,* d 24 Oct 1823 æ. 75 *WdT1;* m 18 May 1769 *WdC*—Lent Sperry.

vii Jane, b 22 Apr 1753 *NHV,* d 20 Jan 1830 æ. 78 *WdT1,* 19 Jan *WdC,* 21 Jan *WdD.*

2 HANNAH, b 15 Feb 1711 *NHV,* bp 5 July 1719 *NHC1,* d 1798; m 20 Dec 1733 *NHV*—Amos Sperry.

3 MARY, b 2 Nov 1714 *NHV,* bp 5 July 1719 *NHC1,* d c. 1790; m 5 June 1740 *NHV*—Peter Perkins.

4 JOSEPH, b 28 Mar 1718 *NHV,* bp 5 July 1719 *NHC1,* d 1 Mar 1788 æ. 70 *WdT1,* 2 Mar *WdC;* m 12 Jan 1742/3 *NHV*—Amy da. Seth & Elizabeth (Munson) Perkins, b 3 Sep 1726 *NHV,* d 2 June 1799; Census, Amy (Wd) 0-0-1.

i Bathsheba, b 20 Mar 1745/6 *NHV,* bp 8 July 1750 *WdC,* d 26 Dec 1832 æ. 87 *WdC;* m 18 Sep 1775 *WdC*—Roswell Palmer of Farm; Census, Bathsheba Palmer (Wd) 0-0-2.

ii Seth, b 11 Nov 1747 *NHV,* bp 8 July 1750 *WdC,* d 10 Feb 1831; res. Bristol; m 4 Dec 1771 *WdC* —Hannah da. Samuel & Kezia (Lines) Alling, b 27 Nov 1751 *NHV,* d 31 Dec 1821.

iii Joseph, b c. 1749, bp 8 July 1750 *WdC,* d 24 May 1800 in 51 yr. (at NH) *ConnJournal;* gaolkeeper; Census (NH) 1-2-4; m 27 Dec 1774 *NHC2*—Sarah da. Thomas & Sarah (Ingraham) Alcott, b 28 Aug 1751 *NHV.* FAM. 33.

iv Amy, bp 28 July 1751 *WdC;* m 24 Dec 1775 *WdC*—Wilmot Bradley.

v Dan, bp 17 June 1753 *WdC,* d 26 Aug 1815; Census (Wd) 1-1-4; rem. to Bristol; m (1) 1 Feb 1776 *WdC*—Eunice da. Richard Russell; m (2) Lois Yale; m (3) Mary Roberts.

vi John, b c. 1756, d 8 Mar 1825 æ. 69 *NHT1,* 9 Mar æ. 70 *(NHC2) NHV;* Census (NH) 1-2-2; m 12 Mar 1780 *NHC2*—Lois da. Jonathan & Mehitabel (Maltby) Osborn, b 19 Jan 1757 *NHV,* d 15 Mar 1845 æ. 88 *NHV.* FAM. 34.

vii Dorcas; m 10 Dec 1777 *NHC2*—William Osborn.

viii Asenath, b 19 Sep 1760 *OT,* d 10 Dec 1838 *OT;* m 27 Sep 1781 *WdC*—Stephen Russell.

ix Electa, b 23 Oct 1761 *F;* m 5 Nov 1783 John Alling.

x Henry, b 7 Mar 1764 *F;* Census (Wd) 1-1-2; m 9 Apr 1787 *WdC*—Elizabeth Clark.

xi Rhoda, b c. 1768, d 4 Jan 1770 æ. 2 *WdT1.*

5 RACHEL, b 1 Aug 1721 *NHV,* bp Aug 1721 *NHC1;* m Thomas Perkins.

FAM. 18. EBENEZER & ELIZABETH (WILMOT) PECK:

6 AMBROSE, b 5 Mar 1725 *NHV* [1725/6], bp Mar 1726 *NHC1;* m Rhoda da. Zebulon & Sarah (Johnson) Carrington.

7 LYDIA, b 11 Dec 1728 *NHV* [1727], bp 11 Feb 1727/8 *NHC1,* d young.

8 EUNICE, b 6 Aug 1730 *NHV,* bp 27 Sep 1730 *NHC1,* d young.

9 BATHSHEBA, b 27 Sep 1732 *NHV,* bp 7 Jan 1732/3 *NHC1,* d young.

10 BENAJAH, b 1 June 1735 *NHV,* bp 13 July 1735 *NHC1,* d 19 May 1785 æ. 50 *BT1,* bu. 22 May *NHx;* m 25 Jan 1757 *WdC*—Sarah da. Jonathan & Mary (Dorman) Mansfield, b 14 Jan 1735/6 *NHV;* Census, Sarah (Wd) 0-0-1.

i Jonathan Mansfield, b c. 1758, d 21 Apr 1788 *BD,* æ. 30 *BT1,* bu. 23 Apr (k. by falling of a tree in B) *NHx;* Lt.; m Elizabeth da. Elnathan & Hannah (Hitchcock) Andrews, b 21 June 1758 *WV;* Census, Elizabeth (Wd) 1-2-4; she m (2) Chauncey Tuttle. FAM. 35.

ii Eunice; m Asel Brooks.

iii Elizabeth Mary, b c. 1772, d 27 Dec 1819 æ. 48 *WdC,* æ. 47 *WdT1;* m 16 Nov 1788 *WdC*—Roger Newton.

11 BENJAMIN, b 14 Aug 1737 *NHV,* bp 2 Oct 1737 *NHC1,* d soon.

12 BENJAMIN, b 10 Mar 1746/7 *NHV* [error for 1739/40], bp 20 Apr 1739/40 *NHC1,* d 14 Mar 1812 æ. 72 *WdC,* 13 Mar *WdD;* Census (Wd) 1-0-4; m 23 July 1761 *NHV, WdC*—Thankful da. William & Thankful (Collins) Russell, b 11 Jan 1742 *NHV,* d 24 Mar 1823 æ. 81 *WdC.*

i Elizabeth, b 25 Jan 1763 *NHV,* d 1 Sep 1843 æ. 81 *WdT3;* m 20 Feb 1782 *WdC*—Elisha Osborn.

ii Thankful, b 24 Apr 1768 *NHV,* prob. d s. p.

iii Martha, b c. 1773, d 24 Feb 1839 æ. 68 *WdC;* Sarah Lucinda, adopted da. of Martha, bp 6 Nov 1829 *WdC.*

13 STEPHEN, b 5 Aug 1742 *NHV,* bp 10 Oct 1742 *NHC1,* d 13 June 1830 æ. 88 *WdT1, WdC;* Census (Wd) 2-2-5; m 29 Dec 1763 *NHV, WdC*—Eunice da. Timothy & Mercy (Baldwin) Bradley, b 3 May 1746 *NHV,* d 16 Dec 1831 *WdC,* 17 Dec æ. 86 *WdT1.* [*ColR* says Stephen d 13 June 1830 æ. 88; lived with w. 66 yrs.; 7 children, 28 gr. children, 35 gr. gr. children.]

i Silas, b 23 May 1765 *NHV*, d 6 Apr 1841 æ. 76 *WdT1, WdC;* Census (Wd) 1-1-2; m Electa da. Samuel & Mary (Johnson) Carrington, b c. 1767, d 8 Jan 1835 æ. 68 *WdT1,* 3 Jan *WdC*. FAM. 36.

ii Hezekiah, b 7 July 1767 *NHV*, d 2 May 1840 æ. 73 *WdT1, WdC;* m Sarah da. Seth & Sarah (Wilmot) Downs, b c. 1771, d 19 June 1851 æ. 80 *WdT1, WdD*. A son, Horace, b c. 1791, d 8 June 1868 æ. 77 *WdT1, WdD;* Dea.; m Sarah ———, who d 21 June 1855 æ. 65 *WdT1, WdD*.

iii Stephen, b 30 Dec 1774 *F*, d 28 Jan 1832 æ. 57 *WdT1,* 29 Jan *WdC;* m (1) Jeannette ———; m (2) Eunice da. Amos & Abiah (Downs) Perkins, b [19 May 1773 *NHV*], d 29 July 1869 æ. 92 *WdT1*.

iv Edward, b c. 1778, d s. p. 24 Jan 1841 æ. 62 *WdT1, WdC*.

v Eunice, b c. 1781, d 21 Nov 1818 æ. 38 *WdT1, WdC;* m David Smith.

vi Sally, b c. 1783; m 15 Dec 1802 *F*—John Hubbard.

vii Polly Barbara, b c. 1787, d 23 Oct 1859 æ. 72 *WdD;* m David Perkins.

14 EUNICE, b 28 Sep 1744 *NHV*, bp 18 Oct 1744 *WdC*, d 26 Mar 1830 æ. 86 *WdT1,* 27 Mar æ. 87 *WdD;* m 2 Dec 1765 *WdC*—Jesse Ford.

FAM. 19. PETER & ESTHER (SMITH) PECK:

1 POLLY, b 14 Apr 1768 *WV*.

2 DAVID, b 13 July 1770 *WV*, d 15 Oct 1794 æ. 23 (at sea) *WHD*.

3 ABEL, b 9 May 1773 *WV*.

4 MOSES, b 23 Oct 1776 *WV*.

5 HULDAH, b 23 Oct 1776 *WV;* m 15 May 1803 *NHC1*—Peter Noe of N. Y. City.

6 EUNICE, b 21 Aug 1779 *WV*.

7 ESTHER, b 16 Apr 1789 *WV*.

FAM. 20. JAMES & ELIZABETH (HALL) PECK (family incomplete):

1 GAD, b 12 Oct 176[4] *WV*, d 3 June 1853 æ. 89 *NHT1;* Capt.; Census (NH) 1-0-1; m 6 Feb 1787 *NHV, NHC1*—Asenath da. Stephen & Desire (Shattuck) Osborn, b 1 Feb 1768 *WV*, d 13 Dec 1823 æ. 55 *Meadville, Pa.,T*.

i William Ward, b 23 Jan 1791 *NHV*, "Bilious Ward" bp 5 May 1793 *NHC1*.

ii Charles, b 10 Aug 1793 *NHV*, bp 27 Oct 1793 *NHC1*, d 23 Aug 1795 *NHV*, "son" 24 Aug æ. 3 *NHC1*.

iii Amelia, b 24 Aug 1798 *NHV,* bp 16 Sep 1798 *NHC1.*
iv Caroline, b 7 Aug 1802 *NHV,* bp 5 Sep 1802 *NHC1.*
v Robert, b 5 Apr 1806 *NHV.*
2 LYDIA, b 14 June 1767 *WV,* d 17 Feb 1846 æ. 79 *WT1;* m James Humiston.
3 HULDAH, b 26 Aug 1774 *WV.*
4 JAMES, b 31 Jan 1777 *WV.*
5 CHARLES, b 14 Nov 1780 *WV.*

FAM. 21. ABNER & SARAH [COOK] PECK:
1 BELA, b 8 Dec 1774 *WV;* m 6 Nov 1796 *NoBC2*—Eunice da. Lud & Lois (Johnson) Munson, b 30 June 1775 *WV.*
2 DAN, b 29 Aug 1777 *WV.*
3 SARAH, b 2 Sep 1779 *WV.*
4 LUCY, b 6 Dec 1781 *WV,* d 30 Apr 1842 æ. 60 *NHV;* m (1) 25 Oct 1801 *WC1*—Ambrose Culver; m (2) 1 Dec 1818 *WC1*—William Mansfield of NH.

FAM. 22. STEPHEN & SARAH (IVES) PECK:
1 COLLIER, b 5 Nov 1774 *WV,* d s. p. c. 1797.

FAM. 22. STEPHEN & MARGERY (PARKER) PECK:
2 ELIADA, b c. 1778, d 18 Sep 1833 æ. 55 *WT1;* m Justina ———.
3 SARAH IVES, b 30 Sep 1780 *WV.*
4 JEMIMA, b 23 Feb 1783 *WV.*
5 HANNAH; m Aaron Culver.

FAM. 23. TITUS & REBECCA (HITCHCOCK) PECK:
1 TITUS; res. Cornwall, Vt., 1796; m Mabel da. Nathaniel & Elizabeth (Bassett) Tuttle.
2 MARY; m 4 Mar 1790 James Parker.
3 REBECCA.

FAM. 24. Roger & PHILENA (HINE) PECK:
1 BETSEY; m 24 June 1795 Edward Perkins.
2 ROGER; m Mary [Camp], who d 23 Oct 1815 æ. 31 *BT2.*
3 LEVI, b 8 Oct 1779 *BT2,* d 14 Jan 1852 (at Wd) *BT2;* m Polly da. Ezra & Abigail (Crittenden) Sperry, b 20 June 1791 *BT2,* d 8 Oct 1874 *BT2,* 7 Oct æ. 83 *WdD.*
4 LYDIA, b 15 Oct 1782; m Lyman Sperry.
5 LEVIRUS, lost at sea.
6 MARY PHILENE, d s. p.
7 CHARLES, d 1854.
8 JOHN A.; m Ann Ruggles.
9 GEORGE.

FAM. 25. AMOS & LOIS (CHATTERTON) PECK:
1 JEREMIAH, b 18 Dec 1773 *NHV,* bp 12 Oct 1777 *HC1;*

m (1) 23 Jan 1800 *HV*—Mary da. James & Elizabeth (Osborn) Miles, b c. 1777, d 23 Mar 1830 æ. 53 *HT3;* m (2) 23 Aug 1830 *HV*—Ruth da. Rufus & Ruth (Peck) Hoadley, wid. Linus Todd, b 2 Nov 1782 (Northford).

(By 1): *i* Otis, d s. p. 1830; res. H.
ii Miles.
iii Willis.
iv Eliza; m ——— Bradley.
v Lucius.

2 Benjamin, b 30 Mar 1776 *NHV,* d 22 Feb 1837 æ. 62 *HT3;* m 16 June 1797 Lucy da. Chauncey & Rebecca (Bradley) Dickerman, b 5 June 1776 *NHV,* d 10 Nov 1858 æ. 82 *HT3.*

i Sophia, b 7 Dec 1797, d 8 Oct 1837 æ. 41 *HT2;* m Merrit Alling.
ii Lewis, b 4 Jan 1799, d 28 Mar 1856 æ. 57 *HT3;* m 3 Apr 1821 *HV*—Eunice da. Elijah & Eunice (Bradley) Wooding, b c. 1799, d 16 June 1859 æ. 60 *HT3.*
iii Rebecca, b 20 Jan 1802, d 18 Aug 1868 æ. 68 *BT(Meth);* m Anan Atwater.
iv Henry, b 21 Feb 1804, d 17 Dec 1861 æ. 58 *HT3;* m (1) 19 Apr 1826 *HV*—Perlina da. William & Thankful (Wolcott) Shares, bp 1802 *HC2,* d 8 May 1847 æ. 45 *HT3;* m (2) 15 Aug 1847 *HV*—Emeline da. Stephen & Damaris (Sanford) Hitchcock, wid. Gilbert Root of D, b [Jan 1809], d 22 Nov 1895 æ. 86-10 *HV.*
v Francis, b 26 Sep 1806, d 20 Sep 1887 (Jacksonville, Ill.); m 2 Mar 1835 *NHV*—Mary Andrus of Simsbury.
vi Frederick, b 8 May 1809, d 19 Dec 1870; m 5 Jan 1829 Sarah Sperry.
vii Lois, b 29 Dec 1811, d 20 Jan 1873; m 1 Dec 1831 *HV*—Lewis Perkins.
viii Edson, b 3 Oct 1814; m (1) 18 Mar 1837 Hannah Talmadge; m (2) 13 Oct 1850 *HV*—Polly A. Minor.
ix Chloe, b 1 June 1817; m Edwin Church Austin.
x Sylvia C., b 11 Feb 1820, d 6 Aug 1875; m 1840 Andrew Hills.

3 Mary, b 28 Jan 1779, d c. 1865; m Jesse Bradley.

4 Lois, bp May 1782 *HC1,* d 12 Nov 1822 æ. 41 *HT3;* m 21 Mar 1805 Samuel Dickerman.

5 Chloe, b 13 Mar 1786, d 20 Oct 1879 æ. 94 *BT4;* m Oct 1827 Seymour Tuttle.

6 AMOS, b 14 Nov 1794 *HV*, bp 5 Apr 1795 *HC1*, d 26 Apr 1866 æ. 71 *HT3*; m 19 Feb 1817 *HV*—Lovisa da. Eli & Bede (Todd) Todd, b 11 Oct 1797, d 23 Nov 1865 æ. 68 *HT3*.

i Jennet Lovisa, b 24 Dec 1818, d 30 Aug 1888; m 9 Apr 1838 Bazel Munson.

FAM. 26. MOSES & ABIGAIL ESTHER (JOHNSON) PECK:

1 NABBY ESTHER, b c. 1779, bp 27 Dec 1789 *HC1*; m 6 Apr 1800 *HV*—Jared Alling.

2 NANCY, d 13 Sep 1789 *HC1*.

3 ELIZABETH, b c. 1785, bp 27 Dec 1789 *HC1*; m 14 Feb 1808 Robert Buell.

FAM. 27. ELIJAH & SARAH (BRADLEY) PECK:

1 JOB BRADLEY, b 22 Apr 1782 *CV*, bp 23 June 1782 *CC*.

2 AMARILLA, b 10 Jan 1785 *CV*.

3 AMOS, b 7 Sep 1787 *CV*, bp 5 Nov 1787 *CC*.

4 SALLY, b 2 Aug 1789 *CV*, bp 11 Oct 1789 *CC*.

5 MABEL, b 5 Jan 1792 *CV*, bp 25 Mar 1792 *CC*.

6 ELIJAH JABEZ, b 4 Aug 1794 *CV*, bp 21 Sep 1794 *CC*.

7 SARAH LUE, b 1 May 1796 *CV*, bp 26 June 1796 *CC*.

8 DESIRE, b 14 Aug 1798 *CV*.

FAM. 28. JESSE & HULDAH [? ATWATER] PECK:

1 CHAUNCEY, b c. 1790, bp 23 June 1793 *HC1*, d 8 July 1832 æ. 42 *NHT1*, 9 July æ. 42 *(NHx) NHV*; m Laura ———, who d 2 Oct 1827 æ. 45 *NHT1*.

2 CYNTHIA, b [31 Oct 1795], bp 5 Apr 1795 *HC1*, d 6 Apr 1883 æ. 87-5-6 *NHV*; m W. Baldwin.

3 JESSE WHITING, bp 30 Sep 1798 *HC1*, d 18 Apr 1859 æ. 60 *NHT1*, *NHV*; m 3 July 1827 *ConnH*—Mary Ann da. Isaac & Mary (Dodd) Mix, who d 5 Apr 1891 æ. 86 *NHT1*.

4 LAURA, bp 8 Mar 1801 *HC1*.

FAM. 29. JOSEPH & OLIVE (CHATTERTON) PECK:

1 SARAH; m ——— Moss.

2 OLIVE, b c. 1787, d 5 Oct 1827 æ. 40 *HT1*; m 8 May 1805 *HV*—Seymour Goodyear.

3 JULIA.

4 HANNAH; m ——— Rowe.

5 FANNY; m ——— Hall.

6 ZERI, b c. 1794, d 29 May 1867 æ. 73 *HT3*, æ. 72 (suicide) *HV*; m Alma da. Jonah & Olive (Sanford) Warner, b [Dec 1803], d 7 Nov 1893 æ. 89-11 *HV*, 6 Nov æ. 90 *HT3*.

FAM. 30. EBENEZER & REBECCA (DICKERMAN) PECK:

1 EBENEZER, b 23 Aug 1791 *NHV*.

2 JAMES, b 6 Mar 1793 *NHV*, bp 1 June 1794 *NHC1*, d 1865 (Jeffersonville, Ind.); m 12 Sep 1813 (at Middleborough, Mass.) *ColR*—Ann Atwater of Bd.

3 Rebecca, b 5 Jan 1795 *NHV,* bp 1 Feb 1795 *NHC1,* d 2 Apr 1863 æ. 67 *NHV.*

4 Mary, b 30 Jan 1797 *NHV,* bp 19 Feb 1797 *NHC1,* d 7 Mar 1807 æ. 10 *NHC1.*

5 Martha, b 15 Sep 1799 *NHV,* bp 10 Nov 1799 *NHC1,* d 1841; m Cornelius Hogeboom.

6 Grace, b 1 Sep 1801 *NHV,* bp 8 Nov 1801 *NHC1,* d 8 Apr 1870; m Wm. C. Butler.

7 Emeline, b 24 Oct 1803 *NHV,* bp 11 Dec 1803 *NHC1,* d 28 Oct 1869; m Rev. Judson Adoniram Root.

8 Harriet, b 14 Jan 1806 *NHV,* d 29 Sep 1895.

FAM. 31. Henry & Hannah (Lewis) Peck:

1 Esther, b 19 Dec 1783 *F,* 1787(?) *NHT1,* bp 3 Oct 1790 *NHC1,* d 1832 *NHT1;* m (1) 1 July 1804 *NHC1*—Daniel Goffe Phipps; m (2) Solomon Phipps.

2 Polly, b 5 Feb 1785 *F,* bp 3 Oct 1790 *NHC1,* d 5 Nov 1865 æ. 80 *NHV;* m 19 Apr 1804 *NHC1*—Thomas Dougal.

3 Grace, b 2 Dec 1786 *F,* bp 3 Oct 1790 *NHC1;* m 5 June 1808 *NHV*—Eli Mix.

4 Elisha, b 27 May 1788 *F,* bp 13 Oct 1789 *NHC1,* d 18 Oct 1789 æ. 0-20 *NHT1,* "child" 19 Oct æ. 2 *NHC1.*

5 Elisha, b 5 May 1790 *NHV,* bp 3 Oct 1790 *NHC1,* d 11 June 1866; m 14 June 1831 *NHV*—Grace Bonticou.

FAM. 32. John & Mary (Lewis) Peck:

1 Nehemiah Lewis, b 4 Aug 1789 *F,* bp 23 Aug 1789 *NHC1,* d 2 Feb 1821 (in South) *F.*

2 Nancy, b 9 Sep 1791 *F,* bp 1 Apr 1792 *NHC1,* d 10 Jan 1858 æ. 66 *NHT1.*

3 Elizabeth, b 29 Jan 1793 *F,* bp 10 Mar 1793 *NHC1,* d 27 July 1847 æ. 54 *NHT1.*

4 Mary, b 19 Dec 1798 *F,* bp 14 Apr 1799 *NHC1,* d 4 Nov 1859 æ. 60 *NHT1.*

FAM. 33. Joseph & Sarah (Alcott) Peck:

1 Lyman, b c. 1776, bp 28 May 1780 *NHC2.*

2 Joseph, b c. 1778, bp 28 May 1780 *NHC2,* d 11 Mar 1781 æ. 4 *NHT1.*

3 Sally, b c. 1780, bp 28 May 1780 *NHC2.*

4 Joseph, bp 18 Aug 1782 *NHC2,* d Apr 1813 æ. 31 *ColR;* prob. m 23 Sep 1804 *NHx*—Hannah Cook, who m (2) Newton Wheeler. Only child: Mary, b 2 Jan 1812 *NHT1,* d 12 Dec 1854 *NHT1.*

5 Nancy, b c. 1785; [? m 27 Sep 1807 Thaddeus Atwater].

6 Bela, bp 28 Mar 1788 *NHC2,* d 18 Apr 1791 æ. 3 *NHT1.*

7 Thomas Basil, bp 21 Nov 1790 *NHC2,* d 13 Sep 1792 æ. 2 *NHT1.*

8 Bela Thomas, bp 23 Sep 1792 *NHC2,* d 21 Sep 1837 æ. 43 *NHV;* m 20 Dec 1825 *NHV*—Maria Atwater.

FAM. 34. John & Lois (Osborn) Peck:

1 Charlotte, b c. 1781, d 17 Sep 1870 æ. 90 *NHT1;* m 24 Nov 1823 *NHV*—Dennis Covert.

2 [John, d s. p.].

3 Ezekiel Osborn, b c. 1787, d 4 July 1795 æ. 8 *NHT1.*

4 Mary Elizabeth, b c. 1789, d 20 Aug 1866 æ. 77 *NHT1.*

5 Francis Sidney, b [June 1791], d 13 Aug 1792 æ. 0-14 *NHT1.*

FAM. 35. Jonathan Mansfield & Elizabeth (Andrews) Peck:

1 Roxana, bp 27 Sep 1780 *NHx;* m Jacob Tolles.

2 George Frederick, b 5 Jan 1781 *F,* bp 10 Jan 1781 *NHx,* d 25 Mar 1860; m 19 Oct 1800 Fanny Ball.

3 Amilla, b c. 1784; m Reed Bosworth.

4 Benajah, b c. 1786.

5 Betsey Mansfield, b c. 1788; m Jesse Byington.

FAM. 36. Silas & Electa (Carrington) Peck:

1 Almira, b c. 1788, d 22 Nov 1838 æ. 50 *WdT1;* m Simeon Sperry.

2 Ansel, b c. 1790, d 1 Sep 1866 æ. 76 *WdD.*

3 Lauren, rem. to Vt.; m 24 Oct 1815 *WdC*—Sally Baldwin.

4 Amanda, b c. 1794, d 20 May 1880 æ. 86 *WdV;* m James Perkins.

5 Lewis, b 6 June 1796 *F,* d 10 Apr 1857 æ. 61 *WdD;* m 10 Nov 1824 *WdV*—Elizabeth Ann da. Ephraim Beecher.

6 Eunice, b c. 1800, d 28 Feb 1885 æ. 85-3 *WdD;* m 22 Oct 1823 *WdV, WdC*—Elionai Clark.

7 Electa, b c. 1802, d 13 Sep 1835 æ. 33 *WdT1;* m 29 Dec 1824 *NHV*—Linus Gilbert Thomas.

8 Garry, b c. 1804, d 19 June 1855 æ. 51 *WdD.*

9 Sabra [Seabury, of Westville].

10 Mary, b c. 1809, d 2 Oct 1850 æ. 41 *WdT1.*

11 Naaman, of Seymour.

(*Continued on page 1409*)

BOOK REVIEWS

This department of the New Haven Genealogical Magazine offers to compilers and publishers of genealogical books the opportunity to secure fair and honest reviews of their productions. The reviewer will do his utmost to point out the good features of every book which is presented for review, but in fairness to readers will mention striking deficiencies, such as the lack of an index, unusually poor arrangement of material, or gross inaccuracies. Those who wish books reviewed should send one copy to the address below.

Donald L. Jacobus, Editor,
554 Central Avenue,
Westville, Conn.

KELSEY A Genealogy of the Descendants of William Kelsey, Volume II. By Edward A. Claypool and Azalea Clizbee and concluded by Earl Leland Kelsey from data collected by many. Edited by Chester Caulfield Kelsey. Ten illustrations, three maps. Pub. 1929. 424 p. 8°. Order from Dwight C. Kelsey, 53 Hillcrest Ave., Hamden, Conn. Price, $7.25 postpaid.

The second volume of this work maintains the high standard set by the first, and indicates to an even greater extent the tremendous amount of work that has been required to collect these records and prepare them for publication. The present volume is devoted to the fifth and sixth generations, including the births of the children of the seventh generation. On some lines this brings the work down to the births of Kelseys who are still living, while in other branches intervening generations have still to appear.

The pictures of old Kelsey houses and sawmills increases the attractiveness of this second volume, which genealogically shows the same conscientious care which we found pleasure in commending in our review of the first volume.

The index is quite adequate and fills nearly fifty pages. On the female lines, among the families to which considerable space is devoted are Chapman, Griswold, Hubbard, Hull, Lane, Stevens, and Wilcox.

The format of the book is the same as that of the first volume, and the difference in price is caused by the larger number of pages in this volume. The work is recommended to genealogical libraries, and Kelsey descendants should be eager to buy each volume as it appears. The second volume does not complete the work, and the backers of the publication are underwriting a large expense, in the discharging of which all members of the family should share to the extent of purchasing copies.

Families of Ancient New Haven

(Continued from page 1407)

PECK. FAM. 37. WILLIAM, s. of Jonathan, b Nov 1702 (Bristol, R. I.), d 1758 *NHC1;* m (1) 13 May 1725 *Bristol*—Elizabeth Throop, who d 18 Apr 1731; m (2) Elizabeth ———, who d 12 Nov 1740; m (3) (intention 24 Oct 1741) *Bristol*—Rebecca Talbott.

(By 1): 1 ELIZABETH, b 15 Sep 1726 *NHV,* bp 25 Dec 1726 *NHC1.*

2 MARY, b 3 Dec 1727 *NHV,* bp 3 Dec 1727 *NHC1.*

3 MARTHA, b 1 Feb 1730/1 *Newport.*

4 NICHOLAS, b 23 Mar 1731/2 *Newport,* d 22 July 1793 æ. 64 *NHC1;* Census (NH) 1-0-2; m 12 Nov 1753 *NHV*—Abigail da. James & Dinah (Sherman) Atwater, b 19 Nov 1727 *NHV.*

i Abigail, b 13 Dec 1754 *NHV,* bp 15 Dec 1754 *NHC1.*

ii Mary, bp 27 Aug 1758 *NHC1.*

iii Pamela, bp 25 Jan 1761 *NHC1.*

iv William, bp 27 Mar 1763 *NHC1,* d 6 Dec 1781 (k. at Yorktown) *NHC1.* Also, William entered as k. in Army 25 Feb 1782 *NHC1.*

v Elijah, b 14 Mar 1765 *NHV.*

vi Mary Dinah, b 31 Oct 1767 *NHV,* bp 1768 *NHC1.*

vii Sarah, b 10 Mar 1770 *NHV,* bp 6 May 1770 *NHC1,* "infant son" d Mar 1770 æ. 2 wks. *NHC1.*

(By 2): 5 CHLOE.

6 BENJAMIN, b 13 Sep 1741 *Bristol.*

(By 3?): 7 SETH; rem. to Northfield, Mass.; m 15 Nov 1780 Elizabeth Peck.

WILLIAM (the above or a son?) m 9 Feb 1748/9 *NHV*—Dorothy Tuttle.

ELIZABETH of Bristol, R. I., m 4 Dec 1729 *NHV*—John Bradley.

PECK. For the unusually full account we are able to give of the family of Joseph Peck of M, we are very largely indebted to the generosity of George C. Bryant, Esq., of Ansonia, Conn.

FAM. 38. JOSEPH, the settler, adm. to Milford Church, May 1652, d 26 Feb 1700/1 *MV;* m (1) 12 Sep 1650 *NHV*—Alice, wid. John Burwell, who d 19 Dec 1666 *MC1;* m (2) Mary da. Thomas Richards of Wat, who was adm. to Milford Church, 26 Nov 1669.

(By 1): 1 ELIZABETH, bp 27 July 1651 *MC1;* m 29 Dec 1677 *MV*—Sgt. Thomas Hayes; rem. to Newark, N. J.

2 JOSEPH, bp 20 Mar 1652/3 *MC1,* d 1 Mar 1731 in 79 yr. *MT;* m 27 Jan 1678/9 *MV*—Mary da. Nicholas & Sarah (Beard) Camp, b 12 July 1660 *MV.*

i Joseph, b 25 Feb 1680 *MV, NewtownV* [1680/1]; m 14 Jan 1706 *NewtownV* [1706/7]—Abigail da. Theophilus & Elizabeth (Canfield) Baldwin.

ii Mary, b 15 Dec 1682 *MV;* m 14 Feb 1704 *MV*—Timothy Botsford.

iii John, b 4 Sep 1685 *MV,* d 27 Nov 1709 *MV.*

iv Jeremiah, bp 5 Feb 1687/8 *MC1,* d 1768; m 20 Aug 1713 *MV*—Hannah da. Dr. John & Hannah (Baldwin) Fiske. FAM. 39.

v Samuel, bp 13 July 1690 *MC1,* d 1728; m 5 May 1714 *MV*—Martha da. Ens. George & Deborah (Gold) Clark, bp 26 May 1695 *MC1,* d 3 Dec 1747 æ. 52 (St); she m (2) James Booth. FAM. 40.

vi Ephraim, bp 11 Sep 1692 *MC1,* d 23 July 1760 ; m 7 Nov 1716 (at M) *NewtownV*—Sarah da. John & Sarah (Fitch) Ford, bp 26 Oct 1701 *MC1.*

vii Henry, bp 24 Mar 1695 *MC1,* d 19 Nov 1762; m (1) 28 Feb 1722/3 *MV*—Ann da. John & Sarah (Fitch) Ford, bp 26 Oct 1701 *MC1,* d 28 Dec 1726 *MV;* m (2) Mary da. Jobamah Gunn, wid. Amos Northrup, bp 24 May 1691 *MC1,* d c. 1770. FAM. 41.

viii Elizabeth, bp 22 Aug 1697 *MC1.*

ix Nathaniel, bp 7 Jan 1699/1700 *MC1,* d 1776; m Phebe ———. FAM. 42.

x Abigail, b 25 Sep 1701 *MV,* d 14 Sep 1764 in 64 yr. *New MilfordT;* m 1 June 1725 *NMV*—Samuel Canfield.

xi Heth, b 3 Oct 1703 *MV,* d 4 May 1797 ; m 26 Feb 1729/30 *MV,* 19 Feb *NewtownV*—Hannah da. Samuel & Mary (Baldwin) Camp, bp 3 July 1709 *MC1.* FAM. 43.

3 JOHN, b 4 Mar 1654 *MV,* bp 1654 *MC1.*

(By 2): 4 MARY, b 29 Apr 1670 *MV,* bp 1 May 1670 *MC1;* m William Northrup.

5 ANNA, bp 25 Aug 1672 *MC1.*

FAM. 39. JEREMIAH & HANNAH (FISKE) PECK:

1 HANNAH, b 6 May 1716 *MV;* m 15 Jan 1741/2 *MV*—David Clark.

2 JOHN, b 9 Dec 1718 *MV,* d 21 Oct 1790 æ. 72 *MD;* m (1) 15 Feb 1750/1 *MV*—Sarah da. Joseph & Mehitabel (Fenn) Platt, b 4 Sep 1721 *MV,* d 21 June 1783 æ. 62 *MD;* m (2) Elizabeth da. Ebenezer

& Elizabeth Tibbals, wid. Nathan Prince, bp 7 May 1727 *MC1*.

(By 1): *i* Sarah, b 15 Oct 1751 *MV,* d 11 May 1786 æ. 36 *MD;* m Samuel Andrew.

ii Mehitabel, b 15 Feb 1753 *MV,* d Aug 1833 æ. 80 *F;* m (1) David Camp; m (2) Lazarus Northrup.

iii John, b 26 June 1755 *MV,* d 2 Dec 1831 æ. 67 *LT;* m Mary da. Nathaniel & Philena (Prince) Camp, b c. 1764, d 29 Aug 1861 æ. 97 *LT*.

iv Joseph, b 26 Aug 1757 *MV,* d 5 Mar 1829 (Onondaga, N. Y.); m 16 Feb 1778 *F*—Hannah da. Jesse & Anna (Peck) Lambert, b 22 Aug 1756.

3 Jeremiah, b 20 Jan 1720/1 *MV,* d 18 Mar 1786 æ. 66 (at Wtn); m 26 Oct 1743 *MV*—Frances da. Josiah & Sarah (Burwell) Platt, b 23 Apr 1717 *MV,* d 16 Oct 1794 æ. 78 (at Wtn).

4 Phineas, b 10 Apr 1723 *MV,* bp 14 Apr 1723 *MC1,* d 28 Jan 1803 *WdC,* æ. 81 *WdT3;* dea.; Census (Wd) 2-0-2; m (1) 18 Feb 1745/6 *MV*—Deborah da. George & Mary (Coley) Clark, bp 20 Apr 1718 *MC1,* d 15 June 1789 *WdC,* in 72 yr. *WdT3;* m (2) 17 Apr 1794 *WdC*—Susanna da. Peter & Elizabeth (Hale) Smith, wid. Stephen Hine, b 20 Sep 1736 *NHV,* d 22 Nov 1810 æ. 74.

i Phineas, b 1 Jan 1746/7 *MV;* d 14 Oct 1776 in 30 yr. *WdT2;* m 16 Nov 1769 *WdC*—Elizabeth da. Alexander & Mary (Lines) Hine, bp 21 Apr 1745 *WdC;* she m (2) 9 Sep 1782 *WdC*—Joseph Smith. FAM. 44.

ii Samuel Fiske, b 25 Mar 1750 *MV,* d 15 May 1835 *F,* æ. 85 *WdT;* m 18 Nov 1773 *WdC*—Elizabeth da. Nathan & Elizabeth (Peck) Platt, b 19 Mar 1748/9 *MV,* d 9 June 1841 æ. 92 *WdC,* æ. 92-2-21 *WdD*. FAM. 45.

iii Deborah, b 3 Oct 1752 *F,* bp 19 Nov 1752 *MC2,* d 2 Feb 1786 æ. 34 *WdT2;* m 23 June 1774 *WdC*—Nathan Platt.

iv Zenas, b 11 June 1755 *F,* bp 31 Aug 1755 *MC2,* d 11 Sep 1788 *WdC,* æ. 34 *WdD,* in 34 yr. *WdT3;* m Hannah da. Joseph & Mary (Merwin) Treat, bp 12 Aug 1750 *MC1,* d 11 Feb 1840 æ. 89 *WdT3,* 12 Feb. *WdD;* Census, Hannah (Wd) 0-2-3; she m (2) Nov 1802 *WdC*—Enoch Clark, & (3) 9 Jan 1811 *WdC*—Samuel Newton. FAM. 46.

v Naomi, b 8 May 1758 *F,* d 5 Oct 1818 æ. 60 *NMT;* m 19 June 1782 *WdC*—Stephen Hine.
vi Bezaleel, b 8 Mar 1761 *F,* d 1837; Census (D) 1-1-3; m 15 May 1783 *WdC*—Martha da. Andrew & Dennis (Wilmot) Bradley, b 9 Oct 1763 *NHV.* FAM. 47.
vii Anon, b 20 Sep 1763 *F,* d 18 Nov 1788 æ. 25 *WdD;* m Betsey da. Joseph & Martha (Augur) Beecher, b c. 1767, d. 5 Feb 1788 *WdC,* æ. 21 *WdD.* FAM. 48.

5 SARAH, b 25 May 1726 *MV.*
6 SIBELLA, b 24 June 1728 *MV,* bp 30 June 1728 *MC1,* d 21 May 1787 æ. 59 *MD;* m Jireh Bull.
7 LUCY, b 23 Oct 1730 *MV.*
8 COMFORT, b 1 Apr 1734 *MV,* bp 7 Apr 1734 *MC1.*
9 CONTENT, b 1 Apr 1734 *MV,* bp 7 Apr 1734 *MC1,* d 16 July 1737 in 4 yr. *MT.*

FAM. 40. SAMUEL & MARTHA (CLARK) PECK:

1 MARTHA, b 31 Jan 1714/5 *MV.*
2 SAMUEL, b 21 May 1716 *MV,* d 30 Dec 1801 æ. 86 *MD;* m (1) 18 Aug 1735 *MV*—Hannah da. Michael & Elizabeth Jennings, b 13 Dec 1717 *FV,* bp 20 Dec 1719 , d 24 Aug 1783 æ. 66 *MD;* m (2) ———, who d 14 Nov 1796 æ. 73 *MD.*

(By 1): *i* Samuel, b 22 Aug 1736 *MV,* d 14 June 1822 æ. 86 *OC;* m 7 July 1762 *MV*—Mehitabel da. Ephraim & Sarah (Newton) Smith, who d Jan 1826 æ. 85 [Peck Gen.]. FAM. 49.
ii Michael, b 10 Aug 1738 *MV,* d 1829 æ. 90 *MD;* m Sybil da. Samuel & Sarah (Fenn) Merchant, b 15 Dec 1750 *MV.*
iii (prob.) Sarah, b 23 Jan 1742; m Nehemiah Lewis [Hist. of So. Britain, p. 154].

3 MARY, b 30 July 1718 *MV,* bp 3 Aug 1718 *MC1,* d 2 May 1804 æ. 86 *MD;* m 4 Nov 1741 *MV*—Benjamin Fenn.
4 JOB, b 15 Sep 1720 *MV,* bp 18 Sep 1720 *MC1,* d 9 Sep 1782 in 62 yr. *StT;* m 31 July 1744 *StV*—Betty da. James & Martha (Lewis) Judson, b 25 Sep 1725 *StV,* d 21 Dec 1780 in 56 yr. *StT.*
5 ABIGAIL, bp 17 Mar 1722/3 *MC1;* m Oct 1743 *StV*—David Clark.
6 NATHAN, bp Jan 1727 *MC1;* m 12 Sep 1750 *StV*—Tabitha da. Josiah & Elizabeth (Ufford) Beers, bp July 1732 *StC.*

FAM. 41. HENRY & ANN (Ford) PECK:

1 HENRY, b 7 Dec 1723 *MV,* bp 19 Feb 1726/7 *MC1,* d 8 Oct 1808 in 85 yr. *HawleyvilleT;* m (1) Rachel

da. Jesse & Mary (Gillet) Lambert, b 15 Feb 1728/9 *MV*, d 29 Jan 1792 in 63 yr. *HawleyvilleT;* m (2) Abiah da. Joseph & Mary (Clark) Smith, wid. Gideon Peck, b 28 Sep 1728 *MV*, d 15 July 1819 æ. 92 *NewtownT*.

2 Ann, b 15 Aug 1725 *MV*, bp 19 Feb 1726/7 *MC1*, d 3 July 1809 æ. 84; m 28 Oct 1745 Jesse Lambert.

3 Benjamin, b 16 Nov 1726 *MV*, bp 19 Feb 1726/7 *MC1*, d 12 Oct 1803 æ. 77 *MD;* Capt.; m (1) 3 Feb 1757 *MC2*—Amy da. Abraham & Amy (Whitmore) Smith, bp 4 June 1738 *MC1*, d c. 1764; m (2) 21 Nov 1764 *MC2*—Sarah da. Caleb & Abigail (Clark) Smith, b 24 Sep 1734 *MV*, d 23 July 1809 æ. 75 *MD*. fam. 50.

fam. 41. Henry & Mary (Gunn) Peck:

4 Mehitabel, b 3 Oct 1735 *MV*, bp 5 Oct 1735 *MC1*, d [11 Aug 1805 æ. 68 *MD*]; m (1) Phineas Baldwin; m (2) Edward Allen.

fam. 42. Nathaniel & Phebe (———) Peck (incomplete):

1 Phebe, b 22 Feb 1732/3 *MV*, bp 25 Feb 1732/3 *MC1*.

2 Nathaniel, b 9 Oct 1734 *MV*, bp 13 Oct 1734 *MC1*.

3 Ezra, bp 25 Mar 1738 *MC1*.

fam. 43. Heth & Hannah (Camp) Peck:

1 Heth, b 29 May 1731 *MV*, *NewtownV*, d 4 Jan 1816 æ. 84 *NewtownT;* m Mary Skidmore, who d 6 Oct 1810 æ. 75 *NewtownT*.

2 Hannah, b 5 July 1733 *MV*, *NewtownV*.

3 Mary, b 31 Dec 1735 (at M) *NewtownV*.

4 Sarah, b 14 Apr 1738 (at M) *NewtownV*.

5 Ammiel, b 24 July 1740 *NewtownV*.

6 Hephzibah, b 23 July 1742 *NewtownV*.

7 Samuel, b 20 Aug 1744 *NewtownV*.

8 Amos, b 12 Jan 1746/7 *NewtownV*.

9 David, b 17 Nov 1748 *NewtownV*.

fam. 44. Phineas & Elizabeth (Hine) Peck:

1 Eunice; m Joseph Nichols Beecher.

2 Elizabeth, b 11 Feb 1774 *F*, d 3 Sep 1820; m 12 July 1797 *WdC*—Jared Munson.

3 Lucy; m 9 Oct 1803 *WdC*—Jerry Riggs.

fam. 45. Samuel Fiske & Elizabeth (Platt) Peck:

1 Elizabeth, b 25 Aug 1774 *F*, d 28 July 1858 æ. 84 *WdD;* m Oct 1798 *WdC*—Camp Newton.

2 Sarah, b 20 Feb 1776 *F*, d 3 Jan 1845 æ. 69 *WdT2;* m 1 June 1794 *WdC*—Edward Hine.

3 Phineas, b 2 Jan 1778 *F*, d 20 Nov 1856 æ. 79 *WdD;* m 4 Apr 1799 *F*—Anna da. David & Huldah (Beecher) Smith, b [3 Oct 1776], d 21 Mar 1869 æ. 92-5-18 *WdD*.

i Louisa, b 1 Nov 1799 *F*, bp 26 Apr 1812 *WdC*, d 27 Nov 1876 æ. 77-0-27 *WdD;* m Lewis Thomas.

ii Phineas Earl, b 3 Nov 1801 *F*, bp 26 Apr 1812 *WdC;* res. Colebrook; m (1) Nancy Beecher; m (2) Electa, wid. Mood. PAGE 1789

iii William, b 8 Sep 1803 *F*, bp 26 Apr 1812 *WdC*, d 16 Aug 1879 æ. 75-11-7 *WdV;* Dea.; m Elizabeth Tolles, who d 23 Nov 1886 æ. 82-4 *WdT*.

iv Sidney Wells, b 30 Aug 1805 *F;* bp 26 Apr 1812 *WdC*, d s. p. 3 July 1844 æ. 39 (at Melmore, Ohio) *WdD*.

v Silas Julius, b 1 Feb 1808 *F*, bp 26 Apr 1812 *WdC*, d 16 Nov 1875 æ. 67 *WdD;* m Adaline M. Baldwin.

vi John, b 20 Oct 1810 *F*, bp 26 Apr 1812 *WdC*, d 21 Aug 1883 æ. 72 *WdD;* m (1) Jenette Baldwin; m (2) Louisa Baldwin.

4 Huldah, b 27 Jan 1780 *F*, d 11 Feb 1780 *F*.

5 Samuel, b 15 Feb 1781 *F*, d 20 Feb 1865 æ. 84-0-5 *WdV;* m Rebecca [da. Burr & Eunice (Smith)] Beecher, [b 25 Apr 1784 *WdV*], d 6 Oct 1851 æ. 66 *WdD*, æ. 67 *WdT*.

FAM. 46. Zenas & Hannah (Treat) Peck:

1 Mary, b c. 1780, d 9 Feb 1870 æ. 90 *WdD;* m 3 Oct 1799 *WdC*—Jonah Newton.

2 Jerry, b c. 1782, d 14 Apr 1854 æ. 72 *WdD;* m 19 Aug 1807 *WdC*—Amelia da. Jesse & Eunice (Peck) Ford, bp 1786 *WdC*, d 5 Dec 1864 æ. 78 *WdV*.

3 Hannah, b 4 June 1785 *F*, d 1 Sep 1879 æ. 94-3 *WdD;* m 1 May 1816 *WdC*—Russell Johnson of Oxf. PAGE 1529

4 Zenas, bp 10 Oct 1788 *WdC*, d 5 Sep 1864 æ. 76 *WdV;* m 1813 *WdC*—Sophia Lines, who d 2 Jan 1823 æ. 29 *WdC*.

FAM. 47. Bezaleel & Martha (Bradley) Peck:

1 Debby, bp 29 Mar 1783 *WdC;* m Jonathan O'Cain.

2 Martha, bp 22 Nov 1784 *WdC*, d 4 Dec 1835 æ. 51 *WdT3;* m ——— Johnson.

3 Harriet, b c. 1791, d 26 Aug 1853; m (1) 1 May 1816 *WdC*—Russell Johnson of Oxf.; m (2) Harry French. PAGE 1529

FAM. 48. Anon & Betsey (Beecher) Peck:

1 Jerre Beecher, b 8 Nov 1787 *WdT2*, bp 6 Apr 1788 *WdC*, d 15 Jan 1830 æ. 42 *WdT2*, 14 Jan *WdC;* m Betsey da. Daniel & Thankful (Smith) Smith, b 14 June 1787 *F*, d 23 Nov 1877 æ. 90 *WdT2*.

FAM. 49. SAMUEL & MEHITABEL (SMITH) PECK:

1 MEHITABEL, b 13 Feb 1763 *F*, d 13 Dec 1851 æ. 89 *MT;* m Abraham Clark.

2 SAMUEL, b 19 Oct 1764 *F*, d 28 Nov 1841 æ. 77 *MT;* m 13 Jan 1796 *MC1*—Mehitabel Ingersoll, who d 21 Aug 1842 *MT*.

3 EPHRAIM, b 19 Nov 1766 *MT*, d 2 Apr 1839 æ. 72 *MT;* m Rachel Bennett, b c. 1767, d 23 July 1806 æ. 39 *MT*.

4 HEZEKIAH, b 25 Dec 1768 *F;* m (1) Sally da. Benjamin & Ann (Platt) Bull, who d 1837 æ. 69 *MD;* m (2) Charlotte da. John & Mary (Read) Herpin wid. Benjamin Bull, Jr., b 18 Jan 1762 *MV*, d 22 July 1851 æ. 89 *MT*.

5 NATHAN, b 20 Mar 1771 *F*, bp 24 Mar 1771 *MC1*, d 31 May 1854 æ. 83-2-11 *NHV;* m Mehitabel da. Samuel & Mehitabel (Lambert) Tibbals.

6 MICHAEL, b 12 Aug 1773 *F*, bp 22 Aug 1773 *MC1*, d 27 Dec 1861 *F;* m 1 Jan 1797 *MC1*—Mary da. Jonathan & Elizabeth (Bristol) Marshall, bp 12 Dec 1773 *MC1*.

7 DAN, b 28 Nov 1775 *F*, bp 7 Jan 1776 *MC1*, d 6 Jan 1861 æ. 85 *MV;* m Mary da. John & Jane (Green) Miles, bp 8 June 1778.

FAM. 50. BENJAMIN & AMY (SMITH) PECK:

1 ABRAHAM, b 29 June 1761 *MV;* m Mercy da. Philosebius & Elizabeth (Baldwin) Treat.

2 BENJAMIN, b 24 Apr 1764 *MV*, d 5 Jan 1838 æ. 72 *MT;* m 14 Nov 1797 *HuntingtonC*—Nancy da. Enoch & Maria (Curtis) Buckingham, who d 20 Nov 1854 æ. 82 *MT*.

FAM. 50. BENJAMIN & SARAH (SMITH) PECK:

3 SARAH, b 25 Nov 1765 *MV*, d 5 Apr 1826 æ. 60 *MT;* m 5 Nov 1794 *MC2*—Stephen Gunn.

4 ANNE, b 12 Mar 1768 *MV;* m John Prudden Strong.

PECK. MISCELLANEOUS. THOMAS m Catharine da. Jesse & Catharine (Conkling) Leavenworth, wid. Samuel Dennis, who d June 1815 æ. 46 (at NH) *ColR*....... ADONIRAM had w. who d 10 Jan 1824 æ. 62 *WdD;* & a s. Allen, b c. 1796, d 10 Mar 1837 æ. 41 *WdD*, m Julia da. Jared Sperry, who d 14 Mar 1874 æ. 72 *WdD*....... MITCHELL, b c. 1784, d 29 June 1843 æ. 59 *BT2;* Capt; m Harriet Sperry, who d 20 July 1828 æ. 37 *BT2;* Mitchell had bro. Rufus or Austin & sister Julia w. John Russell....... ELIZABETH prob. da. Paul of Hartford m 29 Oct 1674 *WV*—Jeremiah How....... RUTH da. Paul m 12 May 1680 *WV*—Thomas Beach....... RUTH of Hartford m 28 Jan 1714 *WV*—Solomon Moss....... ABIGAIL m 24 Nov 1774 *NHC1*—Joseph Cook....... OLIVE m 6 Mar 1811 *NHx*—John Beers....... ELI m 1 Feb 1804 *NoHV*—Martha Rogers.

PECKHAM. GEORGE, b c. 1711, d 26 Oct 1807 æ. 96 *NHT1;* Census (H) 1-0-1; m 1 May 1766 *WC1*—Rachel da. Samuel & Eunice (Munson) Bradley, b 20 Dec 1733 *NHV,* d 16 Nov 1810 æ. 77 *NHT1.*

1 SARAH, b c. 1767; m 20 Oct 1785 *NHC1*—John Orshall.

2 GEORGE, b c. 1769, d 29 June 1821 æ. 52 *NHT1,* 1 July æ. 53 *(NHx)NHV;* Census (H) 2-0-2; m (1) Azuba ———, b c. 1771, bp (adult) 30 Jan 1794 *NHx,* d 4 Aug 1805 æ. 34 *NHT1;* m (2) Sarah Welch, b c. 1776, d 6 Mar 1840 æ. 64 *NHV.*

(By 1): *i* Rachel, b 22 Sep 1790 *NHT1,* bp 30 Jan 1794 *NHx,* d 25 Feb 1857 *NHT1,* æ. 67 *NHV;* m 26 Apr 1807 *NHx*—Henry Parmelee.

ii George, b [Oct 1792], bp 30 Jan 1794 *NHx,* d 29 Jan 1794 æ. 0-16 *NHT1,* 31 Jan æ. 0-15 *NHx.*

iii Sarah, b [May 1795], bp 22 Aug 1796 (æ. 0-15) *NHx,* d 23 Sep 1796 *NHx,* 21 Sep æ. 0-20 *NHT1.*

iv George A.; m 18 Jan 1824 *NHV*—Rhoda Hunter.

v Jennet, b [Dec 1799], d 6 Sep 1882 æ. 82-8 *NHV;* m (1) Sidney Twitchell; m (2) ——— Barney.

vi Sally; m Enoch Burwell.

vii Amanda, b [Nov 1804], d 6 Oct 1805 æ. 0-11 *NHT1.*

(By 2): *viii* Charles Welch, bp 27 Nov 1808 *NHx,* d 3 May 1843 æ. 35 *NHV;* m 15 June 1828 *NHV*—Elizabeth P. da. Freegift & Polly Coggshall of M, who d 16 May 1882 æ. 77-3 *NHV.*

ix Jane Minerva, b [May 1810], bp 23 June 1811 *NHx,* d 7 Nov 1811 æ. 0-18 *NHT1.*

x William Merwin, b [Dec 1813], d 18 Sep 1815 æ. 0-21 *NHT1.*

xi William A.

xii Harry, b c. 1818, d 30 May 1825 æ. 7 *NHT1.*

3 WILLIAM, b c. 1770, d s. p. 19 Jan 1825 æ. 55 *NHT1,* 24 Jan *(NHx)NHV;* m Elizabeth ———, who d 24 Sep 1824 æ. 55 *NHT1.*

4 PHILEMON, b c. 1772, d 1 Sep 1849 æ. 77 *NHT1,* 2 Sep *NHV;* m (1) 19 Apr 1794 *NHx*—Anne da. Nicholas & Mabel Howell, b c. 1776, d 27 Nov 1805 æ. 30 *NHT1;* m (2) Martha da. Samuel & Esther Wooding, b c. 1778, d 25 June 1816 æ. 39 *NHT1;* m (3) 23 Feb 1819 *ColR*—Anna Maria da. John & Elizabeth (Tomline) Hunt, wid. Justus Potter, b 5 Dec 1777 *NHV,* d 27 Dec 1853 æ. 76 *NHT1, NHV.*

(By 1): *i* John, b c. 1794, bp 26 June 1803 (æ. 9) *NHx,* d 25 Dec 1805 æ. 11 *NHT1.*

ii James, b c. 1797, bp 26 June 1803 (æ. 6) *NHx.*

iii Anna, b c. 1799, bp 26 June 1803 (æ. 4) *NHx,* d 25 June 1861 æ. 62 *NHT3;* m James R. Hunt.

iv Nancy, b [6 July 1801], bp 26 June 1803 (æ. 2) *NHx,* d 28 July 1895 æ. 94 *HT4,* æ. 94-0-22 *HV;* m Horace Potter.

v Phebe, b [June 1803], bp 27 Sep 1803 (æ. 0-3) *NHx;* m 27 Feb 1823 *NHV*—Ebenezer Deming.

vi William, b [Aug 1805?], d 15 Mar 1816 [? 1806] æ. 0-7 *NHT1.*

(By 2): *vii* Caroline, bp 26 May 1808 *NHx.*

viii John, bp 23 June 1811 *NHx;* m 2 Jan 1836 Anna Louisa Thomas.

ix William, bp 11 July 1813 *NHx,* d 29 Apr 1846 æ. 33 *NHV.*

x Elizabeth, b [Jan. 1816], d 10 Feb 1816 æ. 6 wks. *NHT1.*

(By 3): *xi* Emeline; m 18 June 1840 Lucius Augustus Thomas.

5 MUNSON; m (1) 16 Aug 1796 *NH SupCt*—Abigail Clark of D; he div. her 1800; m (2) c. 1800 *NH SupCt*—Hannah Thompson, b 1776, d 1856 *NHT1,* d 29 Feb 1856 æ. 80 *BAlm;* she div. him 1810; he rem. to Newbern, N. C.

(By 2): *i* Maria, b [3 July 1802], b 1802, d 1880 *NHT1,* d 28 Feb 1880 æ. 77-7-25 *NHV;* m Merritt Newhall.

ii Hannah B., b 22 July 1805 *F,* d 3 Dec 1882 æ. 78-5 *NHV;* m 7 Oct 1823 *NHV*—Job Mansfield Atwater.

PENFIELD. FAM. 1. SAMUEL, d 30 Nov 1711 *GV;* m (1) 30 Nov 1675 *Lynn, Mass.*—Mary Lewis; m (2) Ann ———; m (3) Mary ———.

(By 1): 1 SAMUEL, b 17 Sep 1676 *Lynn,* d 22 Nov 1714 *GV;* m Hannah ———.

i Samuel, b 19 July 1700 *Bristol, R. I.;* m 1 Dec 1727 *BdV*—Bethia Rose. Children recorded *BdV:* Hannah, b 8 Sep 1728; Lydia, b 4 Sep 1733; Abigail, b 11 Nov 1736; Samuel, b 17 Apr 1740 (FAM. 3); Bethia, b 31 May 1744.

ii Peter, b 14 July 1702 *Bristol;* m 28 May 1730 *FdV*—Mary Allen & had family in Fairfield.

iii Abigail, b 22 Dec 1704 *Bristol;* m James Wadsworth of Durham.

iv Nathaniel, b 10 Feb 1706/7 *Bristol;* d 5 Jan 1776 æ. 79 (?) *WT2;* m 4 May 1731 *BdV*—

Hannah da. Joseph & Abigail (Royce) Cole, b 11 Apr 1706 *WV,* d 5 June 1777 æ. 72 *WT2.* FAM. 2.

v Mary; m Benjamin Hand of G.

vi Hannah; m Cornelius Johnson of Bd.

2 MARY, b 24 Oct 1678 *Lynn;* m 14 Apr 1698 *Taunton*—Jeremiah Fairbanks of Bristol, R. I.

3 JOHN, b 30 May 1681 *Rehoboth;* res. Mid; m Ann da. Thomas Cornwall; had s. Stephen of Mid who m 13 June 1738 *Bristol, R. I.*—Jerusha Brewer.

4 SARAH; m Joseph Wilson of Newport, R. I.

5 ISAAC, b 27 July 1685 *Bristol,* d 21 Oct 1754 æ. 70 *EHT;* m (1) Hannah da. William & Mercy (Whitehead) Luddington, b 13 Mar 1693 *EHV,* d 11 June 1719 æ. 27 *EHT;* m (2) Elizabeth da. John & Hannah (Hemingway) How, b 19 Dec 1702 *NHV,* d 8 Jan 1767 æ. 65 *EHT;* she m (2) Caleb Chidsey.

(By 1): *i* Elizabeth, b 24 Jan 1717 *EHV;* m 31 Aug 1737 *NHV*—Isaac Goodsell.

(By 2): *ii* Hannah, b 19 Feb 1724 *EHV,* d s. p.

6 HANNAH, b 29 Oct 1687 *Bristol;* m John Turner of G.

7 JONATHAN, b 21 Nov 1689 *Bristol,* d s. p. 11 Apr 1735 *WV;* m 29 Mar 1722 *WV*—Mary da. Samuel & Hope (Parker) Cook, wid. Nathaniel Ives, b 23 Apr 1675 *WV.*

(By 2): 8 ABIGAIL, b 23 Oct 1692 *Bristol;* m (1) 4 Feb 1711 *DurhamV*—Timothy Rossiter; m (2) 6 Sep 1727 *DurhamV*—Gideon Leete.

9 REBECCA, b 23 Oct 1692 *Bristol,* d 3 Oct 1714 *GV.*

(By 3): 10 BENJAMIN, b 26 Apr 1696 *Bristol;* res. Durham.

FAM. 2. NATHANIEL & HANNAH (COLE) PENFIELD:

1 NATHANIEL, b 6 Apr 1732 *BdV,* d 18 May 1777 (New Britain); m Jan 1755 *WC2*—Lydia Barnes, who d 31 Jan 1811 æ. 76; she m (2) 23 Apr 1778 Jeremiah H. Osgood.

i Phineas, b 6 June 1756 *WV,* bp 13 June 1756 *WC2.*

ii Lydia, b 19 Aug 1758 *NHV,* bp 27 Aug 1758 *NHC1.*

iii Nathaniel, b 14 Nov 1760 *NHV,* bp 25 Jan 1761 *NHC1.*

iv Rebecca Rena, b 10 May 1763 *NHV,* bp 29 May 1763 *NHC1.*

v Amelia, b 26 May 1766 *NHV,* bp 8 June 1766 *NHC1.*

vi Elizabeth.

vii Phebe, bp 19 Aug 1772 *New BritainC.*

viii Sylvia, bp 31 July 1774 *New BritainC.*

2 Isaac, b 4 July 1733 *BdV;* m 1 Aug 1755 *GV*—Esther Hollabird [Hurlbut].
3 Samuel, b 7 Mar 1734/5 *BdV;* m 1 June 1758 *WV, WC2*—Rebecca da. James & Rebecca Scovill, b 24 July 1741 *WV* [1740]. A child, Abigail, b 18 Nov 1761 *WV.*
4 Lois, b 10 Oct 1736 *BdV;* m 8 Feb 1759 *WC2*—Hezekiah Warner of Mid.
5 Hannah; m (1) 6 Apr 1758 *WV, WC2*—Isaac Royce; m (2) 18 Dec 1766 *MidV*—Josiah Boardman.
6 Sarah, b 23 Nov 1740 *BdV;* m 11 Feb 1762 *WC2*—James Churchill of Mid.
7 Peter; m 19 Dec 1770 *WV*—Huldah Hand of E. Guilford.
8 Rebecca, d 14 Oct 1762 *WV, WC2.*
9 Elizabeth, b 15 Sep 1747 *WV,* bp 25 Oct 1747 *WC2,* d 20 Nov 1765 æ. 18 *WT2.*
10 Child, "a monster," b c. 1749, d 12 Dec 1749 *WC2.*

FAM. 3. Samuel, s. of Samuel & Bethia (Rose) Penfield, b 17 Apr 1740 *BdV,* d c. 1763; m 15 Dec 1762 *NHC1*—Esther da. Andrew & Eunice (Sherman) Tuttle, b 8 July 1742 *NHV,* d 11 May 1821 æ. 82 *NHT1;* she m (2) 25 Sep 1774 *NHC1*—James Bradley.

1 Abigail, b 7 Nov 1763 *F,* bp 25 Dec 1763 *NHC1,* d 29 Dec 1844 æ. 81 *LT;* m 20 Dec 1789 Ebenezer Bolles.

PENNINGTON. Ephraim, of NH, d 1660.

1 Ephraim, b 1645 *NHC1,* bp 22 Oct 1648 *NHC1;* res. M & Newark, N. J.; m 25 Oct 1667 *NHV*—Mary da. John Brockett, bp 28 Sep 1646 *NHC1.*
2 Mary, b 1646 *NHC1,* bp 22 Oct 1648 *NHC1;* m 12 Apr 1666 *NHV*—Jonathan Tompkins; rem. to Newark.

PERIT. [Assistance received on this family from George C. Bryant, Esq., of Ansonia.] Peter, b c. 1707, d 8 Apr 1791 æ. 84 *MD, NHT1;* m 31 Oct 1734 *MV*—Abigail da. John & Abigail (Allen) Shepard, b 22 Oct 1713 *MV,* d 27 Sep 1794 æ. 81 *NHT1,* 26 Sep *NHx.*

1 Peter, b c. 1735, d 24 Sep 1803 æ. 68 *MD;* "Wid." Perit d 1805 *MD.*
2 John, b c. 1738, d 1795 æ. 57 (at Philadelphia) *MD;* res. Norwich 1774; m Ruth da. Pelatiah Webster.
   i John W.
   ii Maria.
   iii Rebecca.
   iv Pelatiah, b c. 1786 (at Norwich), d 8 Mar 1864 æ. 78 *NHV.*
3 Mary, b c. 1740, d 4 Feb 1816 æ. 76 *NHT1;* m 8 Sep 1761 *MC2*—Ralph Isaacs.

4 Samuel, b c. 1744, d 1808 æ. 64 *MD;* m.

5 Anthony, b c. 1744, d s. p. 15 July 1816 æ. 72 *NHT1;* Census (NH) 1-0-1; m (1) 31 Jan 1773 *NHx*—Mary da. Benjamin & Mary (Brown) Sanford, b c. 1757, d 4 Mar 1774 *NHx,* 4 Apr æ. 17 *NHT1;* m (2) 11 Nov 1784 *NHx*—Betsey da. Isaac & Lucretia (Burroughs) Quintard, b 21 Feb 1763 *StamV,* d before 1831.

6 Job, b c. 1751, d 2 Oct 1794 æ. 43 *NHT1, NHx;* Census (NH) 1-0-2; m 17 Nov 1782 *NHx*—Sarah da. Benjamin & Mary (Brown) Sanford, b c. 1760, d 26 July 1829 æ. 69 *NHT1;* she m (2) 24 Nov 1804 *NHx*—Eneas Munson.

i Benjamin Sanford, bp 30 Nov 1783 (sponsors, Benj. & Hannah Brown & Anthony Perit) *NHx,* d 29 Jan 1784 *NHx,* æ. 0-3 *NHT1.*

ii Elizabeth Sanford, bp 14 Aug 1785 (sponsors. Anthony & Elizabeth Perit & Desire Sanford) *NHx,* d 8 Jan 1858 æ. 72 *F;* m 27 Apr 1806 Elihu Munson.

iii Sarah Sanford, b c. 1789, bp 11 July 1791 *NHx,* d 11 July 1791 *NHx,* æ. 2 *NHT1.*

iv Sophia Caroline, bp 11 June 1794 (sponsors, Lucy Sanford & Thadeus Perit) *NHx,* d 22 June 1794 *NHx,* æ. 3 wks. *NHT1.*

7 Thaddeus, b c. 1755, d 3 Aug 1806 æ. 51 *NHT1;* Census (NH) 1-1-1; m (1) 16 Mar 1782 *NHx*—Sophia da. Pelatiah Webster, b c. 1760 (at Philadelphia), d 22 May 1784 æ. 24 *NHT1,* bu. 23 May *NHx;* m (2) 26 Nov 1789 *NHx*—Desire da. Benjamin & Mary (Brown) Sanford, b c. 1768, d 27 Aug 1838 æ. 70 *NHT1.*

(By 1): *i* Pelatiah Webster, bp 30 Mar 1783 *NHx,* d 16 Apr 1811 æ. 28 *NHT1;* m 19 Sep 1808 *NHx*—Frances Hall.

PERKINS. fam. 1. Edward, d after 1688; m 20 Mar 1649 *NHV*—Elizabeth Butcher.

1 John, b 18 Aug 1651 *NHV,* d after 1727; m (1) 16 May 1677 *NHV*—Mary ——— (name omitted); m (2) c. 1703 Rebecca da. John & Dorothy Thompson, wid. Daniel Thomas, b 26 Jan 1651 *NHV,* d after 1727.

(By 1): *i* John, b 3 June 1678 *NHV,* bp 8 July 1688 *NHC1,* d 1749; m (1) 15 May 1701 *NHV*—Sarah Warner, who d 11 Mar 1706 *NHV;* m (2) 3 Feb 1707/8 *NHV*—Elizabeth da. Thomas & Ruth Hayward of Enfield. fam. 2.

ii Stephen, b 7 Apr 1680 *NHV,* bp 8 July 1688 *NHC1,* d after 1755; m (1) 27 Aug 1700 *NHV*—Elizabeth da. Samuel & Elizabeth (Hipkins) Ford, b 19 Feb 1679 *NHV;* m (2) 12 Nov 1729 *NHV*—Anna da. Elijah & Mary (Bellamy) How, b 18 Oct 1704 *WV,* d after 1755. FAM. 3.

iii Peter, b 18 May 1682 *NHV,* bp 8 July 1688 *NHC1,* d 14 Feb 1738/9 *NHV;* m Hannah da. Samuel & Elizabeth (Hipkins) Ford, b 16 Sep 1687 *NHV.* FAM. 4.

iv James, b 23 Aug 1684 *NHV,* bp 8 July 1688 *NHC1.*

v Elisha, bp 8 July 1688 *NHC1,* d c. 1720; m 27 Feb 1713 *HadleyV*—Sarah da. Samuel & Sarah (Bliss) Smith, b 10 Apr 1689 *HadleyV;* she m (2) 29 May 1724 *HadleyV*—Benjamin Church. FAM. 5.

vi Mary, b 9 Oct 1689 *NHV,* bp 6 (?) Oct 1689 *NHC1;* m Abraham Tomlinson of D.

vii Nathan, bp 9 Sep 1694 *NHC1,* d 1748; m 23 May 1718 *NHV*—Abigail da. Ebenezer & Abigail (Wooding) Hill, b c. 1693, bp (adult) 24 July 1737 *NHC1,* d after 1775. FAM. 6.

viii Aaron, bp 29 Nov 1700 *NHC1,* d 1763; m (1) 2 Oct 1719 *NHV*—Silence da. Samuel & Hannah (Johnson) Humiston, b 7 Feb 1690/1 *NHV;* m (2) 18 Dec 1723 *NHV*—Mary nat. da. John Alling & Jane Holmes, b 26 Aug 1693 *NHV,* d 1784. FAM. 7.

2 MEHITABEL, b 21 Sep 1652 *NHV.*

3 JONATHAN, b 12 Nov 1653 *NHV;* m 14 June 1682 *NHV*—Mary da. Anthony Elcock, b 22 July 1661 *NHV,* bp (adult) 7 Apr 1689 *NHC1,* d 9 Nov 1718 *NHV.*

i Seth, b 4 Sep 1685 *NHV,* bp 7 Aug 1689 *NHC1,* d 1733; m 28 Feb 1716/7 *NHV*—Elizabeth da. John & Sarah (Cooper) Munson, b 15 May 1695 *NHV;* she m (2) 7 June 1733 *NHV*—Nicholas Russell. FAM. 8.

ii Sarah, bp 7 Aug 1689 *NHC1,* d soon.

iii Ann, b 5 Nov 1690 *NHV,* bp 8 Sep (?) 1690 *NHC1;* m 25 June 1711 *NHV*—Ebenezer Hitchcock.

iv Jonathan, b 6 May 1694 *NHV,* bp May 1694 *NHC1.*

v Sarah, b 6 Dec 1696 *NHV,* bp Dec 1696 *NHC1;* m 4 Jan 1720/1 *NHV*—John Sperry.

vi Thomas, b 11 Aug 1699 *NHV,* bp 13 Aug 1699 *NHC1.*

vii Eleanor, bp 13 Aug 1699 *NHC1,* d soon.

viii Eleanor, b 7 Mar 1702 *NHV,* d 11 May 1769 æ. 65 *NHC1;* m 15 Dec 1726 *NHV*—Abraham Dickerman.

4 David, b 3 Oct 1656 *NHV,* d 27 Oct 1732 *NHV;* m (1) 8 June 1682 *NHV*—Deliverance da. Thomas & Elizabeth Bliss [name of bride omitted; marriage also recorded *NorwichV*], b Aug 1655 [at Saybrook] *NorwichV;* m (2) 19 June 1729 *NHV*—Sarah da. John & Hannah (Parmelee) Johnson, wid. John Wolcott & Benjamin Bradley, b 26 Aug 1664 *NHV,* d 1 Nov 1732/3 *NHV.*

(By 1): *i* David, b 14 May 1683 *NHV,* d 25 Nov 1685 *NHV.*

ii Elizabeth, b 23 Jan 1684 *NHV* [1684/5], bp 26 July 1685 *NHC1,* d 27 Nov 1686 *NHV.*

iii Rebecca, b 9 Jan 1686 *NHV* [1686/7], bp 12 Feb 1686/7 *NHC1,* d 9 Mar 1693 *NHV.*

iv Daniel, b 4 Apr 1689 *NHV,* bp 7 Apr 1689 *NHC1,* d 1760 *NHC1;* m 5 May 1714 *NHV*—Martha da. Thomas & Martha (Munson) Elcock, b July 1693 *NHV,* bp Feb 1717/8 *NHC1,* d 22 Jan 1767 æ. 74 *NHC1.* FAM. 9.

v Experience, b 31 Jan 1690 *NHV* [1690/1], bp 8 Sep 1690 *NHC1,* d 24 Apr 1691 *NHV.*

vi Mehitabel, b 29 Oct 1692 *NHV,* bp 16 (?) Oct 1692 *NHC1,* d 1751; m 23 May 1717 *NHV*—William Punchard.

vii Rebecca, b 28 Nov 1694 *NHV,* bp 9 Dec 1694 *NHC1,* d bef. 1733; m Caleb Thomas.

viii Samuel, b 16 May 1698 *NHV,* bp Aug 1698 *NHC1,* d young.

ix Experience, b 5 Dec 1699 *NHV,* bp 30 Jan 1700 *NHC1,* d 14 Sep 1748 ; m 28 May 1724 *NHV*—David Gilbert.

FAM. 2. John & Sarah (Warner) Perkins:

1 Phineas, b 25 Feb 1701/2 *NHV,* d Oct 1705 *NHV.*

2 Roger, b 25 Mar 1704 *NHV,* d 1751; res. D; m (1) Ann da. Timothy & Anna (Perry) Wooster, wid. Daniel Hawkins, b 27 Jan 1705 *DV;* m (2) Mary ———, who d 2 July 1789 *OxfC.*

(By 1): *i* Ithiel, b 10 Jan 1733/4 *DV,* d Feb 1826; res. Oxf, & Fair Haven, Vt.; insane; m 26 Oct 1767 *DV*—Esther da. John & Elizabeth (Johnson) Chatfield, wid. Benjamin Fox, b 21 Aug [1734] *DV.* FAM. 10.

ii Mary, b c. 1736.

iii Anna, bp 9 July 1738 *DC,* d 1753.
iv Damaris.
v Ann.
(By 2): *vi* Sarah, b 7 Oct 1748 *DV;* m 19 Jan 1774 *WV*—Samuel Kingsley. [In 1789 Sarah Kingsley was called only child of Mary Perkins *NHPro.*]
vii Eunice, b 22 June 1749 *DV* [error for 1750?], d 25 Apr 1777 æ. 27 *OxfC.*

3 SARAH, b 27 Nov 1705 *NHV;* m John Crawford of D.

FAM. 2. JOHN & ELIZABETH (HAYWARD) PERKINS:

4 MIRIAM, b 2 Nov 1708 *NHV,* d 22 Aug 1794 æ. 86 *NoHT1;* m 5 Feb 1735/6 *NHV*—Joy Bishop.

5 JOHN, b 21 June 1710 *NHV;* m (1) 17 May 1739 *NHV*—Ruth da. James & Abigail (Bennett) Bishop, b 19 May 1709 *NHV,* d 15 Dec 1742 æ. 32 *NHT1;* m (2) 3 Dec 1744 *NHV*—Thankful Chamberlin, "old Widow Perkins of West Woods" d 9 May 1801 *GilbertDrec.*

(By 2): *i* Reuben, b 27 Sep 1745 *NHV,* bp 24 Nov 1745 *WdC,* d 13 Apr 1804 æ. 59 *HT3,* 13 Apr 1805 *GilbertDrec.;* Census (Wd) 2-3-4; m 19 Nov 1767 *WdV*—Thankful da. Joseph & Esther (Ives) Smith, b c. 1746, d 6 Sep 1831 æ. 85 *BT4.* FAM. 11.
ii Titus, b 27 Aug 1747 *NHV,* bp 11 Oct 1747 *WdC,* d 12 Jan 1752 *NHV.*
iii John, b 30 Aug 1749 *NHV,* bp 10 Dec 1749 *WdC,* d 8 Oct 1832 æ. 82 *GilbertDrec.;* Census (H) 1-2-5; m 24 July 1776 *NHV*—Jerusha da. Ephraim & Rachel (Wheeler) Turner, "wife of John" d 17 May 1824 *GilbertDrec.* FAM. 12.
iv Ruth, b 4 July 1751 *NHV,* d soon.
v Elizabeth, b 8 Nov 1753 *NHV;* m 8 Jan 1774 *WatV*—Ephia Warner.
vi Aaron, Census (H) 1-0-1; m Odice ———, who d 5 June 1826 æ. 63 (at H) *ColR.* They prob. had issue: Levi, m Clarissa Hitchcock; & Ambrose, res. 1818 Burton, O.
vii Ruth, b 7 Sep 1758 *NHV;* m 27 Dec 1784 *HC1*—Hezekiah Brockett.
viii Thankful; m Amos Guernsey of Wat.
ix Elias, b c. 1763, d 6 May 1837 æ. 74 *WdC;* Census (Wd) 1-3-2; m (1) Lucy ——, who d 24 Dec 1810 æ. 50 *WdD;* m (2) 8 Apr 1812 *WdV*—Phebe Baldwin, who d 23 Jan 1840 æ. 71 *WdD.* By 1st w. he had: Amos, b c. 1796, d Jan 1809 æ. 12 *WdD;* by 2d w.: Temperance, b 24 Dec 1812 *WdV;* prob. others.
x Titus, d 1783 (in Rev. Army).

6 ANN, b 12 Nov 1711 *NHV*, d 5 Dec 1774 æ. 64 *NoHT1*.

7 ELIZABETH, b 12 Aug 1713 *NHV*, d 2 Feb 1806 æ. 92 *SC;* m 21 Mar 1739 *WV*—Samuel Merriam.

8 LOIS, b 1 May 1715 *NHV*, d 11 Jan 1804 æ. 90 *HT2;* m 8 Nov 1739 *NHV*—Joseph Dickerman.

9 AZARIAH, b 2 Apr 1718 *NHV*, d 14 June 1794 æ. 76 *BT4;* Census, "Adonijah" (Wd) 2-1-2; m 12 Oct 1743 *NHV*—Anna da. Lambert & Rebecca (Curtis) Johnson, b c. 1724, d 15 Mar 1793 *BD*, æ. 69 *BT4*.

i Azariah, b 2 Nov 1744 *NHV;* m 28 Dec 1769 *NHV*—Elizabeth da. Joseph & Lydia (Jones) Moss, b 31 May 1750 *WV*. Children recorded *NHV:* Francis Newman, b 24 Oct 1770; Eliakim, b 8 Mar 1773; Amos Mix, b 10 Mar 1775.

ii Thaddeus, b 9 Sep 1746 *NHV*, bp 14 Feb 1748 *WdC*, d soon.

iii Elijah, b 19 Apr 1748 *NHV*, bp 22 May 1748 *WdC*, d soon.

iv Moses, b 30 Nov 1749 *NHV*, bp 21 Jan 1750 *WdC*.

v Aaron, b 30 Nov 1749 *NHV*, bp 21 Jan 1750 *WdC*.

vi Thaddeus, b 6 Mar 1752 *NHV*, bp 3 May 1752 *WdC*.

vii Anna, b 28 Feb 1754 *NHV;* m 4 Aug 1774 *WV*—Dan Hitchcock.

viii Elijah, b 17 July 1756 *NHV*, d 22 Nov 1842 æ. 86 *WashingtonT;* m (1) 12 Feb 1782 *WashingtonV*—Sarah Castle; m (2) 11 Dec 1803 *WashingtonV*—Mary Clark, who d 12 Sep 1833 æ. 63 *WashingtonT*.

ix Archibald, b 31 Dec 1758 *NHV*, d 2 Mar 1842 æ. 83 *BT2;* Census (Wd) 1-3-3; m (1) Huldah da. John & Desire (Sperry) Wooding, b c. 1763, d 28 Jan 1797 æ. 33 *BT4;* m (2) 19 Apr 1797 *F*—Sarah da. David & Hannah (Lines) French, wid. Nathan Nettleton, b 5 Aug 1766 *F*, d 27 Sep 1846 æ. 80 *BT2*. FAM. 13.

x Rebecca, b 24 Sep 1765 *NHV*.

10 PHINEAS, b 7 Feb 1719/20 *NHV*, bp Feb 1719/20 *NHC1*, d 5 Sep 1793 æ. 73 *HartlandC;* m 13 Dec 1744 *NHV*—Susanna da. John & Sarah (Holt) Bradley, b 21 Jan 1722/3 *NHV*.

i Eliphaz, b 7 Dec 1746 *NHV*, d c. Feb 1813 æ. 66 *ConnH;* Census (L) 1-5-4; m 11 Jan 1776 *Hartland*—Mary Daniels.

ii Eunice, b 27 Nov 1748 *NHV;* m Simeon Couch of Hartland.

iii Phineas, b 4 Sep 1750 *NHV;* Census (L) 3-1-1; m 4 May 1779 *HartlandC*—Phebe Hall.
iv Susanna, b 22 May 1752 *NHV;* m 22 Apr 1776 *HartlandC*—Elisha Giddings.
v Gideon, b 17 Feb 1754 *NHV;* m 14 Oct 1783 *HartlandC*—Sarah Harger, who d 1 Feb 1804 æ. 43 *HartlandC.*
vi Jason, b 31 Aug 1756 *NHV.*
vii Patience, b 16 May 1758 *NHV;* m Edward Garman of Windsor.

11 EUNICE, b 5 Mar 1721/2 *NHV,* bp 13 May 1722 *NHC1,* d 7 Oct 1744 *HadleyV;* m Elisha Perkins.

12 BENJAMIN, b 26 Oct 1724 *NHV,* bp 27 Dec 1724 *NHC1,* d 1750; m 3 Apr 1745 *NHV*—Rebecca da. Lambert & Rebecca (Curtis) Johnson, who m (2) 13 Mar 1752 *NHV*—John Wilmot, (3) 3 Aug 1756 *WdC*—Samuel Thomas, & (4) 11 Sep 1766 *WdC*—Ebenezer Morris.
i Benjamin, b 12 Feb 1745/6 *NHV,* bp 30 June 1751 *WdC.*
ii Simeon, b 25 June 1749 *NHV,* bp 30 June 1751 *WdC,* d c. 1807; m 22 Feb 1771 *WV, NHx*—Tryphena da. John & Dorothy (Pardee) Benham, b c. 1751, d 2 Mar 1832 æ. 81 *WT2;* she m (2) Archelaus Alling. FAM. 14.

13 RUTH, b 30 May 1726 *NHV,* bp 24 July 1726 *NHC1,* d 31 Oct 176[2] æ. 37 *BT1;* m 4 Apr 1751 *NHV, WdC*—John Lounsbury.

FAM. 3. STEPHEN & ELIZABETH (FORD) PERKINS:

1 JOSEPH, b 18 Sep 1701 *NHV;* m 23 Feb 1728/9 *NHV*—Phebe da. Samuel & Sarah (Barnes) Moulthrop, b 15 Oct 1711 *EHV.* Family incomplete.
i Phebe, b 17 Feb 1730/1 *NHV,* bp 27 June 1736 *NHC1;* m 10 Jan 1754 *NHV*—Joseph Wooding.
ii Joseph, b 23 Sep 1733 *NHV,* bp 27 June 1736 *NHC1,* d soon.
iii Timothy, bp 27 June 1736 *NHC1.*
iv Joseph, bp 7 Jan 1738/9 *NHC1.*
v (perhaps) Lydia, bp 12 July 1741 *NHC1.*
vi Abial, bp 1 June 1746 *WdC;* m 4 Mar 1771 *OxfC, WatV*—Mark Porter.
vii Tryphena, bp 6 Nov 1748 *WdC.*
viii Child, bp 22 Oct 1752 *WdC;* [perhaps she was Amy who m 30 Jan 1776 *WatV*—Abel Scott].

2 ELIZABETH, b 10 Nov 1703 *NHV;* m 27 Feb 1728/9 *NHV*—James Bishop.

3 LYDIA, b 24 Nov 1705 *NHV,* d 22 Dec 1767 æ. 63 *OxfC;* m 23 Dec 1725 *NHV*—William Wilmot.

4 THANKFUL, b 17 Apr 1708 *NHV*, d 24 Dec 1788 æ. c. 82 *BD*.

5 MARY, b 31 Mar 1712 *NHV;* m 13 May 1736 *NHV*—Daniel Ford.

6 STEPHEN, b 14 June 1716 *NHV*, bp 29 July 1716 *NHC1*, d young.

FAM. 3. STEPHEN & ANNA (HOW) PERKINS:

7 ANNA, b 26 Mar 1731 *NHV*, bp 16 May 1731 *NHC1;* m (1) 3 June 1752 *WV*, *WC2*—Thomas Berry; prob. m (2) 15 May 1759 *BethlehemC*—Abijah Mitchell.

8 STEPHEN, b 6 July 1732 *NHV*, bp 20 Aug 1732 *NHC1*, d 1815; m 12 May 1756 *WV*—Susanna da. Benjamin & Miriam (Cook) Curtis, b 9 Nov 1732 *WV*.

i Tabitha, b 7 Oct 1757 *WV*, d 24 Aug 1790 æ. 33 *EHT;* m 1779 Philemon Augur.

ii Lois, b 26 Sep 1760 *WV*, d 23 Jan 1852 æ. 94 *WT1;* m 12 Jan 1789 *WV*, *CV*—Justus Royce.

iii Fletcher, b 15 Aug 17[63] *WV*, d 15 Jan 1831 *ColR;* rem. to Atwater, O.; m 26 Sep 1790 *WC2*—Damaris Curtis.

iv Philo, b 16 Jan 176[6] *WV*.

v Violet, b 3 Mar 1769 *WV*, d 22 Dec 1776 *WV*.

vi Lucretia, b 9 Sep 1771 *WV*, d 9 Oct 1776 *WV*.

vii Agnes, b 30 Apr 1774 *WV*, d 8 Nov 1776 *WV*.

viii Liberty, b 31 July 1776 *WV;* m Sarah ———.

9 SYBIL, b 28 May 1734 *NHV*, bp 7 July 1734 *NHC1*.

10 TABITHA, b 12 Apr 1736 *NHV*, bp 13 June 1736 *NHC1*, d 24 Apr 1755 *WC2;* m 6 Feb 1754 *WV*, *WC2*—Eldad Curtis.

11 ELISHA, b 8 Oct 1739 *NHV* [error for 1738?], bp 13 May 1739 *NHC1;* m 9 June 1768 *WV*—Mehitabel Merriam.

12 KERAN, b 8 Oct 1740 *NHV*, "Caron" bp 5 July 1741 *NHC1*.

13 CONTENT, b 31 July 1745 *NHV*.

FAM. 4. PETER & HANNAH (FORD) PERKINS:

1 SAMUEL, b 4 July 1706 *NHV*, d s. p. 15 Apr 1762 *NHV*, æ. 55 *BT1*.

2 HANNAH, b 22 July 1708 *NHV*, bp 3 Sep 1738 *NHC1;* m 5 July 1733 *NHV*—Isaac Sperry.

3 DINAH, b 3 Aug 1710 *NHV*, bp 24 Nov 1734 *NHC1*, d 1774; m 6 Jan 1741/2 *NHV*—Daniel Sanford.

4 MABEL, b 21 Sep 1712 *NHV*, d 8 Sep 1799 æ. 88 *WdT1;* m 17 June 1742 *NHV*—Samuel Johnson.

5 PETER, b 19 June 1714 *NHV*, d 2 Mar 1766 æ. 52 *BT1;* m 5 June 1740 *NHV*—Mary da. Ebenezer & Hannah (Hotchkiss) Peck, b 2 Nov 1714 *NHV*, d c. 1790.

i Peter, b 11 Nov 1741 *NHV,* bp 2 Dec 1750 *WdC,* d 23 Nov 1799 æ. 58 *BT1;* Dea.; Census (Wd) 4-1-4; m 12 Dec 1765 *NHV*—Elizabeth da. Joel & Mabel (Dorman) Perkins, b 9 Sep 1744 , d 17 Apr 1798 æ. 53 *BT1.* FAM. 15.

ii Edward, b 25 Oct 1743 *NHV,* bp 2 Dec 1750 *WdC,* d 1787; m (1) Mary da. Israel & Martha (Hine) Thomas, b 21 Nov 1747 *NHV;* m (2) Rosanna Judd, who d 9 Nov 1821; Census, Rosanna (Wd) 0-0-3; she m (2) James Brown. FAM. 16.

iii Hannah, b 1 Feb 1746/7 *NHV,* bp 2 Dec 1750 *WdC,* d 1829; m 18 Feb 1769 *NHV*—David Beecher.

iv Ebenezer, b 11 Apr 1749 *NHV,* d soon.

v Ebenezer, b c. 1753, "child" bp 21 July 1753 *WdC,* d 7 Sep 1836 æ. 83 *BethlehemC;* Dr.; m Mercy [da. Joseph & Margaret (Clinton)] Stilson, b c. 1755, d 14 Nov 1825 æ. 70 *BethlehemC.* FAM. 17.

vi Samuel, b 11 Sep 1756 *NHV;* m 26 Nov 1777 *CC*—Amy Beecher.

6 ICHABOD, b 26 Feb 1715/6 *NHV,* d s. p. 15 Jan 1741/2 *NHV;* m 9 Oct 1741 *NHV*—Sarah da. John & Mehitabel (Wolcott) Ford, b c. 1720, d c. 1743.

FAM. 5. ELISHA & SARAH (SMITH) PERKINS:

1 SON, b & d 1713 *Hadley.*

2 SON, b & d 1715 *Hadley.*

3 ELISHA, b 5 Jan 1717 *Hadley,* d June 1757 *CC;* m (1) Eunice da. John & Elizabeth (Hayward) Perkins, b 5 Mar 1721/2 *NHV,* d 7 Oct 1744 *Hadley;* m (2) 9 Sep 1745 *NHV, WdC*—Dinah da. Moses & Anna (Blakeslee) Sperry, b 24 June 1717 *NHV,* d 1747 *CC;* m (3) 20 Jan 1747/8 *NHV*—Deborah da. Israel & Elizabeth (Clark) Cook, b 1 Oct 1725 *WV,* d Mar 1758 *CC.*

(By 1): *i* Sarah, b 28 Aug 1741 *Hadley;* m Josiah Hotchkiss.

ii Eunice, b 12 Sep 1742 *Hadley;* m 30 July 1761 *WV*—David Curtis.

iii Sybil, b 28 Feb 1744 *Hadley,* d 14 Mar 1794 *CC,* æ. 51 *CT1;* m 12 Oct 1771 *WV,* 12 Dec *CC*—Benjamin Bristol. She had a nat. child by Simeon Miles: Simeon, b 1 Mar 1764 *WV.*

(By 2): *iv* Abigail, b 13 June 1746 *NHV;* m 23 Jan 1768 *WV,* 1766 *WC2*—John Miles.

v Moses, b 16 Sep 1747 *NHV;* Census (Hampton, N. Y.) 1-5-7; m 23 Mar 1769 *WV, EHC*—Mary da. John & Mary (Cook) Smith, b 29 Aug 1751 *WV*. FAM. 18.

(By 3): *vi* Elisha, b 8 Nov 1748 *NHV*, bp Dec 1748 *CC*, d 13 Feb 1834 æ. 87 *W. Springfield, Mass., V;* Census (H) 2-1-6; m 8 Mar 1771 *CC*—Lois da. Josiah & Lois (Kellogg) Smith, b 9 Oct 1755 *WV*. A child d 22 Apr 1777 *CC*. His children Israel, Lowly, Lois, Sarah, Eunice & Elisha, bp 22 June 1788 [*Hx* ?].

vii Israel, d 23 June 1767 *CC*.

viii Dinah, bp May 1752 *CC*, "wid. of Asa" d 8 Aug 1826 æ. 73 *(NHx) NHV;* m 24 May 1773 *WV*—Asa Austin.

4 JOHN, b 9 Sep 1719 *Hadley*, d after 1790; Census (C) 1-1-1; m (1) 19 May 1746 *NHV*—Dorcas [perhaps da. Nathaniel & Mary (Allis)] Brooks, b [at Deerfield], d 9 Apr 1757 *NHV;* m (2) 11 Feb 1762 *WV*—Eunice da. Ebenezer & Lydia (Hotchkiss) Johnson, b 5 Sep 1728 *WV*.

(By 1): *i* Mercy, b 7 Jan 1747/8 *NHV*, d 6 Oct 1750 *NHV*.

ii Joel, b 1 Mar 1749/50 *NHV*.

iii Rebecca, b 28 July 1752 *NHV;* m 16 Oct 1777 *WV*—William Morris.

iv William, b 6 Jan 1755 *NHV;* rem. to Pomfret, Vt.; m 20 Dec 1775 *CC*—Ruth da. Lent & Abigail (Chauncey) Hotchkiss, b 29 Oct 1751 *WV*. Family incomplete; had (2) Lent Hotchkiss, b 31 Jan 1778 *WV;* (3) Elias, b 4 Aug 1780 *WatV;* also Dorcas Brooks & Rebecca.

(By 2): *v* Samuel, b 26 Jan 1763 *WV;* m Sarah ——— & had s. William Johnson, b 20 Jan 1787 *CV*, who m 9 June 1808 *WatV*—Nancy da. Joseph Bronson & had Lodema, b 11 May 1810 *WatV*.

vi Hannah, b 4 Apr 1765 *WV*, d 19 Apr 1765 *WV*.

vii Eunice, b 6 Nov 1767 *WV*.

FAM. 6. NATHAN & ABIGAIL (HILL) PERKINS:

1 NATHAN, b 23 Feb 1718/9 *NHV*, d 24 Dec 1722 *NHV*.

2 JOEL, b 29 Jan 1720/1 *NHV*, bp 24 July 1737 *NHC1*, d 1748; m 10 Nov 1743 *NHV*, *WdC*—Mabel da. Joseph & Sarah (Lines) Dorman, b 26 Oct 1720 *NHV*, d 18 Mar 1787 æ. 67 *BT1;* she m (2) 26 Apr 1749 *WdC*—Gershom Thomas.

i Elizabeth, b 9 Sep 1744 , d 17 Apr 1798 æ. 53 *BT1;* m 12 Dec 1765 *NHV*—Peter Perkins.

ii Mabel, bp 12 Apr 1747 *WdC*, d 23 Sep 1786 æ. 40 *BT1;* m Jesse Terrell.

3 ABIGAIL, b 8 Dec 1723 *NHV*, bp 24 July 1737 *NHC1*,

d 18 Oct 1756 æ. 24 *WdT1;* m 13 Nov 1746 *NHV, WdC*—David Sperry.

4 SUSANNA, b 13 May 1726 *NHV,* bp 24 July 1737 *NHC1,* d 2 Feb 1789 *BD;* m 20 Sep 1748 *WdC*—Thomas Johnson.

5 MEHITABEL, b 30 Oct 1728 *NHV,* d young.

6 HANNAH, b 14 Nov 1731 *NHV,* bp 24 July 1737 *NHC1,* d c. 1809; m 5 Mar 1761 *WdC*—David Beers.

7 NATHAN, b 28 Apr 1734 *NHV,* bp 24 July 1737 *NHC1,* d young.

FAM. 7. AARON & MARY (ALLING) PERKINS:

1 AARON, b 6 May 1725 *NHV,* bp 20 June 1725 *NHC1.*

2 RACHEL, b 3 Mar 1726/7 *NHV,* bp 23 Apr 1727 *NHC1.*

3 MARTHA, bp 20 Aug 1728 *NHC1;* m 15 Sep 1748 *NHV, WdC*—Moses Brooks.

4 [MOSES, bp 11 Sep 1731 *NHC1.*]

5 MARY, bp 22 Sep 1734 *NHC1,* d 4 Feb 1806 *CC;* m 26 July 1757 *NHV*—Nicholas Russell. [Was Amy who m June 1754 *WdC*—Nicholas Russell a sister of Mary, or is this a variant record or misreading of Mary's marriage?]

FAM. 8. SETH & ELIZABETH (MUNSON) PERKINS:

1 THOMAS, b 20 Dec 1717 *NHV,* bp 13 Oct 1723 *NHC1,* d 1758; m Rachel da. Ebenezer & Hannah (Hotchkiss) Peck, b 2 Aug 1721 *NHV;* Census, Rachel (Wd) 0-0-1.

i Rachel, b 11 Nov 1741 *NHV,* d 11 Nov 1741 *NHV.*

ii Rachel, b 26 Sep 1742 *NHV,* bp 7 Aug 1743 *WdC,* d 26 Nov 1827 æ. 87 *WatT3;* m 19 Apr 1770 *NHC1*—Lemuel Potter.

iii Mary, b 20 Aug 1744 *NHV;* m 25 Jan 1763 *WdC*—Jacob Hotchkiss.

iv Thomas, b 8 May 1746 *NHV,* d 9 May 1746 *NHV.*

v Jonathan, b 28 Apr 1747 *NHV,* bp 7 June 1747 *WdC,* d 30 Jan 1832 æ. 87 *WdC;* Census (Wd) 2-1-2; m 10 Jan 1771 *NHC1*—Lydia da. Noadiah & Hannah (Moulthrop) Carrington, bp 16 June 1745 *WdC,* d 17 Dec 1834 æ. 89 *WdD.* FAM. 19.

vi Thomas, bp 3 Sep 1749 *WdC,* d 1790; m 4 Sep 1775 *WdC*—Eunice da. Elisha & Lois (Gilbert) Wood; Census, Eunice (Wd) 0-3-4; she m (2) Shadrack Minor. FAM. 20.

vii Lucy, bp 1 Dec 1751 *WdC,* m 11 June 1772 *WdC*—Jesse Johnson.

2 Amy, b 3 Sep 1726 *NHV,* bp 23 Oct 1726 *NHC1,* d 2 June 1799 ; m 12 Jan 1743/4 *NHV,* 1744 *WdC*—Joseph Peck.

3 Eleanor, b 3 Sep 1726 *NHV,* bp 23 Oct 1726 *NHC1,* d 9 May 1816 æ. 90 *WdT1;* m 16 Dec 1748 *NHV,* 15 Dec *WdC*—Solomon Hotchkiss.

FAM. 9. Daniel & Martha (Elcock) Perkins:

1 Mary, b 12 June 1715 *NHV;* m 25 Nov 1740 *NHV*—Samuel Hitchcock.

2 Samuel, b 20 Jan 1716/7 *NHV,* d 1749; m 17 Feb 1742/3 *NHV*—Hannah da. John & Hannah (Rowe) Leek, b 2 Mar 1723/4 *NHV;* she m (2) 2 July 1751 *NHV*—Stephen Hunnewell.

i Sarah, b 21 Aug 1746 *NHV;* m 1 Dec 1768 *NHx*—William Harrison.

ii Samuel, b 10 Oct 1748 *NHV,* bp (adult) 30 July 1775 *NHx,* d 2 July 1778 *F;* Capt.; m 17 Oct 1773 (witnesses, Joseph Brown & Sarah Perkins) *NHx*—Sarah da. Joseph & Prudence (Alling) Brown, b 13 July 1754 *F,* d 19 Aug 1834 *F;* she m (2) 27 Apr 1783 *NHx*—Benjamin Matthews. Child: Sarah, b 9 Nov 1776 *F,* d 2 Jan 1778 *F.*

3 Daniel, b 8 Apr 1719 *NHV,* bp Apr 1719 *NHC1,* d 1746; m 7 Sep 1743 *NHV*—Elizabeth da. Joseph & Elizabeth (Trowbridge) Miles, b 26 Oct 1720 *NHV.*

i Elizabeth, b 10 Aug 1744 *NHV,* bp 12 Aug 1744 *NHC1;* m 11 Jan 1764 *NHC1*—Peleg Sanford.

ii Jabez, b 17 May 1746 *NHV.*

4 Amos, b 19 Jan 1720/1 *NHV,* bp Jan 1720/1 *NHC1,* d 9 Dec 1793 æ. 72 *WdT1, WdV;* Dea.; Census (Wd) 2-1-2; m 23 Jan 1744/5 *NHV*—Hannah da. Samuel & Abigail (Atwater) Bishop, b 16 Apr 1725 *NHV,* d 22 Aug 1793 æ. 68 *WdT1, WdV.*

i Mary, b 12 Nov 1745 *NHV,* d s. p.

ii Amos, b 21 Nov 1746 *NHV,* bp 30 Nov 1746 *WdC,* d 26 Mar 1819 æ. 73 *WdT1;* Capt.; Census (Wd) 1-4-2; m 10 June 1772 *WdC*—Abiah da. Seth & Sarah (Wilmot) Downs, b 3 Nov 1752 *NHV,* d 30 Dec 1823 æ. 71 *WdT1.* FAM. 21.

iii Daniel, b 1 Mar 1748/9 *NHV,* bp 5 Mar 1749 *WdC,* d 15 Aug 1841 æ. 91 *LT;* Census (D) 2-1-2; m 8 June 1773 *WdC*—Elizabeth da. Thomas & Elizabeth (Terrell) Beecher, bp 19 Feb 1753 *WdC,* d 4 Aug 1793 æ. 38 *OxfT1.* FAM. 22.

iv Abram, b 6 June 1752 *NHV,* bp 7 June 1752 *WdC;* m 16 Oct 1774 *WdC*—Patience Clark. Child: Elias, b 20 Oct 1774 *WdV.*

v Elijah, b 28 Jan 1755 *NHV;* Census (Wd) 1-4-2; m 9 Aug 1774 *WdC*—Lydia da. Jacob & Lydia (Tuttle) Sperry, b 16 Nov 1754 *NHV.* Children bp 1 May 1788 *WdC:* Abraham, Lyman, Mark & Hannah.

vi Silas, b 4 Apr 1758 *NHV.*

vii Hannah, b 24 Mar 1765 *NHV, BT3,* d 8 Feb 1800 *BT3;* m 20 Oct 1785 Thaddeus Thompson.

5 [Martha, bp 10 Mar 1722/3 *NHC1,* d young.]

6 David, b c. 1725, d 3 Oct 1776 æ. 52 *WdT1;* m 19 Nov 1747 *NHV*—Lydia da. Abraham & Sarah (Wilmot) Bradley, b 1 May 1725 *NHV,* d 7 May 1781 æ. 56 *WdT1.*

i David, b 30 Dec 1749 *NHV,* bp 9 Apr 1750 *WdC,* d 1 Dec 1818 æ. 69 *WdT1, ColR;* m 19 June 1772 *WdC*—Anna da. Caleb & Abigail (Wheeler) Beecher, b 9 Feb 1753 *NHV,* d 28 Oct 1846 æ. 94 *WdT1.* FAM. 23.

ii Lydia, b 16 Mar 1750/1 *NHV,* bp 12 May 1751 *WdC,* d 19 May 1839 æ. 89 *WdT1;* m 31 July 1771 *WdC*—Roger Alling.

iii Sarah, b 24 Oct 1752 *NHV,* d 25 Nov [1834] æ. 83 *WatT1;* m 1 Sep 1773 *WatV, WdC*—Jacob Sperry.

iv Isaac, b c. 1755, d 10 May 1777 æ. 22 *WdT1.*

v Martha, b 10 Oct 1757 *NHV,* d 6 Jan 1838; m 25 Feb 1778 *WtnV*—David Baldwin.

vi Mary, b c. 1759, d 17 Feb 1812 æ. 53 *BT2;* m 1 Jan 1777 *WdC*—Joel Hine.

vii Huldah, b c. 1763, d 20 Sep 1805 æ. 42 *BT4;* m 24 Dec 1781 *WdC*—Alling Carrington.

7 Martha, b 20 Oct 1728 *NHV,* bp 13 July 1729 *NHC1.*

8 Mercy, b 30 Jan 1730 *NHV* [1730/1], bp 31 Jan 1730/1 *NHC1,* d 14 Feb 1797 æ. 66 *NHT1;* m 16 Nov 1758 *NHV*—Obadiah Hotchkiss.

9 Jabez, b 18 Feb 1732/3 *NHV,* bp 25 Feb 1732/3 *NHC1,* d bef. 1756.

10 [Hannah, bp 30 Mar 1735 *NHC1,* d young.]

FAM. 10. Ithiel & Esther (Chatfield) Perkins:

1 Roger, b 5 Apr 1769 *DV,* d c. 1834; rem. to Fair Haven, Vt., & London, Ontario; m 2 June 1790 *OxfC*—Betsey Candee & had issue.

2. David, b 20 Apr 1771 *DV;* m Abigail Smith & had issue.

3 JOSEPH, b 30 Oct 1773 *DV;* m 16 Jan 1793 *OxfC*—Sarah Candee & had issue.

4 ANNA, b 21 July 1776 *DV,* bp 15 Sep 1776 *OxfC;* m 4 Sep 1793 *OxfC*—Joseph Tuttle of Castleton, Vt.

FAM. 11. REUBEN & THANKFUL (SMITH) PERKINS:

1 HULDAH, b 12 Sep 1768 *WdV.*

2 HETTY [MEHITABEL], b 8 Dec 1770 *WdV,* d 1 Oct 1856 æ. 86 *HT3,* æ. 85-9-15 *HV;* m Simeon Todd.

3 DAVID, b 5 Feb 1772 *WdV,* d 16 Nov 1852 æ. 80 *BT4;* m (1) Lowly da. Joel & Elizabeth (Peck) Todd, b c. 1776, d 13 Mar 1814 *BT4;* m (2) Mar 1818 (at Wd) *ColR*—Sarah da. Simeon & Patience (Smith) Sperry, wid. Fletcher Merwin, b c. 1776, d 8 Feb 1861 æ. 85 *WdD,* æ. 84-10 *WdV.*

(By 1): *i* Seymour, b c. 1799.

ii Reuben, b c. 1802.

iii Emily, b c. 1803, d 20 June 1881 æ. 78; m 12 Sep 1824 Abram Lounsbury.

iv Willis, b 17 July 1805 *F,* d 10 Jan 1892; m 7 Feb 1828 *HV*—Laura Dickerman.

v Alvin, b c. 1810, d 9 Aug 1847 æ. 37 *WdD;* m Lucretia da. Henry Sanford.

vi David Allen, b c. 1813, d 16 Mar 1814 æ. 0-13 *BT4.*

4 REUBEN, b 9 July 1774 *WdV.*

5 ELIZABETH, b 2 Oct 1776 *WdV;* m 2 Dec 1799 Jotham Tuttle.

6 THANKFUL ASENATH, b 16 Jan 1783 *WdV,* d 21 Apr 1861 æ. 76 *HT3;* m 28 Sep 1806 *HC1*—Eli Tuttle.

7 AMASA, b 10 Mar 1787 *WdV,* d 31 Jan 1853 æ. 66 *HT3;* m 23 Nov 1808 Esther Hitchcock.

8 BENONI, b 19 Apr 1790 *WdV,* 12 Apr 1789 *BT4,* d 26 Dec 1840 *BT4;* m Polly da. Eli & Comfort (Rogers) Nettleton, b 27 June 1787.

9 ASAEL, b 26 Jan 1793 *WdV.*

PAGE 2049

FAM. 12. JOHN & JERUSHA (TURNER) PERKINS:

1 EUNICE, b 25 June 1777 *NHV,* d May 1849 æ. 73 *HV,* bu. 2 May æ. 73 (of H) *Bx.*

2 REBECCA, b 18 Sep 1780 *NHV,* prob. d 5 Oct 1848 æ. 70 *HV.*

3 JERUSHA, b 29 Oct 1782 *NHV,* d 23 Oct 1801 æ. 19 *HT3.*

4 JOHN.

5 [IRA, b c. 1789, d 12 May 1857 æ. 68 *HT6;* m Mary da. Thaddeus & Penina (Brockett) Todd, b c. 1792, d 28 Nov 1861 æ. 69 *HT6.*]

6 [ELECTA, b c. 1795, d 15 Oct 1879 æ. 84 *CT1;* m John Sears.]

FAM. 13. ARCHIBALD & HULDAH (WOODING) PERKINS:
1 LIBBENE, b 28 Dec 1782 *F*.
2 ARCHIBALD ABNER, b 19 Aug 1784 *F*, bp 28 Nov 1784 *NHx*, d 10 Jan 1869 æ. 84 *BT2;* m (1) 16 Mar 1806 *CC*—Molly adopted da. Ephraim Hotchkiss, b 29 May 1784 *CV*, d 1 Oct 1818 æ. 34 *BT2;* m [? (2)]; m (3) 23 Feb 1843 *WatV*—Malvina Andrews of Mid; m (4) Lois ———, who d 4 Aug 1852 æ. 51 *BT2;* m (5) 20 May 1855 Minerva da. Walter & Hannah (Johnson) Wilmot, wid. Chester Scovill, b 21 Feb 1802, d 4 Dec 1891. Family incomplete.
(By 1): *i* Elizabeth, b [26 Aug 1807], d 30 May 1881 æ. 73-9-4 *NHV;* m 1826 Burton Sperry.
ii Ephraim L., b c. 1810, d 4 Mar 1842 æ. 32 *BT2*.
iii Huldah, b c. 1812, d 8 June 1881 æ. 70 *NHV;* m ——— Myers.
iv Benjamin P., b c. 1818, d 14 Aug 1845 æ. 27 *BT2*.
(By 2): *v* Jennette; m 6 Oct 1844 Benjamin Bronson.
3 JESSE, b 17 Aug 1786 *F;* m Charlotte Hotchkiss.
4 HANNAH, b 18 Nov 1788 *F*.
5 GUY, b 30 May 1791 *F*, d 19 May 1794 *F*.
6 ANNA, b 4 Apr 1793 *F;* m 25 Apr 1811 *WatV*—Elijah Frisbie Merrill.

FAM. 13. ARCHIBALD & SARAH (FRENCH) PERKINS:
7 GUY, b 6 Mar 1798 *F*, b 1798 d 1887 *BT2;* m Laura Doolittle, b 1801 d 1885 *BT2*.
8 REBECCA, b 26 July 1799 *F*.
9 JAMES, b 26 Feb 1800 *F*, d 27 Aug 1800 *F*.
10 BURR; m 21 Dec 1826 *WatV, WdV*—Clarinda Grilley.
11 CHARLES.
12 JAMES, b 23 Oct 1808 *F*, d 23 Oct 1824 æ. 16 *BT2*.

FAM. 14. SIMEON & TRYPHENA (BENHAM) PERKINS:
1 ANNA, b 28 July 1772 *WV;* m Joel Merriman.
2 REBECCA, b 29 Apr 1773 *WV*, "da." d 15 May 1789 æ. 16 *WC2*.
3 LUCINDA, b 31 May 1775 *WV*, d bef. 1797; m 5 Nov 1794 William Olds.
4 JARED, b 25 Apr 1777 *WV*.
5 HULDAH, b 14 May 1779 *WV*.
6 TRYPHENA, b c. 1781, d May 1855; m 13 Oct 1804 Joseph Farrington.
7 SIMEON, b c. 1783; m 13 May 1807 *MeridenV*—Fanny Parker.
i Harriet Pluymert, b 3 Oct 1808 *MeridenV*.
ii Fanny, b 20 Aug 1810 *MeridenV*.
iii Anna, b 20 Aug 1810 *MeridenV*.
iv Wm. Sherlock, b 29 July 1812 *MeridenV*.

8 Benjamin, b c. 1786; res. S; m (1) Polly Baxter Wilson; m (2) 31 Mar 1851 *HV*—Asenath, wid. Barnes, who d 14 Sep 1862 æ. 78 (b at NoH) *CV*.
9 Child, b c. 1789, "infant" d 19 Nov 1789 *WC2*.
10 Sherlock; m (1) Catherine Brockett; m (2) Amanda ———.

FAM. 15. Peter & Elizabeth (Perkins) Perkins:

1 Peter, b 27 Sep 1766 *NHV*, d 25 Mar 1829 æ. 63 *BT2;* m Asenah da. Jesse & Abigail (Sperry) Beecher, b 4 Nov 1767 *NHV*, 4 Dec 1767 *BT2*, d 28 Jan 1858 æ. 90 *BT2*.

PAGE 1790

i Peter, b c. 1789, d 4 July 1870; res. L; m Sally Hotchkiss.
ii Abigail, b c. 1792, d 23 Nov 1827 æ. 35 (at Norfolk, Va.) *BT2;* m Clark Hotchkiss.
iii Enos, b c. 1794, d 1 Nov 1863 æ. 70 *BT2;* m Alma da. Reuben Doolittle, who d 28 Aug 1878 æ. 80 *BT2*.
iv Anson, b 9 Mar 1796 *BT2*, d 18 Apr 1876 *BT2*.
v Betsey, b c. 1798, d 3 Nov 1805 æ. 7 *BT1*.
vi Mabel; m Chauncey Sperry.
vii Sally; m Lyman Beecher.
viii Lucy, b c. 1804, d 13 Nov 1886 æ. 82 *NHV;* m (1) ——— Barnes; m (2) Alva Bunnell.
ix Isaac S.
x Beecher, b 3 May 1811 *LT*, d 20 Aug 1882 æ. 71 *LT;* m Mary Ann ———, who d 1 Sep 1875 æ. 60 *LT*.

2 Elizabeth, b 14 Nov 1767 *NHV*, d 1 Dec 1849 æ. 81 *BT1;* m Demas Sperry.
3 Sarah, b c. 1774, d 15 July 1827 æ. 53 *BT1;* m Ebenezer Downs Thomas.
4 Hannah, b c. 1775, d 24 Apr 1804 æ. 29 *LT;* m Moses Wheeler of Oxf.
5 Mabel, b c. 1777, d 18 Jan 1844 æ. 67 *WolT;* m Isaac Downs.
6 Joel, b c. 1779, d 26 May 1831 æ. c. 40 *ColR*, 27 May æ. 60 (!) *(NHx) NHV*.
7 Harvey, b c. 1781, d 11 Mar 1856 æ. 75 *LT;* m (1) 1802 Abigail da. John & Abigail Russell, b c. 1782, d 13 June 1820 æ. 38 *LT;* m (2) 24 June 1821 Barthena Moss.

(By 1): *i* Julia, b 6 Oct 1803 (at Wd) *F*.
ii Lewis, b 1 Apr 1804 (at L) *F;* m 16 Aug 1826 Orilla Morse.
iii Orrin, b 27 July 1805; res. N. J.; m 14 Sep 1829 Lucinda Wheeler, who d 1897.
iv Henry, b 27 July 1807; m 12 Mar 1834 Harriet McNeil.

v Edwin, b 5 Jan 1809.
vi Abigail, b 8 May 1813.
vii Eliza, b 24 July 1816.
(By 2): *viii* Norman B., b 3 June 1822; m 25 Nov 1847 Sophia Davis.
ix Delia A.
x Harvey B.; m 17 Apr 1856 Olive B. Spencer.
xi Harriet, d 26 Feb 1836 æ. 5 *LT*.

FAM. 16. EDWARD & MARY (THOMAS) PERKINS:

1 ISRAEL, b 30 Dec 1767 *NHV*, d 8 Sep 1846; Census (Wd) 2-0-2; m Millie Judd.
i Celeste, b c. 1789, d 8 June 1810 æ. 21 *BT4*.
ii Leonora; m Isaac Warren.

2 EDWARD, b 7 Feb 1769 *NHV;* res. Medina, Ohio; m (1) 14 Oct 1793 Lois da. Daniel & Lois (Smith) Abbott; m (2) 24 June 1795 Betsey Peck.
(By 1): *i* Child, d young.
(By 2): *ii* Edward, b 21 July 1804 *F;* m 11 May 1828 Delight da. Samuel Smith. Children: Betsey Louisa, b 18 Feb 1829; Edward Smith, b 7 July 1833; Harriet Delight, b 18 Dec 1835; Hannah Eliza, b 4 Dec 1838; Sarah Orilla, b 14 Sep 1841.
iii Israel, b 1 May 1808 *F*, d s. p.; m 7 Sep 1830 Orilla Hurlbut.

3 MARY, b 13 Jan 1771 *NHV*, d 5 Jan 1859 æ. 88 *BT4;* m Elias Lounsbury.

4 ELECTA, b 31 Oct 1775 *NHV*, d 11 July 1856; m Uri Tuttle.

FAM. 16. EDWARD & ROSANNA (JUDD) PERKINS:

5 ROSANNA, b 14 Jan 1780 *WatV;* m 1797 *WatV*—Henry Grilley.

6 ANNA; m Elijah Crook.

FAM. 17. EBENEZER & MERCY (STILSON) PERKINS:

1 EBENEZER PECK, b 13 Apr 1776 *NHV*, d 14 Feb 1794 æ. 18 *BethlehemC*.

2 MERCY SENA, b 25 June 1778 *NHV;* m ——— French.

3 DARIUS, b c. 1783, d 20 Apr 1842 æ. 59 *BethlehemC;* m Olive ———, who d 16 Feb 1847 æ. 59 *Bethlehem C*. Children: John P., Ebenezer, Mercy H., Susan L. & Sarah O.

4 ESTHER, b c. 1789, d 11 Feb 1794 æ. 5 *BethlehemC*.

5 MELINDA, b c. 1793, d 14 Mar 1842 æ. 49 *BethlehemC;* m [Israel or Jeriel?] Hayes. Children: Stephen, Samuel, Hannah & Betsey Ann.

FAM. 18. MOSES & MARY (SMITH) PERKINS:

1 ABIGAIL, b 27 Oct 1769 *WV*, bp 20 Jan 1771 *CC*.

2 HANNAH, b 11 Feb 1771 *WV*.

3 SALLY, b 5 June 1773 *WV*, bp 4 July 1773 *CC*.

4 MARY COOK, b 18 Mar 1775 *WV*, bp 26 Mar 1775 *CC*.
5 MOSES, b 10 Mar 1777 *WV*, bp 4 May 1777 *CC*.
6 SYLVESTER, b 21 Feb 1779 *WV*, bp 4 Apr 1779 *CC*.
7 CHESTER, bp 25 Feb 1781 *CC*.
8 ELAM, bp 26 Jan 1783 *CC*.
9 ANSON ABIRAM, bp 2 Jan 1785 *CC*.
10 CATA, bp 21 Jan 1787 *CC*.
11 AURILLA, bp 10 Oct 1790 *CC*.
12 LUCY, bp 5 Oct 1794 *CC*.

FAM. 19. JONATHAN & LYDIA (CARRINGTON) PERKINS:

1 REBECCA, b [19 Aug 1771], d 25 June 1859 æ. 87-10-6 *WdD;* m ——— Peck.
2 SETH, b c. 1774, d 25 Mar 1854 æ. 80 *WdD;* m (1) Feb 1798 *WdC*—Dennis da. Richard & Rebecca (Baldwin) Sperry, b 31 Mar 1773 *MV*, d 8 Mar 1827 æ. 50 *WdD;* m (2) Mary da. Daniel & ——— Smith, b 27 Oct 1773 *F*, d 1863. Family incomplete.
(By 1): *i* Lewis, b c. 1798, d 14 Nov 1809 æ. 11 *WdD*.
ii Lucy, b [May 1801], d 4 May 1849 æ. 47-11 (at DeWitt, N. Y.) *WdD;* m Alanson Osborn.
iii Lyman, b c. 1810, d 15 Aug 1825 æ. 15 (at M) *WdD*.
iv Merrit R., b c. 1815, d 2 Oct 1857 æ. 42 *WdD*.
3 BELA.

FAM. 20. THOMAS & EUNICE (WOOD) PERKINS:

1 MARY, b Feb 1778 *WdV*, bp 15 May 1791 *WdC;* m Bailey Plumb.
2 THOMAS, b Oct 1779 *WdV*, bp 15 May 1791 *WdC;* m 16 Jan 1812 Susan Beers.
3 ELI, b Jan 1781 *WdV*, bp 15 May 1791 *WdC*, d 4 Feb 1809 æ. 26 *WdC;* m 1805 Content Downs.
4 JESSE, b Feb 1787 *WdV*, bp 15 May 1791 *WdC*, d 12 Mar 1828 æ. 41 (at Wd) *ColR;* m.
5 JEREMIAH, b Nov 1789 *WdV*, bp 15 May 1791 *WdC*, d 1818; res. EH.

FAM. 21. AMOS & ABIAH (DOWNS) PERKINS:

1 EUNICE, b 19 May 1773 *NHV*, d young.
2 SARAH, b 14 Oct 1774 *NHV*.
3 EUNICE, b c. 1777, bp 1788 *WdC*, d 29 July 1869 æ. 90 *WdD*, æ. 92 *WdT1;* m Stephen Peck.
4 SAMUEL, b c. 1780, bp 1788 *WdC*, d 11 Aug 1843 æ. 63 *WdT1, WdC;* m Sep 1804 *WdC*—Sarah da. Eliakim & Molly (Clark) Sperry, b c. 1786, d 22 July 1843 æ. 57 *WdD*.
i Lucretia, b [June 1806], d 7 Apr 1888 æ. 81-10 *WdD;* m Leverett Carrington.
ii Edwin W., b c. 1809, d 21 Mar 1884 æ. 74 *WdD*.

iii Samuel Farrand, b 10 May 1811 *WdT1,* d 23 Oct 1886 *WdT1,* æ. 75 *WdD;* m Mehitabel da. Isaac & Mehitabel (Smith) Stowe, b 4 July 1811 *WdT1,* d 26 Mar 1880 *WdT1,* æ. 62 *WdD.*
iv Sally M.; m ——— Robinson.
v Lewis; m Mary ———, who d 3 Apr 1856 æ. 30 *WdD.*
vi Elizur, b [Jan 1825], d 27 Oct 1861 æ. 36-9 (at Havana, Cuba) *WdD.*
5 Amos, b c. 1782, bp 1788 *WdC,* d 19 Dec 1856 æ. 74 *WdD;* m.
6 James, b c. 1785, bp 1788 *WdC,* d 22 Feb 1862 æ. 77 *WdV;* m Amanda da. Silas & Electa (Carrington) Peck, b c. 1794, d 20 May 1880 æ. 86 *WdV.*
7 William, b c. 1788, d 19 Nov 1820 æ. 33 *WdT1, WdC.*
8 Farren, b c. 1791, d 29 May 1809 æ. 18 *WdD.*

FAM. 22. Daniel & Elizabeth (Beecher) Perkins:
1 Enoch, b 20 Oct 1774 *NHV,* 22 Oct 1773 *Jack's Hill T,* bp 28 Oct 1788 *OxfC,* d 14 May 1857 æ. 84 *OxfV,* 12 May *Jack's HillT;* m. Nancy da. Ebenezer & Ann (Thompson) Riggs, b 4 July 1778, d 2 Aug 1857 *Jack's HillT.*
i Elizabeth, b c. 1798 (at Wtn), d 10 Oct 1885 æ. 87 *NHV;* m Enos Candee.
ii Nancy, b 28 Sep 1802 *Jack's HillT,* d 1 Jan 1806 *Jack's HillT.*
iii Charlotte, b 12 Apr 1805 *Jack's HillT,* d 2 Aug 1891 *Jack's HillT.*
iv Charles D. R., b 7 July 1815 *Jack's HillT,* d 12 Apr 1886 *Jack's HillT;* m Lydia Ann Whittlesey, b 14 Jan 1816, d 1 Feb 1857 *Jack's HillT.*
2 Daniel, b c. 1782, bp 28 Oct 1788 *OxfC,* d 3 July 1847 æ. 66 *LT;* res. Cornwall 1810; m Rachel ———, who d 13 June 1876 æ. 95 *LT.*

FAM. 23. David & Anna (Beecher) Perkins:
1 Thaddeus, b [Jan 1773], d 9 Sep 1774 æ. 1-8 *WdT1.*
2 Anna, b [25 Apr 1777], d 5 May 1777 æ. 0-0-10 *WdT1.*
3 Anna, b 29 May 1778 *WdV,* d 14 July 1801 *WdV,* æ. 23 *WdT1;* m 19 July 1797 *WdV*—Lazarus Clark.
4 Betsey, b c. 1780, d 6 June 1851 æ. 71 *WdD;* m 8 Jan 1800 John Lines.
5 David, b c. 1782, d 29 May 1856 æ. 74 *WdD, WdT1;* m Polly Barbara da. Stephen & Eunice (Bradley) Peck, b c. 1787, d 23 Oct 1859 æ. 72 *WdD.*
i Stephen P., b c. 1806, d 27 Sep 1890 æ. 84 *WdD, WdT1;* m Julia Ann da. Richard & Alice

(Yorke) Pettit, b c. 1807, d 6 June 1874 æ. 67 *WdT1*.

ii Anna, b [May 1810], d 4 Mar 1862 æ. 51-9 *WdD;* m Elihu Gorham.

iii Isaac, b c. 1813, d 21 Mar 1874 æ. 60 (at NH) *WdD*.

iv Betsey, b c. 1815, d 10 Apr 1830 æ. 15 *WdD, WdT1*.

v David, b [Sep 1818], d 3 Feb 1819 æ. 0-4 *WdD, WdT1*.

vi Charles, b c. 1820, d 25 Apr 1879 æ. 59 (at Meriden) *WdD*.

6 Isaac, bp 1786 *WdC*, "child" d 3 Aug 1786 *WdC*.

7 Isaac, bp 29 Aug 1790 *WdC*, d 6 Oct 1812 (at Baltimore) æ. 22 *WdT1*.

PERKINS. miscellaneous. Eliphaz & Lydia had: 1 Chauncey Fitch, bp 6 Nov 1785 *NHC2;* 2 Julia, bp 6 Nov 1785 *NHC2*. ......Peggy m 14 Aug 1769 *NHC1*—Caleb Mix.......Rachel, b c. 1802, d 17 Mar 1888 æ. 86; m Russell Humiston.......Child of U, bp 25 Jan 1784 (at B) *NHx*.......Joel, b c. 1801, d 27 July 1853 æ. 52 *WdD;* m Almyra da. George W. & Patty Morgan, b c. 1803, d 13 June 1867 æ. 64 *WdD*.

PERKINS. Thomas of Enfield m Sarah Richards; their s. Thomas, b 22 Sep 1695, d 1770, m (1) 23 July 1718 Mary Allen, who d 9 Dec 1739 æ. 42, & m (2) 10 Mar 1740/1 Mary Standish. By his 1st w. he had 8 children, including:

2 Thomas, b 15 Dec 1720 *Enfield*, d 7 Oct 1768 *Enfield;* m Eunice Bedell of Springfield; she m (2) 4 June 1778 *OxfC*—Samuel Chatfield.

i Reuben, b 28 Oct 1740 *Enfield;* m (1) 6 Jan 1763 *Enfield*—Lucy Pease; m (2) Lois da. Nathaniel & Margaret (Kirby) Wooster, b c. 1747. He had by 1st w.: Reuben, b 5 Nov 1763 *Enfield;* Lucy, b 28 May 1765 *Enfield;* Thomas, b 7 Dec 1766 *DV*, bp 1 May 1768 *DC;* Benjamin, b 1 May 1769 *DV*.

ii Abner, b 8 Dec 1745 *Enfield*.

iii Abner, b 13 Mar 1748/9 *Enfield*.

iv Eunice, b 26 May 1752 *Enfield;* m 5 Jan 1775 *OxfC*—Hezekiah Wooding.

6 Mary, b c. 1732, d 16 Oct 1788 æ. 56 *SeymourT (Meth);* m 19 Dec 1754 *Enfield*—Bradford Steele.

8 Elias, b 1 Dec 1739 *Enfield;* m Elizabeth da. John & Hannah (Davis) Hawkins, b 14 Feb 1736 *DV*.

i Sarah, b 28 Jan 1764 *DV*.

ii Hannah, b 27 Oct 1765 *DV*, bp 8 Dec 1765 *Dx*.

iii John Hawkins, b 2 Jan 1768 *DV*, bp 17 Apr 1768 *Dx*.

iv Tryphena, bp 15 July 1770 *Dx.*
v Ned Allen, bp 18 Oct 1772 *Dx.*

PERRY. Richard m Mary Malbone. Children bp *NHC1;* Mary, 4 Oct 1640; Micajah, 31 Oct 1641; Samuel, 8 June 1645; John, 11 July 1647; Grace, 2 Sep 1649.

PETTIT. Richard m Alice da. Henry & Susanna (Chatterton) Yorke, b 10 Apr 1789 *F,* d 20 Apr 1852 æ. 62 *WdD.*

1 Julia Ann, b c. 1807, d 6 June 1874 æ. 67 *WdD;* m Stephen P. Perkins.
2 Henry, b c. 1809, d 15 May 1862 æ. 53 (at D) *WdD.*
3 Earl, b c. 1811, d 22 Feb 1876 æ. 65 *WdD.*

PHELPS. Timothy, Census (NH) 1-0-0; m (1) 21 Mar 1795 *NHx*—Jennet da. Samuel Broome, b c. 1774, d 25 Apr 1802 æ. 28 *NHT1;* m (2) Sep 1802 (at NH) *Conn Journal*—Henrietta Broome, who d Aug 1811 *NHT1.*

(By 1): 1 Samuel Broome, bp 1 May 1796 *NHx,* d 1 Sep 1829 æ. 33 (at N. Y. City) *NHT1.*
2 Amelia Maria, bp 16 May 1798 *NHx.*
3 [Timothy.]
(By 2): 4 Caroline Broome, bp 9 Oct 1803 (sponsor, Caroline Broome) *NHx,* d 5 Nov 1805 æ. 2-2 *NHT1.*
5 John, b [Aug 1805], d 16 Feb 1807 æ. 0-18 *NHT1.*
6 Grace Hubbard, d 17 June 1810 *NHT1.*

PHIPPS. Danforth of Falmouth, Me., m Elizabeth Skillon. Family incomplete.

1 Roger Dearing, b c. 1735, d 11 Sep 1770 æ. 35 *NHT1;* m 12 Oct 1758 *NHV,* 15 Nov 1759 (?) *NHC2*—Phebe da. John & Phebe (Munson) Brown, b 28 Sep 1735 *NHV,* bp (adult) 1 Aug 1773 *NHC2;* she m (2) 22 Jan 1775 *NHC2*—Asa Todd.
i Miriam, b 8 Nov 1759 *NHV,* bp 1 Aug 1773 *NHC2,* d 14 Sep 1794 æ. 35 *NHx;* m 30 July 1781 *NHC2*—John Gilbert.
ii Elizabeth, b 18 Feb 1763 *NHV,* bp 1 Aug 1773 *NHC2;* m 30 Oct 1781 *NHC2*—Isaac Munson.
iii Phebe, b 18 Feb 1763 *NHV,* bp 1 Aug 1773 *NHC2,* d 13 Apr 1766 æ. 3-2 *NHT1.*

2 David, b 2 Aug 1741 *NHT1,* d 26 Mar 1825 *NHT1,* 25 Mar æ. 84 *(NHx) NHV;* Capt.; Census (NH) 1-2-4; m 13 June 1771 *NHV, NHC1*—Mary da. Benjamin & Sarah (Dayton) English, b 29 Sep 1744 *NHV,* d 27 Oct 1794 æ. 50 *NHT1,* æ. 51 *NHC1.*
i Mary, b 21 Aug 1772 *NHV,* bp 30 Aug 1772 *NHC1,* d c. 1821; m 20 Oct 1805 *NHC1*—Samuel Bird.
ii Sarah, b 26 Nov 1774 *NHV,* bp 4 Dec 1774 *NHC1,* d s. p.; m 11 Mar 1797 *NHC1*—Joseph Mix of Suffield.

iii Elizabeth, b 8 Apr 1776 *NHV, NHT1,* bp 2 June 1776 *NHC1,* d 12 Apr 1850 (at Fishkill, N. Y.) *NHT1;* m 2 Mar 1800 Jared Mansfield.

iv David, b 16 Jan 1778 *NHV,* bp 8 Mar 1778 *NHC1,* d s. p. Aug 1822.

v Roger Dearing, b 28 July 1782 , bp 11 Aug 1782 *NHC1,* d 25 Sep 1794 æ. 13 *NHT1,* 25 Sep æ. 12 *NHx,* 26 Sep æ. 12 *NHC1.*

vi Son, d 15 Mar 1785 æ. 1 hr. *NHC1.*

3 SOLOMON, b 17 Aug 1745, d 1 June 1813 æ. 68 *NHT1;* Capt.; Census (NH) 1-0-4; m (1) 26 Mar 1772 *F*—Elizabeth da. Asa & Mary (Tuttle) Todd, b 13 Apr 1749 *NHV,* d 7 May 1785 æ. 36 *NHT1;* m (2) 3 Feb 1788 *NHC2*—Hannah da. Caleb & Hannah (Alling) Alling, wid. Hamlin Dwight, b 23 Oct 1752 *NHV,* d 7 Sep 1789 æ. 37 *NHT1.*

(By 1): *i* Asa Todd, b 16 June 1774 *F,* d 2 Sep 1774 *F.*

ii Elizabeth Mary, b 27 Nov 1776 *F,* bp 1 Dec 1776 *NHC2,* d 15 Apr 1849 æ. 72 *NHT1;* m (1) 11 Feb 1795 *NHSupCt*—Webster Brown; she div. him 1800; m (2) 5 Aug 1800 *F*—Jonathan Mix.

iii Joanna, b 8 July 1779 *F,* bp 29 Aug 1779 *NHC2,* d 19 Dec 1826 æ. 47 *NHT1;* m Olney Burr.

iv Asa Todd, b 16 Nov 1781 *F,* bp 10 Feb 1782 *NHC2,* d 13 May 1782 *F.*

v Lucretia, b 11 Apr 1784 *F,* bp 5 Apr 1784 *NHC2,* d 6 Nov 1865 (at N. Y. City) æ. 82 *NHT1;* m 11 Sep 1807 *F*—Gaines Fenn.

(By 2): *vi* Hannah Alling, b 10 Mar 1789 *F,* bp 16 Mar 1794 (ae. 5) *NHx;* m Joel Augur of Northford.

4 DANIEL GOFFE, b c. 1752, d 3 Dec 1838 æ. 87 *NHV;* Capt.; Census (NH) 1-3-3; m 3 Mar 1776 *NHC2*—Anna da. Ebenezer & Elizabeth (Larmon) Townsend, b 24 June 1756 *F,* d 3 Nov 1837 æ. 82 *NHV.*

i Betsey, bp 14 Oct 1787 *NHC2.*

ii Daniel Goffe, bp 14 Oct 1787 *NHC2;* m 1 July 1804 *NHC1*—Esther da. Henry & Hannah (Lewis) Peck, b 19 Dec 1783 *F,* d 1832 *NHT1;* she m (2) Solomon Phipps.

i Grace Ann, b c. 1806, d 8 Apr 1880 æ. 74 *NHV.*

iii Solomon, b 1782 d 1833 *NHT1,* d 12 Oct 1834 æ. 52 *(NHC1) NHV;* m Esther da. Henry & Hannah (Lewis) Peck, wid. Daniel Goffe Phipps.

PIERPONT. FAM. 1. REV. JAMES, s. of John & Thankful (Stow), b 4 Jan 1659 *Roxbury, Mass.* [1659/1660], bp 8 Jan

1659 *RoxburyC,* d 22 Nov 1714 *NHV,* æ. 55 *NHT1;* B.A. (Harvard 1681); m (1) 27 Oct 1691 *NHV*—Abigail da. John & Abigail (Pierson) Davenport, b 20 Aug 1672 *Boston,* d 3 Feb 1691/2 *NHV,* 1691 æ. 20 *NHT1;* m (2) 30 May 1694 (at Hartford) *NHV*—Sarah da. Joseph & Sarah (Lord) Haynes, b c. 1673, d 7 Oct 1696 *NHV,* æ. 23 *NHT1;* m (3) 26 July 1698 *NHV*—Mary da. Samuel & Mary (Willet) Hooker, b 3 July 1673, d 1 Nov 1740 *NHV,* æ. 68 *NHT1.*

(By 2): 1 Abigail, b 19 Sep 1696 *NHV,* bp 20 Sep 1696 *NHC1,* d 10 Oct 1768 *NHV,* 22 Sep 1768 æ. 73 *NHC1;* m 6 Nov 1716 *NHV*—Joseph Noyes.

(By 3): 2 James, b 21 May 1699 *NHV,* bp 21 May 1699 *NHC1,* d 18 June 1776 æ. 78 *NHT1;* m (1) 1 Nov 1727 *Boston*—Sarah da. Nathaniel & Martha Breck, b Nov 1710 *Boston,* d 28 Sep 1753 *NHV,* æ. 43 *NHT1;* m (2) 28 Mar 1754 *NHV, WdC*—Ann [? da. Jabez] Sherman, b c. 1738, d 22 Dec 1803 æ. 65 *EHC;* she m (2) 15 Oct 1780 *EHC*—John Davenport.

(By 2): *i* Evelyn, b 16 Mar 1755 *NHV,* bp 16 Mar 1755 *NHC2,* d 7 Feb 1808; m Mar 1780 Rhoda Collins.

ii Robert, b 13 June 1757 *NHV,* bp 19 June 1757 *NHC2,* d 16 Aug 1835; res. Manchester, Vt.; m 11 Oct 1780 Lois Collins.

iii James, b 27 July 1761 *NHV,* bp 6 Sep 1761 *NHC2,* d 23 Apr 1840 æ. 79 *LT;* m (1) 24 Sep 1782 Elizabeth Collins; m (2) 16 Dec 1817 Lucy Crossman.

iv David, b 26 July 1764 *NHV,* bp 9 Sep 1764 *NHC2,* d 16 Feb 1826 æ. 62 *LT;* m Sarah Phelps.

v William, b 11 Jan 1772 *NHV,* bp 22 Mar 1772 *NHC2,* d 16 Feb 1841 æ. 69 *LT;* m (1) Huldah ———; m (2) Abigail, wid. Smith.

3 Samuel, b 30 Dec 1700 *NHV,* d 15 Mar 1722/3 *NHV;* B.A. (Yale 1718); Rev.

4 Mary, b 23 Nov 1702 *NHV,* d 24 June 1740; m 19 Aug 1719 William Russell of Mid.

5 Joseph, b 21 Oct 1704 *NHV,* d 24 Nov 1748 æ. 45 *NoHT1;* m c. 1725 Hannah da. Noadiah & Mary (Hamlin) Russell, b 23 Feb 1705/6 *MidV,* d 5 June 1791 æ. 84 *NoHT1,* 6 June æ. 86-3 *NoHC;* she m (2) 5 Aug 1752 *NHV*—Samuel Sackett.

i James, b c. 1726 *F,* d c. 1727 *F.*

ii Samuel, b 16 Apr 1729 *NHV,* d 22 Dec 1820 æ. 92 *NoHT1;* Census (NoH) 2-1-4; m 5 Nov 1751 *NHV*—Elizabeth da. Ebenezer & Mary (Tuttle) Frost. fam. 2.

iii Joseph, b 13 Sep 1730 *NHV,* d 8 Feb 1824 æ. 94 *NoHT1,* 7 Feb æ. 93 *NoHD;* Census (NoH) 2-0-1; m (1) 21 Oct 1756 *NHV, NoHV*—Lydia da. Joseph & Miriam (Bradley) Bassett, b 1 Aug 1736 *NHV,* d 9 Nov 1783 æ. 48 *NoHV;* m (2) 26 Oct 1791 *NoHV*—Annis da. John & Mary (Hickox) Warner, wid. Ebenezer Curtis & Noah Blakeslee, b 13 Jan 1734/5 *WatV,* d 4 Sep 1800 æ. 66 *NoHV, NoHT1.* FAM. 3.

iv James, b 2 Oct 1732 *NHV,* d 27 Dec 1815 æ. 83-2 *NoHC;* Census (NoH) 2-1-4; m Lydia [da. John & Sarah (Brockett) Mansfield], b c. 1731, d 15 Dec 1814 æ. 84 *NoHT1.* FAM. 4.

v Dorothy, d infant *F.*

vi Benjamin, b 7 Jan 1734/5 *NHV,* d 20 Sep 1812 *NoHV,* æ. 78 *NoHT1;* Census (NoH) 2-1-1; m 17 Oct 1765 *NHV*—Sarah da. Isaac & Mary (Frost) Blakeslee, b 13 May 1738 *NHV,* d 10 Sep 1794 æ. 57 *NoHT1,* 19 Sep *NoHV.* FAM. 5.

vii Hannah, b 12 Nov 1736 *NHV,* d 16 Apr 1816 æ. 79 *NoHT2;* m 24 July 1755 *NHV*—Abel Brockett.

viii Mary, b 20 Oct 1738 *NHV,* d 21 June 1773 æ. 34 *NoHT2;* m 31 Mar 1756 *NHV*—Richard Brockett.

ix Giles, b 4 June 1741 *NHV,* d 16 Jan 1832 *NoHV,* æ. 91 *NoHT1;* Sgt; Census (NoH) 1-2-4; m 22 Jan 1766 *NoHV, NoHC*—Elizabeth da. Jude & Mehitabel (Brockett) Cooper, b 20 Mar 1743/4 *NHV,* d 1 Nov 1832 *NoHV,* æ. 89 *NoHT1.* FAM. 6.

x Abigail, b 6 June 1743 *NHV,* d 13 Feb 1815 æ. 72 *NoHT1;* m 23 Dec 1762 *NHV*—Noah Ives.

xi Hezekiah, b 27 Sep 1745 *NHV;* Census (NoH) 1-1-3; res. Rowe, Mass., 1796; m 26 Sep 1771 *NoHC*—Mehitabel da. Jude & Mehitabel (Brockett) Cooper, b 12 July 1750 *NHV.* FAM. 7.

xii Sarah, b 31 July 1747 *NHV,* d 21 Jan 1801 æ. 53-5 *NoHC;* m Peter Eastman.

6 BENJAMIN, b 18 July 1706 *NHV,* d 17 Dec 1706 *NHV.*

7 BENJAMIN, b 15 Oct 1707 *NHV,* d s. p. 1733.

8 SARAH, b 9 Jan 1709/10 *NHV,* d 2 Oct 1758; m 20 July 1727 Rev. Jonathan Edwards.

9 HEZEKIAH, b 26 May 1712 *NHV,* d 22 Sep 1741 æ. 29 *NHT1;* m 9 Feb 1736/7 *NHV*—Lydia da. Jacob & Lydia (Ball) Hemingway, b 2 Sep 1716 *NHV,* d 27 May 1779 (at Killingworth); she m (2) 2 Mar 1745 Theophilus Morgan.

i Jacob, b 11 Feb 1737/8 *NHV*, bp 12 Feb 1737/8 *NHC1*, d 1 Apr 1761 *F&IWRolls*.

ii John, b 21 May 1740 *NHV*, bp 25 May 1740 *NHC1*, d 8 Oct 1805 *NHV*, æ. 66 *NHT1*; Census (NH) 2-3-3; m 26 Dec 1767 *NHV*, 28 Dec 1766 *NHC2*—Sarah da. Nathan & Hannah (Nichols) Beers, b 29 Oct 1744, d 15 Apr 1835 æ. 91 *NHV, NHT1*. FAM. 8.

FAM. 2. SAMUEL & ELIZABETH (FROST) PIERPONT:

1 ELIZABETH, b 3 July 1752 *NHV*, d 18 Dec 1811 æ. 60 *NoHT1*; m Jonah Blakeslee.

2 HANNAH, b 16 June 1754 *NHV*; m ——— Collins.

3 SAMUEL, b 16 May 1756 *NHV*; loyalist, reported dead at N. Y. 1778, living there 1779 *NHTaxLists*; m 12 Jan 1777 *NoHC*—Sarah da. Ebenezer & Rhoda (Todd) Wolcott.

4 THEODOSIA, b 22 Feb 1758 *NHV*, d 15 July 1806 æ. 48 *NHT1*; m 17 Nov 1777 *NoHC*—William Walter.

5 MABEL, b 28 June 1760 *NHV*, bp 1760 *NoHx*, d 12 Nov 1795 æ. 35 *NoHV, NoHT1*; m 1 Feb 1787 *NoHV, NoHC*—Abraham Blakeslee.

6 ELI, b 5 Aug 1763 *NHV*, bp 1763 *NoHx*; Census (C) 1-0-0.

7 ABIGAIL, bp 1766 *NoHx*, d 9 Mar 1839 æ. 73 *NoHT1*.

8 BETHIA, b c. 1768, d 19 June 1806 æ. 39 *NHT1*; m Samuel Sackett.

9 EBENEZER, bp 1771 *NoHx*, d 4 Mar 1854 æ. 83 *NoHT1*; m Lydia da. Joel & Elizabeth (Sackett) Blakeslee, b 2 July 1768 *NHV*, d 22 July 1863 æ. 95 *NoHT1*.

i Roxana, b c. 1795, d 10 Jan 1821 æ. 26 *NoHT1*.

FAM. 3. JOSEPH & LYDIA (BASSETT) PIERPONT:

1 EZRA, b 11 July 1757 *NHV, NoHV*, d 6 Jan 1842 æ. 84 *WatT2*; m 31 Mar 1783 *NoHC*—Mary da. Isaac & Lydia (Alcott) Blakeslee, b 10 Oct 1762 *NHV*, d 27 Sep 1827 æ. 65 *WatT2*, 28 Sep *Watx*.

i Chloe, b 15 Aug 1783 *WatV*, d 21 Feb 1816 æ. 33 *CT2*; m 17 Oct 1805 Lemuel Hall.

ii Luther, b 8 Feb 1785 *WatV*, d 14 Apr 1862 æ. 77 *WatT2*; m 6 June 1814 *WatV*—Delia Maria da. Thaddeus Waugh of L, who d 1 Dec 1861 æ. 70 *WatT2*.

iii Seabury, b 13 Mar 1787 *WatV*, d 1 Mar 1829 æ. 42 *WatT2*; m 16 Dec 1813 *WatV*—Clorana da. Jared & Lucy (Hull) Hall, b 26 June 1785 *CV, WatT2*, d 6 Aug 1856 *WatT2*.

iv Austin, b 19 May 1791 *WatV*, d 23 June 1848 æ. 57 *WatT2*; m (1) 20 Feb 1812 *WatV*—Sally da. Enos Beecher, who d 20 Dec 1846 æ. 52

WatT2; m (2) 19 May 1847 *WatV*—Emily, wid. Sperry of B.

v Lucy, b 26 July 1793 *WatV.*

vi Ezra Stiles, b c. 1796, d 12 Aug 1828 æ. 32 *WatT2.*

vii Joseph E., b c. 1800, d 1 Nov 1821 æ. 21 *WatT2.*

2 Joseph, b 28 Apr 1760 *NHV, NoHV,* d 30 June 1833 æ. 73 *NoHT1,* 30 July *NoHV;* Census (NoH) 1-0-2; m 26 Oct 1789 *NoHV*—Esther da. Abel & Chloe (Todd) Bishop, b 2 Apr 1767 *NHV,* d 16 Aug 1826 æ. 59 *NoHT1.*

i Lydia, b 30 Oct 1790 *NoHV,* bp 1791 *NoHx;* m ——— Heald.

ii Dennis, b 1 Dec 1793 *NoHV,* bp 1794 *NoHx,* d 29 Sep 1794 *NoHV,* æ. 0-10 *NoHT1.*

iii Asahel, b 16 Oct 1796 *NoHV,* bp 1797 *NoHx,* d 6 Mar 1880 æ. 84 *NHT1;* m (1) 19 Nov 1823 *NoHV*—Lois Thorpe, who d 21 Oct 1826 æ. 25 *NoHD;* m (2) 24 Oct 1830 *NoHV*—Mary Thorpe, who d 11 Aug 1847 æ. 44 *NHT1;* m (3) 29 Nov 1849 *NHV*—Sarah Ann Coon, who d 22 June 1853 æ. 41 *NHT1;* m (4) Frances Ann Hall of C, who d 1 Jan 1886 æ. 72 *NHT1.*

iv Son, d 28 Feb 1800 (infant) *NoHT1.*

v Mary, b 28 Feb 1802 *NoHV;* m 13 Sep 1820 *NoHV*—John S. Bunnell of NoB.

vi Belinda, b 29 Dec 1804 *NoHV;* m 3 May 1825 *NHV*—Levi S. Bigelow.

vii George, b 15 Oct 1808 *NoHV.*

viii Lucy, b 1 Dec 1810 *NoHV.*

3 Russell, b 17 May 1763 *NHV, NoHV,* bp 19 June 1763 *NoHC,* d 12 Dec 1844 æ. 82 *HT1;* m 3 Dec 1790 *HV*—Sarah Miles da. Samuel & Bethia (Miles) Tuttle, b 2 Feb 1770 *F,* d 25 Aug 1841 æ. 72 *HT1.*

i Nancy, b 9 Jan 1792 *HV,* d 8 July 1878 æ. 86 *HT1;* m Jan 1814 Leonard Pierpont.

ii Ammi Miles, b 20 Mar 1799 *HV,* d 23 June 1850 æ. 51 *HT1.*

iii Bethia, b 2 Feb 1805 *HV,* d 25 Apr 1843 æ. 39 *EHC;* m 2 Nov 1826 *HV*—John Thompson.

iv Sally Rosetta, b 13 Nov 1808 *HV,* d 9 May 1893 æ. 84 *HV;* m 24 Dec 1834 *HV*—Elias Ford.

v Russell, b 11 June 1814 *HV,* d 11 June 1814 *HV.*

4 Lydia, b 18 Nov 1766 *NHV, NoHV,* bp 11 Jan 1767 *NoHC,* d 9 Sep 1788 æ. 22 *NoHV, NoHC.*

5 Lucy, b 21 Oct 1771 *NHV, NoHV,* bp 15 Dec 1771 *NoHC,* d 4 Nov 1792 æ. 21 *NoHV, NoHT1.*

6 DANIEL, b 16 May 1775 *NHV, NoHV,* bp 1775 *NoHx,* d 16 Nov 1851 æ. 76-6 *NoHT1;* m 26 Sep 1799 *NoHV*—Esther da. Samuel & Mary (Gill) Humiston, b 23 May 1774 *HV,* d 17 Aug 1864 æ. 90 *NoHT1.*

i Bede, b 10 Dec 1800 *NoHV,* bp 1800 *NoHx,* d 21 Feb 1851 (?), "Mrs. Beda" d Spring 1842 *NoHD;* m 15 June 1823 *NoHV*—Merritt Pierpont.

ii Elias, b 21 Apr 1803 *NoHV,* d 12 Aug 1883 æ. 80-3-22 *NHV;* m (1) 28 Sep 1821 *NHV*—Sophronia Lucy da. John & Lucy (Foote) Gill, b c. 1809, d 18 Oct 1841 æ. 32 *NoHT3;* m (2) 24 Aug 1842 *NHV*—Grace Bradley.

iii Esther, b 1 Sep 1805 *NoHV,* d 26 Sep 1836 *NoHV,* æ. 30 *NoHT1;* m 30 Apr 1829 *NoHV*—Ezra Stiles.

iv Harriet, b 13 Feb 1808 *NoHV,* d 4 May 1886 æ. 78-2-21 *NoHT3.*

v Sally, b 10 Dec 1811 *NoHV,* d 27 July 1831 æ. 20 *NoHV, NoHT1.*

vi Jared, b 24 June 1814 *NoHV,* d 19 Dec 1846 æ. 32 ("of Smithville, N. Y.") *NoHT3;* m Fanny T. ———.

vii Rufus, b 5 Mar 1818 *NoHV,* d 30 July 1855 æ. 37 *NoHD;* Capt.; m 14 Sep 1847 *Watx*—Harriet da. Luther Abijah Richards of Vt.

FAM. 4. JAMES & LYDIA [Mansfield] PIERPONT:

1 (perhaps) MARY, b c. 1757, d 27 June 1832 æ. 75 *WT1;* m (1) 20 Oct 1774 *NoHC*—Timothy Andrews; m (2) 6 Jan 1799 *NoHC*—Lent Hough.

2 THOMAS, b c. 1760, d 28 Mar 1795 (in W. Indies) *NoHC;* Census (NoH) 2-1-3; m 13 Dec 1781 *NoHC*—Elizabeth da. James & Patience (Todd) Bishop, b 16 Oct 1759 *NHV,* d 21 Mar 1829 æ. 70 *NoHC;* she m (2) Peter Hall.

i Hannah, b c. 1786, bp 1793 *NoHC,* d 24 Jan 1816 æ. 30 *NoHC.*

ii Andrew, b 13 Dec 1788 *NoHV,* bp 1793 *NoHC,* d 31 Dec 1819 æ. 31 *NoHT1, NoHC;* m 31 Dec 1811 *NoHC*—Mercy da. Joshua & Mercy (Tuttle) Barnes, b 30 May 1789 *NoHV,* d 20 May 1840 æ. 51 *NoHT1.*

iii Edward, b c. 1791, bp 1793 *NoHC,* d 5 Sep 1794 æ. 3 *NoHC.*

iv Noyes, bp 16 Mar 1794 *NoHC,* d 5 Sep 1794 æ. 1 *NoHC.*

v Thomas, bp 22 Nov 1795 (as son of Wid. Elizabeth) *NoHC,* d 20 Oct 1812 æ. 17 *NoHT1.*

3 JOHN, bp 4 Apr 1762 *NoHC,* d 30 Dec 1851 æ. 91 *NoHT3;* Census (NoH) 1-1-1; m 26 Feb 1789 *NoHC*—Ruth da. Isaac & Mabel (Clark) Stiles, b 1 Apr 1760 *F,* d 2 Feb 1847 æ. 87 *NoHT3, NoHD.*

i Leonard, b c. 1789, bp 9 Nov 1794 *NoHC,* d 12 Sep 1855 æ. 66 *NoHT3;* m Jan 1814 Nancy da. Russell & Sarah M. (Tuttle) Pierpont, b 9 Jan 1792 *HV,* d 8 July 1878 æ. 86 *HT1.*

ii Polly, b [July 1791], bp 9 Nov 1794 *NoHC,* d 19 Feb 1888 æ. 96-7 *NoHV, NHV;* m 29 Nov 1813 *NoHC*—Augustus Munson.

iii Child, d 5 Sep 1793 (infant) *NoHC.*

iv Alfred, bp 5 Apr 1795 *NoHC,* d 22 Sep 1870 æ. 74 *NoHV, NoHT3;* m 4 Dec 1821 *HV*—Eliza da. Eli & Martha (Davenport) Potter, bp 1802 *HC2.*

v Elisa, bp 21 Jan 1798 *NoHC;* m Hervey Treat.

vi Almira, bp 21 June 1801 *NoHC,* d 12 Mar 1880 æ. 79 *HT4;* m 14 Feb 1821 *NoHV*—Jabez Potter.

vii Emilia, bp 29 July 1804 *NoHC,* d 7 May 1891 æ. 88-11 *NoHT2;* m 15 Feb 1825 *NoHV*—Erastus Robinson.

4 JAMES, bp 22 July 1764 *NoHC,* d 1830; m (1) Lucinda da. Gideon & Prudence (Tuttle) Todd, b 22 Apr 1770 *F,* d 24 Mar 1804 *F;* m (2) 15 June 1806 *NoHV*—Esther da. Lawrence & Elizabeth (Todd) Clinton, wid. Solomon Jacobs, b 5 Aug 1760 *NHV,* d 14 May 1842 æ. 82 *NoHT2.* Family incomplete.

(By 1): *i* Noyes, b c. 1794, d 4 Sep 1834 æ. 40 *WT1;* m Belinda da. Levi Parker, who d 2 Jan 1881 æ. 85 *WT1.*

ii Fidelia, b [10 July 1800], d 12 Aug 1885 æ. 85-1-2 *NHV;* m James P. Hart.

5 BEDE, bp 26 June 1768 *NoHC,* d 9 June 1810 æ. 42 *NoHT2,* æ. 43 *NoHC;* m 29 May 1794 *NoHC*—Newbury Button.

6 SUSANNA, bp 24 Feb 1771 *NoHC,* d 2 Nov 1858 æ. 88 *NoHT1;* m 25 Nov 1796 *NoHV*—Nathan Marks.

7 SARAH, bp 28 Mar 1773 *NoHC,* d 28 Mar 1773 æ. 0 *NoHC.*

8 ELIADA, bp 20 Aug 1775 *NoHC.*

FAM. 5. BENJAMIN & SARAH (BLAKESLEE) PIERPONT:

1 BENJAMIN, b 4 Sep 1766 *NHV,* d 2 Feb 1821 æ. 54 *NoHT1;* m 4 Nov 1795 *NoHV*—Susanna da. Benjamin & Althea (Ray) Brockett, b c. 1772, d 9 May 1844 æ. 72 *NoHT1.*

i Sarah, b 24 Sep 1796 *NoHV,* bp 1796 *NoHx,* d 15 June 1797 *NoHV.*

ii Miles, b 15 Dec 1798 *NoHV,* bp 1799 *NoHx,* d s. p. 2 Jan 1878 æ. 79 *NoHV, NoHT3.*

iii David, b 23 Feb 1801 *NoHV,* d s. p. 22 May 1857 æ. 56 *NoHT3.*

iv Lavinia, b 14 Feb 1804 *NoHV,* d 26 Sep 1874 æ. 70 *NoHT3,* æ. 70½ *NoHV.*

v Lois, b 13 Jan 1806 *NoHV;* m 9 Nov 1834 *NoHV*—Horace Stiles.

vi Eunice, b 21 Jan 1808 *NoHV,* d 26 Dec 1808 *NoHV.*

vii Sala, b 25 Dec 1809 *NoHV,* bp 1810 *NoHx,* d 26 Aug 1848 æ. 38 *NoHT3;* m 10 Oct 1832 *NoHV* —Hannah da. Jude & Hannah Smith, bp 7 Jan 1814 *NoHC,* d 2 Aug 1864 æ. 50 *NoHT3.*

viii Charlotte, b 1 Jan 1812 *NoHV;* m 1 May 1834 *NoHV*—Henry M. Blakeslee.

ix Bela, b 1 Jan 1815 *NoHV,* d 8 Apr 1870 æ. 55 *NoHT3.*

2 PHILEMON, bp 1780 *NoHx,* d 23 Feb 1865 æ. 85 *NoHT1,* æ. 84 *NoHV;* m (1) 22 Jan 1801 *NoHV*—Mehitabel da. Eli & Sarah Sackett, b [3 Aug 1782], d 16 May 1834 æ. 52 *NoHT1,* æ. 51-9-13 *NoHV;* m (2) 28 May 1835 *NHV*—Bede da. Joel & Elizabeth (Sackett) Blakeslee, wid. Thomas Brockett, bp 1780 *NoHx,* d 28 Mar 1842 æ. 62 *NoHT2.*

(By 1): *i* Merritt, b 8 Oct 1799 [out of wedlock] *NoHV;* rem. to Oxford, N. Y.; m 15 June 1823 *NoHV* —Bede da. Daniel & Esther (Humiston) Pierpont, b 10 Dec 1800 *NoHV.*

ii Child, b 1 May 1802 *NoHV,* d 25 July 1802 *NoHV.*

iii Jared, b 13 Jan 1809 *NoHV,* d 13 Aug 1872 æ. 63 *NoHT3;* m 25 Mar 1833 Anna Loisa Todd, b 30 Sep 1807 *NoHV,* d 13 Dec 1892 æ. 88 *NoHT3.*

iv Betsey, b 1 Mar 1813 *NoHV,* d 2 Jan 1894 *F;* m 28 Aug 1834 *NHV*—George Todd.

v Jason, b 11 Sep 1819 *NoHV;* m 23 Feb 1845 *NoHV*—Martha A. Crowell.

FAM. 6. GILES & ELIZABETH (COOPER) PIERPONT:

1 LUCINDA, b 1 Dec 1766 *NoHV,* bp 7 Oct 1771 *NoHC,* d 15 Jan 1841 æ. 74 *NoHV.*

2 JOEL, b 9 Oct 1768 *NoHV,* bp 7 Oct 1771 *NoHC,* d 21 May 1815 æ. 49 *NoHT1;* m (1) 20 Sep 1790 *NoHC*—Hannah da. Lawrence & Elizabeth (Todd) Clinton, bp 1 Nov 1772 *NoHC,* d 15 Jan 1861 æ. 88

NoHT3; he div. her 1802; m (2) 9 Sep 1804 *EHC*—Mehitabel da. James Adkins & Abigail (Nails) Broughton, wid. ——— Talmadge, bp 25 Oct 1767 *EHC,* d 16 Aug 1826 æ. 59 *NoHD.*

(By 1): *i* Lewis, b c. 1792, d Summer 1841 *NoHD;* res. Lanesborough, Mass., 1833; m & had Capt. Lewis who d 11 May 1857 (lost on Charleston Bar) *NHT3;* the younger Lewis m 7 Oct 1838 *NoHV*—Rosetta E. Jacobs who d 18 Jan 1903 æ. 83 *NHT3.*

ii Lewey, b c. 1795, d 10 Mar 1887 æ. 92 *NoHT3;* m 29 Nov 1813 *NoHC*—John Todd.

(By 2): *iii* Lucy, b c. 1814; m 1 May 1834 *NoHV*—Nathan Beach of W.

3 Esther, b 27 Oct 1771 *NoHV,* bp 15 Dec 1771 *NoHC,* d 11 Nov 1857 æ. 86 *NoHT3;* m 30 Sep 1795 *NoHV, NoHC*—Jesse Tuttle.

4 Eunice, b 24 Feb 1775 *NoHV,* bp 9 Apr 1775 *NoHC,* d 3 Aug 1807 æ. 33 *NoHT1.*

5 Zerah, b 20 July 1779 *NoHV,* bp 29 Aug 1779 *NoHC,* d 10 Nov 1802 æ. 23-4 *NoHC.*

6 Giles, b 31 May 1783 *NoHV,* bp 27 July 1783 *NoHC,* d 28 Dec 1842 æ. 59 *NoHT3;* m (1) 26 Oct 1808 *NoHV*—Eunice da. Jonathan & Mary (Taintor) Munson, bp 3 June 1792 *WC1,* d 23 June 1814 æ. 23 *NoHT1;* m (2) 13 Dec 1814 *NoHV*—Sarah da. Jesse & Esther (Bassett) Bassett.

(By 1): *i* Sally, b 21 Aug 1810 *NoHV, NoHT3,* d 14 June 1893 *NoHT3.*

ii Munson, b 4 Nov 1813 *NoHV;* assumed the name "Edwards Pierrepont"; d 6 Mar 1892 (N. Y. City); m Margaretta Willoughby.

(By 2): *iii* Elmon, b 19 Jan 1816 *NoHV,* d 19 Mar 1816 *NoHV.*

iv Zerah, b 25 Feb 1817 *NoHV,* d 30 Nov 1842 æ. 26 *NoHT3.*

v Guy, b 23 Apr 1820 *NoHV,* d 1870 (Rockford, Ill.); m 21 May 1845 *CV*—Jerusha Gaylord.

vi Eunice, b 23 Mar 1822 *NoHV,* d 17 Sep 1851 æ. 29-6; m 1 May 1844 Samuel Anson Tuttle.

vii Sylvia, b 17 Mar 1824 *NoHV,* d 29 Mar 1853 æ. 29 *NoHT3;* m 13 Nov 1843 *NoHV*—Henry M. Bradley.

viii Laura, b 12 Aug 1826 *NoHV,* d 3 Jan 1843 æ. 16 *NoHT3.*

ix Elmon, b 3 Dec 1828 *NoHV;* rem. to Kansas; m Caroline S. Warner.

FAM. 7. HEZEKIAH & MEHITABEL (COOPER) PIERPONT:
1 SARAH, b c. 1773, bp 11 July 1779 *NoHC.*
2 HANNAH, b [July 1775], d 14 Sep 1776 æ. 1-2 *NoHC.*
3 ISAAC, b c. 1777, bp 11 July 1779 *NoHC.*
4 AZUBAH, bp 5 Mar 1780 *NoHC.*

FAM. 8. JOHN & SARAH (BEERS) PIERPONT:
1 HEZEKIAH BEERS, b 3 Nov 1768 *NHV,* bp 12 Feb 1786 (adult) *NHx,* d 11 Aug 1838 (N. Y. City); m 21 Jan 1802 Anna Maria da. William Constable of N. Y.
2 SALLY, b 22 June 1770 *F,* d 11 Nov 1772 æ. 3 *NHT1.*
3 SALLY, b [28 Feb 1773], d 3 Mar 1773 æ. 0-0-3 *NHT1.*
4 SARAH, b 3 Apr 1774 *NHV,* d 12 Feb 1788 æ. 14 *NHT1.*
5 HANNAH, b 13 Feb 1776 *NHV,* d 10 July 1859; m 17 Mar 1802 (at NH) *ConnJournal*—Claudius Herrick.
6 MARY, b 13 Feb 1776 *F,* d 20 Sep 1776 æ. 0-7 *NHT1.*
7 POLLY, b 3 Apr 1778 *NHV,* d 29 Jan 1852 æ. 73 *NHT1;* m (1) 11 Nov 1796 *NHV,* 12 Nov *NHC1*—Edward J. O'Brien; m (2) 12 Jan 1806 *NHV*—Eleazer Foster.
8 JOHN, b 8 Aug 1780 *NHV,* d 12 Apr 1836 æ. 57 *NHT1.*
9 NATHAN, b 18 Oct 1782 *NHV,* d 12 Jan 1803.
10 HENRY, b 18 Jan 1785 *NHV,* d 8 Aug 1790 æ. 6 *NHT1.*

PIERPONT. MISCELLANEOUS. PHILENA m 27 May 1804 *EHC*—Hezekiah Davenport.

PIGG. ROBERT of NH d c. 1660; m Margaret ———, who m (2) 8 Oct 1662 *NHV*—William Thorpe.
1 ALICE; m John Jenner.

PINION. NICHOLAS of Lynn, Mass., rem. to EH, d Apr 1676 *NHV;* m (1) Elizabeth ———, who d [1667] *NHV;* m (2) Mary, wid. Thomas Dickerson & Daniel Finch of Fairfield.
(By 1): 1 RUTH; m (1) 28 Dec 1657 *Lynn*—James Moore; m (2) c. 1664 Peter Briggs of Killingworth; she deserted him 1665.
2 ROBERT.
3 MARY.
4 THOMAS, d 10 Oct 1710 *EHV;* m Mercy ———.
i Christian; m 1 July 1691 *NHV*—Samuel Downs.
ii Mercy; m Joseph Mallory.
iii Experience, b c. 1679, bp 29 July 1688 *NHC1,* d 27 Aug 1753 æ. 74 *WHT1;* m Samuel Humphreville.
iv Abigail, b c. 1680, bp 29 July 1688 *NHC1,* d 9 Jan 1743 æ. 63 *WHT1;* m 28 Apr 1703 *NHV*—Samuel Candee.
5 HANNAH, b c. 1649.

PINTO. FAM. 1. JACOB, b 26 Jan 1723/4 *StV,* d 1806; Census (NH) 1-1-3; m (1) Thankful da. James & Mary (Hitchcock) Peck, b 6/9 Apr 1741 *NHV,* d 28 July 1768 æ. 28 *NHT1;* m (2) Abigail da. James & Mary (Hitchcock) Peck, b 6 Mar 1748/9 *NHV,* d 9 Mar 1798 æ. 49 *NHT1.*

(By 1): 1 ABRAHAM, b 8 Mar 1757 *NHV;* m 30 Dec 1779 *NHV, NHC2*—Mary Gault of Boston; Census, Polly (NH) 0-1-1. Family incomplete.

i Miriam Myers, bp 8 Nov 1781 *NHx.*

ii Abraham, bp 13 Jan 1793 (æ. 4) *NHx.*

2 SOLOMON, b 29 Dec 1758 *NHV,* d 29 Mar 1824 æ. 65 *(NHC1) NHV.*

3 WILLIAM, b 16 Dec 1760 *NHV;* m (1) 24 Dec 1789 *NHSupCt*—Fanny Hamilton of N. Y. City; he div. her 1799; m (2) 29 Nov 1802 *NHC1*—Urania Parmalee da. Hezekiah Clark, who d 30 Aug 1815 æ. 33 *ColR.*

(By 2): 4 THANKFUL, b 22 Dec 1769 *NHV.*

5 SAMUEL, b 18 Aug 1771 *NHV;* res. Jefferson, Me., 1824; m Ann ———.

6 ISAAC, b 21 Dec 1777 *NHV;* res. Chilicothe, Ohio, 1829; m 7 Sep 1806 *NHC2*—Maria da. Samuel Bryan Marshall.

7 SARAH, b 3 Feb 1780 *NHV.* [Sally m c. Oct 1807 *ConnH*—Jesse West.]

FAM. 2. SOLOMON (brother of Jacob), b 23 Feb 1725/6 *StV,* d 22 Dec 1775 æ. 50; m 4 Oct 1762 *NHV, NHC1*—Anna Green, b c. 1741, d 25 Apr 1825 æ. 84; she m (2) 8 June 1777 Giles Meigs of Mid.

1 ELIZABETH, b 9 Feb 1772 *NHV,* bp 16 Feb 1772 *NHC1.*

2 JOHN DIXWELL, b 12 Oct 1774 *NHV,* bp 4 Dec 1774 *NHC1,* d 29 Sep 1775 æ. 1 *NHC1.*

3 POLLY, bp 16 June 1776 *NHC1.*

PINTO. MISCELLANEOUS. SOLOMON m 28 Apr 1807 *NHC1*—Clarissa Smith, who d 10 Oct 1884 æ. 96 *NHT1*....... ANN SOPHIA, b 10 June 1795 (at W. Indies) *NHT1,* d 30 Nov 1890 *NHT1;* m Caleb Mix.

PLANT. MISCELLANEOUS. JAMES m 9 Jan 1772 *NHV*—Lucy Judd; had 1 Lucy, b 14 May 1773 *NHV;* 2 Joseph, b 26 Mar 1775 *NHV*....... TIMOTHY had: Mary Ann & Benjamin Dickinson, bp 18 Oct 1801 *NHC1,* & Susan bp 27 Mar 1803 *NHC1.*

PLATT. FAM. 1. JOSIAH, s. of Josiah & Sarah (Burwell), b 13 Oct 1707 *MV,* bp 3 July 1709 *MC1,* d 19 Mar 1795 æ. 88 *WHD;* Dea.; Census (NH) 1-0-0; m (1) 25 Nov 1731 *NHV*—Mary Arnold, who d 5 Jan 1745/6 *NHV, WHT1;* m (2) 3 Mar 1745/6 *NHV*—Mehitabel da. Samuel & Abigail (Clark) Stevens, b 6 July 1705 *NHV,* d 11 Feb 1746/7 *NHV, WHT1;* m (3) 14 May 1747 *NHV*—Mary Newton, who d 13 Sep 1780 *NHV, WHD.*

(By 1): 1 MARY, b 16 Oct 1732 *NHV,* d 18 July 1743 *NHV,* æ. 11 *WHT1.*
2 ELIZABETH, b 6 Jan 1733/4 *NHV.*
3 JOSIAH, b 6 May 1735 *NHV;* m 13 Nov 1758 *Newtown V*—Sarah Sanford.
4 TEMPERANCE, b 18 Feb 1736/7 *NHV,* bp 19 June 1737 *NHC1,* d 3 May 1821 æ. 84 *WHD;* m Benjamin Downs.
5 ABIGAIL, b 3 Oct 1739 *NHV,* d 17 June 1817 æ. 76 *WHD.*
6 SARAH, b 17 Feb 1741/2 *NHV,* d 7 Apr 1825 æ. 83 OC; m Daniel Hodge.
7 MARY, b 17 Jan 1743/4 *NHV.* [A Mary, Census (NH) 0-0-1.]
8 ALICE, b 10 Sep 1745 *NHV.*
(By 3): 9 NATHAN, b 22 Mar 1748 *NHV,* d 11 Oct 1760 *NHV.*
10 MEHITABEL, b 9 Sep 1749 *NHV,* d 30 May 1785 *WHD,* bu. 3 June *NHx;* m Benajah Thomas.
11 ANN, b 7 Oct 1751 *NHV;* m 22 Aug 1779 *WdV*—Ezekiel Smith.
12 JOHN, d 16 July 1782 *WHD;* m Anna ———.
i Mary, b c. 1776, d 29 July 1833 æ. 57 *WHT2;* m Nathan Smith.
ii Anna; m Jonathan Beers of Trumbull.
iii Susanna; m Jonathan Alling.
iv Phebe; m Philo Beers of Trumbull.
v Nathan, b c. 1780; m Cata Merrick.
vi John; res. Litchfield Co.; m Eunice ———, who d 4 Dec 1800 in 27 yr. (at WH) *ConnJournal.*

PLATT. FAM. 2. NATHAN, s. of Nathan & Elizabeth (Peck), b 20 Oct 1750 *MV,* d 7 Oct 1813 æ. 63 *WdT2;* Dea.; m 23 June 1774 *WdC*—Deborah da. Phineas & Deborah (Clark) Peck, b c. 1752, d 2 Feb 1786 æ. 34 *WdC.*
1 DEBORAH, b [24 Jan 1775], d 15 Aug 1863 æ. 88 *WdT2,* æ. 88-6-22 *WdD;* m Lewis Sperry.
2 POLLY, b c. 1777, d 5 Apr 1863 æ. 86 *WdD;* m Justus Thomas.
3 NAOMI, b c. 1779, d 13 Sep 1848 æ. 69 *WdD;* m Eliakim Sperry.
4 CLARINDA, b c. 1782, d 16 Feb 1786 æ. 4 *WdT2.*

PLATT. MISCELLANEOUS. MARY da. Richard m 1 May 1651 *NHV*—Luke Atkinson.......JOHN of Norwalk m 20 Nov 1722 *NHV*—Mary Smith.......NATHAN, b c. 1700, d 9 Oct 1778 æ. 78 *WdT2;* m Ann ———, b c. 1710, d 6 Nov 1778 æ. 68 *WdT2.* ......ELIZABETH m 18 Nov 1773 *WdC*—Samuel Fiske Peck.

PLUMB. FAM. 1. JOHN, s. of Robert & Mary (Baldwin), b 1646, d 1728; m 24 Nov 1668 *MV*—Elizabeth da. John & Elizabeth (Clark) Norton.

PAGE 1529

1 ELIZABETH, b 1 Nov 1669 *MV,* d 17 Oct 1749 *WatV;* m 16 Apr 1690 *WatV*—Samuel Hickox.

2 JOHN, b 29 July 1671 *MV,* d 1716; m Rachel da. Benjamin & Rebecca (Mallory) Bunnell, b 16 Dec 1683 *NHV,* d 21 July 1728 æ. 45 *MT.*

i John, bp 30 July 1704 *MC1,* d 1763; m 27 May 1723 *MV*—Kezia da. Samuel & Abigail (Grannis) Alling.

ii Samuel, bp 30 July 1704 *MC1,* d 1790; m Mary Lobdell.

iii Jemima, bp 25 Nov 1705 *MC1,* d Sep 1744 *CC;* m bef. 1734 William Wheeler [proof, M Deeds, 8:269]. She had a nat. child by Samuel Adams: Samuel Adams, b 1726 *NHCCt.*

iv Zuriel, bp 22 Feb 1707/8 *MC1,* d 24 Mar 1828 æ. 21 *MT.*

v Seth, bp 23 July 1710 *MC1,* d Nov 1783; m (1) Hannah da. Joseph & Mary (Parker) Clark, b 11 July 1716 *NHV,* d 29 June 1759 *SC;* m (2) Beulah da. Samuel & Phebe (Tyler) Beach, wid. Enos Abernathy, b 19 Mar 1719 *WV,* d 1785. FAM. 2.

vi Benjamin, b c. 1713, d 1746; m Mar 1737 *MV*—Elizabeth Camp.

vii Rachel, bp 4 Mar 1715/6 *MC1,* d Jan 1789 æ. 73 *SC;* m (1) 6 June 1739 *WV*—Enoch Curtis; m (2) Silas Clark.

3 MARY, b 15 May 1673 *MV;* m 17 Oct 1704 *NHV*—Joseph Kirby.

4 SARAH, b 1675 , d 1712; m 1702 Joseph Kellogg.

5 HANNAH, b 1677 , d 16 Nov 1716 *NMV;* m Benjamin Bunnell.

6 DOROTHY, b 1679 ; m 1699 Samuel Prindle.

7 JOSEPH, b c. 1683, d 27 May 1742 *MT;* m (1) 5 Dec 1709 *MV*—Elizabeth Bailey; m (2) Thankful Gaylord.

8 RUTH, b 1685 , d c. 1744; m Hezekiah Bunnell.

9 JOSIAH, b 1687 , d s. p.

10 ROBERT, b 1691 , d 1699.

FAM. 2. SETH & HANNAH (CLARK) PLUMB:

1 LYDIA, bp May 1736 *CC,* d 5 May 1762 *SC.*

2 ESTHER, b c. 1741, bp 9 Jan 1743 *WdC;* m Nathaniel Alling; res. Cornwall 1786.

3 RACHEL, b 19 Aug 1743 *NHV,* bp 18 Sep 1743 *WdC;* m 1764 *WV*—Jonathan Page; res. L 1786.

4 Hannah, b 19 Aug 1743 *NHV,* bp 18 Sep 1743 *WdC;* m 14 June 176[-] *WV*—Jesse Merwin; res. Cornwall, 1786.

5 Jemima, b 14 Nov 1745 *NHV,* bp 29 Dec 1745 *WdC;* m 1 May 1766 *WV*—Ebenezer Merwin; res. Pittsfield, Mass., 1786.

6 Lucy, b 15 June 1748 *NHV,* bp 3 Mar 1751 *WdC,* d soon.

7 Deborah, b 2 Nov 1749 *NHV,* bp 3 Mar 1751 *WdC;* m James Travis; res. Cornwall, 1786.

8 Lucy, b c. 1755, d 22 Jan 1825 æ. 69 *WT1;* m (1) 8 Mar 1779 *WV*—Jedediah Dudley; m (2) Dan Johnson.

FAM. 2. Seth & Beulah (Beach) Plumb:

9 Phebe, d s. p. c. 1793.

10 Seth, d s. p. 23 Nov 1801; m 11 June 1792 *NoHC*—Sarah Tuttle.

PLUYMERT. William, Census (NH) 1-2-3; m 4 June 1757 *NHV*—Sarah da. Benjamin & Sarah (Dayton) English, b 27 Aug 1738 *NHV,* d 27 Sep 1794 *NHx.*

1 Sarah, b 28 Oct 1757 *NHV,* bp 12 Nov 1769 *NHC1;* m 22 Apr 1781 *NHC2*—Cebria Chaplin.

2 John, b c. 1763, bp 12 Nov 1769 *NHC1,* d 12 Mar 1826 æ. 63 *CT3;* m (1) 10 Sep 1782 *BdV,* 5 Sep *NoBC2*—Abigail da. Joseph & Abigail (Winchell) Foote, who d 14 Feb 1802 æ. 40 *WC2,* 15 Feb *CT3;* m (2) c. Nov 1807 *ConnH*—Rachel (———) Doolittle, b 16 May 1775 *CT3,* d 26 Feb 1858 æ. 83 *CT3.*

(By 1): *i* William Champlin, b 2 May 1783 *BdV,* d s. p.

ii John, b 24 Dec 1784 *BdV,* d s. p.

iii Sarah, b 29 Dec 1786 *BdV;* m ——— Hough.

iv Harriet, b 19 Nov 1788 *BdV;* m 5 Sep 1810 *CC*—Luzon Whiting.

v Joseph F., b 11 July 1791 *BdV;* m Eliza ———.

vi Abigail Amelia, b 14 May 1793 *BdV,* d s. p.; [Amelia m 5 Feb 1821 (at Meriden) *ColR*—Joseph Warner of Mid.]

vii Maria.

viii Ann; m.

ix Lucretia, b 1800, d 1877 *WolT;* m Samuel Butler, b 1808, d 1888 *WolT.*

3 Emilia, bp 12 Nov 1769 *NHC1;* m ——— Patterson.

4 William Milner, bp 29 Oct 1775 *NHC2.*

POLLARD. Jonathan & Mary had: Henry Johnson, bp 9 Feb 1777 *NHx,* d 13 Feb 1777 *NHx.*

POND. FAM. 1. Samuel of Windsor, d 14 Mar 1654; m 18 Nov 1642 Sarah ———; she m (2) 6 July 1655 John Linsley of Bd. She was not named Ware, as by misreading is often falsely stated.

1 ISAAC, b 16 Mar 1646 *Windsor,* d 15 Nov 1668 *Windsor;* m 10 May 1667 Hannah Griffen, b 4 July 1649 *Windsor.*

i Hannah, b 10 Feb 1667 *Windsor* [1667/8].

2 SAMUEL, b 4 Mar 1648 *Windsor,* d 30 Jan 1718 æ. 69 *GV;* Lt.; m 3 Feb 1669 *BdV* [1670]—Miriam da. Thomas & Susanna Blatchley.

i Nathaniel, b 14 Feb 1676 *BdV,* d 23 Aug 1716 *StamfordV;* m (1) Elizabeth da. John & Sarah (Tuttle) Slauson, b 30 Jan 1672, d 11 May 1711; m (2) Sarah, wid. Benjamin Ferris. FAM. 2.

ii Abigail, d 19 Oct 1679 *BdV.*

iii Samuel, b 1 July 1679 *BdV,* d 1726; m. 8 June 1704 *BdV*—Abigail da. Bartholomew & Mary (Bartholomew) Goodrich, b c. 1686. FAM. 3.

iv Abigail; m (1) 6 Nov 1704 *BdV*—Isaac Tyler; m (2) [Josiah] Arnold of Haddam.

v Josiah, b 25 Sep 1688 *BdV,* d s. p.

vi Lois, b 1690; m 24 June 1730 Joseph Lee of E. Guilford.

vii Moses, b 1693, d 1747; res. Haddam & Bd; m 7 Jan 1718/9 *Haddam*—Mary da. Elijah & Mary (Bushnell) Brainerd, b 20 June 1700 *Haddam,* d 21 Nov 1770 *NoBC2;* she m (2) John Pardee of NoH. FAM. 4.

viii Miriam, b 1696.

ix Mindwell, b 1698, d 1 Apr 1777 *Haddam;* m 26 Oct 1731 *Haddam*—Joseph Brainerd.

3 NATHANIEL, b 2 Sep 1650 *Windsor,* d 19 Dec 1675 *Windsor* (in K. Philip's War).

4 SARAH, b 11 Feb 1651/2 *Windsor;* m Jonathan Hoyt of G.

FAM. 2. NATHANIEL & ELIZABETH (SLAUSON) POND:

1 ABIGAIL, b 18 Apr 1698 *StamfordV;* not mentioned in brother Josiah's will.

2 ELIZABETH, b 22 Nov 1699 *StamV,* d 17 Dec 1706 *StamV.*

3 JOSIAH, b 13 Jan 1701 *StamV,* d s. p. 25 Nov 1726 *GV.*

4 HANNAH, b 13 Feb 1703 *StamV,* d 28 Dec 1706 *StamV.*

5 NAOMI, b 22 Mar 1705 *StamV.*

6 THANKFUL, d Feb 1747; m (1) 1727 James Bishop (1678-1739) of G; m (2) Nathan Moody.

FAM. 2. NATHANIEL & SARAH (———) POND:

7 NATHANIEL, b 18 Nov 1712 *StamV;* not mentioned in brother Josiah's will.

8 ISRAEL, b 7 Dec 1714 *StamV,* d 3 Apr 1715 *StamV.*

FAM. 3. SAMUEL & ABIGAIL (GOODRICH) POND:

1 SAMUEL, b 7 May 1705 *BdV*, d s. p.

2 PHILIP, b 5 June 1706 *BdV*, d 19 May 1750 æ. 44 *NoBT1;* Lt.; m 13 Apr 1726 *BdV*—Thankful da. Edward & Martha (Pardee) Frisbie, b 9 Apr 1708 *BdV;* she m (2) 15 May 1753 *NoBC2*—Ens. Wm. Stebbins.

i Dan, b 4 Nov 1726 *BdV*, d 27 May 1783; rem. to Poultney, Vt.; m 29 Aug 1750 *BdV*—Mabel da. Abel & Sarah (Peck) Munson, b 2 June 1730 *WV*, d 8 Jan 1793. FAM. 5.

ii Timothy, b 7 Oct 1730 *BdV*, d 22 May 1801 *Clinton,N.Y.,T;* Capt.; m (1) 19 June 1751 *WatV*, 20 June *NoBC2*—Mary da. Abel & Sarah (Peck) Munson, b 2 May 1732 *WV*, d 16 Jan 1763; m (2) 30 Aug 1764 *WatV*—Sarah Bartholomew, b 28 Dec 1740 *BdV*, d 7 July 1826 æ. 86 *Clinton,N.Y.,T.* FAM. 6.

iii Thankful, b 27 Apr 1733 *BdV;* m 5 Oct 1752 *NoBC2*—Abiel Linsley.

iv Bartholomew, b 13 Apr 1736 *BdV;* m 9 Sep 1755 *WatV*—Lucy da. Daniel Curtis. FAM. 7.

v Rebecca, b 13 Apr 1736 *BdV*, d 19 Dec 1754 æ. 19 *NoBT1.*

vi Philip, b 7 Feb 1740/1 *BdV*, d 24 Apr 1776 *Wy;* m Experience ———; she m (2) Isaiah Gilbert. Children: Philip, Experience, Lorinda.

vii Samuel; res. Wy.

viii Edward; res. Wy; m 7 Nov 1765 *Wy*—Mary Judson.

3 BARTHOLOMEW, b 19 Jan 1708 *BdV.*

4 JOSIAH, b 19 Mar 1710/1 *BdV*, d 1745; m 9 Dec 1736 *BdV*—Abigail da. Thomas & Margaret Harrison, b 17 Nov 1696 *BdV.*

i Roswell, b 10 Oct 1738 *BdV*, d 8 July 1776 *Harwinton;* m 22 Nov 1764 Lydia Rogers.

5 ABIGAIL, b 7 July 1713 *BdV;* m 22 Nov 1739 *BdV*—Abraham Page.

6 PHINEAS, b 9 June 1715 *BdV*, d 12 May 1750 (at Wat); m Martha ———.

i Phineas, b 15 June 1737 *BdV*, d 16 Oct 1756 *F&IWRolls.*

ii Jonathan, b 24 June 1740 *BdV*, d 16 Dec 1817 æ. 78 *BristolT;* m (1) Susanna Hungerford; (2) Jerusha Jerome.

iii Abigail, b 6 Mar 1746/7 *BdV.*

iv Martha, [d 20 Feb 1774 *PC;* m Isaac Curtis].

7 Peter, b 22 Jan 1718/9 *BdV*, d 1765; res. M; m c. 1739 Mary Hubbard.
8 Mene Mene Tekel Upharsin, b 5 Mar 1720/1 *BdV*, d young.
9 Elizabeth; m 6 Feb 1745/6 *WV*—Daniel Cook.

FAM. 4. Moses & Mary (Brainerd) Pond:
1 Aaron, b 1 Oct 1719 *Haddam*, d 21 Apr 1776 *Wol*; m 23 Jan 1745 *Haddam*—Martha ———. Of their children, Naomi d 3 Mar 1827 æ. 72 *ST*; Lois d 22 May 1826 æ. 69 *ST*.
2 Moses, b c. 1721, d young.
3 Mary, b c. 1723; m 15 Jan 1746 *BdV*—Nathaniel Goodrich.
4 Bathsheba, b 2 Jan 1724/5 *BdV*, d after 1795; m 17 Oct 1753 *BdV*—Daniel Johnson; res. S.
5 Gad, b 12 Aug 1727 *BdV*, d 1791; res. C & Jewett, N. Y.; m Mary da. Moses & Mary (Hotchkiss) Atwater, b 1 Aug 1737 *WV*.
i Lucy, b 5 July 1758 *WV*.
ii Allethea, b 29 Dec 1762 *WV*.
iii Samuel, b 1 Jan 1764 *WV*.
iv Mary Sophia, b 14 Feb [1766] *WV*.
v Clara, b 3 Mar 1768 *WV*; m 16 Dec 1790 *CV*—Gideon Brooks.
vi Moses, b 13 Aug 1770 *WV*, bp 30 Sep 1770 *CC*; rem. to Ohio.
vii Aaron, b 14 Jan 1773 *WV*, bp 21 Mar 1773 *CC*.
viii Phineas, b 28 Feb 1776 *WV*, bp 5 May 1776 *CC*; rem. to Ohio.
ix David, b 15 Apr 1778 *WV*, bp 14 June 1778 *CC*; res. Hiram, Portage Co., Ohio; m Miriam Atwater.
6 Asher, b 12 Aug 1727 *BdV*, d s. p. 1759.
7 Lois, b 20 June 1730 *BdV*; m Jonathan Linsley.
8 Rachel, b 26 May 1733 *BdV*; m Joseph Lane of Killingworth.
9 Paul, b 12 May 1736 *BdV*, d s. p. 1759.
10 Samuel, b 24 June 1739 *BdV*, d s. p. 1759.
11 Mindwell, b 12 July 1742 *BdV*; m Jacob Linsley.

FAM. 5. Dan & Mabel (Munson) Pond:
1 Dan, b 22 Apr 1751 *BdV*, d 7 Feb 1838; res. Shoreham, Vt.; m Esther Ward.
2 Philip, d (in Rev.).
3 Abel, b 27 Oct 1753, d 29 Dec 1828; res. Poultney, Vt.; m (1) Eunice Curtis; m (2) Jerusha Barnes.
4 Rebecca, b 1755; m George Leonard.
5 Josiah, b 20 Dec 1756, d 3 Aug 1842; res. Shoreham, Vt.; m (1) Lydia Belden; m (2) Olive Marrells.

6 PHINEAS, b May 1758, d Apr 1846; res. Tioga Co., Pa.; m Rhoda Wood.
7 SILAS, b 1759, d 17 Nov 1827; res. Panton, Vt.; m Lucinda Lee.
8 NATHANIEL, b 1760, d 16 July 1835; res. Crawford Co., Pa.; m Polly Landers.
9 JARED, b 27 June 1762, d 12 Aug 1817; res. Panton, Vt.;. m (1) Esther Merrell; m (2) Mary, wid. Halsted.
10 WILLIAM, b 2 Sep 1763, d 5 July 1838; res. Schroon, N. Y.; m Ruth Wood.
11 ASAHEL, b 10 Jan 1765, d 12 Oct 1830; res. Poultney, Vt.; m 9 Dec 1792 Lovisa Ward.
12 IRA, b 10 Nov 1766, d 11 Mar 1837; res. Shoreham, Vt.; m (1) 22 Feb 1802 Olive Bateman; m (2) 9 Jan 1815 Wealthy, wid. Douglass.
13 BENJAMIN, b 1768, d 6 Oct 1814; res. Schroon, N. Y.; m Abigail Ashley.
14 THANKFUL, b 25 Sep 1770, d 17 July 1839; m Zebulon Ashley of Middlebury, O.
15 MONSON, b 18 Sep 1772, d 10 Nov 1861; res. White Peek, Ogle Co., Ill.; m (1) June 1796 Anna Allen; m (2) 1800 Ruth Bateman.

FAM. 6. TIMOTHY & MARY (MUNSON) POND:
1 BARTHOLOMEW, b 7 June 1754 *WatV*, d 31 Mar 1850 æ. 95-8 *Camden,N.Y.,T;* m Elizabeth Dunbar, who d 8 Nov 1839 æ. 78 *Camden,N.Y.,T.*
2 BARNABAS, b 29 Oct 1755 *WatV*, d 9 May 1841 *Clinton T;* Maj.; m 17 Feb 1784 *PC*—Thankful da. Moses Foote, b 30 June 1762, d 8 Oct 1814 *ClintonT.*
3 THANKFUL, b 16 Feb 1757 *WatV*, d 9 Jan 1848 *ClintonT;* m 7 May 1782 *PC*—Bronson Foote.
4 TIMOTHY, b 3 Aug 1758 *WatV*, d c. 1813 (at Sackett's Harbor, N. Y.); m 17 Feb 1784 *PC*—Marina Meggs.
5 SARAH, b 21 Feb 1760 *WatV;* m 11 Jan 1782 *PC*—William Cook.
6 MARY, b 8 June 1761 *WatV;* m 2 Apr 1782 *PC*—Ira Foote.
7 MUNSON, b 17 Dec 1762 *WatV*, k. 23 May 1780 (in Rev. at Horse Neck).

FAM. 6. TIMOTHY & SARAH (BARTHOLOMEW) POND:
8 JERUSHA, b 24 June 1765 *WatV*, d (Syracuse, N. Y.); m ——— Fay.
9 LYDIA, b 29 Apr 1767 *WatV.*
10 ADA, b 7 Apr 1770 *WatV;* m ——— Richards.
11 ISAAC, b 2 Apr 1772 *WatV*, d 4 Nov 1835; res. Camden, N. Y., returned to Conn.; m Sybil Scott, who d 27 Jan 1830.

12 Lowly, b 20 Oct 1774 *WatV*, d 1822; m Timothy Hinman.
13 Dice, b 1 Sep 1778 *WatV*, d 15 Sep 1850; m 4 Mar 1798 Henry Kinney.
14 Munson, b 26 Nov 1780 *WtnV*, d July 1830; m Phebe Chapin, b 11 Nov 1782, d Apr 1829.
[15 Patty; m ——— Gage.]

fam. 7. Bartholomew & Lucy (Curtis) Pond:
1 Beriah, b 10 Aug 1757 *WatV;* m 3 June 1784 *PC*—Sue Sanford.
2 Ire, b 27 Nov 1759 *WatV*, d 26 Sep 1792 *PC;* m c. 20 May 1782 *PC*—Lettice Blakeslee.
3 Content, b 23 Nov 1761 *WatV;* m 18 Feb 1779 *PC*—Benjamin Curtis.
4 Zerah, b 24 Nov 1763 *WatV*.
5 Sally, b 20 Mar 1766 *WatV;* m 22 Mar 1784 *PC*—Luther Foot.
6 Rebecca, b 5 June 1768 *WatV*.
7 Lucy, b 10 May 1770 *WatV*.
8 Jesse, b 17 July 1772 *WatV;* m 8 Mar 1795 *PC*—Anna Griggs.
9 Samuel, b 24 Jan 1775 *WatV*.

PORTER. Richard, s. of Daniel & Mary, b 24 Mar 1658, d 1740; Dr.; res. Wat & WH; m (1) Ruth [da. Joshua & Ruth (Sherwood) Holcomb], who d 9 Jan 1709/10 *WatV;* m (2) Mary, wid. John Thomas of WH; she m (3) Deliverance Downs of M.

(By 1): 1 Daniel; res. Simsbury.
2 Joshua, b 7 Aug 1688 *WatV*, d 19 Nov 1709 *WatV*.
3 Mary, b 14 Jan 1690/1 *WatV;* m ——— Northrop.
4 Ruth, b Oct 1692 *WatV;* m ——— Cossett.
5 Samuel, b 30 Mar 1695 *WatV*, d 1727; m 9 May 1722 *WatV*—Mary Bronson.
6 Hezekiah, b 29 Jan 1696/7 *WatV*, d Aug 1702 *WatV*.
7 John, b 11 June 1700 *WatV*.
8 Timothy, b 21 Dec 1701 *WatV;* m (1) 18 Dec 1735 *WatV*—Mary Baldwin; m (2) 27 Aug 1767 *WatV*—Hannah Winters.
9 Hezekiah, b 27 July 1704 *WatV;* res. Wy.

(By 2): 10 Lydia, b c. 1716, d after 1795; m 19 Dec 1734 *NHV*—Daniel Pardee.
11 Joshua, b 5 Nov 1718 *NHV*, bp Mar 1719 *NHC1*, d 1803; Dr.; res. S; m (1) Mercy ———, who d 1796; m (2) c. 1797 Mabel da. John & Mary (Forbes) Russell, wid. Stephen Pardee, b 7 May 1729 *EHV*, d 1807.
12 Richard, b 22 Aug 1722 *NHV*, bp 14 Oct 1722 *NHC1*.

PORTER. MISCELLANEOUS. MARY da. Nathaniel of St m 2 June 1692 *WV*—Robert Royce....... ELIZABETH m 28 Nov 1732 *WV*—Benjamin Atwater....... COMFORT m 20 Apr 1737 *WV*—Abel Thompson....... HANNAH m 10 Jan 1740 *WV*—Caleb Munson....... ABIGAIL m 23 Dec 1742 *WV*—Josiah Mix.

POST. SAMUEL s. Samuel & Susanna (Grant), b c. 1763, d 29 Sep 1794 æ. 31 *NHx*, æ. 34 *NHT1;* m 21 Aug 1784 *NHx*—Mary da. Thomas & Lois (Tuttle) Davis, b c. 1763, d 29 Jan 1836 æ. 73 *NHT1;* she m (2) Thomas Canby of Philadelphia. Child: Samuel bp Aug 1785 *NHx*, bu. 28 Apr 1786 (æ. 0-9) *NHx*. Samuel had also a nat. da. Lucy. [Proof, NHPro. 17:174.]

POTTER. FAM. 1. ——— m Hannah ———, who d 1659; she m (2) [John?] Beecher.

1 JOHN, d 1643; m Elizabeth ———, who d 28 July 1677 *NHV;* she m (2) Edward Parker; (3) Robert Rose. [Was he the John Potter who m 14 Apr 1630 *Chesham, co. Bucks, Eng.*—Elizabeth Wood & had da. Elizabeth bp 16 Feb 1631 *Chesham?*]

i John, b c. 1636, d 24 Dec 1706 *NHV;* Sgt.; m (1) c. 1660 Hannah da. John Cooper, b 1638 *NHC1*, bp 15 Aug 1641 *NHC1*, d 15 June 1675 *NHV;* m (2) 29 Dec 1679 *NHV*—Mary da. Edward & Mary Hitchcock, wid. Ralph Russell, b 2 Feb 1638 *NHC1*, bp 15 Dec 1644 *NHC1*. FAM. 2.

ii Hannah, d 7 Nov 1723 *NHV;* m (1) 3 Dec 1650 *NHV*—Samuel Blakeslee; m (2) 21 Dec 1676 *NHV*—Henry Brooks.

iii Samuel, bp 7 Oct 1641 *NHC1*, d 1696; m (1) 21 Nov 1670 *NHV*—Anna da. William & Sarah (Davis) Russell, b 29 July 1650 *NHV*, d 9 May 1676 *WV;* m (2) 6 Dec 1676 *WV*————. FAM. 3.

2 WILLIAM, b c. 1608, d June 1662; m Frances ———.

i Joseph, b c. 1635, d 17 Aug 1669 *NHV;* m Phebe da. William & Hannah Ives, bp 2 Oct 1642 *NHC1;* she m (2) Aug 1670 *NHV*—John Rose. FAM. 4.

ii Mary, b c. 1637, bp 22 Aug 1641 *NHC1;* m c. 1657 Joseph Mansfield.

iii Sarah, b c. 1639, bp 22 Aug 1641 *NHC1;* m (1) Robert Foote; m (2) 1686 Aaron Blatchley.

iv Hope, bp 3 Oct 1641 *NHC1;* m 3 Feb 1663 *NHV*—Daniel Robinson.

v Rebecca, bp Jan 1643 *NHC1;* m 27 Nov 1667 *NHV*—Thomas Adams. She had a nat. child by John Thorpe, b 1666.

vi Nathaniel, bp 22 Dec 1644 *NHC1;* m 1 Apr 1675 *NHV*—Elizabeth Hawes. FAM. 5.

FAM. 2. JOHN & HANNAH (COOPER) POTTER:

1 HANNAH, b c. 1661, d 13 June 1662 *NHV.*

2 JOHN, b 13 June 1663 *NHV,* d 10 Aug 1664 *NHV.*

3 HANNAH, b 26 June 1665 *NHV;* m 17 Nov 1684 *BdV* —John Butler.

4 JOHN, b 4 Aug 1667 *NHV,* d 12 Mar 1712/3 *EHV;* m 23 Feb 1691/2 *NHV*—Elizabeth da. John & Elizabeth (Thomas) Holt, b 28 Sep 1674 *NHV,* d 19 Dec 1751 æ. 78 *EHV.*

i John, b 14 June 1695 *NHV,* bp 26 Nov 1699 *NHC1,* d 18 Feb 1784 *SC;* m (1) Abigail ———, b c. 1696, d 27 July 1753 æ. 57; m (2) 16 May 1754 *WC2*—Elizabeth, wid. Spenser, who d 10 Jan 1766 *SC;* m (3) 22 Apr 1767 *SC*—Elizabeth Strickland, wid. Samuel Neal. FAM. 6.

ii Elizabeth, b 24 Sep 1697 *NHV,* bp 26 Nov 1699 *NHC1,* d 3 Sep 1746 *EHV;* m (1) John Luddington; m (2) 2 Oct 1734 *BdV*—Thomas Wheaton.

iii Gideon, b 3 June 1700 *NHV,* bp 28 July 1700 *NHC1,* d 30 Dec 1758 æ. 57 *EHT;* m 24 Oct 1723 *EHV*—Mary da. Matthew & Mary (Brockett) Moulthrop, b 4 June 1701 *EHV,* d Nov 1786 æ. 85 *EHC;* she m (2) 7 Apr 1767 *EHC*—Samuel Thompson. FAM. 7.

iv Daniel, b 15 Jan 1701 *NHV* [1701/2], d 20 Jan 1746/7 *EHV;* m 12 Sep 1728 *NHV*—Hannah da. Pelatiah & Martha (Sanford) Holbrook, bp 18 May 1701 *MC1,* d 15 Sep 1742 *EHV.* FAM. 8.

v Joseph, res. Wat; m Thankful da. Samuel & Margaret (Old) Jacobs, b 2 Feb 1709/10 *NHV.* FAM. 9.

vi Enos, b 12 Dec 1706 *NHV;* m Sarah da. Abraham & Sarah (Talmadge) Hemingway, b 12 Apr 1712 *NHV.* FAM. 10.

vii Samuel, b c. 1708, d 22 Nov 1756 æ. 47 *ThomastonT;* m 1 June 1738 *BdV*—Dorothy da. Matthew & Mary (Brockett) Moulthrop, b 1 Dec 1712 *EHV,* d 30 Dec 1793 æ. 82 (Episcopalian) *PC,* 31 Dec *ThomastonT.* FAM. 11.

5 SAMUEL, b 23 July 1669 *NHV,* d 16 Nov 1669 *NHV.*

6 SAMUEL, b 25 Dec 1670 *NHV,* d 1 Jan 1670 *NHV* [1670/1].

7 Son, b 1 Feb 1671 *NHV* [1671/2], d Feb 1671 *NHV* [1671/2].
8 Mary, b 16 Mar 1672/3 *NHV*.
9 Samuel, b 3 June 1675 *NHV*, d s. p. 26 Nov 1707 *EHV*.

FAM. 2. John & Mary (Hitchcock) Potter:
10 Abigail, b 23 Sep 1680 *NHV*, bp 15 Dec 1689 *NHC1*, d 1755; m (1) Samuel Thompson; m (2) Thomas Smith.

FAM. 3. Samuel & Anna (Russell) Potter:
1 Samuel, b 19 Sep 1671 *WV*, d 5 Feb 1756; rem. to N. J.
2 John, b 20 Nov 1673 *WV*.
3 Hannah, b 29 Dec 1675 *WV*.

FAM. 3. Samuel & ——— (———) Potter (incomplete):
4 Nathaniel; res. Huntington, L. I.; m.
i Gilbert, b 8 Jan 1725, d 4 Feb 1786; Lt.-Col.; res. Huntington; m 23 Feb 1748 Elizabeth Williams.
ii Zebediah; res. Md.

FAM. 4. Joseph & Phebe (Ives) Potter:
1 Joseph, b 8 Oct 1661 *NHV*, d young.
2 Rebecca, b 26 May 1663 *NHV;* m (1) Samuel Frisbie of Bd; m (2) Charles Tyler.
3 Phebe, b c. 1665, d 12 July 1738 *BdV;* m John Palmer of Bd.
4 Joseph, "son" b Mar 1667/8 *NHV*, d 22 Nov 1742 æ. 75 *NHT1;* m Mary da. Daniel & Abiah (Street) Sherman, b 28 Oct 1670 *NHV*.
i Joseph, b 15 Mar 1702 *NHV*, d 1743; m 11 Mar 1728/9 *NHV*—Thankful da. Joseph & Anna (Heaton) Bradley, b 17 Mar 1704 *NHV*, bp 24 Nov 1734 (adult) *NHC1*, d 4 Nov 1789 æ. 87 *NHC1*. FAM. 12.
ii Elizabeth, b 2 Sep 1704 *NHV*, d 1754 æ. 50 *NHT1;* m 31 Jan 1723/4 *NHV*—Timothy Clark.
iii John, b Aug 1706 *NHV*, d 10 Nov 1784 æ. 78 *HT4;* m 4 Feb 1730/1 *NHV*—Esther da. Joseph & Hannah (Bradley) Lines, b c. 1709, d 21 Dec 1773 æ. 64 *HT4*. FAM. 13.
iv Mary, b 19 May 1710 *NHV*, d 27 Mar 1770 æ. 61 *NoHT1;* m 15 Oct 1733 *NHV*—James Todd.

FAM. 5. Nathaniel & Elizabeth (Hawes) Potter:
1 Nathaniel, b 20 Feb 1675 *NHV* [1675/6], d 1740; m 19 Dec 1706 *NHV*—Lydia da. John & Lydia (Parker) Thomas, b c. 1681, d 4 Apr 1765 æ. 84 *NoHC;* she m (2) Thomas Beach.

i James, b 6 Sep 1707 *NHV;* m 19 Mar 1729/30 *NHV*—Sarah da. Joseph & Anna (Heaton) Bradley, b 24 Sep 1709 *NHV*. FAM. 14.
ii Lydia, b 15 July 1709 *NHV;* m 31 July 1736 *NHV*—Benjamin Beach.
iii Thankful, b c. 1714, d 11 Nov 1798 æ. 85 *Amenia,N.Y.,T;* m 10 Dec 1740 *NHV*—Enos Talmadge.
iv Sarah, bp (adult) 28 Mar 1736 *NHC1;* m 3 Jan 1738/9 *NHV*—Stephen Ford.
v Anna, bp (adult) 17 Aug 1735 *NHC1;* m 7 Sep 1749 *NHV*—Asa Alling.

2 ELIZABETH, b 30 Aug 1677 *NHV*, d 21 Oct 1736 *NHV;* m 6 Aug 1724 *NHV*—John Blakeslee.

3 SAMUEL, b 3 Oct 1679 *NHV*, d July 1740 æ. 60 *NHT1;* m 10 Jan 1710/1 *NHV*—Abigail da. John & Hannah (Grannis) Hill, b 24 Dec 1681 *NHV*, d Aug 1759 *NHC1*.
i Samuel, b 18 Sep 1711 *NHV*, bp (adult) 6 Dec 1730 *NHC1*, d 23 Nov 1788 æ. 78 *NoHC*.
ii Moses, b 10 Nov 1713 *NHV*.
iii Aaron, b 1 Mar 1715/6 *NHV*, bp 8 July 1716 *NHC1;* m 3 Apr 1740 *NHV*—Dorcas da. John & Esther (Clark) Munson, b 18 Nov 1720 *NHV*, d 22 Sep 1761 *NHV*. FAM. 15.
iv David, b 26 Nov 1717 *NHV*, bp Feb 1717/8 *NHC1*, d 1794; Census (H) 1-0-1; m 17 Nov 1748 *NHV*—Sarah da. Stephen & Elizabeth (Sherman) Gilbert, b 10 Apr 1730 *NHV*. FAM. 16.
v Abigail, b 28 Aug 1719 *NHV*, bp Oct 1719 *NHC1;* m 3 Apr 1740 *NHV*—David Munson.
vi Hannah, b 7 Nov 1721 *NHV;* m 11 Nov 1742 *NHV*—Joseph Ball.
vii Joel, b 31 Jan 1723/4 *NHV*, bp 22 Mar 1723/4 *NHC1;* m 13 Oct 1746 *NHV*—Susanna da. Joseph & Hannah (Skeath) Stacey, b [at Boston?]. FAM. 17.

4 SARAH, b 31 Oct 1681 *NHV*, d young.

5 STEPHEN, b 11 July 1684 *NHV*, d 26 Oct 1763 æ. 80 *NHC1;* m (1) Mary da. Ebenezer & Mercy (Brooks) Hill; m (2) Patience ——.
(By 1): *i* Mercy, b 9 Sep 1711 *NHV;* m 2 Aug 1733 *NHV*—Isaac Turner.
ii Stephen, b 18 Sep 1714 *NHV*, d 30 Aug 1759 *NHV;* m 25 May 1737 *NHV*—Joanna da. Benjamin & Azuba (Tuttle) Fox, b c. 1714, d 3 Jan 1799 æ. 85 *HT2 list*. FAM. 18.

iii Amos, b 29 Dec 1715 *NHV,* d Jan 1772 æ. 52 (?) *NHC1.*

iv Hannah, b 4 Apr 1718 *NHV.*

6 Mary, b 8 Oct 1686 *NHV,* d 3 Sep 1751 æ. 65 *NoHT1;* m Joseph Gilbert.

7 Daniel, b 1 Jan 1688/9 *NHV;* m (1) 30 Mar 1714 *NHV*—Mary Ray; m (2) Lydia da. Samuel Sanford, wid. Reuben Batchelor, b 22 July 1698 *NHV,* d 24 Oct 1769 æ. 70 *NoHC.* Family incomplete.

(By 1): *i* Thomas, b 15 Sep 1714 *NHV,* d 1762; m Abigail da. James & Abigail (Morris) Peck, b 1 July 1713 *NHV.* FAM. 19.

ii Daniel, b 9 June 1718 *NHV,* d 29 Oct 1773 *PC,* æ. 55 *PT;* m 11 Mar 1740/1 *NHV*—Martha da. Ebenezer & Mary (Atwater) Ives, b 1 May 1717 *NHV,* d 13 July 1770 *PC,* æ. 54 *WatV.* FAM. 20.

iii Mabel, b 9 Nov 1720 *NHV,* d 25 June 1787 æ. 67 ; m 8 Jan 1738/9 *NHV*—James Grannis.

iv (perhaps) Enos, d 7 Aug 1759 *F&IWRolls;* m 12 Apr 1750 *NHV*—Abigail da. Eleazer & Sarah (Rowe) Brown, b 12 June 1730 *NHV,* d after 1799. Children: (1) William, b 21 Nov 1750 *NHV;* (2) Ezra, b 10 May 1752 *NHV;* (3) Abigail, b 23 June 1754 *NHV;* the last two bp (as children of Wid. Abigail) 7 Nov 1762 *NHC1.*

v Noah, b c. 1725, d c. Oct 1807 æ. 82 (at NH) *ConnH;* Census (NH) 1-0-2; m Thankful da. James & Thankful (Hotchkiss) Gilbert, b 8 Mar 1726/7 *NHV,* d 2 Feb 1802 æ. 75 (at NH) *ConnJournal.* Family unknown except s. Asa, d bef. 1829; Capt.; Census (NH) 1-1-3; m 4 Sep 1783 *NHC2*—Mary Mansfield. Asa had a da. Grace who d Aug 1829 (at Washington, D. C.) *ColR,* w. of ——— Hurst.

(By 2): *vi* Meeké, b 14 June 1742 *NHV;* res. Claremont, N. H.; m Mary ———.

8 Deborah, b 1 Mar 1694/5 *NHV,* d s. p. 1741; m John Clark.

9 Sarah, b 1 Mar 1698/9 *NHV,* bp (adult) 19 May 1728 *NHC1,* d 30 Nov 1778 æ. 79 *NHC1;* m 14 Apr 1729 *NHV*—John Harris. She had a nat. child by Thomas Gill:

i John Gill, b 1724 *NHCCt,* bp 16 June 1728 *NHC1;* see Gill.

10 Abigail, b 1 Sep 1701 *NHV,* d 6 June 1765 æ. 62 *NHT1;* m 13 May 1730 *NHV*—James Tuttle.

FAM. 6. JOHN & ABIGAIL (———) POTTER:

1 JOHN, b 1 Apr 1721 *NHV*, d 1 Nov 1791 æ. 71 *NoBT1*, 1 Nov 1792 *BdV*; Lt.; m 14 Nov 1746 *BdV*—Mary da. Samuel & Sarah (Wheeler) Beers, b c. 1721, d 30 May 1780 *BdV*, æ. 59 *NoBC2*.

i Achsah, b 26 Sep 1747 *BdV*, d s. p.

ii Ard, b 26 Dec 1748 *BdV*, d 26 May 1766 æ. 18 *NoBT1*.

iii Mary.

iv Hannah; m ——— Foote.

v Sarah; m 30 Nov 1772 *WV*—Asa Todd.

vi John, b c. 1760, d 14 Apr 1843 æ. 83 *NoBT1*; m (1) 27 Nov 1781 *EHC*—Asenath da. Ebenezer & Sarah (Wilford) Linsley, b 15 May 1757 *BdV*, d 15 June 1797 æ. 41 *NoBT1*, æ. 44 *NoBC2*; m (2) 15 Jan 1798 *NoHC*—Mabel Bassett. Children by 1st w. recorded *BdV*: 1 James, b 3 Jan 1782; 2 Bela, b 18 Mar 1785; 3 Jonathan Beers, b 9 —— 1787; 4 John, b 29 Apr 1789; 5 Merrit, b 17 Oct 1792; 6 Priscilla, b 1 Oct 1795.

2 ABIGAIL, b 26 Jan 1723 *NHV*; m 12 Jan 1743/4 *SC*—Gideon Andrews.

3 JOEL, b 11 Apr 1727 *NHV*, d bef. 1785; m 18 Mar 1752 *SC*—Rhoda ———, who d 5 Sep 1801 æ. 67 *SC*.

i Asahel, bp 23 July 1753 *SC*, d 21 May 1775.

ii Philemon, bp 31 Mar 1754 *SC*.

iii Lemuel.

iv Rhoda, bp 9 Apr 1758 *SC*, d 1 Apr 1795; m Martin Deming.

v John, bp 8 June 1760 *SC*; Dr.; res. Wol; m (1) 11 Sep 1783 Lydia Harrison; m (2) 30 Mar 1797 Hila Clark.

vi Paulinus, bp 11 Apr 1762 *SC*; m 24 June 1784 *SC*—Abigail Barnes.

vii Joel, bp 20 May 1764 *SC*.

viii Elizabeth, bp 23 Mar 1766 *SC*; m 26 Oct 1789 *SC*—Harvey Smith.

ix Martin, bp 21 Oct 1767 *SC*, d 4 June 1821 æ. 54 *ST*, *SC*; Capt.; m 25 Nov 1790 *SC*—Phebe Barrett, who d 25 Dec 1858 æ. 91 *ST*.

x Phebe, bp 18 Feb 1770 *SC*.

xi Daniel, bp 8 Feb 1773 *SC*, d Feb 1773 *SC*.

xii Lydia; m 1 Jan 1799 *SC*—Palmer Neal.

FAM. 7. GIDEON & MARY (MOULTHROP) POTTER:

1 MARY, b 17 Aug 1724 *EHV*, d 16 July 1804 æ. 80 *SC*; m David Smith.

2 Gideon, b 24 Apr 1726 *EHV,* d 19 Mar 1767 æ. 41 *EHT;* m 27 Aug 1752 *EHV*—Kezia da. David & Mary Leavit, b 5 Mar 1728 *WV;* she m (2) 6 Sep 1768 *EHC*—Abner Bean.

i Thankful, b 10 Nov 1753 *EHV,* bp 13 Jan 1754 *BdC,* d 2 Feb 1761 æ. 8 *EHT.*

ii Lois, b 15 July 1756 *EHV,* bp 8 Aug 1756 *EHC,* d 16 June 1792 æ. 36 *EHT;* m 22 May 1775 *EHC*—Nehemiah Smith.

iii Lydia, bp 9 July 1759 *EHC;* res. Bristol 1790 & New Hartford 1792.

iv Thankful; m James Spencer; res. New Hartford 1794.

v Gideon, bp [———] 1764 *EHC,* d 9 Sep 1767 æ. 3 *EHT.*

3 Thankful, b 16 July 1728 *EHV,* d 25 Aug 1743 *EHV.*

4 David, b 12 Jan 1730/1 *EHV,* d 11 Sep 1760 *F&IW Rolls;* m 8 Nov 1750 *EHV*—Mary Wright; she m (2) 28 Jan 1762 *EHC*—John Shepard.

i Levi, b 26 Nov 1751 *EHV,* d 26 May 1752 *EHV,* æ. 0-6 *EHT.*

ii Desire, b 25 Jan 1755 *EHV,* bp 2 Feb 1755 (at EH) *BdC;* m 18 Mar 1782 *EHC*—Dan Goodsell.

iii Levi, b 1 Jan 1757 *EHV,* bp 6 Feb 1757 *EHV,* d 8 Oct 1835 æ. 78-9 *EHC;* Ens.; Census (EH) 2-0-4; m 1778 *EHC*—Sarah da. Samuel & Elizabeth (Denison) Thompson, b 27 May 1749 *NHV,* d 12 Sep 1835 æ. 86 *EHC.* fam. 21.

iv Isaac, bp 9 July 1759 *EHC,* d 1 Dec 1777.

5 Dorothy, b 15 Dec 1733 *EHV,* d 1736 æ. 3 *EHV,* 11 Nov 1736 *EHT.*

6 Desire, b 1 May 1736 *EHV,* d 24 Dec 1744 æ. 9 *EHV, EHT.*

7 Stephen, b 12 Jan 1738/9 *EHV,* d 18 Sep 1810; m 3 July 1766 *BdV*—Sarah Linsley.

i Lucinda, b 4 Apr 1767.

ii Sarah; m 16 Nov 1789 *BdC*—Thomas Norton.

iii James.

iv Matilda.

v Mary.

vi Frederick ["Wm. F." bp 9 Jan 1785 *BdC*].

8 Jerusha, b 31 July 1741 *EHV,* d 21 Oct 1741 *EHV,* æ. 0-3 *EHT.*

9 Jared, b 25 Sep 1742 *EHV,* d 11 July 1810 æ. 68 *WT1;* Dr.; B.A. (Yale 1760); m 19 Apr 1764 *EHC*—Sarah da. Samuel & Mary (Thompson) Forbes, b c. 1744, d 6 May 1831 æ. 87 (at W) *ColR.*

i Sarah, b 5 Oct 1767, d 4 Nov 1805 æ. 39 *WT1;* m Billious Kirtland.
ii Mary, b 10 Feb 1772, d 21 Mar 1850; m 19 June 1793 Turhand Kirtland.

FAM. 8. DANIEL & HANNAH (HOLBROOK) POTTER:

1 NATHAN, b 28 July 1729 *NHV;* m 29 Apr 1760 *BdV*—Hannah Foote.
i Isaac, b 23 Aug 1762 *BdV*.
2 EUNICE, b c. 1731, d 9 Sep 1742 *EHV*.
3 PHINEAS, b 7 Jan 1732/3 *NHV;* m 10 Mar 1757 *Wy*—Dorcas Hinman; had children in Wy.
4 HOSEA, b 29 Mar 1735 *NHV,* d 20 Sep 1742 *EHV*.
5 LOIS, b 15 Dec 1737 *NHV,* d 15 Sep 1742 *EHV*.
6 ELAM, b 1 Jan 1741/2 *NHV,* "child" d 9 Sep 1742 *EHV*.

FAM. 9. JOSEPH & THANKFUL (JACOBS) POTTER:

1 MERCY, b 18 Dec 1737 *EHV*.
2 THOMAS, b 26 Aug 1739.
3 SYBIL, b 1 Sep 1741 *EHV*.
4 JESSE, b 21 May 1743 *EHV*.
5 ELIZABETH, b 1 Aug 1745 *EHV*.
6 DESIRE, b 28 Dec 1748 *WatV,* d soon.
7 ENOS, b 31 May 1751 *WatV*.
8 DESIRE, b 1 Oct 1755 *WatV*.

FAM. 10. ENOS & SARAH (HEMINGWAY) POTTER:

1 SARAH, b c. 1732, d 1 Sep 1743 *EHV,* æ. 11 *EHT*.
2 ANNA, d s. p.
3 ISAAC, d 7 Feb 1756 *EHV*.
4 ISRAEL, b c. 1738, d 9 Mar 1815 æ. 77 *LT;* Capt.; Census (L) 1-3-3; m 4 Feb 1761 *EHC*—Mary da. Thomas & Hannah (Robinson) Dawson.
i Sarah, bp 22 May 1774 *EHC;* m 9 June 1777 *EHC*—Eliphalet Luddington.
ii Hannah, bp 22 May 1774 *EHC*.
iii Anna, bp 22 May 1774 *EHC*.
iv Joel, bp 22 May 1774 *EHC*.
v Asahel, bp Apr 1776 *EHC*.
vi Amy, bp [———] 1778 *EHC*.
vii Enos, b c. 1782, d 8 Feb 1826 æ. 44 *LT;* m Polly ———.
viii Israel, b c. 1784, d 12 Oct 1785 æ. 1 *LT*.
5 ABNER.
6 HANNAH, b c. 1744, d 4 Nov 1821 æ. 77 (at Wy) *NHT3;* m 10 Sep 1770 *EHC*—Levi Chidsey.

FAM. 11. SAMUEL & DOROTHY (MOULTHROP) POTTER:

1 SAMUEL, b 10 Sep 1739 *BdV;* m 8 Jan 1765 *WatV*—Lydia da. John & Abigail (Sutlief) How, b 10 Apr 1744 *WatV,* d 20 Apr 1796 æ. 52 *ThomastonT*.

i Eunice, b 6 Sep 1765*Wat V*.
ii Lucy, b 11 Nov 1766 *WatV*.
iii Mary, b 15 June 1768 *WatV*.
iv Jared, b 21 July 1770 *WatV*.
v Samuel, b 30 July 1772 *WatV*.
vi Betty, b 25 July 1774 *WatV*.
vii Enos, b 2 Mar 1777 *WatV*.
viii Daniel, b 13 Feb 1779 *WatV*.
ix Polly, b 20 Jan 1783 *WtnV*.
x Asher, b 10 Sep 1786 *WtnV*.

2 JACOB, b 26 June 1741 *BdV;* m 2 July 1762 *WatV*—Abigail da. Thomas & Mary (Scott) Blakeslee, b 22 Dec 1741 *WatV*. Family incomplete.
i Demas, b 29 Jan 1763 *WatV*.
ii Zenas, b 5 Mar 1765 *WatV;* m 15 Nov 1789 *PV*—Betty Blakeslee; had Sherman, b 2 Aug 1790 *PV*, & Sheldon, b 18 Mar 1795 *PV*.
iii Thomas, b 14 Mar 1767 *WatV*.
iv Mabel, b 3 Apr 1769 *WatV*.
v Dolly, b 21 Mar 1772 *WatV*.
vi Arza, b 2 Apr 1774 *WatV*.
vii Chester, b 23 Oct 1787 *WtnV*.

3 EUNICE, bp 4 Sep 1743 *SC*, d 13 Nov 1756 *WatV*.
4 LUCY, bp 20 July 1746 *SC*, d 7 Nov 1756 *WatV*.
5 MARY, bp 18 Dec 1748 *SC*, d 7 Nov 1756 *WatV*.
6 (perhaps) ZEBULON, who had a s. Samuel, b 23 Oct 1773 *WV*.

FAM. 12. JOSEPH & THANKFUL (BRADLEY) POTTER (all bp 8 Jan 1743/4 *NHC1* as children of Wid. Thankful):

1 JOSEPH, b 6 Aug 1730 *NHV*, d 10 Apr 1800 æ. 70 *HT2;* Census (H) 2-1-4; m 26 Apr 1759 *NHC2*—Jemima da. Joseph & Rebecca [Wooding] Smith, b 28 May 1735 *NHV*, d 29 May 1801 æ. 66 *HT2*.
i Medad, b 4 Feb 1760 *NHV;* m Mehitabel da. David & Hannah (Johnson) Ball.
ii Rebecca, b 5 Apr 1761 *NHV*, d 10 Feb 1828 æ. 67 *HT4;* m Abraham Cooper.
iii Thaddeus, b 4 Jan 1763 *F*, d 4 Mar 1836 *F;* m Sarah Ferris.
iv Lucy; m (1) Joseph Ball; [m (2) Thomas Pardee].
v Chauncey; m Dorcas Bradley.
vi Rhoda; m ———.
vii Thomas; m (1) 16 Sep 1793 *EHC*—Amy da. Stephen & Amy (Grannis) Shepard; m (2) 23 July 1801 *EHC*—Polly Edwards. Children by 1st w. unknown; one may have been Lucinda, b c. 1794, d 30 Mar 1867 æ. 73 *HV;*

m Edward Nichols. Children by 2d w.: 1 Warren, b c. 1802, d 22 Feb 1887 æ. 85 *NHV;* m Elizabeth Farren, wid. Edmund H. Monroe, who d 7 Feb 1874 æ. 61 *NHT3*. 2 Wealthy Ann, b c. 1804, bp 23 July 1808 (æ. 4) *NHx*. 3 Willard, b c. 1806, bp 23 July 1808 (æ. 0-18) *NHx;* m 24 Mar 1833 *EHV*—Mary Ann Russell.

2 Timothy, b 12 Feb 1731/2 *NHV,* d 24 Oct 1799 æ. 69 *HT4;* Census (H) 2-1-3; m (1) 15 Feb 1756 *NHV*—Esther da. George & Katherine (Tuttle) Mix, b 22 Nov 1732 *NHV;* m (2) 2 Aug 1768 *NHV*—Susanna da. David & Thankful (Todd) Punderson, b 16 Aug 1744 *NHV;* m (3) Keturah ——.

(By 1): *i* Timothy, b 30 Oct 1756 *NHV,* bp 27 Oct 1787 (adult) *NHx,* d 15 Nov 1816 æ. 60 *HT4;* Census (H) 1-1-4; m 14 Mar 1781 *NHC1*—Martha da. Abraham & Rebecca (Seeley) Turner, b 10 Mar 1758 *NHV,* d 28 Oct 1838 æ. 81 *HT4*. FAM. 22.

ii Titus, bp 27 Oct 1787 (adult) *NHx*.

iii Katharine, b c. 1763, bp (adult) 27 Oct 1787 *NHx,* d 28 Mar 1833 æ. 70 *NHV*.

(By 2): *iv* Jared, b 11 July 1769 *NHV,* bp 27 Oct 1787 (adult) *NHx;* m Betsey ——, b c. 1769, bp 7 May 1793 (æ. 24) *NHx*. FAM. 23.

v Allen, b 2 June 1771 *NHV,* bp 13 Dec 1790 (æ. 16 or 17) *NHx,* d 1 Nov 1831 æ. 60 *HT4;* m Patty ——. FAM. 24.

vi John, b c. 1773, bp 27 Oct 1787 (adult) *NHx,* d 25 July 1813 æ. 40 *HT4;* m Eunice ——; she m (2) —— Phelps. FAM. 25.

vii Esther; m John Camp.

viii James, b c. 1778, bp 27 Oct 1787 *NHx,* d s. p. 24 Apr 1833 æ. 55 *HT4*.

ix Susanna, bp 27 Oct 1787 *NHx;* m —— Peck.

3 Titus, b 1 Apr 1734 *NHV,* d s. p. 1757.

4 Philemon, b 31 Mar 1737 *NHV,* d 11 Jan 1817 æ. 80 *HT4;* Census (H) 3-3-2; m (1) 13 Aug 1761 *NHC2*—Phebe da. Joseph & Phebe (Bassett) Mansfield, b c. 1740, d 2 May 1809 æ. 69 *HT4;* m (2) Pamela [Peck], wid. Samuel Smith & Benajah Thomas, b c. 1760, d 6 Oct 1815 æ. 55 *HT4,* Aug 1815 æ. 58 *ColR;* m (3) Lois ——.

(By 1): *i* Obedience, b c. 1761, d 3 Sep 1813 æ. 52 *HT4;* m 1781 *EHC*—David Potter.

ii Jesse, b c. 1763, d 15 July 1815 æ. 52 *HT4;* Census (H) 1-0-5; m Sybil da. Joseph & Esther

(Potter) Beecher, b 23 June 1763 *NHV,* d 24 Dec 1834 æ. 74 *HT4.* FAM. 26.

iii Eli, b c. 1766, d 2 Apr 1850 æ. 84 *HT4,* æ. 85 *HV;* m 1793 *EHC*—Martha da. Samuel & Mary (Street) Davenport, b 16 Dec. 1771 *NHV,* d 21 June 1743 æ. 72 *HT4.* FAM. 27.

iv Justus, b c. 1772, d 23 Dec 1809 æ. 37 *HT4;* m 5 June 1798 *EHC*—Ann Maria da. John & Elizabeth (Tomline) Hunt, b 5 Dec 1777 *NHV,* d 27 Dec 1853 æ. 76 *NHT1;* she m (2) 23 Feb 1819 *ColR*—Philemon Peckham. FAM. 28.

v Amelia [Pamela], b c. 1776, d 16 June 1864 æ. 88 *HT2;* m 6 July 1795 *EHC*—Willis [Austin] Heaton.

vi Lemuel; m Jemima da. Elijah Scovill. A son, Henry Justus, b [6 Dec 1810], d 19 Nov 1883 æ. 72-11-13 *NHV.*

vii Chester, b c. 1781, d 22 June 1858 æ. 77 *HT4;* m 12 Feb 1803 *NHx*—Hephzibah da. Alexander & Lydia (Bradley) Bradley, b c. 1785, d 2 Apr 1871 æ. 86 *HT4.* Children: 1 Luther, b c. 1806, d 18 Feb 1882 æ. 76 *NHV;* m 19 Oct 1828 *NHV*—Elizabeth Smith; 2 Sherman B., b 10 Nov 1821 *HV,* d 28 Oct 1908 *HV;* prob. others.

5 BETTY, b c. 1739, bp 8 Jan 1743/4 *NHC1,* d 4 Feb 1799 æ. 60 *HT2;* m (1) 26 Apr 1759 *NHC2*—Michael Gilbert; m (2) Ezra Dorman.

FAM. 13. JOHN & ESTHER (LINES) POTTER:

1 JOHN, b 16 Nov 1731 *NHV,* bp 20 June 1736 *NHC1,* d 2 Dec 1742 æ. 11 *NHT1.*

2 THOMAS, b 15 June 1733 *NHV,* bp 20 June 1736 *NHC1,* d young.

3 ESTHER, b 8 Apr 1735 *NHV,* bp 20 June 1736 *NHC1,* d 31 Mar 1789 *WolC;* m 28 Feb 1754 *NHV, NHC2*—Joseph Beecher.

4 MARY, b 2 Mar 1736/7 *NHV,* bp 5 June 1737 *NHC1,* d soon.

5 PHEBE, b 8 Oct 1739 *NHV,* d 4 Dec 1742 æ. 3 *NHT1.*

6 MARY, b 23 Sep 1741 *NHV,* bp 1 Nov 1741 *NHC1.*

7 PHEBE, b 8 Aug 1743 *NHV,* bp 11 Sep 1743 *NHC1;* m 14 Mar 1765 *NoHC*—Nathaniel Beach.

8 THANKFUL, b 19 June 1745 *NHV,* bp 21 July 1745 *NHC1;* m 15 Mar 1764 *NHV, NHC2*—Joel Ford.

9 SYBIL, b 4 Nov 1747 *NHV,* bp 27 Dec 1747 *NHC1.*

10 JOHN, b 29 Sep 1749 *NHV,* bp 19 Nov 1749 *NHC1.*

11 JOB, b 20 Nov 1751 *NHV,* bp 12 Jan 1751/2 *NHC1;* Census (H) 1-3-7; m 16 Nov 1775 *NHC2*—Mary

da. Joseph & Miriam (Gilbert) Bradley, b c. 1754.
i Mary.
ii John.
iii Miriam, b 26 May 1780 *NHV,* d 14 Sep 1834 *F.*
iv Esther, b 18 Mar 1782 *NHV,* d 28 Oct 1820 *F.*
v Polly, b 18 Mar 1782 *NHV,* d 11 Mar 1848 *F.*
vi Adah, b 4 Apr 1784 *NHV.*
vii Herman Bradley, b 8 Jan 1786 *NHV,* d 7 Oct 1854 *F.*
viii Robert Lines, b 21 Jan 1788 *F,* d 5 Feb 1841 *F.*
ix Sarah, b 11 May 1790 *F,* d 29 Apr 1860 *F;* m 9 Nov 1820 Emanuel Coryell.
x Thomas, d soon.
xi Frances, b 16 Apr 1795 *F,* d 5 Apr 1872 *F;* m George Kirby.
xii Thomas Gilbert, b 5 Jan 1797 *F;* m Eliza Jordan Harrison.

12 THOMAS, b 18 Jan 1754 *NHV,* bp 17 Mar 1754 *NHC1,* d 18 Dec 1823 *F;* Maj.; Census (H) 1-3-3; res. Cassewago, Pa., 1818; m 5 Feb 1778 *NoHC*—Abigail da. Elias & Abigail (Shepard) Forbes.
i Esther, b 12 Jan 1778 *F,* d 21 July 1809 æ. 31 *HT4;* m ——— Kimberly.
ii Obadiah, b 1781, d 1828; m 1808 Eliza W. Jones.
iii Elihu, d s. p.
iv Aaron Forbes, bp 6 Feb 1791 *NHC2;* m 1814 Lydia Gilbert.
v Job, b 16 Apr 1793 *F,* bp 7 July 1793 *NHC2,* d 13 Nov 1869 *F;* res. Crawford Co., Pa.; m 14 Mar 1816 Amelia Ford.

FAM. 14. JAMES & SARAH (BRADLEY) POTTER:

1 RHODA, b 22 Feb 1730/1 *NHV,* "Sybil" bp 17 Aug 1735 *NHC1,* d s. p. 1757; m 11 Feb 1756 *NHV,* 12 Feb *NHC2*—Dennis Covert.

2 JONAH, b 5 Feb 1733/4 *NHV,* bp 17 Aug 1735 *NHC1,* d s. p.

3 SARAH, b 19 Nov 1736 *NHV,* bp 13 Mar 1736/7 *NHC1,* d 8 Feb 1820 æ. 84 *HT2;* m Timothy Turner.

4 EUNICE, b 13 Nov 1742 *NHV,* bp 5 Dec 1742 *NHC1,* d 7 May 1833 æ. 93 *HT2;* m 17 Nov 1763 *NHC2*—Moses Ford.

5 LYDIA, bp 3 Aug 1746 *NHC1,* d s. p.

FAM. 15. AARON & DORCAS (MUNSON) POTTER:

1 MOSES, b 8 Jan 1740/1 *NHV,* bp 15 Oct 1752 *NHC2,* d 3 Feb 1822 æ. 82 *HT2 list;* m 24 Nov 1762 *WdC*—Rebecca da. Nathaniel & Thankful (Bassett) Yale, b 4 Oct 1737 *NHV,* d 9 Dec 1817 æ. 77 *HT2 list.*
i Silas.

ii Ithiel, b c. 1766, d 8 Mar 1796 æ. 30 *HT2 list;* m Rebecca da. Isaac & Lois (Bishop) Bradley, bp 16 Dec 1770 *NHC2,* d 21 Dec 1857 æ. 87 *NHT1;* she m (2) 8 Apr 1798 *NHC1*—Daniel Talmadge. Child: 1 Betsey, b c. 1792, d 30 Jan 1871 æ. 79 *HT2;* m 12 Apr 1810 Benjamin Mix.

iii Ruth, b c. 1768, d 26 Dec 1829 æ. 62 (at H) *ColR.*

iv Ezra.

v Lois, b c. 1775; m 7 Jan 1796 *NHC1*—Aaron Sperry.

vi Jason, b c. 1777, d 18 Feb 1866 æ. 89 *NHT2;* m 25 Nov 1803 *SC*—Betsey da. Caleb & Betsey (Davis) Ray, bp 19 Mar 1786 *NHx,* d 10 Apr 1857 æ. 71 *NHT2.* Children: 1 James, bp 1817 *HC2;* 2 Edwin Davis, bp 1817 *HC2;* m ——— Candee; 3 Elizabeth Mary, bp 1817 *HC2;* m ——— Frost; 4 Ithiel.

vii Rebecca. [Eliza Benton, da. of Rebecca Potter, b c. 1802 (at H), d 13 Oct 1884 æ. 82 *NHV.*]

viii James, d 9 Sep 1796 *HT2 list.*

2 Dorcas, b 4 Apr 1743 *NHV,* bp 15 Oct 1752 *NHC2,* d 6 May 1790 æ. 47 *NHC1;* m 5 Mar 1764 *WdC*—Ebenezer Peck.

3 Aaron, b 1 July 1745 *NHV,* bp 15 Oct 1752 *NHC2;* m 5 Feb 1767 *NHV, NHC2*—Mary [da. Timothy & Mary (Humphreville) ?] Alling.

i Mary, b 28 Nov 1767 *NHV,* bp 7 Feb 1768 *NHC2.*

4 Lemuel, b 8 July 1747 *NHV,* bp 15 Oct 1752 *NHC2,* d c. 1801; res. Naugatuck; m 19 Apr 1770 *NHC1*—Rachel da. Thomas & Rachel (Peck) Perkins, b 26 Sep 1742 *NHV,* d 26 Nov 1827 æ. 87 *WatT3.*

i Thomas.

ii Lemuel, b c. 1776, d 16 Aug 1860 æ. 84 *WatT3;* m Lois ———, who d 28 May 1859 æ. 83 *WatT3.*

iii Samuel, b 23 Sep 1779 *F;* m (1) 9 May 1799 *F*—Leva Judd; m (2) 14 Mar 1803 *F*—Chloe Brockett.

iv Aaron, b c. 1781, d 3 Oct 1863 æ. 82 *WatT3;* m Laura ———, who d 28 Feb 1866 æ. 79-6 *WatT3.*

v Anna.

5 Esther (name changed from Abigail), b 13 May 1749 *NHV,* bp 15 Oct 1752 *NHC2;* m 12 June 1771 *WdC*—Ebenezer Hine.

6 DOROTHY, b 29 Nov 1750 *NHV,* bp 15 Oct 1752 *NHC2;* m (name stated as Deborah) 29 Nov 1770 *WdC*—Eli Baldwin.

7 ABIGAIL, bp 13 Apr 1755 *NHC2.*

8 SAMUEL, b 13 Dec 1758 *NHV,* bp 17 June 1759 *NHC2.*

FAM. 16. DAVID & SARAH (GILBERT) POTTER:

1 ABEL, b 15 June 1749 *NHV,* d 29 Aug 1818 æ. 69 *NoBT1;* Census (H) 1-1-2; m Mary da. Abraham & Rebecca [Seeley] Turner, b c. 1764, d 7 Oct 1831 æ. 68 *NoBT1.*

i Sarah Gilbert, b 24 Apr 1783 *F,* d s. p. 11 Oct 1864 *F.*

ii Abel, b 21 Apr 1785 *F,* d 12 Apr 1860; res. Charlemont, Mass.; m (1) 25 June 1809 Vincey da. Solomon Todd; m (2) 14 Dec 1831 Anna Louisa Foote; m (3) 24 Aug 1836 Clarissa Giles.

iii Elam, b 11 June 1787 *F,* d s. p. 28 May 1801 *F.*

iv Rhoda Turner, b 20 Oct 1791 *F,* d 26 July 1875; m Benjamin Buell of W.

v Samuel, b 24 Oct 1794 *F,* d 19 Feb 1880; res. Charlemont, Mass.; m 21 Feb 1819 Sophia Rice.

vi Mary A., b 1 Dec 1797 *F,* d 14 Aug 1821 æ. 24 *NoBT1.*

vii Mary Eliza, b 5 Apr 1801 *F,* d s. p. c. 1854.

viii Elam, b 18 May 1803 *F,* d 12 Nov 1839; m 20 June 1824 Amelia da. Leonard Ives.

ix Rebecca Maria, b 28 June 1807 *F,* d 14 Dec 1885; m 14 Feb 1825 Hollister Baker Thayer.

2 DAVID, b 10 June 1751 *NHV,* d 22 Apr 1761 *NHV.*

3 ELIZABETH, b c. 1754, d s. p. 6 Jan 1817 æ. 63 *HT5.*

4 SARAH, b c. 1756, d 27 May 1790 æ. 34 *HT4.*

5 SAMUEL, b c. 1759, d 1779 (k. by British) *F.*

6 DAVID, b 28 May 1762 *NHV,* d 13 Mar 1846 (Bridgeport); m (1) 1781 *EHC*—Obedience da. Philemon & Phebe (Mansfield) Potter, b c. 1761, d 3 Sep 1813 æ. 52 *HT4;* m (2) 7 Dec 1823 *DanburyV*—Hannah Hoyt.

(*Continued on page 1473*)

Families of Ancient New Haven

(Continued from page 1472)

FAM. 17. JOEL & SUSANNA (STACEY) POTTER:

1 BENJAMIN, b c. 1747, d 13 Sep 1753 æ. 6 *NHT1*.

2 POLLY; [?m 11 Jan 1779 *EHC*—William Broughton].

3 STACEY; Census (NH) 1-0-1; m 24 Jan 1785 *NHC1*—Sarah da. James & Thankful (Sperry) Lines, b 31 Dec 1764 *NHV*.

4 JOEL, b c. 1761, bp 26 Dec 1784 *NoBC*, d 18 July 1827 æ. 66 *LT;* m 1784 Thankful Stone; had issue.

5 BENJAMIN, b c. 1763, bp 26 Dec 1784 *NoBC*, d 18 June 1837 æ. 74 *LT;* m 1783 Rachel Stone.

6 JOSEPH SKEATH, d 7 June 1795 *F;* Census (NH) 1-0-0; m 14 Nov 1790 *NHx*, 10 Nov *F*—Alice da. Zephaniah & Mary (Smith) Hatch, bp 1 July 1770 *NHC2*, d 19 Aug 1831 æ. 61-2 *F;* she m (2) 17 June 1797 *NHC1*—Henry Yorke.

i Alice, b 15 Mar 1791 *F;* m 1805 *F*—Alexander Grant.

ii Harriet, b 10 Apr 1795 *F*, bp 2 Aug 1795 *NHC1;* m 1818 *F*—Lyman Augustus Sisson.

FAM. 18. STEPHEN & JOANNA (FOX) POTTER:

1 LOIS, b 29 Jan 1738 *NHV;* [m 30 May 1758 *NHC2*—William Mansor].

2 MOSES, b 8 Feb 1740 *NHV*.

3 MABEL, b 3 Apr 1742 *NHV;* she had a nat. child b c. 1765.

4 HANNAH, b 29 July 1745 *NHV;* m 9 Jan 1766 *NHC1*—Daniel Ford.

5 STEPHEN, b 20 Mar 1748 *NHV*.

6 LEVI, b 17 Mar 1751 *NHV*, d Apr 1800 in 50 yr. (at NH) *ConnJournal;* Census (NH) 1-1-1; m 15 Oct 1773 *F*—Pamela da. James & Thankful (Sperry) Lines, b 15 Apr 1756 *NHV*, d 3 Aug 1815 *F*.

i William, b 25 Mar 1787 *F*, bp 2 Oct 1791 (æ. 4) *NHx*.

ii Pamela, b 5 Sep 1790 *F*, bp 2 Oct 1791 (æ. 1) *NHx;* m ——— Ufford.

7 AMOS, b 14 June 1754 *NHV;* m 11 Aug 1774 *NHC1*—Sarah da. Benjamin & Sarah (Tuttle) Warner, b 12 Mar 1755 *NHV*.

FAM. 19. THOMAS & ABIGAIL (PECK) POTTER:

1 MORRIS, bp 11 Feb 1749/50 *NHC1*, d 25 Dec 1761 *NoHC*.

2 JOHN, b [June 1747], bp 11 Feb 1749/50 *NHC1*, d 15 Mar 1767 æ. 19-9 *NoHC*.

3 THOMAS, bp 25 Feb 1749/50 *NHC1*.

[Leonard s. John (?) Potter bp 11 Feb 1749/50 with the two children of Thomas perhaps also belongs to him. No record of other children found.]

FAM. 20. DANIEL & MARTHA (IVES) POTTER:

1 ELAM, b 1 Feb 1741/2 *WatV*, d 17 Jan 1794; m.

2 AMBROSE, b 28 Apr 1743 *WatV*, d 17 Apr 1822; m.

3 ELIAKIM, b 6 Jan 1744/5 *WatV*, d 11 Mar 1822 æ. 77 *PT*; Dea.; m 18 Feb 1777 *WtnV*, 20 Feb *PC*—Temperance (———) Blakeslee, who d 3 Apr 1824 æ. 67 *PT*.

4 ISAIAH, b 23 July 1746 *WatV*, d 5 July 1817 (Lebanon, N. H.); m 15 Nov 1774 Elizabeth Barrett.

5 LYMAN, b 14 Mar 1747/8 *WatV*, d 20 July 1827; m. 1770 Abigail Payne.

6 MARY, b 20 Dec 1749 *WatV*, d 31 Aug 1750 *WatV*.

7 MARY, b 9 Mar 1751 *WatV*, d 18 July 1827; m 26 Mar 1773 *WatV*, 25 Mar *PC*—Aaron Dunbar.

8 MABEL, b 5 Nov 1752 *WatV*, d 6 June 1813 æ. 62 *PT*; m 8 Apr 1776 *WatV*, *PC*—Eliasaph Doolittle.

9 MARTHA, b 16 Mar 1754 *WatV*, d 21 June 1827; m 15 Jan 1778 *WatV*, *PC*—Jason Fenn.

10 SON, b & d c. 1756.

11 SON, b & d c. 1756.

12 DANIEL, b 15 Feb 1758 *WatV*, d 27 Apr 1842 æ. 84 *ThomastonT*; m 25 Jan 1781 *WtnV*, *PC*—Martha Humiston.

13 LUKE, b 13 Aug 1759 *F*, d 30 June 1834 æ. 75 *PT*; m 16 Jan 1786 Lois Royce, who d 1 Feb 1832 æ. 67 *PT*.

FAM. 21. LEVI & SARAH (THOMPSON) POTTER:

1 SAMUEL, b [May 1779], "only child" d 18 Mar 1780 æ. 0-10 *EHC*.

2 LEVI, b 24 Feb 1781 *F*, bp 7 Sep 1788 *EHC*, d 29 Aug 1814 æ. 33 *EHC*, 28 Aug æ. 34 *EHT*; m 5 Jan 1803 *NHx*—Polly da. Ichabod & Mehitabel (Bradley) Bishop, b c. 1782, d 3 May 1817 æ. 35 *EHC*.

i Samuel T., b c. 1804, d 28 Apr 1820 æ. 16 *EHC*, æ. 17 *EHT*.

ii Levi, b [Mar 1809], d 27 Sep 1809 æ. 0-6 *EHT*.

iii Levi, b [Feb 1812], d 2 Aug 1813 æ. 1-5 *EHT*.

iv Levi Bradley, b [19 July 1814], d 4 June 1815 æ. 0-10-15 *EHT*, "child of Wid. Polly" æ. 1 *EHC*.

3 Sarah, b 24 Feb 1781 *F,* bp 7 Sep 1788 *EHC,* d 28 Oct 1810 æ. 30 *EHC.*
4 Polly, b 9 Apr 1783 *F,* bp 7 Sep 1788 *EHC,* d 29 July 1826 æ. 43 *EHC;* m Roswell Bradley.
5 Elizabeth, b [Oct 1785], "child" d 28 Feb 1786 æ. 0-4 *EHC.*
6 Elizabeth, b 17 Jan 1787 *F,* d 4 Feb 1818 æ. 31 *EHT;* m 3 Dec 1807 *NoHC*—Benjamin Smith.
7 James, b 19 Sep 1789 *F,* bp 22 Nov 1789 *EHC,* d 11 Jan 1815 æ. 25 *EHC, EHT.*
8 Anna, b 4 Feb 1792 *F,* bp 1 Apr 1792 *EHC,* d June 1811 æ. 19 *EHC.*

fam. 22. Timothy & Martha (Turner) Potter:
1 Anna, b c. 1782, bp 27 Nov 1787 *NHx.*
2 Nancy, b 14 Sep 1784 *F,* bp 27 Nov 1787 *NHx,* d 14 Apr 1856; m 27 Dec 1802 Samuel Shipman.
3 Fanny, bp 27 Nov 1787 *NHx;* m David Heath.
4 Daniel Levi, b [Mar 1790], bp 13 Dec 1790 (æ. 0-9) *NHx;* m ——— Cleaver.
5 Timothy, b 14 Feb 1792 *F* [error for 1793], bp 7 May 1793 *NHx,* d 30 Apr 1854 æ. 61 *NHV;* m Aug 1815 Julia Smith.
i Jane H., b [Feb 1816], d 10 Sep 1887 æ. 71-7 *NHV;* m John M. Wilson.
6 Sena; m 14 Jan 1805 *NHx*—Elias Hull.
7 Jabez Turner, b 17 Jan 1796 *F,* d 1 Sep 1871 æ. 75 *HT4;* m 14 Feb 1821 *NoHV*—Almira da. John & Ruth (Stiles) Pierpont, bp 21 June 1801 *NoHC,* d 12 Mar 1880 æ. 79 *HT4.*
8 Rachel, b 8 Dec 1798 *F,* d 16 Apr 1891 æ. 92 *HT4;* m 17 Feb 1823 (at H) *ConnH*—Philo Curtis.
9 George Washington, b 6 May 1802 *F,* d 10 Oct 1879; m Lydia Bradley.

fam. 23. Jared & Betsey (———) Potter:
1 Susanna, b c. 1790, bp 7 May 1793 (æ. 2) *NHx;* m 11 Oct 1807 *NoHC*—Aaron Fuller of Norwalk & NH.
2 Oliver Bradley, b [July 1792], bp 7 May 1793 (æ. 0-10) *NHx,* d 12 Jan 1872 æ. 79-6 *HV;* res. Norfolk 1830, Canaan & H; m.
3 Anna; m Lewis C. Lawrence.

fam. 24. Allen & Patty (———) Potter:
1 Maria, b 7 June 1798 *F,* d 11 Aug 1866 *F;* m 9 Feb 1823 *HV*—Philip Frazier of Rainham, Mass.
2 Henry P., b 15 Apr 1800 *F,* d 6 Nov 1876 *F.*
3 Seymour, b 25 Dec 1801 *F,* d 18 Dec 1880 *F.*
4 Allin, b 11 Mar 1804 *F,* d s. p. 9 Aug 1863 æ. 59 *NHV;* m.
5 Jennet, b 28 Feb 1806 *F,* d 23 July 1896 *F;* m 16 May 1825 *HV*—Henry Barnes of NH.

6 Elihu, b 15 Mar 1808 *F,* d 10 Sep 1815 æ. 7 *HT4.*
7 Timothy, b 11 June 1810 *F,* d 25 June 1810 *F;* "infant" æ. 0-0-14 *HT4.*
8 Abigail Stow, b 11 July 1812 *F,* d 7 Dec 1891 *F;* m 14 Nov 1830 John E. Beers.
9 Adaline, b 7 Aug 1814 *F,* d 11 Sep 1892 *F;* m.
10 Mariett, b 1 Jan 1817 *F,* d 13 July 1845 *F;* m ——— Sabin.
11 Julia A., b 7 July 1821 *F,* d s. p. 20 July 1913; m James B. Munson.

FAM. 25. John & Eunice (———) Potter:
1 Joseph; res. H 1832.
2 Alfred.
3 Laura, b c. 1791, "Loriana" bp 7 May 1793 (æ. 2) *NHx;* m ——— Cooper.
4 Almira, b c. 1794, bp 7 Mar 1796 (æ. 2) *NHx,* d between 1819 & 1825; m Jacob Watson of Canaan.
5 John; res. H 1832.
6 Nelson.

FAM. 26. Jesse & Sybil (Beecher) Potter:
1 Hester; m Eliphalet Smith.
2 Aurelia [or is this a misreading for Amelia (of NH) who m Apr 1809 *ConnH*—Seth Galpin of Berlin?].
3 Sybil.
4 Sally.
5 Jesse.
6 Sylvester, b c. 1805, d 25 Feb 1863 æ. 58 *NHV;* m.

FAM. 27. Eli & Martha (Davenport) Potter:
1 Charlotte, bp 1 Mar 1795 *EHC,* d 17 Nov 1854 æ. 60 *NoHT3;* m Richard Mansfield.
2 Lyman.
3 Eliza, bp 1802 *HC2;* m Alfred Pierpont.

FAM. 28. Justus & Ann Maria (Hunt) Potter:
1 Horace, b c. 1799, bp 22 June 1803 (æ. 4) *NHx,* d 8 Mar 1869 æ. 70 *HT4;* m (1) Emma ———; m (2) Nancy Peckham.
2 Elias, b [27 Apr 1800], bp 22 June 1803 (æ. 3) *NHx,* d 11 Oct 1878 æ. 78-5-14 *NHV;* m 18 Apr 1830 *NHV*—Sally F. Curtis of O.
3 Pamela [Amelia], b c. 1802, bp 22 June 1803 (æ. 1½) *NHx;* m 21 Jan 1824 Stephen Gilbert.

POTTER. MISCELLANEOUS. Rachel bp 5 Apr 1741 *NHC1.* ......Abigail m 12 Feb 1786 *NHC1*—Aner Adee.

POWELL. Thomas d 3 Oct 1681 *NHV;* m Priscilla ———.
1 Hannah, b Aug 1641 *NHC1,* bp 1643 *NHC1,* d 15 Oct 1710 *NHV;* m 21 May 1661 *NHV*—Thomas Tuttle.

2 PRISCILLA, b Dec 1642 *NHC1,* bp 1644 *NHC1,* d 18 Apr 1726 *EHV;* m 22 May 1666 (at Bd) *NHV*—John Thompson.

3 MARY, bp 20 July 1645 *NHC1;* m (1) 18 Nov 1669 *NHV*—Ephraim Sanford; m (2) Nathaniel Baldwin.

4 MARTHA, bp 28 Jan 1648 *NHC1,* d soon.

5 MARTHA, bp Jan 1650 *NHC1,* d s. p.

6 HESTER, b 6 June 1653 *NHV,* bp 6 June 1653 *NHC1,* d s. p.

POWELL. MISCELLANEOUS. ABIGAIL m 4 Apr 1721 *WV*—Israel Hall.......ROBERT d 2 June 1748 *WV, WC2*.......JOHN m 14 Mar 1749 *WV*—Ruth Atkins; had Ruth, b 26 Jan 1749/50 *WV*.......WILLIAM, b c. 1745, d 4 Feb 1830 æ. 85 *(NHx) NHV;* Capt.; Census (NH) 2-0-2; m 28 Oct 1773 *NHx*—Miriam Tyler, b c. 1750, d 12 Mar 1807 æ. 57 *NHx.*

POWERS. JAMES, of NH, rem. to Farm; m 30 July 1765 *WdC*—Lois [da. George & Anne (Bristol)] Clinton.

1 JAMES, bp 14 June 1772 (sponsors, Enos Alling, Stephen Mansfield & Freelove Adams) *NHx.*

PRATT. NICHOLAS m Dinah [da. Jared & Dinah (Thomas) Belden, bp 28 Oct 1748 *WHx*].

1 DAVID, bp 16 July 1775 *NHx.*

2 DINAH, bp 11 May 1777 *NHx.*

PRENTICE. JONAS, b c. 1741, d 16 Oct 1817 æ. 76 *NHT1;* Col.; Census (NH) 2-1-5; m Amy da. Jabez & Amy Smith, b c. 1747, d 11 Mar 1814 æ. 67 *NHT1.* Family incomplete.

1 JONAS, b c. 1768, d 16 Apr 1804 æ. 36 *NHT1, NHx;* m Rebecca A. ———, who d 2 Dec 1809 æ. 34 *NHT1.*

2 AMY, b c. 1771, d Aug 1808; m May 1807 *NHC1,* 14 June *NHC2*—Elisha Colt of Hartford.

3 EUNICE, bp 29 Aug 1773 *NHC1,* d 18 Aug 1810 æ. 36 *HT1;* m [14] Aug 1806 *NHC1*—Simeon Goodyear.

4 JULIA ANNA, bp 15 Oct 1780 *NHC1,* d 6 Jan 1787 æ. 7 *NHT1,* "Nancy" æ. 6 *NHC1.*

5 MARIA SMITH, bp 25 June 1786 *NHC1,* d 4 Dec 1786 *NHC1,* æ. 0-6 *NHT1.*

6 NANCY MARIA, bp 9 Mar 1788 *NHC1,* d 14 Mar 1876 æ. 88 *NHT1.*

7 ELIZA, bp 30 May 1790 *NHC1,* d Feb 1867; m Aner Bradley.

PRESCOTT. FAM. 1. JAMES, s. of Benjamin & Rebecca (Minot), b 15 Mar 1749, d 25 May 1842 æ. 93 *NHT1, NHV;* rem. to NH 1771; Census (NH) 4-3-4; m (1) 28 Oct 1783 Rebecca da. James & Miliscent (Estabrook) Barrett, b 30 Aug 1763 (Concord, Mass.), d 3 May 1795 æ. 32 *NHT1;* m (2) 6 Feb 1796 *NHC1*—Rebecca da. David & Elizabeth (Bassett) Atwater, b 27

Apr 1760 *NHV*, d 17 July 1834 æ. 74 *NHT1*, 18 July *(NHC1) NHV*.

(By 1): 1 Rebecca, b c. 1785, d 13 Apr 1859 æ. 74 (at Concord, Mass.) *NHT1*.

2 Miliscent, bp 20 Jan 1788 *NHC2*, d 17 Apr 1838 æ. 50 *NHT1*.

3 James, bp 30 Jan 1790 *NHC2*, d Mar 1812 æ. 22 *NHT1*.

4 Minot, bp 23 Sep 1792 *NHC2*, d 4 Nov 1795 æ. 3 *NHT1*.

5 Child, d stillborn *NHT1*.

(By 2): 6 James Minot, b 12 Jan 1797 *F;* m (1) Lucy Bissett Tyler, who d 10 July 1874 (bu. at Philadelphia) *NHT1;* m (2) Ann R. Latimer, who d Jan 1891 *NHT1*.

7 Elizabeth, b 8 Apr 1798 *F;* m George Barrett of Concord, Mass.

8 David William, b 16 Mar 1800 *F;* m Susan Austin of Norwich.

fam. 2. Benjamin Prescott (bro. of above), b c. 1757, d 23 Oct 1839 æ. 82 *NHT1;* Census (NH) 4-3-2; m Hannah da. Tilley & Hannah (Alling) Blakeslee, b 24 Sep 1761 *NHV*, d 10 May 1824 æ. 62 (at Calais, Me.), 14 Nov 1824 æ. 62 *(NHC2) NHV*, but death reported in 31 May 1824 issue of *Conn Mirror*.

1 Henry, b c. 1784, d 16 Mar 1807 æ. 23 (at St. Thomas) *NHT1;* m Alida Frink, who d 14 May 1864 æ. 77 *NHT1*.

2 Enos Alling, b 19 Feb 1787 *F;* m 27 Dec 1807 *NHC2*—Polly Carrington.

3 Rebecca; m Apr 1809 *ConnH*—Forbes Kyle.

4 Hannah, b c. 1791, d 10 Apr 1866 æ. 75 *NHT1;* m Ira Bulford.

5 Mercy Gibbs, b c. 1793, d 28 Mar 1843 æ. 49 *NHT1;* m Joseph A. Bishop.

6 Benjamin, b c. 1795, d 16 July 1818 æ. 23 (at St. Eustace) *NHT1*.

7 Martha Goodhue; m James Frink.

8 Elizabeth Daggett; m 22 May 1823 *NHV*—Henry Hotchkiss.

9 Roger Sherman, b 27 Jan 1799 *F*, d 12 June 1856; m (1) 10 July 1822 *NHV*—Sally Jeannette Tomlinson, who d 30 May 1836 æ. 34 *NHV;* m (2) 12 Oct 1837 Rebecca Carrington.

10 Mary Barret; m 14 Feb 1819 John Beach.

PRESTON. fam. 1. William [s. of Adam & Isabel (Braithwait), bp 23 Jan 1590 [1590/1] *Giggleswick, co. York*], d 1647; m (1) 11 Oct 1613 *Chesham, co. Bucks*—Elizabeth Sale, bp 8 June 1590 *Chesham*, bu. 22 Feb 1634 *Chesham;* m (2) Mary da.

Robert Seabrook, b c. 1601, d after 1680; she m (2) Thomas Kimberly.

(By 1): 1 WILLIAM, bp 5 Oct 1614 *Chesham,* bu. 4 June 1633 *Chesham.*

2 JOHN, b c. 1617, bu. 18 Nov 1623 *Chesham.*

3 EDWARD, bp 14 Nov 1619 *Chesham,* d 1699; res. NH & Boston; m Margaret Hurst, "wife of Edward" d 28 Dec 1690 *NHV.* Family incomplete.

i William, b 30 Nov 1651 *BostonV.*

ii Mary, b 1 Jan 1653 *BostonV.*

iii Hannah, b 14 Sep 1653 *NHV,* d May 1669 *NHV.*

iv Elizabeth, b 29 Sep 1655 *NHV;* m (1) 23 Nov 1674 *NHV*—John Levins of St & Woodstock; m (2) 24 Mar 1699 Peter Aspinwall.

v Abigail, b Jan 1664 *NHV;* m 21 Mar 1687/8 *NHV*—Joseph Thomas.

vi Samuel, b June 1668 *NHV,* d c. 1693; m Abigail [? da. John & Lydia (Parker) Thomas; she m (2) Richard Lounsbury]. A child b 1693 *NHCCt.*

PAGE 1790

4 DANIEL, bp 3 Mar 1621 *Chesham,* d 10 Nov 1707 *Dorchester, Mass.;* m Mary ———; had issue.

5 ELIZABETH, bp 18 Jan 1623 *Chesham,* d 29 Aug 1693 æ. 68 *NHT1;* m Joseph Alsop.

6 SARAH, bp 18 July 1626 *Chesham;* m William Meeker.

7 MARY, bp 13 Dec 1629 *Chesham;* [m Peter Mallory].

8 JOHN, bp 4 Mar 1632 *Chesham;* res. Mass.; m.

(By 2): 9 JEHIEL, bp 14 June 1640 *NHC1,* d 1684; m (1) Sarah da. Thomas & ——— (Seabrook) Fairchild, b 19 Feb 1641 *StV* [1641/2]; m (2) Temperance da. Isaac & Margery Nichols, b 17 May 1662 *StV;* she m (2) 17 Apr 1688 Samuel Hubbell.

(By 1): *i* Samuel, b 1 July 1663 *StV,* d s. p. 1707.

ii Joseph, b 10 July 1666 *StV,* d young. (The above are the only children of Jehiel recorded in St; the Hist. of Stratford erroneously adds births of other children.)

(By 2): *iii* Mary, d Aug 1734; m Daniel Jackson of Stratfield & Newtown.

10 HACKALIAH, bp 9 Apr 1643 *NHC1,* d 20 Nov 1692 *Wy;* m 20 Apr 1676 *StV*—Emm da. Thomas & ——— (Seabrook) Fairchild, b 23 Oct 1653 *StV,* d 25 Feb 1733 *Wy;* had issue.

11 ELIASAPH, bp 9 Apr 1643 *NHC1,* d 1707; Dea.; m (1) Mary ———; m (2) c. 1675 Elizabeth da. John & Mary Beach, b 20 Mar 1652 *FPro;* m (3) c. 1694 Martha da. William & Alice (Pritchard) Bradley, wid. Samuel Munson, bp Oct 1648 *NHC1;* she m (3) Daniel Sherman.

(By 1): *i* Mary, b 12 Apr 1674 *StV*, 24 Apr *WV*, d 28 Nov 1755 *WV;* m 10 Mar 1708 *WV* [1708/9]—Samuel Munson.

(By 2): *ii* Elizabeth, b 29 Jan 1676 *WV* [1676/7]; m Daniel Kellogg of Norwalk.

iii Hannah, b 12 July 1678 *WV*, d s. p.

iv Eliasaph, b 26 Jan 1679 *WV* [1679/80], d 4 Jan 1763 *WV;* m (1) 31 Jan 1704 *WV* [1704/5]—Rebecca da. Timothy & Johanna (Birdsey) Wilcoxson, wid. Benjamin Royce, b 13 July 1680 *StV*, d 2 Sep 1716 *WV;* m (2) 2 Jan 1717 *WV*—Deborah da. Samuel & Sarah (Wooding) Merwin, bp 15 Mar 1691 *MC1*. FAM. 2.

v Joseph, b 10 Mar 1681/2 *WV*, d after 1762; m 7 July 1708 *WV*—Jane da. Henry & Mary (Hall) Cook. FAM. 3.

vi Esther, b 28 Feb 1683 *WV* [1683/4], d 4 July 1764 *WV;* m 9 Dec 1702 *WV*—James Benham.

vii Lydia, b 5 May 1686 *WV;* m James Dorchester of Springfield, Mass.

viii Jehiel, b 25 Aug 1688 *WV*, d 24 Nov 1689 *WV*.

12 JOSEPH, bp 24 Jan 1646 *NHC1*, d s. p. 1733; Sgt.; m Joanna da. Philip Leek, wid. Henry Stevens, b 22 Jan 1657 *NHV*.

FAM. 2. ELIASAPH & REBECCA (WILCOXSON) PRESTON:

1 EPHRAIM, b 8 Sep 1709 *WV*, d 8 Apr 1778 *WV*, æ. 69 *WT1;* Capt.; m (1) 11 Mar 1730 *WV*—Patience Dayton, who d 14 May 1753 *WV;* m (2) 25 Mar 1754 *WV*—Eunice da. Eliasaph & Abigail (Hull) Merriman, wid. Samuel Doolittle, b 24 Nov 1721 *WV*.

(By 1): *i* Mary, b 8 Jan 1731 *WV*, d 27 Oct 1754 *WV;* m Nicholas Jones.

ii Phebe, b 3 Oct 1732 *WV*, d 2 Aug 1758 *WV;* m 8 June 1757 *WV*—Moses Beach.

iii Ephraim, b 6 Aug 1734 *WV*, d 22 Apr 1786 *CC;* m 5 Apr 1762 *WV*—Esther da. Eliasaph & Abigail (Hull) Merriman, b 2 Dec 1734 *WV*, "Wid." d 25 May 1787 *CC*. FAM. 4.

iv Reuben, b 27 May 1736 *WV*, d 5 Aug 1765 *WV;* m 25 May 1756 *WV*—Elizabeth da. Eliasaph & Abigail (Hull) Merriman, b 27 July 1732 *WV*. FAM. 5.

v Patience, b 30 Mar 1738 *WV*, d 18 Apr 1738 *WV*.

vi Lent, b 5 Mar 1739 *WV*, d young.

vii Eliasaph, b 25 Nov 1740 *WV*, d s. p. 12 Apr 1777 *WV*, æ. 37 *WT1;* m 17 Feb 1764 *WV*—Phebe Hart; she m (2) 24 Feb 1780 *WV*—Stephen Yale.

viii Titus, b 29 Jan 1743/4 *WV*, d 7 June 1770 *WV;* m 5 May 1767 *WV*—Thankful da. Stephen & Thankful (Cook) Hotchkiss, b 14 Mar 1744/5 *WV*, d 20 Sep 1776 *WV;* she m (2) 21 Mar 1771 *WV*—Stephen Cook.

ix Benjamin, b 27 Dec 1745 *WV*, d 17 Apr 1813 æ. 68 *WV;* m.

x Elizabeth, b 7 Dec 1750 *WV*.

(By 2): *xi* Eunice; m 11 June 1788 *CV*—Jehiel Merriman.

2 Elizabeth, b 8 Aug 1711 *WV*, d Dec 1715 *WV*.

3 Joanna, b 18 Mar 1714 *WV*, d 18 Jan 1781 æ. 67 *WT1;* m 24 Dec 1734 *WV*—Daniel Johnson.

FAM. 2. Eliasaph & Deborah (Merwin) Preston:

4 Jehiel, b 11 Sep 1719 *WV*, d 22 Nov 1758 *WV;* Sgt.; m 21 Oct 1741 *WV*—Thankful da. Samuel & Ruth (Peck) Sedgwick, b 21 Apr 1721 *HartfordV*, d 5 Oct 1806 æ. 85 *CT1;* she m (2) 16 Dec 1761 *WV*—Ephraim Tuttle; (3) 17 Feb 1774 *WV*—Jason Hotchkiss; (4) 4 June 1778 *CC*—John Hall.

i Sarah, b 23 Aug 1742 *WV*, d 11 Mar 1817 æ. 75 *CT1;* m 17 Jan 1765 *WV*—Augustus Bristol.

ii Esther, b 1 Apr 1744 *WV*, d 23 July 1822 æ. 80 *WT1;* m 27 Apr 1762 *WV*—Ebenezer Moss.

iii Samuel, b 24 Apr 1746 *WV*, d 15 Aug 1815 *F;* res. P; m 7 Sep 1769 *WV*—Lucy da. Amos & Abigail (Holt) Johnson, b 11 Sep 1747 *WV*, d 23 Jan 1808 æ. 61 *WV*. FAM. 6.

iv Caleb, b 24 Apr 1746 *WV*, d 27 Feb 1813 æ. 67 (Camden, N. Y.); m 15 June 1765 *WV*—Amy da. Caleb & Eunice (Welton) Lewis, b 31 Jan 1745/6 *WV*, d 1 June 1817 æ. 73 (Camden, N. Y.). FAM. 7.

v Hannah, b 5 July 1748 *WV;* m Jesse Hull.

vi Rebecca, b 11 Sep 1750 *WV*, d 10 July 1793 *CC*, æ. 43 *CT1;* m 7 Dec 1772 *WV*—William Hall.

vii Thankful, b 10 Dec 1752 *WV*, d 24 May 1817 æ. 65 *WT1;* m (1) 21 Sep 1772 *WV*—Andrew Hall; m (2) 18 Jan 1781 *WV*—John McCleave.

viii Jehiel, b 4 Mar 1755 *WV*, d 11 Aug 1820 æ. 65 *WT2;* m 9 Sep 1779 *WV*—Molly da. Reuben & Kezia (Moss) Royce, b c. 1759, d 15 June 1833 æ. 74 *WT2*. FAM. 8.

ix Ruth, b 28 Jan 1757 *WV*, d 1762.

5 REBECCA, b 25 Sep 1721 *WV*, d 14 May 1739 *WV*.
6 ELIZABETH, b 28 Dec 1727 *WV*, d 23 Mar 1794 æ. 67 *CT1;* m 19 Feb 1745/6 *WV*—Abner Bunnell.

FAM. 3. JOSEPH & JANE (COOK) PRESTON:

1 ELIASAPH, b 9 May 1709 *WV*, d soon.
2 ELIASAPH, b 1 May 1710 *WV*, d Apr 1750 *CC;* m 22 Nov 1726 *WV*—Hannah Mott, bp (adult) Aug 1734 *CC*.
i Isaac, b 1 Oct 1727 WV, bp Aug 1734 *CC;* res. New Lebanon, Mass., 1772; m Sarah ———. Children bp 25 Sep 1772 *Gt.Barrington x:* Amasa, Hannah, John Williams, Moses & Sarah.
ii Moses, d 8 Apr 1733 *WV*, "child" Apr 1733 *CC*.
iii Mary, b 8 Jan 1731 [*WV* ?].
iv Moses, b 30 Oct 1734 *WV*, bp 1 Dec 1734 *CC;* Census (Wells, Vt.) 1-1-2.
v Lois, b 3 Feb 1737/8 *WV*, bp 29 Jan (?) 1737/8 *CC;* m 19 Nov 1756 *Goshen*—Caleb Beach.
vi Eliasaph, bp Oct 1741 *CC*.
3 JOSEPH, b 7 Apr 1711 *WV*, d 1763; rem. to Winchester; m 30 Jan 1734 *WV*—Sarah da. Jeremiah & Mary (Cook) How, b 16 Apr 1709 *WV*. Family incomplete.
i Dinah, b 19 Nov 1734 *WV;* m 13 Jan 1759 *TorringtonC*—William Filley.
ii Samuel, b 30 Sep 1737 *WV*.
iii Joseph, b c. 1744, d 6 June 1824 æ. c. 80 *Conn Mirror;* res. Winchester; m Kezia ———.
iv Benjamin; m (1) 3 May 1775 Sarah Videto; m (2) 20 Aug 1782 Mary Curtis. Children at Winchester, by 1st w.: Thankful, b 31 Dec 1775; Eliasaph, b 17 Aug 1777, d 17 Aug 1777; Patience, b 16 Mar 1779, d 16 Mar 1779; by 2d w.: Benjamin, b 29 Dec 1783; Ephraim, b 22 Feb 1787, d 12 Mar 1794; Seth, b 25 Apr 1789.
(Samuel s. of Joseph bp 4 Sep 1749 *SC*. John s. of Joseph & Mary (?) b 13 Jan 1750 *WyV*.)
4 JONATHAN, b 8 Jan 1713 *WV*, d 18 Aug 1777 *PC;* m (1) 28 July 1740 *WV*, 29 July *WC2*—Sarah Williams, who d 17 Mar 1761 *WatV;* m (2) 18 July 1761 *WatV*—Katharine da. Ebenezer Elwell, wid. Abraham Luddington, who d 24 June 1784 *PC*.
(By 1): *i* Tabitha, b 31 Oct 1741 *WatV*, d 30 Jan 1742.
ii Thankful, b 7 June 1743 *WatV*.
iii John, b 26 Oct 1745 *WatV*.
iv Hannah, b 25 Aug 1747 *WatV*.

v Hackaliah, b 29 Nov 1749 *WatV*, "missing" 1776; res. Torrington; m Sarah Cook, b 12 May 1753 *Windsor;* she m (2) Samuel Oviatt of Ohio. Children: 1 Esther, b 6 Aug 1772 ; 2 Aaron, b 16 Nov 1775 *Goshen;* res. Westford, Otsego Co., N. Y.; m Lydia Johnson, b 28 Oct 1781, d 8 Jan 1833; 3 Jeremiah, b c. 1777.

vi Amasa, b 22 Apr 1752 *WatV;* prob. m [Aug] 1782 *PC*—Mary Curtis.

vii Sarah, b 2 May 1755 *WatV*.

viii Jonathan, b 2 Oct 1758 *WatV;* m 28 Sep 1779 *ConnSupCt*—Mary ——— of Danbury; div. 1785. Child: Abram.

ix Martha, b 22 Aug 1760 *WatV*.

(By 2): *x* Moses, b 19 May 1762 *WatV;* m 1 Jan 1783 *PC*—Thankful Curtis.

xi Abraham, b 2 Sep 1765 *WatV*.

5 Samuel, b 27 Aug 1715 *WV* [d 1747; res. St; m 19 Apr 1741 *Stx*—Susan Wilcoxson; had Mary, bp Feb 1744 *Stx*].

6 John, b 22 June 1718 *WV*.

7 (perhaps) Jesse of St, m Hannah ———; had Sarah, b 14 Dec 1746 *StV*.

8 Ebenezer, b 17 Sep 1723 *WV;* res. Bd & Winchester; m (1) Martha ———, wid. Abel Hoadley & John Howd; m (2) 20 Feb 1771 *Winchester*—Martha Catlin.

(By 1): *i* Samuel, b 27 Mar 1746 *BdV;* m 4 Jan 1770 *Winchester*—Elizabeth Gleason.

ii Lydia, b 22 Mar 1748 *BdV*, d 13 Feb 1814; m Aaron Cooke.

(By 2): *iii* Phebe, b 20 July 1773 *Winchester*.

iv Rebecca, b 27 Aug 1774 *Winchester*, bp 18 Sep 1774 *TorringtonC*.

FAM. 4. Ephraim & Esther (Merriman) Preston:

1 Jesse, b 25 Dec 1762 *WV*, d s. p. 28 Mar 1790.

2 Joel, b Dec [1763] *WV*, d 11 Dec 1763 *WV*.

3 Ebenezer, b Dec [1763] *WV*, d 11 Dec 1763 *WV*.

4 Titus, b 27 Nov 1764 *WV*, d 1 May 1842 æ. 78 *WT1;* m 31 Dec 1787 *CC*—Abigail da. Eliasaph & Jerusha (Mattoon) Merriman, b 6 July 1764 *WV*, d 2 Oct 1835 æ. 74 *WT1*.

i Almon, b 12 Jan 1789 *WT1*, d 2 Apr 1852 æ. 63 *WT1;* m Nancy ———, b 9 Dec 1790 *WT1*, d 19 July 1878 æ. 87 *WT1*. FAM. 9.

ii Laura, b c. 1791, d 8 Oct 1866 ; m Elias Dudley.

iii Sally, b c. 1794, d 23 Sep 1800 æ. 6 *WT1*.

iv Esther; m 8 Apr 1829 Joel Hunt.
v Sally, b 18 May 1802 *CT2,* d 23 Mar 1857 *CT1;* m 15 June 1829 *CV*—Amasa Preston.

5 Reuben, b 29 Oct 176[6] *WV,* d 22 Oct 1845 æ. 79 *CT1;* Census (C) 3-1-2; m 11 Mar 1792 *CV, CC*—Laura da. Amasa & Sarah (Bradley) Hitchcock, b 22 June 1766 *WV,* d 15 July 1829 æ. 63 *CT1.*
i Laurin, b 12 Feb 1793 *CV,* bp 21 Sep 1794 *CC,* d s. p. 20 Aug 1869 æ. 76 *CT1;* m 15 Nov 1812 *CV*—Anna Sanford, who d 5 Mar 1863 æ. 70 *CT1.*
ii Amasa, b 2 Nov 1795 *CV,* bp 10 Jan 1796 *CC,* d 26 Aug 1866 æ. 70 *CT1;* m (1) 20 Nov 1815 *CV*—Phila Sanford, b 31 Dec 1795 , d 12 Mar 1829 æ. 33 *CT1;* m (2) 15 June 1829 *CV*—Sally da. Titus & Abigail (Merriman) Preston, b 18 May 1802 *CT2,* d 23 Mar 1857 *CT2;* m (3) Lois A. Dickerman, b 12 June 1816 *CT2,* d 3 Apr 1876 æ. 59 *CT2.* fam. 10.
iii Eliza, bp 12 Apr 1801 *CC;* m 14 Oct 1818 *CV*—Jesse A. Humiston.

6 Ephraim, b 15 Feb [1769] *WV,* d Dec 1845 ; m 10 Apr 1794 *CC*—Mary Ann da. Dan & Esther (Miles) Hitchcock, b 9 Feb 1774 *WV.*
i Rufus, bp 18 Sep 1803 *CC.*
ii Lyman, bp 18 Sep 1803 *CC.*
iii Ephraim, bp 18 Sep 1803 *CC.*

7 Benajah, b 7 July 1771 *WV.*

8 Eliasaph Merriman, b 9 Apr 1776 *WV,* bp 14 Apr 1776 *CC;* rem. to Freehold, N. Y.; m 23 Sep 1801 *CC*—Hannah Tuttle.

fam. 5. Reuben & Elizabeth (Merriman) Preston:

1 Mary, b 13 Jan. 1757 *WV,* d 19 Oct 1776 æ. 20 *WV.*

2 Charles, b 17 May 1758 *WV,* d 17 May 1758 *WV.*

3 Charles, b 19 June 1761 *WV,* d 8 Oct 1803 *BarkhamstedV;* m 30 July 1783 *WV*—Lucy da. Abel & Temperance (Hough) Austin, b 23 Nov 1755 *WV.*
i Nathaniel, b 14 Mar 1784 *WV.*
ii Polly, b 11 Nov 1785 *BarkhamstedV.*
iii James, b 10 Sep 1787 *BarkV;* m 5 Oct 1806 *BarkV*—Lydia Bushnell.
iv Lyman, b 2 Feb 1790 *BarkV.*
v Merriman, b 4 Oct 1792 *BarkV.*
vi Reuben, b 2 Nov 1795 *BarkV.*
vii Deney, b 27 Nov 1797 *BarkV.*
viii Austin, b 24 Nov 1800 *BarkV,* d 18 Sep 1803 *BarkV.*
ix Lucy Austin, b 30 Oct 1803 *BarkV.*

4 Nathaniel, b 16 Jan 1764 *WV,* d 16 Nov 1776 *WV.*

FAM. 6. SAMUEL & LUCY (JOHNSON) PRESTON:

1 SAMUEL, b 20 July 1770 *WV*, d 21 Mar 1832 ; m 9 Oct 1794 *CC*—Boadice da. Amos & Thankful (Tuttle) Bristol, b 11 Aug 1775 *WV*.

i Child, d 22 Oct 1797 *CC*.

ii Child, d 31 July 1801 *CC*.

iii Child, d 28 Apr 1802 *CC*.

iv Samuel Sidney; res. Calif.

v Orrin; m Julana Kimberly.

vi Lynde Bristol, b 1815, d s. p. 6 Jan 1886; m Betsey Ann Tyler.

vii Amanda Juliette; m Orin Atkins.

2 JEHIEL, b 22 Mar 1772 *WV;* m Lydia Morgan.

3 BETSEY, b 31 Dec 1773 *F*, d 16 July 1817 æ. 44 *CT1;* m Aaron Cook.

4 LUCY, b 7 July 1776 *F*, d Jan 1810 æ. 36 *F;* m 14 Jan 1798 *CC*—Rufus Merriam.

5 LUMAN, b 5 May 1778 *F*, d 31 Oct 1845 ; m 25 Dec 1800 *PV*—Betsey Blackney.

i Florilla, b 25 Aug 1802 *PV*, d 24 Feb 1835.

ii Linus, b 23 May 1804 *PV*, d 12 Oct 1834; m Hannah Morris.

iii Betsey, b 26 Dec 1805 *PV*.

iv Lorenda, b 30 June 1807 *PV*.

v Luman, b 8 Mar 1809 *PV*.

vi Junius, b 18 Sep 1811 *PV*.

vii Lucy, b 31 Dec 1813 *PV;* m Wm. Gaylord Curtis.

viii Sophronia, b 1 Nov 1822 *F*.

6 SEDGWICK, b 23 Oct 1780 *F*, d 30 Sep 1807 æ. 26 *F*.

7 IRA, b 9 Mar 1785 *F;* m Deborah Goff.

8 MILLY, b 1787 *F*, d 4 July 1821 æ. 34 *F;* m ——— Doolittle

FAM. 7. CALEB & AMY (LEWIS) PRESTON:

1 AMY, b 5 June 1767 *WV;* m 7 June 1792 Salathiel Chapman of Vernon, Conn., Springfield, Mass., & Simsbury. She had a nat. child by James Curtis: Salmon, b 24 July 1787 *F*.

2 LURINDA, b 15 Jan 176[9] *WV*.

3 EUNICE WELTON, b 18 June 1771 *WV*.

4 CALEB, b 10 Sep 1772 *WV*, d 28 May 1867 æ. 96 *Camden,N.Y.;* m ———, who d 18 Apr 1851 æ. 76 *Camden*.

i Amanda, b 29 Sep 1796 (?), d Sep 1865; m Abram Eliphalet Johnson.

ii Merrit, b 21 Jan 1797; Rev.

iii Eliasaph, b 29 Mar 1798; res. Pompey, N. Y.

iv Phebe, b 4 July 1799.

v Ruth, b 13 Apr 1802; m Samuel Leffingwell of Wis.
vi Lucius, b 14 Oct 1805; res. Wis.
vii Sarah, b 11 Apr 1810; m James Whaley of Mich.
viii Clarissa, b 30 Dec 1813, d 28 Dec 1856; m David Coe.

5 ELIASAPH, b 29 July 1775 *WatV,* d 13 Feb 1859 æ. 83 *Ppt;* m 23 Sep 1801 Hannah Tuttle.

6 ABNER, b c. 1781, d 24 Nov 1833 æ. 52 *Camden,N.Y.;* m Hannah ———.

FAM. 8. JEHIEL & MOLLY (ROYCE) PRESTON:

1 BETSEY, b 2 Feb 1781 *WV,* d 2 May 1831 æ. 50 *WT2;* m 8 Feb 1797 Samuel Way.

2 CHARLOTTE, b 7 Apr 1785 *WV,* d 18 May 1838 æ. 53 *WT2;* m Matthew Foster.

3 POLLY, b 28 Apr 1787 *WV.*

4 CHAUNCEY, b c. 1790, d 11 Nov 1841 æ. 51 *HT3;* m (1) Roxy da. Daniel & Dinah (Chatterton) Doolittle, b c. 1792, d 27 Aug 1837 æ. 45 *GilbertDlist,* m (2) Deborah da. Daniel & Deborah (Morgan) Chatterton, b 9 Oct 1793 *HV.*

(By 1): *i* Mary A., b c. 1817, d 24 Aug 1834 æ. 17 *HT3.*
ii Horace C., b c. 1820, d 15 Nov 1844 æ. 24 *HT3.*

5 PERMELIA, b 3 Feb 1792 *WV,* d [———] *WT2.*

6 IRA, b 28 Sep 1796 *WV.*

7 LUCINDA, b 25 Dec 1798 *WV,* d 26 Feb 1847 æ. 58 *HT3.*

8 NANCY, b c. 1800, d 10 Sep 1844 æ. 44 *HT3.*

FAM. 9. ALMON & NANCY (———) PRESTON:

1 ABIGAIL, b 24 Aug 1812 ; m 4 Apr 1833 William Williams.

2 LYDIA ANN, b 18 July 1814.

3 CORNELIA, b 11 May 1816 ; m 15 Dec 1843 Lambert Dickerman.

4 ANDREW, b 23 Oct 1820.

5 JAMES, b 31 Aug 1824.

6 ALMON JEROME, b 18 Jan 1830.

FAM. 10. AMASA & PHILA (SANFORD) PRESTON:

1 SUSAN EMERIT, b 6 Aug 1816 *CV,* d 17 Aug 1816 *CV.*

2 SUSAN E., b 25 Mar 1818 *CV,* d 8 Feb 1851 *CV;* m 17 Sep 1837 *CV*—Samuel A. Atwater.

3 CHARLES SIDNEY, b 9 Sep 1825 *CV,* d 4 Jan 1826 *CV.*

4 JULIUS AMASA, b 5 Nov 1828 *CV,* d 20 Oct 1887 ; m 29 May 1850 *CV*—Elizabeth Barnes.

FAM. 10. AMASA & SALLY (PRESTON) PRESTON:

5 FRANCES L., b 13 Mar 1832 *CV.*

PRESTON. MISCELLANEOUS. Mary & Sarah, children of MARY, bp 24 July 1664 *NHC1*.......ROBERT (no relative of Wm.) d 1648.

*PRINDLE. FAM. 1. WILLIAM, d 1690; m 7 Dec 1655 *NHV*—Mary Desborough, who d c. 1700.

1 PHEBE, b 16 Mar 1656/7 *NHV;* m 5 Nov 1677 *NHV*—Eleazer Beecher.

2 JOHN, b 5 Oct 1658 *NHV,* d 25 Nov 1734 *DV;* m (1) 23 Dec 1685 *DV*—Mary da. John & Mary [Beach] Hull, b 31 Oct 1666 *StV,* d 5 Sep 1696 *DV;* m (2) 1 Mar 1696/7 *DV*—Abigail da. Joseph & Abigail (Holbrook) Hawkins, b 2 Feb 1672 *DV,* d 1 July 1698 *DV;* m (3) 21 Dec 1699 *DV*—Hannah Botsford, b Apr 1673 ; she m (2) Nov [1735] *DV*—Joseph Hull.

(By 1): *i* John, b 1 Oct 1686 *DV,* d 4 Oct 1712 *DV;* m 31 May 1709 *DV*—Deborah Booth. Children recorded *DV:* Edmund, b 28 Feb 1709 [1709/10]; Nathaniel, b 23 Aug 1711.

ii Samuel, b 18 July 1691 *DV,* d 25 May 1718 *StV;* m 1 Dec 1715 *StV*—Abigail Lewis; had Samuel, b 28 June 1718 *StV.*

iii Ebenezer, b 15 July 1693 *DV,* d 10 Jan 1772 *WV;* m Abigail da. David & Abigail (Peck) Austin, b 5 Apr 1699 *NHV.* FAM. 2.

iv Mary, b 5/6 Sep 1696 *DV,* d 26 Dec 1696 *DV.*

(By 2): *v* Hannah, b 4 Dec 1700 *DV,* d c. 1784; m (1) Nathan Smith; m (2) 27 July 1726 *NHV*—Samuel Botsford.

vi Elnathan, b 13 July 1702 *DV,* d 11 May 1721 *DV.*

vii Abigail, b 17 Oct 1704 *DV;* m 20 Nov 1728 *DV*—Ebenezer Chatfield.

viii Mary, b 20 Sep 1708 *DV;* m 31 Dec 1730 *DV*—Edward Washburn.

3 MARY, b 8 Mar 1659/60 *NHV;* m 23 Jan 1683 *NHV*—John Roach of M.

4 EBENEZER, b 10 Sep 1661 *NHV,* d 1740; rem. to Newtown; m Elizabeth Hobby.

5 JOSEPH, b 11 June 1663 *NHV,* d 18 Mar 1737/8 *NHV,* 1738 æ. 65 [75] *WHT1;* m 19 Aug 1686 *NHV*—Mary da. John & Mary (Walker) Brown, b 2 May 1664 *NHV,* bp (adult) 27 June 1686 *NHC1.*

i Daughter, d July 1688 *NHV.*

ii John, b c. 1691; m 28 May 1717 *NHV*—Hannah Clark. Child: William, b 27 June 1718 *NHV.*

iii Samuel, b 11 Nov 1693 *NHV,* bp 26 Nov 1693 *NHC1,* d 1767; res. Danbury; m (1) 24 Apr

1718 *NHV*—Mary da. Ebenezer & Mary Smith, b 1 Aug 1699 *NHV;* m (2) Hannah ———. Children by 1st w.: Esther, b 1 Feb 1718/9 *NHV;* Moses, b 4 Aug 1724 ; Joseph, b 17 July 1730.

iv Joel, b 28 Jan 1695/6 *NHV*, bp 15 Mar 1695/6 *NHC1*, d 23 Feb 1725/6 *NHV*, 21 Feb 1726 æ. 34 *WHT1;* m 15 Oct 1718 *NHV*—Jemima da. Nathan & Sarah (Beecher) Benham, b 21 Sep 1700 *NHV*, d 8 Aug 1752 *CC;* she m (2) 9 Jan 1729 *WV*—John Morgan. FAM. 3.

v Hephzibah, b 15 May 1698 *NHV*, bp May 1698 *NHC1;* m 24 June 1724 *WV*—Abiel Roberts.

vi Mary, b 1 Feb 1701/2 *NHV*, d c. 1733; m 21 Dec 1726 *NHV*—John Bristol.

vii Joseph, b 7 Mar 1704 *NHV*, d 10 Nov 1771 ; m 27 July 1727 *NHV*—Elizabeth da. Daniel & Eunice (Brown) Thomas, b c. 1705, d 25 Mar 1783 *WHD*. FAM. 4.

6 JONATHAN, b 7 June 1665 *NHV*, d [1665] *NHV*.

7 SARAH, b 19 Oct 1666 *NHV*, d s. p.

8 SAMUEL, b 15 Apr 1668 *NHV*, d 20 Sep 1750 ; rem. to NM; m.

9 ELEAZER, b 7 June 1669 *NHV*, d c. 1713; res. M; m Elizabeth da. Thomas & Elizabeth (Porter) Andrews, b 4 Nov 1678 *MV;* she m (2) John Bronson of Wat.

10 HANNAH, b 10 Mar 1670/1 *NHV;* [perhaps m John Miles].

11 JOANNA, b 2 Feb 1672 *NHV* [1672/3], d 23 July 1673 *NHV*.

FAM. 2. EBENEZER & ABIGAIL (AUSTIN) PRINDLE:

1 MARY, b 8 Apr 1722 *WV*, d 12 May 1747 *WV*.

2 ABIGAIL, b 30 July 1724 *WV*, "child" d 1728-34 *WC2*.

3 SARAH, b 22 May 1729 *WV*, "da." d 1734-6 *WC2*.

4 ELIZABETH, b 17 Feb 1732 *WV*, bp 20 Feb 1732 *WC2*, d 21 Oct 1802 æ. 71 *WT2;* m 4 May 1749 *WV*—John Hall.

5 JOHN, b 5 Jan 1739 *WV*, bp 7 Jan 1738/9 *WC2*, d 14 Feb 1739 *WC2*.

FAM. 3. JOEL & JEMIMA (BENHAM) PRINDLE:

1 WILLIAM, b 2 Oct 1719 *NHV*.

2 SARAH, b 9 July 1721 *WV;* m 2 Oct 1744 *WV*—Andrew Ives.

3 LOIS, b 21 Feb 1724 *WV*, d Jan 1756 *CC;* m 1743 *WV*—Henry Bristol.

4 JOEL, b 16 Jan 1725/6 *NHV;* m.

FAM. 4. JOSEPH & ELIZABETH (THOMAS) PRINDLE:

1 BETTY, b 7 Oct 1728 *NHV*, d 1809; m 8 June 1758 Ebenezer Knibloe of Amenia, N. Y.

2 ELIZABETH, b 9 Aug 1730 *NHV*, d 30 Aug 1809 æ. 79 *WHD;* Census (NH) 0-0-1.

3 JOSEPH, b 14 Feb 1731/2 *NHV*, d 20 Apr 1814 æ. 82 *WHT2;* Dea.; Census (NH) 2-1-3; m (1) Lois da. Ebenezer & Anna (Thompson) Clark, b c. 1730, d 12 May 1767 æ. 38 *WHT2;* m (2) Elizabeth da. William & Mehitabel (Blakeslee) Trowbridge, b 16 Nov 1731 *NHV*, d 28 Apr 1806 æ. 74 *WHT2*.

(By 1): *i* Joseph, b 28 Aug 1757 *F*, d 4 Sep 1824 æ. 67 *WHD;* m 9 Apr 1788 *NHx*—Lois da. Isaac & Esther (Hodge) Beecher, b 20 Sep 1760 *F*, d 28 Aug 1819 æ. 59 *WHT2*. Child: Elizabeth, b 5 Sep 1789 *F*, d 9 Dec 1875 *F;* m Bryan Clarke.

ii Asahel, b c. 1759, d 1 May 1785 (at sea) *WHD*, 8 May æ. 26 *WHT2*.

iii Lois, b 1 Feb 1761 *F*, d 28 Dec 1842 *F;* m 7 Apr 1784 *NHx*—David Lambert.

iv Charles, b 27 May 1763 *F*, d 4 Mar 1841; res. Sharon; m 6 Jan 1785 *NHx*—Sybil da. Samuel & Abigail (Farrand) Clark. FAM. 5.

v Stephen, b c. 1765, d 4 Aug 1822 æ. 57 *WHD;* m 25 Jan 1795 (at M) *NHx*—Mary Andrew, who d 5 June 1821 æ. 47 *WHD*. FAM. 6.

(By 2): *vi* Martha, b 10 June 1771 *F*, d 26 Feb 1840 *F;* m 8 Oct 1790 Josiah Merrick of Seymour.

4 CHARLES, b 19 Mar 1733/4 *NHV*, d 24 Dec 1806 æ. 72 *NHT1;* Census (NH) 2-1-5; m (1) 12 Jan 1758 *F*—Martha da. Ebenezer & Anna (Thompson) Clark, b c. 1732, d 28 July 1764 æ. 32 *NHT1;* m (2) 19 Mar 1766 *NHC2*—Ruth [da. John & Mary (Griffin)] Storer, b c. 1740, d 11 Aug 1785 æ. 46 *NHT1*, bu. 12 Aug *NHx;* m (3) 21 May 1787 *F*—Phebe da. Joseph & Lydia (Gilbert) Thompson, wid. William Punchard, b c. 1753, d 6 Apr 1837 æ. 84 *NHT1*.

(By 3): *i* Martha, b 4 Dec 1787 *F*, bp 14 Sep 1788 *NHx*, d 18 Aug 1794 æ. 7 *NHT1*, d 17 Aug *NHx*.

ii Ruth, b 8 Jan 1790 *F*, bp 17 Feb 1790 (æ. 5 wks) *NHx*, d 3 Apr 1834 æ. 43 *NHT1;* m 22 Nov 1808 *NHx*, 22 Nov 1809 *NHV*—Daniel Brown.

5 ASAHEL, b 27 Oct 1736 *NHV*, d 21 Aug 1751 *F*.

6 JOHN, b 20 Sep 1739 *F*, d 7 Jan 1806 (Washington, N. Y.); m 17 Feb 1768 *NHx*—Susanna Smith.

i Sarah, b 26 Dec 1768 *F*, d 27 Sep 1773 *F*.
ii Susanna, b 22 May 1770 *F*, d 29 Sep 1773 *F*.
iii Lodima, b c. 1772, d 25 Sep 1773 *F*.
iv Sarah Susanna, b 29 Aug 1774 *F*, d 23 Mar 1843 *F;* m John Oakley.
v John, b 6 Dec 1776 *F*, bp 16 Feb 1777 (sponsor, Edward Smith) *NHx*, d 23 Mar 1843 *F;* m (1) 2 Nov 1812 Elizabeth Northrop; m (2) 27 Oct 1822 Elizabeth (? Pardy).
vi Susanna Sarah, b 10 Jan 1779 *F*, bp 4 Apr 1779 (sponsor, Joseph Prindle) *NHx*, d 6 Dec 1835; m c. 1800 Allen Mix.
vii Anson, b 15 Sep 1781 *F*, d 22 Sep 1844; m Sybil Ann Prindle.
viii Ezra, bp 16 Jan 1785 (sponsor, Joseph Prindle) *NHx*, d 17 Jan 1816 (Tower Hill, N. Y.); m Polly Coffin.

7 Mary, b 16 May 1742 *NHV*, d 28 July 1767 *F*.

8 Elijah, b 2 Apr 1744 *NHV*, d 23 Oct 1803 (Washington, N. Y.); Census (NH) 2-2-4; m 1766 Elizabeth da. John & Dorothy (Pardee) Benham, who d 21 Dec 1822 (Washington, N. Y.).
i Elizabeth, b 2 Sep 1767 *F*, d 29 Aug 1773 *F*.
ii Mary, b 26 Sep 1769 *F*, d 1842 (Ohio); m David Bristol.
iii Elijah, b 17 Jan 1772 *NHT1*, d 1 Apr 1854 *NHT1;* m 17 July 1795 *F*—Sally da. Titus & Amy (Smith) Ward, b 26 May 1776.
iv Ebenezer, b 17 Aug 1774 *F*, d 23 Nov 1852; m (1) 27 Apr 1802 Obedience Chatfield; m (2) 19 June 1839 Rhoda (———) Dorrance.
v Elizabeth, b 17 Aug 1774 *F;* m Merritt Bristol.
vi Zada, b 5 Apr 1777 *F*, bp 11 May 1777 (sponsor, John Jones) *NHx;* m (1) Ephraim Tobey; m (2) Ebenezer Pope of Lebanon.
vii Elias, b 18 Jan 1781 *F*, d 17 Mar 1852 (Johnstown, N. Y.); m 17 Mar 1804 *F*—Polly Fitch.
viii Huldah, b 4 Mar 1784 *F*, "da." bp 18 Apr 1784 *NHx;* m (1) Charles Hall; m (2) Jonathan Butts.
ix Rebecca, b 15 Oct 1789 *F*, bp 6 Dec 1789 (æ. 8 wks.) *NHx;* m Wheeler Gay.

9 Stephen, b 27 Dec 1746 *NHV*, d 13 Aug 1751 *F*.

FAM. 5. Charles & Sybil (Clark) Prindle:

1 Asahel, b 1 May 1786, d s. p. 22 Aug 1864.

2 Esther Abigail, b 25 Nov 1789, d 15 Oct 1873.

3 Sybil Ann, b 11 Apr 1791, d 16 Mar 1858; m Anson Prindle.

4 Samuel J., b 7 Mar 1793, d 11 Dec 1886; m 3 Dec 1846 Mary A. Brown.
5 Julia, b 18 Apr 1795, d s. p. 4 Jan 1892, m Joseph Lord.
6 Lydia, b c. 1797, d 3 Nov 1879.
7 Charles Leonard, b 25 June 1799, d 18 Sep 1885 (Hornellsville, N. Y.); m Sally Lines.

FAM. 6. Stephen & Mary (Andrew) Prindle:
1 Lyman, b 12 Sep 1799, d 31 Dec 1835 (Sharon); m 22 Mar 1823 Durand Downs.
2 Mary Ann, b 19 Aug 1801, d 18 Feb 1881 (Meriden); m Lancelot Smith.
3 Esther Camp, b c. 1803, d 11 Oct 1843; m 2 Sep 1827 Josiah Boardman.
4 Horatio Nelson, b 4 Oct 1805, d 7 Sep 1879; m 1837 Abigail D. (Downs) Prindle.

FAM. 7. Jonathan, s. of Ebenezer (Fam. 1, 4), bp 4 July 1703, d 9 Feb 1778 *CC;* m 1 Mar 1731 *WV*—Elizabeth da. Joseph & Hannah (Clark) Thompson, b 28 Oct 1710 *WV.*
1 Ebenezer, b 7 Oct 1731 *WV,* bp Mar 1736 *CC,* d 7 Apr 1769 *CC.*
2 Kezia, b 14 Mar 1733 *WV;* bp Apr 1736 *CC;* m 19 Mar 1759 *WV*—Isaiah Moss.
3 Phebe, b 14 Jan 1735 *WV,* bp Apr 1736 *CC,* d c. 1760; m 29 Jan 1755 *WatV*—Moses Frost.
4 Ezra, b 23 Jan 1737 *WV,* bp Mar 1737 *CC,* d 31 May 1804 *CC.*
5 Damaris, b 17 Dec 1738 *WV,* bp Feb 1738/9 *CC,* d 24 Oct 1808 æ. 71 *PptC;* m (1) 15 May 1760 *WatV*—Bela Lewis; m (2) 15 May 1764 *WatV*—Oliver Terrell.
6 Anna, b 30 Dec 1740 *WV,* bp Mar 1740/1 *CC;* m (1) 19 Nov 1761 *WV*—Lot Hudson; m (2) 6 Jan 1783 *CC*—Elihu Atwater.
7 Jotham, b 16 Jan 1742/3 *WV,* bp Mar 1742/3 *CC.*
8 Jonathan, b 13 June 1745 *WV,* bp 22 July 1745 *CC,* "child" Oct 1746 *CC.*
9 Elizabeth, b 15 June 1747 *WV,* bp 21 June 1747 *CC,* "Wid." d 1831 æ. 84 *Wat x;* m 13 July 1767 *WV*—James Benham.
10 Jonathan, b 23 Oct 1749 *WV,* bp 25 Dec 1749 *CC.*
11 Sarah, b 25 May 1752 *WV,* bp 11 July 1752 *CC;* Census (C) 0-0-1.
12 Patience, b 20 Sep 1755 *WV.*

PRITCHARD. Variant, Prichard. Roger, d 26 Jan 1670 *NHV* [1670/1]; m (1) Frances ———; m (2) 18 Dec 1653 *MV*—Elizabeth da. James Prudden, wid. William Slough. He was at Wethersfield 1640, Springfield 1643, M 1653. Family incomplete.

(By 1): 1 ALICE; m 18 Feb 1645 *Springfield*—William Bradley.
2 JOAN; m 1 Sep 1647 *Springfield*—John Lambert.
3 NATHANIEL, d 11 Nov 1710 *NHV;* m 1652 *Springfield* —Hannah Langton.
(By 2): 4 JOSEPH, b 2 Oct 1654 *MV,* d 1676 (King Philip's War).
5 BENJAMIN, b last Jan 1657 *MV* [1657/8]; m 14 Nov 1683 Rebecca Jones.

PROUT. JOHN, s. of Timothy & Margaret, b 4 Feb 1649 *F,* bp 11 Feb 1648/9 *BostonC,* d 20 Sep 1719 *NHV,* æ. 70 *NHT1;* Capt.; m 23 Aug 1681 *NHV*—Mary da. Henry & Sarah Rutherford, wid. Daniel Hall, b 23 Feb 1649 *NHV,* d 1724.

1 MARGARET, b 7 June 1682 *NHV,* bp 7 Apr 1689 *NHC1;* m 3 Nov 1702 *NHV*—Moses Mansfield.
2 SARAH, b 7 Jan 1683 *NHV* [1683/4], bp 7 Apr 1689 *NHC1,* d 18 Apr 1745 æ. 62 *New London T;* m 22 Jan 1711/2 *NHV*—Christopher Christophers.
3 MARY, b 16 Apr 1686 *NHV,* bp 7 Apr 1689 *NHC1;* m 1 Sep 1708 *NHV*—John Dixwell.
4 SUSANNA, b 8 May 1688 *NHV,* bp 7 Apr 1689 *NHC1,* d s. p.
5 JOHN, b 19 Nov 1689 *NHV,* bp Nov 1689 *NHC1,* d 4 Apr 1776 æ. 86 *NHT1, NHC1;* B.A. (Yale 1708); Treasurer, Yale Coll. 1717-65; m 1712 Sybil da. John Howell, b 9 Aug 1691 Southampton, L. I., d 5 Feb 1782 æ. 90 *NHT1, NHC1.*
i John, b 8 July 1713 *NHV,* bp 1716 *NHC1,* d 25 Sep 1736 æ. 23 *NHT1.*
ii Mary, b 17 Mar 1716 *NHV,* bp 1716 *NHC1;* m Robert Sloan.
iii Susanna, b 1 Apr 1718 *NHV,* bp 30 Mar 1718 *NHC1,* d 8 Oct 1755 æ. 38 *NHT1;* m 5 Nov 1747 *NHV*—Timothy Bontecou.
iv Sybil, b 13 Oct 1719 *NHV,* bp Oct 1719 *NHC1,* d s. p.
v Timothy, b 3 July 1722 *NHV,* bp July 1722 *NHC1,* d 12 Sep 1741 æ. 19 *NHT1.*
vi Margaret, bp 26 July 1725 *NHC1,* d 20 Aug 1794 æ. 69 *NHT1, NHC1;* Census (NH) 0-0-1.
vii William, bp 8 Mar 1726/7 *NHC1,* d s. p.
viii Sarah, bp 29 June 1729 *NHC1,* d 1802; m Samuel Bird.
ix Henry, bp 21 Sep 1735 *NHC1,* d s. p.

PROUT. MISCELLANEOUS. SARAH bp 17 June 1724 *NHC1.* ......THANKFUL m 17 Dec 1745 *NHV*—Hezekiah Talmadge. ......JOHN, of Mid & W, d 23 Dec 1751 *WC2;* m [2 ?] c. 1736 Abigail da. Ebenezer & Elizabeth (Parker) Clark, wid. Josiah Royce, b 8 June 1705 *WV.* Children: Joseph, b 12 July 1746

WV; Sherman, b 15 Feb 1747 *WV* [1747/8].....JOHN m 1 Jan 1756 *WV*—Sarah Corbet. Children: Jesse, b 10 May 1756 *WV;* Eunice, b 3 June 1758 *WV;* James, b 12 Aug 1760 *WV;* William, b 11 Feb 1763 *WV;* Rachel, b 21 Mar 1765 *WV;* Huldah, b 10 May 1768 *WV;* John, b 15 Oct 1770 *WV;* Sherman, b 10 May 1774 *WV.*

PUNCHARD. FAM. 1. WILLIAM, s. of William & Abigail (Waters), b 11 Nov 1677 *Salem, Mass.,* d 16 Dec 1748 *NHV;* m (1) 21 Apr 1703 *NHV*—Hannah da. Eleazer & Sarah (Bulkeley) Brown; m (2) 23 May 1717 *NHV*—Mehitabel da. David & Deliverance Perkins, b 29 Oct 1692 *NHV,* d 1751.

(By 1): 1 WILLIAM, b 1 Aug 1704 *NHV,* d soon.

2 ABIGAIL, b 20 July 1708 *NHV,* bp 6 June 1725 *NHC1,* d 26 Oct 1774 æ. 67 *HT3;* m 2 Feb 1726/7 *NHV*—Daniel Bradley.

3 HANNAH, b 2 Oct 1711 *NHV,* bp (adult) 20 June 1736 *NHC1;* m (1) 23 Mar 1737/8 *NHV*—Hezekiah Beecher; m (2) 7 May 1752 *NHV*—Enos Pardee.

(By 2): 4 SARAH, b 19 Feb 1717/8 *NHV,* d s. p. c. 1761; m (1) 27 Feb 1739/40 *NHV*—Joseph Todd; m (2) 8 Sep 1757 *NHC2*—Charles Sabin.

5 WILLIAM, b 29 Oct 1719 *NHV,* bp 1 Nov 1719 *NHC1;* m 12 Feb 1746/7 *NHV*—Mary da. Isaac & Hannah (Miles) Gorham, b 10 Oct 1721 *NHV,* d 1 Apr 1773 *NHx.*

i Mary, b 10 May 1749 *NHV,* bp 18 Feb 1749/50 (at NH) *Dx,* d 25 Sep 1823 æ. 74 *NHT1;* m (1) William Sherman; m (2) 23 Nov 1793 *NHx*—Abraham Bradley.

ii William, bp May 1752 (at NH) *Dx;* m Phebe da. Joseph & Lydia (Gilbert) Thompson, b c. 1753, d 6 Apr 1837 æ. 84 *NHT1;* she m (2) 21 May 1787 Charles Prindle. FAM. 2.

6 MARY, b 23 Mar 1721/2 *NHV,* bp Mar 1722 *NHC1,* d c. 1748/9; m 12 Mar 1746/7 *NHV*—Timothy Gorham.

7 MEHITABEL, b 4 Oct 1726 *NHV,* bp 23 Oct 1726 *NHC1,* d s. p.

FAM. 2. WILLIAM & PHEBE (THOMPSON) PUNCHARD:

1 MARY, bp 30 July 1780 *NHC2;* m before 1805 Ralph Hervey.

2 PHEBE, bp 30 July 1780 *NHC2,* "P——— da. ——— Punchard now Mrs. Prindle" bu. 28 Jan 1791 æ. 10 *NHx.*

3 BETSEY, bp 18 Aug 1782 *NHC2.*

4 WILLIAM, bp 13 Apr 1783 *NHC2,* d ("son of Phebe w. Charles Prindle") 16 June 1793 æ. 10-3 *NHx.*

PUNDERFORD. JOHN, Census (NH) 1-3-3; m Content ———, who d 23 Nov 1793 *NHx*. Children: Thomas, b c. 1782, bp 14 Dec 1789 (æ. 8) *NHx*, d 4 Sep 1795 æ. 10 or 11 *NHx;* Mary, b c. 1788, bp 14 Dec 1789 (æ. 1½) *NHx*, "Polly" d 31 Aug 1832 æ. 43 *NHV*.......JAMES, m (1) Clarissa Morgan, who d 25 Dec 1827 æ. 23 *NHT1;* m (2) Anna da. Isaac & Anna (Mix) Gilbert, b 14 Aug 1783 *F*, d 24 June 1844 æ. 62 *NHT1*. A child, Clarissa M., d 13 May 1828 æ. 0-4 *NHT1*.

PUNDERSON. FAM. 1. JOHN, d 11 Feb 1680 *NHV* [1680/1]; m Margaret ———.

1 HANNAH, bp May 1642 *NHC1*, d 18 Jan 1715/6 *NHV;* m (1) 27 Oct 1670 *NHV*—John Gibbs; m (2) [John] Slauson of Stamford.

2 JOHN, bp Oct 1644 *NHC1*, d 23 Jan 1729/30 *NHV;* Dea.; m 5 Nov 1667 *NHV*—Damaris da. David & Damaris (Sayre) Atwater, b 2 Nov [1649] *NHV*, bp 21 Oct 1649 *NHC1*, d 14 Dec 1711 *NHV*, æ. 62 *NHT1*.

i Abigail, b 15 Sep 1671 *NHV*, d prob. s. p.

ii John, b 10 Dec 1673 *NHV*, d 3 July 1742 *NHV*, æ. 69 *NHT1;* m (1) 3 Aug 1699 *NHV*—Abigail da. John & Susanna (Coe) Alling, b 23 Nov 1673 *NHV*, d 8 Mar 1738/9 *NHV;* m (2) 6 Mar 1739/40 *NHV*—Mary da. Thomas & Mary (Sanford) Tuttle, wid. John Ball, b 6 May 1693 *NHV*, d 23 Sep 1771 æ. 78 *NHC1*, æ. 79 *NHT1*. FAM. 2.

iii Hannah, b 29 July 1676 *NHV*, d s. p. after 1740.

iv Thomas, b 15 Jan 1678 *NHV*, d 29 July 1742 *NHV*, æ. 64 *NHT1;* m 21 Sep 1704 *NHV*—Lydia da. Abraham & Hannah (Thompson) Bradley, b 28 Nov 1685 *NHV*, d 1757. FAM. 3.

v Damaris, b 25 Dec 1680 *NHV;* m 19 Sep 1710 *DurhamV*—William Seward.

vi Mary, b 1 Aug 1683 *NHV*, bp 19 July 1685 *NHC1*, d 17 Sep 1713 *NHV*.

vii David, b 3 Nov 1686 *NHV*, bp 9 Jan 1686/7 *NHC1*, d 18 Sep 1731 æ. 45 *NHT1;* m 27 Dec 1716 *NHV*—Sarah da. Samuel & Sarah (Chidsey) Alling, b 17 Jan 1685 *NHV*, bp 18 July 1686 *NHC1*, d 27 Nov 1761 æ. 75 *NHT1*. FAM. 4.

viii Samuel, b 20 Sep 1691 *NHV*, bp 27 Sep 1691 *NHC1*, d s. p. 26 Oct 1731 æ. 40 *NHT1*.

ix Ebenezer, b 18 Oct 1694 *NHV*, bp Oct 1694 *NHC1*, d 21 Nov 1702 *NHV*.

FAM. 2. JOHN & ABIGAIL (ALLING) PUNDERSON:

1 ABIGAIL, b 3 Dec 1700 *NHV*, bp Dec 1700 *NHC1;* m 6 June 1732 *NHV*—Benjamin Munson.

2 SUSANNA, b 29 July 1703 *NHV,* d 14 Dec 1741 æ. 38 *NHT1;* m Stephen Munson.

3 HANNAH, b 21 Dec 1704 *NHV,* d 1759; m David Austin.

4 JOHN, b 25 July 1709 *NHV,* d 26 Nov 1742 *NHV;* m 27 Apr 1738 *NHV*—Ann da. Theophilus & Esther (Mix) Munson, b 4 Jan 1717/8 *NHV,* d 18 Oct 1739 *NHV,* æ. 22 *NHT1.*

i Abigail, b 21 Apr 1739 *NHV,* bp 22 Apr 1739 *NHC1,* d 13 May 1739 *NHV.*

FAM. 3. THOMAS & LYDIA (BRADLEY) PUNDERSON:

1 EBENEZER, b 12 Sep 1705 *NHV,* d c. 1764; Rev.; res. Groton, & Rye, N. Y.; m 1732 Hannah Minor, b c. 1712, d 1792.

i Hannah, b 1733, d 1775; m Solomon Avery of Groton.

ii Ebenezer, b 1735, d Apr 1809 æ. 73 (at Preston) *ConnH;* res. Groton & Norwich; Census (New London Co.) 1-0-2; m 1756 Prudence Geer.

iii Cyrus, b 1737; res. Brookhaven, L. I.; m Gloriana ———; their s. George Munson, bp 18 Sep 1768 *NHx.*

iv Clarina; m c. 1762 Basil Bartow.

2 LYDIA, b 1 Mar 1708 *NHV;* m 9 Jan 1728/9 *NHV*—Gideon Thompson.

3 ESTHER, b c. 1711, d Apr 1743 *NHV;* m 14 Dec 1732 Wait Chatterton.

4 THOMAS, b 24 Aug 1713 *NHV,* d 22 Feb 1781 æ. 68 *NHT1;* m Mary da. Joseph & Elizabeth (Trowbridge) Miles, b 18 Dec 1719 *NHV,* d 9 Sep 1795 æ. 78 *NHT1.*

i Mary, b 28 Jan 1737/8 *NHV,* bp 11 Feb 1738/9 *NHC1,* d 1 Mar 1821 æ. 84 *NHT1;* m Joshua Hotchkiss.

ii Joseph, b 30 Jan 1739/40 *NHV,* bp 17 Feb 1739/40 *NHC1.*

iii Lydia, b 2 Nov 1741 *NHV,* d s. p.

iv Esther, b 24 Sep 1743 *NHV,* bp 25 Sep 1743 *NHC1,* d 12 July 1824 æ. 81 *NHT1;* m 11 Jan 1769 *WdC*—Ebenezer Johnson.

v Lydia, b 28 Aug 1745 *NHV,* bp 8 Sep 1745 *NHC1,* d 18 Oct 1832 æ. 87 *NHT1,* 20 Oct (at Orange) *(NHC1) NHV.*

vi Elizabeth, b 2 Sep 1747 *NHV,* bp 6 Sep 1747 *NHC1,* d 29 Jan 1837 æ. 90 *HT2 list;* m (1) 2 July 1767 *NHC2*—Samuel Wooding; m (2) 16 Oct 1783 *NHC2*—John Mansor.

vii Hannah, b 18 Aug 1749 *NHV,* bp 20 Aug 1749 *NHC1,* d 10 July 1828 æ. 78 *NHT1;* m David Hull.

viii Thomas, b 11 Apr 1752 *NHT1,* d 5 Jan 1829 æ. 77 *NHT1,* 6 Jan *(NHC2) NHV;* Census (NH) 3-3-3; m 24 Feb 1779 *NHC1*—Hannah da. Elisha & Sarah (Sackett) Booth, b 1 Apr 1755 *NHT1,* d 25 Aug 1836 æ. 81 *NHT1,* 26 Aug *RiptonC.* FAM. 5.

ix Damaris, b 14 May 1754 *NHV,* bp 26 May 1754 *NHC2,* d 25 Nov 1800 æ. 46 *NHT1;* she had a nat. child: Mary, bp 5 June 1774 *NHC2;* m Hezekiah Lounsbury.

x Samuel, b 4 Oct 1756 *NHV, NHT1,* bp 10 Oct 1756 *NHC2,* d 20 Oct 1826 *NHT1;* Capt.; Census (NH) 1-2-5; m 1 May 1781 *NHC1*—Eunice da. Matthew & Ruth (Sackett) Gilbert, b 1 June 1755 *NHT1,* d 4 Nov 1828 *NHT1,* æ. 73 *(NHC2) NHV.* FAM. 6.

5 MARY, b 8 Oct 1716 *NHV,* bp 1716 *NHC1,* d 7 Oct 1729 æ. 13 *NHT1.*

6 DAMARIS, b 12 July 1719 *NHV,* bp July 1719 *NHC1,* d 9 Sep 1742 *NHV;* m 9 June 1739 *NHV*—Joseph Mix.

7 MABEL, b 26 June 1724 *NHV,* bp 25 June 1724 *NHC1,* d soon.

8 MABEL, b 19 Mar 1725/6 *NHV,* bp 27 Mar 1726 *NHC1,* d c. 1765; m (1) 28 Dec 1743 *NHV*—Lazarus Ives; m (2) 11 June 1764 *NHC1*—Samuel Hitchcock.

9 ELIZABETH, b 20 Sep 1727 *NHV,* bp 24 Sep 1727 *NHC1.*

FAM. 4. DAVID & SARAH (ALLING) PUNDERSON:

1 DAVID, b 29 June 1718 *NHV,* bp 29 June 1718 *NHC1,* d 5 May 1777 æ. 59 *NHT1;* m 20 Dec 1739 *NHV*—Thankful da. John & Hannah (Butler) Todd, b 18 July 1717 *NHV,* d 7 Mar 1798 æ. 81 *WtnD,* 6 Mar *ConnJournal.*

i Hannah, b 21 Oct 1740 *NHV,* bp 2 Nov 1740 *NHC1,* d 22 Aug 1826 æ. 86 *LT;* m 27 May 1761 *NHV,* 28 May *NHC2*—Joseph Mansfield.

ii Charles, b 14 July 1742 *NHV,* d s. p.

iii Susanna, b 16 Aug 1744 *NHV;* m 2 Aug 1768 *NHV*—Timothy Potter.

iv Sarah, b 30 May 1746 *NHV,* 10 June *LT,* bp 4 June 1749 *NHC2,* d 16 Jan 1831 *LT;* m 26 Nov 1771 *WatV*—Zechariah Thompson.

v John, b 1 Jan 1747/8 *NHV,* bp 4 June 1749 *NHC2;* Census (Queensburg, N. Y.) 1-1-2; m

(1) ———; m (2) Rhoda Alger, who d 1 June 1830 æ. 63 (Chenango Co., N. Y.).

vi David, b 9 Sep 1749 *NHV;* Census (Easton, N. Y.) 1-2-6; m 23 Feb 1774 *WatV*—Dinah [da. Peter & Abigail (Porter)] Welton, [b 1 June 1759 *WatV*]; she m (2) 20 May 1794 *NMC*—David Mallory. FAM. 7.

vii Daniel, b 15 Dec 1752 *NHV*, bp 17 Dec 1752 *NHC2*, d s. p. 5 July 1829 æ. 78 *NHT1*, (Bapt.) *NHV*; Census (NH) 1-0-0; m 26 June 1803 *NHC1*—Hannah da. Daniel & Mary (Thompson) Talmadge, b 30 Apr 1761 *NHV*, d 30 July 1851 æ. 90 *NHT1*, *NHV*.

viii William Joseph, b 13 Nov 1754 *NHV*, bp 24 Nov 1754 *NHC2;* res. Wtn.

ix Ahimaaz, b 26 Aug 1757 *NHV*, bp 4 Sep 1757 *NHC2*, d s. p.

x Anna, b 17 Feb 1760 *NHV*, bp 17 Feb 1760 *NHC2*, d s. p.

xi Anna, b 5 Oct 1763 *NHV*, bp 9 Oct 1763 *NHC2*, d 1 Apr 1844; m 16 May 1784 *WtnV*—Charles Merriman.

xii Thankful, b 5 Oct 1763 *NHV*, bp 9 Oct 1763 *NHC2;* m 5 Sep 1782 *WtnV*—Thomas Dutton.

2 DANIEL, b 28 Sep 1722 *NHV*, bp 30 Sep 1722 *NHC1*, d s. p. 1761.

3 SARAH, b 3 Oct 1725 *NHV*, bp 24 Oct 1725 *NHC1;* m 6 Feb 1744/5 *NHV*—James Thompson.

4 ELIZABETH, d s. p. after 1772.

FAM. 5. THOMAS & HANNAH (BOOTH) PUNDERSON:

1 RUTH, b 12 Mar 1780 *F*, bp 16 July 1780 *NHC2*, d 1857; m 1 Jan 1806 *NHC2*—William Fitch.

2 THOMAS, b 28 Dec 1783 *F*, bp 21 Mar 1784 *NHC2*, d 1 Aug 1848 æ. 64 *HuntingtonT;* Rev.; m Betsey da. Stephen Day, who d 30 Apr 1876 æ. 84 *HuntingtonT*.

3 ELISHA, b Nov 1788 *F*, bp 28 July 1793 *NHC2*, d 5 Feb 1864 æ. 74 *NHT1;* m Eunice da. Samuel & Eunice (Gilbert) Punderson, b 20 Jan 1796 *F*, d 23 Dec 1839 æ. 43 *NHT1*.

FAM. 6. SAMUEL & EUNICE (GILBERT) PUNDERSON:

1 LEMUEL, b 4 Jan 1782 *F*, bp 24 Aug 1782 *NHC2;* rem. to Ohio; m ——— Hickox.

2 MILES, b 6 Jan 1785 *F*, d 1 Sep 1861 æ. 76-7 *NHT1*, æ. 75-7-26 *NHV;* m 25 Feb 1813 *NHx*—Harriet Prudence da. Joseph Isaac & Anna (Brintnall) Brown, b 18 July 1798 *F*, d 25 Jan 1882 æ. 85-6 *NHV*.

3 Elizabeth, b 4 Oct 1786 *F*, bp 29 June 1794 *NHC2*, d 10 Feb 1810 æ. 24 *F*; m 18 Sep 1804 *NHC1*—William Dougal.
4 Samuel, b 22 Jan 1791 *NHT1*, bp 29 June 1794 *NHC2*, d 13 Mar 1870 *NHT1*; m Caroline Swift.
5 Eunice, b 20 Jan 1796 *F*, d 23 Dec 1839 æ. 43 *NHT1*; m Elisha Punderson.

FAM. 7. David & Dinah (Welton) Punderson:
1 Child, stillborn 31 Dec 1774 *WtnD*.
2 Clarissa, b 30 Jan 1776 *WatV*; m ——— Warner.
3 Dinah Lucy, b 29 June 1778 *WatV*; m Truman Bennett of NM.
4 William, b 13 Sep 1780 *WatV*; res. 1829 Lyons, Wayne Co., N. Y.; m Mercy ———.
5 David, b c. 1783, d 5 June 1864 æ. 81 *WashingtonV*; m 22 Apr 1806 *Washington*—Susan Smith.
6 Betsey, b c. 1786, d 8 June 1829 æ. 43 *Roxbury*; m 22 July 1807 *RoxburyC*—John Montcalm.
7 Abigail.
8 Sally; m Jacob DeVoe; res. 1829 Portage, N. Y.

PURCELL. Thomas m 20 Mar 1752 *NHV*, 30 Mar *NHC2*—Mary Newell.
1 Thomas Richmond, b 13 May 1753 *NHV*.

PURCHASE. [Information contributed by Mrs. Wm. H. Lewin of New Britain.] Thomas, b 29 Jan 1680 *(Lynn, Mass.)*, d 27 Dec 1758 *SpringfieldV*; res. W, Enfield & W. Springfield, Mass.; m Hannah Cook, who d 5 Apr 1753 *SpringfieldV*.
1 Elizabeth; m 26 Dec 1728 *SomersC*—Thomas Roe.
2 Jonathan, bp 21 May 1727 *SomersC*, res. W. Springfield; m 10 Nov 1734 *SomersC*—Margaret Worthington.
3 Thomas, b c. 1713, d 15 Nov 1806 æ. 94; res. Somers; m 7 Apr 1738 *SomersC*—Sarah Parsons.
4 John, b 16 Sep 1716 *WV*, d 15 Oct 1716 *WV*.
5 Mary, b 30 Aug 1717 *WV*, bp 18 Jan 1727 *SomersC*; [m Jonathan Worthington].
6 Hannah, b c. 1719, bp 18 Jan 1727 *SomersC*; m 23 July 1747 *CanaanV*—Samuel Trescott.
7 Lydia, bp 18 Jan 1727 *SomersC*; m Lemuel Roberts.

QUINTARD. Isaac of Stamford & NH; m 10 Oct 1754 *NHC2*, *StamV*—Lucretia da. Joseph & Lydia (Munson) Burroughs, b 6 July 1732 *NHV*.
1 Hannah, b 14 Feb 1756 *StamV*.
2 Lydia, b 23 June 1758 *StamV*.
3 Lucretia Burroughs, b 10 Feb 1760 *StamV*; m Thomas Carpenter.
4 Betsey, b 21 Feb 1763 *StamV*, d s. p. before 1831; m 11 Nov 1784 *NHx*—Anthony Perit.

RALPH. JONATHAN, b c. 1733, d 2 Mar 1823 æ. 90 *NoHC;* Census (NoH) 2-1-4; m 6 Oct 1784 *WV*—Eunice da. Joy & Miriam (Perkins) Bishop, wid. Jacob Thorpe, b 15 Mar 1747/8 *NHV,* d 29 May 1824 æ. 76 *NoHC,* 30 May *NoHD.*

1 TILLEY, b 4 Aug 1785 *NoHV,* bp 20 Nov 1785 *NoHC;* res. 1819 Salem, New London Co. (NoH Deeds 4: 264).

RAMSDALE. HARTHAN, s. of Zephaniah, b c. 1754 (Lynn, Mass.), d 6 Oct 1823 æ. 69 *(NHC1) NHV,* 4 Oct *NHT1;* m (1) 20 June 1782 *NHC2*—Sarah Danielson; m (2) 1 Jan 1784 *NHV, NHC2*—Catherine da. James & Martha (Bell) Burn, b c. 1756 (at M), d 17 Oct 1847 æ. 91 *NHV,* 16 Oct *NHT1.* Family incomplete.

(By 2): 1 WILLIAM, b 22 Aug 1784 *NHV.*

2 [JAMES B., b c. 1786, d 29 Mar 1838 æ. 52 *NHV;* m (1) Phebe ———; m (2) 10 Oct 1824 *NHV*—Betsey Warner, who prob. d 26 Oct 1839 æ. 48 *NHV.* A child by 1st w.: Harriet Eliza, b 26 May 1821 *NHV;* m 29 Apr 1838 *NHV*—Harvey Seward.]

3 CHILD, bp 12 Oct 1788 *NHC2.* [A child d 12 Mar 1796 *WdD.*]

4 WILLIAM, bp 24 Oct 1790 *NHC2,* d 23 Aug 1858 æ. 68 *NHT2;* m Persis ———, who d 24 Feb 1873 æ. 81 *NHT2.*

5 HARRIET E., bp 28 Oct 1792 *WdC.*

6 KNEELAND, bp 19 Apr 1795 *WdC,* d 5 June 1841 æ. 47 *NHV;* m.

7 CATHERINE, b [Jan 1797], bp 7 May 1797 *WdC,* d 6 Apr 1881 æ. 84 *NHT2,* æ. 84-3 *NHV;* m Willis Sperry.

8 DAVID, bp Apr 1799 *WdC,* d 5 Jan 1836 æ. 37 *NHT1, NHV.*

9 MARY LUCAS, bp 17 May 1801 *WdC,* d 4 Aug 1854 æ. 52 *NHT1;* m ——— Thompson.

RANDALL. WILLIAM had: 1 Daughter, bu. 5 Sep 1785 æ. 0-18 *NHx;* 2 William, bu. 9 Oct 1785 æ. 0-18 *NHx.*

RANNEY. MISCELLANEOUS. KATHARINE of Mid m 24 Oct 1728 *NHV*—Stephen Clark....... WILLIAM of Mid m 20 Apr 1720 *NHV*—Anne Johnson....... RUTH m 13 Apr 1738 *WV*—Theophilus Moss....... JOHN of NH m 25 Nov 1773 *NHV*—Hannah Tiley of Saybrook.

RAY. FAM. 1. JOSHUA, b [Feb 1688], d 13 Jan 1770 æ. 81-11 *NoHC;* m (1) 29 Mar 1716 *NHV*—Abigail da. Thomas & Abigail (Frost) Barnes, b 10 June 1693 *NHV;* m (2) Mar 1743/4 *NHV*—Anna da. John & Elizabeth (Daniel) Winston, b 23 May 1697 *NHV,* d 1762 *NHC1.*

(By 1): 1 THOMAS, b 5 Jan 1717/8 *NHV,* d 24 Apr 1805 æ. 87-3 *NoHC;* Lt.; Census (NoH) 1-0-0; m 16 Dec 1742

NHV—Abigail da. Phineas & Abigail (Bassett) Clark, b 27 Feb 1718 *NHV*, d 7 Sep 1784 æ. 66 *NoHC*.

i Allethea, b 28 Nov 1743 *NHV*, d 23 Aug 1828 æ. 85 *NoHT2;* m (1) 3 Jan 1770 *NoHC*—Benjamin Brockett; m (2) ——— Todd.

ii Levi, b 19 Dec 1744 *NHV*, d 10 Aug 1831 æ. 87 *NoHT2;* Census (NoH) 3-1-5; m 30 Oct 1768 *NoHV*, *NoHC*—Mary da. Jude & Mehitabel (Brockett) Cooper, b 11 May 1748 *NHV*, d 25 Mar 1830 æ. 82 *NoHT2*. FAM. 2.

iii Enoch, b 4 Sep 1746 *NHV*, d 31 May 1825 æ. 79 *NoHT1;* Census (NoH) 2-0-3; m 7 Jan 1773 *NoHC*—Abigail da. John & Martha (Pardee) Frost, b 14 Sep 1749 *NHV*, d 21 Sep 1833 æ. 84 *NoHT1*. FAM. 3.

iv Lois, b 29 Aug 1751 *NHV;* m 31 Dec 1777 *NoHC*—John Heaton.

2 CALEB, b 3 Aug 1726 *NHV*.

3 ABIGAIL, b 15 Aug 1729 *NHV*, d 18 Dec 1802 æ. 74 *NoHT1;* m 19 Oct 1752 *NHV*—Thomas Humiston.

4 JOSHUA; m 4 Oct 1757 *NHV*—Martha da. Richardson & Elizabeth (Munson) Minor, b 13 Feb 1736/7 *TrumbullC*, d 27 Sep 1793 æ. 56 *NHx;* Census, Martha (NH) 0-0-2.

i Caleb, b 12 Aug 1758 *NHV;* m 26 May 1784 *NHx*—Betsey da. Thomas & Lois (Tuttle) Davis, who d 11 July 1791 *NHx*. FAM. 4.

ii Martha, b 16 June 1760 *NHV*.

iii Richardson, b 1 Mar 1762 *NHV*.

iv Abigail, b 20 July 1763 *NHV*, d 15 June 1796 *F;* m (1) 12 Feb 1791 *NHx*—Richard Hood; m (2) 14 Jan 1795 *F*, 24 Jan *NHx*—Ezra Lines.

v Rebecca, b 19 Aug 1765 *NHV*, d 13 Nov 1836 æ. 72 *CT3;* m (1) ——— Stone; m (2) Stephen Parker of C.

vi Esther, b 16 Apr 1767 *NHV*, d 3 May 1790 æ. 23 *NHx*.

vii Anna, bp 23 July 1769 (sponsors, John Miles, Rebecca Camp & Martha Ray) *NHx*, d 19 May 1832 æ. 63 *NHT1*.

viii Joshua, bp 14 July 1771 (sponsors, John Miles, Benj. & Abigail English) *NHx*.

ix Lucy, bp 2 May 1773 (sponsors, John Miles, Abigail English & Martha Ray) *NHx*.

FAM. 2. LEVI & MARY (COOPER) RAY:

1 DAVID, b 12 July 1770 *NoHV*, bp 16 Nov 1787 *NoHC;* m (1) 1 May 1800 *NoHC*—Lois da. Jesse & Hannah

(Bradley) Goodyear, b 20 Nov 1770 *NHV,* d s. p. 22 Mar 1811 æ. 44 *NHT1;* m (2) 24 May 1812 *WdC* —Charlotte da. Nathan & Mabel Clark, who d 9 May 1864 æ. 84 (at St) *NHV.*

2 LEVI, b 14 July 1772 *NoHV,* bp 16 Nov 1787 *NoHC;* m Tryphena ——— & had Levi, Fanny & Lovicy bp 4 Apr 1802 *NoHC.*

3 THOMAS, b 19 Dec 1774 *NoHV,* bp 16 Nov 1787 *NoHC,* d 24 Feb 1856 æ. 80 *NoHT2.*

4 JOEL, b 6 Oct 1776 *NoHV,* bp 16 Nov 1787 *NoHC,* d 19 Sep 1848 æ. 72 *NoHT3;* m 19 Mar 1801 *NoHV, NoHC*—Harriet da. Justus Johnson & Susanna (Beach) Fitch, b 8 Sep 1775 *NHV,* d 6 Aug 1852 æ. 77 *NoHT3.*

i Susan Charlotte, b 13 Jan 1804 *NoHV,* d s. p.

ii Harriet Angeline, b 31 May 1808 *NoHV;* m 12 July 1827 *ConnH*—Rev. Samuel H. Riddell of Glastonbury.

iii Joel Luzerne, b 22 Dec 1811 *NoHV.*

5 POLLY, b 19 Jan 1779 *NoHV,* bp 16 Nov 1787 *NoHC,* d 19 Aug 1841 æ. 62-7 *NoHT2;* m 20 Nov 1799 *NoHC,* 19 Nov *NoHV*—Melicu Todd.

6 LOVICY, b 10 May 1782 *NoHV,* bp 16 Nov 1787 *NoHC,* d 27 Mar 1801 æ. 19 *NoHT3;* m 21 Aug 1800 *NoHC* —Benajah Tuttle.

7 BETSEY, b 4 Feb 1785 *NoHV,* bp 16 Nov 1787 *NoHC,* d 23 Jan 1844 æ. 60 *NoHT3;* m 24 June 1802 *NoHV* —Benajah Tuttle.

8 RHODA, b 24 Aug 1788 *NoHV,* bp 16 Nov 1787 *NoHC;* m 25 Dec 1808 *NoHC*—Justus Johnson Fitch.

9 COOPER, b 29 June 1790 *NoHV,* bp 9 Aug 1789 *NoHC.*

FAM. 3. ENOCH & ABIGAIL (FROST) RAY:

1 DAUGHTER, b c. 1774, d 5 Feb 1774 *NoHC.*

2 PATTY, b c. 1775, d 26 Feb 1852 æ. 77 *NoHT2;* m 14 Oct 1802 *NoHV*—Joel Beach.

FAM. 4. CALEB & BETSEY (DAVIS) RAY:

1 CALEB, bp 27 Nov 1784 *NHx,* bu. 28 Nov 1784 *NHx.*

2 JOSHUA, bp 27 Nov 1784 *NHx,* bu. 21 Dec 1784 *NHx.* [He & bro. erroneously called children of Caleb & *Mary.*]

3 BETSEY, bp 19 Mar 1786 (sponsors, Zina Denison & Sarah Forbes) *NHx,* d 10 Apr 1857 æ. 71 *NHT2;* m 25 Nov 1803 *SC*—Jason Potter.

4 SAMUEL, bp 10 Aug 1788 (sponsor, Zina Denison & Solomon Davis) *NHx.*

RAY. MISCELLANEOUS. HANNAH, b c. 1693, d 20 Nov 1786 ; m 23 June 1711 *NHV*—John Humiston....... MARY m 30 Mar 1714 *NHV*—Daniel Potter....... SARAH of EH, d 1759; willed whole estate to Sarah da. Jonathan Goodsell of Bd.......MARY, b 14 Sep 1777 *NHT1,* d 20 Nov 1829 æ. 52 *NHT1;* m Abel Denison.......LYDIA m Daniel Sackett.

READ. Variant, REED. FAM. 1. Daniel, s. of Daniel & Mary (White), b 2 Nov 1757 (Rehoboth, Mass.), d 4 Dec 1836 æ. 79 *NHV;* m Jerusha Sherman, b c. 1763, d 7 Jan 1840 æ. 77 *NHV.*

1 GEORGE FREDERICK HANDEL, b 21 May 1788 *NHV;* m (1) 5 Sep 1810 *NHx*—Eunice Dummer; m (2) Rebecca da. William Sherman, who d 1 Sep 1845 æ. 56 *NHV.*

2 NATHAN SHERMAN, b 31 Jan 1792 *NHV,* d 7 Aug 1821 æ. 29-6 (near Cape Cod) *NHT1;* B.A. (Yale 1811); m Apr 1814 *ColR*—Hannah Merriman.

3 ELIZA, b 12 Dec 1799 *NHV,* d 16 Sep 1800 *NHV, NHT1.*

4 MARY WHITE, b 30 June 1802 *NHV;* m 14 Nov 1821 *NHV*—Jonathan Nicholson.

READ. FAM. 2. Peter, of Rehoboth, Mass., H, & Ludlow, Vt.; Rev.; Census (H) 1-1-2; m (1) in 1776 (Rehoboth) Molly Pitcher; m (2) Lydia da. John & Lydia (Ives) Gilbert, b 4 Mar 1760 *NHV.* Family incomplete.

(By 2): 1 MARY, b 11 Sep 1787 *HV,* bp 14 Oct 1787 *NHC2,* d 6 May 1789 *HV.*

2 RUFUS, b 10 July 1789 *HV.*

3 JESSE, b 2 Oct 1790 *HV,* bp 1 May 1791 *NHC2.*

READ. FAM. 3 MATTHEW, b 3 Nov 1776 (at Ashford) *NHT1,* d 28 Sep 1860 æ. 84 (at Albany, N. Y.) *NHT1;* m 28 Nov 1801 *NHV*—Lydia da. Silas & Esther (Gilbert) Hotchkiss, who d 10 Oct 1813 æ. 32 *NHT1.*

1 ELIZABETH, b 24 Oct 1802 *NHV,* d 21 Aug 1809 *NHV.*

2 MATTHEW HENRY, b 2 Sep 1804 *NHV.*

3 ELIZUR BURDINE, b 12 Sep 1808 *NHV,* d 7 Oct 1881 æ. 73 *NHT1;* m 9 Oct 1836 *NHV*—Rebecca Gorham.

4 TIMOTHY, b 19 May 1817 *NHV.*

READ. MISCELLANEOUS. JOHN m 26 Aug 1730 *NHV*—Desire [da. Joseph & Elizabeth (Sanford)] Tuttle, wid. Daniel Todd, bp 1 Aug 1697 *NHC1*.......SARAH had a son James b 18 Dec 1733 *WV;* she m 25 Mar 1736 *WV*—Abel Ives.......SUSANNA, Census (NH) 0-0-3; James Neil (s. of Susanna) bp 28 Oct 1774 *NHC1;* 2 children of Susanna bp June 1782 (at house of Nancy Doyle) *NHx*.......MARY m 5 Sep 1764 *NHC1*—Edward Downee....... ZECHARIAH, b c. 1753, d 22 Sep 1811 æ. 58 *NHT1;* m Sarah ———, who d 9 Oct 1833 æ. 77 *NHT1;* of their children, Zechariah d 14 Mar 1796 æ. 6 *NHT1;* Charles, bp 17 June 1794 *NHC1,* d 18 June 1794 æ. 0-18 *NHT1.*

*REDFIELD. JAMES, of NH, rem. to Fairfield; m May 1669 *NHV*—Elizabeth da. Jeremy & Elizabeth How, bp 30 Mar 1645 *NHC1.*

1 ELIZABETH, b 31 May 1670 *NHV.*

REXFORD. FAM. 1. ARTHUR, d 1 Feb 1727/8 *NHV;* m 3 Sep 1702 *NHV*—Elizabeth da. Henry & Joanna (Leek) Stevens, b 10 Dec 1678 *NHV*.

1 ARTHUR, b 13 July 1703 *NHV*, d 15 Mar 1781 *Sharon;* m Jemima ———.

i Samuel, b 21 Mar 1728 *WV*, bp 21 July 1734 *WC2;* m & had children bp *WashingtonC:* Sarah 5 June 1757, Theoda 11 Nov 1758, Susanna 17 Oct 1762, & Levi 7 Feb 1767.

ii Arthur, b 4 May 1730 *WV*, bp 21 July 1734 *WC2*, d 25 Feb 1797 æ. 67 *SharonT*.

iii Joseph, b 11 June 1732 *WV*, bp 21 July 1734 *WC2;* m 28 Nov 1753 *WC2*—Lydia Spencer.

iv John, b 1 June 1734 *WV*, bp 21 July 1734 *WC2;* m Ruth ———; she m (2) 2 Mar 17[58] *WV*—Joseph Munson & (3) 3 Oct 1766 *WV*—Job Clark. A child John, b 14 Feb 1756 *WV*.

v Daniel, b 27 Oct 1736 *WV*, bp 2 Jan 1736/7 *WC2*.

vi Benjamin, b 1 June 1739 *WV*, bp 15 July 1739 *WC2;* m 1 July 1760 *WV*, *WC2*—Esther Hall. FAM. 2.

vii Abigail, b 20 Aug 1741 *WV*, bp 23 Aug 1741 *WC2*.

viii Jemima, b 2 Jan 1746/7 *WV*, bp Mar/Apr 1746 *WC2*.

2 SARAH, b 6 Sep 1705 *NHV*, d c. 1770; m 10 Aug 1727 *WV*—Jedediah Cook.

3 PHILIP, b 19 June 1708 *NHV*, bp (adult) 22 Sep 1734 *NHC1*, d May 1798 æ. 90 (at NH) *ConnJournal;* m (1) 15 Apr 1734 *NHV*—Anna da. Joseph & Lydia (Roberts) Beecher; m (2) 4 May 1766 *NHC2*—Mary da. John & Lydia Blakeslee, wid. John Ball, b 5 Apr 1720 *NHV*, d c. 1799.

(By 1): *i* Elisha, b 9 Jan 1735 *NHV* [1735/6], bp 11 Jan 1736 *NHC1*, d soon.

ii Elisha, b 24 Oct 1737 *NHV*, bp 30 Oct 1737 *NHC1*, d 3 Apr 1808 æ. 71 *MonroeT;* Rev.; m (1) 30 Jan 1765 *NHC1*—Lydia da. Samuel & Abigail (Hollingsworth) Munson, b 8 Mar 1742/3 *NHV*, d 31 Mar 1785 æ. 42 *MonroeT;* m (2) Sarah ———. Child: Ann Abigail [called Nancy]; m 19 May 1793 *WatV*—Abijah Fenn.

iii Hezekiah, bp 12 Oct 1740 *NHC1*.

iv Hezekiah, b 9 Oct 1742 *NHV*, prob. identical with above, & error as to birth year, d young.

4 DANIEL, b 27 May 1711 *NHV*, d 12 Jan 1799 *Barkhamsted;* m Desire da. Samuel & Sarah (Bradley) Hotchkiss.

i Sarah; m 10 Jan 1760 *NHV*—Ezekiel Tuttle.

ii Daniel, b c. 1742, bp (adult) 25 Oct 1767 *NHC1*, d 28 July 1793 *BarkhamstedV;* m (1) 9 Sep 1766 *NHV*, 9 Oct *NHC1*—Martha da. Samuel & Mary (Perkins) Hitchcock, b 19 Dec 1744 *NHV*, d 1 Apr 1774 æ. 29 *HT1;* m (2) 23 Feb 1775 *BarkhamstedV*—Sarah da. Nathan & Hannah (Todd) Alling, b 20 Oct 1745 *NHV*, d Feb 1837. FAM. 3.

iii William, b 18 Jan 1746 *F*, d 5 June 1827 (Lebanon, N. Y.); m 30 Dec 1772 *BarkhamstedV*, *NoHC*—Dennis da. Richard & Elizabeth (Bradley) Sperry, b 6 Dec 1746 *NHV*. FAM. 4.

iv Betsey; m Amaziah Alling of Smyrna, N. Y.

v Joel, b c. 1751, d 22 Mar 1821 æ. 70 (Smyrna, N. Y.); m 23 Jan 1774 *BarkhamstedV*—Rhoda Spencer. FAM. 5.

[perhaps] *vi* Anna; m 9 Feb 1768 *NHV*—William Stiles.

5 ELIZABETH, b c. 1718, d July 1799 æ. 80 *WdC;* m 11 Feb 1741/2 *NHV*—Amos Sherman.

6 MARY, b c. 1720, d 2 Aug 1770 æ. 50 *NHC1;* m 8 Nov 1739 *NHV*—Nehemiah Hotchkiss.

FAM. 2. BENJAMIN & ESTHER (HALL) REXFORD:

1 BENJAMIN, b 15 May 1761 *WV;* m 11 Sep 1779 *WV*—Katharine Royce.

2 MARTHA b 10 Feb 1764 *WV;* m 11 Dec 1783 *WV*, *WC2*—Lamberton Clark.

3 ISAAC, b 16 Sep 1765 *WV;* res. 1787 Charlotte, Vt.; m Lucretia da. Divan Berry.

4 THOMAS, b 6 Oct 176[6] *WV*.

5 SAMUEL, b 15 June 1768 *WV*.

6 ELISHA, b 15 Sep 1770 *WV*.

7 ABRAHAM, b 6 June 1772 *WV*.

8 BENAJAH, b 2 Sep 1774 *WV*.

FAM. 3. DANIEL & MARTHA (HITCHCOCK) REXFORD:

1 JARED, b 7 Nov 1767 *NHV*, bp 25 Oct 1767 *NHC1*, d 1844; m 17 Aug 1794 *BarkhamstedV*—Rachel Lewis, who d 19 Apr 1796 *BarkV*.

i Son, b 9 Sep 1795 *BarkV*, d 12 Nov 1795 *BarkV*.

2 JOEL, b 5 Feb 1770 *NHV*, bp 11 Feb 1770 *HC1*, d 1828; rem. to Sherburne, N. Y.; m 2 July 1792 *BarkV*—Susanna Weed.

i Polly, b 20 July 1794 *BarkV*.

ii Rachel, b 27 July 1797 *BarkV*, d 20 Jan 1819 *BarkV*.

iii Harriet, b 20 Aug 1806 *BarkV*, d 18 Dec 1871 *BarkV*.

3 MILLA, b 5 Mar 1772 *NHV*, bp 15 Mar 1772 *HC1*; m ——— Tiffany.

FAM. 3. DANIEL & SARAH (ALLING) REXFORD:

4 BENJAMIN, b 1 Jan 1776 *BarkV*, bp 14 Jan 1776 *HC1*, d 1825; res. Sherburne, N. Y.; m 1806 Mary Clark.

5 ZINA, b 17 Sep 1777 *BarkV*, d 6 Sep 1855 (Fabius, N. Y.) *BarkV*; m 1828 Lucy C. Rose.

6 MICAH, b 1 Feb 1780 *BarkV*, d 3 June 1820 (Lima, N. Y.) *BarkV*; m 1803 Paulina Holden.

7 SARAH, b 16 Jan 1784 *BarkV*, d 11 Apr 1872 *BarkV*; m Salmon Howd.

8 JOHN, b 10 or 27 Apr 1786 *BarkV*, d 12 June 1862 *BarkV*; m (1) 1813 Ursula Hitchcock; m (2) 1837 Henrietta M. Allen.

9 MARTHA, b 22 Apr 1789 *BarkV*, d 11 Jan 1864 *BarkV*; m Luke Hayden.

10 ALLEN, b 9 Sep 1791 *BarkV*, d 5 Dec 1875 (Sherburne, N. Y.) *BarkV*; m 1818 Almira Hart.

FAM. 4. WILLIAM & DENNIS (SPERRY) REXFORD:

1 WILLIAM, b 22 Dec 1773 *BarkV*.

2 JASON, b 7 May 1776 *BarkV*, d 11 Sep 1778 æ. 2-4 *BarkV*.

3 Son, b 23 Dec 1779 *BarkV*, d 25 Dec 1779 æ. 0-0-2 *BarkV*.

4 WILLIAM, b 23 Dec 1779 *BarkV*, d 14 Sep 1778 [? 1784] æ. 4-9 *BarkV*.

5 BETSEY, b 15 Aug 1781 *BarkV*.

6 LEVERETT, b 21 Feb 1787 *BarkV*.

FAM. 5. JOEL & RHODA (SPENCER) REXFORD:

1 SIMEON, b 7 Mar 1776 *BarkV*.

2 MARTHA, b 9 Dec 1779 *BarkV*, d 9 Aug 1780 æ. 0-8 *BarkV*.

3 LYMAN, b 24 Apr 1784 *BarkV*.

REYNOLDS. WILLIAM of Bd m Elizabeth da. John & Mercy (Payne) Frost, b 1673 *NHV*; she div. him & m (2) Wm. Hoadley.

1 MARY, b 24 Mar 1694/5 *NHV*.

REYNOLDS. JAMES, b c. 1731, d May 1818 æ. 87 *WHT1*, *WHD*; Census (NH) 1-0-1; m Mehitabel ———, b c. 1732, d 3 Nov 1810 æ. 78 *WHT1*, 2 Nov *WHD*.

1 JAMES B., b c. 1754, d 1 Jan 1834 æ. 80 *WHT1*, *WHD*; Census (NH) 1-1-2; m Mary da. Israel & Mary (Tolles) Kimberly, wid. Seth Thomas, b c. 1753, d 1 Jan 1834 æ. 80 *WHT1*, *WHD*.

i Mary, b c. 1789, d 9 Mar 1863 æ. 74 *WHT3;* m 1809 Newton Stevens.

ii James; m Mehitabel ———, who d 30 Nov 1835 æ. 41 *WHD.*

2 SAMUEL, b c. 1762, d 10 Mar 1845 æ. 83 (at WH, of Long Meadow, Mass.) *WHT2, WHD;* m Lucy ———, who d 12 Feb 1849 æ. 84 *WHT2,* æ. 85 *WHD.*

3 FREDERICK, b c. 1764, d 16 Oct 1821 æ. 57 *WHD;* Capt.; Census (NH) 1-1-2; m Mehitabel da. Benjamin & Abigail (Smith) Smith, b c. 1765, d 19 Apr 1830 æ. 65 *WHD.*

i Fanny.

ii Jeannette.

iii Hetty; m Oct 1819 *ColR*—William Richards.

iv Laura.

v Caroline.

vi Roswell ["Russell" d 16 Jan 1854 æ. 64 *OC*]; "wife of Roswell" d 1 Dec 1826 æ. 40 *WHD.*

vii Frederick.

viii William, b c. 1805, d 6 Jan 1837 æ. 32 *WHT2.*

4 WILLIAM AUGUSTUS, d s. p. 25 Feb 1794 (at sea) *WHD.*

RHODES. JOHN, bu. 26 Jan 1775 *NHx;* Dr.; m 23 Sep 1756 *NHV*—Rebecca da. Joseph & Sarah (Southmayd) Starr, wid. Thomas Tyler, b 8 June 1733 *MidV,* d 6 Apr 1802; she m (3) 12 Sep 1775 *NHx*—Daniel Bonticou & (4) 23 Dec 1787 Ephraim Pease of Enfield. [Traditionally, he was a Prussian, named Rohde.]

1 JOHN, b 4 Mar 1757 *NHV,* d s. p.

2 FREDERICK, b 14 Jan 1759 *NHV, NHT1,* d 22 Nov 1759 *NHT1.*

3 THOMAS, b 10 Sep 1760 *NHV.*

4 JOSEPH, b c. 1763, d 3 Jan 1776 æ. 12 *NHx.*

5 WILLIAM FREDERICK, b c. 1765; m Hannah ———, bp 16 Apr 1794 æ. 16 or 17 *NHx.*

i Wm. Scranton, bp 16 Aug 1795 *NHx.*

6 ANDREW SOUTHMAYD, bp 3 July 1768 (sponsor, Stephen Mansfield) *NHx.*

7 KATHARINE, b 27 Jan 1770 *NHT1,* bp 17 Apr 1770 *NHx,* d 14 Jan 1773 *NHT1.*

8 SON, d 8 July 1772 (stillborn) *NHT1.*

RHODES. WILLIAM m 1 June 1698 *NHV*—Sarah da. Moses & Mercy (Glover) Mansfield, b 14 June 1677 *NHV.*

RICH. FAM. 1. DAVID, b 1694 F, d 4 June 1748 æ. 54 (at Bristol) *F;* m Elizabeth ———.

1 ABIGAIL, b 18 Sep 1717 *WV;* m Jan 1737 *WC2*—Joseph Atkins of Mid.

2 David, b 12 Jan 1720 *WV,* d 6 Mar 1794 æ. 75 *Claremont,N.H.,T;* m 10 Nov 1743 *WC2*—Mehitabel da. Samuel & Phebe (Royce) Ives, b 27 Mar 1724 *WV,* d 22 July 1757 *FarmV.*

i Josiah, b 6 Sep 1744 *WV, FarmV,* bp 9 Sep 1744 *WC2.*

ii Rebecca, b 21 Jan 1746 *FarmV,* "child" bp 22 Jan 1746 *WC2.*

iii Phebe, b 22 Dec 1747 *FarmV;* m 19 Nov 1767 *WV*—Joseph Royce.

iv Mehitabel, b 12 Nov 1749 *FarmV;* m 29 Nov 1769 Ebenezer Hawley.

v Elizabeth, b 20 Aug 1751 *FarmV,* d 21 Mar 1752 *FarmV.*

vi Samuel, b 26 Feb 1753 *FarmV.*

vii Jerusha, b 4 Mar 1757 *FarmV,* d 26 Aug 1832 æ. 76 *WT2;* m 25 Feb 1776 *WV*—Benjamin Hart.

3 Elizabeth, b 8 Jan 1722 *WV;* m 9 Nov 1738 *WV, WC2*—Joseph Gaylord.

4 Rebecca, b 17 Aug 1723 *WV,* d 7 Feb 1741 *WC2.*

5 William, b 12 Mar 1724 *WV* [1724/5], d 27 Mar 1785 æ. 60 (at Bristol) *F;* m Mary ———, who d 4 Dec 1798 æ. 75 (at Bristol) *F.* Their son William, b July [1752] *F,* d 29 Apr 1822 (Meredith, N. Y.) *F;* m Abigail ———, who d 29 Mar 1826 æ. 67-5 (Meredith) *F,* & had (from Bible record):

i Samuel, b 30 Apr 1779 (Bristol), d 11 Sep 1845 æ. 66 (NH); m 7 May 1806 Angelina Painter, b 8 Aug 1784 (NH), d 24 July 1856 æ. 72 (NH). FAM. 2.

ii Parthena, b 29 Mar 1781, d Mar 1838 (Bristol).

iii Almena, b 11 May 1783, d 20 Mar 1872 (Bristol).

iv Sylvester, b 31 May 1785, d July 1867 (Croton, N. Y.).

v William, b 4 Apr 1788, d 24 Sep 1828 (Bristol).

vi Abigail, b 14 Mar 1790, d 4 Apr 1862 (Bristol).

vii George, b 22 Mar 1792, d Sep 1825 (Warm Springs, Va.).

viii Nancy, b 16 Apr 1794, d 10 May 1794.

ix Nancy, b 27 Dec 1795, d Aug 1850 (Croton, N. Y.).

x Sally, b 11 Sep 1797.

xi Emeline, b 27 Apr 1800, d 18 Sep 1822.

xii Franklin, b 7 Apr 1803.

xiii Julia, b 11 May 1808, d 4 June 1856 (Croton, N. Y.).

6 PHEBE, b 5 Feb 1726 *WV* [1726/7]; m 24 May 1744 *WC2*—Benjamin Hart.
7 SAMUEL, b 27 Dec 1729 *WV*, bp 25 Jan 1729/30 *WC2*.
8 SARAH, b 20 Feb 1733 *WV*.

FAM. 2. SAMUEL & ANGELINA (PAINTER) RICH:
1 CHILD, b 7 Mar 1807 (Sangerfield, Oneida Co., N. Y.), d æ. 0-0-12.
2 GEORGE BERKLEY, b 25 Jan 1808 (Sangerfield), d 5 Sep 1877 æ. 59 (NH); m 27 Aug 1831 Catherine E. Brown, b 6 June 1812 (NH).
3 AMELIA PAINTER, b 16 Jan 1810 (Sangerfield); m June 1832 Smith Merwin, who d 21 Jan 1873 æ. 63 (NH).
4 CYNTHIA, b 23 Feb 1812 (Sangerfield), d 1 Sep 1816 (Westfield, Mass.).
5 HARRIET NEWELL, b 12 Nov 1814 (Sangerfield), d 9 Dec 1876 æ. 62 (Brooklyn, N. Y.); m 25 July 1832 Thomas Davis, who d 25 July 1843 æ. 36 (NH).
6 ABIGAIL, b 7 Sep 1819 (Columbia Society, Cheshire), d 19 Aug 1863 æ. c. 44 (WH); m 22 Aug 1839 Lucius E. Clark.
7 EMELINE, b 7 Mar 1823 (Columbia); m 25 Nov 1841 Cornelius Smith, who d 6 Dec 1859 æ. 42 (WH).

RICHARDS. JOHN, s. of John, b c. 1737, d 31 May 1800 æ. 64 *WHD*, fell from boat in harbor *ConnJournal; Census* (NH) 2-3-5; m Lydia da. Charles & Lydia (Augur) Thomas, b 27 May 1744 *NHV*, d 22 Jan 1822 æ. 77 *WHD*.
1 LYDIA, b c. 1764; m (1) 9 June 1785 *NHx*—Ebenezer Thompson; m (2) 14 Mar 1790 *NHx*—Eli Smith.
2 EUNICE, b c. 1766, d 17 Oct 1838 æ. 70 (or 73) *WHD;* m 14 Feb 1788 *NHx*—John Ward.
3 JOHN, b c. 1768, d 27 Mar 1800 (at sea) *WHD;* m Amarilla da. Samuel & Dinah (Sherman) Smith, b c. 1770, d 28 Apr 1848 æ. 78 *WHT2;* she m (2) Timothy Talmadge; m (3) Levi Curtis.
i Gerard.
ii William, b c. 1794, d 14 Apr 1861 æ. 67 *WHT3;* m Mehitabel ———, who d 12 Nov 1875 æ. 81 *WHT3*.
iii Amarilla; m Falane Meloy.
4 LOIS; m 2 Oct 1791 *NHx*—Clark Sage.
5 BENJAMIN, b c. 1771, d 13 July 1796 æ. 30 (drowned) *WHD*.
6 MARTHA, b 5 Oct 1773 *F*, d 1850 æ. 77 *WHD*, 12 Nov *WHT3;* m Ichabod Smith.
7 ZEBIAH, b 7 Mar 1776 *F*, bp 5 May 1776 *NHx;* m (1) James Miller; m (2) James Leete.
8 STEPHEN, b 3 Aug 1778 *F*, "son" bp 18 Oct 1778

NHx, d 9 Oct 1856 æ. 56 *WHV;* m Mabel Thomas, who d 18 Apr 1862 æ. 81-4 *NHV*.

9 Bathsheba, bp 2 July 1780 *NHx*, d 30 Oct 1847 æ. 67 *WHT2;* m Laban Smith.

10 Seth Thomas, bp 15 Sep 1782 (sponsor, Benajah Thomas) *NHx*, d 12 Mar 1813 *WHD*.

11 Charles, b c. 1786, d 18 Oct 1865 æ. 80 (at WH) *BAlm;* m Amelia Smith.

RICHARDS. Nathaniel of Norwalk m 15 Mar 1663/4 *NHV*—[Rosamond] wid. Henry Lindon.

RICHARDSON. Thomas, d 11 June 1761 *WV;* m 1700 *WV*—Rachel da. John & Hannah (Bassett) Parker, b 16 June 1680 *WV*, d 8 Sep 1763 *WV*. Moses Doolittle of W & Dorcas Thomas of NH petitioned Nov 1747 for conservator for Tho. Richardson & wife. Adm'n on Est. of Tho. granted July 1761 to John Royce in right of w., da. of dec'd, the widow Rachel desiring it.

1 Dorcas, b 2 Dec 1700 *WV*, d 21 Mar 1790 æ. 89-3-19 *BD;* m 17 Apr 1723 *WV*—Joseph Thomas.

2 Lydia, b c. 1703, d 30 Jan 1747/8 *WV*, 31 Jan æ. 45 *CT1;* m 29 Mar 1729 *WV*—Moses Doolittle.

3 Abigail, d 1776; m John Royce. Adm'n on Est. of Wid. Abigail Roys of W granted Oct 1776 to Mrs. Dorcas Thomas of NH.

RICHARDSON. Thomas, b c. 1773, d 29 Sep 1825 æ. 52 (choked) *WdD;* m Hannah Smith, b [31 July 1771], d 9 Jan 1858 æ. 86-5-9 *WdD*.

1 Abigail, b c. 1800, d 8 Nov 1836 æ. 36 *WdD*.

2 Lucy, b c. 1802, d 22 Mar 1871 æ. 69 *WdD;* m Aurelius Beecher.

3 Nancy R., b [Nov 1804], d 2 May 1884 æ. 80-7 *WdD;* m Jeremiah Lines.

4 Henry, b c. 1807, d 26 Apr 1874 æ. 67 *WdD;* m Maria C., wid. Wm. Manville.

RILEY. Ebenezer, s. of Wid. Abigail, bp 26 Sep 1773 *NHC1*.

RITTER. John, s. of Thomas of E. Hartford, b 2 Nov 1750 *F*, d 4 Dec 1802 *NHT1;* stone cutter; m 4 Nov 1774 *F*—Hannah da. Eliphalet & Elizabeth (Ritter) Brown of Coventry, b 11 Mar 1745 *F*, d 18 Aug 1823 æ. 79 *NHT1*.

1 David, b 21 Sep 1776 *F*, d Sep 1778 *F*.

2 David, b 13 Jan 1779 *F*, d 14 Oct 1842 *NHT1;* m (1) Anna T. ———, who d 8 Nov 1820 æ. 40 *NHT1;* m (2) 25 Mar 1821 *NHV*—Julia Mansfield, who d 9 Oct 1850 æ. 66 *NHT1*.

The Ritter monument *(NHT1)* contains these inscriptions relating to David's family: Elizabeth Inness d 10 Mar 1831 æ. 19; David Ritter d 9 Dec 1865 æ. 47; Nathan Ritter d 22 Dec 1891 æ. 82 & Elizabeth Hotchkiss his w. d 27 Jan 1886 æ. 73; John Ritter, 47 yrs. in marble business, d 13 Sep 1872 æ. 68, & Wealthy

Hilliard his w. d 13 May 1834 æ. 26, & Grace L. Chapman his wid. d 30 Jan 1880 æ. 75; Sarah M. Ritter w. John B. Yale d 28 July 1885 æ. 77; Grace Ritter w. Watson Adams d 28 May 1893 æ. 77.

ROACH. John of M m 23 Jan 1683 *NHV*—Mary da. Wm. & Mary (Desborough) Prindle, b 8 Mar 1659/60 *NHV*.

ROBERTS. fam. 1. William, b c. 1617, d 6 Aug 1689 æ. 72 *MT;* m Joanna ——.

1 Elizabeth, b c. 1650, bp 14 May 1653 *MC1,* [d 4 Aug 1722 æ. 72 *NHT1;* m John Beecher].

PAGE 1790

2 Zachariah, bp 14 May 1653 *MC1;* rem. to Bedford, Mass.; m 8 Feb 1677 *MV*—Mary Lawrence.

i Zachariah, b 7 Mar 1678 *MV*.

3 Joanna, b 26 June 1657 *MV,* [d 24 Feb 1732 æ. 77 *NHT1;* m Isaac Beecher].

4 Phebe, b 6 Oct 1659 *MV,* d s. p.

5 Phebe, b 13 Mar 1661 *MV*.

6 William, b 24 Aug 1663 *MV;* rem. to Durham; m Elizabeth Lobdell.

7 Alice, b 12 Aug 1666 *MV*.

8 Lydia, b 27 Aug 1672 *MV;* m Joseph Beecher.

ROBERTS. fam. 2. William, of EH, m —— da. Robert & Mary Abbot. Records of this family very incomplete.

1 Son, b Dec 1681 *NHV*.

2 Ann, b 2 Feb 1688 *NHV;* m 21 Mar 1713/4 *BdV*—Samuel Butler.

3 Abigail, b 29 Jan 1696/7 *NHV*.

fam. 3. Thomas of EH, perhaps s. of above William; m ——.

1 Joseph, b 14 Dec 1727 *EHV,* d 1736 æ. 9 *EHV*.

2 John, b 14 Nov 1729 *EHV,* d soon.

3 Ebenezer, b 4 Dec 1731 *EHV;* m 15 Dec 1756 *EHV, BdC*—Elizabeth da. Samuel & Margaret (Old) Jacobs, b c. 1728, d 8 Dec 1787 æ. 60 *EHC*.

i Susanna, b c. 1757, d 7 Nov 1791 æ. 34 *EHC*.

ii Anna, bp 25 Jan 1760 *EHC;* no further record; perhaps an error for Susanna above.

4 Elizabeth, b 17 Oct 1733 *EHV*.

5 Mary, d 10 Oct 1742 *EHV*.

6 Joseph, b 17 Apr 1738 *EHV*.

7 Eunice, d 5 Oct 1742 *EHV*.

8 Ann, d 28 Sep 1742 *EHV*.

9 John, b 21 June 1744 *EHV*.

10 Thomas, b 27 Jan 1745/6 *EHV*.

fam. 4. Jonathan of Meriden & EH, m c. 1716 Bridget da. John & Elizabeth (Harris) Hunnewell, b 2 Oct 1691 *Wethersfield*. "Aged Wid." Roberts d between 1728 & 1734 *WC2,* perhaps mother of Jonathan.

1 Molly, b c. 1717, d 6 Mar 1794 æ. c. 77 *EHC*.

2 Rebecca, b c. 1721, d 9 Sep 1796 æ. 75 *EHC*.

3 Thankful, b 24 Mar 1729 *WV*, bp 8 Mar 1729/30 *WC2*, d 30 July 1773 æ. 43 *EHC;* m Joseph Mallory.

4 Jonathan, b 1 June 1734 *WV*, bp 2 June 1734 *WC2*, d 16 Oct 1788; m Jemima Abbot.

i William, bp 23 May 1756 *EHC*, d soon.

ii William, bp 6 Nov 1757 *EHC*.

iii Hannah, bp 30 Sep 1759 *EHC*.

iv Pamela, bp 27 Sep 1761 *EHC*.

v Child [probably Rebecca], bp 1764 *EHC*.

vi Mima [Jemima], bp 3 Mar 1776 *EHC*.

ROBERTS. fam. 5. Eli, of WH, d c. June 1693; m Mary da. Peter & Mary [Preston] Mallory, b 28 Nov 1656 *NHV*, d 17 Sep 1752 æ. 96 *CT1;* she m (2) 14 July 1696 *WV*—Henry Cook; (3) 9 Apr 1705 *WV*—Jeremiah How.

1 Mary, b 2 Sep 1679 *NHV*.

2 Peter, b 25 Nov 1681 *NHV;* m 5 Apr 1703 *NHV*—Lydia da. Joseph & Lydia (Bristol) Smith, b 26 Apr 1683 *NHV*. A deed [NH Land, 25: 391] indicates that Peter was living in Wy 1763, but no record of family found there. A Peter d at Windsor 26 May 1752 æ. 72; his only children were Peter & Luke Roberts of Boston [i. e. Boston Neck in Suffield] & John Roberts of Windsor. Luke of Boston d c. 1791 leaving sons Elijah, Benjamin & Samuel, & gr. dau. Hannah Herring. John of Windsor (see Hist. of Windsor, II. 646) d 11 Dec 1775 æ. 62, & in 1791 his surviving children were James, Oliver, Peletiah, Paul, Henry, Mary w. Elijah Andruss, Lucy w. Eben Bissell, Sarah w. Ozias Loomis, Ann w. Timothy Loomis, & Ruhamah Roberts.

3 Elizabeth, b 28 Sep 1683 *NHV*, d young.

4 Susanna, b 14 Oct 1685 *NHV*, bp 31 July 1698 *NHC1*.

5 John, b 6 Aug 1688 *NHV*, bp 31 July 1698 *NHC1*.

6 Alexander, b 5 Mar 1689/90 *NHV*, bp 31 July 1698 *NHC1*, d 4 Jan 1764 *SC;* m (1) 6 Jan 1715 *WV*—Hannah [? da. Walter & Tryntie (Henerig)] Johnson; m (2) 17 Feb 1759 *SC*—Abigail da. Samuel & Mary (Brown) Clark, wid. Jonathan Bronson & [Ephraim] Squires; she m (4) 10 Dec 1765 *SC*—Daniel Sperry; (5) 14 Feb 1769 *SC*—James Beckwith.

(By 1): *i* John, b 11 Dec 1715 *WV*, d 31 Oct 1716 *WV*.

ii Mary, b 5 Sep 1717 *WV;* m 21 Mar 1734 *WV*—Isaac Clark.

iii John, b 25 Mar 1720 *WV*, d 29 Dec 1751 *WV*.

iv Thankful, b 10 Oct 1726 *WV*.
v Anna, b 28 Mar 1731 *WV*, bp May 1731 *CC*.
vi Susanna, b 28 Mar 1731 *WV*, bp May 1731 *CC*. (Was Elisha s. Alexander & Anna *Johnson*, b 20 July 1722 *WV*, intended for a son of Alexander & Hannah (Johnson) *Roberts*?)

7 ELI, b 14 Feb 1691 *NHV* [1691/2], d 23 Sep 1754 æ. 63 *NMT*; m 2 Dec 1718 *WV*—Mary da. John & Mary (Thorpe) McKay, b 16 June 1696 *Wethersfield*, d 3 July 1757 æ. 63 *NMT*.
i Susanna, b 11 Sep 1719 *WV*, d soon.
ii Peter, b 1 Feb 1721 *WV*; m 1 July 1746 *WV*—Mary da. Matthew & Elizabeth (Winston) How, b 21 Dec 1721 *WV*. Family incomplete. Children: 1 Anna, b 2 Oct 1747 *WV*, bp 28 Sep 1755 *NMC*; 2 Matthew How, b 31 Aug 1749 *WV*, bp 28 Sep 1755 *NMC*; 3 Elizabeth, b 15 Sep 1752 *NMV*, d 15 Aug 1753 *NMV*. 4 Samuel, b 30 Sep 1754 *NMV*. 5 Eliakim, b 6 Dec 1761 *NMV*.
iii Susanna, b 29 Sep 1722 *WV*; m 8 Dec 1768 *NMC*—Deliverance Wakelee.
iv Benjamin, b 1 May 1724 *WV*; m 15 Nov 1756 *NMV*—Ann Bostwick, b 7 July 1733, d 29 Aug 1789; she m (2) 30 Apr 1783 Ebenezer Hotchkiss. FAM. 6.
v Lydia, b 30 Mar 1726 *WV*, bp May 1726 *CC*; m (1) 31 July 1744 *WV*—John Moss; m (2) James Bradshaw.
vi Anna, b 31 Dec 1727 *WV*, bp Feb 1727/8 *CC*, d 8 June 1792; m 29 May 1746 *WV*—Isaac Moss.
vii Eunice, b 21 Apr 1730 *WV*, bp May 1730 *CC*, m Simeon Chandler.
viii Tabitha, b 27 Nov 1732 *WV*, bp Jan 1732/3 *CC*; m 6 Mar 1755 *NMC*—Oliver Canfield.
ix Eli, b 14 Apr 1736 *WV*, bp May 1736 *CC*, d 11 Feb 1805 (Vergennes, Vt.); m 31 May 1761 *NMV*—Abigail Durand, b 12 July 1744 *F*. FAM. 7.
x Mary, b 26 Nov 1738 *WV*, d young.

8 ABIEL, b 10 Dec 1693 *NHV*, d 14 June 1786 *CC*; m (1) 17 Jan 1723 *WV*—Elizabeth da. Isaac & Sarah (Foote) Curtis, b 10 Aug 1701 *WV*, d 21 Nov 1723 *WV*; m (2) 24 June 1724 *WV*—Hephzibah da. Joseph & Mary (Brown) Prindle, b 15 May 1698 *NHV*.

(By 1): *i* Elizabeth, b 1 Nov 1723 *WV*, d 1 May 1724 *WV*.
(By 2): *ii* Abiel, b 25 Apr 1725 *WV*, d 25 May 1725 *WV*.
iii Abiel, b 26 Apr 1726 *WV;* m (1) 14 Aug 1750 *FarmV*—Martha da. Miles & Mary (Tuttle) Hull, b 29 Nov 1730 *WV*, d 14 June 1769 *WatV;* m (2) 11 Feb 1771 *WatV*—Susanna da. Samuel & Elizabeth (Scott) Warner, wid. Ephraim Bissell, b 3 Aug 1738 *WatV*. FAM. 8.
iv Elizabeth, b 15 Nov 1727 *WV;* m 16 Apr 1751 *WV*—Benjamin Hotchkiss.
v Hephzibah, b 10 Dec 1729 *WV;* m 22 Jan 1755 *WatV*—Seth Bartholomew.
vi Joseph, b 27 Sep 1731 *WV*.
vii Ebenezer, b 2 Oct 1733 *WV*, d 29 Jan 1734 *WV*.
viii Mary, b 4 Jan 1735 *WV;* m 30 Apr 1761 *WatV*—Samuel Sperry.
ix Joel, b 4 July 1736 *WV*, d 10 Feb 1815 æ. 79 *WatT1;* m 10 July 1766 *WatV*—Abigail Foote of Newtown.
x Ebenezer, b 13 Mar 1739 *WV;* Census (H) 1-1-1; m 10 Apr 1766 *WV*—Rebecca da. Abraham & Mary (Hotchkiss) Barnes, b 2 Feb 1738 *WV* [1738/9], d 4 Dec 1801 æ. 63 *HC1*. FAM. 9.
xi Moses, b 19 Feb 1741 *WV*, d 13 Mar 1741 *WV*.
xii Martha, b 13 Sep 1742 *WV*.

FAM. 6. BENJAMIN & ANN (BOSTWICK) ROBERTS:

1 HANNAH, b 27 Nov 1757, d 14 Apr 1776; m 16 Mar 1775 Abraham Peet.
2 ABRAHAM, b 7 Oct 1759, d 21 Feb 1821; m Annis ———, who d 28 Sep 1831 æ. 70.
3 JOHN, b 30 Mar 1762, d 24 June 1836; m (1) 1 Jan 1788 Jane Camp, b 14 Nov 1764, d 26 Jan 1812; m (2) 3 July 1816 Sarah Noble, wid. Gershom Bennett.
4 BENJAMIN, b 21 June 1765, d 5 Jan 1771.
5 ELI, b 28 June 1769, d (St. Lawrence Co., N. Y.); m 21 June 1820 Jerusha Booth.

FAM. 7. ELI & ABIGAIL (DURAND) ROBERTS:

1 DURAND, b 17 Feb 1764 *NMV*, d 19 Sep 1817 (Ferrisburg, Vt.); m 5 Oct 1794 Abigail da. Zebulon & Lucy (Root) Sackett.
2 ADRIAN, b 29 Mar 1767 *NMV;* res. Livingston & Ingham Cos., Mich.; m Cynthia Webster.
3 SETH; m Sarah Hunt.

FAM. 8. ABIEL & MARTHA (HULL) ROBERTS:

1 MOSES, b 23 May 1751 *FarmV*, bp Apr 1751 *CC*, d 16 June 1777 *WatV*.

2 MIRIAM, b 8 Feb 1753 *FarmV,* bp 1 Apr 1753 *SC.*
3 HEPHZIBAH, b 9 Feb 1755 *FarmV,* bp 16 June 1755 *SC.*
4 MARTHA, b 30 July 1757 *WatV;* m 4 Feb 1778 *WatV*—Enos Root.
5 HESTER, b 27 July 1759 *WatV,* d 11 Apr 1840 æ. 81 *Salem x;* m 26 Dec 1780 *WatV*—Uri Scott.
6 MARY, b 31 Dec 1761 *WatV;* m 29 Apr 1784 *WatV*—Sele Scovill.
7 SARAH, b 12 Apr 1764 *WatV.*
8 JOSEPH, b 21 Nov 1766 *WatV.*
9 ELIZABETH, b 4 June 1769 *WatV.*

FAM. 8. ABIEL & SUSANNA (WARNER) ROBERTS:
10 RUTH, b 22 Apr 1772 *WatV.*
11 PHEBE, b 9 Apr 1779 *WatV.*

FAM. 9. EBENEZER & REBECCA (BARNES) ROBERTS:
1 JOSEPH, b 31 Jan 1767 *WV,* d 30 Nov 1786 *HC1.*
2 MARY, b 18 Nov 1769 *WV.*
3 DIMON, bp 18 June 1775 *HC1;* res. Greene, N. Y.; m Hannah da. Samuel & Lowly (Pardee) Dickerman, b 17 Aug 1777, d 25 Oct 1843; had 7 children.

ROBERTS. FAM. 10. ELIAS, s. of David & Thankful (Bow) of Mid; m 26 July 1746 *WV*—Susanna da. Gideon & Mary (Royce) Ives, b 26 May 1727 *WV.*
1 ELIAS, b 25 Feb 1747 *WV,* bp 17 Mar 1751 *WC2,* d 11 Sep 1777 æ. 31 *BristolT.*
2 GIDEON, b 5 Mar 1749 *WV,* bp 17 Mar 1751 *WC2,* d 20 June 1813 æ. 64 *BristolT;* m Fally ———.
3 SETH, b 29 Jan 1752 *WV,* "child" bp Jan 1752 *WC2.*
4 PHEBE, b 27 Apr 1755 *WatV.*
5 (perhaps) JABEZ, b c. 1760, d 20 Feb 1833 æ. 73 *BristolT;* m Charlotte ———, who d 27 May 1834 æ. 71 *BristolT.*

ROBERTS. FAM. 11. JOSIAH, b c. 1739, bu. 11 Oct 1810 æ. 71 *NHx;* Census (NH) 1-1-4; m Mary ———, who d Nov 1818 æ. 72 *ColR.*
1 WILLIAM, bp 26 Jan 1776 *NHx.*
2 KATHARINE; m 29 Apr 1795 (at house of Josiah Roberts) *NHx*—Josias Wiggins of N. Y.
3 JOSIAH, bp 2 July 1786 *NHx.*
4 RUTH, bp 7 Aug 1788 *NHx,* bu. 5 Sep 1794 æ. 6 *NHx.*

ROBERTS. MISCELLANEOUS. ABEL & Joanna had Jacob, b 15 May 1732 *WV*.......SARAH of Durham m 19 June 1744 *NHV*—Phineas Clark.......THANKFUL [of Mid] m 29 Jan 1737 *WV*—Ebenezer Cooper.......MARY m 25 July 1749 *WV*—Joseph Holt.......ELIZABETH m 5 Sep 1758 *WatV*—Ebenezer Sexton.

ROBINS. JOHN, m (1) 4 Nov 1659 *BdV*—Mary, wid. Robert Abbot; m (2) 23 June 1670 *BdV*—Jane [wid. ?] Tillison.

(By 1): 1 Benjamin, b 24 Oct 1660 *BdV*, d 1689; m 29 Aug 1687 *NHV*—Sarah da. John Brooks, b 9 Apr 1661 *NHV;* she m (2) 10 Dec 1692 *NHV*—Nathaniel Thorpe.

2 John, b 2 July [1662] *BdV*.

ROBINSON. fam. 1. Jacob, d after 1747; res. EH; m Sarah da. Eliakim & Sarah (Merrick) Hitchcock, b 16 Oct 1669 *NHV*.

1 John, b 3 Dec 1691 *NHV*, d 1760; m 23 Nov 1720 *NHV*—Mary da. Daniel & Mary (Tappen) Barnes, b 15 May 1698 *NHV*.

i Jacob, b 20 Oct 1721 *NHV*, d 24 Nov 1762 *F&IWRolls;* m 14 July 1747 *NHV*—Elizabeth da. Moses & Lydia (Humiston) Brockett, b 9 Aug 1718 *NHV*, d 1772. fam. 2.

ii Mary, b 5 Sep 1724 *NHV;* m 29 Sep 1746 *NHV*—Moses Sanford.

iii John, b 16 Aug 1729 *NHV*, d c. 1810-12; Census (EH) 3-1-3; m 8 Mar 1755 *NHV*—Lois da. William & Desire (Bunnell) Sanford, b 3 June 1737 *NHV*. fam. 3.

iv Miriam, b 1 Dec 1731 *NHV*, d 20 Dec 1802 æ. 72 *NoHT1;* m Joel Bradley.

2 Thomas, b 5 Dec 1693 *NHV*, d 9 June 1766 æ. 73 *EHT;* m (1) Esther da. Thomas & Mary (Sanford) Tuttle, b 19 Feb 1694/5 *NHV*, d c. 1721; m (2) Hannah da. John & Hannah (Hemingway) How, b 9 Feb 1693 *NHV;* perhaps m (3) 11 Nov 1755 *EHC*—Mary Butler.

(By 1): *i* Benjamin, b 23 Dec 1716 *EHV*, d 1759; m Katharine [Durand], b c. 1721, d 17 Oct 1801 æ. 80 *EHC*. fam. 4.

ii Esther, b 7 July 1720 *EHV*, d 17 Feb 1790 æ. 69 *EHT;* m 18 June 1741 *NHV*—Stephen Morris.

(By 2): *iii* Thomas, b 7 Apr 1723 *EHV*, d 16 Oct 1760 *F&IWRolls;* Cpl.; m Ann da. Abraham & Mary (Walker) Wooster, b (at St). fam. 5.

iv Child, d 1745 *EHR*.

v Child, d 1745 *EHR*.

vi Hannah, b Sep 1731 *EHV*, d 1736 æ. 5 *EHV*, 17 Nov 1736 in 6 yr. *EHT*.

vii Andrew, b 5 Dec 1733 *EHV*, d Oct 1736 æ. 3 *EHV*, 27 Oct in 3 yr. *EHT*.

3 Sarah, b 24 Dec 1695 *NHV*, d 18 Jan 1778 æ. 82 *EHC;* m 27 Jan 1714/5 *EHV*—Samuel Bradley.

4 Hannah, b 24 Feb 1697/8 *NHV*, d 7 July 1781 æ. 82 *EHC;* m Thomas Dawson.

5 ELIAKIM, b Apr 1706 *NHV,* 2 Apr *EHV,* d 1756; Sgt.; m Lydia da. Samuel & Sarah (Barnes) Moulthrop, b 5 May 1707 *EHV;* she m (2) Roger Tyler of Bd.

i Jared; Lt.; m 24 Dec 1760 *EHC*—Mary da. Samuel & Hannah (Hemingway) Thompson. They are said to have had children: Chandler, Jemima, Anna, Sarah & Ziba. Chandler m 26 Dec 1781 *EHC*—Lois Grannis. In 1810 Chandler, Eliakim & Jared Robinson of Braintrim, Luzerne Co., Pa., conveyed land as heirs of Moses Thompson.

ii Sarah; m 24 May 1758 *EHC, WV*—Aaron Williams.

iii Zerviah; m (1) 16 Mar 1757 *EHC*—Joshua Sperry; m (2) June 1762 *WdC,* 17 June *NHV* —Caleb Tuttle.

iv Jehu; m 1769 *EHC*—Elizabeth da. Abraham & Elizabeth (Bradley) Augur, bp 11 June 1749 *WdC,* d 19 July 1785 æ. 37 *NHC1.* FAM. 6.

v Ziba.

vi Lydia, b c. 1743, d 2 June 1836 æ. 93 *LT;* m 1769 Elihu Hotchkiss.

vii Amasa.

FAM. 2. JACOB & ELIZABETH (BROCKETT) ROBINSON:

1 MOSES, b 14 July 1754 *NHV.*

2 ADAH, b 18 Aug 1760 *NHV,* bp 19 Apr 1761 *NoHC;* m 23 July 1789 *NoHC*—Ebenezer Buck.

FAM. 3. JOHN & LOIS (SANFORD) ROBINSON:

1 MARY, b 8 Aug 1755 *NHV,* bp 14 Nov 1764 *NoHC,* d 1841; m 24 Nov 1774 *NoHC,* 25 Nov *WV*—Andrew Clark of W.

2 DESIRE, b 2 Jan 1758 *NHV,* bp 14 Nov 1764 *NoHC;* m ——— Andrews. She had a nat. child by Justus Bradley:

i Abigail, b 24 Jan 1777 *NHV.*

3 JOHN, b 12 Nov 1760 *NHV,* bp 14 Nov 1764 *NoHC,* d 25 Nov 1840 æ. 80 *NoHT2;* m 13 Mar 1784 *EHV,* 11 Mar *WC*—Laura Spencer.

i Mary, b 2 Aug 1784 *EHV.*

ii Uriah, b 6 July 1787 *EHV,* d 20 Nov 1809 æ. 23 *NoHT2.*

iii Desire, b 6 July 1787 *EHV.*

iv Clarissa.

v Abigail.

vi Susan.

vii Salmon.

viii Erastus.

4 Justus, b 6 Dec 1765 *NHV*, bp 8 June 1766 *NoHC;* m 15 Dec 1790 *NoHV*—Lucy Barnes.
i John S.
ii Sylvester.

5 Harman, b 7 July 1768 *NHV* (by a duplicate entry, 6 July 1767), bp 21 Aug 1768 *NoHC*, d 30 Mar 1853 æ. 86 *NoHT2;* m (1) Dency ———, who d 3 Nov 1831 æ. 66 *EHC;* m (2) Clarinda Baldwin, who d 5 Feb 1853 æ. 88 *NoHT2*.
(By 1): *i* Harmon (proof, EH Deeds 6-126).
ii Samuel R. (proof, EH Deeds 6:127).

6 Medad, b 19 July 1770 *NHV*, bp 7 Oct 1771 *NoHC*, d s. p.

7 Linus, b 14 Feb 1774 *NHV*, bp 19 June 1774 *NoHC;* res. Bd 1814.

8 Lois, b 19 Mar 1776 *NHV*, bp 16 June 1776 *NoHC;* m ——— Barnes.

FAM. 4. Benjamin & Katharine [Durand] Robinson:

1 Esther, b c. 1749, d 19 Oct 1800 *NHC1*, æ. 51 *NHT1;* m 13 Feb 1771 *NHC1*—Leverett Hubbard.

2 Andrew.

3 Mary; m 24 Nov 1774 *EHC* [called "Richards" at marriage]—Freeman Hughes.

4 Levi, bp 30 Oct 1757 *EHC*.

5 Benjamin, bp 18 Mar 1759 *EHC*.

Benjamin had a nat. child by Bathsheba da. John & Hannah (Hemingway) How: ———, b 1739.

FAM. 5. Thomas & Ann (Wooster) Robinson:

1 Abraham, b 19 June 1751 *EHV*.

2 Hannah, b 18 Sep 1753 *EHV;* probably m Joseph Fairman of "Shaticok," N. Y.; they conveyed 1796 right from her gr. father Tho. Robinson.

3 David, b 23 May 1756 *EHV*, bp 6 June 1756 *EHC*, bu. 23 Dec 1776 æ. 21 *NHx*.

FAM. 6. Jehu & Elizabeth (Augur) Robinson:

1 Betsey, b c. 1770, bp 2 Oct 1774 *NHC1*.

2 Billy, b c. 1772, bp 2 Oct 1774 *NHC1*.

3 Chloe, bp 2 Oct 1774 *NHC1*, d 2 Apr 1782 æ. 8 *NHC1*.

4 James, bp 6 July 1777 *NHC1*.

5 Elihu, bp 21 Aug 1779 *NHC1*, d 21 Aug 1779 æ. 0-0-2 *NHC1*.

6 Chloe, bp 3 Nov 1782 *NHC1*.

7 Elihu, bp 3 July 1785 *NHC1*, d 10 June 1849 æ. 64 (at B); m Laura da. Noah & Mary (Tolles) Thomas.

ROBINSON. FAM. 7. DAVID m 20 July 1724 *WV*—Dorcas da. Jabez & Dorothy (Lyman) Brockett; prob. div. as she m (2) under her maiden name, 8 Jan 1736 *WV*—Joseph Marks.

1 DAVID, son of "Darcos" Robinson formerly Brockett, b 3 Dec 1727 *WV*, d 3 Jan 1769 *WV;* m ———. Probate refers to wid., also to mother Dorcas Marks.

ROBINSON. FAM. 8. JOSIAH, b c. 1700, d 2 Apr 1766 *WV, WC2,* æ. 67 *WT2;* Capt.; m 29 Mar 1725 *WV*—Ruth da. John & Rebecca Merriam, b 12 Feb 1706 *Lynn,Mass.,V,* d 4 July 1776 *WV, CC;* she m (2) 2 Feb 1768 *WV*—Caleb Hull.

1 JOSIAH, b 19 Dec 1725 *WV*, d 17 Apr 1771 *WV*, æ. 45 *WT2;* Lt.; m 23 Feb 1748/9 *WV, WC2*—Eunice da. John & Hannah (Royce) Ives, b 13 May 1727 *WV*, d 26 July 1787 æ. 61 *WT2;* she m (2) 5 Dec 1776 *WV*—John Miles.

i Ruth, b 7 Oct 1750 *WV*, bp 26 July 1754 *WC2;* m 18 Feb 1768 *WV*—Caleb Bull.

ii John, b 2 Apr 1752 *WV*, bp 26 July 1754 *WC2.*

iii Huldah, b 12 June 1754 *WV*, bp 26 July 1754 *WC2,* d 14 Aug 1778 *WV;* m 6 Jan 1774 *WV*—Nathaniel Beadles Johnson.

iv Eunice, b 12 Dec 1756 *WV*, bp Dec 1756 *WC2,* d 11 Apr 1775 *WV.*

v Howell, b 20 June 1759 *WV*, d 25 June 1761 *WV.*

vi Sarah, b 5 Jan 1762 *WV.*

vii Hannah, b 25 June 176[4] *WV.*

viii Lucy, b 10 Oct 1767 *WV*, d 28 Dec 1775 *WV.*

2 MARGARET, b 26 June 1729 *WV;* m 12 May 1747 *WV, WC2*—Caleb Merriman.

3 JOHN, b 16 Apr 1733 *WV*, d 14 July 1739 *WV, WC2.*

4 CHRISTOPHER, b 6 June 1735 *WV*, bp 8 June 1735 *WC2,* d 6 Dec 1760 *WV, WC2;* m 14 Apr 1757 *WV*—Sarah da. Theophilus & Damaris (Olmstead) Mix, b 26 Aug 1732 *WV;* she m (2) 21 Nov 1766 *WV*—Yale Bishop.

i Theophilus Mix, b 26 Jan 1758 *WV;* m 3 Feb 1780 *WV*—Huldah Couch.

ii Levi, b 7 Dec 1759 *WV;* res. Lee, Mass., 1799; m ——— da. John & Eunice (Andrews) Yale.

ROBINSON. MISCELLANEOUS. DANIEL, of NH, rem. to Crosswicks, N. J.; m 3 Feb 1663 *NHV*—Hope da. William & Frances Potter, bp 3 Oct 1641 *NHC1*...Children recorded *NHV*: 1 Mary, b 14 Dec 1664; 2 Daniel, b 27 Nov 1666.......CAPT. JOHN d 27 Aug 1828 æ. 89 (at Wd, formerly of NH) *ColR*.......THOMAS m 31 Oct 1776 *NHx*—Hannah [da. Abraham & Lydia (Humiston) Tuttle], wid. William Warner.

ROGERS. William, d 26 July 1770 *PC;* m 14 Nov 1729 *BdV*—Abigail da. Isaac & Rebecca Bartholomew.
1 Jerusha, b 13 Apr 1732 *NHV.*
2 Hezekiah, b 8 Jan 1734/5 *NHV;* m 29 Jan 1763 *WatV*—Martha Scott; she m (2) 27 May 1773 *WatV*—Aaron How.
3 Freelove, b 18 Nov 1737 *NHV.*
4 Abigail, b 30 July 1740 *NHV,* d soon.
5 Abigail, b 2 Jan 1742/3 *NHV.*
6 Jerusha, b 28 July 1745 *NHV.*
7 Desire, b 20 Mar 1747/8 *NHV.*

ROGERS. Elihu m 23 Nov 1768 *BdV*—Elizabeth Baldwin.
1 Thankful, b 30 Aug 1770 *NHV.*

ROOT. Joel, s. of Elisha, b 30 Aug 1770 (at S), d 12 Jan 1847 æ. 76 *NHV;* m Eleanor Strong, b [Jan 1771 at Torrington], d 5 July 1853 æ. 82-5 *NHV.*
1 Olivia Ann, b c. 1788, bp 1 July 1804 (æ. 16) *NHx,* d 1827 æ. 38 (at Philadelphia, Pa.) *ConnH;* m Alderman Badger.
2 Lucy Curtis, b c. 1790, bp 1 July 1804 (æ. 14) *NHx,* d 10 Dec 1824 æ. 32 *NHT1;* m Charles Atwater.
3 Eliza Maria, b c. 1792, bp 1 July 1804 (æ. 12) *NHx;* m ——— Norton.
4 Eleanor Paris, b c. 1794, bp 1 July 1804 (æ. 10) *NHx;* m ——— Rice.
5 Jennet Frances, b c. 1796, bp 1 July 1804 (æ. 8) *NHx;* m ——— Bliss.
6 Charlotte Antoinette, b c. 1798, bp 1 July 1804 (æ. 6) *NHx;* m (1) Wm. Forbes; m (2) ——— Laignoux.
7 Susan Augusta, b c. 1800, bp 1 July 1804 (æ. 4) *NHx,* d 2 Oct 1846 æ. 46 *NHT1;* m 5 Sep 1822 *NHV*—Eleazer Thompson Fitch.

ROOT. Josiah, d 1805; Dr.; Census (S) 1-2-3; res. H; m Merab ———. Children recorded *HV:* 1 James, b 2 Apr 1796; 2 William, b 10 June 1798; 3 Nancy, b 4 May 1801; 4 Emily, b 20 May 1805.

ROSBOTTOM. Benjamin m 29 Dec 1724 *NHV*—Sarah da. Gershom & Hannah (Mansfield) Brown, b Mar 1699 *NHV;* s. p.

ROSE. fam. 1. Robert, b c. 1594, d 1665; res. Wethersfield & Bd; m (1) Margery ———, b c. 1594; m (2) Elizabeth, wid. John Potter & Edward Parker, who d 28 July 1677 *NHV.*

(By 1): 1 John, b [c. 1616 ?], d 1683; res. Bd & EH; m (1) ———; m (2) [Mar/Apr 1663] *NHV*—Ellen Moulthrop, wid. William Luddington; m (3) after 1675 Phebe da. Thomas & Phebe (Bisby) Bracey, wid. Joseph Dickinson of Northfield, Mass. His will gave legacies to gr. child Elizabeth, da. Martha

Luddington, son John Jordan, & residue to son John Rose, da. Mary Bates & da. Hannah Frisbie.

(By 1): *i* John, d 27 Dec 1722 *BdV;* Dea.; m (1) [perhaps Deborah, da. or relative of Robert Usher of Stamford who in 1669 left legacy by will to "Debra Rose"]; m (2) Aug 1670 *NHV*—Phebe [Ives], wid. Joseph Potter, [bp 2 Oct 1642 *NHC1*]; m (3) Elizabeth da. William Curtis, wid. Mercy Moss, b 16 Sep 1654 *StV*, d 21 Jan 1719/20 *BdV;* m (4) Hannah ——. FAM. 2.

ii Mary; m —— Bates.

iii Hannah; m Benoni Frisbie.

iv [Martha; m William Luddington.]

v [perhaps a da. m John Jordan.]

2 ROBERT, b c 1619; d 1683; res. St; m Rebecca ——; she m (2) Henry Allyn of St.

i Mary, b 15 Apr [1655] *BdV*, 20 Apr 1655 *StV;* m Moses Johnson of Wy.

ii Rebecca, b 14 July 1657 *StV;* m Obadiah Stevens of Stamford.

iii Elizabeth, b Feb 1658/9 *StV;* m 2 June 1683 *StV*—Isaac Bennett.

iv Dorcas, b Apr 1661 *StV*, d young.

v Sarah, b Aug 1664 *StV;* m John Minor of Wy.

vi Hannah, b c. 1666; m (1) Isaac Stiles; m (2) 9 May 1693 *DV*—Samuel Harger of D; m (3) 28 Mar 1700 *DV*—John Tibbals.

vii Mercy, b 3 Mar 1672 *StV*.

3 ELIZABETH, b c. 1621; m Micah Taintor.

4 SAMUEL, b c. 1625, d c. 1698; res. Newark, N. J.; m Mary Tompkins.

5 SARAH, b c. 1627.

6 DANIEL, b c. 1631; res. Wethersfield; m Elizabeth da. John Goodrich, b 2 Nov 1645 *WethV;* children, see Hist. Weth. 2:590.

7 DORCAS, b c. 1633; m 1653 Daniel Swayne of Bd.

8 MARY.

9 HANNAH.

10 JONATHAN, d 1684; m [1669] *BdV*—Delivered da. John Charles.

i Lydia, b 20 Sep 1671 *BdV*, d young.

ii John, d 17 Apr 1712 *BdV;* m 9 Dec 1702 *BdV*—Hannah Williams.

iii Hannah, bp 15 Mar 1676 *BdC;* m Caleb Frisbie.

iv Jonathan, d 1736; Capt.; m 15 Aug 1697 *BdV*—Abigail, wid. Samuel Foote.

v Samuel, d 1715; m 18 Apr 1705 *BdV*—Joanna

Baldwin; she m (2) 13 Sep 1715 *BdV*—Ebenezer Frisbie.

FAM. 2. JOHN & [? DEBORAH (USHER)] ROSE:

1 ELIZABETH, b 28 Apr 1668 *BdV,* d s. p. 1690; m 15 Feb 1687/8 *NHV*—Samuel Newman.

FAM. 2. JOHN & PHEBE [IVES] ROSE:

2 DEBORAH, b 6 June 1671 *BdV;* m George Baldwin.

3 SARAH, b 26 Nov 1673 *BdV;* m Joseph Foote.

4 HANNAH, b 15 Mar 1676/7 *BdV;* m 5 Jan 1703/4 *BdV*—Samuel Harrington.

5 JOHN, b 28 Oct 1679 *BdV,* d young.

6 DANIEL, b 11 Mar 1682/3 *BdV.*

FAM. 2. JOHN & ELIZABETH (CURTIS) ROSE:

7 SAMUEL, b 1 Dec 1690 *BdV,* d 15 Apr 1763 æ. 73 *BdT;* Dea.; m 6 June 1716 *BdV*—Lydia Butler.

ROSEWELL. WILLIAM, d 1696; Capt.; res. NH & Bd; m (1) ——— ; m (2) Katharine da. Richard Russell, who d 1698.

(By 1): 1 RICHARD, b c. 1652, d Mar 1702 *NHV,* 24 Mar æ. 50 *NHT1;* m 22 Dec 1681 *NHV*—Lydia da. Thomas & Sarah (Rutherford) Trowbridge, b 7 June 1666 *NHV,* bp 12 Aug 1688 *NHC1,* d 10 Dec 1731 *NHV,* 9 Dec æ. 66 *NHT1.*

i Sarah, b 5 Dec 1682 *NHV,* bp 12 Aug 1688 *NHC1,* d 20 Oct 1720 æ. 37 *NHT1;* m John Woodward.

ii Dorcas, b 21 Dec 1684 *NHV,* bp 12 Aug 1688 *NHC1,* d 2 Sep 1715 *DV;* m 10 Feb 1714/5 *NHV,* 20 Feb 1714 *DV*—Rev. Joseph Moss.

iii Lydia, b 21 Aug 1687 *NHV,* bp 12 Aug 1688 *NHC1,* d 21 May 1732 *NHV;* m 9 Apr 1713 *NHV*—Jeremiah Atwater.

iv Elizabeth, b 5 Sep 1690 *NHV,* bp Sep 1690 *NHC1,* d 3 Oct 1742 æ. 53 *NHT1;* m 22 Dec 1726 *NHV*—Francis Brown.

v Katharine, b 26 Dec 1695 *NHV,* bp 19 Jan 1695/6 *NHC1,* d 4 Nov 1758 æ. 63 *NHT1;* m William Greenough.

(By 2): 2 MAUD, b 21 Aug 1668 *NHV,* "da." d Sep 1668 *NHV.*

3 WILLIAM, b 16 June 1670 *NHV,* d s. p.

4 ELIZABETH, b 1 Oct 1679; m Gov. Gurdon Saltonstall.

ROSS. GEORGE m 7 Dec 1658 *NHV*—Constance Little.

1 JOHN, b 23 Feb 1660 *NHV,* bp 13 May 1662 *NHC1.*

2 DANIEL, b 10 Oct 1663 *NHV,* bp 17 Nov 1663 *NHC1.*

3 ELIZABETH, b 26 Dec 1665 *NHV.*

4 HANNAH, b 14 Aug 1668 *NHV.*

ROWE. FAM. 1. MATTHEW, d 27 May 1662 *NHV;* m [Sarah da. Robert Abbott], who d 7 Dec 1693 *NHV.*

1 ELIZABETH, b 10 Aug 1650 *NHV,* d 2 Jan 1650 *NHV* [1650/1].

2 Daniel, b 4 Jan 1651 *NHV* [1651/2], d 3 Sep 1652 *NHV*.

3 John, b 30 Apr 1654 *NHV*, d 1724; m 14 July 1681 *NHV*—Abigail da. Joseph & Elizabeth (Preston) Alsop, b 4 Sep 1656 *NHV*, bp 26 Apr 1657 *NHC1*, d c. 1738.

i John, b 23 Oct 1681 *NHV*, d 1757; m 22 June 1736 *NHV*—Hannah da. Daniel & Hannah (Sanford) Tuttle, wid. Dan Carrington, bp 27 June 1697 *MC1*, d c. 1784. FAM. 2.

ii Matthew, b 14 Feb 1683 *NHV*, d 29 Dec 1750 æ. 67 *EHT*; m 1 Feb 1710/1 *NHV*—Rebecca da. Nathaniel & Mary (Pantry) Mix, b 23 Nov 1684 *NHV*, bp (adult) 29 June 1718 *NHC1*, d 6 Dec 1760 æ. 76 *EHT*. FAM. 3.

iii Stephen, b 6 June 1687 *NHV*, d 15 Nov 1724 *NHV*; m Mary da. Joseph & Sarah (Alling) Peck, b 6 Oct 1689 *NHV*, d 22 Jan 1747/8 *WV*; she m (2) 9 June 1729 *NHV*—Timothy Tuttle. FAM. 4.

iv Abigail, b 13 Aug 1689 *NHV*; m 24 Feb 1714/5 *NHV*—James Morris.

v Hannah, b 11 Feb 1691 *NHV*, d 16 May 1770 æ. 78 *NHC1*; m (1) 1 Sep 1720 *NHV*—John Leek; m (2) 10 July 1729 *NHV*—James Peck.

vi Sarah, b 15 Oct 1700 *NHV*, bp 30 Nov 1724 *NHC1*, d 5 May 1779 æ. 79 *NHC1*; m 21 Jan 1724/5 *NHV*—Eleazer Brown.

4 Hannah, b 6 Oct 1656 *NHV*.

5 Joseph, b 20 Feb 1658 *NHV*, d [1659] *NHV*.

6 Stephen, b 28 Aug 1660 *NHV*.

FAM. 2. John & Hannah (Tuttle) Rowe:

1 John, b 1 July 1737 *NHV*, bp 4 July 1737 *NHC1*; rem. to D; m Esther ———. Family incomplete.

i John, b 13 Dec 1765 *NHV*.

ii Esther, b 7 Mar 1768 *NHV*, d 15 Feb 1848 æ. 80 *LT*; m Isaac Baldwin.

2 Hannah, b 27 Sep 1739 *NHV*, bp 30 Sep 1739 *NHC1*, d s. p.

3 Mary, b 7 Oct 1741 *NHV*, bp 11 Oct 1741 *NHC1*; m (1) 15 Sep 1766 *NHV*, *EHC*—Michael Todd; m (2) 10 June 1779 *NHC1*—Samuel Dwight.

4 Katharine, b 28 Oct 1744 *NHV*, bp 3 June 1744 *NHC1*; m 5 Nov 1772 *WC*—Jonathan Brooks; res. NH 1774 & Ludlow, Vt., 1786.

FAM. 3. Matthew & Rebecca (Mix) Rowe:

1 Mary, b 27 Jan 1711 *NHV*, bp 29 June 1718 *NHC1*, d 8 Apr 1778 æ. 67 *HT3*; m 13 Dec 1733 *NHV*—Amos Bradley.

2 Abigail, b 17 Jan 1712/3 *NHV,* bp 29 June 1718 *NHC1;* m (1) 13 May 1736 *NHV*—Stephen Ives; m (2) Joseph Sackett.

3 John, b 5 May 1715 *NHV,* bp 29 June 1718 *NHC1,* d 11 Jan 1790 æ. 74 *EHT,* 12 Jan 1789 æ. 74 *EHC;* m 9 July 1741 *NHV*—Hannah da. John & Martha (Tuttle) Smith, b 26 Dec 1718 *NHV,* d 7 Sep 1790 æ. 71 *EHT,* [———] 1789 æ. 71 *EHC.*

i Matthew, b 20 Feb 1741/2 *NHV,* d 20 Sep 1743 *NHV.*

ii Mary, b 22 Mar 1744 *NHV,* d 16 Nov 1778 æ. [—] *EHT,* 17 Nov æ. 37 *EHC;* m 10 Oct 1765 *EHC*—Samuel Holt.

iii Lois, b 21 Mar 1746 *NHV,* d 8 Sep 1791 æ. 45 *EHC;* m 10 Oct 1765 *EHC*—Solomon Moulthrop.

iv Matthew, b 18 Mar 1748 *NHV,* d 28 Apr 1748 *NHV.*

v Hannah, b 6 June 1749 *NHV,* d young.

vi Ezra, b 5 Apr 1752 *NHV,* d 17 Sep 1834 æ. 84 *NHT3,* 16 Sep æ. 83 *EHC;* Census (EH) 1-5-4; m 1773 *EHC,* 1 Feb 1773 *EHR*—Huldah da. Samuel & Hannah (Grannis) Chidsey, b 24 Nov 1751 , d 14 Aug 1832 æ. 80 *NHT3,* æ. 80-8 *EHC.* FAM. 5.

vii John, b 31 May 1754 *NHV,* d s. p. 5 Dec 1840 æ. 87 *NHT3,* æ. 86½ *EHC;* Census (EH) 2-0-2; m 29 [Oct] 1778 *EHC*—Esther Hotchkiss.

viii Matthew, b 28 Nov 1756 *NHV,* bp 12 Dec 1756 *EHC,* d 23 Feb 1813 æ. 56 *EHC,* æ. 57 *NHT3;* Census (EH) 1-2-4; m 4 Oct 1781 *EHV*—Eunice da. Nathaniel & Eunice (Russell) Luddington, b c. 1759, d 13 Apr 1838 æ. 79 *NHT3.* FAM. 6.

ix Stephen, b 6 May 1759 *NHV,* bp 10 June 1759 *EHC,* d 15 Sep 1816 æ. 57 *NHT3;* Census (NH) 2-1-3; m (1) 6 Dec 1781 *EHC*—Abigail da. Henry Freeman & Lydia (Tuttle) Hughes, b 2 Oct 1761 *NHV,* d 16 Sep 1813 æ. 52 *NHT3;* m (2) Elizabeth Miles; she m (2) c. 1836 ———. FAM. 7.

x Hannah, b 9 June 1762 *NHV,* bp 25 July 1762 *EHC,* d 10 Jan 1826 æ. 63 *EHC;* m 1781 *EHC*—Jesse Mallory.

4 Sarah, b 20 Oct 1716 *NHV,* bp 29 June 1718 *NHC1;* m 7 Jan 1759 *EHC*—Daniel Olds.

5 Rebecca, b 22 Oct 1718 *NHV*, bp Apr 1719 *NHC1*, d 7 Jan 1806 æ. 87 *EHT;* m 17 Feb 1742/3 *NHV*—Joel Tuttle.

6 Hannah, b 8 Aug 1724 *NHV*, bp Oct 1724 *NHC1*, d 12 Nov 1776 æ. 52 *EHT;* m 16 Jan 1745/6 *NHV*—Stephen Thompson.

7 Lydia, b 10 June 1726 *NHV*, bp 24 July 1726 *NHC1;* m 5 Aug 1747 *NHV*—Job Smith.

FAM. 4. Stephen & Mary (Peck) Rowe:

1 Stephen, b 7 Sep 1716 *NHV*, bp 1716 *NHC1*, d s. p. 16 Nov 1751 *NHV*.

2 Joseph, b 7 Oct 1718 *NHV*, bp 12 Oct 1718 *NHC1*, d 1801 æ. 83 *BristolC;* m 21 Dec 1743 *NHV*—Abigail da. John & Elizabeth (Barnes) Beecher, b 6 Feb 1726 *NHV*.

i Joseph, b 27 Sep 1744 *NHV;* bp 17 Feb 1744/5 *NHC1*.

ii Abigail, b 29 July 1746 *NHV*, bp 28 Sep 1746 *NHC1;* m (1) 25 Dec 1771 *WV*, *CC*—Ephraim Atwater; m (2) 20 Mar 1783 *CC*—Elnathan Conner [proof, C. Deeds, 3: 542].

iii Ebenezer, b 2 Sep 1748 *NHV*, d s. p. 1772; m Lydia da. Daniel & Lydia (Parker) Humiston; she m (2) 17 Mar 1774 *WV*—Peter Hall.

iv Rebecca, b 29 June 1750 *NHV*, bp 2 Sep 1750 *NHC1;* m 9 Nov 1767 *WV*—Ebenezer Merriam.

v Mary, b 28 Jan 1753 *NHV;* m 23 Sep 1779 *WV*—David Morgan.

vi Eunice, b 29 June 1755 *NHV*, bp 6 June 1756 *NHC1;* m 2 Nov 1775 *CC*—Reuben Bunnell.

vii Stephen, b 31 Jan 1758 *NHV*, bp 3 June 1759 *NHC2;* m Lurenda ———. Children recorded *BristolV:* 1 Truman, b 22 Mar 1784; 2 Ira, b 25 Dec 1785; 3 Stephen, b 7 Feb 1788; 4 Lurenda, b 3 July 1790; 5 John, b 21 Feb 1795.

viii Solomon, bp 6 Apr 1760 *NHC2;* m Jerusha ———.

ix Eli.

x Ari; m & had children recorded *BristolV:* 1 Levi, b 8 Sep 1791; 2 Loysa, b 7 May 1793.

xi Esther, b c. 1768, d 1830 æ. 62 *BristolC*.

3 Daniel, b 7 Nov 1720 *NHV*, bp Dec 1720 *NHC1;* m (1) Thankful da. Samuel & Mary (Hitchcock) Bassett, b 24 Dec 1721 *NHV;* m (2) c. 1766 Rhoda ———.

(By 1): *i* Mary, bp 6 Jan 1748 *Bristol x*, d 27 Dec 1777 *WatV;* m 7 Dec 1769 *WatV*—Samuel Camp.

ii Thankful, bp 6 Jan 1748 *Bristol x*.

iii Daniel, bp 30 Apr 1750 *Bristol x,* 1 May 1750 (at Bristol) *Dx,* d 26 May 1811 *PV;* m Thankful ———, b c. 1750, d 12 June 1820 æ. 70 *PT.*
iv Stephen, bp 12 May 1753 *Bristol x.*
v Isaiah, bp 10 Aug 1755 *Bristol x.*
vi David, bp 8 Dec 1757 *Bristol x.*
vii Susan, bp 31 Aug 1760 *Bristol x.*
viii Samuel, bp 7 Aug 1763 *Bristol x.*

4 Mary, b 21 Dec 1722 *NHV,* bp Feb 1722/3 *NHC1,* d 21 Jan 1806 *CC;* m 3 Dec 1740 *WV*—Moses Bradley.

5 Ebenezer, b 18 Feb 1724/5 *NHV,* bp 28 Mar 1725 *NHC1,* d July 1748 *CC;* m 20 Apr 1746 *WV*—Mindwell da. Samuel & Elizabeth (Frederick) Curtis, b 8 Jan 1727 ; she m (2) 29 Aug 1749 *WV*—William Clark.
i Lois, b 6 Apr 1747 *WV,* bp Feb (?) 1746 *CC,* d after 1801; she had a nat. child b c. 1764 (Ebenezer Badger reputed father); m Gideon Webb [proof, H. Deeds, 5:134].

FAM. 5. Ezra & Huldah (Chidsey) Rowe:

1 Elizabeth, b 11 July 1774 *EHV,* 12 July 1774 *NHT3,* bp 9 May 1779 *EHC,* d 5 Dec 1851 *NHT3;* m 28 July 1793 *EHC*—Heman Hotchkiss.

2 Elijah, b 18 June 1776 *EHV,* bp 9 May 1779 *EHC,* d 16 Feb 1841 æ. 65 *NHT3;* Dea.; res. Wol 1799; m c. 1798 Mary da. Elihu & Mary (Hotchkiss) Moulthrop, b [July 1776], d 9 Nov 1862 æ. 86-4 *NHT3.*
i John H.
ii Mary, b c. 1803, d 14 Aug 1880 æ. 77 *NHV;* m Harvey Barnes.
iii Betsey; m 30 Jan 1831 *NHV*—Willis Mallory.
iv Ezra C.
v Henry M.
vi Statira, b c. 1800, d 29 Feb 1872 æ. 72 *NHT3;* m 26 Feb 1823 *NHV*—Eli H. Farren.
vii Elijah R.

3 Samuel, b 8 Apr 1778 *EHV,* bp 9 May 1779 *EHC,* d 14 Jan 1832 æ. 54 *NHT3,* 1832 æ. 54 *EHC.*

4 Levi, b 5 Mar 1780 *EHV,* d 6 Feb 1858 æ. 78 *NHT3;* m 28 Dec 1803 *EHC*—Eunice Grannis.

5 Huldah, b 22 Apr 1783 *EHV* [1782], bp 1 Sep 1782 *EHC;* m 19 Sep 1805 *NoHC*—Morgan Fowler of NH.

6 Ezra, b 25 Feb 1786 *EHV* [1785], bp 17 Apr 1785 *EHC,* d s. p. 9 July 1852 æ. 67 *NHT3;* Capt.; m 1806 *EHC*—Betsey da. Joseph & Sarah (Fields)

Pardee, b 22 Dec 1786 *F*, d 16 Feb 1873 æ. 86 *NHT3*.

7 Harvey, b 26 Oct 1788 *EHV* [1787], bp 3 Feb 1788 *EHC*, d 25 Dec 1861 æ. 74 *NHT3;* Dea.; m 29 Oct 1810 *EHC*—Wealthy da. Isaac & Mary (Fields) Bradley, b 22 Feb 1792 *F*, d 7 Jan 1867 æ. 75 *NHT3*.

8 Sarah, b 26 June 1790 *EHV*, bp 8 Aug 1790 *EHC*, d 13 Aug 1875 æ. 85 *NHT3;* m 18 Nov 1810 *EHC*—Willet Hemingway.

9 Frances, b 13 Oct 1792 *EHV;* m ——— Parmalee.

FAM. 6. Matthew & Eunice (Luddington) Rowe:

1 Daniel, b 5 Aug 1782 *EHV*, bp 16 Sep 1787 *EHC*, d 10 Aug 1860 æ. 78 *NHT3;* Capt.; m 19 Apr 1805 *EHC*—Elizabeth da. Jedediah & Abigail (Barnes) Andrews, b c. 1786, d 18 Sep 1862 æ. 76 *NHT1*.

i Stephen, b 12 Sep 1805 *NHT3*, d 27 Sep 1886 *NHT3;* m Charlotte Tuttle, b 8 Aug 1808 *NHT3*, d 17 Oct 1889 *NHT3*.

ii Barney Nelson, b c. 1807, d 1 Nov 1815 æ. 8 *NHT3*.

iii Eliza, b c. 1810, d 3 May 1872 æ. 62 *NHT3;* m Robert Linsley, who d 1 May 1893 æ. 88 *NHT3*.

iv Daniel, b c. 1812, d 6 Nov 1830 æ. 18 *NHT3*.

v Ann Maria, b [Dec 1814], d 1 Sep 1815 æ. 0-8 *NHT3*.

vi Barney Nelson, b 22 Mar 1823 *NHT3*, d 7 Aug 1903 *NHT3*.

2 Mary, b 14 Mar 1785 *EHV*, bp 16 Sep 1787 *EHC;* m 28 Nov 1811 *EHC*—Eli Sanford.

3 Hannah, b 21 Oct 1786 *EHV*, bp 16 Sep 1787 *EHC*, d 9 Sep 1873; m 4 Sep 1805 *NoHC*—Jedediah Harmon Norton.

4 Matthew, b 19 Sep 1788 *EHV*, d 7 Oct 1877 æ. 89 *NHT3;* m 23 Nov 1813 *EHC*—Fanny da. Amos & Huldah (Chidsey) Luddington, b c. 1793, d 12 Apr 1844 æ. 51 *EHC*.

5 Lois, b 28 Feb 1791 *EHV*, bp 17 Apr 1791 *EHC*, d 10 May 1791 *EHV*, "infant" d 11 May *EHC*.

6 Stephen, b 22 Mar 1792 *EHV*, "John" bp 13 May 1792 *EHC*, "son" d 16 [June] 1801 æ. 9 (drowned) *EHC*.

7 Eunice, b 22 Jan 1795 *EHV*, bp 15 Mar 1795 *EHC;* m 27 Nov 1820 *EHV*—Thomas Sanford.

8 Elizabeth, b 26 May 1797 *EHV*, bp 16 July 1797 *EHC*, d 2 Sep 1798 *EHV*, æ. 2 *EHC*.

9 Russell, b 7 Aug 1800 *EHV*, bp 5 Oct 1800 *EHC*, d 13 Feb 1843 æ. 42 *EHC*.

10 ROSWELL, b 7 Aug 1800 *EHV*, bp 5 Oct 1800 *EHC*, d 7 Jan 1833 æ. 32 *NHT3, EHC*; m.

11 ELIZA LOISA, bp 22 May 1803 *EHC*, d 16 Oct 1805.

FAM. 7. STEPHEN & ABIGAIL (HUGHES) ROWE:

1 STEPHEN, b 6 Dec 1782 *NHV*, "child" d 4 Feb 1787 æ. c. 5 *EHC*.

2 LOIS, b 17 Oct 1783 *NHV*, d 3 Feb 1788 *NHV*, in 5 yr. *EHT*.

3 JOHN, b 11 Nov 1785 *NHV*, bp 27 May 1787 *EHC*, d 9 June 1825 æ. 40-7 *NHT3*; m Rachel da. Elam & Rachel (Tuttle) Luddington, b 4 Sep 1780 *EHV*, d 14 Sep 1864 æ. 82 *NHT3* [marriage proved by EH Deeds 5:392].

4 LYDIA, b 14 Dec 1786 *NHV*, bp 27 May 1787 *EHC*, d 1 Dec 1866 æ. 80 *NHT3*; m 20 Sep 1807 *NHC2*—Levi Grannis.

5 STEPHEN, bp 13 Jan 1789 *EHC*, d 15 Jan 1789 æ. 0-0-3 *EHC*.

6 CHILD, d [Dec] 1789 æ. 0-0-2 *EHC*.

7 CHILD, d 27 Dec 1790 æ. 0-0-3 *EHC*.

8 CHILD, d Jan 1793 æ. c. 4 wks *EHC*.

9 LUEY, b 11 Nov 1793 *NHV*, "Lue" bp 10 Jan 1796 *EHC*, d 15 May 1880; m Chancellor Kingsbury.

10 ESTHER, b 14 Dec 1795 *NHV*, d 1 June 1812 æ. 19 *NHT3*; m 17 Dec 1809 Eliphaz Gillet.

11 ELIADA, b 12 Aug 1798 *NHV*, bp [———] 1798 *EHC*, d 22 Apr 1852 æ. 54 *NHT3*; m (1) 5 July 1818 Thankful ["Tenty"] Talmadge; m (2) 19 Oct 1828 *NHV*—Elizabeth, wid. Broughton. Children (incomplete): 1 Amasa, b 24 May 1819, d 30 May 1819 *NHT3*; 2 Juline, b 15 June 1820, d 14 Apr 1821 *NHT3*.

12 CHILD, d 18 Dec 1799 æ. 3 wks. *EHC*.

FAM. 7. STEPHEN & ELIZABETH (MILES) ROWE:

13 WILLIS STEPHEN; m Abby da. Joshua Brooks of C.

(*Continued in Volume VII, page 1549*)

ADDITIONS AND CORRECTIONS

BLAKESLEE. (Page 227.) Gad, b 10 Jan 1770 *WatV*, rem. 1818 to Medina, Ohio; m Anna Lattin. Children (prob. b at P): Burritt (1806-1866), m Caroline Lowly Welton; Chauncey (1809-1868), m ———; Sarah, m Charles Camp of Cleveland. [Contributed by Mrs. C. W. Ellenwood, Wooster, Ohio.]

BUNNELL. (Page 360.) FAM. 2, 4. The family of Solomon was furnished by a correspondent, and as printed contains errors which are now corrected by Mrs. James H. Stansfield, Washington, D. C. Solomon m. Mary Holdren (not Holdern). Their son Isaac m Lana [Helena] Barcaloo.

FAM. 2, 5, *v*. Joseph of Wy & Milton m a da. of Roger Kirby. One of his brothers, prob. Isaac, m Jerusha Sherwood.

(Page 364.) FAM. 4, 12, *vi* did not m Jesse Wilmot, as suggested hypothetically. Instead, he m Hannah Bunnell (FAM. 2, 5, *xi*, 2). [Corrected by George Scoles, Esq., New York City.]

GOODSELL. (Page 664.) N. Goodsell, a grandson of Isaac (FAM. 1, 1, *iii*), wrote from Oswego County, N. Y., in 1866 as follows: that his grandfather died before his sons were grown up; that his widow, Elizabeth Penfield, married Deacon Mallory of Southbury. He d about 1794, and she went to live with her son Timothy in Washington. In 1807, N. Goodsell was in Connecticut, found that his grandmother was tired of living with son Timothy, so he took her home with him to Oneida Co., N. Y., where he was then living. She d about 1816, aged 100 yrs. 6 mos., and is buried at Clinton, N. Y. [Contributed by Miss Helen D. Love, South Kent, Conn.]

GORHAM. (Page 679.) FAM. 7. The third child, Richard, had w. Ann, who d 21 Aug 1821 æ. 34-9. The fifth child, Elizabeth, d 23 Nov 1839; m 17 Feb 1814, George Adam Ash, b 23 Dec 1793 (Savannah, Ga.), d 26 May 1861. The eighth child, Mary, d 21 Oct 1840; m William Rahn. The death records are from Laurel Grove Cemetery, Savannah, Ga. [Contributed by Mrs. Lindsey P. Henderson, Savannah, Ga.]

LITTLE. (Page 1106.) FAM. 2, 1, *ii*. William's wife was Susan da. Timothy & Martha (Thompson?) Talmadge. [Transposition corrected by Mrs. J. Ross Bowdre, Macon, Ga.]

MANSFIELD. (Page 1140.) FAM. 5, 6, *ii*. Margaret; add, m 11 Feb 1767 *NHC2*—Benedict Arnold.

MERRIMAN. (Page 1175.) FAM. 10, 5. For Mabel (Andrews), read Mabel (Foster).

NASH. (Page 1312.) Mary, d 16 Aug 1683; her marriage to Roger Alling was accidentally omitted.

OSBORN. (Page 1332.) FAM. 9, 4. Emma Maria m David DeForest Swift. [Corrected by Jessie P. Andrews, New Haven, Conn.]

PARKER. (Page 1371.) FAM. 4, 11. Benjamin, b 12 Feb 1729, rem. from W to Simsbury; m 18 June 1751, Mercy da. Moses & Sarah (Merriman) Atwater, b 15 Aug 1731; rem. c. 1775 to Hartland, later to Barkhamsted, where he d 9 Feb 1807 æ. 78, and his wife d 3 Apr 1812 æ. 81. Deacon and Rev. soldier. Children:

1 ABIGAIL, b 5 Apr 1752; m Benjamin Brown.
2 MERCY, b 8 June 1754; m Oliver Hitchcock, Jr.
3 BENJAMIN, b 26 July 1757, d 8 Nov 1776.
4 SARAH, b 23 Apr 1759; m Daniel Rose.
5 LOVEL, b 5 July 1762.
6 EUNICE, b 16 Jan 1766; m Stephen Parker.
7 JOEL, b 2 May 1768.

[Contributed by Joseph M. Kellogg, Esq., Lawrence, Kans.]

PECK. (Page 1414.) FAM. 46, 3, Hannah, and her cousin Harriet (FAM. 47, 3) are both stated to have m 1 May 1816 *WdC* Russell Johnson. This regrettable error, called to our attention by Lt. Col. H. S. Terrell of Norfolk, Conn., was caused by an error in the Woodbridge church records as printed by Miss Louise Tracy in the Connecticut Quarterly, Hannah's name being misprinted there as Harriet; and this old error was inadvertently retained on our books after the correct entry had been made under Hannah. The Woodbridge Mortality List states that Hannah, relict of Russell Johnson of Oxford, and da. Zenas & Hannah Peck, d at West Haven 1 Sep 1879 æ. 94-3. From a printed source we find: Hannah Peck, b 4 June 1785, d 1 Sep 1879; m Russell Johnson, b 4 Oct 1789, d 15 Nov 1830. Also: Harriet Peck, b c. 1791, d 26 Aug 1853; m 12 Oct 1811 Harry French, b 25 Dec 1791, d 17 May 1866.

PLUMB. (Page 1451.) John m Elizabeth da. John & Dorothy Norton. Her mother was not Elizabeth Clark, who was John Norton's third wife. [Corrected by Mrs. Maud Sloan Baum, Pine Bluff, Ark.]

NOTE ON GILBERT'S MORTUARY LIST

(New Haven Genealogical Magazine, Vol. V, pp. 1259 and 1265)
By George Sherwood Dickerman.*

The List contains two allusions to the family of my father, Ezra Dickerman, which do not quite agree with our own records as given in the Dickerman Genealogy, pp. 458-460.

The List has this entry: "February 1, 1835, Died child of Ezra Dickerman, aged 1 year."

Our record gives the date January 30, and the age a little over 13 months.

The difference here is unimportant.

* Mr. Dickerman wrote us: "I find Mr. Gilbert's records generally good and think you did well to print them."

The other entry is for 1845 as follows, "June 25 or 27, Infant of Ezra Dickerman."

To find out what this means, we may glance at the story of the family as a whole. On the date given, the children with their several ages in order were as follows:

Edward Dwight, aged 18.
Elizabeth Hall, aged 16.
Abbie Ann, aged 13.
Henry Street, aged 9.
Sarah Frances, aged 7.
Ezra Day, aged 4.
George Sherwood, aged 2.

Another child, Watson Bradley, was born on the ensuing 4th of January 1846, but does not belong to the record of this date. The Infant then to whom Mr. Gilbert alludes, is manifestly George Sherwood.

And now, eighty-four years after, the task falls to me of trying to show in a convincing manner that putting me on a mortuary list in 1845 was a bit premature.

But how did it happen? The date points to a story of measles that my mother used to tell. It was thought in those times to be a good thing to have this liability over with while children were young. That month of June in 1845 looked like a favorable time for it. All of the family were quite well, summer was coming on, and the measles were in the neighborhood. So Elizabeth, the eldest daughter, was sent to call at a house where the boon could be got. She brought it home with her and after a little had experience of what it meant herself. Then in due course all her brothers and sisters shared in the experience. Mother had assumed that she was immune, and would be able to devote herself to taking care of the children, but this was a mistake, and she too came down with all the others. According to her account, I was put to sleep in the cradle as usual with no signs of what was coming, till in the night I felt bad, clambered out of the cradle and found my way to her bedside, when she lifted me in and found me cold as a stone. After that I was terribly sick, worse than anyone else of them all. Still, somehow or other, I pulled through, like all the rest.

Some twenty years after this, when I was in college and mother was living with me in New Haven, my youngest brother, Watson Bradley, then just starting as a broker in Wall Street, caught the measles there and came up to our home with his fianceé to be taken care of. That was the hour of mother's triumph: "See what all the rest of you escaped from!"

I seem to have been the only one to get into the Mortuary List.

NEW HAVEN CENSUS, 1704

On 3 Apr. 1704 a drawing was made for lots in the ''Half Division'' of New Haven lands, recorded in the volume of Proprietors' Records which is labeled 4, at pages 108 to 116. This list gives the number of persons in the family of each proprietor, and hence is equivalent to a census. It is very useful in checking the genealogical statistics. Those with none in their families were either non-residents or deceased early proprietors.

Dauid Atwater	5
Hannah Alsope	2
Mr Harriman	0
John Miles	6
John Johnson Ju^{n}	6
Mrs Dauids & Ling	3
M^{rs} falcanar	3
M^{rs} abig^{ll} Jones	4
Thom^{s} Barnes	10
S^{rg} John Thompson	8
Dan^{ll} Brown	4
Joseph pardee	6
Joseph Bradly	5
S^{rg} John Ball	9
Lt John Munson	6
Mrs Morrison	6
Mr Jer Osborne	4
Japhet Mansfield	2
Dan^{ll} Bristoll	6
Jededia Andrews	1
Joseph Becher	5
John Hill	8
Mr John Gibbs	0
Capt Andrews	5
Benj Bunnell	4
Thom^{s} sanford	5
Nath^{ll} Potter jun	1
elipha^{tt} Bristoll	3
Henry Tooles	6
Thom^{s} Hotchkis	9
John Buttler	2
Coledg estate	0
M^{r} sam^{ll} Bassett	11
Dan^{ll} Johnson	1
ensigne Holt	7
[—]g elia^{z} Browne	5
Natha^{ll} mix	7
Samuell smith Ju	3
John Holt	4
Joseph Thomas	8
John Payne	11
Joseph Jues	3
Mr Mather	2
Joseph hull	3
Sam^{ll} Todd seno^{r}	7
sam^{ll} Smith sen^{or}	3
Daniell Hotchkis	8
John Brocket	7
Willm Thomson	10
John Tuttle Jun	3
edmond Tapp	0
Thom^{s} Leek	9
Joseph Thomson	3
Jsaac Johnson	3
Thom^{s} Tuttle Ju^{n}	7
Capt John Miles	4
Benj Willmott	3
James Pierpont	6
William Tuttle	4
Theophilus Munson	5
John Hancock	1
Edward Scot	4
Joseph Prindle	6
John Mix Jun	2
Thom^{s} Tuttle sen^{or}	3
John Dunbar	5
Sarg^{nt} Will Willmott	2
Thom^{s} Trowbridg	8
Seth Heaton	3
Daniell Sperry	7
Thom^{s} Sperry	9
John Becher	7
Sam^{ll} Clark Jun	6
ebenezer frost	2
Thomas Gilbert	4
John Mix Sen^{or}	6
John Gilbert	5
Henry Brooks	4
Gershom Browne	5
Sam^{ll} Browne	3
Willm Collins	7
M^{r} sam^{ll} Bishop	6
Joseph Morris	10
Mr Caleb Trowbridg	1
Joseph Goodwin	4
John Malary	7
Mr John Prout	7
Lt John Sackett	6
John Johnson seni	9
Thom^{s} Beech	1
John Thomas Jun	1
Thom^{s} panter	7
Robbert auger	3
Nathan Benham	4
M^{rs} elizabeth eyer	5
John glouer	3
Joseph Mansfield	4
Mrs Dauenport	1
Joseph Turner	1
Joseph How	2
Sam^{ll} Gilbert	5
John Punderson	3

Daniell Bradly	3
Serg Benjamin Bradly	9
Mr Moses Mansfield	2
Josiah Thomas	1
Peter Mallary	10
Mr Jonathan Atwater	11
Widow Willmott	2
Nathll Bradly	7
enos Talmadge	4
Steuen Hotchkis	0
Lt Thoms Talmadge	9
Mercy Moss	0
Francis Browne	1
Recomp Thomas	1
Daniell Sherman	2
Widow How	1
Mrs Anne Collins	4
Mr John Winston	8
John Perkins Seni	7
Mr Joseph Moss Jun	2
Mr John Alling	9
John Graniss	1
Jacob Robison	8?
John Perkins Jr.	3
Thoms biggs	3
Mr James Heaton	2
Samll Clark sen	9
Mrs Coster	0
John steuens	5
Mr Thom Yale	1
Thoms Trowbridge farmer	7
Stephen Munson	1
Jonath Sackitt	3
Jonat Lampson	0
Samll Thomas	5
Benjn Wooden	4
Willm Wooden	7
John Thomas farmer	4
Capt Thoms Munson	0
Samuell ford	4
Zacheus Cande	3
Joseph Chidsey	5
ebenezer Brown sen	3
Willm Hoadly	4
Maj John Nash / Mrs Hannah Ball	2
Daniell Abutt	6
John Benham	6
Samll Johnson Jun	1
John Hull	5
John & Samll Umberfield	7
John Bracket Junor	1
Thoms Humberston	4
samll Mix	4
John Willmott	5
a Lot for ye Ministry	0
edmond Dorman	3
Capt Jsack & Nathl Turner	5
Joseph Smith senior	5

ebenezer Smith	7
Benjamin Peck	5
Lidiah Bristoll	3
The Heires of John Sperry	4
Mr John Yale	6
Hezikiah Bunill	2
Nathall Tharp senior	7
Nathall Tutle Jun	3
Joseph Bradly Jun	3
Nathanll Kimberly Jun	6
John Barnes	7
ebenzr Brown Junor	5
Nathanll Poter Senior	12
Nathan Andrewes	5
Joseph Moss senior	3
Mr Thoms Nash	0
John Thomas sen	6
Gidion Andrewes	3
elizabeth Hitchcock	5
Moses Blackley	3
Theophilus Heaton	1
Laurane Clenton	3
eliazer Becher	8
Willm Johnson senior	5
Mr Will Tuttle	0
ebenezr Blackly	10
John Watson	5
Samuell Horton	3
John Bristoll	3
Jonathan Tutle	1
Mr John Hudson	3
Joseph Clark sen	6
Mrs Mary Jues	6
Samuell Lines	2
Samll Jacobs	1
Major Moses Mansfield	4
John Cooper Junor	5
samuell Tutle sen	9
William Johnson Jr	7
Samuell Burwell	8
Samll Humberston	4
John Todd	6
Daniell Thomas	2
Widow Chaterton	5
Stephen Perkins	3
Samll Alling Jun:	7
Joseph Kerbee	5
Nathll Boykin	1
John Newman	3
Samuell & Stephen WhitHead	2
Samll Johnson sen	5
Samll Chaterton	4
Sergnt John Cooper	4
Mr Willm Hook Lot	0
Samll Thomson sen	5
Mr Mathew Gilbert	8
Samll Tuttle Jun	4
Stephen Clark	2
Joseph Peck senior	8

Willm Thomson Jun	1
Thoms Jacobs	1
Joseph Granis	2
Jonath Perkins	8
Thoms Steuens	1
Thoms Willmott	2
John Clark	5
John Rowe	8
Samll fernes	2
Willm Chatterton	2
Benjamin Dorman	4
Joseph Steuens	1
Joseph Tuttle	7
Benjmin Bouden	2
Zachcheus Candee Jr	2
Ralph Lines	9
John How senior	1
Daniell Barnes	6
Josseph Potter	3
Simon Tutle	4
Sergnt Samuell Alling	9
Caleb Mix	9
Mr Jsaac Jones	8
Mr ebenezer Atwater	6
Widow abigall Hill	5
ebenezer Mansfield	1
Mathew ford	4
Richard Miles Jun	5
Mr John Thomson	1
Willm fredrick	0
Jerimiah Wooden	4
Joseph Clark Jun	1
Mr grexson Lot	1
Samll Downe	6
Nathan Smith	5
Lt ab Dickerman	4
John Blackly Jun	5
Thoms Holt	1
Mr John Morris	6
Mr fenns children	0
Widow Hotchkis	5
Capt fowler	1
John sherman	4
Nathanll Heaton	4
Willm Russell	1
Henry steuens	4
Nathanll Tuttle sen	0
John Hotchkis	5
ebenezer Sperry	7
Joseph Dorman	6
sergnt Joseph Sackett	1
Widow ford	8
John Tuttle sen	0
Joseph Lines	5
Peter Carrinton	7
Mr John Bishop	8
ebenezer Downs	5
Daniell Clark	3
Nathaniell Sperry	10

Caleb Mathewes	2
Samuell Sanford	5
John ford	0
James Steuens	3
Joshua Hotchkis Jun	3
Thomas Kimberly	2
John Blackly sen	4
John Smith Jun	1
Samuell Cooper	4
Dauid Perkins	7
Samll Candee	1
John Woolcott	6
Paul Cornwell	3
Thomas Mallary	3
Jsaac Becher	9
Nathll Wooden	7
Samll Blackly	10
John Bradly	4
Thoms Munson	5
Micaell Todd	8
Thoms Hodge	7
Nathll Kimberly sen	2
Samuell Steuens	5
Mr Philip Alcock	3
Mrs Gilbert	1
Samll Todd Junur	5
ensigne Joshua Hotchkis	9
Simon simons	4
Ms Lidiah Rosewell	6
Samuell farrin	3
James Bishop	5
ensigne John Basset	9
John Allcock	2
Capt Daniell Sherman	6
Samuell Atwater	7
Joseph Peck Jun	1
Caleb Tuttle	4
Nathaniell Tharp Jun	8
Mr Nathanll Yale	5
Deacon abraham Bradly	6
John Downes	2
John Lines	3
James Bishop esquir	2
Thoms Alcock	1
Richd Sperry Jun	12
Thoms elcock	6
William Jones esqr Theophilus Eaton esqr	3
Richard Miles senior	0
Joseph osborne	7
Mr John Perry	1
arther Rexford	2
Joseph Smith Jun	7
Richd Hall	4
Abram Dickerman	4
Deacon John Punderson	8
ely Robberts	6
Thoms Powell	0
Sergnt Joseph Preston	2

Samuell Malary 2
Sam[ll] son of Sam[ll] Clark 3
John Smith senior 5
edward granis 3

Here ffoloweth after claimers & no Lott Drawn

John Thomas Jun 0
M[r] John Yale his uncles M[r] Dauid Yale 1st purchas 0
Simon Tuttle 0
John Humerston 1
James Talmadge 1
Sam[ll] gilbert in Right of his wife a 4th part of Rich[d] Littles 83 Right
Danill Trowbridge 1
Henry gibons 0
Will gibons 0
Ensign Sam[ll] Munson 0
the heirs of Capt Thomas Munson 0
edward Preston 0
Rich[d] Higinbothom 0
John Humerstons heirs 5

TOWN POOR, NEW HAVEN, 1786

Contributed by Miss Ethel Lord Scofield

[After the new towns of Hamden and North Haven were set off from New Haven in 1786, an agreement was made dividing the town poor between the original town and the daughter towns. This document is among the collections of the New Haven Colony Historical Society, and the following verbatim copy has been contributed by the librarian, Miss Scofield.]

At a Meeting of the several Committees appointed by the several Towns of New Haven Hamden and North Haven to make an Equal Division of the Poor Persons supported by the said Towns as belonging to them as being heretofore the Towns Poor of said New Haven & now divided to each Town according to their lists on the fifteenth Day of December A. D. 1786 the aboue Division was made and agreed to and the said Poor are divided and set to the several Towns as above & said Towns to take and support them accordingly—in the above division Daniel McNamarra and wife and Francis Claridge and Family are not divided but still remain a charge upon all said Towns according to their sd Lists

Witness our Hands in New Haven
this 15th day of December 1786

Samuel Bishop
David Austin
Timothy Jones
Charles Chauncey
Stephen Ball
} Com^ee^ of New Haven

Simeon Bristol
John Hubbard
Isaac Dickerman
} Com^ee^ of Hamden

Ephraim Humaston
Samuel Mix
Joshua Barns
} Com^ee^ of No Haven

New Haven

Joseph Mix and Wife	0 - 8 - 0
Ebenezer Wilmot	7 - 0
Wid^w^ Culver	4 -10
Andrew Reed	6 - 0
Abigail Tuttle	5 - 0
Timothy Thomas	7 - 0
Widow Fry—(?) and child	12 - 0
Stephen Beecher	6 - 0
Mrs Howes four Children	13 - 0
Easton Sabin	2 - 0
	£ 3 - 10 - 10

Abigail Andrews
Sarah Thompson
Elisabeth Punderson
Thomas Sherman dec'ds Child
Simon King
Wid^w Ruth Gordon
Hannah Bingley
Nathan Smith
Jerom Smith
Anna Gibson
Wid^w Graham
Sol^o Townshends Wives Child

Hampden

Widow Kimberly	0 - 6 - 0
Sarah Wilds	3 - 0
John Melone	7 - 0
Joel Alling	11 - 0
Ichabod Barns Child	3 - 0
Silas Culvers Child	3 - 0
Margaret Doyle	3 - 0
	£ 1 - 16 - 6

Andrew Ives
Thomas Ives
John Melones Wife
Wid^w Mary Potter
Wid^w Sarah H aabard (?)
Lydia Ives

North Haven

Mercy Parker	0 - 4 - 0
Stephen Clark	5 - 0
Enos Blakesley	5 - 0
Rachel Barns	5 - 0
Nancy Doyle and infant	9 - 0
Thankful Tuttle	1 - 0
Wid^w Fryars boy at Tim^o Turners	3 - 6
Oliver Bradleys child	3 - 0
Wid^w Fryars boy at Jocelins	2 - 9
	£ 1 - 18 - 3

Caleb Turner
Thomas Sanford
Elias Forbes
Daniel Hotchkiss
Ebenezer Humistone
Sarah Hunt

BOOK REVIEWS

This department of the New Haven Genealogical Magazine offers to compilers and publishers of genealogical books the opportunity to secure fair and honest reviews of their productions. The reviewer will do his utmost to point out the good features of every book which is presented for review, but in fairness to readers will mention striking deficiencies, such as the lack of an index, unusually poor arrangement of material, or gross inaccuracies. Those who wish books reviewed should send one copy to the address below.

Donald L. Jacobus, Editor,
554 Central Avenue,
Westville, Conn.

TWITCHELL. Genealogy of the Twitchell Family. Record of the Descendants of the Puritan—Benjamin Twitchell—Dorchester, Lancaster, Medfield and Sherborn, Massachusetts, 1632-1927. Compiled and Edited by Ralph Emerson Twitchell. 4°. New York, 1929. Price, $25.00; order from Mrs. Herbert K. Twitchell, Setauket, L. I., N. Y.

This substantial quarto volume, from the press of The Tuttle Company, Rutland, Vt., is a well-made book, with attractive cloth binding, a good grade of book paper, and excellent illustrations. The frontispiece is a picture of Chesham, co. Bucks, Eng., where the Twitchell family originated, and there is also an interesting picture of the market square at Chesham, besides nearly seventy portraits of members of the Twitchell family.

There are 61 pages of introductory matter, giving records of the family in England, ascertained principally through the efforts of Mr. Herbert K. Twitchell, a list of Massachusetts Twitchells in the Revolutionary War, other war lists, and the Twitchell heads of families in the first federal census, 1790. Then follow 619 pages devoted to the genealogical data of descendants of Benjamin Twitchell; and the copious, well-arranged indexes fill the final 87 pages.

Col. Ralph Emerson Twitchell, the compiler, a well-known writer on the history and archaeology of New Mexico, unfortunately died before the publication of the book, which bears evidence, in the citation of authorities for the early generations, of his scholarly care. The financial burden of the undertaking was assumed by Mr. Herbert Kenaston Twitchell, of New York, who also passed away before the book was published.

The Massachusetts lines are traced with requisite thoroughness, and the numerous biographies are extremely well written. The book should be of abiding interest to all Twitchell descendants, and is recommended to all libraries which purchase genealogical books.

The presentation of the earlier generations bears evidence to their being based quite largely on printed sources, and we may surmise that future Twitchell historians may find additional data in original record sources. It is with real regret that we call attention to the inadequate treatment of the Connecticut branch of the family which settled early at Derby. The account of this branch, much less thorough than that of the Massachusetts branches, was drawn chiefly from the printed histories of Derby and Oxford, and in addition to being very incomplete, contains several inaccuracies. The records of St. James's Church, Derby, containing numerous Twitchell entries, were not utilized at all, though printed in the *New England Historical and Genealogical Register* in 1922. Some of the Twitchell entries in Sharpe's *History of Oxford* were overlooked.

It was Hannah (Hinman), widow of Samuel Twitchell (No. 52, page 25) who married 13 Apr. 1749, John Pierce, and not Hannah Twitchell (No.

93, page 48), who instead married Joseph Tuttle. The birth year of this Hannah (1741) has been arbitrarily set back to 1735 in order to enable her to marry in 1749. A Samuel Twitchell born 1744 (No. 95, page 49) is erroneously said to have married in 1801, though the same marriage is correctly attributed to a younger Samuel (No. 236, page 106). It is said of Abijah Twitchell (No. 239, page 107), who was born 1776: ''The census of 1790 . . . . . . does not give this man, and it must be presumed that he had died before that time.'' Since he was only fourteen years old in 1790, one would hardly expect to find him listed then as the head of a family; as a matter of fact, his death is recorded at Oxford in 1811 aged 35. Elizabeth Twitchell (No. 108, page 51), born 1760, is said to have married Ichabod Dean. Actually she married Eliakim Terrell, and the marriage to Ichabod Dean, which took place 1775, belongs to Elizabeth (Hull), widow of Wooster Twitchell (No. 100, page 50). It is said that Mary Twitchell (No. 104, page 51), born 1750, married Benjamin Bunnell, ''who was fourteen years her junior''; it was really her younger sister, also named Mary (twin with Elizabeth, born 10 Feb. 1760, No. 109, page 26) who married Benjamin Bunnell; the older Mary had died young. On page 26, the child of John Twitchell, born 10 Oct. 1737, was not named Edward, as stated, but David (No. 91); he had a first cousin David (No. 103), ten years younger than himself. Both Davids are listed in the 1790 Census, but only one of them is identified in the Genealogy of the Twitchell Family.

It will be seen from the examples given that the Derby branch of the family was accorded very imperfect treatment by the compiler, though the worst errors may be due to the lack of final revision, which apparently he did not live to complete. For these imperfections the publisher can be held in no way responsible, nor do they detract from the great value of the information given on other branches of the family. The book is meritorious in so many respects that the reviewer deeply regrets not being able to praise it in every respect.

THE MAGAZINE OF AMERICAN GENEALOGY. Published monthly by the Institute of American Genealogy, 440-442 Dearborn Street, Chicago, Ill. First issue, August, 1929. Price: $1.50 per issue.

Each issue of the magazine contains several sections, the sections being paged consecutively through the successive issues. The idea seems to be to enable subscribers to bind the sections into so many separate volumes.

The first section consists of editorial matter. The second contains Derivation of Surnames, a subject in which many people are interested, but which belongs rather to the field of etymology than to that of genealogy. Several excellent hand-books on the subject are in existence, which furnish the material, and the Magazine states, ''no originality is claimed for this work.''

The third section treats of Heraldry. The first and second issues contain a verbatim reprint of the history of heraldry and dictionary of terms, from Burke's General Armory. The subsequent issues contain coats-of-arms of various surnames, alphabetically arranged, but without specifying the English families to whom the arms pertain. Some are attributed to certain American families, but the grounds for such attribution are not stated.

Section IV treats of Immigrants to America before 1750, and Section V of Soldiers and Sailors in the American Revolution, both alphabetically arranged. The latter is useful, as it brings into one grouping, with references to the printed sources, the names of those who served in the Revolution, which heretofore were only to be found in separate publications. The sixth section is an Index to American Lineages, the seventh is a Bibliography of American Genealogy, and the final section is devoted to queries sent in by subscribers.

The whole scheme of the Magazine is undeniably pretentious, and the fifth and seventh sections are practical enough to be serviceable to genealogical students. The fourth section (Immigrants to America) might better be omitted, for in it the Magazine gives to the American public one more of those conglomerations of mingled fact and fancy for which the public never seems to lose its appetite. The data given is unverified and for the most part unreferenced. No reputable genealogist would dare quote it as authority. It is anonymous, being apparently the work of a clerical staff untrained in the rudiments of genealogical research, and unskilled in making critical use of available printed sources, evidenced by their inability to discriminate between good genealogical books and poor ones. This section perpetuates old errors and perpetrates new errors. It is distinctly a disservice to the cause of scientific genealogy, and should be discontinued before it injures irretrievably the standing of the Institute in the eyes of all serious genealogical students.

The space of a single review is insufficient to make a detailed criticism of the data that has appeared in the fourth section, but lest the above strictures be deemed too severe, a couple of examples will be given out of the many with which every page in this section teems. On page 33, it is said of Gideon Allen that he ''m. Sarah ———; m. 2d, Ann, dau. of Nathaniel Burr of Fairfield.'' His only wife was Sarah Prudden; it was his son Gideon who settled in Fairfield and married Ann Burr. On the next page, Henry Allen is given a son George (b. 1678) who actually did not belong to him, but to his brother Gideon.

These are examples of old errors, going back to Savage. Of course, Savage was a pioneer, working without the facilities which are open to genealogists to-day; and he displayed marvelous critical acumen and judgment in handling the material that was then accessible. But it cannot be denied that after some seventy years Savage's work is antiquated and must be amplified by that of many searchers who have combed smaller fields with greater thoroughness. The need to-day is not for a new edition of Savage, but for a new Savage who can compile with that pioneer's keen judgment the data which has been made accessible since his day.

But the anonymous compilers of the Immigrants do not succeed in improving matters when they depart from Savage. On page 41 we read of John Alling that he ''m. Oct. 14, 1652, Eleanor Beardsley (Savage says 'Ellen Bradley').'' Obviously this is intended for a correction of Savage. However, Savage is not alone in stating the wife's name as Ellen Bradley; her name is correctly so stated in the excellent verbatim printed copy of the New Haven Vital Records; it is also so stated in the Alling Genealogy published in 1899, as well as in the New Haven Genealogical Magazine. Here are four authorities, from the oldest to the most recent, one of them a verbatim copy of the marriage record itself; all agreeing on the name Bradley. Yet the Magazine of American Genealogy, following some nameless authority, prefers to print an incorrect correction, and thus give currency to a new error which reputable genealogists will have to combat for a century to come. Is this sort of thing a service to genealogy? A thousand times, no!

Granted that in handling an immense amount of data, every genealogist is liable to a very occasional error of fact or of judgment, the quality of work must be judged by what is characteristic, not by what is exceptional. Unfortunately, the examples given are not exceptions, but characterize every page of this compilation, and brand it as a slip-shod piece of work, which any genealogist of standing would repudiate.

In Section VI appear what are called American Lineages, alphabetically arranged. The lineages follow this form: Alling: ''Benjamin (b. 1736)—Nathan—Samuel—John (m. 1652).'' Only males are indexed, and those in the intervening generations are omitted from the alphabetical listing. The first issue of the Magazine contains the estimate that it will require 26 volumes of 500 pages each to complete this index. The number of pages printed in the first five issues indicates that, at the present rate of printing, about 375 pages will be printed each year. At this rate it will therefore require about a third of a century to complete the index, and few of those now interested in genealogy will live to see its completion. However, the value of a lineage index of this type is not clear. Certainly there is value in indexing manuscript collections and unindexed books. But here, to return to our example, are some two pages of Alling lineages. They can all (at least, all the correct ones) be found in the Alling Genealogy, which is indexed. Where would an Alling to-day look for his lineage if not in the Alling Genealogy, and just what benefit is derived from printing two pages of selected Alling lineages? Every issue of the Magazine contains the following conspicuously placed advertisement: "The Institute of American Genealogy is prepared to furnish a typewritten copy, as fully as it is given in the source, of any lineage listed." Aside from this, it is doubtful whether the Index of American Lineages will serve any practical purpose.

When the Institute of American Genealogy was organized, one of its proposed objects was to formulate a code of ethics and standard of practice for professional genealogists. We are still awaiting with curiosity the code of ethics that will be formulated. Genealogy ranks as a profession because the genealogist charges a fee for personal services which his knowledge, training, and ability enable him to render. No conscientious genealogist would consider it ethical to turn over to a clerical staff inquiries for information, knowing that his clerical workers would merely copy matter from genealogical books, without study, verification, or investigation of the accuracy of the books utilized. Few attempts to commercialize genealogy have been successful. Those that have enjoyed moderate success have done so chiefly by capitalizing the ignorance of a portion of the genealogical public regarding what constitutes proper methods of research.

Genealogical research does not mean copying something out of a book, whether right or wrong; anyone able to read and write can do that. It means the employment of special knowledge and training directed towards discovering and establishing a correct lineage, by the critical utilization of dependable printed sources and (when required) by study of unpublished record sources. These remarks would not be apropos in a review, were it not that the advertising which is printed at the beginning of each section in every issue of the Magazine of American Genealogy, and a careful analysis of the type and quality of the data printed, clearly indicate that the Institute which publishes this magazine is a commercial organization, attempting to apply commercial methods to genealogy.

CONNECTICUT GENEALOGY

Having used genealogical books critically for more than a quarter of a century, and having observed the curious mingling of excellence and the opposite which characterize a large proportion of them, the reviewer hopes he may be pardoned for appending a note for the benefit of others who may be compiling histories of Connecticut families. The State Library at Hartford possesses copies (the Barbour collection), unverified but exceedingly useful, of all the *town* vital records in the State, and copies of these entries can be obtained for a very modest fee. Copies of the records of many churches are also on deposit at the State Library, as well as at the Connecticut Historical Society in Hartford, and many Probate Districts have deposited their files at the State Library. Compilers of family histories need not therefore confine their research to printed works, which are usually incomplete and too often inaccurate. If compilers can visit these institutions personally, the officials will be found most courteous in aiding inquirers. It would be proper and advantageous for descendants of Connecticut families who are compiling a history, if they wish to avail themselves fully of the facilities for research offered by the Connecticut Historical Society, to join the Society, the membership fees being very moderate. If compilers cannot make their searches in person, the officials of these institutions, when unable to spare the time to search their records, recommend genealogists or clerical workers who can do so.

If possible, the land records of the town where the family resided should also be searched, for they are full of valuable genealogical data. In this State, each town has possession of its own land records. Some Probate Districts still retain their files, and the record volumes often contain matter not found in the files. These can be searched at least expense (if the compiler cannot do so personally) by a genealogist living in or near the town where the records are located. Since the writer is himself a genealogist, his motives in giving this advice may perhaps be misconstrued. He has, however, compiled and published family histories, and often employs other genealogists for research in other localities; and is convinced from long experience that the best results can be obtained by this method.

The issuing of a family history is a major expense. Printing costs are high, and the sales of the volume are necessarily limited. In an undertaking which involves in total many hundreds, and often several thousands, of dollars, it seems a great pity to save a very small part of the total cost by neglecting to obtain readily accessible records which would add far more to the intrinsic value of the book than a handsome appearance, desirable though the latter be. That family histories so frequently bear witness to a deficiency of research, must be attributed to the compilers' lack of knowledge of the location and accessibility of records. The early generations of a family cannot be traced and arranged adequately without a very considerable amount of research in original record sources; the ordinary methods of scholarship fall far short of producing exact genealogical data.

A large majority of family histories are compiled by some member of the family who, notwithstanding the interest and enthusiasm he brings to the task, and the natural ability he may possess, lacks experience in this type of research. If he happens to live far from the old towns where the early generations of the family resided, the difficulties of his undertaking are increased, and often he is utterly without realization of the many avenues open to research. In addition to those mentioned above, there are many volumes of original documents at the State Library, relating to Colonial and Revolutionary times, and they are well indexed. There are County Court records and Superior Court records. Copies of the inscriptions in many graveyards can be seen at various historical society libraries, while other graveyards have to be visited to secure data. There are also the invaluble federal census records for each decade, in addition to the printed first census (1790). Finally, the files of the Pension Bureau in Washington are teeming with information concerning Revolutionary War soldiers and their families, and record searchers in Washington can be employed to abstract them at very moderate fees.

Yet volume after volume is turned out at large cost of publication, in blissful ignorance of these various record sources,—full of erroneous deductions and inconsistencies,—bearing evidence of rank amateurishness. To be sure, it would be quite expensive to cover *all* these sources thoroughly. It may be necessary to keep this expense within certain limits. That may be taken for granted. But many compilers never even make a beginning, and apparently never even learn that these record sources are available. Every family history is certain to contain something of value, since the compiler obtains information and records from family sources. However, it is rare for family records to extend back much more than 100 years, or 150 years at most; and for the early generations, the compiler is too often satisfied to follow what he finds in print, in total ignorance of its trustworthiness, and to reconcile all difficulties he may encounter by assumptions and guesses. In view of this situation, the wonder is that so many good family histories have been written, and that the average one is even as good as it is.

If this note should prove helpful to compilers or prospective compilers of such works, its purpose will be served.

AT YE EDITOR'S DESK

As announced at the end of the first issue of the present volume, the death of our printer, Mr. Smith, in addition to our feeling of personal loss, placed on the editor the burden of making new arrangements immediately. We are pleased to announce that all difficulties have been satisfactorily met, and that the future of the magazine is not menaced by a financial setback. The subscription list was insufficient to meet printing costs, but the sale of back issues from time to time has made good the deficit and covered all expenses, leaving a very small surplus with which to start the next volume.

The alphabetical appearance of family statistics has now reached well into the letter R, emboldening us to hope that two more volumes will complete the work. This volume has been almost solidly devoted to the Families of Ancient New Haven, with very little space given to other matter. In this issue, we are printing 72 pages instead of 64, so as to make room for book reviews and one or two special features.

In preparing such a mass of data for publication, in addition to extensive genealogical research on which the editor is employed professionally, it is too much to hope that errors can be entirely avoided. We are correcting them at the end of each volume as rapidly as they are discovered or pointed out to us. Not infrequently, they turn out to be old errors taken years ago from inaccurate printed sources and remaining on our books notwithstanding every effort to eliminate unverified matter.

It gives us great pleasure to announce that Mr. Gilbert H. Doane, of the University Library, Lincoln, Nebraska, editor of the Nebraska and Midwest Genealogical Record, will be added to our editorial staff. Beginning with the next issue, Mr. Doane will contribute reviews of current genealogical books or periodicals. Mr. Doane is well known in genealogical circles for the critical judgment and independent expression which characterize his reviews.

YE EDITOR.

NOTICE

It having come to my attention that my name has been used for some time past in connection with the advertising circulars and other literature of the Institute of American Genealogy, I wish to state emphatically that I am not, and never have been, a member of the Council of that organization, and aside from joining as a member at the time it was organized, I have no connection with the Institute and no responsibility for the policies pursued by it.

DONALD LINES JACOBUS.